Hoover's Handbook of

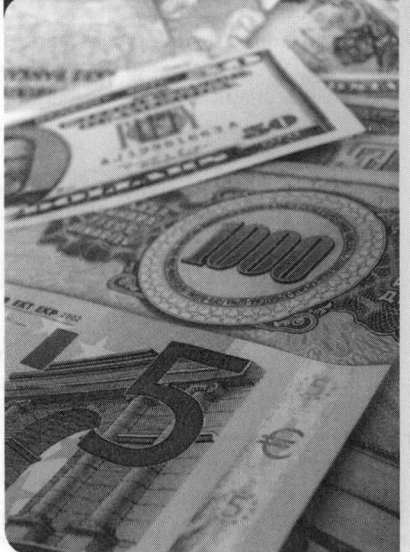

World
Business

2006

Austin, Texas

Hoover's Handbook of World Business 2006 is intended to provide readers with accurate and authoritative information about the enterprises covered in it. Hoover's asked all companies and organizations profiled to provide information. Many did so; a number did not. The information contained herein is as accurate as we could reasonably make it. In many cases we have relied on third-party material that we believe to be trustworthy, but were unable to independently verify. We do not warrant that the book is absolutely accurate or without error. Readers should not rely on any information contained herein in instances where such reliance might cause loss or damage. The publisher, the editors, and their data suppliers specifically disclaim all warranties, including the implied warranties of merchantability and fitness for a specific purpose. This book is sold with the understanding that neither the publisher, the editors, nor any content contributors are engaged in providing investment, financial, accounting, legal, or other professional advice.

The financial data (Historical Financials sections) in this book are from a variety of sources. Hemscott, Inc. provided selected data for the Historical Financials sections of publicly traded companies. For private companies and for historical information on public companies prior to their becoming public, we obtained information directly from the companies or from trade sources deemed to be reliable. Hoover's, Inc., is solely responsible for the presentation of all data.

Many of the names of products and services mentioned in this book are the trademarks or service marks of the companies manufacturing or selling them and are subject to protection under US law. Space has not permitted us to indicate which names are subject to such protection, and readers are advised to consult with the owners of such marks regarding their use. Hoover's is a trademark of Hoover's, Inc.

HOOVERS™
A D&B COMPANY

10 9 8 7 6 5 4 3 2 1

Publishers Cataloging-in-Publication Data

Hoover's Handbook of World Business 2006

    Includes indexes.

    ISBN 1-57311-110-4

    ISSN 1055-7199

    1. Business enterprises — Directories. 2. Corporations — Directories.

HF3010 338.7

Hoover's Company Information is also available on the Internet at Hoover's Online (www.hoovers.com). A catalog of Hoover's products is available on the Internet at www.hooversbooks.com.

The Hoover's Handbook series is edited by George Sutton and is produced for Hoover's Business Press by:

Sycamore Productions, Inc.
5808 Balcones Drive, Suite 205
Austin, Texas 78731
info@sycamoreproductions.com

Cover design is by John Baker. Electronic prepress and printing are by Von Hoffman Corporation, Owensville, Missouri.

U.S. AND WORLD BOOK SALES

Hoover's, Inc.
5800 Airport Blvd.
Austin, TX 78752
Phone: 512-374-4500
Fax: 512-374-4538
e-mail: orders@hoovers.com
Web: www.hooversbooks.com

EUROPEAN BOOK SALES

William Snyder Publishing Associates
5 Five Mile Drive
Oxford OX2 8HT
England
Phone & fax: +44-186-551-3186
e-mail: snyderpub@aol.com

Hoover's, Inc.

Founder: Gary Hoover
President: Dwayne H. Spradlin
EVP International: Russell Secker
EVP Marketing and Product: Paul Pellman
EVP Technology: Jeffrey (Jeff) Guillot
VP US Sales and Support: John Lysinger
VP Finance: Charles (Chuck) Harvey
VP Human Resources: Gillian Felix
VP Product Design and Creative Services: Michael Reiff
VP Acquisition Marketing: Chris Warwick
VP Strategic Accounts and Channel Sales: George Kanuck
VP Subscription Sales and Support: Mel Yarbrough

EDITORIAL

VP Content: Rachel Brush
Director, Content Acquisition and Management: Valerie Pearcy
Senior Editors: Margaret Claughton, Kathleen Kelly, Laurie Najjar, Barbara Redding, Dennis Sutton
Library Research Manager: Gina Leiss
Content Operations Analyst: Alison Stoeltje
Team Leads: Linnea Anderson Kirgan, Larry Bills, Troy Bryant, Carrie Geis, Zack Gonzales, Nancy Kay, Julie Krippel, Greg Perliski
Editors: Sally Alt, Adam Anderson, Alex Biesada, Joe Bramhall, James Bryant, Ryan Caione, Jason Cella, Catherine Colbert, Elizabeth Cornell, Danny Cummings, Jeff Dorsch, Michaela Drapes, Bobby Duncan, Lesley Epperson, Marcus Gould, David Hamerly, Stuart Hampton, Rosie Hatch, Donna Iroabuchi, Jessica Jimenez, Maggie Jimenez, Kenny Jones, Anne Law, Tara LoPresti, Josh Lower, John MacAyeal, Michael McLellan, Rachel Meyer, Barbara Murray, Nell Newton, Kristi Park, Peter Partheymuller, David Ramirez, Melanie Robertson, Belen Rodriguez, Matt Saucedo, Amy Schein, Seth Shafer, Lee Simmons, Joe Simonetta, Katherine Smith, Paula Smith, Betsy Staton, Diane Stimets, Barbara Strickland, Daysha Taylor, Vanita Trippe, Tim Walker, Kathi Whitley, Randy Williams, David Woodruff
Content Manager: Jannell Chester
QA Editors: Jason Cother, Emily Domaschk, Lisa Goodgame, Allan Gill, Diane Lee, John Willis
Financial Editors: Adi Anand, Jim Harris, Chris Huston, Anthony Staats
Editorial Projects Analyst: Karin Marie
Editorial Projects Specialist: Rob Mellett
Editorial Customer Advocates: Amy Davison, Anna Porlas

HOOVER'S BUSINESS PRESS

Distribution Manager: Rhonda Mitchell
Fulfillment and Shipping Manager: Michael Febonio
Shipping Clerk: Paul Olvera

ABOUT HOOVER'S, INC. — THE BUSINESS INFORMATION AUTHORITY™

Hoover's, a D&B company, gives its customers a competitive edge with insightful information about industries, companies, and key decision makers. Hoover's provides this updated information for sales, marketing, business development, and other professionals who need intelligence on U.S. and global companies, industries, and the people who lead them. This information, along with powerful tools to search, sort, download, and integrate the content, is available through Hoover's (www.hoovers.com), the company's premier online service. Hoover's business information is also available through corporate intranets and distribution agreements with licensees, as well as via Hoover's books. The company is headquartered in Austin, Texas.

Abbreviations

AB – Aktiebolag (Swedish)*

ADR – American Depositary Receipts

AG – Aktiengesellschaft (German)*

AFL-CIO – American Federation of Labor and Congress of Industrial Organizations

AMEX – American Stock Exchange

A/S – Aktieselskab (Danish)*

ASA – Allmenne Aksje Selskaper (Norwegian)*

ATM – asynchronous transfer mode; automated teller machine

CAD/CAM – computer-aided design/computer-aided manufacturing

CASE – computer-aided software engineering

CD-ROM – compact disc – read-only memory

CEO – chief executive officer

CFO – chief financial officer

CMOS – complementary metal-oxide semiconductor

COMECON – Council for Mutual Economic Assistance

COO – chief operating officer

DAT – digital audio tape

DOD – Department of Defense

DOE – Department of Energy

DOT – Department of Transportation

DRAM – dynamic random-access memory

DVD – digital versatile disc/digital video disc

EC – European Community

EPA – Environmental Protection Agency

EPS – earnings per share

EU – European Union

EVP – executive vice president

FCC – Federal Communications Commission

FDA – Food and Drug Administration

FDIC – Federal Deposit Insurance Corporation

FTC – Federal Trade Commission

GATT – General Agreement on Tariffs and Trade

GmbH – Gesellschaft mit beschränkter Haftung (German)*

GNP – gross national product

HDTV – high-definition television

HMO – health maintenance organization

HR – human resources

HTML – hypertext markup language

ICC – Interstate Commerce Commission

IMF – International Monetary Fund

IPO – initial public offering

IRS – Internal Revenue Service

KGaA – Kommanditgesellschaft auf Aktien (German)*

LAN – local-area network

LBO – leveraged buyout

LNG – liquefied natural gas

LP – limited partnership

Ltd. – Limited

MFN – Most Favored Nation

MITI – Ministry of International Trade and Industry (Japan)

NAFTA – North American Free Trade Agreement

Nasdaq – National Association of Securities Dealers Automated Quotations

NATO – North Atlantic Treaty Organization

NV – Naamlose Vennootschap (Dutch)*

NYSE – New York Stock Exchange

OAO – open joint stock company (Russian)

OAS – Organization of American States

OECD – Organization for Economic Cooperation and Development

OEM – original equipment manufacturer

OOO – limited liability company (Russian)

OPEC – Organization of Petroleum Exporting Countries

OS – operating system

OTC – over-the-counter

P/E – price-to-earnings ratio

PLC – public limited company (UK)*

RAM – random-access memory

R&D – research and development

RISC – reduced instruction set computer

ROA – return on assets

ROI – return on investment

SA – Société Anonyme (French)*; Sociedad(e) Anónima (Spanish and Portuguese)*

SA de CV – Sociedad Anónima de Capital Variable (Spanish)*

SEC – Securities and Exchange Commission

SEVP – senior executive vice president

SIC – Standard Industrial Classification

SpA – Società per Azioni (Italian)*

SPARC – scalable processor architecture

SVP – senior vice president

VAR – value-added reseller

VAT – value-added tax

VC – venture capitalist

VP – vice president

WAN – wide-area network

WWW – World Wide Web

ZAO – closed joint stock company (Russian)

z o.o. – z ograniczona odpowiedzialnoscia (Polish)*

* These abbreviations are used in companies' names to convey that the companies are limited liability enterprises; the meanings are usually the equivalent of *corporation* or *incorporated*.

Contents

List of Lists

HOOVER'S RANKINGS

THE BIGGEST

INDUSTRY

THE RICHEST

Companies Profiled

Companies Profiled (continued)

About Hoover's Handbook of World Business 2006

This 13th edition of *Hoover's Handbook of World Business* brings you the facts on 300 of the world's most influential companies based outside of the United States, making it one of the most complete sources of in-depth information on large, non-US-based business enterprises available anywhere.

Hoover's Handbook of World Business is one of our four-title series of handbooks that covers, literally, the world of business. The series is available as an indexed set, and also includes *Hoover's Handbook of American Business*, *Hoover's Handbook of Private Companies*, and *Hoover's Handbook of Emerging Companies*. This series brings you information on the biggest, fastest-growing, and most influential enterprises in the world.

HOOVER'S ONLINE FOR BUSINESS NEEDS

In addition to the 2,550 companies featured in our handbooks, coverage of some 40,000 business enterprises is available in electronic format on our Web site, Hoover's Online, at www.hoovers.com. Our goal is to provide one site that offers authoritative, updated intelligence on US and global companies, industries, and the people who shape them. Hoover's has partnered with other prestigious business information and service providers to bring you all the right business information, services, and links in one place.

We welcome the recognition we have received as the premier provider of high-quality company information — online, electronically, and in print — and continue to look for ways to make our products more available and more useful to you.

We believe that anyone who buys from, sells to, invests in, lends to, competes with, interviews with, or works for a company should know all there is to know about that enterprise. Taken together, this book and the other Hoover's products and resources represent the most complete source of basic corporate information readily available to the general public.

HOW TO USE THIS BOOK

This book has four sections:

1. "Using Hoover's Handbooks" describes the contents of our profiles and explains the ways in which we gather and compile our data.

2. "A List-Lover's Compendium" contains lists of the largest, fastest-growing, and most valuable companies of global importance.

3. The company profiles section makes up the largest and most important part of the book — 300 profiles of major business enterprises, arranged alphabetically.

4. Three indexes complete the book. The first sorts companies by industry groups, the second by headquarters location. The third index is a list of all the executives found in the Executives section of each company profile.

As always, we hope you find our books useful. We invite your comments via phone (512-374-4500), fax (512-374-4538), mail (5800 Airport Boulevard, Austin, Texas 78752), or e-mail (custsupport@hoovers.com).

The Editors,
Austin, Texas,
January 2006

Using Hoover's Handbooks

SELECTION OF THE COMPANIES PROFILED

The 300 profiles in this book include a variety of international enterprises, ranging from some of the largest publicly traded companies in the world — DaimlerChrysler AG, for example — to Malaysia's largest and oldest conglomerate, Sime Darby Berhad. It also includes many private businesses, such as Bertelsmann AG and LEGO, as well as a selection of government-owned entities, including the British Broadcasting Corporation and Mexico's Petróleos Mexicanos. The companies selected represent a cross-section of the largest, most influential, and most interesting companies based outside the United States.

In selecting these companies, we followed several basic criteria. We started with the global giants, including Toyota and Royal Dutch/Shell Group, and then looked at companies with substantial activity in the US, such as Vivendi Universal and Diageo. We also included companies that dominate their industries (e.g., Electrolux, the world's #1 producer of household appliances), as well as representative companies from around the world (one Indian conglomerate, Tata; one firm from Finland, Nokia; and two companies from Russia, OAO Gazprom and OAO LUKOIL). Companies that weren't necessarily global powerhouses but had a high profile with consumers (e.g., IKEA) or had interesting stories (Virgin Group) were included. Finally, because of their truly global reach, we added the Big Four accounting firms (even though they are headquartered or co-headquartered in the US).

ORGANIZATION

The profiles are presented in alphabetical order. You will find the commonly used name of the enterprise at the beginning of the profile; the full, legal name is found in the Locations section. For some companies, primarily Japanese, the commonly translated English name differs from the actual legal name of the company, so both are provided. (The legal name of Nippon Steel Corporation is Shin Nippon Seitetsu Kabushiki Kaisha.) If a company name starts with a person's first name (e.g., George Weston Limited), it is alphabetized under the first name. We've also tried to alphabetize companies where you would expect to find them — for example, Deutsche Lufthansa is in the L's and Grupo Televisa can be found under T.

The annual financial information contained in the profiles is current through fiscal year-ends occurring as late as August 2005. We have included certain nonfinancial developments, such as officer changes, through November 2005.

OVERVIEW

In the first section of the profile, we have tried to give a thumbnail description of the company and what it does. The description will usually include information on the company's strategy, reputation, and ownership. We recommend that you read this section first.

HISTORY

This extended section reflects our belief that every enterprise is the sum of its history and that you have to know where you came from in order to know where you are going. While some companies have limited historical awareness and were unable to help us much and other companies are just plain boring, we think the vast majority of the enterprises in this book have colorful backgrounds. We have tried to focus on the people who made the enterprises what they are today. We have found these histories to be full of twists and ironies; they make fascinating reading.

EXECUTIVES

Here we list the names of the people who run the company, insofar as space allows. We have shown age and pay information where available, although most non-US companies are not required to report the level of detail revealed in the US.

Although companies are free to structure their management titles any way they please, most modern corporations follow standard practices. The ultimate power in any corporation lies with the shareholders, who elect a board of directors, usually including officers or "insiders" as well as individuals from outside the company. The chief officer, the person on whose desk the buck stops, is usually called the chief executive officer (CEO) in the US. In other countries, practices vary widely. In the UK, traditionally, the Managing Director performs the functions of the CEO without the title, although the use of the term CEO is on the rise there. In Germany it is customary to have two boards of directors: a managing board populated by the top executives of the company and a higher-level supervisory board consisting of outsiders.

As corporate management has become more complex, it is common for the CEO to have a "right-hand person" who oversees the day-to-day operations of the company, allowing the CEO plenty of time to focus on strategy and long-term issues. This right-hand person is usually designated the chief operating officer (COO) and is often the president of the company. In other cases one person is both chairman and president.

We have tried to list each company's most important officers, including the chief financial officer (CFO), the chief legal officer, and the chief human resources or personnel officer. For companies with US operations, we have included the names of the US CEO, CFO, and top human resources executive, where available.

The people named in the Executives section are indexed at the back of the book.

The Executives section also includes the name of the company's auditing (accounting) firm, where available.

LOCATIONS

Here we include the company's full legal name and its headquarters, street address, telephone and fax numbers, and Web site, as available. We also list the same information for the US office for each company, if one exists. Telephone numbers of foreign offices are shown using the standardized conventions of international dialing. The back of the book includes an index of companies by headquarters location.

In some cases we have also included information on the geographic distribution of the company's business, including sales and profit data. Note that these profit numbers, like those in the Products/Operations section below, are usually operating or pretax profits rather than net profits. Operating profits are generally those before financing costs (interest income and payments) and before taxes, which are considered costs attributable to the whole company rather than to one division or part of the world. For this reason the net income figures (in the Historical Financials section) are usually much lower, since they are after interest and taxes. Pretax profits are after interest but before taxes.

PRODUCTS/OPERATIONS

This section lists as many of the company's products, services, brand names, divisions, subsidiaries, and joint ventures as we could fit. We have tried to include all its major lines and all familiar brand names. The nature of this section varies by company and the amount of information available. If the company publishes sales and profit information by type of business, we have included it (in US dollars).

COMPETITORS

In this section we have listed enterprises that compete with the profiled company. This feature is included as a quick way to locate similar companies and compare them. Because of the difficulty in identifying companies that only compete in foreign markets, the list of competitors is still weighted to large international companies with a strong US presence.

HISTORICAL FINANCIALS

Here we have tried to present as much data about each enterprise's financial performance as we could compile in the allocated space. Financial data for all companies is presented in US dollars, using the appropriate exchange rate at fiscal year-end.

While the information presented varies somewhat from industry to industry, it is less complete in the case of private companies that do not release data (although we have always tried to provide annual sales and employment). The following information is generally present.

A 10-year table, with relevant annualized compound growth rates, covers:

- Sales — fiscal year sales (year-end assets for most financial companies)
- Net income — fiscal year net income (before accounting changes)
- Net profit margin — fiscal year net income as a percent of sales (as a percent of assets for most financial firms)
- Employees — fiscal year-end or average number of employees
- Stock price — the fiscal year close
- P/E — high and low price/earnings ratio
- Earnings per share — fiscal year earnings per share (EPS)
- Dividends per share — fiscal year dividends per share
- Book value per share — fiscal year-end book value (common shareholders' equity per share)

The information on the number of employees is intended to aid the reader interested in knowing whether a company has a long-term trend of increasing or decreasing employment. As far as we know, we are the only company that publishes this information in print format.

The numbers on the left in each row of the Historical Financials section give the month and the year in which the company's fiscal year actually ends. Thus, a company with a September 30, 2005, year-end is shown as 9/05.

In addition, we have provided in graph form a stock price history for companies that trade on the major US exchanges. The graphs, covering up to 10 years, show the range of trading between the high and the low price as well as the closing price for each fiscal year. For public companies that trade on the OTC or Pink Sheets or that do not trade on US exchanges, we graph net income. Generally, for private companies, we have graphed net income, or, if that is unavailable, sales.

Key year-end statistics in this section generally show the financial strength of the enterprise, including:

- Debt ratio (long-term debt as a percent of shareholders' equity)
- Return on equity (net income divided by the average of beginning and ending common shareholders' equity)
- Cash and cash equivalents
- Current ratio (ratio of current assets to current liabilities)
- Total long-term debt (including capital lease obligations)
- Number of shares of common stock outstanding
- Dividend yield (fiscal year dividends per share divided by the fiscal year-end closing stock price)

- Dividend payout (fiscal year dividends divided by fiscal year EPS)
- Market value at fiscal year-end (fiscal year-end closing stock price multiplied by fiscal year-end number of shares outstanding)
- Fiscal year sales for financial institutions.

Per share data has been adjusted for stock splits. The data for public companies with sponsored American Depositary Receipts has been provided to us by Hemscott, Inc. Other public company information was compiled by Hoover's, which takes full responsibility for the content of this section.

In the case of private companies that do not publicly disclose financial information, we usually did not have access to such standardized data. We have gathered estimates of sales and other statistics from numerous sources.

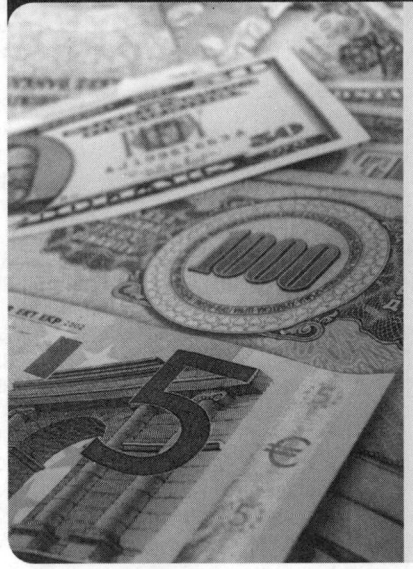

Hoover's Handbook of

World Business

A List-Lover's Compendium

The 100 Largest Companies by Sales in
Hoover's Handbook of World Business 2006

Rank	Company	Sales ($ mil.)	Rank	Company	Sales ($ mil.)	Rank	Company	Sales ($ mil.)
1	BP p.l.c.	285,059	36	Vodafone Group	64,505	71	Saint-Gobain	43,682
2	Royal Dutch/Shell	265,190	37	Munich Re	64,419	72	EADS	43,322
3	DaimlerChrysler	192,433	38	Electricité de France	64,010	73	Petróleos de Venezuela S.A.	42,580
4	Toyota Motor	172,749	39	Credit Suisse	63,989	74	Telecom Italia	42,314
5	TOTAL S.A.	166,209	40	France Telecom	63,879	75	Telefónica, S.A.	42,278
6	AXA	132,547	41	Crédit Agricole	61,696	76	Philips Electronics	41,070
7	Allianz AG	129,536	42	British American Tobacco	60,988	77	Auchan S.A.	40,983
8	Volkswagen AG	121,346	43	Deutsche Post	60,743	78	CNP Assurances	40,514
9	ING Groep	115,324	44	Deutsche Bank	60,631	79	Bayer AG	40,310
10	Samsung Group	101,459	45	BNP Paribas	60,495	80	Barclays PLC	40,016
11	NTT	100,990	46	BMW	60,473	81	Nokia	39,645
12	Carrefour SA	99,119	47	UBS AG	59,878	82	GlaxoSmithKline	39,032
13	Siemens AG	90,670	48	Prudential plc	59,685	83	AEGON N.V.	38,624
14	Hitachi, Ltd.	84,365	49	Zurich Financial Services	59,678	84	Mitsubishi	38,548
15	Fortis SA/NV	82,819	50	Repsol YPF	56,472	85	PETROBRAS	37,452
16	Matsushita	81,298	51	RWE	55,919	86	ALDI Group	37,000
17	Honda Motor	80,705	52	Renault S.A.	55,535	87	Gazprom	36,395
18	Assicurazioni Generali	79,882	53	Sojitz	55,487	88	Banco Santander Central Hispano	36,059
19	Eni S.p.A.	79,084	54	SUEZ S.A.	55,186	89	Deutsche Bahn	35,432
20	Deutsche Telekom	78,404	55	Robert Bosch	54,570	90	Centrica plc	35,255
21	Aviva plc	77,955	56	Unilever	54,413	91	BT Group	35,194
22	Peugeot	77,800	57	Toshiba	54,264	92	LUKOIL	33,845
23	METRO AG	76,942	58	HBOS plc	51,817	93	Tengelmann	33,840
24	Nestlé S.A.	76,660	59	BASF AG	51,573	94	Veolia Environnement	33,423
25	HSBC Holdings	70,860	60	Hyundai Motor	50,695	95	Canon Inc.	33,345
26	Ifi	70,762	61	Statoil ASA	50,332	96	PPR SA	33,026
27	Royal Ahold	70,439	62	Enel S.p.A.	49,428	97	Mitsui & Co.	32,951
28	Petróleos Mexicanos	70,110	63	Royal Bank of Scotland	48,729	98	RALLYE S.A.	32,511
29	Nissan Motor	70,087	64	ThyssenKrupp	48,489	99	Bouygues SA	31,920
30	Nippon Life Insurance	68,261	65	Tokyo Electric Power	45,946	100	Volvo	31,813
31	Legal & General Group	68,099	66	NEC Corporation	45,298			
32	Sony	66,912	67	NTT DoCoMo	45,184			
33	E.ON AG	66,515	68	ABN AMRO	45,139			
34	Fiat S.p.A.	66,140	69	Fujitsu Limited	45,123			
35	Tesco PLC	65,176	70	Japan Tobacco	43,782			

SOURCE: HOOVER'S, INC., DATABASE, DECEMBER 2005

The 100 Most Profitable Companies in
Hoover's Handbook of World Business 2006

Rank	Company	Net Income ($ mil.)	Rank	Company	Net Income ($ mil.)	Rank	Company	Net Income ($ mil.)
1	Royal Dutch/Shell	18,183	36	LUKOIL	4,248	71	SUEZ S.A.	2,444
2	BP p.l.c.	15,731	37	Banco Santander		72	Henkel KGaA	2,367
3	TOTAL S.A.	13,020		Central Hispano	4,247	73	National Australia Bank	2,311
4	HSBC Holdings	11,840	38	BBVA	4,193	74	Royal Bank of Canada	2,311
5	Toyota Motor	10,907	39	Statoil ASA	4,129	75	Robert Bosch	2,285
			40	Telefónica, S.A.	3,898			
6	Eni S.p.A.	9,854				76	AEGON N.V.	2,254
7	Royal Bank of Scotland	8,691	41	Mizuho Financial	3,853	77	Deutsche Post	2,166
8	GlaxoSmithKline	8,248	42	Philips Electronics	3,842	78	British American Tobacco	2,105
9	ING Groep	8,084	43	AstraZeneca	3,813	79	Norsk Hydro	2,081
10	Gazprom	7,227	44	France Telecom	3,771	80	Hutchison Whampoa	2,074
			45	POSCO	3,685			
11	UBS AG	7,088				81	KPN	2,047
12	NTT DoCoMo	6,972	46	Enel S.p.A.	3,666	82	Aviva plc	2,036
13	NTT	6,637	47	Peugeot	3,469	83	TeliaSonera	1,960
14	BHP Billiton	6,398	48	BT Group	3,442	84	Bank of Montreal	1,928
15	BNP Paribas	6,367	49	AXA	3,412	85	Toronto-Dominion Bank	1,895
			50	Telstra	3,377			
16	Deutsche Telekom	6,277				86	Carrefour SA	1,892
17	Barclays PLC	6,265	51	Deutsche Bank	3,349	87	Nippon Life Insurance	1,880
18	PETROBRAS	6,190	52	DaimlerChrysler	3,340	88	Electricité de France	1,829
19	Nestlé S.A.	5,935	53	Canon Inc.	3,301	89	Canadian Imperial Bank	
20	HBOS plc	5,888	54	BMW	3,031		of Commerce	1,804
			55	Allianz AG	2,979	90	SAP	1,775
21	E.ON AG	5,878						
22	Roche Holding	5,867	56	RWE	2,915	91	Imperial Oil	1,710
23	Novartis AG	5,767	57	Anglo American	2,913	92	Mitsubishi	1,696
24	Samsung Group	5,632	58	Ericsson	2,876	93	YPF, S.A.	1,653
25	ABN AMRO	5,566	59	Siemens AG	2,702	94	Hyundai Motor	1,610
			60	Centrica plc	2,662	95	Sony	1,531
26	Crédit Agricole	5,414						
27	L'Oréal SA	4,946	61	Repsol YPF	2,641	96	Gaz de France	1,507
28	Credit Suisse	4,932	62	Tesco PLC	2,621	97	Saint-Gobain	1,477
29	Renault S.A.	4,844	63	Petróleos de Venezuela S.A.	2,590	98	Allied Irish Banks	1,425
30	Nissan Motor	4,752	64	Zurich Financial Services	2,587	99	Tokyo Electric Power	1,416
			65	BASF AG	2,551	100	Volvo	1,414
31	Mittal Steel	4,701						
32	Fortis SA/NV	4,581	66	Unilever	2,541			
33	Honda Motor	4,536	67	Bank of China	2,527			
34	A.P. Møller - Mærsk	4,464	68	Munich Re	2,500			
35	Nokia	4,344	69	Telmex	2,498			
			70	Diageo plc	2,460			

SOURCE: HOOVER'S, INC., DATABASE, DECEMBER 2005

The 100 Most Valuable Public Companies in
Hoover's Handbook of World Business 2006

Rank	Company	Market Value* ($ mil.)	Rank	Company	Market Value ($ mil.)	Rank	Company	Market Value ($ mil.)
1	BP p.l.c.	209,520	36	Honda Motor	46,317	71	Alcatel	20,404
2	HSBC Holdings	190,238	37	Deutsche Bank	46,045	72	Infosys Technologies	19,949
3	Vodafone Group	181,620	38	ABN AMRO	45,297	73	Norsk Hydro	19,746
4	GlaxoSmithKline	140,694	39	Diageo plc	45,216	74	Cadbury Schweppes	19,529
5	TOTAL S.A.	139,500	40	PETROBRAS	43,620	75	Allied Irish Banks	18,957
6	Novartis AG	122,651	41	Sony	39,864	76	Alcan Inc.	18,141
7	Toyota Motor	121,540	42	BASF AG	38,922	77	Novo Nordisk	18,020
8	Sanofi-Aventis	113,053	43	British American Tobacco	37,072	78	Volvo	17,480
9	Eni S.p.A.	100,783	44	Anglo American	35,538	79	YPF, S.A.	17,306
10	Deutsche Telekom	95,211	45	Vivendi Universal	34,399	80	STMicroelectronics	17,232
11	Telefónica, S.A.	93,331	46	Statoil ASA	34,398	81	Fuji Photo Film	16,258
12	UBS AG	85,796	47	Philips Electronics	33,960	82	Imperial Tobacco Group	15,984
13	BHP Billiton	82,666	48	BT Group	33,623	83	Nortel Networks	14,826
14	France Telecom	81,619	49	Royal Bank of Canada	33,287	84	Veolia Environnement	14,814
15	NTT DoCoMo	77,506	50	Matsushita	33,243	85	Mitsui & Co.	14,575
16	Banco Santander Central Hispano	77,366	51	Repsol YPF	31,865	86	Scottish Power	14,550
17	Barclays PLC	73,705	52	National Australia Bank	30,395	87	Wipro Limited	14,367
18	Nokia	73,081	53	SUEZ S.A.	26,961	88	POSCO	14,339
19	Siemens AG	68,907	54	Nomura Holdings	26,906	89	Kyocera	13,394
20	ING Groep	66,693	55	Toronto-Dominion Bank	26,354	90	WPP Group	12,961
21	Telecom Italia	65,874	56	Millea Holdings	24,940	91	Stora Enso Oyj	12,479
22	NTT	65,292	57	Mittal Steel	24,843	92	Akzo Nobel	12,158
23	Enel S.p.A.	60,352	58	Bayer AG	24,817	93	Royal Ahold	12,077
24	BBVA	60,154	59	Danone	24,718	94	ABB Ltd.	11,718
25	E.ON AG	59,977	60	Bank of Montreal	23,677	95	NEC Corporation	11,614
26	AstraZeneca	59,862	61	Thomson Corporation	23,120	96	Energias de Portugal	11,054
27	SAP	55,882	62	Telmex	22,670	97	Reuters Group	10,276
28	Ericsson	50,800	63	BCE Inc.	22,343	98	Gallaher Group	9,943
29	Allianz AG	48,756	64	KPN	22,269	99	Pearson plc	9,768
30	DaimlerChrysler	48,666	65	BSkyB	22,092	100	Kirin Brewery	9,563
31	Nissan Motor	48,407	66	AEGON N.V.	21,287			
32	Telstra	48,155	67	Canadian Imperial Bank of Commerce	20,995			
33	Canon Inc.	48,121	68	Hitachi, Ltd.	20,926			
34	AXA	47,235	69	Imperial Oil	20,743			
35	Credit Suisse	46,865	70	Prudential plc	20,662			

*Market value at the latest available fiscal year-end

SOURCE: HOOVER'S, INC., DATABASE, DECEMBER 2005

The 100 Largest Employers in
Hoover's Handbook of World Business 2006

Rank	Company	Employees	Rank	Company	Employees	Rank	Company	Employees
1	Carrefour SA	430,695	36	Allianz AG	162,180	71	Jardine Matheson	100,000
2	Compass Group	402,375	37	Philips Electronics	161,586	72	RWE	97,777
3	DaimlerChrysler	384,723	38	SUEZ S.A.	160,700	73	ABN AMRO	97,276
4	Deutsche Post	346,410	39	Fiat S.p.A.	160,549	74	Sanofi-Aventis	96,439
5	Volkswagen AG	342,502	40	Fujitsu Limited	156,169	75	PPR SA	95,397
6	Tesco PLC	335,750	41	Electricité de France	156,152	76	BNP Paribas	94,900
7	Gazprom	332,800	42	Auchan S.A.	155,000	77	KPMG	93,983
8	Sodexho Alliance	312,975	43	J Sainsbury	154,900	78	Karstadt Quelle	92,546
9	METRO AG	261,438	44	George Weston	148,000	79	Telecom Italia	91,365
10	HSBC Holdings	253,000	45	Woolworths	140,000	80	Lufthansa	90,673
11	Deutsche Bahn	250,913	46	Petróleos Mexicanos	137,722	81	IKEA	90,000
12	Nestlé S.A.	247,000	47	Crédit Agricole	135,502	82	Danone	89,449
13	Deutsche Telekom	244,645	48	Renault S.A.	130,573	83	Schneider Electric	85,000
14	Robert Bosch	242,348	49	PricewaterhouseCoopers	130,203	84	Seiko Epson Corporation	84,899
15	SNCF	229,877	50	VINCI	128,000	85	Alcan Inc.	82,500
16	Unilever	223,000	51	Michelin	126,474	86	BASF AG	81,955
17	Tata Group	220,219	52	Royal Bank of Scotland	126,100	87	Novartis AG	81,392
18	Casino Guichard-Perrachon	212,603	53	RALLYE S.A.	124,223	88	Volvo	78,196
19	Anglo American	209,000	54	Nissan Motor	123,748	89	Barclays PLC	77,000
20	Peugeot	207,200	55	Deloitte	115,000	90	Bertelsmann	76,266
21	France Telecom	206,524	56	Bayer AG	113,825	91	InBev NV/SA	74,694
22	Royal Ahold	206,441	57	Bridgestone	113,699	92	BAE SYSTEMS	73,300
23	NTT	201,486	58	Bouygues SA	113,300	93	Fuji Photo Film	73,164
24	Samsung Group	195,000	59	ING Groep	113,039	94	Ricoh	73,137
25	ThyssenKrupp	187,678	60	Royal Dutch/Shell	112,000	95	Electrolux	72,382
26	Tengelmann	183,050	61	TOTAL S.A.	111,401	96	Air France	71,654
27	Hutchison Whampoa	182,000	62	EADS	110,662	97	Eni S.p.A.	71,497
28	Bank of China	181,894	63	Wal-Mart de México	109,057	98	Kingfisher plc	70,811
29	Saint-Gobain	181,228	64	Canon Inc.	108,257	99	Marks and Spencer	70,550
30	Ifi	179,790	65	Ernst & Young	106,650	100	Nippon Life Insurance	70,073
31	Coles Myer	176,108	66	BMW	105,972			
32	Telefónica, S.A.	173,554	67	BP p.l.c.	102,900			
33	Accor	168,619	68	ABB Ltd.	102,500			
34	Toshiba	165,000	69	BT Group	102,100			
35	Mittal Steel	164,393	70	GlaxoSmithKline	100,019			

SOURCE: HOOVER'S, INC., DATABASE, DECEMBER 2005

The 100 Fastest-Growing Companies in Five-Year Sales Growth in
Hoover's Handbook of World Business 2006

Rank	Company	Annual % Change*	Rank	Company	Annual % Change	Rank	Company	Annual % Change
1	Mitsubishi	68.5	36	TeliaSonera	21.2	71	San Miguel	15.1
2	Mitsui & Co.	64.1	37	Tesco PLC	21.1	72	Tata Group	15.0
3	Mittal Steel	44.5	38	POSCO	20.8	73	Millea Holdings	15.0
4	Atos Origin	41.5	39	Gazprom	20.2	74	IKEA	15.0
5	SABMiller plc	40.6	40	Securitas AB	20.1	75	Telstra	14.9
6	Hilton Group	40.4	41	Enel S.p.A.	19.8	76	METRO AG	14.9
7	Infosys Technologies	40.0	42	Novo Nordisk	19.7	77	SAS AB	14.8
8	Sanofi-Aventis	38.0	43	Deutsche Telekom	19.4	78	RALLYE S.A.	14.7
9	HBOS plc	35.0	44	France Telecom	19.1	79	SAP	14.7
10	Publicis Groupe	32.8	45	Deutsche Bahn	19.0	80	British American Tobacco	14.7
11	Vodafone Group	32.0	46	Rogers Communications	18.9	81	Eni S.p.A.	14.5
12	Aviva plc	31.7	47	Electricité de France	18.6	82	Ernst & Young	14.3
13	MOL	30.8	48	Hyundai Motor	18.5	83	SUEZ S.A.	14.1
14	MAN	30.2	49	Deutsche Post	18.5	84	National Australia Bank	14.0
15	Imperial Tobacco Group	30.1	50	Statoil ASA	18.0	85	Anglo American	13.9
16	A.P. Møller - Mærsk	30.1	51	Sinopec Shanghai Petrochemical	18.0	86	Munich Re	13.8
17	Wipro Limited	29.5	52	BP p.l.c.	17.8	87	Petróleos de Venezuela S.A.	13.6
18	BHP Billiton	29.4	53	VINCI	17.7	88	L'Oréal SA	13.5
19	Royal Bank of Scotland	28.8	54	Carlsberg A/S	17.3	89	George Weston	13.5
20	Alcan Inc.	28.4	55	Cadbury Schweppes	17.2	90	Reed Elsevier	13.3
21	Energias de Portugal	28.2	56	Peugeot	16.9	91	Wal-Mart de México	13.1
22	Compass Group	27.7	57	Fortis SA/NV	16.7	92	Toyota Motor	13.0
23	OMV	27.0	58	Auchan S.A.	16.7	93	Telecom Italia	13.0
24	LUKOIL	26.4	59	WPP Group	16.6	94	Carrefour SA	12.9
25	Koç Holding	26.1	60	BMW	16.1	95	Prudential plc	12.8
26	Formosa Plastics	24.9	61	Robert Bosch	16.1	96	VNU N.V.	12.8
27	Centrica plc	24.2	62	Crédit Agricole	15.8	97	Barclays PLC	12.8
28	BSkyB	24.1	63	Allianz AG	15.7	98	Lufthansa	12.8
29	EADS	24.1	64	Asahi Shimbun	15.6	99	SNCF	12.7
30	Hutchison Whampoa	24.0	65	Heineken	15.6	100	Saint-Gobain	12.6
31	Gaz de France	23.7	66	Bouygues SA	15.5			
32	Gallaher Group	23.6	67	Royal Dutch/Shell	15.5			
33	Volvo	23.2	68	Fuji Photo Film	15.3			
34	PKN ORLEN	22.7	69	Casino Guichard-Perrachon	15.2			
35	Porsche	22.1	70	CNP Assurances	15.2			

*These rates are compounded annualized increases, and may have resulted from
 acquisitions or one time gains. If less than 5 years of data are available, growth
 is for the years available.

SOURCE: HOOVER'S, INC., DATABASE, DECEMBER 2005

The 100 Fastest-Growing Companies in Five-Year Employment Growth in
Hoover's Handbook of World Business 2006

Rank	Company	Annual % Change*	Rank	Company	Annual % Change	Rank	Company	Annual % Change
1	Mittal Steel	74.3	36	Placer Dome	9.7	71	Kao Corporation	4.7
2	Royal Bank of Scotland	59.2	37	Tommy Hilfiger	9.6	72	Novartis AG	4.6
3	Mitsui & Co.	56.6	38	Volvo	9.6	73	NTT DoCoMo	4.6
4	Wipro Limited	49.9	39	Statoil ASA	9.2	74	Swatch Group	4.3
5	Millea Holdings	44.3	40	Rogers Communications	9.2	75	Kyocera	4.2
6	Gallaher Group	42.6	41	PETROBRAS	8.4	76	BNP Paribas	4.2
7	Infosys Technologies	39.1	42	Pioneer	8.1	77	Schneider Electric	4.2
8	Hutchison Whampoa	38.4	43	Allianz AG	7.9	78	Airbus S.A.S.	4.2
9	Sanofi-Aventis	34.8	44	Pearson plc	7.8	79	George Weston	4.1
10	Imperial Tobacco Group	33.5	45	SAP	7.6	80	Royal Bank of Canada	4.1
11	Japan Airlines	30.7	46	Electricité de France	7.4	81	LVMH	4.0
12	Publicis Groupe	22.5	47	Dentsu Inc.	7.1	82	Nippon Life Insurance	4.0
13	Alcan Inc.	22.2	48	Toyota Motor	7.0	83	Telefónica, S.A.	3.9
14	InBev NV/SA	21.6	49	SABMiller plc	6.9	84	Virgin Group	3.9
15	Casino Guichard-Perrachon	20.4	50	Koç Holding	6.9	85	AstraZeneca	3.9
16	VNU N.V.	20.4	51	Lufthansa	6.9	86	Accor	3.8
17	Seiko Epson Corporation	18.9	52	Carrefour SA	6.9	87	Qantas Airways	3.8
18	Fuji Photo Film	18.5	53	Ernst & Young	6.8	88	Nippon Steel	3.7
19	All Nippon Airways	17.9	54	IKEA	6.5	89	RALLYE S.A.	3.6
20	Asahi Shimbun	17.8	55	Deloitte	6.3	90	Gaz de France	3.5
21	Compass Group	17.5	56	CNP Assurances	6.3	91	Auchan S.A.	3.5
22	San Miguel	15.5	57	Porsche	5.8	92	Nikon	3.4
23	HBOS plc	15.1	58	Canon Inc.	5.7	93	STMicroelectronics	3.2
24	Atos Origin	14.7	59	EADS	5.6	94	BMW	3.1
25	Heineken	13.0	60	Royal Dutch/Shell	5.6	95	BBC	3.0
26	Veolia Environnement	12.9	61	adidas-Salomon	5.6	96	Coles Myer	2.9
27	Cadbury Schweppes	12.5	62	Robert Bosch	5.3	97	Woolworths	2.9
28	Centrica plc	11.3	63	Mitsubishi	5.3	98	METRO AG	2.8
29	Munich Re	10.5	64	Carlsberg A/S	5.0	99	Legal & General Group	2.8
30	Tesco PLC	10.5	65	Reed Elsevier	5.0	100	Bridgestone	2.7
31	HSBC Holdings	10.5	66	Samsung Group	4.9			
32	Crédit Agricole	10.5	67	Air France	4.9			
33	Novo Nordisk	10.2	68	Honda Motor	4.8			
34	Energias de Portugal	9.9	69	Tokyo Electric Power	4.7			
35	Wal-Mart de México	9.9	70	Peugeot	4.7			

*These rates are compounded annualized increases, and may have resulted from
acquisitions or one time gains. If less than 5 years of data are available, growth
is for the years available.

SOURCE: HOOVER'S, INC., DATABASE, DECEMBER 2005

Forbes' 100 Largest Public Companies by Market Value

Rank	Company	Country	Market Value* ($ mil.)	Rank	Company	Country	Market Value ($ mil.)
1	ExxonMobil	US	405,250	51	Nokia	Finland	73,140
2	General Electric	US	372,140	52	Comcast	US	72,060
3	Microsoft	US	273,750	53	Abbott Laboratories	US	71,620
4	Citigroup	US	247,660	54	Merck & Co	US	70,300
5	BP	UK	231,880	55	Barclays	UK	70,220
6	Royal Dutch/Shell Group	Netherlands/UK	221,490	56	Siemens Group	Germany	69,940
7	Wal-Mart Stores	US	218,560	57	Gazprom	Russia	69,900
8	Pfizer	US	197,990	58	Nippon Telegraph & Telephone	Japan	68,380
9	Johnson & Johnson	US	194,680	59	ING Group	Netherlands	68,040
10	Bank of America	US	188,770	60	Oracle	US	67,660
11	HSBC Group	UK	186,740	61	American Express	US	67,630
12	American International Group	US	173,990	62	Tyco International	Bermuda	67,400
13	Vodafone	UK	170,290	63	Unilever	Netherlands/UK	65,570
14	IBM	US	152,760	64	3M	US	64,930
15	Total	France	151,130	65	AstraZeneca	UK	64,740
16	Intel	US	149,390	66	Telecom Italia	Italy	64,690
17	Toyota Motor	Japan	140,890	67	BNP Paribas	France	64,390
18	GlaxoSmithKline	UK	140,390	68	China Mobile (HK)	Hong Kong/China	64,190
19	Berkshire Hathaway	US	138,740	69	Eli Lilly and Co	US	63,370
20	Altria Group	US	134,750	70	Medtronic	US	63,000
21	Procter & Gamble	US	133,920	71	HBOS	UK	62,130
22	ChevronTexaco	US	131,520	72	Morgan Stanley	US	61,410
23	JPMorgan Chase	US	129,980	73	Hewlett-Packard	US	60,480
24	Novartis Group	Switzerland	122,070	74	Mitsubishi Tokyo Financial	Japan	59,880
25	Sanofi-Aventis	France	113,150	75	UnitedHealth Group	US	59,580
26	Cisco Systems	US	112,600	76	Viacom	US	59,510
27	PetroChina	China	111,030	77	E.ON	Germany	59,440
28	Royal Bank of Scotland	UK	108,950	78	Qualcomm	US	59,330
29	Nestlé	Switzerland	108,040	79	Enel	Italy	58,860
30	Roche Group	Switzerland	107,990	80	BBVA-Banco Bilbao Vizcaya	Spain	58,830
31	ENI	Italy	104,710	81	Mizuho Financial	Japan	58,410
32	Coca-Cola	US	103,120	82	E.I. du Pont de Nemours	US	57,580
33	Wells Fargo	US	100,460	83	Walt Disney	US	57,200
34	Verizon Communications	US	99,640	84	eBay	US	56,800
35	Dell	US	99,600	85	Fannie Mae	US	56,580
36	BHP Billiton	Australia/UK	91,940	86	Rio Tinto	UK/Australia	56,340
37	Telefónica	Spain	91,440	87	U.S. Bancorp	US	55,260
38	PepsiCo	US	90,430	88	Merrill Lynch	US	54,580
39	UBS	Switzerland	89,160	89	Wyeth	US	54,460
40	Deutsche Telekom	Germany	88,090	90	Lloyds TSB Group	UK	52,780
41	Home Depot	US	87,880	91	Dow Chemical	US	52,590
42	United Parcel Service	US	86,850	92	Goldman Sachs Group	US	52,470
43	Wachovia	US	84,180	93	Telstra	Australia	51,960
44	SBC Communications	US	79,420	94	AXA Group	France	51,450
45	Time Warner	US	79,060	95	Google	US	51,400
46	Amgen	US	78,250	96	United Technologies	US	51,120
47	Banco Santander	Spain	77,700	97	L'Oréal Group	France	51,060
48	Samsung Electronics	South Korea	77,130	98	SAP	Germany	50,690
49	ConocoPhillips	US	76,540	99	News Corp	US	50,560
50	France Telecom	France	74,660	100	Honda Motor	Japan	49,940

*As of February 28, 2005.

SOURCE: *FORBES*, MARCH 31, 2005

The *FORTUNE* Global 500

Rank	Company	Country	2004 Sales ($ mil.)
1	Wal-Mart Stores	US	287,989.0
2	BP	UK	285,059.0
3	Exxon Mobil	US	270,772.0
4	Royal Dutch/Shell Group	UK/Netherlands	268,690.0
5	General Motors	US	193,517.0
6	DaimlerChrysler	Germany	176,687.5
7	Toyota Motor	Japan	172,616.3
8	Ford Motor	US	172,233.0
9	General Electric	US	152,866.0
10	Total	France	152,609.5
11	Chevron	US	147,967.0
12	ConocoPhillips	US	121,663.0
13	AXA	France	121,606.3
14	Allianz	Germany	118,937.2
15	Volkswagen	Germany	110,648.7
16	Citigroup	US	108,276.0
17	ING Group	Netherlands	105,886.4
18	Nippon Telegraph & Telephone	Japan	100,545.3
19	American International Group	US	97,987.0
20	IBM	US	96,293.0
21	Siemens	Germany	91,493.2
22	Carrefour	France	90,381.7
23	Hitachi	Japan	83,993.9
24	Assicurazioni Generali	Italy	83,267.6
25	Matsushita Electric Industrial	Japan	81,077.7
26	McKesson	US	80,514.6
27	Honda Motor	Japan	80,486.6
28	Hewlett-Packard	US	79,905.0
29	Nissan Motor	Japan	79,799.6
30	Fortis	Belgium/Netherlands	75,518.1
31	Sinopec	China	75,076.7
32	Berkshire Hathaway	US	74,382.0
33	ENI	Italy	74,227.7
34	Home Depot	US	73,094.0
35	Aviva	UK	73,025.2
36	HSBC Holdings	UK	72,550.0
37	Deutsche Telekom	Germany	71,988.9
38	Verizon Communications	US	71,563.3
39	Samsung Electronics	South Korea	71,555.9
40	State Grid	China	71,290.2
41	Peugeot	France	70,641.9
42	Metro	Germany	70,159.3
43	Nestlé	Switzerland	69,825.7
44	U.S. Postal Service	US	68,996.0
45	BNP Paribas	France	68,654.4
46	China National Petroleum	China	67,723.8
47	Sony	Japan	66,618.0
48	Cardinal Health	US	65,130.6
49	Royal Ahold	Netherlands	64,675.6
50	Altria Group	US	64,440.0
51	Pemex	Mexico	63,690.5
52	Bank of America Corp.	US	63,324.0
53	Vodafone	UK	62,971.4
54	Tesco	UK	62,458.7
55	Munich Re Group	Germany	60,705.5
56	Nippon Life Insurance	Japan	60,520.8
57	Fiat	Italy	59,972.9
58	Royal Bank of Scotland	UK	59,750.0
59	Zurich Financial Services	Switzerland	59,678.0
60	Crédit Agricole	France	59,053.8
61	Credit Suisse	Switzerland	58,825.0
62	State Farm Insurance Cos.	US	58,818.9
63	France Télécom	France	58,652.1
64	Électricité De France	France	58,367.2
65	J.P. Morgan Chase & Co.	US	56,931.0
66	UBS	Switzerland	56,917.8
67	Kroger	US	56,434.4
68	Deutsche Bank	Germany	55,669.5
69	E.ON	Germany	55,652.1
70	Deutsche Post	Germany	55,388.4
71	BMW	Germany	55,142.2
72	Toshiba	Japan	54,303.5
73	Valero Energy	US	53,918.6
74	AmerisourceBergen	US	53,179.0
75	Pfizer	US	52,921.0
76	Boeing	US	52,553.0
77	Procter & Gamble	US	51,407.0
78	RWE	Germany	50,951.9
79	Suez	France	50,670.1
80	Renault	France	50,639.7
81	Unilever	UK/Netherlands	49,960.7
82	Target	US	49,934.0
83	Robert Bosch	Germany	49,759.2
84	Dell	US	49,205.0
85	ThyssenKrupp	Germany	48,756.1
86	Costco Wholesale	US	48,107.0
87	HBOS	UK	47,755.7
88	Johnson & Johnson	US	47,348.0
89	Prudential	UK	47,055.8
90	Tokyo Electric Power	Japan	46,962.7
91	BASF	Germany	46,686.6
92	Hyundai Motor	South Korea	46,358.2
93	Enel	Italy	45,530.4
94	Marathon Oil	US	45,444.0
95	Statoil	Norway	45,440.0
96	NEC	Japan	45,175.5
97	Repsol YPF	Spain	44,857.5
98	Dai-ichi Mutual Life Insurance	Japan	44,468.8
99	Fujitsu	Japan	44,316.0
100	Time Warner	US	42,869.0

SOURCE: *FORTUNE*, JULY 25, 2005

Rank	Company	Country	2004 Sales ($ mil.)	Rank	Company	Country	2004 Sales ($ mil.)
101	ABN AMRO Holding	Netherlands	42,319.0	151	Merrill Lynch	US	32,467.0
102	SBC Communications	US	41,098.0	152	Société Générale	France	32,411.2
103	Tyco International	US	41,042.0	153	DZ Bank	Germany	32,261.9
104	Dow Chemical	US	40,161.0	154	Canon	Japan	32,071.5
105	Albertson's	US	40,052.0	155	Santander Central Hispano Group	Spain	31,803.6
106	Saint-Gobain	France	39,831.5	156	Mitsubishi Electric	Japan	31,735.4
107	Morgan Stanley	US	39,549.0	157	Nippon Steel	Japan	31,536.9
108	MetLife	US	39,535.0	158	Sumitomo Life Insurance	Japan	31,000.2
109	EADS	Netherlands	39,503.1	159	Walt Disney	US	30,752.0
110	Barclays	UK	39,347.2	160	Veolia Environnement	France	30,687.7
111	Telecom Italia	Italy	39,228.2	161	CVS	US	30,594.3
112	AEON	Japan	38,943.6	162	AT&T	US	30,537.0
113	Meiji Yasuda Life Insurance	Japan	38,835.1	163	Caterpillar	US	30,251.0
114	Telefónica	Spain	38,188.0	164	Franz Haniel	Germany	30,244.5
115	LG Electronics	South Korea	37,757.5	165	Groupe Pinault-Printemps	France	30,114.8
116	Royal Philips Electronics	Netherlands	37,709.6	166	Northrop Grumman	US	29,868.0
117	SK	South Korea	37,691.6	167	Goldman Sachs Group	US	29,839.0
118	Arcelor	Luxembourg	37,531.7	168	Deutsche Bahn	Germany	29,803.0
119	Walgreen	US	37,508.2	169	Foncière Euris	France	29,666.2
120	United Technologies	US	37,445.0	170	Indian Oil	India	29,643.2
121	Groupe Auchan	France	37,370.1	171	Sysco	US	29,335.4
122	GlaxoSmithKline	UK	37,304.2	172	PepsiCo	US	29,261.0
123	UnitedHealth Group	US	37,218.0	173	Groupe Caisse d'Épargne	France	29,174.9
124	Bayer	Germany	37,011.9	174	American Express	US	29,115.0
125	Petrobrás	Brazil	36,987.7	175	Bouygues	France	29,106.5
126	CNP Assurances	France	36,942.9	176	Swiss Reinsurance	Switzerland	29,045.1
127	Microsoft	US	36,835.0	177	Lloyds TSB Group	UK	28,925.0
128	United Parcel Service	US	36,582.0	178	Lukoil	Russia	28,810.0
129	Lowe's	US	36,464.0	179	Delphi	US	28,700.0
130	Nokia	Finland	36,401.2	180	Volvo	Sweden	28,643.1
131	Archer Daniels Midland	US	36,151.4	181	Rabobank	Netherlands	28,513.2
132	Sears Roebuck	US	36,099.0	182	J. Sainsbury	UK	28,427.8
133	Petronas	Malaysia	36,064.8	183	Prudential Financial	US	28,348.0
134	Safeway	US	35,822.9	184	Mizuho Financial Group	Japan	28,278.7
135	Lockheed Martin	US	35,526.0	185	Marubeni	Japan	28,273.7
136	Aegon	Netherlands	35,463.4	186	Novartis	Switzerland	28,247.0
137	Medco Health Solutions	US	35,351.9	187	Wachovia Corp.	US	28,067.0
138	Motorola	US	35,349.0	188	DuPont	US	27,995.0
139	OAO Gazprom	Russia	35,089.5	189	A.P. Møller-Mærsk Group	Denmark	27,920.7
140	BT	UK	34,672.7	190	SNCF	France	27,436.1
141	Intel	US	34,209.0	191	Best Buy	US	27,433.0
142	Nippon Oil	Japan	34,150.7	192	Sprint	US	27,428.0
143	Allstate	US	33,936.0	193	New York Life Insurance	US	27,175.5
144	Wells Fargo	US	33,876.0	194	KDDI	Japan	27,170.1
145	Ito-Yokado	Japan	33,631.9	195	HVB Group	Germany	27,140.1
146	Centrica	UK	33,536.9	196	Viacom	US	27,054.8
147	Sumitomo Mitsui Financial Group	Japan	33,318.2	197	Millea Holdings	Japan	26,978.7
148	Mitsui	Japan	32,805.9	198	International Paper	US	26,722.0
149	Mitsubishi	Japan	32,735.0	199	Vivendi Universal	France	26,651.3
150	Freddie Mac	US	32,564.0	200	Johnson Controls	US	26,553.4

Rank	Company	Country	2004 Sales ($ mil.)	Rank	Company	Country	2004 Sales ($ mil.)
201	Tyson Foods	US	26,441.0	251	Samsung Life Insurance	South Korea	22,347.9
202	JFE Holdings	Japan	26,087.6	252	William Morrison Supermarkets	UK	22,264.3
203	Denso	Japan	26,052.7	253	Mittal Steel	Netherlands	22,197.0
204	Caremark Rx	US	25,801.1	254	Cisco Systems	US	22,045.0
205	J.C. Penney	US	25,678.0	255	Suzuki Motor	Japan	22,010.9
206	Honeywell International	US	25,601.0	256	Endesa	Spain	21,969.8
207	Ingram Micro	US	25,462.1	257	Coca-Cola	US	21,962.0
208	Bunge	US	25,168.0	258	ABB	Switzerland	21,886.0
209	Roche Group	Switzerland	25,166.3	258	Bristol-Myers Squibb	US	21,886.0
210	Vinci	France	25,106.3	260	Hilton Group	UK	21,792.5
211	Mazda Motor	Japan	25,081.4	261	Legal & General Group	UK	21,769.8
212	China Life Insurance	China	24,980.6	262	China Telecommunications	China	21,561.8
213	Anglo American	UK	24,930.0	263	T&D Holdings	Japan	21,556.9
214	Alcan	Canada	24,885.0	264	UFJ Holdings	Japan	21,450.8
215	FedEx	US	24,710.0	265	Adecco	Switzerland	21,441.2
216	Norsk Hydro	Norway	24,552.9	266	Idemitsu Kosan	Japan	21,434.9
217	Mitsubishi Tokyo Financial Group	Japan	24,457.5	267	AstraZeneca	UK	21,426.0
218	Almanij	Belgium	24,401.1	268	Banco Bilbao Vizcaya Argentaria	Spain	21,335.5
219	Kansai Electric Power	Japan	24,317.7	269	National Australia Bank	Australia	21,313.9
220	British American Tobacco	UK	24,201.3	270	Lehman Brothers Holdings	US	21,250.0
221	Mitsubishi Heavy Industries	Japan	24,106.0	271	Bertelsmann	Germany	21,163.8
222	Air France-KLM Group	France	24,011.3	272	Compass Group	UK	21,103.8
223	Alcoa	US	23,960.0	273	Lufthansa Group	Germany	21,100.4
224	China Mobile Communications	China	23,957.6	274	Electronic Data Systems	US	21,033.0
225	Sharp	Japan	23,632.6	275	Plains All American Pipeline	US	20,975.5
226	East Japan Railway	Japan	23,610.5	276	POSCO	South Korea	20,929.1
227	Fuji Photo Film	Japan	23,516.4	277	Korea Electric Power	South Korea	20,914.2
228	HCA	US	23,502.0	278	Old Mutual	UK	20,892.1
229	Industrial & Commercial Bank of China	China	23,444.6	279	Manulife Financial	Canada	20,855.4
230	TIAA-CREF	US	23,411.3	280	Wellpoint	US	20,815.1
231	TUI	Germany	23,293.9	281	Landesbank Baden-Württemberg	Germany	20,807.5
232	RAG	Germany	23,254.9	282	News Corp.	US	20,802.0
233	La Poste	France	23,229.7	283	Magna International	Canada	20,653.0
234	Sunoco	US	23,226.0	284	Nationwide	US	20,558.0
235	Coles Myer	Australia	23,184.4	285	Abbott Laboratories	US	20,473.1
236	Massachusetts Mutual Life Ins.	US	23,159.2	286	Halliburton	US	20,466.0
237	Sanyo Electric	Japan	23,118.8	287	Sinochem	China	20,380.7
238	George Weston	Canada	23,015.4	288	Mitsubishi Chemical	Japan	20,372.3
239	Merck	US	22,938.6	289	Woolworths	Australia	20,334.5
240	St. Paul Travelers Cos.	US	22,934.0	290	Comcast	US	20,307.0
241	BHP Billiton	Australia	22,887.0	291	Dexia Group	Belgium	20,292.0
242	Delhaize Group	Belgium	22,793.0	292	Raytheon	US	20,245.0
243	Duke Energy	US	22,779.0	293	Groupama	France	20,237.2
244	BellSouth	US	22,729.0	294	Michelin	France	20,148.2
245	Hartford Financial Services	US	22,693.0	295	3M	US	20,011.0
246	Weyerhaeuser	US	22,665.0	296	Deere	US	19,986.1
247	MCI	US	22,615.0	297	Cendant	US	19,979.0
248	UES of Russia	Russia	22,602.9	298	Aetna	US	19,904.1
249	Gaz de France	France	22,548.2	299	Georgia-Pacific	US	19,876.0
250	Bridgestone	Japan	22,350.0	300	Chubu Electric Power	Japan	19,849.0

Rank	Company	Country	2004 Sales ($ mil.)	Rank	Company	Country	2004 Sales ($ mil.)
301	Japan Airlines	Japan	19,817.8	351	Groupe Danone	France	17,039.5
302	Tech Data	US	19,790.3	352	SHV Holdings	Netherlands	17,022.7
303	Liberty Mutual Insurance Group	US	19,754.0	353	Daiei	Japan	17,020.5
304	Mitsubishi Motors	Japan	19,750.4	354	Aisin Seiki	Japan	17,018.9
305	AutoNation	US	19,734.1	355	Lear	US	16,960.0
306	Kmart Holding	US	19,701.0	356	Ricoh	Japan	16,879.7
307	Sara Lee	US	19,566.0	357	Rite Aid	US	16,816.4
308	General Dynamics	US	19,552.0	358	Sun Life Financial Services	Canada	16,705.8
309	Shanghai Baosteel Group	China	19,543.3	359	BAE Systems	UK	16,664.9
310	Supervalu	US	19,543.2	360	Royal & Sun Alliance	UK	16,536.7
311	UniCredito Italiano	Italy	19,527.8	361	Royal Mail Holdings	UK	16,522.8
312	Royal Bank of Canada	Canada	19,103.8	362	Skanska	Sweden	16,508.2
313	Sumitomo	Japan	19,068.1	363	Bayerische Landesbank	Germany	16,435.1
314	McDonald's	US	19,064.7	364	Electrolux	Sweden	16,424.9
315	China Construction Bank	China	19,047.9	365	Dior (Christian)	France	16,418.9
316	China Southern Power Grid	China	18,928.8	366	UAL	US	16,391.0
317	Otto Group	Germany	18,870.3	367	Migros	Switzerland	16,338.4
318	Nippon Mining Holdings	Japan	18,817.0	368	Nippon Express	Japan	16,314.0
319	Mitsui Sumitomo Insurance	Japan	18,813.3	369	Alliance Unichem	UK	16,304.7
320	Japan Tobacco	Japan	18,739.0	370	Gap	US	16,267.0
321	Sanofi-Aventis	France	18,709.9	371	Hon Hai Precision Industry	Taiwan	16,239.5
322	Publix Super Markets	US	18,686.4	372	Sumitomo Electric Industries	Japan	16,192.0
323	Power Corp. of Canada	Canada	18,683.8	373	PTT	Thailand	16,023.3
324	Visteon	US	18,657.0	374	Washington Mutual	US	15,962.0
325	AMR	US	18,645.0	375	Flextronics International	Singapore	15,908.2
326	MAN Group	Germany	18,590.5	376	Banco Bradesco	Brazil	15,899.0
327	Itochu	Japan	18,527.9	377	Taisei	Japan	15,892.0
328	Commerzbank	Germany	18,463.6	378	Computer Sciences	US	15,849.1
329	Swiss Life	Switzerland	18,434.8	379	Bombardier	Canada	15,839.0
330	Goodyear Tire & Rubber	US	18,370.4	380	Akzo Nobel	Netherlands	15,780.8
331	Sabic	Saudi Arabia	18,329.4	381	Xerox	US	15,722.0
332	ConAgra Foods	US	18,178.7	382	National Grid Transco	UK	15,720.2
333	Cigna	US	18,176.0	383	TNT	Netherlands	15,714.9
334	Coca-Cola Enterprises	US	18,158.0	384	Kajima	Japan	15,700.6
335	Banca Intesa	Italy	18,155.2	385	Continental	Germany	15,668.2
336	L'Oréal	France	18,076.7	386	Cepsa	Spain	15,650.0
337	Japan Post	Japan	18,006.4	387	Federated Department Stores	US	15,630.0
338	L.M. Ericsson	Sweden	17,966.1	388	Emerson Electric	US	15,615.0
339	Bank Of China	China	17,960.4	389	Koc Holding	Turkey	15,578.8
340	Lafarge	France	17,954.9	390	Mediceo Holdings	Japan	15,499.9
341	Wolseley	UK	17,816.5	391	Vattenfall	Sweden	15,433.1
342	Northwestern Mutual	US	17,806.3	392	Stora Enso	Finland	15,417.4
343	KarstadtQuelle	Germany	17,782.2	393	Hanwha	South Korea	15,406.3
344	Sompo Japan Insurance	Japan	17,677.1	394	Kimberly-Clark	US	15,400.9
345	Lagardère Groupe	France	17,384.3	395	Premcor	US	15,334.8
346	Wyeth	US	17,358.0	396	Cosmo Oil	Japan	15,296.5
347	Hutchison Whampoa	China	17,280.8	397	Agricultural Bank of China	China	15,284.6
348	Alstom	France	17,194.8	398	CRH	Ireland	15,273.5
349	Amerada Hess	US	17,126.0	399	Alcatel	France	15,254.7
350	Corus Group	UK	17,099.2	400	KFW Bankengruppe	Germany	15,218.9

Rank	Company	Country	2004 Sales ($ mil.)
401	Telstra	Australia	15,193.1
402	Chinese Petroleum	Taiwan	15,189.5
403	William Hill	UK	15,185.7
404	Gasunie	Netherlands	15,117.2
405	Express Scripts	US	15,114.7
406	Commonwealth Bank of Australia	Australia	15,083.9
407	Hochtief	Germany	15,066.3
408	Delta Air Lines	US	15,002.0
409	Tohoku Electric Power	Japan	14,994.2
410	Nippon Yusen	Japan	14,944.3
411	Anheuser-Busch	US	14,934.2
412	Manpower	US	14,930.0
413	TJX	US	14,913.5
414	KT	South Korea	14,901.1
415	San Paolo IMI	Italy	14,899.0
416	BCE	Canada	14,841.5
417	Reliance Industries	India	14,841.0
418	Royal KPN	Netherlands	14,828.1
419	Banco Do Brasil	Brazil	14,768.5
420	U.S. Bancorp	US	14,705.7
421	Marks & Spencer	UK	14,652.6
422	AMP	Australia	14,600.8
423	Loews	US	14,584.2
424	Exelon	US	14,515.0
425	Fortum	Finland	14,508.5
426	CFE	Mexico	14,465.0
427	Staples	US	14,448.4
428	May Department Stores	US	14,441.0
429	Bharat Petroleum	India	14,436.9
430	Edeka Zentrale	Germany	14,418.5
431	British Airways	UK	14,414.1
432	GUS	UK	14,366.1
433	American Electric Power	US	14,357.0
434	COFCO	China	14,189.4
435	ACS	Spain	14,152.9
436	Hindustan Petroleum	India	14,114.9
437	United States Steel	US	14,108.0
438	Kingfisher	UK	14,060.9
439	Countrywide Financial	US	14,050.7
440	Dominion Resources	US	13,980.0
441	Eurohypo	Germany	13,952.5
442	Samsung	South Korea	13,919.2
443	Sodexho Alliance	France	13,899.8
444	Isuzu Motors	Japan	13,897.2
445	Eli Lilly	US	13,857.9
446	SK Networks	South Korea	13,844.3
447	Eastman Kodak	US	13,829.0
448	China First Automotive Works	China	13,825.4
449	AREVA	France	13,816.9
450	Shimizu	Japan	13,811.2
451	Qwest Communications	US	13,809.0
452	Progressive	US	13,782.1
453	Seiko Epson	Japan	13,768.6
454	Oil & Natural Gas	India	13,751.7
455	Accenture	US	13,673.6
456	Asahi Glass	Japan	13,647.8
457	Onex	Canada	13,614.8
458	Nordea Bank	Sweden	13,580.6
459	Office Depot	US	13,564.7
460	WestLB	Germany	13,548.3
461	Fuji Heavy Industries	Japan	13,459.2
462	Kobe Steel	Japan	13,433.8
463	Nextel Communications	US	13,368.0
464	Komatsu	Japan	13,350.3
465	AFLAC	US	13,281.0
466	OfficeMax	US	13,270.2
467	Dai Nippon Printing	Japan	13,258.6
468	Whirlpool	US	13,220.0
469	Chubb	US	13,177.2
470	Henkel	Germany	13,173.9
471	Toppan Printing	Japan	13,152.9
472	Central Japan Railway	Japan	13,114.9
473	Kyushu Electric Power	Japan	13,107.8
474	Humana	US	13,104.3
475	Obayashi	Japan	13,069.7
476	FirstEnergy	US	12,949.0
477	Westpac Banking	Australia	12,943.3
478	Solectron	US	12,903.2
479	Schneider Electric	France	12,892.0
480	Danske Bank Group	Denmark	12,890.3
481	Centex	US	12,859.7
482	Iberdrola	Spain	12,828.8
483	Asahi Kasei	Japan	12,819.0
484	Williams	US	12,814.7
485	Thales Group	France	12,796.3
486	Sekisui House	Japan	12,719.5
487	Daiwa House Industry	Japan	12,709.4
488	Canadian Imperial Bank of Commerce	Canada	12,661.8
489	Scottish Power	UK	12,635.2
490	Australia & New Zealand Banking	Australia	12,618.4
491	Texas Instruments	US	12,580.0
492	Constellation Energy	US	12,549.7
493	Waste Management	US	12,516.0
494	Bank of Nova Scotia	Canada	12,504.2
495	Tenet Healthcare	US	12,496.0
496	Yamaha Motor	Japan	12,471.5
497	Heineken	Netherlands	12,443.8
498	SCA (Svenska Cellulosa)	Sweden	12,433.4
499	EnCana	Canada	12,433.0
500	Masco	US	12,431.0

Business Week's Information Technology 100

Rank	Company	Country	Revenue ($ mil.)	Rank	Company	Country	Revenue ($ mil.)
1	América Móvil	Mexico	11,940.3	51	CACI	US	1,551.6
2	Hon Hai	Taiwan	16,237.0	52	Intel	US	35,552.0
3	LG Electronics	Korea	37,773.2	53	Cisco Systems	US	24,146.0
4	Google	US	3,794.1	54	Deutsche Telekom	Germany	71,987.6
5	Samsung	Korea	71,584.8	55	VimpelCom	Russia	2,146.6
6	Apple Computer	US	11,097.0	56	China Telecom	China	19,465.8
7	Dell	US	51,051.0	57	EMC	US	8,601.0
8	Mobile Telesystems	Russia	3,887.0	58	SAP	Germany	9,674.7
9	Nextel Communications	US	13,873.0	59	ASML Holding	Netherlands	3,393.8
10	Infosys	India	1,592.0	60	Amphenol	US	1,584.6
11	High Tech Computer	Taiwan	1,068.8	61	NCR	US	6,037.0
12	Tata Consultancy	India	2,167.9	62	Canon	Japan	33,697.9
13	BT Group	UK	34,356.1	63	Qualcomm	US	5,213.0
14	Turkcell	Turkey	3,353.2	64	Atos Origin	France	6,594.3
15	Telefónica Móviles	Spain	16,191.6	65	Applied Materials	US	8,081.3
16	Telefónica	Spain	39,654.3	66	Texas Instruments	US	12,616.0
17	China Mobile (Hong Kong)	Hong Kong	23,229.2	67	MiTAC International	Taiwan	1,782.1
18	Nokia	Finland	38,284.6	68	Taiwan Semiconductor Mfg.	Taiwan	7,730.4
19	Bharti Tele-Ventures	India	1,790.7	69	First Data	US	10,234.7
20	Telekom. Indonesia	Indonesia	3,802.2	70	Telus	Canada	6,074.7
21	Western Wireless	US	1,991.5	71	L-3	US	7,337.9
22	Acer	Taiwan	6,745.9	72	Anteon	US	1,330.0
23	Wipro	India	1,865.0	73	LG TeleCom	Korea	2,803.1
24	Nextel Partners	US	1,466.4	74	Research In Motion	Canada	1,350.4
25	Teléfonos de México	Mexico	12,299.7	75	SRA International	US	821.6
26	Novatek Microelectronics	Taiwan	524.7	76	Logitech	Switzerland	1,482.6
27	Microsoft	US	38,919.0	77	Network Appliance	US	1,598.1
28	NII Holdings	US	1,362.4	78	Advantest	Japan	2,229.5
29	Asustek Computer	Taiwan	7,496.2	79	Chi Mei Optoelectronics	Taiwan	3,534.8
30	Western Digital	US	3,447.2	80	ZTE	China	2,562.2
31	Accenture	Bermuda	16,144.5	81	Activision	US	1,405.9
32	Cognizant	US	648.6	82	VeriSign	US	1,338.3
33	Autodesk	US	1,291.5	83	Ingram Micro	US	26,238.4
34	Yahoo!	US	3,990.5	84	Flserv	US	3,794.0
35	LM Ericsson	Sweden	18,724.7	85	Satyam Computer Services	India	793.6
36	TPV Technology	Bermuda	3,738.2	86	KT Freetel	Korea	5,190.4
37	Lam Research	US	1,478.3	87	Tokyo Electron	Japan	5,919.3
38	Oracle	US	10,997.0	88	BenQ	Taiwan	5,238.7
39	MEMC Electronic Materials	US	1,057.1	89	Marvell Technology	Bermuda	1,319.8
40	Motorola	US	32,043.0	90	ATI Technologies	Canada	2,285.7
41	Verizon Communications	US	72,406.0	91	CommScope	US	1,226.7
42	NIDEC	Japan	4,524.0	92	Nikon	Japan	5,944.9
43	Lite-On Technology	Taiwan	6,432.2	93	Compal Electronics	Taiwan	6,889.2
44	IBM	US	97,026.0	94	SunGard	US	3,661.7
45	France Telecom	France	58,651.0	95	Harris	US	2,901.5
46	Adobe Systems	US	1,716.2	96	Hoya	Japan	2,869.5
47	KT	Korea	16,489.6	97	Anixter	US	3,387.5
48	Powerchip Semiconductor	Taiwan	1,721.9	98	KLA-Tencor	US	2,043.7
49	Telecom Cp New Zealand	New Zealand	3,784.6	99	Symantec	US	2,582.8
50	Seagate	Cayman Islands	6,710.0	100	SanDisk	US	1,841.1

Note: Rank based on shareholder return, return on equity, revenue growth, and total revenue (revenue for the most recent four quarters available; most recent FY for those companies that do not report quarterly results).

SOURCE: *BUSINESSWEEK*, JUNE 20, 2005

The World's 100 Largest Public Financial Companies

Rank	Company	Country	Assets* ($ mil.)	Rank	Company	Country	Assets ($ mil.)
1	UBS	Switzerland	1,520,191	51	AEGON	Netherlands	323,071
2	Citigroup	US	1,484,101	52	Nomura Holding	Japan	321,664
3	Allianz	Germany	1,347,418	53	Toronto-Dominion Bank	Canada	309,296
4	Mizuho Financial Group	Japan	1,330,323	54	Washington Mutual	US	307,918
5	HSBC Holdings	UK	1,276,778	55	National Australia Bank	Australia	299,186
6	Crédit Agricole	France	1,244,848	56	Munich Re	Germany	292,975
7	BNP Paribas	France	1,235,699	57	Legal & General Group	UK	292,079
8	ING Groep	Netherlands	1,173,356	58	Sanpaolo Imi	Italy	285,850
9	JPMorgan Chase	US	1,157,248	59	Bank of Nova Scotia	Canada	265,948
10	Deutsche Bank	Germany	1,137,956	60	Hartford Financial Services Group	US	259,735
11	Royal Bank of Scotland	UK	1,123,874	61	Bear Stearns Companies	US	255,950
12	Bank of America	US	1,110,457	62	Bank of Montreal	Canada	251,980
13	Mitsubishi UFJ Financial Group	Japan	1,011,578	63	Commonwealth Bank of Australia	Australia	250,560
14	Fannie Mae	US	1,009,569	64	CNP Assurances	France	248,538
15	Barclays	UK	1,000,949	65	Skandinaviska Enskilda Banken	Sweden	240,607
16	Sumitomo Mitsui Financial Group	Japan	967,569	66	Canadian Imperial Bank of Commerce	Canada	237,445
17	Credit Suisse Group	Switzerland	954,716	67	Crédit Industriel et Commercial	France	233,439
18	HBOS	UK	853,077	68	DEPFA BANK	Ireland	218,361
19	ABN AMRO Holding	Netherlands	824,441	69	Svenska Handelsbanken	Sweden	203,982
20	Société Générale	France	819,885	70	Westpac Banking Corporation	Australia	198,088
21	American International Group	US	798,660	71	U.S. Bancorp	US	195,104
22	Freddie Mac	US	795,284	72	American Express	US	192,638
23	Banco Santander Central Hispano	Spain	779,434	73	Erste Bank	Austria	190,526
24	Fortis	Belgium	778,364	74	Natexis Banques Populaires	France	190,031
25	Morgan Stanley	US	775,410	75	Berkshire Hathaway	US	188,874
26	General Electric	US	750,330	76	Australia and New Zealand Banking	Australia	188,648
27	AXA	France	651,510	77	Capitalia	Italy	181,114
28	Merrill Lynch & Co	US	648,059	78	Banca Monte dei Paschi di Siena	Italy	176,458
29	HVB Group	Germany	637,545	79	Deutsche Postbank	Germany	174,885
30	Commerzbank	Germany	579,535	80	Kookmin Bank	South Korea	171,516
31	Lloyds TSB Group	UK	536,515	81	Bank of Ireland	Ireland	163,872
32	Goldman Sachs Group	US	531,379	82	Swiss Reinsurance	Switzerland	162,999
33	Dexia NV/SA	Belgium	530,807	83	ERGO Versicherungsgruppe	Germany	160,079
34	Wachovia	US	493,324	84	SunTrust Banks	US	158,870
35	Aviva	UK	447,399	85	Allianz	Germany	157,799
36	Wells Fargo	US	427,849	86	FöreningsSparbanken	Sweden	154,293
37	Banco Bilbao Vizcaya Argentaria	Spain	425,819	87	Manulife Financial	Canada	153,551
38	Prudential Financial	US	401,058	88	Allstate	US	149,725
39	Royal Bank of Canada	Canada	397,637	89	Swiss Life Holding	Switzerland	146,319
40	KBC Group	Belgium	384,668	90	Sumitomo Trust and Banking	Japan	145,506
41	Danske Bank	Denmark	380,989	91	State Bank of India	India	143,567
42	Resona Holdings	Japan	377,143	92	Standard Chartered	UK	141,688
43	Nordea Bank	Sweden	376,519	93	National City Corporation	US	139,280
44	Banca Intesa	Italy	374,552	94	Shinhan Financial Group	South Korea	138,642
45	UniCredit	Italy	362,626	95	Allied Irish Banks	Ireland	138,494
46	Lehman Brothers Holdings	US	357,168	96	Assurances Générales de France	France	130,954
47	MetLife	US	356,808	97	Countrywide Financial	US	128,496
48	Zurich Financial Services	Switzerland	346,083	98	Old Mutual	UK	127,630
49	Prudential	UK	334,628	99	Woori Finance Holdings	South Korea	126,475
50	Assicurazioni Generali	Italy	326,115	100	T&D Holdings	Japan	124,097

*Assets at the latest available fiscal year-end

SOURCE: HOOVER'S INC. DATABASE, JANUARY 2006

The World's Top 20 Electronics Companies

Rank	Company	Electronics Revenue ($ mil.)	Total Revenue ($ mil.)
1	IBM	96,293	96,293
2	Hewlett-Packard	81,845	81,845
3	Matsushita Electric Industrial	80,435	80,435
4	Siemens	56,607	95,944
5	Samsung Electronics	56,197	56,197
6	Dell	49,205	49,205
7	Hitachi	47,021	83,966
8	NEC	46,703	46,703
9	Fujitsu	45,123	45,123
10	Sony	43,913	69,703
11	Nokia	39,932	39,932
12	Microsoft	38,474	38,474
13	Toshiba	38,027	52,816
14	Intel	34,209	34,209
15	Motorola	31,323	31,323
16	Canon	29,677	33,345
17	Philips Electronics	28,957	41,367
18	Ingram Micro	25,462	25,462
19	LG Electronics	24,045	24,045
20	Cisco Systems	23,579	23,579

*For the four quarters ending closest to December 31, 2004

SOURCE: *ELECTRONIC BUSINESS*, AUGUST 1, 2005

The World's Top 20 Motor Vehicle and Parts Manufacturers

Rank	Company	Country	2004 Revenue ($ mil.)
1	General Motors	US	193,517
2	DaimlerChrysler	Germany	176,688
3	Toyota Motor	Japan	172,616
4	Ford Motor	US	172,233
5	Volkswagen	Germany	110,649
6	Honda Motor	Japan	80,487
7	Nissan Motor	Japan	79,800
8	Peugeot	France	70,642
9	Fiat	Italy	59,973
10	BMW	Germany	55,142
11	Renault	France	50,640
12	Robert Bosch	Germany	49,759
13	Hyundai Motor	South Korea	46,358
14	Delphi	US	28,700
15	Volvo	Sweden	28,643
16	Johnson Controls	US	26,553
17	Denso	Japan	26,053
18	Mazda Motor	Japan	25,081
19	Bridgestone	Japan	22,350
20	Suzuki Motor	Japan	22,011

SOURCE: *FORTUNE*, JULY 25, 2005

The World's Top 20 Telecommunications Companies

Rank	Company	Country	2004 Revenue ($ mil.)
1	Nippon Telegraph & Telephone	Japan	100,545
2	Deutsche Telekom	Germany	71,989
3	Verizon Communications	US	71,563
4	Vodafone	UK	62,971
5	France Télécom	France	58,652
6	SBC Communications	US	41,098
7	Telecom Italia	Italy	39,228
8	Telefónica	Spain	38,188
9	BT	UK	34,673
10	AT&T	US	30,537
11	Sprint	US	27,428
12	KDDI	Japan	27,170
13	Vivendi Universal	France	26,651
14	China Mobile Communications	China	23,958
15	BellSouth	US	22,729
16	MCI	US	22,615
17	China Telecommunications	China	21,562
18	Comcast	US	20,307
19	Telstra	Australia	15,193
20	KT	South Korea	14,901

SOURCE: *FORTUNE*, JULY 25, 2005

The World's Top 20 Marketing Organizations

Rank	Company	Headquarters	Revenue ($ mil.)
1	Omnicom Group	New York	9,747.2
2	WPP Group	London	9,370.1
3	Interpublic Group of Cos.	New York	6,200.6
4	Publicis Groupe	Paris	4,777.3
5	Dentsu	Tokyo	2,851.0
6	Havas	Suresnes, France	1,866.0
7	Aegis Group	London	1,373.6
8	Hakuhodo DY Holdings	Tokyo	1,372.4
9	Asatsu-DK	Tokyo	473.3
10	Carlson Marketing Group	Minneapolis	346.9
11	MDC Partners	Toronto/New York	316.8
12	Incepta Group	London	279.8
13	Monster Worldwide	New York	251.6
14	Digitas	Boston	251.6
15	HealthSTAR Communications	Woodbridge, NJ	203.0
16	Alloy	New York	194.1
17	Cheil Communications	Seoul	185.9
18	Aspen Marketing Services	West Chicago, IL	180.0
18	G2R	Seoul	180.0
20	Tokyu Agency	Tokyo	176.0

SOURCE: *ADVERTISING AGE*, May 2, 2005

The World's Top 10 Aerospace and Defense Companies

Rank	Company	Country	2004 Revenue ($ mil.)
1	Boeing	US	52,553
2	EADS	Netherlands	39,503
3	United Technologies	US	37,445
4	Lockheed Martin	US	35,526
5	Northrop Grumman	US	29,868
6	Honeywell Intl.	US	25,601
7	Raytheon	US	20,245
8	General Dynamics	US	19,552
9	BAE Systems	UK	16,665
10	Bombardier	Canada	15,839

SOURCE: *FORTUNE*, JULY 25, 2005

The World's Top 10 Petroleum Refining Companies

Rank	Company	Country	2004 Revenue ($ mil.)
1	BP	UK	285,059
2	Exxon Mobil	US	270,772
3	Royal Dutch/Shell Group	UK/Netherlands	268,690
4	Total	France	152,610
5	Chevron	US	147,967
6	ConocoPhillips	US	121,663
7	Sinopec	China	75,077
8	ENI	Italy	74,228
9	China National Petroleum	China	67,724
10	Valero Energy	US	53,919

SOURCE: *FORTUNE*, JULY 25, 2005

The World's Top 10 Energy Companies

Rank	Company	Country	2004 Revenue ($ mil.)
1	E.ON	Germany	55,652
2	RWE	Germany	50,952
3	Suez	France	50,670
4	OAO Gazprom	Russia	35,090
5	Duke Energy	US	22,779
6	Plains All American Pipeline	US	20,976
7	Gasunie	Netherlands	15,117
8	American Electric Power	US	14,357
9	AREVA	France	13,817
10	Williams	US	12,815

SOURCE: *FORTUNE*, JULY 25, 2005

The World's Top 10 Electric and Gas Utilities

Rank	Company	Country	2004 Revenue ($ mil.)
1	State Grid	China	71,290
2	Électricité De France	France	58,367
3	Tokyo Electric Power	Japan	46,963
4	Enel	Italy	45,530
5	Centrica	UK	33,537
6	Veolia Environnement	France	30,688
7	Kansai Electric Power	Japan	24,318
8	UES of Russia	Russia	22,603
9	Gaz de France	France	22,548
10	Endesa	Spain	21,970

SOURCE: *FORTUNE*, JULY 25, 2005

The World's Top 10 Pharmaceutical Companies

Rank	Company	Country	2004 Revenue ($ mil.)
1	Pfizer	US	52,921
2	Johnson & Johnson	US	47,348
3	GlaxoSmithKline	UK	37,304
4	Novartis	Switzerland	28,247
5	Roche Group	Switzerland	25,166
6	Merck	US	22,939
7	Bristol-Myers Squibb	US	21,886
8	AstraZeneca	UK	21,426
9	Abbott Laboratories	US	20,473
10	Sanofi-Aventis	France	18,710

SOURCE: *FORTUNE*, JULY 25, 2005

Forbes' "Richest People in the World" by Net Worth

Rank	Name	Net Worth ($ bil.)	Country	What
1	William Gates III	46.5	US	Microsoft
2	Warren Buffett	44.0	US	Berkshire Hathaway
3	Lakshmi Mittal	25.0	India	Steel
4	Carlos Slim Helu	23.8	Mexico	Telecom
5	Prince Alwaleed Bin Talal Alsaud	23.7	Saudi Arabia	Investments
6	Ingvar Kamprad	23.0	Sweden	IKEA
7	Paul Allen	21.0	US	Microsoft/investments
8	Karl Albrecht	18.5	Germany	Supermarkets
9	Lawrence Ellison	18.4	US	Oracle
10	S. Robson Walton	18.3	US	Wal-Mart
11	Jim Walton	18.2	US	Wal-Mart
11	John Walton *	18.2	US	Wal-Mart
13	Alice Walton	18.0	US	Wal-Mart
13	Helen Walton	18.0	US	Wal-Mart
15	Kenneth Thomson & family	17.9	Canada	Publishing
16	Liliane Bettencourt	17.2	France	L'Oréal
17	Bernard Arnault	17.0	France	LVMH
18	Michael Dell	16.0	US	Dell
19	Sheldon Adelson	15.6	US	Casinos/hotels
20	Theo Albrecht	15.5	Germany	Supermarkets
21	Roman Abramovich	13.3	Russia	Oil
22	Li Ka-shing	13.0	Hong Kong	Diversified
23	Amancio Ortega	12.6	Spain	Zara
24	Steven Ballmer	12.1	US	Microsoft
25	Silvio Berlusconi	12.0	Italy	Media
25	Abigail Johnson	12.0	US	Fidelity
27	Barbara Cox Anthony	11.7	US	Cox Enterprises
27	Anne Cox Chambers	11.7	US	Cox Enterprises
29	Stefan Persson	11.2	Sweden	Hennes & Mauritz
30	John Kluge	11.0	US	Metromedia
31	Raymond, Thomas & Walter Kwok	10.9	Hong Kong	Real estate
32	Forrest Mars Jr.	10.4	US	Candy
32	Jacqueline Mars	10.4	US	Candy
32	John Mars	10.4	US	Candy
35	Luciano Benetton & family	9.9	Italy	Benetton
35	Pierre Omidyar	9.9	US	eBay
35	Galen Weston & family	9.9	Canada	Retail
38	Lee Shau Kee	9.3	Hong Kong	Real estate
38	Azim Premji	9.3	India	Software
40	Nasser Al-Kharafi & family	9.0	Kuwait	Construction
41	Kirk Kerkorian	8.9	US	Investments/casinos
42	Sumner Redstone	8.8	US	Viacom
43	Leonardo Del Vecchio	8.5	Italy	Eyewear
43	Michele Ferrero & family	8.5	Italy	Chocolates
45	Michael Otto & family	8.3	Germany	Retail
46	Susanne Klatten	8.2	Germany	BMW/pharmaceuticals
46	Philip Knight	8.2	US	Nike
46	Hans Rausing	8.2	Sweden	Packaging
49	Serge Dassault & family	7.8	France	Aviation
49	Carl Icahn	7.8	US	Leveraged buyouts

*John Walton died in a plane crash in June 2005

SOURCE: FORBES, MARCH 28, 2005

Hoover's Handbook of

World

Business

The Companies

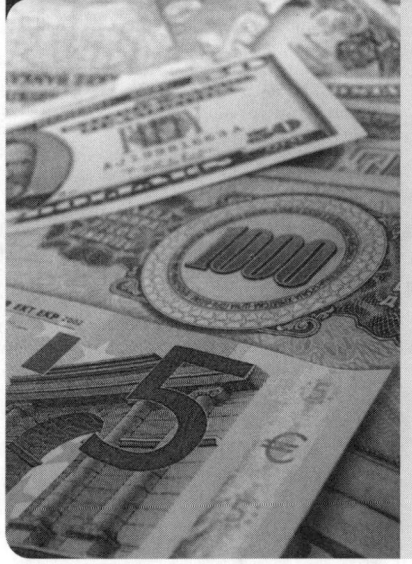

ABB Ltd.

You could be forgiven for thinking that ABB is short for "A Bunch of Businesses" — though the bunch is smaller than it once was. ABB (which used to be called Asea Brown Boveri) operates through two major divisions — power technologies and automation technologies — and serves a broad base of utility, industrial, and commercial customers. The power technologies division provides the power supply industry with equipment and services for transmission, distribution, and automation. The automation technologies unit offers equipment used to monitor and control processes in plants and utilities.

ABB has undergone an extensive program of restructuring after years in which it overdiversified, racked up huge debts, alienated investors, and faced the threat of bankruptcy. The company hived off many of its far-flung businesses, including units that dealt in wind energy, capital finance, high-voltage cables, export banking, metering equipment, and marine switchgear. Over the course of two years the company pared its enormous workforce by a quarter.

ABB consolidated its remaining businesses into two areas. Its power technologies division comprises the former power technology products and utilities divisions, and its automation technologies division comprises its former automation technology products and industries divisions. The company retains an important presence in many sectors: for example, ABB claims the largest installed base of industrial robots in the world, and says that it equips and services three-quarters of all pulp and paper mills worldwide.

The company has sought to settle an asbestos liability case related to a US subsidiary. A final settlement — which could involve payment of more than $1 billion in obligations — would remove another huge headache for the company, but ABB has faced legal setbacks to its settlement plan.

HISTORY

Asea Brown Boveri (ABB) was formed in 1988 when two giants, ASEA AB of Sweden and BBC Brown Boveri of Switzerland, combined their electrical engineering and equipment businesses. Percy Barnevik, head of ASEA, became CEO.

ASEA was born in Stockholm in 1883 when Ludwig Fredholm founded Electriska Aktiebolaget to manufacture an electric dynamo created by engineer Jonas Wenstrom. In 1890 the company merged with Wenstrom's brother's firm to form Allmanna Svenska Electriska Aktiebolaget (ASEA), a pioneer in industrial electrification. Early in the 1900s ASEA began its first railway electrification project. By the 1920s it was providing locomotives and other equipment to Sweden's national railway, and by the next decade ASEA was one of Sweden's largest electric equipment manufacturers. In 1962 it bought 20% of appliance maker Electrolux. ASEA created the nuclear power venture ASEA-ATOM with the Swedish government in 1968 and bought full control in 1982.

BBC Brown Boveri was formed in 1891 as the Brown, Boveri, and Company partnership between Charles Brown and Walter Boveri in Baden, Switzerland. It made power generation equipment and produced the first steam turbines in Europe in 1900. BBC entered Germany (1893), France (1894), and Italy (1903) and diversified into nuclear power equipment after WWII.

By 1988 BBC, the bigger company, had a West German network that ASEA, the more profitable company, coveted. Both had US joint ventures. In an unusual merger, ASEA (which became ABB AB) and BBC (later ABB AG) continued as separate entities sharing equal ownership of ABB. Barnevik crafted a unique decentralized management structure under which national subsidiaries were closely linked to their local customers and labor forces. In six years ABB took over more than 150 companies worldwide.

An ABB-led consortium built one of the world's largest hydroelectric plants in Iran in 1992, and in 1995 ABB merged its transportation segment into Adtranz (a joint venture with Daimler-Benz, now DaimlerChrysler) to form the world's #1 maker of trains.

Tragedy struck in 1996. Robert Donovan, CEO of ABB's US subsidiary, died in a plane crash along with Commerce Secretary Ron Brown and other executives on a trade mission. Donovan's death hastened the US unit's restructuring.

In 1997 Barnevik gave up the title of CEO, remaining as chairman, and was succeeded by Göran Lindahl, an engineer who had worked his way up the ranks at ASEA. (Barnevik remained chairman until 2001.)

In 1999 ABB acquired Elsag Bailey, a Dutch maker of industrial control systems, for about $1.5 billion, and sold its 50% stake in Adtranz to DaimlerChrysler. ABB and France's Alstom combined their power generation businesses to form the world's largest power plant equipment maker. That year ABB AB and ABB AG were at last united under a single stock.

ABB scaled back its power plant-related activities in 2000. It sold its nuclear power business to BNFL for $485 million and its 50% stake in ABB Alstom Power to ALSTOM for $1.2 billion. In 2001 Lindahl resigned and Jörgen Centerman, head of the company's automation business, replaced him. With economic slowdowns occurring in the company's key markets, ABB announced plans in July 2001 to cut 12,000 jobs, or about 8% of its workforce, over 18 months. Later that year, amid rising numbers of asbestos claims against US subsidiary Combustion Engineering, ABB took a $470 million fourth-quarter charge to cover asbestos liabilities. The claims charged asbestos exposures stemming from products supplied before the mid-1970s by Combustion Engineering, which ABB had acquired in 1990.

In 2002 ABB agreed to sell part of its financial services unit to GE Commercial Finance for $2.3 billion. The day after the company sold its structured finances unit, ABB's chief executive, Jörgen Centerman, resigned and was replaced by the chairman, Jürgen Dormann.

ABB sold its upstream oil, gas, and petrochemicals unit to Candover Partners, 3i, and J.P. Morgan Partners for $925 million in 2004. (To clear the way for the sale, ABB also agreed to pay US regulators $16 million in fines to settle bribery cases at US-based ABB Vetco Gray and Scotland-based ABB Vetco UK. The subsidiaries — part of the petroleum business that was sold — had allegedly paid off government officials in Angola, Kazakhstan, and Nigeria in order to win oil contracts between 1998 and 2003.)

Sulzer CEO Fred Kindle succeeded Dormann as ABB's CEO in January 2005. (Dormann remains chairman.)

EXECUTIVES

Chairman: Jürgen Dormann, age 65
President and CEO: Fred Kindle, age 44
EVP, Human Resources: Gary Steel, age 53
EVP, Power Technologies: Peter Smits, age 54
CFO: Michel Demaré
Head of Corporate Development: Ulrich Spiesshofer
EVP, Automation Technologies; President, ABB Inc.: Dinesh C. Paliwal, age 47
SVP, Corporate Communications: Björn Edlund
SVP, Sustainability Affairs: Christian Kornevall
VP, Risk Management: Charles Salek
CTO: H. Markus Bayegan
CIO: Haider Rashid
Deputy CFO and Head, Corporate Finance and Taxes: Alfred Storck
CFO, Automation Technologies: Herbert Parker
CFO, Power Technologies: Victor Bolt
General Counsel and Head, Legal and Compliance: John G. Scriven, age 60
Corporate Communications: Thomas Schmidt
Investor Relations: Michel Gerber, age 39
Auditors: Ernst & Young Ltd.

LOCATIONS

HQ: ABB Ltd.
Affolternstrasse 44, 8050 Zurich, Switzerland
Phone: +41-43-317-7111   **Fax:** +41-43-317-4420
US HQ: 501 Merritt 7, Norwalk, CT 06851
US Phone: 203-750-2200   **US Fax:** 203-750-2263
Web: www.abb.com

ABB operates in more than 100 countries worldwide.

2004 Sales

	% of total
Europe	52
Asia	21
The Americas	17
Middle East & Africa	10
Total	**100**

PRODUCTS/OPERATIONS

2004 Sales

	% of total
Automation technologies	51
Power technologies	41
Non-core activities	8
Total	**100**

Major Operations and Products

Automation Technologies
  Automation products
    Instrumentation
      Actuators and positioners
      Analytical instruments
      Flowmeters
      Pressure transmitters
      Recorders and indicators
      Temperature sensors
    Low- and high-voltage motors
    Low- and medium-voltage drives
    Motor control systems
    Power electronics systems
    Wire management equipment
  Manufacturing automation
    Control systems
    Industrial robots
  Process automation
    Collaborative production management systems
    Marine propulsion equipment
    Process control systems
    Product quality sensors
    Turbochargers

Power Technologies
  High-voltage products
    Cables
    Gas-insulated switchgear
    Generator circuit breakers
  Medium-voltage products
    Circuit breakers
    Fuses
    Sensors
    Switches
    Vacuum interrupters
  Power systems
    Flexible alternating current
      transmission systems (FACTS)
    High-voltage direct current (HVDC) systems
    Power lines
  Transformers
    Converter transformers
    Distribution transformers
    Phase-shifting transformers
    Reactors
    Single-phase transformers
  Utility automation systems
    Distributed control systems
    Substation automation equipment
    Utility communication networks
Other operations
  Building systems
  Equity ventures
  Structured finance

COMPETITORS

Aker Kværner
ALSTOM
Bechtel
Cooper Industries
Emerson Electric
Endress + Hauser
Fluor
Foster Wheeler
GE
Halliburton
Hitachi
Honeywell ACS
Invensys
JGC
McDermott
Samsung
Schneider
Siemens
Technip
Toshiba
VA Technologie

HISTORICAL FINANCIALS

Company Type: Public

Income Statement

FYE: December 31

	REVENUE ($ mil.)	NET INCOME ($ mil.)	NET PROFIT MARGIN	EMPLOYEES
12/04	20,721	(35)	—	102,500
12/03	18,795	(767)	—	116,500
12/02	18,295	(783)	—	139,051
12/01	23,726	(691)	—	156,865
12/00	22,967	1,443	6.3%	160,818
12/99	24,681	1,614	6.5%	164,154
12/98	30,872	1,305	4.2%	199,232
12/97	31,265	572	1.8%	213,057
12/96	33,767	1,233	3.7%	214,894
12/95	33,738	1,315	3.9%	209,637
Annual Growth	(5.3%)	—	—	(7.6%)

2004 Year-End Financials

Debt ratio: 173.5%
Return on equity: —
Cash ($ mil.): 3,676
Current ratio: 1.17
Long-term debt ($ mil.): 4,901
No. of shares (mil.): 2,070
Dividends
  Yield: 0.0%
  Payout: —
Market value ($ mil.): 11,718

12/95 12/96 12/97 12/98 12/99 12/00 12/01 12/02 12/03 12/04

	STOCK PRICE ($) FY Close	P/E High/Low	PER SHARE ($) Earnings	Dividends	Book Value
12/04	5.66	337 243	0.02	0.00	1.36
12/03	5.08	— —	(0.63)	0.00	1.46
12/02	2.87	— —	(0.83)	0.00	0.91
12/01	9.41	— —	(0.61)	0.00	1.81
Annual Growth	(15.6%)	— —	—	—	(9.0%)

ABN AMRO

When the tulip bed got a little too crowded, ABN AMRO Holding decided to cultivate more exotic acreage, concentrating on Asia, the US, and the rest of Europe for much of its growth. One of the Netherlands' largest financial services firms, ABN AMRO performs retail banking services mainly in its home country, Brazil (through Banco ABN AMRO Real), and the US, where it runs LaSalle Bank in Illinois, Indiana, and Michigan, and is one of the largest foreign banks by assets. Other lines of business, which operate worldwide, include private banking, asset management, and investment banking. All told, ABN AMRO and its subsidiaries operate more than 3,800 offices in some 60 countries.

To unify its stateside brands ABN AMRO changed the name of Standard Federal Bank in Michigan and Indiana to LaSalle Bank in 2005. However, the company has divested some other US business, such as trust, professional brokerage, and prime brokerage. Elsewhere, the company owns nearly 30% of Banca Antoniana Popolare Veneta (Banca Antonveneta), a regional bank in northeastern Italy, and has arranged to buy about another 40%, including Banca Popolare Italiana's 30% stake after that company had originally tried to block ABN AMRO's takeover bid for Banca Antonveneta.

Thailand's "one presence" rule, which prevents foreign banks from holding a major stake in a local bank while also maintaining their own branches, forced ABN AMRO to sell its majority stake in Bank of Asia to Singapore-based United Overseas Bank in 2004.

ABN AMRO has also arranged to purchase UK-based mental health care provider The Priory Group from private equity firm Doughty Hanson.

HISTORY

ABN AMRO comes by its initials honestly. It is the product of a 1991 merger between the Netherlands' #1 and #2 banks — Algemene Bank Nederland (ABN) and Amsterdam-Rotterdam Bank (AMRO), respectively — and a final amalgamation of what were the four top banks in the Netherlands.

The Netherlands Trading Society was founded in 1824 to finance business ventures in the Dutch colonies, operating from an office in what is now Jakarta, Indonesia. The company prospered, moving into agricultural financing and commercial banking and acquiring banks in the early 1900s. Although the firm weathered WWI and the Depression, WWII was catastrophic — Germany occupied the homeland and Japan took over the Dutch East Indies.

The Netherlands Trading Society never recovered, and in 1964 it merged with Twentsche Bank (founded in 1861 as an agricultural bank) to form Algemene Bank Nederland. ABN's chief rival was AMRO, product of the 1964 merger of Amsterdam Bank and Rotterdam Bank. Founded in 1863, Rotterdam Bank financed commercial activity in the colonies before refocusing on the shipping business through Rotterdam. Amsterdam Bank was founded in 1871 by several Dutch and German banks and was the largest Dutch bank when it merged with Incasso Bank in 1948. In 1964 the new entity added the operations of Hollandsche Bank — Unie.

ABN was smaller than AMRO until it bought merchant bank Mees & Hope (1975) followed by the purchase of Chicago-based LaSalle National Bank (1979). ABN had retreated so far from its colonial roots that it was largely unscathed by the mass default of Third World banks in 1987. Instead, AMRO financed oil and gas exploration and construction on the English Channel Tunnel.

ABN and AMRO merged in 1991, and the new company turned its attention to overseas markets like the American Midwest, where LaSalle National Bank was gobbling up competitors like Talman Home Federal Savings (1991). ABN AMRO also took control of European American Bank (EAB), which had sustained heavy losses on bad real estate and Third World loans. The company bought investment banks Chicago Corp. and Alfred Berg in 1995.

Expansion brought internal oversight problems during the next few years: in 1995 Swiss banking authorities asked ABN AMRO to better police its branches there after the bank lost as much as $124 million to embezzlement. In 1997 the firm closed its diamond office after losing about $100 million to fraud.

In 1998 ABN AMRO bought Brazil's Banco Real and Bandepe banks (and then closed their European and US offices). The next year it began buying minority interests in Italian banks. Also in 1999 the company elected to become a major force in European real estate with the acquisition of Bouwfonds Nederlandse Gemeenten, the Netherlands' #5 mortgage lender. As part of this effort, it expanded its mortgage servicing portfolio with the purchase of Pitney Bowes subsidiary Atlantic Mortgage and Investment Corp.

ABN AMRO cut 150 branches in its overbanked home market (and about 10% of its Dutch workforce) in 2000. It bought the energy-derivative business of Merrill Lynch, Barclays' Dial car-leasing unit, and Alleghany Corporation's asset management unit.

In 2001 ABN AMRO sold EAB to Citigroup and bought US-based Michigan National Corporation from National Australia Bank and merged it with another Michigan holding, Standard Federal Bancorporation, to form Standard Federal Bank, one of the largest banks in Michigan. It also bought the US brokerage and corporate finance operations of Dutch rival ING Groep in a quarter-billion dollar deal.

EXECUTIVES

Chairman, Supervisory Board:
 Jonkheer Aarnout Loudon, age 68
Vice Chairman: Maarten C. van Veen, age 70
Chairman, Managing Board: Rijkman W. J. Groenink,
 age 56
**Chairman, Executive Committee, Consumer and
 Commercial Clients (Brazil and New Growth Markets)
 and Private Clients:** Dolf Collee, age 53
**Chairman, Executive Committee, Wholesale Clients and
 Asset Management:** Wilco G. Jiskoot, age 55
**Chairman, Executive Committee, Consumer &
 Commercial Clients (the Netherlands and North
 America):** Joost Ch. L. Kuiper, age 58
COO: Hugh Y. Scott-Barrett, age 47
CFO and Head of Risk Management: Tom de Swaan,
 age 59
**SEVP; CEO, Consumer and Commercial Clients, The
 Netherlands:** Jan Peter Schmittmann
**SEVP; CEO, Consumer and Commercial Clients,
 Brazil; President, ABN AMRO Brazil:** Fabio C. Barbosa
**SEVP; CEO, Consumer and Commercial Clients,
 United States; President and CEO, LaSalle Bank
 Corporation:** Norman R. (Norm) Bobins, age 62
SEVP; CEO, Asset Management:
 Huibert G. Boumeester
SEVP; CEO, Transaction Banking Group: Ann Cairns
SEVP; CEO, Wholesale Clients Services: David A. Cole
**SEVP; CEO, Consumer and Commercial Clients, New
 Growth Markets and Private Clients:** Lex Kloosterman
SEVP; CEO, Group Shared Services: Ron Teerlink
SEVP, Group Legal and Compliance: Jaap J. Kamp
SEVP, Group Human Resources: Eltjo H. Kok
Head of Investor Relations: Richard P. Bruens
Head of Corporate Communications: Robin Boon
Chairman, Bouwfonds: Henk Rutgers
President, ABN AMRO Services: Sam Halim
Auditors: Ernst & Young Accountants

LOCATIONS

HQ: ABN AMRO Holding N.V.
 Gustav Mahlerlaan 10,
 1082 PP Amsterdam, The Netherlands
Phone: +31-20-628-9393   **Fax:** +31-20-629-9111
US HQ: 135 S. La Salle St., Chicago, IL 60603
US Phone: 312-904-2000   **US Fax:** 312-904-2579
Web: www.abnamro.com

PRODUCTS/OPERATIONS

2004 Sales

	% of total
Interest	68
Commission revenue	16
Financial transactions	7
Securities & participating interests	5
Other	4
Total	**100**

COMPETITORS

Citigroup
Credit Suisse
Deutsche Bank
Dresdner Bank
Fifth Third Bancorp
Harris Bankcorp
HSBC Holdings
ING
JPMorgan Chase
National City
Northern Trust
Société Générale

HISTORICAL FINANCIALS

Company Type: Public

Income Statement

FYE: December 31

	ASSETS ($ mil.)	NET INCOME ($ mil.)	INCOME AS % OF ASSETS	EMPLOYEES
12/04	824,441	5,566	0.7%	97,276
12/03	704,581	3,974	0.6%	110,201
12/02	583,986	2,318	0.4%	107,416
12/01	532,430	2,879	0.5%	112,206
12/00	511,557	2,353	0.5%	115,098
12/99	462,097	2,594	0.6%	108,689
12/98	503,896	2,132	0.4%	105,826
12/97	412,867	1,902	0.5%	74,935
12/96	346,741	1,911	0.6%	66,172
12/95	339,773	1,626	0.5%	63,694
Annual Growth	**10.4%**	**14.6%**	**—**	**4.8%**

2004 Year-End Financials

Equity as % of assets: 2.3%
Return on assets: 0.7%
Return on equity: 32.2%
Long-term debt ($ mil.): 196,920
No. of shares (mil.): 1,703

Dividends
 Yield: 4.6%
 Payout: 37.0%
Market value ($ mil.): 45,297
Sales ($ mil.): 45,139

Stock History

NYSE: ABN

	STOCK PRICE ($) FY Close	P/E High/Low		PER SHARE ($) Earnings	Dividends	Book Value
12/04	26.60	8	6	3.32	1.23	11.91
12/03	23.48	10	5	2.43	0.99	9.98
12/02	16.18	14	7	1.45	0.82	7.12
12/01	16.28	14	8	1.86	0.86	6.84
12/00	22.75	17	13	1.53	0.86	7.85
12/99	25.31	15	11	1.73	0.65	8.24
12/98	21.75	19	10	1.42	0.29	8.67
12/97	19.50	19	14	1.29	0.00	14.73
Annual Growth	**4.5%**	**—**	**—**	**14.5%**	**—**	**(3.0%)**

Accor

Accor est l'hospitalité. The company is one of
the world's leading hotel operators, owning or
managing almost 4,000 properties throughout
the world. It serves travelers in Europe through
its flagship chains Mercure, Novotel, and Sofitel,
as well as its economy chains Ibis and Formule
1. In the US it operates budget brands Motel 6
and Red Roof Inns. Accor also owns half of travel
services giant Carlson Wagonlit, a 30% stake in
resorts operator Club Méditerranée, and 30% of
casino hotel company Groupe Lucien Barrière.
In addition, Accor operates or owns stakes in
several hospitality and food services; its Accor
services unit provides outsourced benefits services to more than 300,000 corporate customers.

More than 70% of Accor's revenue comes from
its hotel operations, which are anchored by its
upscale and mid-market chains in Europe. Many
of these hotels are either owned or operated by the
company. In contrast, its US economy brands (accounting for less than 20% of sales) boast more
than 1,200 properties, most of which are franchised. Accor has embarked on a sale and lease-
back strategy for its upscale properties to reduce
its exposure to slowdowns in the market and it is
working to transition many of its midscale hotel
leasing agreements to variable cost arrangements.

Accor plans to use the cash from its restructuring, and a $1.3 billion investment from US-
based Colony Capital, to boost its expansion
efforts. It hopes to increase room capacity by
about 20% over three years, with a particular
focus on the emerging markets of India and
other parts of Asia. Accor hopes to double the
number of hotels it has in China over that span.

In 2005 veteran chairman and CEO Jean-
Marc Espalioux announced he would leave the
company at the end of his term early in 2006.
Gilles Pélisson, head of Bouygues Telecom
(France's #3 mobile carrier controlled by conglomerate Bouygues), has been recommended
as a possible replacement.

HISTORY

Until Gérard Pélisson and Paul Dubrule built
their first hotel in 1967, French hotels were generally quaint old inns or expensive luxury hotels.
Pélisson and Dubrule's Novotel introduced mid-
priced hotels based on the American model. The
pair opened the Ibis Hotel in 1973 and bought
the Mercure chain in 1975. By 1979, when it
opened its first US hotel in Minneapolis, Novotel was Europe's #1 hotel chain, operating 184
hotels on four continents.

Dubrule and Pélisson married their growing
hotel business to Jacques Borel International,
forming publicly traded Accor in 1983. Jacques
Borel had started out with one restaurant in
1957 and was Europe's #1 restaurateur by 1975,
when he took over Belgium's Sofitel chain of
luxury hotels. Losses in the hotel game
prompted Borel to sell Sofitel to Dubrule and
Pélisson in 1980, making their company one of
the world's top 10 hotel operators — a list traditionally dominated by US chains. They picked
up the rest of Borel's empire in 1983, launching
Accor into the restaurant business.

Accor began offering packaged vacations in
1984, after buying a majority stake in Africatours
(Africa's largest tour operator), then expanded
into the South Pacific, Asia, and the Americas by
buying Islands in the Sun (1986), Asietours
(1987), and Americatours (1987).

The company opened its first budget hotels
(Formule 1) in France in 1985. Accor started
marketing Paquet cruises in 1986 and formed
the Hotelia and Parthenon chains (Brazilian residential hotels) the next year.

Faced with a mature European market and
eager to take advantage of favorable exchange
rates, Accor bought Dallas-based budget chain
Motel 6 (along with its high debts and poor reputation, which Accor began remedying with an
expensive renovation program) in 1990. The next
year Accor bought US-based Regal Inns (now
part of Motel 6).

Also in 1990 Accor joined Société Générale de
Belgique to buy 26.7% of Belgium's Wagons-
Lits, owner of about 300 hotels in Europe, Thailand, and Indonesia, as well as restaurants,
caterers, and travel agencies in Europe. After a
battle involving both Belgian and EC antitrust officials, Accor was allowed to buy a majority stake
of Wagons-Lits (later called Wagonlit Travel).

This buy — along with Accor's attempt to increase its share of the luxury market, the continuing burden of its US purchases, and a recession in the travel business — took a financial toll. In response, it began selling assets in 1994, ridding itself of expensive hotel real estate. The company also joined with US-based Carlson Companies to form a joint travel venture called Carlson Wagonlit Travel.

In 1997 co-chairmen Dubrule and Pélisson retired from active management and were succeeded by Jean-Marc Espalioux, formerly of Générale des Eaux (now Vivendi Universal). As part of its strategy to continue to expand internationally, Accor reached an agreement that year with the Moroccan government to develop that country's hotel industry. In 1999 Accor continued hotel acquisitions with US chain Red Roof Inns and hotels in Finland, France, the Netherlands, Poland, and Sweden.

The following year the company opened a luxury Sofitel hotel in downtown Manhattan and began developing other Sofitels in Dallas, Chicago, and Washington, DC. It also sold its EuropCar stake to Volkswagen. In 2001 the company announced plans for a 370-room Sofitel in the high-tech center of Shenyang, China. Early in 2002 Accor bought a 22% stake in Compagnie Européenne de Casinos, an operator of 24 casinos mostly in France, in a bid to buy out the company. However, after a two-month bidding war with competitor Groupe Partouche, Accor sold its stake to Partouche. The bidding war had driven up Compagnie Européenne's stock dramatically, and Accor ended up pocketing some £12 million from the sale. Also in 2002, Accor opened 261 new hotels, largely Ibis, Etap, and Mercure properties. Later that year the company acquired a 30% stake in Dorint AG, a German hotel group.

Accor acquired a 29% stake in resorts operator Club Méditerranée in 2004. Later that year it merged its casino operations with Société Hôtelière de la Chaîne Lucien Barrière and Société des Hôtels et Casinos de Deauville to form Group Lucien Barrière, with Accor holding a 30% stake in the new business. US-based investment firm Colony Capital made a $1.3 billion investment in Accor the following year.

EXECUTIVES

Director, Supervisory Board: Serge Weinberg, age 54
Chairman, Management Board, and CEO:
 Jean-Marc Espalioux, age 53
Chairman, Management Board: Gilles Pélisson
Executive Vice Chairman, Management Board:
 Benjamin Cohen, age 66
Senior Vice Chairman, Management Board:
 John Du Monceau, age 67
Director of Hotel Operations, Europe, Africa, and Middle East, and Management Board Member:
 André Martinez, age 52
CFO and Director, Management Board: Jacques Stern, age 41
Human Resources: Cathy Kopp
General Secretary: Pierre Todorov
Communications and External Relations:
 Jacques Charbit
Corporate Legal Services: Catherine Bertini
Marketing and Development, Accor Services:
 Thierry Gaches
Investor Relations and Financial Communication:
 Éliane Rouyer
CEO, Club Méditerranée: Henri Giscard d'Estaing, age 49

President and CEO, Accor North America:
 Georges Le Mener
President and CEO, Carlson Wagonlit Travel:
 Hubert Joly, age 46
Finance, Administration, and Human Resources, Accor Services: Olivier de Surville
Auditors: Deloitte Touche Tohmatsu

LOCATIONS

HQ: Accor
 2, rue de la Mare-Neuve, 91021 Évry, France
Phone: +33-1-69-36-80-80   **Fax:** +33-1-69-36-79-00
US HQ: 4001 International Pkwy., Carrollton, TX 75007
US Phone: 972-360-9000   **US Fax:** 972-360-2821
Web: www.accor.com

2004 Sales

	$ mil.	% of total
Europe		
France	3,301	34
Other countries	3,376	35
North America	1,682	17
Latin America & Caribbean	597	6
Other regions	760	8
Total	**9,716**	**100**

2004 Locations

	No.
Europe	
France	1,319
Other countries	879
North America	1,257
Asia Pacific	225
Latin America & Caribbean	158
Africa & the Middle East	135
Total	**3,973**

PRODUCTS/OPERATIONS

2004 Sales

	$ mil.	% of total
Hotels		
Upscale & midscale	3,908	40
Economy	1,704	18
Economy US	1,258	13
Services	691	7
Other	2,155	22
Total	**9,716**	**100**

2004 Locations

	No.
Leased	1,562
Franchised	949
Owned	927
Managed	535
Total	**3,973**

Selected Operations

Hotels
 Upscale and mid-scale hospitality
 Economy lodging services
Services
 Compliance services
 Employee benefits programs
 Employee training programs
 Expense management
 Facilities management
 Family and personal assistance programs
 Relationship marketing
 Social programs
Other business units and subsidiaries
 Carlson Wagonlit Travel (50%, travel services, US)
 Club Méditerranée (29%, resorts)
 Compagnie des Wagons-Lits
  (railway hospitality services)
 Gemeaz Cusin (Italy, contract food service)
 GR Brasil (50%, contract food service)
 Lenôtre (catering, retail foods, and restaurants)
 Groupe Lucien Barrière (30%, casino hotels)

COMPETITORS

Best Western	Hilton International
Carlson Hotels	Hyatt
Cendant	InterContinental Hotels
Choice Hotels	Marriott
Hilton	Société du Louvre
Hilton Group	Starwood Hotels & Resorts

HISTORICAL FINANCIALS
Company Type: Public

Income Statement

FYE: December 31

	REVENUE ($ mil.)	NET INCOME ($ mil.)	NET PROFIT MARGIN	EMPLOYEES
12/04	9,716	326	3.4%	168,619
12/03	8,571	339	4.0%	158,023
12/02	7,482	451	6.0%	157,412
12/01	6,458	420	6.5%	146,748
12/00	6,596	421	6.4%	145,347
12/99	6,145	354	5.8%	128,850
12/98	6,561	347	5.3%	126,908
12/97	5,298	251	4.7%	121,396
12/96	5,409	202	3.7%	124,378
12/95	6,317	188	3.0%	120,668
Annual Growth	**4.9%**	**6.3%**	**—**	**3.8%**

2004 Year-End Financials

Debt ratio: 89.8%   Current ratio: 1.16
Return on equity: 6.8%   Long-term debt ($ mil.): 4,598
Cash ($ mil.): —

Net Income History

Euronext Paris: AC

Acer Inc.

Acer's plan: divide and conquer. The company is a leading manufacturer of notebook, tablet, handheld, and desktop computers. Other Acer products include servers, storage systems, projectors, and displays. The company also provides IT support services. Acer has streamlined its operations in recent years, spinning off its contract manufacturing operations (now Wistron), as well as its consumer electronics and peripherals business (now BenQ). It still holds stakes in both companies. Acer now outsources its manufacturing. It sells through resellers and distributors worldwide.

Slumping sales in a weakening computer hardware market prompted Acer's restructuring efforts. In addition to clarifying the structure of Acer's sizable operations, the separation of Acer's branded operations and Wistron serves to eliminate possible customer concerns about a conflict of interest between the two businesses. The company has made China and other Asian markets the primary target for its ongoing business, although it has also seen its market share grow considerably in European countries. Acer pulled out of the US retail market in 1999, and it now focuses on serving corporate customers through distributors in the US.

HISTORY

Acer founder and chairman Stan Shih, respected enough for his business acumen to once be considered for the premiership of Taiwan, designed that country's first desktop calculator in the early 1970s. The company's precursor, Multitech International, was launched in 1976 with $25,000 by Shih and four others who called themselves the "Gardeners of Microprocessing." In 1980 Multitech introduced the Dragon Chinese-language terminal, which won Taiwan's top design award; in 1983 it introduced an Apple clone and its first IBM-compatible PC. Multitech set up AcerLand, Taiwan's first and largest franchised computer retail chain, in 1985.

The company changed its name to Acer (the Latin word for "sharp, acute, able, and facile") in 1987 and went public on the Taiwan exchange the next year. Acer got into the semiconductor market in 1989 when it entered into a joint venture with Texas Instruments (named TI-Acer) to design and develop memory chips in Taiwan. In 1990 Acer's US subsidiary, Acer America, paid $90 million for Altos Computer Systems, a US manufacturer of UNIX systems.

During the prosperous 1980s Acer increased its management layers and slowed the decision making process. In late 1990 the company restructured, trimming its workforce by 8% (about 400 employees), including two-thirds of headquarters. The layoff was unprecedented — being asked to resign from a job in Taiwan carries a social stigma. Shih wrote a letter to all those affected, explaining the plight of the company. The following year Acer began its decentralization plan to create a worldwide confederation of publicly owned companies.

Acer suffered its first loss in 1991 on revenues of almost $1 billion, partly because of increased marketing budgets in the US and Europe and continuing investment in TI-Acer. The company bounced back in 1993, with 80% of its profit coming from that joint venture.

The Aspire PC, available in shades of gray and green, was unveiled in 1995. In 1996 the company expanded into consumer electronics, introducing a host of new, inexpensive videodisc players, video telephones, and other devices in order to boost global market share. In 1997 Acer purchased TI's notebook computer business. A slowdown in memory chip sales, plus a financial slide at Acer America, cost the firm $141 million, but Acer finished the year in the black.

Shih stepped down as president in 1998 to focus on restructuring. The company ended its venture with TI, buying TI's 33% stake and renaming the unit Acer Semiconductor Manufacturing. The company also began making information appliances, introducing a device able to play CD-ROMs via TV sets and perform other task-specific functions. Continued losses due to a highly competitive US market caused a drop in profits for 1998.

In 1999 Acer sold a 30% stake in its struggling Acer Semiconductor Manufacturing affiliate to Taiwan Semiconductor Manufacturing Corp. (TSMC completed its purchase of the remaining 70% of the business, which was renamed TSMC-Acer Semiconductor Manufacturing, the following year.) The competitive heat and the rise of under-$1,000 PCs took a toll that year when Acer cut US jobs, streamlined operations, and withdrew from the US retail market. The company intensified its focus on providing online software, hardware, and support for users, launching a digital services business and a venture capital operation to invest in promising Internet startups.

The company suffered a financial blow in 2000 when large customer IBM cancelled an order for desktop computers. Late that year, after continued losses in a slowing PC market, the company announced it would cut more jobs in the US and Germany and close an unspecified number of plants worldwide.

In 2001 the company spun off its contract manufacturing and peripherals units, and renamed them Wistron and BenQ, respectively. Acer's restructuring efforts continued the following year, when it merged with its distribution unit, Acer Sertek. (Although Sertek was the surviving entity, the company immediately revived the Acer name to maintain its stronger brand.)

In 2005 president J.T. Wang succeeded Shih as CEO.

EXECUTIVES

Chairman and CEO: J. T. Wang
President: Gianfranco Lanci
CFO: Howard Chan
Associate Director, Investor Relations: Andrew Chang
Auditors: KPMG Peat Marwick

LOCATIONS

HQ: Acer Inc.
   9F, 88 Hsin Tai Wu Rd., Sec 1,
   Hsichih, Taipei 221, Taiwan
Phone: +886-2-696-1234   **Fax:** +886-2-696-3535
US HQ: 2641 Orchard Pkwy., San Jose, CA 95134
US Phone: 408-432-6200   **US Fax:** 408-922-2933
Web: www.acer.com

PRODUCTS/OPERATIONS

Selected Products

Computers
   Desktop (home and business)
   Notebook
   Personal digital assistants (PDAs)
   Servers
   Tablet

Displays
   Digital projectors
   Monitors (cathode-ray tube and liquid-crystal display)
   Plasma displays

COMPETITORS

Apple Computer
Dell
eMachines
Founder Holdings
Fujitsu
Fujitsu Siemens
 Computers
Gateway
Hewlett-Packard
Hitachi
IBM
Lenovo
Matsushita
NEC
Samsung
Samsung Electronics
Sharp Electronics
Siemens
Sony
Sun Microsystems
Tatung
Toshiba
TriGem

HISTORICAL FINANCIALS

Company Type: Public

Income Statement

FYE: December 31

	REVENUE ($ mil.)	NET INCOME ($ mil.)	NET PROFIT MARGIN	EMPLOYEES
12/04	7,036	219	3.1%	6,560
12/03	4,623	214	4.6%	6,368
12/02	3,070	247	8.1%	6,240
12/01	3,226	30	0.9%	—
12/00	4,764	205	4.3%	—
12/99	5,779	233	4.0%	33,912
12/98	5,269	77	1.5%	—
12/97	4,220	115	2.7%	4,401
12/96	4,191	111	2.7%	4,394
12/95	3,924	203	5.2%	—
Annual Growth	6.7%	0.9%	—	5.1%

2004 Year-End Financials

Debt ratio: 0.4%   Current ratio: 1.42
Return on equity: 11.6%   Long-term debt ($ mil.): 8
Cash ($ mil.): 996

Net Income History

Taiwan: ACER

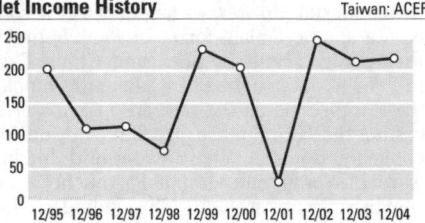

adidas-Salomon

Jesse Owens and Muhammad Ali broke records in their adidas athletic shoes. The heart of the adidas product line is athletic shoes, but the three-stripe logo appears on apparel and other jock accoutrements. Bankruptcy once had it on the ropes, but it made a comeback by shifting production to Asia and beefing up its marketing. The #2 maker of sporting goods worldwide, behind NIKE, it owns sponsorship deals with US football and basketball stars, as well as the New York Yankees. Its purchase of Salomon, the French maker of ski and golf gear, was short-lived. It sold the unit to Amer Sports Corp. and is buying Reebok for $3.8 billion.

Having already put a stamp on athletic shoe history and widely recognized for its expertise in engineering footwear, adidas has been missing two integral components: a brand as strong and as global as Nike's and a sturdy foundation in the US market. With its acquisition of Reebok (expected to be completed in the first half of 2006), adidas will have the traction it needs to cross both components off its wish list. To boot, adidas, through its purchase of Reebok, will greatly expand its portfolio of licensed brands, get a leg up on the urban market, and begin to chip away at Nike's long-running status as the world's #1 footwear firm that controls more than 20% of the US athletic shoe market. The deal also offers adidas and Reebok, as a combined entity, more bargaining muscle with suppliers and marketers.

adidas makes athletic clothing and gear such as TaylorMade golf clubs and Mavic bike components. (adidas products account for nearly 80%

of sales.) adidas is also repositioning its adidas brand, marketing its products as both performance and lifestyle wear. And the firm expects to boost brand awareness in Germany, as the country hosts the World Cup in 2006. The firm has also won sponsorship rights to the 2008 Olympic Games in Beijing.

Although the purchase of Salomon was intended to create economies of scale and an advantage in emerging markets for trendy sports, integrating the company has been difficult. adidas sold its Salomon division to equipment maker Amer Sports Corp., a unit of Amer Group, in late 2005. The company plans to change its name in May 2006 to adidas AG.

HISTORY

adidas grew out of an infamous rift between German brothers Adi and Rudi Dassler, who created athletic shoe giants adidas and Puma. As WWI was winding down, Adi scavenged for tires, rucksacks, and other refuse to create slippers, gymnastics shoes, and soccer cleats at home. His sister cut patterns out of canvas. By 1926 the shoes' success allowed the Dasslers to build a factory. At the 1928 Amsterdam Olympics, German athletes first showcased Dassler shoes to the world. In 1936 American Jesse Owens sprinted to Olympic gold in Dassler's double-striped shoes.

Business boomed until the Nazis commandeered the Dassler factory to make boots for soldiers. Whereas both Rudi and Adi were reportedly members of the Nazi party, only Rudi was called to service. Adi remained at home to run the factory. When Allied troops occupied the area, Adi made friends with American soldiers — even creating shoes for a soldier who wore them at the 1946 Olympics. Rudi came home from an American prison camp and joined his brother; together they scavenged the war-torn landscape for tank materials and tents to make shoes.

Soon a dispute between the brothers split the business. Rumors circulated that Rudi resented that Adi had failed to use his American connections to help spring him from prison camp. Rudi set up his own factory facing Adi across the River Aurach. The brothers never spoke to each other again, except in court. Rudi's company was named Puma, and Adi's became adidas. Adi added a third stripe to the Dassler's trademark shoe, while Rudi chose a cat's paw in motion. Thus began one of the most intense rivalries in Europe. The children of Puma and adidas employees attended separate elementary schools, and the employees even distinguished themselves by drinking different beers.

With Adi's innovations throughout the late 1940s and 1950s (such as the replaceable-cleat soccer shoe), adidas came to dominate the world's athletic shoe market. In the late 1950s it capitalized on the booming US market, overtaking the canvas sneakers made by P.F. Flyers and Keds. The company also initiated the practice of putting logos on sports bags and clothing.

In the 1960s and 1970s, adidas continued to expand globally to maintain its dominant position. However, a flood of new competitors following the 1972 Munich Olympics and the death of Adi in 1978 signaled the end of an era. As NIKE and Reebok captured the US market during the 1980s, adidas made one of its biggest missteps — it turned down a sneaker endorsement offer from a young Michael Jordan in 1984.

French politician and entrepreneur Bernard Tapie bought the struggling company in 1989, but he stepped down in 1992 amid personal, political, and business scandals. The next year Robert Louis-Dreyfus became CEO. He shifted production to Asia, pumped up the advertising budget, and brought in former NIKE marketing geniuses to re-establish the company's identity.

adidas became adidas-Salomon in 1997 with its $1.4 billion purchase of Salomon, a French maker of skis and other sporting goods. The company also opened its first high-profile store in Portland, Oregon, that year. In a 1998 reorganization, Louis-Dreyfus sacked Jean-Francois Gautier as Salomon's president in the wake of disappointing sales, particularly from TaylorMade Golf, Salomon's golf subsidiary.

Amid a 10% slide in revenue, several key executives decided to leave the company in 2000, including adidas America CEO Steve Wynne. Citing poor health, Louis-Dreyfus soon followed (but remained as chairman); he was replaced by the new CEO of adidas America, Ross McMullin, who soon after was diagnosed with cancer.

In 2001 Louis-Dreyfus retired as chairman and in March COO Herbert Hainer became chief executive. In 2003 a senior executive in the US division pleaded guilty to conspiracy to commit fraud. Top sales executive Timothy McCool admitted to cooking the books for adidas by reporting to auditors that the company owed $2.2 million to footwear retailer Just For Feet, when the actual number was less than $50,000.

In 2004 adidas bought collegiate and pro athlete apparel maker Valley Apparel Company. Valley Apparel holds licenses for some 140 colleges and universities and for an additional 100 athletes and was previously an adidas licensee.

Barclays Bank PLC became adidas' largest shareholder in 2004, raising its stake to 5.4%.

EXECUTIVES

Chairman and CEO: Herbert Hainer, age 49
Deputy Chairman and Chief Investment Officer: Fritz Kammerer, age 58
CFO: Robin Stalker, age 46
President and CEO, adidas America: Erich Stamminger, age 47
President, adidas Golf: John Kawaja
President, adidas North America: Rob Langstaff, age 42
Managing Director, Central Area: Ulli Gritzhuhn
Managing Director, India: Andreas Gellner
Head of Asia/Pacific Region: Christophe Bezu, age 46
SVP, Sales, adidas America: Russ Hopcus
Head of Corporate and Global Public Relations: Jan Runau
Head of Investor Relations: Natalie M. Knight
Director of Global Operations: Glenn Bennett, age 40
Director of Human Resources & Administration: Michel Perraudin, age 57
Director of Retail, adidas USA: Kerry Barnes
Director of Marketing Communications: Britt Jorgenson
Director of Sports Marketing: Kevin Wulff
Business Event Manager, Digital: Adam Milne
Communication and Marketing Manager, adidas Italy: Marco Bona
Internet Business Developer: Tara Moss
Investor Relations: Charlotte Brigitte Loos
Investor Relations: Kathrin Bibro
Public Relations, adidas America: Nicole Vollebregt
Auditors: KPMG Deutsche Treuhand-Gesellschaft AG

LOCATIONS

HQ: adidas-Salomon AG
  Adi-Dassler-Strasse 1-2,
  91074 Herzogenaurach, Germany
Phone: +49-9132-84-0   **Fax:** +49-9132-84-2241
US HQ: 5055 N. Greeley Ave., Portland, OR 97217
US Phone: 971-234-2300   **US Fax:** 971-234-2450
Web: www.adidas-group.com

2004 Sales

	% of total
adidas	80
Salomon	10
TaylorMade-adidas golf	10
Total	**100**

2004 Sales

	% of total
Footwear	42
Apparel	39
Hardware	19
Total	**100**

Selected Brands

adidas (footwear and apparel for basketball, cycling, running, soccer, and tennis)
Maxfli (golf balls and accessories)
TaylorMade (golf clubs, accessories)

COMPETITORS

Amer Sports	Mizuno
Benetton	New Balance
Callaway Golf	NIKE
Converse	PUMA
Fila USA	Reebok
Fortune Brands	Rollerblade
Head	Rossignol
Head-Tyrolia-Mares	Sara Lee
Huffy	Trek
K2	Under Armour
K-Swiss	

HISTORICAL FINANCIALS

Company Type: Public

Income Statement

FYE: December 31

	REVENUE ($ mil.)	NET INCOME ($ mil.)	NET PROFIT MARGIN	EMPLOYEES
12/04	8,836	429	4.9%	16,342
12/03	7,866	327	4.2%	15,686
12/02	6,837	240	3.5%	14,716
12/01	5,414	185	3.4%	13,941
12/00	5,494	171	3.1%	13,157
12/99	5,392	229	4.3%	12,433
12/98	5,911	239	4.0%	12,036
12/97	3,724	259	6.9%	7,993
12/96	3,055	204	6.7%	6,986
12/95	2,434	170	7.0%	5,730
Annual Growth	**15.4%**	**10.8%**	**—**	**12.3%**

2004 Year-End Financials

Debt ratio: 53.0%   Current ratio: 1.80
Return on equity: 21.9%   Long-term debt ($ mil.): 1,177
Cash ($ mil.): 267

Net Income History

OTC: ADDDY

AEGON N.V.

Not only has AEGON expanded across Europe, it has also spread Transamerica. The Dutch life insurance giant is using its expertise in acquisition (US rival Transamerica was its largest catch) and consolidation to build a transnational collection of financial services businesses. Its subsidiaries operate primarily in the US, the Netherlands, and the UK, offering personal and commercial life and accident insurance, as well as retirement and savings advice and management services. Its US operations also offer life, nonmedical health, and long-term insurance, and sell annuities and other retirement products. AEGON also has banking operations in the Netherlands.

The company, which derives about 80% of its revenues from life insurance, is expanding in Asia and the Pacific including its Beijing-based insurance joint venture with the Chinese National Offshore Oil Corporation (CNOOC). AEGON also operates in the Czech Republic, Hungary, and Spain. It agreed to acquire the Polish operations of Nationwide Insurance in mid-2005.

AEGON has sold its German subsidiary AEGON Lebensversicherngs-AG, which operates as MoneyMaxx, to Deutscher Ring.

Focusing on life insurance and pensions, the company has sold most of the business of its Transamerica Finance subsidiary (which had been on the market since 1999) to GE Commercial Finance; Transamerica Finance's real estate tax unit was sold to First American, and the company has sold the European trailer leasing business of Transamerica Finance to a joint venture held by Goldman Sachs and Cerberus Capital Management. AEGON has also been focusing on broadening its distribution channels, which include independent agents, brokers, direct response, workplace marketing, banks, and other financial institutions.

Vereniging AEGON, an independent trust, owns 12% of AEGON.

HISTORY

AEGON traces its roots to 1844, when former civil servant and funeral society agent J. Oosterhoff founded Algemeene Friesche, a burial society for low-income workers. The next year a similar organization, Groot-Noordhollandsche, was founded. These companies later became insurers and expanded nationwide. Meanwhile Olveh, a civil servants' aid group, was founded in 1877. The three companies merged in 1968 to form AGO Holding.

AEGON's other operations came from different traditions. Vennootschap Nederland was founded in 1858 as a *tontine* (essentially a death pool, with the survivors taking the pot) by Count A. Langrand-Dumonceau, an ex-French Foreign Legionnaire from Belgium. In 1913 the company merged with Eerste Nederlandsche, whose accident and health division had been previously spun off as Nieuwe Eerste Nederlandsche.

A year after Vennootschap was founded, C. F. W. Wiggers van Kerchem founded a similar scheme, Nillmij, in the Dutch East Indies. The government promoted Nillmij to colonial civil servants and military people, and for a while the company enjoyed a monopoly in the colony. Nillmij's Indonesian operations were nationalized after independence in 1957, but its Dutch subsidiaries continued to operate. All insurers were hit by fast-growing postwar government social programs. As a result, industry consolidation came early to the Netherlands. In 1969 Eerste Nederlandsche, Nieuwe Eerste Nederlandsche, and Nillmij merged to form Ennia.

The shrinking Dutch insurance market forced companies to look overseas. AGO moved into the US in 1979 by buying Life Investors; by 1982 half of its sales came from outside the Netherlands. Ennia, meanwhile, expanded in Europe (it entered Spain in 1980) and the US (buying Arkansas-based National Old Line Insurance in 1981).

AGO and Ennia merged in 1983 to form AEGON. The company made more purchases at home and abroad and spent much of the rest of the decade assimilating operations.

AEGON's US units accounted for about 40% of sales in the mid-1980s, and the firm increased that figure with acquisitions. In 1986 it bought Baltimore-based Monumental Corp. (life and health insurance) and expanded the company's US penetration.

This left AEGON underrepresented in Europe, as deregulation paved the way for economic union, and social service cutbacks spurred opportunities in private financial planning in the region. So in the 1990s AEGON began buying European companies, including Regency Life (UK, 1991) and Allami Biztosito (Hungary, 1992). It formed an alliance with Mexico's Grupo Financiero Banamex in 1994. This reduced its reliance on US sales. It continued buying specialty operations in the US, particularly asset management lines.

In 1997 AEGON began to concentrate on life insurance and financial services and shed its other operations. It bought the insurance business of Providian (now part of Washington Mutual) and sold noncore lines, such as auto coverage. The next year it sold FGH Bank (mortgages) to Germany's Bayerische Vereinsbank (now Bayerische Hypotheken und Vereinsbank) and in 1999 sold auto insurer Worldwide Insurance.

That year AEGON expanded further in the US with the $9.7 billion purchase of Transamerica and bought the life and pensions businesses of the UK's Guardian Royal Exchange. In 2000 the company sold Labouchere N.V., a Dutch banking subsidiary, to Dexia. Also in 2000 AEGON acquired UK-based third-party administrator HS Administrative Services.

EXECUTIVES

Chairman of the Supervisory Board:
Dudley G. (D.G.) Eustace, age 69
Vice Chairman of the Supervisory Board: O. John Olcay, age 69
Chairman of the Executive Board: Donald J. Shepard, age 59, $3,658,248 pay
Member of the Executive Board and CFO:
Joseph B.M. Streppel, age 56, $1,107,568 pay
Member of the Executive Board and CEO, AEGON Nederland N.V.: Johan G. van der Werf, age 53, $968,440 pay
Member of the Executive Board:
Alexander R. Wynaendts, age 45, $911,152 pay
EVP, Group Legal and Compliance: Erik Lagendijk
EVP, Group Finance and Information:
Ruurd A. van den Berg
EVP, Group Corporate Affairs and Investor Relations, and Group Treasury: C. Michiel van Katwijk
SVP, Group Business Development: Marc A. van Weede, age 38
SVP, Group Tax: Adri D. J. Verzijl
SVP, Group Risk: Tom M. P. Grondin
SVP, Group Corporate Affairs: Guy Nielsen
VP, Group Corporate Responsibility: Charles Henderson, age 43
Company Secretary: Peter Tuit
President and CEO, AEGON USA, Inc.:
Patrick S. (Pat) Baird, age 51
CEO, AEGON UK: Otto Thoresen, age 49
CFO, AEGON UK: Mark Laidlaw, age 39
Auditors: Ernst & Young Accountants

LOCATIONS

HQ: AEGON N.V.
AEGONplein 50,
2501 CE The Hague, The Netherlands
Phone: +31-70-344-3210   **Fax:** +31-70-347-5238
US HQ: 1111 N. Charles St., Baltimore, MD 21201
US Phone: 410-576-4571   **US Fax:** 410-347-8685
Web: www.aegon.com

AEGON operates worldwide, but primarily in the Netherlands, the UK, and the US.

2004 Sales

	$ mil.	% of total
Americas	19,978	52
UK	8,358	22
The Netherlands	7,817	20
Spain	699	2
Hungary	471	1
Other countries	849	2
Other revenues	452	1
Total	**38,624**	**100**

PRODUCTS/OPERATIONS

2004 Sales

	$ mil.	% of total
Gross premiums		
Life insurance	22,174	57
Accident & health insurance	3,140	8
General insurance	1,101	3
Investment income	9,688	25
Fees & commissions	1,685	5
Income from banking activities	385	1
Other income	451	1
Total	**38,624**	**100**

Selected Subsidiaries and Affiliates

ÁB-AEGON Általános Biztosító Rt. (Hungary)
AEGON Asset Management UK plc
AEGON Bank N.V.
AEGON España S.A. (99.98%; Spain)
AEGON Financiële Diensten B.V.
AEGON International N.V.
AEGON Levensverzekering N.V.
AEGON Life Insurance (Taiwan) Inc.
AEGON NabestaandenZorg N.V.
AEGON Nederland N.V.
AEGON Schadeverzekering N.V.
AEGON Spaarkas N.V.
AEGON UK Distribution Holdings Ltd.
AEGON UK plc
AEGON USA, Inc. (US)
AEGON Vastgoed Holding B.V.
AEGON-CNOOC Life Insurance Company Ltd.
   (50%, insurance joint venture)
Commonwealth General Corporation (US)
First AUSA Life Insurance Company (US)
Guardian Assurance plc (UK)
Guardian Linked Life Assurance Limited (UK)
Guardian Pensions Management Limited (UK)
HS Administrative Services Limited (UK)
Life Investors Insurance Company of America (US)
Meeùs Groep B.V.
Monumental Life Insurance Company (US)
Peoples Benefit Life Insurance Company (US)
Scottish Equitable International Holdings plc (UK)
Scottish Equitable plc (UK)
Spaarbeleg Kas N.V.
Stonebridge Casualty Insurance Company (US)
Stonebridge Life Insurance Company (US)
TKP Pensioen B.V.
Transamerica Corporation (US)
Veterans Life Insurance Company (US)
Western Reserve Life Assurance Co. of Ohio (US)

HISTORICAL FINANCIALS

Company Type: Public

Income Statement

FYE: December 31

	ASSETS ($ mil.)	NET INCOME ($ mil.)	INCOME AS % OF ASSETS	EMPLOYEES
12/04	323,071	2,254	0.7%	27,446
12/03	294,155	2,254	0.8%	27,707
12/02	250,188	1,625	0.6%	26,659
12/01	235,358	2,136	0.9%	25,663
12/00	230,003	1,946	0.8%	28,928
12/99	230,913	1,584	0.7%	24,316
12/98	153,070	1,385	0.9%	20,723
12/97	134,623	1,089	0.8%	23,429
12/96	105,027	929	0.9%	19,346
12/95	93,660	823	0.9%	19,806
Annual Growth	14.7%	11.8%	—	3.7%

2004 Year-End Financials

Equity as % of assets: 6.0%	Dividends
Return on assets: 0.7%	Yield: 3.6%
Return on equity: 12.1%	Payout: 35.2%
Long-term debt ($ mil.): 4,695	Market value ($ mil.): 21,287
No. of shares (mil.): 1,553	Sales ($ mil.): 38,624

Stock History

NYSE: AEG

	STOCK PRICE ($) FY Close	P/E High	P/E Low	PER SHARE ($) Earnings	PER SHARE ($) Dividends	PER SHARE ($) Book Value
12/04	13.71	11	7	1.42	0.50	12.57
12/03	14.80	10	4	1.45	0.23	11.95
12/02	12.34	24	8	1.09	0.73	9.95
12/01	25.75	27	13	1.50	0.69	9.22
12/00	39.86	34	22	1.40	0.58	8.62
12/99	45.94	50	27	1.25	0.52	9.84
12/98	58.80	50	18	1.21	0.66	7.64
12/97	21.55	24	16	0.92	0.00	7.43
12/96	15.21	19	13	0.79	0.36	5.87
12/95	10.58	15	8	0.73	0.19	4.66
Annual Growth	2.9%	—	—	7.7%	11.4%	11.7%

Agrium Inc.

It's no bull that Agrium is a top producer and marketer of fertilizers in North America. A leader in the production of nitrogen, the company has 11 plants in Canada, the US, and Argentina that produce mostly nitrogen products. The plants have the capacity to produce more than 7 million tons of nitrogen per year. Agrium also produces and markets phosphate and potash, as well as micronutrients used primarily in fertilizers. In addition to supplying wholesalers, Agrium operates more than 200 fertilizer retail outlets in the US in 22 states and nearly 40 retail farm centers in South America. The company also owns 50% of Profertil, a joint venture with Spain's Repsol YPF that runs Argentina's largest nitrogen plant.

In early 2005 Agrium expanded its operations in Argentina, Bolivia, and Chile by acquiring retail businesses of United Agri Products (UAP) South America. The retail outlets focus on selling branded crop protection chemicals. It operates 33 of the retail farm centers in Argentina, four in Chile, and two in Bolivia. The company integrated its North and South American retail segments into one retail segment in 2004.

Agrium plans to expand its retail business even more in the US with a bid to take over the outstanding Income Deposit Securities of Royster-Clark ULC and Royster-Clark Ltd. Royster-Clark is a major distributor of agricultural nutrients and seed and crop protection products in the US.

In 2005 Agrium also agreed to acquire two divisions of US-based Spectrum Brands' Nu-Gro subsidiary.

HISTORY

Agrium was formed in 1992 to facilitate the reorganization of Cominco's fertilizer division and to acquire the fertilizer business of the Alberta Energy Company (1993). Cominco was founded in 1896 as the Smelting and Refining Company when Fritz Heinze fired up his first smelter at Trail Creek Landing, British Columbia. Using the ores of the nearby Rossland mines, the company soon diversified into other products (such as fertilizers) and new metallurgical technologies. In 1906 the Smelting and Refining Company, the Rossland mines, and the nearby St. Eugene Mine merged to form the Consolidated Mining and Smelting Company of Canada Limited.

During WWI the Canadian government conscripted all the company's lead, zinc, and chemical production and instructed the company to make explosive-grade ammonium nitrate at its fertilizer plants. Cominco became the company's official name in 1966.

Alberta Energy was formed in 1973 to lessen Alberta's dependence on foreign oil, in response to the OPEC oil embargo. In 1989 its petrochemical division established fertilizer (ammonium nitrate) subsidiaries in the US.

Agrium was established to compete in the rapidly consolidating fertilizer market (the number of North American ammonia producers fell from 55 in 1980 to 26 at the end of 1996). The phosphate and potash industries also consolidated, albeit on a smaller scale.

Between 1993 and 1996 the company expanded its US operations by acquiring Crop Protection Services and Western Farm Service (both retail operations), AG-BIO (the phosphate-based fertilizer business of Imperial Oil), and Nu-West

Industries. Agrium expanded into South America in 1995 by opening retail sales units for selling fertilizer, agricultural chemicals, and other services in the farming regions of Argentina.

In 1996 Agrium acquired Viridian, a Canadian fertilizer producer with nitrogen- and phosphate-based fertilizer plants in Alberta. Expanding its supply base, the company bought a phosphate mine in Alberta in 1997. The company also bought back 10% of its shares in 1998.

Agrium opened a phosphate rock mine in Ontario in 1999 to replace its reliance on phosphate rock imported from West Africa. In 2000 Agrium bought Unocal's nitrogen-based fertilizer operations for around $325 million. That year Agrium's Profertil nitrogen plant, a joint venture with Spain's industrial giant Repsol-YPF, began production in Argentina, but the plant was shut down by a government agency following an accidental discharge of ammonia. The plant was reopened later in 2000. Agrium also increased its nitrogen production capacity some 60% with the acquisition of Unocal's agricultural products division.

EXECUTIVES

Chairman: Frank W. Proto, age 61
President, CEO, and Director: Michael M. (Mike) Wilson
SVP, Finance and CFO: Bruce G. Waterman
SVP: John D. Yokley
SVP, Corporate Development and Strategy: Andrew K. Mittag
SVP, Wholesale: Ronald A. (Ron) Wilkinson
SVP, Retail: Richard L. Gearheard
VP and Treasurer: Patrick J. Freeman
VP, General Counsel, and Corporate Secretary: Leslie A. O'Donoghue
VP, Human Resources: James M. Grossett
VP, Manufacturing: William C. McClung
VP, Strategic Development and Planning: Dorothy E. A. Bower
VP, Supply Management: Christopher W. (Chris) Tworek
Manager, Investor Relations: Christine Gillespie
Auditors: KPMG LLP

LOCATIONS

HQ: Agrium Inc.
13131 Lake Fraser Dr. SE,
Calgary, Alberta T2J 7E8, Canada
Phone: 403-225-7000   **Fax:** 403-225-7609
US HQ: 4582 S. Ulster St., Ste. 1700, Denver, CO 80237
US Phone: 303-804-4400   **US Fax:** 303-804-4482
Web: www.agrium.com

Agrium has operations in Argentina, Bolivia, Canada, Chile, and the US.

PRODUCTS/OPERATIONS

2004 Sales

	$ mil.	% of total
Wholesale		
Nitrogen	1,317	45
Phosphate	309	10
Potash & other operations	220	7
Retail		
Fertilizers	556	19
Chemicals	416	14
Seed & other products	142	5
Adjustments	122	—
Total	**2,838**	**100**

Air France

It's clear skies ahead for Air France. Europe's new leading airline serves more than 200 destinations in 90 countries. Though still about 20% owned by the state, the carrier has been for the most part privatized and has been enjoying growth with an increasing number of flights to major destinations in Asia, South America, and the US. Air France Cargo is a world-leading air cargo carrier. Aided in part by expansions at its Charles de Gaulle hub in Paris, Air France has also benefited from its SkyTeam alliance with Delta, AeroMéxico, and Korean Air Lines. On top of its growth the carrier has leapfrogged into being Europe's largest carrier through the acquisition of Dutch carrier KLM in 2004.

Air France and KLM will continue to operate under their own names while they work through the daunting task of combining operations under the newly created Air France-KLM holding company. Since the completion of the merger the two carriers have managed to wring considerable savings from their combined operations, even despite high fuel prices. The two companies hope to achieve a $2.6 billion savings in the first two years of operation.

In an industry increasingly defined by global marketing alliances, the addition of KLM will help Air France's Skyteam better compete with Oneworld (anchored by British Airways and American Airlines) and Star (anchored by United Airlines and Lufthansa).

At a time when other airlines are abandoning transatlantic routes, Air France has increased the frequency of popular routes to places such as Los Angeles, Montreal, New York, and Tokyo. Air France has also acquired regional carriers that have helped bolster the airline's domestic and European presence. The airline owns a 23% interest in the computer reservation system Amadeus.

HISTORY

Société Air France was founded in 1933, the product of consolidation during the adolescence of French aviation. The government that year forced a four-way merger of France's competing airlines: Air Union, Air Orient, Société Générale de Transport Aérien, and Compagnie Internationale de Navigation Aérienne.

Air France expanded during the 1930s to become one of the world's leading airlines, but its ascent was interrupted by WWII and the German occupation, during which the carrier shuttered operations.

Air France resumed flight after the war, and as the French state began nationalizing some industries to quickly rebuild the postwar economy, it took control of the airline in 1948. Renamed Compagnie Nationale Air France, the carrier enjoyed government-backed financing that allowed it to launch its expansion.

With the era of big jets dawning, Air France began adding Boeing 707s to its fleet in 1960. Then France and the UK agreed in 1962 to jointly develop a supersonic transport — the Concorde. The next year French authorities realigned France's airline industry: International flights to Africa, Australia, and the Pacific were granted to a private carrier, Union de Transports Aériens (UTA); Air France controlled the remaining international routes. The domestic market was closed to both.

Air France added more jets to its fleet in the early 1970s and launched its cargo transport services. The company began flying the Concorde in 1976. Though spiraling development costs had made the Mach 2 jetliner a debatable investment, the supersonic transport served as a symbol of national pride.

In 1987 Air France joined in creating the Amadeus computer reservation system (launched 1989). The late 1980s were boom times in the industry, with Air France scoring healthy profits. But its attempt to take control of the domestic market by buying Air Inter was challenged by UTA, which increased its Air Inter stake in opposition. The battle was resolved in 1990: Air France bought control of both airlines.

But this French consolidation came just as the Gulf War, high oil prices, and an economic downturn began to wreak havoc on airlines. Air France fell into a money-losing streak just as deregulation in Europe was about to unleash new levels of competition. The government slapped down chairman Christian Blanc's attempt to cut wages and jobs in 1993 in the face of massive strikes. The airline eventually slimmed down and achieved net profits in 1997; Blanc, however, resigned in 1997 as the state dragged its feet on privatization.

With the 1998 signing of a US-France open skies agreement, Air France boosted flights to the US and struck code-sharing deals with Delta and Continental. The government finally launched a public offering of Air France in 1999 (keeping 63%, later reduced).

To better compete with members of the Star and Oneworld global airline marketing alliances, Air France joined Delta Air Lines, AeroMéxico, and Korean Air Lines to form the SkyTeam alliance in 2000. Also that year Air France further consolidated the domestic market by acquiring or upping stakes in regional carriers Proteus Airlines, Flandre Air, and Regional Airlines.

An Air France Concorde jet crashed shortly after takeoff from Paris in 2000, killing all 109 people on board and four more on the ground. Concorde flights were grounded after the crash, but resumed the following year.

Air France fared better than most airlines in the wake of September 2001 terrorist attacks on the US. The airline curbed its expansion plans and streamlined its fleet, but did not cut back on routes or resort to layoffs to stay aloft. Instead, Air France began looking for ways to grow, and it began talks with Dutch carrier KLM in 2002. Initially the carriers discussed forming an alliance, but discussions soon developed into the merger kind. By 2003 the two carriers were looking into how to combine their respective operations and announced their intent to merge.

The European Commission threw a wrench in the deal when it launched an investigation in early 2004 into potential anti-competitive elements of the merger. The investigation could have taken months to complete and slowed the roll-out of the new airline. The Commission, however, approved the merger rather quickly when the two airlines agreed to give up 94 slots per day between their airports to ensure a competitive market amongst European airlines. That same year it signed a codeshare agreement with Australia's Qantas Airways.

In 2005 Air France became the first European airline to say it would add the new Airbus A380 super jumbo to its fleet. Passengers will be able to take flight in the A380 in April 2007. That same year Air France sold its 30% stake in Air Austral to French bank Credit Agricole.

HISTORICAL FINANCIALS

Company Type: Subsidiary

Income Statement

FYE: March 31

	REVENUE ($ mil.)	NET INCOME ($ mil.)	NET PROFIT MARGIN	EMPLOYEES
3/04	15,018	113	0.8%	71,654
3/03	13,696	130	0.9%	71,525
3/02	10,899	133	1.2%	70,156
3/01	10,790	370	3.4%	64,717
3/00	9,861	338	3.4%	59,190
3/99	9,766	268	2.7%	55,199
3/98	9,810	303	3.1%	46,385
3/97	7,693	66	0.9%	44,874
3/96	8,269	(436)	—	45,084
3/95	13,558	(722)	—	47,343
Annual Growth	1.1%	—	—	4.7%

2004 Year-End Financials

Debt ratio: 100.7%
Return on equity: 2.4%
Cash ($ mil.): 402

Current ratio: 2.78
Long-term debt ($ mil.): 4,980

Net Income History

400									
200									
0									
-200									
-400									
-600									
-800									
	3/95	3/96	3/97	3/98	3/99	3/00	3/01	3/02	3/03	3/04

Airbus S.A.S.

Can you imagine 550-800 people in one airplane? Airbus, which has moved past Boeing as the world's #1 commercial aircraft maker, is betting that airlines will love its gigantic double-decker A380 (maiden flight completed in 2005; due out in 2007) for hub airports. The company's current planes include single-aisle (A318, A319, A320, A321) and wide-body (A300, A310, A330, A340) models with capacities ranging from about 110 to 400 passengers. Airbus has also announced that it will build a new mid-sized plane, the A350. Due out in 2010 and based on the A330 platform, the A350 will compete directly against Boeing's upcoming 787 Dreamliner. EADS owns 80% of Airbus; UK-based BAE SYSTEMS owns the other 20%.

Airbus, which had opted for big (the A380) vs. Boeing's small (the 787 Dreamliner) announced in December of 2004 that it wanted it both ways. To complement its gigantic A380 — and, not incidentally, compete head-to-head against Boeing's 787 — the company would build a new mid-size plane, the A350.

Before the A350 announcement Airbus had been banking on its jumbo A380 (which received brisk orders even before it was formally approved — so much so that Boeing scrapped plans for a competing plane), a steady increase in passenger air travel and air cargo transport, new flight routes, and the need for more mid-sized, long-range aircraft for future success.

With the A350, the company has hedged its bets. Based on the A330 and due in 2010 — two years behind behind the 787 — the A350 will reportedly come in two configurations: the A350-800 will seat 245 passengers and have a range of 8,600 miles; the A350-900 will seat 285 passengers and have a range of 7,500 miles. Boeing returned Airbus' A350 vs. Dreamliner favor in November 2005 when it announced that it built a stretch 450-passenger 747-8 to compete more directly with Airbus' A380.

EADS consists of DaimlerChrysler Aerospace (Germany), Aerospatiale Matra (France), and CASA (Spain). Each company oversees part of the production; for example, aircraft wings hail from the UK, cockpits are from France, and interiors come from Germany. Airbus plants in France and Germany assemble the parts.

Airbus CEO Noël Forgeard left to become co-CEO of EADS in mid-2005. Former Airbus chief operating officer Gustav Humbert replaced Forgeard as Airbus' CEO.

HISTORY

In the 1970s three US companies, Boeing, Lockheed, and McDonnell Douglas, dominated the commercial aircraft market. France and the UK had been discussing an alliance to build competing jets since 1965, but political infighting stalled the talks. Finally, in 1969 France and West Germany committed to building the Airbus A300. Airbus Industrie was born in 1970 as a *groupement d'intérêt économique* (grouping of economic interest, a structure used by allied French vineyards). Seed money came from partners Aerospatiale Matra and Deutsche Airbus. CASA joined in 1971.

The A300 entered service with Air France in 1974, but Airbus had trouble selling it outside member countries. The following year the firm hired former American Airlines president George

Warde to help market the A300 in the US. His efforts paid off when Eastern Air Lines decided to buy the A300. Also in 1975 Airbus launched the A310, a smaller, more fuel-efficient version of the A300. The UK joined the consortium in 1979.

By 1980 Airbus trailed only Boeing among the world's commercial jet makers. The A320 was introduced in 1984 — it featured a ground-breaking "fly-by-wire" system that allowed pilots to adjust the aircraft's control surfaces via a computer, helping to make it the fastest-selling jetliner in history. The firm launched the A330 and A340, larger planes designed for medium- and long-range flights, in 1987. Two years later Airbus introduced the A321, an elongated version of the A320, and received a $6 billion order from Federal Express.

The German government sold its 20% stake in Deutsche Airbus to Daimler-Benz (now Daimler-Chrysler) in 1992, giving Daimler-Benz 100% ownership of the German partner (it now holds about 38%).

In 1993 Airbus sold only 38 planes, about one-sixth as many as Boeing. Sales rebounded in 1995, and the next year the firm won a contract worth about $5 billion to provide planes to USAir (now US Airways). The four Airbus partners agreed in 1997 to restructure the consortium as a limited liability company, possibly as a first step toward taking it public.

Seeking more customers in Asia, Airbus signed parts contracts with Japanese suppliers in 1999 and launched production of its A318, a 107-seat short-haul passenger jet designed to compete with Boeing's 717. Also that year Airbus won a contract worth $946 million to provide British Airways with up to 24 of its A318s. For the first time ever, the company recorded more plane orders than Boeing.

In 2000 the UK government pledged $836 million in loans to back consortium partner BAE SYSTEMS' participation in the A3XX project, an ambitious plane that would seat more than 550 passengers. That year the German government announced plans to purchase up to 75 Airbus A400M transports valued at around $9.8 billion. In June the company announced that it had finally inked a deal to turn Airbus into a corporation. It also committed to producing the superjumbo A3XX and soon received 17 firm orders from Air France and Emirates Airlines. Around the same time, the European Aeronautic Defence & Space Company, which owns 80% of Airbus, launched its own IPO.

Airbus officially launched the A3XX — and renamed it the A380 — late in 2000. Early in 2001 Airbus announced that it would become a stand-alone corporation (rather than a consortium) before the end of the year. The company also announced that it was setting up a subsidiary in Japan — where Boeing traditionally dominates. In July Airbus Industrie was incorporated in France as Airbus S.A.S.

Faced with the drastic downturn in the commercial aviation market due to the September 11 attacks, in 2002 the company announced that it would cut full-time equivalent work hours by around 13% (equal to about 6,000 jobs) through voluntary retirement, reduction in part-time work, and cancellation of temporary contracts.

Airbus unveiled the first A380 to press and buyers in 2005. The A380 made a maiden test flight of nearly four hours on April 27, 2005. Just over a month later, Airbus announced that deliveries of the first A380s would be delayed by up to six months.

EXECUTIVES

President, CEO, and COO: Gustav Humbert, age 55
CFO: Andreas Sperl, age 58
Chief Commercial Officer and EVP, Commercial Affairs: John J. Leahy, age 55
EVP, Customer Services: Patrick Gavin, age 56
EVP, Government Relations, Communications, and External Affairs: Philippe Delmas, age 51
EVP, Engineering: Alain Garcia, age 62
EVP, Human Resources: Erik Pillet, age 48
EVP, Operations: Karl-Heinz Hartmann, age 54
EVP, Procurement: Henri Courpron, age 42
EVP, Programmes: Tom Williams, age 53
EVP, Special Advisor to the CEO: Jürgen Thomas
Managing Director, Airbus Military SL: Francisco Fernández Sáinz, age 60
SVP; Chairman, Airbus North America Holdings, Inc.: T. Allan (Allan) McArtor
SVP; General Manager, Airbus España: Manuel Hita-Romero, age 60
SVP; General Manager, Airbus France: Jean-Marc Thomas
SVP; General Manager, Airbus Germany: Gerhard Puttfarcken, age 59
SVP; General Manager, Airbus UK: Iain Gray, age 48
SVP; President, Airbus China: Laurence Barron, age 54
President and CEO, Airbus Japan: Glen S. Fukushima, age 55

LOCATIONS

HQ: Airbus S.A.S.
1, Rond point Maurice Bellonte,
31707 Blagnac, France
Phone: +33-5-61-93-33-33 **Fax:** +33-5-61-93-49-55
US HQ: 198 Van Buren St., Ste. 300, Herndon, VA 20170
US Phone: 703-834-3400 **US Fax:** 703-834-3341
Web: www.airbus.com

Airbus S.A.S. has offices in China, North America, and Singapore, and it manufactures airplanes in factories throughout Europe, with final assembly carried out in France and Germany.

PRODUCTS/OPERATIONS

Selected Aircraft

Single-aisle twin-engine jets
  A318
  A319
  A320
  A321
Superjumbo four-engine jets
  A380 (555-passenger, scheduled for delivery in 2007)
Wide-body twin-engine jets
  A300-310
  A300-600F
Wide-body two- and four-engine jets
  A330 (two-engine)
  A340 (four-engine)
  A340-500
  A340-600
  A350-800
    (245-passenger, scheduled for delivery in 2010)
  A350-900
    (285-passenger, scheduled for delivery in 2010)

Selected Customers

Aer Lingus	Japan Air System
Air Canada	Korean Airlines
Air France	Lufthansa
Alitalia	Northwest
America West	SilkAir (Singapore
American Airlines	Airlines)
China Southern	United
Delta	US Airways
Federal Express	Virgin Atlantic Airways
Iberia	

COMPETITORS

Boeing
Boeing Commercial Airplanes
Boeing UK
Bombardier
Bombardier Aerospace
Embraer
Gulfstream Aerospace
Sextant Avionique

HISTORICAL FINANCIALS

Company Type: Joint venture

Income Statement

FYE: December 31

	REVENUE ($ mil.)	NET INCOME ($ mil.)	NET PROFIT MARGIN	EMPLOYEES
12/04	27,280	—	—	53,000
12/03	24,225	—	—	50,000
12/02	20,333	—	—	46,000
12/01	18,159	—	—	45,000
12/00	17,200	—	—	45,000
12/99	16,817	—	—	45,000
12/98	13,300	—	—	2,700
12/97	11,600	—	—	2,289
12/96	8,800	—	—	2,207
12/95	9,600	—	—	2,182
Annual Growth	**12.3%**	**—**	**—**	**42.5%**

Revenue History

(Revenue in $ mil., 12/95–12/04, rising from about 9,600 to 27,280)

Akzo Nobel

Akzo Nobel is the world's largest paint maker, but it can do more than paint a pretty picture. The company is among the world's largest chemical manufacturers and also is a major salt producer. Akzo Nobel is organized along three business lines. The company's coatings group makes paints, automotive finishes, and decorative coatings. Its chemical unit produces pulp and paper chemicals, functional chemicals (including flame retardants and crop nutrients), surfactants (used in detergents and personal care products), polymers, and catalysts. A third unit, pharmaceuticals, produces contraceptives, fertility treatments, antidepressants, antipsychotics, over-the-counter drugs, and veterinary medicines.

Coming off a difficult 2003, Akzo Nobel spent much of 2004 trimming down, divesting three businesses (phosphorous chemicals, catalysts, and coating resins) from its chemicals segment. The three units netted the company $1 billion, which it intends to use to buffer the coatings segment.

That came to fruition in 2005 with acquisitions in Germany, France, and Switzerland. That last purchase, of Swiss Lack, made Akzo Nobel the largest paint company in Switzerland as well.

The company's pharmaceutical business, too, has been hurt by the end of patent protection in the US on its top-selling drug, the antidepressant

Remeron. A management reorganization in the unit led to a rethinking of strategy. Akzo Nobel now actively seeks out partnerships in the manufacture and marketing of its drugs. While 2005 will likely be a down year for the segment, the company is pointing to potential drug launches in 2006 to boost sales greatly.

Late in 2005 Akzo Nobel decided to further pare down its operations with an agreement to sell its inks and adhesive resins business to Hexion Specialty Chemicals. The business is concentrated in Europe but has strong international operations as well. The deal should net the company about $100 million.

Akzo Nobel has operations in 80 countries; about half its sales are in Europe.

HISTORY

The Akzo side of Akzo Nobel traces its roots to two companies — German rayon and coatings maker Vereinigte Glanzstoff-Fabriken (founded in 1899) and Dutch rayon maker Nederlandsche Kunstzijdebariek (founded in 1911 and known as NK or Enka). In 1928 NK built a plant near Asheville, North Carolina, in what later became the town of Enka. The two companies merged in 1929 to create Algemene Kunstzijde-Unie (AKU).

In 1967 two Dutch companies merged to form Koninklijke Zout-Organon (KZO). In 1969 KZO bought US-based International Salt and merged with AKU to form Akzo. In the 1980s Akzo focused on building its chemicals, coatings, and pharmaceuticals businesses. Akzo sold its paper and pulp business to Nobel in 1993. A few months later the company reclaimed that business when it bought Nobel.

Best remembered for the prizes that bear his name (which were first awarded in 1901 through a bequest in his will), Alfred Nobel invented the blasting cap in 1863, making it possible to control the detonation of nitroglycerin. He then persuaded Stockholm merchant J. W. Smitt to help him finance Nitroglycerin Ltd. to make and sell the volatile fluid (1864). Nobel's quest to improve nitroglycerin led to his invention of dynamite in 1867.

After Nobel's death in 1896, Nitroglycerin Ltd. remained an explosives maker, and in 1965 it changed its name to Nitro Nobel. In 1978 Swedish industrialist Marcus Wallenberg bought Nitro Nobel for his KemaNord chemical group, known afterward as KemaNobel. Within six years industrialist Erik Penser controlled both armaments maker Bofors and KemaNobel, and he merged them in 1984 as Nobel Industries.

Risky investments led Penser to ruin in 1991. His holdings, including Nobel, were taken over by a government-owned bank and conveyed into Securum, a government-owned holding company (which still owns 18% of Akzo Nobel). In 1992 Nobel spun off its consumer-goods segment.

Akzo bought Nobel in 1994. Although the company had good financial results in 1995, it faced pressure from rising costs for raw materials and a difficult foreign-exchange environment. Akzo announced major closings and layoffs — it sold its polyethylene packaging resin business and moved some clothing-grade rayon operations to Poland.

The merger between Akzo and Nobel was legally completed in 1996. That year the company introduced Puregon, a fertility drug, and Remeron, touted as a replacement for Prozac, in the US and other countries. In 1997 Akzo Nobel put most of its worst-performing segment, fibers, into a joint venture with Turkish conglomerate

Sabanci. It also sold its North American salt unit to Cargill.

Akzo Nobel acquired Courtaulds (coatings, sealants, and fibers) in 1998 and changed the firm's name to Akzo Nobel UK. Akzo Nobel also bought BASF deco, the European decorative-coatings business of BASF Coatings. Akzo Nobel combined its fiber business with Akzo Nobel UK to form a new division, Acordis. Akzo Nobel then sold Acordis to investment firm CVC Capital Partners in 1999 for $859 million (Akzo Nobel retains a minority share). Also in 1999 Akzo Nobel bought Hoechst's animal-health unit, Hoechst Roussel Vet, for $712 million. The next year the company bought Dexter Corporation's aircraft coatings business.

In 2001 Akzo Nobel sold its medical diagnostics division to French drugmaker bioMérieux-Pierre Fabre. Later that year the company picked up the vehicle refinishes business of MAC Specialty Coatings of the US. In November Akzo Nobel agreed to sell its printing inks business to a private equity firm.

CEO Cees van Lede retired in May 2003, succeeded by Hans Wijers, who immediately set about restructuring, cutting costs, and erasing debt. By the end of that year more than 3,300 jobs were cut and Akzo Nobel had sold off three big chemical units: catalysts (to Albemarle for about $750 million), coating resins, and phosphorous chemicals (to Ripplewood Holdings for another $270 million).

In late 2005 Akzo Nobel acquired a 60% stake in Egypt-based powder coatings manufacturer Coatech For Chemical Industries SAE; the new joint venture will change its name to Akzo Nobel Powder Coatings.

EXECUTIVES

Chairman, Supervisory Board:
Jonkheer Aarnout Loudon, age 68
Chairman, Board of Management and CEO:
G. J. (Hans) Wijers, age 54
Member, Board of Management and CFO: Rob Frohn, age 43
Member, Board of Management, Chemicals: Leif Darner
Member, Board of Management, Pharma; President, Organon: A.T. M. (Toon) Wilderbeek, age 55
SVP, Finance: Frits H. Hensel, age 62
SVP, Human Resources: Heiko Hutmacher, age 46
General Counsel: A. Jan A. J. Eijsbouts
Secretary: G.H. (Han) Jalink
Senior Group Director, Chemicals; President and Treasurer, Akzo Nobel, Inc.: Conrad S. Kent
Senior Group Director, Coatings; General Manager, Car Refinishes: M. (Rinus) Rooseboom, age 58
Senior Group Director, Pharmaceuticals: Jan H. Dopper
Corporate Information Officer: Bill Stubbins, age 50
Corporate Director, Corporate Social Responsibility and Health, Safety, and Environment: André Veneman, age 45
Director, Internal Auditing: Paul Grimmelikhuizen, age 51
Director, Corporate Strategy: Derek Welch
Auditors: KPMG Accountants N.V.

LOCATIONS

HQ: Akzo Nobel N.V.
Velperweg 76, 6800 SB Arnhem, The Netherlands
Phone: +31-26-366-4433 **Fax:** +31-26-366-3250
US HQ: 525 W. Van Buren St., Chicago, IL 60607
US Phone: 312-544-7000
Web: www.akzonobel.com

Akzo Nobel has operations in roughly 80 countries.

2004 Sales

	$ mil.	% of total
Europe		
Germany	1,570	9
UK	1,126	7
The Netherlands	1,119	6
Sweden	685	4
Other	5,435	32
US & Canada	3,309	19
Asia	2,079	12
Latin America	983	6
Other	881	5
Total	**17,187**	**100**

PRODUCTS/OPERATIONS

2004 Sales and Operating Income

	Sales		Operating Income	
	$ mil.	% of total	$ mil.	% of total
Coatings	7,110	41	488	24
Chemicals	5,852	34	1,032	50
Pharma	4,397	25	539	26
Adjustments	(152)	—	(298)	—
Total	**17,187**	**100**	**1,761**	**100**

Selected Products

Coatings
Car refinishes
Decorative coatings
Industrial finishes
Industrial products
Marine and protective coatings
Powder coatings
Chemicals
Base chemicals
Energy
Functional chemicals
Polymer chemicals
Pulp and paper chemicals
Salt
Surface chemistry
Pharmaceuticals
Drugs for human health care (including oral contraceptives, antidepressants, and infertility treatments)
Pharmaceutical ingredients
Veterinary medicines (including antibiotics, vaccines, and anti-infectives)

COMPETITORS

Abbott Labs	Huntsman
Alfa	Imperial
Asahi Kasei	Chemical Industries
BASF AG	Johnson & Johnson
Bayer	Kemira
Bristol-Myers Squibb	Merck
Compass Minerals	Novartis
Degussa	Novo Nordisk
Dow Chemical	Orica
DuPont	PPG
Eastman Chemical	Roche
Eli Lilly	Rohm and Haas
Engelhard	RPM
Ferro	Sherwin-Williams
Formosa Plastics	Solvay
GlaxoSmithKline	TOTAL
H.B. Fuller	Valspar
Hercules	Wyeth

HISTORICAL FINANCIALS

Company Type: Public

Income Statement

FYE: December 31

	REVENUE ($ mil.)	NET INCOME ($ mil.)	NET PROFIT MARGIN	EMPLOYEES
12/04	17,187	1,160	6.7%	60,350
12/03	16,408	757	4.6%	66,400
12/02	14,706	859	5.8%	67,900
12/01	12,576	598	4.8%	66,300
12/00	13,188	909	6.9%	68,400
12/99	14,565	206	1.4%	68,000
12/98	14,557	711	4.9%	85,900
12/97	11,872	797	6.7%	68,900
12/96	12,882	757	5.9%	70,700
12/95	13,363	817	6.1%	69,800
Annual Growth	**2.8%**	**4.0%**	**—**	**(1.6%)**

2004 Year-End Financials

Debt ratio: 78.8%
Return on equity: 32.0%
Cash ($ mil.): 2,453
Current ratio: 1.81
Long-term debt ($ mil.): 3,240
No. of shares (mil.): 286
Dividends
Yield: 2.9%
Payout: 30.6%
Market value ($ mil.): 12,158

Stock History

NASDAQ: AKZOY

	STOCK PRICE ($) FY Close	P/E High/Low		Earnings	PER SHARE ($) Dividends	Book Value
12/04	42.49	11	8	4.05	1.24	14.37
12/03	38.21	15	7	2.64	1.25	10.99
12/02	31.89	16	9	3.00	1.08	7.70
12/01	44.85	19	11	2.10	1.10	8.17
12/00	53.25	17	12	3.19	0.93	8.06
12/99	49.75	19	13	0.71	2.11	6.57
12/98	44.63	26	13	2.49	1.06	7.44
12/97	43.44	17	11	2.80	0.78	31.28
12/96	33.75	13	10	2.66	0.90	31.07
12/95	29.00	12	9	2.88	0.83	28.89
Annual Growth	**4.3%**	**—**	**—**	**3.9%**	**4.6%**	**(7.5%)**

Alcan Inc.

Its Alcan-do attitude has helped make Alcan one of the world's largest aluminum producers, behind the US's Alcoa. The company controls 13% of the world's aluminum production capacity. It mines bauxite (aluminum ore) and makes and recycles aluminum sheet, foil, wire and cable, and extrusions (doors, windows, auto parts). Alcan also generates hydroelectric power and makes aluminum-related specialty chemicals and packaging products. This decade has proved busy for Alcan. It bought Algroup in 2000, Pechiney in 2003, and spun off its aluminum rolled products unit into a public company called Novelis in early 2005.

Finally settled down following the additions of Algroup and Pechiney and the divestiture of Novelis, Alcan runs its business through six segments:

Packaging, Engineered Products, Rolled Products Americas & Asia, Rolled Products Europe, Primary Metal, and Bauxite and Alumina.

Alcan's packaging segment includes aluminum, plastic, paperboard, glass, and steel products for a variety of industries. The engineered products group makes cable and wire along with composite materials. The rolled products segments make aluminum sheet and light gauge products for the automotive and beverage can markets. The primary metal division runs smelting operations, power generation, and manufacture of anodes and fluoride. Lastly, the bauxite and alumina unit mines bauxite and then refines it, making alumina.

The US accounts for close to a third of company sales.

The company's purchase of VAW Flexible Packaging from Norsk Hydro ASA appreciably bolstered Alcan's packaging sector. The move was part of Alcan's strategic push to expand the global reach of its packaging business. The company also acquired a Polish flexible packaging plant that furthers its Central and Eastern European interests even more. Another move designed to increase its international business was the 2005 acquisition of the Malaysian tobacco packaging company CM Printing. The deal raised Alcan's presence in a region where many tobacco companies are ramping up production.

HISTORY

In 1886 American chemist Charles Hall and a French chemist simultaneously discovered an inexpensive process for aluminum production. Two years later Hall, with an investor group led by Captain Alfred Hunt, formed the Pittsburgh Reduction Company. It became the Aluminum Company of America (Alcoa) in 1907.

As mandated by a US antitrust divestment order, in 1928 Alcoa organized its Canadian and other foreign operations as a separate company, Aluminium Limited (which used the British spelling for *aluminum*). The company retained close ties with Alcoa and appointed Edward Davis, brother of former Alcoa chairman Arthur Davis, its first chief executive.

After narrowly surviving the Depression, Aluminium Limited expanded globally, building plants in Asia and Europe. Aluminum demand during WWII made it the world's largest smelter by war's end.

US courts in 1950 ordered the Mellon and Davis families to end their joint ownership of Alcoa and Aluminium Limited. Both families opted to stay with Alcoa.

In 1961 the company began fabricating its own products in Oswego, New York. Aluminium Limited changed its name to Alcan in 1966. Alcan had to readjust its strategy when Guyana nationalized its raw resources in 1971. Six years later Jamaica (a major bauxite producer) acquired 70% of Alcan's assets, and the two formed joint venture Jamalcan.

David Culver became the company's CEO (the first non-Davis family member to hold the position) in 1979 and led Alcan through an early 1980s recession with a massive cost-cutting campaign. In 1989 Alcan built the world's largest aluminum beverage-can recycling plant in Berea, Kentucky.

The entrance of former Soviet republics and other Eastern Bloc countries into the international aluminum market in 1991 caused a drastic drop in aluminum prices worldwide. That year

Alcan shut down 8% of its smelting capacity and began selling off less-profitable operations.

By 1994 increased global demand for aluminum and cutbacks in production spurred industrywide recovery, and Alcan's operations returned to the black for the first time in four years. In 1998 Alcan signed a 10-year pact to supply aluminum to General Motors. As market conditions in Asia soured, Alcan reduced its ownership of Nippon Light Metal Company from 45% to about 11%. Also that year it sold Handy Chemicals Limited.

In 1999 the company agreed to acquire Pechiney and Alusuisse Lonza Group (Algroup) in a three-way merger to create Alcan-Pechiney-Algroup. In 2000 the European Commission approved a proposed merger between Alcan and Algroup, but Alcan's plan to include Pechiney in a three-way merger had to be withdrawn because of antitrust concerns. Pechiney pulled out of the deal entirely after Alcan voted against selling its 50% stake in a German aluminum plant (Norf). The same year Alcan acquired Algroup in a $5.3 billion deal.

Company president and CEO Jacques Bougie resigned in 2001 and was replaced by former ITT Industries CEO Travis Engen. To reflect its broader array of products, the company changed its name from Alcan Aluminium to Alcan Inc. that year.

In 2002 Alcan increased its stake from 20% to 40% in Aluminerie Alouette (aluminum smelter, Canada) from Corus Group; Alcan also sold certain parts of its molded glass operations to Glass Group Inc.

Alcan acquired VAW Flexible Packaging from Norsk Hydro for around $545 million in 2003. Mid-year Alcan launched a hostile bid for French competitor Pechiney for roughly $3.9 billion in cash and stock. Pechiney's board members unanimously rejected Alcan's takeover bid indicating the offer was undervalued. Alcan raised its offer to $4.3 billion but Pechiney rejected that offer as well. The company countered a third time with a proposal of roughly $5 billion, which about 92% of Pechiney's shareholders accepted. Soon after, Alcan reopened its offering and gained another 7%, making its total ownership in Pechiney approximately 99%. In 2004 Alcan was granted the last remaining percentage, giving it full ownership in Pechiney.

In 2005 Alcan spun off its aluminum rolled products unit, known as Novelis, as a publicly traded company.

EXECUTIVES

Chairman: L. Yves Fortier, age 69
President, CEO, and Director: Travis Engen, age 61, $2,830,000 pay
EVP, COO, and Director: Richard B. (Dick) Evans, age 57, $872,500 pay (prior to promotion)
EVP (Office of the President) and CFO: Michael Hanley, age 39
EVP, Corporate Development and Chief Legal Officer: David L. McAusland, age 51
SVP, Corporate and External Affairs: Daniel Gagnier, age 58
SVP, Human Resources: Gaston Ouellet, age 62
SVP; President and CEO, Alcan Primary Metal Group: Cynthia Carroll, age 48, $1,176,433 pay
SVP; President and CEO, Alcan Packaging: Christel Bories, age 40
SVP; President and CEO, Alcan Engineered Products: Michel Jacques, age 52
SVP; President and CEO, Alcan Bauxite and Alumina: Jacynthe Côté, age 47
VP and Controller: Cesidio Ricci, age 40
VP and Treasurer: Rhodri J. Harries, age 41

VP, International Relations and Government Affairs: Thierry Berthoud
Corporate Secretary: Roy Millington, age 45
VP, Communications: Elizabeth Vassallucci
VP, Corporate Procurement: Jacques Barrailler
VP, Investor Relations: Corey B. Copeland
Chief Tax Officer: Michael O'Connor
Deputy Chief Legal Officer: Pierre Chenard
Auditors: PricewaterhouseCoopers LLP

LOCATIONS

HQ: Alcan Inc.
 1188 Sherbrooke St. West,
 Montreal, Quebec H3A 3G2, Canada
Phone: 514-848-8000   **Fax:** 514-848-8115
US HQ: 8770 W. Bryn Mawr Ave.,
 Chicago, IL 60631
US Phone: 773-399-8000
Web: www.alcan.com

Alcan operates bauxite mines in Australia, Brazil, and Ghana; alumina plants in Australia, Brazil, Canada, and the UK; and manufacturing plants or sales offices in more than 38 countries in Africa, Asia, Australia, Europe, and the Americas.

2004 Sales

	$ mil.	% of total
Europe		
Germany	2,267	9
France	2,197	9
UK	2,099	8
Switzerland	235	1
Other	4,453	18
US	7,620	31
Asia & Other Pacific	3,051	12
Canada	1,117	4
Brazil	527	2
Australia	429	2
Other	890	4
Total	**24,885**	**100**

PRODUCTS/OPERATIONS

2004 Sales

	$ mil.	% of total
Packaging	6,119	24
Engineered Products	5,162	21
Rolled Products Americas & Asia	4,388	18
Primary Metal	4,275	17
Rolled Products Europe	3,217	13
Bauxite & Alumina	1,501	6
Other	263	1
Adjustments	(40)	—
Total	**24,885**	**100**

Selected Products and Services

Fabrication Group
 Castings (automobile engine components, aluminum alloys)
 Extrusions (automobile components, doors, and windows; extrusion ingots)
 Flat-rolled products (foil and sheet)
 Flexible packaging
 Recycling
 Wire and cable (electrical wire and cable, screen wire, cable coverings)

Primary Metal Group
 Alumina refining
 Aluminum activities
 Bauxite mining
 Power generation

HISTORICAL FINANCIALS

Company Type: Public

Income Statement

FYE: December 31

	REVENUE ($ mil.)	NET INCOME ($ mil.)	NET PROFIT MARGIN	EMPLOYEES
12/04	24,885	258	1.0%	82,500
12/03	13,640	167	1.2%	88,000
12/02	12,540	374	3.0%	48,100
12/01	12,626	5	0.0%	52,000
12/00	9,148	618	6.8%	37,000
12/99	7,324	460	6.3%	36,000
12/98	7,789	399	5.1%	36,000
12/97	7,777	485	6.2%	33,000
12/96	7,614	410	5.4%	34,000
12/95	9,287	263	2.8%	39,000
Annual Growth	11.6%	(0.2%)	—	8.7%

2004 Year-End Financials

Debt ratio: 60.1%
Return on equity: 2.4%
Cash ($ mil.): 184
Current ratio: 1.02
Long-term debt ($ mil.): 6,345

No. of shares (mil.): 370
Dividends
  Yield: 1.2%
  Payout: 87.0%
Market value ($ mil.): 18,141

Stock History

NYSE: AL

	STOCK PRICE ($) FY Close	P/E High/Low	PER SHARE ($) Earnings	Dividends	Book Value
12/04	49.04	76 53	0.69	0.60	28.99
12/03	46.95	97 53	0.50	0.47	29.34
12/02	29.52	37 20	1.14	0.54	26.83
12/01	35.93	— —	(0.01)	0.60	27.39
12/00	34.19	19 12	2.45	0.60	28.38
12/99	41.38	20 11	2.06	0.60	25.38
12/98	27.06	20 11	1.71	0.60	24.42
12/97	27.63	20 13	2.09	0.60	22.32
12/96	33.63	21 16	1.74	0.60	21.46
12/95	31.13	35 22	1.06	0.45	21.40
Annual Growth	5.2%	— —	(4.7%)	3.2%	3.4%

Alcatel

Alcatel found its calling. One of France's largest industrial companies, Alcatel is a leading global supplier of high-tech equipment for telecommunications networks. Core network switching and transmission systems for wireline and wireless networks for carriers and enterprises account for most of its sales. Other communications products include cell phones, communications cable, and satellite equipment. The company also manufactures transport automation equipment and provides a wide array of services. Alcatel's clients include top European telecom service providers Orange and Deutsche Telekom.

Chairman and CEO Serge Tchuruk (pronounced "cha-RUK") has honed a once lumbering Alcatel with broad industrial interests into a focused telecom heavyweight. He has overseen an extensive restructuring that included the sale of noncore businesses such as electrical power, engineering, nuclear power, and defense electronics. Alcatel's operations are now organized into three main divisions: fixed communications, mobile communications, and private communications.

A global leader in the markets for optical and DSL network infrastructure equipment, Alcatel trails its competitors in sales of wireless equipment. The company's attempts to remedy that situation include the acquisition of mobile network switching products maker Spatial Wireless for $250 million in 2004. Alcatel also turned its attention to its IP routing product lines with the acquisitions of eDial and TiMetra that year. The company bought iMagic and PacketVideo in 2003 as part of an effort to gain ground in the video networking market.

Alcatel has teamed up with Finmeccanica to form two joint ventures — Alcatel Alenia Space and Telespazio Holding. Alcatel Alenia Space, in which Alcatel owns 67% and Finmeccanica 33%, combines Alcatel Space and Alenia Spazio and is focused on the design, development, and manufacture of space systems, satellites, and related systems for civilian and military use. Telespazio Holding is 67% owned by Finmeccanica and 33% by Alcatel, is meant to concentrate on operations and services for satellite systems, and combines Alcatel Space Services with Telespazio.

Alcatel, which makes half of its sales in Europe, is firming up its presence in the US through acquisitions as well as pursuing contracts in burgeoning Asia markets such as China. The company's key customers include Verizon, AT&T (formerly SBC Communications), BellSouth, and China Telecom.

HISTORY

In 1898 Pierre Azaria combined his electric generating company with three others to form Compagnie Générale d'Électricité (CGE). As one of Europe's pioneer electric power and manufacturing companies, CGE expanded operations in France and abroad through acquisitions. After the French government nationalized electric utilities in 1946, CGE diversified into the production of telecommunications equipment, consumer appliances, and electronics.

In 1970 CGE bought Alcatel, a French communications pioneer founded in 1879 that had introduced digital switching exchanges. CGE combined its telecom division with Alcatel to form CIT Alcatel.

The Mitterrand government nationalized CGE in 1982. The next year the company traded its electronics units for Thomson's communications businesses, making CGE the world's fifth-largest telephone equipment maker. Later, CGE combined Alcatel with ITT's phone equipment operations to form Alcatel NV, a Brussels-based company that started off as the world's second-largest telecom enterprise, after AT&T.

In 1987 the government sold CGE to the public. Two years later CGE and UK-based The General Electric Company, plc (GEC, now Marconi plc) combined their power systems and engineering businesses to create GEC Alsthom NV. The company adopted the Alcatel Alsthom name in 1991 (shortened to Alcatel in 1998) and purchased the transmission equipment unit of US-based Rockwell International (now Rockwell Automation).

Turnaround specialist Serge Tchuruk, the former head of French oil giant TOTAL, was chosen to lead the company in 1995. Deregulation and intense competition in the European telecom market, along with massive writeoffs of bad investments dating back to the 1980s, led to a $5 billion loss in 1995, Alcatel's first loss and one of the largest to date by a French company. As a result Alcatel divested nonstrategic assets and cut its workforce by more than 12,500 employees. The company bounced back with a profit in 1996.

Following the recommendation of the French government, in 1998 Alcatel, Dassault Industries, and Aerospatiale joined forces to buy part of the state's stake in defense electronics group Thomson-CSF (now Thales). Intensifying its telecommunications focus, Alcatel sold its main engineering unit (Cegelec) to GEC Alsthom in 1998 and then spun off the venture as ALSTOM.

In 2000 Alcatel swapped all but 10% of its stake in nuclear power company Framatome for an additional 10% of Thomson-CSF. The company pressed further into the US that year with the purchases of Genesys Telecommunications (computer-telephony software) and Canadian equipment maker Newbridge Networks. Also that year Alcatel sold 20% of its optical components unit to create the first European tracking stock.

In 2001 Genesys acquired IBM's CallPath computer-telephony software unit. A market slowdown that year led Alcatel to announce staff cuts of about 10%. In 2002 Alcatel sold its enterprise distribution and services operations in Europe to Platinum Equity.

The company added to its optical transport products for metro networks with the acquisition of startup Astral Point that year, and it announced that it would acquire privately held Telera, a US-based provider of software for making Web content accessible by phone, in order to strengthen Genesys' contact center software business. That year it sold its semiconductor business, Alcatel Microelectronics, to STMicroelectronics for about $345 million; the two companies will jointly develop chipsets for DSL networking equipment.

Alcatel in 2003 began a series of acquisitions intended to build its presence in the wireless, IP routing, and video markets. The company that year also sold its power systems unit, which comprised AEG SVS Power Supply Systems, Alcatel Converters, Harmer & Simmons, and the Saft Power Systems business lines.

EXECUTIVES

Chairman and CEO: Serge Tchuruk, age 67, $3,142,124 pay
President and COO: Mike Quigley, age 52
CFO: Jean-Pascal Beaufret, age 54
CTO: Olivier Baujard
Chief Marketing Officer: Alan Mottram
EVP; President, Alcatel Europe and South: Jacques Dunogué, age 54
EVP; President, Mobile Communications Group: Etienne Fouques, age 56
EVP; President, Private Communications Group; Chairman, Telespazio Holding: Olivier Houssin, age 52
EVP; President, Alcatel Asia-Pacific: Christian Reinaudo, age 50
SVP, Corporate Human Resources: Thomas Edig, age 43
SVP, Corporate Communications: Caroline Mille
SVP, Corporate Operations: Christian Tournier, age 60
VP, Internal Communications and Corporate Image: Cyril Déchelette
VP and General Manager, Mobile Solutions, North America: Matthieu Cornillault
President, IP: Basil Alwan
President, Enterprise Solutions: Jean-Christophe Giroux
President, Submarine Networks: Jean Godeluck
President, Mobile Solutions, North America: David Owen
President, Alcatel Iberia and Latin America; CEO, Alcatel España: Alfredo Redondo
President, Optical Networks: Romano Valussi
VP, Investor Relations: Pascal Bantegnie
VP, Investor Relations, North America: Charlotte Laurent-Ottomane
General Counsel: Pascal Durand-Barthez
SVP, Communications, Alcatel North America: Hilary Mine
Auditors: Barbier Frinault & Autres; Deloitte & Associés

LOCATIONS

HQ: Alcatel
54, rue La Boétie, 75008 Paris, France
Phone: +33-1-40-76-10-10   **Fax:** +33-1-40-76-14-00
US HQ: 3400 W. Plano Pkwy., Plano, TX 75075-8011
US Phone: 972-519-3000   **US Fax:** 972-519-3999
Web: www.alcatel.com

2004 Sales

	% of total
Europe	
France	36
Germany	10
Other Western Europe	18
Other Europe	2
Asia Pacific	12
North America	15
Other countries	7
Total	**100**

PRODUCTS/OPERATIONS

2004 Sales

	% of total
Fixed communications	41
Private communications	32
Mobile communications	27
Total	**100**

Selected Operations

Access systems
Core optical transmission equipment
Data switching and routing equipment
Enterprise networking systems
Metro optical transmission equipment
Mobile network transmission and switching equipment and software
Modems (ADSL, SHDSL)
Optical components
Optical fiber, cable, and connectivity hardware
Professional services
 Consulting
 Deployment
 Design
 Integration
 Maintenance
 Operation
 Planning
Satellite systems
Software
 Call center
 Messaging and billing
 Network management
 Operation support systems
 Service creation
Submarine systems
Telephones
Transport automation equipment
Video delivery products
Voice and multimedia switching equipment
Wireless access and transmission systems

Selected Subsidiaries and Affiliates

Alcatel SEL AG (Germany)
Alcatel USA, Inc.
Genesys Telecommunications Laboratories, Inc. (US)
Thales (9%)

COMPETITORS

3Com	Marconi
ADC Telecommunications	Motorola
Avaya	NEC
Cisco Systems	Nokia
Corning	Nortel Networks
DIRECTV	Oki Electric
ECI Telecom	Panasonic Mobile
Ericsson	Communications
Fujitsu	SAFRAN
Harris Corp.	Siemens
Hitachi	Tellabs
Juniper Networks	Toshiba
Lucent	

HISTORICAL FINANCIALS

Company Type: Public

Income Statement

FYE: December 31

	REVENUE ($ mil.)	NET INCOME ($ mil.)	NET PROFIT MARGIN	EMPLOYEES
12/04	16,614	381	2.3%	55,718
12/03	15,731	(2,444)	—	60,486
12/02	17,379	(4,984)	—	75,940
12/01	22,597	(4,424)	—	99,314
12/00	29,580	1,247	4.2%	131,598
12/99	23,235	650	2.8%	115,712
12/98	24,906	2,741	11.0%	118,000
12/97	30,854	774	2.5%	189,500
12/96	31,269	526	1.7%	190,600
12/95	32,709	(5,216)	—	191,830
Annual Growth	**(7.3%)**	**—**	**—**	**(12.8%)**

2004 Year-End Financials

Debt ratio: 129.4%
Return on equity: 9.1%
Cash ($ mil.): 3,533
Current ratio: 1.88
Long-term debt ($ mil.): 5,905
No. of shares (mil.): 1,305
Dividends
 Yield: 0.0%
 Payout: —
Market value ($ mil.): 20,404

Stock History

NYSE: ALA

12/95 12/96 12/97 12/98 12/99 12/00 12/01 12/02 12/03 12/04

	STOCK PRICE ($) FY Close	P/E High/Low		PER SHARE ($) Earnings	Dividends	Book Value
12/04	15.63	65	38	0.28	0.00	3.49
12/03	12.85	—	—	(1.84)	0.00	2.97
12/02	4.44	—	—	(4.39)	0.14	4.16
12/01	16.55	—	—	(3.86)	0.43	6.92
12/00	55.94	76	33	1.13	0.39	11.76
12/99	45.00	67	30	0.69	0.00	62.70
12/98	24.44	15	5	3.08	0.39	62.99
12/97	25.31	29	16	0.97	0.00	44.71
12/96	16.00	27	20	0.70	0.31	48.30
12/95	17.50	—	—	(0.65)	0.61	46.32
Annual Growth	**(1.2%)**	**—**	**—**	**—**	**—**	**(25.0%)**

ALDI Group

ALDI keeps it cheap so shoppers can, too. How has discount food retailer ALDI Group become one of the world's biggest grocery chains, running about 7,500 stores worldwide? By offering deeply discounted prices on about 700 popular food items (a typical grocery store has 25,000). No frills ALDI (short for "Albrecht Discounts") buys cheap land mostly on city outskirts, builds cheap warehouses, keeps a tiny staff, and carries mostly private-label items, displaying them on pallets rather than shelves. ALDI has more than 780 stores in 26 US states, but Germany (where ALDI has a 40% share of the grocery market) accounts for about two-thirds of sales. Brothers and co-founders Theo and Karl Albrecht own the company.

Although Spartan-like, the company's stores do sell housewares, textiles, electronic equipment, and garden supplies. But ALDI is better known for the products and services it doesn't offer, such as in-store banking, pharmacies, liquor, fresh meats and fish, and checkout newsstands. As penny-pinching as its customers, ALDI doesn't advertise and about 85% of ALDI's products are private labels. A pair of reclusive billionaires, the Albrecht brothers also own US specialty food retailer Trader Joe's, as well as a minority stake in supermarket operator Albertson's.

ALDI's discount market dominance is being challenged by its European competitors, including compatriot Lidl & Schwarz, who have emulated its low-cost operating methods while offering brand-name products and stolen customers from ALDI. In response, ALDI has changed its private label strategy to begin offering more branded items from consumer goods makers such as Procter & Gamble and Unilever.

While ALDI operates in Germany, the US, and 14 other countries, it is missing out on the fast-growing markets in Eastern Europe, where it is not present. However, ALDI is growing rapidly in Australia, where it has about 100 outlets in New South Wales and Victoria, and in Ireland.

The international limited-assortment grocery chain is also mulling over a move into the New Zealand market.

In the UK, where ALDI operates more than 275 stores, the discount retailer plans to open as many as 200 more outlets over the next five to seven years. The chain may also expand its Scandinavian business by expanding into Sweden. (ALDI already does business in Denmark.)

ALDI entered the US market in 1976 and has annual sales in North America of about $3.7 billion. The discount grocery chain is expanding into new markets here, including Detroit, Michigan, and Oklahoma City. It is also building a new regional headquarters and distribution center in Frederick, Maryland to serve its stores in the Baltimore-Washington area.

HISTORY

Brothers Karl and Theo Albrecht began running their first grocery store in 1948 in the Ruhr Valley, Germany. By the late 1950s the quickly growing company ran about 350 Albrecht Discount stores in Germany, which were later abbreviated to ALDI. As business progressed in the early 1960s, Karl and Theo decided to go their separate ways and divided the company in half. (The company also introduced self-service stores at this time.) Karl began overseeing ALDI Sud (South), which would eventually encompass Australia, Austria, parts of Germany, Ireland, the UK, and the US. Brother Theo took ALDI Nord (North), which would grow to include Belgium, Denmark, France, parts of Germany, Luxembourg, and the Netherlands. (Austrian ALDI stores run under the Hofer banner.)

The firm remained notoriously private and secretive, especially following the 1971 kidnapping of Theo, who was taken by an Italian terrorist group known as the Red Brigade. He was released after the family paid the group's ransom demands.

ALDI broke US ground in 1976 when it opened its first store across the Atlantic. In 1979 the Albrecht brothers bought grocery store Trader Joe's (formerly Pronto Markets) from founder Joseph Coulombe.

The chain opened its first store in the UK in 1990 and had grown to about 250 stores there by the end of the 1990s. In 1999 Karl crossed over the Irish Sea, opening stores in Dublin and Cork. ALDI intends to dot its stores all over the Emerald Isle.

In February 2000 top cereal maker Kellogg agreed to make five cereals under ALDI's own Gletscher Krone brand. The cereals will be called Schoko Chips, Schoko Flakes, Honey Nut Flakes, Honey Balls, and White Flakes.

ALDI Sud went south literally in 2000, opening its first Australian location in Sydney. Another 100 stores are planned over the next couple of years. The company has also opened stores in Spain.

In protest over a new German law imposing a mandatory deposit on aluminum cans and small bottles, ALDI stopped selling canned beer and soft drinks on January 1, 2003. To eliminate inventory the discounter cut the price of beer to as little as five cents a can at the end of 2002.

Co-founders Theo and Karl Albrecht stepped down as co-CEOs in 2003 and turned over the day-to-day operation of ALDI Sud to Ulrich Wolters and Norbert Podschlapp. Theo's son Theo Albrecht Jr. is the chief executive of ALDI Nord.

In November 2004 ALDI opened a distribution center in Scotland to support its expansion in the UK.

Alitalia

With airline deregulation and the subsequent arrival of low-cost European airlines, Alitalia's skies have been cloudy for some time. Once a monopoly, Alitalia - Linee Aeree Italiane now competes for the 22 million passengers that it carries each year. It operates a fleet of about 190 aircraft, has hubs in Rome and Milan, and, including codeshare flights, flies to about 500 destinations in more than 100 countries. Subsidiaries offer regional airline services. Since 2003 the carrier has struggled to keep financially afloat, battled with disgruntled employees, and undergone management shake-ups. The Italian government controls 62% of Alitalia, but is in the process of decreasing its stake to less than 50%.

As European competition grew, Alitalia launched regional carrier Alitalia Express, which took over the operations of Gandalf, a previously independent regional carrier. Alitalia also had low-cost carrier operations that it later spun off; the company is now known as Eurofly.

Early in 2004, the company was plagued with labor disputes, facing several strikes within a few-weeks period over a restructuring plan proposed by the board. The plan called for a reduction of 2,700 jobs, forcing it to cancel hundreds of flights and leading to long delays and dismayed passengers. The crisis level was enough to force the government to intervene.

The government drafted its own plan for restructuring the airline, which led to the resignation of then CEO Francesco Mengozzi. The plan was to include a loan instead of complete or partial privatization, something that had been suggested as one way to clean up the carrier's ailing operations. However, any loan would be heavily restricted by EU rules, so the Italian government announced that it would not help the airline directly. Instead it would contribute aid to Italy's air sector in general.

Another management shake-up occurred just months after the first when layoffs were once again put on the table. The government called for the resignations of Marco Zanichelli, who had replaced Mengozzi as CEO, and chairman Giuseppe Bonomi. The majority of the company's board of directors resigned shortly after it accepted Zanichelli's resignation.

The Italian government received approval in 2004 from the EU to grant the carrier a bridge loan of up to €400 million, which could be supplemented by private banks. The carrier would never be allowed to receive aid from the Italian government, which also will have to reduce its stake from 62% to 49%.

The latest plan offered by management calls for eliminating about one-third of Alitalia's workforce, while splitting the remaining employees between two new companies. The new companies would no longer use the Alitalia name. The carrier has received hard-fought approval from unions, but some of the agreements have helped pave the way for a government loan to help the airline operate.

In 2005 Alitalia sold off its loss-making ground service unit, Alitalia Servizi, to holding company Fintecna. Alitalia also announced plans to issue new shares, more than half of which the Italian government, with the approval of the European Commission, has agreed to purchase to insure that the company remains afloat.

HISTORY

Alitalia got off the ground in 1946 as Alitalia Aerolinee Italiane Internazionali. The airline was 40%-owned by BEA (British European Airways, later part of British Airways) and 60%-owned by the Italian government. Alitalia was intended to be an international carrier; TWA and the Italian state set up Linee Aeree Italiane (LAI) for domestic flights.

Alitalia began flying in 1947 with a Turin-Rome-Catania route, and service to Africa and Brazil was launched from Rome in 1948. To better compete with other European carriers, Alitalia and LAI merged in 1957 and took the name Alitalia - Linee Aeree Italiane. The government bought the shares held by BEA and TWA and assigned Alitalia to IRI, the Italian state holding company. The new airline's fleet had 37 aircraft.

By 1960 Alitalia carried a million passengers and had introduced its first jets. By 1968 it had an all-jet fleet. The stylized "A" tailfin logo appeared a year later, and in 1970 Alitalia adopted use of the Boeing 747. But Alitalia began losing money in the 1970s. Facing rising fuel prices, inflation, and labor strikes, it responded by cutting underused routes and buying fuel-efficient Boeing 727s.

In the early 1980s Alitalia diversified by creating Sigma (travel-related information systems) and Italiatour (tour operator). Diversification came, however, at the expense of the airline's expansion, and it began losing market share to rivals Air France and Lufthansa. In 1988 Alitalia brought in Carlo Verri from the private sector to deal with labor and structural problems. He secured labor contracts and developed aircraft financing, but his auspicious start ended with a fatal car crash in 1989. Alitalia limped through the early 1990s with losses, aging equipment, and a reputation for poor service.

IRI hired former IBM executive Renato Riverso as chairman in 1994. With deregulation fast approaching, Alitalia penned code-sharing partnerships with Continental (1994) and Canadian Airlines (1995). In 1995 several labor strikes flared up amid talk of restructuring and cost-cutting measures. After receiving little government support, Riverso resigned in 1996. His short-lived reign laid a foundation: Labor tensions were eased with the promise of an employee-owned share in the company.

Europe's air transportation market was opened to competition in 1996 (after a long process that began in 1983). Alitalia began low-fare carrier Alitalia Team, signed on Italian regional airline Azzurra as a code-share partner the next year, and set up its own regional carrier, Alitalia Express.

IRI reduced its stake in Alitalia to 53% in 1998, and employees got their 20% stake. IRI was liquidated in 2000, and the state holding company's stake in Alitalia was transferred to the Treasury Ministry. Another chance at an alliance hatched when Alitalia signed partnership agreements with Delta and Air France, which led to full membership in the SkyTeam alliance near the end of 2001. In 2002 the Italian government raised its stake in the airline from 53% to 62%.

Alitalia in late 2003 cut some 1,500 jobs from its workforce of 21,000. In 2004 workers struck to protest the lack of government assistance (although EU rules prohibited the government from aiding the airline) in conjunction with an announcement to cut a further 16% of it workforce on top of the cuts made in 2003. The government began transferring Alitalia employees to other state-controlled jobs.

EXECUTIVES

Chairman and CEO: Giancarlo Cimoli, age 66
CFO: Gabriele Spazzadeschi
Director Engineering & Maintenance: Renzo Lunardi
Director Ground Activities: Alberto Gaudino
Director Human Resources: Massimo Chieli
Director Human Resources: Vito Mangano
Director Industrial Relations: Marco Sarti
Director People Care: Massimo Pinzarrone
Director Quality: Luciano Sorvillo
Director Safety: Carlo Occhiato
Director Security: Sergio Micheli
Manager Media Relations: Simone Cantagallo
Corporate Finance: Pierluigi Ceschia
Institutional Relations: Genaro Schettino
Management Committee: Mario Russo
Strategic Projects: Nicola Shiavone
Auditors: Deloitte & Touche S.p.A.

LOCATIONS

HQ: Alitalia - Linee Aeree Italiane S.p.A.
Viale Alessandro Marchetti, 111, 00148 Rome, Italy
Phone: +39-06-6562-21   **Fax:** +39-06-6562-4733
US HQ: 666 5th Ave., 6th Fl., New York, NY 10103
US Phone: 212-903-3300   **US Fax:** 212-903-3535
Web: www.alitalia.it

2004 Sales

	% of total
Europe	
Italy	26
Other countries	31
Americas	20
Far East	14
Other regions	9
Total	**100**

PRODUCTS/OPERATIONS

2004 Sales

	% of total
Passenger	87
Cargo	11
Mail & other	2
Total	**100**

Selected Subsidiaries

Alitalia Express (regional airline)
Alitalia Servizi (group services)
   Alitalia Airport (airport services)
   Alitalia Maintenance Systems
    (60%, airline maintenance)
Atitech (maintenance)
Aviofin (holding company)
GA 2000 Travel Service Ltd. (ticket sales, connection services)
Global Executive Travel Selections (ticket sales, connection services)

Selected Code-Sharing Partnerships

AeroMexico
Air France
Czech Airlines
Delta Air Lines
Korean Air

COMPETITORS

Aer Lingus
Air France
AMR Corp.
British Airways
Delta Air Transport
easyJet
Eurofly
Iberia
Lufthansa
Ryanair
SAS
UAL
US Airways
Virgin Atlantic Airways

HISTORICAL FINANCIALS

Company Type: Public

Income Statement

FYE: December 31

	REVENUE ($ mil.)	NET INCOME ($ mil.)	NET PROFIT MARGIN	EMPLOYEES
12/04	5,553	(1,108)	—	20,575
12/03	5,405	(652)	—	22,200
12/02	4,966	98	2.0%	22,536
12/01	4,875	(803)	—	22,948
12/00	5,330	(241)	—	23,478
12/99	5,104	6	0.1%	20,497
12/98	5,513	247	4.5%	19,600
12/97	4,949	252	5.1%	15,740
12/96	5,309	(797)	—	16,507
12/95	4,936	(57)	—	17,982
Annual Growth	**1.3%**	**—**	**—**	**1.5%**

2004 Year-End Financials

Debt ratio: 363.1%   Current ratio: 0.78
Return on equity: —   Long-term debt ($ mil.): 2,240
Cash ($ mil.): 116

Net Income History

Italian: AZA

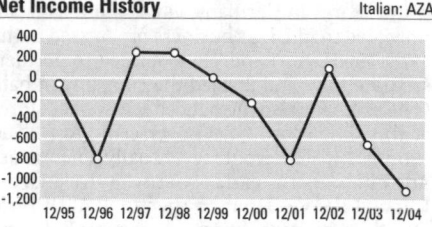

All Nippon Airways

Nippin' at the heels of Japan Airlines, All Nippon Airways (ANA) is Japan's second-largest airline overall (Japan Airlines is #1). With a fleet of more than 180 airliners (mostly Boeings), ANA flies more than 130 Japanese routes and more than 30 international routes in more than 10 countries. Seeking strength in numbers, ANA is also a member of the global Star Alliance. The company is additionally involved in related businesses, including maintenance and ground support. It also operates hotels and provides international and domestic travel packages through ANA Hallo Tour and ANA Sky Holiday.

ANA has been doubly challenged by Japan's lingering recession and the sweeping deregulation that has led to greater domestic and international competition. It's fighting back with a one-two punch of its own in the form of two new systems for increasing efficiency, FAM and PROS, which respectively determine demand for aircraft and seats, and thereby guide downsizing and other operational decisions. The company recently exhibited confidence in its business prospects, however, by ordering 50 Boeing aircraft in 2005.

ANA also faces increased competition with Japan Airlines, which has a strong domestic foothold and a growing presence in China. ANA, however, has signed a codesharing deal with Air China, which should give it a boost.

In order to develop its own cargo business, ANA plans to sell its 27%-plus stake in Nippon Cargo Airlines to Nippon Yusen Kabushiki Kaisha.

HISTORY

Two domestic Japanese air carriers that started in 1952 — Nippon Helicopter and Aeroplane Transport and Far East Airlines — consolidated operations in 1957 as All Nippon Airways (ANA).

Throughout the 1960s ANA developed a domestic route network linking Japan's largest cities — Tokyo, Osaka, Fukuoka, and Sapporo — and its leading provincial centers, including Nagoya, Nagasaki, Matsuyama, and Hakodate. During this period domestic traffic grew at an annual rate of 30% to 60%.

In 1970 the Japanese cabinet formulated routes for its major airlines, giving ANA scheduled domestic service and unscheduled international flights. That year Tokuji Wakasa became ANA's chairman, and the company began a program of diversification that led to the establishment of ANA Trading, international charter service (starting with Hong Kong), and a hotel subsidiary. Air Nippon, a regional domestic airline, was started in 1974.

The company established Nippon Cargo Airlines, a charter service set up jointly with four steamship lines, in 1978. ANA carried 19.5 million passengers that year, but its growth slowed between 1978 and 1980. High jet fuel prices caused a $45.6 million loss in 1979, but ANA rebounded a year later. In 1982 ANA opened international charter service to Guam. The company founded ANA Sports in 1984 to manage the company soccer team.

Japan deregulated air routes in 1985, allowing ANA to offer scheduled international flights. The airline offered its first regular flight from Tokyo to Guam in 1986 and soon added service to Los Angeles and Washington, DC. Flights to China, Hong Kong, and Sydney began a year later.

Between 1988 and 1990 ANA added flights to Bangkok, London, Moscow, Saipan, Seoul, Stockholm, and Vienna. In 1988 ANA bought a minority stake in Austrian Airlines and set up the domestic computer reservation system (CRS). The company's international CRS, INFINI (a joint venture with CRS co-op ABACUS), went online in 1990.

ANA started World Air Network Charter (WAC) in 1991 to serve travelers from Japan's smaller cities. That year ANA opened its first European hotel (in Vienna), was listed on the London Stock Exchange, and opened a flight school in the US for its pilots.

In 1992 ANA premiered a hotel in Beijing. In 1995 the airline announced that it would increase its international traffic by more than 30%. As part of this strategy ANA and Air Canada began a code-sharing service in 1996 between Osaka and Vancouver, and a year later ANA became the first Japanese airline to operate a Boeing 777 on an international route (between Tokyo and Beijing).

As the Asian financial crisis sent Japanese airlines to the brink, a pilot strike in 1998 dashed ANA's hopes for a 15% pay cut. To cope, ANA formed alliances with UAL's United Airlines, Lufthansa, and Brazil's VARIG. ANA extended those partnerships in 1999 by joining the global Star Alliance. To shore up its financial strength, ANA reorganized domestic routes, dropping some unprofitable ones and shifting others to its Air Nippon unit; it also announced plans to launch low-cost air service for international routes in Asia. Competition intensified when Japan fully deregulated domestic fares in 2000, sparking a fare war.

The following year ANA avoided a potentially costly strike and began working toward expanding through partnerships. However, terrorist attacks on the US caused a slump in worldwide air travel, and ANA was forced to cut back on its flights. Then ANA had to trim more routes in response to a worldwide slump in air travel in 2003 due to the SARS outbreak.

EXECUTIVES

Chairman: Yoji Ohashi
President and CEO: Mineo Yamamoto
SEVP: Suguru Omae
SEVP: Hiromichi Toya
EVP: Kenichiro Hamada
EVP: Shinichiro Ito
EVP: Katsuhiko Kitabayashi
EVP: Shin Nagase
EVP: Koshichiro Kubo
SVP: Minoru Aimono
EVP: Masao Nakano
SVP: Osamu Asakawa
SVP: Kenkichi Honbo
SVP: Hiroyuki Ito
SVP: Katsuyori Kikuchi
SVP: Isamu Komatsu
SVP: Shinsuke Maki
SVP: Junji Onishi
SVP: Atsuro Takahashi
Corporate Auditor: Koichiro Ono
Corporate Auditor: Masahiko Takada
Auditors: Shin Nihon & Co.

LOCATIONS

HQ: All Nippon Airways Co., Ltd.
(Zen Nippon Kuyu Kabushiki Kaisha)
Shiodome City Center, 1-5-2 Higashi-Shimbashi,
Minato-ku, Tokyo 105-7133, Japan
Phone: +81-3-6735-1000   **Fax:** +81-3-6735-1005
US HQ: 1251 Avenue of the Americas, Ste. 820,
New York, NY 10020
US Phone: 212-840-3700   **US Fax:** 212-840-3704
Web: www.ana.co.jp

PRODUCTS/OPERATIONS

2005 Sales

	% of total
Air transportation	70
Travel services	13
Hotel operations	5
Other	12
Total	**100**

COMPETITORS

Accor
Air France
AMR Corp.
British Airways
Carlson
Cathay Pacific
Central Japan Railway
China Airlines
Continental Airlines
Delta Air
Dragonair
East Japan Railway
Evergreen Marine
FlightSafety
Hyatt
Japan Airlines
Kintetsu Corp.
KLM
Northwest Airlines
Qantas
Singapore Airlines
Virgin Atlantic Airways

HISTORICAL FINANCIALS

Company Type: Public

Income Statement
FYE: March 31

	REVENUE ($ mil.)	NET INCOME ($ mil.)	NET PROFIT MARGIN	EMPLOYEES
3/05	12,021	251	2.1%	29,098
3/04	11,526	234	2.0%	28,870
3/03	10,146	(236)	—	29,001
3/02	9,081	(71)	—	29,095
3/01	10,130	(319)	—	29,831
3/00	11,465	(144)	—	14,919
3/99	8,990	(40)	—	15,273
3/98	8,120	(41)	—	15,200
3/97	8,254	35	0.4%	15,996
3/96	9,019	(80)	—	14,649
Annual Growth	**3.2%**	**—**		**7.9%**

2005 Year-End Financials

Debt ratio: 344.3%
Return on equity: 14.7%
Cash ($ mil.): 1,471
Current ratio: 0.83
Long-term debt ($ mil.): 6,860

Net Income History   Pink Sheets: ALNPY

Allianz AG

Allianz is hoping its alliances will take it to the top. One of the world's biggest insurers, Allianz has join forces with Dresdner Bank, creating the world's fourth-largest financial group (Citigroup is #1). Allianz offers a range of insurance products and services through some 100 subsidiaries and affiliates, including life, health, and property & casualty. Other businesses include risk consulting and public investment funds. Making its mark in the high-profile world of asset management, the company's Allianz Global Investors (formerly Allianz Dresdner Asset Management, or ADAM) manages private and institutional funds.

Allianz is part of a web of interlocking German corporate ownership. It holds stakes in the country's top corporations (including Deutsche Bank and Lufthansa), as well as 22% of the world's largest reinsurer, Munich Re (which has an equal stake in Allianz).

Allianz paid out claims of some $1.3 billion relating to the terrorist attacks on the World Trade Center. The company has set up a terrorism insurance unit, offering coverage primarily for companies within the European Union.

After a year of record losses (primarily due to investment losses and Dresdner's struggles), former CEO Henning Schulte-Noelle stepped down and assumed the chair post in 2003. Allianz' stock lost more than 75% of its value in 2002.

Getting out of the red, Allianz rebounded some in 2003, thanks to the upturn in the stock markets and the streamlining of its operations (the company shrunk its employee total by some

8,000 people). Allianz has also raised some $5 billion to improve its capital base.

The company in 2004 sold most of its Canadian property and casualty operations to ING Canada.

HISTORY

Carl Thieme founded Allianz in Germany in 1890. That year the company took part in the creation of the Calamity Association of Accident Insurance Companies, a consortium of German, Austrian, Swiss, and Russian firms, to insure international commerce.

By 1898 Thieme had established offices in the UK, Switzerland, and the Netherlands. His successor, Paul von der Nahmer, expanded Allianz into the Balkans, France, Italy, Scandinavia, and the US. After a hiatus during WWI, Allianz returned to foreign markets.

In WWII, Allianz insured Auschwitz, Dachau, and other death camps. Company documents show Allianz wasn't worried about risk at the SS troop-guarded camps. After the German defeat, the victors seized Allianz's foreign holdings, except for a stake in Spain's Plus Ultra. In the 1950s Allianz repurchased confiscated holdings in Italian and Austrian companies.

Allianz saturated the German market and began a full-scale international drive in the late 1950s and 1960s. It became Europe's largest insurer through a series of acquisitions beginning in 1973. Allianz formed Los Angeles-based Allianz Insurance in 1977.

In 1981 Allianz launched a takeover (which turned hostile) of the UK's Eagle Star insurance company. After a 1983 bidding joust with Britain's B.A.T Industries (now part of Zurich Financial Services), Allianz withdrew.

The firm consoled itself by shopping. In 1984 it won control of Riunione Adriatica di Sicurtà (Ras), Italy's second-largest insurance company. Two years later the firm bought Cornhill in the UK (on its third try). As the Iron Curtain crumbled, Allianz in 1989 acquired 49% of Hungaria Biztosito. Its *drang nach Osten* continued the next year after national reunification, when it gained control of Deutsche Versicherungs AG, East Germany's insurance monopoly. Allianz that year became the first German insurer licensed in Japan; it also bought the US's Fireman's Fund Insurance.

Natural disasters led to large claims and set the company back in 1992, the first time in 20 years it lost money from its German operations. Allianz restructured operations that year; profits surged in 1993, mostly from international business.

Allianz expanded in Mexico in 1995, forming a life and health insurance joint venture with Grupo Financiero BanCrecer (now owned by Grupo Financiero Banorte). The company set up an asset management arm in Hong Kong in 1996 with an eye to further Asian expansion, getting a license in China the next year. In 1997 after Holocaust survivors sued Allianz and other insurers for failing to pay on life policies after WWII, Allianz agreed to participate in a repayment fund.

In 1998 Allianz bought control of Assurances Générales de France; it was the white knight that prevented Assicurazioni Generali from taking the company. In 1999 Allianz said it would restructure some of its insurance operations, including spinning off its marine and aviation lines, to better compete in the multinational market. That year US subsidiary Allianz Life bought Life USA Holding. In 2000 Allianz bought 70% of PIMCO Advisors Holdings to strengthen its asset management operations. That year the

company continued its push into Asia, buying a 12% stake in Hana Bank of South Korea and planning to boost its ownership of Malaysia British Assurance Life. Also in 2000, Allianz acquired Dutch insurer Zwolsche Algemeene.

Allianz remained acquisitive in 2001, buying US investment manager Nicholas-Applegate and taking a majority stake in ROSNO, one of Russia's largest insurers.

EXECUTIVES

Chairman of the Supervisory Board:
Henning Schulte-Noelle, age 63
Deputy Chairman of the Supervisory Board:
Norbert Blix, age 56
Chairman of the Management Board:
Michael Diekmann, age 50, $3,486,384 pay
Member of the Management Board (Group Finance):
Paul Achleitner, age 49, $2,652,980 pay
Member of the Management Board (Europe II, Reinsurance, Alternative Risk Transfer, Allianz Global Risks): Detlev Bremkamp, age 61, $2,305,160 pay
Member of the Management Board (Americas); Chairman, Fireman's Fund Insurance and Allianz Life Insurance Company of North America; President and CEO, Allianz of America: Jan R. Carendi, age 60, $2,376,088 pay
Member of the Management Board (Allianz Dresdner Asset Management); CEO, Allianz Global Investors: Joachim Faber, age 55, $2,135,095 pay
Member of the Management Board (Europe I): Reiner Hagemann, age 58, $2,988,524 pay
Member of the Management Board (Group Controlling, Accounting, Taxes, Compliance): Helmut Perlet, age 58, $2,296,976 pay
Member of the Management Board (Group Information Technology; Life Insurance Germany): Gerhard Rupprecht, age 57, $2,247,872 pay
Member of the Management Board (Allianz Dresdner Banking); Chairman, Dresdner Bank: Herbert Walter, age 52, $3,141,292 pay
Member of the Management Board (Growth Markets): Werner Zedelius, age 48, $1,795,024 pay
Auditors: KPMG Deutsche Treuhand-Gesellschaft AG

LOCATIONS

HQ: Allianz AG
Königinstrasse 28, D-80802 Munich, Germany
Phone: +49-89-3800-0   **Fax:** +49-89-3800-3425
US HQ: Allianz of America, Inc.
55 Greens Farms Rd. Ste. 3, Westport, CT 06880
US Phone: 203-221-8500   **US Fax:** 203-221-8529
Web: www.allianz.com

Allianz operates in more than 70 countries in Africa, Asia, Europe, North and South America, and the Pacific Rim.

PRODUCTS/OPERATIONS

2004 Sales

	$ mil.	% of total
Premiums earned (net)	76,926	59
Interest & similar income	28,518	22
Fee, commission & service activities income	9,242	7
Income from investments Associated enterprises & joint ventures	1,053	1
Other income from investments	6,524	5
Trading income (net)	3,810	3
Other income	3,463	3
Total	**129,536**	**100**

Selected Holdings

Adriática de Seguros C.A. (Venezuela)
AGF Allianz Argentina Compañia de Seguros Generales S.A.
AGF Brasil Seguros S.A. (Brazil)
Allianz Compañía de Seguros S.A. (Chile)
Allianz Cornhill Insurance (Far East) Ltd. (Hong Kong)
Allianz Elementar Versicherung-AG (Austria)
Allianz Fire and Marine Insurance Japan Ltd.
Allianz First Life Insurance Co. Ltd. (South Korea)
Allianz Globus Marine Versicherungs-AG
Allianz Insurance Company (US)
Allianz Insurance Ltd. (South Africa)
Allianz Insurance of Namibia Ltd.
Allianz Insurance (Singapore) Pte. Ltd.
Allianz Irish Life Holdings
Allianz Lebensversicherungs-AG
Allianz Life Insurance Company of North America (US)
Allianz México S.A. Compañía de Seguros
Allianz Nederland N.V. (The Netherlands)
Allianz poist'ovna, a.s. (Slovakia)
Allianz pojist'ovna, a.s. (Czech Republic)
Allianz Subalpina Società di Assicurazioni e Riassicurazioni S.p.A. (Italy)
Allianz Tiriac Insurance (Romania)
Allianz Versicherung (Schweiz) AG (Switzerland)
Assurances Générales de France (65%)
Assurances Générales de Laos
P.T. Asuransi Allianz Utama Indonesia
Banque AGF (France)
Bayerische Versicherungsbank AG (90%)
Cornhill Insurance PLC (UK)
Deutsche Lebensversicherungs-AG
Domus-Forsikringsaktieselskab (Denmark)
Dresdner Bank AG
ELVIA Assurances S.A. (Belgium)
ELVIA Reiseversicherungen (Switzerland)
Fireman's Fund Insurance Company (US)
France Life (South Korea)
Frankfurter Versicherungs-AG
Hungária Biztosító Rt (Hungary)
International Reinsurance Company S.A. (Luxembourg)
Jefferson Insurance Company (US)
Koç Allianz Hayat Sigorta T.A.S. (Turkey)
Les Assurances Fédérales IARD (France)
Malaysian British Assurance Berhad
Manufacturers' Mutual Insurance Group (Australia)
Monticello Insurance Company
Münchener Rückversicherungs-Gesellschaft AG (Munich Re, 22%)
National Insurance Company Berhad (Brunei)
Ost-West Allianz Insurance Company (Russia)
Portugal Previdente Companhia de Seguros S.A.
Rhin et Moselle Assurances Françaises Compagnie d'Assurances sur la Vie (France)
Royal Nederland Schade (The Netherlands)
T.U. Allianz BGZ Polska Zycie S.A. (Poland)
Zwolsche Algemeene Levensverzekering N.V. (The Netherlands)

COMPETITORS

AEGON	Mitsui Sumitomo
AIG	Insurance
Allstate	Munich Re
AMB Generali	New York Life
Aviva	Nippon Life Insurance
AXA	Prudential
Citigroup	Prudential plc
ERGO	Royal & Sun
Fortis SA/NV	Alliance Insurance
Generali	Sompo Japan Insurance
ING	State Farm
Legal & General Group	Winterthur
MetLife	Zurich Financial Services
Millea Holdings	

HISTORICAL FINANCIALS

Company Type: Public

Income Statement

	ASSETS ($ mil.)	NET INCOME ($ mil.)	INCOME AS % OF ASSETS	EMPLOYEES
				FYE: December 31
12/04	1,347,418	2,979	0.2%	162,180
12/03	1,176,678	2,032	0.2%	173,750
12/02	894,914	(1,226)	—	181,651
12/01	840,429	1,447	0.2%	179,146
12/00	414,387	3,259	0.8%	119,683
12/99	385,486	2,249	0.6%	113,584
12/98	399,865	2,123	0.5%	105,676
12/97	212,165	1,133	0.5%	73,290
12/96	200,554	1,062	0.5%	65,836
12/95	199,835	1,133	0.6%	69,236
Annual Growth	**23.6%**	**11.3%**	**—**	**9.9%**

2004 Year-End Financials

Equity as % of assets: 3.1%
Return on assets: 0.2%
Return on equity: 7.7%
Long-term debt ($ mil.): 318,009
No. of shares (mil.): 3,669
Dividends
  Yield: 1.4%
  Payout: 22.2%
Market value ($ mil.): 48,756
Sales ($ mil.): 129,536

Stock History

NYSE: AZ

12/95 12/96 12/97 12/98 12/99 12/00 12/01 12/02 12/03 12/04

	STOCK PRICE ($) FY Close	P/E High/Low		PER SHARE ($) Earnings	Dividends	Book Value
12/04	13.29	18	11	0.81	0.18	11.38
12/03	12.72	21	8	0.60	1.14	9.81
12/02	9.55	—	—	(0.51)	0.13	9.46
12/01	23.60	64	31	0.59	0.14	11.70
12/00	37.50	28	25	1.33	0.00	13.64
Annual Growth	**(22.8%)**	**—**	**—**	**(11.7%)**	**—**	**(4.4%)**

Allied Irish Banks

Allied Irish Banks (AIB), one of Ireland's largest banks and private employers, is looking beyond the Emerald Isle for its proverbial pot o' gold. The company offers retail and commercial accounts and loans, life insurance, financing, leasing, pension, and trust services through some 280 branches in Ireland and another 60 in Northern Ireland, where it operates First Trust Bank. In England and Scotland, AIB focuses on commercial clients through about 40 locations, while in Poland, AIB operates from 387 branches and outlets. The company's capital markets division offers commercial treasury services, corporate banking, asset management, and stock brokerage.

The bank's four operating divisions are divided into the following categories: AIB Bank Republic of Ireland, AIB Bank Great Britain and Northern Ireland, Capital Markets, and Poland.

The small Irish market and its inevitable ties to the UK's economy have made AIB look overseas to remain competitive. (Its home turf also faces intruders — namely European banks free to do business in the EU-opened Irish market.) The firm has positioned itself as an international bank with a presence in Eastern Europe where it owns a majority stake in Poland-based Bank Zachodni and its 387 branches. About 40% of AIB's shareholders, assets, and pre-tax profits now come from outside of the country.

HISTORY

Allied Irish Banks was formed in 1966 by the "trinity" of Provincial Bank (founded 1825), The Royal Bank (founded 1836), and Munster and Leinster (founded 1885 but with origins back to the late 1600s). Both AIB and its then-larger rival, Bank of Ireland, had to consolidate in order to compete with North American banks entering Ireland. From its start, AIB sought to expand overseas, and by 1968 it had an alliance with Canada's Toronto-Dominion Bank.

In the 1970s AIB expanded its branch network to England and Scotland. The 1980s saw AIB boost its presence in the US market (it had already debuted AIB branches) with the acquisition of First Maryland Bancorp.

The Irish Parliament's Finance Act of 1986 instituted a withholding tax known as the Deposit Interest Retention Tax (DIRT) for Irish residents. Consequently (with a wink and a nod) AIB and other banks let customers create bogus non-resident accounts to avoid paying DIRT. An investigation indicated that, at one point, AIB's branch in Tralee had 14,700 non-resident accounts on its rolls — more than half the local population. After tax authorities began probing, many of the accounts in question were reclassified as "resident," and customers had to pay the taxes on them. In 1991 AIB was reprimanded, but neither the bank nor its customers have paid the remaining $100 million tax bill.

Tom Mulcahy, who integrated AIB's treasury, investment, and international banking activities, became chief executive in 1994. Mulcahy, a respected leader, envisioned AIB as an international, Ireland-based bank.

In 1995 AIB bought UK-based investment fund manager John Govett from London Pacific Group (now Berkeley Technology Limited). Mulcahy moved AIB the same year into Eastern Europe with a stake in Poland-based Wielkopolski Bank Kredytowy (or WBK, of which it now owns 60%).

AIB was busy in 1999. It gained a toehold in Asia by entering a cross-marketing agreement with Singapore's Keppet TatLee bank, a survivor of the region's financial crisis. Liberalized Singapore banking laws allowed AIB the right to buy one-quarter of the bank by 2001. AIB also bought an 80% stake of Bank Zachodni in Poland in 1999.

That year AIB merged First Maryland Bancorp and its other US holdings into the renamed Allfirst Financial, a sizable mid-Atlantic states bank.

In 2001 AIB merged Wielkopolski Bank Kredytowy and Bank Zachodni into Bank Zachodni WBK in Poland to consolidate its power in Eastern Europe. That year Mulcahy retired but then was appointed by the Irish government to take over as chairman of troubled airline Aer Lingus.

In 2003 AIB sold troubled Maryland-based bank Allfirst Financial to M&T Bank Corporation. As part of the deal, AIB assumed ownership of more than 20% of M&T, becoming the company's largest shareholder. Under AIB's direction Allfirst grew into a major regional player with about 250 branches in Maryland, Virginia, Pennsylvania, and Washington, DC. However, AIB lost nearly $700 million from 1996 to 2002, apparently from bogus foreign exchange transactions made by rogue trader John Rusnak, who pleaded guilty to bank fraud.

EXECUTIVES

Chairman: Dermot Gleeson, age 56
Group Chief Executive and Director: Eugene J. Sheehy, age 51
Group Director, Finance and Enterprise Technology: Gary E. Kennedy, age 47, $886,600 pay
Group Chief Risk Officer: Shom Bhattacharya, age 54
Group Finance Director: John O'Donnell
Managing Director, AIB Bank, Republic of Ireland: Donal Forde, age 43
Managing Director, AIB Capital Markets: Colm E. Doherty, age 46, $1,033,912 pay
Managing Director, AIB Group (UK) p.l.c.: Aidan McKeon, age 57, $815,672 pay
Managing Director Designate AIB Group (UK) p.l.c.: Robbie Henneberry
Managing Director, AIB Poland Division: Gerry Byrne, age 49
Secretary: W. M. Kinsella
Director, Operations: Steven Meadows
Head of Corporate Relations: Catherine Burke
Head of Group Investor Relations: Alan Kelly
Head of Strategic Human Resources: Michael J. (Mike) Lewis, age 56
Group Internal Auditor: Tony Schatzel
Auditors: KPMG

LOCATIONS

HQ: Allied Irish Banks, p.l.c.
  Bankcentre, Ballsbridge, Dublin 4, Ireland
Phone: +353-1-660-0311   **Fax:** +353-1-660-9137
US HQ: 405 Park Ave., New York, NY 10022
US Phone: 212-339-8000   **US Fax:** 212-339-8008
Web: www.aibgroup.com

Allied Irish Banks has operations in Ireland, Poland, the US, and the UK.

2004 Assets

	% of total
AIB Bank ROI	42
AIB Bank GB & NI	15
Capital Markets	32
Poland	6
Group	5
Total	**100**

PRODUCTS/OPERATIONS

Selected Subsidiaries

AIB Asset Management Holdings Limited (85%; UK, funds management)
AIB Bank (CI) Ltd. (Jersey, Channel Islands, banking services)
AIB Bank (Isle of Man) Ltd. (Isle of Man, banking services)
AIB Capital Markets p.l.c. (banking and financial services)
AIB Corporate Finance Ltd. (company financial advice)
AIB Finance Ltd. (industrial banking)
AIB International Financial Services Ltd. (financial services)
AIB Investment Managers Limited (investment management)
AIB Leasing Ltd.
Allied Irish Banks, p.l.c.
Allied Irish Capital Management Ltd. (91%)
Ark Life Assurance Company Ltd. (insurance and pensions business)
AIB Group (UK) p.l.c. d/b/a Allied Irish Bank (GB) in England and Scotland and d/b/a First Trust Bank p.l.c. in Northern Ireland (banking and financial services)
Bank Zachodni WBK S.A. (70%; Poland, banking and financial services)
Goodbody Holdings Ltd. (corporate finance)
  Goodbody Stockbrokers

Anglo Irish Bank
Bank Millennium
Bank of America
Bank of Ireland
Bank Pekao
Barclays
Citigroup
First Active
HSBC Holdings
Lloyds TSB
RBS
SunTrust
Wachovia

HISTORICAL FINANCIALS

Company Type: Public

Income Statement

FYE: December 31

	ASSETS ($ mil.)	NET INCOME ($ mil.)	INCOME AS % OF ASSETS	EMPLOYEES
12/04	138,494	1,425	1.0%	22,800
12/03	101,783	857	0.8%	23,300
12/02	90,377	1,079	1.2%	31,300
12/01	79,180	476	0.6%	32,397
12/00	75,050	736	1.0%	31,778
12/99	67,687	784	1.2%	26,264
12/98	62,929	796	1.3%	23,749
12/97	53,724	543	1.0%	23,921
12/96	43,231	449	1.0%	15,882
12/95	38,201	396	1.0%	15,274
Annual Growth	15.4%	15.3%	—	4.6%

2004 Year-End Financials

Equity as % of assets: 5.5%
Return on assets: 1.2%
Return on equity: 20.3%
Long-term debt ($ mil.): 21,680
No. of shares (mil.): 459

Dividends
  Yield: 3.4%
  Payout: 41.9%
Market value ($ mil.): 18,957
Sales ($ mil.): 7,090

Stock History

NYSE: AIB

12/95 12/96 12/97 12/98 12/99 12/00 12/01 12/02 12/03 12/04

	STOCK PRICE ($) FY Close	P/E High/Low		PER SHARE ($) Earnings	Dividends	Book Value
12/04	41.28	13	8	3.32	1.39	16.46
12/03	31.74	17	12	1.97	1.12	14.23
12/02	26.88	12	7	2.44	0.83	10.87
12/01	23.10	26	17	1.00	0.73	11.31
12/00	23.50	15	9	1.66	0.68	9.77
12/99	21.13	23	12	1.78	0.70	9.08
12/98	36.75	21	11	1.75	0.58	2.76
12/97	19.31	15	9	1.37	0.63	2.71
12/96	13.07	10	8	1.27	0.49	2.25
12/95	10.86	11	7	1.09	0.37	2.01
Annual Growth	16.0%	—	—	13.2%	15.8%	26.4%

AMP Limited

AMP is on top — down under. Formerly known as Australian Mutual Provident Society, the company is Australia's largest life insurance and investment management group. More than 2,000 representatives sell the company's insurance and financial products, which include life insurance; retirement products; financial planning and advice; superannuation products (professionally managed retirement investment funds); banking; and investment management. The company's AMP Financial Services (AFS) division serves individual and corporate clients throughout Australia and New Zealand; AMP Capital Investors provides investment management to AFS and to other individual and institutional investors.

AMP demutualized in 1998 to gain cash and stock to use in making itself more competitive on the world stage, but the stage proved to be a less-than-salutary spot for the company. Expansion in its UK operations led to losses and executive bloodbaths, until AMP eventually decided to stop the bleeding and restore value to the company by splitting off its UK-based operations as HHG at the end of 2003 (retaining a 10% share). HGG eventually changed its name to Henderson Group plc in 2005. AMP sold its shares in Henderson later in the year.

Even though the company ultimately expects positive results, the extreme makeover was painful: AMP took a $4 billion hit that year.

Even before the UK separation, AMP had been working to sharpen its focus and divest costly operations. Local rival Suncorp-Metway bought AMP's domestic general insurance unit, and Churchill Insurance (a subsidiary of Credit Suisse) acquired its similar operations in the UK.

J.P. Morgan Chase owns 12% of AMP; fellow Aussie WestPac owns more than 10%.

HISTORY

AMP was conceived in Sydney in 1848 by W. S. Walsh (a clergyman), Thomas Mort (a businessman), and Thomas Holt (a wool trader), who convened with two others to discuss forming a mutual life insurance company in Australia. The next year Australian Mutual Provident Society was born; it opened for business with a staff of two: secretary William Perry and a small boy. In its first year the company sold only 42 policies. Luckily, no one died in the first three years of operations and the company was able to build up some reserves. The company grew slowly over the next decade, appointing just two agents — in Auckland, New Zealand, and Hobart, Australia.

Sales took off with the 1860 appointment of the company's first full-time agent, Benjamin Short, who had the novel idea of actively recruiting customers and actually *selling* policies. The company opened an office in New Zealand in 1871; it opened a branch in the UK in 1908.

In the next few decades, the company helped build the Australian economy through investment of its reserves. It funded industry and infrastructure, including farming communities, as part of the South Australian Land Development Scheme. The company grew free of foreign competition, protected by regulations severely restricting the activities of foreign companies in the banking and financial industries in Australia. In 1958 the company formed AMP Fire and General Insurance (changed to AMP General in 1990).

In 1988 AMP moved abroad with the acquisition of London Life Assurance. The following year it made history with its acquisition of funds management group Pearl Assurance, then the largest takeover of a British financial firm by a foreign company.

The company founded AMP Asset Management in 1991 to manage its overseas assets. In 1995 the company expanded its international presence through a joint venture with the financial services arm of UK-based Virgin Group. The company also began offering mortgage and banking products in Australia through a new unit, Priority One.

After a careful inquiry, in 1996 AMP's board recommended demutualization; policyholders approved in 1997, and the conversion was completed the next year with the company taking the name AMP Limited. AMP has since expanded aggressively. It launched AMP Banking in Australia and bought Citibank's New Zealand retail banking business and UK fund manager Henderson in 1998. The next year AMP battled to buy general insurer GIO Australia Holdings, picking up 57% after resistance to its original low-ball offer; it also bought UK mutual insurer National Provident Institution (NPI).

The company streamlined all of its investment-management operations into a single unit in 1999 and expanded Asian operations with offices in Beijing and Tokyo. In 2000 the problems arising from the GIO takeover resulted in a board shakeup; chairman Ian Burgess resigned.

AMP in 2003 demerged its UK and Australian operations, splitting the former off into a new entity called HHG (eventually named Henderson Group plc in 2005).

EXECUTIVES

Chairman: Peter Mason
CEO and Director: Andrew Mohl, age 49, $2,736,396 pay
CFO: Paul Leaming, $1,003,345 pay
Managing Director, AMP Capital Investors:
  Stephen Dunne, $1,042,325 pay
General Manager, AMP Australian Financial Services:
  Craig Dunn, age 38, $1,042,325 pay
General Manager, Corporate and Public Affairs:
  Matthew Percival, age 50
General Manager, Human Resources and Strategy:
  Peter Hodgett, $733,604 pay
General Counsel: David Cohen, $694,624 pay
Auditors: Ernst & Young

LOCATIONS

HQ: AMP Limited
  Level 24, 33 Alfred St., Sydney 2000, Australia
Phone: +61-2-9257-5000   **Fax:** +61-2-9257-7178
Web: www.ampgroup.com

AMP Limited operates primarily in Australia and New Zealand, with limited operations in India and other countries.

PRODUCTS/OPERATIONS

2004 Sales

	% of sales
AMP Financial Services	95
AMP Capital Investors	3
Other	2
Total	**100**

Selected Operations

AMP Banking
AMP Capital Investors (investment management)
AMP Financial Services (wealth management
  products and services)
Arrive Wealth Management (distribution)
Cobalt/Gordian (run-off general insurance business)
Hillross Financial Services (distribution)
Magnify (distribution)

COMPETITORS

AIG	Fortis SA/NV
Australia and New Zealand	ING
Banking	Macquarie Bank
Aviva	National Australia Bank
AXA Asia Pacific	Royal & Sun Alliance
Commonwealth Bank	Insurance
of Australia	St. George Bank

HISTORICAL FINANCIALS

Company Type: Public

Income Statement

FYE: December 31

	ASSETS ($ mil.)	NET INCOME ($ mil.)	INCOME AS % OF ASSETS	EMPLOYEES
12/04	55,418	728	1.3%	3,464
12/03	52,596	(4,151)	—	3,961
12/02	89,190	(506)	—	11,403
12/01	88,624	353	0.4%	15,000
12/00	99,061	2,508	2.5%	22,000
12/99	86,133	2,187	2.5%	22,400
12/98	68,895	(394)	—	12,000
Annual Growth	**(3.6%)**	**—**		**(18.7%)**

2004 Year-End Financials

Equity as % of assets: 5.8% Long-term debt ($ mil.): 1,608
Return on assets: 1.3% Sales ($ mil.): 8,498
Return on equity: 15.9%

Net Income History

Australian: AMP

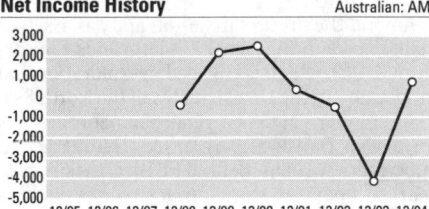

Anglo American

Anglo American's name might be a little misleading — it's never been American. The UK-based company owns stakes in leading global producers of gold (51%, AngloGold Ashanti), platinum (75%, Anglo Platinum), and diamonds (45%, De Beers Consolidated). In addition, Anglo American has interests in paper and packaging goods (more than 20% of sales), ferrous and base metals, and industrial minerals. It also is one of the world's largest independent coal miners. The company controls assets around the world. Descendants of the founding Oppenheimer family no longer control Anglo American, although Nicky Oppenheimer, who chairs De Beers, sits on the company's board.

The company, formerly Anglo American Corporation of South Africa, moved to the UK and began trading on the London Stock Exchange in an effort to reach international investors. When it was based in South Africa, Anglo American was unable to send its money overseas (the result of boycotts connected to that country's apartheid policies), so it bulked up on South African interests. Anglo American now depends on product and geographic diversity to weather global economic turmoil.

In 2004 the company sold its 20% stake in Gold Fields Limited to Norilsk Nickel. The following year Anglo American and partner BHP Billiton sold their joint venture, chrome miner and manufacturer Samancor, to US investment firm the Kermas Group for $469 million. Also in 2005 Anglo American rid itself of subsidiary Boart Longyear selling the mining machinery and services company in two parts for a total of $635 million.

The divestitures continued late in 2005 when Anglo American made several announcements about the direction it hopes to move. First the company is selling its 80% stake in Highveld Steel. Next up, and more significantly, Anglo American has decided to dispose of a portion of its stake in gold, reducing its stake in Anglo Gold Ashanti to below the current 51%. The company seems to be capitulating to market demands and the idea that the gold industry is sufficiently different from the rest of the mining industry as to necessitate separate management. Anglo American also will rid itself of its paper and packaging businesses.

HISTORY

In 1905 the Oppenheimers, a German family with a major interest in the Premier Diamond Mining Company of South Africa, began buying some of the region's richest gold-bearing land. The family formed Anglo American Corporation of South Africa in 1917 to raise money from J. P. Morgan and other US investors. The name was chosen to disguise the company's German background during WWI.

Under Ernest Oppenheimer the company bought diamond fields in German Southwest Africa (now Namibia) in 1920, breaking the De Beers hegemony in diamond production. Oppenheimer's 1928 negotiations with Hans Merensky, the person credited with the discovery of South Africa's "platinum arc," led to Anglo American's interest in platinum.

The diamond monopoly resurfaced in 1929 when Anglo American won control of De Beers, formed by Cecil Rhodes in 1888 with the help of England's powerful Rothschild family.

Anglo American and De Beers had become the largest gold producers in South Africa by the 1950s. They were also major world producers of coal, uranium, and copper. In the 1960s and 1970s, Anglo American expanded through mergers and cross holdings in industrial and financial companies. It set up Luxembourg-based Minorco to own holdings outside South Africa and help the company avoid sanctions placed on firms doing business in the apartheid country.

Minorco sold its interest in Consolidated Gold Fields in 1989, and in 1990 it bought Freeport-McMoRan Gold Company (US). In 1993 Minorco bought Anglo American's and De Beers' South American, European, and Australian operations as part of a swap that put all of Anglo American's non-African assets, except diamonds, in Minorco's hands. Some analysts claimed the company had moved the assets to protect them from possible nationalization by the new, black-controlled South African government. The company spun off insurer African Life to a group of black investors in 1994.

Anglo American bought a stake in UK-based conglomerate Lonrho (now Lonmin) in 1996. In 1997 Anglo American made mining acquisitions in Zambia, Colombia, and Tanzania and began reorganizing its gold and diamond operations. In 1998 the company's First National and Southern Life financial units merged with Rand Merchant Bank's Momentum Life Assurers to form FirstRand. (Anglo American has divested most of its interest in FirstRand.)

The company left its homeland for London in 1999, changed its name to Anglo American plc, and wrapped up the acquisitions of many of its minority interests including Amcoal, Amgold, Amic, and Minorco.

In 2000 the company bought UK building materials company Tarmac plc and later sold Tarmac America to Greece-based Titan Cement for $636 million. That year De Beers paid $590 million for Anglovaal Mining's stake in De Beers' flagship Venetia diamond mine and $900 million for Royal Dutch/Shell's Australian coal mining business. On the disposal side, Anglo American sold its 68% stake in LTA and its 14% stake in Li & Fung, a Hong Kong trading company. Harry Oppenheimer died that year at the age of 92.

In a surprising move, in early 2001 Anglo American announced that it had formed a consortium with Central Holding (the Oppenheimer family) and Debswana Diamond to acquire De Beers. In February De Beers agreed to be acquired in a deal worth about $17.6 billion. The deal — giving Anglo American and Central Holding 45% each and Debswana a 10% stake — was completed in June 2001.

In 2002 Anglo American and Japan-based conglomerate Mitsui pooled their Australian coal resources; Anglo American owns 51% of the joint venture. The company also completed a $1.3 billion deal that year for Chilean copper assets formerly owned by Exxon Mobil. In 2003 the company eyed the red hot iron ore market when it acquired a controlling stake in South Africa-based iron producer Kumba Resources.

EXECUTIVES

Chairman: Sir Mark Moody-Stuart, age 65, $376,560 pay
CEO and Executive Director: Anthony J. (Tony) Trahar, age 56, $1,621,719 pay
EVP, Group Human Resources and Business Development: Russell King, age 47
Director, Finance and Executive Director: René Médori, age 47
Executive Chairman, Anglo Platinum Corp.; Executive Director: Barry E. Davison, age 60
Chairman, Base Metals and Industrial Minerals and Executive Director: Simon Thompson, age 45
Chief Executive, Mondi Group and Executive Director: David Hathorn, age 43
Chief Executive, South Africa: Lazarus Zim, age 44
Group Technical Director and Chairman, Coal: Tony Redman, age 46
COO, South Africa: Godfrey Gomwe
SVP, Russia: Richard Witt
Auditors: Deloitte & Touche LLP

LOCATIONS

HQ: Anglo American plc
  20 Carlton House Terrace,
  London SW1Y 5AN, United Kingdom
Phone: +44-20-7968-8888 **Fax:** +44-20-7968-8500
Web: www.angloamerican.co.uk

Anglo American's operations include subsidiaries in Australia, Austria, Brazil, Canada, Chile, the Czech Republic, France, Germany, Ireland, Namibia, Peru, Poland, South Africa, Spain, the UK, and Venezuela.

2004 Sales by Origin

	% of total
Africa	
South Africa	37
Other countries	9
Europe	33
South America	11
Australia & Asia	6
North America	4
Total	**100**

2004 Sales by Destination

	% of total
Europe	44
Africa	
South Africa	16
Other countries	2
Australia & Asia	17
North America	16
South America	5
Total	**100**

PRODUCTS/OPERATIONS

2004 Sales

	% of total
Paper & Packaging	22
Ferrous Metals & Industries	20
Industrial Minerals	12
Base Metals	11
Diamonds	10
Platinum	10
Gold	8
Coal	7
Total	**100**

Selected Industries and Subsidiaries

Paper and Packaging
Frantschach Packaging AG (70%, industrial packaging, Austria)
Mondi Limited (paper and packaging, South Africa)
Mondi Packaging (Europe) SA (corrugated packaging, Luxembourg)
Neusiedler AG (graphic paper, Austria)

Ferrous Metals and Industries
Highveld Steel (80%; steel, vanadium, and ferroalloys)
Kumba Resources Limited (67%; Coal, iron ore, heavy minerals; South Africa)
Scaw Metals (iron, steel, and engineering works; South Africa)
The Tongaat-Hulett Group Limited (53%; sugar, starch, and aluminum; South Africa)

Industrial Minerals
Bilfinger Berger Baustoffe GmbH (construction materials, Germany)
Copebras Limitada (73%, phosphate products, Brazil)
Lausitzer Grauwacke GmbH (construction materials, Germany)
Midland Quarry Products Limited (50%, construction materials, UK)
Steetley Iberia SA (construction materials, Spain)
Tarmac France SA (construction materials, France)
Tarmac Group Limited (construction materials, UK)
Tarmac Severokamen AS (96%, construction materials, Czech Republic)
WKSM SA (construction materials, Poland)

Base Metals
Black Mountain (copper, lead, and zinc; South Africa)
Codemin SA (90%, nickel, Brazil)
Empresa Minera de Mantos Blancos SA (copper, Chile)
Gamsberg Zinc Corporation (zinc, South Africa)
Hudson Bay Mining and Smelting Co. (copper and zinc, Canada)
Minera Loma de Níquel, CA (91%, nickel, Venezuela)
Minera Quellaveco SA (80%, copper, Peru)
Minera Sur Andes Limitada (copper, Chile)
Namakwa Sands (mineral sands, South Africa)

Diamonds
De Beers Consolidated (45%)

Platinum
Anglo Platinum Corporation Limited (75%, South Africa)

Gold
AngloGold Ashanti (51%, gold mines, South Africa)

Coal
Anglo Coal (South Africa)
Anglo Coal (Callide) Pty Limited (Australia)

COMPETITORS

ASARCO	Norilsk Nickel
Barrick Gold	Peñoles
BHP Billiton	Phelps Dodge
Brookfield	Placer Dome
Centromin	Rio Tinto
CRH	Sappi
Falconbridge	Shell Transport and
Freeport-McMoRan	Trading
Grupo México	Stora Enso Oyj
Hanson	Teck Cominco
Harmony Gold	Umicore
Impala Platinum	UPM-Kymmene
Inco Limited	Vale do Rio Doce
International Paper	Weyerhaeuser
Mitsubishi Materials	Xstrata
Newmont Mining	

HISTORICAL FINANCIALS

Company Type: Public

Income Statement

FYE: December 31

	REVENUE ($ mil.)	NET INCOME ($ mil.)	NET PROFIT MARGIN	EMPLOYEES
12/04	24,930	2,913	11.7%	209,000
12/03	18,637	1,592	8.5%	193,000
12/02	15,145	1,563	10.3%	177,000
12/01	14,786	3,176	21.5%	204,000
12/00	14,824	1,957	13.2%	249,000
12/99	11,578	1,552	13.4%	113,000
12/98*	6,907	789	11.4%	—
3/98	10,269	1,169	11.4%	—
3/97	3,207	1,607	50.1%	—
3/96	2,633	1,101	41.8%	—
Annual Growth	**28.4%**	**11.4%**	**—**	**13.1%**

*Fiscal year change

2004 Year-End Financials

Debt ratio: 29.1%
Return on equity: 12.8%
Cash ($ mil.): 2,086
Current ratio: 1.16
Long-term debt ($ mil.): 7,278
No. of shares (mil.): 1,494
Dividends
  Yield: 2.4%
  Payout: 28.6%
Market value ($ mil.): 35,538

Stock History

NASDAQ (SC): AAUK

	STOCK PRICE ($) FY Close	P/E High/Low		PER SHARE ($) Earnings	Dividends	Book Value
12/04	23.79	14	10	1.96	0.56	16.73
12/03	22.12	20	12	1.10	0.55	13.81
12/02	14.60	18	10	1.10	0.54	11.07
12/01	15.11	14	4	2.13	0.53	9.15
12/00	13.56	14	7	1.23	0.44	9.53
12/99	16.28	18	7	1.00	0.34	10.50
12/98*	7.00	18	7	0.83	0.27	9.69
3/98	11.47	13	6	1.25	0.38	9.83
3/97	15.31	10	7	1.72	0.33	8.32
3/96	16.09	16	11	1.18	0.32	6.88
Annual Growth	**4.4%**	**—**	**—**	**5.8%**	**6.4%**	**10.4%**

*Fiscal year change

A.P. Møller - Mærsk

Danish maritime giant A.P. Møller - Mærsk (formerly A.P. Møller) has been on a roll since its start as a steamship company in 1904. Now Denmark's largest industrial group, A.P. Møller - Mærsk owns one of the world's top container shipping lines, Maersk Sealand, and has acquired Netherlands-based Royal P&O Nedlloyd. The group's fleet includes container carriers, bulk carriers, supply and specialty ships, and tankers. A.P. Møller - Mærsk also drills for oil and gas (primarily in the North Sea) and owns a stake in one of Denmark's largest grocery and general merchandise chains. In addition, it builds ships and shipping containers, operates domestic airline Maersk Air, and provides information technology services.

The reshuffling due to the acquisition of Royal P&O Nedlloyd is scheduled to be completed by the end of 2006; in February 2006 Maersk Sealand and P&O Nedlloyd will operate under the name Maersk Line, while P&O Nedlloyd Logistics will be integrated into Maersk Logistics.

The former A.P. Møller was a group made up of two separately listed companies: Aktieselskabet Dampskibsselskabet Svendborg and Dampskibsselskabet af 1912, Aktieselskab. The group reorganized in 2003 and wound up with A.P. Møller - Mærsk A/S, a single publicly traded company, at its head. A.P. Møller - Mærsk owns direct and indirect interests in other group companies.

Maersk Sealand's fleet includes more than 250 container carriers and about 800,000 containers. The shipping line has operations in more than 100 countries.

Among the group's major oil and gas assets is a 39% stake in the Dansk Undergrunds Consortium (DUC), which is engaged in exploration and production in the Danish sector of the North Sea.

A.P. Møller - Mærsk 's retail segment includes a stake in Dansk Supermarked, Denmark's #2 supermarket chain (behind FDB). Dansk Supermarked operates stores under names such as Føtex, Bilka, and Netto in Denmark, Germany, Poland, Sweden, and the UK.

The company has received approval from the Indian government to convert a bulk terminal into a container terminal. The project is estimated to cost A.P. Møller - Mærsk nearly $70 million.

The company has agreed to sell its IT services unit Mærsk Data to the IBM Danmark. It has also ordered two LNG (liquefied natural gas) carriers to accommodate anticipated growth in that market.

HISTORY

Arnold Peter Møller and his father, sea captain Peter Mærsk Møller, founded Aktieselskabet Dampskibsselskabet Svendborg (Steamship Company Svendborg) in 1904 in Svendborg, Denmark. Their first ship, a second-hand steamer, bore on its funnel a white seven-pointed star on a blue background, which had been on Peter's first ship. Later known as the Maersk star, the logo adorned all subsequent ships of the company, as well as ships of a second company formed eight years later — Dampskibsselskabet af 1912, Aktieselskab (Steamship Company of 1912). At that point, six ships were in the Maersk fleet.

In 1917 the company began building its own ships after establishing the Odense Steel Shipyard. It launched regular liner service between the US and the Far East in 1928, calling the operation the Maersk Line. With the addition of its first tankers that year, Maersk owned 35 ships.

Mærsk Mc-Kinney Møller, A.P.'s son, became a partner in the company in 1940. That year, with Germany occupying Denmark, he fled to the US with his bride on one of the last ships out. Refusing to take orders from the Nazis, A.P. transferred control of the company to the US, where the 26-year-old Mærsk had established operations. Most of the Maersk fleet flew under British or US flags during the war, which took the life of 148 Maersk seamen and claimed 25 ships. Mærsk Mc-Kinney Møller returned to Denmark in 1947.

A.P. Møller formed the Maersk Company in 1951 in London as a shipbroker, which became one of the world's largest shipowners. The early 1960s saw A.P. Møller diversifying as it moved into oil and gas exploration and production in Denmark in 1962 and established supermarket chain Dansk Supermarked in 1964. A.P. died the next year, having run the company for more than 60 years. Prior to his death, he had created three foundations to hold most of the company's shares. His son Mærsk took command of A.P. Møller and the Maersk fleet, which contained 88 ships. Under his leadership the company expanded even further and became more international; his business savvy became apparent when he sold some of the company's tanker fleet in the 1970s, just prior to prices going down.

In 1970 A.P. Møller established domestic carrier Maersk Air. A.P. Møller began seeing its first oil production in the North Sea in 1972. The next year the company acquired its first container vessel, the *Svendborg Maersk*.

Maersk Container Industri was formed in 1991 to produce intermodal containers. That year Maersk and rival Sea-Land entered into a transpacific vessel-sharing agreement, which was expanded into a global alliance in 1995. In 1999, just months after buying South Africa's Safmarine Container Lines, Maersk bought Sea-Land's international liner services and 18 terminals. The Maersk Line and Sea-Land operations were merged to form Maersk Sealand.

In 2000 A.P. Møller planned to extend its Bilka grocery chain into southern Sweden. That year Maersk Sealand decided to shift its transshipment hub in Singapore to a Malaysian port. In 2001 Maersk Air and Scandinavian Airlines System (SAS) were together fined $45 million by the European Commission for infringing on the EC's competition rules by entering a secret deal to monopolize certain air routes in Scandinavia. As a result, Maersk Air's chairman and managing director stepped down and were replaced.

With the shipping industry in a slump, A.P. Møller in 2003 sold Maersk Medical, a maker of catheters and continence products. A.P. Møller purchased the majority of Kerr-McGee's North Sea oil assets in late 2005.

EXECUTIVES

Chairman; Vice Chairman, Olie og Gas:
Michael Pram Rasmussen, age 48
Partner and CEO; Chairman, Olie og Gas:
Jess Søderberg
Partner; CEO, Mærsk Sealand: Knud E. Stubkjær
Partner: Tommy Thomsen
CEO, Olie og Gas: Thomas T. Andersen, age 49
EVP, Olie og Gas: Jep Brink, age 51
SVP, Corporate Communications: Jette Clausen
Managing Director, Maersk España S.A.: Eric A. Sisco

Managing Director, Kraks Forlag and PFA Holding:
Svend-Aage Nielsen
Managing Director, T&W Holding and A-huset Holding:
Jan Tøpholm
Managing Director: Jørn Steen Nielsen, age 49
SVP and CFO, Maersk Container Business:
Michael T. Jørgensen
Auditors: KPMG C. Jespersen

LOCATIONS

HQ: A.P. Møller - Mærsk A/S
Esplanaden 50, DK-1098 Copenhagen K, Denmark
Phone: +45-3363-3363   **Fax:** +45-3363-4108
Web: www.apmoller.com

2004 Sales

	% of total
Europe	49
North & South America	23
Asia	11
Other regions	17
Total	**100**

PRODUCTS/OPERATIONS

Selected Subsidiaries

A.P. Møller Finance S.A., Switzerland (holding company)
A.P. Møller Singapore Pte. Ltd. (shipping)
A/S Em. Z. Svitzer Group (salvage and towing)
A/S Roulunds Fabriker Group (automotive parts)
Danbor Service A/S Group (service, transport, production)
Dansk Industri Syndikat A/S (industrial air purification equipment)
Dansk Supermarked Group (supermarkets, hypermarkets, general merchandise)
Maersk Air A/S Group (airline services)
Maersk A/S Group (agency activities, drilling operations)
Maersk Company Canada Ltd. (anchor-handling, platform supply vessels)
Maersk Company Limited, UK (shipping, floating production)
Maersk Data A/S Group (electronic data processing)
Maersk Gulf Ltd. (agency activities, container repair, terminal operations, trucking; Central America and the Caribbean)
Maersk Hong Kong Ltd. (agency activities)
Maersk Inc. Group (agency activities, container terminals, land transport, distribution centers, liner-related businesses)
Maersk Olie og Gas AS Group (oil and gas production)
Maersk Sealand (container shipping services)
Maersk Singapore Pte. Ltd (agency activities, feeder services, logistics and terminal operations)
Maersk South America Ltd. (agency activities, container terminals, land transport, container-related activities)
Norfolkline B.V., The Netherlands (door-to-door transport and ferry services, rail freight)
Odense Staalskibsvaerft A/S Group (shipbuilding)
Rosti A/S Group (plastics)

COMPETITORS

Amerada Hess	ICA
Bolloré	John Swire & Sons
BP	Mitsui O.S.K. Lines
CMA CGM	Neptune Orient
COSCO Group	Norsk Hydro
CP Ships	NYK Line
Evergreen Marine	Orient Overseas
FDB	P&O
Hanjin Shipping	SAS
Hapag-Lloyd	Statoil

HISTORICAL FINANCIALS

Company Type: Public

Income Statement

FYE: December 31

	REVENUE ($ mil.)	NET INCOME ($ mil.)	NET PROFIT MARGIN	EMPLOYEES
12/04	30,421	4,464	14.7%	62,300
12/03	26,489	2,912	11.0%	63,161
12/02	21,388	1,701	8.0%	61,294
12/01	17,865	1,003	5.6%	—
12/00	10,630	662	6.2%	—
12/99	6,632	279	4.2%	—
12/98	6,725	462	6.9%	—
12/97	6,028	367	6.1%	—
12/96	5,605	383	6.8%	—
12/95	5,123	333	6.5%	—
Annual Growth	21.9%	33.4%	—	0.8%

2004 Year-End Financials

Debt ratio: 24.1%   Current ratio: 1.56
Return on equity: 24.5%   Long-term debt ($ mil.): 5,040
Cash ($ mil.): 3,075

Net Income History   Copenhagen: MAERSKA

Asahi Shimbun

The Asahi Shimbun Company helps the Japanese wake up informed. The company's flagship *Asahi Shimbun* is the #2 newspaper in Japan (behind *Yomiuri Shimbun*). With a daily circulation of 8 million, it is noted for its in-depth political coverage and investigative reporting. Asahi Shimbun also publishes books and magazines, including *AERA* and *Shukan Asahi*. The firm's English-language *Asahi Evening News* has been replaced by the *International Herald Times/The Asahi Shimbun*, published in cooperation with International Herald Tribune. The founding Murayama and Ueno families control Asahi Shimbun.

In addition to publishing, Asahi Shimbun operates in television broadcasting (as the largest shareholder of Asahi National Broadcasting, known as TV Asahi). The company also publishes content on the Internet.

Kotaro Akiyama replaced Shinichi Hakoshima as president of Asahi Shimbun in 2005 after a scandal involving paid editorial content in one of the company's publications. A second scandal broke later that year when a reporter for the newspaper was accused of fabricating information used in stories.

In addition to its domestic operations, Asahi Shimbun has publishing operations in several international locations, including Hong Kong, London, Los Angeles, New York, and Singapore.

HISTORY

Ryohei Murayama, the son of a wealthy merchant in Osaka, published the first issue of *Asahi Shimbun* in 1879. The four-page paper was intended to provide news in an easy-to-read format for the general public. Riichi Ueno later joined Murayama, and together in 1881 they purchased the paper outright from their backers. By 1883 it was the most widely read newspaper in Japan. It expanded to Tokyo in 1888 and became the first Japanese newspaper publisher to have foreign correspondents in Europe and the US.

A sharp critic of the government and the military, Asahi Shimbun defied the government censorship during the Rice Riots of 1918 (when housewives plundered the warehouses of rice merchants who were speculating on rice prices). The company successfully launched two weeklies in the 1920s, *Shukan Asahi* (1922) and *Asahi Graph* (1923). Its criticism of the armed forces led to a military boycott of *Asahi Shimbun* in the 1930s, culminating in an assault on its Tokyo office by army officers in 1936. Military censorship stifled the newspaper's reporting during WWII, and following the war the company's executives admitted their complicity in publishing misleading information and resigned.

Regaining its standing as the "people's organ," the company launched its English-language *Asahi Evening News* and the English-language review, *Japan Quarterly,* in the 1950s. Asahi Shimbun became the first publisher in the world to use facsimile and offset printing to publish daily newspapers in 1959.

Major investigative pieces became the hallmark of *Asahi Shimbun* in the 1970s and 1980s. The paper exposed collusion between government, big business, and the civil service, such as the Lockheed scandal involving under-the-table payments to Japanese politicians. In 1988 *Asahi Shimbun* broke the "Recruit Affair," another bribery scandal that led to the resignation of then Prime Minister Noboru Takeshita and other top politicians. Its journalistic drive continued into the 1990s, breaking the 1992 story of 500 million yen in kickbacks to Japanese political kingmaker Shin Kanemaru in connection to scandals centering on parcel delivery service Tokyo Sagawa Kyubin. (The news touched off a nationwide political reform movement.)

In 1995 Asahi Shimbun scored an exclusive when it was the first to beam images of the Sakhalin (Russia) earthquake around the world. SOFTBANK and News Corp. sold their shares of Asahi National Broadcasting (TV Asahi) to Asahi Shimbun in 1997 to promote future cooperation of Japanese TV programming for Japan Sky Broadcasting (JSkyB), a satellite broadcasting network started by the two heavyweights. Asahi Shimbun president Muneyuki Matsushita died in 1999 and was replaced by Shinichi Hakoshima, the company's senior managing director. The next year TV Asahi went public to finance its conversion to digital broadcasting standards. In 2001 the firm joined the *International Herald Tribune* to publish a new English-language paper to replace the *Asahi Evening News*.

Kotaro Akiyama replaced Hakoshima as president in 2005.

EXECUTIVES

President, CEO, and Director: Kotaro Akiyama, age 60
Senior Managing Director: Aihiko Bando, age 61
Senior Managing Director: Norio Utsumi
Managing Director, Advertising: Yukio Hirose, age 62
Managing Director: Fumio Ikeuchi, age 59
Managing Director and Internal Auditor: Yasuhiro Kobayashi, age 59
Managing Director, Editorial: Shin-ichi Yoshida, age 55
Director, Sales: Ikutaro Hama, age 59
Director, Administrative and Legal: Yoshio Honsawa, age 59
Director, Business Strategy: Hideo Jintoku, age 55
Director, International: Ryoichi Satoh, age 61
Auditors: KPMG AZSA & Co.

LOCATIONS

HQ: The Asahi Shimbun Company
　5-3-2 Tsukiji, Chuo-ku, Tokyo 104-8011, Japan
Phone: +81-3-3545-0131　　**Fax:** +81-3-3545-8450
US HQ: 845 3rd Ave., 11th Fl., New York, NY 10022
US Phone: 212-317-3030　　**US Fax:** 212-317-3039
Web: www.asahi.com

PRODUCTS/OPERATIONS

Selected Operations
Book publishing
Magazines
　AERA (news)
　Ronza (business)
　Shukan Asahi (news)
Newspapers
　Asahi Shimbun
　International Herald Times/The Asahi Shimbun
　Shukan Asahi
Other investments
　Asahi National Broadcasting (TV Asahi)
　Daiko Advertising

COMPETITORS

Dow Jones
Fuji Television
International
　Herald Tribune
Kodansha
Nihon Keizai Shimbun
Nippon Television
Tokyo Broadcasting
　System
Yomiuri Shimbun

HISTORICAL FINANCIALS

Company Type: Private

Income Statement

FYE: March 31

	REVENUE ($ mil.)	NET INCOME ($ mil.)	NET PROFIT MARGIN	EMPLOYEES
3/05	5,700	179	3.1%	14,407
3/04*	5,701	120	2.1%	14,122
3/01	5,716	—	—	10,733
3/00	3,954	—	—	7,543
3/99	3,187	—	—	7,470
3/98	3,135	—	—	7,543
3/97	3,376	—	—	7,580
3/96	3,785	—	—	7,698
3/95	4,651	—	—	7,832
Annual Growth	2.6%	49.5%	—	7.9%

*Irregular reporting interval

2005 Year-End Financials

Debt ratio: 6.1%　　　Current ratio: 1.47
Return on equity: 7.3%　　Long-term debt ($ mil.): 154
Cash ($ mil.): 839

Net Income History

Assicurazioni Generali

Italy's largest insurance company (and one of the largest in Europe), Assicurazioni Generali writes insurance for risks as varied as space launches and corporate package policies. Some 175 companies make up the Generali group, which also holds interests in many more companies. About 100 of the core companies are involved primarily in insurance (including life, accident, health, motor, fire, marine/aviation, and reinsurance); the rest concentrate on other financial services and real estate. Generali is noted for being a leading insurer of satellite and space missions, which it has been covering since 1964. In more earthbound realms, the company targets individuals and small to mid-sized businesses.

Italy and Germany are Generali's largest markets. The insurer is further establishing itself in Germany, having acquired a controlling interest in one of the country's largest insurers, AMB Generali (formerly Aachener und Munchener), and establishing an alliance with Commerzbank.

Generali shareholders include Italy's secretive and powerful MEDIOBANCA (14%), as well as Banca d'Italia and Unicredito (each about 4%).

HISTORY

Assicurazioni Generali was founded as Assicurazioni Generali Austro-Italiche in 1831 by a group of merchants led by Giuseppe Morpurgo in the Austro-Hungarian port of Trieste. Formed to provide insurance to the city's bustling trade industry, the company offered life, marine, fire, flood, and shipping coverage. That year Morpurgo established what he intended to be Generali's headquarters in Venice. (While the company maintained offices in both cities, Trieste ultimately won out.)

By 1835 Generali had opened 25 offices in Central and Western Europe; it had also expelled Morpurgo. The firm moved into Africa and Asia in the 1880s. In 1900 Generali began selling injury and theft insurance. In 1907 Generali's Prague office provided the young, experimental writer Franz Kafka his first job. (He found it disagreeable and quit after a few months.)

During WWI, the firm's Venice office pledged allegiance to Italy, while the office in Trieste (still part of Austria-Hungary) stayed loyal to the Hapsburgs. After the war Trieste was absorbed by the new Italian republic. Under Edgardo Morpurgo, Generali expanded further in the 1920s, managing 30 subsidiaries and operating in 17 countries. As fascist Italy aligned itself with Germany in the 1930s, adoption of anti-Semitic laws caused Morpurgo and a number of other high-ranking Jewish employees to flee the country. In 1938 Generali moved its headquarters to Rome (but moved them back to Trieste after WWII).

The firm maintained steady business both before and during Nazi occupation in WWII; in 1945, however, the Soviets seized all Italian properties in Eastern Europe, including 14 Generali subsidiaries. In 1950 Generali invaded the US market, offering shipping and fire insurance and reinsurance. Generali established a cooperative agreement with Aetna Life and Casualty (now Aetna Inc.) in 1966, further cementing its US connections.

In 1988 Generali tried to acquire French insurer Compagnie du Midi. Foreshadowing Generali's later dealings with Istituto Nazionale delle Assicurazioni (INA), Midi escaped Generali's grasp through a merger with AXA. As the Iron Curtain frayed in 1989, Generali formed AB Generali Budapest through a joint venture with a Hungarian insurer. In 1990 the firm opened an office in Tokyo through an agreement with Taisho Marine and Fire Insurance (which became Mitsui Marine & Fire Insurance and is now Mitsui Sumitomo Insurance). By 1993 Generali had become Italy's largest insurer.

In 1997 the firm was accused, along with other major European insurers, of not paying on policies of Holocaust victims. (It moved to settle claims in 1999.)

The company focused on the German and Swiss markets in 1998, acquiring controlling interests in insurer AMB Aachener und Munchener (now AMB Generali) and in Banca della Svizzera Italiana. Also that year Generali and Commerzbank established an alliance that gave the companies more access to each other's markets.

In 1999 Generali succeeded in a hostile takeover of INA, its largest domestic competitor. The move pre-empted INA's proposed merger with San Paolo IMI, which would have knocked Generali to second place among the country's insurers.

Avoiding violation of the EU's antitrust laws in connection with the INA acquisition, the company sold four subsidiaries (including Italian insurers Aurora and Navale) in 2000.

In 2002 Generali rolled together three securities investments firms — Altinia, Ina Sim, and Prime Consult Sim — into Banca Generali.

EXECUTIVES

Chairman: Antoine Bernheim, age 81
Deputy Chairman: Gabriele Galateri di Genola, age 58
Managing Director and Board Member: Sergio Balbinot, age 47
Managing Director and Board Member: Giovanni Perissinotto, age 52
General Manager, Italian Operations: Fabio Buscarini
Secretary and Deputy General Manager, Legal, Corporate Affairs, and Privacy: Vittorio Rispoli
General Manager: Raffaele Agrusti, age 48
Deputy General Manager, Corporate Development and Risk Management: Mel Carvill
Deputy General Manager: Aldo Minucci
CEO and Director General, Genertel: Davide Passero
Chief Executive, AMB Generali Holding: Walter Thiessen
Chairman and CEO, Generali France: Claude Tendil, age 59
CEO, Generali Holding Vienna: Karl Stoss, age 48
CEO, Generali Switzerland: Alfred Leu
CEO, Migdal: Izzy Cohen
General Manager, Generali Espana: Monica Mondardini
Assistant General Manager, Human Resources: Lodovico Floriani
Corporate Communications: Mauro Giusto
Tax: Stefano Meroi
Auditors: PricewaterhouseCoopers SpA

LOCATIONS

HQ: Assicurazioni Generali SpA
Piazza Duca degli Abruzzi, 2, 34132 Trieste, Italy
Phone: +39-040-671-111   **Fax:** +39-040-671-600
US HQ: 1 Liberty Plaza, New York, NY 10006
US Phone: 212-602-7600   **US Fax:** 212-616-6399
Web: www.generali.com

Assicurazioni Generali has operations in Argentina, Austria, Belgium, Brazil, China, Colombia, Croatia, the Czech Republic, Ecuador, France, Germany, Greece, Guatemala, Hong Kong, Hungary, Ireland, Israel, Italy, Mexico, Netherlands, Panama, Peru, the Philippines, Poland, Portugal, Romania, Slovakia, Slovenia, Spain, Switzerland, Thailand, Turkey, the UK, and the US.

PRODUCTS/OPERATIONS

Selected Subsidiaries and Affiliates

Aachener und Münchener Lebensversicherung Aktiengesellschaft (Germany)
Adriavita S.p.A.
AdvoCard Rechtsschutzversicherung AG (Germany)
Alleanza Assicurazioni S.p.A.
Allgemeine Immobilien-Verwaltungs-Gesellschaft A.I.V. (Austria)
Altegia S.A. (France)
Am Prudence S.A. (France)
AMB Generali Holding AG (Germany)
AMB Generali Immobilien GmbH (Germany)
AMB Generali Pensionsfonds AG (Germany)
AMB Generali Pensionskasse AG (Germany)
ASSITALIA — Le Assicurazioni d'Italia S.p.A.
Banca BSI Italia S.p.A.
Banca Generali S.p.A.
Banca Svizzera Italiana SA (Switzerland)
Banco Vitalicio De España (Spain)
Central Krankenversicherung AG (Germany)
Continent Assistance S.A. (France)
Continent Holding S.A. (France)
Cosmos Lebensversicherungs-AG (Germany)
Cosmos Versicherung Aktiengesellschaft (Germany)
Deutsche Bausparkasse Badenia AG (Germany)
Dialog Lebensversicherungs-AG (Germany)
ENVIVAS Krankenversicherung AG (Germany)
Europ Assistance — Companhia Portuguesa de Seguros de Assistencia S.A. (Portugal)
Europ Assistance (Ireland) Ltd.
Europ Assistance (Suisse) S.A. (Switzerland)
Europ Assistance Belgium
Europ Assistance France S.A. (France)
Europ Assistance G.M.B.H. (Austria)
Europ Assistance Holding (France)
Europ Assistance Holdings Ltd. (UK)
Europ Assistance Magyarország Kft. (Hungary)
Europ Assistance Nederland (The Netherlands)
Europ Assistance Polska SP. Z.O.O. (Poland)
Europ Assistance RU (Russia)
Europ Assistance s.r.o. (Czech Republic)
Europai Utazasi Biztosito RT. (Hungary)
Europäische Reiseversicherung-AG (Austria)
Europ-Assistance España (Spain)
Europ-Assistance Italia S.P.A.
Europ-Assistance Luxembourg
Europ-Assistance Versicherungs-AG (Germany)
Europeenne De Protection Juridique S.A. (France)
F.A.T.A. — Fondo Assicurativo Tra Agricoltori S.p.A.
Finagen S.p.A.
Fortuna Investment AG (Switzerland)
G.G.L. S.p.A.
Genagricola S.P.A.
Generali (Schweiz) Holding (Switzerland)
Generali Asigurari S.A. (Romania)
Generali Asset Management SGR
Generali Assurances iard (France)
Generali Assurances vie (France)
Generali Bank AG (Austria)
Generali Belgium S.A.
Generali Direct (Switzerland)
Generali Dommages (France)
Generali Employee Benefits Bruxelles (Belgium)
Generali Employee Benefits G.m.b.H. Frankfurt (Germany)
Generali Employee Benefits London (UK)
Generali Epargne (France)

Generali España, Holding De Entidades De Seguros, S.A. (Spain)
Generali Finance B.V. (The Netherlands)
Generali Finances S.A. (France)
Generali France S.A. (France)
Generali Hellas A.E.A.Z. Property and Casualty Insurance Co. (Greece)
Generali Holding Vienna AG (Austria)
Generali International Ltd. (Guernsey)
Generali Lebensversicherung AG (Germany)
Generali Levensverzekering Mij N.V. (The Netherlands)
Generali Life Hellenic Insurance Company A.E. (Greece)
Generali Lloyd AG (Germany)
Generali Luxembourg S.A.
Generali Osiguranje D.D. (Croatia)
Generali PanEurope Limited (Ireland)
Generali Personenversicherungen (Switzerland)
Generali Poist'ovna A.S. (Slovakia)
Generali Pojistovna a.s. (Czech Republic)
Generali Portfolio Management Limited (Guernsey)
Generali Powszechne Towarzystwo Emerytalne S.A. (Poland)
Generali Protection Vie S.A. (France)
Generali Rueckversicherung A.G. (Austria)
Generali Schadeverzekering Mij N.V. (The Netherlands)
Generali Servizi S.r.l.
Generali Sigorta A.S. (Turkey)
Generali Towarzystwo Ubezpieczen S.A. (Poland)
Generali Versicherung AG (Austria)
Generali Versicherung AG (Germany)
Generali Verzekeringsgroep NV (The Netherlands)
Generali Vida Companhia de Seguros S.A. (Portugal)
Generali Vita S.p.A.
Generali Worldwide Group (Guernsey)
Generali Worldwide Insurance Company Ltd. (Guernsey)
Generali Zavarovalnica d.d. (Slovenia)
Generali Zivotno Osiguranje D.D. (Croatia)
Generali Zycie Towarzystwo Ubezpieczen S.A. (Poland)
Generali-Providencia Biztosito RT. (Hungary)
GeneraliVoyages.com (France)
Genertel S.p.A.
GPA-IARD S.A. (France)
GPA-VIE S.A. (France)
Gruppo Generali Immobiliare Spa
Ina Vita S.p.A.
Interunfall Versicherung Aktiengesellschaft (Austria)
La Estrella, S.A. De Seguros Y Reaseguros (Spain)
La Federation Continentale S.A. (France)
La Venezia Assicurazioni S.p.A.
L'equité (France)
Middlesea Insurance p.l.c. (Malta)
Prudence Vie (France)
Risparmio Assicurazioni S.p.A.
UMS Generali Marine S.p.A.
Uni One Assicurazioni S.p.A.
Uni One Vita S.p.A.
Union Generale Du Nord (France)

COMPETITORS

AGF
AIG
Allianz
AXA
ERGO
Eureko
Fineco
FonSai
Fortis SA/NV
ING
Lloyd Adriatico
Milano Assicurazioni
Ras
Swiss Re
Toro Group
UniCredit
Unipol
Zurich Financial Services

HISTORICAL FINANCIALS

Company Type: Public

Income Statement

FYE: December 31

	ASSETS ($ mil.)	NET INCOME ($ mil.)	INCOME AS % OF ASSETS	EMPLOYEES
12/04	383,718	1,793	0.5%	58,000
12/03	326,115	1,274	0.4%	60,638
12/02	246,014	(791)	—	59,753
12/01	203,417	974	0.5%	58,445
12/00	206,202	1,342	0.7%	57,443
12/99	176,747	1,596	0.9%	56,593
12/98	34,491	773	2.2%	54,598
12/97	29,481	585	2.0%	41,417
12/96	88,551	947	1.1%	40,003
12/95	79,598	438	0.6%	38,236
Annual Growth	**19.1%**	**17.0%**	**—**	**4.7%**

2004 Year-End Financials

Equity as % of assets: 3.3%
Return on assets: 0.5%
Return on equity: 13.7%
Long-term debt ($ mil.): 1,841
Sales ($ mil.): 107,213

Net Income History

Italian: G

(Chart showing net income from 12/95 to 12/04, y-axis from -1,000 to 2,000)

AstraZeneca

AstraZeneca's products run the gamut from A (breast cancer drug Arimidex) to Z (migraine treatment Zomig). One of the world's top pharmaceutical firms, AstraZeneca specializes in drugs for gastrointestinal, cardiovascular, and oncology therapeutic areas. The firm's biggest seller is acid reflux remedy Nexium. For matters of the heart, AstraZeneca makes hypertension and heart failure drug Atacand and cholesterol reducer Crestor. The company's oncology drugs include Nolvadex (breast cancer) and Zoladex (prostate cancer), and lung cancer growth-inhibitor Iressa. The company also makes drugs for respiratory and central nervous system conditions and pain control.

Faced with patent expirations of such top-selling drugs such as Prilosec, Nolvadex, and Zestril, the company answered the challenge with several promising new drugs. Its purple Prilosec follow-up, Nexium, rocketed to the top of the company's offerings. In addition, cholesterol medication Crestor and lung cancer therapy Iressa had impressive debuts, but the company's hopes for these two drugs have dimmed. Clinical trial results announced in 2004 revealed Iressa failed to help lung cancer patients live longer and pulled the drug from the approval queue in Europe and ceased selling it in the US. Iressa also took another blow in early 2005 when it was announced that it had no significant effect on breast cancer survival rates in a study sponsored by the National Cancer Institute. Additionally, in early 2005 the FDA ordered AstraZeneca to note on Crestor's label that the drug can cause

life-threatening muscle damage to some patients, particularly those of Asian descent.

To keep new drugs coming, AstraZeneca is investing heavily in research and development in its core areas of expertise, spending $3.8 billion on drug development in 2004. The company's pipeline is stocked with projects such as diabetes therapy Galida. Its thrombosis medication Exanta, however, was rejected by the FDA in 2004. Other projects include drugs for gastrointestinal disorders, psychiatric diseases, cancer, and pain.

Not surprisingly, the company earns 45% of its sales from the US. Its top US customers, together accounting for 80% of its nearly $10 billion in US sales, are drug distributors McKesson, AmerisourceBergen, and Cardinal Health.

AstraZeneca's other businesses include Aptium Oncology (formerly Salick Health Care), which operates cancer treatment centers in the US, and Astra Tech, which manufactures such medical devices as urinary catheters and dental implant systems.

The company was fined $73 million by the European Commission in mid-2005 in the first case that used EU antitrust laws to punish a company for manipulating patent laws to prevent generic competition. The Commission decided that AstraZeneca did just that to prevent generic versions of Losec (known as Prilosec in the US) from coming to market in Denmark, Sweden, and Norway.

Asset management firm The Capital Group Companies owns almost 15% of the company.

HISTORY

AstraZeneca forerunner Imperial Chemical Industries (ICI) was created from the 1926 merger of four British chemical companies — Nobel Industries; Brunner, Mond and Company; United Alkali; and British Dyestuffs — in reaction to the German amalgamation that created I. G. Farben. ICI plunged into research, recruiting chemists, engineers, and managers and forming alliances with universities. Between 1933 and 1935, at least 87 new products were created, including polyethylene.

Fortunes declined as competition increased after WWII. In 1980 ICI posted losses and cut its dividend for the first time. In 1982 turnaround artist John Harvey-Jones shifted ICI from bulk chemicals to high-margin specialty chemicals such as pharmaceuticals and pesticides. That business became Zeneca, which ICI spun off in 1993.

The takeover specter loomed large over the company during its first year. Zeneca had several drugs in its pipeline, but it also had expiring patents on others, making them fair game for competitors. Bankrolled by its agrochemical business, Zeneca forged alliances with other pharmaceutical firms. In 1994 it entered a marketing alliance with Amersham International (now Amersham) to sell Metastron, a nuclear-medicine cancer agent. The next year Zeneca formed a joint venture with Chinese companies Advanced Chemicals and Tianli to make textile-coating chemicals.

In 1995 Glaxo was forced to sell a migraine drug candidate to complete its merger with Wellcome. Zeneca's gamble in buying the then-unproven drug (Zomig) paid off when the product gained US FDA approval two years later.

By 1997 Zeneca completed its gradual acquisition of Salick Health Care, formed to create more humane cancer treatment programs. The purchase followed a trend of large drug firms

moving into managed care, which raised concerns that centers might be pressured to use their parent companies' drugs, but Zeneca maintained that Salick would remain independent except to the extent that it offered an opportunity to evaluate treatments.

In 1998 Zeneca got the FDA's OK to sell its brand of tamoxifen (Nolvadex) to women at high risk of contracting breast cancer. In 1999 it sued Eli Lilly to protect Nolvadex against Lilly's marketing claim that its osteoporosis treatment Evista reduced breast cancer risk, a use for which it was not approved.

In 1999 Zeneca completed its purchase of Sweden's Astra to form AstraZeneca. That year the firm sold its specialty chemicals unit, Zeneca Specialties, to Cinven Group and Investcorp. With its agricultural business stagnated due to crippled markets in Asia and Europe, AstraZeneca announced plans to merge the unit with the agrochemicals business of Novartis and spin it off as Syngenta. In 2000 Sweden approved ulcer drug Nexium, as well as Symbicort Turbuhaler, an asthma inhaler.

In 2001 AstraZeneca sold its genetic diversity testing services subsidiary, Cellmark Diagnostics, to Orchid Cellmark (with whom the company also announced a multi-year collaborative research agreement).

EXECUTIVES

Chairman: Louis Schweitzer, age 63
Deputy Chairman: Håkan Mogren, age 60, $53,000 pay
CEO and Executive Director:
Sir Thomas F.W. (Tom) McKillop, age 61, $2,524,000 pay
Executive Director, Development: John Patterson
CFO and Executive Director: Jonathan Symonds, age 45, $1,587,000 pay
EVP, Product Strategy and Licensing and Business Development: Martin Nicklasson
EVP, Discovery Research: Jan Lundberg
EVP, Human Resources: Tony Bloxham
EVP, Europe, Japan, Asia Pacific, and the Rest of the World: Bruno Angelici
EVP, North America and Executive Director; President and CEO, AstraZeneca US: David R. Brennan
EVP, North America; President and CEO, AstraZeneca US: Tony P. Zook
EVP, Operations: Barrie Thorpe
VP, Federal Government Affairs: Richard (Rich) Buckley
VP, Medical Affairs: Les Paul
VP, Public Policy: Robert Perkins
VP, Global Compensation and Benefits: Peter Brown
Group Secretary and Solicitor: Graeme H. R. Musker
Senior Director, Medical Science: Peter Langmuir
Commercial Brand Leader: Don Bearnish
Auditors: KPMG Audit Plc

LOCATIONS

HQ: AstraZeneca PLC
15 Stanhope Gate,
London W1Y 1LN, United Kingdom
Phone: +44-20-7304-5000 **Fax:** +44-20-7304-5183
US HQ: 1800 Concord Pike,
Wilmington, DE 19850
US Phone: 302-886-3000 **US Fax:** 302-886-2972
Web: www.astrazeneca.com

AstraZeneca's principal facilities are in Australia, Canada, France, Germany, Italy, Japan, Puerto Rico, Sweden, the UK, and the US.

2004 Sales

	$ mil.	% of total
The Americas		
US	9,604	45
Canada	876	4
Other countries	420	2
Europe		
France	1,569	7
UK	1,108	5
Germany	961	5
Italy	922	4
Sweden	723	3
Spain	709	3
Belgium	325	2
The Netherlands	205	1
Other countries	1,419	7
Asia, Africa & Australasia		
Japan	1,364	6
Australia	451	2
Other countries	770	4
Total	**21,426**	**100**

PRODUCTS/OPERATIONS

2004 Sales

	$ mil.	% of total
Gastrointestinal		
Nexium	3,883	18
Losec/Prilosec	1,947	9
Other	88	—
Cardiovascular		
Seloken	1,387	6
Crestor	908	4
Atacand	879	4
Other	1,593	8
Neurology		
Seroquel	2,027	9
Local anesthetics	542	3
Other	927	4
Oncology		
Casodex	1,012	5
Zoladex	917	4
Other	1,447	7
Respiratory & Inflammation		
Pulmicort	1,050	5
Symbicort	797	4
Rhinocort	361	2
Other	375	2
Infection	539	3
Other products	737	3
Total	**21,426**	**100**

Selected Products

Gastrointestinal
  Entocort (anti-inflammatory for
    inflammatory bowel disease)
  Losec/Prilosec/Omepral (acid reflux disease)
  Nexium (acid reflux disease)

Cardiovascular
  Atacand (hypertension and heart failure)
  Crestor (cholesterol-lowering drug)
  Plendil (hypertension and angina)
  Seloken ZOK/Toprol-XL (beta-blocker)
  Zestril (ACE inhibitor)

Oncology
  Arimidex (breast cancer)
  Casodex (prostate cancer)
  Faslodex (breast cancer)
  Iressa (anti-tumor)
  Nolvadex (breast cancer)
  Zoladex (prostate and breast cancer)

Respiratory and Inflammation
  Accolate (asthma)
  Oxis (asthma)
  Pulmicort (anti-inflammatory)
  Rhinocort (topical nasal anti-inflammatory)
  Symbicort (anti-inflammatory and
    bronchodilator in one inhaler)

Neurology
  Diprivan (general anesthetic)
  Naropin (local anesthetic)
  Seroquel (schizophrenia)
  Xylocaine (local anesthetic)
  Zomig (migraines)
Infection
  Merrem/Meronem (antibiotic)

COMPETITORS

Abbott Labs	Merck
Bayer	Novartis
Bristol-Myers Squibb	Pfizer
Elan	Roche
Eli Lilly	Sanofi-Aventis
GlaxoSmithKline	Schering
Hoffmann-La Roche	Schering-Plough
Johnson & Johnson	Wyeth
Memorial Sloan-Kettering	

HISTORICAL FINANCIALS

Company Type: Public

Income Statement

FYE: December 31

	REVENUE ($ mil.)	NET INCOME ($ mil.)	NET PROFIT MARGIN	EMPLOYEES
12/04	21,426	3,813	17.8%	64,000
12/03	18,849	3,036	16.1%	60,000
12/02	17,841	2,836	15.9%	58,000
12/01	16,480	2,967	18.0%	54,600
12/00	15,804	2,538	16.1%	55,000
12/99	17,791	1,143	6.4%	58,000
12/98	9,144	1,185	13.0%	34,000
12/97	8,579	1,205	14.0%	31,400
12/96	9,184	1,101	12.0%	31,100
12/95	7,597	521	6.9%	30,800
Annual Growth	**12.2%**	**24.7%**	**—**	**8.5%**

2004 Year-End Financials

Debt ratio: 7.1%
Return on equity: 27.6%
Cash ($ mil.): 1,055
Current ratio: 1.86
Long-term debt ($ mil.): 1,030
No. of shares (mil.): 1,645
Dividends
  Yield: 2.3%
  Payout: 36.8%
Market value ($ mil.): 59,862

Stock History

NYSE: AZN

	STOCK PRICE ($) FY Close	P/E High/Low		Earnings	PER SHARE ($) Dividends	Book Value
12/04	36.39	24	17	2.28	0.84	8.76
12/03	48.38	28	17	1.78	0.78	7.78
12/02	35.09	28	15	1.64	0.78	6.50
12/01	46.60	29	23	1.69	0.26	5.61
12/00	51.50	30	18	1.44	0.78	5.39
12/99	41.75	30	22	0.64	0.76	5.80
12/98	44.88	40	25	1.25	0.28	4.38
12/97	35.96	10	7	3.82	0.00	1.21
12/96	27.97	25	16	1.16	0.56	1.22
12/95	19.44	38	24	0.55	0.49	1.02
Annual Growth	**7.2%**	**—**	**—**	**17.1%**	**6.2%**	**27.1%**

Atos Origin

Atos Origin has a firm toehold on Europe's information technology (IT) services mountain. The company provides services such as facilities management, e-commerce consulting, and systems design, implementation, and integration. Atos Origin also offers data and transaction processing services, Web site hosting, and outsourcing services for such functions as customer relationship management and enterprise resource planning. In early 2004 Atos Origin acquired the IT services arm of Schlumberger for about $1.5 billion, a purchase that will significantly increase its annual revenues. Philips Electronics had owned more than one-third of Atos Origin, but sold off its stake in 2004 and 2005.

Formed from the 2000 combination of Atos and Origin (the computer services division of Philips Electronics), Atos Origin targets clients in the financial services, automotive, manufacturing, and telecommunications industries. The company, which derives about 90% of its sales from customers in Europe, the Middle East, and Africa, has acquired KPMG International's British and Dutch operations, moving the company into high-end consulting and the realm of Capgemini and IBM.

Philips is one of the company's largest clients; it and KPN each accounted for about 5% of revenues in 2004. Other customers include Vivendi Universal, BNP Paribas, and Unilever.

HISTORY

Atos Origin's lineage is a story of mergers. The company's predecessor, Groupe Sligos, was itself the product of a merger — the 1973 union of Sliga (Crédit Lyonnais' data processing services subsidiary) with Cegos Informatique, a management systems development and consulting company started in 1962.

In 1981 Sligos debuted the first bank/retailer network switching system. It acquired Soliac, France's largest credit card maker, in 1983. Sligos went public in 1986 and two years later acquired a majority stake in CMG (acquired by rival Logica plc to form LogicaCMG in 2002), one of France's leading computer engineering companies.

During the early 1990s Sligos focused on international growth, gaining majority interests in banking systems companies. It bought a controlling interest in Marben Group, a systems integration and networking firm, in 1993.

In 1996 Sligos joined with CyberCash, a (now-defunct) US-based transaction processing company, to develop a secure Internet payment method for the European market. It sold CMG (by then a PC retailing subsidiary) to Infopoint and its Soliac magnetic strip and smart card unit to Schlumberger.

In late 1997 Sligos merged with French IT services company Axime. (Axime was created by the 1991 merger of IT service providers FITB, Segin, and Sodinforg. Bernard Bourigeaud joined Axime that year and became its chairman and CEO in 1992.)

Following the Sligos-Axime merger the company changed its name to Atos, with Axime's Bourigeaud assuming the role of chairman. Atos spent the last half of 1997 (and the first half of 1998) reorganizing its operations around four key areas: systems integration, outsourcing, multimedia, and services.

In 1998 Atos pared off its networking services and direct marketing subsidiaries. That year the company doubled the size of its Italian operation by acquiring IT services firm Sesam from Fiat and Digital Equipment (later acquired by Compaq), and it bought French customer relationship management specialist Statilogie. Atos in 1999 bought a controlling interest in France-based Odyssée, a consulting specialist in the financial services market. The next year the company developed a joint venture with ParisBourse to offer online stock trading and electronic banking.

In 2000 the company merged with Origin, the computer services arm of Philips Electronics. Bourigeaud became chairman and CEO of the new company, named Atos Origin. In 2002 Atos Origin acquired KPMG's British and Dutch operations for $617 million. Late the same year, Philips ended up taking a sizeable write-off on its stake in Atos Origin.

In early 2004 the company acquired the IT services arm of Schlumberger for about $1.5 billion.

EXECUTIVES

Chairman: Didier Cherpitel
CEO: Bernard Bourigeaud, age 61, $2,563,447 pay
CFO: Eric Guilhou, $1,361,831 pay
Director, UK, Americas, Asia Pacific, and Coordinating Global Markets and Accounts and Olympics: Xavier Flinois, $1,522,047 pay
Director, France, Germany, Central Europe, AtosEuronext, Atos Worldline, and Coordinating Global Managed Operations: Dominique Illien, $1,522,047 pay
Director, Netherlands, Belgium, Luxembourg, and the Nordic Region, and Coordinating Global Consulting and Global Systems Integration: Wilbert Kieboom, $1,522,047 pay
Director, Italy, Spain, Portugal, Andorra, Middle East and Africa: Giovanni Linari, $1,361,831 pay
Director, Corporate Human Resources, Internal Communications, Marketing Communications, and Public Relations: Jans Tielman, $1,281,723 pay
Managing Director, Consulting Division: Keith Rowling
Finance Director, Atos Origin UK: John Campbell
Director, Communication and Public Relations: Marie-Tatiana Collombert
Director, Managed Services: Gerhard Fercho
Director, Investor Relations: John White
Head of Applications Maintenance Services: Patrice Dannenberg
Sales Manager, Banking and Telecom, Argentina; Business Manager, Chile: Victor Rodriguez Cubero
Financial Communications: Bertrand Labonde
Auditors: Amyot Exco; Deloitte & Associés

LOCATIONS

HQ: Atos Origin S.A.
Tour Les Miroirs — Bâtiment C, 18, avenue d'Alsace, 92926 Paris, France
Phone: +33-1-55-91-20-00   **Fax:** +33-1-55-91-20-05
US HQ: 5599 San Felipe, Ste. 300, Houston, TX 77056
US Phone: 713-513-3000   **US Fax:** 713-403-7204
Web: www.atosorigin.com

Atos Origin has operations in more than 40 countries.

2004 Sales

	% of total
Europe, Middle East & Africa	
France	27
UK	23
Benelux	20
Germany & Central Europe	6
Italy	6
Spain	5
Other	5
Americas	5
Asia/Pacific	3
Total	**100**

PRODUCTS/OPERATIONS

2004 Sales

	% of total
Managed Operations	52
Consulting & Systems Integration	48
Total	**100**

2004 Sales

	% of total
Public Sector & Utilities	27
Finance	19
Telecom & Media	19
Discrete Manufacturing	12
Process Industries	8
CPG & Retail	7
Other	8
Total	**100**

Selected Services

Systems Integration
  Application and data migration
  Application lifecycle management
  Configuration management
  Enterprise architecture
  Enterprise resource planning
  eServices
  Operations design, roll-out, and support
  Systems development
Managed Operations
  Business continuity
  Data and application hosting
  IT support outsourcing
  On-demand services
  Security services
Consulting
  Business intelligence
  Business strategy
  Customer relationship management
  Enterprise security
  Financial management solutions
  Knowledge services
  Supply chain management
  Transformation management

COMPETITORS

Altran Technologies
ARES
Aubay
BT
Bull
Capgemini
CBGI
Computacenter
Computer Sciences Corp.
CS Communication
Devoteam
Diagonal
Dimension Data
EDS
Finsiel
Fujitsu Services
Getronics
GFI Informatique
HP Technology Solutions Group
IBM Global Services
LogicaCMG
Morse
Parity
Siemens Business Services
Sogeti-Transiciel
Sopra
Steria
TEAMLOG
Triple P
Umanis
Unilog
Unisys
Xansa

HISTORICAL FINANCIALS

Company Type: Public

Income Statement

FYE: December 31

	REVENUE ($ mil.)	NET INCOME ($ mil.)	NET PROFIT MARGIN	EMPLOYEES
12/04	7,232	174	2.4%	46,584
12/03	3,809	(212)	—	26,345
12/02	3,189	74	2.3%	28,602
12/01	2,691	109	4.1%	26,278
12/00*	1,802	46	2.5%	26,916
9/99	1,154	51	4.4%	9,983
9/98	1,120	43	3.8%	9,400
9/97	968	30	3.1%	8,742
9/96	408	26	6.4%	2,702
9/95	415	26	6.2%	2,593
Annual Growth	**37.4%**	**23.6%**	**—**	**37.8%**

*Fiscal year change

2004 Year-End Financials

Debt ratio: 50.7%
Return on equity: —
Cash ($ mil.): 636
Current ratio: 3.34
Long-term debt ($ mil.): 1,049

Net Income History

Euronext Paris: ATO

Auchan S.A.

Auchan's mammoth markets make room for more than meals. France's third-largest supermarket chain (behind Carrefour and ITM Entreprises), Auchan operates about 320 hypermarkets and 600-plus supermarkets in a dozen countries. France is Auchan's largest market, but it has stores throughout Europe and in China, Morocco, Russia, and Taiwan. (Auchan exited the US and Mexico markets in 2003.) Its hypermarkets carry up to 100,000 products including groceries, apparel, consumer electronics, and fast food. They also provide travel services. Auchan runs Leroy Merlin, a leading home improvement retail chain in France. The founding Mulliez family owns about 84% of Auchan; employees own the rest.

The Mulliez family, one of the richest in the world, also owns Tapis Saint-Maclou, France's largest carpet company, and about 80 Kiabi clothing stores in France, Spain, and Italy.

Auchan is expanding in Europe — Poland, Hungary, Italy, and Russia — and in China and Taiwan. In Hungary, where Auchan has nine hypermarkets, the French retailer plans to have up to 20 hypermarkets there by 2008. Through a partnership with Morocco's ONA group, Auchan plans to open eight hypermarkets and 25 supermarkets there in the next five years. In Italy, Auchan acquired the food retailing operations of La Rinascente for about $1.4 billion. La Rinascente is splitting its department store and food businesses. (Auchan already owns part of La Rinascente.)

The company's hypermarkets operate under the names Auchan and Alcampo; its supermarkets operate under the banners Atac, Expresso, and Sabeco. In addition to its 600 company-owned supermarkets, another 1,250-plus supermarkets are operated as partnerships or franchises. Auchan's Leroy Merlin home improvement chain has about 150 stores in France, Italy, and Spain. The do-it-yourself retailer plans to acquire Brico DIY stores in France, Spain, and Portugal. Other holdings include French retailers Decathlon, warehouse-style sporting goods stores, and Boulanger, a consumer electronics chain.

HISTORY

Gerard Mulliez opened his first grocery store in Roubaix, France, in 1961. Seven years later he opened a store (under the Auchan banner) in Roncq — the store was the first modern hypermarket. For the next decade Mulliez expanded his retail operations across France, opening 26 stores.

In 1967 he started an employee shareholding program. Reaching outside the grocery and basic consumer goods market, the company acquired a 50% stake in home improvement retailer Leroy Merlin in 1979.

Auchan entered the international market in 1981, opening an Alcampo hypermarket in Spain. By 1988 the company had one store in the US and a few in Italy. In 1996 Auchan opened hypermarkets in Poland, Mexico, Portugal, and Luxembourg. Also that year Auchan doubled in size by acquiring French grocery retailer Docks de France (including Mammouth hypermarkets and Atac supermarkets) and bought Pao de Acucar, which added more stores in Spain and Portugal. In 1997 it opened stores in Thailand and Argentina, followed by a hypermarket in Hungary in 1998. In 1999 Auchan opened its first store in China.

In April 2000 the company sold 407 small grocery and convenience stores to rival French food retailer Casino Guichard-Perrachon (the stores were obtained when Auchan bought Docks de France). Also in 2000 Auchan opened its second US store (also in Houston) and it bought 68% of retailer RT Mart Taiwan.

Though having announced plans for expansion into Morocco and Russia, Auchan agreed in April 2001 to sell its only hypermarket in Thailand to its rival Casino. Also in 2001 Auchan launched e-commerce sites in France and Spain and acquired Billa, a Polish chain of 11 supermarkets. Overall, the company added 44 supermarkets and 51 hypermarkets that year.

In 2002 Auchan expanded into Russia with the opening of two hypermarkets in the Moscow area.

Auchan closed its hypermarkets in Mexico and shuttered its two remaining US outlets in Houston in March 2003, citing a sharp rise in competition in the Houston area. Overall in 2003, the company opened 31 new stores (nine hypermarkets and 22 supermarkets) in Europe and two hypermarkets in Beijing and Chengdu, China.

EXECUTIVES

Chairman and Managing Director, Hypermarkets: Christophe Dubrulle
Director, Support Services, Hypermarkets; Vice Chairman, France: Henri Mathias
Director, Finance, Hypermarkets: Xavier de Mézerac
Director, Business Development; Chairman, Innochan: Vianney Mulliez
Director, Training and Human Resources; Chairman, Hypermarkets, Poland: Phillipe Saudo
Chairman, Hypermarkets, France: Arnaud Mulliez

Chairman, Hypermarkets, Hungary and Russia: Jean Mailly
Chairman, Hypermarkets, China and Taiwan: Christian Clerc-Batut
Chairman and Managing Director, Supermarkets; Chairman, France: Benoist Cirotteau
Director, Finance, Supermarkets: Philippe Delalande
Chairman, Supermarkets, Spain: Miguel Ganuza
Auditors: KPMG Audit

LOCATIONS

HQ: Auchan S.A.
200 rue de la Recherche,
59650 Villeneuve d'Ascq, France
Phone: +33-3-28-37-67-00   **Fax:** +33-3-20-67-55-20
Web: www.auchan.com

2004 Stores

	No.
Hypermarkets	
France	120
Spain	45
Italy (La Rinascente)	39
Poland	19
Taiwan	19
China	13
Portugal	17
Morocco	11
Hungary	9
Russia	6
Luxembourg	1
Supermarkets	
France	264
Italy (La Rinascente)	212
Spain	121
Morocco	17
Poland	13
Total	**926**

COMPETITORS

Carrefour
Casino Guichard
Castorama Dubois
E.Leclerc
Galeries Lafayette
Guyenne et Gascogne
ITM Entreprises
J Sainsbury
Kingfisher
Lidl & Schwarz Stiftung
Migros
PPR
Royal Ahold
Tengelmann
Tesco
Wal-Mart

HISTORICAL FINANCIALS

Company Type: Private

Income Statement				FYE: December 31
	REVENUE ($ mil.)	NET INCOME ($ mil.)	NET PROFIT MARGIN	EMPLOYEES
12/04	40,983	649	1.6%	155,000
12/03	36,032	722	2.0%	156,000
12/02	28,888	306	1.1%	143,000
12/01	23,196	292	1.3%	136,000
12/00	22,124	288	1.3%	135,000
12/99	22,178	—	—	116,413
12/98	23,532	—	—	110,000
12/97	24,536	—	—	107,000
Annual Growth	7.6%	22.5%	—	5.4%

2004 Year-End Financials

Debt ratio: 100.3%
Return on equity: 11.4%
Cash ($ mil.): 1,619
Current ratio: 0.74
Long-term debt ($ mil.): 5,778

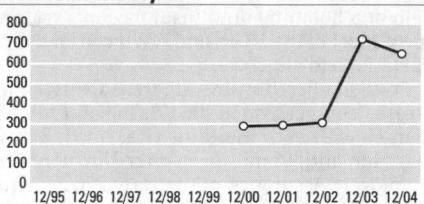

Net Income History

Aviva plc

In the consolidating European insurance industry, no acronym can last for long. Originally formed as CGNU after the merger of insurer CGU and nonlife specialist Norwich Union, the company has reinvented itself as Aviva. A major insurance force in the UK and a leading firm throughout Europe, Aviva offers both life and general insurance. Its long-term savings segments focuses on life insurance, pensions, unit trusts, and other products; its general insurance segment includes home, auto, and fire coverage. Financial services include international fund management. Aviva acquired UK-based automotive-service company RAC in 2005.

RAC will be combined with Aviva's Norwich Union operations, and about 1,700 jobs are slated to be lost in the UK (800 of the 1,700 to go overseas). RAC had already tentatively entered the financing and insurance arena.

As part of its strategy of exiting unprofitable insurance markets, Aviva sold its US general insurance operations to White Mountains Insurance Group. The company is instead focusing on smaller acquisitions in emerging markets: Aviva bought insurers in Belgium, Hungary, and the Netherlands. The company also purchased Fortis' Australian operations, making Aviva one of that country's top 10 insurers. Extending its distribution channels, Aviva has teamed up with banks all across Europe (including tie-ups with ABN AMRO and Royal Bank of Scotland).

Aviva is focused on growing its long-term savings business (including the launch of online wealth management services in the UK) and on expanding into central and eastern Europe.

The insurer also looks to the East for operational strategies as it moves more and more of its back-office operations to India and Sri Lanka. Aviva expects to employ as many as 7,000 offshore workers by the end of 2007.

HISTORY

When insurers hiked premiums after the 1861 Great Tooley Street Fire of London, merchants formed Commercial Union Fire Insurance (CU). It opened offices throughout the UK and in foreign ports and soon added life (1862) and marine (1863) coverage.

Over the next 20 years, CU's foreign business thrived. The firm had offices across the US by the 1880s. In the 1890s CU entered Australia, India, and Southeast Asia. Foreign business eventually accounted for some 75% of CU's sales.

CU went shopping in the 20th century, adding accident insurer Palatine Insurance Co. of Manchester in 1900 and rescuing two companies ruined by San Francisco's 1906 earthquake and fire. CU recovered from the Depression with the help of a booming auto insurance market, and spent most of the 1930s and WWII consolidating operations to cut costs.

Profits suffered in the 1950s as CU faced increased competition in the US. To boost sales, it merged with both multiline rival North British and Mercantile and life insurer Northern and Employers Assurance in the early 1960s. While US business continued to lag in the 1970s, the company's European business grew.

From 1982 to 1992, CU cut its operations in the US, entered new markets (Poland, 1992; South Africa and Vietnam, 1996), and sold its New Zealand subsidiaries (1995). As competition in the UK increased, the company in 1997 reorganized and merged with General Accident in 1998.

General Accident & Employers Liability Assurance Association (GA) was formed in 1885 in Perth, Scotland, to sell workers' compensation insurance. Within a few years, GA had branches in London and Scotland. It diversified into insurance for train accidents (1887), autos (1896), and fire (1899); in 1906 its name changed to General Accident Fire and Life Assurance.

GA expanded into Australia, Europe, and Africa at the turn of the century. After WWI, the company's auto insurance grew along with car ownership. During the 1930s the company entered the US auto insurance market. WWII put a stop to GA's growth.

The company expanded after the war, forming Pennsylvania General Fire Insurance Association (1963) and acquiring the UK's Yorkshire Insurance Co. (1967). By the 1980s about one-third of its sales came from the US.

After 1986 GA acquired some 500 real estate brokerage agencies to cross-sell its home and life insurance. To increase presence in Asia and the Pacific, the company in 1988 acquired NZI Corp., a New Zealand banking and insurance company whose failing operations cost GA millions. At the same time, new US government regulations and a series of damaging storms hammered the company.

In response GA cut costs, posting a profit by 1993. As the industry consolidated, the company bought nonstandard auto insurer Sabre (1995), life insurer Provident Mutual (1996), and General Insurance Group Ltd. in Canada (1997). Unable to compete on its own, GA merged with Commercial Union to form CGU in 1998.

After the merger, CGU added personal pension plans and entered alliances to sell insurance in Italy and India. Merger costs and exceptional losses for 1998 hit operating profits hard. In 1999 CGU upped its stake in French bank Société Générale to about 7% to help it fend off a hostile takeover attempt by Banque Nationale de Paris (now BNP Paribas).

In 2000 the company merged with rival Norwich Union to form CGNU and made plans to exit the Canadian life and the US general insurance businesses. In 2001 CGNU sold its US property/casualty operations to White Mountains Insurance.

In an attempt to strengthen its brand name, the company changed its name to Aviva in 2002.

EXECUTIVES

Chairman: Pehr G. Gyllenhammar, age 69
Deputy Chairman: George Paul, age 65
Group Chief Executive and Director: Richard Harvey, age 54
Group Finance Director and Director: Andrew Moss, age 47
Group Executive Director, UK Life and Long-Term Savings: Philip Scott, age 51

Group Executive Director, UK General Insurance; Chief Executive, Norwich Union: Patrick Snowball, age 54
Managing Director, Norwich General Insurance; Finance Director, Norwich Union: Mark Hodges
Chief Executive, Norwich Union Life (UK): Gary Withers
CEO, Russia: Andrei Doubinine, age 42
Managing Director, RAC: Simon Machell
Group Company Secretary: Richard Whitaker
Investor Relations Director: Charles Barrows, age 43
Director of External Affairs: Hayley Stimpson
Head of Group Media Relations: Sue Winston
Auditors: Ernst & Young

LOCATIONS

HQ: Aviva plc
St. Helen's, 1 Undershaft,
London EC3P 3DQ, United Kingdom
Phone: +44-20-7283-2000   **Fax:** +44-20-7662-2753
Web: www.aviva.com

Aviva has offices in more than 50 countries in Africa, the Asia/Pacific region, Europe, the Middle East, and North and South America.

2004 Sales

	% of total
Continental Europe	53
UK	43
Other	4
Total	**100**

PRODUCTS/OPERATIONS

Selected Subsidiaries and Affiliates

Aseguradora Valenciana, SA de Seguros y Reaseguros (50%, Spain)
Aviva Asigurari de Viata SA (Romania)
Aviva Australia Holdings Limited
AVIVA COFCO Life Insurance Company Limited (50%, China)
Aviva Canada Inc
Aviva Eletbiztosito Rt. (Hungary)
Aviva Hayat ve Emeklilik (Turkey)
Aviva Insurance Berhad (51%, Malaysia)
Aviva Insurance (Thai) Co. Limited (68%, Thailand)
Aviva Italia Holding SpA (Italy)
Aviva Life Insurance Company India Pvt. Limited (26%)
Aviva Life Insurance Company Limited (Hong Kong)
Aviva Limited (Singapore)
Aviva Participations SA (France)
Aviva Sigorta AS (99%, Turkey)
Aviva USA Corporation
Aviva Vida y Pensiones, SA de Seguros y Reaseguros (50%, Spain)
Aviva zivotni pojist'ovna a.s. (Czech Republic)
Bank Nagelmackers 1747 NV (99.6%, Belgium)
Bia Galicia de Seguros y Reaseguros (50%, Spain)
The British Aviation Insurance Company Limited (38%)
Caja Espana Vida, Compania de Seguros y Reaseguros (50%, Spain)
CGNU Life Assurance Limited
CGU Bonus Limited
CGU Insurance plc
CGU International Insurance plc
CGU Underwriting Limited
Commercial Union International Life SA (Luxembourg)
Commercial Union Life Assurance Company Limited
Commercial Union Polska Towarzystwo Ubezpieczen na Zycie SA (90%, Poland)
Commercial Union Polska Towarzystwo Ubezpieczen Ogolnych SA (90%, Poland)
Commercial Union Powszechne Towarzystwo Emerytalne BPH CU WBK SA (75%, Poland)
Curepool Limited (Bermuda)
Delta Lloyd Deutschland AG (Germany)
Berlinische Lebensversicherung AG (99.5%, Germany)
Delta Lloyd Life NV (Belgium)
Delta Lloyd NV (Netherlands)
Delta Lloyd ABN AMRO Verzekeringen Holding BV (51%, Netherlands)
Eurovida BNC Companhia de Seguros de Vida S.A. (50%, Portugal)
General Accident plc

General Vida Sociedad de Agencia de Seguros (25%, Spain)
Hibernian Group plc (Ireland)
London & Edinburgh Insurance Group Limited
Morley Fund Management International Limited
Morley Fund Management Limited
Morley Investment Services Limited
Morley Pooled Pensions Limited
Morley Properties Limited
The Northern Assurance Company Limited
Norwich Union Annuity Limited
Norwich Union Equity Release Limited
Norwich Union Healthcare Limited
Norwich Union Insurance Limited
Norwich Union Investment Funds Limited
Norwich Union Life & Pensions Limited
Norwich Union Linked Life Assurance Limited
Norwich Union Personal Finance Limited
ProCapital SA (44%, France)
RBS Life Investments Limited (49.99%)
RBSG Collective Investments Limited (49.99%)
Unicorp Vida, Compania de Seguros y Reaseguros (50%, Spain)

COMPETITORS

Abbey National
Allianz
AXA UK
Chubb
Cox Insurance Holdings
Guardian Royal Exchange plc
Highway Insurance
Legal & General Group
Lloyd's
Lloyds TSB
Millea Holdings
Prudential plc
QBE Insurance
Royal & Sun Alliance Insurance
Standard Life
Zurich Financial Services

HISTORICAL FINANCIALS

Company Type: Public

Income Statement

	ASSETS ($ mil.)	NET INCOME ($ mil.)	INCOME AS % OF ASSETS	EMPLOYEES
12/04	447,399	2,036	0.5%	55,872
12/03	371,012	1,687	0.5%	60,740
12/02	296,598	(857)	—	64,562
12/01	273,128	1,634	0.6%	68,107
12/00	288,566	(2,582)	—	72,749
12/99	296,117	1,621	0.5%	68,250
12/98	175,597	826	0.5%	51,965
12/97	151	2,494	1,652.9%	51,756
Annual Growth	213.3%	(2.9%)	—	1.1%

FYE: December 31

2004 Year-End Financials

Equity as % of assets: 3.6%   Long-term debt ($ mil.): 246,253
Return on assets: 0.5%   Sales ($ mil.): 77,955
Return on equity: 14.7%

Net Income History

London: AV

AXA

The insurance world revolves around this AXA. AXA, which started as a sleepy collection of mutual insurance companies, is today one of the world's largest insurers (alongside Allianz and ING) and a financial management powerhouse. In the US, AXA owns AXA Financial, which owns a majority of investment manager Alliance Capital Management. The company also has major subsidiaries in the UK (AXA UK, formerly Sun Life and Provincial Holdings), Australia (AXA Asia Pacific, formerly National Mutual), and Belgium (AXA Belgium, formerly Royale Belge). The companies offer life insurance; personal and commercial property and casualty insurance; reinsurance; financial services; and real estate investment services.

Mutuelles AXA (a group of eight mutuals) controls AXA through its 20% stake.

Rather than trying to run a cross-border organization, AXA instead buys and builds up businesses in each country, rebranding them under the AXA name.

Through former executive chairman (now supervisory board chairman) Claude Bébéar, acquisitive AXA brought a North American style to the once-genteel practice of business in France. The company wielded its power in the bank takeover struggle that resulted in the formation of BNP Paribas.

AXA has discontinued its slumping US-based reinsurance operations (AXA Corporate Solutions Reinsurance and AXA Corporate Solutions Life Reinsurance); the company still sells reinsurance in the US through Paris-based AXA Re.

In an attempt to strengthen its US retail insurance and annuity business, AXA, through subsidiary AXA Financial, bought MONY Group for some $1.5 billion. The deal was opposed by some of MONY's shareholders, but ultimately gained approval.

Another planned deal fell apart in 2004 when AXA failed to come to terms with 52%-owned subsidiary AXA Asia Pacific Holdings over its plans to buy the subsidiary's remaining stock.

HISTORY

AXA dates to the 1817 formation of regional fire insurer Compagnie d'Assurances Mutuelles contre l'incendie in Rouen, France (northwest of Paris). In 1881 France's first mutual life insurer was founded: Mutuelle Vie.

In 1946 these two operations and the younger Anciennes Mutuelles Accidents (founded 1922) were brought together by Sahut d'Izarn (general manager of Compagnie d'Assurances) as the Groupe Ancienne Mutuelle. Later members included Ancienne Mutuelle of Calvados (1946), Ancienne Mutuelle of Orleans (1950), Mutualité Générale (1953), and Participation (1954).

A long-term thinker, d'Izarn named not only his successor, Lucien Aubert, but also Aubert's successor: Claude Bébéar, a 23-year-old friend of d'Izarn's son. Never having held a job, Bébéar found the whole thing amusing and decided to try it.

Groupe Ancienne Mutuelle prospered during the 1960s, thanks to d'Izarn's disciplined management, but his technophobia kept the company from entering the computer age.

D'Izarn died in 1972. Aubert capitulated to worker demands during a series of strikes in the early 1970s; Bébéar ended a 1974 strike by threatening to use force against an employee sit-in, then ousted Aubert.

Bébéar spent the rest of the 1970s upgrading the firm's technology. During this period the company became known as Mutuelles Unies.

Bébéar then began building the firm through a series of spectacular acquisitions. In 1982 Mutuelles Unies gained control of crisis-ridden stock insurer Drouot. Two years later the company's name became AXA (which has no meaning and was chosen because it is pronounced the same in most Western languages). When another old-line insurer, Providence, went on the market, AXA went after it. Providence's management was entertaining another offer when AXA bought tiny, inactive Bayas Tudjus, which held the right to a seat on the Providence board. Bébéar capitalized on small stockholders' dissatisfaction to spark a bidding war and used a new issue of Drouot stock in 1986 to buy Providence — France's first hostile takeover.

AXA bought lackluster US firm Equitable (now AXA Financial) in 1991, infusing $1 billion into the firm in return for the right to own up to 50% of its stock upon demutualization in 1992. AXA moved into Asia with the purchase of Australia's National Mutual in 1995.

Bébéar consolidated the operations into a global organization. In 1996 AXA bought the ailing Union des Assurances de Paris, which had done poorly since its 1994 privatization. It bought the 52% of Belgian insurer Royale Belge SA it didn't already own, as well as Belgian savings bank Anhyp in 1998.

Bébéar raised hackles when he supported the Société Générale-Paribas bank merger, then supported BNP's hostile takeover attempt of both (which garnered only Paribas). In 1999 AXA bought Guardian Royal Exchange, then sold the life and pensions business to Dutch insurer AEGON; Bébéar announced his retirement in 1999. In 2000 he stepped down from the management board but took over as Chairman of the Supervisory Board.

That year AXA took control of Japan's Nippon Dantai Life Insurance. It also bought the remaining shares of AXA Financial and the 44% of AXA UK (formerly Sun Life and Provincial Holdings) it didn't already own. The next year AXA unloaded its debt-heavy subsidiary Banque Worms to Deutsche Bank.

EXECUTIVES

Chairman of the Supervisory Board: Claude Bébéar, age 70
Vice Chairman of the Supervisory Board: Jean-René Fourtou, age 66
Chairman of the Management Board and CEO: Henri de Castries, age 51
Member of the Management Board in charge of Transversal Operations, Communications, and Human Resources: Claude Brunet, age 48
Member of the Management Board in charge of Finance, Control, and Strategy: Denis Duverne, age 52
Member of the Management Board and CEO and President, AXA Financial: Christopher M. (Kip) Condron, age 58
Member of the Management Board and CEO, AXA France: François Pierson, age 58
Chairman, AXA Seguros, and Head, Mediterranean Region: Jean-Raymond Abat
CEO, AXA Japan; President of the Board of Directors, AXA RE: Philippe Donnet
CEO, AXA UK: Dennis Holt, age 57
CEO, AXA Investment Managers: Nicolas Moreau, age 41
CEO, AXA Re: Hans-Peter Gerhardt, age 48
Group CEO, AXA Asia Pacific Holdings; Head of Asia Pacific Region (excluding Japan): Les Owen

Group CEO, AXA Northern Europe; CEO, AXA Royale Belge: Alfred J. (Freddy) Bouckaert, age 59
Chairman, Management Board, AXA Konzern: Eugène Teysen
Vice Chairman and CFO, AXA Financial: Stanley B. (Stan) Tulin, age 55
Chief Procurement Officer: Alain Page-Lecuyer
Regional CFO, AXA Northern Europe: Christophe Dupont Madinier
President, COO, and Director, Alliance Capital Management L.P.: Gerald M. (Jerry) Lieberman, age 58
Head of Brand and Communications: Claire Dorland-Clauzel
Auditors: PricewaterhouseCoopers Audit

LOCATIONS

HQ: AXA
    25 Avenue Matignon, 75008 Paris, France
Phone: +33-1-4075-5700   **Fax:** +33-1-4075-5795
US HQ: 1290 Avenue of the Americas, New York, NY 10104
US Phone: 212-314-2902   **US Fax:** 212-707-1805
Web: www.axa.com

AXA has operations in more than 60 countries in the Asia/Pacific region, Europe, and North and South America.

2004 Insurance Gross Premiums

	% of total
Life & Savings	
US	20
France	18
UK	10
Japan	9
Germany	5
Belgium	3
Other countries	7
Property/casualty	
France	8
UK	7
Germany	4
Belgium	2
Other countries	7
Total	**100**

PRODUCTS/OPERATIONS

2004 Sales

	$ mil.	% of total
Gross written premiums	91,381	69
Net investment results	34,653	26
Revenues from banking activities	1,072	1
Change in unearned premiums reserve	64	—
Other revenues	5,377	4
Total	**132,547**	**100**

2004 Sales

	$ mil.	% of total
Insurance		
Life & Savings	63,801	48
Property/casualty	24,201	18
International	4,571	4
Financial services		
Asset management	4,185	3
Other financial services	1,072	1
Other revenues	34,717	26
Total	**132,547**	**100**

Selected Subsidiaries and Affiliates

Alliance Capital Management (56%, US)
ASA Portugal Life (95%)
AXA Art (91%, Germany)
AXA Asia Pacific Holdings
AXA Assicurazioni (Italy)
AXA Assistance
AXA Assurance Maroc (51%, Morocco)
AXA Assurances (Canada)
AXA Assurances (Switzerland)
AXA Aurora (Spain)
AXA Bank (91%, Germany)
AXA Bank Belgium
AXA Banque

AXA Bausparkasse (91%, Germany)
AXA Belgium
AXA China Region (52%, Hong Kong)
AXA Corporate Solutions Assurance (99%)
AXA Credit
AXA Financial (US)
AXA France Assurances
AXA Germany
AXA Insurance (96%, Japan)
AXA Insurance (Canada)
AXA Insurance (Singapore)
AXA Insurance (UK)
AXA Investment Managers (93%, US)
AXA Ireland
AXA Japan
AXA Konzern (91%, Germany)
AXA Life (52%, Singapore)
AXA Luxembourg
AXA Non-Life Insurance (Japan)
AXA Oyak (50%, Turkey)
AXA Portugal (99%)
AXA PPP Healthcare (UK)
AXA Re
AXA Real Estate Investment Managers (93%, US)
AXA Rosenberg (75%, US)
AXA Sun Life (UK)
AXA UK Holdings
AXA Verzekeringen (The Netherlands)
Compagnie Financiere de Paris
Direct Seguros (50%, Spain)

COMPETITORS

AEGON
AGF
AIG
Allianz
CIGNA
Citigroup
Dai-ichi Mutual Life
Fortis SA/NV
Generali
The Hartford
Highway Insurance
ING
Legal & General Group
Merrill Lynch
MetLife
Munich Re
Nationwide
New York Life
Nippon Life Insurance
Prudential
Sumitomo Life

HISTORICAL FINANCIALS

Company Type: Public

Income Statement

FYE: December 31

	ASSETS ($ mil.)	NET INCOME ($ mil.)	INCOME AS % OF ASSETS	EMPLOYEES
12/04	651,510	3,412	0.5%	76,339
12/03	564,776	1,263	0.2%	74,584
12/02	467,023	997	0.2%	78,142
12/01	432,814	463	0.1%	90,151
12/00	446,993	3,677	0.8%	90,357
12/99	512,149	2,040	0.4%	92,008
12/98	450,849	1,794	0.4%	78,943
12/97*	400,723	1,315	0.3%	80,613
12/94	149,525	425	0.3%	—
12/93	141,166	229	0.2%	—
Annual Growth	**18.5%**	**35.0%**	**—**	**(0.8%)**

*Irregular reporting interval

2004 Year-End Financials

Equity as % of assets: 5.4%
Return on assets: 0.6%
Return on equity: 10.5%
Long-term debt ($ mil.): 19,516
No. of shares (mil.): 1,908
Dividends
Yield: 0.2%
Payout: 2.8%
Market value ($ mil.): 47,235
Sales ($ mil.): 132,547

Stock History NYSE: AXA

12/93 12/94 12/97 12/98 12/99 12/00 12/01 12/02 12/03 12/04

	STOCK PRICE ($) FY Close	P/E High/Low		PER SHARE ($) Earnings	Dividends	Book Value
12/04	24.75	14	11	1.79	0.05	18.57
12/03	21.47	31	14	0.70	0.42	16.55
12/02	13.45	40	16	0.58	0.50	14.13
12/01	21.02	131	53	0.29	0.50	12.74
12/00	35.91	18	13	2.29	1.08	27.52
12/99	35.50	30	20	1.36	0.00	23.16
12/98	36.13	29	14	1.25	0.00	22.64
12/97	19.50	21	15	0.95	0.00	19.71
Annual Growth	**3.5%**	**—**	**—**	**9.5%**	**—**	**(0.8%)**

Axel Springer

The paper trail has been a path to success for Axel Springer Verlag. One of Europe's leading publishers, the company owns hundreds of newspapers and magazines throughout the continent, including *Bild* (Germany's #1 newspaper), *Die Welt,* and *Hamburger Abendblatt.* Its magazine portfolio boasts titles such as *Bild der Frau* (women's monthly), *Hörzu* (television guide), and *Sport Bild.* Axel Springer is also one of Germany's leading book publishers, owns about a dozen commercial printing plants (for company and third-party use), and has investments in on-line bookseller Buecher.de and TV production company Schwartzkopff TV. The family of the late founder owns about 60% of the firm.

Axel Springer publishes more than 150 newspapers and magazine titles in total, with distribution to nearly 30 countries worldwide.

Axel Springer has been making several investments in new print titles and online publishing ventures, including the youth-targeted *Yam!* (launched in 2000) and an online site for *Hamburger Abendblatt.* It also created a new Web portal around its *Bild* banner with Deutsche Telekom's T-Online. In addition, the company has created online marketing firm Interactive Media through a joint venture with T-Online. In 2004, it took a 49% stake in Stepstone Deutschland, a Web-based employment agency in Germany. However, Axel Springer's investments have reduced the bottom line at a time when advertising revenue is under pressure, causing some consternation in the boardroom.

In early 2003 it agreed to sell the paperback unit of its Ullstein Heyne List book group to Random House. The company has also sold off several of its stakes in TV production companies as it seeks to focus on its main publishing unit.

Widening its reach, Springer has had success with publications in Eastern Europe and has published its first Russian magazine. The company launched a Russian edition of licensed business magazine *Forbes* in 2004. In 2005 the company announced plans to expand content and distribution of its reduced-format daily newspaper *'Welt*

Kompakt'. Part of the reasoning behind it is to stem competition such as Sweden's *Metro* from getting a foothold on the dailies market.

Axel Springer also took a new in-road to success: the company acquired German cable television producer ProSiebenSat.1, of which it already owned about 12%. The deal is likely to change the landscape of German media and therefore had to undergo governmental examination of all antitrust issues. The acquisition closed in August 2005.

HISTORY

Hinrich Springer, whose newspaper business had been closed by the Nazi government in 1941, and his son Axel launched Axel Springer Verlag in 1946 with the magazine *Nordwestdeutsche Hefte.* In 1948 the company unveiled *Hamburger Abendblatt,* which became Hamburg's best-selling newspaper by 1950. Axel Springer eventually took over the business and introduced the tabloid *Bild Zeitung* (later renamed *Bild*) in 1952. The success of the paper helped fund the company's expansion.

Axel Springer bought the daily *Die Welt* in 1953 and *Berliner Morgenpost* in 1959. The company moved its headquarters to Berlin in 1966. Fiercely supportive of the reunification of Germany, Springer built the company's headquarters immediately next to the Berlin Wall. In the 1970s the company expanded into the regional newsletter and magazine market. Axel Springer's growing control over German media did not go unnoticed, however, and opposition to the company's power was demonstrated when its Hamburg office was bombed in 1972 (the company was the target of arson again in 1998). Springer considered selling the entire company, but opted to sell several individual publications instead.

The company expanded beyond print media in 1984, investing in satellite consortium SAT.1 Satelliten Fernsehen. In 1985 it acquired stakes in cable TV and bought two Munich radio stations. After taking the company public that year, founder Axel Springer died. In 1989 German media firm KirchGruppe (since renamed TaurusGroup) began buying shares in Axel Springer Verlag.

In 1996 Axel Springer entered the Czech and Slovak newspaper markets with the purchase of a 49% stake in Dutch firm Ringier-Taurus. The company formed a joint venture in 1998 with Infoseek (later absorbed by Walt Disney Internet Group) and other partners to launch a German-language Web search service. It also bought 95% of German book publisher ECON + LIST Verlagsgesellschaft. August Fischer, former chief executive of News Corp.'s News International, was appointed chairman and CEO that year. A 1998 bid to buy UK-based media firm Mirror Group (now Trinity Mirror) proved unsuccessful.

In 1999 Axel Springer acquired stakes in several TV production companies, including a 90% interest in Schwartzkopff TV-Productions. The following year the company merged its 41%-owned TV station SAT.1 with German TV station operator Pro Sieben Media to create ProSiebenSAT.1 Media, Germany's largest commercial TV group. (Axel Springer now owns 12% of the company.) Fischer retired at the end of 2001 and was replaced by Mathias Döpfner. The company began investing in new online ventures, including a portal built around *Bild.* TaurusGroup sold its shares in the company in 2003 to Deutsche Bank.

EXECUTIVES

Chairman: Giuseppe Vita, age 70
CEO; Head, Newspaper Division: Mathias Döpfner, age 42
Deputy Chairman of the Management Board and Head of Printing and Logistics Division: Rudolf Knepper, age 60
COO and CFO: Steffen Naumann, age 39
Head of Magazines and International Division: Andreas Wiele, age 43
Head of Investor Relations: Diana Ioana Grigoriev
Investor Relations: Claudia Thomé
Auditors: PwC Deutsche Revision AG

LOCATIONS

HQ: Axel Springer Verlag AG
Axel-Springer-Str. 65, 10888 Berlin, Germany
Phone: +49-30-2591-0
Web: www.asv.de

2004 Sales

	% of total
Germany	84
Other countries	16
Total	**100**

PRODUCTS/OPERATIONS

2004 Sales

	% of total
Newspapers	58
Magazines	32
Printing	6
Services/holding	4
Total	**100**

Selected Magazines

Allegra
Auto Bild
Bild der Frau
Bildwoche
Computer Bild
Familie & Co
Finanzen
Funk Uhr
HAMMER
Hörzu
Journal für die Frau
musikexpress
Popcorn
Sport Bild
TVneu
Yam!

Selected Newspapers

Berliner Morgenpost
Bild
Bild am Sonntag
B.Z.
Die Welt
Euro am Sonntag
Hamburger Abendblatt
Welt am Sonntag

Selected Electronic Media and TV Investments

Buecher.de (25%, online bookseller)
ProSiebenSat.1 Media (12%, TV group)
Schwartzkopff TV (90%, TV production)

COMPETITORS

American Institute Of Physics	Modern Times Group
Bertelsmann	News Corp.
Dow Jones	Pearson
Edipresse	Reed Elsevier Group
Editis	Reuters
Emap	Schibsted
Financial Times	Time
Hachette Filipacchi Médias	Verlagsgruppe Georg von Holtzbrinck
IPC Group	VNU
METRO AG	

HISTORICAL FINANCIALS

Company Type: Public

Income Statement
FYE: December 31

	REVENUE ($ mil.)	NET INCOME ($ mil.)	NET PROFIT MARGIN	EMPLOYEES
12/04	3,276	201	6.1%	10,700
12/03	3,056	164	5.3%	11,694
12/02	2,910	64	2.2%	13,203
12/01	2,537	(175)	—	13,500
12/00	2,732	92	3.4%	13,590
12/99	2,683	152	5.7%	11,687
12/98	2,870	165	5.7%	13,331
12/97	2,566	118	4.6%	12,195
12/96	2,845	105	3.7%	12,346
12/95	2,875	99	3.4%	12,646
Annual Growth	**1.5%**	**8.2%**	**—**	**(1.8%)**

2004 Year-End Financials

Debt ratio: 30.1%
Return on equity: 18.4%
Cash ($ mil.): 620
Current ratio: 1.15
Long-term debt ($ mil.): 354

Net Income History
German: SPR

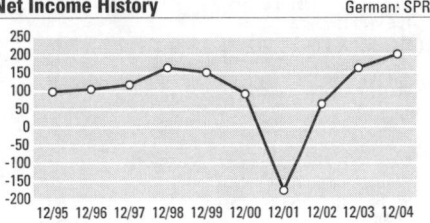

Bacardi

You want proof? The folks at Bacardi Limited will pour it for you — from a bottle. One of the world's leading wine and spirits groups, Bacardi produces a dozen varieties of its rum, selling more than 200 million bottles per year in nearly 200 countries. Other brands include Bombay Sapphire gin, Martini & Rossi vermouth, Dewar's Scotch whisky, DiSaronno Amaretto, and B&B and Benedictine liqueurs. Other drinks by Bacardi include vodka, tequila, cognac, sparkling wine, and Hatuey beer. About 600 descendants of founder Facundo Bacardi y Massó own Bacardi.

Steeped in liquor lore, Bacardi claims the first Cuba Libre (rum and cola) was made with its product in 1898. Its bottles feature Bacardi's trademark bat logo, said to have been inspired by bats (an omen of good luck) that lived in the company's first distillery. To round out its white liquor portfolio, the distiller has been expanding its line of premium liquors through acquisitions, including one of Mexico's leading premium tequilas, Tequila Cazadores. It also holds distribution rights in Mexico to Brown-Forman's Jack Daniel's, Southern Comfort, and other popular brands. In 2004 Bacardi topped off its liquor offerings with the purchase of premium vodka brand Grey Goose.

Though a well-known family operation, Bacardi may go public. Shareholders have approved the creation of two classes of company stock — one for family members and one for the public. While family members would maintain a controlling interest in the company, it is believed the company needs outside investment to grow its business. It has yet to actually issue any new stock.

HISTORY

Facundo Bacardi y Massó immigrated to Cuba from Spain in 1830. He started in the liquor business as a rum salesman for John Nunes, an Englishman who owned a small distillery in Santiago, Cuba. In 1862 Facundo, his brother José, and a French wine merchant bought Nunes' distillery and began producing a smoother rum from a formula created by Facundo after years of trial and error. The more mixable quality of Bacardi's rum proved to be a key to its success. In 1877 Facundo passed company leadership to his sons; the eldest, Emilio, took over running the company (and spent some of his spare time in jail for his anti-Spanish activities).

Bacardi Limited struggled during the 1890s as Cuba's economy foundered. The business was thrown into even greater turmoil when revolutionary leader José Marti began what would be the final fight for Cuban independence. One of Marti's biggest supporters was Emilio, who earned another stay in jail and then exile for his sympathies. After Cuba gained its independence in 1902, Bacardi grew rapidly, getting a further boost from Prohibition as Havana became "the unofficial US saloon." (Prohibition did, however, end a venture in the US.)

The company moved into brewing in the 1920s and expanded its rum operations in the 1930s, opening a distillery in Mexico (1931) and another in Puerto Rico (1935). In 1944 it opened Bacardi Imports in the US and built up its overseas operations during the 1950s.

Amid all its success, Bacardi again became embroiled in Cuban politics during the late 1950s. Although some company leaders showed open opposition to Cuban leader Fulgencio Batista and support for Fidel Castro, others opposed Castro. As a result of the 1959 revolution, the Bacardi family was forced into exile, fleeing to the US and Europe. Castro seized Bacardi's assets in 1960. However, the expropriation was not a fatal blow since both the Mexican and Puerto Rican operations had been outearning the Cuban operations since the 1940s. Bacardi continued to enjoy explosive growth during the 1960s and 1970s. In 1977 some family members sold about 12% of the Bacardi empire to Hiram Walker.

By 1980 Bacardi was the #1 liquor brand in the US, but family squabbles and bad decisions threatened the company. Bacardi Capital, set up to manage the empire's money, lost $50 million in 1986. That year the empire's leadership started to buy up shares in Bacardi companies, including those sold to Hiram Walker and the 10% of Bacardi Corporation that had been sold to the public in 1962.

In an effort to diversify and to increase its European markets, the company bought a majority stake in Martini & Rossi in 1993. Two years later it launched Bacardi Limon, a citrus-flavored rum, and Hatuey (pronounced "ahtway") beer. In 1996 family lawyer George Reid became president and CEO, the first nonfamily member to head the company.

Bacardi acquired the rights to the Havana Club trademark in 1997 from the Arechabala family. The move exacerbated a dispute with France's Pernod Ricard, which had partnered with the Cuban government to use the Havana Club name (the dispute lives on in the US, spearheaded by

Bacardi U.S.A.). Bacardi bought the Dewar's Scotch whisky and Bombay gin brands from Diageo in 1998.

In 2000 Reid resigned and Ruben Rodriguez was named president and CEO. Rodriguez added chairman to his titles when Manuel Jorge Cutillas retired later in the year. In 2000 Bacardi (along with partner Brown-Forman) also lost the bidding war for Seagram's alcoholic drinks business (Glenlivet, Sterling Vineyards, Martell Cognac) to rival bidding duo Diageo and Pernod Ricard.

In 2002 Bacardi acquired Tequila Cazadores, a leader in Mexico's Agave Reposado segment. Javier Ferran, an 18-year company veteran, left Bacardi in 2004 after serving as CEO for only about 18 months. Ferran was replaced by Andreas Gembler, a Philip Morris veteran.

Rodriguez retired in 2005 as the company's chairman. Bacardi named Facundo Bacardi, a great-grandson of the company's founder, as chairman. Rodriguez remained a board member.

EXECUTIVES

Chairman: Facundo L. Bacardi, age 38
President, CEO, and Director: Andreas Gembler, age 62
VP, Operations and Sales: Guillermo Rodriguez
VP, Packaging Global Manufacturing: Yousef Zaatar
President and CEO, Bacardi North America:
  Eduardo M. Sardina
CEO, Bacardi Canada: Paul Beggan
President, Bacardi Puerto Rico: Angel Torres
Global Chief Marketing Officer: Stella David, age 42
Director, Barcardi-Martini BV Northern Europe:
  Luis Bach
Director, Global Operations: Jon Grey
Director, IT: Ron Stan
Director, Marketing: Andrew Carter
Director, Trade Marketing: Brue Ray
Manager, Bacardi Global Project: Richie DiFranco
Manager, Marketing: Joe Metevier

LOCATIONS

HQ: Bacardi & Company Limited
  65 Pitts Bay Rd., Pembroke HM 08, Bermuda
Phone: 441-295-4345   **Fax:** 441-292-0562
Web: www.bacardi.com

Bacardi Limited has production facilities in the Bahamas, Brazil, Canada, Martinique, Mexico, Panama, Puerto Rico, Spain, and Trinidad.

PRODUCTS/OPERATIONS

Selected Brands
Bacardi
  8
  151
  1873
  Solera
  Anejo
  Black
  Carta Blanca
  Exclusiv
  Gold
  Light
  Limón
  Select
  Solera
  Spice
Castillo
  Anejo
  Gold
  White
Estelar Suave
Ron Bacardi Anejo

Other Spirits and Beverages
Alcohol-based aperitif
  Pastis Casanis
  Pastis

Amaretto
  DiSaronno Amaretto
Beer
  Hatuey
Brandy
  Gran Reserva Especial
  Vergel
  Viejo Vergel
Champagne
  Charles Volner
  Veuve Amiot
Cognac
  Exshaw
  Gaston de la Grange
  Otard
Gin
  Bombay
  Bombay Sapphire
  Bosford, Martini
Liqueur
  B&B
  Benedictine
  China Martini
  Kalyr
  Nassau Royale
Low-alcohol beverage
  Bacardi Breezer
  Bacardi & Cola
  Caribbean Classics
  Martini Brand Jigger
Scotch whisky
  Dewar's
  Glen Deveron
  William Lawson's Finest Blend
  William Lawson's Scottish Gold
Sparkling wine
  Grande Auguri
  Martini & Rossi Asti Spumante
  Montelera Riserva
  Martini Brand Asti
  Martini Brand Riesling
Tequila
  Camino Real
  Tequila Cazadores
Vodka
  Eristoff
  Grey Goose
  Martini
  Natasha
  Russian Prince

COMPETITORS

Allied Domecq	Highland Distillers
Angostura	Jim Beam Brands
Blavod Extreme Spirits	Jose Cuervo
Brown-Forman	LVMH
Cabo Wabo	Pernod Ricard
Constellation Brands	Rémy Cointreau
Diageo	Sebastiani Vineyards
Fortune Brands	Suntory Ltd.
Gallo	William Grant & Sons
Heaven Hill Distilleries	

HISTORICAL FINANCIALS

Company Type: Private

Income Statement

FYE: March 31

	REVENUE ($ mil.)	NET INCOME ($ mil.)	NET PROFIT MARGIN	EMPLOYEES
3/04	3,300	—	—	6,000
3/03	3,100	—	—	6,300
3/02	2,900	—	—	6,300
3/01	2,700	—	—	6,200
3/00	2,600	—	—	6,000
3/99	2,464	—	—	6,200
3/98	2,400	—	—	6,200
Annual Growth	**5.5%**	—	—	**(0.5%)**

Revenue History

3,500
3,000
2,500
2,000
1,500
1,000
500
0

3/95 3/96 3/97 3/98 3/99 3/00 3/01 3/02 3/03 3/04

BAE SYSTEMS

BAE SYSTEMS, which helped win the Battle of Britain with its Mosquito and Spitfire fighters, is now Europe's largest defense contractor and the largest foreign player in the US defense market. BAE's offerings include avionics, military aircraft, armored vehicles, air-defense systems, missiles, artillery locators, communications and navigation systems, radar, ships, space systems, and aerospace electronics. BAE's fighter aircraft include the Harrier, Hawk, Tornado, and the next-generation Eurofighter Typhoon. BAE also owns 20% of Airbus, Boeing's only competitor for large commercial aircraft. The company acquired armored vehicle maker Alvis in 2004 and United Defense Industries the following year.

BAE — which derives about about 80% of sales from support services, systems and software, and Airbus — has been leveraging its airborne technology know-how in its land systems and has beefed up its defense electronics operations by buying units from Lockheed Martin. The company's interest in expanding its North American operations has been spurred by the underperformance by its UK Ministry of Defence programs.

BAE was selected as the prime contractor for the next-generation UK aircraft carrier program in 2003, but in 2004 prime contractor status was taken away and BAE agreed to build the ships in conjunction with Thales. The controversy was racheted up a notch in 2005 when Halliburton subsidiary Kellogg Brown & Root was brought in as the physical integrator of the project.

BAE SYSTEMS took a 29% stake in Alvis, maker of the Challenger main battle tank in August 2003. In March 2004 General Dynamics made a 280 pence a share bid for Alvis; BAE topped that offer in early June with a bid of 320 pence a share (about $650 million) and a deal was struck. BAE then combined Alvis with its RO Defence group to form a new business unit, Land Systems. In 2005 BAE acquired — through its North American subsidiary — US-based United Defense Industries (UDI) as part of its push to get more US defense contracts. Now part of the company's BAE Systems Land and Armaments business, UDI made armored vehicles (including the Bradley Fighting Vehicle), landing craft, and weapons systems. Upon closing the UDI deal, BAE SYSTEMS North America changed its name to BAE Systems Inc.

Prior to the Alvis deal, BAE had reportedly been in merger talks with US contractors (including General Dynamics). Since the company closed its commercial aerospace unit, which made Avro jet aircraft, BAE is basically a pure defense contractor with a 20% stake in Airbus. In fact, the company has begun seeking buyers for its aerostructures business, declaring that the unit isn't core to BAE's business.

HISTORY

Post-Wright brothers and pre-WWII, a host of aviation companies sprang up to serve the British Empire — too many to survive after the war when the empire contracted. Parliament took steps in 1960 to save the industry by merging companies to form larger, stronger entities — Hawker-Siddeley Aviation and British Aircraft Corporation (BAC).

Hawker-Siddeley, made up of aircraft and missiles divisions, was created by combining A.V. Roe, Gloster Aircraft, Hawker Aircraft, Armstrong Whitworth, and Folland Aircraft. It attained fame in the 1960s for developing the Harrier "jump jet."

BAC was formed from the merger of Bristol Aeroplane, English Electric, and Vicker-Armstrong. In 1962 it joined France's Aerospatiale to build the supersonic Concorde and became a partner in ventures to develop the Tornado and Jaguar fighters. The cost of these ventures, plus the commercial failure of the Concorde, was more than the company could bear. Realizing British aviation was again in trouble, the British government nationalized BAC and Hawker-Siddeley in 1976 and merged them in 1977 with Scottish Aviation to form British Aerospace (BAe).

BAe joined the Airbus consortium in 1979. A partial privatization of the company began in 1981 when the government sold 52% to the public (the remaining stake sold in 1985). Also in 1981 BAe announced a joint venture with Comsat General and announced that it would be the prime contractor for L-SAT-1, the European Space Agency's telecommunications satellite.

In 1987 BAe bought Steinheil Optronik (optical equipment) and Ballast Nedam Groep (civil and marine engineering). In 1990 BAe formed Ballast Nedam Construction.

BAe began to restructure its troubled regional aircraft division in 1992 by laying off thousands of workers and closing a major plant. The company sold Ballast Nedam and its corporate jet business to Raytheon and won a $7.5 billion contract from Saudi Arabia for Tornado jets in 1993. BAe sold its satellite business in 1994.

Matra BAe Dynamics, the world's third-largest maker of tactical missiles, was formed in a 1996 merger between BAe and Lagardère subsidiary Matra Hachette.

BAe's emphasis on large jetliners led to the 1998 breakup of Aero International, its two-year-old regional-aircraft joint venture with Aerospatiale (France) and Alenia (Italy). Shortly thereafter, BAe spent $454 million for a 35% stake in Swedish military jet maker Saab AB. In 1999 BAe bought the electronic systems defense unit of Marconi Electronic Systems (MES) for $12.7 billion (including US-based Tracor). The company changed its name to BAE SYSTEMS to remove the British influence from its name.

In 2000 the UK government agreed to loan BAE about $836 million to support the Airbus A3XX superjumbo airliner project. The same year BAE acquired Lockheed Martin's control-systems unit. The prime contractor for the UK's new Type 45 destroyer, BAE was named to build two of the first three Type 45s. Late in the year BAE spent about $1.67 billion for a group of Lockheed Martin's defense electronics businesses, including its Sanders airborne electronics unit.

Early in 2001 the company sold its 54% stake in BAE SYSTEMS CANADA (now known as CMC Electronics) to Oncap, a Toronto-based investment fund. The same year BAE announced that it would phase out its regional-aircraft business.

It was revealed in January 2005 that BAE was seeking buyers for its aerostructures business, which makes airframe components for such customers as Airbus, Boeing, Raytheon, and Cessna. Around the same time the Ministry of Defence selected Kellogg Brown & Root to work on the UK aircraft carrier project along with BAE and Thales. In February of 2005 BAE reduced its stake in SAAB AB from 35% to 22%.

In the summer of 2005 BAE acquired US armored vehicle maker United Defense Industries (UDI) in a deal worth about $4.2 billion. UDI was combined with BAE operations to form BAE Systems Land and Armaments.

EXECUTIVES

Chairman: Richard L. (Dick) Olver, age 58, $493,107 pay (partial-year salary)
CEO: Michael J. (Mike) Turner, age 56, $2,777,580 pay
COO: Chris V. Geoghegan, age 51, $1,583,337 pay
COO: Steven L. (Steve) Mogford, age 49, $1,612,230 pay
COO; President and CEO, BAE Systems Inc.:
Mark H. Ronald, age 63, $2,061,034 pay
Chief of Staff: George Mayhew
Group Communications Director: Charlotte Lambkin
Group Finance Director: George W. Rose, age 52, $1,750,916 pay
Group Legal Director: Michael Lester, age 64, $1,939,684 pay
Group Marketing Director: Mike Rouse
Group Managing Director, Air Systems:
Nigel Whitehead
Group Managing Director, Command/Control, Communications, Computing, Intelligence, Surveillance, and Reconnaissance: Phill Blundell
Group Managing Director, Customer Solutions and Support and Land Systems: Ian King
Group Managing Director, International Partnerships: Stephen Henwood
Group Managing Director, Sea Systems:
Brian Phillipson
Group HR Director; Group Managing Director, Shared Services: Alastair Imrie
Group Strategic Development Director: Alison Wood, age 41
VP, Homeland Security: Harris Belman
VP and General Counsel, BAE Systems Inc.:
Sheila C. Cheston
VP, Human Resources, BAE Systems Inc.:
Curtis L. (Curt) Gray
Senior Military Adviser: Sir John Day
Managing Director, Marketing, US: Bob Fitch
Investor Relations Director: Andrew Wrathall
Auditors: KPMG Audit Plc

LOCATIONS

HQ: BAE SYSTEMS plc
6 Carlton Gardens,
London SW1Y 5AD, United Kingdom
Phone: +44-1252-373-232   **Fax:** +44-1252-383-000
US HQ: 1601 Research Blvd., Rockville, MD 20850
US Phone: 301-738-4000   **US Fax:** 301-738-4643
Web: www.baesystems.com

BAE SYSTEMS has operations in Africa, Asia, Australia, Europe, and North America.

2004 Sales

	$ mil.	% of total
Europe		
UK	4,713.4	27
Other countries	2,448.2	14
US & Canada	6,019.4	34
Middle East	3,303.4	19
Asia & Pacific	809.0	5
Africa, Central & South America	225.4	1
Total	**17,518.8**	**100**

PRODUCTS/OPERATIONS

2004 Sales

	$ mil.	% of total
Programmes	5,359.8	28
North America	5,338.6	28
Customer Solutions & Support	3,961.1	21
Avionics	2,100.0	11
HQ & other businesses	1,063.5	6
Commercial Aerospace	668.5	4
International partnerships	381.5	2
Adjustments	(1,354.2)	—
Total	**17,518.8**	**100**

Selected Products and Services

Avionics
Airborne electronic systems
Flight control systems

Commercial Aerospace
Airbus commercial jets (20% stake in EADS)

Customer Solutions and Support
Military services and support

International Partnerships
Air-to-air missiles
Combat and radar systems
Naval sonar

Land Systems
All terrain vehicles (Bv206)
Armored personnel carriers (Warrior, Piranha)
Battle tanks (Challenger 2)
Combat vehicles/light tanks (Combat Vehicle 90)
Mine clearer (Viking Mine Clearing System)
Recovery vehicles (Beach Recovery Vehicle)
Weapons platforms (Alvis Moelv Mortar Platform)

Programmes
Astute class submarine
Eurofighter Typhoon
Hawk
Nimrod
Type 45 destroyers

COMPETITORS

Astronautics
Beretta
Boeing
Bombardier
Colt's
EADS
General Dynamics
General Dynamics UK
Glock
Honeywell International
Horstman Defence Systems
L-3 Storm
Lockheed Martin
Lockheed Martin Aeronautics
Lockheed Martin Missiles
Lockheed Martin UK
Meggitt USA
Northrop Grumman
Northrop Grumman Integrated Systems
Northrop Grumman Ship Systems
Park Air Systems
Rockwell Collins (UK)
SEPI
Smiths Group
Thales
Ultra Electronics

HISTORICAL FINANCIALS

Company Type: Public

Income Statement

FYE: December 31

	REVENUE ($ mil.)	NET INCOME ($ mil.)	NET PROFIT MARGIN	EMPLOYEES
12/04	17,519	(900)	—	73,300
12/03	14,911	11	0.1%	68,400
12/02	12,953	(1,100)	—	68,100
12/01	13,119	(194)	—	70,100
12/00	14,399	(19)	—	85,000
12/99	14,434	524	3.6%	83,400
12/98	14,283	1,148	8.0%	47,900
12/97	14,098	266	1.9%	43,400
12/96	10,982	525	4.8%	47,000
12/95	8,896	214	2.4%	45,400
Annual Growth	7.8%	—	—	5.5%

2004 Year-End Financials

Debt ratio: 35.2%
Return on equity: —
Cash ($ mil.): 1,901
Current ratio: 0.84
Long-term debt ($ mil.): 3,207

Net Income History

Pink Sheets: BAESY

1,500	
1,000	
500	
0	
-500	
-1,000	
-1,500	

12/95 12/96 12/97 12/98 12/99 12/00 12/01 12/02 12/03 12/04

Banco Santander Central Hispano

Banco Santander Central Hispano (SCH) is the leader in the running of Spanish banks. The company offers retail banking and consumer finance in Spain, Portugal, and other parts of Europe. Subsidiaries such as Banco Santander-Chile, Banco Río de la Plata in Argentina, and Mexico's Grupo Financiero Santander Mexicano, make it a top banking group in Latin America, where it has operations in about 10 countries. Through other subsidiaries, SCH offers asset management, private banking, corporate and investment banking, and insurance. In one of Europe's largest cross-border bank mergers ever, SCH paid more than $15 billion for British bank Abbey National in 2004.

SCH owns nearly 90% of Puerto Rico's Santander BanCorp and plans to make its first serious foray into the US via its pending purchase of a 20% stake in Sovereign Bancorp, which is active in the Northeast. All told, SCH has more than 62 million customers and nearly 10,000 locations in a dozen countries.

The company is selling its 22% stake in Unión Fenosa to ACS for more than €2.2 billion (about $2.7 billion).

The Botín family has led SCH since its founding in 1857. Emilio Botín, Spain's richest man (depending on who you ask), has been chairman since 1986.

HISTORY

Banco Santander Central Hispano (BSCH) was created by the 1999 merger of Banco Santander and Banco Central Hispano (BCH).

In 1857 a group of Basque businessmen formed Banco Santander to finance Latin American trade. The emergence of Cantabria as a leading province after WWI helped the bank expand, first regionally, then nationally.

The Botín family has been closely identified with the bank for decades. Before his death in 1923, Emilio Botín served as a board member, then for a few years as chairman. The post was held by his son Emilio Botín-Sanz de Sautuola from 1950 to 1986, when *his* son Emilio Botín Ríos (known as Don Emilio) took over.

Spanish banks were spared the worst of the Great Depression (thanks to their isolation and the country's shunning the gold standard), but Spain's civil war was draining. In the early 1940s Santander expanded into Madrid and other major Spanish cities and merged with a few rivals. In the 1950s and 1960s, as interest rates were controlled and mergers halted, banks competed by building branch networks and investing overseas, particularly in Latin America. In 1965 Santander joined with Bank of America to form Bankinter (it divested most of its stake by the mid-1990s).

Tight economic controls were relaxed in the 1970s after Franco's death. Despite global recession, Santander continued to invest in Latin America through the mid-1980s.

In the late 1980s Santander prepared to compete in a deregulated Spain and Europe, forming alliances with Royal Bank of Scotland, Kemper (now part of Zurich Financial Services), and Metropolitan Life Insurance. In 1989 the bank jump-started competition by introducing Spain's first high-interest account.

Santander focused on home in the 1990s. Spurned by Banco Hispano Americano (BHA), Santander acquired a 60% stake in the ailing Banco Español de Crédito (Banesto); Banesto became wholly owned in 1998. The bank took a hit when Latin America plunged into an economic crisis that year. With profit margins falling, the bank merged with BCH in 1999.

BCH was formed by the 1991 merger of Banco Central and BHA. BHA was established in 1900 by investors in Latin America; Central was founded in 1919. The mixed banks offered both commercial and investment banking; they funded industrialization and investment in Latin America and became two of Spain's largest banks before the civil war.

After the war BHA sold its Latin American assets when the currency dried up, while Central used mergers and acquisitions to expand across Spain. Isolated from WWII by Franco, the two banks used their dual strategies to fund overseas investment and domestic-branch growth.

After Franco's death, the banks faced increased competition at home and abroad. Central bought BHA in 1991 to remain competitive as Spain entered the European Economic Community (now the EU) in 1992.

Following the merger, BCH trimmed 20% of its branches, fired some 10,000 employees, and sold unprofitable holdings. Focused on Latin America, the bank took small stakes in small banks. Losing its edge, BCH merged with Santander in 1999.

In 2000 BSCH focused on expanding in Europe and Latin America. Among its European moves was its alliance with Société Générale to buy investment-fund management firms, particularly in the US. In Latin America the bank bought Brazil's Banco Meridional, Banco do Estado de São Paulo (Banespa), and Grupo Financiero Serfin, Mexico's #3 bank. Critics question the $5 billion price tag BSCH paid for Banespa, charging that the formerly state-run bank was overvalued in 2001. Executive infighting saw ex-Santander chairman Emilio Botín triumph over ex-BCH chairman José María Amusátegui for control of BSCH's helm. Soon after, the bank started doing business as simply Santander Central Hispano (SCH). The following year the bank sold off its shares of Germany's Commerzbank and France's Société Générale.

EXECUTIVES

Chairman: Emilio Botín
Second Vice Chairman and CEO: Alfredo Sáenz
Director; Chairwoman, Banesto: Ana P. Botín
Third Vice Chairman: Matías Rodríguez Inciarte
CEO, Abbey National: Francisco Gómez Roldán
Director; EVP, America: Francisco Luzón
EVP, America: Marcial Portela
EVP, America: Jesús M. Zabalza, age 46
EVP, Asset Management and Insurance: Jorge Morán
EVP, Communications and Research: Juan Manuel Cendoya
EVP, Europe and Consumer Lending: Juan Rodríguez Inciarte
EVP, Financial Accounting: José Manuel Tejón
EVP, Financial Management: José A. Alvarez
EVP and General Secretary: Ignacio Benjumea
EVP, Industrial Portfolio: Joan-David Grimà
EVP, Internal Auditing: David Arce
EVP, Portugal: Antonio Horta Osorio
EVP, Resources and Costs: Pedro Mateache
EVP, Resources and Costs: Serafin Méndez
EVP, Retail Banking: Enrique García Candelas
EVP and Vice-Secretary General: Juan Guitard

LOCATIONS

HQ: Banco Santander Central Hispano, S.A.
Santander Group City, Boadilla del Monte,
28660 Madrid, Spain
Phone: +34-91-659-75-17
Web: www.gruposantander.com

Banco Santander Central Hispano is mainly active in Argentina, Brazil, Chile, Colombia, Germany, Italy, Mexico, Portugal, Puerto Rico, Spain, the UK, and Venezuela.

PRODUCTS/OPERATIONS

2004 Sales

	% of total
Interest income	56
Fees collected	23
Fixed-income securities	14
Gains on financial transactions	4
Equity securities & other	3
Total	**100**

COMPETITORS

Banco Comercial Português
Banco de la Nación
Banco do Brasil
Banco Galicia
Banco Popular
Bank of America
Bankinter
BBVA
BBVA Chile
Citigroup
Deutsche Bank
Dresdner Bank
Espírito Santo
HSBC Holdings
Itaúsa
JPMorgan Chase

HISTORICAL FINANCIALS

Company Type: Public

Income Statement

FYE: December 31

	ASSETS ($ mil.)	NET INCOME ($ mil.)	INCOME AS % OF ASSETS	EMPLOYEES
12/04	779,434	4,247	0.5%	126,488
12/03	442,271	3,282	0.7%	103,038
12/02	340,516	2,360	0.7%	104,178
12/01	319,208	2,216	0.7%	114,927
12/00	328,620	2,127	0.6%	126,757
12/99	258,439	1,587	0.6%	95,442
12/98	181,777	1,392	0.8%	73,964
12/97	171,353	1,086	0.6%	72,740
12/96	149,954	919	0.6%	—
12/95	135,243	837	0.6%	—
Annual Growth	21.5%	19.8%	—	8.2%

2004 Year-End Financials

Equity as % of assets: 6.2%
Return on assets: 0.7%
Return on equity: 4.9%
Long-term debt ($ mil.): 141,151
No. of shares (mil.): 6,254
Dividends
 Yield: 3.2%
 Payout: 36.4%
Market value ($ mil.): 77,366
Sales ($ mil.): 36,059

Stock History

NYSE: STD

12/95 12/96 12/97 12/98 12/99 12/00 12/01 12/02 12/03 12/04

	STOCK PRICE ($) FY Close	P/E High/Low		PER SHARE ($) Earnings	Dividends	Book Value
12/04	12.37	12	9	1.07	0.39	7.70
12/03	12.01	20	9	0.59	0.32	26.53
12/02	7.05	19	9	0.50	0.27	4.66
12/01	8.30	24	13	0.49	0.26	4.37
12/00	10.56	24	17	0.50	0.23	4.31
12/99	11.69	29	19	0.43	0.19	2.68
12/98	9.88	32	14	0.45	0.00	2.56
12/97	7.98	22	13	0.38	0.00	2.25
12/96	5.18	15	10	0.35	0.16	2.39
12/95	4.02	13	8	0.32	0.12	2.75
Annual Growth	13.3%	—	—	14.4%	14.0%	12.1%

Bank of China

Issuer of Great Wall credit cards, the Bank of China (BOC) is China's oldest bank and one of its top four state-owned commercial banks. BOC operates more than 13,000 domestic branches and has more than 550 offices in 25 countries and regions. Commercial banking makes up the majority of its business, including corporate and retail banking and banking with financial institutions. The bank also provides investment banking, insurance, and credit card operations. BOC recently received another multibillion-dollar bailout from the Chinese government; the bank plans to go public.

China has had to bail out two of the country's top banks, BOC and China Construction Bank, three times in the last six years. For decades, money in China's state banks was used to support failing state companies, leaving the banks with a mountain of bad loans.

The Chinese government is now scrambling to turn debt-laden BOC and CCB into profitable, self-supporting corporations as the country prepares to open its financial doors to foreign competition by 2006 as promised to the World Trade Organization. Many see the most recent $45 billion bailout (split roughly in half between BOC and CCB) as preparation for initial public offerings overseas; both banks are expected to trade on Western exchanges in the near future.

BOC is already building networks with other economies. In the first move of its kind, BOC, the Korea Exchange Bank, and Japan's Sumitomo Mitsui signed an accord on foreign exchange cooperation in 2003. The agreement focuses on settlement systems and network channels, which should smooth electronic transactions among the three banks. The banks also agreed to share human and intellectual resources.

China developed a credit card system culminating in the 1986 debut of the BOC's Great Wall card. An estimated 570 million cards have been issued since then, although almost all are debit cards that draw money directly from consumers' bank accounts. BOC faces new competition from Citibank and HSBC Holdings, who now offer credit cards to the growing population of newly affluent Chinese who might adopt the credit habits of their neighbors.

HISTORY

The Bank of China (BOC) has always had strong ties to the government of China. Established as a central bank in 1912, right after the establishment of the Provisional Government of the Republic of China, BOC became a government-chartered international exchange bank in 1928. Their first overseas branch was opened in London in 1929, leading to a global network of 34 overseas branches over the next two decades.

After WWII the bank specialized in foreign exchange, supporting foreign trade and the development of China's national economy. Between 1984 and 2001 BOC issued bonds in the international capital market 27 times. In 1993, when China initiated reform in its foreign exchange system, BOC played a key role in the unification of exchange rates, foreign exchange purchases and sales, and the incorporation of foreign-funded enterprises into the foreign exchange sales system.

In 1994 BOC began to transform from a specialized bank to a wider-based, state-owned commercial bank by issuing its first BOC Hong Kong dollar notes and then Macao pataca notes. The issue of both notes helped stabilize their respective markets.

BOC International Holdings, a wholly owned subsidiary of BOC specializing in investment banking, was incorporated in Hong Kong in 1998. Three years later Bank of China restructured its Hong Kong operations by merging 10 of its member banks into Bank of China (Hong Kong) Limited, a locally registered bank that successfully listed on the Hong Kong Stock Exchange in July 2003.

The bank is not free of scandal. A 2002 probe into BOC's New York branch by the US Office of the Comptroller of the Currency revealed that preferential treatment was given to certain customers who had personal relationships with some members of the bank's previous management. Regulators from the US and China fined BOC $20 million for "unsafe and unsound" business practices.

EXECUTIVES

Chairman and President: Xiao Gang, age 45
Vice Chairman and CEO: Liu Jinbao, age 50
Vice Chairman and EVP: Sun Changji, age 61
Vice Chairman and EVP: Jiang Zuqi
Vice Chairman: Yang Huiqiu
EVP and Managing Director: Hua Qingshan, age 50
EVP and Managing Director: Zhang Yanling, age 52
EVP and Managing Director: Zhou Zaiqun, age 51
EVP and Managing Director: Li Zaohang, age 48
Managing Director: He Guangbei, age 49
Managing Director: Zhuang Shiping, age 92
EVP: Zhu Min, age 51
EVP: Wang Yongli, age 72
COO, Bank of China and BOC Hong Kong: Raymond Lee Wing Hung, age 55
Senior Advisor: Anthony F. Neoh
Executive Assistant President: Zhu Xinqiang, age 52
Executive Assistant President: Wang Yongli, age 39
Auditors: Shenzhen Pengcheng Certified Public Accountants

LOCATIONS

HQ: Bank of China
 (Zhongguo Yinhang)
 1 Fuxingmen Nei Dajie, Beijing 100818, China
Phone: +86-10-6659-6688   **Fax:** +86-10-6659-3777
US HQ: 410 Madison Ave., New York, NY 10017
US Phone: 212-935-3101   **US Fax:** 212-593-1831
Web: www.bank-of-china.com

PRODUCTS/OPERATIONS

Selected Subsidiaries

BOC International (China) Ltd.
BOC International Holdings Ltd.
BOC International (Singapore) Pte Ltd.
Chiyu Banking Corp. Ltd.
Nanyang Commercial Bank Ltd.

COMPETITORS

Bank of East Asia
China Construction Bank
China Development Bank
Hang Seng Bank
HSBC Holdings
Mitsui Trust

HISTORICAL FINANCIALS

Company Type: Government-owned

Income Statement

FYE: December 31

	ASSETS ($ mil.)	NET INCOME ($ mil.)	INCOME AS % OF ASSETS	EMPLOYEES
12/04	515,443	2,527	0.5%	181,894
12/03	463,748	554	0.1%	188,716
12/02	433,785	1,140	0.3%	192,468
12/01	405,747	955	0.2%	201,590
12/00	382,696	553	0.1%	192,279
12/99	350,794	534	0.2%	200,000
12/98	338,209	684	0.2%	197,547
12/97	269,591	475	0.2%	198,487
12/96	250,881	628	0.3%	197,079
12/95	236,926	563	0.2%	—
Annual Growth	**9.0%**	**18.1%**	**—**	**(1.0%)**

2004 Year-End Financials

Equity as % of assets: 4.8%
Return on assets: 0.5%
Return on equity: 10.7%
Long-term debt ($ mil.): 11,563
Sales ($ mil.): 18,007

Net Income History

3,000										
2,500										
2,000										
1,500										
1,000										
500										
0	12/95	12/96	12/97	12/98	12/99	12/00	12/01	12/02	12/03	12/04

Bank of Montreal

Bank of Montreal, Canada's oldest and fifth-largest bank, has about 1,100 branches serving individuals, government agencies, institutions, and businesses large and small at home and abroad. The company, which also goes by BMO Financial Group, provides mortgages, insurance, asset management services, and mutual funds. In the US, it owns Chicago's Harris Bankcorp, which provides retail and corporate banking in the Midwest. Subsidiaries BMO Nesbitt Burns and US-based Harris Nesbitt offer brokerage, mergers and acquisitions advice, and investment and merchant banking services.

Organized along operational lines (Personal and Commercial Client Group, Private Client Group, and Investment Banking Group), the company is focused on building its business through acquisitions as well as organic growth. With more than a quarter of its revenue coming from south of the border, it would like to build on its successful Harris Bank franchise. The bank has already made modest forays into Florida and Arizona.

Continuing its southward push, it bought Chicago-area community banks Lakeland Community Bank, New Lenox State Bank, and Villa Park Trust and Savings Bank, as well as Indiana-based Mercantile Bancorp. The company is now looking to expand its market area and is on the prowl for a larger US bank in other parts of the Midwest.

Bank of Montreal sold US-based online brokerage Harrisdirect to E*TRADE in 2005; the company continues to operate its BMO InvestorLine online brokerage.

HISTORY

Montreal was a key port for fur and agriculture trade by the early 1800s. To finance these activities, the Montreal Bank (Canada's first) opened in 1817. Chartered in 1822, the bank officially became Bank of Montreal. Its ties with the US were strong, and nearly 50% of its original capital came from Yanks.

When the fur trade shifted northward to Hudson Bay in the 1820s, the bank diversified. In 1832 Bank of Montreal financed Canada's first railroad, the Champlain & St. Lawrence. The bank also grew through acquisitions, including the Bank of Canada (1831) and the Bank of the People (1840). It opened a branch in New York in 1859.

Canada united in confederacy in 1867, and Bank of Montreal expanded west. During the 1860s, it became Canada's de facto central bank until the 1935 creation of the Bank of Canada. By 1914 Bank of Montreal was the nation's largest bank. It bought the British Bank of North America (1918), Merchants Bank of Canada (1922), and Molsons Bank (1925). During the Depression, however, its growth ground to a halt.

WWII pumped up Canada's economy and the company's finances. Bank of Montreal enjoyed even greater growth during the postwar boom. It began expanding internationally, particularly in Latin America. But the bank failed to capitalize on the growth of consumer and small-business lending during the 1960s and was the last major Canadian bank to issue a credit card (in 1972). In 1975 Bank of Montreal hired William Mullholland, a Morgan Stanley veteran, to run the company. Mullholland closed unprofitable branches and modernized operations.

The bank bought Chicago-based Harris Bankcorp in 1984. As Canada's banking industry deregulated, Bank of Montreal moved into investment banking, acquiring one of Canada's largest brokerage firms, Nesbitt Thomson, in 1987.

The Latin American debt crisis and the recession of the late 1980s and early 1990s hit Bank of Montreal hard. It tumbled into the red in 1989, partly because of loan defaults. The next year Matthew Barrett replaced Mullholland as chairman and began overhauling operations, focusing on consumer and middle-market business banking and on cutting costs.

By 1994 nonperforming assets were down, and Bank of Montreal began growing again. It bought brokerage Burns Fry and merged it with Nesbitt Thomson to form Nesbitt Burns, thus increasing its presence in merchant and investment banking and securities. It added to its Harris Bank network with the purchase of Suburban Bancorp. The next year Bank of Montreal expanded its private banking business for wealthy individuals; it also began targeting aboriginal Canadians.

Eyeing international growth, Bank of Montreal bought an interest in Mexico's Grupo Financiero Bancomer in 1996 (now called BBVA Bancomer) and opened branches in Beijing (1996) and Dublin, Ireland (1997). It agreed in 1998 to merge with Royal Bank of Canada, but Canada's finance minister rejected the merger.

Barrett stepped down as CEO and chairman in 1999; the firm named F. Anthony Comper its new CEO. The bank realigned its operations to focus on retail and commercial banking, investment

banking, and wealth management and cut some 2,450 jobs. Eyeing growth in the US, in 2000 Bank of Montreal agreed to buy Florida's Village Banc of Naples, as well as Seattle brokerage Freeman Welwood. Also that year subsidiary Harris Bank began offering wireless banking.

In 2001 Bank of Montreal took its southern expansion one step further when it announced it would buy the 18-branch First National Bank of Joliet (Illinois) and merge it into Harris Bank. Later, Bank of Montreal sold its stake in BBVA Bancomer to Banco Bilbao Vizcaya Argentaria. The next year Bank of Montreal picked up online brokerage CSFBdirect.

EXECUTIVES

Chairman: David A. Galloway, age 61
President, CEO, and Director:
F. Anthony (Tony) Comper, age 58, $2,460,900 pay
Deputy Chair; CEO, BMO Nesbitt Burns and Harris Nesbitt: William A. (Bill) Downe, $3,400,000 pay
Deputy Chair, Enterprise Risk and Portfolio Management Group: Ronald G. Rogers, age 57
President, Québec; Chairman, BMO Nesbitt Burns:
L. Jacques Ménard, age 59
President and CEO, Technology and Solutions:
Lloyd F. Darlington, age 60
President and CEO, Private Client Group; Deputy Chair, BMO Nesbitt Burns: Gilles G. Ouellette, $1,886,690 pay
President and CEO, Personal and Commercial Client Group: Robert W. (Rob) Pearce, age 50
President and CEO, Harris Bankcorp and Harris Trust & Savings Bank: Franklin J. (Frank) Techar, age 45
President and COO, BMO Nesbitt Burns:
Yvan J.P. Bourdeau, $2,624,960 pay
SEVP, Group Development: Maurice A. D. Hudon
SEVP and CFO: Karen E. Maidment, $1,184,404 pay
SEVP, Human Resources and Head of Office of Strategic Management: Rose M. Patten
EVP; Chief Economist, BMO Nesbitt Burns; Global Economic Strategist, Harris Bank: Sherry S. Cooper
EVP, Finance and Treasurer: Thomas E. Flynn
EVP and Chief Economist; Chief Economist, Harris Bank: Timothy J. (Tim) O'Neill
EVP, Taxation and General Counsel: Ronald B. Sirkis
SVP, Investor Relations: Susan Payne
VP, Corporate Communications, BMO Financial Group and Harris Bank: Andrew (Andy) Plews
VP and Secretary: Robert V. Horte
Auditors: KPMG LLP

LOCATIONS

HQ: Bank of Montreal
1 First Canadian Place, 100 King St. West,
Toronto, Ontario M5X 1A1, Canada
Phone: 416-867-5000   **Fax:** 416-867-6793
US HQ: 111 W. Monroe St., Chicago, IL 60603
US Phone: 312-461-2121   **US Fax:** 312-461-3869
Web: www.bmo.com

PRODUCTS/OPERATIONS

2004 Sales

	$ mil.	% of total
Interest		
Loans	5,530.5	51
Securities	1,210.6	11
Deposits with banks	359.2	3
Noninterest		
Securities commissions & fees	865.3	8
Deposit & payment service charges	611.9	6
Mutual fund revenues	310.0	3
Underwriting & advisory fees	281.3	3
Lending fees	260.0	2
Investment management & custodial fees	251.8	2
Other	1,152.4	11
Total	**10,833.0**	**100**

2004 Assets

	$ mil.	% of total
Cash & equivalents	14,800.5	7
Trading securities	29,071.2	13
Other securities	26,390.7	12
Residential mortgages	46,295.3	21
Business & government loans	41,026.4	19
Consumer installment & other personal loans	20,412.3	9
Derivative financial instruments	20,872.4	10
Other assets	18,643.2	9
Total	**217,512**	**100**

Selected Subsidiaries

Bank of Montreal Assessoria e Serviços Ltda. (Brazil)
Bank of Montreal Capital Markets (Holdings) Limited (UK)
  BMO Nesbitt Burns Limited (UK)
Bank of Montreal Finance Ltd.
Bank of Montreal Global Capital Solutions Ltd.
Bank of Montreal Holding Inc.
  Bank of Montreal Holding Investments Inc.
  Bank of Montreal Insurance (Barbados) Limited
  Bank of Montreal Securities Canada Limited
    BMO Nesbitt Burns Corporation Limited
  BMO Holding Finance, LLC (US)
  BMO Investments Limited (Bermuda)
  BMO Nesbitt Burns Trading Corp. S.A. (Luxembourg)
  BMO Service Inc.
Bank of Montreal Ireland plc
Bank of Montreal Mortgage Corporation
BMO Capital Corporation
BMO Investments Inc.
BMO InvestorLine Inc.
BMO Ireland Finance Company
BMO Life Insurance Company
BMO Nesbitt Burns Equity Partners Inc.
BMO Trust Company
Harris Financial Corp. (US)
  BMO Financial, Inc. (US)
  BMO Global Capital Solutions, Inc. (US)
  BMO Nesbitt Burns Corp. (US)
  BMO Nesbitt Burns Equity Group (U.S.), Inc.
  EFS (U.S.), Inc. and subsidiaries
  Harris Bancorp Insurance Services, Inc. (US)
  Harris Bankcorp, Inc.
  Harris Nesbitt Financing, Inc. (US)
  Harris RIA Holdings, Inc. and subsidiaries (US)
  Harris*direct* LLC (US)
MyChoice Inc.

COMPETITORS

Bank of America	RBC Dain Rauscher
CIBC	RBC Financial Group
Citigroup	Scotiabank
JPMorgan Chase	TD Bank
Laurentian Bank	Washington Mutual
Northern Trust	Wells Fargo

HISTORICAL FINANCIALS

Company Type: Public

Income Statement

FYE: October 31

	ASSETS ($ mil.)	NET INCOME ($ mil.)	INCOME AS % OF ASSETS	EMPLOYEES
10/04	217,512	1,928	0.9%	33,593
10/03	194,499	1,384	0.7%	33,993
10/02	162,339	910	0.6%	33,000
10/01	150,852	927	0.6%	33,000
10/00	153,248	1,219	0.8%	33,200
10/99	156,749	939	0.6%	32,844
10/98	144,216	875	0.6%	33,400
10/97	147,586	927	0.6%	34,286
10/96	126,949	873	0.7%	33,468
10/95	113,435	737	0.6%	33,341
Annual Growth	**7.5%**	**11.3%**	**—**	**0.1%**

2004 Year-End Financials

Equity as % of assets: 4.6%
Return on assets: 0.9%
Return on equity: 21.0%
Long-term debt ($ mil.): 1,964
No. of shares (mil.): 501
Dividends
  Yield: 2.4%
  Payout: 30.9%
Market value ($ mil.): 23,677
Sales ($ mil.): 10,833

Stock History

NYSE: BMO

	STOCK PRICE ($) FY Close	P/E High/Low		PER SHARE ($) Earnings	Dividends	Book Value
10/04	47.27	13	10	3.63	1.12	21.60
10/03	37.44	15	9	2.61	0.88	18.95
10/02	24.59	15	11	1.72	0.75	15.50
10/01	21.37	17	12	1.71	0.71	13.76
10/00	23.19	11	7	2.16	0.67	15.00
10/99	19.03	14	10	1.61	0.62	13.98
10/98	20.44	20	11	1.51	0.61	13.00
10/97	21.56	14	9	1.64	0.59	12.09
10/96	15.19	10	7	1.55	0.52	10.91
10/95	11.13	9	7	1.27	0.47	9.96
Annual Growth	**17.4%**	**—**	**—**	**12.4%**	**10.1%**	**9.0%**

Barclays PLC

An old hand at banking in Britain, Barclays traces its origins to the 17th century. The bank sports more than 2,000 branches in the UK and some 500 branches in Europe, Africa, Asia, Australia, and the US. Its operations include personal financial services (savings, checking, and consumer loans); corporate banking; asset management for wealthy individuals; mortgage lender Woolwich; and Barclaycard, a leading credit card issuer in Europe. US-based Barclays Global Investors is one of the world's largest institutional fund managers, while Barclays Capital handles foreign exchange, derivatives, and fixed-income business. Barclays also runs one of the UK's largest online banks, with nearly 4 million registered users.

The company entered the US credit card market when it bought Juniper Financial from Canadian Imperial Bank of Commerce (CIBC) in 2004. In a previous hook-up with CIBC, it merged its Caribbean banking business with that company's to create an 85-branch regional bank, FirstCaribbean International Bank, with each company owning an equal stake.

After exiting the South African market in 1987 over apartheid concerns, Barclays returned in a big way in 2005, buying a majority stake in the Absa Group, one of the country's largest retail banks. The deal also represented the largest-ever direct foreign investment there.

Barclays has an alliance with London-based Legal & General Group to market that company's life insurance products; it sells general insurance from Aviva.

HISTORY

Barclays first spread its wings in 1736 when James Barclay united family goldsmithing and banking businesses. As other family members joined the London enterprise, it became known as Barclays, Bevan & Tritton (1782).

Banking first became regulated in the 19th century. To ward off takeovers, 20 banks combined with Barclays in 1896. The new firm, Barclay & Co., began preying on other banks. Within 20 years it bought 17, including the Colonial Bank, chartered in 1836 to serve the West Indies and British Guiana (now Guyana). The company, renamed Barclays Bank Ltd. in 1917, weathered the Depression as the UK's #2 bank.

Barclays began expanding again after WWII, and by the late 1950s it had become the UK's top bank. It had a computer network by 1959, and in 1966 it introduced the Barclaycard in conjunction with Bank of America's BankAmericard (now Visa).

In 1968 the UK's Monopolies Commission barred Barclays' merger with two other big London banks, but had no objections to a two-way merger, so Barclays bought competitor Martins.

Barclays moved into the US consumer finance market in 1980 when it bought American Credit, 138 former Beneficial Finance offices, and Bankers Trust's branch network.

During the 1980s, London banks faced competition from invading overseas banks, local building societies, and other financial firms. Banking reform in 1984 led to formation of a holding company for Barclays Bank PLC.

To prepare for British financial deregulation in 1986, Barclays formed Barclays de Zoete Wedd (BZW) by merging its merchant bank with two other London financial firms. Faced with sagging profits, Barclays sold its California bank in 1988 and its US consumer finance business in 1989.

In 1990 Barclays bought private German bank Merck, Finck & Co. and Paris bank L'Européenne de Banque. The company countered 1992's bad-loan-induced losses by accelerating a cost-cutting program begun in 1989. To appease stockholders, chairman and CEO Andrew Buxton (a descendant of one of the bank's founding families) gave up his CEO title, hiring Martin Taylor (previously CEO of textile firm Courtaulds) for the post.

The company sold its Australian retail banking business in 1994, then began trimming other operations, including French corporate banking and US mortgage operations. However, it bought the Wells Fargo Nikko Investment Company to boost Asian operations.

Barclays' piecemeal sale of BZW signaled its failure to become a global investment banking powerhouse. In 1997 it sold BZW's European investment banking business to Credit Suisse First Boston, retaining the fixed-income and foreign exchange business. (Credit Suisse bought Barclays' Asian investment banking operations in 1998.)

Losses in Russia and a $250 million bailout of US hedge fund Long-Term Capital Management hit Barclays Capital in 1998. Taylor resigned that year in part because of his radical plans for the bank. Sir Peter Middleton stepped in as acting CEO; Barclays later tapped Canadian banker Matthew Barrett for the post. (Middleton also became chairman upon Buxton's retirement.)

Barclays in 1999 started a move toward online banking at the expense of traditional branches. The company announced free lifetime Internet access for new bank customers.

In 2000 the bank ruffled feathers when it announced the closure of about 170 mostly rural UK branches. Also in 2000 the company sold its Dial auto leasing unit to ABN AMRO and bought Woolwich plc. The following year Barclay's closed its own life insurance division, opting instead to sell the life insurance and pension products of London-based Legal & General Group.

EXECUTIVES

Chairman: Matthew W. (Matt) Barrett, age 61, $1,113,125 pay
Deputy Chairman: Sir Nigel Rudd, age 58
Group Chief Executive and Executive Director: John S. Varley, age 48, $1,455,625 pay
President and Executive Director; Chief Executive, Investment Banking and Investment Management: Robert E. (Bob) Diamond Jr., age 53
COO and Executive Director: Paul Idzik, age 44
Group Finance Director and Executive Director: Naguib Kheraj, age 41, $856,250 pay
Chairman, UK Banking and Barclaycard and Executive Director: Gary A. Hoffman, age 44, $856,250 pay (prior to promotion)
Chief Executive, International Retail and Commercial Banking and Executive Director: David Roberts, age 43, $856,250 pay
Chief Administrative Officer: Mike Foley
CIO: Dominic Trotta
Group Financial Controller: Jonathon Britton
Group Secretary: Lawrence Dickinson
Group Treasurer: Chris Grigg, age 45
General Counsel: Mark Harding
Head of Compliance: Brian Harte
Director of Corporate and External Affairs: Stephen Whitehead, age 39
Corporate Responsibility Director: Alistair Camp
Director of Finance: Colin Walklin
Director of Global Servicing: Wai Au
Investor Relations Director: Cathy Turner
Public Policy Director: Mike Davis
Public Relations Director: Chris Tucker
Risk Director: Robert Le Blanc
Tax Director: Heather Devine
Chief Executive, Juniper Financial: Richard W. Vague
Human Resources Director, International Retail and Commercial Banking: Allan Fielder, age 43
Auditors: PricewaterhouseCoopers

LOCATIONS

HQ: Barclays PLC
  1 Churchill Place,
  London E14 5HP, United Kingdom
Phone: +44-20-7116-1000
US HQ: 200 Park Ave., New York, NY 10166
US Phone: 212-412-4000
Web: www.barclays.com

Barclays has operations in Australia, Botswana, Egypt, France, Germany, Ghana, Gibraltar, Hong Kong, India, Ireland, Italy, Japan, Kenya, Mauritius, Portugal, Singapore, South Africa, South Korea, Spain, Switzerland, Tanzania, Uganda, the UK, the United Arab Emirates, the US, Zambia, and Zimbabwe.

PRODUCTS/OPERATIONS

2004 Sales

	% of total
Interest	66
Fees & commissions	24
Dealing profits	7
Other	3
Total	**100**

COMPETITORS

Bank of New York
CIBC
Citigroup
Credit Suisse
Deutsche Bank
HBOS
HSBC Holdings
JPMorgan Chase
Lloyds TSB
Mizuho Financial
RBC Financial Group
RBS
Standard Chartered
UBS
Vanguard Group

HISTORICAL FINANCIALS

Company Type: Public

Income Statement

FYE: December 31

	ASSETS ($ mil.)	NET INCOME ($ mil.)	INCOME AS % OF ASSETS	EMPLOYEES
12/04	1,000,949	6,265	0.6%	77,000
12/03	790,690	4,894	0.6%	74,420
12/02	649,541	3,594	0.6%	77,570
12/01	519,352	3,590	0.7%	78,400
12/00	472,767	3,698	0.8%	75,300
12/99	411,695	2,842	0.7%	74,300
12/98	364,250	2,222	0.6%	78,600
12/97	387,583	1,866	0.5%	83,200
12/96	318,528	2,807	0.9%	87,400
12/95	262,187	2,118	0.8%	89,300
Annual Growth	**16.0%**	**12.8%**	**—**	**(1.6%)**

2004 Year-End Financials

Equity as % of assets: 3.3%
Return on assets: 0.7%
Return on equity: 19.8%
Long-term debt ($ mil.): 153,535
No. of shares (mil.): 1,614
Dividends
  Yield: 1.4%
  Payout: 15.9%
Market value ($ mil.): 73,705
Sales ($ mil.): 40,016

Stock History

NYSE: BCS

12/95 12/96 12/97 12/98 12/99 12/00 12/01 12/02 12/03 12/04

	STOCK PRICE ($) FY Close	P/E High	P/E Low	PER SHARE ($) Earnings	PER SHARE ($) Dividends	PER SHARE ($) Book Value
12/04	45.68	12	8	3.91	0.62	20.70
12/03	36.35	12	7	3.00	1.32	18.21
12/02	24.70	18	10	2.15	1.13	14.90
12/01	33.64	16	10	2.14	0.98	12.67
12/00	32.19	13	9	2.42	0.90	11.86
12/99	28.78	17	11	1.87	0.56	9.17
12/98	22.50	22	10	1.47	0.92	6.58
12/97	27.30	24	13	1.22	0.79	6.30
12/96	17.19	10	6	1.79	0.83	6.23
12/95	11.31	11	8	1.18	0.45	6.69
Annual Growth	**16.8%**	**—**	**—**	**14.2%**	**3.6%**	**13.4%**

BASF AG

The world is BASF's ester. BASF is the world's largest chemical company, ahead of Dow and DuPont. BASF has more than 100 major manufacturing facilities and does business worldwide through five business segments: plastics (including polyolefins and polystyrene), performance products (value-added chemicals, coatings, and dyes), basic chemicals (plasticizers, catalysts, solvents), oil and gas exploration and production (through subsidiary Wintershall AG), and agricultural products and nutrition (additives, herbicides, and fertilizers). BASF and Shell combined their petrochemical businesses into joint-venture Basell in 2000 and sold the JV to a private investment group in 2005.

BASF uses what it calls *Verbund* strategy throughout its facilities — plants are both customers and suppliers of each other. While the company still gets more than half its sales from Europe, it continues to expand overseas, particularly in Asia. It saw early on that the chemicals market in Asia will be the equal of that in Europe and wanted a healthy piece of the action.

Toward that end, the company has opened two Verbund sites in Asia — one in Nanjing, China and the other in Kuantan, Malaysia. The Chinese site delivered its first product in early 2005 and began operating fully in the middle of that year. It's the centerpiece and primary operation of a joint venture with Sinopec that was formed in 2000, BASF-YPC.

In early 2005 BASF added Merck KGaA's electronic chemicals unit for nearly $500 million. Later in the year it acquired Swiss fine chemicals maker Orgamol, which supplies pharmaceutical companies with raw ingredients.

The company said in late 2004 that it would cut employment at its main plant in Ludwigshafen — the world's largest chemicals plant — by 10%, or 3,600 jobs. The move is to take place over three years and be handled without layoffs.

BASF and Shell exited the polyolefins business with the sale of Basell to Access Industries for about $5.7 billion in late 2005.

HISTORY

Originally named Badische Anilin & Soda-Fabrik, BASF AG was founded in Mannheim, Germany, by jeweler Frederick Englehorn in 1861. Unable to find enough land for expansion in Mannheim, BASF moved to nearby Ludwigshafen in 1865. The company was a pioneer in coal tar dyes, and it developed a synthetic indigo in 1897. Its synthetic dyes rapidly replaced more expensive organic dyes.

BASF scientist Fritz Haber synthesized ammonia in 1909, giving BASF access to the market for nitrogenous fertilizer (1913). Haber received a Nobel Prize in 1918 but was later charged with war crimes for his work with poison gases. Managed by Carl Bosch, another Nobel Prize winner, BASF joined the I.G. Farben cartel with Bayer, Hoechst, and others in 1925 to create a German chemical colossus. Within the cartel BASF developed polystyrene, PVC, and magnetic tape. Part of the Nazi war machine, I.G. Farben made synthetic rubber and used labor from the Auschwitz concentration camp during WWII.

After the war I.G. Farben was dismantled. BASF regained its independence in 1952 and rebuilt its war-ravaged factories. Strong postwar domestic demand for basic chemicals aided its recovery, and in 1958 BASF launched a US joint venture with Dow Chemical (BASF bought out Dow's half in 1978). The company moved into petrochemicals and became a leading manufacturer of plastic and synthetic fiber.

In the US the company purchased Wyandotte Chemicals (1969), Chemetron (1979), and Inmont (1985), among others. To expand its natural gas business in Europe, in 1991 the company signed deals with Russia's Gazprom and France's Elf Aquitaine. BASF bought Mobil's polystyrene-resin business and gained almost 10% of the US market.

BASF bought Imperial Chemical's polypropylene business in 1994 and became Europe's second-largest producer of the plastic. The next year the company paid $1.4 billion for the pharmaceutical arm of UK retailer Boots.

In 1997 BASF formed a joint venture with PetroFina (now TOTAL S.A.); in 2001 the venture opened the world's largest liquid steam cracker, in Port Arthur, Texas.

In 1999 the US fined the company $225 million for its part in a worldwide vitamin price-fixing cartel (in 2001 the European Commission fined it another $260 million, bringing the total expected cost of fines, out-of-court settlements, and legal expenses to about $800 million); BASF also faced a class-action suit as a result of the scheme. That year the company moved into oil and gas exploration in Russia through a partnership agreement with Russia's Gazprom. BASF also merged its textile operations into Bayer and Hoechst's DyStar joint venture, forming a $1 billion company that is a world leading dye maker.

BASF completed its acquisition of Rohm and Haas' industrial coatings business in 2000 and bought the Cyanamid division (herbicides, fungicides, and pesticides) of American Home Products (now Wyeth). That year BASF expanded its superabsorbents business by paying $656 million for US-based Amcol International's Chemdal International unit. Rather than attempt to compete in the rapidly consolidating pharmaceutical industry, in 2001 BASF sold its mid-sized Knoll Pharmaceutical unit to Abbott Laboratories for about $6.9 billion. It also announced that it was closing 10 plants and cutting about 4,000 jobs (4% of its workforce).

BASF sold its fibers unit in 2003 to focus on core chemical operations, which it added to throughout the next few years. To begin with, it bought a portion of Bayer's agchem businesses for $1.3 billion when European antitrust regulators mandated the Bayer divestment following its acquisition of Aventis CropScience. BASF also acquired Honeywell Specialty Materials' engineering plastics business in exchange for its fibers division.

That year also brought chairman Jürgen Hambrecht's announcement that the company would push forward with a restructuring of its North American business. Included among the steps were job cuts of approximately 1,000.

EXECUTIVES

Chairman, Supervisory Board: Jürgen F. Strube, age 65
Chairman, Board of Executive Directors:
Jürgen Hambrecht, age 58
Vice Chairman, Board of Executive Directors:
Eggert Voscherau, age 61
Member, Board of Executive Directors and CFO:
Kurt W. Bock, age 46
Member, Board of Executive Directors: John Feldman, age 55
Member, Board of Executive Directors:
Andreas Kreimeyer, age 49

Member, Board of Executive Directors; CEO, BASF Corp.: Klaus Peter Löbbe, age 58
Member, Board of Executive Directors:
Stefan Marcinowski, age 51
Member, Board of Executive Directors: Peter Oakley, age 51
President, Asia Pacific: Wolfgang Hapke
President, Asia Pacific: Harald Lauke
President, Europe: Walter Seufert
President, NAFTA: Hans-Ulrich Engel
President, Chemicals, Plastics, and Performance Products North America: Joseph (Joe) Breunig
President, South America: Rolf Dieter Acker
President, Accounting: Eckard Müller
President, Communications: Felix Gress, age 43
President, Global Human Resources: Dietmar Kokott
President, Investor Relations: Magdalena Moll
President, Legal, Taxes, and Insurance: Eckart Sünner
Auditors: Deloitte & Touche GmbH

LOCATIONS

HQ: BASF Aktiengesellschaft
   Carl-Bosch St. 38, 67056 Ludwigshafen, Germany
Phone: +49-621-60-0   **Fax:** +49-621-60-42525
US HQ: 100 Campus Dr., Florham Park, NJ 07932
US Phone: 973-245-6000   **US Fax:** 973-245-6002
Web: www.basf.com

BASF AG has operations in more than 100 countries.

2004 Sales

	% of total
Europe	
Germany	20
Other countries	36
North America	22
Asia/Pacific & Africa	17
South America	5
Total	**100**

PRODUCTS/OPERATIONS

2004 Sales and Operating Income

	Sales $ mil.	Sales % of total	Operating Income $ mil.	Operating Income % of total
Plastics	14,471	28	913	13
Performance Products	10,998	21	1,457	21
Chemicals	9,645	19	1,693	24
Oil & Gas	7,231	14	2,233	32
Agricultural Products & Nutrition				
Agricultural Products	4,608	9	671	9
Fine Chemicals	2,463	5	65	1
Other	2,157	4	(408)	—
Total	**51,573**	**100**	**6,624**	**100**

Selected Products

Plastics
  Engineering plastics
  Foams
  Polyurethane
  Polyamide and intermediates
  Styrenics
Performance Products
  Automotive coatings
  Automotive fluids
  Decorative paints
  Industrial coatings
  Pigments
  Printing systems
  Surfactants
  Textile chemicals
Chemicals
  Inorganics (ammonia, formaldehyde, melamine, sulfuric acid, and urea)
  Intermediates
  Petrochemicals (feedstocks, industrial gases, and plasticizers)
  Specialty chemicals

Oil and Gas
  Crude oil and natural gas exploration
  Natural gas distribution and trading
Ag Products and Nutrition
  Agricultural products (fungicides, herbicides, and insecticides)
  Fine chemicals (fragrances, pharmaceutical ingredients, UV absorbers, and vitamins)

COMPETITORS

3M	Formosa Plastics
Air Products	Henkel
Akzo Nobel	Hercules
Ashland	Hoffmann-La Roche
Bayer	Honeywell International
BP	Honeywell Specialty
Cargill	Materials
Celanese AG	Huntsman Corp
Ciba Specialty Chemicals	LG Group
Clariant International	Lyondell Chemical
Cognis	Mitsubishi Chemical
Degussa	Monsanto
Dow Chemical	NewMarket
DSM	PPG
DuPont	Royal Dutch/Shell Group
Dynea	RWE
Eastman Chemical	Sony
Eni	Syngenta
Exxon Mobil	Teknor Apex
FMC	TOTAL

HISTORICAL FINANCIALS

Company Type: Public

Income Statement

FYE: December 31

	REVENUE ($ mil.)	NET INCOME ($ mil.)	NET PROFIT MARGIN	EMPLOYEES
12/04	51,573	2,551	4.9%	81,955
12/03	42,576	1,144	2.7%	87,159
12/02	34,155	1,580	4.6%	89,398
12/01	29,206	5,221	17.9%	92,545
12/00	33,989	1,164	3.4%	103,273
12/99	31,539	1,246	3.9%	104,628
12/98	32,255	1,983	6.1%	105,945
12/97	31,125	1,806	5.8%	104,979
12/96	31,642	1,842	5.8%	103,406
12/95	32,153	1,718	5.3%	106,565
Annual Growth	**5.4%**	**4.5%**	**—**	**(2.9%)**

2004 Year-End Financials

Debt ratio: 8.2%
Return on equity: 12.6%
Cash ($ mil.): 2,826
Current ratio: 2.18
Long-term debt ($ mil.): 1,713
No. of shares (mil.): 540
Dividends
  Yield: 2.4%
  Payout: 37.0%
Market value ($ mil.): 38,922

Stock History

NYSE: BF

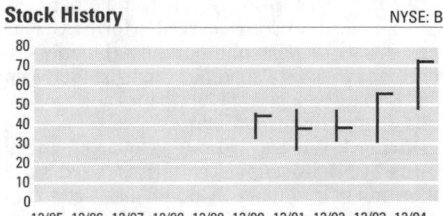

12/95 12/96 12/97 12/98 12/99 12/00 12/01 12/02 12/03 12/04

	STOCK PRICE ($) FY Close	P/E High/Low	PER SHARE ($) Earnings	PER SHARE ($) Dividends	PER SHARE ($) Book Value
12/04	72.02	16 10	4.65	1.72	38.68
12/03	55.75	27 15	2.04	1.54	34.99
12/02	38.22	17 12	2.73	1.14	30.47
12/01	37.91	6 3	8.66	1.21	26.22
12/00	44.44	24 18	1.90	0.00	21.35
Annual Growth	**12.8%**	**—**	**25.1%**	**—**	**16.0%**

Bayer AG

You could get a headache trying to name all of the Bayer Group's products. The company, which created aspirin in 1897, makes health care products (diagnostic equipment and pharmaceuticals), agricultural products (crop protection and animal health), and specialty materials (plastics and synthetic rubber). It operates in the US through Bayer Corporation. Bayer has reorganized, spinning off its divisions and becoming a management holding company. It also has separated its former chemicals subgroup, which was spun off as a publicly traded company called Lanxess in early 2005. In November 2004 Bayer closed a deal for Roche's consumer health unit for nearly $3 billion.

Besides its line of Bayer aspirins, the company's best-known brands include Alka-Seltzer and One-A-Day vitamins. Bayer spends about 10% of revenues on R&D, with much of that money going to fuel advances in its health care unit. The success of drugs such as Cipro, Levitra, and Avalox (used to treat infectious diseases) has prompted the company to expand its biotechnology and genetic research efforts.

The Roche deal created one of the top three non-prescription drugs companies in the world, combining Bayer's aspirin, Alka-Seltzer, and Midol brands with Roche's Aleve pain relievers, among others.

That acquisition is in line with Bayer's intention to focus its health care group on becoming the world's #1 OTC drug company, and part of that process is to divest noncore assets. In December 2004 the company sold off Bayer HealthCare's blood products unit. Bayer sold the business, which makes plasma products, to venture capital groups Cerberus and Ampersand for nearly $600 million.

HISTORY

Friedrich Bayer founded Bayer in Germany in 1863 to make synthetic dyes. Research led to such discoveries as Antinonin (synthetic pesticide, 1892), aspirin (1897), and synthetic rubber (1915).

Under Carl Duisberg, Bayer allegedly made the first poison gas used by Germany in WWI. During the war the US seized Bayer's US operations and trademark rights and sold them to Sterling Drug.

In 1925 Bayer, BASF, Hoechst, and other German chemical concerns merged to form I.G. Farben Trust. Their photography businesses, combined as Agfa, also joined the trust. Between wars Bayer developed polyurethanes and the first sulfa drug, Prontosil (1935).

During WWII the trust took over chemical plants of Nazi-occupied countries, used slave labor, and helped make Zyklon B gas used to kill people at Auschwitz. At war's end Bayer lost its 50% of Winthrop Laboratories (US) and Bayer of Canada (to Sterling Drug). The 1945 Potsdam Agreement called for the breakup of I.G. Farben, and Bayer AG emerged in 1951 as an independent company with many of its original operations, including Agfa.

After rebuilding in West Germany, Bayer AG and Monsanto formed a joint venture (Mobay, 1954); Bayer AG later bought Monsanto's share (1967). In the 1960s the company offered more dyes, plastics, and polyurethanes, and added factories worldwide. Agfa merged with Gevaert (photography, Belgium) in 1964; Bayer AG retained 60%. Over the next decades it acquired Miles Labs (Alka-Seltzer, US, 1978), the rest of Agfa-Gevaert (1981), Compugraphic (electronic imaging, US, 1989), and Nova's Polysar (rubber, Canada, 1990).

Bayer AG integrated its US holdings under the name Miles in 1992 (renamed Bayer Corporation in 1995). The next year it introduced its first genetically engineered product, Kogenate hemophilia treatment. It regained US rights to the Bayer brand and logo in 1994 by paying SmithKline Beecham $1 billion for the North American business of Sterling Winthrop.

Bayer AG formed a joint venture with Swiss rival Roche Holding in 1996 to market over-the-counter Roche drugs in the US. In 1997 Bayer, Baxter International, Rhône-Poulenc Rorer, and Green Cross agreed to a $670 million settlement over blood products that infected thousands of hemophiliacs with HIV during the 1980s.

In 1998 the company sold the food-ingredients arm of its Haarmann & Reimer unit to Tate & Lyle. Bayer bought US-based Chiron's diagnostics operations for $1.1 billion, created a North American joint venture with Crompton & Knowles' seed-treatment unit, and formed a research alliance with Millennium Pharmaceuticals (giving Bayer a 14% stake in Millennium). The firm spun off all but 30% of its photographic and electronic prepress business as Agfa-Gevaert (it plans to sell its remaining stake to Goldman Sachs).

Bayer, Hoechst, and BASF merged their textile activities in 1999 to form the world's largest dye-making company. The next year Bayer boosted its polyurethane business by paying $2.5 billion for US-based Lyondell Chemical's polyols unit. The company also formed a joint venture with Exelixis Pharmaceuticals to develop gene-based insecticides and announced it would develop an anti-impotence drug to rival Pfizer's Viagra (which drug launched in 2003 as Levitra).

In 2001 Bayer agreed to invest as much as $874 million on two drug-development deals with US genomics company CuraGen (Bayer will take a 7% stake). The company's summer was marred by the one-two punch of sharply lower profits and the recall of Baycol (known as Lipobay in Europe), its popular cholesterol-lowering drug that has been linked to more than 100 deaths worldwide. Bayer announced in September 2001 that it was separating its health care and agrochemical operations from the chemicals and polymers businesses, but that it was keeping its pharmaceuticals business.

In a bid to bolster its agrochemical business, Bayer acquired Aventis CropScience in 2002 for about $5 billion plus $2 billion in debt. The company was combined with Bayer Crop Protection to form Bayer CropScience.

That change precipitated a series of restructurings and realignments of Bayer's divisions. The successive restructurings were meant to pave the way for the sale of individual operations — such as its household insecticide business, which Bayer sold to S.C. Johnson & Son in October 2002. Late in 2003 Bayer finally settled on the holding company structure and the sale of what is now Lanxess.

In mid-2003 the company, along with partner GlaxoSmithKline, launched Levitra, its rival to Pfizer's $1 billion-earning Viagra.

EXECUTIVES

Chairman, Supervisory Board: Manfred Schneider, age 66
Deputy Chairman, Supervisory Board: Erhard Gipperich, age 63
Chairman, Management Board: Werner Wenning, age 59
Member, Management Board, Finance: Klaus Kühn, age 53
Member, Management Board, Human Resources: Richard Pott, age 52
Member, Management Board, Innovation, Technology and Environment: Udo Oels, age 61
Member, Management Board; President and CEO, Bayer Corporation: Attila Molnar, age 57
Chairman, Management Board, Bayer CropScience: Friedrich Berschauer, age 55
Chairman, Management Board, Bayer MaterialScience: Hagen Noerenberg, age 58
Chairman and CEO, Bayer HealthCare: Arthur J. Higgins, age 49
Managing Director, Bayer Business Services: Andreas Resch, age 52
Managing Director, Bayer Technology Services; CTO, Bayer Corporation: Achim Noack
Managing Director, Bayer Industry Services: Jürgen Hinz, age 59
Head of Investor Relations: Alexander Rosar
Auditors: PwC Deutsche Revision AG

LOCATIONS

HQ: Bayer AG
51368 Leverkusen, Germany
Phone: +49-214-30-1 **Fax:** +49-214-30-66328
US HQ: 100 Bayer Rd., Pittsburgh, PA 15205-9741
US Phone: 412-777-2000 **US Fax:** 412-777-2034
Web: www.bayer.de

Bayer Group operates primarily in Canada, France, Germany, Japan, the UK, and the US.

2004 Sales

	$ mil.	% of total
Europe	17,494	43
North America	11,212	30
Asia/Pacific	6,700	16
Latin America/Africa/Middle East	4,904	11
Total	**40,310**	**100**

PRODUCTS/OPERATIONS

2004 Sales

	$ mil.	% of total
MaterialScience		
Systems	7,246	18
Materials	4,400	11
HealthCare		
Pharmaceuticals & Biological Products	5,944	15
Consumer Care & Diagnostics	4,485	11
Animal Health	1,065	3
Lanxess	8,199	20
CropScience	8,054	20
Adjustments	917	2
Total	**40,310**	**100**

Selected Operations and Products

MaterialScience
Cellulose products (Wolff Walsrode)
Coatings
Colorants
Plastics
Polyurethanes
Specialty metals (H. C. Starck)

HealthCare
Diagnostics (laboratory products)
Pharmaceuticals
Pharmaceutical research and development
Consumer care products (over-the-counter drugs)

CropScience
BioScience (biotechnology and seeds)
Crop protection (insecticides and herbicides)
Environmental Science (lawn care and non-agricultural pesticides)

Selected Brands

Adalat (cardiovascular medication)
Alka-Seltzer (analgesic and antacid)
Aspirin (analgesic)
Cipro (antibiotic)
Dralon (acrylic staple fiber)
Glucometer (blood sugar monitor)
Levitra (impotence drug)
Makrolon (polycarbonate resin)
One-A-Day (vitamins)

COMPETITORS

3M
Abbott Labs
Akzo Nobel
AstraZeneca
BASF AG
Baxter
Boehringer Ingelheim
Bristol-Myers Squibb
Degussa
Dow Chemical
DSM
DuPont
Eastman Chemical
Eli Lilly
Eni
E.ON
GlaxoSmithKline
Henkel
Hercules
Honeywell International
Huntsman
Imperial Chemical Industries
International Flavors
ITOCHU
Johnson & Johnson
Lyondell Chemical
Merck
Merck KGaA
Mitsubishi Chemical
Monsanto
Norsk Hydro
Novartis
Perrigo
Pfizer
Rhodia
Roche
Sanofi-Aventis
Schering-Plough
Syngenta
Wyeth

HISTORICAL FINANCIALS

Company Type: Public

Income Statement

	REVENUE ($ mil.)	NET INCOME ($ mil.)	NET PROFIT MARGIN	EMPLOYEES
12/04	40,310	817	2.0%	113,825
12/03	35,914	(1,585)	—	118,280
12/02	30,415	1,113	3.7%	122,600
12/01	25,792	860	3.3%	116,900
12/00	27,764	1,564	5.6%	122,100
12/99	27,511	2,016	7.3%	120,400
12/98	32,744	1,884	5.8%	145,100
12/97	30,580	1,635	5.3%	144,600
12/96	31,533	1,768	5.6%	142,200
12/95	31,006	1,665	5.4%	142,900
Annual Growth	3.0%	(7.6%)	—	(2.5%)

FYE: December 31

2004 Year-End Financials

Debt ratio: 58.0%
Return on equity: 5.1%
Cash ($ mil.): 4,836
Current ratio: 1.98
Long-term debt ($ mil.): 9,641
No. of shares (mil.): 730
Dividends
  Yield: 1.8%
  Payout: 54.5%
Market value ($ mil.): 24,817

	STOCK PRICE ($) FY Close	P/E High/Low		PER SHARE ($) Earnings	Dividends	Book Value
12/04	33.98	31	21	1.12	0.61	22.75
12/03	29.41	—	—	(2.34)	0.97	21.02
12/02	21.65	24	11	1.52	0.79	22.05
Annual Growth	25.3%	—	—	(14.2%)	(12.1%)	1.6%

BBC

The dominant broadcaster in the UK, British Broadcasting Corporation (BBC) operates two public TV channels, a 24-hour cable news channel, digital channels, national and digital radio networks, and an online news service. The BBC World Service broadcasts radio programming in more than 40 languages and is the sole source of news in some parts of the world. Subsidiary BBC Worldwide offers international TV channels (BBC Prime, BBC America) and program distribution. In addition, the company (often called The Beeb) operates a number of Web sites and publishes about 40 magazines.

Established by royal charter, the BBC (once fondly referred to by Brits as "Auntie" for its once prudish image) is governed by a 12-member board appointed by the Queen. It derives 75% of its sales from annual mandatory license fees paid by TV set owners in the UK. In early 2005, the government seriously reexamined the role of the company in the widest-ever review of the BBC. Although the UK renewed the BBC's royal charter until 2016, it demanded that the company restructure its management operations by replacing the board of governors with a more independent body that does not also run the BBC's day-to-day management. (The current charter expires at the end of 2006.)

The BBC's growing involvement in commercial ventures under its controversial former director general Greg Dyke has prompted public grumbling that the broadcaster is straying from its public service role. It increased license fees to fund a move into digital television, which also drew fire. To prove that it is serious about controlling costs, the company is cutting 3,800 jobs, or 19% of its workforce, over a three-year period (the cuts began in 2005). The BBC also launched a new children's channel as a way to profitably expand the broadcaster's operations.

More controversy flared in 2004 when a British judge debunked a BBC news story from a year before that accused Prime Minister Tony Blair of exaggerating the threat of Iraqi weapons of mass destruction during the run up to the US' and UK's invasion of the Middle Eastern country. BBC chairman Gavyn Davies and Dyke stuck by the main thrust of the story but acknowledged that there were problems with the report. Both men resigned as a result. The BBC appointed television executive Michael Grade as the new chairman and Mark Thompson, former Channel Four CEO, as the new director general.

HISTORY

Established as the British Broadcasting Company Limited in 1922, the BBC was founded by a group of radio manufacturers aiming to block any single manufacturer from grabbing a broadcasting monopoly. Under general manager John Reith, BBC radio programming grew to include news, cultural events, sports, and weather. A burgeoning social and cultural presence led to its re-establishment in 1927 under a new royal charter. The organization was renamed the British Broadcasting Corporation, and the charter ensured it would remain outside the control of the British Parliament.

By 1935 BBC radio had reached about 95% of the British population. TV broadcasting debuted the next year, but the cost of TV sets limited audience numbers to about 20,000. Those who could afford a TV got to see the coronation of King George VI and Wimbledon. TV broadcasting would be short-lived, however: Beginning in 1939 and throughout WWII, the signal was blacked out when the transmitter proved a good aircraft direction finder.

Although TV screens went dark, BBC radio served a vital role during WWII. Its broadcasts to occupied territories and the airing of Prime Minister Winston Churchill's wartime speeches elevated the BBC's reputation as a news broadcaster.

BBC TV transmission resumed in 1946. The 1953 broadcast of the coronation of Queen Elizabeth II helped launch the television age of the 1950s. In 1955 commercial broadcaster Independent Television Network became the BBC's first rival for viewers. The BBC introduced its second public TV channel (BBC Two) in 1964. By 1969 both BBC One and BBC Two were broadcasting in color.

The corporate culture of the BBC during the 1970s and 1980s was dominated by financial upheaval. Budget cuts combined with growing competition prompted the formation of a committee to review the BBC's financing alternatives. Although the committee's 1986 report did not permit commercial advertising on the BBC, it did lead to more flexibility in funding.

Sir John Birt was appointed the BBC's director general in 1992, and the reorganization and cost-cutting program he instituted fueled the debate over the company's move toward commercialization. Through BBC Worldwide, the BBC inched away from its public service roots. In 1997 the BBC privatized its domestic TV and radio transmission business and launched a 24-hour cable news channel. UKTV (a commercial TV joint venture with Flextech) also went on the air that year. In 1998 the BBC teamed with Discovery Communications to launch BBC America, a US cable channel, and teamed with Scottish Power to provide free Internet access.

In 1999 Greg Dyke, who had been chief executive of Pearson Television, was named to succeed Birt, who left in January 2000. Shortly after Dyke took the reins, he announced a massive restructuring of the organization designed to cut costs (eliminating hundreds of jobs), foment more partnerships with private entities, and increase the amount spent on programming. In 2001 the BBC received approval for five digital radio and four digital TV channels. Dyke announced that he would explore privatizing parts of the company, such as its magazine and book operations.

In 2002 the company started commercial subsidiary BBC Broadcast, which offers channel management services. (The BBC sold that business in 2005.)

The BBC started 2005 with a renewal of its royal charter that will keep the company in business until 2016. However, the UK government has demanded that it abolish its board of governors with a more independent body that is not also responsible for the BBC's day-to-day managment.

EXECUTIVES

Chairman: Michael Grade, age 62, $180,355 pay (partial-year salary)
Vice Chairman: Anthony Salz, $45,089 pay (partial-year salary)
Director General: Mark Thompson, age 48, $851,051 pay (partial-year salary)
Deputy Director-General: Mark Byford, age 47, $832,264 pay
COO; CEO, BBC Worldwide: John Smith, age 45, $674,453 pay
Group Finance Director: Zarin Patel, $129,630 pay (partial-year salary)
Creative Director and Director of Drama, Entertainment, and CBBC: Alan Yentob, age 58
Director of BBC People: Stephen Dando, age 43, $573,004 pay
Director of BBC World Service and Global News Division: Richard Sambrook, age 49
Director of Factual and Learning: John Willis
Director of Governance: Nicholas Kroll, age 50
Director of Marketing, Communications, and Audiences: Tim Davie, age 37
Director of Nations and Regions: Pat Loughrey
Director of New Media and Technology: Ashley Highfield, age 40, $302,000 pay
Director of Policy, Strategy, Legal, and Distribution: Caroline Thomson, age 48, $514,764 pay
Director of Radio and Music: Jenny Abramsky, age 59, $546,702 pay
Director of Television: Jana Bennett, age 48, $597,427 pay
Auditors: KPMG LLP; PricewaterhouseCoopers LLP

LOCATIONS

HQ: British Broadcasting Corporation
Broadcasting House, Portland Place,
London W1A 1AA, United Kingdom
Phone: +44-20-7580-4468   **Fax:** +44-20-7765-1181
US HQ: 7475 Wisconsin Ave., Ste. 110,
Bethesda, MD 20814
US Phone: 301-347-2233   **US Fax:** 301-656-8591
Web: www.bbc.co.uk

PRODUCTS/OPERATIONS

Selected Television Operations
BBC America (US cable channel)
BBC Four (digital channel focusing on culture and the arts)
BBC Japan (Japan cable channel)
BBC News (news bureau)
BBC News 24 (24-hour news programming)
BBC One (news and entertainment programming)
BBC Parliament (unedited coverage of the Parliament)
BBC Prime (international entertainment programming)
BBC Three (digital channel featuring youth-oriented programming)
BBC Two (entertainment and informational programming)
CBBC (children's digital channel)
CBeebies (children's digital channel)

Selected Radio Operations
1Xtra (digital channel aimed at hip-hop audiences)
BBC 6 (music, music news, and documentary programming)
BBC 7 (speech-based digital service)
BBC Asian Network (broadcasts in English to Asian audiences in the UK)
BBC World Service & Global News (international news programming)
Radio 1 (news and music programming)
Radio 2 (news and music programming)
Radio 3 (classical, jazz, and world music programming)
Radio 4 (news, educational, dramatic, and documentary programming)
Radio 5 Live (news and sports radio programming)
Five Live Sports Extra (digital channel focusing on live sports events)

Selected BBC Worldwide Magazines
BBC Good Food
BBC History
BBC Music
BBC Parenting
BBC Wildlife
Easy Gardening
HOT!
Radio Times
Songs of Praise
Top Of The Pops

Selected Subsidiaries and Units
BBC Resources (broadcast facilities)
BBC Online (Internet site)
BBC Technology Holdings (tech support)
BBC Worldwide Limited (oversees international operations)

Regional Operations
BBC Northern Island (radio and television)
BBC Scotland (radio and television)
BBC Wales (radio and television)

COMPETITORS

BSkyB	Liberty Media
Channel 4	International
Daily Mail and	Pearson
General Trust	RTL Group
Emap	Scottish Radio
Flextech	SMG
Future	Time Warner
GCap Media	Yorkshire-Tyne Tees
ITV	Television Holdings

HISTORICAL FINANCIALS
Company Type: Government-owned

Income Statement
FYE: March 31

	REVENUE ($ mil.)	NET INCOME ($ mil.)	NET PROFIT MARGIN	EMPLOYEES
3/05	7,205	(354)	—	27,264
3/04	6,766	(454)	—	27,632
3/03	5,559	(495)	—	27,148
3/02	4,823	(23)	—	25,568
3/01	4,482	11	0.2%	24,219
3/00	4,781	(19)	—	23,640
3/99	4,593	—	—	23,119
3/98	4,159	—	—	21,023
3/97	3,825	—	—	19,517
3/96	2,776	—	—	19,000
Annual Growth	**11.2%**	—	—	**4.1%**

2005 Year-End Financials
Debt ratio: 28.4%   Current ratio: 1.44
Return on equity: —   Long-term debt ($ mil.): 282
Cash ($ mil.): 72

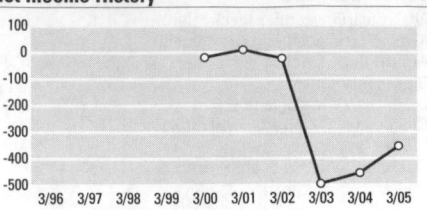

BBVA

Don't tell Banco Bilbao Vizcaya Argentaria (BBVA) that we're in a post-colonial era. It's not Cortez revisited, but BBVA, one of Spain's top banks (alongside Santander Central Hispano), is conquering Latin America, where it controls key banks in about 10 countries in the region. With some 7,500 offices in nearly 40 countries, its services include retail, corporate, and institutional banking; investment banking; asset management; insurance; and Internet banking. Beyond its activities in Spain and Latin America, BBVA also operates elsewhere in Europe, mainly in Portugal, France, and Italy. It's also expanding its reach into the US.

BBVA controls Banco Bilbao Vizcaya Argentaria, Chile and BBVA Banco Francés in Argentina. In 2004 BBVA bought the 40% of Mexico's BBVA Bancomer that they did not already own. To finance about half of the approximately $4 billion bid, they issued 195 million new shares.

In Italy, the company owns about 15% of Banca Nazionale del Lavoro (BNL) and tried to buy the remaining shares for more than $8 billion. BNL's board approved the deal, as did the Bank of Italy. But Italian insurer Unipol, which also holds around 15% of BNL, stepped in with a better bid and more allies with voting shares. BBVA decided to forgo the takeover and announced it will sell its stake in BNL to Unipol.

Eager to tap into the burgeoning Spanish-speaking market in the US, BBVA bought Texas bank Laredo National Bancshares (LNB) in 2005. LNB is part of a new US unit that will focus on money transfers to Latin American countries. BBVA also set up a private equity fund that will invest in US-based Hispanic-owned small and medium-sized enterprises with annual sales between $25 million and $500 million.

HISTORY

Banco Bilbao Vizcaya Argentaria (BBVA) is the progeny of the 2000 merger of Banco Bilbao Vizcaya (BBV) and Argentaria, Caja Postal y Banco Hipotecario. BBV formed when Banco de Bilbao and Banco de Vizcaya merged in 1988, while Argentaria, Caja Postal y Banco Hipotecario coalesced from the 1991 merger of six government-owned banks.

In 1857 a group of Basque businessmen banded together to offer loans and other banking services to businesses. The bank — eventually Banco de Bilbao — helped fund the region's industrialization. Its first foray beyond the Basque region was Paris, not Madrid, in 1902. It later entered London, Madrid, and other major European cities.

Franco's rise to power and the isolation of WWII deterred industrial growth. In protectionist Spain, Bilbao bought 16 banks between 1941 and 1943 and formed a unit to focus on US and Latin American partnerships.

In the 1960s Bilbao reorganized and formed a unit focused on industrial growth. It rolled with the punches as banking rules continued to change in the 1970s and 1980s. The bank expanded consumer services, began issuing credit cards (1971), and bought banks that couldn't cope with changing regulations.

To compete in financially deregulated Europe, Spain's overpopulated banking industry began to consolidate in the early 1990s. After #3 Bilbao failed to take over #2 Banco Español de Crédito, it merged with regional rival Banco de Vizcaya.

Formed in 1901 by Basque merchants, Banco de Vizcaya expanded through purchases and had some 200 branches by 1935, including offices in Europe's leading cities. During the post-WWII bust, it bought weaker banks and invested in Spain's industrial complex.

In the 1960s and 1970s, Vizcaya added industrial banking, insurance, personal investment management, and leasing. The bank refocused on international growth, opening branches in London, Mexico City, New York, and other cities. It entered consumer banking and became another participant in the branch race; by 1980 Vizcaya had some 900 offices. Looking to be a strong player in deregulated Europe, the bank merged with Bilbao in 1988; together, the two banks had nearly 3,400 branches.

The merger almost unraveled after Vizcaya chair Pedro Toledo (set to lead the new bank with Bilbao chair José Ángel Sánchez Asiain) died in 1989. The two banks fought over Toledo's replacement until the Bank of Spain suggested in 1990 Bilbao executive Emilio Ybarra y Churruca become the only chair.

Until 1992 government regulations and strong unions prevented BBV from cutting some 5,000 jobs and 600 branches. After Europe's 1992 deregulation, the company targeted Latin America, buying banks in Mexico and Peru (1995); Argentina, Colombia, and Venezuela (1996); and Brazil and Chile (1997). The merger of rivals Banco Santander and Banco Central Hispanoamericano in 1999 prompted BBV to merge with Argentaria in 2000.

After the merger, BBVA teamed with top Spanish telecom Telefónica to develop online banking services. The duo later bought first-e, one of Europe's first Internet-only banks, and merged it with BBVA's Uno-e online bank to form UnoFirst. BBVA bought 30% of Grupo Financiero Bancomer, Mexico's #2 bank, and merged it into its existing Mexican bank, Grupo Financiero BBV-Probursa; the resulting Grupo Financiero BBVA-Bancomer is the country's largest bank. The bank completed the renaming of its subsidiaries to reflect their position as BBVA subsidiaries in 2002.

EXECUTIVES

Chairman and CEO: Francisco González Rodríguez, $4,928,132 pay
President, COO, and Director:
José Ignacio Goirigolzarri Tellaeche, age 51, $3,932,412 pay
Company Secretary and Director:
José Maldonado Ramos, $1,410,376 pay
CFO: Manuel González Cid
Managing Director, Americas: Vitalino M. Nafría Aznar
Managing Director, BBVA Foundation: Rafael Pardo
Managing Director, Business Development:
Manuel Castro

Managing Director, Corporate Relations:
José Ignacio Wert
Managing Director, Human Resources and General Services: Ángel Cano Fernández
Managing Director, Innovation and Development:
Javier Bernal
Managing Director, Retail Banking, Spain and Portugal:
Julio López Gómez
Managing Director, Risk Management:
Manuel Méndez del Río
Managing Director, Systems and Operations:
Ignacio Sánchez-Asiaín Sanz
Managing Director, Wholesale and Investment Banking:
José María Abril Pérez
Director, Communications and Image: Javier Ayuso
Head of the Office of the Chairman: José Sevilla Álvarez
General Counsel: Eduardo Arbizu Lostao
Auditors: Deloitte SL

LOCATIONS

HQ: Banco Bilbao Vizcaya Argentaria, S.A.
Plaza San Nicolás, 4, 48005 Bilbao, Vizcaya, Spain
Phone: +34-944-875-555   **Fax:** +34-944-876-161
US HQ: 1345 Avenue of the Americas, 45th Fl.,
New York, NY 10105
US Phone: 212-728-1500   **US Fax:** 212-333-2906
Web: www.bbv.es

2004 Sales

	% of total
Europe	
Spain	53
Other	4
Latin America	40
US	1
Other regions	2
Total	**100**

PRODUCTS/OPERATIONS

2004 Sales

	$ mil.	% of total
Financial revenues	12,422.7	51
Fees collected	5,645.1	23
Fixed-income portfolio	4,496.6	19
Equities portfolio	955.1	4
Market operations	821.2	3
Other	24.8	—
Total	**24,365.5**	**100**

2004 Assets

	% of total
Cash & equivalents	3
Government debt securities	6
Due from credit institutions	5
Debentures & other debt securities	17
Other investments	4
Net loans	55
Other	10
Total	**100**

Selected Subsidiaries

Banco Bilbao Vizcaya Argentaria, Chile S.A. (Chile)
BBVA Banco Continental (Perú)
BBVA Banco Francés (Argentina)
BBVA Banco Ganadero (Columbia)
BBVA Banco Provincial (Venezuela)
BBVA Bancomer (México)
BBVA Panamá
BBVA Paraguay
BBVA Puerto Rico
BBVA Uruguay

COMPETITORS

ABN AMRO
Banamex
Banco Comercial Português
Banco de la Nación
Banco do Brasil
Banco Galicia
Banco Popular
Banco Río de la Plata
Banco Zaragozano
Bankinter
Banorte
Barclays
Credit Suisse
DEPFA BANK
Deutsche Bank
Espírito Santo
HSBC Holdings
JPMorgan Chase
SCH
Société Générale
Unibanco
Wells Fargo

HISTORICAL FINANCIALS

Company Type: Public

Income Statement

FYE: December 31

	ASSETS ($ mil.)	NET INCOME ($ mil.)	INCOME AS % OF ASSETS	EMPLOYEES
12/04	425,819	4,193	1.0%	84,117
12/03	361,005	2,799	0.8%	86,197
12/02	293,603	1,806	0.6%	93,093
12/01	275,631	2,106	0.8%	98,588
12/00	282,515	2,099	0.7%	108,082
12/99	240,023	1,759	0.7%	89,235
12/98	157,084	1,153	0.7%	69,999
12/97	138,616	1,181	0.9%	60,282
12/96	130,080	795	0.6%	44,064
12/95	115,123	690	0.6%	34,178
Annual Growth	**15.6%**	**22.2%**	**—**	**10.5%**

2004 Year-End Financials

Equity as % of assets: 7.5%
Return on assets: 1.1%
Return on equity: 16.5%
Long-term debt ($ mil.): 67,813
No. of shares (mil.): 3,391
Dividends
Yield: 2.8%
Payout: 39.2%
Market value ($ mil.): 60,154
Sales ($ mil.): 24,366

Stock History

NYSE: BBV

	12/95	12/96	12/97	12/98	12/99	12/00	12/01	12/02	12/03	12/04

	STOCK PRICE ($) FY Close	P/E High/Low		Earnings	Dividends	Book Value
12/04	17.74	14	10	1.25	0.49	9.37
12/03	13.85	16	8	0.88	0.38	5.93
12/02	9.71	23	12	0.57	0.27	5.09
12/01	12.45	25	13	0.66	0.31	5.06
12/00	14.69	23	17	0.69	0.39	5.24
12/99	14.19	27	18	0.64	0.27	4.27
12/98	16.00	38	16	0.56	0.07	3.24
12/97	10.76	19	10	0.58	0.00	2.68
12/96	5.92	15	10	0.39	0.17	2.78
12/95	3.96	12	8	0.34	0.11	2.64
Annual Growth	**18.1%**	**—**	**—**	**15.6%**	**18.1%**	**15.1%**

BCE Inc.

The ABCs for BCE are three Cs: content, connectivity, and commerce. Canada's biggest communications company, BCE owns Bell Canada, the provider of long-distance and local access in Ontario and Quebec that also owns stakes in local phone companies across the nation, and wireless carrier Bell Mobility. Other BCE services include Internet access, data and e-commerce services, and satellite communications. BCE owns 68% of Bell Globemedia, which includes broadcaster CTV, Internet portal Sympatico, and *The Globe and Mail* newspaper (it is reducing its stake to 20% pending regulatory approval of the unit's proposed new ownership structure). BCE has spun off its 64% stake in e-commerce firm BCE Emergis to shareholders.

BCE (for Bell Canada Enterprises) operates more than 13 million local access lines and provides wireless services to nearly 5 million customers. It also provides dial-up Internet access (nearly 1 million subscribers) and broadband Internet access (to 1.5 million), as well as direct-to-home satellite TV (1.4 million customers).

The company has sold its Bell Canada directories business to Kohlberg Kravis Roberts & Co. and a unit of the Ontario Teachers' Pension Plan. In the deal, valued at C$3 billion, BCE kept a 10% stake in the new company. BCE has used the proceeds from this sale to buy back the 16% of Bell Canada owned by Texas-based AT&T Inc. (formerly SBC Communications). It also bought the 40% of Bell West it did not own. Bell Canada has heard the call of the Web, too. Its Bell Nexxia unit operates an Internet protocol network that stretches across Canada.

Reaching for the sky, units Telesat and TMI Communications provide satellite services. Bell ExpressVu has more than 1.3 million direct-to-home satellite TV customers. BCE took full ownership of Internet portal Sympatico in 2002, acquiring the 29% formerly held by Lycos. Bell Canada and ExpressVu have teamed up with Microsoft to develop Internet protocol TV (IPTV).

The company's Ventures division handles investments in other telecom and media firms, including troubled Bell Canada International, which held interests in telecom and cable TV providers in Latin America.

A lack of demand for its broadband services forced BCE to reconsider the value of its Teleglobe unit. In 2002 BCE discontinued long-term funding for Teleglobe, which began working to restructure its debt under bankruptcy protection. As 2002 ended Teleglobe was sold to a unit of Ernst & Young, the court-appointed creditors' monitor. But in 2004 the company agreed to acquire the Canadian fiber network of 360networks, including its GT Group Telecom unit.

BCE also is dismantling 62%-owned Bell Canada International, which held interests in Latin American telecom companies. The Bell Canada unit, on the other hand, has agreed to buy back the shares in residential phone installation and repair services provider Entourage Technology Solutions. Bell Canada spun off the unit in 1996 and sold a 57% stake to private entrepreneur Adrien Pouliet. An Entourage workers' cooperative owns 10% and Bell Canada kept a 33% stake. The recent agreement allows Bell Canada to buy back the 57% stake from the Pouliet family and the company has plans to acquire the rest.

HISTORY

Alexander Graham Bell experimented with the telephone in his native Canada before moving to the US in the mid-1870s. His father sold his Canadian patent rights to National Bell Telephone (which became AT&T Corp.), which combined with Canada's Hamilton District Telegraph to form Bell Telephone Company of Canada. Known as Bell Canada, it received a charter in 1880 and settled in Montreal. By 1882 it had 40 exchanges. AT&T owned 48% of the company in 1890, but by 1925 Canadians owned 95% of Bell Canada. (AT&T severed all ties in 1975).

As telecommunications needs grew, the company began buying smaller exchanges (1954). It acquired a 90% stake in telecom equipment maker Northern Electric in 1957 and the rest in 1964. After Bell Canada reduced the stake in 1973, Northern became Northern Telecom in 1976 (now Nortel Networks). Bell Canada also invested in a satellite joint venture (Telesat, 1970) and formed Bell Canada International (BCI) to provide international telecom consulting (1976).

In 1983, responding to proposed legislation that would have calculated manufacturing profits in phone rate formulas, Bell created Bell Canada Enterprises (renamed BCE in 1988) as a holding company to separate unregulated businesses from phone carriers. BCE branched out with stakes in gas pipelines (1983) and real estate (1985) but dropped out of the ventures to focus on its core telecom business (1989). It began providing wireless phone service in 1985.

As deregulation rolled into Canada in the 1990s, Bell Canada had to maintain high long-distance rates to subsidize its regulated local service. In 1993 it was denied a rate increase and took a large loss. That year it bought stakes in cable operator Jones Intercable and the UK's Cable & Wireless (C&W). In 1994 regulators allowed local rate increases. The next year BCE announced 10,000 jobs cuts and began offering Internet access.

BCE took a loss in 1997, writing down assets in preparation for full competition. Also that year it floated part of BCI, following contracts for cellular systems in Brazil and India. BCE began staging a comeback in 1998 when it sold its shares in Jones Intercable and C&W. It made new investments, including 100% of Telesat Canada, a part of fONOROLA's fiber network, and more than 40% of computer consulting firm CGI Group. Insider Jean Monty (who had steered Nortel's turnaround) became CEO.

Through an alliance with MCI WorldCom (now WorldCom), the company gained access to a global network in 1999. Also that year Ameritech (now part of AT&T Inc., formerly SBC Communications) bought a 20% stake in Bell Canada, which snapped up the 35% of its wireless subsidiary that it didn't already own and a 20% stake in Manitoba Telecom Services (it sold its stake in MTS in 2004).

In 2000 Bell Canada spun off nearly all of its 40% Nortel stake to shareholders. That year it bought broadcaster CTV, and went on to buy global broadband services provider Teleglobe in a $5 billion stock deal. BCE combined its broadcasting and Internet portal assets with Thomson's *The Globe and Mail* newspaper to form a new company, Bell Globemedia, in 2001 (Thomson sold its stake in 2003).

EXECUTIVES

Chairman: Richard J. (Dick) Currie, age 67
President, CEO, and Director; CEO, Bell Canada: Michael J. Sabia, $590,863 pay
CFO: Siim A. Vanaselja
EVP and Chief Strategy Officer: Francis P. Crispino
EVP Communications and Marketing Services, BCE and Bell Canada: Peter Daniel
EVP Regulatory and Competitive Affairs: Lawson A.W. Hunter, age 60
EVP; Group President, Corporate Performance and National Markets, Bell Canada: Stephen G. Wetmore, age 52, $631,506 pay (prior to promotion)
SVP and Treasurer: Michael T. Boychuk, age 49
SVP Audit and Risk Management: Mahes S. Wickramasinghe
SVP; President, BCE Corporate Services Inc.: Alain Bilodeau
Group President, Operations, Bell Canada: David A. Southwell
Group President, Systems and Technology, Bell Canada: Eugene Roman
President and CEO, Bell Globemedia; CEO, CTV Inc.: Ivan Fecan, $754,698 pay
President and CEO, Telesat Canada: Laurier J. (Larry) Boisvert
CEO, Bell Mobility and Bell Distribution, Bell Canada: Robert Odendaal
Chief Legal Officer: Martine Turcotte
Auditors: Deloitte & Touche LLP

LOCATIONS

HQ: BCE Inc.
1000, rue de La Gauchetière Ouest, Ste. 3700, Montreal, Quebec H3B 4Y7, Canada
Phone: 514-870-8777　　　**Fax:** 514-870-4385
Web: www.bce.ca

PRODUCTS/OPERATIONS

2004 Sales

	$ mil.	% of total
Bell Canada		
Local & access	4,641	28
Data	3,032	19
Wireless	2,347	14
Long-distance	1,938	12
Video	708	4
Terminal sales & other	1,316	8
Bell Globemedia	1,183	7
CGI	849	5
Telesat	302	2
Other revenues	50	1
Adjustments	(371)	—
Total	**15,995**	**100**

Selected Subsidiaries and Affiliates

BCE Emergis (64%, e-commerce)

Bell Canada Holdings Inc.
　Aliant (54%, local phone service, Atlantic Canada)
　Bell Canada (telecommunications services)
　Bell Distribution Inc. (retail outlets)
　Bell ExpressVu L.P. (direct-to-home satellite TV)
　Bell Mobility Inc. (wireless phone and paging)
　Bell Nexxia Inc. (data services for businesses)
　Bell West Inc. (competitive local-exchange carrier)
　Nexxlink Technologies Inc. (IT services)
　NorthernTel L.P. (63%, local phone service, Ontario)
　Northwestel Inc. (local phone service, northwestern Canada)
　Sympatico Inc. (Internet portal)
　Télébec ltée (63%, local phone service, Quebec)

BCE Ventures
　Bell Canada International (BCI, 62%, telecom investments outside Canada)
　CGI Group Inc. (30%, IT services)
　Telesat Canada (satellite communications)

Bell Globemedia (68%, broadcast, print, and Internet)
　CTV Inc. (broadcast TV)
　The Globe and Mail (newspaper)

HISTORICAL FINANCIALS

Company Type: Public

Income Statement			FYE: December 31
	NET	NET	
REVENUE	INCOME	PROFIT	EMPLOYEES
($ mil.)	($ mil.)	MARGIN	
12/04	15,995	1,328	8.3%	61,739
12/03	14,793	1,409	9.5%	64,054
12/02	12,561	1,573	12.5%	66,266
12/01	13,639	329	2.4%	75,000
12/00	12,065	3,242	26.9%	56,608
12/99	9,825	3,773	38.4%	55,000
12/98	17,735	2,970	16.7%	58,000
12/97	23,217	(1,074)	—	122,000
12/96	20,554	841	4.1%	118,450
12/95	18,059	574	3.2%	121,000
Annual Growth	(1.3%)	9.8%	—	(7.2%)

2004 Year-End Financials

Debt ratio: 95.5%
Return on equity: 13.6%
Cash ($ mil.): 317
Current ratio: 0.68
Long-term debt ($ mil.): 9,842

No. of shares (mil.): 926
Dividends
Yield: 3.7%
Payout: 65.2%
Market value ($ mil.): 22,343

Stock History

NYSE: BCE

	STOCK PRICE ($)	P/E		PER SHARE ($)		
	FY Close	High/Low	Earnings	Dividends	Book Value
12/04	24.13	19	14	1.38	0.90	12.63
12/03	22.36	16	12	1.47	0.84	11.41
12/02	18.01	13	8	1.72	0.76	8.93
12/01	22.80	82	57	0.36	1.20	13.20
12/00	28.94	28	4	4.95	1.18	14.38
12/99	90.19	17	6	5.77	1.25	19.21
12/98	37.94	10	6	4.57	1.36	13.77
12/97	33.31	—	—	(1.77)	1.36	10.79
12/96	23.88	20	14	1.24	1.00	13.74
12/95	17.25	21	18	0.82	0.99	13.19
Annual Growth	3.8%	—	—	6.0%	(1.1%)	(0.5%)

Benetton Group

If Benetton had a theme song, it could be "We Are the World." Italy's largest clothing maker, The Benetton Group pushes a global attitude in its ads while dressing customers in 120 countries through more than 5,000 franchised Benetton stores, department stores, and megastores. Benetton's clothing — primarily casual knitwear and sportswear for men, women, and children — bears labels such as United Colors of Benetton and Sisley (nearly 20% of sales). Not content with selling sunglasses, watches, clothes, and shoes, Benetton once branched out into sporting goods, but withdrew to hone in on its clothing division. The Benetton family, through Edizione Holding, owns about 67% of Benetton.

The company's controversial ads, a mix of provocative images and political stances (bloody soldiers, death-row inmates, a priest and a nun kissing), have won a following as well as a fair share of critics. Benetton has since parted ways with the agency responsible for the shocking campaign.

The Italian apparel maker has teamed up with America's largest toymaker Mattel to launch a new line of clothing called "Barbie Loves Benetton." The Barbie-inspired brand appeared in stores in September 2005.

The group's multimedia enterprises fall under the Fabrica umbrella, which Benetton describes as a "communication research and development center," that the company founded in 2000. Fabrica produces films, funds avant-garde music projects, and publishes the magazine "Colors."

In early 2003, the company pared down its branches and returned to its fashion roots by selling off its Nordica and Rollerblade subsidiaries. Tennis racket and sportswear maker Prince was sold off soon thereafter.

Despite its global outlook, about 85% of Benetton Group's sales come from Europe, which is plagued by a sluggish economy. Consequently, Benetton is looking to foreign markets for growth, especially China and India. Benetton plans to open about 40 stores in China this year (including flagship stores in Beijing and Shenzhen), and would like to have as many as 200 stores there by 2008. The Italian retailer also recently formed a joint venture with Turkey's Boyner Group to boost sales in that country. Benetton is also focusing on attracting younger customers to its stores. To that end, the retailer has expanded its low-priced collections of denim, polo shirts, and sweatshirts.

HISTORY

Luciano Benetton began selling men's clothing while still in his teens in post-WWII Treviso, Italy. His younger, artistic sister, Giuliana, knitted colorful and striking sweaters for a small, local clientele. In 1955 the two pooled their skills. Giuliana sold Luciano's accordion and a younger brother's bicycle, raising enough money to purchase a knitting machine. Luciano then marketed her moderately priced sweaters.

Demand for their clothes grew, and the pair did so well that 10 years later they built a factory in Ponzano, near Treviso. Siblings Gilberto and bicycleless Carlo joined the business, and the first Benetton store opened in Belluno, in the Alps, in 1968. By 1975 Benetton had 200 stores in Italy and had set up headquarters in a 17th-century villa. In 1979 the company opened five stores in the US.

Through the early to mid-1980s, the company averaged one store opening a day; Benetton was the first Western retailer to enter Eastern Europe. The company's controversial advertising program began in 1984 with ads depicting such provocative images as then-president Ronald Reagan with AIDS lesions.

When it went public in 1986, Benetton had almost 600 stores in the US. That year it established a factory in the US. In the late 1980s Edizione Holding, the family's investment firm, also bought a hotel chain and ski equipment maker Nordica.

Benetton began losing US market share in the late 1980s. Competition from The Gap and The Limited hurt and overexpansion brought complaints from franchisees that the stores were cannibalizing each other's sales. (In New York City there were seven stores on Fifth Avenue alone.) In the early 1990s The Gap established stores in the already-mature European market, and Benetton began looking for new markets.

Edizione increased its investments in those years, acquiring 80% of Prince Manufacturing, a US maker of tennis equipment, and purchased a 50% interest in the TWR group, a racecar manufacturer. The company formed Benetton Legs in 1991 to produce and sell pantyhose in Europe.

In 1995 Benetton won its second lawsuit against German retailers who refused to pay for merchandise because they said sales had been hurt by the company's shock advertising. The next year it opened a United Colors of Benetton megastore on Fifth Avenue in New York City, the first to combine Edizione's clothing, sporting goods, and accessories under one roof.

Benetton bought Edizione's sports equipment and apparel collection, Benetton Sportsystem, and renamed the division Playlife in 1998. Benetton began selling the sporting goods through specialty sports stores and a new chain of Playlife megastores.

Trying to win back US consumers, Benetton in 1998 cut a deal to sell Benetton USA-brand clothing in Sears, Roebuck & Co. stores. In early 2000, however, Sears yanked the Italian goods from its store after customers complained about Benetton's anti-death penalty ad campaign. Soon after, Benetton and controversial ad man Oliviero Toscani parted ways. Benetton's ads are now produced by an ad agency Toscani founded.

In 2001 Benetton announced plans to recapture the US market share it once held by opening megastore formats (starting with three new stores in Manhattan). Later, Carlo Gilardi stepped down as joint managing director and Luigi de Puppi (former CEO of Electrolux Zanussi) was named his successor.

Just weeks before its 2003 shareholders meeting, the company announced that de Puppi would step down since his mandate to clear out of Benetton's ailing sports divisions was completed with sales of Rollerblade, Nordica, and Prince. In late 2003 Benetton reorganized its internal operations — production and logistics are handled by Benind, trademarks and commercial activities by Bencom, and IT services and systems by United Web (under the name Bentec).

In May 2005 Alessandro Benetton, son of Chairman Luciano Benetton, was named deputy chairman of the company's board, a title he now shares with his uncle Carlo.

EXECUTIVES

Chairman: Luciano Benetton, age 70
Deputy Chairman: Alessandro Benetton
Deputy Chairman: Carlo Benetton, age 61
Benneton Group Managing Director, and Director:
Silvano Cassano, age 48
Tax, Legal, and Corporate Affairs Officer; Secretary:
Pierluigi Bortolussi, age 57
COO: Biagio Chiarolanza, age 41
CFO: Pier Francesco Facchini
Chief Information Technology: Adolfo Pastorelli
Chief Commercial Officer: Fabrizio de Nardis
Benneton Group Marketing and Strategy Director:
Maximo Ibarra
Art Director, United Colors of Benetton: Joel Berg
Chairman and Editorial Director, Colors Magazine:
Kurt Andersen
CEO, Benetton India: Madhu Kumar
Director of Media and Corporate Communication:
Federico Sartor
Sales and Marketing Manager, North and Central
America: Paola Ugolini
Head of Investor Relations: Mara Di Giorgio
Senior Investor Relations: Barbara Ferrante
Junior Investor Relations: Giada De Mattia
Investor Relations: Silvia Cadamuro
IT Manager: Mike Wainwright
Human Resources Officer: Andrea Negrin
Auditors: PricewaterhouseCoopers SpA

LOCATIONS

HQ: Benetton Group S.p.A.
Villa Minelli, 31050 Ponzano Veneto, Treviso, Italy
Phone: +39-0422-519111   **Fax:** +39-0422-969501
US HQ: 597 5th Ave., 11th Fl., New York, NY 10017
US Phone: 212-593-0290   **US Fax:** 212-371-1438
Web: www.benetton.com

Benetton Group sells its products in more than
120 countries.

2004 Sales

	% of total
Europe	85
Asia	10
The Americas	4
Other regions	1
Total	**100**

PRODUCTS/OPERATIONS

2004 Sales

	% of total
Casual apparel	89
Manufacturing & other	6
Sportswear & equipment	5
Total	**100**

Selected Brands

Casual wear
Sisley (higher-fashion men's and women's clothing)
United Colors of Benetton

Sportswear
Killer Loop (snowboarding clothing)
Playlife (sporty leisure wear)

Selected Products

Baby products
Dresses
Handbags
Hats
Knitwear
Perfume
Shirts
Shoes
Socks
Sportswear
Sunglasses
Underwear
Watches

COMPETITORS

Abercrombie & Fitch	K2
adidas-Salomon	Lands' End
Aéropostale	Levi Strauss
Amer Sports	Limited Brands
American Eagle Outfitters	Liz Claiborne
AnnTaylor	Marks & Spencer
Burberry	Mossimo
C&A	Nautica Enterprises
Calvin Klein	NIKE
Columbia Sportswear	Polo Ralph Lauren
Cortefiel	Quiksilver
Esprit Holdings	Rossignol
French Connection	Swatch
Gap	Tommy Hilfiger
H&M	Variflex
Head-Tyrolia-Mares	Vendex
Inditex	Warnaco Group
J. Crew	Wet Seal

HISTORICAL FINANCIALS

Company Type: Public

Income Statement

FYE: December 31

	REVENUE ($ mil.)	NET INCOME ($ mil.)	NET PROFIT MARGIN	EMPLOYEES
12/04	2,284	167	7.3%	7,424
12/03	2,337	136	5.8%	6,949
12/02	2,092	(10)	—	7,162
12/01	1,870	132	7.1%	7,666
12/00	1,899	229	12.1%	6,672
12/99	1,996	168	8.4%	6,585
12/98	2,318	177	7.6%	7,235
12/97	2,055	164	8.0%	7,421
12/96	1,890	162	8.6%	5,973
12/95	1,866	139	7.4%	6,018
Annual Growth	**2.3%**	**2.0%**	**—**	**2.4%**

2004 Year-End Financials

Debt ratio: 45.5%
Return on equity: 10.6%
Cash ($ mil.): 353
Current ratio: 2.18
Long-term debt ($ mil.): 759
No. of shares (mil.): 91
Dividends
Yield: 3.5%
Payout: 50.5%
Market value ($ mil.): 2,429

Stock History

NYSE: BNG

	STOCK PRICE ($) FY Close	P/E High/Low		PER SHARE ($) Earnings	Dividends	Book Value
12/04	26.76	15	11	1.84	0.93	18.36
12/03	23.07	19	9	1.48	0.81	16.26
12/02	17.90	—	—	(0.11)	0.71	13.20
12/01	22.30	29	12	1.46	0.81	12.18
12/00	40.75	20	14	2.52	2.00	1.22
12/99	45.44	25	17	1.85	2.21	1.24
12/98	39.75	25	14	1.96	0.00	14.78
12/97	32.63	22	14	1.52	0.00	12.64
12/96	23.93	13	10	2.10	0.52	13.21
12/95	22.25	14	9	1.65	0.32	11.53
Annual Growth	**2.1%**	**—**	**—**	**1.2%**	**12.6%**	**5.3%**

Bertelsmann

Bertelsmann is so big, it needs space in the bookcase, CD rack, and magazine stand. One of the world's top media firms, Bertelsmann has publishing, music, and broadcasting operations in nearly 60 countries. It owns #1 trade book publisher Random House and 50% of #2 music company Sony BMG Music Entertainment. It also has a 75% stake in magazine publisher Gruner + Jahr, owns 90% of RTL Group, Europe's #1 over-the-air broadcaster, and owns media services firm arvato. In addition, Bertelsmann owns several book and music clubs, and online retail channels. Carl Bertelsmann founded the company in 1835. His descendants, the Mohn family, and company execs control the firm. Groupe Bruxelles Lambert owns a 25% stake.

Bruxelles bought its stake in the company in 2001 with the understanding that it would eventually float its interest to the public, bringing an end to Bertelsmann's longtime status as a private company. (The Mohns own 17% and the Bertelsmann Foundation owns 57%.) The company's plans for an IPO and a massive expansion onto the Internet were the brainchild of former CEO Thomas Middelhoff. In mid-2002 the board unexpectedly fired Middelhoff citing differences of opinion in the company's direction. He was replaced by arvato's chairman Gunter Thielen.

For a time, Thielen embarked on an e-commerce selloff at the company. The firm sold such assets as its 36% stake in barnesandnoble.com, among others. And instead of directly owning all or parts of retail Web sites, Bertelsmann has cut deals in which other companies operate the sites for the firm in exchange for a profit percentage (such as Amazon.com's takeover of CDNOW). But in 2005, Bertelsmann's BMG Direct subsidiary acquired mail order entertainment retailer Columbia House, largely to gain a foothold in the fast-growing DVD sales business.

Bertelsmann had agreed to buy defunct Internet music company Napster, which it wanted to use as a subscription music service. However, a bankruptcy court refused to approve the deal, which hammered the last nail in the original Napster's coffin. The music service has since reemerged with help from Roxio as a paid music site, but the damage had already been done and music publishers have brought suit against Bertelsmann on the grounds that its initial funding of the Internet company contributed to copyright violations.

But Bertelsmann has bigger fish to fry in the music world than Napster. It hopes to bring new life into the doldrums of the industry with the 2004 creation of Sony BMG Music Entertainment, a 50-50 joint venture with consumer electronics and media giant Sony. The new music company is now the world's second largest, behind Universal Music.

Bertelsmann sold BertelsmannSpringer, its science and trade publishing subsidiary, to UK investment firms Cinven Group and Candover Investments for an estimated $1.2 billion. Bertelsmann has earmarked about $2.4 billion for possible expansion in China, India, and Eastern Europe.

In addition, the company entered the book retailing industry with the 2005 purchase of France's Privat chain for $64 million.

HISTORY

Carl Bertelsmann founded his publishing company C. Bertelsmann Verlag in Gütersloh, Germany, in 1835. The company primarily published hymnals and religious materials, expanding into newspapers during the 1860s. Heinrich Mohn, a fourth-generation descendant, took over the company in 1921 and expanded its operations to include popular fiction, which helped Bertelsmann expand to more than 400 employees by 1939.

During WWII the company published books and propaganda material for the German army, but was closed by the Nazi government in 1944 as it was not considered important to the war effort. (The company had maintained for decades it was closed because it produced religious materials, but contrary evidence was uncovered in 2000 by historians working at the behest of the company.) After WWII Mohn's son, Reinhard (who had been captured by the Allies and interned in a Kansas POW camp), returned to Germany determined to rebuild the company.

Bertelsmann boosted book sales by launching book clubs in Germany during the 1950s and bought Germany's UFA (TV and film production) in 1964. It took a minority interest in publisher Gruner + Jahr in 1969, taking a controlling stake in 1973. In the US, Bertelsmann bought 51% of Bantam Books in 1977 (and the rest in 1981) and Arista Records in 1979. In 1986 it took control of Doubleday Publishing and bought RCA Records (forming Bertelsmann Music Group the next year). Mohn transferred substantial non-voting shares in the company to the Bertelsmann Foundation in 1993.

The company teamed up with America Online in 1995 to form AOL Europe, and with Luxembourg broadcaster CLT it launched CLT-Ufa in 1997. Bertelsmann acquired book publisher Random House the next year. The company also took a 50% stake in online bookseller barnesandnoble.com (retaining nearly 40% after an IPO in 1999). In addition, Thomas Middelhoff became chairman and CEO in 1998. The next year Bertelsmann acquired some 85% of scientific publisher Springer Verlag. Also in 1999 Reinhard Mohn transferred his controlling shares in the company to Bertelsmann Verwaltungsgesellschaft, a firm controlled by Bertelsmann executives and the Mohn family.

In 2000 Bertelsmann announced that it would sell its half-interest in AOL Europe back to AOL (now part of Time Warner) by mid-2002. It later merged CLT-Ufa with Pearson TV to form RTL Group. (Bertelsmann got a 37% stake.) That year Bertelsmann bought online music retailer CDnow. Late in 2000 the company formed an alliance with online music service Napster, loaning the company start-up cash and allowing it to use the BMG music catalog to develop a subscription-based service.

Bertelsmann bought Groupe Bruxelles Lambert's 30% stake in RTL Group in 2001. As part of the deal Bruxelles gained a 25% stake in Bertelsmann with the understanding that it would be able to float its interest to the public in four years. Also that year, it bought Pearson's 22% stake in RTL Group.

The company's board fired Middelhoff in 2002 citing disagreements over the direction of the company. He was replaced by Gunter Thielen, chairman of Bertelsmann's arvato business unit.

In 2004, Bertelsmann combined BMG with Sony Music to create Sony BMG Music Entertainment, a joint venture with Sony that is now the world's #2 music company.

EXECUTIVES

Honorary Chairman; Founder, Bertelsmann Foundation: Reinhard Mohn, age 84
Chairman and CEO: Gunter Thielen, age 63
Deputy Chairman and CFO; Chairman, RTL Group: Siegfried Luther, age 61
CFO: Thomas Rabe, age 39
Chief Creative Officer; Chairman, Sony BMG Music Entertainment: Rolf Schmidt-Holtz, age 57
EVP Corporate Communications: Jasmine Borhan, age 41
SVP Media Relations and Chief Press Officer: Oliver Herrgesell, age 43
Auditing: Klaus-Peter Blobel
Corporate Center New York: Rob Sorrentino
Human Resources: Detlef Hunsdiek
Legal Department: Urlich Koch
Media Technology: Johannes Mohn, age 55
Treasury and Finance: Verena Volport
Chairman, BMG Music Publishing: Nicholas Firth
Chairman, arvato: Harmut Ostrowski, age 47
Vice Chairman, RTL Group: Martin Taylor
Chairman, President, and CEO, Gruner + Jahr: Bernd Kundrun, age 48
Chairman and CEO, Sony BMG Music North America: Clive Davis, age 72
Chairman and CEO, Random House: Peter W. Olson, age 55
CEO, DirectGroup Bertelsmann: Ewald Walgenbach, age 46
CEO, RTL Group: Gerhard Zeiler, age 50
CEO, Sony BMG Music Entertainment: Andrew R. (Andy) Lack, age 58
Auditors: KPMG Deutsche Treuhand-Gesellschaft AG

LOCATIONS

HQ: Bertelsmann AG
Carl-Bertelsmann-Strasse 270,
D-33311 Gütersloh, Germany
Phone: +49-5241-80-0   **Fax:** +49-5241-80-9662
US HQ: 1540 Broadway #24, New York, NY 10036-4098
US Phone: 212-782-1000   **US Fax:** 212-782-7600
Web: www.bertelsmann.de

Bertelsmann has operations in nearly 60 countries.

2004 Sales

	$ mil.	% of total
Europe		
Germany	6,962.9	30
Other countries	9,748.2	42
US	5,106.2	22
Other regions	1,392.5	6
Total	**23,209.8**	**100**

PRODUCTS/OPERATIONS

2004 Sales

	$ mil.	% of total
RTL Group	6,655.5	28
arvato	5,124.6	22
BMG	3,475.1	14
Gruner + Jahr	3,327.7	14
DirectGroup	2,967.5	12
Random House	2,451.8	10
Adjustments	(792.4)	—
Total	**23,209.8**	**100**

Selected Operations

arvato (media services)
  AZ Direct (direct marketing)
  Bertelsmann Financial Group
    (credit reports and risk management)
  empolis (content management)
  handy.de (wireless services)
  TJ-Net (wireless services)

DirectGroup Bertelsmann
  (book and music clubs, e-commerce)
  Media Communities
    Bertelsmann Book Club (China)
    The Bookclub (Korea)
    Bookspan (50%US)
    Circulo de Lectores (Spain)
    Der Club (Denmark)
    ECI (The Netherlands)
    France Loisirs
    Québec Loisirs (Canada)
  Online Shops
    BMG Direct
    Book of the Month Club
Gruner + Jahr (75%, magazine and newspaper publishing)
  Magazines
    Brigitte
    Capital
    Eltern
    Geo
    Fast Company
    Inc.
    Muy Interesante
    Stern
  Newspapers
    Blic
    Evenimentul Zilei
    Financial Times Deutschland
    Novy Cas
    Sächsische Zeitung
Random House (book publishing)
  Alfred A. Knopf
  C. Bertelsmann
  Doubleday
  Fodors
  Pantheon
RTL Group (90%, broadcasting)
  Internet
    M6 Web (48.4%, France)
    RTL iMedia (The Netherlands)
    RTL NEWMEDIA (Germany)
    RTL NET (France)
  Radio
    104.6 RTL (Germany)
    Antenne Bayern (16%, Germany)
    Bel RTL (43%, Belgium)
    Fun Radio (France)
    HITRADIO RTL (48.9%, Germany)
    Radio 21 (17%, Germany)
    Radio Contact (35%, Belgium)
    Radio Hamburg (29.2%, Germany)
    RTL (France)
    RTL2 (France)
    RTL RADIO Lëtzebuerg (Luxembourg)
    Radio NRW (17%, Germany)
    Sud Radio (20%, France)
    WIT FM (20%, France)
    Yorin FM (The Netherlands)
  Television
    Antena 3 (17%, Spain)
    Bel RTL (43%, Belgium)
    Blu (television production
      and distribution, Denmark)
    Club RTL (66%, Belgium)
    Channel 5 (UK)
    FreemantleMedia (television
      production and distribution)
    Grundy Productions France
      (television production and distribution)
    M6 (48.4%, France)
    Plug TV (66%, Belgium)
    REN TV (30%, Russia)
    RTL 4 (The Netherlands)
    RTL 5 (The Netherlands)
    RTL 9 (35%, France)
    RTL Klub (49%, Hungary)
    RTL SHOP (Germany)
    RTL Télé Lëtzbuerg (Luxembourg)
    RTL Television (Germany)
    RTL Televizija (65.5%, Croatia)
    SUPER RTL (50%, Germany)
    TVI (11%, Portugal)
    VOX (99.7%, Germany)
    Yorin (The Netherlands)

Sony BMG Music Entertainment (50%, music
  publishing)
  Ariola (record label)
  Arista (record label)
  BMG Classics (record label)
  BMG Music Publishing
  BMG Online
  Columbia Records (record label)
  Epic Records (record label)
  Private Music (record label)
  RCA Music Group (record label)
    Arista Records (record label)
  Sony Music International (record label)
  Sony Music Nashville (record label)
  Windham Hill (record label)
  Zomba Label Group (record label)

COMPETITORS

Advance Publications
Amazon.com
Axel Springer
Columbia House
Disney
Editis
Hachette Filipacchi Médias
Hearst
IWCO Direct
Lagardère
McGraw-Hill
News Corp.
Pearson
PRIMEDIA
Reed Elsevier Group
Schibsted
Sony
Time Warner
Universal Music Group
Verlagsgruppe Georg von Holtzbrinck
Viacom
Virgin Group
VNU
Wolters Kluwer

HISTORICAL FINANCIALS

Company Type: Private

Income Statement

FYE: December 31

	REVENUE ($ mil.)	NET INCOME ($ mil.)	NET PROFIT MARGIN	EMPLOYEES
12/04	23,210	1,408	6.1%	76,266
12/03	21,089	193	0.9%	73,221
12/02*	19,193	973	5.1%	80,632
6/01	17,011	824	4.8%	82,162
6/00	15,785	641	4.1%	76,257
6/99	13,721	480	3.5%	64,937
6/98	12,700	621	4.9%	57,807
6/97	12,860	585	4.5%	57,173
6/96	14,126	594	4.2%	57,996
6/95	14,889	592	4.0%	57,397
Annual Growth	5.1%	10.1%	—	3.2%

*Fiscal year change

2004 Year-End Financials

Debt ratio: 25.0%
Return on equity: 15.1%
Cash ($ mil.): 2,853
Current ratio: 1.68
Long-term debt ($ mil.): 2,564

Net Income History

BHP Billiton

Two heads — or headquarters — are better than one. Aussie mining and oil company BHP Limited acquired UK miner Billiton plc in 2001. The result is a dual-listed company with two head-quarters that is run as a single entity with the same board of directors and management. The Melbourne-based operation is BHP Billiton Limited; the London-based side is BHP Billiton Plc; collectively they're known as BHP Billiton.

The company ranks among the world's top producers of iron ore and coal (thermal and metallurgical) and is a major producer of petroleum products such as crude oil and natural gas. Other units produce aluminum, base metals, diamonds, manganese, and stainless steel. BHP Billiton has operations on six continents.

BHP Billiton is experiencing eyebrow-raising growth thanks in part to high commodity prices and the emerging Asian economies. China, for example, represented 10% and 12% of the company's sales in 2004 and 2005, respectively. Due to the strong demand, BHP Billiton is increasing production of iron ore, coking coal, and manganese over the next year. On the petroleum side, the company is continuing to acquire oil and gas exploration leases in the Gulf of Mexico.

With Anglo American, BHP Billiton had a South African joint venture called Samancor. In early-2005 the two companies sold Samancor's chrome mining and manufacturing business to the Kermas Group for $469 million.

In mid-2005 BHP Billiton acquired 100% of the shares in metals and minerals company WMC Resources, which had been the subject of much takeover speculation and the target of the Swiss mining heavyweight Xstrata. BHP Billiton opened talks with WMC's board and made an offer for the Australian company in early 2005. Its offer of $7.3 billion surpassed Xstrata's and was accepted and endorsed by the WMC board, which had turned down the two earlier proposals by Xstrata. The addition of WMC added significantly to BHP Billiton's copper, nickel, and uranium operations.

HISTORY

In 1883 Charles Rasp, a boundary rider for the Mount Gipps sheep station, believed valuable ore lay in the Broken Hill outcrop in New South Wales, Australia. He gathered a few young speculators, and The Broken Hill Proprietary Company (BHP) was incorporated in 1885. BHP immediately found a massive lode of silver, lead, and zinc. None of the founders knew how to run a mine, so they recruited US engineers William Patton and Herman Schlapp. From the beginning, labor and management clashed. The founding directors set up the head office in Melbourne, far from the mine, and gambled with gold sovereigns in the boardroom. But the miners worked in dangerous conditions. An 1892 labor strike was the first of BHP's bitter strikes.

In 1902 the new general manager, Guillaume Delprat, invented a flotation process that recovered valuable metals from iron ore waste. Delprat also foresaw a future in steel, although Australia had no steel industry. BHP commissioned the Newcastle steelworks in 1915 and soon became the country's largest steel producer. BHP's 1935 purchase of Australian Iron and Steel, its only competitor, gave it a virtual steel monopoly, while high tariffs protected it from outside competition. Its exhausted Broken Hill mine was closed that year.

In the 1960s BHP got into oil when it partnered with Esso Standard, the Australian subsidiary of Standard Oil of New Jersey, for offshore exploration. In 1967 the partners found oil in the Bass Strait, which soon supplied 70% of Australia's petroleum. In the 1960s and 1970s, BHP began expanding its iron ore, manganese, and coal interests. Meanwhile, public opposition mounted to BHP's market power and labor practices, and in 1972 the government took steps to limit BHP's power, removing some subsidies and tax breaks.

The weak steel market of the 1970s and 1980s caused BHP to lay off almost a third of its steelworkers in 1983, but with government intervention, BHP radically improved its steel productivity. In 1984 BHP bought Utah International's mining assets from General Electric (including Chile's rich Escondida copper mine). In 1986 corporate raider Robert Holmes à Court took a run at BHP; BHP decided to become an international mining company to prevent further raids. Its acquisitions in the late 1980s included ERG Inc. and Monsanto Oil (combined into BHP Americas), Aquila Steel, and Pacific Refining in Hawaii.

A peace deal with Holmes à Court gave BHP about 37% of Foster's Brewing, but in 1992 BHP took a $700 million write-down after Foster's stock declined. BHP also bought Arizona-based Magma Copper in 1996, but plunging world copper prices forced a $420 million write-down.

With new worries over Asia's economic troubles, BHP soon was struggling. In 1997 BHP sold most of its stake in Foster's, and three senior executives resigned. In 1998 the company unloaded Pacific Refining, which was acquired by Tesoro Petroleum for about $275 million.

As BHP's woes continued, CEO John Prescott resigned; Paul Anderson was recruited from Duke Energy to succeed Prescott. In 1999 D. R. Argus took over as chairman, replacing Jeremy Ellis. In a restructuring move, the company sold its engineering, power, insurance and information technology businesses in 1999 and 2000. BHP began to sell $2 billion worth of steel operations (including its long product unit, OneSteel). In 2000 the company shortened its official name to BHP Limited.

BHP acquired Billiton in 2001, forming BHP Billiton Ltd. and BHP Billiton plc. The combined BHP Billiton had sales of almost $20 billion and a market capitalization approaching $30 billion. In addition, BHP paid $436 million for Dia Met Minerals, which owned 29% of Canada's only producing diamond mine, Ekati.

Also in 2001 BHP Billiton and Alcoa combined their North American metals distribution businesses as joint venture Integris Metals. In order to focus on its minerals and oil and gas operations, in 2002 BHP Billiton spun off its steel business as BHP Steel. After a revolving door of CEOs during the past five years, BHP named Charles Goodyear to the position after the ouster of Brian Gilbertson in early 2003.

EXECUTIVES

Chairman: Don R. Argus, age 67
Chief Executive and Director:
  Charles W. (Chip) Goodyear, age 47, $3,241,196 pay
Executive President and Director:
  Miklos (Mike) Salamon, age 50
Special Advisor and Head of Group Secretariat:
  Karen J. Wood, age 48
CFO and Director: Christopher J. (Chris) Lynch, age 52

Chief Human Capital and Excellence Officer:
Marcus P. Randolph, age 49
Group President, Non-Ferrous Businesses and Director: Marius Kloppers, age 43
Group President, Carbon Steel Materials:
Robert W. (Bob) Kirkby, age 58, $1,327,231 pay
Group President, Energy: Philip S. (Phil) Aiken, age 56, $1,525,143 pay
President, Marketing: Tom Schutte, age 40
VP, Investor and Media Relations (South Africa):
Michael Campbell
VP, Investor Relations and Communications (UK and US): Mark Lidiard
Project Director, Business Excellence and Corporate Alignment: Greg Robinson, age 43
Chief Legal Counsel and Head of External Affairs:
John Fast, age 56, $1,230,670 pay
COO, Aluminum, Southern Africa: Xolani Mkhwanazi, age 50
President and COO, Western Australia Iron Ore:
Ian Ashby
Auditors: KPMG Audit Plc

LOCATIONS

HQ: BHP Billiton
180 Lonsdale St., Melbourne 3000, Australia
Phone: +61-1300-55-4757   **Fax:** +61-3-9609-3015
US HQ: 1360 Post Oak Blvd., Ste. 150,
Houston, TX 77056-3020
US Phone: 713-961-8500   **US Fax:** 713-961-8400
Web: www.bhpbilliton.com

BHP Billiton primarily has production operations in Africa, Australia, and South America. It maintains corporate offices in Houston, Johannesburg, London, Melbourne, and Santiago.

2005 Sales

	$ mil.	% of total
Asia		
China	3,628	12
Japan	3,620	12
South Korea	1,876	6
Other countries	2,100	7
Europe	9,825	33
Australia	2,637	9
North America	2,092	7
Southern Africa	1,584	6
Other	2,225	8
Total	**29,587**	**100**

PRODUCTS/OPERATIONS

2005 Sales

	$ mil.	% of total
Carbon steel materials	7,606	24
Petroleum	5,970	19
Aluminum	5,265	17
Base metals	5,071	16
Energy coal	3,390	11
Stainless steel materials	2,274	7
Diamonds & specialty products	1,544	5
Other	798	3
Adjustments	(2,331)	—
Total	**29,587**	**100**

Selected Divisions
Carbon steel materials
  Iron ore
  Manganese
  Metallurgical coal
Petroleum
  Crude oil
  Ethane
  LPG
  Natural gas
Aluminum
  Alumina
  Aluminum

Base metals
  Cathode
  Copper
  Gold
  Lead
  Silver
  Zinc
Energy coal
Stainless steel materials
  Cobalt
  Ferrochrome
  Nickel
Diamonds and specialty products
  Diamonds
  Integris metals

COMPETITORS

Alcan
Alcoa
Anglo American
BP
Chevron
Codelco
ConocoPhillips
Corus Group
Exxon Mobil
Falconbridge
Freeport-McMoRan
Inco Limited
Koch
Marathon Oil
Newmont Mining
Nippon Steel
Norsk Hydro
Ormet
Phelps Dodge
Placer Dome
Rio Tinto
Royal Dutch/Shell Group
ThyssenKrupp
TOTAL
Xstrata

HISTORICAL FINANCIALS

Company Type: Public

Income Statement

FYE: June 30

	REVENUE ($ mil.)	NET INCOME ($ mil.)	NET PROFIT MARGIN	EMPLOYEES
6/05	29,587	6,398	21.6%	36,468
6/04	22,887	3,403	14.9%	35,070
6/03	15,608	1,900	12.2%	34,801
6/02	15,896	1,648	10.4%	50,224
6/01	10,558	1,024	9.7%	58,953
6/00*	12,841	971	7.6%	69,491
5/99	12,553	(1,509)	—	50,000
5/98	13,264	(923)	—	55,000
5/97	15,983	313	2.0%	61,000
5/96	15,271	835	5.5%	60,000
Annual Growth	**7.6%**	**25.4%**	**—**	**(5.4%)**

*Fiscal year change

2005 Year-End Financials

Debt ratio: 46.8%
Return on equity: 39.7%
Cash ($ mil.): 916
Current ratio: 1.10
Long-term debt ($ mil.): 8,024
No. of shares (mil.): 3,028
Dividends
  Yield: 1.7%
  Payout: 22.1%
Market value ($ mil.): 82,666

Stock History   NYSE: BHP

	STOCK PRICE ($) FY Close	P/E High/Low		Earnings	Dividends	Book Value
6/05	27.30	15	8	2.08	0.46	5.66
6/04	17.52	19	10	1.09	0.48	4.84
6/03	11.59	20	14	0.62	0.27	4.11
6/02	11.80	24	14	0.55	0.26	4.24
6/01	10.53	20	15	0.59	0.26	3.03
6/00*	11.50	27	17	0.52	0.31	3.34
5/99	10.04	—	—	(0.84)	0.30	3.13
5/98	8.32	—	—	(0.53)	0.17	4.12
5/97	13.98	86	70	0.17	0.39	5.61
5/96	14.61	31	24	0.50	0.18	5.82
Annual Growth	**7.2%**	**—**	**—**	**17.2%**	**11.0%**	**(0.3%)**

*Fiscal year change

BMW

Bayerische Motoren Werke (better known as BMW) is one of Europe's top automakers. BMW models include the 1 Series, the 3 Series (coupe, sedan, convertible, and compact) 5 Series (sedan and touring), 6 Series (coupe and convertible), and 7 Series sedan. Other models include the M3 coupe and convertible; the X3 and X5 sport utilities; and the Z4 roadster. In addition to its BMW automobiles, the company's operations include motorcycles (K 1200 GT, R 1200 CL, and R 1150 R models, among others), the MINI automotive brand, Rolls-Royce Motor Cars, and software (softlab GmbH). BMW's motorcycle division also offers a line of motorcycling apparel such as leather suits, gloves, and boots.

While its North American counterparts are struggling BMW is thriving. 2004 marked a record year for BMW, despite less-than-ideal global economic conditions (high raw materials costs — namely oil). The company managed to increase car sales, revenue, and earnings. The only low point in BMW's product mix was the soft market for motorcycles, but bikes only account for about 3% of the company's total sales.

BMW has opened up a joint-venture in China (with local partner Brilliance China Automotive Holdings Ltd.) for production of BMWs for that market. The company is also looking out for opportunities in Eastern Europe as nations there join the European Union.

Germany's Quandt family controls BMW.

HISTORY

BMW's logo speaks to its origin: a propeller in blue and white, the colors of Bavaria. In 1913 Karl Rapp opened an aircraft-engine design shop near Munich. He named it Bayerische Motoren Werke (BMW) in 1917. The end of WWI brought German aircraft production to a halt, and BMW shifted to making railway brakes until the 1930s. BMW debuted its first motorcycle, the R32, in

1923, and the company began making automobiles in 1928 after buying small-car company Fahrzeugwerke Eisenach.

In 1933 BMW launched a line of larger cars. The company built aircraft engines for Hitler's Luftwaffe in the 1930s and stopped all auto and motorcycle production in 1941. BMW chief Josef Popp resisted and was ousted. Under the Nazis, the company operated in occupied countries, built rockets, and developed the world's first production jet engine.

With its factories dismantled after WWII, BMW survived by making kitchen and garden equipment. In 1948 it introduced a one-cylinder motorcycle, which sold well as cheap transportation in postwar Germany. BMW autos in the 1950s were large and expensive and sold poorly. When motorcycle sales dropped, the company escaped demise in the mid-1950s by launching the Isetta, a seven-foot, three-wheeled "bubble car."

Herbert Quandt saved the enterprise in 1959 by buying control for $1 million. Quandt's BMW focused on sports sedans and released the first of the "New Range" of BMWs in 1961. Success of the niche enabled BMW to buy automaker Hans Glas in 1966.

In the 1970s BMW's European exports soared, and the company set up a distribution subsidiary in the US. The company also produced larger cars that put BMW on par with Mercedes-Benz.

Rapid export growth in the US, Asia, and Australia continued in the 1980s, but Japanese bikes and poor demand hurt motorcycle sales. The launch of the company's luxury vehicles in 1986 heated up the BMW-Mercedes rivalry. US sales peaked that year and fell 45% by 1991. However, in 1992 BMW outsold Mercedes in Europe for the first time and became the first European carmaker to operate a US plant since Volkswagen pulled out in 1988.

BMW teamed with the UK's Rolls-Royce aerospace firm in 1990 to make jet engines for planes that included executive business-travel jets such as the Gulfstream V.

The company bought UK carmaker Rover from British Aerospace and Honda in 1994 and introduced a cheaper vehicle, the four-wheel-drive Discovery. It launched Highlander Land Rover in 1996 to meet a growing demand for 4x4 utility vehicles.

BMW offered to buy the luxury Rolls-Royce auto unit (including the Bentley) from UK-based Vickers in 1998, but lost out when Volkswagen (VW) countered with a higher offer. The company fared better, however, when aircraft engine maker Rolls-Royce sold the Rolls brand name and logo to BMW for $66 million. (VW got to use the name until 2003.) Also in 1998 BMW was hit by a class-action lawsuit brought by Holocaust survivors seeking compensation for their work as slave laborers during WWII.

In mid-1998 BMW began cutting jobs at its money-losing Rover unit. As Rover's plants continued their downward trend in 1999, BMW's board forced out chairman Bernd Pischetsrieder, who spearheaded the Rover acquisition in 1994. The UK later pledged to help pay for renovations at Rover's Longbridge plant to save about 14,000 jobs and prevent it from moving operations to Hungary.

The company in 2000 sold its Land Rover SUV operations to Ford in a deal worth about $2.7 billion. Also that year BMW handed over its Rover Cars operations and MG brand to the Phoenix Consortium, a UK-based group led by former Rover CEO John Towers, for a lesser sum — about $15.

In 2001 BMW launched its MINI brand in the UK; other European markets soon followed. BMW brought the MINI Cooper to US shores in 2002. The following year BMW took control of the Rolls-Royce brand from Volkswagen, and began making Rolls-Royce Phantoms in Goodwood in the south of England.

EXECUTIVES

Chairman, Supervisory Board: Joachim Milberg, age 62
Chairman of the Board of Management: Helmut Panke, age 59
Member, Management Board, Finance: Stefan Krause
Member, Management Board, Development: Burkhard Göschel
Member, Management Board, Human Resources and Industrial Relations Director: Ernst Baumann
Member, Management Board, Production: Norbert Reithofer
Member, Management Board, Sales and Marketing: Michael Ganal
General Counsel: Dieter Löchelt
VP, Brand Management, MINI: Kay Segler
VP, Central Marketing and Brand Management, BMW: Torsten Müller-Oetvoes
Chairman and CEO, BMW Financial Services: John Christman
Regional Director, Asia Pacific, Africa, and Eastern Europe: Klaus Berning
Regional Director, Europe: David Barry Panton
Regional Director, Germany: Ludwig Willisch
Regional Director, USA; Chairman and CEO, BMW of North America: Tom Purves
Director of Design: Chris Bangle
Regional Director, China: Christoph Stark
Auditors: KPMG Deutsche Treuhand-Gesellschaft AG

LOCATIONS

HQ: Bayerische Motoren Werke AG
Petuelring 130, D-80788 Munich, Germany
Phone: +49-89-382-0   **Fax:** +49-89-382-2-44-18
US HQ: 300 Chestnut Ridge Rd.,
Woodcliff Lake, NJ 07677
US Phone: 201-307-4000   **US Fax:** 201-307-4095
Web: www.bmw.com

The BMW Group operates globally, with 23 production and assembly plants in seven countries.

2004 Sales

	$ mil.	% of total
Europe		
Germany	16,315	27
Other countries	21,583	36
The Americas	14,524	24
Africa, Asia & Oceania	8,051	13
Total	**60,473**	**100**

PRODUCTS/OPERATIONS

2004 Sales

	$ mil.	% of total
Automobiles	49,648	82
Financial services	9,315	15
Motorcycles	1,394	3
Adjustments	116	—
Total	**60,473**	**100**

Selected Products

Automobiles
  BMW models
    1 Series
    3 Series Convertible
    3 Series Coupe
    3 Series Sedan
    3 Series Touring
    5 Series Sedan
    5 Series Touring
    6 Series Convertible
    6 Series Coupe
    7 Series
    M Models
    X3 Models
    X5 Models
    Z4 Models

MINI
  MINI Cooper
  MINI Cooper Convertible
  MINI Cooper S
  MINI Cooper S Convertible
  MINI One
  MINI One Convertible
  MINI One D
Rolls-Royce
  Phantom
Motorcycles
  Cruiser
    R 1200 C Classic
    R 1200 C Independent
    R 1200 CL
    R 1200 Montauk
  Enduro
    F 650 GS
    F 650 Dakar
    R 1150 GS Adventure
    R 1200 GS
  Roadster
    F 650 CS
    K 1200 R
    R 850 R
    R 850 R Comfort
    R 1150 R
    R 1150 R Rockster
  Sports Bikes
    K 1200 S
  Sports Tourer
    K 1200 RS
    R 1100 S
    R 1200 ST
  Tourer and Luxury Tourer
    K 1200 GT
    K 1200 RT
    R 1200 LT

COMPETITORS

DaimlerChrysler
Ducati
Fiat
Ford
General Motors
Harley-Davidson
Honda
Kawasaki Heavy Industries
Mazda
Nissan
Peugeot Motors of America, Inc.
Renault
Saab Automobile
Suzuki Motor
Toyota
Ultra Motorcycle
Volkswagen
Yamaha

HISTORICAL FINANCIALS

Company Type: Public

Income Statement

FYE: December 31

	REVENUE ($ mil.)	NET INCOME ($ mil.)	NET PROFIT MARGIN	EMPLOYEES
12/04	60,473	3,031	5.0%	105,972
12/03	52,122	2,444	4.7%	104,342
12/02	44,316	2,117	4.8%	101,395
12/01	34,071	1,653	4.9%	97,275
12/00	33,291	966	2.9%	93,624
12/99	34,643	(2,504)	—	114,874
12/98	37,666	539	1.4%	115,927
12/97	33,556	695	2.1%	109,600
12/96	33,648	523	1.6%	116,112
12/95	32,094	478	1.5%	115,763
Annual Growth	**7.3%**	**22.8%**	**—**	**(1.0%)**

2004 Year-End Financials

Debt ratio: 88.6%   Current ratio: 2.17
Return on equity: 13.7%   Long-term debt ($ mil.): 21,171
Cash ($ mil.): 5,401

4,000	
3,000	
2,000	
1,000	
0	
-1,000	
-2,000	
-3,000	

12/95 12/96 12/97 12/98 12/99 12/00 12/01 12/02 12/03 12/04

BNP Paribas

No Napoleon complex here. One of Europe's largest banks, BNP Paribas operates some 2,200 retail branches in France and has operations in more than 85 other countries. The company and its many subsidiaries specialize in corporate, retail, and investment banking. Other activities include private banking, real estate financing (through its UCB subsidiary), private equity (BNP Capital), wealth and asset management (Cardif and BNP Paribas Asset Management), and insurance (Natio, a joint venture with AXA). BNP Paribas also controls consumer lender Cetelem, online brokerage CortalConsors, merchant bank Cobepa, and property management firm Klépierre.

The company is focused on growing its international retail banking operations, particularly in the US, where it owns BancWest (the parent of Bank of the West and First Hawaiian Bank). It expanded there with its purchases of Community First Bankshares in 2004 and Commercial Federal Corporation in 2005.

HISTORY

BNP Paribas Group's predecessor Banque Nationale de Paris (BNP) is the progeny of two state banks with parallel histories; each was set up to jump-start the economy after a revolution in 1848.

For a century, Paris-based Comptoir National d'Escompte de Paris (CNEP) bounced between private and public status, depending on government whim. It was the #3 bank in France from the late 19th century through the 1950s.

Banque National pour le Commerce et l'Industrie (BNCI) started in Alsace, a region that was part of Germany from the Franco-Prussian War until WWI. BNCI served as an economic bridge between Germany and France, which had to give the bank governmental resuscitation during the Depression. By the 1960s BNCI had passed CNEP in size.

French leader Charles de Gaulle expected banking to drive post-WWII reconstruction, and in 1945 CNEP and BNCI were nationalized. In 1966 France's finance minister merged them and they became BNP. That year the company started an association with Dresdner Bank of Germany, under which the two still operate joint ventures, primarily in Eastern Europe.

By 1993 privatization was again in vogue, and BNP was cut loose by the government. It expanded outside France to ameliorate the influences of the French economy and government. Even before it was privatized, BNP was involved in such politically charged actions as the bailout of OPEC money repository Banque Arabe and the extension of credit to Algeria's state oil company Sonatrach.

The privatized BNP looked overseas in the late 1990s. In 1997 alone, it won the right to operate in New Zealand, bought Laurentian Bank and Trust of the Bahamas, took control of its joint venture with Egypt's Banque du Caire, and opened a subsidiary in Brazil.

BNP bought failed Peregrine Investment's Chinese operations in 1998. That year the bank also expanded in Peru, opened an office in Algeria, opened a representative office in Uzbekistan, set up an investment banking subsidiary in India, and bought Australian stock brokerage operations from Prudential.

After a decade of globe-trotting, BNP brought it on home in 1999 and set off a year of tumult in French banking. As France's other two large banks (Société Générale and Paribas) made plans to merge, BNP decided it would absorb both banks as a means to get a bigger chunk of the to-be-privatized Crédit Lyonnais and to protect France from Euro-megabank penetration by creating the globe's largest bank.

Executives at Société Générale (SG) had other ideas, forming a cartel called "Action Against the BNP Raid." Meanwhile, BNP tried to boost to controlling stakes its holdings in the two banks. (In Europe's cross-ownership tradition, the target banks also owned part of BNP.) France's central bank tried unsuccessfully to negotiate a deal (the government supported the triumvirate merger). A war of words was played out in the media, and finally shareholders had to vote on the proposals. In the end, BNP won control of Paribas, but not SG. As BNP prepared to integrate a reluctant Paribas into its operations, regulators ordered BNP to relinquish its stake in SG. The newly merged company was dubbed BNP Paribas Group.

In 2000 BNP Paribas and Avis Group launched a fleet-management joint venture. BNP also bought 150 shopping centers from French retailer Carrefour and the 40% of merchant bank Cobepa that it didn't already own. In 2001 BNP Paribas took full control of US-based BancWest.

The company bought United California Bank from UFJ Holdings (now part of Mitsubishi UFJ Financial Group) in 2002.

EXECUTIVES

Chairman: Michel Pébereau, age 63
Vice Chairman: Jean-Louis Beffa, age 64
President, CEO, and Director: Baudouin Prot, age 54
Co-COO: Georges Chodron de Courcel, age 55
Co-COO: Jean Clamon, age 53
Head of Asset Management and Services: Alain Papiasse, age 49
Head of Compliance: Vivien Lévy-Garboua, age 57
Head of Corporate and Investment Banking: Philippe Blavier
Head of French Retail Banking: Jean-Laurent Bonnafé
Head of Group Development and Finance: Philipe Bordenave
Head of Group Human Resources: Bernard Lemée
Head of Group Information Systems: Hervé Gouëzel
Head of International Retail Banking and Financial Services: Pierre Mariani, age 46
Head of BNP Paribas Capital: Amaury-Daniel de Seze
Auditors: Barbier Frinault & Autres; Mazars & Guérard; PricewaterhouseCoopers Audit

LOCATIONS

HQ: BNP Paribas
16, boulevard des Italiens, 75009 Paris, France
Phone: +33-1-40-14-45-46   **Fax:** +33-1-40-14-69-73
US HQ: 787 7th Ave., New York, NY 10019
US Phone: 212-841-3000   **US Fax:** 212-841-2146
Web: www.bnpparibas.com

PRODUCTS/OPERATIONS

2004 Sales

	% of total
Interest	64
Commission income	16
Net gains on trading account securities	11
Insurance companies	4
Other banking income	2
Other	3
Total	**100**

COMPETITORS

ABN AMRO
Banco Popular
Bank of America
Barclays
BBVA
Caisses d'Epargne
Citigroup
Crédit Agricole
Deutsche Bank
Generale de Belgique
HSBC France
HSBC Holdings
JPMorgan Chase
Natexis
Société Générale
UBS
U.S. Bancorp
Wells Fargo

HISTORICAL FINANCIALS

Company Type: Public

Income Statement

FYE: December 31

	ASSETS ($ mil.)	NET INCOME ($ mil.)	INCOME AS % OF ASSETS	EMPLOYEES
12/04	1,235,699	6,367	0.5%	94,900
12/03	982,917	4,721	0.5%	89,100
12/02	744,485	3,454	0.5%	87,700
12/01	731,047	3,559	0.5%	85,000
12/00	653,505	3,883	0.6%	80,464
12/99	703,515	1,494	0.2%	77,472
12/98	379,047	1,362	0.4%	56,286
12/97	339,213	994	0.3%	52,702
12/96	355,647	737	0.2%	52,762
12/95	324,653	363	0.1%	53,600
Annual Growth	16.0%	37.5%	—	6.6%

2004 Year-End Financials

Equity as % of assets: 3.3%   Long-term debt ($ mil.): —
Return on assets: 0.6%   Sales ($ mil.): 60,495
Return on equity: 16.6%

Net Income History

Euronext Paris: BNP

7,000	
6,000	
5,000	
4,000	
3,000	
2,000	
1,000	
0	

12/95 12/96 12/97 12/98 12/99 12/00 12/01 12/02 12/03 12/04

Bombardier

Bombardier makes the goods to get people moving. Its Bombardier Aerospace subsidiary is the world's #3 maker of civil aircraft behind Boeing and Airbus; the #1 regional aircraft maker (Canadair, de Havilland), ahead of Embraer; and one of the two largest makers of business jets (Challenger, Learjet), just behind Gulfstream. Its Bombardier Transportation division — which added DaimlerChrysler's Adtranz rail systems unit in 2001 — is the world's largest railway equipment maker. The company, which may build a family of 110- to 135-seat planes, has sold its recreation vehicle business, which made Ski-Doo and Lynx snowmobiles, ATV's, and Sea-Doo personal watercraft. The Bombardier family controls Bombardier.

After announcing that it would sell units that can't generate 30% growth earnings per share, Bombardier sold its Recreational Products group (which previously accounted for about 10% of sales) in December 2003. It also agreed to sell its inventory finance division, which provides equipment financing, to GE Commercial Finance for $2.4 billion ($1.4 billion in cash and $1 billion in assumed liabilities).

The company is focusing on its aerospace operations, which account for just over half of sales (down from 65% in 2001); and its transportation operations, which account for about 40% of sales. Bombardier's rail operations became the largest producer of railway equipment in the world — ahead of ALSTOM and Siemens AG — when the company acquired DaimlerChrysler's Adtranz rail systems unit.

On the aerospace front, Bombardier cut thousands of jobs in response to the plunge in commercial aircraft demand in 2002 and 2003. As things began looking up in 2004, however, Bombardier announced that it was considering building a family (C Series) of 100- to 130-seat jets that would compete directly with Boeing and Airbus. Early in 2005 the company's board approved the larger C Series planes, but it deferred its final decision until late November 2005 at the earliest. Sales of business jets increased nearly 70% in 2004.

Meanwhile, Bombardier is interested in pursuing international growth outside of North America and Western Europe. The company is also in the midst of restructuring its Transportation segment; the changes are expected to cut about 4,000 jobs. The Bombardier family owns more than 50% of Bombardier.

HISTORY

Bombardier got its start in the 1920s when mechanic Joseph-Armand Bombardier began converting old cars into snowmobiles. He founded L'Auto-Neige Bombardier Limited in 1942 to make commercial snow vehicles. In 1959 Bombardier introduced the first personal snowmobile, the Ski-Doo.

At age 27, Laurent Beaudoin became the company's president in 1966. Bombardier went public in 1969. When the bottom dropped out of the snowmobile business due to the energy crisis in 1973, Beaudoin diversified, and in 1974 Bombardier won its first mass-transit contract to

build Montreal subway cars. Expanding further into mass transportation, Bombardier merged with MLW-Worthington Limited, a builder of diesel engines and diesel-electric locomotives. In 1978 the company became Bombardier Inc.

During the 1980s Bombardier continued to diversify. It expanded into military vehicles and became the leading supplier to the North American rail transit industry. The company entered the European railcar market in 1986, the same year it acquired Canadair, Canada's largest aerospace company, from the national government.

Founded in 1920 as the aircraft division of Canadian Vickers, Canadair became a separate company producing military and civilian aircraft in 1944. Acquired by Electric Boat (which became part of General Dynamics) in 1947, it was nationalized by the Canadian government in 1976. In 1978 Canadair introduced its Challenger 600 business jet, which became a major seller.

Bombardier began development of a commuter aircraft, the Canadian Regional Jet (a 50-seat derivative of the Challenger), in 1989.

In 1990 the company bought US-based Learjet and its service centers, and two years later it acquired a stake in de Havilland, a regional aircraft maker, which it jointly owns with the Province of Ontario. The company bought German railroad-equipment maker Waggonfabrik Talbot in 1995.

In 1996 Amtrak selected an international consortium headed by Bombardier to produce high-speed trains, electric locomotives, and train-maintenance facilities. Also that year the Global Express business jet made its first flight.

Bombardier doubled the size of its European operations in 1998 by buying German railcar maker Deutsche Waggonbau. In 1999 Bombardier announced the launch of its all-new business jet, the eight-passenger Continental.

The company sold its 50% stake in Shorts Missile Systems to Thomson in 2000. Also that year Bombardier landed an $817 million contract to supply Spanish carrier Air Nostrum with 44 planes. It also inked a $2 billion deal to make 94 regional jets for Delta Air Lines; the Delta order includes options for an additional 406 aircraft through 2010.

To start off 2001, Bombardier signed a deal with SkyWest worth about $1.4 billion for 64 Canadair regional jets. It was also selected by a bankruptcy court as winning bidder for Outboard Marine's Evinrude and Johnson outboard marine engine assets. Completing an agreement made the year before, Bombardier acquired DaimlerChrysler's Adtranz rail systems unit for about $725 million, making it part of its Bombardier Transportation division. In September the company announced that it would take a charge of about $600 million and lay off about 10% of its aerospace workforce (it also said that it would cut another 7% of that workforce if demand did not grow).

In 2002 Bombardier sought about $870 million in damages from DaimlerChrysler over the Adtranz deal, claiming that the level of equity in Adtranz was overstated and that the costs related to third-party contracts were higher than stated at the time of the deal. Late in 2002 Bombardier temporarily suspended business jet production. Bombardier divested its Recreational Products unit in December 2003.

CEO Paul Tellier resigned in December 2004 amid rumored boardroom differences with Laurent Beaudoin, who assumed the CEO duties.

EXECUTIVES

Chairman and CEO: Laurent Beaudoin, age 66
Vice Chairman: J.R. André Bombardier
Vice Chairman: Jean-Louis Fontaine, $917,062 pay
SVP and CFO: Pierre Alary, $814,104 pay
SVP and Treasurer: François Lemarchand
SVP, Strategy and Corporate Audit Services and Risk Assessment: Richard C. Bradeen
SVP, General Counsel, and Assistant Secretary: Daniel Desjardins
SVP, Public Affairs: John Paul MacDonald
SVP: Carroll L'Italien, $791,490 pay
VP, Investor Relations: Réjean Bourque
Corporate Secretary: Roger Carle
Executive Assistant to the Chairman: Marie-Claire Simoneau
President and COO, Bombardier Aerospace: Pierre Beaudoin, $1,330,000 pay
President and COO, Bombardier Capital: Brian Peters
President, Bombardier Transportation: André Navarri, age 56, $1,701,404 pay
COO, Bombardier Transportation: Wolfgang Toelsner
Auditors: Ernst & Young LLP

LOCATIONS

HQ: Bombardier Inc.
800 René-Lévesque Blvd. West,
Montreal, Quebec H3B 1Y8, Canada
Phone: 514-861-9481   **Fax:** 514-861-7053
Web: www.bombardier.com

Bombardier's principal production facilities are located in Canada, the UK, and the US.

2005 Sales

	$ mil.	% of total
The Americas		
US	6,557	41
Canada	485	3
Other countries	383	2
Europe		
UK	2,167	14
Germany	1,585	10
Switzerland	609	4
France	541	3
Spain	407	3
Italy	391	2
Austria	375	2
Sweden	331	2
Netherlands	323	2
Portugal	100	1
Other countries	661	4
Asia		
China	265	2
Japan	100	1
Other countries	107	1
Other regions	452	3
Total	**15,839**	**100**

PRODUCTS/OPERATIONS

2005 Sales

	% of total
Aerospace	50
Transportation	48
Bombardier Capital	2
Total	**100**

Selected Operations

Aerospace
Amphibious aircraft
  Canadair-415 turboprop
Business aircraft
  Canadair SE
  Challenger 604
  Continental
  Global Express
  Learjet 31A, 45, 60
Defense services
  Flying training
  Military aircraft technical service
  Special defense products (Unmanned Aerial Vehicle)
Regional aircraft

CRJ 200	Q200
CRJ 700	Q300
CRJ 900	Q400
Q100	

Transportation
Freight cars
Locomotives for passenger trains
Monorails
Rapid-transit cars
Single-level and bi-level railcars
Subway cars
Trams
Tram-trains
Turbotrains
Vehicles with tilting systems

Bombardier Capital
Aircraft and industrial equipment
  financing and leasing
Consumer financing
Inventory financing
Mortgage financing
Ski industry financing

COMPETITORS

Airbus	Lockheed Martin
ALSTOM	NetJets
BMW	Northrop Grumman
Boeing	Polaris Industries
Brunswick	Raytheon
Cessna	Safire
Cirrus Design	Siemens
Eclipse Aviation	Suzuki Motor
Embraer	Textron
Fiat	Trinity Industries
Gulfstream Aerospace	Yamaha

HISTORICAL FINANCIALS

Company Type: Public

Income Statement

FYE: January 31

	REVENUE ($ mil.)	NET INCOME ($ mil.)	NET PROFIT MARGIN	EMPLOYEES
1/05	15,839	(85)	—	59,550
1/04	16,025	(67)	—	64,600
1/03	15,482	(403)	—	70,411
1/02	13,614	246	1.8%	74,879
1/01	10,705	649	6.1%	58,000
1/00	9,419	497	5.3%	56,000
1/99	7,607	367	4.8%	53,000
1/98	5,853	289	4.9%	47,778
1/97	5,917	301	5.1%	41,150
1/96	5,170	112	2.2%	40,000
Annual Growth	13.2%	—	—	4.5%

2005 Year-End Financials

Debt ratio: 300.4%
Return on equity: —
Cash ($ mil.): 2,355
Current ratio: 1.21
Long-term debt ($ mil.): 6,904

Net Income History   Toronto: BBD.B

Bouygues SA

Bouygues (pronounced "bweeg") is très beeg in both construction (buildings and civic works, roads, and property development) and services (media, public utilities management, and telecommunications). The group runs more than 40 subsidiaries and affiliates in 80 countries, including Colas (road construction) and the African and Italians businesses of Saur (utilities management). The company has increased its stake in Bouygues Telecom (France's #3 mobile phone carrier) to 83%, and it also owns 41% of TF1 (France's #1 TV channel). Brothers Martin and Olivier Bouygues together control more than 22% of Bouygues.

Although Bouygues has felt the squeeze of the global economic slowdown, its diversified international holdings have kept the company in the black. One of Europe's largest industrial groups, Bouygues separates its global network of subsidiaries and affiliates into three main business sectors: construction, services, and telecoms-media.

Construction services generate more than 60% of Bouygues' total sales. Bouygues Construction is composed of building and civil works firms. The Colas subsidiary provides road construction and maintenance internationally; it also produces emulsions. Other construction subsidiaries include ETDE (power and data transmission networks construction) and Bouygues Immobilier (property management). The construction division has been expanding in Western Europe, especially the UK and the Netherlands, while slowing down in the Asia/Pacific region.

On the services side of the business, utilities management firm Saur designs, constructs, and manages water and sewage systems, and it provides solid waste management services. In 2005, Bouygues sold several divisions of Saur (Coved, Saur France, Saur International and Stereau) to French private equity firm PAI Partners; it still owns the African and Italian (Sigesa-Crea) divisions of the firm. Bouygues is slowly pulling out of this line of business in order to concentrate on its telecom and construction businesses.

The group's media holdings include a stake in Société Télévision Française 1 (TF1), France's oldest and leading TV channel. TF1 owns 66% of TPS, France's second-largest satellite operator. Bouygues also has been steadily upping its stake in Bouygues Telecom, which has 6.9 million customers.

Chairman Martin Bouygues and his brother Olivier, sons of the company's founder, together own the controlling stake in Bouygues through holding company SCDM.

HISTORY

With $1,700 in borrowed money, Francis Bouygues, son of a Paris engineer, started Entreprise Francis Bouygues in 1952 as an industrial works and construction firm in the Paris region of France. Within four years his firm had expanded into property development.

By the mid-1960s Bouygues had entered the civil engineering and public works sectors and developed regional construction units across France. In 1970 it was listed on the Paris stock exchange. Four years later the company established Bouygues Offshore to build oil platforms.

In 1978 the firm built Terminal 2 of Paris' Charles de Gaulle airport. Three years later it won the contract to construct the University of Riyadh in Saudi Arabia (then the world's largest building project at 3.2 million sq. ft.), which was completed in 1984. That year Bouygues acquired France's #3 water supply company, Saur, and power transmission and supply firm ETDE.

Expansion continued in 1986 with the purchase of the Screg Group, which included Colas, France's top highway contractor. The next year the company led a consortium to buy 50% of newly privatized network Société Télévision Française 1 (TF1), France's leading TV channel. Bouygues became the largest shareholder with a 25% stake (increased to 40% by 1999). In 1988 the company began building the Channel Tunnel (completed in 1994) and moved into ultramodern headquarters, dubbed Challenger, in Saint-Quentin-En-Yvelines, outside Paris.

After rumors of failing health, Francis Bouygues resigned as chairman in 1989. His youngest son, Martin, took over as chairman and CEO, although the patriarch, called France's "Emperor of Concrete," remained on the board until his death in 1993.

Despite fears that the group would suffer without its founder's leadership, Bouygues continued to grow with the 1989 acquisition of a majority interest in Grands Moulins de Paris, France's largest flour milling firm (sold in 1998). In 1990 it purchased Swiss construction group Losinger.

The company entered the telecom industry in 1993 with a national paging network and added a mobile phone license a year later. In 1996 the group listed 40% of Bouygues Offshore's shares on the New York and Paris stock exchanges. Also that year it launched mobile phone operator Bouygues Telecom and entered a partnership with Telecom Italia.

By 1999 Bouygues Telecom had reached 2 million customers, and Bouygues bought back a 20% share held by the UK's Cable and Wireless to increase its stake to nearly 54%. That year Bouygues Offshore bought Norwegian engineering firm Kvaerner, and the group spun off its construction sector, creating Bouygues Construction.

After word circulated that Deutsche Telekom wanted to acquire the group's telecom unit, Bouygues became the target of takeover rumors. Francois Pinault, France's richest businessman, became Bouygues' largest non-family shareholder when he increased his stake to 14%. Then Pinault's biggest rival, Bernard Arnault, upped his stake to more than 9% of the group, fueling speculation of a battle over control of the board.

In 2001 the company pulled out of France's auction for a third-generation wireless license and remained the only European incumbent mobile carrier without a major domestic investment in 3G technology. The next year the company agreed to buy Telecom Italia's stake in Bouygues Telecom, increasing Bouygues' ownership in the mobile operator from 54% to more than 65%. In 2002 the company sold its 51% stake in oil field platform construction unit Bouygues Offshore to Italian oil services group Saipem, which announced plans to bid for the remaining shares.

However, talks with German utility giant E.ON over the sale of Bouygues' Saur subsidiary failed that year, after E.ON decided to focus instead on its electricity and gas operations.

EXECUTIVES

Chairman and CEO: Martin Bouygues, age 53, $3,137,200 pay
Deputy CEO: Olivier Poupart-Lafarge, age 63, $2,948,968 pay
Deputy CEO: Olivier Bouygues, age 55, $2,635,248 pay
EVP, Information Systems and New Technologies: Alain Pouyat, age 61, $1,969,616 pay
SVP, Cash Management and Finance: Lionel Verdouck
EVP, Telecommunications Division and Chairman, Bouygues Telecom: Philippe Montagner, age 61
SVP Group Human Resources and Administration: Jean-Claude Tostivin, age 57
Chairman and CEO, Bouygues Construction: Yves Gabriel, age 55, $2,148,300 pay
Chairman and CEO, Bouygues Telecom: Gilles Pélisson
Chairman and CEO, Colas: Alain Dupont, age 65, $3,074,456 pay
Chairman and CEO, Bouygues Immobilier: François Bertière, age 54
Chairman and CEO, TF1: Patrick Le Lay, age 63, $2,799,838 pay
CEO, Saur: Hervé Le Bouc
Corporate Secretary: Jean-François Guillemin
Group Corporate Communications Director: Blandine Delafon
Investor Relations: Anthony Mellor
Auditors: Ernst & Young Audit; Mazars & Guérard

LOCATIONS

HQ: Bouygues SA
1, avenue Eugène Freyssinet, 78061 Saint-Quentin-en-Yvelines, France
Phone: +33-1-30-60-23-11   **Fax:** +33-1-30-60-48-61
Web: www.bouygues.fr

2004 Sales

	% of total
Western Europe	
France	73
Other countries	9
North America	6
Africa	5
Eastern Europe	4
Asia/Pacific & other regions	3
Total	**100**

PRODUCTS/OPERATIONS

2004 Sales

	% of total
Construction	62
Telecoms & media	28
Services	10
Total	**100**

Selected Subsidiaries and Affiliates

Construction
  Bouygues Bâtiment SA (99.9%)
  Bouygues Construction SA (99.9%)
  Bouygues Immobilier Group
  Bouygues TP SA (99.9%)
  Bouygues UK Ltd (99.9%)
  Colas SA (96%)
  ETDE SA (99.9%)
  O.F. Construction (formerly SB Ballestrero SA)
  O.F. Equipement (formerly Olin-Lanctuit SA)
Telecoms and Media
  Bouygues Telecom SA (83%)
  Télévision Française 1 SA (TF1, 41%)
  Télévision Par Satellite SNC (TPS, 66%)

COMPETITORS

AMEC	France Telecom
Autostrade	Halliburton
AWG	HOCHTIEF
Balfour Beatty	Hyundai Engineering and
Bechtel	Construction
Bilfinger Berger	MWH Global
Bovis Lend Lease	Severn Trent
CANAL+	SFR Cegetel
CSCEC	Skanska
Dragados	SUEZ
EIFFAGE	SUEZ Environnement
FCC	Technip
Fluor	VINCI
Foster Wheeler	

HISTORICAL FINANCIALS

Company Type: Public

Income Statement

FYE: December 31

	REVENUE ($ mil.)	NET INCOME ($ mil.)	NET PROFIT MARGIN	EMPLOYEES
12/04	31,920	1,170	3.7%	113,300
12/03	27,391	565	2.1%	124,300
12/02	23,317	698	3.0%	121,604
12/01	18,135	305	1.7%	125,034
12/00	17,942	396	2.2%	118,645
12/99	16,916	62	0.4%	109,588
12/98	17,957	248	1.4%	103,350
12/97	15,320	126	0.8%	94,400
12/96	14,021	125	0.9%	94,895
12/95	15,042	(593)	—	93,857
Annual Growth	**8.7%**	—	—	**2.1%**

2004 Year-End Financials

Debt ratio: 111.6%
Return on equity: 19.7%
Cash ($ mil.): 608
Current ratio: 1.09
Long-term debt ($ mil.): 6,063

Net Income History

Euronext Paris: EN

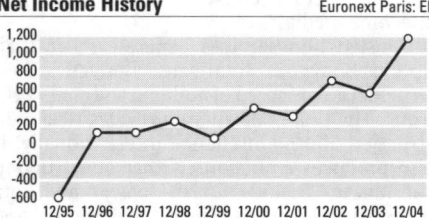

1,200	
1,000	
800	
600	
400	
200	
0	
-200	
-400	
-600	

12/95 12/96 12/97 12/98 12/99 12/00 12/01 12/02 12/03 12/04

BP p.l.c.

BP is also BO (Big Oil). It is the world's largest integrated oil concern, ahead of Exxon Mobil. The company, which was formed in 1998 from the merger of British Petroleum and Amoco, grew by buying Atlantic Richfield Company. BP has proved reserves of 14.6 billion barrels of oil equivalent, including large holdings in Alaska. BP is the largest oil and gas producer in the US and also a top refiner. BP operates about 27,000 gas stations worldwide, including approximately 14,200 in the US. In 2003 BP, the Alfa Group, and Access-Renova combined their Russian oil assets to create TNK-BP, one of Russia's largest oil companies. BP has announced plans to sell its petrochemical unit, Innovene, to INEOS for $9 billion.

Outside of the US, BP has significant production activities in Canada, the Gulf of Mexico, the North Sea, Trinidad, and now India. The company

has announced plans for a joint venture with the India-based Hindustan Petroleum to build a $3 billion refinery in the city of Bhatinda. BP has also dedicated $615 million to develop two fields in the Gulf of Suez through its joint venture with Egyptian General Petroleum. The company has agreed to purchase nearly a quarter (23%) of China Aviation Oil, a jet fuel importer. In order to concentrate on in Russia and Asia, BP will deemphasize its exploration and production activities in Brazil.

BP has swapped control of its stake in German natural gas supplier Ruhrgas, with E.ON, in return for ownership of Veba Oel, which operates Germany's largest gas station chain. To recoup some of BP's investment, Veba Oel's exploration and production operations were sold to Petro-Canada.

In 2003 BP agreed to sell some of its mature oil and gas assets in the US and the North Sea (including its Forties field, where oil was discovered in 1970) to Apache for $1.3 billion, as part of a strategy to focus on more profitable production assets. It also sold its Boqueron field and Desarrollo Zulia Occidental assets, both located in Venezuela, to Europe's Perenco. In 2004 the company sold its minority stakes in Chinese entities Sinopec and PetroChina. It also announced plans to sell its one-third stake in Singapore Refining Company.

With the success of its BP Solar International subsidiary, BP has created BP Alternative Energy (hydrogen, solar, and wind power generation) with an initial investment of $1.8 billion.

HISTORY

Today's BP (formerly BP Amoco) was born on two sides of the Atlantic. In the US, Amoco emerged from Standard Oil Trust, organized by John D. Rockefeller in 1882. In 1886 he bought Lima (Ohio) oil, a high-sulfur crude, anticipating the discovery of a sulfur-removing process. Such a process was, indeed, patented in 1887, and in 1889 Standard organized Standard Oil of Indiana, which later established such innovations as company-owned service stations and a research lab at the refinery.

Overseas, British Petroleum (BP) was a twinkle in the eye of English adventurer William D'Arcy, who began oil exploration of Persia in 1901. In 1908, bankrolled by Burmah Oil, D'Arcy's firm was the first to strike oil in the Middle East. D'Arcy and Burmah Oil formed Anglo-Persian Oil in 1909, and the British government took a 51% stake in 1914.

Back in the US, Standard was broken up into 34 independent oil companies in 1911. Standard Oil of Indiana kept its oil refining and US marketing operations. In 1925 it added a few Mexican and Venezuelan firms, including Pan American Petroleum and Transport, which held half of American Oil Co., known for Amoco antiknock gasoline. It began Amoco Chemicals in 1945.

Anglo-Persian took the BP name in 1954 and bought its own Standard Oil: After making a strike in Alaska in 1969, BP swapped Alaskan reserves for a 25% interest (later upped to 55%) in Standard Oil of Ohio (SOHIO). BP also struck North Sea oil in 1970. But falling oil and copper prices in the mid-1980s and a dry hole in the Beaufort Sea hurt earnings. Under Robert Horton, SOHIO sold off units. BP also bought livestock feed producer Purina Mills (1986, sold 1998) and the rest of SOHIO (1987).

Standard Oil of Indiana had its own problems, including being kicked out of Iran after the Islamic revolution and causing a major oil spill off the French coast in 1978. The firm, which became Amoco in 1985, bought Canada's Dome Petroleum in 1988, making it the largest private owner of North American gas reserves, but the big purchase proved hard to swallow.

In 1992 Amoco hurled itself into overseas oil exploration. It was the first foreign oil company to explore the Chinese mainland. John Browne, often compared to Rockefeller, became BP's CEO in 1995. In 1996 BP and Mobil merged their European fuel and lubricants operations, and the British government sold its remaining stake in BP.

As oil prices tumbled in 1998, BP merged with Amoco in a $52 billion deal that formed BP Amoco. The new oil major agreed the next year to buy US-based Atlantic Richfield in a deal that closed in 2000. BP Amoco sold ARCO's Alaskan properties to Phillips (later ConocoPhillips) for $7 billion to gain regulatory approval for the purchase.

Its stake in Siberian oil fields was nearly taken away in a controversial 1999 bankruptcy sale before BP Amoco and Russia's Tyumen Oil agreed to cooperate. In 2000 BP Amoco and Shell Oil sold their stakes in Altura Energy to Occidental Petroleum for $3.6 billion. Also that year BP Amoco bought motor-oil maker Burmah Castrol for $4.7 billion. It paid $1.5 billion for the 18% of former ARCO exploration and production unit Vastar Resources that it didn't already own.

The company adopted BP as its main worldwide brand in 2000, and it officially shortened its name the next year.

In 2001 BP agreed to swap control of its stake in German natural gas supplier Ruhrgas, plus $1.6 billion in cash and $950 million in assumed debt, to German utility giant E.ON for a majority interest in Veba Oel, owner of Germany's largest gas station chain. Regulators moved to keep E.ON from acquiring the Ruhrgas stake, but BP agreed to make up the difference in cash if necessary, and the deal proceeded. The agreement allowed BP to take full ownership of Veba Oel in 2002. That year BP increased it stake in Russian oil and gas producer Sidanco from 10% to 25%.

In 2003 BP sold its Boqueron field and Desarrollo Zulia Occidental assets, both located in Venezuela, to Europe's Perenco. BP purchased the outstanding shares of Olympic Pipe Line in late 2005, making it a wholly owned subsidiary.

EXECUTIVES

Chairman: Peter D. Sutherland, age 59
Deputy Chairman: Sir Ian Prosser, age 61
Group Chief Executive and Director:
  Lord E. John P. Browne, age 57, $7,053,744 pay
Group Executive Officer: Iain C. Conn, age 42,
  $963,100 pay
CFO and Director: Byron E. Grote, age 57,
  $4,050,798 pay
EVP, Group Chief of Staff, and Managing Director:
  David C. Allen, age 50, $1,974,355 pay
EVP and Group General Counsel: B. Peter Bevan, age 61
EVP, Human Resources: Sara (Sally) Bott, age 56
EVP; Chief Executive, Refining and Marketing, and Managing Director: John A. Manzoni, age 45,
  $1,974,355 pay
EVP, Gas, Power, and Renewables, and Integrated Supply and Trading: Vivienne Cox, age 45
Group VP and CIO: John Leggate

Deputy CEO, Exploration and Production:
  Andrew G. Inglis
President, BP America: Ross J. Pillari, age 55
President and General Manager, BP Egypt:
  Hesham Mekawi
President and CEO, BP Energy Company:
  Cameron Byers, age 46
Chief Executive Exploration and Production, and Managing Director: Anthony B. (Tony) Hayward, age 48, $1,974,355 pay
Chief Executive, International Marine Division:
  Kevin L. James
Chief Executive, Petrochemicals: Ralph C. Alexander, age 50
Company Secretary: David J. Jackson
Chief Scientist: Steven E. Koonin
Head of Investor Relations: Fergus MacLeod
Refinery Manager, Texas City: Don Parus
US Press Office: Neil Chapman
Auditors: Ernst & Young

LOCATIONS

HQ: BP p.l.c.
  1 St. James's Square,
  London SW1Y 4PD, United Kingdom
Phone: +44-20-7496-4000   **Fax:** +44-20-7496-4630
US HQ: 28100 Torch Pkwy., Warrenville, IL 60555-3938
US Phone: 630-821-2222   **US Fax:** 630-836-5513
Web: www.bp.com

2004 Sales

	$ mil.	% of total
US	127,049	45
Europe		
UK	52,671	18
Other countries	47,494	17
Other regions	57,845	20
Total	**285,059**	**100**

PRODUCTS/OPERATIONS

2004 Sales

	$ mil.	% of total
Refining & marketing	179,587	56
Gas, power & renewables	83,320	26
Exploration & production	34,914	11
Petrochemicals	21,209	7
Other	546	—
Adjustments	(34,517)	—
Total	**285,059**	**100**

Major Operations

Refining and Marketing
  Marketing
  Refining
  Supply and trading
  Transportation and shipping
Gas and Power
  Natural gas marketing and trading
  Natural gas liquids
Exploration and Production
  Field development
  Gas processing and marketing
  Oil and gas exploration
  Pipelines and transportation
    Alyeska Pipeline Service Co. (47%)
    Trans Alaska Pipeline System
    Valdez terminal
Chemicals
  Chemical intermediates
  Feedstock
  Performance products
  Polymers
Other
  Coal mining
  Solar power

COMPETITORS

Amerada Hess	ICI American
Apache	Imperial Oil
Ashland	Kerr-McGee
BASF AG	Koch
Bayer	Lyondell Chemical
BG Group	Norsk Hydro
BHP Billiton	Occidental Petroleum
Cargill	PDVSA
Chevron	PEMEX
Chevron Stations	PETROBRAS
Dow Chemical	Royal Dutch/Shell Group
DuPont	Shell Aviation
Eni	Shell Petroleum
Exxon Mobil	Sinclair Oil
Hercules	Sunoco
Huntsman	TOTAL

HISTORICAL FINANCIALS

Company Type: Public

Income Statement

FYE: December 31

	REVENUE ($ mil.)	NET INCOME ($ mil.)	NET PROFIT MARGIN	EMPLOYEES
12/04	285,059	15,731	5.5%	102,900
12/03	232,571	10,267	4.4%	103,700
12/02	178,721	6,845	3.8%	115,250
12/01	174,218	8,010	4.6%	110,150
12/00	148,062	11,870	8.0%	107,200
12/99	83,566	4,686	5.6%	80,400
12/98	68,304	3,260	4.8%	96,650
12/97	71,783	4,080	5.7%	56,450
12/96	76,602	4,370	5.7%	53,150
12/95	56,000	1,740	3.1%	56,650
Annual Growth	**19.8%**	**27.7%**	**—**	**6.9%**

2004 Year-End Financials

Debt ratio: 16.8%
Return on equity: 20.6%
Cash ($ mil.): 1,156
Current ratio: 0.99
Long-term debt ($ mil.): 12,907

No. of shares (mil.): 3,588
Dividends
  Yield: 2.9%
  Payout: 40.2%
Market value ($ mil.): 209,520

Stock History

NYSE: BP

	STOCK PRICE ($) FY Close	P/E High	P/E Low	Earnings	Dividends	Book Value
12/04	58.40	15	11	4.25	1.71	21.37
12/03	49.35	18	13	2.75	1.66	20.60
12/02	40.65	30	20	1.82	1.57	18.61
12/01	46.51	26	20	2.13	1.43	19.89
12/00	47.88	22	16	2.72	1.35	19.55
12/99	59.31	41	26	1.44	1.38	13.33
12/98	45.38	48	36	1.02	0.00	12.95
12/97	39.84	22	15	2.13	0.00	6.07
12/96	35.34	15	10	2.34	0.66	5.82
12/95	25.53	28	20	0.94	0.68	4.93
Annual Growth	**9.6%**	**—**	**—**	**18.3%**	**10.8%**	**17.7%**

Bridgestone

Although stone bridges may be increasingly rare, Bridgestone can help most vehicles traverse almost any type of terrain. Bridgestone is the world's largest tire maker, but in addition to supplying tires to most major car manufacturers, the company also makes tires for heavy equipment (off-road mining vehicles) and aircraft. Non-tire products include building materials (roof tiles), sporting goods (golf balls), industrial rubber products (conveyor belts and automotive hoses), marine components (dredging hoses, marine fenders, oil booms, and silt barriers), and switches.

Bridgestone is working hard to address some emerging trends in the global tire business. Demand for tires is growing on a worldwide basis and Bridgestone's increased sales reflect that demand. In industrialized regions demand is shifting to high-performance and oversized tires. Meanwhile Bridgestone has increased production in emerging markets such as China, Thailand, and Eastern Europe.

Despite increased sales, Bridgestone's earnings are being negatively impacted by rising material costs which the company partially offset by raising prices. Exchange rates between the dollar and the yen have also been unfavorable to Bridgestone's results.

HISTORY

In 1906 Shojiro Ishibashi and his brother Tokujiro assumed control of the family's clothing business. They focused on making *tabi*, traditional Japanese footwear, and in 1923 began working with rubber for soles. In 1931 Shojiro formed Bridgestone (Ishibashi means "stone bridge" in Japanese) to make tires, and during that decade the company began producing auto tires, airplane tires, and golf balls. Bridgestone followed the Japanese military to occupied territories, where it built plants. The company's headquarters moved to Tokyo in 1937.

Although Bridgestone lost all of its overseas factories during WWII, its Japanese plants escaped damage. The company began making bicycles in 1946 and signed a technical assistance pact with Goodyear five years later, enabling Bridgestone to import badly needed technology. In the 1950s and 1960s, Bridgestone started making nylon tires and radials and again set up facilities overseas, mostly elsewhere in Asia. The company benefited from the rapid growth in Japanese auto sales in the 1970s. Shojiro died at age 87 in 1976.

In 1983 Bridgestone bought a plant in La-Vergne, Tennessee, from tire maker Firestone. Five years later Bridgestone topped Italian tire maker Pirelli's bid and bought the rest of Firestone for $2.6 billion, valuing the tire manufacturer at a lofty 26 times its earnings. Bridgestone/Firestone (now Bridgestone Americas Holding) became Bridgestone's largest subsidiary. Harvey Firestone had founded his tire business in 1900 and expanded with the auto industry in the US. In the 1920s he leased one million acres in Liberia for rubber plantations and established a chain of auto supply and service outlets. After WWII Firestone started making synthetic rubber and automotive components, expanded overseas, and acquired US tire producers Dayton Tire & Rubber and Seiberling.

At the time of Firestone's purchase, General Motors (GM) dropped it as a supplier. Bridgestone/Firestone compensated for this loss in volume by selling more tires through mass-market retailers. It began selling tires to GM's Saturn Corporation in 1990.

The following year new Bridgestone/Firestone chairman Yoichiro Kaizaki moved to cut production costs, alienating union workers. He became company head in 1993. During the early 1990s Bridgestone bought Colonial Rubber Works, a US roofing material manufacturer, and America Off The Road Company, which makes tires for heavy equipment. To improve its distribution, in 1992 Bridgestone renamed its 1,550 North American MasterCare auto service centers "Tire Zone at Firestone" and took the unheard-of step of selling rival Michelin's tires. It expanded operations in Brazil, Indonesia, Mexico, Thailand, and the US the next year.

Bridgestone's US operations have been plagued with problems, such as disputes with the United Rubber Workers (URW) union. Tensions rose in 1995 when the company hired 2,300 permanent replacement workers during a plant strike. In 1996, after URW members had become part of United Steelworkers of America, the two sides approved a new contract. In 1997 Bridgestone built a South Carolina plant to help reduce Japanese imports.

Expanding its markets, Bridgestone opened a retail outlet in Moscow in 1999 and acquired a radial tire plant in China from South Korea's Kumho Industrial Company in 2000. That year it recalled approximately 6.5 million Firestone ATX, ATX II, and Wilderness AT tires after dozens of incidents where the tires came apart at road speeds. The affected tires have been used on light trucks and SUVs since 1990, many of them as original equipment on the Ford Explorer. Not long after the recall, Bridgestone/Firestone chairman and CEO Masatoshi Ono retired and was replaced by John Lampe. The fallout and ensuing blame-game (improper inflation guidelines/unstable vehicle vs. faulty tires) virtually ended Bridgestone's 95-year relationship with Ford (Bridgestone still does business with Ford outside the Americas).

In 2001, while revealing that it would face its first loss since listing 30 years ago, Bridgestone announced that it would close the Decatur, Illinois, plant at which many of the recalled tires were made. The plant employed about 1,500 workers. Later in the year the company announced that it would recall an additional 3.5 million tires at a cost of nearly $30 million.

Near the end of 2001 Bridgestone announced it would inflate its beleaguered Bridgestone/Firestone subsidiary with $1.3 billion in cash. The company also announced the restructuring of its Bridgestone/Firestone operations.

Bridgestone and Continental AG entered into an agreement in early 2002 whereby the two companies will adapt run-flat technology to conventional wheel systems (conventional systems utilize special wheels). In early 2003 the company's US subsidiary changed its name from Bridgestone/Firestone Americas Holding to Bridgestone Americas Holding. Later in the year the company was awarded a contract to supply tires for the Airbus A380 aircraft; the deal was reportedly worth $84.3 million.

In 2005 Bridgestone purchased the Indonesian rubber plantations business (Goodyear Sumatra Plantations) of Goodyear Tire & Rubber for about $62 million.

EXECUTIVES

Chairman, President, and CEO: Shigeo Watanabe
SVP, International Operations and Director: Shoshi Arakawa
VP, CFO, and Senior Officer, Finance, Purchasing, IT and Network and Director: Shoji Mizuochi
VP and Senior Officer, Diversified Products; Director, Chemical Division and Director: Yasuo Asami
VP and Senior Officer, Original Equipment and Director: Tatsuya Okajima
VP and Senior Officer, Replacement Tire Sales and Director: Giichi Miyakawa
VP and Senior Officer, Technology and Director: Akira Inoue
VP and Senior Officer, Tire Production and Distribution and Safety, Quality, and Environment and Director: Masaharu Oku
VP, Chief Compliance Officer, and Senior Officer, Corporate Administration and Director: Tomuyuki Izumisawa
VP and Senior Officer; Chairman and President, Bridgestone (China) Investment Co., Ltd.: Hiromichi Odagiri
VP and Senior Officer; CEO and President, Bridgestone Europe NV/SA: Minekazu (Mike) Fujimura
VP; Vice Chairman and President, Bridgestone Americas Holding, Inc.: Asahiko (Duke) Nishiyama
VP, Commercial Tire Business: Junya Satou
VP, Consumer Tire Business: Shuichi Ishibashi
VP, Human Resources and General Affairs: Masayuki Okabe
Director; Chairman, President, and CEO, Bridgestone Americas Holding, Inc.: Mark A. Emkes, age 52
Auditors: Deloitte Touche Tohmatsu; Tohmatsu & Co.

LOCATIONS

HQ: Bridgestone Corporation
10-1, Kyobashi 1-chome, Chuo-ku,
Tokyo 104-8340, Japan
Phone: +81-3-3567-0111   **Fax:** +81-3-3535-2553
US HQ: 535 Marriott Dr., Nashville, TN 37214
US Phone: 615-937-1000   **US Fax:** 615-937-3621
Web: www.bridgestone.co.jp

Bridgestone operates tire factories and diversified products plants in 24 countries.

2004 Sales

	$ mil.	% of total
The Americas	9,830	42
Japan	7,901	34
Europe	3,120	13
Other regions	2,588	11
Total	**23,439**	**100**

PRODUCTS/OPERATIONS

2004 Sales

	$ mil.	% of total
Tires	18,699	80
Other products	4,740	20
Total	**23,439**	**100**

Selected Products

Tires and Tubes
  Agricultural machinery
  Aircraft
  Buses
  Cars
  Commercial vehicles
  Construction and mining vehicles
  Monorails
  Motorcycles
  Race cars
  Scooters
  Subways
  Trucks

Industrial Rubber Products
  Belts
  Hoses
  Inflatable rubber dams
  Marine products
  Multi-rubber bearings
  Rubber tracks
  Silt barriers
  Vibration-isolating and noise-insulating materials
  Waterproofing materials
Chemical Products
  Building materials
  Ceramic foam
  Flexible polyurethane foam products
  Office equipment components
  Thermal insulating polyurethane foam
Sporting Goods
  Bicycles
  Golf balls
  Golf clubs
  Tennis balls
  Tennis rackets
  Tennis shoes

COMPETITORS

3M	Huffy
Acushnet	K2
Ansell	Kumho Tire
Armstrong Holdings	Marangoni
Avon Rubber	Michelin
Brunswick	Newell Rubbermaid
Callaway Golf	Sime Darby
Continental AG	Sumitomo Rubber
Cooper Tire & Rubber	TBC
Goodyear	Wingate Partners

HISTORICAL FINANCIALS

Company Type: Public

Income Statement

FYE: December 31

	REVENUE ($ mil.)	NET INCOME ($ mil.)	NET PROFIT MARGIN	EMPLOYEES
12/04	23,439	1,110	4.7%	113,699
12/03	21,512	828	3.9%	108,315
12/02	18,962	383	2.0%	106,846
12/01	16,270	133	0.8%	104,700
12/00	17,532	155	0.9%	102,165
12/99	20,403	868	4.3%	101,489
12/98	19,689	921	4.7%	97,767
12/97	16,624	300	1.8%	96,204
12/96	16,923	608	3.6%	92,458
12/95	16,294	523	3.2%	89,418
Annual Growth	4.1%	8.7%	—	2.7%

2004 Year-End Financials

Debt ratio: 32.9%
Return on equity: 12.8%
Cash ($ mil.): 2,558
Current ratio: 1.67
Long-term debt ($ mil.): 2,986

Net Income History

OTC: BRDCY

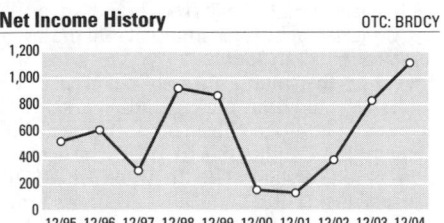

British Airways

A member of the royal family of European airlines, British Airways (BA) has had to relinquish its throne. Europe's #2 carrier (newly formed Air France-KLM is #1) flies from its hubs in London's Heathrow and Gatwick airports, the airline flies about 290 aircraft to more than 150 destinations in some 75 countries. It owns a minority stake in Spain's Iberia. BA and AMR's American Airlines have formed the Oneworld global marketing alliance, which also includes Cathay Pacific Airways, Finnair, Qantas, and Iberia, among others. BA has survived reduction in tourism and increased terrorist threats, but it is looking to cut more costs, including continued reduction of its workforce through 2006.

BA has built a global network through partnerships. However, in 2004 it sold its 19% stake in Qantas Airways to help cut down on its debt, but it maintains a 9% stake in Iberia. It has also signed a codeshare agreement with Swiss.

BA is beefing up its local coverage by moving to an all-jet fleet for its regional routes under its British Airways CitiExpress banner. The regional arm of BA carries more than 5 million passengers a year to 26 destinations in the UK. The move is an effort to better compete with up-and-coming low-fare carriers which have been undercutting BA's sales through more simplified routes and pricing structures.

Britain's flagship carrier has also enjoying regulatory approval for expansion of its codesharing agreement with American Airlines; the two companies now carry joint codes on 200 flights.

The carrier announced cost-cutting measures in 2004 that include a reduction of employee and operating costs. The reductions would take place over the next two years.

BA has also expressed an interest in acquiring its Irish competitor Aer Lingus as rumors of the Irish government considering the sale of its majority stake in the struggling airline increase.

Former Aer Lingus boss and current British Airways chief Willie Walsh announced in late 2005 that British Airways would trim its management ranks by 35% in order to reduce costs and invest in the business. The cuts, to be completed by 2008, will save the English flagship carrier an estimated $85.9 million.

HISTORY

British Airways has a jet trail winding back to 1916 and its biplane-flying ancestor, Aircraft Transport and Travel, which in 1919 launched the world's first daily international air service (between London and Paris). Concerned about subsidized foreign competition, British authorities in 1924 merged Aircraft Transport and Travel successor Daimler Airways with other fledgling British carriers — British Air Marine Navigation, Handley Page, and Instone Air Line — to form Imperial Airways.

Imperial pioneered routes from London to India (1929), Singapore (1933), and — in partnership with Qantas Empire Airways — Australia (1934). Competition on European routes emerged in the 1930s from upstart British Airways; in 1939 the government, troubled by the threat to Imperial, nationalized and merged the two airlines to form British Overseas Airways Corporation (BOAC).

After WWII, BOAC continued as the UK's international airline, but state-owned British European Airways (BEA) took over domestic and European routes. In 1972 the government combined the duo to form British Airways (BA).

BA and Air France jointly introduced supersonic passenger service in 1976 with the Concorde — a PR victory that contributed to years of losses. Colin Marshall became CEO in 1983 and reduced manpower and routes.

In 1987 the government sold BA to the public, and the airline bought chief UK rival British Caledonian. Hoping to become a globe-spanning carrier, in 1992 BA tried to gain a 44% stake in USAir (which became US Airways). American Airlines, United, and Delta strongly objected, demanding equal access to UK markets. BA settled for a 25% stake, the maximum foreign ownership allowed by US law, in 1993. It also bought 25% of Qantas.

That year BA settled a libel suit brought by UK competitor Virgin Atlantic Airways, which accused BA of waging a smear campaign against it. The settlement cost BA about $5 million, and Virgin Atlantic followed with a $1 billion antitrust suit in the US (dismissed in 1999). In 1994 BA paid out $4 million to settle yet another Virgin Atlantic suit, this one claiming BA had done sloppy maintenance on Virgin aircraft. BA also sold British Caledonian.

In 1996 Marshall turned over the CEO job to Bob Ayling, who had joined BA in 1985. BA and American Airlines agreed to coordinate prices and schedules and to share market data for their transatlantic routes. Though the deal met regulatory obstacles from the start, in 1997 BA sold its stake in US Airways. BA and American also took the lead in forming the Oneworld global alliance (which took effect in 1999).

The next year BA launched low-fare European carrier Go. Ayling resigned in 2000, and Marshall stepped in as temporary CEO before Rod Eddington, a veteran of Cathay Pacific and Ansett, was appointed. Also that year BA took a 9% stake in Iberia and sold its interest in France's Air Liberté.

BA grounded its Concordes in 2000 (flights resumed in 2001), three weeks after the crash of an Air France Concorde outside Paris in which 113 people were killed. The airline put its no-frills carrier Go up for sale that year, and in 2001 sold the airline to venture capital firm, 3i Group.

That year BA laid off 5,200 employees as a result of decreased demand for air travel after the terrorist attacks in New York and Washington, DC. The layoffs were on top of 1,800 job cuts the airline made earlier in the year, reducing BA's workforce by 10%.

BA's long-negotiated transatlantic alliance with American Airlines received tentative approval from the US Department of Transportation in 2002.

2003 saw the retirement of the BA's Concorde fleet, a longtime symbol of the airline's transatlantic dominance. Threats of terrorist attacks have caused the airline to cancel several flights between London and Washington, DC, as well as services to Saudi Arabia. The issue has led the BA to agree to the use of armed guards on certain flights, but the European Union has yet to agree on the subject.

Lord Colin Marshall, a 20-year veteran of British Airways, stepped down in 2004. From privatization to reviving the carrier after September 11, Lord Marshall had been instrumental in keeping Britain's flag carrier aloft.

EXECUTIVES

Chairman: Martin F. Broughton, age 58
Chief Executive: William M. (Willie) Walsh, age 43
CFO: Keith Williams, age 49
EVP Sales and Marketing, Americas: Robin Hayes
CIO: Paul Coby, age 49
Secretary: Alan Buchanan, age 45
Director Brands and Marketing: Kelly Reed
Director Commercial: Martin George, age 43
Director Commercial Planning: Robert Boyle, age 40
Director Customer Service, Operations and Director: Mike Street, age 57, $809,720 pay
Director Engineering: Alan McDonald, age 54
Director Flight Operations: Lloyd Cromwell Griffiths, age 60
Director Ground Operations: Geoff Want
Director Investments and Alliances: Roger Maynard, age 62
Director People: Neil Robertson, age 52
General Counsel: Robert Webb, age 57
Auditors: Ernst & Young

LOCATIONS

HQ: British Airways Plc
Waterside, Harmondsworth,
London UB7 0GB, United Kingdom
Phone: +44-0870850 9850   **Fax:** +44-20-8759-4314
US HQ: 75-20 Astoria Blvd., Jackson Heights, NY 11370
US Phone: 347-418-4000
Web: www.british-airways.com

British Airways serves about 220 destinations
in some 94 countries.

2005 Sales

	$ mil.	% of total
Europe		
UK	7,412	50
Other countries	2,221	15
The Americas	2,613	18
Africa, Middle East &		
Indian sub-continent	1,419	10
Asia/Pacific and Australia	1,100	7
Total	**14,765**	**100**

PRODUCTS/OPERATIONS

Major Subsidiaries and Affiliates

British Airways Capital Ltd. (airline finance)
British Airways Finance B.V. (airline finance, The Netherlands)
British Airways Holidays Ltd. (package holidays)
Comair Ltd. (18%, South Africa)
Deutsche BA Luftfahrtgesellschaft mbH (German airline)
Iberia Lineas Aéreas de España SA (9%, Spain)

COMPETITORS

Air France
All Nippon Airways
Delta Air
Delta Air Transport
easyJet
Japan Airlines
KLM
Lufthansa
Northwest Airlines
Ryanair
SAS
Singapore Airlines
UAL
Virgin Atlantic Airways

HISTORICAL FINANCIALS

Company Type: Public

Income Statement

FYE: March 31

	REVENUE ($ mil.)	NET INCOME ($ mil.)	NET PROFIT MARGIN	EMPLOYEES
3/05	14,765	474	3.2%	49,490
3/04	13,933	240	1.7%	51,939
3/03	12,150	114	0.9%	57,014
3/02	11,887	(202)	—	61,460
3/01	13,151	162	1.2%	62,175
3/00	14,245	(33)	—	65,157
3/99	14,367	332	2.3%	64,051
3/98	14,447	769	5.3%	60,770
3/97	13,705	907	6.6%	58,210
3/96	11,843	722	6.1%	55,296
Annual Growth	**2.5%**	**(4.6%)**	**—**	**(1.2%)**

2005 Year-End Financials

Debt ratio: 164.1%
Return on equity: 10.8%
Cash ($ mil.): 147
Current ratio: 0.95
Long-term debt ($ mil.): 7,644
No. of shares (mil.): 108
Dividends
Yield: 0.0%
Payout: —
Market value ($ mil.): 5,439

Stock History

NYSE: BAB

	STOCK PRICE ($) FY Close	P/E High/Low		Earnings	PER SHARE ($) Dividends	Book Value
3/05	50.23	13	8	4.35	0.00	43.01
3/04	51.00	28	7	2.23	0.00	37.75
3/03	16.85	34	13	1.06	0.00	21.56
3/02	35.10	—	—	(1.88)	2.02	26.53
3/01	45.75	46	26	1.49	2.90	42.10
3/00	53.75	—	—	(0.32)	6.28	46.36
3/99	68.63	37	17	3.09	0.00	50.38
3/98	104.06	18	12	7.02	2.20	53.44
3/97	104.75	13	9	8.32	2.73	48.80
3/96	82.00	12	9	6.75	1.75	39.63
Annual Growth	**(5.3%)**	**—**	**—**	**(4.8%)**	**—**	**0.9%**

British American Tobacco

When people pick up smoking, British American Tobacco (BAT) picks up steam. Spun off in the reorganization of B.A.T Industries, BAT is the world's #2 tobacco firm (behind Marlboro maker Altria Group) with about 15% of the market. It sells nearly 855 billion cigarettes in more than 190 countries. BAT's international cigarette brands include Dunhill, Kent, Lucky Strike, and Pall Mall; it also makes loose tobacco and regional cigarette brands. Its former US unit, Brown & Williamson (Kool and GPC cigarettes), merged with R.J.

Reynolds Tobacco (RJRT) in July 2004. Companies controlled by South African billionaire Anton Rupert own about 28% of BAT.

BAT owns 42% of Reynolds American, which was created by the Brown & Williamson/RJRT merger. Not surprisingly, BAT now looks to emerging markets in Korea, Vietnam, and Nigeria for growth. In early 2005, the tobacco company ruled out speculation that it was eyeing Gallaher or Altadis, saying it was considering a smaller buy.

Moreover, BAT would like to build a factory in China, the world's top tobacco market, and would move its Asian headquarters to Hong Kong if that were to happen. Meanwhile, it's scaling back in the UK and Canada. In 2004 it closed a manufacturing plant in Darlington, cutting about 500 jobs. In 2005 it's closing the doors on a Southampton, UK, plant and eliminating some 530 positions (and more than 65 in Ireland). Its subsidiary, Imperial Tobacco Canada (not affiliated with the UK's Imperial Tobacco), cut almost 850 jobs after closing a Montreal plant and other Canadian facilities. Imperial Tobacco says it controls about 60% of the Canadian cigarette market.

In response to health concerns and lawsuits brought against the tobacco industry in the US, BAT is test-marketing a Swedish product called snus, a pasteurized tobacco product that resembles a small teabag. BAT plans to market it in South Africa under the Peter Stuyvesant brand and in Sweden under the Lucky Strike brand as more than 100 times less harmful than cigarettes.

HISTORY

After a year of vicious price-cutting between Imperial Tobacco (UK) and James Buchanan Duke's American Tobacco in the UK, Imperial counterattacked in the US. To end the cigarette price war in the UK, the firms created British American Tobacco (BAT) in 1902. The truce granted Imperial the British market, American the US market, and they jointly owned BAT in the rest of the world.

With Duke in control, BAT expanded into new markets. In China it was selling 25 billion cigarettes a year by 1920. When the Communist revolution ended BAT's operations in China, the company lost more than 25% of its sales (although China later reemerged as a major export market for the company's cigarettes).

A 1911 US antitrust action forced American to sell its interest in BAT and opened the US market to the company. BAT purchased US cigarette manufacturer Brown & Williamson in 1927 and continued to grow through geographical expansion until the 1960s. In 1973 BAT and Imperial each regained control of its own brands in the UK and Continental Europe. Imperial sold the last of its stake in BAT in 1980.

Fearing that mounting public concern over smoking would limit the cigarette market, BAT acquired nontobacco businesses; it changed its name to B.A.T Industries in 1976. The acquisitions of retailers Saks (1973), Argos (UK, 1979), Marshall Field (1982), and later, insurance firms, diversified the company's sales base. After a 1989 hostile takeover bid from Sir James Goldsmith, it sold its retail operations, and retained its tobacco and financial services.

In 1994 B.A.T acquired the former American Tobacco for $1 billion. In 1997 the company acquired Cigarrera de Moderna (with 50% of Mexico's cigarette sales) and formed a joint venture with the Turkish tobacco state enterprise, Tekel.

B.A.T's tobacco operations were spun off in 1998 as British American Tobacco (BAT). The financial services operations were merged with Zurich Insurance in a transaction that created two holding companies: Allied Zurich (UK) and Zurich Allied (Switzerland). With the changes, Martin Broughton became chairman of BAT.

The company in 1999 paid $8.2 billion to buy Dutch cigarette company Rothmans International (Rothmans, Dunhill) from Switzerland's Compagnie Financiere Richemont and South Africa's Rembrandt Group — both controlled by Anton Rupert. With the purchase, BAT received a controlling stake in Canada's Rothmans, Benson & Hedges (RBH).

In early 2000 BAT bought the 58% of Canada's Imasco it didn't already own. Imasco sold off its financial services and BAT received Imasco's Imperial Tobacco unit (not related to the UK's Imperial Tobacco Group) in the deal. (Formerly called Imperial Tobacco Company of Canada, Imasco was created in 1908 with help from BAT.) BAT also unloaded its share of RBH via public offering.

In 2001 BAT bought the 40.5% of its BAT Australasia subsidiary (formed in 1999 through the Rothmans merger) it didn't already own. Broughton announced that year that the Chinese government had approved development plans that would allow the company to build a factory in China. The company also announced it would build the first foreign-owned cigarette factory in South Korea, at that time the world's #8 tobacco market.

Increasing its Latin American regional presence, BAT purchased a controlling stake in Peru's top tobacco company, Tabacalera Nacional, and several of its suppliers in 2003. However, two months later BAT said it would not make the million-dollar investment in the company. The announcement came soon after Peru raised taxes on cigarettes. By the end of the year, BAT had purchased tobacco manufacturer Ente Tabacchi Italiani S.p.A. from the Italian government. In 2004, BAT sold the distribution end of its Italian business to Compañía de Distribución Integral Logista.

EXECUTIVES

Chairman: Jan P. du Plessis, age 51, $88,895 pay (prior to promotion)
Deputy Chairman: Rt. Hon. Kenneth H. Clarke, age 64, $224,673 pay
CEO and Director: Paul Adams, age 50, $975,750 pay (prior to promotion)
COO and Director, America/Pacific; Director, British American Tobacco: Antonio Monteiro de Castro, age 59, $830,712 pay
Director, Finance; Director, British American Tobacco: Paul Rayner, age 49, $785,000 pay
Director, Africa and Middle East: Jacques Kruger, age 53
Regional Director, Asia/Pacific: John Daly
Director, Corporate and Regulatory Affairs: Michael Prideaux, age 52
Director, Human Resources: Rudi Kindts, age 47
Director, Europe: Ben Stevens, age 44
Director, Latin America and Caribbean: Flávio de Andrade, age 55
Director, Legal and General Counsel: Neil Withington, age 47
Director, Marketing: Jimmi Rembiszewski, age 53
Director, Operations and IT: Peter Taylor, age 51
Director, US: Susan M. Ivey, age 46
Manager, UK Social Reporting Manager: Nicky Donnelly
Head, Investor Relations: Ralph Edmondson
Head, Science and Regulation: Christopher Procter
Auditors: PricewaterhouseCoopers LLP

LOCATIONS

HQ: British American Tobacco p.l.c.
Globe House, 4 Temple Place,
London WC2R 2PG, United Kingdom
Phone: +44-20-7845-1000   **Fax:** +44-20-7240-0555
Web: www.bat.com

2004 Sales

	% of total
Europe	40
America/Pacific	25
Asia/Pacific	14
Africa & Middle East	11
Latin America	10
Total	**100**

PRODUCTS/OPERATIONS

Selected International Cigarette Brands
Barclay
Benson & Hedges (Asia Pacific, Middle East, Africa)
Capri
Carlton
Dunhill
John Player Gold Leaf
Kent
Kool
Lucky Strike
Misty
Pall Mall
Peter Stuyvesant
Player's
Rothmans
State Express 555
Viceroy
Winfield

Selected Regions and Brands
Argentina (Jockey Club)
Asia/Pacific (Holiday)
Australia (Stradbroke)
Canada (du Maurier)
Europe (Golden American)
Finland (North State)
Germany (HB)
Hungary (Sopianae)
India (Wills)
Indonesia (Ardath)
Ireland (Carrolls)
Latin America (Belmont, Derby, Free, Hollywood)
Mexico (Boots)
Peru (Hamilton)
Poland (Jan III Sobieski)
Russia (Yava Gold)
South Africa (Courtleigh)
Switzerland (Parisienne)
US (GPC)
Uzbekistan (Xon)

Selected Other Products and Brands
Cigars (Dunhill, Mercator, Schimmelpenninck)
Fine cut tobaccos (Ajja, Belgam, Javaanse Jongens, Samson, Schwarzer Krauser)
Pipe tobaccos (Captain Black, Clan, Dunhill, Erinmore)

COMPETITORS

Altadis
Carolina Group
Gallaher
Imperial Tobacco
Japan Tobacco
Philip Morris International
Reemtsma
Santa Fe Natural Tobacco
Swedish Match
Swisher International
Tiedemanns
Universal Corporation
Vector

HISTORICAL FINANCIALS

Company Type: Public

Income Statement

FYE: December 31

	REVENUE ($ mil.)	NET INCOME ($ mil.)	NET PROFIT MARGIN	EMPLOYEES
12/04	60,988	2,105	3.5%	90,249
12/03	43,071	1,125	2.6%	86,941
12/02	37,596	1,856	4.9%	85,819
12/01	35,627	1,471	4.1%	81,425
12/00	35,254	1,002	2.8%	86,805
12/99	30,374	898	3.0%	107,620
12/98	24,202	574	2.4%	101,081
12/97	11,766	852	7.2%	117,339
Annual Growth	**26.5%**	**13.8%**	**—**	**(3.7%)**

2004 Year-End Financials

Debt ratio: 119.6%
Return on equity: 23.4%
Cash ($ mil.): 3,629
Current ratio: 1.31
Long-term debt ($ mil.): 11,967

No. of shares (mil.): 1,070
Dividends
  Yield: 4.3%
  Payout: 75.9%
Market value ($ mil.): 37,072

Stock History

AMEX: BTI

	STOCK PRICE ($) FY Close	P/E High/Low		Earnings	PER SHARE ($) Dividends	Book Value
12/04	34.65	18	14	1.95	1.48	9.35
12/03	27.67	29	18	0.95	1.24	7.70
12/02	19.70	15	10	1.61	1.09	7.66
12/01	17.00	15	10	1.28	0.95	6.35
12/00	15.81	19	9	0.86	0.86	7.11
12/99	10.25	26	12	0.87	1.05	7.16
12/98	17.50	27	21	0.73	0.00	0.14
Annual Growth	**12.1%**	**—**	**—**	**17.8%**	**—**	**102.6%**

BSkyB

The lofty British Sky Broadcasting Group (BSkyB) is the UK's #1 pay-TV provider. BSkyB distributes entertainment, news, and sports programming which reaches 16.6 million homes in the UK and Ireland, including the 7.8 million that subscribe to its digital direct-to-home (DTH) satellite service. Responding to the success of Freeview in the UK, BSkyB quietly introduced its own free-to-air TV service, in hopes of capturing some of that growing market. BSkyB also offers interactive TV services, holds broadcast rights to the leading football (soccer) leagues in England and Scotland, and has minority stakes in several clubs. Rupert Murdoch's News Corp. owns 37% of BSkyB, and Rupert's son James Murdoch is CEO.

BSkyB also currently resells fixed-line phone service, and now plans to acquire Easynet, which would allow BSkyB to offer a triple play of TV, phone, and broadband services. While about 73% of BSkyB's revenues come from its DTH satellite customers base, the company also wholesales some of its channels to cable providers NTL and Telewest (which are now set to merge).

To boost brand awareness, BSkyB broadcasts three channels — Sky News, Sky Sports News, and Sky Travel — over Freeview, a free-to-air TV service jointly owned by the BBC, BSkyB, and Crown Castle. (Freeview and services like it are also referred to as digital terrestrial television, or DTT, services.) With millions of untapped homes in the UK, the company is hoping increased brand awareness will bring in more subscriber revenue.

In order to compete with the very popular Freeview, BSkyB quietly introduced its own free-to-air satellite TV offering in 2004. With the purchase of a set of reception equipment, customers have access to about 200 TV and radio channels with no subscription fees. From there, it would be easy to upgrade and add pay-TV service so BSkyB hopes it will gain more monthly subscribers in the long run. The company is also planning to offer a high definition TV (HDTV) service in 2006.

The company scored big points when it acquired exclusive broadcasting rights to the Premier League football (soccer) games in 2003, but the deal prompted the European Commission to scrutinize the situation as a possible violation of European competition rules.

HISTORY

Australian-born media czar Rupert Murdoch, after taking control of several British newspapers, moved into satellite TV service in the UK in 1989 when his News Corp. holding company started Sky Network Television. Broadcasting SkyTV's four channels via satellites owned by the Luxembourg-based Astra group allowed Murdoch to avoid restrictions of the British Broadcasting Act, which prohibited owners of national newspapers from owning more than 20% of a TV company.

In 1990 a consortium of companies, including Chargeurs, Granada, and Pearson, set up rival service British Satellite Broadcasting. The rivals faced a consumer market slow to adapt to new technology and a shrinking advertising base caused by an economic recession; both companies posted huge losses (SkyTV's weekly losses grew to more than $20 million in 1990). In the wake of such financial hemorrhaging, the firms merged that year and became British Sky Broadcasting (BSkyB), a slimmer operation with five channels. The small stake held by Chargeurs was later transferred to its Pathé communications unit.

In 1993 BSkyB teamed up with US media group Viacom to produce a Nickelodeon channel (children's programming) for the UK market. Then the firm allied with home shopping channel QVC to launch QVC UK (BSkyB sold its stake in the company in 2004). By the end of 1993, more than 3 million UK homes were receiving BSkyB's programs.

BSkyB sold about 20% of itself to the public in 1994, dropping News Corp.'s stake from 50% to 40%. That year it reinforced its position as the top UK sports broadcaster by launching Sky Sports 2. BSkyB teamed with rival BBC in 1995 to acquire more sports programming. It also formed an alliance with international news agency Reuters in an effort to strengthen its Sky News Channel.

In 1997 BSkyB began developing digital satellite TV and interactive services in the UK through British Interactive Broadcasting, a joint venture with British Telecommunications (now BT Group), HSBC Holdings, and Matsushita Electric Industrial. (The service, Sky Digital, was launched in 1998 and offers subscribers about 150 channels.)

Managing director Sam Chisholm and his deputy, David Chance, resigned in 1997, opening the door for Murdoch's 29-year-old daughter, Elisabeth, to take a greater role at BSkyB. (She left the company in 2000.) Mark Booth (formerly with Murdoch's Japanese Sky Broadcasting) became CEO. BSkyB launched digital pay-per-view TV in the UK in 1997.

Fox/Liberty Networks CEO Tony Ball replaced Booth as CEO in 1999 after Booth was named to head a News Corp.-backed new media company. French conglomerate Vivendi (now Vivendi Universal) bought Pathé's stake in BSkyB, along with those of Granada and Pearson, and Rupert Murdoch took over as chairman of BSkyB, replacing Pathé's Jerome Seydoux. Vivendi announced in 2000 that it would sell its BSkyB stake to clear regulatory hurdles in its bid to acquire Canada's Seagram and take over the Universal entertainment group. That year BSkyB paid $1 billion for a 24% stake (which was then sold off in 2002) in Germany's KirchPayTV.

News Corp. in 2000 spun off its satellite holdings, including BSkyB, to form a new company, Sky Global Networks, in large part to accommodate Murdoch's acquisition of US-based DIRECTV. A planned IPO was postponed in 2001 after Murdoch pulled out of the bidding for the market-leading satellite operator.

That same year BSkyB completed the transition to an all-digital network and discontinued analog service, and acquired both British Broadcasting Limited, which operates the OpenTV interactive service, and Sports Internet Group, a sports-related Web site operator.

Ball stepped down as CEO in 2003. Eyebrows were raised when Rupert Murdoch's son James was brought in to fill the CEO spot. At least in part because he was only 30 years old at the time, there were many grumblings about nepotism.

EXECUTIVES

Chairman: K. Rupert Murdoch, age 74, $81,911 pay
Deputy Chairman: Lord Jacob Rothschild, age 69, $53,747 pay
CEO and Director: James R. Murdoch, age 32, $3,518,190 pay
COO: Richard Freudenstein, age 40
CFO and Director: Jeremy Darroch, age 43, $1,948,536 pay
Chief Marketing Officer: Jon Florsheim, age 45
Managing Director, Sky Media: Nick Milligan, age 44
Managing Director, Sky Networks: Dawn Airey, age 44
Managing Director, Sky Sports: Vic Wakeling, age 62
Company Secretary: David (Dave) Gormley, age 42
Group Director Engineering and Platform Technology: Alun Webber, age 39
Director, IT and Strategy: Jeff Hughes, age 35
Director, Communications: Matthew Anderson
Director, People and Organisational Development: Beryl Cook, age 44
Director, Strategy: Mike Darcey, age 40
Head of Public Affairs: Martin Le Jeune
Head of Regulatory Affairs: Michael Rhodes, age 41
General Counsel: James Conyers, age 40
Strategic Adviser, Technology: Robin Crossley, age 47
Auditors: Deloitte & Touche LLP

LOCATIONS

HQ: British Sky Broadcasting Group plc
Grant Way, Isleworth,
London TW7 5QD, United Kingdom
Phone: +44-20-7705-3000   **Fax:** +44-20-7705-3453
Web: www.sky.com

British Sky Broadcasting operates in the UK and Ireland.

PRODUCTS/OPERATIONS

2005 Sales

	% of total
Direct-to-home subscribers	73
Advertising	8
Sky Bet	7
Cable subscribers	6
Sky Active	2
Other	4
Total	**100**

Selected Channels

The Amp (music programming)
Artsworld
Flaunt (music programming)
Scuzz (music programming)
Sky Box Office (pay-per-view programming)
Sky Cinema (classic cinema programming)
Sky Movies
Sky News
Sky One (general entertainment programming)
Sky Sports
Sky Travel (travel programming)
Sky Vegas Live (interactive entertainment)

Selected Subsidiaries and Affiliates

Attheraces Holdings Limited (50%, broadcast horse racing and related services)
Australian News Channel Pty Limited (33%, 24-hour news)
British Interactive Broadcasting Holdings Limited (interactive TV services)
British Sky Broadcasting Limited (pay-TV broadcasting)
British Sky Broadcasting SA (satellite transponder leasing, Luxembourg)
Granada Sky Broadcasting Limited (80%, general entertainment channels)
The History Channel (UK) (50%, history programming)
MUTV (33%, Manchester United football channel)
National Geographic Channel UK (50%, natural history and adventure programming)
Nickelodeon UK (50%, children's programming)
Paramount UK (25%, comedy programming)
Sky In-Home Service Limited (supply, installation, and maintenance of satellite TV receiving equipment)
Sky Subscribers Services Limited (satellite broadcasting support services)
Sky Television Limited (holding company)
Sky Ventures Limited (joint ventures holding company)

COMPETITORS

BBC	SMG
Channel 4	Telewest
Flextech	UGC Europe
Freeview	UnitedGlobalCom
ITV	Yorkshire-Tyne Tees
NTL	Television Holdings
RTL Group	

HISTORICAL FINANCIALS

Company Type: Public

Income Statement

FYE: June 30

	REVENUE ($ mil.)	NET INCOME ($ mil.)	NET PROFIT MARGIN	EMPLOYEES
6/05	7,241	760	10.5%	9,958
6/04	6,646	585	8.8%	9,500
6/03	5,273	315	6.0%	9,132
6/02	4,251	(2,117)	—	9,083
6/01	3,260	(761)	—	9,948
6/00	2,801	(412)	—	10,730
6/99	2,439	(450)	—	8,271
6/98	2,390	415	17.4%	4,634
6/97	2,114	480	22.7%	4,580
6/96	1,563	362	23.2%	4,025
Annual Growth	18.6%	8.6%	—	10.6%

2005 Year-End Financials

Debt ratio: —
Return on equity: 1,475.7%
Cash ($ mil.): 1,150
Current ratio: 1.18
Long-term debt ($ mil.): 1,925

No. of shares (mil.): 467
Dividends
Yield: 2.2%
Payout: 52.8%
Market value ($ mil.): 17,527

Stock History

NYSE: BSY

	STOCK PRICE ($) FY Close	P/E High/Low		PER SHARE ($) Earnings	Dividends	Book Value
6/05	37.54	29	21	1.59	0.84	(0.13)
6/04	45.51	45	30	1.21	0.00	0.34
6/03	45.10	71	41	0.64	0.00	(0.36)
6/02	38.36	—	—	(4.50)	0.00	(0.65)
6/01	40.02	—	—	(1.65)	0.00	2.17
6/00	77.46	—	—	(0.95)	0.00	1.43
6/99	37.44	—	—	(1.04)	0.23	(1.52)
6/98	28.43	33	23	0.97	0.48	(0.78)
6/97	29.81	40	24	1.12	0.45	(1.09)
6/96	27.10	34	20	0.85	0.35	(1.46)
Annual Growth	3.7%	—	—	7.2%	10.2%	—

BT Group

Once upon a time, BT Group rivals could have fit into one of the company's signature red phone booths. Though competition has taken a toll, BT Group still wears the crown as the UK's leading telecommunications carrier. Formerly known as British Telecommunications, the BT Group offers local and long-distance phone service through about 30 million access lines to 19 million consumer customers and more than 1 million business clients. It also provides Internet access and other data services.

In a major reorganization, BT Group has turned itself into a holding company. Ordered to upgrade and open its domestic networks, it has split its UK fixed-line network operations into separate wholesale and retail businesses.

BT Group operates primarily in the UK, but the BT Group empire stretches into other parts of Western Europe and across the pond to North America. The company has introduced a new corporate identity, its first change since 1991, which, the company said, better reflects the range of activities that BT Group now encompasses. It also has rolled out Openreach, a new entity that contains the company's local network services unit.

The company also has expanded its information communications technology services offered to multi-site corporations in the US. It has signed its largest IT services deal to date, valued at $3 billion over eight-and-a-half years, with the Reuters Group. BT Group also has acquired financial services extranet provider Radianz from Reuters for $175 million.

It has acquired Infonet, a leading provider of corporate managed voice and data network services. The company, renamed BT Infonet, will be a part of the BT Global Services unit. It also has expanded its multi-protocol label switching (MPLS) capacity in North America. BT Group also has acquired SkyNet Systems, a provider of Internet protocol-based LAN systems.

BT is refocusing its other international holdings to concentrate on Europe. It has teamed up with Microsoft to deliver broadband applications using the MSN 8 Web browser and the company has created separate units for its broadband Internet protocol business and its consumer ISP (BT Openworld). Data transmission makes up more and more of BT's network traffic.

Once the leading wireless telecoms operator in the UK, BT Group has reentered that market through BT Mobile, wireless services marketed by the parent company using the Vodafone Group network. BT Group had countered mounting debt woes in 2001 with the spinoff (named O2) of its wireless businesses, including its UK operations.

The group has also reduced its workforce by about 15% in recent years.

HISTORY

In 1879 the British Post Office (now known as Royal Mail and formerly Consignia) got the exclusive right to operate telegraph systems. When private firms tried to offer phone service, the government objected, arguing in court that its telegraph monopoly was imperiled. The courts agreed, and the Post Office was empowered to license private phone companies, collect a 10% royalty, and operate its own systems.

The private National Telephone Company emerged as the leading phone outfit, competing with the Post Office. When National's license expired in 1911, the Post Office took over and became the monopoly phone company. In 1936 the phone system introduced its familiar red public call offices (phone booths), designed for King George V's jubilee.

Under a 1981 law, telecommunications were split from the Post Office and placed under the new British Telecommunications (BT). The government also allowed competitor Mercury Communications (Formerly One 2 One, now known as T-Mobile (UK)) to compete. The Thatcher government soon called for BT's privatization.

After the Telecommunications Act of 1984, BT went public in one of the largest UK stock offerings in history. The act set up the regulatory Office of Telecommunications (OFTEL). The next year Cellnet, BT's joint venture with Securicor, launched its mobile phone network. To become a multinational concern, BT bought control of Canadian phone equipment maker Mitel (1986, sold in 1992) and 20% of firm McCaw Cellular (1989, sold to AT&T in 1994).

In 1990 the British government opened the UK to more phone competition and BT responded with improvements to its network and a workforce reduction. The government sold almost all of its remaining shares in BT in 1993. The next year the company bought a 20% stake in MCI, the #2 US long-distance carrier.

In 1999 BT expanded in continental Europe, Latin America (a 20% stake in IMPSAT), Asia (with AT&T, a 30% stake in Japan Telecom), and the US, where it bought systems integration firm Syntegra (USA) (formerly Control Data Systems) and Yellow Book USA. At home BT bought out Securicor's stake in Cellnet. UK regulators also ordered the company to upgrade its UK phone network and open it to rivals by 2001.

BT bought Ireland's Esat Telecom in 2000. That year the government sold its remaining stake in BT and the company bought Telenor's stake in VIAG Interkom; early the next year the company took full ownership of the German mobile phone company. Also in early 2001, BT sold its stakes in Japan Telecom and J-Phone Communications to Vodafone, which later that year bought BT's Airtel Móvil (now known as Vodafone España) interest.

BT Group countered increasing competition and mounting debt woes through restructuring that included the 2001 spinoff of its domestic and international wireless businesses, combined under the mmO2 brand (formerly BT Wireless), which included BT Cellnet, a leading UK mobile phone operator. The decision left BT Group as the only top-tier European telecom firm without a wireless network.

To further its restructuring, BT in 2002 sold its Yellow Pages unit, Yell, to two buyout firms, Hicks, Muse, Tate & Furst and Apax Partners. The company also sold a 77% stake in Brightstar, its technology incubator, to private equity investment firm Coller Capital and New Venture Partners in a deal valued at $77 million. BT Group held a 23% stake and remained a limited partner in a new venture (NVP Brightstar) that continued to work closely with its BT Exact unit.

In 2002 BT sold its 26% stake in France's Cegetel to Vivendi Universal. It also has unloaded other noncore assets including its 21% stake in Hong Kong wireless carrier SmarTone Telecommunications in its continuing effort to reduce debt.

EXECUTIVES

Chairman: Sir Christopher Bland, age 67, $912,900 pay
Deputy Chairman: Sir Anthony Greener, age 65, $209,967 pay
Chief Executive and Director: Bernardus J. (Ben) Verwaayen, age 53, $2,096,018 pay
Group Finance Director and Board Member: Hanif Lalani, age 43, $375,740 pay
Group Strategy Director and Regional Director, London: Clive R. Ansell
Chief Executive, BT Global Services, and Director: Andy Green, age 50, $1,183,118 pay
Chief Executive, BT Retail, and Director: Ian P. Livingston, age 40, $1,253,093 pay
Chief Executive, BT Wholesale, and Director: Paul Reynolds, age 48, $1,119,215 pay
CIO; Chief Executive, BT Exact: Al-Noor Ramji, age 51
Chief Executive, BT Infonet: José A. Collazo, age 60
Chief Executive, Openreach: Steve Robertson
CTO: Matthew W. (Matt) Bross, age 44
Futurologist: Ian Pearson
Company Secretary: Larry Stone, age 48
President, BT International: François Barrault, age 44
Managing Director, BT Openworld: Duncan Ingram
Managing Director, Products and Enterprises, BT Retail: Steve Andrews
Director, Customer Contact Centre, BT Retail: Carol Borghesi
Director, Syntegra and Americas Regiona, BT Global Services: Tim Smart
President, Customer Service, BT Global Services: Roel M.M. Louwhoff, age 38
VP, International Affairs: Aad Van Waveren
Director of HR and Management Services, BT Retail: Joe McDavid
Auditors: PricewaterhouseCoopers LLP

LOCATIONS

HQ: BT Group plc
BT Centre, 81 Newgate St.,
London EC1A 7AJ, United Kingdom
Phone: +44-20-7356-5000   **Fax:** +44-20-7356-5520
US HQ: 40 E. 52nd St., New York, NY 10022
US Phone: 212-418-7787
Web: www.btplc.com

2005 Sales

	$ mil.	% of total
Europe		
UK	32,064	91
Other countries	2,638	7
Americas	359	1
Asia/Pacific	133	1
Total	**35,194**	**100**

PRODUCTS/OPERATIONS

2005 Sales

	$ mil.	% of total
Business		
Major corporate	11,530	33
Small & midized	4,657	13
Consumer	10,653	30
Wholesale	8,308	24
Other	46	—
Total	**35,194**	**100**

2005 Sales

	% of total
BT Retail	45
BT Wholesale	32
BT Global Services	23
Total	**100**

Selected Operating Units

BT Exact (research, technology, and information
technology (IT) operations)
BT Global Services (formerly BT Ignite, international
data and IP (Internet protocol) services)
  BT International (BT Global Services operations in
  Europe, the Americas, and the Asia Pacific regions,
  and BT Group's international sales
  and marketing operations)
  Syntegra (business transformation and change
  management services)
BT Retail (consumer communications
services and products)
  BT Broadband (high-speed Internet access)
  BT Openworld (Internet access and portal services)
BT Wholesale (carrier-level network and
communications services and products)
Openreach (local network services)

COMPETITORS

Accenture
Bush Telegraph
Cable & Wireless
Centrica Telecommunications
COLT Telecom
Deutsche Telekom
Energis
Euphony Communications
France Telecom
Integrated Communications for Business
KPN
MCI
O2
PTV
T-Com
Telecom Italia
Telefónica
Telewest
Verizon
Virgin Mobile UK
Wanadoo UK
Xfone

HISTORICAL FINANCIALS

Company Type: Public

Income Statement

FYE: March 31

	REVENUE ($ mil.)	NET INCOME ($ mil.)	NET PROFIT MARGIN	EMPLOYEES
3/05	35,194	3,442	9.8%	102,100
3/04	34,131	2,612	7.7%	99,900
3/03	29,596	4,245	14.3%	104,700
3/02	26,293	1,418	5.4%	108,600
3/01	28,953	(2,565)	—	137,000
3/00	29,820	3,275	11.0%	136,800
3/99	27,322	4,808	17.6%	124,700
3/98	26,145	2,852	10.9%	129,200
3/97	24,486	3,405	13.9%	127,500
3/96	22,048	3,031	13.7%	130,700
Annual Growth	**5.3%**	**1.4%**	**—**	**(2.7%)**

2005 Year-End Financials

Debt ratio: 210.1%
Return on equity: 53.0%
Cash ($ mil.): 389
Current ratio: 0.83
Long-term debt ($ mil.): 15,290

No. of shares (mil.): 863
Dividends
  Yield: 4.3%
  Payout: 41.5%
Market value ($ mil.): 33,623

Stock History

NYSE: BT

	STOCK PRICE ($) FY Close	P/E High	P/E Low	PER SHARE ($) Earnings	PER SHARE ($) Dividends	PER SHARE ($) Book Value
3/05	38.94	12	9	4.00	1.66	8.43
3/04	33.39	11	8	3.01	1.25	6.60
3/03	25.44	19	10	4.90	0.71	4.81
3/02	40.18	11	4	1.70	0.00	(0.59)
3/01	74.30	—	—	(3.93)	3.55	30.28
3/00	188.13	50	29	4.92	3.54	38.68
3/99	164.19	33	19	7.30	5.46	37.22
3/98	109.38	26	14	4.46	0.00	28.12
3/97	70.00	14	9	5.38	1.85	28.68
3/96	56.63	14	11	4.82	2.97	30.75
Annual Growth	**(4.1%)**	**—**	**—**	**(2.1%)**	**(6.3%)**	**(13.4%)**

Cable and Wireless

Telegraph cables and short-wave radio have given way to webs of optical fiber and satellites, but Cable and Wireless nonetheless promotes its famous name like never before. The company has been rerouting its corporate strategy and is taking on the business world's data needs, focusing on the demand for business data and Internet services. Cable and Wireless serves customers in about 300 cities in 80 countries with wireless and fixed-line voice and data services. The company has its primary operations in the Caribbean, Macao, Panama, and the UK.

Cable and Wireless intended to rid itself of noncore holdings and to invest in the develop-

ment of IP (Internet protocol) networks and Web hosting facilities, but overcapacity in the market forced the company to withdraw from many fronts and refocus on its UK operations and those in the Caribbean.

The company in 2003 announced that it would exit the US market. It sold its bankrupt US operations, which included Cable & Wireless Internet Services and Cable & Wireless USA, to SAVVIS in 2004 as part of this strategy. Later that year Cable and Wireless bought Monaco Telecom from Vivendi Universal as part of an effort to expand its presence in Europe.

HISTORY

British cable and telegraph veteran John Pender began Eastern Telegraph in 1872. When he died in 1896, Eastern and associated companies owned one of every three miles of telegraph cable on the planet.

As the new century began, telecommunications expanded to include the wireless radio communications promoted by inventor Guglielmo Marconi, head of the UK's Marconi Wireless Telegraph. After WWI, the industry grew in importance, and, partly to counter a threat from a new US company called ITT, UK companies, including Marconi Wireless and Eastern Telegraph, joined in 1929 to form Cable and Wireless (C&W).

C&W began providing telegraph and telephone services in the UK's far-flung colonies, from Hong Kong to the Philippines to the Cayman Islands. It was nationalized in 1947, and in the 1950s C&W began losing franchises in former colonies or had local governments strip it of its monopolies.

The Thatcher government returned C&W to private ownership in 1985. C&W began building a network of undersea fiber-optic cables and satellites to link the Caribbean, Hong Kong, Japan, the UK, and the US. To complete the task, C&W assembled the world's largest commercial fleet of cable ships.

C&W joined British Petroleum (BP) and Barclays Merchant Bank in 1982 to form Mercury Communications as a rival to giant British Telecommunications (BT, now BT Group). C&W bought out BP and Barclays in 1984. The next year Mercury won the right to interconnect with BT.

As the 1990s began, C&W was adrift. In 1993 C&W and U S WEST's cable unit (later MediaOne) launched a digital cellular service — One 2 One — in the UK, but overall C&W wasn't making much headway in Europe. In 1996 merger talks with BT to build the world's largest telecom company failed. At this low point, Dick Brown, an American, was named C&W's CEO. Under Brown's direction C&W disposed of underperforming assets and created Cable & Wireless Communications (CWC) by combining Mercury with cable firms NYNEX CableComms, Bell Cablemedia, and Videotron.

When the UK handed over Hong Kong to China in 1997, C&W — in a bid to get access to the mainland market — sold a stake in Hong Kong Telecom to China Telecom. When MCI agreed to merge with WorldCom in 1998, C&W bought MCI's Internet business in a major step toward its emerging data-centric strategy. The company later sold the US dial-up business to Prodigy and the remaining data hosting and services operations later became C&W USA Inc.

Hong Kong Telecom became Cable & Wireless HKT in 1999. Brown left that year and was succeeded by Graham Wallace, former boss of CWC. C&W won a bidding war with NTT for Japan's International Digital Communications (now Cable & Wireless IDC). But selling was generally the order of the day: C&W sold its Global Marine undersea-cable operations to Global Crossing and struck a deal (which closed in 2000) to sell its UK consumer phone and cable TV business to rival NTL. It also sold One 2 One for about $11 billion to Deutsche Telekom.

In 2000 C&W announced plans to build a fiber-optic network in Japan. It took an 11% stake in Japanese ISP Garnet Connections and continued to acquire European ISPs. That year the company completed the sale of Cable & Wireless HKT, Hong Kong's dominant telecom carrier, to Pacific Century CyberWorks (now called PCCW).

The company sold its controlling interest in Cable & Wireless Optus, and in 2001 Optus was acquired by Singapore Telecommunications. Also that year Cable and Wireless bought US-based Digital Island, and in 2002 it completed the acquisition of assets from bankrupt Exodus Communications. But the Exodus purchase has proved unwise and the company is cutting 30% of its workforce from C&W Global, its Internet unit. The division is now focusing on multinational clients and is supported by the company's international connections and fiber-optic networks.

The company has also cut jobs in Europe and sold some operations in that region, including businesses offering domestic-only services in Belgium, the Netherlands, Russia, Sweden, and Switzerland. Cable and Wireless also sold its 14% stake in Hong Kong operator PCCW.

Also Cable and Wireless purchased bankrupt PSINet's Japan unit in 2002 and announced plans to build a fiber-optic network in Japan. It also teamed up with Alcatel to lay a new transatlantic cable for Internet traffic.

EXECUTIVES

Chairman: Richard D. Lapthorne, age 61
Deputy Chairman: Lord George Robertson, age 57
CEO: Francesco Caio, age 47
COO: Kevin Loosemore, age 45
Group CFO: Charles E. N. Herlinger, age 48
Group Director, Corporate and Public Affairs: Lesley Smith
Group Director, Mobile: Barbara Poggiali
CEO, Caribbean Mobile: Stephen Brewer
CEO, Cable & Wireless USA: Simon Cunningham
CEO, Cable & Wireless Japan/Asia: Phil Green
VP, Investor Relations: Virginia Porter
VP, Marketing, Cable & Wireless America: Laurie Probst
Managing Director, Retail & Industry: Robin Morgan
Company Secretary: Ken Claydon, age 59
Auditors: KPMG Audit Plc

LOCATIONS

HQ: Cable and Wireless plc
124 Theobalds Rd.,
London WC1X 8RX, United Kingdom
Phone: +44-20-7315-4000   **Fax:** +44-20-7315-5198
US HQ: 8219 Leesburg Pike, Vienna, VA 22182
US Phone: 703-790-5300   **US Fax:** 571-203-3993
Web: www.cw.com/new

Cable and Wireless has operations in the Asia/Pacific region, the Caribbean Basin, Europe, the Indian Ocean, the Middle East, Panama, and the UK.

2005 Sales

	% of total
Europe	
UK	53
Other countries	9
Caribbean	18
Panama	8
Asia	
Macao	4
Other countries	2
Other regions	6
Total	**100**

PRODUCTS/OPERATIONS

Selected Subsidiaries and Affiliates

Cable & Wireless (Barbados) Limited (81%)
Cable & Wireless (Cayman Islands) Limited
Cable & Wireless Global Limited (formerly Cable & Wireless Global Markets Limited)
Cable & Wireless IDC Inc. (98%, Japan)
Cable & Wireless Jamaica Limited (82%)
Cable & Wireless Panama SA (49%)
Cable & Wireless UK (formerly Cable & Wireless Communications Mercury)
Cable & Wireless (West Indies) Limited
Companhia de Telecomunicações de Macau S.A.R.L. (51%)
Dhivehi Raajjeyge Gulhun Private Limited (45%)
Yemen International Telecommunications Company LLC (51%)

COMPETITORS

AT&T
BT
BT Infonet
Bush Telegraph
Check Communications
Deutsche Telekom
Equant
France Telecom
Global Crossing
Level 3 Communications
MCI
NTT

HISTORICAL FINANCIALS

Company Type: Public

Income Statement

FYE: March 31

	REVENUE ($ mil.)	NET INCOME ($ mil.)	NET PROFIT MARGIN	EMPLOYEES
3/05	6,089	571	9.4%	14,781
3/04	6,766	(437)	—	17,430
3/03	6,940	(10,383)	—	23,152
3/02	8,425	(7,302)	—	35,561
3/01	11,480	3,731	32.5%	47,904
3/00	14,661	12,905	88.0%	54,919
3/99	12,803	1,463	11.4%	50,671
3/98	11,704	2,153	18.4%	46,550
3/97	9,919	1,110	11.2%	37,488
3/96	8,420	926	11.0%	39,636
Annual Growth	(3.5%)	(5.2%)	—	(10.4%)

2005 Year-End Financials

Debt ratio: 44.1%
Return on equity: 17.2%
Cash ($ mil.): 255
Current ratio: 2.15
Long-term debt ($ mil.): 1,514
No. of shares (mil.): 798
Dividends
Yield: 3.3%
Payout: 34.3%
Market value ($ mil.): 5,811

Stock History

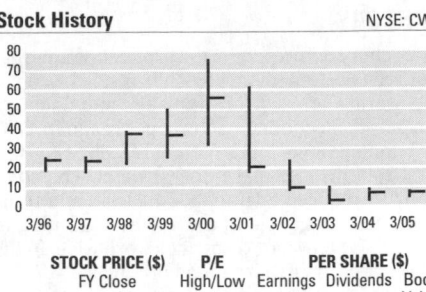

NYSE: CWP

	STOCK PRICE ($) FY Close	P/E High/Low		Earnings	PER SHARE ($) Dividends	Book Value
3/05	7.28	11	7	0.70	0.24	4.30
3/04	7.12	—	—	(0.56)	0.00	4.04
3/03	3.31	—	—	(13.29)	0.26	4.28
3/02	9.84	—	—	(8.01)	0.68	16.20
3/01	20.60	—	—	4.10	1.35	23.34
3/00	56.00	10	4	7.21	0.68	15.86
3/99	36.94	31	16	1.82	0.20	9.70
3/98	37.75	14	8	2.86	0.00	6.82
3/97	23.75	17	12	1.49	0.61	6.74
3/96	24.25	16	12	1.57	0.49	6.72
Annual Growth	(12.5%)	—	—	(8.6%)	(7.6%)	(4.8%)

Cadbury Schweppes

Drop a melted Cadbury chocolate bar on your favorite white shirt? Not to worry, Schweppes club soda will get it right out. A leading global confectioner, Cadbury Schweppes is also the world's #3 soft-drink producer, after The Coca-Cola Company and PepsiCo. Its beverage brands are sold mainly in North America and Western Europe and include 7 UP (US only), A&W Root Beer, Canada Dry, Dr Pepper, and Hawaiian Punch. It also makes Mott's apple products and Clamato juice. The company's confections are the market leaders in the UK. Along with the famous Cadbury Créme Egg, its candy brands include Trebor and Bassett. Cadbury Schweppes' gum brands include Bubbas, Trident, and Dentyne.

Cadbury Schweppes' US candy brands — which include Cadbury, Peter Paul, and York — are licensed to The Hershey Company. Subsidiary Cadbury Schweppes Americas represents about 25% of company sales.

Cadbury's UK division, Cadbury Trebor Bassett, has one of the strongest confectionery brands in Dairy Milk. In other countries, the firm markets its powerful Cadbury name with regional brands. Its 2003 purchase of Pfizer's consumer brand, Adams, brought with it Bubblicious, Certs, Chiclets, Dentyne, Halls, and Trident to the company's roster.

In 2005 the company announced the sale of its European beverage business to a group of private investors managed by The Blackstone Group and Lion Capital for $2.2 billion in cash. The sale does not include Cadbury's US drinks business. Brands involved include Schweppes, Orangina, Oasis, Apollinaris, and La Casera. Cadbury will continue to own Dr Pepper, 7 UP, and Snapple.

HISTORY

Cadbury Schweppes is the product of a merger between two venerable British firms: Schweppes, the world's first soft-drink maker, and Cadbury, a candy confectionery. Schweppes began in 1783 in London, where Swiss national Jacob Schweppe first sold his artificial mineral water. The company introduced a lemonade in 1835 and tonic water and ginger ale in the 1870s. Beginning in the 1880s Schweppes expanded worldwide. In the 1960s it diversified into food products.

John Cadbury opened a coffee and tea shop in Birmingham, England, in 1824. He sold cocoa for drinking, which proved so popular that in 1831 he began making cocoa and was producing 15 varieties of chocolates by 1841.

The companies merged in 1969. Under Dominic Cadbury (great-grandson of founder John), Cadbury Schweppes acquired Peter Paul (Mounds, Almond Joy) in 1978 while increasing beverage sales in Europe and Asia. In 1982 it acquired applesauce and juice maker Duffy-Mott.

The company sold its noncandy and nonbeverage businesses in 1986. It then acquired Canada Dry, the rights to Sunkist soda, and 34% of Dr Pepper (reduced to 18% when Dr Pepper merged with Seven Up in 1988).

Fatigued by Mars' and Hershey's US dominance, Cadbury Schweppes signed a licensing agreement with Hershey in 1988, ending its direct involvement in the US candy market. The company added the Orange Crush and Hires brands in 1989, and it acquired candy makers Trebor and Bassett and the noncola soft-drink operations of Source Perrier in 1990.

The Camelot Group, a UK consortium that includes Cadbury Schweppes, was picked in 1994 to operate the UK's National Lottery. Cadbury Schweppes bought the rest of Dr Pepper/Seven Up for $2.5 billion in 1995, and became the world's #3 soft-drink company. John Sunderland was appointed CEO of Cadbury Schweppes in 1996 and named executive chairman in 2003. Todd Stitzer succeeded Sunderland as Cadbury's CEO that same year.

Cadbury Schweppes and The Carlyle Group investment firm created American Bottling through acquisitions in 1998. In 1999 Cadbury Schweppes and Carlyle bought the Dr Pepper Bottling Company of Texas for $691 million, combining it with American Bottling to form Dr Pepper/Seven Up Bottling Group.

In 1999 Cadbury Schweppes sold its beverage operations in more than 160 countries (excluding Australia, Continental Europe, and the US) to The Coca-Cola Company for $973 million.

In 2000 the company acquired Snapple Beverage Group from Triarc Companies in a deal worth about $1.45 billion. Deciding to continue soft-drink operations in Australia, that month Cadbury Schweppes also bought Pepsi Cola Bottlers Australia (a joint venture between Lion Nathan and Pepsi Cola). It also bought France's largest chewing gum maker, Hollywood, for $170 million, making it the world's #4 confectioner.

In 2001 the company sold Royal Crown Cola's international division to Canada's Cott Corporation for $94 million. (It retained the RC business in the US, Canada, Puerto Rico, and Mexico.) Expanding further into soft drinks, the firm agreed to buy Pernod Ricard's soft-drink businesses (including the Orangina and Yoo-Hoo brands) in Continental Europe, North America, and Australia in September for about $640 million.

The next year Cadbury Schweppes acquired Squirt, a leading carbonated soft-drink brand in Mexico. In May the company bought Nantucket Allserve (Nantucket Nectars) from Ocean Spray Cranberries and folded Nantucket's brands into its Snapple group in order to bolster its noncarbonated drinks business. In September of the same year it also purchased Denmark's Dandy chewing gum company, further bolstering its global status as the world's #4 gum company. Later in 2002 Cadbury and Nestlé made a joint $10.5 billion bid for Hershey but Hershey subsequently called the sale off.

Cadbury Schweppes revised its organizational structure in 2003 by reducing its number of reporting units from 10 to five. The units included Americas Beverages, Americas Confectionery, EMEA Confectionery (Europe, Middle East, and Africa), Europe Beverages, and Asia/Pacific. Later that year, Cadbury Schweppes completed its purchase of Pfizer Inc.'s Adams confectionery business for $4.2 billion.

While still busy integrating the Adams production and products, Cadbury Schweppes added a new functional division to the company structure. Joining finance, human resources, legal, global commercial, and global supply chain in 2004, was a science and technology unit, headed by David Macnair.

In 2005 Cadbury bought UK organic chocolate maker Green & Black's.

EXECUTIVES

Executive Chairman: John M. Sunderland, age 59
Deputy Chairman: Roger M. Carr, age 58
CEO and Director: Todd Stitzer, age 53, $1,296,333 pay
CFO and Director: Ken Hanna, age 51, $681,875 pay
VP, Government Affairs: Deborah L. Louison
VP, HR: Pippa Greenslade
Chief Human Resources Officer and Director:
 Robert J. (Bob) Stack, age 54, $728,104 pay
CIO: Christine Connolly
Chief Science and Technology Officer: David Macnair
Chief Executive, Bebidas de Espana: Patrick Falgas
Group Secretary, Chief Legal Officer, and Director:
 Michael A. C. (Mike) Clark, age 57
President and CEO, Americas Beverages:
 Gil M. Cassagne
President and CEO, Americas Confectionery:
 Matt Shattock
President and CEO, Asia/Pacific: Rajiv Wahi
President and CEO, Europe Beverages:
 Marie-Bernard Trannoy, age 56
Director, Finance Confectionary UK: James Reed
**Director, Investor Relations and Finance Global
 Commercial:** Sally Jones
Director, Media: Erika Knight
Director, New Product Development: David Sheperd
Director, Sales: Louise Cook
Manager, Secretariat: Matthew Jones
Head of Group Public Relations: Dora McCabe
Auditors: Deloitte & Touche LLP

LOCATIONS

HQ: Cadbury Schweppes plc
 25 Berkeley Sq., London W1J 6HB, United Kingdom
Phone: +44-20-7409-1313   **Fax:** +44-20-7830-5200
US HQ: 5301 Legacy Dr., Plano, TX 75024
US Phone: 972-673-7000   **US Fax:** 972-673-7980
Web: www.cadburyschweppes.com

Cadbury Schweppes' confections are sold in more than 190 countries. Cadbury Schweppes sells beverages in nine countries and licenses the sale of its beverages in about 20 others.

2004 Sales

	% of total
Americas Beverages	33
Europe, Middle East, Africa	25
Americas Confectionery	16
Asia/Pacific	16
Europe Beverages	10
Total	**100**

PRODUCTS/OPERATIONS

Selected Brand Names

Beverages
 7 UP (US & Puerto Rico)
 A&W Root Beer
 Canada Dry
 Clamato
 Country Time (licensed, US)
 Crush
 Crystal Light (licensed, US)
 Diet Rite
 Dr Pepper (Australia, Canada, Europe, Mexico, US)
 Hawaiian Punch
 La Casera
 Mauna La'i
 Mistic (fruity beverages)
 Mott's
 Nantucket Nectars
 Nehi
 Oasis
 Orangina (France)
 RC Cola
 Schweppes
 Snapple
 Squirt
 Stewart's (sodas)
 Sunkist (licensed)
 Sun Valley Squeeze
 Welch's (licensed, US)
 WhipperSnapple
 YooHoo

Chewing Gum
 Bazooka
 Beldent
 Bubbas
 Chiclets
 Clorets
 Dentyne
 Dirol
 Hollywood
 Sportlife
 STIMOROL
 Trident
 V6

Confections
 Allan (Canada, US)
 Bassett
 Beldent
 Bim Bim (Egypt)
 Bouquet d'Or (France)
 Butterkist (UK)
 Cadbury
 Carambar (France)
 Elegan
 Fuzzy Peach
 Green & Black's
 Halls
 Jelibon (Turkey)
 La Pie Qui Chante (France)
 Maynards (UK)
 Miss
 Olips (Turkey)
 Peter Paul
 Piasten (Germany)
 Picnic
 Poulain (France)
 Red Tulip (Australia)
 Relax (Turkey)
 Sour Patch Kids
 Swedish Fish
 Trebor
 Turbo (Turkey)
 Wedel (Poland)
 York

COMPETITORS

Associated British Foods	National Beverage
Britvic	National Grape
Campbell Soup	Cooperative
Coca-Cola	Nestlé
Cott	Northern Foods
CSM	Ocean Spray
Ferolito, Vultaggio	PepsiCo
Heinz	PepsiCo International
Hershey	Pernod Ricard
Jelly Belly Candy	Russell Stover
Jones Soda	See's Candies
Kellogg	Thorntons
Kraft Foods International	Tootsie Roll
Lindt & Sprüngli	Virgin Group
Mars	Wrigley

HISTORICAL FINANCIALS

Company Type: Public

Income Statement

FYE: Saturday nearest December 31

	REVENUE ($ mil.)	NET INCOME ($ mil.)	NET PROFIT MARGIN	EMPLOYEES
12/04	12,918	826	6.4%	58,442
12/03	11,487	653	5.7%	55,799
12/02	8,538	883	10.3%	42,848
12/01	8,037	789	9.8%	38,489
12/00	6,841	742	10.8%	36,460
12/99	6,950	1,037	14.9%	37,425
12/98	6,814	589	8.6%	38,656
12/97	6,893	1,143	16.6%	41,320
12/96	8,759	591	6.7%	42,911
12/95	7,417	480	6.5%	—
Annual Growth	6.4%	6.2%	—	3.9%

2004 Year-End Financials

Debt ratio: 125.4%
Return on equity: 15.4%
Cash ($ mil.): 385
Current ratio: 0.92
Long-term debt ($ mil.): 6,875

No. of shares (mil.): 518
Dividends
  Yield: 2.4%
  Payout: 56.5%
Market value ($ mil.): 19,529

Stock History

NYSE: CSG

12/95 12/96 12/97 12/98 12/99 12/00 12/01 12/02 12/03 12/04

	STOCK PRICE ($) FY Close	P/E High/Low	PER SHARE ($) Earnings	Dividends	Book Value
12/04	37.70	15 12	1.61	0.91	10.58
12/03	29.89	13 9	1.30	0.82	10.20
12/02	25.61	18 14	1.75	0.73	9.46
12/01	25.72	19 15	1.56	0.68	8.20
12/00	29.00	20 14	1.47	0.71	7.74
12/99	24.19	17 11	2.02	0.66	7.16
12/98	34.56	30 17	1.16	0.46	6.01
12/97	20.69	6 4	3.52	0.27	5.46
12/96	17.06	15 12	1.17	1.08	4.41
12/95	16.63	18 13	0.97	1.22	4.12
Annual Growth	9.5%	— —	5.8%	(3.2%)	11.0%

Canadian Imperial Bank of Commerce

Canadian Imperial Bank of Commerce (CIBC) is both Canadian and imperial when it comes to growing its business. CIBC's nearly 1,100 branches offer a range of consumer and business services, including deposit accounts, loans, brokerage, mutual funds, and trust services. It operates in three segments: CIBC Retail Markets (credit cards, consumer and small business banking); CIBC World Markets (corporate banking, securities, foreign exchange trading); and CIBC Wealth Management. Subsidiary Amicus Bank provides electronic banking in Canadian grocery stores under the name of President's Choice Financial.

Operating units within CIBC's business lines include trust and custody services provider CIBC Mellon, a joint venture with Mellon Financial; CIBC Wood Gundy, the asset management arm of CIBC World Markets; and institutional fund manager TAL Global Asset Management.

The company tried to grow through megamergers and diversification in the past, but both moves were nixed by the government for fear of excessive industry consolidation. Now CIBC faces the prospect of good, old-fashioned organic growth with a piecemeal acquisition here and there.

To build its customer base, the bank is focusing on its core banking operations, targeting small businesses in Canada and retail banking customers in growing cities in the US. However, not all of its ventures south of the border have been successful. In 2003 CIBC chose to close down all of its Amicus electronic banking operations in the US. The following year it sold Juniper Financial, a Delaware-based credit card issuer, to Barclays for some $293 million.

CIBC took a hit in mid-2005 when it agreed to pay some $2.4 billion in an investor class-action suit to resolve claims that the company helped notorious energy trader Enron to conceal losses.

HISTORY

In 1858 Bank of Canada was chartered; Toronto financier William McMaster bought the charter in 1866 when investors failed to raise enough money to open it and changed the name to Canadian Bank of Commerce.

Canadian Bank of Commerce opened in 1867, bought the Gore Bank of Hamilton (1870), and expanded within seven years to 24 branches in Ontario, as well as Montreal and New York. Led by Edmund Walker, the bank spread west of the Great Lakes with the opening of a Winnipeg, Manitoba, branch in 1893 and joined the Gold Rush with branches in Dawson City, Yukon Territory, and Skagway, Alaska, in 1898.

As the new century began, the bank's purchases spanned the breadth of Canada, from the Bank of British Columbia (1901) to Halifax Banking (1903) and the Merchants Bank of Prince Edward Island (1906). More buys followed in the 1920s; the bank's assets peaked in 1929 and then plunged during the Depression. It recovered during WWII.

In 1961 Canadian Bank of Commerce merged with Imperial Bank of Canada to become Canadian Imperial Bank of Commerce. Imperial Bank was founded in 1875 by Henry Howland; it went west to Calgary and Edmonton and became known as "The Mining Bank." It bought Barclays Bank (Canada) in 1956.

As the energy and agriculture sectors declined in the early 1980s, two of CIBC's largest borrowers, Dome Petroleum and tractor maker Massey-Ferguson, defaulted on their loans. Deregulation opened investment banking to CIBC, which in 1988 bought a majority share of Wood Gundy, one of Canada's largest investment dealers; CIBC also purchased Merrill Lynch Canada's retail brokerage business.

In 1992 CIBC added substantially to its loss reserves (resulting in an earnings drop of 98%) to cover real estate losses from developer Olympia & York and others. This launched more cost-cutting as the company reorganized by operating segments.

Deregulation allowed CIBC to begin selling insurance in 1993; the company built a collection of life, credit, personal property/casualty, and nonmedical health companies.

In 1996 the bank formed Intria, a processing and technical support subsidiary. The next year CIBC Wood Gundy became CIBC World Markets, and CIBC bought securities firm Oppenheimer & Co. and added its stock underwriting and brokerage abilities to CIBC World Markets.

In 1998, increasing foreign competition prompted CIBC and Toronto-Dominion to plan a merger (as did Royal Bank of Canada and Bank of Montreal); the government halted both plans citing Canada's already highly concentrated banking industry.

Spurned, the bank overhauled its operations to spark growth in the late 1990s. To cut costs it eliminated some 4,000 jobs and sold its more than $1 billion real estate portfolio. It teamed with the Winn-Dixie (1999) and Safeway (2000) supermarket chains to operate electronic branches in the US. The firm scaled back its disappointing international operations and began selling its insurance units.

In 2000 CIBC created Amicus as a holding company for CIBC World Markets' retail electronic banking business. The following year the bank sold its merchant card services business to US-based Global Payments.

In 2002 the company snagged US-based Merrill Lynch's Canadian retail brokerage, asset management, and securities operations, renaming it CIBC Asset Management Inc. That same year CIBC merged its Caribbean banking business with that of UK-based Barclays to create FirstCaribbean Bank.

EXECUTIVES

Chairman: William A. Etherington, age 63
President, CEO, and Director: Gerald T. (Gerry) McCaughey, age 48, $3,185,625 pay (prior to promotion)
Vice Chairman and CIO: Michael D. (Mike) Woeller
SEVP, Retail Markets: Sonia A. Baxendale
SEVP, Chief Administrative Officer, and Chief Privacy Officer: Ron A. Lalonde
SEVP and Chief Risk Officer: Steven R. McGirr, age 49
SEVP, Corporate Development; Managing Director and Deputy Chairman, CIBC World Markets: Richard E. Venn, age 54
SEVP and CFO: Tom D. Woods, $1,148,420 pay
EVP and General Counsel: Michael G. Capatides
EVP, Wealth Management: Victor Dodig
EVP, Technology Solutions: Phil Emond

EVP, CIBC Mortgages and Insurance Services Division, CIBC Retail Markets: W. E. (Ed) Gettings
EVP, Personal and Small Business Banking and Chief Marketing Officer: Stephen D. Graham
EVP and Treasurer: Michael G. Horrocks
EVP, Credit and Investment Portfolio Management and Adjucation: P. Kenneth M. (Ken) Kilgour
EVP, Branch and Small Business Banking, CIBC Retail Markets: Kenn W. Lalonde
EVP, Imperial Service and Private Wealth Management: Steven M. McNair
EVP; CEO, Amicus Bank: John Orr
EVP, Human Resources: Joyce M. Phillips
EVP and Chief Auditor: Pankaj Puri
SVP, Investor Relations: Kathryn A. (Kathy) Humber
SVP, Communications and Public Affairs: Robert E. (Bob) Waite
VP, Corporate Secretary, and Associate General Counsel: Michelle Caturay
Auditors: Ernst & Young LLP

LOCATIONS

HQ: Canadian Imperial Bank of Commerce
Commerce Court,
Toronto, Ontario M5L 1A2, Canada
Phone: 416-980-2211 **Fax:** 416-980-5028
US HQ: 425 Lexington Ave., New York, NY 10017
US Phone: 212-856-4000 **US Fax:** 212-667-4776
Web: www.cibc.com

PRODUCTS/OPERATIONS

2004 Sales

	$ mil.	% of total
Interest income		
Loans	6,193	45
Securities	2,038	15
Deposits with banks	125	1
Noninterest income		
Commissions on		
securities transactions	732	5
Underwriting & advisory fees	654	5
Deposit & payment fees	623	5
Trading activities	507	4
Mutual fund fees	504	4
Other fees	1,025	7
Other	1,300	9
Total	**13,701**	**100**

2004 Assets

	% of total
Cash & equivalents	4
Trading securities	19
Investment securities	6
Securities purchased under resale agreements	7
Derivative instruments	8
Loans	
Residential mortgages	26
Personal	9
Credit card	3
Business & government	11
Other	7
Total	**100**

Selected Subsidiaries

Amicus Bank
CIBC Australia Holdings Limited
CIBC Asia Limited
CIBC Asset Management Holdings Inc.
CIBC BA Limited
CIBC Capital Funding, L.P.
CIBC Capital Funding II, L.P.
CIBC Financial Planning Inc.
CIBC Holdings (Cayman) Limited

CIBC Investor Services Inc.
CIBC Life Insurance Company Limited
CIBC Mortgages Inc.
CIBC Offshore Banking Services Corporation
CIBC Securities Inc.
CIBC Trust Corporation
CIBC World Markets Inc.
CIBC World Markets (Japan) Inc.
CIBC World Markets plc (UK)
INTRIA Items Inc. (90%)
TAL Global Asset Management Inc.

COMPETITORS

Bank of America	JPMorgan Chase
Bank of New York	Lehman Brothers
Barclays	Merrill Lynch
Bear Stearns	Mizuho Financial
BMO Financial Group	Morgan Stanley
Citigroup	National Bank of Canada
Credit Suisse	RBC Financial Group
Deutsche Bank	Scotiabank
Goldman Sachs	TD Bank
HSBC Holdings	UBS Financial Services

HISTORICAL FINANCIALS

Company Type: Public

Income Statement

FYE: October 31

	ASSETS ($ mil.)	NET INCOME ($ mil.)	INCOME AS % OF ASSETS	EMPLOYEES
10/04	228,642	1,804	0.8%	37,281
10/03	210,161	1,564	0.7%	36,630
10/02	175,454	419	0.2%	42,552
10/01	181,137	1,062	0.6%	41,000
10/00	175,773	1,353	0.8%	44,215
10/99	170,150	699	0.4%	45,998
10/98	182,339	684	0.4%	47,171
10/97	168,996	1,101	0.7%	42,446
10/96	148,688	1,020	0.7%	41,606
10/95	133,336	755	0.6%	39,329
Annual Growth	**6.2%**	**10.2%**	**—**	**(0.6%)**

2004 Year-End Financials

Equity as % of assets: 3.7%
Return on assets: 0.8%
Return on equity: 22.0%
Long-term debt ($ mil.): 3,190
No. of shares (mil.): 347
Dividends
Yield: 3.2%
Payout: 42.3%
Market value ($ mil.): 20,995
Sales ($ mil.): 13,701

Stock History

NYSE: BCM

70					
60					
50					
40					
30					
20					
10					
0					

10/95 10/96 10/97 10/98 10/99 10/00 10/01 10/02 10/03 10/04

	STOCK PRICE ($) FY Close	P/E High/Low		PER SHARE ($) Earnings	Dividends	Book Value
10/04	60.42	13	10	4.54	1.92	31.21
10/03	44.87	12	6	3.93	1.15	28.86
10/02	25.37	42	25	0.87	1.02	22.05
10/01	30.82	14	11	2.56	0.94	20.65
10/00	31.75	11	7	3.18	0.98	19.79
10/99	21.50	19	13	1.51	0.80	18.68
10/98	19.94	28	11	1.46	0.82	17.36
Annual Growth	**20.3%**	**—**	**—**	**20.8%**	**15.2%**	**10.3%**

Canon Inc.

Canon is still banging away at the document reproduction market. The company makes printers and other computer peripherals for home and office use. Its other well-known lines include copiers, fax machines, and scanners. Canon's optical segment features products used in such diverse applications as semiconductor manufacturing equipment, television broadcast lenses, and devices used for eye examinations. The company still operates its original camera business, which makes digital cameras, camcorders, liquid-crystal display projectors, lenses, and binoculars.

Canon's imaging products, its largest segment, include printers, copiers, scanners, and multifunction devices for the consumer and enterprise markets. Canon sells branded products and supplies partners such as Hewlett-Packard that resell under their own brands. The company is targeting color office products for growth in this segment.

Perhaps still best known for its cameras, Canon has seen its photographic business drop to about 20% of revenues. However, the company is a leader in the digital camera market, where it is concentrating on high-end single lens reflex (SLR) devices.

Canon has teamed with Toshiba to develop surface-conduction electron-emitter display (SED) products, an alternative to liquid-crystal display (LCD) and plasma technologies.

Canon adheres to the *kyosei* philosophy (living and working together for the common good), which stresses respect for local cultures and customs and more local control of subsidiaries. The company, which generates about two-thirds of its revenues outside of Japan, continues to emphasize its product development and marketing efforts in Europe and the US.

HISTORY

Takeshi Mitarai and a friend, Saburo Uchida, formed Seiki Kogaku Kenkyusho (Precision Optical Research Laboratory) in Tokyo in 1933 to make Japan's first 35mm camera. In 1935 the camera was introduced under the brand name Kwanon (the Buddhist goddess of mercy) — but later renamed Canon. In response to a pre-World War II military buildup, the company made X-ray machines for the Japanese.

In 1947 the company became Canon Camera Company as the brand name gained popularity. Canon opened its first overseas branch — in New York — in 1955. It diversified into business equipment by introducing the first 10-key electronic calculator (1964) and a plain-paper photocopier (1968) independent of Xerox's patented technology. Canon dropped "Camera Company" from its name in 1969.

The company invented the "liquid dry" copying system, which uses plain paper and liquid developer, in 1972. It failed to produce new cameras and was surpassed by Minolta as Japan's top camera exporter. Sales were sluggish in the early 1970s, and in 1975 Canon suspended dividends for the first time since World War II.

At that time Canon's managing director, Ryuzaburo Kaku, convinced Mitarai that the company's problems stemmed from indecisive leadership and weak marketing. Kaku turned Canon around, unleashing the electronic AE-1 in a media blitz that in 1976 included the first-ever

TV commercials for a 35mm camera. With automated features, the AE-1 appealed to the clumsiest photographers. Its success catapulted Canon past Minolta as the world's #1 camera maker.

In 1979 Canon introduced the first copier to use a dry developer. As the copier market matured in the early 1980s, Canon shifted to making other automated office equipment, including laser printers and fax machines.

Mitarai died in 1984. Minolta the next year again displaced Canon as the world's #1 camera maker, when it introduced a fully automated model. But Canon came back in 1987 with the electronic optical system (EOS) auto-focus camera, which returned the company to preeminence in 1990. That year the company initiated an ink cartridge recycling program. Canon teamed up with IBM in 1992 to produce portable PCs. In 1993 Takeshi Mitarai's son Hajime, who had joined Canon in 1974, was named president and began expanding product development.

In 1995 Canon introduced the world's first color ferroelectric liquid-crystal display designed to replace cathode-ray tubes in computer and TV screens as the industry standard. When Hajime died that year, cousin Fujio Mitarai, a 34-year Canon employee who served as the head of Canon U.S.A. in the 1980s, was named president and CEO. In 1996 the company made Canon Latin America a direct subsidiary of Canon U.S.A., with the *kyosei* idea that regionalized control would make the subsidiary more efficient.

Canon stopped making PCs in 1997. The next year the company unveiled its Hyper Photo System, which combines a scanner, PC server, and printer to produce photo prints, and expanded its copier remanufacturing operations. In 1999, after 16 years of production, Canon stopped making optical memory cards. The company also opened a research and development facility in the US.

In 2000 Canon and Toshiba began working together to develop technology for flat-panel displays. Canon expanded its line of digital cameras in 2001; the company's sales in that segment almost doubled that year.

The next year the company announced that it would merge two of its office equipment subsidiaries, Copyer and Canon Aptex, in an effort to improve operating efficiency.

EXECUTIVES

President and CEO: Fujio Mitarai, age 70
Senior Managing Director; Chief, Global Marketing Promotion Committee; Group Executive, Human Resources Management and Organization: Yukio Yamashita, age 66
Senior Managing Director; Chief Executive, Image Communications Products: Tsuneji Uchida, age 64
Senior Managing Director; Group Executive, Finance and Accounting: Toshizo Tanaka, age 65
Managing Director; Group Executive, Corporate Intellectual Property and Legal; Senior General Manager, Legal Affairs Coordination: Nobuyoshi Tanaka, age 59
Managing Director; Group Executive, Corporate Strategy and Development: Kunio Watanabe, age 61
Managing Director; Group Executive, General Affairs and Information and Communication Systems: Akiyoshi Moroe, age 61
Managing Director; Group Executive, Global Environment Promotion: Yusuke Emura, age 60
Managing Director; Chief Executive, Optical Products HQ: Junji Ichikawa, age 62
Managing Director; President and CEO, Canon U.S.A.: Yoroku Adachi, age 57
Managing Director; President, Canon Europa N.V.: Hajime Tsuruoka, age 62

Director; Chief Executive, Inkjet Products: Katsuichi Shimizu, age 59
Director; Chief Executive, Peripheral Products: Yasuo Mitsuhashi, age 55
Managing Director; Group Executive, Core Technology Development and Display Development; Group Executive, Display Development: Hironori Yamamoto, age 61
Director; EVP, Canon USA: Ryoichi Bamba, age 58
Director; Deputy Group Executive, Finance and Accounting: Masahiro Ohsawa, age 58
Director; Deputy Group Executive, Human Resource Management and Organization: Keijiro Yamazaki, age 57
Auditors: KPMG

LOCATIONS

HQ: Canon Inc.
30-2, Shimomaruko 3-chome, Ohta-ku, Tokyo 146-8501, Japan
Phone: +81-3-3758-2111   **Fax:** +81-3-5482-5135
US HQ: 1 Canon Plaza, Lake Success, NY 11042
US Phone: 516-328-5000   **US Fax:** 516-328-5069
Web: www.canon.com

2004 Sales

	% of total
Europe	32
Americas	31
Japan	24
Other regions	13
Total	**100**

PRODUCTS/OPERATIONS

2004 Sales

	% of total
Business machines	
Computer peripherals	33
Office imaging	32
Business information	4
Cameras	22
Optical & other	9
Total	**100**

Selected Products

Business Machines
  Computer peripherals
    Consumables
    Printers (bubble jet and laser)
    Scanners
  Office imaging
    Consumables
    Office
    Personal
  Business information
    Document scanners
    Fax machines
    Handy terminals
Camera segment
  Cameras
    Digital
    Film
  Lenses
  Liquid-crystal display projectors
  Video camcorders
Optical
  Broadcasting equipment
  Digital radiography
  Encoders
  Eye care systems
  Medical imaging systems
  Semiconductor production equipment
  Transceivers

COMPETITORS

Agfa	NEC
ASML	Nikon
Eastman Kodak	Océ
Epson	Oki Electric
Fuji Xerox	Olympus
Fujifilm	Pentax
Fujitsu	Philips Electronics
Hewlett-Packard	Polaroid
Hitachi	Ricoh
IBM	SANYO
Imagistics	Sharp
Konica Minolta	Sony
Kyocera	Toshiba
Lexmark	Victor Company of Japan
Matsushita	Xerox

HISTORICAL FINANCIALS

Company Type: Public

Income Statement

FYE: December 31

	REVENUE ($ mil.)	NET INCOME ($ mil.)	NET PROFIT MARGIN	EMPLOYEES
12/04	33,345	3,301	9.9%	108,257
12/03	29,889	2,577	8.6%	102,567
12/02	24,501	1,590	6.5%	97,802
12/01	22,027	1,269	5.8%	93,620
12/00	24,272	1,170	4.8%	86,673
12/99	25,709	689	2.7%	81,009
12/98	24,364	945	3.9%	79,799
12/97	21,239	914	4.3%	78,767
12/96	22,054	812	3.7%	75,628
12/95	21,026	534	2.5%	72,280
Annual Growth	5.3%	22.4%	—	4.6%

2004 Year-End Financials

Debt ratio: 1.3%	No. of shares (mil.): 887
Return on equity: 17.1%	Dividends
Cash ($ mil.): 8,536	Yield: 0.0%
Current ratio: 2.27	Payout: —
Long-term debt ($ mil.): 276	Market value ($ mil.): 48,121

Stock History

NYSE: CAJ

	STOCK PRICE ($) FY Close	P/E High/Low		PER SHARE ($) Earnings	Dividends	Book Value
12/04	54.26	15	12	3.72	0.00	23.96
12/03	47.64	18	12	2.90	0.26	19.82
12/02	36.85	23	17	1.79	0.21	15.11
12/01	35.06	31	18	1.43	0.18	12.61
12/00	33.69	39	23	1.32	0.16	12.95
12/99	40.56	52	25	0.78	0.14	13.52
12/98	21.50	23	16	1.07	0.15	2.27
12/97	23.35	31	19	1.04	0.14	1.95
12/96	22.00	25	19	0.92	0.11	1.98
12/95	18.28	31	24	0.61	0.12	1.97
Annual Growth	12.8%	—	—	22.2%	—	32.0%

Capgemini

Technology and outsourcing are the twin pillars of this business. Capgemini is one of the world's leading providers of systems integration and consulting services, with operations in more than 30 countries. It offers enterprise systems development and implementation, as well as analysis and consulting services to help businesses choose the technology best suited to their needs. It also offers a range of business process outsourcing (BPO) services in such functional areas as customer relationship management (CRM), finance, human resources, and supply chain management. Capgemini also provides traditional management consulting services.

Like other consultancies, the firm was hit hard by the long technology downturn, but the effects were felt especially hard at Capgemini in part because of its 2000 acquisition of Ernst & Young's consulting arm. Both chairman Serge Kampf and CEO Paul Hermelin came under fire for pursuing the $11 billion deal, but under their leadership Capgemini has weathered the storm and emerged as a more streamlined company.

Reorganization efforts in 2004 (including a name change from Cap Gemini Ernst & Young) helped focus the company along the functional lines of consulting, outsourcing, and technology services. Its Sogeti-Transiciel division provides support and consulting to smaller customers through local offices, primarily in Europe. As a result, local professional services and outsourcing have become Capgemini's growth areas as the company diversifies its revenue base.

The company continues to focus efforts on streamlining its operations, especially in the North America (which accounts for more than 20% of revenue). In 2005 Capgemini sold its North American health care consulting practice to Accenture for about $175 million and it continues to look for areas to trim non-essential or non-core operations. Later that year, however, COO Pierre Danon, credited with helping to turn around Capgemini's North American operations, was fired after news leaked he was seeking the CEO position at hotelier Accor.

HISTORY

Serge Kampf founded software house Sogeti in 1967 in Grenoble, France. He had an economics degree and had held a variety of jobs — from selling bakery ovens and computers to working for the French national telephone company. Frustrated as an executive with French computer company Groupe Bull, he resigned and started Sogeti.

Believing the future of information technology (IT) would be in support rather than hardware, Kampf focused on providing computer services to companies outside Paris that were being overlooked by his larger competitors. He was immediately successful, and three years later opened a Paris branch. In 1973 Kampf changed the focus of the company, abandoning the more specialized activities of data processing for general consulting, software, and technical assistance.

Cap Gemini Sogeti was created two years later by merging Sogeti with two French software service companies, C.A.P. (Computerized Applications Programming, started in 1962) and Gemini (1969). At first it operated as a "body shop," a loose organization of freelance programmers offering temporary help to computer users. It set up a consulting team in the US in 1978 and began a series of US acquisitions that led to the formation of Cap Gemini America (1981).

The company acquired a 42% stake in French competitor Sesa in 1982; six years later it bought the rest as part of a new strategy to become a global operator with a range of services. Cap Gemini Sogeti's 1990 purchase of Hoskyns Group, the UK's largest computer services company, was just one of a string of acquisitions aimed at fulfilling that goal. (Over a five-year period, it bought 22 European and American companies for $1.1 billion.) To raise money for his international expansion plans, Kampf sold 34% of the company to German carmaker Daimler-Benz (now DaimlerChrysler) in 1991.

As Cap Gemini Sogeti expanded around the world, its decentralized network of operations rarely shared business or expertise. In 1993, on the heels of its first loss, the company launched a restructuring program that set up seven strategic business areas with dual regional and segment roles and modified product lines. Cap Gemini Sogeti returned to profitability in 1995.

The mid-1990s brought more than a dozen partnerships, including deals with French chemical conglomerate Rhône-Poulenc (now Sanofi-Aventis, 1995) and British Steel (now Corus Group, 1996). Also in 1996 the company launched its year 2000 date fixing software. It completed the reorganization, creating holding company Cap Gemini, and moved its corporate headquarters to Paris.

In 1997 Daimler-Benz sold its stake (then 24%) in Cap Gemini to Compagnie Générale d'Industrie et de Participations (CGIP, now controlled by Wendel Investissement). The next year Cap Gemini bought the UK finance and commerce arm of AT&T. The company sold its UK training unit in 1999 to focus its UK operations on IT services. Expanding further into the US that year, the company bought telecommunications specialist Beechwood.

In 2000 Cap Gemini solidified its US presence with the $11 billion purchase of the consulting business of Ernst & Young, changing its name to Cap Gemini Ernst & Young. Geoff Unwin took over as CEO that year; Kampf remained as chairman.

Stung by a slowdown in IT spending (primarily in the US), in 2001 the company announced it was cutting 5,400 jobs. Later that year Unwin announced his retirement as CEO, and was succeeded by COO Paul Hermelin. In 2002 another 5,500 jobs (about 10% of its workforce) were cut, mainly in its telecom and financial services units. The appointment of Alexandre Haeffner as COO launched major managerial restructuring.

In April 2004 the company simplified its name to Capgemini as part of an overall reorganization effort. Soon after, the company's struggling US division got a shot in the arm when it signed a 10-year, $3.5 billion business and computer consulting services with power company TXU Corp. Capgemini also acquired consulting firm Transiciel (now Sogeti-Transiciel) for about $435 million.

EXECUTIVES

Chairman: Serge Kampf, age 71
Vice Chairman: Ernest-Antoine Sellière
CEO and Director: Paul Hermelin, age 49
CFO: Nicolas Dufourcq
General Secretary and Human Resources:
 Alain Donzeaud
Managing Director, Central and Southern Europe and Consulting Services Global Coordination:
 Antonio Schnieder
Managing Director, France and Technology Services Global Coordination: Philippe Donche-Gay
Managing Director, Local Professional Services; Chairman, Sogeti-Transiciel: Luc-François Salvador
Managing Director, Northern Europe and Asia Pacific: Henk W. Broeders, age 52
Managing Director, Outsourcing Services: Paul Spence
CEO, North America: Chell Smith, age 51
CEO, Capgemini Americas, and Director: Terrence (Terry) Ozan
General Manager, Capgemini North America: Salil Parekh
Group Director of Communication: Philippe Grangeon
Global Marketing Manager and Global Energy & Utilities Leader: Colette Lewiner
Global Sales and Alliances Manager: Patrick Nicolet
Head of Investor Relations: Manuel Chaves d'Oliveira, age 41
Head of Press Relations: Sylvie Haurat, age 41
Auditors: PricewaterhouseCoopers

LOCATIONS

HQ: Capgemini
 Place de l'Etoile, 11, rue de Tilsitt,
 75017 Paris, France
Phone: +33-1-47-54-50-00 **Fax:** +33-1-47-54-50-86
US HQ: 750 7th Ave., Ste. 1800, New York, NY 10019
US Phone: 212-314-8000 **US Fax:** 212-314-8001
Web: www.capgemini.com

Capgemini has operations in more than 30 countries.

2004 Sales

	$ mil.	% of total
Europe	6,543	76
North America	1,911	22
Asia/Pacific	127	2
Total	**8,581**	**100**

PRODUCTS/OPERATIONS

Selected Services

Application management
Customer relationship management
Enterprise resource planning
Finance and employee transformation
Information technology consulting
Knowledge management
Management consulting
Outsourcing
Program management
Software development
Strategy consulting
Supply chain management
Systems integration
Training

COMPETITORS

Accenture
Affiliated Computer
 Services
Atos Origin
Bain & Company
BearingPoint
Booz Allen
Bull
Capita
CGI Group
Computer Sciences Corp.
Deloitte Consulting
Dimension Data
EDS
Fujitsu Services
Getronics
HP Technology Solutions
 Group
IBM Global Services
Infosys
LogicaCMG
McKinsey & Company
Perot Systems
Tata Consultancy
Unisys
Wipro Technologies

HISTORICAL FINANCIALS

Company Type: Public

Income Statement

FYE: December 31

	REVENUE ($ mil.)	NET INCOME ($ mil.)	NET PROFIT MARGIN	EMPLOYEES
12/04	8,581	(490)	—	59,324
12/03	7,222	(247)	—	49,805
12/02	7,386	(539)	—	52,683
12/01	7,455	135	1.8%	57,760
12/00	6,526	406	6.2%	59,549
12/99	3,098	117	3.8%	39,626
12/98	4,615	219	4.8%	34,606
12/97	3,364	127	3.8%	31,094
12/96	2,832	54	1.9%	25,950
12/95	2,308	11	0.5%	22,079
Annual Growth	15.7%	—	—	11.6%

2004 Year-End Financials

Debt ratio: 21.8%
Return on equity: —
Cash ($ mil.): 342
Current ratio: 1.49
Long-term debt ($ mil.): 891

Net Income History

Euronext Paris: CAP

Carlsberg A/S

If any company has thirst quenching down to a science, it's Carlsberg A/S, the owner of Carlsberg Breweries. In addition to the worldwide brewing operations of its flagship subsidiary, Carlsberg A/S also operates the Carlsberg Research Center, which houses 80 beer brewing laboratories. In 2004 the group acquired Swedish conglomerate Orkla's 40% stake in Carlsberg Breweries and the Germany-based beer brewer and distributor Holsten-Brauerei. Carlsberg has more than 90 production sites in nearly 50 countries. However, it plans to close 14 of its European breweries to improve profitability. The group is controlled by the Carlsberg Foundation, established in 1876 by founder J.C. Jacobsen.

Although most of the company's revenue comes from the sale of Carlsberg beers, the group also sells the Tuborg brand. Tuborg is one of the best-selling beers in Norway. Carlsberg also has a 50/50 joint venture, Baltic Beverages Holding (BBH), with UK brewer Scottish & Newcastle.

Carlsberg's soft drink sales are generated mainly from licenses to produce drinks from Coca-Cola and Pepsi, but the company also produces regional beverages. In Denmark, Norway, and Sweden, Carlsberg produces leading brands of mineral water. It has divested its mineral water operations in Switzerland. Its portfolio also includes a number of local brands, such as Feldschlösschen (Sweden), Okocim (Poland), Pripps (Sweden), Ringnes (Norway), Koff (Finland), and Tetley's (the UK).

In addition to its beverage operations, the group is also involved to a lesser extent in property development and sales, primarily in Denmark.

Carlsberg is expanding through its Baltic Beverages Holding unit and other Eastern European businesses and through acquisitions in China and Germany. A declining beer market in Western Europe, however, has prompted Carlsberg's decision to close about half of its breweries there.

HISTORY

Carlsberg stems from the amalgamation of two proud Danish brewing concerns. Captain J. C. Jacobsen founded the first of these in Copenhagen; his father had worked as a brewery hand before acquiring his own small brewery in 1826. Studious and technically minded, J. C. inherited the brewery in 1835. He opened the Carlsberg Brewery (named for his son Carl) in 1847 and exported his first beer (to the UK) in 1868. J. C. established the Carlsberg Foundation in 1876 to conduct scientific research and oversee brewery operations.

Carl, who conflicted with his father over brewery operations, opened a new facility (New Carlsberg) adjacent to his dad's in 1881. Both men bestowed gifts upon their city, such as a church, an art museum, a royal castle renovation, and Copenhagen Harbor's famous Little Mermaid statue. Father and son willed their breweries to the foundation, which united them in 1906.

Tuborgs Fabrikker was founded in 1873 by a group of Danish businessmen who wanted to establish a major industrial project (including a brewery) at Tuborg Harbor. Philip Heyman headed the group and in 1880 spun off all operations but the brewery.

Carlsberg and Tuborg became Denmark's two leading brewers. After WWII, both began marketing their beers outside the country. Between 1958 and 1972 they tripled exports and established breweries in Europe and Asia. Both brewers' desire to grow internationally influenced their decision to merge, which they did in 1969 as United Breweries.

During the 1980s the firm diversified, forming Carlsberg Biotechnology in 1983 to extend its research to other areas. It strengthened its position in North America through licenses with Anheuser-Busch (1985) and John Labatt (1988). United Breweries reverted to the old Carlsberg name in 1987.

Carlsberg and Allied-Lyons (now Allied Domecq) combined their UK brewing, distribution, and wholesaling operations under the name Carlsberg-Tetley (now Carlsberg UK) in 1992, creating the UK's third-largest brewer (behind Bass and Courage).

The firm teamed up with India's United Breweries in 1995 to distribute Carlsberg beer on the subcontinent. Bass acquired Allied's 50% of Carlsberg-Tetley in 1996 but upon orders from regulators sold its stake to Carlsberg in 1997. Also in 1997 Carlsberg and Coca-Cola set up Coca-Cola Nordic Beverages to bottle and distribute soft drinks in Nordic countries. That year Poul Svanholm retired after 25 years as CEO; he was replaced by Jørn Jensen.

Carlsberg acquired a 60% stake in Finnish brewer Sinebrychoff in 1998. Carlsberg then sold a 60% stake in Vingaarden to Finland's Oy Rettig (1999), sold its remaining 43% share of the Tivoli amusement park to Danish tobacco group Skandinavisk Tobakskompagni (2000), and reduced its 64% holding in Royal Scandinavia to 28% (2000). Carlsberg bought the beverage operations of Swedish firm Feldschlösschen Hürlimann in 2000 and agreed to combine brewing businesses with Norway-based Orkla in a deal worth $1.5 billion; Carlsberg Breweries was

formed in February 2001 after both agreed to divest several brands and distribution rights to gain regulatory approval.

Carlsberg stopped production at Coca-Cola Nordic Beverages (the company still exists but has no operations) in 2001 because of conflicts with Orkla's Pepsi bottling contracts in Sweden and Norway; Carlsberg and Coca-Cola continued to produce and sell Coke in Denmark and Finland. In 2002 Carlsberg sold 32% of its Lithuanian brewery to Russia's Baltic Beverage Holding, a joint venture between Carlsberg and Scottish & Newcastle. That year Carlsberg also signed an agreement giving Carib Brewery Ltd., part of the ANSA McAl Group, the rights to brew and distribute Carlsberg Beer in selected areas of the Caribbean.

In January 2003 Carlsberg Breweries acquired an additional 27.5% stake in Pirinsko Pivo, a Bulgarian brewery, bringing its overall ownership to 94.5%. That same month it purchased the Chinese brewer Kunming in southeast China. Carlsberg bought a second Chinese brewer, Dali, in June 2003.

EXECUTIVES

Chairman: Prof Povl Krogsgaard-Larsen
EVP and CFO; CFO, Carlsberg Breweries: Jørn P. Jensen, age 41
CEO: Nils S. Andersen
Chairman, Carlsberg Sweden: Paul Bergqvist, age 59
EVP, Eastern Europe: Jørgen Buhl Rasmussen, age 50
SVP, UK, Switzerland, Italy, and Portugal: Lars Fellman
SVP, Asia, Malawi, Balkan, and Export and Licence: Jesper Bjørn Madsen
SVP, Supply Chain and Procurement: Kasper Madsen, age 42
SVP, Sales and Marketing: Alex Myers, age 41
CEO, Carlsberg Sweden: Stig Sunde, age 42
VP, IT: Torben Melskens
VP, Human Resources: Vibeke Frank
VP, Corporate Communications: Anne-Marie Skov
Manager, Investor Relations: Mikael Bo Larsen
VP, Group Accounting: Jan Rasmussen
VP, Controlling: Morten Leth
VP, Treasury and Risk Management: Jørgen Andersen
VP, Business Development and Projects: Geir Nesheim
VP, Legal Counseling: Ulrik Andersen
Auditors: KPMG; PricewaterhouseCoopers

LOCATIONS

HQ: Carlsberg A/S
1, Valby Langgade, DK-2500 Valby, Denmark
Phone: +45-3327-2727   **Fax:** +45-3327-4850
Web: www.carlsberg.com

2004 Sales

	% of total
Western Europe	74
Eastern Europe	
Baltic Beverages Holding	14
Other Eastern European operations	8
Asia	4
Total	**100**

COMPETITORS

Heineken
InBev
SABMiller
Scottish & Newcastle

HISTORICAL FINANCIALS

Company Type: Public

Income Statement

FYE: December 31

	REVENUE ($ mil.)	NET INCOME ($ mil.)	NET PROFIT MARGIN	EMPLOYEES
12/04	6,596	87	1.3%	31,703
12/03	5,838	161	2.8%	31,531
12/02	5,015	143	2.8%	28,466
12/01	4,082	142	3.5%	27,368
Annual Growth	17.3%	(14.9%)	—	5.0%

2004 Year-End Financials

Debt ratio: 150.6%
Return on equity: 3.8%
Cash ($ mil.): 322
Current ratio: 0.99
Long-term debt ($ mil.): 3,979

Net Income History

Copenhagen: CARC

Carrefour SA

At the junction of groceries, merchandise, and services, you'll find Carrefour (which means "crossroads"). The world's second-largest retailer (behind Wal-Mart), Carrefour operates more than 11,000 stores under some two dozen names, including hypermarkets (Carrefour), supermarkets (Champion), convenience stores (Shopi, Marché Plus), discount stores (Dia, Ed), and cash-and-carry stores (Promocash) in more than 30 countries in Europe, Latin America, and Asia. France accounts for about half of the retailer's sales. Carrefour secured its spot as the #1 European retailer (based on sales) when it merged with food retailer Promodès early in 2000 and raised its banner over those stores.

Carrefour is an originator of hypermarkets — huge department store and supermarket combinations that sell food, clothing, electronics, and household appliances, among other items, at a discount. It is consolidating many of its banners under the Carrefour name for hypermarkets and Champion for supermarkets.

The French retail giant is in the express lane toward growth. Unable to build new stores in its homeland due to regulations protecting smaller stores, Carrefour expands through acquisitions at home and abroad. It has about 850 hypermarkets, supermarkets, and discount stores in Latin America (including the 110-plus store Norte grocery chain in Argentina, and about 360 outlets in Brazil where it continues to expand), and about 340 hypermarkets in eight Asian countries, including China, South Korea, and Taiwan. In South Korea Carrefour is investing $800 million over the next four years to shore up its competitive position there.

Carrefour is China's largest foreign retailer (ahead of Wal-Mart), with about 225 hypermarkets, supermarkets, and discount stores in some

20 cities. Overall, it is China's fifth-largest retailer with sales of $1.26 billion there.

Closer to home, Carrefour is in the midst of an expansion drive in Italy, where it is already the second-largest retailer via subsidiary Carrefour Italia. It is also expanding in Poland where it recently acquired a dozen Hypernova hypermarkets from Royal Ahold.

The global retailer has pledged to improve the performance of its French hypermarket division, which is facing stagnant sales and competition from deep discount chains. To that end, Carrefour plans to sell $1.2 billion worth of assets — including its stores in Japan and Mexico — in order to lower prices and attract new shoppers, and to fund the construction of new stores.

Carrefour's board of directors has proposed separating the offices of chairman and CEO. The move led to a management shakeup and the resignation of longtime chairman and CEO Daniel Bernard in February 2005.

HISTORY

Although its predecessor was actually a supermarket opened by Marcel Fournier and Louis Defforey in a Fournier's department store basement in Annecy, France, the first Carrefour supermarket was founded in 1963 at the intersection of five roads (Carrefour means "crossroads"). That year Carrefour opened a vast store, dubbed a hypermarket by the media, in Sainte-Genevieve-des-Bois, outside Paris.

The company opened outlets in France and moved into other countries, including Belgium (1969), Switzerland (1970 — the year it went public), Italy and the UK (1972), and Spain (1973). Carrefour stepped up international expansion during the mid-1970s after French legislation limited its growth within the country.

Carrefour imported its French-style hypermarkets to the US (Philadelphia) in 1988. Scant advertising, limited selection, and a union strike led Carrefour to close it US operations in 1993. Carrefour opened its first hypermarket in Taiwan in 1989. The next year it formed Carma, a 50-50 joint venture with Groupama, to sell insurance. Carrefour paid over $1 billion for two rival chains (the bankrupt Montlaur chain and Euromarche) in 1991.

Daniel Bernard replaced Michel Bon, the hard-charging expansion architect, in 1992 after a 50% drop in first-half profits. A year later Carrefour partnered with Mexican retailer Gigante to open a chain of hypermarkets in Mexico. (In 1998 Carrefour bought Gigante's share of the joint venture.) In 1996 the company bought a 41% stake in rival GMB (Cora hypermarket chain) and sold its 11% stake in US warehouse retailer Costco (it now owns 20% of Costco UK). It expanded into Poland in 1997 and the Czech Republic in 1998. Its biggest acquisition to that time came in 1998 when Carrefour acquired French supermarket operator Comptoirs Modernes (with about 800 stores under the Stoc, Comod, Marché Plus flags).

In August 1999 Carrefour announced a deal even bigger than the one for Comptoirs Modernes — a $16.3 billion merger with fellow French grocer Promodès, which operated more than 6,000 hypermarkets, supermarkets, convenience stores, and discount stores in Europe. Paul-Auguste Halley and Leonor Duval Lemonnier founded Promodès in Normandy, France, in 1961. Initially a wholesale food distributor, Promodès opened its first supermarket in 1962. This was followed by a cash-and-carry wholesale

outlet (1964), a hypermarket (1970), and convenience stores (Shopi and 8 à Huit, during the 1970s). To gain regulatory approval for the acquisition, Carrefour divested its stake in the Cora chain and sold nearly 40 other stores in France and Spain. The Promodès acquisition was completed in 2000.

Also in 2000 Carrefour bought Belgian retailer GB (about 500 stores). The grocer sold its 10% stake in PETsMART in a public offering in 2002.

In 2003 Carrefour entered the Scandinavian market through a franchise partnership and supply agreement with Norwegian grocer NorgesGruppen. In 2004 Carrefour opened its first Champion supermarket in Beijing. In September it entered Norway with six Meny Champion discount supermarkets in Oslo, in partnership with Norway's NorgesGruppen.

In 2005 Luc Vandevelde, the former chairman of troubled British retailer Marks and Spencer, succeeded Daniel Bernard as nonexecutive chairman of Carrefour. Bernard had been with Carrefour for 13 years. Concurrently, ex-CFO José-Luis Duran was named CEO. Carrefour exited the Japanese market that year with the sale of its eight hypermarkets there to Japanese retail giant AEON CO. On the plus side, Carrefour completed the acquisition of Chris Cash & Carry of Cyprus through its Greek subsidiary Carrefour Marinopoulos.

EXECUTIVES

Chairman: Luc Vandevelde, age 54
CEO: José-Luis Duran, age 40
Managing Director, Human Resources, Communication and Secretary General: Jacques Beauchet, age 55
Managing Director, DIA International/Hard Discount: Javier Campo, age 49
Managing Director, Europe (except France): José Maria Folache, age 44
Managing Director, Hypermarkets for France: Guy Yraeta, age 52
CFO, Managing Director of Information Systems: Eric Reiss, age 36
General Director, Merchandise: Jean-François Domont, age 53
Managing Director, Asia: Philippe Jarry, age 55
Managing Director for Americas and Group Merchandise and Marketing: Eric Uzan, age 46
Managing Director, Supermarkets, France: Thierry Garnier, age 39
Managing Director, Supermarkets Group: Philippe Pauze
President, Carrefour China: Jean-Luc Chereau
Director, Korea: Philippe Broianigo
Executive Director, Maxidiscompte (Dia), Spain: Santiago Gimeno
Director, Business-to-Business: Jeremy Hollows
General Counsel and Secretary: Etienne van Dyck
Media Relations: Christian d'Oléon
Investor Relations Contact: David Shriver
Manager, Champion, China: Xavier Piesvaux
Auditors: KPMG Audit

LOCATIONS

HQ: Carrefour SA
6, avenue Raymond Poincaré, 75016 Paris, France
Phone: +33-1-53-70-19-00   **Fax:** +33-1-53-70-86-16
Web: www.carrefour.com

Carrefour has operations in more than 30 countries, including Argentina, Bahrain, Belgium, Brazil, China, Colombia, the Czech Republic, Dominican Republic, Egypt, France, Greece, Indonesia, Italy, Malaysia, Norway, Oman, Poland, Portugal, Qatar, Romania, Saudi Arabia, Singapore, Slovakia, South Korea, Spain, Switzerland, Taiwan, Thailand, Tunisia, Turkey, and the United Arab Emirates.

2004 Stores

	No.
Europe	
France	3,675
Other countries	6,156
Latin America	909
Asia	340
Total	**11,080**

2004 Sales

	% of total
Europe	
France	49
Other countries	37
Asia	7
Latin America	7
Total	**100**

PRODUCTS/OPERATIONS

2004 Stores

	No.
Hard discount stores	4,934
Supermarkets	2,376
Hypermarkets	868
Other stores	2,902
Total	**11,080**

2004 Sales

	% of total
Hypermarkets	58
Supermarkets	25
Hard discount stores	8
Other stores	9
Total	**100**

Selected Operations and Banners

Hypermarkets
 Carrefour

Supermarkets
 Champion
 GB
 Globi
 GS
 Marinopoulos
 Norte
 Super GB
 Super GS
 Unic

Hard discount stores
 Dia
 Ed
 Minipreco

Other stores
 Cash-and-carry stores
 Docks Market
 Promocash
 Puntocash

Convenience stores
 8 à Huit
 Di per Di
 GB Express
 Marché Plus
 Proxi
 Shopi

Other Operations

Carfuel (petroleum products)
Comptoirs Modernes (supermarkets)
Costco UK (20%, warehouse club)
Erteco (hard-discount stores)
Financiera Pryca (46%, consumer credit, Spain)
Fourcar B.V. (investments, The Netherlands)
GlobalNetXchange (Internet-based supply
 exchange joint venture)
Immobiliere Carrefour (real estate)
Ooshop (online shopping)
Prodirest (catering)
Providange (auto centers)
S2P (60%, consumer credit)

COMPETITORS

AEON
ALDI
Auchan
Brasileira de Distribuição
Casino Guichard
Comerci
Dairy Farm International
Delhaize
Disco
Edeka Zentrale
E.Leclerc
Eroski
Falabella
Galeries Lafayette
Generale Supermercati
Globex Utilidades
ITM Entreprises
Ito-Yokado
Lidl & Schwarz Stiftung
Marui
METRO AG
Migros
PPR
Primisteres Reynoird
Rallye
REWE-Zentral
Rinascente
Royal Ahold
SHV Holdings
Tengelmann
Tesco
Wal-Mart

HISTORICAL FINANCIALS

Company Type: Public

Income Statement

FYE: December 31

	REVENUE ($ mil.)	NET INCOME ($ mil.)	NET PROFIT MARGIN	EMPLOYEES
12/04	99,119	1,892	1.9%	430,695
12/03	88,474	2,045	2.3%	419,040
12/02	72,035	1,440	2.0%	396,662
12/01	61,551	1,121	1.8%	382,821
12/00	61,018	1,004	1.6%	330,247
12/99	37,626	761	2.0%	297,290
12/98	31,985	755	2.4%	132,875
12/97	28,217	597	2.1%	113,289
12/96	29,602	597	2.0%	103,600
12/95	29,459	720	2.4%	102,900
Annual Growth	14.4%	11.3%	—	17.2%

2004 Year-End Financials

Debt ratio: 184.2%
Return on equity: 20.7%
Cash ($ mil.): 3,997

Current ratio: 0.82
Long-term debt ($ mil.): 17,304

Net Income History

Euronext Paris: CA

Casino Guichard-Perrachon

You won't hit the jackpot at Casino Guichard-Perrachon, but odds are you'll go home with the groceries. The company owns and operates 9,000-plus hypermarkets (mostly Géant), supermarkets (Casino, Franprix, and Monoprix, to name a few), restaurants (Casino Cafétéria), convenience stores, and discount stores (Leader Price). Casino is the #1 convenience store operator in France (primarily Petit Casino, but other banners include Vival and Spar). Most of its stores are in France, but it has more than 2,000 outlets in 14 countries worldwide, including Brazil, Mexico, Poland, Taiwan, and the US (where Casino owns 57% of the Smart & Final warehouse grocery chain). France's Rallye SA owns about 50% of Casino.

About 60% of Casino's sales are made at home in France. The company's 120 Géant hypermarkets (warehouse-style stores that sell groceries and other merchandise) contribute about 40% of revenues, with supermarkets and convenience stores a close second. Casino is France's fifth-largest supermarket company. Casino Cafétéria operates about 240 eating places in varying size and cuisines, including Poncholito (Tex-Mex) and La Pastaria (Italian). Casino is also active in e-commerce (Caly-online).

Casino has an option until the end of 2008 to increase to 51% the 38% stake it purchased in 2002 in Dutch supermarket operator Laurus.

Price competition from discounters has hurt Casino and rival Carrefour as French shoppers eschew their traditional hypermarkets and supermarkets for discount stores. Flat sales preceded the abrupt departure of CEO Pierre Bouchut who was replaced by Casino's chairman and controlling shareholder Jean-Charles Naouri. Taking on both jobs Naouri said will accelerate decision making.

Casino has plans to establish a new publicly-traded subsidiary for part of its real estate assets in France, including shopping mall properties adjacent to its hypermarket and supermarkets as wll as the land under its cafeterias. Following the IPO, planned for the second half of 2005, Casino will own a majority of the new company's shares.

HISTORY

Frenchman Geoffroy Guichard married Antonia Perrachon, a grocer's daughter, in 1889 in Saint-Etienne, France. Three years later Geoffroy took over his father-in-law's general store (a converted "casino" or musical hall). In 1898 the company became Société des Magasins du Casino. By 1900, when it became a joint stock company, Casino had 50 stores; it opened its 100th store in 1904. That year the company introduced its first private-label product: canned sardines. In 1917 Guichard named his two sons, Mario and Jean, as managers.

By WWI there were about 215 branches, more than 50 in Saint-Etienne. From 1919 to the early 1920s the company opened several factories to manufacture goods such as food, soap, and perfumes. In 1925 the elder Guichard retired, leaving the day-to-day operations of Casino to his two sons. (Geoffroy died in 1940.) WWII took a heavy toll on the company: About 70 Casino stores were leveled and another 450 were damaged.

The company began opening cafeterias in 1967, and in 1976 it formed Casino USA to run them. Casino USA bought an interest in the California-based Thriftimart volume retailer in 1983, renaming the company after Thriftimart's Smart & Final warehouse stores.

Casino grew by acquiring companies across France, including CEDIS (16 hypermarkets, 116 supermarkets, and 722 smaller stores in eastern France; 1985) and La Ruche Meridionale (18 hypermarkets and 112 supermarkets in southern France, 1990). Casino bought nearly 300 hypermarkets and supermarkets from Rallye SA in 1992, giving Rallye about 30% of the company. The company opened its first hypermarket in Warsaw, Poland, in 1996.

Rival Promodès made a roughly $4.5 billion hostile takeover bid for Casino in 1997. Guichard family members voted against the Promodès offer, instead backing a $3.9 billion friendly offer from Rallye (increasing their stake to nearly 50%). Casino also launched a massive counterattack — buying more than 600 Franprix and Leader Price supermarket stores from food manufacturer TLC Beatrice and acquiring a 21% stake in hypermarket chain Monoprix. Promodès withdrew its bid four months later.

Casino expanded internationally in the late 1990s, acquiring stakes in food retailers in Argentina (Libertad), Uruguay (Disco), Colombia (Exito), Brazil (Companhia Brasileira de Distribuicao), and Thailand (Big C, the country's largest retailer). It also opened its first hypermarket in Taichung, Taiwan.

Expansion in France included a joint venture (called Opera), formed in 1999 with retailer Cora SA to buy food and nonfood goods for the Casino and Cora stores, and the acquisition of 100 convenience stores (converted to the Petit Casino banner) in southwest France from retailer Guyenne et Gascogne.

Casino acquired 100 Proxi convenience stores in southeast France in 2000 from Montagne (most became Vival franchises) and more than 400 convenience stores (Eco Service and others) from Auchan. Casino also bought 51% of French online retailer CDiscount.com (CDs, videos, CD-ROMs, and DVDs), and it upped its ownership in several of its international supermarket operations, including gaining 100% ownership of Libertad. It also increased its ownership of Monoprix to 49%.

In July 2002, Casino bought a 38% stake in Laurus NV, its financially troubled Dutch rival. Laurus operates nearly 2,000 supermarkets in the Netherlands, Spain, and Belgium. (Soon after, Casino sold Laurus's unprofitable stores in Spain and Belgium.) Also in 2002, the company sold its wine division, Les Chais Beaucairois, to wine and spirits company Marie Brizard for $22 million.

In March 2005 chief executive Pierre Bouchut unexpectedly left Casino. Jean-Charles Naouri, the company's chairman and controlling shareholder, replaced him. In May Casino took joint control of Brazil's leading food retailer, Companhia Brasileira de Distribuição, along with the family of Abilio Diniz. Previously, Casino held a minority stake in the supermarket chain.

EXECUTIVES

Chairman and CEO: Jean-Charles Naouri, age 56
Executive Deputy Managing Director: Jacques-Edouard Charret
Executive Deputy Managing Director, Finance and Administration: Jacques Tierny
Deputy Managing Director, European Hypermarkets (France and Poland): Daniel Sicard
EVP, Human Resources and Communication: Thierry Bourgeron, age 51
Director, Planning and Strategy: Hervé Daudin
Manager, Supply Chain: Jean-Michel Duhamel
General Director, Convenience Stores and Supermarkets: François Duponchel
Director, Real Estate and Expansion: Jacques Ehrmann
Director, Non-food Activities: Joël Mornet
Deputy Managing Director, European Supermarkets (France and the Netherlands), and Restaurants: Jean-Brice Hernu, age 52
Director, Business Development, Asia: Christian P. Couvreux, age 53
Director, Finance: Pascal Announ, age 40
President and CEO, Smart & Final: Etienne Snollaerts
Director, Asian and Indian Ocean region (Thailand, Taiwan, Vietman, Reunion Island, Madagascar, Mauritius and Mayotte): André Mercier
Director, Business Development and Real Estate: Daniel Pain
Director, Customer Care: Philippe Marxgut
Director, Latin American region (Argentina, Uruguay, Venezuela, Brazil, and Colombia): Francis Mauger
Director, Financial Communications: Marc Maillet
Auditors: Bernard Roussel; Ernst & Young Audit

LOCATIONS

HQ: Casino Guichard-Perrachon S.A.
24, rue de la Montat, 42100 Saint-Etienne, France
Phone: +33-4-77-45-31-31   **Fax:** +33-4-77-45-38-38
Web: www.casino.fr

Casino Guichard-Perrachon has operations in France and 14 other countries, Argentina, Brazil, Colombia, Madagascar, Mauritius, Mexico, the Netherlands, Poland, Taiwan, Thailand, Uruguay, the US, Venezuela, and Vietnam.

2004 Sales

	% of total
France	61
Latin America	15
Netherlands	11
North America	5
Asia	4
Indian Ocean	2
Poland	2
Total	**100**

2004 Stores

	No.
France	6,977
Netherlands	721
Brazil	488
Poland	179
US	176
Colombia	96
Argentina	63
Mexico	58
Venezuela	55
Uruguay	46
Thailand	44
Indian Ocean	44
Taiwan	13
Total	**9,078**

PRODUCTS/OPERATIONS

Selected Operations

Banque du Groupe Casino (financial services)
Big C (68%, Thailand)
Caly-online (40%, online services)
 Cdiscount (51%; discount-priced books, CDs, DVDs, CD-ROMs, videos online)
 C-mesCourses (40%, Internet grocery shopping)
 C-online (40%, shopping hub for stores and services)

Casino (supermarkets)
Casino Cafétéria (restaurants, cafeterias, catering)
Casino Enterprise (non-food operations)
Casino USA (99.7%, with a 57% stake in Smart & Final)
Cativen (58%)
 Cada (supermarkets, Venezuela)
 Super Maxy's (hypermarkets, Venezuela)
Companhia Brasileira de Distribuição (34%)
 Barateiro (discount stores, Brazil)
 Eletro (specialty shops, Brazil)
 Extra (hypermarkets, Brazil)
 Pão de Açúcar (supermarkets, Brazil)
Disco (50%, supermarkets, Uruguay)
 Devoto (48%, supermarkets, Uruguay)
Eco Service (convenience stores)
Exito (27%, supermarkets, Colombia)
Franprix (70%, supermarkets)
Géant (hypermarkets)
Imagica (photo and digital imaging processing)
Komogo (multimedia specialist in PCs, software and video games, telephony, books)
Leader Price (70%, supermarkets)
Les Chais Beaucairos (wine production, bottling, and sales)
Libertad (hypermarkets, Argentina)
Monoprix (49%, supermarkets)
Opera (50%, joint-purchasing venture with Cora SA)
Petit Casino (convenience stores)
Spar (convenience stores)
Vival (convenience stores)

COMPETITORS

ALDI	ITM Entreprises
A.P. Møller - Mærsk	Kingfisher
Auchan	METRO AG
Carrefour	Migros
Costco Wholesale	PPR
E.Leclerc	Primisteres Reynoird
Groupe Flo	Royal Ahold
Guyenne et Gascogne	Tesco
IGA	Wal-Mart

HISTORICAL FINANCIALS

Company Type: Public

Income Statement

FYE: December 31

	REVENUE ($ mil.)	NET INCOME ($ mil.)	NET PROFIT MARGIN	EMPLOYEES
12/04	31,603	666	2.1%	212,603
12/03	28,848	618	2.1%	206,760
12/02	23,957	467	1.9%	115,757
12/01	19,473	336	1.7%	106,736
12/00	17,959	344	1.9%	101,061
12/99	15,748	297	1.9%	82,548
12/98	16,519	252	1.5%	70,418
12/97	12,694	185	1.5%	58,626
12/96	12,774	160	1.3%	54,856
12/95	13,064	129	1.0%	52,482
Annual Growth	10.3%	20.0%	—	16.8%

2004 Year-End Financials

Debt ratio: 158.0%   Current ratio: 1.00
Return on equity: 15.9%   Long-term debt ($ mil.): 7,129
Cash ($ mil.): 693

Net Income History

Euronext Paris: CO

CASIO COMPUTER

CASIO COMPUTER wants a watch on every arm and a handheld computer in every pocket. The company makes a wide range of electronics products for consumers, including calculators, cell phones, digital cameras, portable TVs, watches, and musical keyboards. CASIO COMPUTER also manufactures computing and communications devices, like PDAs, and electronic cash registers. The company like to seek superlatives in its products: the G-Shock watch (1983) boasted that it was the toughest (able to survive a fall from a three-story building), and the EXILIM camera (2002) claimed to be the world's thinnest (roughly the size of a credit card). The three younger brothers of late founder Tadao Kashio continue to run CASIO COMPUTER.

CASIO COMPUTER generates most of its sales from consumer electronic products (calculators, digital cameras, and electronic dictionaries) while the rest of revenues are derived from electronic components. To combat sluggish consumer electronics sales, the company is focusing on three primary product categories: digital cameras, electronic dictionaries, and cell phones.

The company launched a joint venture with Hitachi in 2004; the new business unit, Casio Hitachi Mobile Communications Co., produces mobile phone handsets.

HISTORY

In 1942 Tadao Kashio started a Tokyo-based machine shop, Kashio Manufacturing. His brother, Toshio, later joined him. After reading about a 1946 computing contest in which an abacus bested an electric calculator, Toshio, an inventor, wrote a note to himself: "Abacus is human ability; calculator is technology." In 1950 he began developing a calculator. The other Kashio brothers — Yukio, a mechanical engineer, and Kazuo, who took over sales — joined the company in the 1950s.

The brothers incorporated in 1957 as CASIO COMPUTER, an anglicization of the family name. That year the company launched its first product, an electric calculator featuring an innovative floating decimal point display; it was the first Japanese-built electric calculator. CASIO COMPUTER took advantage of new transistor technology to create electronic calculators, and in 1965 it introduced the first electronic desktop calculator with memory. The company began exporting to the US in 1970.

In the 1970s only CASIO COMPUTER and Sharp emerged as significant Japanese survivors of the fierce "calculator war." CASIO COMPUTER's strategy of putting lots of new functions on a proliferation of small models and selling them at rock-bottom prices worked not only with calculators but with digital watches as well. The company introduced its first digital watch in 1974 and went on to dominate that market.

CASIO COMPUTER expanded its product line into electronic music synthesizers (1980), pocket TVs (1983), and thin-card calculators (1983). Determined to break away from the production of delicate timepieces, CASIO COMPUTER introduced shock-resistant (G-Shock) digital watches in 1983. In the mid-1980s sales were hurt by a

rising yen and stiff price competition from developing Asian nations. The company responded by releasing sophisticated calculators for such specialized users as architects and insurance agents. To offset the effects of the yen's heightened value in the late 1980s, CASIO COMPUTER moved manufacturing to Taiwan, Hong Kong, South Korea, California, and Mexico. Kazuo Kashio was named president in 1988.

In 1990 CASIO COMPUTER established CASIO COMPUTER Electronic Devices to sell LCDs and chip-on-film components. In 1991 the company acquired a capital interest in Asahi, a producer of communications equipment and light electrical appliances. CASIO COMPUTER moved much of its production overseas in 1994, primarily to Thailand and Malaysia, after the high yen contributed to a nearly 28% drop in exports.

The company introduced its first digital camera in 1995. The next year CASIO COMPUTER launched its CASSIOPEIA handheld PC, and in 1997 it entered the US pager market. In 1998 the company formed subsidiary CASIO Soft to develop Microsoft-based software for handheld PCs and other mobile devices.

In 2000 the company restructured its management system, and cut expenses (particularly research and development). The following year it instituted a three-year plan designed to strengthen its digital imaging, mobile networking, and electronic components businesses.

EXECUTIVES

Chairman: Toshio Kashio
President and CEO: Kazuo Kashio
EVP and Director: Yukio Kashio
Managing Director: Fumitsune Murakami
Managing Director: Yoshio Ono
Managing Director: Yozo Suzuki
Managing Director: Akinori Takagi
Corporate Officer and Director: Katsuhiro Endo
Corporate Officer and Director: Akira Kashio
Corporate Officer and Director: Atsushi Mawatari
Corporate Officer and Director: Tadashi Takasu
Corporate Officer and Director: Kouichi Takeichi
Corporate Officer: Harunori Fukase
Corporate Officer: Kiyotaka Hachiya
Corporate Officer: Ichiro Ohno
Corporate Officer: Naomitsu Satoh
Corporate Officer and Director: Susumu Takashima
Corporate Officer: Eiichi Takeuchi
Corporate Officer: Tomimoto Umeda
Auditors: KPMG AZSA & Co.

LOCATIONS

HQ: CASIO COMPUTER CO., LTD.
(Casio Keisanki Kabushiki Kaisha)
6-2, Hon-machi 1-chome, Shibuya-ku,
Tokyo 151-8543, Japan
Phone: +81-3-5334-4111   **Fax:** +81-3-5334-4608
US HQ: 570 Mount Pleasant Ave., Dover, NJ 07801
US Phone: 973-361-5400   **US Fax:** 973-537-8910
Web: www.casio.co.jp

CASIO COMPUTER has subsidiaries in Canada, China, France, Germany, Hong Kong, India, Japan, Malaysia, Mexico, Singapore, South Korea, Taiwan, Thailand, the UK, and the US.

2005 Sales

	% of total
Asia	
Japan	78
Other countries	3
Europe	12
North America	7
Total	**100**

PRODUCTS/OPERATIONS

2005 Sales

	% of total
Electronics	80
Electronic components	20
Total	**100**

Selected Products

Electronics
Consumer Products
Calculators
Digital cameras
Electronic dictionaries
Electronic musical instruments
Label printers
Mobile Network Solutions
Cell phones
Pocket PCs
System Equipment
Electronic cash registers
Office computers
Printers
Data projectors
Timepieces
Analog watches
Clocks
Digital watches
Electronic Components and Other Products
Electronic Components
Bump processing consignments
Carrier tape
LCDs
TCP assembly and processing consignments
Other
Factory automation
Molds
Toys

COMPETITORS

Canon	Ricoh
Fujitsu	Roland
Hewlett-Packard	Samsung
Hitachi	SANYO
IBM	Seiko
Matsushita	Sharp
Motorola	Sony
NEC	Timex
Nikon	Toshiba
Palm	Yamaha
Philips Electronics	

HISTORICAL FINANCIALS

Company Type: Public

Income Statement

FYE: March 31

	REVENUE ($ mil.)	NET INCOME ($ mil.)	NET PROFIT MARGIN	EMPLOYEES
3/05	5,198	200	3.9%	12,140
3/04	4,956	134	2.7%	12,929
3/03	3,676	47	1.3%	12,691
3/02	2,881	(188)	—	14,670
3/01	3,514	52	1.5%	18,119
3/00	3,889	59	1.5%	19,325
3/99	3,788	(72)	—	17,783
3/98	3,773	88	2.3%	18,668
3/97	3,709	30	0.8%	18,725
3/96	3,841	7	0.2%	18,797
Annual Growth	**3.4%**	**46.4%**	**—**	**(4.7%)**

2005 Year-End Financials

Debt ratio: 70.3%
Return on equity: 13.9%
Cash ($ mil.): 777
Current ratio: 1.68
Long-term debt ($ mil.): 1,061

Centrica plc

Centrica is not as centered on natural gas supply as it once was. Still the UK's largest gas supplier, Centrica provides gas to 12.6 million households under the British Gas, Scottish Gas, and Nwy Prydain brands. The company also serves 6.2 million residential electricity customers, and it supplies electricity and gas to more than 900,000 businesses. Other operations include gas and electricity production, wholesale energy marketing, international retail energy marketing, telecommunications, and gas heating and cooking equipment sales. The company has divested its Goldfish Bank subsidiary (financial services and credit cards); it has also sold its insurance and roadside services unit, Automobile Association.

In 2005 the company announced intent to sell its One.Tel telecom interest in order to focus on its energy businesses.

Centrica's natural gas production interests — the company has proven and probable reserves of 2.6 trillion cu. ft. — account for about 25% of its supply. The company is expanding its gas production operations in the UK and North America to support its supply businesses; it also has gas storage operations. Through its aggressive acquisition strategy in North America, Centrica has gained some 5.1 million retail power and gas supply customers, including more than 800,000 in the purchase of two Texas retail electric providers from American Electric Power and 1 million through the purchase of Canadian Utilities' retail businesses.

Centrica has also acquired Electricity Direct, a UK commercial retail supplier serving nearly 1 million customers. The company has entered continental Europe by investing in Belgium energy supplier Luminus, and it has entered the Spanish retail market. Centrica has purchased several power plant interests in the UK to support its supply business, and it is buying plants in North America as well. It has also agreed to pay Kerr-McGee more than $500 million dollars for stakes in North Sea natural gas fields.

The company has completed the sale of its Goldfish financial services operations to partner Lloyds TSB, and it has sold its Automobile Association business to equity firms CVC and Permira for $3.2 billion.

HISTORY

William Murdock invented gas lighting in 1792. In 1812 the Gas Light and Coke Company of London was formed as the world's first gas supplier to the public, and by 1829 the UK had 200 gas companies.

In the second half of the 19th century, the gas industry began looking for new outlets for its fuel. Gas stoves were introduced in 1851, the geyser water heater was invented in 1868, and in 1880 the first gas units to heat individual rooms were developed.

Gas companies countered the emerging electricity industry by renting gas stoves at low prices and installing gas fittings (stove, pipe, and lights) in poor homes with no installation charges or deposits. By 1914 the UK had 1,500 gas suppliers.

The electricity industry soon made major strikes against the gas industry's dominance. In 1926 the government began reorganizing the fragmented electricity supply industry, building a national power grid and establishing the Central Electricity Generating Board to oversee it.

The gas industry was nationalized in 1949, and 1,050 gas suppliers were brought under the control of the British Gas Council. Still, the gas industry was losing. Supplying gas was more expensive than generating electricity: Gas was seen as a power supply of the past. The Gas Council sought to change that image through an aggressive marketing campaign in the 1960s, touting gas as a modern, clean fuel. Other factors played a part in its re-emergence: The Clean Air Act of 1956 steadily reduced the use of coal for home heating, liquefied natural gas was discovered in the North Sea, and OPEC raised oil prices in the 1970s. When natural gas was introduced, most of the old gasworks were demolished, and the British Gas Council (which became the British Gas Corp. in 1973) set about converting, free of charge, every gas appliance in the UK to natural gas.

As Margaret Thatcher's government began privatizing state industries, the British Gas Corp. was taken public in 1986. Freed from government control, British Gas expanded its international exploration and production activities. When the US gas industry began deregulating, British Gas formed joint venture Accord Energy in 1994 with US gas trader Natural Gas Clearinghouse (now NGC) to sell gas on the wholesale market.

With the opening of the UK gas-supply market (which began regionally in 1996 and went nationwide in 1998), British Gas split into two public companies to avoid a conflict of interest between its supply business and its monopoly transportation business. In 1997 it spun off Centrica, the retail operations, and BG (now BG Group), which received the transportation business and the international exploration and production operations.

The UK electricity supply market began opening up to competition in 1998, and Centrica won 750,000 UK electricity customers, most of them also gas customers. In 1999 it bought the Automobile Association, which provided roadside service to motorists and sells insurance, from AA members. In 2000 Centrica began offering telecom services in the UK.

Centrica moved into North America in 2000 by purchasing two Canadian companies: natural gas retailer Direct Energy Marketing and gas production company Avalanche Energy. It gained a 28% stake in US marketing firm Energy America through the Direct Energy transaction and purchased the remaining 72% from US firm Sempra Energy the next year. Continuing its non-domestic strategy, Centrica bought a 50% interest in Belgium energy supplier Luminus.

The firm purchased 60% of the 1,260-MW Humber Power station in 2001, its first domestic power plant interest. It also acquired the UK operations of Australia's One.Tel, and it bought Enron's European retail supply business, Enron Direct, for $137 million.

In 2002 Centrica purchased the retail energy services business of Canadian pipeline company Enbridge for $637 million; it also agreed to acquire another Enron-controlled company, US retail energy supplier NewPower Holdings, for $130 million. But Centrica withdrew its offer to buy NewPower a month after the deal was announced because of concerns about NewPower's potential Enron-related liabilities. Later that year Centrica acquired 200,000 retail customer accounts in Ohio and Pennsylvania from NewPower.

EXECUTIVES

Chairman: Roger M. Carr, age 58
Chief Executive: Sir Roy A. Gardner, age 59, $2,542,397 pay
Group Finance Director: Phillip K. (Phil) Bentley, age 46, $1,450,766 pay
CIO: Peter Brickley
CEO, North America: Deryk I. King
Managing Director, British Gas Business: Ian Peters
Managing Director, British Gas Home Services: Chris Weston
Deputy Chief Executive; Managing Director, British Gas Residential Energy: Mark S. Clare, age 46, $1,344,092 pay
Managing Director, Centrica Energy and Director: Jake Ulrich
Managing Director, One.Tel: Ian El-Mokadem
Group Director Human Resources: Anne Minto
Corporate Affairs Director: Michael Young
Group General Counsel and Company Secretary: Grant Dawson
Director Investor Relations: Kath Kyle
Auditors: PricewaterhouseCoopers LLP

LOCATIONS

HQ: Centrica plc
Millstream, Maidenhead Road,
Windsor SL4 5GD, United Kingdom
Phone: +44-1753-494-000   **Fax:** +44-1753-494-001
Web: www.centrica.co.uk

Centrica has operations in Belgium, Canada, Spain, the UK, and the US.

PRODUCTS/OPERATIONS

Selected Subsidiaries and Affiliates

AA Corporation Limited
  Automobile Association Developments Limited (roadside and financial services)
  Automobile Association Insurance Services Limited (financial services)
  Automobile Association Underwriting Services Limited (roadside and financial services)
AccuRead Limited (49%, meter reading)
British Gas Services Limited (installation and servicing of gas heating systems)
British Gas Trading Limited (energy supply)
Centrica Business Services (British Gas Business, commercial energy supply)
Electricity Direct (UK) Ltd (retail energy supply)
Centrica Energía SL (Luseo Energía, retail energy supply, Spain)
Centrica Energy Management Group (industrial sales and wholesaling, gas production, and energy trading)
  Accord Energy Limited (wholesale energy trading)
  Centrica Resources Limited (gas production)
  Hydrocarbon Resources Limited (gas production)

Centrica Insurance Company Limited
  (insurance services)
Centrica North America (retail energy supply)
  CPL Retail Energy LP (energy sales, US)
  Direct Energy LP (energy sales, US)
  Direct Energy Marketing Limited
    (energy sales, Canada)
  Energy America LLC (energy sales, US)
  WTU Retail Energy LP (energy sales, US)
Centrica Storage Holdings Limited (gas storage)
Centrica Telecommunications Limited
  British Gas Communications (local phone service,
    mobile phone service, and Internet access)
  One.Tel (local phone service and Internet access)
Luminus N.V. (50%, retail energy supply, Belgium)

COMPETITORS

AGL Resources
British Energy
Calor
Community Energy
EDF Energy
Electrabel
E.ON Ruhrgas
E.ON UK
Gasunie
Gaz de France
Green Mountain Energy
npower
Scottish and Southern Energy
Scottish Power
STASCO
TNP Enterprises
United Utilities
Viridian Group
Western Power Distribution

HISTORICAL FINANCIALS

Company Type: Public

Income Statement

FYE: December 31

	REVENUE ($ mil.)	NET INCOME ($ mil.)	NET PROFIT MARGIN	EMPLOYEES
12/04	35,255	2,662	7.6%	43,414
12/03	31,880	889	2.8%	42,573
12/02	22,960	767	3.3%	38,051
12/01	18,299	469	2.6%	31,550
12/00	14,827	491	3.3%	28,305
12/99	11,666	294	2.5%	19,600
12/98	12,409	148	1.2%	16,427
12/97	12,936	(1,305)	—	15,423
12/96	13,804	(1,801)	—	19,702
Annual Growth	**12.4%**	**—**	**—**	**10.4%**

2004 Year-End Financials

Debt ratio: 28.1%
Return on equity: 58.9%
Cash ($ mil.): 79

Current ratio: 1.11
Long-term debt ($ mil.): 1,271

Net Income History

Pink Sheets: CPYYY

```
3,000
2,500
2,000
1,500
1,000
 500
   0
-500
-1,000
-1,500
-2,000
     12/95 12/96 12/97 12/98 12/99 12/00 12/01 12/02 12/03 12/04
```

Club Med

Hobbled by a reputation that has become passe, Club Méditerranée (popularly known as Club Med) is struggling to revamp its 1970s "sea, sex, and sun" image and overcome recent losses. With more than 1.5 million guests annually, the company has 150 leisure operations in more than 40 countries, including about 120 resort villages, 12 villas, a cruise ship operation, and a French tour operator. Nearly three-quarters of its visitors come from Europe. Former chairman Philippe Bourguignon, who breathed life into Euro Disney, returned Club Med to profitability and tried new concepts such as Club Med World recreational centers. Worldwide hotel operator Accor owns about 29% of the company.

The company closed 17 of its resorts (12 just for the winter) following September 11, 2001, to help cut costs in a diminished market for tourism. Amid losses for a second consecutive year, Bourguignon resigned in 2002.

In 2004 Accor acquired its 29% equity interest in Club Med, including the 21% of shares held by Exor and 8% held by Caisse des Depots et Consignations. This acquisition makes Accor the core shareholder in Club Méditerranée. In 2005, Richelieu France amassed an 18% stake in Club Med.

HISTORY

Belgian diamond cutter Gérard Blitz dreamed up the Club Méditerranée concept as an escape from the post-WWII doldrums in Europe. In 1950 he convened a gathering of charter members on the island of Majorca, where the group slept in tents, cooked their own food, and had a great deal of fun. The Club Med philosophy was born — vacation villages in exotic locations, combining low prices and simple amenities with community spirit and entertainment.

Frenchman Gilbert Trigano, who provided the tents for that first gathering, came on board as the managing director of the company in 1954 and launched a major expansion drive. Polynesian-style huts replaced the tents at the newly opened location in Greece in 1954, and in 1956 the company set up its first ski resort in Leysin, Switzerland. Club Méditerranée was incorporated the following year.

The Rothschild Group was the company's main shareholder from 1961 until 1988, providing the capital for much of Club Méditerranée's expansion. The company went public in 1966.

Club Méditerranée expanded into the cruise line business during the late 1960s, but surly crews and the outbreak of the Arab-Israeli War in 1967 scuttled plans. In the late 1960s Club Méditerranée gained a foothold in the US, opening an office in New York and a hotel in Northern California. In the 1970s the company became one of the biggest leisure groups in France through a series of mergers and acquisitions. The 1970s and 1980s also saw the company hone its freewheeling, anything-goes image.

Club Med, Inc., was set up in New York in 1984 to handle the company's business in the Americas and Asia. Trigano relaunched the cruise line concept in 1990. Club Méditerranée's expansion came to a crashing halt in 1991 as the company suffered its first-ever loss. Political unrest in its prime tourist locations plagued operations, leading in 1993 to a major loss and Trigano's resignation (though he remained as a director). His

son Serge took over as chairman that year and set about cutting costs. Lawsuits plagued the company in 1996 — one involving the fatal crash of a Club Med plane, the other involving a black-face minstrel show.

Board members looking to turn around losses created a new position for Serge Trigano in 1997 and replaced him as chairman with Philippe Bourguignon, who had helped revive Euro Disney. To boost profits, the company sold its *Club Med 1* cruise ship, as well as other assets that were outside the scope of its core resort business. It also phased out its lower-priced Club Aquarius resorts as part of its efforts to refocus on a single brand. But Club Med suffered record losses in 1997, and Trigano and his father later resigned.

With its restructuring plan in full swing in 1998, Club Med made its way back into the black. The company began renovating its village resorts and consolidating and centralizing its administrative offices. Club Med also implemented a new advertising campaign in 1998 and announced plans to open new ski resorts in the US and Canada, as well as Club Med at Paris Bercy, a recreational center in Paris. In 1999 Club Med bought French travel company Jet Tours Holding.

In 2000 it branched into e-commerce through its creation of Internet subsidiary Club Med On Line. It also purchased its third US village in 2000 in Crested Butte in Colorado. Club Med branched into the body building business in 2001 when it purchased Gymnase Club, a chain of 200 fitness clubs since renamed Club Med Gym.

In 2002 the company struck a licensing deal with Coty Inc. to begin selling beauty products.

EXECUTIVES

Chairman and CEO: Henri Giscard d'Estaing, age 49
SEVP and CFO: Michel Wolfovski
SEVP Europe: François Salamon
SVP Development, Construction, and Assets Management: Bertrand Julien-Laferrière
SVP Human Resources: Olivier Sastre
President, Jet Tours, Club Med Discovery, and Oyyo: Laurence Berman
President and CEO, Americas: John T. A. Vanderslice, age 44
President and CEO, Asia-Pacific: Joël Tiphonnet, age 42
Director of Marketing: Jennifer Vandekreeke
SVP Sales, Club Med North America: Paula Hayes
Marketing Manager: Lauren Funke
VP Marketing, Club Med North America: Mark Wiser
Commercial Director, Club Med Sales Canada: Brenda Kyllo
Press Contact: Thierry Orsoni
Auditors: Cogerco-Flipo; Ernst & Young Audit

LOCATIONS

HQ: Club Méditerranée S.A.
  11 rue Cambrai, 75019 Paris, France
Phone: +33-1-53-35-35-53   **Fax:** +33-1-53-35-32-01
Web: www.clubmed.com

Club Méditerranée has operations in about 40 countries.

2004 Sales

	% of total
Europe	
France	44
Other countries	28
America	16
Asia	12
Total	**100**

Selected Club Med Resort Locations

Australia
Bahamas
Croatia
Cuba
Dominican Republic
Egypt
France
French West Indies
Greece
Haiti
Indonesia
Israel
Italy
Ivory Coast
Japan
Malaysia
Maldives
Mauritius
Mexico
Montenegro
Morocco
New Caledonia
Portugal
Saint Lucia
Saint Martin
Senegal
Spain
Switzerland
Thailand
Tunisia
Turkey
Turks and Caicos
US

PRODUCTS/OPERATIONS

Selected Brands

Club Med
Club Med Business
Club Med Cruises
Club Med Discovery
Club Med Gym
Club Med Voyages
Club Med World
Jet Tours

COMPETITORS

Carlson
Carnival
ClubCorp
Disney
Hilton
Hyatt
Kerzner International
Marriott

Rank
Royal Caribbean Cruises
Sandals Resorts
Société du Louvre
Sol Meliá
Starwood Hotels & Resorts
TUI
Vail Resorts

HISTORICAL FINANCIALS

Company Type: Public

Income Statement

FYE: October 31

	REVENUE ($ mil.)	NET INCOME ($ mil.)	NET PROFIT MARGIN	EMPLOYEES
9/04*	2,004	(54)	—	18,694
10/03	1,914	(109)	—	20,333
10/02	1,758	(61)	—	22,518
10/01	1,829	(63)	—	25,150
10/00	1,636	50	3.0%	23,700
10/99	1,586	41	2.6%	24,200
10/98	1,513	31	2.0%	23,100
10/97	1,423	(224)	—	19,400
10/96	1,562	(145)	—	20,000
10/95	1,734	35	2.0%	—
Annual Growth	1.6%	—	—	(0.8%)

*Fiscal year change

2004 Year-End Financials

Debt ratio: 65.0%
Return on equity: —
Cash ($ mil.): 197

Current ratio: 1.03
Long-term debt ($ mil.): 336

Net Income History

OTC: CLMDY

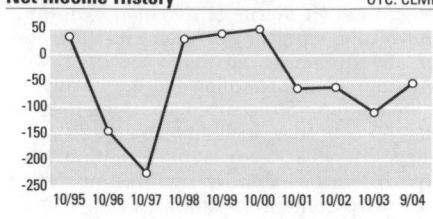

10/95 10/96 10/97 10/98 10/99 10/00 10/01 10/02 10/03 9/04

CNP Assurances

Running to the post office and bank? Buy some insurance while you're out. CNP Assurances is France's top personal life insurer. In addition to life insurance and other savings products, it sells health, death and disability, and other personal risk coverage and pensions. CNP sells its products primarily through La Poste, the French postal service, and La Caisse Nationale des Caisses d'Epargne, the state savings banks; together these two channels account for about 75% of CNP's sales. These partners are also shareholders in the company, together owning about 35%. Another French paragovernmental organization, Caisse des Dépôts et Consignations, owns more than 35%.

CNP's savings products, including life insurance, account for nearly 80% of premiums; personal risk products such as long-term-care, death and disability, and loan insurance make up about 15%.

The firm has distribution deals with France's Treasury and its civil service mutual insurance companies, and such financial institutions as Mutualité Française, the umbrella organization for France's mutual health insurers. CNP has been gradually moving abroad, taking stakes in neighboring countries' leading insurers (primarily in Portugal) as they are privatized.

CNP also controls Caixa Seguros in Brazil. The company's holdings in Argentina were slammed by the economic depression in that country, but CNP is restructuring them for future profitability. The insurer is also working to launch a joint venture with China's postal service.

HISTORY

CNP Assurances traces its origins to three government insurance entities established in the mid-19th century. Caisse nationale d'assurance en cas d'accident ("accident insurance") was formed in 1868. Caisse nationale d'assurance en cas de décès ("death and disability insurance") was formed in 1848, while Caisse de retraite pour la vieillesse ("retirement pensions") followed two years later. These two organizations were merged in 1949, forming Caisse nationale d'assurance sur la vie. Ten years later it was merged with the government's accident insurance bureau to form Caisse Nationale de Prévoyance ("provident society"). CNP was put under the domain of the French government's investment banking arm, Caisse des Dépôts et Consignations (CDC).

Over the years CNP earned a reputation for specializing in certain risks, introducing a variety of life and personal risk insurance and pension and savings products. During the 1980s the company enjoyed a healthy growth rate around 20% annually as more French individuals and companies began investing in insurance products.

In 1987 CNP became a national public establishment, making it independent from, though still owned by, the government. The next year the company teamed with Centre National des Caisses d'Epargne et de Prévoyance (now known as La Caisse Nationale des Caisses d'Epargne or Caisses d'Epargne) to form Ecureuil-Vie, a joint venture to sell CNP's insurance and savings products in the national savings banks. That year it partnered with Portugal's Caixa Geral de Depósitos to create new products.

In the early 1990s CNP was among several entities the government announced it would privatize. To prepare for the change, the company reorganized and became CNP Assurances; the government sold a large chunk of the firm to CDC, La Poste, and Caisses d'Epargne, reducing its stake to 42%. During this time CNP passed rival Union des Assurances de Paris (now part of AXA) to become France's top life insurer.

Privatization lurched along until 1995, when it was put on hold for elections; the Socialist government that came to power was less enthusiastic about the sale of government assets than its predecessor. The process hit another snag two years later when some workers protested, fearing they'd lose their status as civil servants and the perks associated with it. Also in 1997 CNP became the major shareholder of Polish life insurer Polisa-Zycie when it raised its stake from 26% (purchased 1996) to 46%. By 1998 privatization was back on track, and the government sold a 22% stake in CNP to the public. CDC, La Poste, and Caisses d'Epargne raised their interests to their current levels. Before the year's end, CNP bought majority stakes in Portuguese insurers Global and Global Vida.

Expansion abroad continued in 1999 when CNP announced plans to set up operations in China. That year it teamed with the UK's Prudential for cobranded insurance products. In 2000 the company extended its selling arrangement with Caisses d'Epargne to 2005. In 2001 CNP moved into the Brazilian market with the purchase of 51% of insurer Caixa Seguros. In 2003 it sold off its share of Italian life insurance company IntesaVita (formerly Carivita).

EXECUTIVES

Chairman: Edmond Alphandéry
Vice Chairman: Jean-Paul Bailly, age 59
CEO: Gilles Benoist, age 59
CFO: Antoine Lissowski
Director, International Operations: Xavier Larnaudie-Eiffel
Director, Management and Innovation: Jean-Pierre Walbaum, age 59
Director, Partnerships and Business Development: Gérard Ménéroud, age 58
Personnel Director: Dominique Pagant
Secretary to the Advisory Board: Hugues de Vauplane
Investor Relations Officer: Brigitte Molkhou
Auditors: KPMG Audit; Mazars & Guérard; Calan Ramolino & Associés

LOCATIONS

HQ: CNP Assurances SA
4 place Raoul Dautry, 75716 Paris, France
Phone: +33-1-42-18-88-88   **Fax:** +33-1-42-18-86-55
Web: www.cnp.fr

CNP Assurances has operations in Europe and South America.

2004 Premium Sales

	% of total
Europe	
France	96
Other countries	1
Latin America	3
Total	**100**

PRODUCTS/OPERATIONS

2004 Sales

	% of total
Premiums	72
Investment income	27
Other	1
Total	**100**

2004 Premium Sales By Channel

	% of total
Savings banks	40
French Post Office	36
Mutual insurers & local authorities	7
Companies	5
Financial institutions	5
Foreign subsidiaries	4
French Treasury	3
Total	**100**

2004 Premium Sales By Segment

	% of total
Savings	75
Pensions	9
Loan insurance	8
Personal risk insurance	6
Health insurance	1
Property & casualty	1
Total	**100**

Selected Subsidiaries and Affiliates

Age d'Or Expansion
Assurbail (99%; property leasing)
Assurposte (50%; insurance)
Caixa assessoria (52%; services; Brazil)
Caixa capitalização s/a (26%; insurance; Brazil)
Caixa Consorcio S/A (52%; insurance; Brazil)
Caixa Seguros (52%; insurance; Brazil)
Caixa vida e previdência s/a (51%; insurance; Brazil)
Cantis (50%)
CDC Ixis Asset Management (20%; finance company)
Cegape (42%)
CNP Caution
CNP IAM (insurance)
CNP Immobilier (property)
CNP International (reinsurance)
CNP Seguros de Vida (76%; insurance; Argentina)
Ecureuil vie (50%; insurance)
Filassistance (50%)
Fongépar (49%)
Forestière CDC (50%)
Gespré Europe (40%)
Global (84%; insurance; Portugal)
Global Vida (84%; insurance; Portugal)
GPM Assurances SA (33%)
Informatique CDC (30%)
Investissement Trésor Vie (insurance)
Parc de Monfort (50.8%)
Préviposte (insurance)
Previsol AFPJ (30%; insurance; Argentina)
Previsol Seguros de Retiro (30%; insurance; Argentina)
Previsol Seguros de Vida (30%; insurance; Argentina)
Provincia Seguros de Vida (40%; insurance; Argentina)
Sicac (property)

COMPETITORS

AGF
Allianz
AXA
BNP
Crédit Agricole
Eureko
Groupama
ING
Union des Assurances Fédérales

HISTORICAL FINANCIALS

Company Type: Public

Income Statement

FYE: December 31

	ASSETS ($ mil.)	NET INCOME ($ mil.)	INCOME AS % OF ASSETS	EMPLOYEES
12/04	248,538	858	0.3%	4,501
12/03	210,022	731	0.3%	3,998
12/02	161,479	599	0.4%	3,982
12/01	128,722	518	0.4%	—
12/00	124,628	439	0.4%	—
12/99	118,383	438	0.4%	—
12/98	117,349	321	0.3%	—
12/97	95,698	36	0.0%	—
12/96	90,257	303	0.3%	—
12/95	77,998	302	0.4%	—
Annual Growth	**13.7%**	**12.3%**	**—**	**6.3%**

2004 Year-End Financials

Equity as % of assets: 3.0%   Long-term debt ($ mil.): 3,857
Return on assets: 0.4%   Sales ($ mil.): 40,514
Return on equity: 12.4%

Net Income History

Euronext Paris: CNP

Coles Myer

Coles Myer is the top dingo of Australian retailers. The company is Australia's largest retailer with more than 2,500 stores throughout Australia and New Zealand. Accounting for about two-thirds of sales is the food, fuel, and liquor group, which includes about 700 Bi-Lo and Coles supermarkets, some 625 Liquorland outlets, and 600 Coles Express convenience stores. Coles Myer also sells apparel and general merchandise through its department store chain Myer Grace Bros, and the discount chains Target and Kmart. (Coles Myer holds the rights from Kmart and Target Corporation to use the Kmart and Target names in Australia and New Zealand.) The retailer also sells online via e.colesmyer.

CEO John Fletcher is leading a radical five-year restructuring plan to improve the performance of Cole's nonfood operations, which includes the sale of some of the struggling divisions. In a bid to revive business at Myer Grace Bros, Coles has upgraded five key stores and has closed five others in New South Wales. The department store chain has gone upscale and is busy luring fashion labels — including JAG, Ocean Pacific, Sean Jean, and Tommy Hilfiger — to its aisles. The company is renaming about 25 Grace Bros. outlets in New South Wales as Myer department stores in a move designed to establish a unified national brand for its retail operations. Myer has reached an agreement to rebrand CD/DVD/Video departments in Myer stores as Virgin Entertainment departments.

Coles Myer is expanding throughout Australia by acquiring supermarket (Franklins), liquor (Theo's Liquor), and hotel operators, and converting the outlets to its own banners. In Queensland — Australia's fastest-growing state — Coles spent about $100 million on 11 new stores and remodeled 15 others in 2004. The retailer plans to add about 200 stores by 2007 and to refurbish all of its Kmart stores by 2006.

To better compete with rival Woolworths, which sells gasoline at its supermarkets to drive business, Coles Myer has forged a discount fuel alliance with Royal Dutch/Shell Group to become the operator of Shell's network of 584 service stations in Australia.

HISTORY

After studying US and UK chain-store retailing, including the five-and-dime stores of S. S. Kresge, George James Coles opened his first "3d, 6d, and 1/-" discount variety store in 1914 in a working-class neighborhood of Collingwood, Australia. Coles expanded to a larger store five years later. With the formation of G. J. Coles & Coy in 1921, Coles spent the 1920s and 1930s opening stores in other Australian cities. The company went public in 1927.

Following WWII the firm embarked on a major acquisition binge. Coles & Coy bought Selfridges (Australasia — New South Wales, 1950), F&G Stores (Victoria, 1951), and Penneys (Queensland, 1956). The company expanded into food retailing in 1958 with the purchase of the 54-store John Connell Dickins chain. A year later it acquired Beilby's of South Australia and, in 1960, the Matthews Thompson group of 265 outlets in New South Wales.

Coles & Coy opened its first major discount store, Colmart, in 1968 and opened its first Kmart the following year through a joint venture with S. S. Kresge. In 1978 it bought out the renamed Kmart Corporation's interest in return for stock.

The company bought several liquor store chains in 1981, including Liquorland and Mac the Slasher (converted to the Liquorland banner). Coles & Coy began opening Super K food and general merchandise stores in 1982. Two years later it bought Katies, a women's apparel chain with 117 stores.of Melbourne. Founded in 1900 by Sidney Myer, the company went public in 1925 and began opening Target stores in 1970. At the time of the merger, Myer was Australia's #3 retailer and largest department store chain, with 56 department stores, 68 Target stores, 122 Fosseys variety stores, 45 Country Road stores (spun off in 1987), and a number of Red Rooster fast-food outlets.

Coles & Coy became Coles Myer in 1986 when it merged with the Myer Emporium chain. In 1987 Coles Myer entered discount food retailing with the acquisition of 25 Bi-Lo supermarkets. The next year it moved outside Australia when it opened a Kmart in Auckland, New Zealand. Coles Myer shares were listed on the New York Stock Exchange in 1988. In 1989 Myer Direct, the company's new direct mail order business, was established by Myer Stores.

In 1993 the company introduced World 4 Kids toy and recreation stores and a chain of office supply stores, Officeworks. That year Coles Myer repurchased the 21.5% stake owned by Kmart while continuing to use the Kmart name in Australia and New Zealand.

When finance director Philip Bowman was fired in 1995, he sued the company for wrongful dismissal. Bowman claimed he was investigating a 1990 transaction that cost the company $18 million while indirectly benefiting chairman Solomon Lew by the same amount. The "Yannon" deal resulted in Lew's ouster as chairman, though he stayed on the board of directors. Bowman's suit was settled for $1.1 million. In 1997 former chairman and CEO Brian Quinn was found guilty of conspiring to defraud Coles Myer of $3.5 million (used to pay for renovations to his Melbourne home) and sentenced to four years in prison.

In 1997 and 1998 Coles Myer started a dozen concept stores, including Myer Megamart (furniture and electronics), Target Home (home furnishings), and Essentially Me (health and beauty items). The trend continued in 1999 with let's eat (a combination restaurant and grocery).

John Fletcher became CEO in 2001 following the retirement of Dennis Eck. Under Fletcher, Coles Myer began in 2002 its biggest restructuring in more than a decade, but met resistance from dissident board member and former executive chairman Lew. Following a messy public brawl over the future direction of the company, Lew, Coles Myer's largest shareholder, was voted off the board. Fletcher had threatened to quit if Lew was re-elected. Stan Wallis' five-year stint as chairman came to an end prematurely in October when he was replaced by director Rick Allert.

Coles Myer bought the Australian operations of Office Depot in 2003. It sold its Sydney Central Plaza shopping center to Westfield Trust as part of its five-year restructuring plan. The company acquired Australia's biggest online food retailer, ShopFast.

In 2004 Coles Myer's liquor group moved to the Melbourne head office to allow the division to work better with the food group.

EXECUTIVES

Chairman: Richard H. (Rick) Allert, age 62
Managing Director, CEO, and Director:
 John E. Fletcher, age 53, $3,299,153 pay
CFO: Fraser MacKenzie
Chief Officer, Corporate and Property Services:
 Tim Hammon, $1,100,985 pay
Group Managing Director, Food, Liquor, and Fuel:
 Hani Zayadi, age 50, $1,512,176 pay
 (prior to promotion)
Managing Director, Bi-Lo: Peter Merritt
Managing Director, Fuel and Convenience: Joe Barberis
Managing Director, Coles Supermarkets: Gerry Masters
Managing Director, Liquor Group: Peter Scott
Managing Director, Myer: Dawn Robertson,
 $1,575,750 pay
Managing Director, Officeworks: Launa Inman
Managing Director, Target: Larry Davis, $1,324,886 pay
CIO: Peter Mahler
Group General Manager, Corporate Affairs:
 Pamela Catty
Group General Manager, Marketing and Customer Strategy: Tom Lemke
Group General Manager, Human Resources: Ian Clubb
Group General Manager, Supply Chain: Andrew Potter
Auditors: PricewaterhouseCoopers

LOCATIONS

HQ: Coles Myer Ltd.
 800 Toorak Rd., Tooronga, Victoria 3146, Australia
Phone: +61-3-9829-3111   **Fax:** +61-3-9829-6787
Web: www.colesmyer.com

Coles Myer operates more than 1,900 retail stores throughout Australia and New Zealand.

2004 Sales

	% of total
Australia	99
New Zealand	1
Total	**100**

PRODUCTS/OPERATIONS

2004 Sales

	% of total
Food, liquor & fuel	66
Kmart & Officeworks	14
Myer & Megamart	10
Target	9
Emerging businesses	1
Total	**100**

2004 Stores

	No.
Supermarkets (Coles & Bi-Lo)	700
Liquorland	626
Coles Express	598
Kmart & Officeworks	303
Target	253
Myer & Megamart	70
Emerging businesses	9
Total	**2,559**

Selected Banners

Bi-Lo Supermarkets
Coles Supermarkets
Coles Online
Coles Express Service Stations
Harris Technology
Kmart
Kmart Tyre & Auto Service
Liquorland
Liquorland Direct
Megamart
Myer
Officeworks
Shopfast
Target
Theo's Liquor
Vintage Cellars

COMPETITORS

ALDI
Barbeques Galore
Body Shop
David Jones
Esprit Holdings
Foodland Associated
Harris Scarfe Holdings
Harvey Norman Holdings
InterTAN
Metcash
Woolworths Limited

HISTORICAL FINANCIALS

Company Type: Public

Income Statement

FYE: Last Sunday in July

	REVENUE ($ mil.)	NET INCOME ($ mil.)	NET PROFIT MARGIN	EMPLOYEES
7/04	22,655	433	1.9%	176,108
7/03	17,496	278	1.6%	162,414
7/02	13,946	192	1.4%	164,272
7/01	12,100	77	0.6%	155,000
7/00	14,414	174	1.2%	157,000
7/99	14,614	255	1.7%	151,284
7/98	12,499	215	1.7%	148,346
7/97	14,298	290	2.0%	148,000
7/96	14,583	217	1.5%	152,744
7/95	12,396	293	2.4%	143,281
Annual Growth	**6.9%**	**4.4%**	**—**	**2.3%**

2004 Year-End Financials

Debt ratio: 21.0%
Return on equity: 19.7%
Cash ($ mil.): 596
Current ratio: 1.20
Long-term debt ($ mil.): 501
No. of shares (mil.): 153
Dividends
 Yield: 3.0%
 Payout: 57.1%
Market value ($ mil.): 7,668

Stock History

NYSE: CM

	STOCK PRICE ($) FY Close	P/E High/Low		PER SHARE ($) Earnings	Dividends	Book Value
7/04	50.06	20	14	2.66	1.52	18.72
7/03	37.95	23	14	1.72	1.18	16.14
7/02	27.50	31	22	1.19	1.05	12.13
7/01	24.70	69	48	0.50	1.52	11.22
7/00	30.19	39	23	1.20	1.32	11.08
7/99	46.50	27	15	1.77	1.23	12.63
7/98	29.50	28	20	1.51	0.73	11.48
7/97	40.75	21	14	2.02	1.39	13.08
7/96	27.75	20	16	1.49	0.72	14.00
7/95	25.00	19	16	1.45	1.21	14.08
Annual Growth	**8.0%**	**—**	**—**	**7.0%**	**2.6%**	**3.2%**

Compass Group

This is one compass that's really attracted to first-place medals. Compass Group, the world's largest foodservice company with operations in more than 90 countries, managed nearly all of the food-serving operations at the 2002 Winter Olympics in Salt Lake City. It provides contract catering and concession services at airports, hospitals, rest areas, and schools. Compass also operates fine restaurants, including Upper Crust and Caffè Ritazza, and franchises a number of Burger King outlets. In addition, the company provides corporate foodservices for clients such as Avon Products, Bank of America, Nissan, Sony, and Symantec.

Compass Group was a large player in the hotel business through its Forte Hotel Group, which included about 400 hotels operating under the

Le Méridien brand. As part of its plan to focus solely on catering, Compass sold that division to Japanese investment bank Nomura International in 2001. Compass sold its Travelodge budget motel business and Little Chef roadside eateries to London-based private equity firm Permira in 2003.

Despite its size and reach, Compass continues to grow through strategic acquisitions, especially in the fertile US market. Compass enjoys contracts in the UK with the Hampton Court Palace Flower Show, the London Zoo, Madame Tussauds, Royal Albert Hall, and the Wimbledon tennis championships. In the US its customers include Churchill Downs, Walt Disney World, and Wrigley Field. It is penetrating deeper into the Asian market with its purchase of Seiyo Food Systems, Japan's #2 foodservices group.

Compass' success derives from the global scope of its operations and its standardized support structure, which allow it to leverage its strengths in gaining major contracts. Adding to that strength, the company merged in 2000 with UK hospitality and media giant Granada Group (renamed ITV plc in 2004). In conjunction with the merger, Granada spun off its media assets as a separate company, Granada Media. However, in 2001 the new Granada Compass demerged and made Compass Group a public company again. That year Compass purchased Morrison Management Specialists.

In 2005 Sir Roy Gardner, CEO of Centrica, was appointed to the Compass board. He will become chairman of the company sometime during 2006. In addtition, CEO Michael Bailey announced his intention to leave the company in 2006.

HISTORY

Compass Group was formed in 1987 when management bought out the catering business of London-based food and spirits giant Grand Metropolitan (now Diageo) for $260 million. The company went public the next year, listing on the London Stock Exchange. Gerry Robinson, CEO at the time, left in 1991 to take a position with British TV programming giant Granada Group (renamed ITV plc in 2004), where he helped that company diversify into foodservice operations. Finance director Francis Mackay took over as CEO.

Believing that real growth in the catering industry could come from size and economies of scale, Mackay orchestrated a $2.5 billion acquisition plan over the next five years. In 1992 Compass bought Traveller's Fare (now Upper Crust), a railway caterer, from British Rail. The company expanded into airports the following year with the acquisition of Scandinavian Airlines System's catering operations. Then in 1994 Compass bought Canteen Corporation, the US's third-largest vending and foodservice company.

Compass achieved its goal of becoming the world's largest caterer in 1995 with the acquisition of France's Eurest International, putting it ahead of Sodexho and Granada. Mackay calmed London investors nervous about the pace of Compass' acquisitions by selling off its hospital management operations and paying lip service to focusing on organic growth. Later that year Compass was awarded the world's largest foodservice contract, a $250-million, five-year deal with IBM.

By 1996 the company seemed to have forgotten all about organic growth, buying Service America, and then Daka International and France's SHRM in 1997. French subsidiary Eurest later snatched a $40 million contract from

rival Sodexho to supply the staff restaurants at Euro Disney, one of France's top three catering contracts. The next year Compass solidified its position in the airport markets with a five-year licensing deal for use of the T.G.I. Fridays brand, joining Taco Bell, Pizza Hut, Burger King, and Harry Ramsden's fish and chip shops in Compass' quiver of branded airport outlets.

In 1999 CEO Mackay became group chairman, leaving the reins to Compass' chief of North American operations, Michael Bailey. The company's US acquisitions quickly paid off that year with a contract to serve 90% of the food venues at the 2002 Winter Olympics in Salt Lake City. In 2000 the company merged with UK hospitality giant Granada Group (the combined firm became Granada Compass), which then spun off its media operations as a separate company, Granada Media. Late that year it bought Boston-based bakery/café chain Au Bon Pain for about $108 million.

The new company got a quick divorce in 2001 when Granada Compass decided to demerge and make Compass Group public again. Compass Group later sold the Le Méridien hotel operations it gained from the Granada merger to Nomura International for nearly $3 billion. (The firm kept the Travelodge chain but sold it in 2003). The company then began making purchases, including Morrison Management Specialists for $563 million, the 66% it didn't already own in Selecta Group, UK vending machine company Vendepac, and health care services management company Crothall Services. Compass lost seven operating sites during the September 11 terrorist attacks on the World Trade Center. Late in 2001 Compass strengthened its presence in Japan with the $277 million acquisition of Seiyo Food Systems, that country's #2 foodservices group.

In 2002 Compass signed arguably the industry's largest contract ever, a $200 million a year deal to feed Chevron employees around the world. In 2003 the company sold its Travelodge motel business and Little Chef diners to private equity firm Permira for $1.14 billion, a 5% discount to the asking price. Compass became the first non-Chinese company to provide food in stations and on trains operated by the Shanghai Railway Administration in 2004. In addition, the firm bought Creative Host Services in 2004.

The following year, Compass sold a 75% stake in Au Bon Pain to an unidentified buyer. Compass retained 25% of the company.

EXECUTIVES

Chairman: Sir Francis H. Mackay, age 61, $909,800 pay
Group Chief Executive: Michael J. Bailey, age 56, $1,877,947 pay
Group Chief Executive, Commercial Services, and CEO, Selecta: Chris D. Bucknall, age 55
Group Finance Director: Andrew Martin, age 45
Group Human Resources Director: Clive W. P. Grundy, age 53, $564,000 pay
Chairman and CEO, Western Europe: Antoine E. A. Cau, age 56
CEO, Eastern Division: Alain F. Dupuis, age 60, $1,984,076 pay
CEO, Europe and Latin America: Miguel Ramis, age 48
CEO, France: Didier Coutte
CEO, Select Service Partner: Andrew P. Lynch, age 47, $1,219,586 pay
CEO, UK and Ireland: Don A. Davenport, age 60
Group Secretary: Ronald M. Morley, age 52
Director, Corporate Affairs: Paul Kelly
Director, Corporate Strategy and Investor Relations: Sarah Ellis
Auditors: Deloitte & Touche LLP

LOCATIONS

HQ: Compass Group PLC
Compass House, Guildford Street, Chertsey, Surrey KT16 9BQ, United Kingdom
Phone: +44-1932-573-000   **Fax:** +44-1932-569-956
US HQ: 2400 Yorkmont Rd., Charlotte, NC 28217
US Phone: 704-329-4000   **US Fax:** 704-329-4160
Web: www.compass-group.com

Compass Group's food catering and concession services operate in more than 90 countries.

2004 Sales

	% of total
North America	31
UK	23
Other regions	46
Total	**100**

PRODUCTS/OPERATIONS

2004 Sales

	% of total
Business & industry	36
Consessions	24
Healthcare	12
Education	11
Vending	9
Defense offshore & remote site	8
Total	**100**

Selected Operating Units

Canteen Vending (vending machines)
Chartwells (education foodservices)
Eurest (workplace foodservice contracts)
FLIK (upscale foodservices)
Letheby & Christopher (sporting and leisure events)
Medirest (health care services)
Morrison Management Specialists (health care foodservice)
Patina (sporting and leisure events)
Restaurant Associates (sporting and leisure events)
Roux Fine Dining (executive hospitality)
Scolarest (education foodservices)
Select Service Partner (airport foodservice)
Selecta (vending machines)

COMPETITORS

Albert Abela
ARAMARK
Autogrill
Cara Operations
Delaware North
Elior
HDS Services
Morrison Management Specialists
Pret A Manger
Rentokil Initial
Sodexho Alliance
SYSCO
Vistar Corporation

HISTORICAL FINANCIALS

Company Type: Public

Income Statement

FYE: September 30

	REVENUE ($ mil.)	NET INCOME ($ mil.)	NET PROFIT MARGIN	EMPLOYEES
9/04	21,176	324	1.5%	402,375
9/03	18,806	307	1.6%	412,574
9/02	16,574	347	2.1%	392,352
9/01	12,839	215	1.7%	344,830
9/00	7,968	180	2.3%	211,127
9/99	7,924	226	2.8%	191,407
9/98	7,156	194	2.7%	154,758
9/97	5,974	161	2.7%	130,548
9/96	4,144	155	3.7%	107,843
Annual Growth	**22.6%**	**9.6%**	**—**	**17.9%**

2004 Year-End Financials

Debt ratio: 107.4%
Return on equity: 7.4%
Cash ($ mil.): 478
Current ratio: 0.84
Long-term debt ($ mil.): 4,794

Net Income History

London: CPG

Corus Group

Keeping a stiff upper lip is mandatory for Corus Group (formerly British Steel), one of the world's largest steel companies. The company was formed when the UK privatized its major steelworks in 1988. It then changed its name to Corus Group after acquiring most of Dutch rival Koninklijke Hoogovens. Corus makes coated and uncoated strip products, sections and plates, wire rod, engineering steels, and semi-finished carbon steel products. It also manufactures aluminum, including rolled and extrusion products. Customers include companies in the automotive, construction, engineering, and household-product manufacturing industries.

The company manufactures carbon steel using the basic oxygen steelmaking process at its three integrated steelmaking facilities in the UK at Port Talbot, Scunthorpe and Teesside, and one in the Netherlands at IJmuiden. Its engineering steel is manufactured using the electric arc furnace method at two other UK steelmaking facilities in Rotherham and Stocksbridge.

Corus also makes primary aluminum in two smelters in Delfzijl in the Netherlands and Voerde in Germany. Its aluminum rolling mills are located at Koblenz, Germany, Duffel in Belgium, and Cap-de-la-Madeleine in Canada (60% owned). Three locations in Germany, one in Belgium, and one in China (61% owned) produce the company's aluminum extrusions.

French aluminum producer Pechiney had agreed to buy Corus Group's aluminum assets, but the supervisory board of Corus Nederland rejected the sale and their decision was upheld by an Amsterdam court. The deal, worth about $815 million, would have cut debt and help offset losses at the company's UK steel operations.

Russian investor Alisher Usmanov had owned just over 10% of the company, but cut his stake in 2005. Usmanov had plans to have a representative take a seat on the steelmaker's board, but that eventually failed. Credit Suisse First Boston became the owner of about 15% of Corus in April 2005.

HISTORY

It took decades of aggressive government regulation of the UK steel industry to hammer out Corus Group. The process began with price-control measures in the 1930s and in 1950 the Labour government followed up by nationalizing steel producers on the grounds that they represented an unduly powerful oligopoly. A Conservative government took over in 1951 and sold most of the nationalized firms, primarily to their former shareholders. In place of nationalization, an Iron Steel Board — with the power to set maximum steel prices and with the final say on large investments — was formed.

The presence of price controls and an ever-present chance of renationalization discouraged capital investment. Even so, technological innovations such as continuous casting and oxygen-based production enabled UK steelmakers to double production between 1945 and 1960. Meanwhile, competition from European producers stiffened, as did competition from a rebuilt Japan. To add to the UK steel industry's woes, demand began slacking off in the 1960s.

In 1964 the Labour Party, which was committed to renationalizing steel, returned to power. It passed the Iron and Steel Act of 1967, nationalizing about 90% of the UK's steel-making capacity under a new holding company, British Steel Corporation (BSC). However, specialized, nonintegrated companies and rerolling companies remained freestanding, allowing them to benefit from price controls on BSC steel. BSC consisted of 14 crude steel companies' assets with a 475,000 ton annual capacity. The government compensated shareholders based on stock market values, paying much more than the companies were worth. To make matters worse, the companies' return on capital was a meager 3.7%.

BSC began consolidating its small, outdated facilities into larger works with advanced equipment. In the midst of a huge investment program, the mid-1970s' energy crisis hit and steel demand fell; the company began closing its outdated mills. A 1980 strike cost BSC a large chunk of its market share and showed that steel requirements could be met through imports. That year the European Commission (EC) established production limits to reduce the steel glut. It also decided to regulate the amount of state aid steel producers could receive. By the end of 1980, BSC's workforce had been reduced to about 130,000 people — half its size when the companies were nationalized in 1967. During the 1980s BSC disposed of about $1 billion in noncore assets to focus on efficient steelmaking. State aid to European steel producers was largely prohibited in 1985 and the EC's quota system ended in 1988.

The British Steel Act of 1988 privatized BSC, and British Steel was born. The company recorded big profits in 1990, but then a recession hit, and British Steel suffered two years of losses before returning to profitability in 1994. The next year the company announced plans to expand its operations in emerging markets such as Asia, Central Europe, and Latin America. In 1996 British Steel sold about 6,000 tons of rails to Latin America. The next year it built a steel plant in Alabama — its first outside the UK — and sold its British Steel Forgings unit, which made components for the aerospace and automobile industries.

In 1998 British Steel joined other steelmakers in asking the EC to investigate Asian steel dumping. Stiff competition and a strong domestic currency caused the company to suffer a loss for fiscal 1999. That year British Steel paid $2.4 billion for Dutch steelmaker Koninklijke Hoogovens. At the same time, British Steel became Corus, a name chosen because it has no significant meaning in any language. Amid losses, joint chief executives John Bryant and Fokko van Duyne were forced out in 2000.

In 2001 the company announced that it was cutting more than 6,000 jobs in an effort to return to profitability. In 2002 Corus agreed to sell its stainless steel operations to Outokumpu Oyj (Finnish metal producer) for approximately $525 million. That same year, Corus came close to buying Brazil's largest steelmaker, Companhia Siderúrgica Nacional (CSN), but its debt of about $2.6 billion and the weakening Brazilian currency put a stop to the deal.

In 2003 president Anthony Pedder resigned after a tumultuous financial year and a court decision that prevented the sale of its aluminum business to French aluminum maker Pechiney. The next year Corus sold Tuscaloosa Steelworks.

EXECUTIVES

CEO and Executive Director: Philippe Varin, age 51, $2,134,303 pay
Executive Director, Finance: David M. Lloyd, age 40, $858,576 pay
Division Director, Aluminum: Gerhard Buddenbaum
Division Director, Distribution and Building Systems: Scott MacDonald
Division Director, Long Products: Paul Lormor, age 53
Division Director, Strip Products: Rauke Henstra, age 58
Group Director, Technology and Services: Nelson Cunha
Director, Human Resources: J.P. Staf Wouters
Secretary: Richard Shoylekov
Managing Director, Teesside Cast Products: Jon Bolton
Managing Director, Rail Businesses: Joe Guerin
Auditors: PricewaterhouseCoopers LLP

LOCATIONS

HQ: Corus Group plc
30 Millbank, London SW1P 4WY, United Kingdom
Phone: +44-20-7717-4444　　**Fax:** +44-20-7717-4455
Web: www.corusgroup.com

Corus has subsidiaries in more than 20 countries supported by a worldwide trading network and a number of processing and service centers.

2004 Sales

	% of total
Europe	
UK	28
Other Europe	53
North America	10
Other regions	9
Total	**100**

PRODUCTS/OPERATIONS

2004 Sales

	% of total
Carbon steel	89
Aluminum	11
Total	**100**

Selected Products and Operations

Aluminum products
Channels
Columns
Electrical steels
Engineering billets
Joists
Processing
Railway products
Special strip
Steel plate products
Strip products
Wire rod

Selected Subsidiaries

Cogent Power Limited (75%)
Corus LP (60%, Canada)
Norsk Stål AS (50%, Norway)
Norsk Stål Tynnplater AS (50%, Norway)
Orb Electrical Steels Limited (75%)
Thomas Steel Strip Corp. (US)

COMPETITORS

Acesita	Nippon Steel
Allegheny Technologies	Novelis
Arcelor	Nucor
BÖHLER-UDDEHOLM	POSCO
BlueScope Steel	Salzgitter
Carpenter Technology	Sumitomo Metal
Cockerill Sambre	Industries
Gerdau AmeriSteel	ThyssenKrupp
Kobe Steel	United States Steel

HISTORICAL FINANCIALS

Company Type: Public

Income Statement

FYE: December 31

	REVENUE ($ mil.)	NET INCOME ($ mil.)	NET PROFIT MARGIN	EMPLOYEES
12/04	17,891	855	4.8%	48,300
12/03	14,183	(543)	—	49,400
12/02	11,583	(738)	—	50,900
12/01	11,211	(610)	—	55,600
12/00*	17,491	(2,017)	—	64,900
3/99	10,087	(131)	—	46,500
3/98	11,613	378	3.3%	50,000
3/97	11,844	508	4.3%	52,900
3/96	10,757	1,186	11.0%	50,100
3/95	7,755	759	9.8%	—
Annual Growth	**9.7%**	**1.3%**	**—**	**(0.5%)**

*Fiscal year change

2004 Year-End Financials

Debt ratio: 43.2%
Return on equity: 15.2%
Cash ($ mil.): 734
Current ratio: 2.24
Long-term debt ($ mil.): 2,698

No. of shares (mil.): 444
Dividends
Yield: 0.0%
Payout: —
Market value ($ mil.): 4,359

Stock History

NYSE: CGA

	STOCK PRICE ($) FY Close	P/E High/Low		PER SHARE ($) Earnings	Dividends	Book Value
12/04	9.82	6	3	1.80	0.00	14.07
12/03	5.30	—	—	(1.65)	0.00	15.93
12/02	4.17	—	—	(2.36)	0.00	14.01
12/01	10.43	—	—	(1.95)	0.00	14.25
12/00*	10.00	—	—	(6.49)	0.16	16.48
3/99	20.19	—	—	(0.66)	0.62	35.35
3/98	24.25	16	11	1.91	2.06	35.96
3/97	26.63	12	9	2.50	1.97	38.28
3/96	29.50	5	4	5.84	1.59	35.41
3/95	26.25	7	5	3.76	0.58	32.82
Annual Growth	**(10.3%)**	**—**	**—**	**(7.9%)**	**—**	**(9.0%)**

*Fiscal year change

Creative Technology

Creative Technology wants PC audiophiles to get creative. The company is a leading maker of digital entertainment products, including portable audio players (Zen), PC sound cards (Sound Blaster), graphics accelerator cards (the 3D Blaster family), and digital cameras. Creative also makes modems and CD and DVD drives for PCs. Subsidiaries include Cambridge Soundworks (PC speakers), Creative Labs, and E-MU/ENSONIQ (audio chips and electronic musical instruments). Creative's top customers include computer manufacturers Dell, Gateway, and Hewlett-Packard. Co-founder and CEO Sim Wong Hoo owns about 30% of Creative.

Competitive pricing is key to Creative's marketing strategy, particularly in the portable audio market where it runs into the dominant presence of Apple's iPod. The company utilizes low-cost manufacturing at its own facilities in China and Malaysia and through subcontractors in those countries and Singapore.

Late in 2005 Creative released a high-end addition to its Zen line; with 30GB of storage the Zen Vision:M features music, video, and photo capabilities.

HISTORY

In 1981 Sim Wong Hoo (chairman and CEO) and Ng Kai Wa (later joined by Chay Kwong Soon) used a $6,000 stake to found Creative Technology as an engineering services company. It began making Apple II clones for the Chinese market in 1984; two years later it started producing PC clones. From 1983 to 1988 most of Creative's revenues came from PCs.

With stiff competition in the PC market, Sim shifted Creative's focus to sound cards and other PC enhancements. The company introduced its first Sound Blaster audio card in 1989; Sound Blaster soon became the industry standard. That year Creative launched PJS, an artificial intelligence-based Chinese-language operating system, and Views, a complementary word processor and desktop publisher with a more than 70,000-character alphabet. Also in 1989 Tandy (now RadioShack) ordered a large supply of Game Blasters — a sound card targeted at gamers — for its 8,000 Radio Shack stores, giving Creative a strong foothold in the US.

In 1991 Creative launched the first of its market-dominating upgrade kits, the Sound Blaster Multimedia Upgrade Kit, a software package bundled with a high-performance CD-ROM drive and a set of software applications. The company went public in 1992.

The growing popularity of multimedia products was music to Creative's ears. More computers were selling with sound cards and multimedia capabilities pre-installed, so the company signed deals to supply manufacturers including Compaq and Dell. Creative also diversified: In 1993 it acquired ShareVision Technology (videoconferencing products) and E-MU Systems (digital sound production systems).

The company also tried its hand at communication products. In 1994 it acquired modem maker Digicom (now Broadxent). The next year it released Phone Blaster, which combined voice mail, e-mail, and fax transmission functions.

Cracks began to show in Creative's progress in 1995. The slowing of the sound board market caused a steep drop in profits and prompted the company to restructure and refocus on sound products. Ng resigned that year, and Chay left in 1996. Creative introduced Graphics Blaster add-on graphics accelerator cards and signed a deal for Samsung to build its CD-ROM drive products that year.

Opting to add new technology quickly through acquisitions, in 1997 Creative bought speaker maker Cambridge Soundworks; ENSONIQ, maker of audio chips and electronic musical instruments (now part of E-MU/ENSONIQ); and the NetMedia Group of core logic chipset maker OPTi. In 1998 the company acquired Silicon Engineering, a maker of communications, multimedia, and storage integrated circuits. In 1999 Creative debuted the Nomad MP3 player, which plays digitally encoded music downloaded from PCs.

Sharp declines in Creative's Internet investments and the broader electronics market led the company to restructure its operations in 2001. Creative closed a factory, cut its staff by 10%, wrote off substantial losses in its investment portfolio, and recentered its operations on its core lines of digital audio products.

In 2002 the company acquired graphics chip maker 3Dlabs in a deal worth about $105 million.

EXECUTIVES

Chairman and CEO: Sim Wong Hoo, age 50
CFO: Ng Keh Long, age 46
President, 3Dlabs: C. Hock Leow, age 52
President, Cambridge SoundWorks: Michael Sullivan
President, Creative Labs: Craig McHugh
VP, Sales and Marketing and General Manager, E-MU Systems: Bill Wrightson
Director of Corporate Communications: Phil O'Shaughnessy
Director of Latin America Sales: Ricardo Vidal
Director of Product Marketing: Brad Anderson
Director of Product Marketing: Mala Sharma
Senior Brand Manager, Portable Media: Lisa O'Malley
Public Relations Specialist: Jennifer Ellard
Public Relations Specialist: Amy Stojsavljevic
Public Relations Coordinator: Katie Meyer
Auditors: PricewaterhouseCoopers

LOCATIONS

HQ: Creative Technology Ltd.
31 International Business Park,
Creative Resource, 609921, Singapore
Phone: +65-6895-4000 **Fax:** +65-6895-4999
US HQ: 1901 McCarthy Blvd., Milpitas, CA 95035
US Phone: 408-428-6600 **US Fax:** 408-428-6611
Web: www.creative.com

Creative Technology has production and distribution facilities in China, Ireland, Malaysia, Singapore, and the US.

2005 Sales

	$ mil.	% of total
The Americas	522	43
Europe	469	38
Asia/Pacific	233	19
Total	**1,224**	**100**

PRODUCTS/OPERATIONS

2005 Sales

	$ mil.	% of total
Personal digital entertainment	769	63
Speakers	176	14
Audio	166	14
Other	113	9
Total	**1,224**	**100**

Selected Products

Personal digital entertainment
  MP3 players (Zen)

Audio
  Digital sampling systems
  Electronic musical instruments
  Sound cards and chipsets (Sound Blaster)

Speakers (Cambridge Soundworks)

Graphics and video
  2-D/3-D graphic accelerator cards (3D Blaster line)
  Desktop digital camera (Video Blaster WebCam)
  PC digital video disk (DVD) players (Encore)

Multimedia upgrade kits (sound card,
  drive, speakers, software)

Communications
  Bridging and routing devices
  Modems (internal and external)
  Wireless modems

Other
  Rewritable CD drives (Blaster CD-RW)

Selected Subsidiaries

Broadxent, Inc. (formerly Digicom
  Systems; modems, US)
Cambridge Soundworks (speakers, US)
Creative Advanced Technology Center (US)
Creative Future Computer Co., Ltd. (China)
Creative Labs (Portugal)
Creative Labs A/S (Denmark)
Creative Labs GmbH (Germany)
Creative Labs (HK) Limited (Hong Kong)
Creative Labs, Inc. (Canada)
Creative Labs, Inc. (US)
Creative Labs (Ireland) Ltd.
Creative Labs NV (Belgium)
Creative Labs Pty Ltd. (Australia)
Creative Labs (Pty) Ltd. (South Africa)
Creative Labs SA (France)
Creative Labs Sdn Bhd (Malaysia)
Creative Labs SL (Spain)
Creative Labs Srl (Italy)
Creative Labs Taiwan Co., Ltd
Creative Media KK (Japan)
Creative Technologies Scandinavia AB (Sweden)
Cubic Electronics Sdn Bhd (Malaysia)
Data Stream KK (Japan)
E-MU Systems, Inc. (digital sound
  production systems, US)
hifi.com (online audio and video
  equipment shopping, US)

COMPETITORS

Altec Lansing	Harman International
Technologies	Intel
Apple Computer	Iomega
Archos	Logitech
ATI Technologies	Motorola
Bose	NVIDIA
Boston Acoustics	Philips Electronics
Canon	Reigncom
CASIO COMPUTER	Sony
Dell	Toshiba
D-Link	U.S. Robotics
Eastman Kodak	Yamaha
ESS Technology	Zoom Technologies
Guillemot	

HISTORICAL FINANCIALS

Company Type: Public

Income Statement

FYE: June 30

	REVENUE ($ mil.)	NET INCOME ($ mil.)	NET PROFIT MARGIN	EMPLOYEES
6/05	1,224	1	0.0%	7,780
6/04	815	134	16.5%	4,700
6/03	702	23	3.3%	3,900
6/02	806	(20)	—	4,300
6/01	1,229	(130)	—	5,000
6/00	1,344	161	12.0%	5,000
6/99	1,297	115	8.9%	4,000
6/98	1,234	135	10.9%	5,000
6/97	1,233	167	13.5%	3,489
6/96	1,308	(38)	—	4,170
Annual Growth	**(0.7%)**	**—**	**—**	**7.2%**

2005 Year-End Financials

Debt ratio: 36.1%
Return on equity: 0.1%
Cash ($ mil.): 187
Current ratio: 2.79
Long-term debt ($ mil.): 210

No. of shares (mil.): 84
Dividends
Yield: 3.9%
Payout: 2,500.0%
Market value ($ mil.): 540

Stock History

NASDAQ: CREAF

	STOCK PRICE ($) FY Close	P/E High/Low		PER SHARE ($) Earnings	Dividends	Book Value
6/05	6.46	1,729	640	0.01	0.25	6.95
6/04	10.35	8	5	1.61	0.25	8.50
6/03	7.91	37	19	0.29	0.25	5.38
6/02	8.98	—	—	(0.27)	0.25	5.38
6/01	8.46	—	—	(1.65)	0.50	5.16
6/00	23.88	21	5	1.86	0.25	9.69
6/99	13.44	15	6	1.25	0.50	6.67
6/98	12.38	21	8	1.42	0.00	6.70
6/97	17.00	11	2	1.84	0.00	5.88
6/96	6.00	—	—	(0.43)	0.00	3.04
Annual Growth	**0.8%**	**—**	**—**	**—**	**—**	**9.6%**

Crédit Agricole

The name suggests a country farmer's credit union, but Crédit Agricole's scope is much greater. France's largest bank, the company owns a 25% stake each in about 40 regional banks, which in turn own more than half of Crédit Agricole. It offers retail and business banking, lending, and deposit services at more than 9,000 locations throughout the country, including those of subsidiary Le Crédit Lyonnais (LCL), which it acquired in 2003. Crédit Agricole is also involved in investment banking and capital markets (through its Calyon unit), in addition to insurance, leasing, factoring, and asset management.

Formed in 2004, Calyon is the combination of corporate and investment bank Crédit Agricole Indosuez and LCL's corresponding activities. LCL now focuses exclusively on retail banking.

Crédit Agricole acquired Euler Hermes' 49% stake in Eurofactor, the European factoring group, in late 2004. The following year, the bank merged its previously existing factoring subsidiary, Transfact, into Eurofactor. Crédit Agricole's Sofinco subsidiary, the leading consumer finance company in France, has about 100 locations.

Outside of France, Crédit Agricole has partnerships with Italy's Banca Intesa and Banco Espírito Santo in Portugal. It is active in Africa, the Middle East, and Southeast Asia as well.

HISTORY

In the mid-1800s France's farmers were suffering from crop failures and a lack of credit. The government tried to meet the credit crunch without much success until in 1894 it created an agricultural credit company, Crédit Agricole, that was tax-exempt and provided state-subsidized farm loans (a monopoly it enjoyed until 1989). Five years later the government established the regional banks as intermediaries between it and the local banks. By the turn of the century, Crédit Agricole's three-tiered structure was in place.

The first 30 years of the 20th century were a time of growth for the bank. The government allowed Crédit Agricole to expand its lending to include long-term personal loans to encourage the growth of rural farming (1910) and loans to businesses involved in other industries (1919). The bank survived WWI and the drop in farm production largely through government support. After the war Crédit Agricole funded rural electrification and other infrastructure.

After WWII the bank grew as it issued loans to finance the modernization of France's farms. In 1959 the government allowed Crédit Agricole to begin writing mortgages; expansion of the bank's operations continued in the 1960s as it was permitted to broaden its lending scope and create subsidiaries, including one to finance individual investments (Union d'Etudes et d'Investisements). In 1967 it began keeping deposits (before it had transferred them to the French Treasury) and used the assets to fuel its national growth.

The early 1970s saw the bank continue to expand its lending operations. Its diversification came under fire from both the government, which wanted the bank to focus on agriculture, and rival banks, which resented their tax-exempt competitor. Crédit Agricole expanded beyond France in the mid-1970s, offering mainly agricultural loans and funds to export firms. It opened its first international office in Chicago in 1979.

In the early 1980s the government continued to allow Crédit Agricole to broaden its lending scope but at a price: The bank lost its tax-exempt status. It continued diversifying; it established such subsidiaries as Predica (life insurance, 1986) and bought stakes in two brokerage firms (1988). As the 1980s closed, Crédit Agricole became a mutual company when the government sold 90% of the bank to the regional banks.

In 1991 the last restrictions on Crédit Agricole's lending were removed, and the bank began transforming itself into a financial services firm. It expanded its lending operations around the world and added subsidiaries offering a variety of financial services. In 1996 it bought Banque Indosuez (which became Crédit Agricole Indosuez), fueling its growth in international wholesale banking. In the late 1990s the bank sought partnerships to expand its operations.

Its expansion was slowed by financial turmoil in Russia and Asia, and the bank closed its emerging markets business. The next year Crédit Agricole teamed with Spain's Banco Bilbao Vizcaya Argentaria and Commercial Bank of Greece as part of its plans to expand its presence in the Mediterranean and southern Europe; it already owned sizable stakes in Italy's Banca Intesa (now IntesaBci) and major banks in Lebanon, Morocco, and Portugal.

In 2000 the bank bought a majority share in Poland-based Europejski Fundusz Leasingowy, but declined an offer to become the controlling shareholder of fellow French bank Crédit Lyonnais, which it eventually acquired in 2003. Crédit Agricole went public on the Euronext Paris Exchange at the end of 2001.

Under pressure from the US government, Crédit Lyonnais admitted in 2003 to illegally acquiring Executive Life, the Californian insurance company, in the early 1990s. Crédit Lyonnais agreed to pay a $771.75 million fine to avoid criminal prosecution. It was also allowed to keep its US banking license.

EXECUTIVES

Chairman: René Carron, age 63
CEO; Chairman, Crédit Lyonnais: Georges Pauget, age 58
Deputy CEO and Head of Corporate and Investment Banking; Chairman and CEO, Calyon: Edouard Esparbès
Group CFO and Group Chief Risk Management Officer: Gilles de Margerie
Head of Bank Operations Information Systems: Aline Bec
Head of Group Human Resources: Jérôme Brunel
Head of Asset Management: Thierry Coste
Head of Management Control and Planning, Subsidiaries and Affiliates and Head of Strategy and Development: Marc Ghinsberg
Head of General Secretariat: Gilles Guitton
Head of International Retail Banking and Investment Capital: Jean-Frédéric de Leusse
Head of Operations and Logistics: Bernard Michel
Head of Specialised Financial Services; Chairman and CEO, Sofinco: Patrick Valroff
General Manager, Italy: Ariberto Fassati
Corporate Secretary and Head of Strategy and Organisation, Calyon: Jérôme Grivet
Head of Development of the Regional Banks: Alain Strub
CEO, Crédit Lyonnais: Christian Duvillet, age 56
CEO, Crédit Agricole Paris & Ile-de-France: Pascal Célérier
General Secretary, Crédit Lyonnais: Agnès de Clermont Tonnerre
Auditors: Barbier Frinault & Autres; PricewaterhouseCoopers Audit

LOCATIONS

HQ: Crédit Agricole S.A.
91-93 Boulevard Pasteur, 75015 Paris, France
Phone: +33-1-43-23-52-02 **Fax:** +33-1-43-23-34-48
Web: www.credit-agricole-sa.fr

PRODUCTS/OPERATIONS

2004 Sales

	$ mil.	% of total
Interest		
Loans & advances to customers	27,676.9	45
Loans & advances to banks	7,234.7	12
Bonds & other fixed income securities	3,295.4	5
Lease finance	2,361.1	4
Other	178.7	—
Noninterest		
Net commission & fee income	8,897.4	14
Net gains from trading transactions	4,744.0	8
Gross margin on insurance activities	3,809.6	6
Net gains on held-for-sale securities	1,665.4	3
Other	1,833.2	3
Total	**61,696.4**	**100**

COMPETITORS

ABN AMRO
BNP
Caisses d'Epargne
Citigroup
Commerzbank
Credit Suisse
Deutsche Bank
Dresdner Bank
Generale de Belgique
HSBC Holdings
Société Générale
UBS

HISTORICAL FINANCIALS

Company Type: Public

Income Statement

FYE: December 31

	ASSETS ($ mil.)	NET INCOME ($ mil.)	INCOME AS % OF ASSETS	EMPLOYEES
12/04	1,244,848	5,414	0.4%	135,502
12/03	986,568	1,288	0.1%	96,500
12/02	530,043	1,115	0.2%	96,500
12/01	438,530	945	0.2%	96,000
12/00	504,217	2,600	0.5%	91,033
12/99	442,523	2,389	0.5%	93,244
12/98	456,229	2,194	0.5%	86,100
12/97	419,763	1,646	0.4%	85,250
12/96	481,657	1,451	0.3%	85,240
12/95	385,678	1,326	0.3%	72,607
Annual Growth	**13.9%**	**16.9%**	**—**	**7.2%**

2004 Year-End Financials

Equity as % of assets: 4.6%
Return on assets: 0.5%
Return on equity: 12.5%
Long-term debt ($ mil.): 377,181
Sales ($ mil.): 61,696

Net Income History

Pink Sheets: CRARF

6,000									
5,000									
4,000									
3,000									
2,000									
1,000									
0									
	12/95	12/96	12/97	12/98	12/99	12/00	12/01	12/02	12/03 12/04

Credit Suisse

Credit Suisse Group is the second-largest financial services firm in Switzerland, behind rival UBS. The company provides conventional consumer and business banking services within its home market, where it has some 250 locations, but most of its business is done outside the nation. Bulge-bracket investment bank subsidiary Credit Suisse First Boston (CSFB), one of the top IPO underwriters in the world, provides corporate and investment banking services throughout the world. But the unit, which also includes Credit Suisse First Boston (USA), has hit rough waters as it faces a sluggish market and pays off fines levied due to questionable IPO allocation practices.

Credit Suisse is integrating CSFB's operations into its own and will drop the "First Boston" part of the investment bank's name. As a result, CSFB will focus on its most profitable operations and Credit Suisse will be able to keep a closer eye on the unit.

Credit Suisse offers insurance through its Winterthur subsidiary, the heart of its retail bancassurance (banking and insurance) operations in Europe. However, Credit Suisse has made it clear that insurance is not part of its core operations and may sell or spin off the division.

The company's Credit Suisse Private Banking unit serves a global clientele of wealthy individuals about 50 offices in Switzerland and 35 around the world. Credit Suisse Asset Management administers investment portfolios for institutional clients.

Credit Suisse's CEO duties were split between John Mack (who also ran CSFB) and Oswald Grübel, with Walter Kielholz, former CEO of Swiss Re, as chairman. But the company's board of directors, disenchanted with the two-CEO system (Mack was based in New York City, while Grübel is in Zurich), decided not to renew Mack's contract when it expired in July 2004.

Eschewing European merger-mania, Credit Suisse has expressed a desire to remain independent and grow internally.

HISTORY

In 1856, shortly after the creation of the Swiss federation, Alfred Escher opened Credit Suisse (CS) in Zurich. Primarily a venture capital firm, CS helped fund Swiss railroads and other industries. It later opened offices in Italy and helped establish the Swiss Bank Corporation.

CS shifted its focus to commercial banking in 1867 and sold most of its stock holdings. By 1871 it was Switzerland's largest bank, buoyed by the nation's swift industrialization. In 1895 CS helped create the predecessor of Swiss utility Electrowatt. Foreign activity grew in the 1920s. A run on banks in the Depression forced CS to sell assets at a loss and dip into reserves of unreported retained profits.

Trade declined in WWII, but neutrality left Switzerland's institutions intact and made it a major banking center, partly due to CS's role as a conduit for the Nazi's plundered gold. Foreign exchange and gold trading became important activities for CS after WWII. Mortgage and consumer credit acquisitions fueled domestic growth in the 1970s.

In 1978 the bank took a stake in US investment bank First Boston and, with it, formed London-based Credit Suisse-First Boston (CSFB). CS created 44%-owned holding company Credit Suisse

First Boston to own First Boston, CSFB, and Tokyo-based CS First Boston Pacific.

The stock market crash of 1987 led a damaged First Boston to merge with CSFB the next year. In 1990 CS (renamed CS Holding) injected $300 million into CSFB and shifted $470 million in bad loans from its books, becoming the first foreign owner of a major Wall Street investment bank.

In the early 1990s CS Holding strengthened its insurance business with a Winterthur Insurance alliance. In 1993 and 1994 acquisitions helped it gain share in its overbanked home market.

In 1996 CS Holding reorganized as Credit Suisse Group and grew internationally, including further merging the daredevil US investment banking operations into Credit Suisse's more staid and relationship-oriented corporate banking. It bought Winterthur (Switzerland's #2 insurer) in 1997, as well as Barclays' European investment banking business.

Credit Suisse and other Swiss banks came under fire in 1996 for refusing to relinquish assets from Jewish bank accounts from the Holocaust era and for gold trading with the Nazi regime. In 1997 the banks agreed to establish a humanitarian fund for Holocaust victims. A stream of lawsuits by American heirs and boycott threats from US states and cities led in 1998 to a tentative $1.25 billion settlement (unpopular in Switzerland); Credit Suisse is to pay one-third.

CS in 1998 expanded its investment banking by buying Brazil's Banco de Investimentos Garantia; it also moved to expand US money management operations by allying with New York-based Warburg Pincus Asset Management. By 1999 that joint venture — which was to give the investment firm access to CS's mutual fund distribution channels in Europe and Asia — had morphed into CS's $650 million purchase of Warburg Pincus Asset Management.

Japan revoked the license of the company's financial products unit for obstructing an investigation (the harshest penalty ever given to a foreign firm); it also accused the company of helping 60 others hide losses and cover up evidence.

In 2000 the company started a mortgage and home-buying Web site and decided to allow searches of Holocaust-era accounts. The next year, as a part of its European expansion, Credit Suisse acquired Spanish broker and asset manager General de Valores y Cambios.

Under former chairman and CEO Lukas Mühlemann, the company expanded Credit Suisse First Boston when it bought US investment firm Donaldson, Lufkin & Jenrette, now Credit Suisse First Boston (USA), in 2000.

The collapse of Credit Suisse's share price, along with what proved to be an over-ambitious acquisition strategy, brought about the downfall of Mühlemann, who was pressured out by shareholders in 2002.

EXECUTIVES

Chairman: Walter B. Kielholz, age 53
Vice Chairman: Peter Brabeck-Letmathe, age 61
Vice Chairman: Hans-Ulrich Doerig, age 65
CEO: Oswald J. Grübel, age 61
CFO: Renato Fassbind, age 49
Executive Vice Chairman and General Counsel, Credit Suisse First Boston: Gary G. Lynch, age 54
Executive Vice Chairman, Credit Suisse First Boston: Richard E. (Dick) Thornburgh, age 53
CEO, Credit Suisse: Walter Berchtold, age 42
CEO, Credit Suisse First Boston; President and CEO, Credit Suisse First Boston (USA): Brady W. Dougan, age 45
CEO, Winterthur: Leonhard H. Fischer, age 42

President, Credit Suisse First Boston: Brian D. Finn, age 44
COO and CFO, Credit Suisse: Ulrich Körner, age 42
Chairman and CEO, Asia Pacific, Credit Suisse First Boston: Paul Calello, age 43
Chairman and CEO, Europe, Middle East, and Africa, Credit Suisse First Boston: Michael Philipp, age 51
Chief Risk Officer: Tobias Guldimann, age 43
Head of Corporate Center and Group General Counsel: Urs Rohner, age 45
Group Chief Communications Officer: Charles Naylor
Chief of Staff: Philip Hess
Group Chief Accounting Officer: Rudolph A. Bless
Head of Human Resources: Timothy S. Gardner
Head of Tax: Fritz Müller
Head of Group Marketing: Marco Taborelli
Auditors: KPMG Klynveld Peat Marwick Goerdeler SA

LOCATIONS

HQ: Credit Suisse Group
    Paradeplatz 8, 8070 Zurich, Switzerland
Phone: +41-44-212-16-16   **Fax:** +41-44-333-25-87
US HQ: 11 Madison Ave., New York, NY 10010
US Phone: 212-325-2000   **US Fax:** 212-325-6665
Web: www.credit-suisse.com

PRODUCTS/OPERATIONS

2004 Sales

	$ mil.	% of total
Interest & dividend income	27,141.9	42
Insurance net premiums earned	18,292.1	28
Commissions & fees	11,897.7	19
Trading revenue	3,995.1	6
Investment securities	1,013.0	2
Other	1,649.2	3
Total	**63,989.0**	**100**

COMPETITORS

ABN AMRO
Barclays
Bear Stearns
Citigroup
Citigroup Global Markets
Deutsche Bank
Goldman Sachs
HSBC Holdings
Merrill Lynch
Mitsubishi UFJ Financial Group
Mizuho Financial
Nomura Securities
UBS
UBS Financial Services

HISTORICAL FINANCIALS

Company Type: Public

Income Statement

FYE: December 31

	ASSETS ($ mil.)	NET INCOME ($ mil.)	INCOME AS % OF ASSETS	EMPLOYEES
12/04	954,716	4,932	0.5%	60,532
12/03	809,974	622	0.1%	60,477
12/02	691,991	(2,396)	—	78,457
12/01	617,087	958	0.2%	79,699
12/00	655,199	2,780	0.4%	80,538
12/99	454,246	3,356	0.7%	63,963
12/98	473,147	2,225	0.5%	62,300
12/97	473,457	273	0.1%	62,242
12/96	388,503	(1,919)	—	34,821
Annual Growth	**11.9%**	**—**		**7.2%**

2004 Year-End Financials

Equity as % of assets: 3.3%   Dividends
Return on assets: 0.6%   Yield: 0.0%
Return on equity: 16.7%   Payout: —
Long-term debt ($ mil.): 93,117   Market value ($ mil.): 46,865
No. of shares (mil.): 1,111   Sales ($ mil.): 63,989

Stock History

NYSE: CSR

	STOCK PRICE ($) FY Close	P/E High/Low		PER SHARE ($) Earnings	Dividends	Book Value
12/04	42.19	10	7	4.16	0.00	28.61
12/03	36.33	41	17	0.52	0.00	24.25
12/02	21.28	—	—	(2.01)	1.36	18.50
12/01	42.65	54	39	0.80	0.00	18.06
Annual Growth	**(0.4%)**	**—**	**—**	**73.2%**	**—**	**16.6%**

Dai Nippon Printing

Dai Nippon Printing has used the power of the press to become one of the world's top commercial printing companies. At more than 30 Japanese and close to 10 overseas plants, Dai Nippon produces promotional materials, direct mail pieces, books, magazines, business forms, CD-ROMs, catalogs, smart cards, and packaging for consumer products. It also offers electronics, including photomasks used in the manufacture of integrated circuits (ICs) and color filters for liquid crystal displays, as well as artificial wood panels for walls, floors, and kitchen cabinets. In addition, the company owns about 60% of Hokkaido Coca-Cola Bottling.

Dai Nippon is implementing strategies to respond to changing global needs. The company is positioning itself as a complete provider of information communications, offering clients marketing and promotional support, communications software, and cross-media services. It also is emphasizing its environmentally friendly products and has reorganized its production systems and undertaken a number of cost-cutting measures to survive a slowdown caused by a recession in Japan.

HISTORY

In 1876 Shueisha, the predecessor to Dai Nippon Printing (DNP), was established in central Tokyo. As the only modern printing firm in Japan, it was well-positioned to attract the business of the emerging newspaper and book industries. The company originally used a movable-type hand printer, but became the first private industry to use steam power in Japan when it updated its presses in 1884.

Following Japanese victories over China and Russia at the turn of the century, Japan embarked on a period of military and economic expansion. This was matched by a growing demand for printing. In 1927 Japan published 20,000 book titles and 40 million magazines. The country's first four-color gravure printing system was inaugurated the following year. In 1935 Shueisha changed its name to Dai Nippon Printing following its merger with Nisshin Printing.

The 1930s and 1940s were lean times for printers; Japan's repressive military government suppressed publishers and banned books. WWII devastated the publishing industry, along with the rest of the Japanese economy, but the publishing industry recovered soon after the end of the war. DNP was assisted in its recovery by government contracts; in 1946 it was designated by the Ministry of Finance to print 100-yen notes. In 1949 the company entered the securities printing business, and in 1951 it expanded into packaging and decorative interiors production. DNP reemerged in 1958 as Japan's largest printing firm.

In 1963 DNP followed Toppan in setting up an office in Hong Kong. Both Hong Kong and Singapore had become havens for Shanghai printing entrepreneurs who had emigrated in the face of the Communist takeover of China in 1949. These cities became centers for low-cost, high-quality color printing for British and American book publishers. In 1973 DNP overtook R. R. Donnelley as the world's largest printer. The next year the company set up a subsidiary in the US, DNP (America), Inc.

DNP moved into the information processing business in the 1980s, developing a credit card-sized calculator in 1985, a digital color printer system in 1986, and a Japanese-language word processor in 1987. The company launched Hi-Vision Static Pictures in 1989 to market a process that converted data into a form used by high-definition TV. In 1990 DNP bought a controlling stake in Tien Wah Press, the #1 printer in Singapore.

The next year DNP completed the first construction stage of its Okayama plant, dedicated to information media supplies (mainly transfer ribbons for color printers). The second stage, specializing in interior decorative materials, was completed in 1993.

In 1994 the company launched its Let's Go to an Amusement Park! virtual reality software system. Two years later DNP produced an integrated circuit card for about a 10th of current costs, giving it a major competitive edge in the magnetic card market.

In 1999 the company began selling CD-ROMs online through subsidiary TransArt. The following year Dai Nippon formed partnerships or joint ventures with Toshiba (to develop printed circuit boards), Microsoft (to develop Windows-based smart cards), and Numerical Technologies (to develop advanced phase-shifted photomasks). In 2002 the company joined with Toshiba and Takara to develop and promote a lightweight educational computer called an Ex-Pad.

EXECUTIVES

Chairman, President, and CEO: Yoshitoshi Kitajima
Senior Managing Director: Mitsuhiko Hakii
Senior Managing Director: Ryozo Kitami
Senior Managing Director: Kenichi Nakamura
Senior Managing Director: Satoshi Saruwatari
Senior Managing Director: Taira Takahashi
Senior Managing Director: Koichi Takanami
Senior Managing Director and CFO: Masayoshi Yamada
Managing Director: Hiromitsu Ikeda
Managing Director: Kenzo Isumi
Managing Director: Kuniaki Kamei
Managing Director: Yoshinari Kitzjuma

Managing Director: Kosaku Mori
Managing Director: Noriaki Nakamura
Managing Director: Masakazu Sato
Managing Director: Osamu Tsuchida
Managing Director: Teruomi Yoshino
Human Resources, DNP America: Tina Kent
Auditors: Meiji Audit Corporation

LOCATIONS

HQ: Dai Nippon Printing Co., Ltd.
(Dai Nippon Insatsu Kabushiki Kaisha)
1-1-1, Ichigaya Kagacho, Shinjuku-ku,
Tokyo 162-8001, Japan
Phone: +81-3-3266-2111   **Fax:** +81-3-5225-8239
Web: www.dnp.co.jp

PRODUCTS/OPERATIONS

2005 Sales

	% of total
Information Communication	45
Lifestyle & Industrial Supplies	31
Electronics	19
Beverages	5
Total	**100**

Selected Products and Services

Electronic Components & Information Media Supplies
Color filters
Photomasks
Ribbons (fax machines)
Shadowmasks

Information Media

Bank notes
Books
Business forms
Catalogs
CD-ROMs and DVDs
Direct mail
Magazines
Plastic cards
Promotional publications

Lifestyle Products

Decorative materials
Packaging

COMPETITORS

Kodansha
Quebecor World
R.R. Donnelley
Toppan Printing

HISTORICAL FINANCIALS

Company Type: Public

Income Statement

FYE: March 31

	REVENUE ($ mil.)	NET INCOME ($ mil.)	NET PROFIT MARGIN	EMPLOYEES
3/05	13,249	557	4.2%	34,514
3/04	15,658	501	3.2%	34,514
3/03	10,922	240	2.2%	35,182
3/02	9,891	118	1.2%	34,868
3/01	10,624	265	2.5%	34,094
3/00	12,195	370	3.0%	35,347
3/99	10,659	256	2.4%	11,836
3/98	10,044	425	4.2%	14,309
3/97	10,583	454	4.3%	14,427
3/96	11,611	494	4.3%	14,514
Annual Growth	**1.5%**	**1.4%**	**—**	**10.1%**

2005 Year-End Financials

Debt ratio: 5.6%
Return on equity: 6.0%
Cash ($ mil.): 2,728
Current ratio: 1.86
Long-term debt ($ mil.): 524

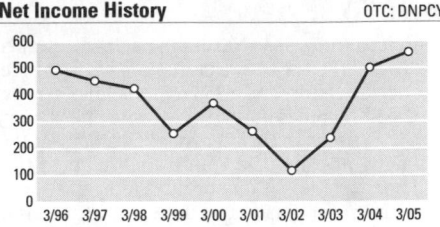

Net Income History   OTC: DNPCY

Daiei

Japan's economic woes put The Daiei on a diet. One of Japan's largest and most troubled retailers, Daiei operates about 3,000 stores through its subsidiaries and franchisees. Its retail businesses include supermarkets, discount stores, department stores, and specialty shops. Other businesses include restaurants, hotels, and real estate services. Domestic sales make up more than 90% of its revenues. Daiei diversified haphazardly during the 1980s loading up on debt and failing to keep up with new, more efficient competitors. The company, which has been on life support for years courtesy of its banks and the Japanese government, is restructuring under the auspices of the Industrial Revitalization Corp. of Japan.

The Daiei's (pronounced die-ay) chronic financial woes are trying the patience of both its lenders and the Industrial Revitalization Corp. Japan (IRCJ), the government agency formed to turn around struggling Japanese companies. The Daiei's debt load exceeds a staggering $9 billion.

Company chairman Heihachiro Yoshino and president Kunio Takagi both announced their resignations just days after Daiei's lenders forced the retailer to seek a government bailout, a move Takagi strongly resisted. The IRCJ rehabilitation plan for Daiei calls for financial aid totaling nearly 600 billion yen from its creditor banks and the closure of more than 50 outlets. Daiei will be allowed to keep its credit card operations.

Top candidates thought to be seeking a piece of Daiei now that it is restructuring include Japanese retailers Ito-Yokado and Aeon. In all, some 50 companies are vying to sponsor parts of Daiei's diverse businesses. Speculation over potential investments by US-retail-giant Wal-Mart Stores was intense following the US retail giant's statement that it is considering additional opportunities in Japan (Wal-Mart already owns 37% of SEIYU); however, Japan's IRCJ rejected the bid.

Prior to the IRCJ's intervention, Daiei tried to reduce its debt by selling stakes in its subsidiaries, including Japan's second-largest convenience store chain, LAWSON, and its department store subsidiary Printemps Ginza. It also closed stores and trimmed its workforce as part of a three-year restructuring plan. The company exited the electronics business, which it once led. It also cleaned its plate of two restaurant units including Wenco Japan, which operates 82 Wendy's restaurants, and its stake in the Big Boy franchise. It has agreed to sell its hotel and ballpark operations in Fukuoka to US investment firm Colony Capital and has agreed to sell its professional baseball team, the Fukuoka Hawks, to Internet service provider Softbank.

HISTORY

Daiei founder Isao Nakauchi narrowly escaped death and the law before launching his first Daiei corner drugstore. As a Japanese soldier serving in the Philippines in WWII, he came under heavy fire but survived. He later thanked sloppy American engineering (the bombs that fell near him did not explode) for his survival. After the war he and his brother made a fortune selling penicillin above the legal price; his brother was arrested for his part in the dealings.

Nakauchi launched his Housewives' Store Daiei in Osaka in 1957 at the depth of the post-Korean War depression. The low prices of a discount drugstore appealed to hard-pressed consumers, and the success of the first store prompted Nakauchi to open others in the Osaka area. He also took advantage of the depression at the wholesale level, buying up surplus goods from cash-strapped manufacturers.

In 1958 the company opened in Sannomiya and introduced the concept of the discount store chain to Japan. Over the next three decades, Daiei diversified its offerings while staying focused on its "for the customers" philosophy, i.e., very low prices.

The company expanded into Tokyo in 1964 with the purchase of Ittoku and opened its first suburban store in 1968 near Osaka. By 1972 Daiei was not only a nationwide chain, it was also Japan's #1 supermarket operator (with 75 stores) and #2 retailer. In 1974 the company overtook Mitsukoshi to become Japan's top retailer. A year later Daiei opened its first convenience store, Lawson.

Showing an increasing interest in sourcing from international businesses, Daiei teamed up with J. C. Penney (1976) and Marks and Spencer (1978) for retailing and Wendy's and Victoria Station (both in 1979) for restaurants. The retailer entered the US market with the 1980 purchase of Holiday Mart, a three-store discount chain in Hawaii, where it also set up its first purchasing office.

Daiei entered the hotel business in 1988 by winning the contract for a $2.2 billion recreation center in Fukuoka. In 1992 the company opened the first American-style membership warehouse in Japan (Kobe), Kuo's Wholesale Membership Club. That year Daiei acquired 42% of major retailer Chujitsuya. The company launched private-label products in 1994. Also that year Daiei merged with retail affiliates Chujitsuya, Uneed Daiei, and Dainaha, establishing Japan's first nationwide network of stores.

When Japan lifted a 50-year ban on holding companies in 1997, Daiei was the first to take advantage of the relaxed laws, forming K.K. Daiei Holding Corporation to oversee its non-retail businesses. The company was hit hard in 1997 and 1998 as Japan's consumer spending slowed just as many of its stores were undergoing renovation. In response, in 1998 Daiei began selling real estate assets, restructuring operations, and closing unprofitable stores.

In 1999 Tadasu Toba became president, replacing founder Nakauchi, who remained chairman of Daiei. Amid allegations of an insider trading scandal, Toba resigned as president and Nakauchi resigned as chairman and CEO in 2000. Hiroshige Sasaki, a former managing director, became acting president and Kunio Takagi was named to replace him as the head of Daiei in 2001.

In 2002 Daiei was rescued by a bank-led bailout and the company announced a three-year restructuring plan that includes 60 store closures and reducing its workforce by about 5,000 employees. The state-run Development Bank of Japan announced a new $480 million funding plan to aid Daiei in its restructuring.

In May 2004 five of the 15 members of the company's board of directors, including chairman Jiro Amagai, left the board. In October Daiei's next chairman — Heihachiro Yoshino — and president Kunio Takagi both announced their resignations, just days after Daiei's lenders forced the struggling retailer to seek a government bailout. Takagi assumed the largely symbolic post of chairman of the company. He was succeeded as president by Toshio Hasumi.

EXECUTIVES

Chairman and CEO: Fumiko Hayashi
President: Yasuyuki Higuchi
Senior Managing Director: Takao Endoh
Senior Managing Director: Shinji Seino, age 53
Managing Director: Shinji Kiyono
Managing Director: Tadahiko Tsuchiya
CFO and Director: Yoshiaki Takahashi, age 49
Director: Mitsuru Hazeyama
Director: Takayuki Itoh, age 51
Director: Mikio Kinohara
Director: Kunio Nishimoto, age 56
Director: Hiroyuki Ogawa
Director: Masahiro Ohta, age 52
Director, Sales Planning: Masakazu Satoh, age 52
Director: Kazuo Takahashi
Director: Keiji Nakamae
Director: Akira Minami
Corporate Auditor: Eisuke Nagai
Auditors: Deloitte Touche Tohmatsu

LOCATIONS

HQ: The Daiei, Inc.
4-1-1, Minatojima Nakamachi,
Chuo-ku, Kobe 650-0046, Japan
Phone: +81-78-302-5001   **Fax:** +81-3-3433-9226
US HQ: 801 Kaheka St., Honolulu, HI 96814
US Phone: 808-973-6600   **US Fax:** 808-941-6457
Web: www.daiei.co.jp

The Daiei operates retail locations throughout Japan and maintains purchasing offices in China and the US.

COMPETITORS

AEON	Marui
Carrefour	Matsuzakaya
Costco Wholesale	Mitsukoshi
Daimaru	MYCAL
Fast Retailing	Seiyu
Isetan	Takashimaya
Ito-Yokado	Tokyu Department Store
Keiyo Company	Uny

HISTORICAL FINANCIALS

Company Type: Public

Income Statement

FYE: Last day in February

	REVENUE ($ mil.)	NET INCOME ($ mil.)	NET PROFIT MARGIN	EMPLOYEES
2/04	18,124	165	0.9%	23,560
2/03*	18,607	1,146	6.2%	26,589
2/00	25,883	(200)	—	—
2/99	25,267	(344)	—	—
2/98	24,868	10	0.0%	—
2/97	26,023	(99)	—	—
2/96	30,095	49	0.2%	—
2/95	33,236	(522)	—	—
2/94	25,517	52	0.2%	—
2/93	21,314	61	0.3%	—
Annual Growth	**(1.8%)**	**11.7%**	**—**	**(11.4%)**

*Irregular reporting interval

2004 Year-End Financials

Debt ratio: (2,718.0%)   No. of shares (mil.): 20
Return on equity: —   Dividends
Cash ($ mil.): 1,778   Yield: 0.0%
Current ratio: 0.51   Payout: —
Long-term debt ($ mil.): 3,430 Market value ($ mil.): 1,045

Stock History   NASDAQ (SC): DAIEY

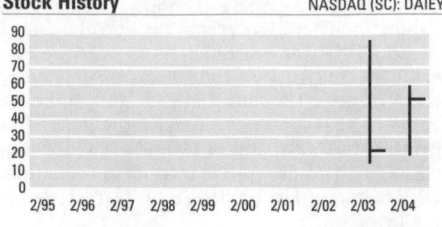

	STOCK PRICE ($) FY Close	P/E High/Low		PER SHARE ($) Earnings	Dividends	Book Value
2/04	51.60	27	9	2.20	0.00	39.75
2/03	22.00	3	1	25.96	0.00	26.30
Annual Growth	**134.5%**	**—**	**—**	**(91.5%)**	**—**	**51.1%**

DaimlerChrysler

DaimlerChrysler is proud of its German-American heritage. Formed by the $37 billion acquisition of Chrysler by Germany's Daimler-Benz in 1998, the company makes about 4.6 million vehicles a year. Chrysler's brands include Dodge, Jeep, and, of course, Chrysler vehicles (the Plymouth line was discontinued); the Mercedes brand includes luxury sedans, commercial vehicles, and SUVs. DaimlerChrysler's Freightliner unit is the US's #1 heavy-truck maker. The carmaker has a 33% stake in EADS, the European aerospace and defense consortium. DaimlerChrysler has sold its 12% stake in Mitsubishi Motors to Goldman Sachs.

DaimlerChrysler's Asian expansion plans have not gone well. The company sought to increase its presence in Asia through stakes in Hyundai Motor and Mitsubishi Motors. After disappointing sales, DaimlerChrysler sold its 10% stake in Hyundai but the two companies maintain a joint development relationship on a project-by-project basis.

Mitsubishi had been the cornerstone of the Asian expansion portion of DaimlerChrysler's strategy to become a global automotive powerhouse. Plagued by quality problems and scandals (covering up defects for years), Mitsubishi was denied a $7 billion cash infusion from DaimlerChrysler in 2004. DaimlerChrysler cut its losses late in 2005 and sold its entire Mitsubishi stake to Goldman Sachs (days later Goldman Sachs sold the stake to undisclosed buyers).

DaimlerChrysler has switched some of its Asian market plans to commercial trucks. It took a 43% stake in Mitsubishi Fuso Truck & Bus Corporation (MFTBC), a new company spun off from Mitsubishi Motors in 2003. (DaimlerChrysler now controls 85%.)

DaimlerChrysler is strengthening its presence in China, the world's fastest-growing car market, through the restructuring of its joint venture with Beijing Automotive Industry Holding Company Ltd. (production of Mercedes-Benz C-Class and E-Class and heavy- and medium-duty trucks). DaimlerChrysler is also forming a joint venture with Chinese Fujian Motor Industry Group and Taiwanese China Motor Corporation with plans to start rolling out the Mercedes-Benz Sprinter and Viano/Vito vans by 2006.

While DaimlerChrysler has been trying to sort out its situation in Asia, problems at home in Germany with Mercedes Car Group have begun to emerge. DaimlerChrysler announced a recall of 1.3 million Mercedes, the brand's largest recall ever. The company also said it would spend $1.56 billion to revamp its smart division. Meanwhile the Chrysler arm of Daimler Chrysler is enjoying a bit of a turnaround with increases in profits and market share and product hits like the Chrysler 300.

Deutsche Bank and the government of Kuwait, both shareholders of former Daimler-Benz, own 10% and 7% of DaimlerChrysler, respectively. Oil rich Dubai, a member of the United Arab Emirates, became DaimlerChrysler's third-largest shareholder late in 2004 when it bought a 1% stake in the company.

HISTORY

Former Buick president and GM VP Walter Chrysler was hired to get Maxwell Motor Car Company out of receivership in 1920. He became president in 1923 and introduced the Chrysler car the next year. He renamed the company for himself in 1925. The company acquired Dodge (1928) and introduced the low-priced Plymouth and the more luxurious DeSoto. Chrysler retired in 1935.

While other carmakers made style modifications, Chrysler kept the same models from 1942 until 1953. It lost market share and for several decades misjudged customer demands in the 1960s by introducing small cars before their time and in the 1970s by holding on to large-car production.

Facing bankruptcy, Chrysler negotiated $1.5 billion in loan guarantees from the US government and brought in former Ford president Lee Iacocca as CEO in 1978. By 1983 it had repaid its loans, seven years ahead of schedule. The company introduced the first minivan in 1984. Iacocca was replaced by GM's head of European operations, Robert Eaton, in 1992. Chrysler sold most of its aerospace and defense holdings in 1996.

Chrysler's acquirer, Daimler-Benz, was formed by the merger of two German motor companies — Daimler and Benz — in 1926. Daimler-Benz bought Auto Union (Audi) in 1958 (sold to Volkswagen in 1966). The company's Mercedes cars gained notoriety and sales expanded worldwide in the 1970s.

Daimler-Benz diversified in the 1980s, buying aerospace, heavy truck (Freightliner), and consumer and industrial electrical companies. Although diversification continued, sales slowed. Losses at its aerospace unit forced Daimler-Benz into the red in 1995. Also that year the company and ABB Asea Brown Boveri formed joint venture Adtranz, the #1 train maker in the world, and Jürgen Schrempp became chairman of the management board (CEO).

In 1998 Daimler-Benz acquired Chrysler. DaimlerChrysler rolled both companies' financial services units into DaimlerChrysler Interservices (DEBIS) and acquired the remaining shares of Adtranz in 1999.

North American influence in the company began to fade in 2000 with the exit of US management, including co-chairman Robert Eaton.

In 2000 DaimlerChrysler agreed to buy a controlling $2.1 billion stake (34%) in Mitsubishi Motors (later upped to 37% when it acquired 3.3% from Volvo). The company also agreed to sell its rail systems unit, Adtranz, to Bombardier (completed in 2001 for about $1.1 billion).

Also in 2000, in an effort to turn things around at its money-losing Chrysler division, James Holden was replaced with Dieter Zetsche, who immediately began making personnel changes. Days after Zetsche was installed, billionaire investor Kirk Kerkorian filed an $8 billion lawsuit seeking to undo the 1998 Daimler-Benz/Chrysler merger on grounds that portraying the deal as a "merger of equals" was misrepresentative.

Zetsche announced early in 2001 that Chrysler would eliminate almost 26,000 North American jobs over three years (largely through retirement and attrition) and make wholesale changes in the group's senior management positions overseeing the Chrysler and Mercedes divisions.

Late in 2004 DaimlerChrysler received Chinese regulatory approval to build cars in China with joint venture partner Beijing Automotive Industry Holding Co. Ltd. (BAIC). The venture plans to build as many as 25,000 C- and E-class Mercedes cars annually.

EXECUTIVES

Chairman of the Supervisory Board: Hilmar Kopper, age 69
Deputy Chairman of the Supervisory Board: Erich Klemm, age 50
Chairman of the Management Board: Prof Jürgen E. Schrempp, age 60
Head of Mercedes Car Group: Dieter Zetsche, age 51
Member of the Board of Management; COO, Chrysler Car Group: Eric R. Ridenour, age 47
Member of the Board of Management; President and CEO, Chrysler Group: Thomas W. LaSorda, age 50
Member of the Board of Management, Commercial Vehicles: Andreas Renschler, age 46
Member of the Board of Management, Corporate Development/China: Rüdiger Grube, age 52
Member of the Board of Management, Finance and Controlling/Financial Services: Bodo Uebber, age 45
Member of the Board of Management, Global Procurement and Supply: Thomas W. Sidlik, age 56
Member of the Board of Management, Human Resources and Labor Relations Director: Günther Fleig, age 56
Member of the Board of Management, Mercedes Car Group: Eckhard Cordes, age 55
Member of the Board of Management, Research and Technology; EVP, Development and Engineering, Mercedes Car Group: Thomas Weber, age 50
SVP and CIO: Susan J. (Sue) Unger
Chairman of the Board of Management, DaimlerChrysler Services AG: Juergen H. Walker, age 56
COO, Mercedes Car Group: Rainer E. Schmueckle, age 45
President and CEO, DaimlerChrysler Services North America LLC: Klaus Entenmann, age 49
EVP and General Counsel: William J. O'Brien, age 62
EVP Global Sales and Marketing, Chrysler Group: Joe W. Eberhardt, age 42
EVP Sales and Marketing, Mercedes Car Group: Klaus Maier, age 51
SVP Human Resources, Chrysler Group: Nancy A. Rae, age 49
Auditors: KPMG Deutsche Treuhand-Gesellschaft AG

LOCATIONS

HQ: DaimlerChrysler AG
  Epplestrasse 225, 70546 Stuttgart, Germany
Phone: +49-711-17-0   **Fax:** +49-711-17-94022
US HQ: 1000 Chrysler Dr., Auburn Hills, MI 48326-2766
US Phone: 248-576-5741   **US Fax:** 248-576-4742
Web: www.daimlerchrysler.com

DaimlerChrysler has manufacturing facilities in 37 countries and sells its products in 200 countries around the world.

2004 Sales

	$ mil.	% of total
Americas		
US	87,009	45
Other countries	15,300	8
European Union		
Germany	30,228	16
Other countries	33,972	18
Asia	13,672	7
Other regions	12,252	6
Total	**192,433**	**100**

PRODUCTS/OPERATIONS

2004 Sales

	$ mil.	% of total
Mercedes Group	67,229	33
Chrysler Group	67,050	33
Commercial vehicles	47,091	23
Services	18,882	9
Other	2,980	2
Adjustments	(10,799)	—
Total	**192,433**	**100**

Selected Divisions and Models

Chrysler Group
  Chrysler
    300 M
    Crossfire
    Pacifica
    PT Cruiser
    Sebring convertible
    Sebring coupe
    Sebring sedan
    Town & Country
  Dodge
    Caravan
    Dakota
    Durango
    Grand Caravan
    Magnum
    Neon
    Ram Pickup
    Sprinter (van)
    SRT-4
    Stratus coupe
    Stratus sedan
    Viper
  Jeep
    Grand Cherokee
    Liberty
    Wrangler
Mercedes Car Group
  Maybach
  Mercedes-Benz
    C-Class
    CL-Class
    CLK-Class
    CLS-Class
    E-Class
    G-Class
    M-Class
    S-Class
    SL-Class
    SLK-Class
    SLR McLaren
  smart
    forfour
    fortwo
    roadster

Commercial Vehicles Division
  Freightliner
  Mercedez-Benz
  Mitsubishi Fuso Truck and Bus
  Setra
  Sterling Trucks
  Western Star Trucks

COMPETITORS

ALSTOM	Navistar
AM General	Nissan
BMW	PACCAR
Boeing	Peugeot
Fiat	Renault
Ford	Saab Automobile
Fuji Heavy Industries	Saturn
General Motors	Scania
Honda	Siemens
Isuzu	Suzuki Motor
Land Rover	Toyota
MAN	Volkswagen
Mazda	Volvo

HISTORICAL FINANCIALS

Company Type: Public

Income Statement

FYE: December 31

	REVENUE ($ mil.)	NET INCOME ($ mil.)	NET PROFIT MARGIN	EMPLOYEES
12/04	192,433	3,340	1.7%	384,723
12/03	171,529	562	0.3%	362,063
12/02	157,107	4,955	3.2%	365,571
12/01	136,256	(590)	—	372,470
12/00	152,446	7,411	4.9%	416,501
12/99	151,035	5,785	3.8%	466,938
12/98	154,615	5,656	3.7%	441,500
Annual Growth	3.7%	(8.4%)	—	(2.3%)

2004 Year-End Financials

Debt ratio: 126.7%
Return on equity: 7.5%
Cash ($ mil.): 10,527
Current ratio: 1.08
Long-term debt ($ mil.): 57,560

No. of shares (mil.): 1,013
Dividends
Yield: 0.0%
Payout: —
Market value ($ mil.): 48,666

Stock History

NYSE: DCX

12/95 12/96 12/97 12/98 12/99 12/00 12/01 12/02 12/03 12/04

	STOCK PRICE ($) FY Close	P/E High/Low	PER SHARE ($) Earnings	Dividends	Book Value
12/04	48.05	15 12	3.29	0.00	44.86
12/03	46.22	79 45	0.55	1.61	42.80
12/02	30.65	10 6	4.90	1.00	36.21
12/01	41.67	— —	(0.59)	2.08	34.65
12/00	41.20	34 16	7.31	2.22	39.68
12/99	78.00	21 13	5.73	2.50	36.19
12/98	96.06	17 13	5.75	0.00	35.57
Annual Growth	(10.9%)	— —	(8.9%)	—	3.9%

Danone

You say Danone, I say Dannon; let's call the whole thing one of the largest food producers in the world. Groupe Danone is the global leader in cultured dairy products (including yogurt, cheese, and dairy desserts) and major producer of biscuits with its LU cookies and crackers. Its Evian, Volvic, Aqua, and other brands make it #2 in bottled water (behind Nestlé). Danone has dozens of regional and international brands, including Dannon yogurt (US), and Amoy, HP and Lea & Perrins sauces. The company is organized around three core activities: fresh dairy products, beverages, and biscuits and cereal.

Acquisitions are a significant part of the company's growth plan. Danone has vigorously snapped up leading home and office water delivery companies around the globe.

Joint ventures have also been part of the company's strategy to expand into new geographic markets. It has become the leading supplier of fresh dairy products in Poland through what was originally a joint venture with a state-owned company. Finding that local milk was of poor quality, Danone arranged to supply farmers with better feeds and deduct the cost from their payments. The result was higher quality milk for which the farmers were paid higher than average.

However, while water and dairy products are helping the company stay liquid, it is pushing brad and water off its tray: In 2005 Danone sold its biscuits businesses in the UK and Ireland. That year it also sold its US home and officer water delivery company, DS Waters of America to investment firm Kelso & Company.

HISTORY

In 1965 Antoine Riboud replaced his uncle as chairman of family-run Souchon-Neuvesel, a Lyons, France-based maker of glass bottles. Antoine quickly made a mark in this field — he merged the firm with Boussois, a major French flat-glass manufacturer, creating BSN in 1966.

Antoine enlarged BSN's glass business and filled the company's bottles by acquiring well-established beverage and food concerns. In 1970 BSN purchased Brasseries Kronenbourg (France's largest brewer), Société Européenne de Brasseries (another French brewer), and Evian (mineral water, France). The 1972 acquisition of Glaverbel (Belgium) gave BSN 50% of Europe's flat-glass market. The next year BSN merged with France's Gervais Danone (yogurt, cheese, Panzani pasta; founded in 1919 and named after founder Isaac Carasso's son Daniel). This moved the company into pan-European brand-name foods.

Rising energy costs depressed flat-glass earnings, so BSN began divesting its flat-glass businesses. In the late 1970s it acquired interests in brewers in Belgium, Spain, and Italy.

BSN bought Dannon, the leading US yogurt maker (co-founded by Daniel Carasso, who had continued making Danone yogurt in France until WWII), in 1982. It established a strong presence in the Italian pasta market by buying stakes in Ponte (1985) and Agnesi (1986). BSN also purchased Generale Biscuit, the world's #3 biscuit maker (1986), and RJR Nabisco's European cookie and snack-food business (1989).

In a series of acquisitions starting in 1986, BSN took over Italy and Spain's largest mineral water companies and several European pasta

makers and other food companies. Adopting the name of its leading international brand, BSN became Groupe Danone in 1994.

Antoine's son, Franck, succeeded him as chairman in 1996. By 1997 Danone had begun shedding non-core grocery products. The company simultaneously stepped up acquisitions of dairy, beer, biscuit, and water companies in developing markets. The 1998 purchase of AquaPenn Spring Water doubled its US water-bottling production capacity. Danone in 1999 completed the sale of part of its BSN Emballage glass-packaging unit to UK buyout firm CVC Capital Partners for $1.23 billion; Danone retained 44% ownership.

Thirsty for the #2 spot in US bottled water sales, Danone gulped down McKesson Water (the #3 bottled water firm in the US after Nestlé and Suntory) for $1.1 billion in 2000. Also that year Danone's joint venture Finalrealm (which includes several European equity firms), with Burlington Biscuits (Nabisco and Hicks, Muse, Tate & Furst), acquired 87% of leading UK biscuit maker United Biscuits. Danone then bought Naya (bottled water, Canada) and sold its brewing operations (#2 in Europe) to Scottish & Newcastle for more than $2.6 billion.

During 2001 Danone announced restructuring would shutter two LU biscuit plants and eliminate about 1,800 jobs; the move met with strikes and legal battles. That same year, having been bumped to the #2 spot in the US yogurt market (after General Mills' Yoplait brand), Danone acquired 40% of Stonyfield Farm, the #4 yogurt brand in the US and ultimately came to own 85% of the company.

In 2002 the company struck a deal handing Coca-Cola the distribution and marketing of Evian in North America, and formed a joint venture with Coke to distribute its lower-end water brands. Antoine Ribaud died that same year, at the age of 83.

Danone continued divesting non-core companies during 2002, including the sale of its Italian meat and cheese business, Galbani, and its Kro Beer Brands (Kronenbourg, 1664 brands) to Scottish & Newcastle.

In 2004 Danone sold its 10% interest in the Australian dairy firm National Foods. Later that year it announced an alliance with Japanese dairy group, Yakult Honsha, to focus both companies' efforts with probiotics. Danone is a 20% shareholder of Yakult and has agreed not to increase its share holdings of Yakult for five years and not to pursue majority control for another five. Also that year Danone acquired the Mexican bottled water company, Arco Iris.

While its dairy and water businesses bubbled along nicely, Danone found its cookies crumbling. Opting for a new recipe, in 2004 it joined with Argentine food giant ARCOR Group to merge both companies' biscuit operations in South America. Later that same year, Danone sold off its W&R Jacob Ltd. biscuit operations in Ireland to local company Fruitfield Foods. It also sold Italaquae, its Italian bottled water business to LGR Holding.

Long after its departure from brewing, in 2004 Danone was fined €1.5 million for forming a beer distribution cartel along with Heineken in 1996. In 2005 Danone and Coca-Cola ended their 2002 water-distribution joint venture.

In 2005 Danone got out of the brewing business altogether, with the sale of its 33% stake in Spanish brewer Mahou. It also sold its HP Foods Group, including Amoy, Lea & Perrins, and HP sauce brands, to Heinz.

EXECUTIVES

Chairman and CEO: Franck Riboud, age 49,
$3,310,237 pay
Vice Chairman: Jacques Vincent, age 59, $2,061,195 pay
EVP, Asia/Pacific: Emmanuel Faber, age 41,
$944,660 pay
EVP, Finance, Strategy, and Information Systems:
Antoine Giscard d'Estaing, age 44
EVP, Fresh Dairy Products: Bernard Hours, age 48
SVP, Beverages: Thomas Kunz, age 47
SVP, Biscuits and Cereal Products: Georges Casala,
age 63
SVP, Human Resources: Franck Mougin, age 46
Chairman, Asia/Pacific: Simon Israël, age 54
President and General Manager, Argentina:
Francisco Camacho
President and General Manager, Evian North America:
Eric Leventhal
General Secretary: Philippe-Loïc Jacob, age 39
Auditors: PricewaterhouseCoopers

LOCATIONS

HQ: Groupe Danone
17, Boulevard Haussmann, 75009 Paris, France
Phone: +33-1-44-35-20-20   **Fax:** +33-1-42-25-67-16
US HQ: 100 Hillside Ave., Greenburgh, NY 10603
US Phone: 914-872-8400
Web: www.danonegroup.com

2004 Sales

	% of total
Europe	68
Asia	15
Other regions	17
Total	**100**

PRODUCTS/OPERATIONS

2004 Sales

	% of total
Fresh dairy products	51
Beverages	25
Biscuits & cereal products	22
Other food	2
Total	**100**

Selected Products and Brands

Biscuits
Argentina (Bagley)
Asia/Pacific (Griffin's)
Colombia (Galletas Noel)
Czech Republic, Slovakia (Opavia)
Greece (Papadopolous)
International (Britannia, Danone, LU, Vitalinea)
Italy (Saiwa)
Pakistan (Continental)
Russia (Bolshevik)
Bottled Water
Asia/Pacific (Aqua)
Argentina (Villa del Sur, Villavicencio)
Canada (Crystal Springs, Evian, Labrador, Naya)
China (Wahaha)
France (Badoit, Salvetat, Arvie)
International (Evian, Volvic)
Italy (Italaquae)
Mexico (Bonafont, Pureza Aga)
Spain (Font Vella)
Turkey (Hayat)
US (CCDA Waters, Great Brands of Europe, DS)
Fresh Dairy
Africa (Clover)
Argentina (La Serenissima, Ser)
China (Bright Dairy, Wahaha)
France (Danone)
International (Actimel, Danone)
Japan (Danone, Yakult)
Latin America (Corpus, La Serenisima, Mastellone)
US (Dannon)
Grocery
France (Blédina)

COMPETITORS

Arla Foods
Bahlsen
Biscuits Gardeil
Coca-Cola
Culligan
Dairy Crest
Fonterra
Friesland Foods
General Mills
Glanbia
Kellogg Snacks
Kerry Group
Kraft Foods
Lactalis
Leche Pascual
Nestlé
Nestlé Waters North America
Owens-Illinois
Parmalat
PepsiCo
Pepsi-Cola North America
Saint-Gobain
Sodiaal
Suntory Ltd.
United Biscuits

HISTORICAL FINANCIALS

Company Type: Public

Income Statement

FYE: December 31

	REVENUE ($ mil.)	NET INCOME ($ mil.)	NET PROFIT MARGIN	EMPLOYEES
12/04	18,558	429	2.3%	89,449
12/03	16,508	1,055	6.4%	88,607
12/02	14,237	1,348	9.5%	92,209
12/01	12,897	118	0.9%	100,560
12/00	13,455	679	5.0%	86,657
12/99	13,415	688	5.1%	75,965
12/98	15,154	701	4.6%	78,945
12/97	14,687	608	4.1%	80,631
12/96	16,041	646	4.0%	81,579
12/95	16,185	435	2.7%	73,823
Annual Growth	**1.5%**	**(0.1%)**	**—**	**2.2%**

2004 Year-End Financials

Debt ratio: 79.0%
Return on equity: 7.0%
Cash ($ mil.): 631
Current ratio: 1.28
Long-term debt ($ mil.): 4,896
No. of shares (mil.): 1,340
Dividends
Yield: 1.6%
Payout: 85.3%
Market value ($ mil.): 24,718

Stock History

NYSE: DA

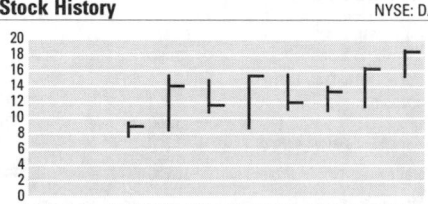

	12/95	12/96	12/97	12/98	12/99	12/00	12/01	12/02	12/03	12/04

	STOCK PRICE ($) FY Close	P/E High/Low		Earnings	Dividends	Book Value
12/04	18.44	55	45	0.34	0.29	4.63
12/03	16.25	20	14	0.81	0.26	4.57
12/02	13.35	14	11	0.99	0.18	4.13
12/01	11.98	172	124	0.09	0.00	3.94
12/00	15.35	32	18	0.48	0.00	4.80
12/99	11.64	31	22	0.48	0.00	4.59
12/98	14.06	32	18	0.48	0.00	5.16
12/97	8.94	22	18	0.42	0.00	4.85
Annual Growth	**10.9%**	**—**	**—**	**(3.0%)**	**—**	**(0.7%)**

Deloitte

This company is "deloitted" to make your acquaintance, particularly if you're a big business in need of accounting services. Deloitte Touche Tohmatsu (now doing business simply as Deloitte) is one of accounting's Big Four, along with Ernst & Young, KPMG, and PricewaterhouseCoopers. Deloitte offers traditional audit and fiscal-oversight services to a multinational clientele. It also provides human resources and tax consulting services, as well as services to governments and international lending agencies working in emerging markets. (China and India are important markets.) Units include Deloitte & Touche (the US accounting arm) and Deloitte Consulting. Consulting services account for 25% of Deloitte's sales.

Deloitte spent the 1980s and 1990s pursuing a strategy of using accountants and consultants in concert to provide seamless service in auditing, accounting, strategic planning, information technology, financial management, and productivity. Deloitte Consulting became Deloitte's fastest-growing line, offering strategic and management consulting, in addition to information technology and human resources services.

Increasingly, though, Deloitte and its peers came under fire for their combined accounting/consulting operations; regulators and observers wondered whether accountants could maintain objectivity when they were auditing clients for whom they also provided consulting services. Criticism mounted after Enron's collapse capsized Arthur Andersen and put the entire accounting industry under scrutiny. (Deloitte picked up new business and members in Andersen's wake.)

Deloitte in 2002 announced it would spin off its consulting business, becoming the last of the big accountants to do so; a year later it called off the split, citing a weakened market for consulting, among other woes.

Deloitte was in the headlines again in late 2003, when auditing client Parmalat filed for bankruptcy in the midst of a $12 billion financial scandal, then dropped Deloitte as its auditor. Parmalat sued Deloitte in 2004, claiming its auditing procedures were inadequate and should have uncovered the fraud at Parmalat earlier.

HISTORY

In 1845 William Deloitte opened an accounting office in London, at first soliciting business from bankrupts. The growth of joint stock companies and the development of stock markets in the mid-19th century created a need for standardized financial reporting and fueled the rise of auditing, and Deloitte moved into the new field. The Great Western Railway appointed him as its independent auditor (the first anywhere) in 1849.

In 1890 John Griffiths, who had become a partner in 1869, opened the company's first US office in New York City. Four decades later branches had opened throughout the US. In 1952 the firm partnered with Haskins & Sells, which operated 34 US offices.

Deloitte aimed to be "the Cadillac, not the Ford" of accounting. The firm, which became Deloitte Haskins & Sells in 1978, began shedding its conservatism as competition heated up; it was the first of the major accountancy firms to use aggressive ads.

In 1984 Deloitte Haskins & Sells tried to merge with Price Waterhouse, but the deal was dropped after Price Waterhouse's UK partners objected.

In 1989 Deloitte Haskins & Sells joined the flamboyant Touche Ross (founded 1899) to become Deloitte & Touche. Touche Ross's Japanese affiliate, Ross Tohmatsu (founded 1968) rounded out the current name. The merger was engineered by Deloitte's Michael Cook and Touche's Edward Kangas, in part to unite the former firm's US and European strengths with the latter's Asian presence. Cook continued to oversee US operations, with Kangas presiding over international operations. Many affiliates, particularly in the UK, rejected the merger and defected to competing firms.

As auditors were increasingly held accountable for the financial results of their clients, legal action soared. In the 1990s Deloitte was sued because of its actions relating to Drexel Burnham Lambert junk bond king Michael Milken, the failure of several savings and loans, and clients' bankruptcies.

Nevertheless, in 1995 the SEC chose Michael Sutton, the firm's national director of auditing and accounting practice, as its chief accountant. That year Deloitte formed Deloitte & Touche Consulting to consolidate its US and UK consulting operations; its Asian consulting operations were later added to facilitate regional expansion.

In 1996 the firm formed a corporate fraud unit (with special emphasis on the Internet) and bought PHH Fantus, the leading corporate relocation consulting company. The next year Deloitte and Thurston Group (a Chicago-based merchant bank) teamed up to form NetDox, a system for delivering legal, financial, and insurance documents via the Internet. In 1997, amid a new round of industry mergers, rumors swirled that a Deloitte and Ernst & Young union had been scrapped because the firms could not agree on ownership issues. Deloitte disavowed plans to merge and launched an ad campaign directly targeted against its rivals.

The Asian economic crisis hurt overseas expansion in 1998, but provided a boost in restructuring consulting. In 1999 the firm sold its accounting staffing service unit (Resources Connection) to its managers and Evercore Partners, citing possible conflicts of interest with its core audit business. Also that year Deloitte Consulting decided to sell its computer programming subsidiary to CGI Group, and Kangas stepped down as CEO to be succeeded by James Copeland; the following year Kangas ceded the chairman's seat to Piet Hoogendoorn.

In 2001 the SEC forced Deloitte & Touche to restate the financial results of Pre-Paid Legal Services. In an unusual move, Deloitte & Touche publicly disagreed with the SEC's findings.

The accountancy put some old trouble to bed in 2003 when it agreed to pay $23 million to settle claims it had been negligent in its auditing of failed Kentucky Life Insurance, a client in the 1980s. Later that year the UK's High Court found Deloitte negligent in audits related to the failed Barings Bank; however, the ruling was considered something of a victory for the accountancy because it essentially cleared Deloitte of the majority of charges against it and effectively limited its financial liability in the matter. Copeland retired from the global CEO's office that year and handed the reins over to Bill Parrett, who had formerly served as managing director for the US and the Americas.

EXECUTIVES

Chairman: Piet Hoogendoorn
CEO; Senior Partner, US: William G. (Bill) Parrett, age 59
CFO and Managing Partner, Global Office: William A. Fowler
CIO: Wolfgang Richter
Global Managing Partner, Reputation, Excellence, and Practice Protection; Managing Partner, Netherlands: Willy A. Biewinga
Global Managing Partner, Innovation and Investment; Managing Partner, Germany and Regional Managing Partner, Europe/Middle East/Africa: Wolfgang Grewe
Global Managing Partner, Client Service Excellence; Tohmatsu Representative to DTT, and Regional Managing Partner, Japan: Shuichiro Sekine
Global Managing Partner, Brand and Eminence; Chief Executive and Managing Partner, Canada and Regional Managing Partner, North America: Colin Taylor
Global Managing Partner, Intellectual Capital, Inclusion, and Development; Chief Executive, France: Philippe Vassor, age 52
Global Managing Partner, Financial Advisory Services: Ralph G. Adams
Global Managing Partner, Audit: Stephen Almond
CEO, Deloitte Consulting: Paul Robinson, age 52
Chairman, Deloitte & Touche LLP: Sharon L. Allen, age 53
CEO, Deloitte & Touche LLP: James H. (Jim) Quigley, age 53
Global Managing Partner, Tax & Legal Services: Alan Schneier
Global Managing Partner, Human Resources: Conrad Venter
Managing Director, Finance and Administration: S. Ashish Bali
General Counsel: Joseph J. Lambert

LOCATIONS

HQ: Deloitte Touche Tohmatsu
1633 Broadway, New York, NY 10019
Phone: 212-436-2000 **Fax:** 212-436-5000
Web: www.deloitte.com

Deloitte Touche Tohmatsu operates through about 670 offices in nearly 150 countries.

2005 Sales

	$ mil.	% of total
Americas	9,100	50
Europe/Middle East/Africa	7,300	40
Asia/Pacific	1,800	10
Total	**18,200**	**100**

PRODUCTS/OPERATIONS

2005 Sales

	$ mil.	% of total
Audit	8,700	48
Consulting	4,300	24
Tax	3,900	21
Financial advisory services	1,300	7
Total	**18,200**	**100**

Selected Products and Services

Audit
  Auditing services
  Global offerings services
  International financial reporting conversion services
Consulting
  Enterprise applications
  Human capital
  Outsourcing
  Strategy and operations
  Technology integration
Enterprise Risk Services
  Capital markets
  Control assurance
  Environment and sustainability
  Internal audit
  Regulatory consulting
  Security services
Financial Advisory
  Corporate finance
  Forensic services
  Reorganization services
  Transaction services
Tax
  Comprehensive tax solutions
  Corporate tax
  European Union services
  Indirect tax
  International assignment services
  International tax
  Mergers and acquisitions
  Research and development credits
  Tax technology solutions
  Transfer pricing

COMPETITORS

Accenture
BDO International
Booz Allen
Boston Consulting
Capgemini
EDS
Ernst & Young
Grant Thornton International
H&R Block
KPMG
Marsh & McLennan
McKinsey & Company
PricewaterhouseCoopers
Towers Perrin
Watson Wyatt

HISTORICAL FINANCIALS

Company Type: Partnership

Income Statement

FYE: May 31

	REVENUE ($ mil.)	NET INCOME ($ mil.)	NET PROFIT MARGIN	EMPLOYEES
5/05	18,200	—	—	121,283
5/04	16,400	—	—	115,000
5/03	15,100	—	—	119,237
5/02	12,500	—	—	98,000
5/01	12,400	—	—	95,000
5/00*	11,200	—	—	90,000
8/99	10,600	—	—	90,000
8/98	9,000	—	—	82,000
8/97	7,400	—	—	65,000
8/96	6,500	—	—	63,440
Annual Growth	**12.1%**	**—**	**—**	**7.5%**

*Fiscal year change

Revenue History

Dentsu Inc.

Unlike Godzilla, Dentsu is one monster that doesn't leave Japan in ruins. One of the largest advertising conglomerates in the world, Dentsu is the #1 ad firm in Japan. Its numerous agencies operate in 27 countries and provide creative services for more than 6,000 clients, although sales outside Japan only account for a small percentage of revenue. Dentsu also offers a host of other services, including public relations, media and event planning, and market research. The company has expanded its operations in Asia through a partnership with US-based Young & Rubicam and owns a 15% stake in ad conglomerate Publicis Groupe. The company completed its IPO on the Tokyo Stock Exchange in late 2001.

As Japan's largest ad conglomerate Dentsu controls more than 30% of Japan's advertising market. While Dentsu has outdistanced its closest domestic rivals, Hakuhodo and Asatsu-DK, the company has designs on becoming a global powerhouse on par with ad conglomerates such as WPP Group and Omnicom, but currently less than 10% of Dentsu's revenues are generated outside of Japan.

Dentsu's strategy for international expansion has been varied and somewhat unfocused; in addition to its partnership with Young & Rubicam, the company owns a handful of US ad agencies and a 15% stake in Publicis (as a result of its investment in Bcom3). Dentsu's future growth plans include expanding its operations in Asia (particularly in China) using the Dentsu brand, and maintaining a grip in the US and Europe through its partnership with Publicis.

Dentsu has organized itself along four business lines representing the company's current position and the lines it would like to grow. Advertising services comprise the bulk of Dentsu's operations, while specialized marketing services, e-solutions services, and overseas operations represent Dentsu's growth objectives.

HISTORY

Seeing a need for a Japanese wire service, Sino-Japanese war correspondent Hoshiro Mitsunaga founded Telegraphic Service Co. in 1901. Mitsunaga let newspapers pay their wire service bills with advertising space, which his advertising agency, Japan Advertising (also founded in 1901) resold. He merged the two companies as Nihon Denpo-Tsushin Sha (Japan Telegraphic Communication Company) in 1907. Known as Dentsu for short (the name was officially changed in 1955), the company gained Japanese rights to the United Press wire in 1908 and began extracting even more favorable advertising rates from its clients.

With its mix of content and advertising, Dentsu became a leading Japanese communications business. But in 1936 Japan's government consolidated all news services into its propaganda machine, Domei, taking half of Dentsu's stock. During WWII, all of Japan's advertising agencies were combined into 12 entities. Following the war, US occupation forces dismantled Domei, and its 50% holding in Dentsu stock was transferred to two new press agencies, Kyodo and Jiji.

Hideo Yoshida, who became president of Dentsu in 1947, began the task of rebuilding the company, currying favor by employing the sons of politicians and business leaders. He also helped build the television industry in Japan by investing in start-up broadcasters. Their gratitude translated into preferential treatment for Dentsu, leading to its decades-long domination of Japanese TV advertising.

By 1973 Dentsu had become the world's largest advertising agency, but the company's growth stalled with the slowing Japanese economy. Slow to expand overseas, foreign billings accounted for just 7% of revenues in 1986 (and despite growth initiatives the company has yet to make lasting progress in this area). The next year Saatchi & Saatchi passed Dentsu as the world's #1 advertising group. Young & Rubicam/Dentsu later joined with Havas' Eurocom to form HDM Worldwide (named after Havas, Dentsu, and Y&R's Marsteller).

Dentsu rebounded with Japan's economic boom in the late 1980s, but the company continued to struggle abroad. Eurocom pulled out of HDM Worldwide in 1990, and the newly named Dentsu, Young & Rubicam Partnerships reorganized to focus on North America, Asia, and Australia. Dentsu joined with Collett Dickenson Pearce to maintain its presence in Europe after HDM's demise. Restructuring in 1996 created several new units, including one to focus on the Olympics, and in 1997 the company set up the Interactive Solution Center to focus on digital media.

The company agreed to buy UK ad agency Harari Page in 1998 and announced plans for its own public offering. Dentsu took a 20% stake in Bcom3 (formerly BDM) in 2000, the new advertising holding company formed by the merger of The Leo Group and MacManus Group. It also formed a Japanese Internet services joint venture with US consulting company marchFIRST. After marchFIRST's demise Dentsu gained full ownership of the company and renamed it DentsuFUSE.

The following year Dentsu reorganized its US and European units and purchased US ad firm Oasis International Group and became a publicly listed company in late 2001.

EXECUTIVES

President and CEO: Tateo Mataki, age 66
EVP: Tetsu Nakamura
EVP: Ko Matsumoto
EVP: Tatsuyoshi Takashima
Senior Managing Director: Isao Maruyama
Senior Managing Director: Takehiko Kimura
Senior Managing Director: Hiromori Hayashi
Managing Director: Haruyuki Takahashi
Managing Director: Ryuichi Mori
Managing Director: Itsuma Wakasugi
Managing Director: Kimiharu Matsuda
Managing Director: Michio Niiyama
Executive Director: Jun Sakakibara
Executive Director: Toyohiko Yamonouchi
Executive Director: Kunihiko Tainaka
Executive Director: Setsuo Kamai
Auditors: KPMG

LOCATIONS

HQ: Dentsu Inc.
1-8-1, Higashi-shimbashi, Minato-ku,
Tokyo 105-7001, Japan
Phone: +81-3-6216-5111   **Fax:** +81-3-5551-2013
US HQ: 488 Madison Ave., 23rd Fl., New York, NY 10022
US Phone: 212-829-5120   **US Fax:** 212-829-0009
Web: www.dentsu.com

Dentsu has offices in 31 cities in Japan and 41 cities in 27 countries.

PRODUCTS/OPERATIONS

Selected Operations
Creative Associates
DentsuFUSE (Internet services)
Dentsu Kosan Service (management services)
Dentsu Management Services
Dentsu Music Publishing
Dentsu Public Relations
Dentsu Research
Dentsu TEC
Dentsu Young & Rubicam (50%, advertising)

COMPETITORS

Asatsu-DK
Grey Global
Hakuhodo
Havas
Interpublic Group
Omnicom
Publicis
Video Research
WPP Group

HISTORICAL FINANCIALS

Company Type: Public

Income Statement				FYE: March 31
	REVENUE ($ mil.)	NET INCOME ($ mil.)	NET PROFIT MARGIN	EMPLOYEES
3/05	2,903	358	12.3%	14,530
3/04	2,750	214	7.8%	14,245
3/03	2,359	(39)	—	13,623
3/02	2,216	204	9.2%	12,167
3/01	2,390	380	15.9%	11,037
3/00	2,462	196	8.0%	10,841
3/99	2,003	37	1.8%	—
3/98	1,812	68	3.8%	—
3/97	1,818	110	6.0%	—
3/96	1,903	131	6.9%	—
Annual Growth	4.8%	11.8%	—	6.0%

2005 Year-End Financials

Debt ratio: 21.7%   Current ratio: 1.21
Return on equity: 8.6%   Long-term debt ($ mil.): 938
Cash ($ mil.): 597

Net Income History   Exchange: Tokyo

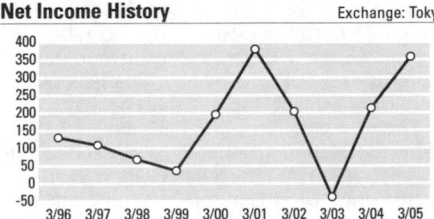

Deutsche Bahn

Deutsche Bahn gets you from Punkt A to Punkt B. The railway's main passenger divisions, DB Fernverkehr (long-distance transportation) and DB Regio (regional and urban transport), carry about 1.7 billion passengers yearly throughout Germany and to neighboring countries. The company's freight transport division, which moves about 280 million tons of freight annually, has been strengthened with the acquisition of logistics provider Stinnes. Other Deutsche Bahn divisions manage the company's train stations and provide track infrastructure services. The company, owned by the German government, is one of Europe's largest transportation providers.

The government had planned to take Deutsche Bahn public by 2003, but financial losses stalled plans for an IPO. However IPO plans may be back on track sooner than later as the German government wants to unload a stake in Deutsche Bahn to raise cash. Deutsche Bahn's agreements with the state of Hamburg to take majority stakes in two businesses there (rail firm Hamburger Hochbahn and port operator Hamburger Hafen und Logistik) may hasten an IPO.

In 2004 Deutsche Bahn partnered with two UK companies, Stagecoach Group and Virgin Group, to bid on UK rail franchises. Deutsche Bahn withdrew from the venture before the bidding got very far, however. Later that year Deutsche Bahn and Russian Railways announced plans to form a joint venture for freight transport.

In 2005 Deutsche Bahn said it would sell its Deutsche Eisenbahn Reklame GmbH advertising subsidiary to Stroer AG for about $168 million. The company is also planning to divest additional, as yet unnamed operations to fund its announced acquisition of US logistics firm Bax Global. Once the transaction is complete Bax Global will be integrated into Deutsche Bahn's shipping unit Schenker.

HISTORY

In 1989 the Federal Cabinet of West Germany adopted a resolution to set up an independent government railway commission. That year the wall between East Germany and West Germany came down, and the two nations became united into one Germany, known as the Federal Republic of Germany, in 1990.

In 1993 the Cabinet approved the legal package on railway reform submitted by the federal minister of transport. Later that year the legislation won the two-thirds majority of the German Parliament and the Federal Council it needed to pass. Deutsche Bahn was then established in 1994 to unify Germany's western (Deutsche Bundesbahn) and eastern (Deutsche Reichsbahn) railway systems as a public company. The Federal Republic of Germany was sole shareholder.

The next year Deutsche Bahn created a subsidiary, DBKom, to offer telecom services in competition with Deutsche Telekom. In 1996 a consortium led by German conglomerate Mannesmann bought a 50% stake in DBKom. By 1997 Deutsche Bahn had been transformed from a government department into a registered company and split into four operating units: tracks, freight, local passenger services, and intercity passenger services. That year Deutsche Bahn also bought Lufthansa's 33% stake in tour operator Deutsches Reisebüro (DER), giving it full ownership of the company as well as DER's 20% stake in tour group TUI.

Trouble came in 1998: Deutsche Bahn sent its 59 first-generation high-speed InterCityExpress (ICE) trains for inspections after one of the trains crashed and killed 98 passengers. Investigators believed a broken wheel caused the crash.

Deutsche Bahn and French state-owned railway SNCF announced plans in 1999 to develop a high-speed train capable of traveling up to 320 km (198 miles) per hour. Also that year Hartmut Mehdorn, credited with turning around printing equipment manufacturer Heidelberger Druck and DaimlerChrysler's aerospace unit, became Deutsche Bahn's new CEO. Tasked with improving the railway's punctuality, Mehdorn pledged to make Deutsche Bahn more efficient by cutting losses and raising productivity. That year the company sold its stake in TUI to conglomerate Preussag and its DER unit to supermarket giant Rewe.

In 2000 the company's DB Cargo unit and Dutch rail freight company N.S. Cargo formed a new group, Railion (joined by Danish State Railways' freight unit DSB Gods in 2001). Also in 2000, Germany's transport minister indefinitely postponed plans to float Deutsche Bahn after it posted losses for the first time since 1994.

Hoping to take advantage of Deutsche Bahn's financial troubles, Connex, then a subsidiary of French conglomerate Vivendi, offered in 2001 to acquire Deutsche Bahn's long-distance express passenger trains. But Mehdorn refused the offer, stating the company did not want to give up its long-distance traffic. Deutsche Bahn did agree in 2001 to form a railway telematics (communications system) joint venture with Mannesmann Arcor, a company controlled by Vodafone. The agreement called for Deutsche Bahn to keep its 18% stake in Arcor but lose its minority veto rights — which Deutsche Bahn had used earlier that year to block an Arcor IPO.

In 2002 the company bought the 65% stake in logistics provider Stinnes held by E.ON. Deutsche Bahn took full ownership of Stinnes the next year.

Deutsche Bahn sold its 83% stake in bus unit Deutsche Touring GmbH to Eurosur SA of Spain for an undisclosed amount in 2005.

EXECUTIVES

Honorary Chairman of the Supervisory Board:
Günther Saßmannshausen
Chairman of the Supervisory Board: Werner Mueller
Deputy Chairman of the Supervisory Board:
Norbert Hansen
Chairman of the Management Board and CEO;
Chairman of the Supervisory Board, Stinnes:
Hartmut Mehdorn
CFO: Diethelm Sack
Director, Infrastructure and Services: Stefan Garber
Director, Marketing and Political Relationships:
Klaus Daubertshäuser
Director, Passenger Transport; Chairman of the
Management Board and CEO of DB Personenverkehr:
Karl-Friedrich Rausch
Director, Personnel: Margret Suckale
Director, Transport and Logistics: Norbert Bensel, age 57
Director, Track Infrastructure; Chairman of the
Management Board and CEO, DB Netz:
Roland Heinisch
Chief Representative, Technology and Procurement:
André Zeug, age 49
Auditors: PwC Deutsche Revision AG

LOCATIONS

HQ: Deutsche Bahn Aktiengesellschaft
Potsdamer Platz 2, D-10785 Berlin, Germany
Phone: +49-30-297-0   **Fax:** +49-30-297-6-19-19
Web: www.bahn.de

COMPETITORS

Air France	Lufthansa
A.P. Møller - Mærsk	National Express Group
British Airways	SNCF
Hamburger Hochbahn	TUI
KLM	Veolia Environnement

HISTORICAL FINANCIALS

Company Type: Government-owned

Income Statement

FYE: December 31

	REVENUE ($ mil.)	NET INCOME ($ mil.)	NET PROFIT MARGIN	EMPLOYEES
12/04	35,314	246	0.7%	233,657
12/03	33,539	(733)	—	250,913
12/02	19,584	(475)	—	250,690
12/01	15,533	(360)	—	214,371
12/00	16,259	80	0.5%	222,656
12/99	17,644	88	0.5%	241,638
12/98	18,011	200	1.1%	252,468
12/97	16,938	217	1.3%	268,273
12/96	19,457	727	3.7%	288,768
12/95	20,806	184	0.9%	349,627
Annual Growth	6.1%	3.2%	—	(4.4%)

2004 Year-End Financials

Debt ratio: 276.7%   Current ratio: 0.40
Return on equity: 2.7%   Long-term debt ($ mil.): 25,977
Cash ($ mil.): 1,043

Net Income History

Deutsche Bank

Deutsche Bank has two primary divisions but one central goal: global domination. The bank's two main operating segments are Corporate and Investment Banking and Private Clients and Asset Management. One of the largest banks in the world, Deutsche Bank offers retail banking services in Germany, but its investment bank and asset management business operate throughout Europe with additional markets in the Pacific Rim and the Americas. It has more than 1,550 locations worldwide, with more than half of those in its home market. In the US, where it hopes to become the "Wal-Mart of asset management," Deutsche Bank owns investment bank Deutsche Bank Alex. Brown and mutual fund manager Scudder Investments.

The latter is part of Deutsche Asset Management, which oversees more than $700 billion for institutional and retail investors worldwide. In

2004 Deutsche Bank acquired Berkshire Mortgage (now Deutsche Bank Berkshire Mortgage), one of the top multifamily residential lenders in the US.

Deutsche Bank is expanding its mutual fund business, DWS, across continental Europe and may scuttle the Scudder name in the US in favor of the DWS brand. However, Deutsche Bank has seen an overall slowdown of business in the UK and sold some of its asset management business there to Aberdeen Asset Management. Deutsche Bank is looking to emerging markets like China, India, and Russia for growth. In 2004 it purchased a 40% stake in Moscow-based investment bank United Financial Group and in late 2005 announced plans to buy the rest.

Deutsche Bank's Corporate and Investment Banking segment, including New York-based Deutsche Bank Securities, performs all manner of capital markets and corporate banking services, including securities underwriting, trading, and research; mergers and acquisition advisory; and trust and cash management.

Deutsche Bank is building its already-massive real estate investment and management business through acquisitions such as RREEF in the US. But Deutsche Bank is selling its nearly 38% stake in mortgage bank Eurohypo, which specializes in commercial property across Europe and in the US, to Commerzbank.

HISTORY

Georg von Siemens opened Deutsche Bank in Berlin in 1870. Three years later the firm opened an office in London and was soon buying other German banks. In the late 1800s Deutsche Bank helped finance Germany's electrification (carried out by Siemens AG) and railroad construction in the US and the Ottoman Empire. Von Siemens ran the bank until his death in 1901.

The bank survived post-WWI financial chaos by merging with Disconto-Gesellschaft and later helped finance the Nazi war machine. After the war, the Allies split the company into 10 banks; it became extinct in Soviet-controlled East Germany.

The bank was reassembled in 1957 and primarily engaged in commercial banking, often taking direct interests in its customers. It added retail services in the 1960s. In 1975, to prevent the Shah of Iran from gaining a stake in Daimler-Benz (now DaimlerChrysler), the bank bought 29% of that company.

The firm opened an investment banking office in the US in 1971 and a branch office in 1978. In the 1980s it expanded geographically, buying Bank of America's Italian subsidiary (1986) and UK merchant bank Morgan Grenfell (1989); it also moved into insurance, creating life insurer DB Leben (1989).

Terrorists killed chairman Alfred Herrhausen, a symbol of German big business, in 1989. After German reunification in 1990, successor Hilmar Kopper oversaw the bank's reestablishment in eastern Germany.

In 1994 Deutsche Bank bought most of ITT's commercial finance unit. That year the company suffered scandal when real estate developer Jurgen Schneider borrowed more than DM1 billion and disappeared; he was later found and returned to Germany.

The company grew its global investment banking operations in 1995 under its Morgan Grenfell subsidiary. Corporate culture clashes prompted Deutsche Bank to take greater control of the unit and restructure it in 1998.

Deutsche Bank's global aspirations suffered a setback in 1998 when losses on investments in Russia trimmed its bottom line. Still trying to put WWII behind it, the bank accepted responsibility for its wartime dealing in gold seized from Jews but has rejected liability to compensate victims of Nazi forced labor who toiled in industrial companies in which it holds stakes.

In 1999 the bank acquired Bankers Trust. Despite a decision to divest its industrial portfolio, in 1999 the company bought Tele Columbus, the #2 cable network in Germany, and Piaggio, the Italian maker of the famed Vespa motor scooter. On the banking front, Deutsche Bank bought Chase Manhattan's Dutch auction business and sought a foothold in Japan through alliances with Nippon Life Insurance and Sakura Bank (now part of Sumitomo Mitsui Banking).

In 2000 the company agreed to merge with Dresdner Bank (after which they would spin off their retail banking businesses), but the merger collapsed, in part over the fate of investment banking subsidiary Dresdner Kleinwort Benson. German mega-insurer Allianz bought Dresdner in 2001. Deutsche Bank's reorganization plans the same year saw the bank eliminate 2,600 jobs worldwide and realign its businesses into two divisions. Deutsche Bank also bought Banque Worms from French insurer AXA.

Looking for a steady supply of cash, in 2001 Deutsche Bank's Morgan Grenfell Private Equity bought 3,000 English pubs owned by UK-based conglomerate Whitbread plc. In 2002 more shuffling of the executive board members allowed Deutsche Bank to grow in the international Anglo-American style, rather than as a domestic player.

EXECUTIVES

Spokesman of the Board of Managing Directors and Chairman of the Group Executive Committee: Josef Ackermann, age 57, $8,410,424 pay
Chairman of the Supervisory Board: Rolf E. Breuer, age 67
CFO and Chief Risk Officer: Clemens Börsig, age 56, $4,140,149 pay
COO: Hermann-Josef Lamberti, age 48, $4,140,149 pay
Chief Administrative Officer: Tessen von Heydebreck, age 59, $4,140,149 pay
Global Head of Compliance: Henry Klehm
Global Head of Deutsche Asset Management: Kevin Parker
Managing Director and Head of Group Accounting: Martin Edelmann
Head of Global Banking: Michael Cohrs
Head of Private Wealth Management: Pierre de Weck, age 55
Head of Regional Management Worldwide; Chairman of the Management Committee, Germany: Jürgen Fitschen
Head of Global Markets: Anshu Jain
Head of Private and Business Clients: Rainer Neske
Head of Equity and Fixed Income Investments: Rami Hayek
Head of Compliance, UK and Western Europe: Andrew Procter
Head of US Private Bank: Patrick Campion
Group Controller: Anthony Di Iorio
General Counsel: Hans-Dirk Krekeler
Auditors: KPMG Deutsche Treuhand-Gesellschaft AG

LOCATIONS

HQ: Deutsche Bank AG
  Taunusanlage 12,
  60262 Frankfurt am Main, Germany
Phone: +49-69-910-00 **Fax:** +49-69-910-38591
US HQ: 60 Wall St., 21st Fl., New York, NY 10005
US Phone: 212-250-2500 **US Fax:** 212-797-0291
Web: www.deutsche-bank.de

PRODUCTS/OPERATIONS

2004 Sales

	% of total
Interest	
Trading assets	28
Loans	16
Central bank funds sold & securities purchased under resale agreements	10
Securities borrowed	4
Interest-earning deposits with banks	2
Other	3
Noninterest	
Net trading revenues	14
Commissions, broker's fees & other securities activities	8
Commissions & fees from fiduciary activities	7
Fees from other customer services	6
Other	2
Total	**100**

COMPETITORS

ABN AMRO
Bankgesellschaft Berlin
Barclays
BNP
Charles Schwab
Citigroup
Citigroup Global Markets
Commerzbank
Cortal Consors
Credit Suisse
Dresdner Bank
DZ BANK
E*TRADE Financial
Goldman Sachs
HSBC Holdings
HVB Group
Intuit
JPMorgan Chase
KfW
Lehman Brothers
Merrill Lynch
Mizuho Financial
Morgan Stanley
National Australia Bank
Rabobank
SCH
Société Générale
TD Bank
UBS

HISTORICAL FINANCIALS

Company Type: Public

Income Statement

FYE: December 31

	ASSETS ($ mil.)	NET INCOME ($ mil.)	INCOME AS % OF ASSETS	EMPLOYEES
12/04	1,137,956	3,349	0.3%	65,417
12/03	1,010,304	1,716	0.2%	67,682
12/02	796,495	416	0.1%	77,442
12/01	818,411	149	0.0%	94,782
12/00	874,927	12,727	1.5%	98,311
12/99	845,744	2,589	0.3%	93,232
12/98	731,151	2,014	0.3%	95,847
12/97	581,974	569	0.1%	76,141
12/96	570,465	1,428	0.3%	74,356
12/95	501,923	1,475	0.3%	74,119
Annual Growth	**9.5%**	**9.5%**	**—**	**(1.4%)**

2004 Year-End Financials

Equity as % of assets: 3.1%
Return on assets: 0.3%
Return on equity: 9.5%
Long-term debt ($ mil.): 144,766
No. of shares (mil.): 517

Dividends
Yield: 0.0%
Payout: —
Market value ($ mil.): 46,045
Sales ($ mil.): 60,631

Stock History

NYSE: DB

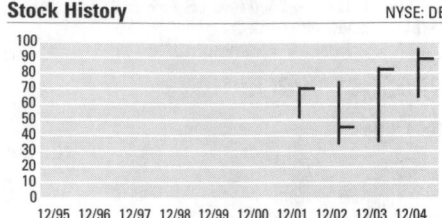

12/95 12/96 12/97 12/98 12/99 12/00 12/01 12/02 12/03 12/04

	STOCK PRICE ($) FY Close	P/E High/Low		PER SHARE ($) Earnings	Dividends	Book Value
12/04	89.01	15	11	6.14	0.00	67.83
12/03	82.21	32	14	2.90	1.53	62.74
12/02	45.43	125	60	0.65	1.20	53.80
12/01	70.15	133	98	0.24	0.00	58.30
Annual Growth	**8.3%**	**—**	**—**	**194.7%**	**—**	**5.2%**

Deutsche Post

Deutsche Post has grown out of its mailbox. Through its DHL unit, the company is one of the world's leading providers of express delivery and logistics services. Deutsche Post, which does business as Deutsche Post World Net, remains Europe's largest postal service provider. Also known as the "Yellow Giant," it provides traditional and same-day letter delivery, online bulk mail management, and mail process outsourcing. In addition, the company offers financial services, through majority-owned Deutsche Postbank. Deutsche Post has acquired the UK-based logistics company, Exel and made plans to purchase a majority stake in the Germany-based financial holding company BHW Holding.

Deutsche Post has gained control of express delivery and logistics operations across Europe and in the US in a series of acquisitions. In 2003 Deutsche Post (through DHL) paid about $1 billion in cash for the ground delivery network of US-based Airborne.

To eliminate overlaps in its operations, Deutsche Post has united its parcel and express delivery services (DHL and Euro Express) and logistics services (Danzas) under the DHL brand. The new DHL consists of four divisions: DHL Express, DHL Freight, DHL Danzas Air & Ocean, and DHL Solutions.

In addition, Deutsche Post is moving to cut costs by centralizing processes such as purchasing and by using ground transportation rather than airplanes for mail in some regions.

HISTORY

The German postal system was established in the 1490s when German emperor Maximilian I ordered a reliable and regular messenger service to be set up between Austria (Innsbruck, where the emperor had his court) and the farther reaches of his Holy Roman Empire: the Netherlands, France, and Rome. The Tassis (later re-named Taxis) family of Italy was responsible for running the network. Members of the von Taxis family settled in major cities across Europe to expand the postal business.

Although the family operated what was officially an exclusively royal mail service, by the early 1500s the company was also delivering messages for private patrons. In 1600 a Tassis family member who served as general postmaster was authorized to collect fees for private mail deliveries. By the early 19th century, Thurn und Taxis, as the company was then called, was the leading postal service in the Holy Roman Empire, serving more than 11 million people.

The dissolution of the Holy Roman Empire, prompted by Napoleon's military adventures, led to creation of a federation of 39 independent German states. Thurn und Taxis had to make agreements with members of the separate states, including Austria and Prussia. After Austria's defeat in 1866 by Prussia, the confederation was dissolved and all Thurn und Taxis postal systems were absorbed by Prussia. When Bismarck's Prussian-led German Reich was established in 1870, the new postal administration (Reichspostverwaltung) began issuing postage stamps valid across Germany.

After Germany was defeated in WWII and split into two nations in 1949, two postal systems were established: Deutsche Post (East Germany) and Deutsche Bundespost (West Germany). The fall of the Berlin Wall in 1989 preceded a reunion of the two German states in 1990. That year Deutsche Post, led by chairman Klaus Zumwinkel, was integrated into Deutsche Bundespost. The merger resulted in losses and a huge backlog of undelivered mail. Zumwinkel initiated the company's first steps to recovery by cutting 140,000 jobs.

The heavy costs of East German reunification (it was 1994 before Deutsche Bundespost posted a profit again) prompted the German government to set the postal system on a course toward full privatization. In 1995 the postal system was restructured as Deutsche Post AG and placed under the management of executives from the private sector.

In 1998 a new postal law reaffirmed Deutsche Post's monopoly on traditional letter delivery until 2002. However, other special mail delivery options (such as same-day delivery of letters) were granted to private companies. That year Deutsche Post acquired shares in parcel delivery companies in Europe and the US, including a stake of nearly 25% in DHL. In 1999 it acquired Deutsche Postbank, the former retail banking arm of Deutsche Bundespost, as part of a strategy to make it more attractive for an IPO.

Continuing its buying spree, Deutsche Post grabbed Swiss-based logistics giant Danzas Holding, Swedish freight forwarder ASG, and the distribution and logistics unit of Dutch transport group Royal Nedlloyd. Undeterred by a European Commission probe into whether it received improper state subsidies, Deutsche Post added more units in 2000, including US-based airfreight forwarder Air Express International, which was integrated into Danzas. It also acquired New York-based QuickMAIL. The German government sold a minority stake in Deutsche Post to the public in 2000.

The German government in 2001 extended Deutsche Post's monopoly over letter delivery until 2007. The next year the postal service took full ownership of DHL. The company sold a minority stake in Deutsche Postbank in an IPO in 2004.

EXECUTIVES

Chairman of the Supervisory Board: Josef Hattig
Chairman of the Board of Management:
Klaus Zumwinkel, age 61, $3,123,815 pay
Member of the Board of Management, Express Americas, Asia, and EMA: John P. Mullen, age 49
Member of the Board of Management, Express Europe: Peter E. Kruse, age 55, $2,073,109 pay
Member of the Board of Management, Finance: Edgar Ernst, $2,380,009 pay
Member of the Board of Management, Financial Services: Prof Wulf von Schimmelmann, age 58, $2,390,155 pay
Member of the Board of Management, Logistics and Corporate Services: Frank Appel, age 44, $1,467,630 pay
Member of the Board of Management, Mail: Hans-Dieter Petram, $2,082,543 pay
Member of the Board of Management, Personnel: Walter Scheurle, $1,882,252 pay
EVP, Global Network Management, Deutsche Post World Net: Christoph Mueller
Auditors: PwC Deutsche Revision AG

LOCATIONS

HQ: Deutsche Post AG
Charles-de-Gaulle-Str. 20, 53113 Bonn, Germany
Phone: +49-228-182-0   **Fax:** +49-228-182-7099
Web: www.dpwn.de

2004 Sales

	% of total
Europe	
Germany	52
Other countries	26
Americas	15
Asia/Pacific	6
Other regions	1
Total	**100**

PRODUCTS/OPERATIONS

2004 Sales

	% of total
Express	41
Mail	28
Financial services	16
Logistics	15
Total	**100**

COMPETITORS

CNF
Exel
FedEx
Finland Post
Geodis
Hays
La Poste
Poste Italiane
Royal Mail
Royal TPG Post
Stinnes
Telair
TNT
UPS
US Postal Service

HISTORICAL FINANCIALS

Company Type: Public

Income Statement

FYE: December 31

	REVENUE ($ mil.)	NET INCOME ($ mil.)	NET PROFIT MARGIN	EMPLOYEES
12/04	60,743	2,166	3.6%	346,410
12/03	51,739	1,643	3.2%	341,572
12/02	44,295	691	1.6%	371,912
12/01	30,963	1,402	4.5%	321,369
12/00	30,798	1,424	4.6%	324,203
12/99	23,697	1,120	4.7%	301,229
12/98	18,295	190	1.0%	258,491
12/97	16,231	(214)	—	266,823
12/96	18,878	217	1.2%	284,889
12/95	17,486	—	—	307,388
Annual Growth	14.8%	33.3%	—	1.3%

2004 Year-End Financials

Debt ratio: 62.4%
Return on equity: 24.7%
Cash ($ mil.): 6,609
Current ratio: 1.47
Long-term debt ($ mil.): 6,142

Net Income History

German: DPW

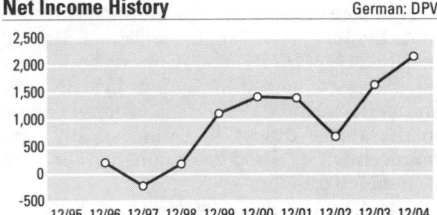

Deutsche Telekom

Deutsche Telekom is leading the charge as Europe's former state-owned telecommunications monopolies confront competition. It is the #1 telecom company in Europe and one of the largest in the world. The company's T-Com unit provides fixed-line network access services and Deutsche Telekom is still Germany's #1 fixed-line phone operator, with about 58 million access lines. T-Mobile International serves wireless phone customers and the company's majority-owned T-Online unit, with 13 million customers, is one of Europe's leading ISPs. The T-Systems division specializes in IT services. The German government has reduced its stake in the company to about 15%. German state-owned development bank KfW owns about 22%.

Deutsche Telekom has announced plans to buy out minority shareholders in T-Online and has acquired a nearly 6% stake in the ISP from media firm Lagardère SCA in a deal valued at more than €500 million.

The company's T-Com division provides access to the traditional fixed-line telecommunications network, including domestic and international long-distance, data transmission, carrier services, and the sales and lease of customer premise equipment. The division is still Germany's #1 fixed-line phone operator, with about 58 million access lines. It also operates through holdings in Eastern Europe.

The T-Mobile division includes Deutsche Telekom's T-Mobile Deutschland unit, one of that country's leading wireless telecom providers (along with Vodafone's German network) serving more than 26 million subscribers. T-Mobile International also includes T-Mobile USA (with more than 13 million subscribers), as well as wireless operations in Austria, the Czech Republic, Russia, Poland, and the UK. The company has said it will boost its T-Mobile USA holdings through the $2.5 billion acquisition of a wireless network serving California and Nevada from Cingular Wireless.

The T-Online division provides dial-up and broadband Internet access as well as Internet portal services to more than 13 million users.

Until 2003 Deutsche Telekom was also Germany's #1 cable provider through the company's six regional cable TV operations, which it sold for $1.87 billion to a group of US investors that includes Apax Partners, the Goldman Sachs Group, and Providence Equity Partners.

With competition flourishing in Germany, Deutsche Telekom is working hard to lose its bureaucratic image and reposition itself as a slimmer, customer-friendly organization. To cut costs and eliminate debt the company plans to reduce its workforce by 22,000 jobs, or 9%, over the next two years. The company has sold a minority stake in T-Online to the public but postponed plans for an IPO of T-Mobile.

HISTORY

Deutsche Telekom was formed by the 1989 separation of West Germany's telecommunications services from the nation's postal system. Dating back to the 15th century (when the Thurn und Taxis private postal system was created for German principalities), the service covered Austria, France, the Netherlands, and most of Germany by the 1850s. After the 1866 Austro-Prussian War, it became part of the North German Postal Confederation. When the German Empire was formed in 1871, the postal operation became the Deutsche Reichspost (later the Bundespost). Shortly thereafter, the newly invented telephone was introduced in Germany.

Post-WWI inflation shook the Bundespost, and the government allowed it to try new organizational structures. A 1924 law allowed the state-run service to operate as a quasi-commercial company.

Hitler came to power in 1933, and the postal service became an instrument of Nazi surveillance. After WWII occupation forces began rebuilding Germany's badly damaged infrastructure. In 1947 the American-British zone returned postal authority to Germans, and in 1949 the USSR established the state of East Germany.

Only by the 1960s did West Germany's postal and phone services meet modern standards. Privatization of the Bundespost became a political cause when many complained about the monopoly's cost and inefficiency. Efforts to privatize the agency (named Deutsche Telekom in 1989) intensified with the 1990 German reunification. Faced with updating the antiquated phone system of the former East Germany, political opposition to taking Deutsche Telekom public faded.

The company began operating T-D1, its mobile phone network, in 1992, and the next year it launched T-Online, now Germany's largest online service provider. In 1996 Deutsche Telekom finally went public and raised more than $13 billion in Europe's largest IPO. It also launched Global One with France Telecom and Sprint; as part of the partnership, Deutsche Telekom took a 10% stake in Sprint.

In 1998 European Union (EU) member countries opened their phone markets to competition, and Deutsche Telekom's long-distance market share quickly eroded. Under EU pressure, in 1999 Deutsche Telekom said it would sell its cable network, which it divided into nine regional units. Deutsche Telekom's plan to merge with Telecom Italia in 1999 blew up in its face: Olivetti butted in and took over Telecom Italia, while an angry France Telecom filed a lawsuit claiming that Deutsche Telekom's merger plan had violated their agreements. (The case was settled in 2000.)

Undaunted, Deutsche Telekom forged ahead with its international expansion plans, buying French fixed-line carrier SIRIS and UK wireless provider One 2 One. In 2000 the company sold its stake in Global One to France Telecom, as did Sprint. (In the fallout from the unwinding of the Global One partnership, Deutsche Telekom in 2001 sold its stake in Sprint PCS and sold its interest in France Telecom the next year.)

Later in 2000 Deutsche Telekom agreed to pay $5.3 billion for a controlling stake in DaimlerChrysler's Debis Systemhaus information technology services unit. It also launched an IPO of its Internet subsidiary, T-Online.

T-Mobile International moved into the US mobile phone market in 2001 with the acquisitions of VoiceStream Wireless and Powertel, now known as T-Mobile USA. The German government's stake in Deutsche Telekom decreased by 17% largely to accommodate US regulators for the VoiceStream and Powertel acquisitions.

EXECUTIVES

Chairman of the Supervisory Board: Klaus Zumwinkel, age 61
Deputy Chairman of the Supervisory Board: Franz Treml
Chairman of the Management Board (CEO): Kai-Uwe Ricke, age 44, $1,562,916 pay
Member of the Management Board, Deputy CEO, and Head of Finance and Controlling (CFO): Karl-Gerhard Eick, age 51, $1,172,187 pay
Member of the Management Board and Head of Human Resources: Heinz Klinkhammer, age 59, $937,750 pay
Member of the Management Board and CEO, T-Mobile International AG: René Obermann, age 42, $937,750 pay
Member of the Management Board, Head of Business Customers, and CEO, T-Systems: Lothar Pauly, age 46
Member of the Management Board and Head of Broadband/Fixed-Network; Chairman, T-Com Board of Management: Walter Raizner, age 51, $213,125 pay (partial-year salary)
CEO, T-Online International AG: Rainer Beaujean, age 37
Auditors: PwC Deutsche Revision AG

LOCATIONS

HQ: Deutsche Telekom AG
Friedrich-Ebert-Allee 140, 53113 Bonn, Germany
Phone: +49-228-181-0   **Fax:** +49-228-181-8872
US HQ: 101 E. 52nd St., New York, NY 10022
US Phone: 212-424-2900   **US Fax:** 212-424-2989
Web: www.telekom.de

Deutsche Telekom operates primarily in Germany, but it holds interests in operations worldwide.

2004 Sales

	% of total
Germany	61
Other countries	39
Total	**100**

PRODUCTS/OPERATIONS

2004 Sales

	$ mil.	% of total
T-Com	33,086	42
T-Mobile	32,630	42
T-Systems	9,805	12
T-Online	2,429	3
Other revenues	454	1
Total	**78,404**	**100**

Operating Divisions

T-Com (fixed-line network voice and data services)
T-Mobile (mobile communications services and equipment sales)
T-Systems (data communications and systems services for large business customers)
T-Online (Internet services)

Selected Subsidiaries and Affiliates

Deutsche Telekom Immobilien und Service GmbH (DeTe Immobilien, facility management services provider)
Deutsche Telekom Network Projects and Services GmbH
GMG Generalmietgesellschaft mbH (group leasing and rental business operations)
Hrvatske telekomunikacije d.d. (Hrvatski Telekom HT, 51%, telecommunications services, Croatia)
MagyarCom Holdings GmbH (holding company)
MagyarTávközlési Rt. (MATÁV, 59%, telecommunications services, Hungary)
Slovak Telecom (formerly Slovenské Telekomunikácie a.s., 51%, telecommunications services, Slovakia)
T-Mobile International AG (wireless telecommunications services)
CMobil B.V. (92%, holding company)
T-Mobile Czech Republic a.s. (formerly RadioMobil, 61%, wireless telecommunications services)
Polska Telefonia Cyfrowa Sp. z o.o. (PTC, 49%, wireless telecommunications services, Poland)
T-Mobile Deutschland GmbH (formerly Deutsche Telekom MobilNet GmbH, or DeTeMobil, wireless telecommunications services)
T-Mobile Global Holding GmbH
T-Mobile Holdings Ltd. (T-Mobile UK, formerly One 2 One Personal Communications Ltd., wireless telecommunications services)
T-Mobile Netherlands B.V. (formerly BEN Nederland, wireless telecommunications services)
T-Mobile Global Holding Nr. 2 GmbH
T-Mobile Austria GmbH (formerly max.mobil.Telekommunikation Service GmbH, wireless telecommunications services)
T-Mobile USA, Inc. (formerly VoiceStream Wireless Corporation, 100%, wireless telecommunications services, US)
Powertel, Inc. (T-Mobile USA)
T-Online International AG (74%, Internet services)
T-Systems International GmbH (formerly debis Systemhaus GmbG, information technology and telecommunications)
T-Systems CDS GmbH

COMPETITORS

America Online	Metromedia
Belgacom	mobilcom
BT	NTT
Cable & Wireless	SFR Cegetel
COLT Telecom	Siemens
EDS	Swisscom
E.ON	TDC
France Telecom	Tele2
Hungarian Telephone and Cable	Telecom Italia
	Telefónica
IBM	Telekom Austria
KPN	Telenor
Lagardère	TeliaSonera
MCI	Vodafone

HISTORICAL FINANCIALS

Company Type: Public

Income Statement

FYE: December 31

	REVENUE ($ mil.)	NET INCOME ($ mil.)	NET PROFIT MARGIN	EMPLOYEES
12/04	78,404	6,277	8.0%	244,645
12/03	70,200	1,575	2.2%	248,519
12/02	56,390	(25,824)	—	255,969
12/01	43,058	(3,079)	—	257,058
12/00	38,556	5,581	14.5%	227,015
12/99	35,796	1,265	3.5%	195,788
12/98	41,868	2,630	6.3%	186,000
12/97	37,559	1,837	4.9%	191,000
12/96	40,917	1,140	2.8%	201,060
12/95	45,997	3,667	8.0%	213,467
Annual Growth	**6.1%**	**6.2%**	**—**	**1.5%**

2004 Year-End Financials

Debt ratio: 125.8%
Return on equity: 15.1%
Cash ($ mil.): 10,905
Current ratio: 0.97
Long-term debt ($ mil.): 57,776

No. of shares (mil.): 4,198
Dividends
  Yield: 0.0%
  Payout: —
Market value ($ mil.): 95,211

Stock History

NYSE: DT

	STOCK PRICE ($) FY Close	P/E High	P/E Low	PER SHARE ($) Earnings	PER SHARE ($) Dividends	PER SHARE ($) Book Value
12/04	22.68	15	10	1.49	0.00	10.94
12/03	18.13	48	26	0.38	0.00	8.92
12/02	12.70	—	—	(6.15)	0.33	7.87
12/01	16.90	—	—	(0.83)	0.56	12.95
12/00	29.25	54	16	1.85	0.57	11.94
12/99	71.00	167	83	0.43	0.65	11.56
12/98	32.75	35	18	0.96	0.67	10.38
12/97	18.63	37	24	0.67	0.35	9.46
12/96	20.38	41	37	0.54	0.00	10.74
Annual Growth	**1.3%**	**—**	**—**	**13.5%**	**—**	**0.2%**

Diageo plc

Diageo's holiday parties must be the talk of the town. Formed by the 1997 merger of alcoholic beverage giant Guinness with food and spirits company Grand Metropolitan, Diageo is the world's largest producer of alcoholic drinks. Its beers and distilled spirits include Guinness Stout, Harp Lager, Johnnie Walker Scotch, José Cuervo tequila, Tanqueray gin, and Smirnoff vodka. Diageo helps stock bars and shelves in 200 countries around the globe. The company gained the Captain Morgan, Crown Royal, and VO Canadian brands through its purchase of Seagram's drinks business from Vivendi Universal.

Diageo also owns 34% of Moët Hennessy. In a rebranding move to emphasize the Diageo name, the company scrapped its Guinness/UDV unit and folded those operations into its premium drinks division. As a result, Diageo plans to cease brewing Guinness in the UK and handle that country's demand for the dark brew from its St. James's Gate brewery in Dublin, Ireland. As many as 90 people will lose their jobs as a result of the consolidation.

HISTORY

Diageo — from the Latin word for "day" and the Greek word for "world" — was born from Guinness and GrandMet's 1997 merger to fight flat liquor sales and spirited competitors.

Guinness began business in 1759 when Arthur Guinness leased a small brewery in Dublin, Ireland. Guinness began specializing in porters in 1799. Managed by the third generation of Guinnesses, the company went public as a London-based firm in 1886.

In the 1950s managing director Hugh Beaver was credited with conceiving the *Guinness Book of World Records*. During the 1970s Guinness bought more than 200 companies, with disappointing results. Guinness refocused on brewing and distilling operations in the late 1980s by selling noncore businesses and acquiring firms such as Schenley (Dewar's). In 1988 and 1989 it bought 24% of LVMH Moët Hennessy Louis Vuitton (later exchanged for 34% of LVMH's wine and spirits business). More acquisitions followed in the 1990s, capped by Guinness' 1997 announcement of its $19 billion merger with Grand Metropolitan.

GrandMet was established by Maxwell Joseph. In 1931 he began acquiring properties for resale, but WWII slowed his progress. He started buying hotels in 1946, and by 1961 GrandMet had gone public.

Diversification began in 1970 with the purchases of catering firms, restaurants, and betting shops. In the early 1970s, in what was the largest British takeover up to that time, GrandMet bought brewer Truman Hanburg, followed by Watney Mann, which owned International Distillers & Vintners, makers of Bailey's, Bombay Gin, and J&B.

GrandMet looked overseas through the 1970s, taking over the Liggett Group, a US cigarette maker (sold in 1986) whose Paddington unit was the US distributor of J&B Scotch. In 1987 it bought Heublein (Smirnoff, Lancers, José Cuervo). Two years later it bought The Pillsbury Company (Burger King and Green Giant) in a hostile takeover.

When Diageo was created, the companies and brands were divided among four divisions: The Pillsbury Company, Burger King, Guinness, and United Distillers & Vintners.

In 2000 COO Paul Walsh, a former Pillsbury CEO, took over as CEO of both Diageo and its newly combined alcoholic beverage division, Guinness/UDV. Also that year Diageo, along with fellow wine and spirits producer Pernod Ricard, agreed to pay $8.2 billion to Vivendi Universal for the Seagram's drinks business that holds several brands, including Crown Royal, VO Canadian whiskies, and Sterling Vineyards.

In 2001 Diageo sold its Guinness World Records business to media company Gullane Entertainment for $63 million. That year the company also completed its sale of Pillsbury to General Mills. After months of wrangling with the FTC, Diageo finally won regulatory approval for the Seagram's drinks purchase in late 2001.

In May 2002 Diageo completed the sale of its Malibu rum brand to Allied Domecq for about

$796 million; the deal also sealed Diageo's ownership of the Captain Morgan rum brand, as Allied Domecq agreed to drop its lawsuit involving Captain Morgan. Later in 2002 Diageo discontinued marketing its Captain Morgan Gold rum drink in the US because of disappointing sales.

Also in 2002 Diageo sold Burger King for $1.5 billion to a group composed of Texas Pacific Group, Bain Capital, and Goldman Sachs Capital Partners. Diageo's decision to sell its Pillsbury unit and its Burger King business (the #2 burger chain, after McDonald's) was part of the company's new focus on its spirits, wine, and beer businesses. The Pillsbury divestiture gave the company a 33% stake in General Mills (Diageo sold nearly half of its shares in October 2004). Also in 2002, Diageo and Pernod Ricard, which together own rights to the Seagram's brand, sold Seagram's line of nonalcoholic mixers to The Coca-Cola Company.

In 2003 Diageo and Jose Cuervo said they would jointly sell Don Julio and Tres Magueyes tequilas. Diageo also joined with Heineken to purchase 30% of InBev's Nambia Breweries in southern Africa. The brewery will make Heineken and Beck's beer.

Diageo said in September 2003 that it would launch a low-alcohol version of its highly popular Baileys Irish Cream. Known as Baileys Glide, the drink still is made with Irish whiskey, but Diageo said it would be manufactured in Germany. Also in September Diageo reopened the George Dickel distillery in Tullahoma, Tennessee. That same year Diageo cut 150 jobs from its Guinness operation amid declining sales of the well-known stout.

In 2005 Diageo and Heineken formed a partnership for the production and distribution of Guinness in Russia. The company also acquired The Chalone Wine Group in 2005 for about $260 million. It added the winery into Diageo's current US wine operations, which are organized under Diageo Chateau & Estate Wines. It also acquired Netherlands distiller Ursus Vodka for an undisclosed amount and added Bushmills Irish whiskey to its stable, with the purchase of the brand from Pernod Ricard for $363 million. It also agreed to stay out of any negotiations regarding the takeover of Allied Domecq.

EXECUTIVES

Chairman: Lord James Blyth of Rowington, age 65, $959,834 pay
CEO and Director: Paul S. Walsh, age 50, $6,468,057 pay
CFO and Director: Nicholas C. (Nick) Rose, age 47, $2,334,634 pay
President and CEO, North America: Ivan M. Menezes, age 46
CEO, Diageo Korea: Song Duck-young
SVP, Public Policy: Carolyn Panzer
VP, Corporate Relations: Virginia Sanchez
VP, Global Marketing SMIRNOFF: Barry Sheridan
VP, Smirnoff: Pamela Bower-Nye
Chairman, Diageo Ireland, and Global Brand Director, Guinness: Brian Duffy
Deputy Chairman, Diageo Africa: Nick Blazquez
President, Diageo Europe: Andrew Morgan, age 47
President, Diageo International: Stuart Fletcher, age 46
President, Global Marketing, Sales and Innovation: Robert M. (Rob) Malcolm, age 51
CIO: Yvonne Harrison
Director, Global Brand Innovation: Syl Saller
Director, Investor Relations: Catherine James
Director, Human Resources: Gareth Williams, age 50
General Counsel: Timothy D. (Tim) Proctor, age 53
Company Secretary: Susanne Bunn
Media Contact: Isabelle Thomas
Auditors: KPMG Audit Plc

LOCATIONS

HQ: Diageo plc
8 Henrietta Place,
London W1G OMD, United Kingdom
Phone: +44-20-7927-5200   **Fax:** +44-20-7927-4600
US HQ: 1301 K St. NW, Ste. 1000, East Tower,
Washington, DC 20005
US Phone: 202-715-1110   **US Fax:** 202-715-1114
Web: www.diageo.co.uk

Diageo has operations in more than 50 countries and sells its products in more than 200. Production takes place in Canada, Ireland, Italy, the UK, and the US.

2005 Sales

	% of total
Europe	43
North America	29
International	28
Total	**100**

PRODUCTS/OPERATIONS

Selected Divisions and Brands

Beer
  Guinness (Draught, Draught Bitter, Draught Extra Cold, Extra Stout, Foreign Extra)
  Harp lager
  Kaliber (nonalcoholic)
  Kilkenny Irish beer
  Malta (nonalcoholic)
  Red Stripe lager
  Smithwick's ale
Wine and Spirits
  American whiskey (Seagram's 7)
  Canadian whiskey (Crown Royal, Seagram's VO)
  Champagne (Moët & Chandon)
  Cognac (Hennessy)
  Gin (Gilbey's, Gordon's, Tanqueray)
  Irish whiskey (Bushmills)
  Liqueur (Baileys Original Irish Cream, Baileys Glide)
  Rum (Bundaberg, Captain Morgan, Myers)
  Scotch whisky (Bell's, Buchanans De Luxe, Cardhu, Dimple, J&B, Johnnie Walker, Old Parr, White Horse, Windsor)
  Single-malt whiskies (Cragganmore, Dalwhinnie, Glenkinchie, Lagavulin, Oban, Talisker)
  Specialty spirits (Pimms)
  Tequila (Don Julio, José Cuervo outside Mexico, Cuervo Clasico, Tres Magueyes)
  Vodka (Gordon's, Popov, Smirnoff, Ursus)
  Wine (Blossom Hill, Beaulieu Vineyard, Chalone Vineyards, Le Piat d'Or, Sterling Vineyards)

Selected Subsidiaries
The Chalone Wine Group, Ltd. (US)
General Mills (7%, US)
Gleneagles Hotel (golf resort)
Moët Hennessy, SNC (34%, France)
The Old Bushmills Distillery Company Limited (UK)
Ursus Vodka Holding NV (The Netherlands)

COMPETITORS

Allied Domecq	Heineken
Angostura	Highland Distillers
Anheuser-Busch	InBev
Asahi Breweries	Jim Beam Brands
Asia Pacific Breweries	Kirin
Bacardi	Lion Nathan
Blavod Extreme Spirits	Martini & Rossi
Brown-Forman	Maxxium
Cabo Wabo	Miller Brewing
Campari	Molson Coors
Carlsberg A/S	Paramount Distillers
Constellation Brands	Pernod Ricard
Edrington	Rémy Cointreau
FEMSA	SABMiller
Fortune Brands	Sapporo
Foster's	Scottish & Newcastle
Future Brands	Scottish Courage
Gallo	Sidney Frank Importing
Grupo Modelo	Skyy
Heaven Hill Distilleries	Yuengling & Son

HISTORICAL FINANCIALS

Company Type: Public

Income Statement

FYE: June 30

	REVENUE ($ mil.)	NET INCOME ($ mil.)	NET PROFIT MARGIN	EMPLOYEES
6/05	16,163	2,460	15.2%	—
6/04	16,161	2,530	15.7%	23,720
6/03	15,624	126	0.8%	38,955
6/02	17,276	2,476	14.3%	62,124
6/01	18,124	1,733	9.6%	71,523
6/00	17,998	1,480	8.2%	72,474
6/99	18,618	1,487	8.0%	72,000
6/98	29,497	2,230	7.6%	77,029
6/97	8,107	1,174	14.5%	20,555
6/96	7,253	922	12.7%	21,533
Annual Growth	**9.3%**	**11.5%**	**—**	**1.2%**

2005 Year-End Financials

Debt ratio: 101.0%
Return on equity: 37.2%
Cash ($ mil.): 1,461
Current ratio: 1.21
Long-term debt ($ mil.): 6,577
No. of shares (mil.): 763
Dividends
  Yield: 3.6%
  Payout: 63.7%
Market value ($ mil.): 45,216

Stock History

NYSE: DEO

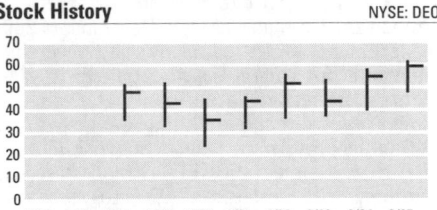

	STOCK PRICE ($) FY Close	P/E High/Low		PER SHARE ($) Earnings	Dividends	Book Value
6/05	59.30	17	14	3.31	2.11	8.54
6/04	54.75	16	11	3.33	1.80	8.78
6/03	43.76	16	12	0.15	1.71	10.58
6/02	51.65	21	14	2.98	1.46	11.43
6/01	43.95	19	13	2.05	1.38	8.60
6/00	35.56	20	11	1.74	1.43	8.35
6/99	43.00	31	20	1.67	1.30	7.42
6/98	48.00	22	16	2.30	5.45	8.59
Annual Growth	**3.1%**	**—**	**—**	**5.3%**	**(12.7%)**	**(0.1%)**

EADS

It's flying alphabet soup! DaimlerChrysler Aerospace (DASA, Germany), Aerospatiale Matra (France), and Construcciones Aeronáuticas SA (CASA, Spain) combined to form the European Aeronautic Defence and Space Company (EADS). EADS is Europe's largest aerospace firm; worldwide it trails only Boeing. EADS' largest holding is an 80% stake in Airbus (BAE SYSTEMS owns the other 20%), which has surpassed Boeing as the world's leading maker of large commercial aircraft. Other operations include helicopters (Eurocopter), business and military jets (46% of Dassault Aviation and 43% of Eurofighter), satellites (Astrium), missiles (38% of MBDA), and commercial satellite launch systems (about 29% of Arianespace).

Airbus, which accounts for about two-thirds of EADS' sales, had been gaining on rival Boeing for years and finally surpassed Boeing in both plane orders and deliveries in 2003. For the future, Airbus is banking on its new super-jumbo A380 jet and the mid-size, long-range A350. Scheduled for delivery in 2006, the A380 will carry up to 800 people in a double-decker configuration; the A350 will seat about 250 and is expected in 2010.

Despite its success against Boeing, the downturn in the civil airline market after the terrorist attacks of September 11 has prompted EADS to increase its focus on its military business. EADS is also focusing more attention on the US defense market through its EADS North America subsidiary. In 2005 the company announced that it was teaming up with Raytheon to compete for the US Army's cargo aircraft contract. EADS North America is also expected to look for a US partner (possibly Northrop Grumman) to compete for the Air Force's refueling tanker project.

After years of negotiations and countless dead ends, the group of Western European aerospace companies that own EADS finally incorporated the company in 2001. As with its Airbus operations, EADS' production takes place in multiple countries; the company's complex ownership and management structure (German and French co-CEOs) is designed to maintain parity between French and German stakes. In December of 2004 replacements for the company's CEOs were announced, but parity was maintained: In 2005 Thomas Enders replaced Rainer Hertich, and Noël Forgeard replaced Phillipe Camus.

DaimlerChrysler owns about 30% of EADS; the French government (SOGEPA), France-based Lagardère, BNP Paribas, and AXA together own about 30%; Spain's state-owned SEPI owns 5.5%.

HISTORY

The short life of the European Aeronautic Defence and Space Company — EADS — is overshadowed by the long history of its components and by the obstacles overcome to cement the deal: The French and the Germans historically aren't overly fond of each other, so how did it come to pass that Germany's DaimlerChrysler Aerospace (DASA) and France's Aerospatiale Matra put aside their differences to band together with Spain's Construcciones Aeronáuticas SA (CASA)?

The US aerospace sector in the 1990s saw many companies consolidate, scrambling to make their way in the post-Cold War era. Boeing, the largest aerospace company in the world, got that way by acquiring a slew of operations, including Rockwell International's aerospace and defense operations (1995) and most importantly, McDonnell Douglas in a $16 billion deal (1997). In the same era, defense giant Lockheed merged with Martin Marietta (1995) and acquired Loral (1997). These US companies had it relatively easy — they all paid taxes to Uncle Sam, but acquisition deals in Europe were stymied by concerns over national security and privatization because much of Europe's defense industry was government-owned.

Spurred into action by their US rivals, in 1997 DASA and British Aerospace (now BAE SYSTEMS) — partners in Airbus — began merger talks. Fearful of being left out in the cold, France's government-owned Aerospatiale — another Airbus partner — began talks to merge with Matra, a French defense company controlled by Lagardère. Weeks after the Aerospatiale-Matra deal was announced in 1998, the chairman of DASA's parent company, Jürgen Schrempp, met with Lagardère's CEO, Jean-Luc Lagardère, and proposed a three-way deal. It never occurred and in 1999 the BAE SYSTEMS and DASA deal fell through as well.

Later that year Schrempp and Lagardère met again and laid the groundwork for a merger between DASA and Aerospatiale Matra. Less than three weeks after the Aerospatiale-Matra merger was completed, Lagardère found himself pitching the DASA/Aerospatiale Matra merger idea to a stunned French government (which still held a 48% stake in Aerospatiale Matra). Marathon negotiations ensued. Late in the year Spain's Construcciones Aeronáuticas SA (CASA) agreed to become part of EADS.

In 2000 EADS went public and Airbus announced that it would abandon its consortium structure in favor of incorporation. The next year EADS began pushing for a consolidation of army and naval equipment manufacturing among EU countries similar to the aerospace consolidation that created EADS. For Airbus, the long-sought switch from consortium to corporation finally occurred in 2001 when Airbus S.A.S. was incorporated.

EADS bought out BAE SYSTEMS' 25% share in their Astrium joint venture in 2003. In October of 2004 EADS agreed to acquire US defense electronics maker Racal Instruments as part of its plan to increase defense sales in the US. The next month, rumors surfaced that EADS was discussing a merger deal with French defense company Thales.

In December of 2004 EADS and BAE SYSTEMS gave Airbus the greenlight to build the A350, a plane that competes directly with Boeing's upcoming 787 Dreamliner. A few months later, in February of 2005, EADS was given preferred bidder status for the UK's Royal Air Force aerial refueling tanker contract. The program is expected to be worth about $25 billion.

EXECUTIVES

Co-Chairman: Manfred Bischoff, age 63
Co-Chairman: Arnaud Lagardère, age 44
Co-CEO and Director: Noël Forgeard, age 59
Co-CEO and Director: Thomas Enders, age 46
CFO and Director: Hans Peter Ring, age 54
CEO, Airbus: Gustav Humbert, age 55
Head, Aeronautics Division: Dietrich Russell, age 64
Head, EADS International: Jean-Paul Gut, age 44
Head, Human Resources: Jussi Itävuori, age 50
Head, Strategic Coordination: Jean-Luis Gergorin, age 59
Chairman and CEO, EADS North America: Ralph D. Crosby Jr., age 58
CFO and VP, Investor Relations, EADS North America: Christopher Emerson
General Counsel, EADS North America: Pierre Cardin
CEO, EADS Space: François Auque, age 49
President, EADS CASA; Head, Military Transport Aircraft: Francisco Fernández Sáinz, age 60
President, EADS UK: Sir Jeremy Blackham
President and CEO, Eurocopter: Fabrice Brégier, age 44
President and CEO, EADS Defence and Security: Stefan Zoller, age 47
VP, Air Force Programs, EADS North America: Charles Coolidge Jr.
Director of Marketing, Advanced Tanker Programs, EADS North America: Silas R. (Si) Johnson Jr.
Auditors: KPMG Accountants N.V.; Ernst & Young Accountants

LOCATIONS

HQ: European Aeronautic Defence and Space Company
EADS N.V.
Le Carré, Beechavenue 130-132,
1119 PR Schiphol-Rijk, The Netherlands
Phone: +31-20655-4800
Web: www.eads-nv.com

2004 Sales

	$ mil.	% of total
Europe	19,816.2	46
North America	11,887.3	27
Asia/Pacific	6,735.4	16
Other regions	4,883.1	11
Total	**43,322.0**	**100**

PRODUCTS/OPERATIONS

2004 Sales

	$ mil.	% of total
Airbus	27,585.5	62
Defence & Security Systems	7,345.1	17
Aeronautics	5,229.6	12
Space Systems	3,022.6	7
Military Transport Aircraft	714.7	2
Adjustments	(575.5)	—
Total	**43,322.0**	**100**

Selected Operations and Interests
Business aircraft (Dassault Aviation, 45.8%)
Commercial airplanes (Airbus, 80%)
Commercial satellite launchers (Arianespace, 28.51%)
Helicopters (Eurocopter SAS)
Jet fighters (Dassault Aviation, 45.8%; Eurofighter, 43%)
Missile systems (MBDA, 37.5%)
Satellites (Astrium)

COMPETITORS

AgustaWestland	Lockheed Martin
BAE SYSTEMS	Lockheed Martin
BAE Systems Electronics	Aeronautics
& Integrated Solutions	Lockheed Martin UK
BAE Systems Inc.	Northrop Grumman
Boeing	Northrop Grumman
Boeing Satellite Systems	Integrated Systems
International	Orbital Sciences
Bombardier	Raytheon
E'Prime Aerospace	Textron
LMCSS	

HISTORICAL FINANCIALS

Company Type: Public

Income Statement				FYE: December 31
	REVENUE ($ mil.)	NET INCOME ($ mil.)	NET PROFIT MARGIN	EMPLOYEES
12/04	43,322	1,405	3.2%	110,662
12/03	37,823	191	0.5%	109,135
12/02	31,339	(313)	—	103,967
12/01	27,281	1,215	4.5%	102,967
12/00	18,293	(850)	—	88,879
12/99	22,711	(1,016)	—	91,940
12/98	24,020	1,387	5.8%	—
Annual Growth	**10.3%**	**0.2%**	**—**	**3.8%**

2004 Year-End Financials

Debt ratio: 26.0%
Return on equity: 6.5%
Cash ($ mil.): 12,527
Current ratio: 1.40
Long-term debt ($ mil.): 6,010

Net Income History   Euronext Paris: EAD

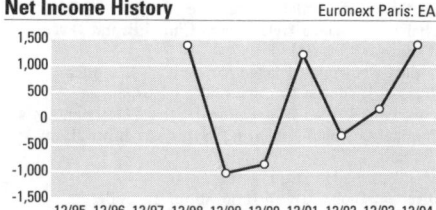

Electricité de France

While France has been slow to open its own doors to competition in the utilities industry, state-owned Electricité de France (EDF) has been quick to expand into global deregulated markets. One of the world's top electric utilities (as well as one of the last major state-owned energy monopolies in Europe), EDF has a generating capacity of more than 100,000 MW and provides power to 27 million French customers. Internationally, the company has interests in electric and gas utilities that serve 15 million customers, and it operates power plants that generate 20,000 MW of capacity in Europe, Africa, the Americas, Asia, and the Middle East. EDF launched an IPO in November 2005, selling as much as 15% of the company.

EDF agreed to acquire Edison SpA (Italy's second-largest power group) in partnership with Italian utility company AEM SpA in 2005 for an estimated $15.4 billion.

Nuclear plants provide more than 60% of EDF's domestic power supply; other sources include hydroelectric and fossil-fueled plants. The company is also developing renewable energy facilities. Making use of its extensive experience, especially in developing nuclear power, EDF builds power plants and provides plant management and consulting services worldwide.

Subsidiary EDF Trading markets electricity, natural gas, coal, and oil throughout Europe. The company's 34%-owned Dalkia unit (Veolia Environnement — formerly Vivendi Environnement — owns 66%) offers energy management and industrial services.

EDF is investing aggressively abroad, including in the liberalized markets of its European neighbors. The firm has grouped its UK retail energy supply operations under the EDF Energy brand; the division serves 5 million customers. EDF also has major utility operations in Germany (EnBW), Italy (EDF Energia Italia and Edison), and Latin America (Light and Edenor).

The company's expansion efforts have spurred criticism since it has been relatively intransigent in opening its own market. However, deregulation of 70% of the French market took effect in July 2004, and full competition is scheduled for 2007. Between 2000 and 2004, only 30% of the market was deregulated, just more than the percentage required by European Union (EU) rulings.

EDF is auctioning off capacity rights to some of its domestic generation facilities to comply with EU regulations; it is also working to create partnerships with other European utilities (including Enel and Electrabel) to allow more access to the French market. To further privatize the industry, the company will divest 49% of its newly formed transmission management firm, RTE.

HISTORY

The French government nationalized hundreds of regional private firms to form Electricité de France (EDF) in 1946 as part of an effort to rebuild the nation's badly shaken post-war economy. This was a marked difference from the notoriously complex and inefficient pre-war electrical industry.

By the 1950s EDF had taken advantage of the centralized control and developed massive hydroelectric projects. Hydroelectric power would account for more than 70% of EDF's power.

But in France as elsewhere, hydro wasn't enough to keep up with the growing demand for electricity, and fossil fuels became an increasingly important power source. Then came the oil shortages of the 1970s, and France — with limited domestic supplies of oil and gas — began searching for alternatives to fossil-fueled plants. Nuclear power was determined to be the answer.

The government moved to invest billions of dollars in developing its relatively small nuclear power production facilities. Muddled with Malthusian predictions of power shortages and a preoccupation with having enough energy to be self-reliant, France found its nuclear operations left the government with more energy than it could use and more debt than it wanted. The company began to build a cable connecting the Continent to the UK in 1981. With the power grids of the two countries connected in 1986, EDF was finally able to start exporting its power to the Brits.

The 1990s brought with them deregulation. EDF fought to keep the UK-France grid closed to other energy sellers. After the government forbade the utility from diversifying into areas other than electricity in 1995, the company turned its attention to foreign investment, especially in Latin America.

The company faced increasing deregulatory pressures from without in the late 1990s. The newly formed European Union required open competition from member states. Begrudgingly and behind schedule, EDF opened about 30% of its market to competition in 2000.

Other members of the EU complained that EDF was trying to play it both ways: It was making aggressive acquisitions in the UK liberalized market (it bought London Electricity in 1999) while resisting a competition-enabling breakup or even allowing a foreign competitor to buy a stake in the French market.

EDF in 2001 expanded its stake in Italy's Montedison, a conglomerate with substantial energy holdings, by forming a consortium (Italenergia) with Italian automaker Fiat and some Italian banks to wrest control of Montedison from Italian bank MEDIOBANCA. Although the consortium owns 94% of Montedison, EDF has only 2% of voting rights. (Montedison changed its name to Edison in 2002.)

EDF also purchased a 35% interest in German utility Energie Baden-Württemberg in 2001, and it merged its energy services unit with Dalkia, a unit of Vivendi Environnement (now Veolia Environnement), taking a 34% stake in Dalkia (which will eventually be increased to 50%). EDF subsidiary London Electricity agreed to buy $2.4 billion in UK assets from TXU Europe that year, including a 2,000 MW power plant, TXU's Eastern Electricity distribution unit, and its interest in TXU/EDF joint venture 24seven; the deals were completed in 2001 and 2002.

In 2002 EDF increased its stake in Brazilian utility Light Serviços de Eletricidade to 88% by swapping Light's interest in Sao Paulo utility Eletropaulo for AES's 24% interest in Light. Later that year EDF purchased UK electric and gas utility SEEBOARD (1.9 million customers) from US utility AEP in a $2.2 billion deal.

EXECUTIVES

Chairman and CEO: Pierre Gadonneix, age 62
SEVP and COO: Gérard Creuzet, age 49
SEVP and CFO: Daniel Camus, age 50

SEVP and Chief Human Resources Officer: Yann Laroche, age 57
EVP, Customers: Jean-Pierre Benqué, age 54
EVP, Development: Robert Durdilly
EVP, Energy Management: Michel Francony
EVP, Generation Engineering: Bruno Lescoeur, age 48
EVP, Local Development and Distribution: Pierre Bart, age 53
EVP, Americas: Fernando Ponasso, age 50
EVP, Asia Pacific: Hervé Machenaud, age 52
EVP, Continental Europe: Marc Boudier, age 47
EVP, Western Europe, Middle East, and Africa: Michel Crémieux, age 53
SVP: Yves Corre
CEO, Dalkia: Olivier Barbaroux, age 49
CEO, R.T.E.: André Merlin, age 60
Corporate Secretary: Marie-Hélène Poinssot
Head of Communications and Public Affairs: Philippe Méchet
Auditors: Deloitte Touche Tohmatsu; Ernst & Young Audit; Mazars & Guérard

LOCATIONS

HQ: Electricité de France
22-30, avenue de Wagram, 75382 Paris, France
Phone: +33-1-4042-2222   **Fax:** +33-1-4042-7940
Web: www.edf.fr

2004 Sales

	% of total
Europe	
France	63
Other countries	33
Other regions	4
Total	**100**

PRODUCTS/OPERATIONS

2004 Generation Mix

	% of total
Nuclear	74
Fossil-fueled	16
Hydroelectric	9
Total	**100**

Selected Subsidiaries and Affiliates

Dalkia Holding (34%, energy services)
EDF Developpement Environnement SA (EDEV, renewable energy and waste services)
EDF International
  Edemsa (23%, electric utility, Argentina)
  Edenor (90%, electric utility, Argentina)
  EDF Energia Italia (energy supply)
  EDF Energy (formerly London Electricity Group, electric and gas supply, UK)
  Energie Baden-Württemberg Aktiengesellschaft (EnBW, 46%, electric and gas utility, Germany)
  Italenergia (18%, Italy)
    Edison (formerly Montedison, 62%, conglomerate, Italy)
  Light Serviços de Eletricidade S.A. (Light Energy, 95%, electric utility, Brazil)
  Shandong Zhonghua Power Company (20%, power generation, China)
EDF Trading (energy marketing and trading)
Electricité de Strasbourg (75%, electric utility)
Réseau de Transport d'Électricité (RTE, transmission system management)

COMPETITORS

Centrica	Nuon
ELETROBRÁS	RWE
Endesa	Scottish and Southern
Enel	Energy
Energias de Portugal	Scottish Power
E.ON	SUEZ
Gaz de France	UES of Russia
Hydro-Québec	Unión Fenosa
IBERDROLA	Vattenfall
International Power	Veolia Environnement

HISTORICAL FINANCIALS

Company Type: Public

Income Statement
FYE: December 31

	REVENUE ($ mil.)	NET INCOME ($ mil.)	NET PROFIT MARGIN	EMPLOYEES
12/04	64,010	1,829	2.9%	156,152
12/03	56,382	1,076	1.9%	167,000
12/02	50,685	504	1.0%	171,995
12/01	36,066	745	2.1%	162,491
12/00	32,403	716	2.2%	117,249
12/99	32,278	720	2.2%	132,550
12/98	34,419	790	2.3%	114,380
12/97	31,664	690	2.2%	116,462
12/96	36,538	1,147	3.1%	116,919
Annual Growth	7.3%	6.0%	—	3.7%

2004 Year-End Financials

Debt ratio: 119.1%
Return on equity: 7.7%
Cash ($ mil.): 4,306
Current ratio: 1.00
Long-term debt ($ mil.): 28,538

Net Income History
Euronext Paris: EDF

| 12/95 | 12/96 | 12/97 | 12/98 | 12/99 | 12/00 | 12/01 | 12/02 | 12/03 | 12/04 |

Electrolux

AB Electrolux has a hunting license for dust bunnies. The world's #1 producer of household appliances cranks out washing machines, stoves, refrigerators, and freezers under the AEG, Electrolux, Eureka, Frigidaire, and Zanussi names. Electrolux is also the world's #1 maker of vacuum cleaners, including the Electrolux and Eureka brands. Electrolux is a presence in the commercial market as well, making products such as foodservice and laundry equipment (Electrolux, Zanussi brands), chainsaws and lawn and garden equipment (Husqvarna and Jonsered brands, which the company plans to spin off), and diamond tools (Dimas and Diamant Boart brands). Electrolux's products are sold in more than 150 countries.

Household appliances account for more than 75% of Electrolux's sales.

In the US 60% of sales are generated through major retail chains; Sears is the largest retailer of Electrolux products, followed by Lowe's, Best Buy, and Home Depot.

Citing production costs, Electrolux will close its Swedish factory in early 2005, moving manufacturing to Hungary. Additional plant closures include its cooker factory in France and facilities in Michigan and Texas. The company announced in 2005 that it would relocate many of its North American and European plants to Asia, Mexico, and Eastern Europe; the company also announced the divestment of its Indian operations. It is also terminating its partnership with Toshiba by 2006 in order to cut down on the number of product lines it is marketing worldwide.

Through Investor AB — which also has stakes in Saab and other multinational companies — the Wallenberg family controls about 26% of Electrolux's voting power.

HISTORY

Swedish salesman Axel Wenner-Gren saw an American-made vacuum cleaner in a Vienna, Austria, store window in 1910 and envisioned selling the cleaners door-to-door, a technique he had learned in the US. Two years later he worked with fledgling Swedish vacuum cleaner makers AB Lux and Elektromekaniska to improve their existing designs. The two companies merged to form AB Electrolux in 1919. When the board of the new company balked at Wenner-Gren's suggestion to mass-produce vacuum cleaners, he guaranteed Electrolux's sales through his own sales company.

In the 1920s the company used the "Every home — an Electrolux home" slogan as Wenner-Gren drove his sales force on and launched new sales companies in Europe and North and South America. He scored a publicity coup by securing the blessing of Pope Pius XI to vacuum the Vatican, gratis, for a year. By the end of the 1920s, Electrolux had purchased most of Wenner-Gren's sales companies (excluding Electrolux US) and had gambled on refrigerator technology and won. By buying vacuum cleaner maker Volta (Sweden, 1934), it gained retail distribution.

Despite the loss of Eastern European subsidiaries during WWII, the company did well until the 1960s, when it backed an unpopular refrigeration technology. Swedish electrical equipment giant ASEA, controlled by Marcus Wallenberg, bought a large stake in Electrolux in 1964, and in 1967 he installed Hans Werthén as chairman. Werthén slashed overhead and sold the company's minority stake in Electrolux US to Consolidated Foods. (The US Electrolux business was taken private in 1987.)

Since 1970 Electrolux has bought more than 300 companies (many of them troubled appliance makers), updated their plants, and gained global component manufacturing efficiencies. Acquisitions included National Union Electric (Eureka vacuum cleaners, US, 1974), Tappan (appliances, US, 1979), Zanussi (appliances, industrial products; Italy; 1984), White Consolidated Industries (appliances, industrial products; US; 1986), and Lehel (refrigerators, Hungary, 1991). By 1996 the company had acquired a 41% interest in Refrigeração Paraná, Brazil's #2 manufacturer of appliances. (Electrolux owned it all by 1998.)

To better focus on its "white goods" (washers, refrigerators, etc.), in 1996 Electrolux began selling noncore businesses. In 1997, under new CEO Michael "Mike the Knife" Treschow, the company launched a restructuring plan involving the closing of about 25 plants and the elimination of more than 12,000 jobs, mostly in Europe. The plan worked: Electrolux's profits more than quadrupled in 1998. Also that year the company launched a joint venture in India with Voltas Limited, forming that country's largest refrigerator manufacturer.

Electrolux acquired the European operations of chainsaw maker McCulloch in 1999. To strengthen its Asian presence, Electrolux teamed up with Toshiba for future collaboration on household appliances. Also that year the company said it would sell its vending machine unit and professional refrigeration business. That year AB Electrolux agreed to buy the major appliance business of E-mail Ltd., Australia's top household appliance maker.

In January 2002 it finalized the sale of its leisure appliance operations — mostly refrigerators for recreational vehicles — to private equity firm EQT Northern Europe. In April 2002 Electrolux CEO Michael Treschow resigned (but remained as a director) and was replaced by board member Hans Sträberg. The firm acquired Diamant Boart International, a world-leading manufacturer and distributor of diamond tools and related equipment, in June 2002.

As part of a restructuring effort to combat the effects of diminishing consumer demand and higher material costs, Electrolux cut nearly 5,000 jobs (about 6% of its workforce) during 2003.

Electrolux relaunched its flagship brand of vacuum cleaners in North America during 2004, having bought the rights from long-unaffiliated vacuum maker Electrolux LLC (now Aerus). Also that year former CEO Michael Treschow reappeared in a leadership position, assuming the role of chairman.

EXECUTIVES

Chairman: Michael Treschow, age 62
Vice Chairman: Peggy Bruzelius, age 56
President, CEO, and Director: Hans Sträberg
CFO: Fredrik Rystedt
Head of Consumer Outdoor Products North America: Robert E. (Bob) Cook
Head of Floor Care Products and Small Appliances: Magnus Yngen
Head of Group Staff Communication and Branding: Lars Göran Johansson
Head of Group Staff Human Resources and Organizational Development: Harry de Vos, age 48
Head of Group Staff Legal Affairs and Secretary: Cecilia Vieweg
Head of Outdoor Products: Bengt Andersson
Head of Pricing Program and Regional Administrative Officer: Lilian Fossum, age 43
Head of Professional Indoor Products: Detlef Münchow
Director, Brand and Marketing, Major Appliances, UK: Andy Mackay
Head of Major Appliances, Europe and Asia Pacific: Johan Bygge
Head of Marketing Services, Outdoor Divison: Rachael Thomson
President, Electrolux Home Products, North America and Latin America: Keith R. McLoughlin
VP, Investor Relations and Financial Information: Åsa Stenqvist
Auditors: PricewaterhouseCoopers AB

LOCATIONS

HQ: AB Electrolux
S:t Göransgatan 143, Stockholm, Sweden
Phone: +46-8-738-6000   **Fax:** +46-8-656-4478
Web: www.electrolux.com

2004 Sales

	$ mil.	% of total
Europe	8,676.1	48
North America	7,103.7	39
Rest of world	2,462.2	13
Total	**18,242**	**100**

PRODUCTS/OPERATIONS

2004 Sales

	$ mil.	% of total
Indoor products		
Europe	6,456.5	35
North America	4,651.9	26
Asia Pacific	1,381.8	7
Latin America	656.2	4
Professional products	973.7	5
Outdoor products		
Consumer products	2,657.8	15
Professional products	1,455.0	8
Other	9.1	—
Total	**18,242**	**100**

Selected Products and Brands

Consumer durables
  Indoor products
    Floorcare products (Electrolux, Eureka, AEG)
    Core A (AEG, Electrolux, Eureka, Frigidaire,
      Simpson, Volta, Westinghouse, Zanussi)
    Outdoor products (Electrolux, Flymo, Husqvarna,
      Partner, McCulloch, Poulan, Pulan Pro, Weed Eater)
Professional products
  Indoor products
    Foodservice equipment (Dito, Electrolux, Molteni,
      Zanussi Professional)
    Laundry equipment (Electrolux)
  Outdoor products
    Chainsaws (Husqvarna, Jonsered)
    Diamond tools (Diamant Boart, Dimas,
      Partner Industrial)
    Lawn and Garden Equipment (Husqvarna, Jonsered)

COMPETITORS

Ali
BISSELL
BSH Bosch und Siemens Hausgeräte
Enodis
Franke
GE Consumer & Industrial
Haier Group
Hobart
Indesit
LG Electronics
Maytag
Miele
Philips Electronics
Royal Appliance
Samsung
SEB
Stihl
Toro
Whirlpool
WinWholesale

HISTORICAL FINANCIALS

Company Type: Public

Income Statement

FYE: December 31

	REVENUE ($ mil.)	NET INCOME ($ mil.)	NET PROFIT MARGIN	EMPLOYEES
12/04	18,242	476	2.6%	72,382
12/03	17,247	664	3.8%	77,140
12/02	15,352	587	3.8%	83,347
12/01	12,956	369	2.8%	85,749
12/00	13,209	473	3.6%	87,128
12/99	14,023	490	3.5%	92,926
12/98	14,503	491	3.4%	99,322
12/97	14,295	45	0.3%	105,950
12/96	15,983	269	1.7%	112,140
12/95	17,312	411	2.4%	112,300
Annual Growth	**0.6%**	**1.7%**	**—**	**(4.8%)**

2004 Year-End Financials

Debt ratio: 16.8%
Return on equity: 12.9%
Cash ($ mil.): 644
Current ratio: 0.75
Long-term debt ($ mil.): 596

Net Income History　　　Pink Sheets: ELUXY

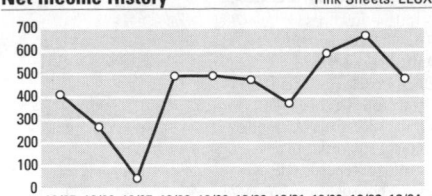

EMI Group

EMI's business is keeping music fans entertained. EMI Group is the #3 major record company (behind Universal Music Group and Sony BMG) in terms of worldwide sales. It distributes CDs, videos, and other music content primarily through its imprints Capitol, EMI Records, and Virgin, which together sport a roster of popular artists such as The Beastie Boys, Norah Jones, Lenny Kravitz, Kylie Minogue, Moby, and Robbie Williams. In addition to recorded music, its EMI Music Publishing division is the world's largest music publishing business, handling the rights to more than a million songs. EMI has operations in more than 50 countries.

While worldwide album sales appear to be recovering after a three-year decline, EMI saw revenue from music sales drop during 2004 in part because of delays in getting new releases to retail. Albums from Coldplay and Gorillaz, two of the company's top artists, that were supposed to be released early in 2005 were held back by creative difficulties in the studio. EMI Music Publishing, meanwhile, has continued to expand with increasing sales coming from synchronization revenue (licensing music for use in movies, television, and advertising) and performance fees. Publishing now accounts for more than 20% of EMI's revenue.

To improve its financial performance, the company is particularly focused on selling more music through digital channels, such as Apple Computer's iTunes and downloadable ringtones licensed to telecommunications carriers. EMI Music Publishing inked a major agreement with Sony BMG in 2004 to jointly develop new digital products and distribution channels. Looking to extend its reach into new international markets, EMI has partnered with Mexico's Grupo Televisa in a 50-50 joint venture label, Televisa EMI Music. However, the real challenge remains for EMI and its labels, particularly Capitol Records and Virgin in the US, to build a more robust stable of artists and generate more hit album releases. To that end, the company brought in former Atlantic Records chief Jason Flom to run Virgin, replacing Matt Serletic.

HISTORY

Electric & Musical Industries (EMI) was established in 1931 as a successor to a 19th-century gramophone producer. It gradually expanded operations to produce everything from radar systems during WWII to the first television system for the BBC. In 1955 the company bought Los Angeles-based Capitol Records (founded in 1942), which featured such artists as Frank Sinatra and Nat "King" Cole. EMI became a major

force in the entertainment industry over the next decades, topping off a string of acquisitions with the purchase of Associated British Picture Corporation in 1969.

EMI suffered through the 1970s with money-losing films and the PR sting of signing the outrageous punk group The Sex Pistols in 1976. (The company canceled its contract with the band in 1978.) The struggling firm was bought by appliance and electronics giant Thorn Electrical Industries (founded by Jules Thorn as the Electrical Lamp Service Company in 1928) for $356 million in 1979. Renamed THORN EMI the next year, the conglomerate lacked strategic focus and continued to suffer losses. Colin Southgate was tapped as CEO in 1985 and streamlined the company's operations to four business sectors. THORN EMI acquired 50% of Chrysalis Records in 1989, and the next year it added Filmtrax music publishing (UK). Also in 1990 the company's HMV stores unit opened its first US superstore in New York City.

In 1992 the company acquired Virgin Records from founder Richard Branson for $960 million. The purchase boosted EMI's US market share and made it one of the world's top music companies. THORN EMI sold its lighting division the next year, and in 1995 it bought UK bookstore business Dillons (later merged with and re-branded Waterstone's).

In 1996 EMI and Thorn split into separately traded companies to maximize the value of its disparate assets; however, share prices plunged when profits failed to materialize. The next year EMI paid $132 million for 50% of Berry Gordy's Jobete companies and its 15,000-song Motown catalog. The Spice Girls, five women brought together by a newspaper ad, became one of Virgin's biggest moneymakers that year.

To focus more on music and less on retail, EMI transferred its HMV and Dillons chains to HMV Media Group, a joint venture with Advent International, in 1998. That year EMI Music head James Fifield resigned with a healthy buyout package after Southgate scotched a succession plan that would have made Fifield CEO. The following year Eric Nicoli, former CEO of United Biscuits, was tapped as Southgate's replacement.

Seeking a bigger presence on the Internet, the company bought an equity stake in music Web site Musicmaker.com in 1999. It also bought music publisher Windswept Pacific for $200 million. The following year the company sold its stake in Musicmaker.com for a hefty profit and later agreed to merge its music operations into a joint venture with Time Warner's Warner Music Group. Its deal with Warner was scrapped, however, to appease European regulators examining the merger of Time Warner and AOL. EMI opened negotiations with Bertelsmann, but the talks broke off in 2001 (again due to pressure from regulators). Also that year, EMI formed online distribution venture MusicNet with Time Warner, BMG, and RealNetworks. (The partners sold their online venture to Baker Capital for about $30 million in 2005.)

EMI's ill-fated five-record contract with pop diva Mariah Carey was a huge embarrassment for the firm. After Carey's first EMI album, *Glitter*, sold a meager 500,000 copies in 2001, the company bought out Carey's deal for $28 million. It subsequently laid off about 20% of its workforce, cut 400 acts from its roster, and took a $340 million charge for the year. Ken Berry, CEO of the EMI Recorded Music division, left the company that year and was replaced by Alain Levy, a former PolyGram executive.

In 2002 the company acquired Mute, a leading European independent record company, for $33.5 million. Also that year it sold off its remaining stake in HMV. EMI turned the tables on an earlier suitor in 2003, making an offer to buy Time Warner's music business. However, the company was outbid by former Vivendi Universal executive Edgar Bronfman, Jr., and Thomas H. Lee Partners.

EXECUTIVES

Chairman: Eric L. Nicoli, age 53, $1,988,296 pay
Deputy Chairman: John Gildersleeve, age 60
CFO and Director: Martin Stewart, age 41
SVP and Financial Controller: Prescott Price
SVP Content Protection: Richard Cottrell
SVP Human Resources: Avery Duff
SVP Industry and Government Affairs: Victoria Bassetti
SVP Information Technology and CIO: James Anderson
VP Legal Affairs: David Widd
VP Marketing: Leonor Villanueva
VP National Sales: Gregg Vickers
VP Operations: Reiner Kirsten
VP Sales: Al Andruchow
Chairman and CEO, EMI Music and Director:
 Alain M. J. I. Levy, age 58, $3,646,123 pay
Chairman and CEO, EMI Music Continental Europe:
 Jean-Francois Cecillon, age 47
Chairman and CEO, EMI Music Publishing and Director: Martin N. Bandier, age 63, $5,668,926 pay
Chairman and CEO, EMI Recorded Music Asia:
 Norman Cheng
Chairman and CEO, Virgin Records America:
 Jason Flom
Vice Chairman, EMI Recorded Music; Chairman and CEO, EMI Recorded Music North America:
 David Munns
Secretary and Group General Counsel:
 Charles P. Ashcroft
Auditors: Ernst & Young LLP

LOCATIONS

HQ: EMI Group plc
 27 Wrights Ln., London W8 5SW, United Kingdom
Phone: +44-20-7795-7000 **Fax:** +44-20-7795-7296
Web: www.emigroup.com

EMI Group has operations in more than 50 countries.

2005 Sales

	$ mil.	% of total
Europe		
UK	575	16
Other countries	1,161	32
North America	1,080	29
Asia Pacific	686	19
Latin America	105	3
Other regions	43	1
Total	**3,650**	**100**

PRODUCTS/OPERATIONS

2005 Sales

	$ mil.	% of total
Recorded music	2,897	79
Music publishing	753	21
Total	**3,650**	**100**

Selected Record Labels

Additive Records
Angel Records (US)
Astralwerks (US)
Back Porch Records (US)
Blue Note Records (US)
Capitol Records Nashville
Capitol Records US
Caroline Records (US)
CCP Records (South Africa)
CyberOctave Music (US)
Delabel (France)
E Sounds (South Africa)
EMI Christian Music Group (US)
EMI Classics
EMI Latin (US)
EMI Music UK
EMI Records
Forefront Records (US)
Heavenly Records
Higher Octave Music (US)
Hostile Records (France)
Manhattan Records (US)
Mute Records
Narada (US)
OmTown Music (US)
Parlophone
Poko Records (Finland)
Positiva Records
Priority Records (US)
Real World
Shakti Records (US)
Sparrow Records (US)
Toshiba-EMI
Virgin Classics
Virgin Records America

COMPETITORS

Sony BMG
Universal Music Group
Warner Music

HISTORICAL FINANCIALS

Company Type: Public

Income Statement

FYE: March 31

	REVENUE ($ mil.)	NET INCOME ($ mil.)	NET PROFIT MARGIN	EMPLOYEES
3/05	3,650	106	2.9%	6,672
3/04	3,872	(131)	—	7,996
3/03	3,424	362	10.6%	8,088
3/02	3,487	(284)	—	9,270
3/01	3,785	137	3.6%	9,996
3/00	3,799	281	7.4%	10,802
3/99	3,829	235	6.1%	10,292
3/98	5,548	383	6.9%	10,452
3/97	6,535	254	3.9%	—
Annual Growth	(7.0%)	(10.4%)	—	(6.2%)

2005 Year-End Financials

Debt ratio: —
Return on equity: —
Cash ($ mil.): 453
Current ratio: 0.81
Long-term debt ($ mil.): 1,958

Net Income History

London: EMI

Enel S.p.A.

Arrivederci, monopolio! Italy's largest electric utility, Enel, has given up its monopoly status and raced into the deregulating power marketplace. Enel distributes electricity to nearly 30 million Italian customers and has some 42,000 MW of primarily fossil-fueled and hydroelectric generating capacity in the country. Enel also owns gas distribution businesses, and it has renewable and international power generation assets. Other operations include information technology, real estate, and engineering and construction services. The Italian government owns about a third of Enel. ENEL sold control of its telecom unit, Wind Telecomunicazioni, in 2005.

Italy's Bersani Decree, passed in 1999, required Enel to divest 25% of its capacity and turn over a portion of its municipal distribution networks to local governments to enhance competition in the country's power market. Enel has completed the required generation asset sales, reducing its capacity by 15,000 MW, and has also reduced its customer count by approximately 1 million through municipal distribution asset sales. It has also transferred management of the national transmission grid to an independent government-owned operator, Gestore della Rete di Trasmissione Nazionale (GRTN).

Italian regulators required Enel divest 80% of its Terna subsidiary, which holds the company's power transmission assets, by 2007. Enel spun off 50% of the unit in an IPO in 2004. The following year it divested another 44%, and the company plans to reduce its holding to about 5% by the end of the year. Grid management and operational functions will also be transferred from GRTN back to Terna.

Enel hasn't just been sipping cappuccino while competitors rush in: The company has moved to become a multi-utility. It has grown to became Italy's second-largest gas distributor (after Italgas) with almost 2 million customers. It also purchased France Telecom's 27% stake in Wind for $1.4 billion in 2003, making the unit a wholly owned subsidiary; Enel had flirted with the idea of taking Wind public but has since sold a majority stake to the Eqypt-based Weather Investments consortium, which has the backing of Orascom Telecom's CEO, Naguib Sawiris.

Internationally, Enel is building and acquiring independent power plants, primarily in Europe and the Americas. The company is also divesting noncore assets, including some real estate holdings and most of its water distribution operations, to focus on its energy operations, and it is also moving back into the nuclear power field.

The Italian government, which floated 32% of the utility in 1999, began the second round of Enel's privatization process in 2003 by selling a 7% stake to Morgan Stanley for more than $2.3 billion. In 2004 the government further reduced its stake by nearly 20% through a public offering of shares. Italy's Ministry of Economy and Finance directly owns approximately 22% of the company, and it owns another 10% indirectly, through the government-controlled bank, Cassa Depositi e Prestiti.

HISTORY

Italy's energy consumption doubled in the 1950s as the country experienced a period of rapid industrialization and urbanization. A tight-knit oligopoly controlled the electric power industry and included Edison, SADE, La Centale, SME, and Finelettrica. The economic boom pushed into the 1960s, and the Italian government created Enel (Ente Nazionale per l'Energia Elettrica) in 1962 to nationalize the power industry. In 1963 Enel began gradually buying some 1,250 electric utilities. About 160 municipal utilities and the larger independents, such as Edison, were left out of the takeover.

The company spent the late 1960s and early 1970s connecting Italy's unwieldy transmission network and building new power plants, including the La Spezia thermoelectric plant (600 MW). Construction costs, coupled with the high prices Enel was required to pay for its takeover targets, caused the utility to become steeped in debt. The Arab oil embargoes of the early 1970s made matters worse, and the Italian government helped Enel with an endowment in 1973.

The energy crisis also prompted Enel to build its first nuclear power plant, Caorso, which came on line in 1980. However, nuclear power was short-lived in Italy: After the 1986 Chernobyl accident, a national referendum forced Enel to de-activate its nukes in 1987. The firm also stepped up its development of renewable energy sources in the 1980s.

Meanwhile, Enel opened its Centro Nazionale de Controllo (CNC) in Rome in 1985 to supervise Italy's power grid. The next year the company turned its first profit.

To begin disassembling Enel's monopoly, the Italian government in 1992 opened the power generation market to outside producers and converted Enel into a joint stock company (with the state holding all of the shares). Following the European Union's 1997 directive to deregulate Europe's power industry, Enel unbundled its utility activities and began trimming its staff. Italy's Bersani Decree (passed in 1999) outlined the restructuring process: Enel was ordered to divest 15,000 MW of its generating capacity, a state-controlled operator was set up to oversee Italy's grid, and large users were allowed to choose their own suppliers.

In response, Enel began to diversify in 1998. It started Wind Telecomunicazioni, a joint venture with France Telecom and Deutsche Telekom. (Deutsche Telekom sold its stake to the other partners in 2000.) Wind began offering fixed-line and mobile telecom services to corporations in 1998 and extended the services to residential users the next year. Enel also began building water infrastructure to serve local distributors and purchased three water operations in southern Italy.

Also in 1999 the government floated 32% of Enel in one of the world's largest IPOs at the time. Enel bought fixed-line telephone company Infostrada from Vodafone in 2001 and sold its 5,400-MW Elettrogen generation unit to Spain's Endesa for $2.3 billion. Enel also put its 7,000-MW Eurogen generation unit on the auction block in 2001. The high bidder, with a $2.6 billion offer, was a consortium backed by Fiat and Électricité de France; the sale was completed in 2002. Also in 2002 Enel purchased Camuzzi Gazometri's gas distribution business (Italy's second-largest) for $870 million from Mill Hill Investments, and it bought Endesa's Viesgo unit (2,400 MW of generating capacity and 500,000 power customers) for about $1.8 billion.

Enel sold its final generation divestment company, Interpower (2,600 MW), to a consortium of utilities (including Belgian utility Electrabel and Italian utility ACEA) for about $880 million in 2003.

EXECUTIVES

Chairman: Piero Gnudi
CEO, General Manager, and Director: Fulvio Conti, age 57
CTO: Francesco Emiliani
Head of Finance Department: Claudio Machetti
Head of Corporate Affairs and Secretary: Claudio Sartorelli, age 59
Head of Accounting: Luciana Tarozzi, age 60
Head of Audit: Antonio Cardani, age 55
Head of Communication: Gianluca Comin, age 42
Head of Generation and Energy Management; Chairman, Enel Produzione S.p.A.: Sandro Fontecedro, age 60
Head of Human Resources: Paolo Ruzzini, age 53
Head of Information and Communication Technology: Alessandro Bufacchi, age 58
Head of International Affairs: Andrea Brentan, age 56
Head of Legal Affairs: Salvatore Cardillo, age 55
Head of Purchasing: Salvatore Sardo, age 52
Head of Regulatory and Institutional Affairs: Massimo Romano, age 45
Head of Sales, Infrastructure, and Networks: Vincenzo Cannatelli, age 52
Head of Telecommunications; CEO, Wind Telecomunicazioni: Tommaso Pompei, age 62
Head of Transmission; CEO and Managing Director, Terna: Sergio Mobili, age 64
Investor Relations Manager: Luca Torchia
Media Relations Manager: Gerardo Orsini
Auditors: KPMG S.p.A.

LOCATIONS

HQ: Enel S.p.A.
    Viale Regina Margherita, 137, 00198 Rome, Italy
Phone: +39-06-8305-1   **Fax:** +39-06-8305-3771
Web: www.enel.it

Enel provides utility services in Italy, has independent power production and distribution operations in other European countries and in the Americas, and has other operations in Africa and Asia.

PRODUCTS/OPERATIONS

2004 Sales

	% of total
Sales, infrastructure & networks	48
Generation & energy management	30
Telecommunications	10
Corporate	3
Transmission	2
Services & other activities	7
Total	**100**

Selected Subsidiaries and Affiliates

Sales, Infrastructure, and Networks
    Electra de Viesgo Distribucion SL (electricity distribution and sale, Spain)
    Enel Distribuzione SpA (electricity distribution)
    Enel Energia SpA (electricity sales)
    Enel Gas SpA (gas sales)
    Enel.si — Servizi Integrati SpA (engineering and energy services)
    Enel Sole Srl (formerly So.l.e. — Società luce elettrica SpA, public lighting)
    Viesgo Energia SL (electricity and gas sales, Spain)

Generation and Energy Management
    Conphoebus SpA (renewable energy-related services)
    Enel Green Power International SA (electricity from renewable resources, Luxembourg)
    Enel Latin America LLC (formerly EGI LLC, renewable electricity generation)
    Enel North America Inc. (formerly CHI Energy, renewable electricity generation, US)
    Enel Produzione SpA (electricity generation)
    Enel Trade SpA (fuel trading and logistics, electricity sales)
    Enel Union Fenosa Renovables SA (80%, renewable electricity generation, Spain)
    Maritza East III Power Holding BV (electricity generation, Bulgaria)
    Viesgo Generaciòn SL (electricity generation and sales, Spain)

Telecommunications
    Wind Telecomunicazioni SpA (fixed-line, mobile, and data services)
National Transmission Network
    T.E.R.N.A. — Trasmissione Elettricità Rete Nazionale SpA (Terna, 50%, transmission assets ownership and maintenance)
Services and Other Activities
    Enel.NewHydro Srl (water distribution)
    Enelpower SpA (power-related engineering and construction)

COMPETITORS

ABB	Hidrocántabrico
ACEA	IBERDROLA
Acque Potabili	International Power
AEM	Italgas
Edison	Risanamento
Electricité de France	RWE
Endesa	SUEZ-TRACTEBEL
Eni	Telecom Italia
E.ON	Unión Fenosa
ERG S.p.A.	Vodafone Omnitel

HISTORICAL FINANCIALS

Company Type: Public

Income Statement

FYE: December 31

	REVENUE ($ mil.)	NET INCOME ($ mil.)	NET PROFIT MARGIN	EMPLOYEES
12/04	49,428	3,666	7.4%	61,898
12/03	39,372	3,154	8.0%	64,770
12/02	31,485	2,109	6.7%	71,204
12/01	25,653	3,767	14.7%	72,660
12/00	24,000	2,000	8.3%	72,647
12/99	21,107	2,362	11.2%	78,511
12/98	22,918	2,598	11.3%	84,938
12/97	21,452	1,889	8.8%	88,957
12/96	23,833	—	—	95,464
12/95	22,225	—	—	—
Annual Growth	9.3%	9.9%	—	(5.3%)

2004 Year-End Financials

Debt ratio: 102.0%	No. of shares (mil.): 1,221
Return on equity: 13.7%	Dividends
Cash ($ mil.): 493	Yield: 8.7%
Current ratio: 0.82	Payout: 144.0%
Long-term debt ($ mil.): 27,418	Market value ($ mil.): 60,352

Stock History

NYSE: EN

12/95	12/96	12/97	12/98	12/99	12/00	12/01	12/02	12/03	12/04

	STOCK PRICE ($) FY Close	P/E High/Low		PER SHARE ($) Earnings	Dividends	Book Value
12/04	49.44	17	11	2.98	4.29	22.02
12/03	34.15	15	11	2.45	2.12	21.90
12/02	25.65	18	13	1.73	1.69	17.99
12/01	27.45	14	9	2.72	1.10	15.41
12/00	38.65	32	25	1.43	1.11	7.01
12/99	41.25	24	22	1.90	0.00	7.30
Annual Growth	3.7%	—	—	9.4%	—	24.7%

Energias de Portugal

If you're from Portugal, you plug into EDP — Energias de Portugal (formerly EDP — Electricidade de Portugal), the state-controlled holding company for utilities that generate, transmit, and distribute electricity. EDP's distribution unit serves more than 5.7 million customers in Portugal. The company also has stakes in Brazilian power distributors that serve another 2.9 million customers, and it owns a controlling stake in Spanish utility Hidrocantábrico. Other EDP operations include telecommunications, information technology, gas distribution, utility metering and billing services, engineering, water and wastewater projects, and real estate management.

EDP has a combined generating capacity of more than 7,900 MW from its domestic hydroelectric, fossil-fueled, and wind-driven plants; the company also has a 30% stake in Portugal's national transmission grid operator, Rede Eléctrica Nacional (REN), a 40% stake in TURBOGÁS Produtora Energética, S.A. (the company behind the construction of gas power station Tapada do Outeiro), and a 27% stake in PORTUGEN Energia, S.A. (which is in charge of operating Tapada do Outeiro).

Branching out across the peninsula, EDP plans to increase its interest in Hidrocantábrico from 40% to 96% by purchasing German utility Energie Baden-Württemberg's 35% stake, as well as Spanish banks Cajastur (17%) and Cáser's (4%) stakes. Capitalizing on its language and cultural connections to Brazil, EDP has also been increasing its Brazilian investments, as well as investing in other Latin American companies.

For diversification at home, EDP has jumped into the telecommunications arena. It owns 56% of Onitelecom (ONI), which provides fixed-line voice and Internet services. The company is also increasing its investments in the Portuguese gas distribution market.

The Portuguese government, which controls 31% of EDP, has been under fire by the European Commission for creating a golden share that allows the state to veto decisions by the utility. The government is reducing its stake in EDP, but it does not plan to sell its entire interest in the company.

HISTORY

EDP — Energias de Portugal has its roots in the several power enterprises that sprouted throughout the country during the infancy of electricity. The first recorded event in Portugal's electrification was the import of six voltaic arc lamps in 1878. The nation's first large-scale project saw the light in 1893 when the city of Braga was illuminated by the Sociedade de Electricidade do Norte de Portugal.

Electricity grew throughout the 1900s in the form of municipal concession contracts for distribution and government-licensed power plants. Large-scale power stations were not in effect in Portugal until after 1947, when Companhia Nacional de Electricidade was formed to interconnect the small generating systems dotting the nation. From the 1950s to mid-1970s, new companies were formed to bring electricity to various parts of Portugal.

The original Electricidade de Portugal was founded in the wake of a leftist revolution during the 1970s in Portugal. In what became known as the Captain's Revolution, military officers overthrew the Portuguese government, which had been a dictatorship since 1933. The new government, dominated by Marxists, nationalized Portugal's industries, including its generation, transmission, and distribution companies, in 1975. The next year the Portuguese government created Electricidade de Portugal to unify the recently nationalized companies.

A new Social Democrat government came to power in 1987 and decided to denationalize Portuguese industry, including EDP. The company reorganized into four major sectors in 1994: production, headed by its CPPE subsidiary, and transmission, distribution, and services, led by its REN subsidiary, which operated the national grid, four regional utilities, and 10 services units. EDP was the holding company.

Seeking opportunities opened up by the privatization of Brazil's state-owned electricity distributor, EDP joined a consortium with Spain's Endesa and Chile's Chilectra to buy 70% of Rio de Janeiro distributor CERJ in 1996. The next year EDP gained a license to help build a hydro plant in Brazil. By 1998 the Endesa-led consortium had gained control of another Brazilian distributor, Coelce.

The Portuguese government floated 30% of EDP in 1997, raising $1.76 billion. In a joint venture with the UK's PowerGen and Germany's Siemens, EDP formed Turbogás to operate a power plant that would produce 20% of Portugal's electricity.

In 1998 EDP forged an alliance with Spain's Iberdrola and bought 80% of Guatemalan utility EEGSA. That year EDP and São Paulo utility CPFL gained control of São Paulo distributor Bandeirante. In 1999 EDP acquired stakes in two other Brazilian distributors. It also joined the UK's Thames Water to develop projects in Portugal, Chile, and Brazil and bought 45% of Chilean water and sewage company Essel. (EDP exchanged its stake in Essel for Thames Water's interest in the Portuguese joint venture in 2002.) The Portuguese state reduced its stake in EDP to about 50% in 1999.

Stepping up its telecommunications activities in 2000, EDP made its telecom unit, Onitelecom (ONI), fully operational and agreed to share a fiber-optic network on the Iberian Peninsula with Spain's Iberdrola. That year the Portuguese government acquired a majority stake in EDP's REN unit. Also in 2000, EDP combined its four power distribution utilities into one unit (EDP Distribuição).

In 2001 EDP and Spanish savings bank Cajastur jointly bid to buy Hidrocantábrico, one of Spain's leading utilities. EDP won control of 20% of Hidrocantábrico, while German utility Energie Baden-Württemberg (EnBW) won control of 60%. The following year, after a fierce bidding war, the two companies agreed that EDP would control the majority share (40%), while EnBW would own only 35%.

The company changed its name from EDP — Electricidade de Portugal to EDP — Energias de Portugal in 2004.

EXECUTIVES

Chairman: Francisco de la Fuente Sánchez, age 63
CEO and Director: João Ramalho Talone, age 53
CFO and Director: Rui M. Horta e Costa, age 44

Head of Business Analysis: Carlos Alves Pereira, age 39
Head of Communication and Image:
Horácio M. Piriquito Casimiro, age 43
Head of Energy Planning: António J. Silva Coutinho, age 36
Head of Environment: António M. Neves de Carvalho, age 55
Head of Financial Management:
Magda Abdool Magid Vakil, age 42
Head of Human Resources:
Eugénio A. Purificação Carvalho, age 51
Head of Information Systems: José A. Abreu Aguiar, age 56
Head of Internal Audit: Vitor M. Silva Leitão, age 51
Head of Investor Relations:
Pedro M. Carreto Pires João, age 35
Head of Legal Affairs and General Secretary:
António P. Alfaia de Carvalho, age 59
Head of Planning and Control, Consolidation, and Tax:
Miguel Ribeiro Ferreira, age 37
Head of Gas Project: José M. Ferrari Bigares Careto, age 42
Head, Information Systems Office:
Luís Pedro Ferraz Flores, age 42
Head of Iberian Articulation:
António Pacheco de Castro, age 46
General Manager and Secretary:
António Manuel Barreto Pita de Abreu, age 55
Auditors: PricewaterhouseCoopers

LOCATIONS

HQ: EDP — Energias de Portugal, S.A.
Praça Marquês de Pombal,
12, 1250-162 Lisbon, Portugal
Phone: +351-21-001-2500   **Fax:** +351-21-002-1403
Web: www.edp.pt

EDP — Energias de Portugal has operations in Brazil, Cape Verde, Guatemala, Macao, Portugal, and Spain.

PRODUCTS/OPERATIONS

Selected Subsidiaries and Affiliates

Bandeirante Energia S.A.
 (96%, electricity distribution, Brazil)
Companhia de Electricidade de Macau, S.A.
 (21%, electricity distribution)
Companhia de Electricidade do Estado do Rio de Janeiro
 (CERJ, 8%, electricity distribution, Brazil)
Edinfor Sistemas Informáticos, S.A.
 (information technology)
EDP Distribuição (electricity distribution)
EDP Produção (electricity generation)
 Companhia Portuguesa de Produção de Electricidade, S.A. (CPPE, electricity generation)
 EDP Energia (electricity marketing and trading)
 Novas Energias, S.A. (ENERNOVA, alternative renewable-energy plants)
Empresa de Electricidade da Guatemala, S.A. (EEGSA, 17%, electricity distribution)
Empresa Energética de Mato Grosso Sul S.A. (Enersul, 36%, electricity distribution, Brazil)
Espirito Santo Centrais Elétricas S.A. (Escelsa, 55%, electricity distribution, Brazil)
Hidroeléctrica Del Cantábrico, S.A. (Hidrocantábrico, 40%, electricity and gas distribution, Spain)
Onitelecom Infocomuniçes (ONI, 56%, telecommunications)
Rede Eléctrica Nacional, S.A. (REN, 30%, national transmission grid operator)

COMPETITORS

AES	E.ON
Cemig	IBERDROLA
Electrabel	Jazztel
Electricité de France	Portugal Telecom
ELETROBRÁS	RWE
Endesa	Unión Fenosa
Enel	Vodafone Portugal

HISTORICAL FINANCIALS

Company Type: Public

Income Statement

FYE: December 31

	REVENUE ($ mil.)	NET INCOME ($ mil.)	NET PROFIT MARGIN	EMPLOYEES
12/04	9,783	596	6.1%	16,057
12/03	8,772	479	5.5%	17,618
12/02	7,419	389	5.2%	12,833
12/01	5,036	402	8.0%	12,071
12/00	3,617	516	14.3%	13,266
12/99	2,956	495	16.7%	13,714
12/98	3,105	539	17.4%	13,932
12/97	3,106	506	16.3%	15,536
12/96	3,525	523	14.8%	16,182
12/95	3,593	442	12.3%	16,449
Annual Growth	11.8%	3.4%	—	(0.3%)

2004 Year-End Financials

Debt ratio: 105.3%
Return on equity: 7.8%
Cash ($ mil.): 377
Current ratio: 0.65
Long-term debt ($ mil.): 9,131

No. of shares (mil.): 366
Dividends
  Yield: 0.0%
  Payout: —
Market value ($ mil.): 11,054

Stock History

NYSE: EDP

12/95 12/96 12/97 12/98 12/99 12/00 12/01 12/02 12/03 12/04

	STOCK PRICE ($) FY Close	P/E High/Low		PER SHARE ($) Earnings	Dividends	Book Value
12/04	30.23	16	13	1.90	0.00	23.72
12/03	26.37	16	9	1.64	0.00	22.20
12/02	16.80	171	112	0.13	1.07	21.27
12/01	21.80	26	16	1.34	0.00	18.11
12/00	33.88	23	15	1.74	0.00	19.45
12/99	34.88	30	17	1.66	0.00	101.54
12/98	44.56	30	21	1.80	0.00	105.35
Annual Growth	(6.3%)	—	—	0.9%	—	(22.0%)

Eni S.p.A.

It's not teeny, it's Eni — and it's huge. One of Italy's largest companies, Eni operates in the oil and natural gas, petrochemicals, and oil field services industries and has expanded into power generation. Its main subsidiaries and affiliates are EniPower (power generation), Italgas (natural gas transmission), Saipem (oil field services), pipeline operator Snam Rete Gas, and Snamprogetti (contracting, engineering). As one of the world's leading oil enterprises, Eni has proved reserves of more than 7.2 billion barrels of oil equivalent, most of it in Italy and in Africa. The Italian government owns about 30% of Eni but is considering selling the holding.

The company's oil and gas holdings and exploration and production efforts extend into more than 30 countries on five continents. Eni has expanded outside its traditional bases of Africa and Italy, with ventures in the Americas, the Asia/Pacific region, Europe, and the Middle East.

In response to the opening up of Italy's energy markets, Eni is increasing its natural gas holdings and adding electricity generating power units. In 2003 Eni acquired Fortum's Norwegian oil and gas business (Fortum Petroleum) for $420 million.

HISTORY

Although the Italian parliament formed Ente Nazionale Idrocarburi (National Hydrocarbon Agency) in 1953, Enrico Mattei is the true father of Eni. In 1945 Mattei, a partisan leader during WWII, was appointed northern commissioner of Agip, a state-owned petroleum company founded in 1926 by Mussolini, and ordered to liquidate the company. Mattei instead ordered the exploration of the Po Valley, where workers found methane gas deposits in 1946.

When Eni was created in 1953, Mattei was named president. His job was to find energy resources for an oil-poor country. He initiated a series of joint ventures with several Middle Eastern and African nations, offering better deals than his large oil company rivals, which he dubbed the Seven Sisters.

Mattei didn't stick to energy: By the time he died in a mysterious plane crash in 1962, Eni had acquired machinery manufacturer Pignone, finance company Sofid, Milan newspaper *Il Giorno,* and textile company Lane Rossi. Eni grew during the 1960s, partly because of a deal made for Soviet crude in 1958 and a joint venture with Esso in 1963. It also expanded its chemical activities.

By the early 1970s losses in Eni's chemical and textile operations, the oil crisis, and the Italian government's dumping of unprofitable companies on Eni hurt its bottom line. Former finance minister Franco Reviglio took over in 1983 and began cutting inefficient operations.

EniChem merged with Montedison, Italy's largest private chemical company, in 1988, but clashes between the public agency and the private company made Montedison sell back its stake in 1990. Eni became a joint stock company in 1992, but the government retained a majority stake.

Franco Bernabe took over Eni following a 1993 bribery scandal and began cutting noncore businesses. The Italian government began selling Eni stock in 1995. In 1996 Eni signed on to develop Libyan gas resources and build a pipeline to Italy. A year later the company merged its Agipa exploration and production subsidiary into its main operations. Eni also took a 35% stake in Italian telecom company Albacom (which has since been sold to British Telecom Group).

The government cut its stake in Eni from 51% to 38% in 1998. That year Vittorio Mincato, a company veteran, succeeded Bernabe as CEO. In 1999 Eni and Russia's RAO Gazprom, the world's largest natural gas production firm, agreed to build a controversial $3 billion natural gas pipeline stretching from Russia to Turkey. Eni agreed to invest $5.5 billion to develop oil and gas reserves in Libya; it also sold interests in Saipem and Nuovo Pignone, as well as some of its Italian service stations.

In 2000 Eni paid about $910 million for a 33% stake in Galp, a Portuguese oil and gas company that also has natural gas utility operations. Also that year Eni bought British-Borneo Oil & Gas in a $1.2 billion deal, and in 2001 it paid $4 billion for UK independent exploration and production company LASMO, topping a bid by US-based Amerada Hess.

The Italian government sold off another 5% of Eni in 2001, reducing its stake to about 30%, and announced that it was considering selling its entire investment. In an effort to reduce noncore holdings, the company sold property management subsidiary Immobiliare Metanopoli to Goldman Sachs. Also that year Eni sold a minority stake in its gas pipeline unit, Snam Rete Gas, to the public.

In 2002 Eni entered discussions to acquire Enterprise Oil, but lost out to a rival bid from Royal Dutch/Shell. Later that year Eni's oil field services unit Saipem gained control of Bouygues Offshore.

EXECUTIVES

Chairman: Roberto Poli, age 67
Managing Director and CEO: Paolo Scaroni, age 59
Group SVP Health, Safety, and Environment: Fabrizio D'Adda, age 63
Group SVP Supply Operations: Vittorio Giacomelli, age 64
Group SVP Legal Affairs: Carlo Grande, age 64
Group SVP Administration: Roberto Jaquinto, age 63
Group SVP Finance and CFO: Marco Mangiagalli, age 56
Group SVP Strategies and International Relations: Leonardo Maugeri, age 41
Group SVP Public Affairs and Communication: Eugenio Palmieri, age 58
Group SVP Human Resources: Renato Roffi, age 58
CTO; Chairman, Snamprogetti: Luigi Patron, age 65
General Manager Exploration and Production Division: Stefano Cao, age 54
General Manager Gas and Power Division: Luciano Sgubini, age 65
General Manager Refining and Marketing Division: Angelo Taraborrelli, age 57
Manager, Corporate Communications: Luciana Santaroni
Corporate Communications: Domenico Negrini
Corporate Communications: Giuseppe Currà
Group SVP Supply Operations: Amedeo Santucci
Auditors: PricewaterhouseCoopers SpA

LOCATIONS

HQ: Eni S.p.A.
  Piazzale Enrico Mattei 1, 00144 Rome, Italy
Phone: +39-06-5982   **Fax:** +39-06-5982-2141
US HQ: 666 Fifth Ave., New York, NY 10103
US Phone: 212-887-0330   **US Fax:** 212-246-0009
Web: www.eni.it

Eni's subsidiaries have operations in more than 70 countries in Africa, Asia, Europe, the Middle East, and North and South America.

2004 Sales

	% of total
Europe	
Italy	47
Other EU countries	23
Other countries	6
The Americas	10
Africa	7
Asia	6
Other regions	1
Total	**100**

PRODUCTS/OPERATIONS

2004 Sales

	% of total
Refining & marketing	36
Gas & power	24
Exploration & production	21
Oil field services & engineering	9
Petrochemicals	7
Corporate & financial	2
Other	1
Total	**100**

Major Subsidiaries and Affiliates

EniPower SpA (power generation)
Italgas SpA (natural gas supply)
Saipem SpA (43%; oil field services)
Snam Rete Gas SpA (50.07%; gas pipeline)
Snamprogetti SpA (contracting and engineering)

COMPETITORS

AEM	ERG S.p.A.
Amerada Hess	Exxon Mobil
Anonima Petroli Italiana	Hellenic Petroleum
Ashland	Koch
BASF AG	Lyondell Chemical
Bayer	Marathon Oil
BG Group	Norsk Hydro
BP	Occidental Petroleum
Chevron	PDVSA
Chiyoda Corp.	PEMEX
ConocoPhillips	PETROBRAS
Dow Chemical	Royal Dutch/Shell Group
DuPont	Sunoco
Edison	TOTAL
E.ON	Unocal

HISTORICAL FINANCIALS

Company Type: Public

Income Statement
FYE: December 31

	REVENUE ($ mil.)	NET INCOME ($ mil.)	NET PROFIT MARGIN	EMPLOYEES
12/04	79,084	9,854	12.5%	71,497
12/03	64,729	7,021	10.8%	76,521
12/02	50,332	4,824	9.6%	80,655
12/01	43,607	6,908	15.8%	70,948
12/00	46,000	5,435	11.8%	69,969
12/99	31,225	2,877	9.2%	72,023
12/98	33,177	2,725	8.2%	78,906
12/97	34,323	2,893	8.4%	75,729
12/96	37,973	2,930	7.7%	83,424
12/95	35,915	2,732	7.6%	86,422
Annual Growth	9.2%	15.3%	—	(2.1%)

2004 Year-End Financials

Debt ratio: 25.3%
Return on equity: 26.4%
Cash ($ mil.): 1,712
Current ratio: 1.09
Long-term debt ($ mil.): 10,395

No. of shares (mil.): 801
Dividends
Yield: 3.6%
Payout: 34.7%
Market value ($ mil.): 100,783

Stock History
NYSE: E

	STOCK PRICE ($) FY Close	P/E High/Low		PER SHARE ($) Earnings	Dividends	Book Value
12/04	125.84	10	7	13.07	4.54	51.31
12/03	94.98	10	7	9.30	3.98	41.92
12/02	78.49	13	10	6.30	3.23	34.46
12/01	61.96	8	6	8.83	1.89	30.61
12/00	64.31	10	7	6.80	1.61	13.18
12/99	55.13	19	15	3.59	1.59	11.58
12/98	67.75	22	15	3.41	1.57	11.82
12/97	57.06	18	13	3.62	1.42	10.48
12/96	51.63	15	9	3.66	1.36	10.42
12/95	34.25	10	9	3.41	0.00	9.09
Annual Growth	15.6%	—	—	16.1%	—	21.2%

E.ON AG

E.ON is on track to transform itself from a conglomerate into a multi-utility. Subsidiary E.ON Energie is one of Germany's top two power companies (running neck and neck with RWE), with some 21 million electricity, natural gas, and water customers in the country; the unit also has 35,000 MW of electric generating capacity and serves energy customers throughout continental Europe. Other utility subsidiaries include E.ON UK, US-based LG&E Energy, and E.ON Nordic. The company has completed its controversial acquisition of Ruhrgas (now E.ON Ruhrgas), Germany's #1 natural gas supplier.

The company is selling noncore operations to focus on its utility businesses. To raise cash for acquisitions (such as its $830 million purchase of Caledonia Oil and Gas), and to comply with US regulations on ownership of utilities, E.ON has sold off some high-profile businesses. It has sold its Veba Oel subsidiary, which explores for and produces oil and gas and operates the Aral service station chain (Germany's largest), to UK-based BP. The company has also sold its stakes in aluminum manufacturer VAW, metals distributor Klöckner, silicon wafer manufacturer MEMC, and logistics provider Stinnes. E.ON has sold its majority stake in chemical maker Degussa (and plans to further decrease its interest in the firm). In addition, the company has completed the sale of its 16% stake in Bouygues Telecom to Bouygues S.A.

E.ON was formed in 2000 from the merger of Germany's VEBA and VIAG conglomerates.

HISTORY

VEBA (originally Vereinigte Elektrizitats-und Bergwerks AG) was formed in 1929 in Berlin to consolidate Germany's state-owned electricity and mining interests. These operations included PreussenElektra, an electric utility formed by the German government in 1927; Hibernia, a coal mining firm founded in 1873; and Preussag, a mining and smelting company founded in 1923.

In the 1930s VEBA produced synthetic gasoline (essential to the German war machine) from coal at its Hibernia plant. In 1938 the company and chemical cartel I. G. Farben set up Chemische Werke Hüls to make synthetic rubber. After WWII, VEBA's assets in western Germany were transferred to the government, and several executives were arrested. Preussag was spun off in 1959.

In 1965 the government spun off VEBA to the public. That year the company entered trading and transportation by buying Stinnes, one of West Germany's largest industrial companies. In 1969 VEBA transferred its coal mining interests to Ruhrkohle and a few years later moved into oil exploration and development. The company shortened its name to VEBA in 1970.

The West German government sold its remaining stake in VEBA in 1987. In a changed regulatory environment, large investors were able to accumulate big portions of stock, and their dissatisfaction with the company's lackluster results made it a takeover target. In response, new chairman Ulrich Hartmann began cutting noncore businesses and reducing staff.

In 1990 VEBA began accumulating mobile communications, networking, and cable TV companies. It allied with the UK's Cable and Wireless (C&W) in 1995 to develop a European mobile phone business, but in 1997 C&W sold its interest to VEBA (as part of the deal, VEBA gained a 10% stake in C&W, which it sold in 1999). In anticipation of the 1998 deregulation of the German telecom market, VEBA and RWE merged their German telecom businesses in 1997.

VEBA acquired a 36% stake in Degussa, a specialty chemicals company, in 1997; two years later Degussa merged with Hüls to form a separately traded chemical company called Degussa-Hüls, in which VEBA took a 62% stake. VEBA sold a 30% stake in Stinnes to the public in 1999. The company's telecom venture sold its fixed-line telephone business, its cable TV unit, and its stake in mobile phone operator E-Plus.

These moves, however, were just the prelude to a bigger deal: a $14 billion merger agreement between VEBA and fellow German conglomerate VIAG. The partners announced plans to dump noncore businesses and beef up their energy and chemicals holdings. VEBA and VIAG completed their merger in 2000, and the combined company adopted the name E.ON. The companies' utilities businesses were combined into E.ON Energie, and their chemicals units were brought together as Degussa.

To gain regulatory approval to form E.ON, VEBA and VIAG agreed to sell their stakes in German electric utilities Bewag and VEAG and coal producer LAUBAG. E.ON sold its VEAG and LAUBAG interests, along with semiconductor and electronics distribution units, in 2000 and sold Bewag in 2001.

That year E.ON agreed to buy UK electricity generator Powergen (now E.ON UK), and it announced plans to sell off nonutility operations, including Degussa and Veba Oel. Later that year E.ON agreed to swap a 51% stake in Veba Oel for BP's 26% stake in German natural gas supplier Ruhrgas (now E.ON Ruhrgas). E.ON also sold Klöckner to UK steel trader Balli and sold its stake in silicon wafer maker MEMC to buyout firm Texas Pacific Group.

In 2002 E.ON sold its VAW Aluminum unit to Norwegian conglomerate Norsk Hydro in a $2.8 billion deal. Regulators moved to prevent E.ON from acquiring BP's stake in Ruhrgas in 2002, but BP agreed to pay for the Veba Oel stake in cash if necessary, and the swap was completed later that year. E.ON also acquired Vodafone and ThyssenKrupp's stakes in Ruhrgas in 2002, and it sold its remaining stake in Veba Oel to BP.

Also in 2002 E.ON completed its purchase of Powergen for about $8 billion, and it sold its 65% stake in logistics company Stinnes to German railroad operator Deutsche Bahn. In late 2002, E.ON acquired the UK energy supply and generation businesses of TXU Europe in a $2.5 billion deal.

The following year E.ON swapped its majority stake in chemical maker Degussa with coal group RAG for RAG's 18% interest in Ruhrgas. It completed its acquisition of Ruhrgas by purchasing the combined 40% stake held by Royal Dutch/Shell, Exxon Mobil, and TUI (formerly Preussag). It also sold subsidiary Viterra's energy services unit (gas and water meters) to CVC Capital Partners.

EXECUTIVES

Chairman of the Supervisory Board: Ulrich Hartmann, age 67
Honorary Chairman: Klaus Liesen, age 73
Deputy Chairman of the Supervisory Board: Hubertus Schmoldt, age 60
Chairman of the Board of Management and CEO; Chairman, E.ON Energie, E.ON Ruhrgas, E.ON UK, and RAG: Wulf H. Bernotat, age 57

Member of the Board of Management, Finance, Accounting, Taxes, and Information Technology and **CFO:** Erhard Schipporeit, age 56

Member of the Board of Management, Controlling and Corporate Planning, Mergers and Acquisitions, and Legal Affairs; **Chairman, Viterra:** Hans Michael Gaul, age 63

Member of the Board of Management, Downstream Business; **CEO, E.ON Energie:** Johannes Teyssen, age 46

Member of the Board of Management, Upstream Business; **CEO, E.ON Ruhrgas:** Burckhard Bergmann, age 62

Member of the Board of Management, Human Resources, Infrastructure and Services, Procurement, and Organization: Manfred Krüper, age 64

EVP Corporate Communications: Peter Blau
EVP Investor Relations: Kiran Bhojani
EVP: Gert von der Groeben
EVP: Heinrich Montag
EVP: Rolf Pohlig
EVP: Hans Gisbert Ulmke
VP, Investor Relations: Mark C. Lewis
Human Resources: Gabriele Blank
Auditors: PwC Deutsche Revision AG

LOCATIONS

HQ: E.ON AG
E.ON-Platz 1, 40479 Düsseldorf, Germany
Phone: +49-211-4579-0 **Fax:** +49-211-4579-501
US HQ: 220 W. Main St., Louisville, KY 40232
US Phone: 502-627-2000 **US Fax:** 502-627-3609
Web: www.eon.com

2004 Sales

	$ mil.	% of total
Europe		
Germany	40,333	60
Other European Union countries	3,189	5
Other European countries	19,375	29
US	3,145	5
Other countries	473	1
Total	**66,515**	**100**

PRODUCTS/OPERATIONS

2004 Sales

	$ mil.	% of total
Public utility	46,737	70
Gas sales	17,913	27
Product sales	1,628	3
Other	237	—
Total	**66,515**	**100**

Selected Subsidiaries and Affiliates

Degussa AG (43%, chemicals)
E.ON Energie AG (power generation and electric, gas, heat, and water distribution in Central European market)
E.ON Nordic AB (Sydkraft; generation, distribution, and sale of electricity and gas in Northern European market; Sweden)
E.ON Ruhrgas AG (natural gas supply)
E.ON UK (formerly Powergen, electric utility and independent power producer, UK)
LG&E Energy LLC (natural gas and electric utility, US)
RAG Aktiengesellschaft (39%, coal production, energy and technology conglomerate)
Viterra AG (residential real estate development, management, and sales)

COMPETITORS

AGIV	Enel
BASF AG	Eni
Bayer	EVN
Bewag	France Telecom
Deutsche Telekom	Nuon
Dow Chemical	RWE
DuPont	SUEZ
Electricité de France	UES of Russia
EnBW	Unión Fenosa
Endesa	Vattenfall

HISTORICAL FINANCIALS

Company Type: Public

Income Statement

FYE: December 31

	REVENUE ($ mil.)	NET INCOME ($ mil.)	NET PROFIT MARGIN	EMPLOYEES
12/04	66,515	5,878	8.8%	69,710
12/03	58,289	5,842	10.0%	66,549
12/02	38,856	2,912	7.5%	107,856
12/01	70,909	1,846	2.6%	151,953
12/00	77,904	3,352	4.3%	186,788
12/99	53,392	2,693	5.0%	131,602
12/98	50,200	1,404	2.8%	132,337
12/97	46,212	1,570	3.4%	126,734
12/96	47,990	1,583	3.3%	123,727
12/95	50,335	1,470	2.9%	125,158
Annual Growth	**3.1%**	**16.7%**	**—**	**(6.3%)**

2004 Year-End Financials

Debt ratio: 35.6%
Return on equity: 14.2%
Cash ($ mil.): 5,657
Current ratio: 1.90
Long-term debt ($ mil.): 16,202

No. of shares (mil.): 1,979
Dividends
Yield: 2.7%
Payout: 27.4%
Market value ($ mil.): 59,977

Stock History

NYSE: EON

	STOCK PRICE ($) FY Close	P/E High/Low		PER SHARE ($) Earnings	Dividends	Book Value
12/04	30.30	10	7	2.99	0.82	22.97
12/03	21.79	7	4	2.98	0.64	19.00
12/02	13.62	14	9	1.49	0.47	13.73
12/01	17.15	18	12	1.15	0.46	10.55
12/00	20.10	11	7	1.80	0.00	12.29
12/99	16.67	11	7	2.00	0.00	9.61
12/98	19.94	26	17	0.93	0.00	9.14
12/97	22.98	22	16	1.04	0.00	8.29
Annual Growth	**4.0%**	**—**	**—**	**16.3%**	**—**	**15.7%**

Ericsson

Ericsson has a way without wires. The company is the world's leading maker of wireless telecom infrastructure equipment. Network operators and service providers use Ericsson's antennas, transmitters, and other wireless infrastructure gear to build and expand networks. The company's other products include corporate networking gear, cable, defense electronics, and software for mobile messaging and commerce. Ericsson is also a top seller of cell phones through Sony Ericsson, a joint venture with Sony. The company is controlled by two groups, the Wallenberg family and Industrivärden, which wield 38% and 28% of the voting power respectively.

To offset the impact of plummeting sales caused by the depressed global telecom market, Ericsson has undergone an extensive reorganization of its product groups and geographic divisions. The company has expanded its professional services business, which now accounts for more than one quarter of its systems segment sales, to take up some of the slack in equipment sales.

Ericsson, which builds products around all the major wireless standards, continues to focus on upgrading carrier networks to the third generation (3G) primarily in Western Europe, Latin America, and the US. To that end, it has increased shipments of products based on interim GPRS technology (an enhancement of the leading GSM standard) to bridge the gap between existing 2G and emerging 3G networks.

Ericsson has combined its mobile phone handset business with that of consumer product expert Sony into a 50%-owned joint venture called Sony Ericsson Mobile Communications. The pair hopes that the endeavor will help them to gain ground on industry leaders Nokia, Motorola, Samsung, and Siemens for a larger share of the cell phone market. However, the company has begun pulling out of the code division multiple access (CDMA) business after failing to gain substantial ground against Lucent Technologies and Nortel Networks. Ericsson shut down the US headquarters for its CDMA business, located in San Diego, cutting 250 jobs.

The company is expanding its telecom network equipment business through an agreement to acquire assets from troubled Marconi. The deal, valued at about $2.1 billion, boosts Ericsson's ability to compete in an increasingly tough global telecoms marketplace.

HISTORY

Lars Magnus Ericsson opened a telegraph repair shop in Stockholm in 1876, the same year Alexander Graham Bell applied for a US patent on the telephone. Within two years Ericsson was making telephones. His company grew rapidly, supplying equipment first to Swedish phone companies and later to other European companies. In 1885 Ericsson crafted a combination receiver-speaker in one handset.

In 1911 Ericsson and SAT, the Stockholm telephone company, merged under the Ericsson banner. The company adopted its present name in 1926. In 1930 international financier Ivar "The Match King" Kreuger, owner of the Swedish Match Co., won control of Ericsson. His triumph was short-lived. Kreuger committed suicide in 1932 and one of his creditors, Sosthenes Behn's ITT, took over.

ITT in 1960 sold its interest in Ericsson to the top Swedish industrialist family, the Wallenbergs. In 1975 Ericsson introduced its computer-controlled exchange, called AXE. Buoyed by AXE's success, the company unveiled the "office of the future" in the early 1980s, diversifying into computers and office furniture.

However, Ericsson's timing was off: The demand for office automation never materialized and profits plunged. Electrolux chairman Hans Werthen was recruited to split his time between the two companies and rescue Ericsson. The company sold its computer business to Nokia in 1988 and refocused on telephone equipment. It dusted off its aging AXE system for the burgeoning cellular market and quickly won key contracts.

The company and aircraft maker Saab merged their military aviation electronics operations as Ericsson Saab Avionics in 1996. (It was dissolved in 1998.) In 1998 manager Sven-Christer Nilsson was appointed CEO. He reorganized the company and laid off 14,000 workers.

After Ericsson fought bitterly with rival QUALCOMM over wireless standards and patents, the companies settled in 1999, agreeing to push for the standardization of third-generation technology based on QUALCOMM's code-division multiple access technology. As a part of the deal, Ericsson purchased QUALCOMM's infrastructure business. To expand its Internet offerings, Ericsson bought Internet router maker Torrent and Internet telephony company Touchwave.

By mid-1999 Nilsson was pushed out for moving too slowly on restructuring plans and was replaced as CEO by chairman Lars Ramqvist, who put many of the duties on president Kurt Hellström. Hellström immediately set out to simplify the company's managerial and accounting structure, trim its workforce and slow-growth businesses, and push new phone models to market.

The next year Ericsson sold noncore businesses including its private radio systems, power supply, and equipment shelter operations. The company also agreed to develop a standard for secure wireless transactions with Nokia and Motorola and formed a joint venture with Web router maker Juniper to sell routers for mobile Internet applications.

Fierce competition, an industrywide slowdown in handset sales, and manufacturing glitches led Ericsson to outsource the manufacture of its phones to Flextronics and form a joint venture (Sony Ericsson Mobile Communications) with Sony to link the development and marketing of their handsets in 2001. Ericsson also sold its direct enterprise sales and service unit, outsourced IT operations in Europe to EDS, and cut more than 20,000 jobs that year. Hellström became CEO in 2001.

Chairman Ramqvist became honorary chairman in 2002; Electrolux CEO Michael Treschow was named as the acting chairman. Ericsson announced 20,000 more layoffs in 2002. That year the company sold its semiconductor unit to Infineon for about $380 million.

Ericsson sold its optoelectronic components business in early 2003. Hellström retired later that year and Carl-Henric Svanberg, former CEO of Assa Abloy, was appointed as company president and CEO.

EXECUTIVES

Chairman: Michael Treschow, age 62
Deputy Chairman: Arne Mårtensson, age 54
Deputy Chairman: Marcus Wallenberg, age 49
President and CEO: Carl-Henric Svanberg, age 53
EVP, CFO, and Head of Group Function Finance: Karl-Henrik Sundström, age 44
EVP, Group Function Sales and Marketing: Bert Nordberg, age 48
EVP and General Manager, Business Unit Access: Kurt Jofs, age 46
EVP and General Manager, Business Unit Systems: Björn Olsson, age 48
EVP and General Manager, Business Unit Global Services: Hans Vestberg, age 39
SVP, CTO, and General Manager, Research and Development: Håkan Eriksson, age 43
SVP, Group Function Communications: Henry Sténson, age 49
SVP, Group Function Human Resources and Organization: Marita Hellberg, age 49
SVP, Group Function Legal Affairs: Carl Olof Blomqvist, age 53
SVP, Group Function Operational Excellence: Joakim Westh, age 43
SVP, Group Function Strategy and Product Management: Torbjörn Nilsson, age 51
SVP and General Manager, Business Unit CDMA: Mats Granryd, age 42

VP and General Manager, Market Unit North America: Angel Ruiz
VP, Market and External Communications: Pia Gideon
Head of Investor Relations: Gary Pinkham
VP, Communications, Ericsson Inc. (Americas): Kathy Egan
Auditors: PricewaterhouseCoopers AB

LOCATIONS

HQ: Telefonaktiebolaget LM Ericsson
Torshamnsgatan 23, Kista,
SE-164 83 Stockholm, Sweden
Phone: +46-8-719-0000   **Fax:** +46-8-18-40-85
US HQ: 6300 Legacy Dr., Plano, TX 75024
US Phone: 972-583-0000   **US Fax:** 972-669-8860
Web: www.ericsson.com

2004 Sales

	$ mil.	% of total
Western Europe		
Sweden	934	5
Other countries	5,195	26
Eastern Europe, Middle East & Africa	4,979	25
Asia/Pacific		
China	1,859	9
Other countries	2,458	12
North America		
US	2,114	11
Other countries	226	1
Latin America	2,189	11
Total	**19,954**	**100**

PRODUCTS/OPERATIONS

2004 Sales

	$ mil.	% of total
Equipment sales		
Construction-type contracts	8,468	42
Delivery-type contracts	8,311	42
Service sales	2,918	15
Other revenues	257	1
Total	**19,954**	**100**

Selected Operations

Mobile systems
  Antennas
  Complete network service hardware platforms
  Fixed cellular terminals
  Microwave and high-speed electronics
    Circuit board
    Interconnect products
    Passive components
    Semiconductor devices
  Point-to-point and point-to-multipoint microwave systems
  Radio base station controllers
  Routers
  Wireless broadband systems
Services
  Consulting
  Customer management
  Network design, integration, management, and migration
  Product support
  Staff training and education
Fixed systems
  ATM and IP routers
  Circuit switching hardware platforms (AXE)
  IP switching hardware platforms (ANS)
Other
  Defense electronics
    Modular airborne computers
    RADAR systems
    Secure wireless communications systems

Enterprise products
  Business communication and call center software
  Network access routers
  PBX systems (BusinessPhone, MD110, WebSwitch)
  Telephones and terminals
  Wireless LAN systems
Software
  Billing
  Customer management
  Network and transmission management
  Service provisioning

COMPETITORS

ADC Telecommunications	Nortel Networks
Alcatel	Oki Electric
Andrew Corporation	Panasonic Mobile
Ciena	Communications
Cisco Systems	Philips Electronics
Fujitsu	QUALCOMM
Harris Corp.	SAFRAN
Hitachi	Samsung Electronics
Kyocera	SANYO
Lucent	Scientific-Atlanta
Marconi	Siemens
Mitsubishi Electric	Tellabs
Motorola	Toshiba
Nokia	

HISTORICAL FINANCIALS

Company Type: Public

Income Statement

FYE: December 31

	REVENUE ($ mil.)	NET INCOME ($ mil.)	NET PROFIT MARGIN	EMPLOYEES
12/04	19,954	2,876	14.4%	50,534
12/03	16,366	(1,507)	—	51,583
12/02	16,808	(2,192)	—	64,621
12/01	22,117	(2,029)	—	85,000
12/00	29,026	2,230	7.7%	105,129
12/99	25,267	1,423	5.6%	103,290
12/98	22,760	1,609	7.1%	103,667
12/97	21,219	1,511	7.1%	100,774
12/96	18,291	1,033	5.6%	93,949
12/95	14,902	813	5.5%	84,513
Annual Growth	3.3%	15.1%	—	(5.6%)

2004 Year-End Financials

Debt ratio: 25.7%
Return on equity: 28.6%
Cash ($ mil.): 1,845
Current ratio: 2.99
Long-term debt ($ mil.): 3,000
No. of shares (mil.): 1,613
Dividends
  Yield: 0.0%
  Payout: —
Market value ($ mil.): 50,800

Stock History

NASDAQ: ERICY

	STOCK PRICE ($) FY Close	P/E High/Low		PER SHARE ($) Earnings	Dividends	Book Value
12/04	31.49	19	10	1.81	0.00	7.25
12/03	17.70	—	—	(0.96)	0.00	5.21
12/02	6.74	—	—	(1.74)	0.00	5.36
12/01	52.20	—	—	(2.57)	0.50	81.12
12/00	111.88	94	37	2.80	0.60	122.98
12/99	164.22	93	28	1.80	0.60	103.65
12/98	59.84	40	18	2.10	0.00	99.78
12/97	46.64	29	16	2.20	0.00	85.39
12/96	37.74	31	17	1.30	0.30	76.44
12/95	24.38	30	15	1.10	0.20	66.86
Annual Growth	2.9%	—	—	5.7%	—	(21.9%)

Ernst & Young

Accounting may actually be the *second*-oldest profession, and Ernst & Young is one of the oldest practitioners. Ernst & Young is also one of the world's largest accounting firms with some 700 offices in 140 countries, offering auditing and accounting services. The firm also provides legal services and services relating to emerging growth companies, human resources issues, and corporate transactions (mergers and acquisitions, IPOs, and the like). Ernst & Young has one of the world's largest tax practices, serving multinational clients that have to comply with multiple local tax laws.

After spending decades building their consultancies, the big accountancies have all moved toward shedding them, because of internal and regulatory pressures, as well as the perceived conflict of interest in providing auditing and consulting services to the same clients. Ernst & Young was the first to split off its consultancy, selling it in 2000 to what is now Cap Gemini Ernst & Young.

Ernst & Young, which gained an impressive amount of weight in former rival Andersen's diaspora, has also boosted its legal services, assembling some 2,000 lawyers in dozens of countries.

But Ernst & Young has faced Andersen-style trouble of its own. Federal regulators in 2002 sued the firm for its alleged role in the failure of Superior Bank FSB, and threatened civil charges for purported fraud relating to Cendant. In the UK, insurer Equitable Life in 2003 sued the accountancy for professional negligence related to work performed when Ernst & Young was its auditor. More problems followed with clients HealthSouth and America Online; Ernst & Young faces a lawsuit in relation to its work for the former company. Rick Bobrow retired as the firm's global CEO after just a year on the job; the departure was presumed to have been related to the airing of previously unpublicized Ernst & Young financial information during Bobrow's divorce proceedings. In 2004 the firm agreed to sell its Ernst & Young Corporate Finance unit to Giuliani Partners (along with its stake in that firm) as part of former New York City mayor Rudolph Giuliani's bid to launch an investment banking firm.

HISTORY

In 1494 Luca Pacioli's *Summa di Arithmetica* became the first published text on double-entry bookkeeping, but it was almost 400 years before accounting became a profession.

In 1849 Frederick Whinney joined the UK firm of Harding & Pullein. His ledgers were so clear that he was advised to take up accounting, which was a growth field as stock companies proliferated. Whinney became a name partner in 1859 and his sons followed him into the business. The firm became Whinney, Smith & Whinney (WS&W) in 1894.

After WWII, WS&W formed an alliance with Ernst & Ernst (founded in Cleveland in 1903 by brothers Alwin and Theodore Ernst), with each firm operating on the other's behalf across the Atlantic.

Whinney merged with Brown, Fleming & Murray in 1965 to become Whinney Murray. In 1979 Whinney Murray, Turquands Barton Mayhew (also a UK firm), and Ernst & Ernst merged to form Ernst & Whinney.

But Ernst & Whinney wasn't done merging. Ten years later, when it was the fourth-largest accounting firm, it merged with #5 Arthur Young, which had been founded by Scotsman Arthur Young in 1895 in Kansas City. Long known as "old reliable," Arthur Young fell on hard times in the 1980s because its audit relationships with failed S&Ls led to expensive litigation (settled in 1992 for $400 million).

Thus the new firm of Ernst & Young faced a rocky start. In 1990 it fended off rumors of collapse. The next year it slashed payroll, even thinning its partner roster. Exhausted by the S&L wars, in 1994 the firm replaced its pugnacious general counsel, Carl Riggio, with the more cost-conscious Kathryn Oberly.

In the mid-1990s Ernst & Young concentrated on consulting, particularly in software applications, and grew through acquisitions. In 1996 the firm bought Houston-based Wright Killen & Co., a petroleum and petrochemicals consulting firm, to form Ernst & Young Wright Killen. It also entered new alliances that year, including ones with Washington-based ISD/Shaw, which provided banking industry consulting, and India's Tata Consulting.

In 1997 Ernst & Young was sued for a record $4 billion for its alleged failure to effectively handle the 1993 restructuring of the defunct Merry-Go-Round Enterprises retail chain (it settled for $185 million in 1999). On the heels of a merger deal between Coopers & Lybrand and Price Waterhouse, Ernst & Young agreed in 1997 to merge with KPMG International. But Ernst & Young called off the negotiations in 1998, citing the uncertain regulatory process they faced.

In 1999 the firm reached a settlement in lawsuits regarding accounting errors at Informix and Cendant and sold its UK and southern African trust and fiduciary businesses to Royal Bank of Canada (now RBC Financial Group).

In 2000 Ernst & Young became the first of the (then) Big Five firms to sell its consultancy, dealing it to France's Cap Gemini Group for about $11 billion. The following year the UK accountancy watchdog group announced it would investigate Ernst & Young for its handling of the accounts of UK-based The Equitable Life Assurance Society. The insurer was forced to close to new business in 2000 because of massive financial difficulties.

Ernst & Young made headlines and gave competitors plenty to talk about in 2002 when closely held financial records were made public during a divorce case involving executive Rick Bobrow (who in 2003 abruptly retired as global CEO after just a year on the job). The firm in 2002 also formed an alliance with former New York City mayor Rudy Giuliani to help launch a business consultancy and an investment firm bearing the Giuliani name.

EXECUTIVES

Global Chairman and CEO; Chairman for the Americas: James S. (Jim) Turley, age 50
COO: Paul J. Ostling
Global Managing Partner — Quality & Risk Management: Sue Frieden
Global Managing Partner — Client Service and Accounts: Thomas P. (Tom) McGrath
Global CFO and Global Managing Partner — Finance and Infrastructure: Jeffrey H. (Jeff) Dworken
Global Managing Partner — People: Pierre Hurstel
Global Managing Partner — Markets: Mike Cullen
Global Managing Partner — Practice Integration: Jean-Charles Raufast
Deputy Global Managing Partner — Infrastructure; VC of Knowledge & Technology, Ernst & Young LLP: John G. Peetz Jr.

Global Director — Business Risk Services: Thomas Bussa
Vice Chairman — Strategy: Beth A. Brooke
Vice Chairman — Assurance and Advisory Business Services: James A. Hassett
Vice Chairman — Global Financial Services: Robert W. (Bob) Stein
Vice Chairman — Tax: Karl Johansson
Vice Chairman — Technology, Communications and Entertainment: Stephen E. Almassy
Vice Chairman — Law: Patrick Bignon
Vice Chairman — Sales: Patrick J.P. Flochel
Vice Chairman — Corporate Finance: Francis Small

LOCATIONS

HQ: Ernst & Young International
5 Times Square, New York, NY 10036
Phone: 212-773-3000   **Fax:** 212-773-6350
Web: www.eyi.com

Ernst & Young International has approximately 700 offices in 140 countries.

2005 Sales

	$ mil.	% of total
Europe, Middle East & Africa	7,636	45
Americas	7,400	44
Asia/Pacific	1,866	11
Total	**16,902**	**100**

PRODUCTS/OPERATIONS

2005 Sales

	$ mil.	% of total
Assurance & advisory business services	11,131	64
Tax & law services	4,489	26
Transaction advisory services	1,667	9
Other	180	1
Adjustment	(565)	—
Total	**16,902**	**100**

Selected Services

Assurance and Advisory
  Actuarial services
  Audits
  Accounting advisory
  Business risk services
  Internal audit
  Real estate advisory services
  Technology and security risk services

Emerging Growth Companies
  Corporate finance services
  Mergers and acquisitions advisory
  Operational consulting
  Strategic advisory
  Transactions advisory

Human Capital
  Compensation and benefits consulting
  Cost optimization and risk management
  Transaction support services

Law
  Corporate and M&A
  Employment
  Finance
  Information technology services
  Intellectual property
  International trade and anti-trust
  Litigation and arbitration
  Real estate

Tax
  Global tax operations
  Indirect tax
  International tax

Transactions
  Capital management
  Corporate development advisory
  Financial and business modeling
  M&A advisory
  Post-deal advisory
  Strategic finance
  Transaction management
  Valuation

COMPETITORS

Bain & Company
BDO International
Deloitte
Grant Thornton International
IBM
KPMG
PricewaterhouseCoopers

HISTORICAL FINANCIALS

Company Type: Partnership

Income Statement

FYE: June 30

	REVENUE ($ mil.)	NET INCOME ($ mil.)	NET PROFIT MARGIN	EMPLOYEES
6/05	16,902	—	—	106,650
6/04	14,547	—	—	100,601
6/03	13,136	—	—	103,000
6/02	10,124	—	—	87,206
6/01	9,900	—	—	82,000
6/00*	9,500	—	—	88,625
9/99	12,500	—	—	97,800
9/98	10,900	—	—	85,000
9/97	9,100	—	—	79,750
9/96	7,800	—	—	72,000
Annual Growth	9.0%	—	—	4.5%

*Fiscal year change

Revenue History

Espírito Santo

Espírito Santo Financial Group (ESFG) wields its earthly powers via two main entities: Banco Espírito Santo and Companhia de Seguros Tranquilidade, one of Portugal's top insurance firms. Its Banco Internacional de Crédito offers mortgage lending and private banking. Although most of its operations are in Portugal, ESFG has banking, insurance, and financial services interests in other European countries, Africa, Brazil, the Caribbean, and the US, where it owns Espírito Santo Bank of Florida. Entities associated with the founding Espírito Santo family are ESFG's major shareholders.

ESFG's other holdings include stockbroker Espírito Santo Dealer (formerly ESER) and investment bank Banco Espírito Santo de Investimento. ESFG sells the lion's share of Tranquilidade's insurance, pension, and investment products through more than 450 bank offices, which also provide consumer and business banking services.

Willing to do what it takes to stay strong in a unifying European economy, ESFG is growing by adding bank branches and new products. The company has benefited from Portugal's position in the EU (the country has been a major recipient of financial aid) and from the privatization of the country's formerly state-controlled economy.

HISTORY

The Espírito Santo financial empire traces its roots to a bank founded by José Maria de Espírito Santo Silva in Lisbon in 1884. After WWI, Portugal underwent a major banking expansion, and in 1920 the Espírito Santo family established Banco Espírito Santo, which grew rapidly thanks to postwar expansion and speculation.

After José Maria's oldest son, José, fled the bank and the country in scandal, his brother, Ricardo, led the massive growth of both the bank and the family's fortune. During the 1930s the Espírito Santos acquired a major interest in insurance company Tranquilidade, and in 1937 Banco Espírito Santo merged with Banco Comercial de Lisboa (founded 1875) to create Banco Espírito Santo e Comercial de Lisboa.

The family's fortunes were aided by dictator Antonio de Oliveira Salazar, who came to power in 1933. During WWII, Salazar declared Portugal neutral, and the country became a sanctuary for many of Europe's elite, who brought the Espírito Santos business and contacts.

The Espírito Santo empire was fostered by Salazar's postwar protectionist policies. Banco Espírito Santo became one of Portugal's largest banks and Tranquilidade one of its largest insurance companies. The family also acquired large coffee, sugar, and palm-oil plantations in Portugal's colonies Angola and Mozambique. At their peak, the Espírito Santo holdings were valued at $4 billion.

But the family's fortunes turned with political upheaval in Portugal during the 1970s. In 1974 the military overthrew Salazar's successor, Marcelo Caetano. A year later the leftist government nationalized Portugal's major corporations, including Banco Espírito Santo and Tranquilidade.

The family fled to London and pooled their savings to create a new company in Luxembourg, Espírito Santo Financial Holding (ESFH). In the late 1970s they got a banking license in Brazil and later set up a fund management company in Switzerland and banks in Miami and Paris. The family's name attracted business and investors.

The Portuguese government reprivatized financial services organizations in 1986. That year ESFH and France's Crédit Agricole opened Banco Internacional de Crédito in Portugal. After raising money on the Eurobond market, ESFH bought back control of Tranquilidade in 1990. A year later the company and a group of investors, including Crédit Agricole, reacquired control of Banco Espírito Santo.

In 1993 ESFH reduced its interest in Banco Internacional de Crédito to 47% (it regained 100% control in 1997). Since then the company has concentrated on Portugal. In the early 1990s recession rocked the economy — and the company. But in the mid-1990s, despite poor commercial demand, consumer-related services rebounded.

ESFH expanded its commercial banking network in 1995 and 1996. In 1997 the company and Brazil's Monteiro Aranha bought more than 60% of that country's Banco Boavista. The firm also dropped "Holding" in favor of "Group," and the next year ESFG, in a vote of confidence in Brazil, moved to raise its holdings in Banco Boavista.

In 1999, amid a flurry of speculation about Spanish/Portuguese banking mergers, the company agreed to buy a majority interest in Spanish brokerage Benito y Monjardin. The company also moved to bolster its asset management operations by inking a deal to buy Portugal-based fund manager Gescapital.

In 2000 ESFG bought the majority stake of French credit institution Via Banque from BNP Paribas (it acquired the rest of Via Banque in 2001). The next year ESFG, in conjunction with Portugal Telecom, launched Banco Electrónico de Serviço Total (Banco Best) as a technologically integrated banking, investment, and brokerage service.

EXECUTIVES

Chairman and President:
Ricardo Espírito Santo Silva Salgado, age 61
Vice Chairman:
José Manuel Pinheiro Espírito Santo Silva, age 60
Director: Manuel de Magalhães Villas-Boas, age 60
SVP: José Carlos Cardoso Castella, age 56
SVP: Erich Dähler, age 53
SVP: Jean-Luc Schneider, age 53
Secretary: Teresa de Souza
Auditors: KPMG

LOCATIONS

HQ: Espírito Santo Financial Group, S.A.
231 Val des Bons Malades,
2121 Luxembourg-Kirchberg, Luxembourg
Phone: +352-434-945   **Fax:** +352-434-9454
US HQ: 320 Park Avenue, 29th Fl., New York, NY 10022
US Phone: 212-702-3400   **US Fax:** 212-750-3888
Web: www.esfg.com

Espírito Santo Financial Group has operations in Angola, Brazil, the Cayman Islands, China, France, Ireland, Luxembourg, Macao, Panama, Portugal, Spain, Switzerland, the UK, and the US.

PRODUCTS/OPERATIONS

Selected Subsidiaries

Bancaire Espírito Santo, SA
  (asset management, Switzerland)
Banco Espírito Santo de Investimento SA (Portugal)
Banco Espírito Santo do Oriente SA
  (BES-ORIENTE, Macao)
Banco Espírito Santo SA (BES, Portugal)
Banco Internacional de Crédito, SA (BIC, Portugal)
Cia. de Seguros Tranquilidade SA (insurance, Portugal)
Espírito Santo Activos Financeiros SGPS,SA (holding
  company, Portugal)
Espírito Santo Bank Ltd. (US)
Espírito Santo Dealer

COMPETITORS

Banco Comercial Português
Banco de Comercio e Industria
Banco Portugues do Atlantico
BBVA
BNP
Citigroup
Crédit Agricole
Credit Suisse
Deutsche Bank
Itaúsa
JPMorgan Chase
Merrill Lynch
SCH
Société Générale
UBS
Zurich Financial Services

HISTORICAL FINANCIALS

Company Type: Public

Income Statement

FYE: December 31

	ASSETS ($ mil.)	NET INCOME ($ mil.)	INCOME AS % OF ASSETS	EMPLOYEES
12/04	68,425	71	0.1%	9,745
12/03	59,922	45	0.1%	9,739
12/02	47,882	(47)	—	10,127
12/01	38,102	10	0.0%	10,969
12/00	35,207	100	0.3%	11,000
12/99	32,821	84	0.3%	11,000
12/98	33,169	71	0.2%	1,076
12/97	25,646	51	0.2%	1,083
12/96	24,838	39	0.2%	1,119
12/95	21,827	30	0.1%	1,112
Annual Growth	13.5%	10.0%	—	27.3%

2004 Year-End Financials

Equity as % of assets: 0.3%
Return on assets: 0.1%
Return on equity: 50.7%
Long-term debt ($ mil.): 20,831
No. of shares (mil.): 48

Dividends
Yield: 0.5%
Payout: 8.1%
Market value ($ mil.): 1,252
Sales ($ mil.): 5,452

Stock History

NYSE: ESF

12/95 12/96 12/97 12/98 12/99 12/00 12/01 12/02 12/03 12/04

	STOCK PRICE ($) FY Close	P/E High/Low	PER SHARE ($) Earnings	Dividends	Book Value
12/04	26.14	18 13	1.49	0.12	3.67
12/03	21.46	22 16	0.99	0.00	2.21
12/02	16.74	— —	(1.09)	0.40	0.88
12/01	17.51	86 70	0.22	0.63	1.87
12/00	17.75	9 7	2.28	0.64	3.33
12/99	15.75	11 8	1.86	0.65	9.28
12/98	19.56	18 8	1.53	0.00	10.59
12/97	20.31	14 8	1.57	0.00	8.73
12/96	13.25	11 9	1.25	0.55	12.22
12/95	11.88	14 9	0.98	1.08	12.58
Annual Growth	9.2%	— —	4.8%	(21.7%)	(12.8%)

Fiat S.p.A.

The country that gave us Sophia Loren and Leonardo da Vinci also gave us century-old Fiat and its plethora of auto offerings, which range from compacts and sedans such as the Fiat Seicento to its Alfa Romeo and Ferrari sports cars. Having sold some noncore businesses, Fiat's refined focus is on cars, CNH Global agricultural and construction equipment, and Iveco commercial vehicles. It has sold its interests in publishing and aerospace. Fiat wants to expand its auto business outside Western Europe. The founding Agnelli family owns about 30% of Fiat.

After several wrong turns on the road back to profitability, Fiat is starting to make some progress. The company has sold its entire 5.1% stake in GM to an unnamed investment bank for nearly $1.2 billion in order to obtain much-needed cash (GM took a 20% stake in Fiat Auto in 2000). Fiat then announced it would cut 12,300 jobs (6.9% of its worldwide workforce) over a three-year period and close 12 factories in hopes of being profitable by 2006. Most of the cuts have come at CNH Global, Iveco, and Fiat Auto. The company also sold its Fiat Avio aviation division as well as its publishing operations to raise cash.

A provision of the 2000 deal that gave GM 20% (later reduced to 10%) of Fiat Auto also gave the Italian automaker the option to force GM to buy the remaining 90% as early as 2004 (or as late as 2009). The "put option" was later backed off by Fiat to 2005 (or as late as 2010). GM claimed the put was rendered invalid when Fiat Auto restructured and GM's stake was reduced to 10%. Fiat insisted GM's claim was false. After a month of very private negotiations early in 2005 GM finally agreed to pay Fiat $2 billion to settle the dispute, and thereby avoid having to buy Fiat Auto.

Fiat (Fiat S.p.A. not Fiat Auto) has bought the unprofitable Maserati nameplate back from Ferrari and is combining the operations of Maserati and Alfa Romeo. Maserati has returned to US shores via Fiat's Ferrari stores and Fiat plans to reintroduce the Alfa Romeo brand to the US by 2007.

HISTORY

Ex-cavalry officer Giovanni Agnelli founded Fabbrica Italiana di Automobili Torino (Fiat) in 1899. Between 1903 and 1918 the automaker expanded into trucks, rail cars, aviation, and tractors. Protected by tariffs, Fiat became Italy's dominant auto company.

WWII boosted Fiat's fortunes, but bombs damaged many of its plants. With US support, Fiat rebuilt and survived by exporting and by building plants abroad. As growth in Italy resumed, Fiat began making steel and construction equipment.

After the European Community forced Italy to lower tariffs in 1961, Fiat lost market share, although foreign sales helped offset its woes. Giovanni Agnelli II (the founder's grandson) became chairman in 1966. Fiat then bought high-end Italian carmakers Lancia and Ferrari in 1969.

The company formed Fiat Auto S.p.A. in 1979, bringing together the Fiat, Lancia, Autobianchi, Abarth, and Ferrari lines. The next year Cesare Romiti became managing director and cut 23,000 jobs and broke union influence at Fiat. The company closed its unprofitable US car operations in 1983. Fiat and British Ford combined their truck operations in 1986, and Fiat also bought Alfa Romeo that year.

In 1989 Fiat purchased 49% of luxury carmaker Maserati (it bought the rest in 1993). Fiat and Ford merged their farm and construction equipment divisions in 1991 to form Fiat subsidiary New Holland (renamed CNH Global in 1999). After posting its biggest loss in 1993, Fiat restructured.

Slow car sales in Italy prompted Fiat to temporarily lay off about 74,000 workers in 1996, and chairman Agnelli stepped down. In 1997 Agnelli's successor, Romiti, and financial director Paolo Mattioli were convicted of falsifying records and illegally financing political parties. They were barred from employment at Fiat.

Paolo Fresco, former vice chairman of General Electric, replaced Romiti as head of Fiat in 1998. Challenged with slumping car sales in Italy and South America, the company sold its chemicals and telecom businesses.

Deals abounded in 1999. Fiat's New Holland subsidiary bought agricultural and construction equipment maker Case Corporation for around $4.3 billion and changed its name to CNH Global. Also, Fiat began making light commercial trucks in China with Yuejin Motor. Other deals in 1999 included Fiat's Comau robotics unit's purchase of a 51% stake in France-based Renault Automation.

To expand its auto business outside Europe, Fiat agreed in 2000 to trade a 20% stake in its car unit for a 5.1% stake in GM. That year ALSTOM agreed to buy a 51% stake in Fiat's rail unit (Fiat Ferrovia). Also in 2000 Fiat began selling off the divisions of Magneti Marelli. These included heating and cooling (to Denso of Japan), rearview mirrors (to Ficosa of Spain), and lubricants (to Doughty Hanson & Co. Ltd. of the UK). Fiat agreed to sell Magneti Marelli's shock absorber and suspension systems units to ThyssenKrupp Automotive in 2000. Fiat's bid (with a consortium including Electricite de France) of about $5.5 billion for control of agro-energy group Montedison was accepted in July.

Toward the end of 2001, Fiat announced that it would postpone selling off any more of Magneti Marelli due to the economic downturn. The company added that the deal to sell its shocks and suspensions unit to ThyssenKrupp Automotive would be renegotiated.

As 2002 came to a close, Fiat announced it would lay off as many as 5,600 workers, and it sold its entire stake in GM to an unnamed investment bank for nearly $1.2 billion. Gianni Agnelli, Fiat's honorary chairman and grandson of the company's founder, died at the age of 81 in 2003. Later that year Fiat sold its Fiat Avio aviation unit to The Carlyle Group and Italian defense group Finmeccanica for about $1.8 billion.

Fiat chairman Umberto Agnelli died in late May of 2004, plunging the company into management chaos. When the board named Ferrari and Maserati chairman Luca Cordero di Montezemolo chairman of Fiat instead of Fiat CEO Giuseppe Morchio, Morchio suddenly quit. The company quickly named turnaround specialist Sergio Marchionne as Fiat S.p.A.'s fifth CEO in two years.

Early in 2005, after a messy divorce from General Motors, Fiat replaced the CEO of beleaguered Fiat Auto, Hebert Demel, with Fiat CEO Sergio Marchionne, marking the first time since 1899 that a single person ran both the Fiat holding company and Fiat Auto. Marchionne also became the fourth executive to run Fiat Auto in a little more than three years.

EXECUTIVES

Chairman; Chairman and CEO, Ferrari:
Luca Cordero di Montezemolo, age 58
Vice Chairman: John Philip Elkann, age 29
CEO; CEO, Fiat Auto and Director: Sergio Marchionne, age 53
SVP, Business Development and Strategies:
Ferruccio Luppi, age 55
SVP, Communications: Simone Migliarino, age 57
SVP, Corporate Initiatives: Roberto Pisa, age 43
SVP, Institutional Relations: Ernesto Auci, age 59
SVP, International Relations: G. Frasca
Interim SVP, Human Resources: Mario Mairano, age 54
Corporate Security: Augusto Ambroso
Secretary of the Board: Franzo Grande Stevens
Senior Counsel: Roberto Russo, age 45
Group Purchasing Coordinator; CEO, Fiat Powertrain Technologies: Domenico Bordone, age 59
Chief Audit Executive and Compliance Officer:
Mauro Di Gennaro, age 43
Social Initiatives: Lodovico Passerin d' Entreves

CEO, Elasis S.c.p.A.: Nevio Di Giusto
CEO, Internazionale Holding Fiat: G. Merlani
CEO, Itedi — Italiana Edzioni S.p.A.:
 Antonello Perricone
CEO, Magneti Marelli: Eugenio Razelli, age 55
CEO, Maserati; COO, Alfa Romeo: Karl-Heinz Kalbfell
VP Communications and Institutional Relations, Fiat
 Auto: Roberto Zuccato
Auditors: Deloitte & Touche S.p.A.

LOCATIONS

HQ: Fiat S.p.A.
 250 Via Nizza, 10126 Turin, Italy
Phone: +39-011-006-1111   Fax: +39-011-006-3798
Web: www.fiatgroup.com

2004 Sales

	$ mil.	% of total
Europe		
Italy	22,118	33
Other countries	25,746	39
North America	8,295	13
Mercosur	4,526	7
Other regions	5,455	8
Total	**66,140**	**100**

PRODUCTS/OPERATIONS

2004 Sales

	$ mil.	% of total
Automobiles (Fiat Auto Holdings)	28,828	44
Agricultural &		
construction equipment	13,866	21
Commercial vehicles	12,689	19
Auto components	3,662	5
Ferrari & Maserati	2,127	3
Production systems	1,819	3
Services	1,136	2
Metallurgical products	1,130	2
Publishing & communications	564	1
Other	319	—
Total	**66,140**	**100**

Selected Brand Names

Automobiles
 Alfa Romeo
 Ferrari
 Fiat
 Lancia
 Maserati

Agricultural and Construction Equipment
 Case
 Case IH
 New Holland
 Steyr

Commercial Vehicles
 Iveco (buses, diesel engines, trucks)

Components
 Magneti Marelli

COMPETITORS

AGCO	Mazda
AUDI	Navistar
BMW	Nissan
Caterpillar	Oshkosh Truck
DaimlerChrysler	PACCAR
Deere	Peugeot
FMC	Porsche
Ford	Renault
Halliburton	Saab Automobile
Honda	Suzuki Motor
Ingersoll-Rand	Toyota
Isuzu	Volkswagen
JLG Industries	Volvo
Kia Motors	

HISTORICAL FINANCIALS

Company Type: Public

Income Statement

FYE: December 31

	REVENUE ($ mil.)	NET INCOME ($ mil.)	NET PROFIT MARGIN	EMPLOYEES
12/04	66,140	(2,148)	—	160,549
12/03	63,298	(2,389)	—	162,237
12/02	61,014	(4,147)	—	186,492
12/01	54,661	(397)	—	198,764
12/00	57,679	625	1.1%	223,953
12/99	48,741	356	0.7%	220,000
12/98	56,535	728	1.3%	234,454
12/97	53,480	1,368	2.6%	239,457
12/96	50,993	1,561	3.1%	237,865
12/95	51,382	1,355	2.6%	237,426
Annual Growth	**2.8%**	**—**	**—**	**(4.3%)**

2004 Year-End Financials

Debt ratio: 319.6%
Return on equity: —
Cash ($ mil.): 4,286
Current ratio: 1.44
Long-term debt ($ mil.): 22,072

No. of shares (mil.): 800
Dividends
 Yield: 0.0%
 Payout: —
Market value ($ mil.): 6,355

Stock History

NYSE: FIA

12/95 12/96 12/97 12/98 12/99 12/00 12/01 12/02 12/03 12/04

	STOCK PRICE ($) FY Close	P/E High	P/E Low	PER SHARE ($) Earnings	PER SHARE ($) Dividends	PER SHARE ($) Book Value
12/04	7.94	—	—	(2.19)	0.00	8.63
12/03	7.74	—	—	(3.03)	0.00	10.67
12/02	7.95	—	—	(6.99)	0.42	18.52
12/01	16.00	—	—	(1.08)	0.55	29.52
12/00	24.25	33	19	1.12	0.56	34.15
12/99	30.13	67	44	0.62	0.64	35.29
12/98	35.25	37	19	1.31	0.00	8.29
12/97	29.50	9	6	4.24	0.60	7.88
12/96	27.95	8	6	4.24	0.58	9.19
12/95	28.63	77	54	0.50	0.18	5.54
Annual Growth	**(13.3%)**	**—**	**—**	**—**	**—**	**5.1%**

Formosa Plastics

Formosa Plastics Corporation (FPC) is foremost in its industry. Taiwan's top petrochemical company and among the world's largest producers of polyvinyl chloride (PVC), FPC is a member of industrial giant Formosa Plastics Group. The company makes acrylic fiber and yarn, polyethylene, caustic soda, chlorine, calcium carbonate, and acrylic acid. FPC subsidiaries include Formosa Plastics Corporation, U.S.A., which produces PVC in the US and is involved in chemical manufacturing (products like caustic soda). Joint ventures include Formosa Komatsu Silicon (with Komatsu Electronic Metals), a maker of silicon wafers, and Formosa Asahi Spandex with Asahi Chemical Industry.

The Taiwanese government fears the country's industry might become too dependent on its

business in China and regulates the issue closely. Despite this fact, Formosa Plastics, along with FPG's other units, have developed a thermal plant in China's Fujian province. The company is planning further Chinese investment, including a PVC plant.

Founder and chairman Yung-Ching Wang is one of Taiwan's wealthiest industrialists.

HISTORY

In 1932 Yung-Ching Wang borrowed $200 from his father, a Taiwanese tea merchant, to buy a rice mill near the town of Jiayi. The mill was destroyed by Allied bombs in 1944, but Wang went on to make a fortune in timber and founded Formosa Plastics, a small polyvinyl chloride (PVC) plant, in 1954. He bought the technology from the Japanese, later joking that he didn't even know then what the "P" in PVC stood for.

At first Wang had trouble finding buyers for his PVC resins. In 1958 he set up his own resin processor, Nan Ya Plastics, and later formed Formosa Chemicals & Fibre to make rayon backing for PVC leather (1965). For the next 15 years, the company grew into the Formosa Plastics Group (FPG), an exclusively Taiwanese enterprise.

Between 1980 and 1988 Wang bought 14 US PVC manufacturers, including Imperial Chemical's vinyl chloride monomer plant (1981), Stauffer Chemical's PVC plant (1981), and Manville Corporation's PVC businesses (1983). He started building a Texas PVC plant in 1981 and cut construction costs up to 40% by importing equipment from Taiwan. When the PVC market became saturated in the mid-1980s, Wang diversified, building plants to make semiconductor chemicals.

Wang bought several Texas-based oil and gas properties in 1988, including 218 producing wells, a gas-processing plant, and a pipeline firm. Faced with stricter pollution controls in Taiwan, Wang began building an ethylene plant in Point Comfort, Texas, in 1988.

In 1992 Wang wanted to build an ethylene complex in mainland China, where there were no pollution controls. Taiwan balked at the proposal, suggesting that FPG build at home. Attempting to circumvent a Taiwanese law against direct investment in the mainland, Wang sought Chinese approval through subsidiary Formosa Plastics Corporation, U.S.A. In 1993 Chinese authorities rejected a plan that would require them to finance up to two-thirds of a $7 billion petrochemical complex.

Formosa Plastics bought bankrupt US computer maker Everex Systems in 1993. Meanwhile, the group's focus again turned to mainland China when Nan Ya Plastics made plans in 1994 to build three plants along China's Long River.

The 1995 death of Wang's mother (at age 108) set off a power struggle between family factions. The company won licenses in 1996 to build power plants, which would make FPG Taiwan's first private-sector power supplier and end a 50-year government utility monopoly. That year, in defiance of Taiwan's policy of limiting investment in China, FPG announced it would build a power plant there. Pressure from the Taiwanese government put the project on hold in 1997.

FPG upped its investment in a new Taiwanese petrochemical complex in 1998. It formed ventures with Asahi Chemical to make spandex fiber and with France's Renault to make hybrid (gasoline/electric) cars. Also that year the group admitted to combining mercury-laden waste with cement and sneaking the toxic mixture to Cambodia disguised as 3,000 tons of cement block. FPG apologized after villagers living near the dump became ill.

Undaunted by a history of animosity between the two countries, Formosa Plastics and FPG's other flagship companies in 1999 invested a 60% stake in the production of power plants in the Chinese province of Fujian.

EXECUTIVES

Chairman: Yung-Ching Wang
President: Chih-Tsuen Lee
EVP: Jason Lin
EVP, Formosa Plastics Corporation U.S.A.: C.L. Tseng
SVP, Polyolefin Division: Chi-Hsiung Hsiao
SVP, Research and Development: Jerome C. L. Ko
SVP, Investor Relations: T. J. Huang
VP, Finance Division: Benny Chang
VP, Construction and Engineering Division: Y. C. Chen
VP, Polypropylene Division: Han-Fu Lin
VP, Tairylan Division: Biing-Chin Chen
VP, Chemicals Division: Guo-Horng Wei
VP, Polyolefin Division: Tze-Long Chang
VP, Plastics Division: Uen-Long Yang
VP, Carbide Division: Wen-Song Chang
Assistant VP, Accounting: Dah-Jye Yu

LOCATIONS

HQ: Formosa Plastics Corporation
(Taiwan Shujiao Gongye Gufeng Youxian Gongsi)
201 Tung Hwa North Rd., Taipei, Taiwan
Phone: +886-22-712-2211   **Fax:** +886-22-717-5287
US HQ: 9 Peach Tree Hill Rd.,
Livingston, NJ 07039-5702
US Phone: 201-992-2090   **US Fax:** 201-992-9627
Web: www.fpc.com.tw

Formosa Plastics has manufacturing operations in Asia and the US.

PRODUCTS/OPERATIONS

Selected Products
Acrylic acid
Acrylic staple fiber
Calcium carbide
Calcium carbonate
Carbon fiber
Esters
Flake caustic soda
Hydrochloric acid
Hydrochlorofluorocarbons
Liquid caustic soda
Petrochemical production
Plastic modifiers
Polyvinyl chloride (PVC) resins
Polypropylene
Vinyl chloride monomer

Selected Affiliates and Subsidiaries
Formosa Asahi Spandex Co., Ltd.
Formosa Daikin Advanced Chemicals Co., Ltd.
Formosa Heavy Industries Corp.
Formosa Komatsu Silicon Corporation
Formosa Petrochemical Corp.
Formosa Plastics Corporation, America (US)
Mailiao Harbor Administration Corp.
Mailiao Power Corp.
Yungchia Chemical Industries Corp.

COMPETITORS

BASF AG	Jilin Chemical
Bayer	LG Group
BP	Lucite
Dow Chemical	Lyondell Chemical
DuPont	Norsk Hydro
Eastman Chemical	Occidental Petroleum
Hercules	Sinopec Shanghai
Imperial	Petrochemical
Chemical Industries	Yizheng Chemical

HISTORICAL FINANCIALS
Company Type: Public

Income Statement
FYE: December 31

	REVENUE ($ mil.)	NET INCOME ($ mil.)	NET PROFIT MARGIN	EMPLOYEES
12/04	3,813	—	—	4,711
12/03	2,477	—	—	4,637
12/02	1,879	—	—	4,471
12/01	1,705	—	—	4,591
12/00	1,566	—	—	4,703
12/99	1,310	—	—	4,577
12/98	1,112	—	—	4,274
12/97	1,472	—	—	4,897
12/96	1,598	—	—	3,891
12/95	1,603	—	—	3,585
Annual Growth	**10.1%**	—	—	**3.1%**

Revenue History
Taiwan: FPC

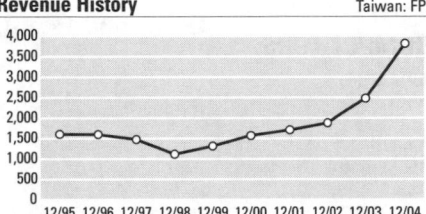

4,000	
3,500	
3,000	
2,500	
2,000	
1,500	
1,000	
500	
0	

12/95 12/96 12/97 12/98 12/99 12/00 12/01 12/02 12/03 12/04

Fortis SA/NV

Fortis earns the "Muscles from Brussels" moniker for its insurance and banking machismo, not for any bad action flicks. The company's operations are focused in banking, insurance, and investment management. The Benelux countries are Fortis' home base and its strength, but the company has operations in other areas, and has aspirations to broaden its brawn further in Europe. Fortis' banking operations include network (retail), commercial, and merchant banking; its insurance products include life, health, and property/casualty lines, as well as employee benefits practices. The company's stock trades through a "twinned share" system — Fortis SA/NV on the Brussels exchange, Fortis N.V. on the Amsterdam exchange.

After 10 years as a joint venture between separately listed Fortis (B) and Fortis (NL), Fortis' parent companies merged their stock listings in 2001 to create the current arrangement. To preserve its binational identity, Fortis operates through a complex holding structure: Fortis SA/NV and Fortis N.V. hold 50/50 stakes in two paper-only entities — Fortis Brussels and Fortis Utrecht — which together form what the company calls the "Fortis Parent Structure." The parent structure, in turn, operates through holding companies Fortis Bank SA/NV and Fortis Insurance N.V. (If you didn't get all of that, don't fret — the same directors and executives govern the various parent and holding entities, and the company calls itself plain old "Fortis.")

Fortis has strengthened its niche operations and solidified its plans to expand its Benelux dominance across other parts of the Continent. The company also has its sights set on further expansion in Asia. In line with its expansion goals, Fortis spent more than $1 billion to acquire Turkey-based Disbank, which it subsequently

renamed Fortis. (The company is in the process of re-branding all its holdings under the Fortis name.) Fortis withdrew a multibillion-dollar bid to purchase NIB Capital, but then paid more than $100 million to acquire Dryden Wealth Management. Subsidiary Fortis UK purchased UK-based insurer OutRight in the second half of 2005.

In 2004, Fortis spun off the majority of its US-based specialty insurer subsidiary Fortis Inc. in an IPO; Fortis retained 35% of the US company, which was renamed Assurant. The following year Fortis announced plans to sell the remainder of its share in Assurant.

Fortis continues to rationalize its overseas operations. In mid-2005 it announced that it would reorganize the sub-Saharan banking operations it has long carried on under the Belgolaise name.

HISTORY

Fortis can trace its roots back to Let op Uw Einde, one of many burial funds set up in the Netherlands in the 19th century. Formed by W. P. Ingenegeren and D. Stolwerk in 1847, the fund allowed impoverished households to prepay funeral expenses and avoid paupers' graves. By 1871 the company had become the country's largest burial fund. More than 10 years later, Let op Uw Einde took advantage of changes in Dutch law to form a life insurance firm, Ultrecht Life, which eventually absorbed the original burial fund.

In the late 19th and early 20th centuries, Ultrecht set up subsidiaries across Europe and became a land developer. It saw investment income shrink during WWI, and the Depression forced it to set aside a reserve that helped it weather WWII. Between the wars, the firm set up holding company N.V. Algemeene Maatschappij tot Exploitatie van Verzekeringsmaatschappijen (AMEV, which became its name in 1968), and afterwards it used its streamlined structure to expand insurance operations primarily at home through purchases in the 1960s and 1970s.

By the late 1970s the Dutch insurance market was saturated, so AMEV focused on expanding in Europe, the US, and Asia. In 1978 it joined with rivals in the UK and West Germany to form the AREA Benefits Network to provide services to multinational corporations in some 40 countries; within 10 years half of AMEV's new business came from this channel. In the 1980s it continued its geographic expansion with such deals as its majority stake in Spain's Bilbao Insurance Group and its purchase of two life insurers and two mutual fund firms from The St. Paul Companies (now St. Paul Travelers) in the US. AMEV, however, was forced to pull out of Australia and New Zealand by poor market conditions and changes in local tax laws. It ended the decade on two high notes: it gradually bought Dutch savings bank Verenigde Spaarbank Groep (VSB) and joined with Belgian life insurer Compagnies Assurances Générales sur la Vie, les Fonds Doutaux et les Survivances (better known as AG 1824) in a 50-50 joint venture to form Fortis.

Windstorms in Europe took their toll on Fortis' first-year results, but the company quickly announced plans to expand its presence in Spain; in 1992 the firm joined with Caja de Ahorros y Pensiones de Barcelona (La Caixa) to form a bancassurance joint venture. The next year, however, the company again took a tumble when its Belgian and Dutch home markets soured, but it fought back by diversifying: Fortis bought half of Algemene Spaar en Lijfrente Kas/Caisse Generale d'apargne et de Retraite (ASLK/CGER), the

Belgian state-owned bank that was being privatized. In 1995 Fortis' parents, which had taken the names Fortis (NL) and Fortis (B), became listed on the London and Luxembourg exchanges.

In 1996 Fortis moved further into its transition from insurer to financial services provider when it bought merchant banking firm MeesPierson from ABN Amro. Two years later the company bought Belgium's Generale de Banque, merging it with its ASLK/CGER, VSB, and MeesPierson operations under the Fortis Bank brand (although MeesPierson kept its name for private banking services). On the insurance side, it bought American Bankers Insurance in the US, Northern Star in the UK, and the Netherlands' ASR Verzekeringsgroep (making it the top Benelux insurer).

In 2000 Fortis' parents began steps to merge their dual structure. The next year Fortis sold Fortis Financial Group, its US life insurance subsidiary, to Hartford Financial. British insurer Aviva (formerly CGNU) bought the company's Australian general insurance subsidiary. Also in 2001, the company merged insurers ASR and AMEV Nederland to create AMEV Stad Rotterdam Verzekeringsgroep.

In 2004 Fortis used an IPO to spin off most of its stake in its US-based specialty insurance provider Fortis Inc., which changed its name to Assurant.

EXECUTIVES

Chairman: Comte Maurice Lippens, age 62, $387,857 pay
Vice Chairman: Jan J. Slechte, age 68, $194,556 pay
CEO: Jean-Paul Votron, age 54
Deputy CEO and COO: Herman Verwilst, age 58
CFO: Gilbert Mittler, age 56
Managing Director, Insurance Belgium: Jozef De Mey, age 62
Managing Director, Insurance International: Peer van Harten, age 43
Managing Director, Insurance Netherlands: Jacques van Ek, age 60
Managing Director, Merchant Banking: Filip Dierckx, age 50
Managing Director, Network Banking: Karel De Boeck, age 56
Managing Director, Retail Banking: Jos Clijsters, age 55
CIO: Alain Deschênes, age 46
CTO: Jean-Pierre Cardinael
Chief Risk Officer: Luc Henrard, age 49
Chief, Institutional Relations and Chairman, Fortis Investments: Joop Feilzer, age 56
General Manager, Communications: Eric Bouwmeester, age 49
General Secretary: Michel van Pée, age 60
Human Resources Director: Michel Deboeck
CEO, Fortis Investments North America: Will Braman
Director, Investor Relations: Robert ter Weijden, age 39
Auditors: PricewaterhouseCoopers Reviseurs d'Entreprises SCCRL

LOCATIONS

HQ: Fortis SA/NV
Rue Royale 20, 1000 Brussels, Belgium
Phone: +32-2-510-52-11   **Fax:** +32-2-510-56-30
US HQ: 1 Chase Manhattan Plaza, New York, NY 10005
US Phone: 212-859-7000   **US Fax:** 212-859-7034
Web: www.fortis.com

Fortis has operations in dozens of countries on six continents.

2004 Sales

	% of total
Benelux countries	
Belgium	40
Netherlands	34
Luxembourg	7
US	3
Other countries	16
Total	**100**

PRODUCTS/OPERATIONS

2004 Sales

	% of total
Interest income	68
Insurance premiums	22
Commissions & fees	3
Results from financial transactions	3
Other	4
Total	**100**

COMPETITORS

ABN AMRO
AEGON
AGF
Allianz
AMP Limited
AXA
Bear Stearns
Citigroup
CSFB
Deutsche Bank
Dexia
Eureko
Generali
Goldman Sachs
ING
Merrill Lynch
Nippon Life Insurance
Rabobank

HISTORICAL FINANCIALS

Company Type: Public

Income Statement

FYE: December 31

	ASSETS ($ mil.)	NET INCOME ($ mil.)	INCOME AS % OF ASSETS	EMPLOYEES
12/04	778,364	4,581	0.6%	49,468
12/03	656,783	2,758	0.4%	54,000
12/02	509,131	557	0.1%	69,000
12/01	427,815	2,302	0.5%	66,210
12/00	412,499	2,606	0.6%	62,881
12/99	408,952	2,332	0.6%	61,109
12/98	394,336	2,084	0.5%	59,481
12/97	166,395	1,002	0.6%	35,229
12/96	177,311	917	0.5%	34,403
12/95	160,064	805	0.5%	30,388
Annual Growth	**19.2%**	**21.3%**	**—**	**5.6%**

2004 Year-End Financials

Equity as % of assets: 2.5%   Long-term debt ($ mil.): 70,851
Return on assets: 0.6%   Sales ($ mil.): 82,819
Return on equity: 24.6%

Net Income History

Euronext Brussels: FOR

Foster's Group

Foster's Group may boast that "Foster's is Australian for beer," but it's wine that now brings in the greater share of revenues. Foster's distributes its beers and wines in about 150 countries. Its Carlton and United Breweries (CUB) division is Australia's #1 brewer, producing beers such as Foster's Lager and Victoria Bitter. Its Foster's Wine States Americas (formerly Beringer Blass Wine Estates) division makes the Mildara Blass wine brands (Wolf Rothbury, Blass, Yellowglen). Beringer Blass also produces the Beringer, Stag's Leap, Meridian, and other wine brands. In 2005 Foster's Group acquired Australian winemaker Southcorp.

In addition to beer, Foster's sells pre-mixed cocktails, bourbon, cider, scotch, and vodka. In the US, the company sells beer through its 50%-owned Foster's USA unit. In 2005 Foster's acquired a total of 91% of its rival premium winemaker Southcorp. It announced a bid to take over all of Southcorp, offering $4.14 per share. Foster's then upped its bid to $4.26 per share (or $2.48 billion) and despite the objections of Southcorp's CEO (who later resigned), the winemaker's board accepted the offer. The merger, which added such brands as Lindemans, Penfolds, and Rosemount wines to Foster's portfolio, created one of the world's biggest global wine companies.

The company has put two of its Australian wineries, acquired during its takeover of Beringer Blass Wine Estates, up for sale: Jamiesons Run and Rothbury Estate.

HISTORY

Upon finding that Australia's only beers were English-styled ales served at room temperature, American emigrants W. M. and R. R. Foster built a lager brewery near Melbourne in 1888 and gave customers ice to chill their Foster's Lager. The brothers began exporting in 1901 when Australians left to serve in the Boer War in South Africa. Carlton and United Breweries Proprietary (CUB) was formed in 1907 when the brothers merged their operations with five other breweries, including Victoria and Carlton.

Over the years CUB acquired stakes in trading company Elder Smith Goldsbrough Mort and Henry Jones (IXL), a diversified food company owned by John Elliott. Faced with a takeover, in 1981 Elder Smith was merged into Henry Jones, forming Elders IXL. CUB became that firm's largest stockholder, with 49%, in 1983. Elders bought the rest of CUB in 1984.

Elders expanded internationally with its purchases of UK's Courage Breweries (1986) and Canada's Carling O'Keefe Breweries (1987). In 1989 Carling O'Keefe and Molson formed a joint venture, Molson Breweries. To fight possible takeover attempts, that year Harlin Holdings (led by Elliott) offered to buy a 17% stake of Elders from two companies, but regulators forced the firm to extend its offer to all shareholders. As a result, Harlin ended up with more than 55% of Elders. The deal saddled Elders with debt, and in 1990 the company began selling its non-brewing assets. Also that year Elliott resigned as chairman and CEO, and Elders changed its name to Foster's Brewing Group.

Foster's purchased the brewing interests of Grand Metropolitan (now Diageo) in 1991. Elliott's investment firm went bankrupt in 1992 and Australian conglomerate Broken Hill Proprietary (BHP), which also owned 19% of Elders, assumed control of its shares. (BHP sold its stake in 1997.) Also in 1992 Molson Breweries chief Ted Kunkel became CEO. He wrote off over $2 billion in non-brewing assets that were still on the books and sold 10% of the brewer's interest in Molson.

In 1995 Foster's sold its UK brewing operations to Scottish & Newcastle. The next year it entered the wine business, buying Mildara Blass and Rothbury Wines, and in 1997 it entered the Australian wine club business with the purchase of Cellarmaster Wines. The next year Foster's bought wine clubs Bourse du Vin International (the Netherlands) and 51% of Germany's Heinrich Maximilian Pallhuber (later acquiring the rest).

Also in 1998 Foster's sold its Canadian brewing interests — 50% of Molson Breweries and 25% of Coors Canada — to The Molson Companies (but retained a 25% interest in Molson USA). In July 1998 Foster's acquired the Austotel Trust hotel chain from Brierly Investments, making it the largest operator of hotels in Australia.

Subsidiary Mildara Blass acquired the US direct wine marketer Windsor Vineyards in 2000; also subsidiary Cellarmaster Wines bought a 25% interest in online wine retailer Wine Planet (increased in mid-2001 to about 90%). Foster's bought Beringer Wine Estates, a leading California winery, for about $1.2 billion. Wine profits for Foster's doubled in the year following the company's 2000 purchase of Beringer.

In 2001 Foster's renamed its wine division Beringer Blass Wine Estates, merging the Beringer and Mildara Blass wine businesses. That year the company dropped "Brewing" from its official name, becoming Foster's Group Limited. In 2002 Beringer Blass Wine Estates agreed to buy the Carmenet brand from Napa-based Chalone Wine Group. In 2002 sales of wine surpassed those of the company's beers for the first time.

Foster's spun off its Australian Leisure and Hospitality group in November 2003, which included pubs, liquor shops, and interests in hotels and real estate development. That division became a separate company known as the Australian Leisure & Hospitality Group Ltd.

In 2004 Foster's said it would expand sales in Russia by distributing through Baltika Breweries, owned by a subsidiary of Carlsberg and Scottish & Newcastle. It also changed the name, Beringer Blass Wine Estates, to Foster's Wine Estates Americas.

EXECUTIVES

Chairman: Frank J. Swan, age 62
CEO and Board Member: Trevor O'Hoy
CFO: Peter F. Scott
SVP, Chief Counsel, and Company Secretary: Martin Hudson, age 59
SVP, Strategy and Business Development, and Managing Director, Wine Clubs and Services: Neville Fielke
SVP, Human Resources: Ben Lawrence
VP, Investor Relations: Chris Knorr
President, North America: Scott A. Weiss
Director, External Communications: Lisa Keenan
Managing Director, Beringer Blass Wine Estates: Jamie Odell
Managing Director, Foster's Australia: John Murphy
Managing Director, Foster's Brewing International: Richard W. Scully
Auditors: PricewaterhouseCoopers

LOCATIONS

HQ: Foster's Group Limited
77 Southbank Blvd.,
Southbank, Victoria 3006, Australia
Phone: +61-3-9633-2000   **Fax:** +61-3-9633-2002
US HQ: 11921 Freedom Dr., Ste. 550, Reston, VA 20190
US Phone: 703-904-4321   **US Fax:** 703-904-4336
Web: www.fostersgroup.com

Foster's Group distributes beer in more than 155 countries and has operations in the Asia Pacific, Europe, the UK, and the US.

PRODUCTS/OPERATIONS

2005 Sales

	% of total
Beer	54
Wine	46
Total	**100**

2005 Sales

	% of total
Carlton & United Beverages	62
Beringer Trade	26
Wine clubs & services	5
Foster's Brewing International	5
Southcorp	2
Total	**100**

Selected Products and Brands

Beer
  Carlton (Cold Filtered Bitter, D-Ale, Diamond Draft, Draught, Lager, Light, Light Bitter, Midstrength, Sterling)
  Carlton and United Premium Dry
  Cascade (Bitter, Diet, Draught, Four Seasons, Lager, Light Bitter, Pale Ale, Premium, Premium Light, Stout, Tiger Head)
  Crown Lager
  Foster's (Extra Lager, Ice, Lager, Light, LightIce, Special Bitter)
  Matilda Bay (Bitter, Draught, Pilsner, Premium)
  Melbourne Bitter
  Powers (Bitter, Gold, Ice, Light)
  Redback (Hefeweitzen, Light, Original)
  Reschs (Dinner Ale, Draught, Pilsner, Real Bitter, Smooth Black Ale)
  sub zero (non-beer alcoholic soda)
  Victoria Bitter

Imported Beer
  Asahi
  Corona Extra
  Guinness
  Harp Lager
  Heineken Lager
  Hoegaarden
  Kilkenny Ale
  Kronenbourg — 1664
  Leffe)
  Miller Genuine Draft
  Mooshead
  Negra Modelo
  Shanghai
  Stella Artois

Wines
  Australian
    Greg Norman Estates
    Southcorp
      Lindemans
      Penfolds
      Rosemount Estate
    Jamiesons Run
    Saltram
    The Rothbury Estate
    Wolf Blass
    Yellowglen
  California
    Beringer
    Chateau St. Jean
    Chateau Souverain
    Etude
    Meridian Vineyards
    Stags' Leap
    St. Clement
  Chilean
    Dallas-Conte, Vina Tarapaca
  Italian
    Catello di Gabbiano
  New Zealand
    Matua Valley

Spirits
  Black Douglas
  Cougar
  Karloff

Selected Affiliates and Subsidiaries

Bourse du Vin International (wine club, Netherlands)
Carlton and United Breweries Limited
Cellarmaster Wines Pty. Ltd. (wine club)
The Continental Spirits Company
Foster's USA (49.9%, beer distribution, US)
Foster's Wine Estates Americas (wine)
Heinrich Maximilian Pallhuber (wine club, Germany)
Southcorp Ltd (wine, Australia)
Wine Planet (Internet wine retailer, US)

COMPETITORS

Accor	Kirin
Allied Domecq	Lion Nathan
Anheuser-Busch	LVMH
Asahi Breweries	Marriott
Asia Pacific Breweries	Molson Coors
Boston Beer	Pabst
Carlsberg	Peerless Importers
Chalone Wine	Premier Pacific
Constellation Brands	Ravenswood Winery
Coors Brewers	SABMiller
Diageo	San Miguel
FEMSA	Scottish & Newcastle
Gallo	Starwood Hotels & Resorts
Gambrinus	Terlato Wine
Geerlings & Wade	Trinchero Family Estates
Heineken	Tsingtao
InBev	V&S
Kendall-Jackson	Wine Group

HISTORICAL FINANCIALS

Company Type: Public

Income Statement

	REVENUE ($ mil.)	NET INCOME ($ mil.)	NET PROFIT MARGIN	EMPLOYEES
6/05	3,025	713	23.6%	10,300
6/04	2,696	551	20.5%	9,300
6/03	3,155	309	9.8%	13,400
6/02	2,576	319	12.4%	12,950
6/01	2,130	239	11.2%	13,700
6/00	2,035	255	12.6%	14,000
6/99	2,066	255	12.3%	12,718
6/98	3,060	253	8.3%	8,207
6/97	1,960	187	9.5%	10,379
6/96	1,850	231	12.5%	10,436
Annual Growth	**5.6%**	**13.3%**	**—**	**(0.1%)**

FYE: June 30

2005 Year-End Financials

Debt ratio: 89.6%   Current ratio: 1.79
Return on equity: 20.5%   Long-term debt ($ mil.): 3,375
Cash ($ mil.): 603

Net Income History

Pink Sheets: FBRWY

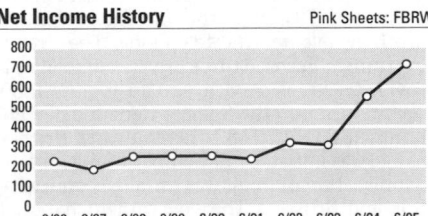

France Telecom

France Telecom hopes it can do for telecommunications services what its countrymen have done for wine: make it the product of choice. The company provides consumer and business fixed-line and wireless voice and data services. Its Orange mobile phone unit has 21 million subscribers in France, another 35 million in other European countries, and more than 63 million subscribers worldwide. France Telecom has nearly 50 million fixed-line customers. It also has acquired the 46% of data network operator Equant it did not yet own; it took full ownership of Orange and Wanadoo, a European directory publisher and ISP, in 2004. The French government has reduced its stake in the company from 56% to about 41%.

France Telecom has brought together its mobile phone operations under the umbrella of its Orange unit, which is France's #1 mobile phone company (Orange is also #2 behind Vodafone in the UK market). The wireless subsidiary also has minority stakes in wireless phone operators throughout Europe and in the Middle East. France Telecom raised about €10 billion in 2001 when it sold a minority stake in Orange to the public but it has bought back what it did not own. Through its Orange unit, France Telecom has agreed to acquire an 80% stake in Spain's Auna, which owns 98% of Spanish mobile carrier Retevisión Móvil, operating as Amena. The deal is valued at €6.4 billion.

To alleviate some of its debt burden, France Telecom cut 28,500 jobs in 2003 and 2004, and has said it will eliminate another 8,000 jobs in 2005. It has sold a stake in its directories business (Pages Jaunes) raising an estimated $2.17 billion, and it has bought out minority shareholders of ISP Wanadoo.

To refocus its attentions on operations in France and the UK, France Telecom has sold its indirect holdings in Telecom Argentina (held through Nortel Inversora) and has agreed to sell its stake in CTE Salvador in separate deals valued at $342 million.

A change in French law that took effect on the first day of 2004 allows the government to decrease its stake in France Telecom to below 50%.

HISTORY

Shortly before he abdicated, King Louis Philippe laid the groundwork for France's state-owned telegraphic service. Established in 1851, the operation became part of the French Post Office in the 1870s, about the time Alexander Graham Bell invented the telephone. The French government licensed three private companies to provide telegraph service, and during the 1880s they merged into the Société Générale de Téléphones (SGT). In 1883 the country's first exchange was initiated in Rheims. Four years later an international circuit was installed connecting Paris and Brussels. The government nationalized SGT in 1889.

By the turn of the century France had more than 60,000 phone lines, and in 1924 a standardized telephone was introduced. Long-distance service improved with underground cabling, and phone exchanges in Paris and other leading cities became automated during the 1930s.

WWII proved a major setback to the French government's telephone operations, Direction Générale des Télécommunications (DGT), because a large part of its equipment was destroyed or damaged. For the next two decades France lagged behind other nations in telephony infrastructure development. An exception to this technological stagnation was Centre National d'Etudes des Télécommunications (CNET), the research laboratory formed in 1944 that eventually became France Telecom's research arm.

In 1962 DGT was a key player in the first intercontinental television broadcast, between the US and France, via a Telstar satellite. The company began to catch up with its peers when it developed a digital phone system in the mid-1970s. In 1974 CNET was instrumental in the launch of France's first experimental communications satellite. In another technological advance, DGT began replacing its paper directories with the innovative Minitel online terminals in 1980.

The French government created France Telecom in 1988. In 1993 France Telecom and Deutsche Telekom (DT) teamed up to form the Global One international telecommunications venture, and Sprint joined the next year. Global One was formally launched in 1996. Also that year France Telecom began providing Internet access, though Minitel still reigned as the country's top online service.

In 1997 the government sold about 20% of France Telecom to the public. With Europe's state telephone monopolies ending in 1998, France Telecom reorganized and brought prices in line with those of its competitors.

In 2001 France Telecom paid $4.3 billion to DT and Sprint to take full ownership of Global One, and it paid $3.6 billion for a 29% stake in Germany's MobilCom (it sold all but 1% of its MobilCom stake in 2005 to Texas Pacific Group). Later in 2000 France Telecom snatched up UK mobile phone operator Orange in a $37.5 billion cash and stock deal after Vodafone was forced to divest the company before merging with Mannesmann.

France Telecom also invested $4.5 billion in UK cable operator NTL and sold its stake in Mexican telecom giant Telmex. In 2001 the company sold its 49.9% stake in Noos, France's #1 cable TV operator, and it made plans to sell its stake in Sprint, which it had acquired when Global One was formed.

To reduce debt, France Telecom sold its Dutch cable unit, Casema, to a group led by US private equity firms Providence Equity Partners and Carlyle Group in a deal valued at €665 million. France Telecom also sold its TDF broadcast unit to a new business controlled by investment funds, retaining a 36% stake in the new entity.

In 2002 the company sold its nearly 11% stake in Greek mobile carrier Vodafone-Panafon to Vodafone Group for €311 million. As it struggled that year to deal with its still burdensome debt, including its stake in troubled MobilCom, CEO Michel Bon resigned. Turnaround specialist Thierry Breton, who was credited with salvaging THOMSON multimedia, became Bon's successor. The company then received a €9 billion loan from the French government and Breton's new management team set out to reduce the nearly €70 billion debt. It announced plans to reduce the number of workers by 22,000, or about 16% of the company's workforce, over three years, and it sold its 5.4% stake in US mobile operator Sprint PCS in a deal valued at $330 million.

EXECUTIVES

Chairman and CEO: Didier Lombard, age 63
SEVP, Financial Rebalancing and Value Creation, and CFO: Michel Combes, age 42
SEVP, Development and Optimization of Human Competencies: Olivier Barberot, age 50
EVP, Enterprise Communication Services; President and CEO, Equant: Barbara Dalibard, age 47
EVP, Home Communication Services; EVP, Groupe Wanadoo SA: Olivier Sichel, age 37
EVP, International Division and TOP Pogram: Jean-Paul Cottet, age 50
EVP, Personal Communication Services; CEO, Orange S.A.: Sanjiv Ahuja, age 48
EVP, Sales and Services France: Michel Davancens, age 57
SVP and Group CTO: Marc Fossier, age 48
SVP, External Communications: Marc Meyer, age 46
SVP, Networks, Carriers, and IT: Jean-Philippe Vanot, age 52
SVP, Sourcing; Chairman, Equant Supervisory Board: Louis-Pierre Wenes, age 56
SVP, Regulatory Affairs: Jacques Champeaux, age 57
SVP, Human Resources: Bernard Bresson, age 55
SVP, Marketing and Branding Coordination; Chairman and CEO, Orange France: Didier Quillot, age 46
SVP, Research and Development: Pascal Viginier, age 47
SVP and General Secretary: Jean-Yves Larrouturou, age 43
Auditors: Ernst & Young Audit; Deloitte & Associés

LOCATIONS

HQ: France Telecom SA
   6, place d'Alleray, 75505 Paris, France
Phone: +33-1-44-44-22-22   **Fax:** +33-1-44-44-95-95
US HQ: 1270 Avenue of the Americas, 28th Fl.,
   New York, NY 10020
US Phone: 212-332-2100   **US Fax:** 212-245-8605
Web: www.francetelecom.fr

France Telecom has investments and operations in more than 75 countries worldwide.

PRODUCTS/OPERATIONS

2004 Sales

	$ mil.	% of total
Fixed-line, distribution, networks, large customers & operators		
Consumer services	14,664	21
Business services	8,379	12
Carrier services	5,586	8
Other services	698	1
Orange	26,535	38
International		
TP Group	5,586	8
Other	2,095	3
Wanadoo	3,491	5
Equant	2,793	4
Adjustments	(5,948)	—
Total	**63,879**	**100**

Company Organization

Operational Divisions
   Enterprise Communication Services (communication services to companies)
   Home Communication Services (residential communication services, especially fixed-line broadband)
   Personal Communication Services (communication services for individuals using mobile devices)
   Sales and Services France (domestic product distribution)
   International (management of international holdings except for subsidiaries of Orange, Wanadoo, and Equant)

Performance Divisions

Networks, Carriers, and IT (management of networks and carriers services and information systems)

Technology and Innovation (R&D)

Sourcing (management of purchasing and operational and investment expenditure)

TOP Program (plan for improved operational performance)

Content Aggregation (management of partnerships with content providers and development of related technology platforms)

Support

COMPETITORS

America Online	Level 3 Communications
AT&T Business	MCI
Belgacom	NCR
Bouygues	O2
BT	SFR Cegetel
Cable & Wireless	Tele2
CANAL+	Telecom Italia
Carrier1	Telefónica
COLT Telecom	Tiscali
CompleTel	T-Mobile International
Deutsche Telekom	T-Online
EDS	UGC Europe
Hewlett-Packard	Unisys
Hutchison Whampoa	Vodafone
IBM Global Services	

HISTORICAL FINANCIALS

Company Type: Public

Income Statement

FYE: December 31

	REVENUE ($ mil.)	NET INCOME ($ mil.)	NET PROFIT MARGIN	EMPLOYEES
12/04	63,879	3,771	5.9%	206,524
12/03	57,983	4,031	7.0%	218,523
12/02	48,892	(21,742)	—	243,573
12/01	38,349	(7,380)	—	206,000
12/00	31,714	3,447	10.9%	188,866
12/99	27,424	2,788	10.2%	174,262
12/98	28,938	2,700	9.3%	165,000
12/97	26,039	2,469	9.5%	159,335
12/96	29,144	406	1.4%	165,200
12/95	30,112	1,873	6.2%	167,660
Annual Growth	8.7%	8.1%	—	2.3%

2004 Year-End Financials

Debt ratio: 229.7%
Return on equity: 20.7%
Cash ($ mil.): 4,339
Current ratio: 0.51
Long-term debt ($ mil.): 48,800

No. of shares (mil.): 2,467
Dividends
Yield: 0.0%
Payout: —
Market value ($ mil.): 81,619

Stock History

NYSE: FTE

	STOCK PRICE ($) FY Close	P/E High/Low	PER SHARE ($) Earnings	Dividends	Book Value
12/04	33.08	22 14	1.52	0.00	8.61
12/03	28.59	14 9	2.01	2.76	6.29
12/02	17.77	— —	(20.04)	0.91	(8.77)
12/01	39.99	— —	(6.69)	0.88	16.29
12/00	85.69	66 25	3.18	0.95	27.06
12/99	133.50	50 25	2.68	0.88	18.58
12/98	78.94	31 13	2.69	1.10	19.47
12/97	36.00	15 13	2.47	0.00	15.57
Annual Growth	(1.2%)	— —	(6.7%)	—	(8.1%)

Fuji Photo Film

Fuji Photo Film enjoys accentuating the negatives. As Japan's #1 photographic film and paper producer, Tokyo-based Fuji leads the film market on its home turf; it has hammered away at rival Eastman Kodak's lead (#1 US), and the two are now virtually tied in the global market. However, Fuji understands the changes wrought by digital technology. The company makes a range of digital imaging products, floppy disks, medical imaging products, office automation systems, and industrial films and chemicals. Fuji has operations in Europe, Australia, Asia, and North and South America, although most of its sales come from Japan. It bought the UK's Sericol in March 2005 from Saratoga Partners for about $230 million.

Like its rival Kodak, Fuji is choosing to invest more in digital technologies and less in traditional film. To meet increasing demand from consumers for digital images, Fuji has adopted what it calls hybrid imaging to combine its expertise in imaging with the latest electronics, such as flat-panel displays and camera-equipped cell phones. In fact, the company has designed lenses for use in cell phones.

In early 2004 Fuji invested $17.5 million in Vitex Systems, a California developer of flexible flat panel display components. Vitex is the commercial spin-off of Battelle Memorial Institute. In October the company consolidated its imaging products operations into a new, wholly owned subsidiary named Fuji Film Imaging. Two other units, Fuji Film Axia and Fuji Color Imaging Service, were consolidated into Fuji Film Imaging as well.

Also in October 2004 Fuji formed a sales subsidiary to handle the recent purchases of firms that have been serving as the company's designated camera and film dealers in Japan. It purchased Asanuma & Co. and Kashimura Co. The acquisitions bring what were dealer wholesale operations into the company, creating a direct sales model.

Fuji acquired a majority of Arch Chemicals' Microelectronic Materials business for about $160 million in late November 2004. The purchase included manufacturing and R&D locations in North America, Asia, and Europe, as well as Arch's 49% share of joint venture company FujifilmArch Co. in Japan.

The company has entered the nucleic acid extraction market with its tabletop DNA/RNA isolation system.

Through a joint venture with Xerox, Fuji generates nearly 40% of its revenues from sales of printers and office copiers.

HISTORY

Mokichi Morita, president of Japan's leading celluloid maker (Dainippon Celluloid Company, founded 1919), decided to start making motion picture film in the early 1930s. Movies were becoming popular in Japan, but there was no domestic film supplier. Working with a grant from the government, Dainippon Celluloid established Fuji Photo Film Co., an independent company, in 1934 in Minami Ashigara Village, near Mount Fuji.

At first the company had trouble gaining acceptance in Japan as a quality film producer. However, German emulsion specialist Dr. Emill Mauerhoff helped Fuji overcome its product deficiencies, producing black-and-white photographic film (1936) and the first Japanese-made color film (1948). In the meantime Fuji added 35mm photographic film, 16mm motion picture film, and X-ray film to its product line. By the early 1940s the company was operating four factories and a research laboratory in Japan. Its first overseas office, opened in Brazil in 1955, was followed by offices in the US (1958) and Europe (1964).

Fuji continued to expand its product line, adding magnetic tape in 1960. Two years later it formed Fuji Xerox, a Japanese joint venture with Xerox, to sell copiers in Japan and the Pacific Rim. It operated as a private-label film supplier in the US and did not market its products under its own brand name until 1972.

International marketing VP Minoru Ohnishi became Fuji's youngest president in 1980 at age 55. To decrease dependence on Japanese film sales, he built sales in the US (agreeing to sponsor the 1984 Los Angeles Olympics, after Eastman Kodak refused to, was key) and pumped money into the production of videotapes, floppy disks, and medical diagnostic equipment. Fuji introduced Fujicolor Quicksnap, the world's first 35mm disposable camera, in 1986. It began establishing manufacturing operations in the US two years later.

The company created the FUJIFILM Microdevices subsidiary to produce image-processing semiconductors in 1990. In 1992 Fuji scientists completed a crude artificial "eye" (a possible forerunner of more efficient eyes for robots). The following year it launched the Pictrostat instant print system, which produces color prints in one minute from photos, slides, and objects.

Fuji was forced to temporarily raise US prices in 1994 after Kodak accused it of illegally dumping its photographic paper exported to the US. But Fuji skirted the problem in 1995 by making the paper at its US plant. That year Kodak asked for economic sanctions against Fuji and the Japanese government, saying that the government encouraged Fuji to use exclusive contracts to control film distribution, thus keeping Kodak from selling film in many stores. (The case was rejected by the World Trade Organization in 1997.)

The firm unveiled the Advanced Photo System (co-developed with Kodak and three other companies) in 1996, combining conventional photography with digital-image processing and printing technology. Also that year Fuji bought six off-site wholesale photofinishing plants from Wal-Mart (the largest US provider of photofinishing services) and won contracts to provide supplies to all of Wal-Mart's in-store one-hour photo labs.

In 1997 it chopped film prices in the US and began making film at its US plant. In 1999 Fuji introduced a high-quality image sensor for digital cameras (Super CCD) and Instax, an instant picture camera. Fuji and Sony launched HiFD, a floppy disk with 140 times the storage capacity of traditional disks, in early 2000. Fuji later announced plans to develop more efficient, low-cost ink jet printers through an alliance with Xerox and Sharp Corp.

In March 2001 Fuji acquired half of Xerox's 50% stake in the companies' Fuji Xerox joint venture. In 2002 the company acquired Japanese film processing company Jusphoto Co. and in 2003 purchased additional shares of Process Shizai Co., renaming it Fujifilm Graphic Systems Co., Ltd.

EXECUTIVES

Chairman: Minoru Ohnishi
President and CEO: Shigetaka Komori
EVP: Kotaro Aso
EVP: Nobuyuki Hayashi
EVP: Akikazu Mikawa
SVP: Hidenobu Fukunaga
SVP: Hisatoyo Kato
SVP: Shigenori Moriuchi
SVP: Keigo Shioya
SVP: Toshio Takahashi
SVP: Takeshi Tanaka
SVP: Yousuke Uchida
SVP; President and CEO, Fuji Photo Film U.S.A.:
 Atsushi (Steve) Yoneda
Chairman, Fuji Photo Film U.S.A.:
 Yasuo (George) Tanaka
Auditors: Ernst & Young

LOCATIONS

HQ: Fuji Photo Film Co., Ltd.
 (Fuji Shashin Film Kabushiki Kaisha)
 26-30, Nishiazabu 2-chome, Minato-ku,
 Tokyo 106-8620, Japan
Phone: +81-3-3406-2111 **Fax:** +81-3-3406-2173
US HQ: 200 Summit Lake Dr., Valhalla, NY 10595
US Phone: 914-789-8100 **US Fax:** 914-789-8295
Web: www.fujifilm.co.jp

2004 Sales

	% of total
Americas	21
Europe	15
Asia	
Japan	52
Other regions	12
Total	**100**

Production Bases

China
 Sanhe
 Shanghai
 Shenzhen
 Suzhou
Europe
 Germany (Kleve)
 Netherlands (Tilburg)
 UK (Hertfordshire)
Japan
 Ashigara
 Ebina
 Fujinomiya
 Odawara
 Taiwa
 Yoshida-Minami
US
 Illinois
 South Carolina

PRODUCTS/OPERATIONS

2004 Sales

	% of total
Document solutions (printers, production systems, etc.)	39
Imaging solutions (cameras, consumer film, etc.)	32
Information solutions (data storage, medical imaging, etc.)	29
Total	**100**

Selected Products

Document Solutions
 Digital color printers
 Digital photo printers
 Photographic papers, equipment, and chemicals
Imaging Solutions
 Electronic imaging systems
  Digital cameras and batteries
  Image scanners
  Photo players
  Photo-video imagers

Magnetic products
 Audio tapes
 Professional videocassettes
 Videocassettes
Motion picture films
Optical products
 Compact cameras
 Instant cameras
 Professional cameras
Photo lab equipment
Photographic films
 Amateur
 Instant
 One-time
 Professional
Information Solutions
 Data storage media
  CD-Rs
  Data storage tape
  DVD-Rs
  Floppy disks
  Magnetic disks
  Zip disks
 Graphic systems
  Chemicals
  Electronic imaging equipment
  Films
  Pre-sensitized plates
 LCD materials
  Cellulose triacetate films
  CV films
  Photosensitive color transfer films
  Wide view films
 Medical imaging products
  Computed radiography systems
  DRI-CHEM analytical systems
  Endoscopes
  Medical X-ray imaging products
 Miscellaneous industrial materials and equipment
  Bio-imaging analyzers
  Industrial chemicals
  Industrial X-ray imaging products
  Lenses and optical equipment
 Office automation systems
  Carbonless copying papers
  Electronic filing systems
  Heat-sensitive papers
  Microfilming systems

COMPETITORS

Agfa	Kyocera
Canon	Mitsubishi Paper Mills
Concord Camera	Nikon
Datapulse Technology	Olympus
Eastman Kodak	Pentax
EFI	Philips Electronics
Hewlett-Packard	Polaroid
Imation	Ricoh
Iomega	Veutron
Konica Minolta	

HISTORICAL FINANCIALS

Company Type: Public

Income Statement

FYE: March 31

	REVENUE ($ mil.)	NET INCOME ($ mil.)	NET PROFIT MARGIN	EMPLOYEES
3/04	24,155	777	3.2%	73,164
3/03	20,881	405	1.9%	72,633
3/02	18,054	612	3.4%	72,569
3/01	11,476	938	8.2%	70,722
3/00	13,658	827	6.1%	37,151
3/99	11,883	591	5.0%	37,551
3/98	10,440	673	6.4%	36,580
3/97	10,098	688	6.8%	33,154
3/96	10,119	680	6.7%	29,903
3/95	5,403	315	5.8%	27,565
Annual Growth	18.1%	10.5%	—	11.5%

2004 Year-End Financials

Debt ratio: 6.7%
Return on equity: 5.1%
Cash ($ mil.): 4,356
Current ratio: 1.98
Long-term debt ($ mil.): 1,102
No. of shares (mil.): 513
Dividends
 Yield: 0.7%
 Payout: 13.9%
Market value ($ mil.): 16,258

Stock History

NASDAQ (SC): FUJIY

	STOCK PRICE ($) FY Close	P/E High/Low		PER SHARE ($) Earnings	Dividends	Book Value
3/04	31.68	23	16	1.51	0.21	32.17
3/03	30.32	42	34	0.79	0.20	27.28
3/02	31.60	37	24	1.19	0.19	24.81
3/01	37.56	24	18	1.83	0.21	25.16
3/00	44.00	30	19	1.61	0.19	28.45
3/99	37.38	38	27	1.15	0.08	23.33
3/98	36.75	33	25	1.31	0.09	21.06
3/97	32.75	26	21	1.34	0.25	21.08
3/96	28.88	25	18	1.23	0.07	11.35
3/95	23.38	41	33	0.59	0.07	13.25
Annual Growth	3.4%	—	—	11.0%	13.0%	10.4%

Fujitsu Limited

Fujitsu Limited's supply of high-tech offerings seems almost limitless. The company provides products ranging from computers and electronic components to air conditioners and barcode scanners to customers worldwide. Fujitsu's computer products include PCs (it competes with NEC for #1 in Japan), servers, storage systems, and peripherals. It also provides consulting, systems integration, and other IT services. Other lines include a wide range of software, telecom transmission equipment, consumer electronics, and semiconductors. Fujitsu also owns one of Japan's top Internet service providers, Nifty.

Fujitsu's software and service operations generate the largest portion of its revenue. In addition to consulting and outsourcing, it provides systems integration, migration, and optimization services. Fujitsu IT Holdings (formerly Amdahl) and Fujitsu Services (formerly ICL) are among the company's key IT services subsidiaries. Fujitsu's software offerings include customer relationship management (CRM), supply chain management (SCM), and enterprise resource planning (ERP) applications.

Fujitsu's computing products range from handheld and notebook PCs to servers and mainframes. Fujitsu and Sun Microsystems have partnered to jointly develop their UNIX-based servers; Fujitsu also offers Linux and Windows-based servers. Fujitsu and Germany's Siemens combined most of their European computer operations to form Fujitsu Siemens Computers. In addition to computers, Fujitsu's hardware products include enterprise and telecom networking equipment, mobile phones, and disk drives. Fujitsu formed an alliance with Cisco late in 2004 to jointly develop networking equipment.

Fujitsu has also pursued a partnership strategy in the electronic components sector, where it has targeted flash memory for devices such as cell phones and digital cameras and system-on-a-chip (SOC) circuits as growth areas. Fujitsu formed a joint venture with AMD called FASL (now Spansion) that manufactures flash memory. Other partners include Lattice Semiconductor and Transmeta. A company formed with Hitachi, Fujitsu Hitachi Plasma Display, develops plasma display panels for televisions, but early in 2005 Fujitsu agreed to sell most of its stake to Hitachi. Fujitsu sold its liquid crystal display (LCD) business, Fujitsu Display Technologies, to Sharp.

HISTORY

Siemens and Furukawa Electric created Fuji Electric in 1923 to produce electrical equipment. Fuji spun off Fujitsu, its communications division, in 1935. Originally a maker of telephone equipment, Fujitsu produced antiaircraft weapons during WWII. After the war it became one of four major suppliers to state-owned monopoly Nippon Telegraph and Telephone (NTT) and continued to benefit from Japan's rapid economic recovery in the 1950s and 1960s.

With encouragement from Japan's Ministry of International Trade and Industry (MITI), Fujitsu developed the country's first commercial computer in 1954. MITI erected trade barriers to protect Japan's new computer industry and in the early 1960s sponsored the production of mainframe computers, directing Fujitsu to develop the central processing unit. The company expanded into semiconductor production and factory automation in the late 1960s. Its factory automation business was spun off as Fujitsu Fanuc in 1972.

Fujitsu gained badly needed technology when it bought 30% of IBM-plug-compatible manufacturer Amdahl in 1972. By 1979 Fujitsu had passed IBM to become Japan's #1 computer manufacturer. In Europe, Fujitsu entered into computer marketing ventures with Siemens (1978) and UK mainframe maker ICL (1981). In the US it teamed with TRW to sell point-of-sale systems (1980), assuming full control of the operation in 1983. Fujitsu released its first supercomputer in 1982.

Fujitsu bought 80% of ICL (from the UK's Standard Telephones & Cables) in 1990 for $1.3 billion. In 1993 it formed a joint venture with Advanced Micro Devices to make flash memory products.

The company doubled its share of Japan's PC market in 1995 to more than 18% and the next year expanded its PC business globally. In 1997 Fujitsu paid about $878 million for the 58% of Amdahl it didn't already own. The next year it bought the 10% of ICL it didn't own. Fujitsu's 1998 earnings suffered from a slump in the semiconductor market, Amdahl-related expenses, and a weak Asian economy.

Also in 1998 Naoyuki Akikusa, son of a former NTT president, became head of Fujitsu. He began trimming some operations while ramping up the company's Internet activities. Fujitsu in 1999 became full owner of online services provider Nifty Serve, making it Japan's largest Internet service provider. It merged Nifty with the operations of another ISP called InfoWeb. Also that year Siemens and Fujitsu combined their European computer operations in a 50-50 joint venture (Fujitsu Siemens Computers) as one part of a larger global alliance. A restructuring of Fujitsu's semiconductor operations caused losses for 1999.

Akikusa's reorganization continued in 2000. Fujitsu overhauled its server business (subsidiary Amdahl ceased production of IBM-compatible mainframes) and accelerated production of flash memory. Responding to a global slump in its markets, in 2001 Fujitsu announced that it would cut more than 16,000 jobs — about 10% of its workforce — to control costs. Soon after, it announced the cutting of an additional 4,500 jobs.

In 2002 Fujitsu moved to outsource its semiconductor test and assembly operations when it agreed to sell its Kyushu Fujitsu Electronics subsidiary to Amkor Technology; the deal was terminated, however, when Amkor and Fujitsu were unable to agree to terms.

EXECUTIVES

Chairman: Naoyuki Akikusa
President: Hiroaki Kurokawa
EVP, Corporate Center: Masamichi Ogura
EVP, Electronic Devices Business: Toshihiko Ono
EVP, Financial Solutions Business Group: Yoshifumi Mita
EVP, Global Business Group and Products Business Operations Group: Kyung-Soo Ahn
EVP, Government & Public Solutions Business Group: Yasuaki Ara
EVP, Industries & Distribution Solutions Business Group: Shinichi Hasegawa
EVP, IT Services Business Group: Yoshihisa Nagano
EVP, Products Business; President, Products Business Operations Group: Chiaki Ito
EVP, Products Business Operations Group: Junichi Murashima
EVP, System Products Business Group: Takashi Nakamura
EVP, Telecom, Utility & Media Industries Business Group: Kazuo Miyata
EVP, Telecom, Utility & Media Industries Business Group: Kazuya Wada
SVP; President, Financial Solutions Business Group: Koichi Hironishi
SVP; President, Global Business Group: Tetsuo Urano
SVP; Group President, Industries and Distribution Solutions Business: Takashi Igarashi
SVP; President, Professional Support Business Group and IT Services Business Unit: Hiromichi Hirata
SVP; President, Regional Business Group: Hirohisa Yabuuchi
SVP; President, Solution Business Support: Michiyoshi Mazuka
SVP; President, System Products Business Group: Yoshiyuki Tanakura
SVP; President, Telecom, Utility, and Media Industries Business Group and Government and Public Solutions Business Group; EVP, System Products Business Group: Hideaki Yumiba
SVP; President, Ubiquitous Products Business Group: Kimihisa Ito
Auditors: Shin Nihon & Co.

LOCATIONS

HQ: Fujitsu Limited
   Shiodome City Center, 1-5-2, Higashi-Shimbashi, Minato-ku, Tokyo 105-7123, Japan
Phone: +81-3-6252-2220   **Fax:** +81-3-6252-2783
US HQ: 1250 E. Arques Ave., Sunnyvale, CA 94085
US Phone: 408-746-6200   **US Fax:** 408-746-6260
Web: www.fujitsu.com

Fujitsu Limited has offices in more than 60 countries.

2005 Sales

	% of total
Japan	70
Europe	13
The Americas	7
Other regions	10
Total	**100**

PRODUCTS/OPERATIONS

2005 Sales

	% of total
Software & Services	44
Platforms	36
Electronic Devices	15
Other	5
Total	**100**

Selected Products

Software and Services
   Services
      Consulting
      Network services
      Outsourcing
      Support and maintenance
      Systems integration
   Software
      Application server
      Database
      ERP systems
      Financial systems
      Groupware
      Internet/intranet
      System/network management
      Translation
Platforms
   ATMs
   Hard disk drives
   IP routers
   Mobile communication base stations
   Mobile phones
   PCs (desktop, handheld, notebook, tablet)
   Point-of-sale (POS) terminals
   Printers
   Servers and mainframes (Linux, UNIX, Windows)
   Storage systems
   Transmission Systems
Electronic Devices
   Plasma display panels
   Semiconductors

COMPETITORS

Alcatel	NEC
Canon	Nokia
Cisco Systems	Nortel Networks
Dell	NTT DATA
EDS	Oki Electric
Epson	Oracle
Ericsson	Philips Electronics
Fujifilm	Ricoh
Hewlett-Packard	Samsung Electronics
Hitachi	SANYO
IBM	Seagate Technology
Infineon Technologies	Sharp
Intel	Siemens
Lucent	Sony
Matsushita	STMicroelectronics
Maxtor	Sun Microsystems
Micron Technology	Texas Instruments
Microsoft	Toshiba
Mitsubishi Electric	Unisys
Motorola	

HISTORICAL FINANCIALS

Company Type: Public

Income Statement

FYE: March 31

	REVENUE ($ mil.)	NET INCOME ($ mil.)	NET PROFIT MARGIN	EMPLOYEES
3/05	44,284	297	0.7%	150,970
3/04	45,123	471	1.0%	156,169
3/03	38,529	(1,019)	—	157,044
3/02	37,748	(2,884)	—	170,111
3/01	43,415	68	0.2%	187,399
3/00	49,808	405	0.8%	188,053
3/99	44,018	(115)	—	188,000
3/98	37,464	42	0.1%	180,000
3/97	36,379	373	1.0%	167,000
3/96	35,075	588	1.7%	164,800
Annual Growth	2.6%	(7.3%)	—	(1.0%)

2005 Year-End Financials

Debt ratio: 101.9%
Return on equity: 3.8%
Cash ($ mil.): 4,226

Current ratio: 1.33
Long-term debt ($ mil.): 8,119

Net Income History

OTC: FJTSY

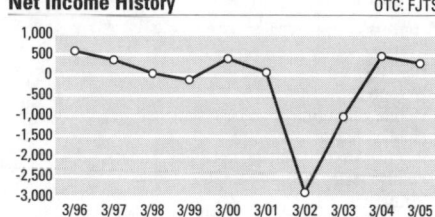

| | 3/96 | 3/97 | 3/98 | 3/99 | 3/00 | 3/01 | 3/02 | 3/03 | 3/04 | 3/05 |

Gallaher Group

When the smoke finally settles over London, Gallaher Group helps kick it up again. The #2 UK cigarette company with about 40% of that country's cigarette market, Gallaher makes tobacco products and sells them in Asia, continental Europe, Ireland, Russia and other former Soviet republics, and the UK. Its premium cigarettes include top UK brands Benson & Hedges and Silk Cut; mid-priced brands include Berkeley; and low-priced brands include Dorchester and Mayfair. Gallaher also makes Hamlet cigars, Amber Leaf hand-rolled tobacco, and Condor pipe tobacco.

Although most of its sales come from cigarettes, Gallaher also controls nearly half of the UK cigar market and a third of all UK sales of hand-rolled tobacco.

Gallaher was spun off in 1997 from Fortune Brands, the result of a flurry of tobacco-related lawsuits in the US. Gallaher and other firms are fighting the European Union's ban on tobacco advertising (scheduled to start in 2006). The company has a European joint venture with R.J. Reynolds and seeks new international markets for its products by also partnering with Indonesian tobacco maker Sampoerna International to sell the ST Dupont Paris luxury cigarette brand in Russia. Gallaher is one of several companies, including British American Tobacco, interested in expanding its share of Chinese smokers, who puff 1.7 trillion cigarettes every year.

The company is involved in some health-related lawsuits from smokers, but to date no court has ordered it to pay damages.

In early 2005 Gallaher announed plans to curb its European production operations, including the closure of facilities in Austria, and reduce production of cigars and cigarettes at two other factories, resulting in a loss of 250 jobs.

The company is looking into expanding its distribution further into Russia, China, and Africa. At the same time, it has announced its intention to acquire Cita, the tobacco company based in the Canary Islands. Cita is one of Spain's biggest cigar-makers and is owned by partly by the Zamorano family and partly by French/Spanish tobacco group Altadis.

HISTORY

Tom Gallaher started his business making and selling pipe tobacco in Londonderry, Ireland, in 1857. By 1873 he had moved his business to Belfast. By 1888 Gallaher was making cigarettes (which had become popular) and flake tobacco. That year Gallaher opened its first London office. The firm was incorporated as Gallaher Limited in 1896. In 1908 it bought Ireland's entire tobacco crop. Gallaher died in 1927.

In 1955 Gallaher bought the UK and Ireland units of cigarette firm Benson & Hedges. Richard Benson and William Hedges launched their firm in England in 1873; they pioneered selling tobacco in sealed tins for freshness. In 1877 Queen Victoria endorsed Benson & Hedges with her Royal Warrant. As more women began smoking in the early 1900s, Benson & Hedges made specialized cigarettes for them, including some with floral designs.

Gallaher bought J. Wix and Sons (Kensitas cigarettes) from American Tobacco in 1962 for a Gallaher stake. American Tobacco had increased its stake to 67% by 1968; it renamed itself American Brands in 1970 as it added nontobacco products.

Diversifying in the 1970s, Gallaher bought Dollond & Aitchison Group (optical services/products, 1970), created retail franchise Marshell Group (tobacco and confectionery concessions, 1971), and bought TM Group (Vendepac and other cigarette and snack vending machines, 1973) and Forbuoys (tobacco, sweets, and newspapers stores; 1973). In 1974 it expanded to Italy through Dollond & Aitchison. American Brands controlled 100% of Gallaher by 1975.

The company continued its acquisitions in the 1980s, including NSS Newsagents in 1986 (550 stores, combined with the 450-store Forbuoys subsidiary). By 1987 Gallaher was the #1 UK tobacco manufacturer. In 1990 the firm acquired Scotland's Whyte and Mackay Distillers.

During the early 1990s Gallaher expanded to France, Spain, and Greece. In 1993 it cut 15% of its workforce, blaming cigarette taxes for lower sales. Gallaher had become Ireland's #1 tobacco firm by 1994.

When parent American Brands sold US subsidiary American Tobacco to British American Tobacco Industries (B.A.T) in 1994, Gallaher sold B.A.T its Silk Cut rights outside Europe in exchange for a manufacturing deal. To focus on tobacco and distilling, Gallaher sold Dollond & Aitchison that year and the next year sold its other noncore units (including Forbuoys and TM Group). It also closed several plants during this period.

Twelve people sued Gallaher and rival Imperial Tobacco in 1996, alleging the firms continued using tar in cigarettes after discovering its link to cancer; the suit was abandoned after the statute of limitations expired.

As US tobacco-related litigation skyrocketed, in 1997 American Brands renamed itself Fortune Brands and spun off Gallaher Group, which floated on the London Stock Exchange in May of that year — the first time a UK firm demerged from a US parent. In 1998 it began exporting to China.

In 1999 Gallaher bought the UK tobacco business of RJR Nabisco (the Dorchester and Dickens & Grant brands and distribution of Camel and More). In a sign of tobacco's fall from favor, the Royal Palace withdrew Queen Victoria's 122-year-old endorsement of Benson & Hedges.

Gallaher entered 2000 with new CEO Nigel Northridge. In August the company bought Russian cigarette maker and distributor Liggett-Ducat from Vector Group for about $400 million. In mid-2001 Gallaher bought 41% of Austria Tabak (90% domestic market share) for more than $700 million and increased its share to more than 99% by the end of the year.

Gallaher announced in May 2003 430 job cuts in Austria and the UK.

EXECUTIVES

Chairman: John Gildersleeve, age 60
Deputy Chairman: Sir Graham J. Hearne, age 67
CEO and Board Member: Nigel Northridge, age 49, $1,610,777 pay
Group Operations Director and Board Member: Nigel Dunlop, age 48, $648,933 pay
Finance Director and Board Member: Mark Rolfe, age 46, $960,066 pay
Group Director, Continental Europe: Nigel Simon, age 48, $896,061 pay
Group Commercial Director: Neil England, age 50, $914,945 pay
Chief Marketing Officer: Yann Tardif, age 44
Group Commercial Director: Stewart Hainsworth, age 36
Managing Director, UK Division: Barry Jenner, age 46
Director, Group Human Resources: Mike Griffiths, age 47
Director, Investor Relations: Claire Jenkins, age 42
Head of Business Development: Suhail Saad, age 50
Head of Corporate Affairs: Jeff Jeffery
Company Secretary and General Counsel: Tom Keevil, age 44
Head of Human Resources: Neil Hayward, age 39
Financial Controller: Jon Moxon, age 41
International Corporate Affairs Manager: Andy Williams
Media: Michelle McKeown
Auditors: PricewaterhouseCoopers LLP

LOCATIONS

HQ: Gallaher Group Plc
Members Hill, Brooklands Road, Weybridge, Surrey KT13 0QU, United Kingdom
Phone: +44-1932-859777   **Fax:** +44-1932-832792
Web: www.gallaher-group.com

2004 Sales

	% of total
Europe	
Continental Europe	52
UK	39
Commonwealth of Independent States (former Soviet republics)	4
Other regions	5
Total	**100**

PRODUCTS/OPERATIONS

Selected Products and Brands

Cigarettes
Benson & Hedges (in UK)	St. George
	Silk Cut
Berkeley	Sovereign
Blend	ST Dupont
Club	Sterling
Dickens & Grant	Cigars
Dorchester	Hamlet
Level	Tobacco
Mayfair	Amber Leaf
Memphis	Condor
Milde Sorte	Old Holborn
Novost	

COMPETITORS

Altadis	Philip Morris International
British American Tobacco	Swedish Match
Carolina Group	Taiwan Tobacco & Wine
Imperial Tobacco	TCHIBO Holding
Japan Tobacco	

HISTORICAL FINANCIALS

Company Type: Public

Income Statement

FYE: December 31

	REVENUE ($ mil.)	NET INCOME ($ mil.)	NET PROFIT MARGIN	EMPLOYEES
12/04	15,558	556	3.6%	11,000
12/03	14,255	440	3.1%	10,212
12/02	12,022	411	3.4%	9,602
12/01	7,944	342	4.3%	6,217
12/00	6,659	372	5.6%	3,519
12/99	7,017	390	5.6%	3,066
12/98	7,061	361	5.1%	—
12/97	7,264	396	5.5%	—
Annual Growth	11.5%	5.0%	—	29.1%

2004 Year-End Financials

Debt ratio: —
Return on equity: —
Cash ($ mil.): 255
Current ratio: 1.02
Long-term debt ($ mil.): 4,178
No. of shares (mil.): 164
Dividends
Yield: 3.6%
Payout: 64.4%
Market value ($ mil.): 9,943

Stock History

NYSE: GLH

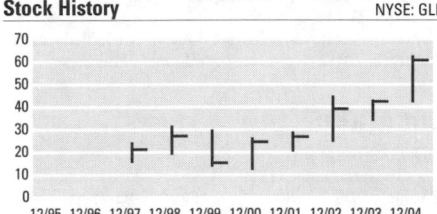

	STOCK PRICE ($) FY Close	P/E High/Low	PER SHARE ($) Earnings	PER SHARE ($) Dividends	PER SHARE ($) Book Value
12/04	60.71	18 13	3.40	2.19	(2.94)
12/03	42.54	16 13	2.70	1.93	(3.35)
12/02	39.20	18 10	2.52	1.71	(3.58)
12/01	26.95	13 10	2.17	1.54	(2.89)
12/00	24.63	11 5	2.34	1.54	(5.36)
12/99	15.38	13 6	2.32	1.49	(4.80)
12/98	27.19	15 9	2.09	0.79	(4.83)
12/97	21.31	10 7	2.31	0.77	(5.10)
Annual Growth	16.1%	— —	5.7%	16.1%	—

Gaz de France

If the Tour de France followed the path of Gaz de France, bikers would ride through Africa, Asia, all the Americas, and most of Europe. The state-owned company's main operation is the distribution of natural gas to more than 10.9 million customers in France; it also serves some 4 million customers abroad. Gaz de France also explores for and produces natural gas; operates gas transmission, storage, and trading businesses; offers energy-related construction and heating, ventilation, and air-conditioning (HVAC) services; runs cogeneration facilities; and supplies fuel for natural gas-powered buses. The French government launched an initial public offering in late June 2005, raising as much as $5 billion.

The government sold about 22% of the utility company, using the majority of the money to help pay for future European expansion. The rest of the money is expected to pay off state debts.

With operations or assets in more than 30 countries, Gaz de France is gearing up in preparation for Europe's liberalization of the gas industry. The company has been acquiring gas distribution companies outside of France, and its Cofathec unit, which provides energy-related services, has also expanded its market share through acquisitions.

Gaz de France has reserves of 670 million barrels of oil equivalent, more than 70% of which comes from natural gas. The company has nearly doubled its reserves through the acquisition of natural gas assets, primarily in the North Sea. Gaz de France produces about 10% of the gas it sells, and it plans to increase its production to 15% of gas sales. It plans to focus its expansion in European markets.

HISTORY

Gaz de France was founded in 1946 by the French government to consolidate the more than 500 (mostly coal-fired) gas works that had existed before WWII. From 1949 on, Gaz de France focused on upgrading gas plants and local transmission networks. Its first long-distance pipeline was built in 1953, linking Paris to the Lorraine coal gas fields. With the development of the Lacq gas field in southwestern France, annual gas sales increased by 300% between 1957 and 1962.

By 1965 nearly half of the French population was supplied with natural gas. Spurred on by the loss of its Algerian colony, which held major oil and gas assets, the French government pushed for new gas supplies to supplement its Lacq resources. Gaz de France was able to secure a contract with Algerian natural gas supplier Sonatrach in 1965, and in 1967 it signed an import contract with Dutch supplier Gasunie. The company also diversified in the 1960s, helping build a natural gas liquefaction plant in Algeria and a receiving terminal in Le Havre. It also helped pioneer gas storage engineering.

Following the price shock of the Arab oil embargo of the early 1970s, Gaz de France stepped up its search for alternative suppliers, including contracts with Russia's largest gas producer Soyouzgazexport (in 1976, 1980, and 1984) and four separate Norwegian producers, Efofisk (1977), Stafjord (1985), Heimdal (1986), and Gullfaks (1987). The company also renewed contracts with its Dutch and Algerian suppliers.

During the 1990s Gaz de France expanded its international operations as deregulation in the industry accelerated. In 1994 the company gained a foothold in eastern Germany's gas sector by buying gas production and storage company Erdgas Erdol GmbH (EEG). Three years later Gaz de France acquired Italian heating and related services firm Agip Servizi and was awarded a joint venture contract to distribute gas in Berlin in 1997 and in the suburbs of Mexico City in 1998.

Through contracts for North Sea oil and gas with Elf Aquitaine (now owned by TOTAL FINA ELF), British-Borneo, and Ruhrgas in 1999, the company increased its natural gas supplies. It also established new gas supply contracts with Nigeria and Qatar.

For the first time in its history, Gaz de France became an offshore field operator in 2000 by acquiring exploration and production company TransCanada International Netherlands and a 39% stake in Noordgastransport BV, an offshore gas pipeline operator.

In 2001, through the purchase of a 10% interest in Petronet LNG, Gaz de France embarked on a project to import liquefied natural gas from Quatar to India.

EXECUTIVES

Chairman and CEO: Jean-François Cirelli, age 47
SEVP Infrastructure and Resources: Yves Colliou, age 58
SEVP Upstream Activities Worldwide: Jean-Marie Dauger, age 52
CFO: Philippe Jeunet
SVP Human Resources: Philippe Saimpert
SVP International: Pierre Clavel
VP Audit and Risks: Georges Bouchard
VP Communication: Raphaële Rabatel, age 42
VP Investments and Acquisitions: Emmanuel Hedde
VP Support Functions: Philippe Charbaut
VP Market Development and Sales: Jean-Pierre Piollat
VP Strategy: Stéphane Brimont
Secretary: Jean Abiteboul
Chairman and CEO, GDF International: Jacques Deyirmendjian, age 60
Chairman and CEO, Cogac; Chairman, Cofathec: Bernard Leblanc
Head of Investor Relations: Valérie Duval
Auditors: Ernst & Young Audit; Mazars & Guérard

LOCATIONS

HQ: Gaz de France
23, rue Philibert Delorme, 75840 Paris, France
Phone: +33-1-47-54-77-25 **Fax:** +33-1-42-54-70-45
Web: www.gazdefrance.com

Gaz de France has operations in 33 countries, including Algeria, Argentina, Austria, Belgium, Canada, Egypt, France, Germany, Hungary, India, Italy, the Ivory Coast, Mexico, the Netherlands, Norway, Poland, Portugal, Russia, Slovakia, Spain, the UK, Ukraine, Uruguay, and the US.

2004 Sales

	% of total
Europe	
France	71
Other countries	28
Other regions	1
Total	**100**

COMPETITORS

BG Group	Gasunie
Centrica	Gazprom
Electricité de France	Italgas
Eni	ITERA
Gas Natural	SUEZ-TRACTEBEL

HISTORICAL FINANCIALS

Company Type: Public

Income Statement
FYE: December 31

	REVENUE ($ mil.)	NET INCOME ($ mil.)	NET PROFIT MARGIN	EMPLOYEES
12/04	24,728	1,507	6.1%	38,251
12/03	20,895	1,230	5.9%	38,101
12/02	15,246	3,831	25.1%	37,853
12/01	12,756	789	6.2%	25,357
12/00	10,546	406	3.8%	33,290
12/99	9,164	447	4.9%	31,100
12/98	10,444	446	4.3%	24,825
12/97	9,205	255	2.8%	25,308
12/96	10,459	494	4.7%	25,081
12/95	10,038	391	3.9%	26,087
Annual Growth	10.5%	16.2%	—	4.3%

2004 Year-End Financials

Debt ratio: —
Return on equity: 11.5%
Cash ($ mil.): —

Current ratio: —
Long-term debt ($ mil.): —

Net Income History
Euronext Paris: GAZ

Gazprom

Gazprom, Russia's largest company, produces 94% of the country's natural gas, controls 25% of the world's reserves, and is also the world's largest gas producer. The company is engaged in gas exploration, processing, transport, and marketing. It operates Russia's domestic gas pipeline network and delivers gas to countries of the former Soviet Union and Europe. Gazprom relies heavily on Western exports and partnerships. It also holds stakes in Russian financial institutions and a polypropylene plant, and has its own telecom network. The Russian government increased its stake in Gazprom from 38% to 51% for a reported $6 billion. Gazprom has acquired a 73% stake in Sibneft for a reported $11 billion.

Millhouse Capital, a holding company controlled by Russian oligarch Roman Abramovich, sold the majority stake in Sibneft (also known as Siberian Oil Company), Russia's fifth-largest oil company. The deal is widely expected to further the Russian government's influence in the energy sector. Gazprom has announced plans to acquire another 20% of Sibneft from YUKOS, once that company's stock is unfrozen.

Gazprom, which evolved from the natural gas ministry of the former Soviet Union, accounts for about 25% of Russia's tax revenues.

Exports to Europe are critical to Gazprom, burdened by debt because of the insolvency of Russian consumers and hordes of nonpaying customers. Gazprom holds strategic partnerships with Western energy companies, including Germany's E.ON Ruhrgas, which owns almost 4% of the company's shares. Other partners in-

clude Royal Dutch/Shell Group, Eni of Italy, and Finland's Fortum. In addition, Gazprom has announced a deal with German chemical conglomerate BASF that grants BASF minority shares in both the proposed North Europe Gas Pipeline and the West Siberia field that will feed it.

Gazprom had announced plans in 2004 to acquire Rosneft (effectively giving the Russian government control of Gazprom), though the deal was complicated by Rosneft's acquisition of the Yugansk assets acquired from YUKOS. In 2005 Gazprom abandoned plans to merge with Rosneft and set its sights on Sibneft in an effort to add significant oil operations to its business.

HISTORY

Following the breakup of the Soviet Union in the early 1990s, one of the first priorities of the Russian government was to move some state monopolies toward a free-market economic system. A presidential decree in 1992 moved the company toward privatization by calling for the formation of a Russian joint-stock company to explore for and produce gas, gas condensates, and oil; provide for gas processing; operate gas wells; and build gas pipelines and storage facilities. By 1993 the government had converted its natural gas monopoly, Gazprom, into a joint-stock company.

The new Gazprom was 15%-owned by Gazprom workers and 28% by people living in Russia's gas-producing regions. The state retained about a 40% share (boosted to 51% in 2003). The company inherited all of the export contracts to Western and Central Europe of the Commonwealth of Independent States.

Thanks to the power of Viktor Chernomyrdin (Gazprom's former Soviet boss and gas industry minister, who became Russia's prime minister in 1992), the company was able to enjoy large tax breaks and maintain its role as a monopoly — even as other industries were being more deeply privatized. However, the privatization of Gazprom was later attacked as being manipulated to profit the company's top management, including Chernomyrdin. Top managers were rumored to have each received 1%-5% of shares — holdings potentially worth $1.2 billion-$10 billion each.

Needing to raise cash, in 1996 Gazprom offered 1% of its stock to foreigners, the first sale of stock to foreign investors. In 1997 Gazprom and Royal Dutch/Shell formally became partners. That year Gazprom began building its Blue Stream pipeline across the Black Sea to Turkey. Italian group Eni helped back the project and became a partner by 1999.

In 1998 Gazprom acquired a stake in Promstroibank, Russia's fourth-largest financial institution. German energy powerhouse Ruhrgas acquired a 3% stake in Gazprom in 1998, which it increased to nearly 4% the next year. Also in 1999 Gazprom started building its Yamal-Europe pipeline, which was to stretch to Germany for exports to Europe.

The next year an attempt by Gazprom to muscle into Hungary's chemicals sector by offering cheaper raw materials was blocked by Hungary's TVK and Borsodchem and their allies. Also in 2000 Gazprom became embroiled in a politically controversial issue when it called for the country's leading private media holding group, Media-MOST, to sell shares to the gas giant in order to settle millions of dollars of debt. Because Media-MOST held NTV television, a major critic of Russian president Vladimir Putin, the deal was alleged

to have been directed by the Kremlin. A government probe into the deal was later ordered.

The alignment of Gazprom's board changed in 2000 after the annual shareholder's meeting. For the first time in Gazprom's history, company managers did not have a majority of seats. A new chairman, Dmitri Medvyedev, second in command to Putin, was elected to replace Chernomyrdin. In 2001 the board fired CEO Rem Vyakhirev and replaced him with deputy energy minister Alexei Miller, a Putin ally.

Gazprom owned a significant stake in Russian independent television channel NTV, which in 2002 it sold in order to focus on its core energy businesses.

EXECUTIVES

Chairman of the Board of Directors: Dmitri A. Medvyedev
Deputy Chairman of the Board of Directors and Chairman of the Executive Board: Alexei B. Miller
Deputy Chairman Executive Board and Chief Accountant: Elena A. Vasilyeva
Deputy Chairman Executive Board: Alexander G. Ananenkov
Deputy Chairman Executive Board: Nikolai N. Guslisty
Deputy Chairman Executive Board: Yury A. Komarov
Deputy Chairman Executive Board; Acting President, Sibneft: Alexander N. Ryazanov
Deputy Chairman Executive Board; General Director of the Security Service: Sergey K. Ushakov
Deputy Chairman Executive Board: Boris D. Yurlov
Head of Capital Construction and Transportation Department: Mikhail A. Axelrod
Head of Gas Transportation, Underground Storage, and Processing Department: Bogdan V. Budzulyak
Head of the Legal Department: Konstantin K. Chuichenko
Head of Department for Relationships with Regions of the Russian Federation: Viktor V. Ilyushin
Head of Finance and Economics Department: Andrei V. Kruglov
Head of Gazexport: Alexander Medvedev
Head of Department of Gas, Gas Condensate and Oil: Vasili G. Podyuk
Head of Department of Strategic Development: Vlada V. Rusakova
Head of Department for Marketing and Processing of Gas and Liquid Hydrocarbons; General Director of Mezhregiongaz: Kirill G. Seleznev
General Director of Gazkomplektimpex: Valeri A. Golubev
General Director of Gazexport: Alexander I. Medvedev
Auditors: ZAO PricewaterhouseCoopers Audit

LOCATIONS

HQ: OAO Gazprom
16 Nametkina, 117997 Moscow V-420, Russia
Phone: +7-95-719-3001   **Fax:** +7-95-719-8333
Web: www.gazprom.ru

OAO Gazprom operates Russia's extensive gas pipeline system and delivers natural gas to 25 countries in Europe and the former Soviet republics.

PRODUCTS/OPERATIONS

Selected Subsidiaries
Gazprom Finance B.V.
Astrakhangazprom
Bashtransgaz
Burgaz
Dagestangazprom
Ecological and Analytical Center of the Gas Industry
Gazexport
Gazflot
Gazkomplektimpex
Gaznadzor
Gazobezopasnost
Gazpromavia
Gazprominvestholding
Gazpromokhrana

Gazpromrazvitiye
Gaztorgpromstroy
Gazsvyaz
Informgaz
IRTsGazprom
Kavkaztransgaz
Kubangazprom
Lentransgaz
Mezhregiongaz
Mostransgaz
Nadymgazprom
Nadymstroygazdobycha
NIIGazekonomika
Novourengoy GCC
Noyabrskgazdobycha
Orenburggazprom
Permtransgaz
Podzemgazprom
Samaratransgaz
Servicegazprom
Severgazprom
Surgutgazprom
Surgutstroygaz
Szhizhenny gas
Tattransgaz
Tomsktransgaz
TyumenNIIGiprogaz
Tyumentransgaz
Ulyanovskgazservice
Uraltransgaz
Urengoygazprom
VNIIgaz
Volgogradtransgaz
Volgotransgaz
Yamburggazdobycha
Yugtransgaz
ZAO Yamalgazinvest

COMPETITORS

BP	LUKOIL
E.ON Ruhrgas	Surgutneftegas
Gasunie	Tatneft
ITERA	Yukos

HISTORICAL FINANCIALS

Company Type: Public

Income Statement

FYE: December 31

	REVENUE ($ mil.)	NET INCOME ($ mil.)	NET PROFIT MARGIN	EMPLOYEES
12/04	36,395	7,227	19.9%	332,800
12/03	28,867	5,841	20.2%	299,717
12/02	19,216	3,807	19.8%	295,487
12/01	19,287	3,290	17.1%	310,700
12/00	17,448	1,712	9.8%	300,000
12/99	12,113	(2,883)	—	298,000
12/98	6,732	1,105	16.4%	278,400
12/97	23,300	6,509	27.9%	362,200
12/96	20,780	1,682	8.1%	398,600
12/95	13,110	3,217	24.5%	375,000
Annual Growth	12.0%	9.4%	—	(1.3%)

2004 Year-End Financials

Debt ratio: 19.3%
Return on equity: 10.5%
Cash ($ mil.): 6,136
Current ratio: 2.31
Long-term debt ($ mil.): 14,323

Net Income History

Exchange: Russian

12/95 12/96 12/97 12/98 12/99 12/00 12/01 12/02 12/03 12/04

George Weston

George Weston Limited fuels Canadians through those long winters. About 85% of the company's sales come from its 62%-owned Loblaw Companies Limited, Canada's largest supermarket operator (with more than a dozen chains such as Loblaws, Provigo, and Zehrs) and the country's largest wholesale food distributor. The rest comes from its food-processing units, with operations in Canada and the US that focus on fresh-baked goods, frozen dough, and other bakery products. (Its Interbake Foods division is a major supplier of Girl Scout cookies in the US.) The units also have fish and dairy operations. Chairman and president Galen Weston owns about 62% of the company, which was founded by his grandfather in 1882.

Already a strong food retailer in most Canadian provinces, Loblaw stepped up its efforts in the lucrative Quebec market when it bought food retailer/wholesaler Provigo. (Loblaw has about a 36% market share in Quebec and a 30% share in Canada.)

The food-processing segment is expanding its bakery and biscuit operations through acquisitions; its purchase of Bestfoods Baking has made it one of the top bakeries in the US. However, it has sold noncore operations, including its forest products business, canned seafood business (Conners), and fisheries operations in Chile. In 2005 the company sold its Heritage Salmon subsidiary, thus exiting the unprofitable fisheries business entirely.

HISTORY

A baker's apprentice, George Weston began delivering bread in Toronto with a single horse in 1882. He added the Model Bakery in 1896 and began making cookies and biscuits in 1908.

Upon George's death in 1924, his son Garfield gained control of the company and took it public as George Weston Limited in 1928. Having popularized the premium English biscuit in Canada, Garfield acquired bakeries in the UK to make cheap biscuits (uncommon at the time). He grouped the bakeries as a separate public company called Allied Bakeries in 1935 (it later became Associated British Foods and is still controlled by the Weston family).

Expansion-minded Garfield led the company into the US with the purchase of Associated Biscuit in 1939. By the late 1930s George Weston was making cakes, breads, and almost 500 kinds of candy and biscuits.

During the 1940s the company made a number of acquisitions, including papermaker E.B. Eddy (1943; sold 1998 to papermaker Domtar, giving it a 20% stake in Domtar), Southern Biscuit (1944), Western Grocers (1944, its first distribution company), and William Neilson (1948, chocolate and dairy products).

In 1953 it acquired a controlling interest in Loblaw Groceterias, Canada's largest grocery chain. George Weston continued its acquisitions during the 1950s and 1960s, adding grocer National Tea and diversifying into packaging (Somerville Industries, 1957) and fisheries (British Columbia Packers, 1962; Conners Bros., 1967).

By 1970, when Garfield's son Galen became president, the company's holdings were in disarray. Galen brought in new managers, consolidated the food distribution and sales operations

under Loblaw Companies Limited, and cut back on National Tea (which shrank from over 900 stores in 1972 to 82 in 1993). When Garfield died in 1978, Galen became chairman.

Ever since Galen, a polo-playing chum of Prince Charles, was the target of a failed kidnapping attempt by the Irish Republican Army in 1983, the family has kept a low public profile.

George Weston became the #1 chocolate maker in Canada with its purchase of Cadbury Schweppes' Canadian assets in 1987. The 1980s concluded with a five-year price war in St. Louis among its National Tea stores, Kroger, and a local grocer. This ultimately proved fruitless, and Loblaw sold its US supermarkets in 1995, ending its US retail presence. As part of its divestiture of underachieving subsidiaries, the company sold its Neilson confectionery business back to Cadbury Schweppes in 1996 and sold its chocolate products company in 1998.

In early 1998 Loblaw set its sights on Quebec, buying Montreal-based Provigo. Other George Weston acquisitions in the late 1990s included Oshawa Foods' 80-store Agora Foods franchise supermarket unit in eastern Canada and its Field-fresh Farms dairy business, the frozen-bagel business of Quaker Oats, Pennsylvania-based Maier's Bakery, and Bunge International's Australian meat processor, Don Smallgoods. It also sold its British Columbia Packers fisheries unit.

Early in 2001 George Weston surprised analysts when it won Unilever's Bestfoods Baking Company (Entenmann's, Oroweat) with a bid of $1.77 billion. The company reduced its stake in Loblaw by 2% and sold its Connors canned seafood business to fund the purchase, which was completed in July 2001. To help pay down debt, in early 2002 the company sold its Orowheat business in the western US to Mexican bread giant Grupo Bimbo for $610 million.

In 2003, Weston's food distribution business introduced about 1,500 private label products.

In 2004 Weston sold its fisheries operations in Chile at a loss for about $20 million. In September of that year the company purchased Quebec-based Boulangerie Gadoua Ltée, a family-owned baking business.

EXECUTIVES

Chairman and President: W. Galen Weston, age 64, $1,734,720 pay
CFO: Richard P. (Rick) Mavrinac, age 52
SVP, Labour Relations: Roy R. Conliffe, age 54
SVP, Secretary, and General Counsel: Stewart E. Green, age 60
SVP, Finance: Louise M. Lacchin, age 47
SVP; President and CEO, President's Choice Bank: Donald G. (Don) Reid, age 55, $767,430 pay
SVP, Corporate Development: Robert G. Vaux, age 56
SVP, Investor Relations and Public Affairs: Geoffrey H. (Geoff) Wilson, age 49
VP, Risk Management and Internal Audit Services: Manny Difilippo, age 45
VP, Taxation: J. Bradley Holland, age 41
VP, Legal Counsel: Michael N. Kimber, age 49
VP, Corporate Systems: Kirk W. Mondesire, age 44
VP, Pension and Benefits: Lucy J. Paglione, age 45
VP, Controller: Rolando Sardellitti, age 37
VP and Treasurer: Lisa R. Swartzman, age 34
VP, Systems Audit and Information Technology: Ann Marie Yamamoto, age 44
President, Weston Foods US: Gary J. Prince, age 53, $1,109,850 pay
President, Weston Foods Canada: Ralph A. Robinson, age 56, $409,604 pay
President, Loblaw Companies: John A. Lederer, age 49, $1,256,667 pay
President, Fisheries: Fraser J. Walsh
President, Interbake Foods: Raymond A. Baxter, age 60
Auditors: KPMG LLP

LOCATIONS

HQ: George Weston Limited
22 St. Clair Ave. East,
Toronto, Ontario M4T 2S7, Canada
Phone: 416-922-2500   **Fax:** 416-922-4395
Web: www.weston.ca

George Weston Limited's Loblaw Companies operates in Canada, and its Weston Foods divisions operate in Canada and the US.

2004 Sales

	% of total
Canada	90
US	10
Total	**100**

PRODUCTS/OPERATIONS

2004 Sales

	% of total
Food distribution	86
Weston Foods	14
Total	**100**

Operating Divisions

Food Distribution (Selected Loblaw Banners)
Atlantic Superstore
Extra Foods
Fortinos
Loblaws
Maxi
Maxi & Co.
no frills
Provigo
The Real Canadian Superstore
The Real Canadian Wholesale Club
SuperValu
valu-mart
Your Independent Grocer
Zehrs Markets

Food Processing (Selected Units)
George Weston Bakeries Inc. (fresh-baked goods, US)
Interbake Foods Inc. (cookies and crackers, US)
Maplehurst Bakeries, Inc. (frozen bakery products, US)
Neilson Dairy (milk processor)
Ready Bake Foods Inc. (frozen bakery products)
Stroehmann Bakeries, LC (fresh-baked goods, US)
Weston Bakeries Limited (fresh-baked goods)
Weston Fruitcake Company

COMPETITORS

Bimbo	Jim Pattison Group
Bridgford Foods	Kellogg Snacks
Campbell Soup	Lanes Biscuits
Canada Safeway	Maple Leaf Foods
Empire Company	METRO
Flowers Foods	Otis Spunkmeyer
IGA	Tasty Baking
Interstate Bakeries	Wal-Mart Canada

HISTORICAL FINANCIALS

Company Type: Public

Income Statement

FYE: December 31

	REVENUE ($ mil.)	NET INCOME ($ mil.)	NET PROFIT MARGIN	EMPLOYEES
12/04	24,732	355	1.4%	148,000
12/03	22,553	612	2.7%	145,860
12/02	17,406	438	2.5%	142,850
12/01	15,499	366	2.4%	139,000
12/00	14,908	321	2.2%	126,000
12/99	14,414	243	1.7%	119,000
12/98	9,588	503	5.2%	124,000
12/97	9,722	170	1.8%	87,330
12/96	9,273	174	1.9%	81,030
12/95	9,502	139	1.5%	76,650
Annual Growth	**11.2%**	**11.0%**	**—**	**7.6%**

2004 Year-End Financials

Debt ratio: 137.1%	Current ratio: 1.02
Return on equity: 10.0%	Long-term debt ($ mil.): 4,983
Cash ($ mil.): 837	

Net Income History

Toronto: WN

GlaxoSmithKline

GlaxoSmithKline (GSK) calms your nerves and helps you breathe easier. One of the top five pharmaceutical firms in the world, GSK's top sellers include central nervous system therapies, respiratory drugs, and anti-infectives. The company's top product is asthma medication Advair, which combines two of the company's other products, Flovent and Serevent, to form a single, twice-daily treatment. Other bestsellers include antidepressants Paxil and Wellbutrin, migraine therapy Imitrex, and antibiotic Augmentin. The company's consumer products include Tums for sour stomachs and cold sore fighter Abreva. For smokers looking to kick the habit, GSK offers several cessation products like Commit, NicoDerm, and Nicorette.

The firm takes almost half its revenues from the US, and maintaining US patent protection for its bestsellers can make or break its future. The company lost patent protection for Paxil in 2003, and in late 2004 it made arrangements with Watson Pharmaceuticals to launch a generic version of Wellbutrin SR. Biovail, the drugmaker that licensed the antidepressant to GSK, is fighting to keep generics of Wellbutrin XL, an extended release version of the drug, off the market.

To alleviate these losses, GSK's development efforts include 140 different projects in the clinical stage of development. Drug candidates nearing the end of the development stage include a rotavirus vaccine and therapies for overactive bladders, osteoporosis, type 2 diabetes, restless leg syndrome, and post-operative bowel disorder.

The British drugmaker is part of the erectile dysfunction craze: The company co-promotes Levitra with Schering-Plough in the US. GSK returned European and international marketing rights for the drug back to its developer, Bayer HealthCare, in late 2004 after it, umm, failed to perform.

In early 2005, the company's vaccine unit, GlaxoSmithKline Biologicals, worked out an exchange of licenses with Merck for a human papillomavirus vaccine. GSK will receive royalties if Merck is able to get the vaccine approved and onto the market. Later that year GSK acquired Corixa in order to gain a factory that produces Monophosphoral Lipid A, a key ingredient in a number of the company's vaccine products and a number of other vaccine-related products.

The company has also announced that it is building a new vaccine production facility in Dresden, Germany, that will effectively double its capacity to manufacture vaccines. Its acquisition of ID Biomedical, a Canadian producer of vaccines, will further boost its capacity to produce the influenza vaccine. Fall of 2005 saw the sale of the company's US dermatology business to the PharmaDerm division of ALTANA; products involved in the deal include Alcovate, Cutivate, Emgel, Oxistat, and Temovate.

HISTORY

Englishman Joseph Nathan started an import-export business in New Zealand in 1873. He obtained the rights to a process for drying milk and began making powdered milk in New Zealand, selling it as baby food Glaxo.

Nathan's son Alec, sent to London to oversee baby food sales in Britain, increased Glaxo's name recognition by publishing the Glaxo Baby Book, a guide to child care. After WWI the company began distribution in India and South America.

In the 1920s Glaxo launched vitamin D-fortified formulations. It entered the pharmaceutical business with its 1927 introduction of Ostelin, a liquid vitamin D concentrate, and continued to grow globally in the 1930s, introducing Ostermilk (vitamin-fortified milk).

Glaxo began making penicillin and anesthetics during WWII; it went public in 1947. A steep drop in antibiotic prices in the mid-1950s led Glaxo to diversify; it bought veterinary, medical instrument, and drug distribution firms.

In the 1970s the British Monopolies Commission quashed both a hostile takeover attempt by Beecham and a proposed merger with retailer and drugmaker Boots. Glaxo launched US operations in 1978.

In the 1980s Glaxo shed nondrug operations to concentrate on pharmaceuticals. A 1981 marketing blitz launched antiulcer drug Zantac (to vie with SmithKline's Tagamet) in the US, where Glaxo's sales had been small. The company boosted outreach by contracting to use Hoffmann-La Roche's sales staff. The Zantac sales assault gave Glaxo leadership in US antiulcer drug sales.

Under CEO Sir Richard Sykes, Glaxo in 1995 made a surprise bid for UK rival Wellcome. Founded in 1880 by Americans Silas Burroughs and Henry Wellcome to sell McKesson-Robbins' products outside the US, Burroughs Wellcome and Co. began making its own products two years later. By the 1990s the company, which fostered Nobel Prize-winning researchers, led the world in antiviral medicines. Its primary drug products were Zovirax (launched 1981) and Retrovir (1987). Though an earlier bid by Glaxo had been rejected, Sykes won the takeover with backing from Wellcome Trust, Wellcome's largest shareholder.

In 1997 the company formed a new genetics division, buying Spectra Biomedical and its gene variation technology. That year it pulled diabetes drug Romozin (Rezulin in the US) from the UK market over concerns that it caused liver damage. Glaxo in 1998 ended its joint venture with Warner-Lambert (begun 1993), selling its former partner the Canadian and US marketing rights to acid blocker Zantac 75.

In 1999 Glaxo trimmed its product line, pulling hepatitis treatment Wellferon because of slow sales and selling the US rights to several anesthesia products. It also cut some 3,400 jobs (half from the UK). Also that year Glaxo threatened to leave the UK after the National Health Service opted not to cover antiflu inhalant Relenza, claiming the drug is not cost-effective.

The FDA in 2000 approved Glaxo's Lotronex for irritable bowel syndrome, but several hospitalizations linked to the drug prompted the FDA to ask the company to withdraw it from the US market. Later that year Glaxo completed its merger with former UK rival SmithKline Beecham to create GlaxoSmithKline (GSK); Jean-Pierre Garnier took over as CEO.

Although GSK has largely escaped the flurry of patent worries afflicting other druggernauts, in 2001 a US court declared invalid three patents protecting Augmentin from generics until 2017 and opened the door for cheaper rivals.

EXECUTIVES

Chairman: Sir Christopher Charles (Chris) Gent, age 56
CEO and Director: Jean-Pierre Garnier, age 57, $3,773,000 pay
CFO and Director: Julian Heslop, age 51
SVP and General Counsel: Rupert Bondy
SVP, Centre of Excellence for External Drug Discovery: Maxine Gowen, age 47
SVP, Human Resources: Daniel (Dan) Phelan
SVP, Corporate Communications and Community Partnerships: Jennie Younger
SVP, Procurement: Joe Meier
VP, Advertising and Promotion Services: Tom Laughery
VP, Corporate Media Relations: Nancy Pekarek
VP, Procurement Global Systems and Operations: R. Gregg Brandyberry
Chairman, Research and Development and Director: Tadataka (Tachi) Yamada, age 59, $1,726,000 pay
Vice Chairman, Pharmaceuticals: Robert A. (Bob) Ingram, age 62
President, Pharmaceuticals Japan: Marc Dunoyer
President, Pharmaceuticals International: Russell Greig
President, Global Manufacturing and Supply: David Pulman
President, Consumer Healthcare, North America: George Quesnelle
President, Pharmaceutical Operations: David M. Stout, age 51
President, US Pharmaceuticals: Chris Viehbacher
CIO: Ford Calhoun
Auditors: PricewaterhouseCoopers LLP

LOCATIONS

HQ: GlaxoSmithKline plc
980 Great West Rd., Brentford,
London TW8 9GS, United Kingdom
Phone: +44-20-8047-5000   **Fax:** +44-20-8047-7807
US HQ: 1 Franklin Plaza, Philadelphia, PA 19101
US Phone: 215-751-5000   **US Fax:** 215-751-3233
Web: www.gsk.com

2004 Pharmaceutical Sales

	% of total
US	44
Europe	29
Asia/Pacific	
Japan	11
Other countries	7
Latin America	4
Middle East & Africa	3
Canada	2
Total	**100**

PRODUCTS/OPERATIONS

2004 Sales

	% of total
Pharmaceuticals	
Respiratory	22
Central nervous system	17
Anti-virals	13
Anti-bacterials	6
Metabolic	6
Vaccines	6
Oncology & emesis	5
Cardiovascular & urogenital	4
Other disease categories	5
Consumer Health Care	
OTC medicines	8
Oral care	5
Nutritionals	3
Total	**100**

Selected Products

Pharmaceuticals
Anti-bacterials
Amoxil (antibiotic)
Augmentin (antibiotic)
Bactroban (skin infections)
Fortum/Fortaz (injectable antibiotic)
Lapdap (malaria)
Malarone (malaria)
Zinnat (community-acquired respiratory infections)
Anti-virals
Agenerase (protease inhibitor for HIV/AIDS)
Combivir/Biovir (reverse transcriptase inhibitor for HIV/AIDS)
Epivir/3TC (reverse transcriptase inhibitor for HIV/AIDS)
Lexiva/Telzir (protease inhibitor for HIV/AIDS)
Retrovir/AZT (reverse transcriptase inhibitor for HIV/AIDS)
Trizivir (reverse transcriptase inhibitors for HIV/AIDS)
Valtrex/Zelitrex (shingles and genital herpes)
Zeffix/Septavir/Heptodin/Epivir HBV (hepatitis B)
Ziagen (reverse transcriptase inhibitor for HIV/AIDS)
Zovirax (herpes infections, shingles, chicken pox, and cold sores)
Cardiovascular
Avodart (prostatic hyperplasia)
Coreg (heart failure and hypertension)
Flolan (blood-clotting inhibitor)
Lacipil (antihypertensive)
Lanoxin (cardiac anti-arrhythmic)
Levitra (erectile dysfunction, with Schering-Plough)
Pritor (hypertension)
Central nervous system disorders
Imigran/Imitrex (migraines)
Lamictal (epilepsy and bipolar disorder)
Naramig/Amerge (migraines)
Requip (Parkinson's disease)
Seroxat/Paxil (depression)
Wellbutrin (depression)
Zyban (smoking-cessation aid)
Metabolic and gastrointestinal
Avandamet (type 2 diabetes)
Avandia (type 2 diabetes)
Zantac (stomach ulcers)
Oncology and emesis
Bexxar (non-Hodgkin's lymphoma)
Hycamtin (ovarian and small cell lung cancers)
Navelbine (lung and breast cancer)
Zofran (cancer therapy-induced nausea)
Respiratory
Beconase (allergies)
Becotide/Beclovent (asthma and chronic obstructive pulmonary disease)
Flixonase/Flonase (allergies)
Flixotide/Flovent (asthma and chronic obstructive pulmonary disease)
Seretide/Advair (asthma and chronic obstructive pulmonary disease)
Serevent (asthma and chronic obstructive pulmonary disease)
Ventolin (asthma and chronic obstructive pulmonary disease)

Vaccines
Engerix-B (hepatitis B vaccine)
Havrix (hepatitis A vaccine)
Infanrix (diphtheria, tetanus, and whooping cough vaccine)
Twinrix (combined hepatitis A and hepatitis B vaccine)
Consumer Products
Over-the-Counter Medicines
Abreva (cold sores)
Abtei (vitamins and nutritional supplements)
Citrucel (laxative)
Commit (smoking-cessation)
Contac (respiratory product)
Nicabate/NicoDerm CQ/NiQuitin CQ (smoking-cessation)
Nicorette (smoking-cessation)
Panadol (analgesic)
Tums (antacid)
Zovirax (cold sores)
Oral Care
Aquafresh (toothpaste and toothbrushes)
Dr Best (toothbrushes)
Macleans (toothpaste)
Odol (toothpaste)
Polident (denture cleaner)
Poli-Grip (denture adhesive)
Sensodyne (toothpaste)
Nutritional Healthcare
Horlicks (milk-based malted food and chocolate drinks)
Lucozade (glucose energy drink)
Ribena (line of juice drinks rich in vitamin C)

COMPETITORS

Abbott Labs	Hoffmann-La Roche
Amgen	Johnson & Johnson
AstraZeneca	Merck
Barr Pharmaceuticals	Mylan Labs
Bayer	Novartis
Bristol-Myers Squibb	Novo Nordisk
Chiron	Pfizer
Elan	Sanofi-Aventis
Eli Lilly	Schering-Plough
Genentech	Wyeth

HISTORICAL FINANCIALS

Company Type: Public

Income Statement

FYE: December 31

	REVENUE ($ mil.)	NET INCOME ($ mil.)	NET PROFIT MARGIN	EMPLOYEES
12/04	39,032	8,248	21.1%	100,019
12/03	38,238	7,997	20.9%	100,919
12/02	34,183	6,341	18.6%	106,166
12/01	29,836	4,504	15.1%	107,899
12/00	27,032	6,295	23.3%	108,201
12/99	13,718	2,926	21.3%	60,726
12/98	13,248	3,047	23.0%	54,350
12/97	13,181	3,056	23.2%	53,068
12/96	14,284	3,420	23.9%	53,808
12/95	15,850	3,691	23.3%	65,702
Annual Growth	**10.5%**	**9.3%**	**—**	**4.8%**

2004 Year-End Financials

Debt ratio: 73.9%	No. of shares (mil.): 2,969
Return on equity: 65.6%	Dividends
Cash ($ mil.): 2,226	Yield: 3.2%
Current ratio: 1.56	Payout: 53.7%
Long-term debt ($ mil.): 8,399	Market value ($ mil.): 140,694

	STOCK PRICE ($)	P/E		PER SHARE ($)		
	FY Close	High/Low	Earnings	Dividends	Book Value
12/04	47.39	17 14	2.87	1.54	3.83
12/03	46.62	18 12	2.75	0.91	4.63
12/02	37.46	24 15	2.13	1.26	3.52
12/01	49.82	27 22	1.47	1.31	3.55
12/00	56.00	32 22	2.02	1.29	3.70
12/99	55.87	47 30	1.61	1.29	2.79
12/98	69.49	41 28	1.70	0.00	2.47
12/97	47.87	28 17	1.72	0.00	1.70
12/96	31.74	18 12	1.93	0.98	1.18
12/95	24.37	24 16	1.05	0.94	0.41
Annual Growth	7.7%	— —	11.8%	5.6%	28.0%

Hanson PLC

Breaking rocks in the hot sun is no punishment for building materials company Hanson PLC. Its Hanson Aggregates and Hanson Building Products operations in the US and the UK produce aggregates, ready-mixed concrete, bricks, and concrete pipe and building products. Other operations include quarries, marine dredging, and recycling. Hanson also has operations in Europe, Asia, and Australia, but the US and the UK account for most sales. The company is what's left of the Hanson Group — a huge industrial conglomerate that was broken into four publicly traded enterprises involving tobacco, coal, chemicals, and building materials.

Hanson has been meeting recent challenges by simplifying its operations. The company has divided its business structure into four regions, with North America as its largest region. In 2003 Hanson disposed of certain noncore operations in Singapore, India, Indonesia, Germany, and the US. Of course, Hanson continues to look for acquisitions within the fragmented building-products industry, especially in high-growth markets.

Its North America operations, formerly Hanson Building Materials America, was divided into Hanson Building Products North America and Hanson Aggregates North America in 2003. The company beefed up its Hanson Australia unit with the acquisition of Pioneer International. Hanson also has a 25% stake in Cement Australia Holdings with Rinker Group and Holcim. Its European unit operates a marine dredging business in a joint venture with Tarmac.

Hanson continued to grow through acquisitions in 2004, spending more than $150 million on a nine new businesses. At the same time, the company sold its Thailand operations and some non-core US operations. Hanson also pledged to spend £200 million–£300 million on acquisitions in 2005.

Mike Welton became chairman in 2005 after Christopher Collins retired.

HISTORY

In the 1950s and 1960s, James Hanson and Gordon White were British *bon vivants*. Hanson was once engaged to Audrey Hepburn, and White dated Joan Collins. However, they later became better known as sharp businessmen.

Through the Wiles Group, a fertilizer business they took over in 1965, Hanson and White sought poorly managed companies in mature industries at low prices. Within 10 years Hanson and White had collected 24 such businesses with sales in excess of $120 million.

Perceiving an antibusiness attitude in the UK, White formed a New York subsidiary, Hanson Industries, in 1973. He made his first American purchase in 1974, buying Seacoast (animal feed). Other purchases in hot dogs, shoes, and batteries followed, including conglomerate US Industries in 1984. That year the company acquired leading UK brick maker London Brick.

In bitterly fought hostile takeovers in 1986, Hanson acquired SCM (Smith-Corona office equipment, Glidden Paints, Durkee's Famous Foods, SCM Chemicals) and Imperial Group (cigarettes, beer, food, hotels, restaurants). It acquired US cement maker Kaiser Cement in 1987. The company changed its name to Hanson PLC that year.

Hanson acquired Peabody (coal) in 1990 and Beazer PLC, a UK construction firm with extensive US holdings, a year later. During 1992 the company sold a number of assets; the next year it bought Quantum Chemicals (propane distribution) for $3.4 billion. Hanson took Beazer Homes (home building materials, US) public in 1994, retaining 30%.

In 1995 the company spun off some of its US operations as U.S. Industries and sold its 62% stake in Suburban Propane, a major US propane distributor. It also reorganized Beazer's US operations as Cornerstone Construction & Materials. In addition, Hanson merged its Butterley Brick and London Brick into one company, Hanson Brick. Also in 1995 founder White died.

The Hanson conglomerate began to split up its operations in 1996, creating four separate public companies focused on chemicals (Millennium Chemicals), tobacco (Imperial Tobacco), energy (Energy Group PLC), and building materials and equipment (Hanson PLC). Founder James Hanson retired as chairman in 1997.

Joining the consolidation of the US building-materials sector, Hanson bought six US firms in 1998 — HG Fenton (aggregates and ready-mix concrete), Becker Minerals (aggregates), Condux (concrete pipe), Gifford-Hill American (aggregates), and Nelson & Sloan (aggregates and ready-mix concrete). That year the company paid $155 million to settle environmental liabilities inherited when it purchased Koppers Company in 1991.

In 1999 Hanson sold Grove Worldwide — a world-leading maker of cranes and materials-handling equipment — to Robert Bass' investment firm, Keystone, and also sold its 24% stake in Westralian Sands (titanium and zircon, Australia). Hanson bought the North American brick business of Canada-based Jannock, as well as San Francisco (Jones Sand) and North Carolina (Brewer Sand) sand businesses.

Hanson acquired Pioneer International, a giant Australian concrete and aggregate company, for about $2.5 billion in 2000. Smaller acquisitions during the year included US concrete pipe and products makers Joelson Taylor, Cincinnati Concrete Pipe, and Milan Concrete Products.

In late 2000 Hanson acquired Davon, another US-based concrete and aggregate company. In early 2001 the company sold its waste management division, part of Hanson Quarry Products Europe, to Waste Recycling Group. Hanson's 2001 acquisitions included Centennial Pipe and Products, a major Canadian pipe maker (from LaFarge), as well as businesses in Mexico, Spain, and the UK.

Early in 2002 Andrew Dougal retired as CEO and was replaced by Alan Murray. Hanson added to its US operations midyear with the purchase of Choctaw Inc. (concrete pipes, corrugated steel pipes, and precast concrete structures) from Amatek Holdings Ltd. That year it sold its 50% stake in North Texas Cement Co. In 2003 Hanson acquired US-based aggregates company Better Materials for $150 million. It also sold various operations in Singapore, India, Indonesia, and Germany as part of its streamlining plan.

The company bought US brick manufacturer Athens Brick in 2004. Founder Lord Hanson died the same year. Early in 2005 Hanson spent about $122 million on UK-based Marshalls Clay Products and $225 million on Thermalite (lightweight concrete blocks).

EXECUTIVES

Chairman: Mike Welton, age 58
CEO: Alan J. Murray, age 51, $1,868,414 pay
Finance Director: Jonathan Nicholls, age 47, $1,163,425 pay
Legal Director: Graham Dransfield, age 52, $847,528 pay
President, Hanson Aggregates North America: James Kitzmiller
President, Hanson Building Products North America: Richard Manning
Managing Director, Continental Europe: Justin Read
Managing Director, Hanson Building Products UK: David J. Szymanski, age 50
Managing Director, Hanson Continental Europe & Asia: Patrick O'Shea
Chief Executive, Hanson Australia: Leslie (Les) Cadzow
Corporate and Investor Relations: Carol Ann Walsh
Secretary: Paul D. Tunnacliffe
Auditors: Ernst & Young LLP

LOCATIONS

HQ: Hanson PLC
1 Grosvenor Place, London SW1X 7JH, United Kingdom
Phone: +44-20-7245-1245 **Fax:** +44-20-7235-3455
US HQ: 1333 Campus Pkwy., Neptune, NJ 07753
US Phone: 732-919-9777 **US Fax:** 732-919-1149
Web: www.hansonplc.com

Hanson has operations in 17 countries including Asia (China, Indonesia, Malaysia, Singapore, and Thailand), Australia, Europe (Belgium, the Czech Republic, France, Germany, the Netherlands, Spain, and the UK), Israel, and North America (Canada, Mexico, and the US).

2004 Sales

	$ mil.	% of total
North America		
Hanson Aggregates	1,657.2	25
Hanson Building Products	1,130.1	17
UK		
Hanson Aggregates	1,531.4	23
Hanson Building Products	532.4	8
Australia & Asia/Pacific		
Hanson Australia	1,010.5	15
Hanson Asia/Pacific	245.8	4
Hanson Continental Europe	484.2	7
Discontinued operations	50.2	1
Total	**6,641.8**	**100**

PRODUCTS/OPERATIONS

Selected Products

Aggregates
Asphalt
Cement
Clay brick
Clay pavers
Concrete products
Crushed rock
Marine aggregates
Ready-mix concrete
Recycled aggregates

Selected Operations

North America
  Hanson Aggregates North America
  Hanson Building Products North America
    Hanson Brick & Tile
    Hanson Pipe & Products
UK
  Hanson Aggregates UK
    Midland Quarry Products
      (joint venture with Tarmac)
  Hanson Building Products UK
Continental Europe and Asia
  Hanson Continental Europe & Marine
    United Marine Holdings (joint venture with Tarmac)
  Hanson Asia Pacific
Australia
  Hanson Australia
    Cement Australia Holdings (25%, with Rinker
      Group and Holcim)
    Pioneer Road Services (joint venture with
      Shell Australia)

COMPETITORS

Aggregate Industries	HeidelbergCement
Aggregate Industries UK	Holcim
Boral	Italcementi
BPB	Lafarge
Castle Cement	Martin Marietta Materials
CBR	Readymix
CEMEX	Rinker Group
CRH	Saint-Gobain
CSR	Siam Cement
Dyckerhoff	Taiheiyo Cement
FCC	Tarmac
FLS Industries	Ube
Foster Yeoman	Vulcan Materials
Franz Haniel	

HISTORICAL FINANCIALS

Company Type: Public

Income Statement
FYE: December 31

	REVENUE ($ mil.)	NET INCOME ($ mil.)	NET PROFIT MARGIN	EMPLOYEES
12/04	6,642	371	5.6%	27,400
12/03	6,454	321	5.0%	24,300
12/02	5,880	302	5.1%	25,600
12/01	5,568	406	7.3%	26,800
12/00	4,689	381	8.1%	24,700
12/99	3,103	540	17.4%	16,800
12/98	3,029	589	19.4%	16,000
12/97	4,993	1,286	25.8%	80,000
12/96	3,995	496	12.4%	76,000
12/95	17,673	1,604	9.1%	75,000
Annual Growth	(10.3%)	(15.0%)	—	(10.6%)

2004 Year-End Financials

Debt ratio: 38.8%
Return on equity: 7.4%
Cash ($ mil.): 2,673
Current ratio: 1.54
Long-term debt ($ mil.): 2,029

No. of shares (mil.): 147
Dividends
  Yield: 2.6%
  Payout: 44.6%
Market value ($ mil.): 6,328

	STOCK PRICE ($) FY Close	P/E High/Low		PER SHARE ($) Earnings	Dividends	Book Value
12/04	42.93	13	10	2.51	1.12	35.45
12/03	36.50	17	10	2.18	1.37	32.94
12/02	22.18	19	10	2.05	1.15	29.08
12/01	33.62	15	10	2.75	1.10	26.92
12/00	34.25	18	9	2.67	1.22	24.58
12/99	40.31	16	10	4.11	2.59	22.89
12/98	39.00	15	7	4.51	0.42	19.60
12/97	23.00	6	5	9.88	0.00	11.11
Annual Growth	9.3%	—	—	(17.8%)	—	18.0%

HBOS plc

Formed by UK-based insurance company Halifax's 2001 acquisition of Bank of Scotland, HBOS provides a host of financial services such as retail banking, consumer credit, savings products, stock brokerage, and asset management. HBOS also owns Bank of Scotland (Ireland), credit insurer St. Andrew's Group, and approximately 60% of UK-based life insurance and financial services provider St. James's Place Capital. Asset management unit Clerical Medical Investment Group serves retail and institutional clients. HBOS Australia oversees Bank of Western Australia (WestBank) and St. Andrew's Australia.

Along with Halifax's Yorkshire origins, HBOS's Scottish roots have impressed UK regulators, who hope the bank will be a strong regional contender against such London city slickers as Barclays, Lloyds TSB, and HSBC. The company hopes to capitalize upon its network of branches, agencies, and real estate agencies, using the organization to cross-sell its various financial and insurance products.

HISTORY

Necessity was the mother of incorporation for Halifax. As urbanization sped up in the mid-19th century, housing shortages led to the rise of building societies, cooperatives that bought land and built houses for their members. Increased demand for urban housing led to the formation of the Halifax Permanent Building and Investment Society in 1853. Because it was a permanent society, members could retain membership in the cooperative after their houses had been built, receiving interest on their invested money.

Initially Halifax kept to its namesake hometown in West Yorkshire, but it eventually expanded with a branch in nearby Huddersfield in 1862. The society got some competition at home in 1871 with the debut of the similarly named Halifax Equitable Benefit Building Society. By 1888 Halifax Permanent was able to offer paid-up shares for the first time to members who finished paying for their houses. The company's

first top officer, Jonas Taylor, died after 50 years of service; he was replaced by Enoch Hill in 1903.

By 1913 Halifax Permanent was the largest building society in the UK. Its lead position was reinforced with the 1928 acquisition of Halifax Equitable; the new company became known simply as the Halifax Building Society. Sir Enoch Hill (having been knighted during his four decades at Halifax) died in 1942.

The Building Societies Act of 1986 allowed Halifax to begin offering banking and financial services.

In 1995 the company merged with Leeds Permanent Building Society. That company's home office became the center for Halifax's financial services operations. Halifax's move into financial services continued with the 1996 acquisition of fund manager Clerical Medical. That year it also established a general insurance subsidiary.

Halifax shuffled off its mutual coil in 1997, converting to stock ownership and instantaneously becoming the eighth-largest publicly traded company in the UK.

Flush with $5 billion from the flotation, Halifax stayed on the acquisition prowl in 1998, outbidding Royal Bank of Scotland for UK mutual banker Birmingham Midshires. It denied rumors that it would buy the UK's top insurer (Prudential plc) or its #2 bank (Barclays).

Halifax launched a reorganization in 1999 to consolidate acquired operations, cut operational costs, and reemphasize customer services. It sold off about 200 of its smaller real estate agencies and invested $150 million to develop online and telephone banking. Halifax also launched an online stock trading service: ShareXpress. That year the company announced it would no longer pursue debtors whose houses had been repossessed more than six years hence but still had leftover debt.

In 2000 the company announced plans for its Internet-based bank. It also bought St. James's Place Capital, whose wealthy clientele would provide Halifax with cross-selling opportunities. The following year Halifax bought the fund management business, sales force, and computer systems of the troubled UK mutual insurer The Equitable Life Assurance Society. Halifax bought Edinburgh-based Bank of Scotland in 2001 to become HBOS plc.

EXECUTIVES

Chairman: Lord Dennis Stevenson, age 59, $1,036,296 pay
Deputy Chairman: Sir Ronald (Ron) Garrick, age 63
Group Chief Executive and Director: James R. Crosby, age 49, $2,584,961 pay
COO and Director: Andy Hornby, age 38
Chief Executive, Corporate Banking and Director: George E. Mitchell, age 54, $1,777,882 pay
Chief Executive, Strategy and International Operations and Director: Colin Matthew, age 54, $1,363,750 pay
Chief Executive, Insurance and Investment Division: John Edwards, age 50
Group Finance Director: Phil Hodkinson, age 46
Group Risk Director: Jo Dawson
Deputy Chief Executive, Corporate Banking: Peter Cummings
Head of Marketing: Philip Hanson
Head of Customer Strategy: Gerald Mclarnon
Head of Media Relations: Mark Hemingway
Head of Risk: Dan Watkins
General Manager, Group Communications: Shane O'Riordain
Director of Investor Relations: Charles Wycks
CEO, HBOS Australia: David S. Willis, age 49
Auditors: KPMG Audit Plc

PRODUCTS/OPERATIONS

2004 Sales

	$ mil.	% of total
Interest receivable & similar income	41,673.3	80
Fees & commissions receivable	5,220.0	10
Long-term assurance business	1,375.3	3
General insurance premium income	1,146.1	2
Dealing profits	400.7	1
Other	2,001.3	4
Total	**51,816.7**	**100**

Selected Subsidiaries

Capital Bank plc
Clerical Medical Investment Group Limited
The Governor & Company of the Bank of Scotland
Halifax General Insurance Services Limited
Halifax Investment Fund Managers Limited
Halifax Life Limited
Halifax plc
Halifax Share Dealing Limited
HBOS Australia Pty Ltd
　Bank of Western Australia Ltd
HBOS Financial Services Limited
HBOS Insurance & Investment Group Limited
HBOS Treasury Services plc
Insight Investment Management Limited
St. Andrews Insurance plc
St. James's Place Capital plc (60%)

COMPETITORS

Abbey National	Lloyds TSB
Alliance & Leicester	Prudential plc
Barclays	RBS
HSBC Holdings	Woolwich

HISTORICAL FINANCIALS

Company Type: Public

Income Statement

FYE: December 31

	ASSETS ($ mil.)	NET INCOME ($ mil.)	INCOME AS % OF ASSETS	EMPLOYEES
12/04	853,077	5,888	0.7%	69,243
12/03	726,118	4,359	0.6%	67,458
12/02	569,513	3,073	0.5%	63,982
12/01	453,111	2,432	0.5%	62,848
12/00	272,448	1,744	0.6%	39,488
12/99	261,999	1,720	0.7%	37,228
12/98	239,805	1,942	0.8%	26,506
12/97	216,262	1,799	0.8%	27,329
12/96	197,212	954	0.5%	25,829
Annual Growth	**20.1%**	**25.6%**	**—**	**13.1%**

2004 Year-End Financials

Equity as % of assets: 4.0%　　Long-term debt ($ mil.): 87,130
Return on assets: 0.7%　　Sales ($ mil.): 51,817
Return on equity: 19.2%

Net Income History

London: HBOS

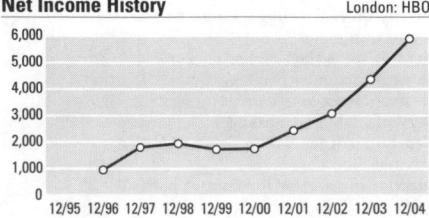

6,000	
5,000	
4,000	
3,000	
2,000	
1,000	
0	

12/95 12/96 12/97 12/98 12/99 12/00 12/01 12/02 12/03 12/04

Heineken

Smaller brewers might be green with envy. Heineken, a global brewing giant, sells its namesake beer in the easily recognized green bottles in just about every country on the planet. The company's other global brands include Amstel and Murphy's — national and regional brands include Buckler (Europe), Quilmes (Argentina), Moretti (Italy), Tiger (Asia's leading regional brew), Zagorka (Bulgaria), and Bochkaryov (Russia). Heineken also distributes soft drinks and other nonalcoholic beverages. Heineken has interests in more than 110 breweries and continues to acquire more worldwide. The founding Heineken family owns 50% of Heineken Holding, which owns 50% of Heineken.

Heineken is the #2 imported beer in the US (behind Grupo Modelo's Corona, which tapped the #1 spot after nearly 65 years of Heineken dominance).

About 75% of Heineken's sales are in Europe, where it has solidified its base by buying breweries in Central Europe, Italy, Spain, and Russia. In 2003 Heineken purchased Austrian brewer BBAG Österreichische Brau-Beteiligungs-AG for $1.7 billion. It combined its regional operations with BBAG, creating Brau Union AG. Heineken also plans to grow steadily in new markets such as Asia and South America. In 2004 it joined its Chinese operations with those of Asia Pacific Breweries to form Heineken Asia Pacific Breweries China (HAPBC); and that year HAPBC bought an approximate 21% stake in China's Kingway Brewery Holding.

Political unrest has impeded Heineken's growth in Africa. However, it joined with Diageo to purchase 30% of InBev's Namibia Breweries in southern Africa and formed a joint venture with Kenya-based East Africa Breweries to introduce Heineken's products in Kenya and Uganda. It also has plans to increase its presence in South Africa.

HISTORY

Every Sunday morning Gerard Heineken's mother was appalled by crowds of drunken Dutchmen who had consumed too much gin the night before. Heineken, who wanted his mother's financial backing, insisted that drunkenness would decrease if people drank beer instead of gin and pointed out that there were no good beers in Holland. His strategy worked. In 1863 Heineken's mother put up the money to buy De Hooiberg (The Haystack), a 271-year-old brewery in Amsterdam.

Gerard proved his aptitude for brewing and within 10 years had established a brewery in Rotterdam. He named the business Heineken in 1873 and launched the company's lucrative foreign trade by exporting beer in 1876 to France. (By the 1950s half the beer brewed by the company was for export.) The company perfected a yeast strain (Heineken A-yeast) in 1886 that is still in use today.

In 1917 Gerard's son Dr. Henri Pierre Heineken inherited the firm and expanded operations to the US. Making a voyage to that country, Henri Pierre met Leo van Munching, a ship's bartender who displayed a remarkable knowledge of beer. Recognizing van Munching's talent, Henri Pierre hired him as Heineken's US importer. Prohibition killed the US operations, although the company entered new markets

elsewhere; after repeal, Heineken was the first foreign beer to re-enter the US market.

After WWII, Henri Pierre sent his son, Alfred, to learn the business under van Munching, who had created a national distribution system in the US. Alfred succeeded his father in 1953 and stepped down in 1989.

Heineken bought the Amstel Brewery in Holland (founded 1870) in 1968. Two years later it became a producer of stout through the acquisition of James J. Murphy in Cork, Ireland. Facing a consolidation of the European market, Heineken launched a campaign in the 1980s to expand its European beer operations, purchasing breweries in France, Greece, Ireland, Italy, and Spain.

In 1991 Heineken bought the van Munching US import business and a majority interest in Hungarian brewer Komaromi Sorgyar, its first Eastern European investment. Two years later Karel Vuursteen was appointed chairman.

The firm cut more than 1,300 jobs in 1993 and sold its spirits and wine operations the next year. In 1995 Heineken began a major spending spree, acquiring Interbrew Italia and 66% of Zlaty Bazant, the largest Slovakian brewery and maltworks (it acquired the rest in 1999). The company bought Birra Moretti, Italy's third-largest brewery, in 1996. It also purchased interests in two African breweries.

To boost its sales in Poland, in 1998 Heineken raised its stake in brewer Zaklady Piwowarskie W. Zywcu (Zywiec) to 75%, bought a minority stake in Brewpole, and merged the companies to create the largest Polish brewer. That year Heineken bought about 25% of Pivara Skopje, the largest brewery in the former Yugoslav republic of Macedonia, through its Brewinvest joint venture. In 1999 the company bought about 18% of Israel's leading brewer, Tempo (Goldstar and Maccabee beers).

In 2000 Heineken bought 99% of Spanish brewer Cruzcampo, most of it from Diageo. Cruzcampo later merged with Heineken's Spanish brewer El Águila to create Heineken España.

In 2002 vice president Anthony Ruys replaced Vuursteen as CEO. Heineken also gained EU approval that year to buy a stake in German brewer Karlsberg. Also in 2002 Heineken agreed to buy stakes in two Central American breweries: Costa Rica's Florida Ice and Farm Company (FIFCO) and Nicaragua's Consorcio Cervecero Centroamericano S.A. (COCECA). With FIFCO and Coca-Cola bottler Panamerican Beverages, Heineken purchased Cervecerías Baru-Panamá, the country's second-largest brewer. The company later purchased Russian brewer Bravo International. Heineken also bought a controlling stake in Egyptian brewer Al Ahram Beverages Co. in 2002. Ak Agram produces Fayrouz, a non-alcoholic beer favored by Muslims. The brewer also agreed to increase its stake in Lebanese brewer Almaza S.A.L. from 10% to 79%.

Making a strong play for the growing US Hispanic market, Heineken inked a three-year deal with FEMSA Cerveza in 2004, making it the sole importer of FEMSA's Mexican beers Tecate, Sol, Dos Equis, Carta Blanca, and Bohemia. Heineken also began an aggressive push into Russia that year, when it purchased Sobol Beer LLC in West Siberia and the Volga and Shikhan breweries.

In 2005 the company formed a partnership with Diageo to produce and distribute Guinness in Russia. It also acquired approximately 91% of German brewer Würzburger Hofbräu AG.

EXECUTIVES

Chairman, Supervisory Board: Cees (C.J.A.) van Lede
Vice Chairman, Supervisory Board:
Jan Maarten (J.M.) de Jong
CEO and Chairman, Executive Board:
Jean François van Boxmeer, age 44, $860,174 pay
(prior to title change)
CFO and Member, Executive Board:
René Hooft (D.R.) Graafland, age 50, $860,174 pay
COO and Member, Executive Board:
Marc J. (M.J.) Bolland, age 46, $860,174 pay
(prior to title change)
President, Africa & Middle East and Member, Executive Committee: Thom de Man, age 57
President, Americas and Member, Executive Committee: Massimo von Wunster, age 48
President, Asia/Pacific and Member, Executive Committee: Siep Hiemstra, age 50
President, Central and Eastern Europe and Member, Executive Committee: Nico Nusmeier, age 44
President, Western Europe and Member, Executive Board: Didier Debrosse, age 49
CEO, Heineken Russia: Roland Pirmez
Group Director, Control and Accounting and Member, Executive Committee: Floris Van Woerkom, age 42
Group Director, Corporate Relations and Member, Executive Committee: Sean O'Neill, age 42
Group Director, Human Resources and Member, Executive Committee: Frans van der Minne, age 57
Group Director, Legal Affairs: Steven van Maasakker
Director, Corporate Finance: David R. Hazelwood
Director, Investor Relations: Jan van de Merbel
Group Director, IT: Paolo Cinelli
Auditors: KPMG Accountants N.V.

LOCATIONS

HQ: Heineken N.V.
Tweede Weteringplantsoen 21,
1017 ZD Amsterdam, The Netherlands
Phone: +31-20-523-9239 **Fax:** +31-20-626-3503
US HQ: 360 Hamilton Ave., Ste. 1103,
White Plains, NY 10601
US Phone: 914-681-4100 **US Fax:** 914-681-1900
Web: www.heinekeninternational.com

Heineken has more than 115 breweries in more than 65 countries.

2004 Sales

	% of total
Western Europe	52
Central & Eastern Europe	22
The Americas	14
Africa & the Middle East	8
Asia/Pacific	4
Total	**100**

PRODUCTS/OPERATIONS

2004 Sales

	% of total
Beer	77
Soft drinks	12
Wines & spirits	8
Other	3
Total	**100**

Selected Brands

33 Export
ABC Stout
Aguila
Alfa
Amstel (regular, 1870, Bock, Dark, Gold, Legend, Light, Malt — alcohol-free)
Buckler
Cruzcampo
Desperados
Fayrouz (alcohol-free)
Fischer
Golden Brau
Guinness (licensed)
Hacker-Pschorr
Havannah
Heineken

Ichnusa
Kaiser
Kaliber
Karlsburg
Kingway
Kriska
Loewenbrau (licensed)
Maccabee
Moretti
Murphy's (Irish Amber, Irish Red Beer, Irish Stout)
Paulaner
Piton
Presidente
Prestige
Primus
Quilmes
Santa Fe
Schneider
Silva
Summer
Star
Stella
Tiger
Victoria
Vos
Warka
Wieckse Witte
Zagorka

COMPETITORS

Allied Domecq	Gambrinus
AmBev	Grolsch
Anheuser-Busch	Grupo Modelo
Asahi Breweries	InBev
Bavaria S.A.	Kirin
Boston Beer	Lion Nathan
Carlsberg	Miller Brewing
Cervecerías Unidas	Molson Coors
Constellation Brands	SABMiller
Diageo	San Miguel
FEMSA	Scottish & Newcastle
Foster's	Taiwan Tobacco & Wine

HISTORICAL FINANCIALS

Company Type: Public

Income Statement

FYE: December 31

	REVENUE ($ mil.)	NET INCOME ($ mil.)	NET PROFIT MARGIN	EMPLOYEES
12/04	13,647	733	5.4%	61,732
12/03	11,617	1,002	8.6%	61,271
12/02	10,788	833	7.7%	48,237
12/01	8,515	679	8.0%	40,025
12/00	7,634	585	7.7%	37,857
12/99	7,198	548	7.6%	36,733
12/98	7,361	522	7.1%	33,511
12/97	6,668	376	5.6%	32,421
12/96	7,053	379	5.4%	31,682
12/95	6,492	413	6.4%	27,379
Annual Growth	**8.6%**	**6.6%**	**—**	**9.5%**

2004 Year-End Financials

Debt ratio: 78.2%
Return on equity: 17.1%
Cash ($ mil.): 857
Current ratio: 1.05
Long-term debt ($ mil.): 3,604

Net Income History

Pink Sheets: HINKY

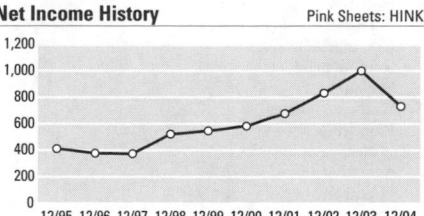

Henkel KGaA

Henkel is focusing on home and hearth. The company sold its chemical operations (Cognis and joint venture Henkel-Ecolab) and its fertilizer and plant care business (Substral) to focus on its branded laundry, home care, cosmetics, toiletries, and adhesive products. Its March 2004 purchase of The Dial Corporation fuels its expansion into these US market segments. Most of Henkel's operations are centered in Europe, where the company is a leading maker of toiletries, cosmetics, detergents, and cleansers. It also makes adhesives and surface care preparation products for industrial use through its Henkel Technologies division. Relatives of the founding Henkel family control the company.

Germany accounts for more than 20% of Henkel's sales, while the rest of Europe, along with Africa and the Middle East, brings in more than 50%. Henkel has operations in more than 75 countries.

Henkel bought US-based Dial Corporation (Dial soap, Purex laundry products, Renuzit air fresheners, Armour Star canned meats) in 2004 for $2.9 billion in cash. The deal gives Henkel a greater presence in the US and allows Henkel to compete with consumer products giants Procter & Gamble and Unilever. Henkel plans to sell all or parts of its share in Ecolab.

Also in 2004 Henkel and US bleach giant Clorox agreed to a deal (in the form of an asset swap) that dissolved Henkel's nearly 30% stake in Clorox. The $2.8 billion transaction involved Henkel's purchase of Clorox's 20% stake in Henkel Iberica, a joint venture between the two in Portugal and Spain. Henkel also bought Clorox's stake in a pesticide company as part of the transaction and added Combat insecticides and Soft Scrub bathroom cleaner to its brand portfolio.

HISTORY

In 1876 Fritz Henkel, a chemical plant worker, started Henkel & Cie in Aachen to make a universal detergent. He moved the business to Düsseldorf in 1878 and launched Henkel's Bleaching Soda, one of Germany's first brand-name products. In the 1880s the company began making water glass, an ingredient of its detergent, which differs from soap in the way it emulsifies dirt. Henkel debuted Persil, a detergent that eliminated the need for rubbing or bleaching clothes, in 1907. Persil became a leading detergent in Germany.

Henkel set up an Austrian subsidiary in 1913. In response to a postwar adhesives shortage, the company started making glue for its own packaging and soon became Europe's leading glue maker. Henkel began making cleansers with newly developed phosphates in the 1920s.

When Fritz died in 1930, Henkel stock was divided among his three children. In the 1930s the company sponsored a whaling fleet that provided fats for its products, and by 1939 the firm had 16 plants in Europe.

During WWII Henkel lost most of its foreign plants and made unbranded soap in Germany. After the war it retooled its plants, branched out into personal care products, and competed with Unilever, Procter & Gamble, and Colgate-Palmolive for control of the German detergent market. (By 1968 Henkel dominated, with close to a 50% share.)

In 1960 Henkel bought its first US company, Standard Chemicals (renamed Henkel Corp. in 1971). Konrad Henkel, who took over in 1961, modernized the company's image by making changes in management structure and marketing techniques. Henkel patented a substitute for environmentally harmful phosphates, acquired 15% of Clorox in 1974, and bought General Mills' chemical business in 1977.

Henkel, owned at the time by 66 family members, went public with nonvoting shares in 1985. It bought US companies Nopco (specialty chemicals) and Parker Chemical (metal surface pretreatment) in 1987 and Emery, the #1 US oleochemicals maker, in 1989.

Henkel reorganized its product lines in 1991 by selling several noncore businesses. That year Henkel formed a partnership with Ecolab (of which it owned 24% — later expanded to 50%); acquired interests in Hungary, Poland, Russia, and Slovenia; and introduced Persil in Spain and Portugal. In 1994 Henkel expanded into China and bought 25% of a Brazilian detergent maker.

The company's 1995 acquisition of Hans Schwarzkopf GmbH made Henkel the #1 hair-coloring manufacturer in Germany. The company bought Novamax Technologies, a US-based maker of metal-surface treatments, in 1996. The next year Henkel paid $1.3 billion for US adhesive giant Loctite, its biggest purchase to date. In 1998 it bought Ohio-based adhesive maker Manco to combine its US and Canadian consumer adhesive businesses (parts of Loctite and LePage, respectively) under Manco. Henkel pushed into the US toiletries market in 1998 by paying $93 million for DEP and creating a new subsidiary, Schwarzkopf & DEP Inc.

In 1999 Henkel formed a joint venture with soap maker Dial (Dial/Henkel LLC); the joint venture later bought the Custom Cleaner home dry cleaning business from Creative Products Resource.

Henkel picked up Yamahatsu Sangyo, a Japanese maker of hair colorants, in 2000. The company sold its Substral unit (fertilizer and plant care) to Scotts Company (now Scotts Miracle-Gro). In 2001 Henkel bought TOTAL's metal-treatment chemicals business. In addition, the company sold its Cognis specialty chemicals unit to private equity funds Schroeder Ventures and Goldman Sachs Capital Partners for about $2.2 billion. Also in 2001 Henkel also said it would cut 2,500-3,000 jobs (about 5% of its workforce) over the next two years. That year the company also sold its stake in joint venture Henkel-Ecolab to Ecolab for about $430 million.

In 2003 Henkel bought a 7% stake in German hair-care company Wella. Later that year Henkel purchased a majority stake in La Luz S.A., a Central American manufacturer and marketer of detergents and household cleaners.

Henkel strengthened its adhesives business in Russia and North, Central, and Eastern Europe when it acquired Makroflex from YIT Construction Ltd. in July 2003. Makroflex, located in Finland and Estonia, develops, makes, and sells sealants and insulation materials for the construction industry.

In 2004 Henkel acquired Advanced Research Laboratories and folded the company into its existing Schwarzkopf & Dep subsidiary. The deal boosts the company's share of the US hairstyling market. Also that year it bought 70% of Coventry's Chemtek, an independent firm that specializes in formulating and manufacturing liquid cleaners.

EXECUTIVES

Chairman: Albrecht Woeste, age 69
President and CEO: Ulrich Lehner, age 59
EVP and Director, Cosmetic and Body Care Division: Hans Van Bylen, age 44
EVP, Consumer and Craftsman Adhesives: Alois Linder, age 58
EVP, Finance: Lothar Steineback, age 57
EVP, Henkel Technologies: Jochen Krautter, age 62
EVP, Human Resources, IT, Logistics, and Purchasing: Kasper B. Rorsted, age 43
EVP, Laundry and Home Care: Klaus Morwind, age 62
VP, Corporate Development, Henkel Merger Corporation: Helmut Nuhn
VP, Henkel Merger Corporation: Kenneth R. Pina
Corporate International VP: Alain Bauwens
President and CEO, Henkel Corporation (US): John E. Knudson
President and CEO, The Dial Corporation: Bradley A. (Brad) Casper, age 45
Chief Technology Officer, Research and Development: Wolfgang Gawrisch
General Counsel: Franz-Josef Acher
Associate General Counsel: Thomas-Gerd Kuehn
Auditors: KPMG Deutsche Treuhand-Gesellschaft AG

LOCATIONS

HQ: Henkel KGaA
    Henkelstrasse 67, D-40191 Düsseldorf, Germany
Phone: +49-211-797-0   **Fax:** +49-211-798-2484
US HQ: 2200 Renaissance Blvd., Ste. 200,
    Gulph Mills, PA 19406
US Phone: 610-270-8100   **US Fax:** 610-270-8104
Web: www.henkel.com

2004 Sales

	% of total
Europe, Africa & Middle East	67
North America	19
Asia-Pacific	7
Latin America	4
Corporate	3
Total	**100**

PRODUCTS/OPERATIONS

2004 Sales

	% of total
Laundry & home care	34
Henkel Technologies	26
Cosmetics/toiletries	23
Adhesives	14
Corporate	3
Total	**100**

Selected Products

Adhesives
  Consumer and craftsmen adhesives
    Adhesive tapes
    Building chemicals
    Ceiling, wall covering, and tile adhesives
    Coatings
    Contact adhesives
    Correction rollers
    Cyanoacrylates
    Flooring adhesives
    Glue rollers
    Glue sticks
    Home-decoration products
    Polyurethane foam fillers
    PVC pipe adhesives
    Roofing products
    Sealants
    Wallpaper pastes
    Wood glues
  Engineering adhesives
    Assembly adhesives
    High-performance sealants
    Reactive sealants
    Sealing systems

Industrial and packaging adhesives
  Adhesives for nonwovens
  Adhesives for the wood-processing industry
  Bookbinding adhesives
  Cigarette adhesives
  Laminating adhesives
  Leather board
  Packaging and labeling adhesives
  Pressure-sensitive adhesives
  Rubber-to-metal bonding agents
  Shoe adhesives
  Wood adhesives
Cosmetics and Toiletries
  Bath and shower products
  Dental care and oral hygiene products
  Deodorants
  Hair colorants
  Hair salon products
  Hairstyling and permanent-wave products
  Perfumes and fragrances
  Shampoos and conditioners
  Skin care products
  Skin creams
  Toilet soaps
Detergents and Household Cleansers
  Bath and toilet cleansers
  Dishwashing products
  Fabric softeners
  Floor and carpet care products
  Furniture and kitchen care products
  Glass cleaners
  Heavy-duty detergents
  Household cleansers
  Plant care products
  Scouring agents
  Shoe care and laundry conditioning products
  Specialty detergents
Industrial and Institutional Hygiene and Surface Technologies
  Industrial and Institutional Hygiene
    Products, appliances, equipment, systems, and services for cleaning, laundry, maintenance, sanitizing, and disinfecting
  Surface Technologies
    Antifreeze agents and corrosion inhibitors for automotive cooling systems
    CFC substitutes for cleaning applications
    Cleaning products
    Corrosion inhibitors
    Corrosion-protection waxes
    Dispersion adhesives
    Elastomer sealants
    Epoxy structural adhesives
    Hotmelt adhesives
    Lubricants
    Polyurethane adhesives
    Process control and metering equipment
    Products and applications for the chemical surface treatment of metals and metal substitutes
    Products for conversion processing
    PVC and polyacrylate plastisols
    Specialty products for the automotive industry

COMPETITORS

3M	Johnson & Johnson
Alticor	Kimberly-Clark
Avon	L'Oréal
Bayer	Playtex
Beiersdorf	Procter & Gamble
Church & Dwight	Reckitt Benckiser
Colgate-Palmolive	Sara Lee
Dow Chemical	Sara Lee Household
Estée Lauder	S.C. Johnson
Gillette	Shiseido
H.B. Fuller	Unilever

HISTORICAL FINANCIALS

Company Type: Public

Income Statement

FYE: December 31

	REVENUE ($ mil.)	NET INCOME ($ mil.)	NET PROFIT MARGIN	EMPLOYEES
12/04	14,448	2,367	16.4%	49,947
12/03	11,844	651	5.5%	48,628
12/02	10,121	456	4.5%	48,638
12/01	11,569	445	3.8%	59,995
12/00	12,033	441	3.7%	60,475
12/99	11,441	407	3.6%	56,396
12/98	12,729	434	3.4%	56,291
12/97	11,196	629	5.6%	53,753
12/96	10,495	332	3.2%	46,665
12/95	9,875	339	3.4%	41,664
Annual Growth	4.3%	24.1%	—	2.0%

2004 Year-End Financials

Debt ratio: 30.2%
Return on equity: 45.4%
Cash ($ mil.): 2,312
Current ratio: 1.67
Long-term debt ($ mil.): 1,889

Net Income History

German: HENKY

2,500									
2,000									
1,500									
1,000									
500									
0									
12/95	12/96	12/97	12/98	12/99	12/00	12/01	12/02	12/03	12/04

Hilton Group

Hilton Group knows how to cover its bets as well as its beds. The company is a major hotel operator through its Hilton International division and is one of the largest betting shop operators in the UK (alongside William Hill). Hilton Group's Ladbrokes unit has more than 2,000 betting shops in Belgium, Ireland, and the UK; it also has telephone, interactive TV, and Internet gambling operations. The company owns rights to the Hilton brand outside the US and operates more than 400 Hilton, Conrad, and Scandic hotels in 80 countries. The company also operates a centralized reservation system and rewards program with US-based Hilton Hotels. In addition, Hilton International owns the LivingWell health clubs.

Hospitality accounts for about 15% of Hilton Group's revenue; its gaming activities make up the remainder. Ladbrokes' Web operations offer online betting on a variety of events, including cricket, soccer, football, rugby, greyhound racing, and golf. Its online casino features roulette, blackjack, craps, video poker, and other games. The division also runs Vernons soccer betting pools.

The company has been paring its hospitality holdings, selling 15 UK hotels and announcing plans for additional UK and international disposals, including a Sydney hotel which had a refurbishment completed in 2005.

The Hilton Group sold off its Ladbroke Casinos in 2000, but has devoted more resources to online gambling opportunities, which in 2004 made up more than 10% of the Ladbrokes' unit sales.

HISTORY

The Hilton Group traces its roots to the village of Ladbroke in central England, where Arthur Bendir, a local racehorse trainer, set up a partnership in 1886 to take bets on horse races. Although off-track betting was illegal, betting on credit was allowed for wealthier members of society. The partnership, Ladbroke and Co., moved to London in 1900 and established itself as a quality credit betting shop in the city's plush West End. Bendir sold the business in 1957 to the Stein family. In 1960 the government legalized cash betting and Ladbroke began to expand. Cyril Stein became chairman in 1966 and took the company public the next year as the Ladbroke Group. It had 109 off-track betting shops in operation; by 1971 it had 660.

Stein pushed to diversify the company into real estate and casinos during the 1970s, and in 1973 Ladbroke bought three hotels. In the late 1970s the company suffered a major setback when its casino ventures in London were closed down and it was found guilty of violating gaming laws. The firm abandoned the casino business in 1979. In 1984 the company bought the Belgian Le Tierce betting shop chain and broke into the US market in 1985 with the acquisition of the Detroit Race Course (sold 1998). In 1987 Ladbroke beat out competitors to buy the 91-hotel Hilton International chain from Allegis Corporation for more than $1 billion. The deal made Ladbroke one of the world's top hotel operators.

Stein retired as chairman in 1994 and was replaced by John Jackson. Peter George, who had been with the company since 1963, was appointed chief executive. That year the company re-entered the casino business, paying $75 million for three London casinos. Though Ladbroke's property and retail division suffered in the 1990s, the hotel chain continued to expand; by 1995 there were 160 in operation. In 1997 Ladbroke entered into a sales and marketing alliance with US-based Hilton Hotels to promote the Hilton brand throughout the world. The next year Ladbroke acquired #3 betting shop operator Coral from leisure group Bass (now split into Mitchells & Butlers and InterContinental Hotel Group). However, UK regulators later forced the company to sell the chain. (A venture capital company backed by Morgan Grenfell Private Equity bought it for about $655 million.)

With its $2 billion acquisition of Stakis in 1999, Ladbroke gained 55 hotels and 20 casinos in the UK and Ireland, as well as the LivingWell health club chain. Stakis' CEO, David Michels, became head of Hilton International. Ladbroke changed its name to Hilton Group that year. In 2000 George resigned from the company and was replaced by Michels. That year Hilton Group sold its casino operations for $373 million to Gala Group Holdings. In 2001 the company bought the Scandic Hotel chain for about $885 million. Also that year Jackson retired as chairman and was replaced by Ian Robinson.

EXECUTIVES

Chairman: Sir Ian Robinson, age 62, $356,347 pay
Group Chief Executive and Director:
David M.C. Michels, age 58, $1,960,872 pay
Deputy Chief Executive and Finance Director:
Brian G. Wallace, age 50, $1,377,233 pay
Director; Chief Executive, Ladbrokes Worldwide:
Christopher (Chris) Bell, age 47, $1,047,853 pay
Director; Chief Executive, Hilton International:
Ian R. Carter, age 43
SVP Marketing, Hilton International: Mike Ashton
HR Director, Ladbrokes Worldwide: Ros Barker

SVP Real Estate, Hilton International: Adrian Bradley, age 39
SVP Distribution and E-Commerce, Hilton International: Tim Davis
Director Corporate Development: Roger Devlin
President, Europe and Africa, Hilton International:
Jürgen Fischer, age 50
SVP Development, Europe and Africa:
Patrick Fitzgibbon
President, The Americas, Hilton International:
Howard Friedman
President, Middle East and Asia Pacific, Hilton International: Koos Klein
President, UK and Ireland, Hilton International:
Wolfgang M. Neumann
Head of Group Human Resources and Legal Services:
Bryan Taker
Head of Investor Relations: Julian Arlett
Secretary: Michael J. Noble
Auditors: Ernst & Young

LOCATIONS

HQ: Hilton Group plc
Maple Court, Central Park, Reeds Crescent, Watford, Hertfordshire WD24 4QQ, United Kingdom
Phone: +44-20-7856-8000   **Fax:** +44-20-7856-8001
Web: www.hiltongroup.com

2004 Sales

	% of total
Europe	
UK	87
Other countries	11
Americas	1
Other regions	1
Total	100

PRODUCTS/OPERATIONS

2004 Sales

	% of total
Betting & gaming	85
Hotels	15
Total	100

COMPETITORS

Camelot	Stanley Leisure
Four Seasons Hotels	Starwood Hotels & Resorts
Gala Group	Thistle Hotels
Hyatt	Whitbread
Marriott	William Hill
Millennium &	Wyndham
Copthorne Hotels	Zetters
Rank	

HISTORICAL FINANCIALS

Company Type: Public

Income Statement

FYE: December 31

	REVENUE ($ mil.)	NET INCOME ($ mil.)	NET PROFIT MARGIN	EMPLOYEES
12/04	22,909	502	2.2%	51,890
12/03	15,878	199	1.3%	49,187
12/02	8,788	156	1.8%	51,637
12/01	6,039	208	3.4%	55,413
12/00	5,898	208	3.5%	53,631
12/99	6,950	155	2.2%	53,483
12/98	7,764	354	4.6%	46,702
12/97	6,295	249	4.0%	71,000
12/96	6,399	35	0.5%	70,000
Annual Growth	17.3%	39.5%	—	(3.7%)

2004 Year-End Financials

Debt ratio: 53.1%
Return on equity: 10.9%
Cash ($ mil.): 931
Current ratio: 0.88
Long-term debt ($ mil.): 2,610

Hitachi, Ltd.

Hitachi, which means "risen sun," is looking for a new dawn of profits from its galaxy of businesses. The company is a world-leading maker of powerful, corporate transaction-oriented mainframes, as well as semiconductors, PCs, and other information system and telecommunications technologies. Hitachi also makes elevators and escalators, industrial robots and control systems, and power plant equipment. The company's power and industrial systems unit is its biggest revenue producer. Other products include metals, wire, and cable. Hitachi's consumer goods range from TVs to refrigerators and washing machines; the company also has operations in financial services, property management, and transportation.

Hitachi's operations are organized into seven divisions: Power & Industrial (power plants, industrial machinery, automotive equipment, heavy machinery), Information & Telecommunication Systems (computer and telecom hardware, software, and services), High-functional Materials & Components (fabricated chemical and metal products), Electronic Devices (LCDs, semiconductor manufacturing equipment, test and measurement equipment, medical electronics), Digital Media & Consumer (optical disk drives, TVs, projectors, mobile phones, home appliances), Financial Services (leasing, lending, insurance), and Logistics, Services & Other.

Hitachi has designated certain businesses within each division for growth. Target operations include outsourcing, data storage hard drives and systems, medical electronics, semiconductor and LCD manufacturing and inspection equipment, automotive products, and plasma display panels.

Decreased demand for PC components and weakness in the telecom sector have hurt Hitachi, and the company is working to cut costs and reduce debt. It also hopes to combine packages of information services with more of its products.

In 2002 Hitachi merged its system chip unit with that of Mitsubishi Electric to form a new company, Renesas Technology. It sold its Hitachi Printing Solutions subsidiary to Ricoh in 2004. The company announced plans for an LCD television joint venture with Toshiba and Matsushita Electric in 2004, and a plasma television joint venture with Matsushita Electric in 2005.

HISTORY

Namihei Odaira, an employee of Kuhara Mining in the Japanese coastal city of Hitachi, wanted to prove that Japan did not have to depend on foreigners for technology. In 1910 he began building electric motors in Kuhara's engineering and repair shop. Japanese power companies were forced to buy Odaira's generators when WWI made imports scarce. Impressed, they reordered, and in 1920 Hitachi (meaning "risen sun") became an independent company.

During the 1920s acquisitions and growth turned Hitachi into a major manufacturer of electrical equipment and machinery. In the 1930s and 1940s, Hitachi developed vacuum tubes and light bulbs and produced radar and sonar for the Japanese war effort. Postwar occupation forces removed Odaira and closed 19 Hitachi plants. Reeling from the plant closures, war damage, and labor strife, Hitachi was saved from bankruptcy by US military contracts during the Korean War.

In the 1950s Hitachi became a supplier to Nippon Telegraph and Telephone Corporation (NTT), the state-owned telecommunications monopoly. Japan's economic recovery led to strong demand for the company's communications and electrical equipment. Hitachi began mass-producing home appliances, radios, TVs, and transistors. The group spun off Hitachi Metals and Hitachi Cable in 1956 and Hitachi Chemical in 1963.

With the help of NTT, the Ministry of International Trade and Industry, and technology licensed from RCA (bought by General Electric in 1986), Hitachi produced its first computer in 1965. Hitachi built factories in Southeast Asia and started manufacturing integrated circuits.

Hitachi launched an IBM-compatible computer in 1974. The company sold its computers in the US through Itel until 1979, when Itel was bought by National Semiconductor, and afterward through National Semiconductor's NAS (National Advanced Systems) unit. In 1982 FBI agents caught Hitachi staff buying documents allegedly containing IBM software secrets. Settlement of a civil lawsuit required Hitachi to make payments to IBM for eight years as compensation for the use of IBM's software.

When in the late 1980s the rising Japanese yen hurt exports, Hitachi focused on its domestic market and invested heavily in factory automation. But a recession at home caused earnings to fall. In 1988 the company and Texas Instruments joined in the costly development and production of 16-megabyte DRAM semiconductor chips. In 1989 Hitachi bought 80% of NAS, giving it direct control of its US distribution.

Despite its rivalry with IBM, in 1991 Hitachi began to resell IBM notebook PCs under its own name in Japan. In a major move to combat sluggish consumer electronics sales, in 1994 Hitachi merged with its marketing subsidiary, Hitachi Sales Corp. Hitachi used joint ventures to beef up its international presence, including a 1995 agreement with India's Tata Group.

Tokyo police in 1997 began investigating Hitachi, charging that the company and others had paid off a corporate racketeer. A slump in microchip prices, coupled with the Asian economic turmoil, hurt Hitachi in 1998. Etsuhiko Shoyama became president the next year, replacing Tsutomu Kanai, who became chairman. Hitachi posted its then-worst loss in history in 1999; the firm combined some subsidiaries and announced layoffs.

In 2000 Hitachi launched the Internet & Network Services Group to focus on Internet business development; the next year it joined NEC Corp. to develop semiconductors for LCD panels and cell phone displays.

The company teamed with Sun Microsystems in 2002 in a multibillion-dollar storage software distribution and cross-licensing agreement. Hitachi also formed a joint venture with IBM for Hitachi to acquire IBM's disk drive operations.

EXECUTIVES

SVP; President and CEO, Information and Telecommunication Systems: Kazuo Furukawa, age 59
President and CEO: Etsuhiko Shoyama, age 69
EVP; General Manager, Information Business Group: Isao Ono
EVP; General Manager, Research and Development Group: Michiharu Nakamura
President, IPS Alpha Technology: Fumiaki Yonai
President and CEO, Hitachi Plant Technologies: Masaharu Sumikawa
SVP; General Manager, Finance: Takashi Miyoshi
SVP; General Manager, Global Business: Hiroaki Nakanishi
SVP; General Manager, Legal and Corporate Communications and Auditing: Takashi Hatchoji
SVP; General Manager, Sales Management Division: Takuya Tajima
VP; CEO, Platform and Network Systems Operation and Information and Telecommunications Systems: Manabu Shinomoto
VP; President and CEO, Automotive Systems: Taiji Hasegawa
VP; President and Director, Hitachi Displays: Kazuhiro Mori
VP; President and CEO, Industrial Systems Group: Gaku Suzuki
VP; President and CEO, Power Systems Group: Shigeharu Mano
VP; President and CEO, Ubiquitous Platform Systems Group: Kazuhiro Tachibana
VP; General Manager, Hitachi Group, Corporate Strategy: Makoto Ebata
VP; General Manager, Human Capital: Iwao Hara
Auditors: Shin Nihon & Co.

LOCATIONS

HQ: Hitachi, Ltd.
(Hitachi Seisakusho Kabushiki Kaisha)
4-6, Kanda-Surugadai, Chiyoda-ku,
Tokyo 101-8010, Japan
Phone: +81-3-3258-1111 **Fax:** +81-3-3258-2375
US HQ: 50 Prospect Ave., Tarrytown, NY 10591
US Phone: 914-332-5800 **US Fax:** 914-332-5555
Web: www.hitachi.com

2005 Sales

	% of total
Asia	
Japan	72
Other countries	14
North America	8
Europe	5
Other regions	1
Total	**100**

PRODUCTS/OPERATIONS

2005 Sales

	% of total
Power & industrial systems	24
Information & telecommunication systems	21
High-functional materials & components	14
Electronic devices	12
Digital media & consumer products	12
Financial services	5
Logistics, services & other	12
Total	**100**

Selected Operations

Power and industrial systems
- Air-conditioning equipment
- Automotive equipment
- Construction machinery
- Elevators
- Environmental control systems
- Escalators
- Hydroelectric power plants
- Industrial machinery and plant construction
- Nuclear power plants
- Rolling stock
- Thermal power plants

Information and telecommunication systems
- Computer peripherals
- Fiber-optic components
- Mainframes
- PCs
- RAID storage systems
- Servers
- Software
- Switches
- Systems integration

High-functional materials and components
- Cables
- Carbon products
- Chemical products
- Components
- Copper products
- Electrical insulating materials
- Fine ceramics
- Magnetic materials
- Malleable cast-iron products
- Printed circuit boards
- Specialty steels
- Synthetic resins
- Wires

Electronic devices
- LCDs
- Medical electronics equipment
- Memories
- Multi-purpose semiconductors
- Semiconductor manufacturing equipment
- System LSIs
- Testing and measurement equipment

Digital media and consumer products
- Batteries
- Fluorescent lamps
- Information storage media
- Kitchen appliances
- LCD projectors
- Mobile phones
- Optical storage drives
- Refrigerators
- Room air conditioners
- TVs
- VCRs
- Videotapes
- Washing machines

Financial services
- Insurance services
- Leasing
- Loan guarantees

Logistics, services, and other
- General trading
- Property management
- Transportation

COMPETITORS

ALSTOM	Nippon Steel
Dell	Nokia
Ericsson	Nortel Networks
Fluor	Oki Electric
Fujitsu	Philips Electronics
GE	Samsung
Hewlett-Packard	SANYO
IBM	Sharp
Intel	Siemens
Matsushita	Sony
McDermott	Texas Instruments
Micron Technology	Toshiba
Mitsubishi Electric	United Technologies
Motorola	Whirlpool
NEC	

HISTORICAL FINANCIALS

Company Type: Public

Income Statement

FYE: March 31

	REVENUE ($ mil.)	NET INCOME ($ mil.)	NET PROFIT MARGIN	EMPLOYEES
3/05	84,365	481	0.6%	323,072
3/04	81,438	150	0.2%	306,876
3/03	69,343	236	0.3%	320,528
3/02	60,104	(3,638)	—	306,989
3/01	67,879	842	1.2%	340,939
3/00	77,956	165	0.2%	337,911
3/99	65,929	(2,800)	—	328,351
3/98	63,764	26	0.0%	331,494
3/97	68,735	712	1.0%	330,152
3/96	75,771	1,322	1.7%	331,852
Annual Growth	1.2%	(10.6%)	—	(0.3%)

2005 Year-End Financials

Debt ratio: 57.2%
Return on equity: 2.3%
Cash ($ mil.): 6,624
Current ratio: 1.31
Long-term debt ($ mil.): 12,327

No. of shares (mil.): 337
Dividends
  Yield: 0.8%
  Payout: 36.6%
Market value ($ mil.): 20,926

Stock History

NYSE: HIT

	STOCK PRICE ($) FY Close	P/E High/Low		PER SHARE ($) Earnings	Dividends	Book Value
3/05	62.13	57	40	1.42	0.52	64.04
3/04	77.55	198	78	0.40	0.53	62.02
3/03	35.15	113	48	0.69	0.00	46.57
3/02	73.55	—	—	(10.90)	0.68	51.89
3/01	87.25	61	31	2.40	0.77	69.13
3/00	121.88	336	137	0.49	0.29	83.95
3/99	72.75	—	—	(8.40)	0.00	71.03
3/98	73.50	1,175	675	0.10	0.00	73.55
3/97	87.88	51	41	2.10	0.43	79.34
3/96	97.63	31	25	3.74	0.54	89.65
Annual Growth	(4.9%)	—	—	(10.2%)	(0.4%)	(3.7%)

Hollinger Inc.

Hollinger makes headlines as one of the largest newspaper groups in the world. It operates through a 17% ownership stake (67% voting interest) in Hollinger International, which publishes more than 200 daily, non-daily, trade, and specialty titles primarily in the UK and the US. Hollinger International owns the *Chicago Sun-Times,* as well as a large number of community newspapers in the Chicago area. It has sold its London-based Telegraph newspaper group and *The Jerusalem Post* (Israeli English-language daily). Embattled former chief Conrad Black controls about 78% of Hollinger through a private holding company. (Black resigned from the holding company in 2005.)

Hollinger has been significantly paring down operations in recent years in an effort to focus on its larger newspapers. The company sold most of its Canadian newspapers in 2000, but kept a 50% stake in the *National Post* until 2002, when it sold out to partner CanWest. It also sold many of its US community papers and in 2004 Hollinger sold *The Jerusalem Post* to Israeli publisher Mirkaei Tikshoret Group, a partner of CanWest.

In 2003 its Hollinger International made a number of management changes, including the removal of Black as CEO after the discovery of certain unauthorized payments (more than $400 million, according to a special committee report) to him and other executives. The SEC is also investigating the controversial payments and has filed civil-fraud charges against Black and former president and COO David Radler. Radler and Mark Kipnis, the company's former legal counsel, have been indicted in federal court on seven counts of fraud.

Black was court-ordered to pay Hollinger International nearly $30 million. A lawsuit filed by Hollinger International accused Black and other company executives of violating racketeering laws and asked for more than $1.2 billion in damages. A judge dismissed the racketeering suit in fall 2004, but left the possibility open for charges to be refiled. Hollinger International filed new charges later in 2004 against Black and another company executive, accusing them of breaching their fiduciary duty. Black ran into more problems in 2005 when Hollinger Inc. sued him and others for more than $525 million.

Another problem arose in 2004 when it was discovered that the *Chicago Sun-Times* had inflated its circulation numbers for several years. Advertisers have started filing lawsuits against the company. The company agreed to pay advertisers $27 million for the overpriced advertising during the period the circulation was misrepresented.

Black's plan to sell his share of Hollinger International to British billionaires, the Barclay brothers, was blocked by a US judge in 2004. Hollinger theb sold its London newspaper group including *The Daily Telegraph* to a group controlled by the Barclay brothers for $1.3 billion.

In 2005, irate shareholders demanded a change in the board of directors, complaining about the direction of the company and the levels of fees the board members were paid. The company agreed to increase the number of board members to seven, comprised of five new members and two remaining members.

HISTORY

A born entrepreneur, Conrad Black bought his first share of stock (in General Motors) at age eight. Some of his early childhood deals weren't quite so constructive: He was expelled from a private school at age 14 for selling exams and was kicked out of one law school after spending all his time playing the stock market.

Black entered publishing in 1969 when he and Peter White founded Sterling Newspapers and bought the *Sherbrooke Record.* The two added to their flagship with a group of small daily papers in British Columbia, Quebec, and Prince Edward Island. In 1975 Black bought his father's 22% of the Ravelston Corporation, which owned Argus, a company formed in 1945 by E. P. Taylor to invest in breweries, malting and bottling operations, and a chemical business. Black took control of the company in the late 1970s by obtaining a loan through Sterling.

After assuming the leadership of Argus (through Ravelston), Black sold off chunks of the company to refine its holdings to key businesses.

The company adopted the Hollinger name (left over from Argus' early investment in Hollinger Consolidated Gold Mines) in 1985 and gained control of struggling newspaper *The Daily Telegraph* (London), which it turned around by cutting staff and modernizing. In 1989 the firm purchased Jerusalem Post Publications.

Hollinger continued to acquire and restore struggling companies during the 1990s. It bought a stake in Southam in 1992 and acquired the Sun-Times Company, publisher of the *Chicago Sun-Times,* in 1994. Hollinger purchased two daily and 12 non-daily papers in 1995 from Armadale, a closely held Canadian firm. Hollinger also bought 19 paid-circulation papers (12 dailies and seven weeklies) and several free publications from Canadian publisher Thomson Corporation.

In 1996 Hollinger International assumed full control of the Telegraph Group, increased its stake in Southam to about 51%. It sold most of its John Fairfax holdings to New Zealand-based Brierley Investments. In 1998 Southam launched Canada's *National Post,* its first national newspaper. Hollinger International finally bought all of Southam in 1999. That year Hollinger combined the smaller publications of Southam, Sterling Newspapers, and UniMedia into Hollinger Canadian Newspapers (in which it holds an 87% stake).

The company had a flurry of activity in 2000. The firm decided to sell off hundreds of its Canadian and American community newspapers and trade magazines in order to concentrate on its larger papers. It sold 13 of its larger Canadian daily newspapers, 136 community newspapers, and a 50% stake in the *National Post,* to CanWest Global Communications for $3.5 billion. (CanWest purchased the rest of the *National Post* in 2002.) It also sold off most of its US community papers. In 2001 the firm sold UniMédia Company, its Quebec-based French-language newspaper group, to Gesca Ltd. That year Black announced that Hollinger would join with a small group of investors to launch a new New York City daily paper in 2002 called the *New York Sun* aimed at a conservative audience. (The *Sun* debuted in April 2002.)

After a scandal involving unauthorized payments, Black stepped down as CEO and chairman of Hollinger International in 2003. He resigned from Hollinger Inc. in 2004. Paul Carroll, a director on the company's board, was named president and CEO in 2005, but his employment was terminated later that same year.

EXECUTIVES

Chairman: Joseph Wright
Chief Restructuring Officer: Randall C. (Randy) Benson
VP and Group Corporate Controller:
Frederick A. Creasey, age 51
Treasurer: Tatiana Samila
Auditors: KPMG LLP

LOCATIONS

HQ: Hollinger Inc.
10 Toronto St., Toronto, Ontario M5C 2B7, Canada
Phone: 416-363-8721 **Fax:** 416-364-2088
US HQ: 401 N. Wabash Ave., Ste. 740, Chicago, IL 60611
US Phone: 312-321-2299 **US Fax:** 312-321-0629
Web: www.hollingerinc.com

Hollinger publishes newspapers in the US and the UK.

COMPETITORS

Bell Globemedia	News Corp.
Dow Jones	Quebecor
Gannett	Torstar
Hearst	Tribune
Knight-Ridder	Washington Post
New York Times	

HISTORICAL FINANCIALS

Company Type: Public

Income Statement

FYE: December 31

	REVENUE ($ mil.)	NET INCOME ($ mil.)	NET PROFIT MARGIN	EMPLOYEES
12/02	1,052	(56)	—	6,249
12/01	1,206	(83)	—	6,660
12/00	2,126	126	5.9%	9,600
12/99	2,254	107	4.7%	17,000
12/98	2,144	72	3.4%	16,500
12/97	2,180	120	5.5%	16,600
12/96	1,372	34	2.5%	12,500
12/95	1,109	8	0.7%	8,700
12/94	906	84	9.3%	8,700
12/93	873	25	2.9%	5,700
Annual Growth	2.1%	—	—	1.0%

2002 Year-End Financials

Debt ratio: — Current ratio: 0.72
Return on equity: — Long-term debt ($ mil.): 618
Cash ($ mil.): 120

Net Income History

Toronto: HLG.C

Honda Motor

*Accord*ing to Honda, a *Ridgeline* might be your *Passport* to *Insight*. Honda is Japan's #3 automaker (after Toyota and Nissan) and the world's largest motorcycle producer. The company's car models include the Accord, CR-V, Civic, Element, Passport, and Ridgeline as well as the luxury Acura brand and the Insight — a gasoline-electric hybrid. Honda's line of motorcycles includes everything from scooters to superbikes. The company also makes a line of ATVs and personal watercraft. Honda's power products division makes commercial and residential-use machinery (lawn mowers, snowblowers), portable generators, and outboard motors.

Honda is enjoying brisk motorcycle sales, particularly in Asia where motorcycles are a popular mode of transportation. The company has announced plans to build a $1 million motorcycle production facility in Argentina to keep up with the growing demand in South America. In North America, Europe, and at home in Japan, Honda has introduced new models of sport bikes. Honda has also completed the conversion of its entire motorcycle lineup to cleaner-burning four-stroke engines.

On the automotive side, Honda gained market share in the US through its entry to the light truck segment with the Ridgeline pickup. In Europe Honda is capitalizing on the popularity of diesel models, and in China the company is selling a lot of cars as the Honda brand grows in popularity. Sales have been flat in Japan, but Honda responded by tightening up its domestic sales organization.

Going forward, Honda is planning on modest growth, primarily in the US and China, but believes growth will be tempered by increasing fuel and raw materials costs as well as fluctuations in foreign currency exhange rates.

Too keep its Asian motorcycle momentum rolling Honda is striving to remain competitive on price while expanding manufacturing capacity at facilities in India, China, and the Philippines. In Europe the company plans to keep delivering on the sport bikes that are popular there.

Based on the Ridgeline's success, Honda's automotive business in the US will see the introduction of additional light truck models, as well as a re-vamping of the stalwart Civic. Honda will also introduce an entry-level vehicle in early 2006 aimed at capturing young, new, and hopefully loyal, Honda customers. While the passenger car market in the US is waning, Honda is confident it can maintain and even grow its share of that market segment.

The automotive market in China is slowing, however the potential for growth is still enormous. The re-vamped Civic will also be brought to China in 2006, and Honda's overall vehicle capacity will grow as well. The company is also targeting Indonesia and India for sales growth with the Jazz and Fit models that have been hits in those markets.

HISTORY

Soichiro Honda spent six years as an apprentice at Tokyo service station Art Shokai before opening his own branch of the repair shop in Hamamatsu in 1928. He also raced cars and in 1931 received a patent for metal spokes that replaced wood in wheels.

Honda started a piston ring company in 1937. During WWII the company produced metal propellers for Japanese bombers. When bombs and an earthquake destroyed most of his factory, Honda sold it to Toyota in 1945.

In 1946 Honda began motorizing bicycles with war-surplus engines. When this proved popular, Honda began making engines. The company was renamed Honda Motor Co. in 1948 and began producing motorcycles. In 1949 Soichiro Honda hired Takeo Fujisawa to manage the company so Honda could focus on engineering. Honda's innovative overhead valve design made its early 1950s Dream model a runaway success. In 1952 the smaller Cub, sold through bicycle dealers, accounted for 70% of Japan's motorcycle production.

Funded by a 1954 public offering and Mitsubishi Bank, Honda expanded capacity and began exporting. American Honda Motor Company was formed in Los Angeles in 1959, accompanied by the slogan "You meet the nicest people on a Honda" in a campaign crafted to counter the stereotypical biker image. Honda added overseas factories in the 1960s and began producing lightweight trucks, sports cars, and minicars.

The company began selling its tiny 600 model in the US in 1970, but it was the Civic, introduced in 1973, that first scored with the US car market. Three years later Honda introduced the

Accord, which featured an innovative frame adaptable for many models. In 1982 Accord production started at the company's Ohio plant.

Ex-Honda engineer Nobuhiko Kawamoto was named president in 1990, a year before Soichiro Honda died. Kawamoto cut costs and continued to expand the company internationally. That year the Big Three US automakers (GM, Ford, and Chrysler), clamoring for trade sanctions against Japanese carmakers, threw Honda out of the US carmakers' trade association.

In 1997 Honda bought Peugeot's plant in Guangzhou, China, and boosted its US vehicle production by opening an all-terrain vehicle (ATV) plant in South Carolina in 1998. American Honda agreed in 1998 to pay $330 million to settle a class-action lawsuit filed by 1,800 dealers who accused Honda of delivering popular models only to dealers who paid bribes (18 executives from American Honda were convicted). That year Hiroyuki Yoshino, an engineer with US management experience, succeeded Kawamoto as CEO.

In 1999 Honda and GM agreed to a deal in which Honda would supply low-emission V6 engines and automatic transmissions to GM, while Isuzu, a GM affiliate, would supply Honda with diesel engines. True to Honda's go-it-alone style, the deal has no equity component.

In 2000 Honda announced that its super low-emission engine (as called for by US regulators) would make its mass-market debut in 2001, well ahead of competitor versions. Also Honda recalled 500,000 cars in Japan due to problems with audio systems and engine oil seals.

Honda announced in 2001 that it would introduce diesel-powered vehicles in Europe by 2003. Later that year Honda's R&D unit set up a solar-powered hydrogen production station in California as part of its efforts to develop renewable-energy fuel cell vehicles.

EXECUTIVES

President, CEO, and Director: Takeo Fukui, age 61
EVP and Director; COO, Business Management Operations: Satoshi Aoki, age 59
Senior Managing Director; President and Director, American Honda Motor Co.; President and Director, Honda North America, Inc.: Koichi Kondo, age 58
Senior Managing Director; COO, Motorcycle Operations: Minoru Harada, age 58
Senior Managing Director; President, Honda R&D Co., Ltd.: Motoatsu Shiraishi, age 59
Senior Managing Director; COO, Production Operations; Risk Management Officer; General Supervisor, Information Systems: Koki Hirashima, age 59
Senior Managing Director; COO, Regional Operations (Asia and Oceania); President and Director, Asian Honda Motor Co., Ltd.: Satoshi Toshida, age 58
Senior Managing Director; COO, Regional Operations (China); President of Honda Motor (China) Investment Co. Ltd.: Atsuyoshi Hyogo, age 56
Senior Managing Director; General Supervisor, Purchasing Policy and Quality: Michiyoshi Hagino, age 61
Senior Managing Director, Government and Industrial Affairs; COO, Regional Sales Operations (Japan); Chief Officer of Driving Safety Promotion Center in Regional Sales Operations (Japan): Satoshi Dobashi, age 58

Managing Director; President and Director, Honda Motor Europe Ltd., COO, Regional Operations (Europe, Middle East and Africa): Shigeru Takagi, age 53
Managing Director; COO, Automobile Operations: Hiroshi Kuroda, age 57
Managing Director; COO, Customer Service Operations: Akira Takano, age 56
Managing Director; COO, Purchasing Operations: Toru Onda, age 56
Managing Officer; President and Director, Honda of America Mfg., Inc.: Akio Hamada
Auditors: KPMG

LOCATIONS

HQ: Honda Motor Co., Ltd.
(Honda Giken Kogyo Kabushiki Kaisha)
2-1-1 Minami-Aoyama, Minato-ku,
Tokyo 107-8556, Japan
Phone: +81-3-3423-1111 **Fax:** +81-3-5412-1515
US HQ: 540 Madison Ave., 32nd Fl.,
New York, NY 10022
US Phone: 212-355-9191 **US Fax:** 212-813-0260
Web: world.honda.com

2005 Sales

	$ mil.	% of total
North America	42,685	53
Asia		
Japan	15,854	20
Other countries	9,115	11
Europe	8,125	10
Other regions	4,926	6
Total	**80,705**	**100**

PRODUCTS/OPERATIONS

2005 Sales

	$ mil.	% of total
Automobiles	64,970	80
Motorcycles	10,242	13
Power products and other	3,107	4
Financial services	2,386	3
Total	**80,705**	**100**

Selected Car and Truck Models

Accord (coupe, sedan)
Accord Hybrid Sedan
Acura (MDX, NSX, RL, RSX, TL, TSX)
Civic (coupe, sedan)
Civic Hybrid
Civic Si
CR-V (SUV)
Element
Insight (gasoline-electric hybrid)
Odyssey (minivan)
Pilot (SUV)
Ridgeline (pickup)
S2000 (roadster)

Selected Motorcycle Models

CBR600F4i
FourTrax (ATV)
Gold Wing
Gold Wing ABS
Interceptor
Nighthawk 750
Rebel
Shadow Spirit 750
Silver Wing (scooter)
Sportrax (ATV)
ST1300
ST1300 ABS
Valkyrie

Selected Power Products

Commercial mowers
Engines
Lawn mowers
Marine motors
Portable generators
Pumps
Snowblowers
Tillers
Trimmers

COMPETITORS

Black & Decker	Kia Motors
BMW	Land Rover
Briggs & Stratton	Mazda
Brunswick	Nissan
Caterpillar	Peugeot
DaimlerChrysler	Renault
Deere	Saab Automobile
Exmark Manufacturing	Suzuki Motor
Fiat	Textron
Ford	Toro
Fuji Heavy Industries	Toyota
General Motors	Triumph Motorcycles
Harley-Davidson	Volkswagen
Isuzu	Volvo
Kawasaki Heavy Industries	Yamaha Motor

HISTORICAL FINANCIALS

Company Type: Public

Income Statement

FYE: March 31

	REVENUE ($ mil.)	NET INCOME ($ mil.)	NET PROFIT MARGIN	EMPLOYEES
3/05	80,705	4,536	5.6%	137,827
3/04	78,222	4,450	5.7%	131,600
3/03	67,479	3,612	5.4%	126,900
3/02	55,253	2,722	4.9%	120,600
3/01	52,170	1,874	3.6%	114,300
3/00	57,455	2,472	4.3%	112,400
3/99	51,688	2,530	4.9%	112,200
3/98	45,418	1,973	4.3%	109,400
3/97	42,654	1,782	4.2%	91,300
3/96	39,984	666	1.7%	96,800
Annual Growth	**8.1%**	**23.8%**	**—**	**4.0%**

2005 Year-End Financials

Debt ratio: 47.4%
Return on equity: 15.6%
Cash ($ mil.): 7,217
Current ratio: 1.07
Long-term debt ($ mil.): 14,550
No. of shares (mil.): 1,850
Dividends
Yield: 0.8%
Payout: 8.6%
Market value ($ mil.): 46,317

Stock History

NYSE: HMC

	STOCK PRICE ($) FY Close	P/E High/Low		PER SHARE ($) Earnings	Dividends	Book Value
3/05	25.04	11	8	2.43	0.21	16.59
3/04	23.14	10	7	2.33	0.15	14.64
3/03	16.60	13	9	1.86	0.12	11.57
3/02	21.17	16	10	1.40	0.10	9.91
3/01	20.53	24	17	0.96	0.11	2.31
3/00	20.31	19	13	1.27	0.09	2.33
3/99	22.28	18	10	1.30	0.00	1.88
3/98	17.75	19	14	1.01	0.00	1.56
3/97	14.63	18	11	0.92	0.03	1.44
3/96	10.75	34	20	0.34	0.03	1.38
Annual Growth	**9.9%**	**—**	**—**	**24.4%**	**24.1%**	**31.8%**

Hopewell Holdings

Hopewell Holdings springs eternal in the mind of its founder and chairman, Sir Gordon Wu. Undeterred by the collapse of several projects in the wake of the Asian economic crisis, Wu has good reason to be hopeful about the future of his real estate and infrastructure development company as the market stabilizes. Hopewell has extensive holdings in real estate in Hong Kong (including Hopewell Centre and Panda Hotel) and is a major infrastructure developer. The company built toll roads and bridges, primarily in mainland China, but has spun off its Hopewell Highway Infrastructure Limited subsidiary (HHI) as a public company. It retains a majority stake (75%).

Although its property and hotel businesses are concentrated mainly in Hong Kong, where it gets most of its sales, Hopewell has worked on infrastructure projects (toll roads and bridges) primarily in China's fast-growing Guangdong province. Mainland toll roads had been one of Hopewell's primary operations, contributing heavily to its earnings. However, the group decided to spin off its mainland infrastructure projects to finance a controversial bridge that would link Hong Kong with Macao and Zhuhai on China's Pearl River delta. It has decided to focus its construction expertise on project management of its own property developments.

One of the first companies outside China to invest in that country's infrastructure projects, Hopewell has been involved in building in China since the 1970s. In addition to the Hopewell Centre and Panda Hotel, the group's Hong Kong holdings include the Hongkong International Trade and Exhibition Centre, Mega Tower Hotel, and Nova Taipa Gardens. The group also operates the China Hotel in Guangzhou, the capital of Guangdong in southern China. And it is constructing a property development project in Huadu, Guangzhou called the Hopewell New Town, which will consist of apartment units, townhouses, and commercial facilities.

Asian economic instability, coupled with a few missteps in the region, has cost the company dearly. Hopewell had to halt construction on a 1,320-MW power plant in Indonesia after it was 80% complete. The company has disposed of its interest in the power station. In addition, the Thai government canceled Hopewell's participation in the Bangkok Elevated Road and Train System (BERTS) project after several delays, changes, and rising costs.

HISTORY

Sir Gordon Wu's Hopewell Holdings empire grew from humble beginnings. His father started out as a Hong Kong taxi owner and driver and helped finance Gordon's first-class education — he received an engineering degree from Princeton University.

On his return to Hong Kong in 1962, Wu took a job in the government's land department. He later left to help his father develop a property business. When his father retired in 1969, cus-

tom forbade Wu Sr. from handing the company over to Gordon, the seventh of nine children. Instead, he liquidated the firm and guaranteed a $2.5 million loan to his son to start a property company of his own.

By 1972 Wu's company was large enough to be listed on the Hong Kong Stock Exchange as Hopewell Holdings Limited. But his American-style "can-do" approach gained him some enemies. He took on the Hong Kong government after it banned him from building a towering headquarters in central Hong Kong — and won. The result was the 66-floor Hopewell Centre.

While visiting nearby Guangzhou in China to promote a hotel project in the early 1980s, Wu spotted opportunity in the region's frequent power outages. Realizing that the province would boom in the 1980s and 1990s, Wu dropped the hotel idea and persuaded China to let him build a power plant. By 1987 the 700-MW plant was on line.

Other major Chinese infrastructure projects followed, including contracts for two more power stations in Guangdong province and a contract to build China's first modern highway, a six-lane toll road linking the cities of Guangzhou and Hong Kong. Wu attributed his success in negotiating with the Chinese authorities to 11 years of lobbying and consuming gallons of *mao tai* (a very potent liquor served at formal dinners in China).

In 1990 Wu gained a contract with the Thai government for a mass transit system, the Bangkok Elevated Road and Train System (BERTS) project. But the project was soon delayed, first by political unrest and then by bureaucratic red tape.

Hopewell spun off 40% of its power subsidiary, Consolidated Electric Power Asia (CEPA), in 1993. The sale helped fund other projects, including the Guangdong toll road and a power plant in the Philippines. But the Philippines project ran into problems in 1995: Although the plant was completed, the local electric utility refused to take the power.

By late 1995 Hopewell was hemorrhaging money. After failing to raise funds by spinning off several transport projects as a public company in 1996, Hopewell sold CEPA to US utility Southern Company. The Asian financial contagion of 1997-98 didn't help matters. In 1998 the elevated train project in Bangkok was halted by the Thai government, and Hopewell lost its $153 million stake in Peregrine Investment Holdings when the Hong Kong-based firm collapsed. Hopewell also stopped work on a major Indonesian power plant that it was building in a venture. The firm fell into the red in 1998.

That year, however, the company gained a contract to help build a toll road in southern China, and in 1999 it won another contract for a toll road in the Philippines. In fiscal 1999 Hopewell regained profitability, although it lost its listing on the Hong Kong index in 2000. In 2002 the company made plans to spin off its major toll road, the Guangzhou-Shenzhen Superhighway, and to rebid for the BERTS project. Also that year Sir Gordon stepped down from his duties as managing director but remained chairman of the group.

In 2003 the company listed its Hopewell Highway Infrastructure Limited subsidiary, which held most of its mainland-China transportation infrastructure interests, on the Hong Kong stock exchange. It also divested its interest in the Tanjung Jati B power project in Indonesia.

EXECUTIVES

Honorary Chairman: James M. H. Wu
Chairman: Sir Gordon Y. S. Wu, age 68
Vice Chairman and Managing Director: Eddie P. C. Ho, age 71
Deputy Managing Director: Josiah C. L. Kwok, age 52
Deputy Managing Director; Managing Director, Hopewell Highway Infrastructure Limited: Thomas J. Wu, age 32
Executive Director, Finance: Robert V. J. Nien, age 57
Executive Director: Albert K. Y. Yeung, age 53
Executive Director: David Y. G. Lui, age 59
Executive Director: Andy L. M. Cheung, age 38
Executive Director: Eddie W. C. Ho Jr., age 35
Company Secretary: Peter Y. W. Lee
Executive Director: Barry C. T. Mok, age 47
Auditors: Deloitte Touche Tohmatsu

LOCATIONS

HQ: Hopewell Holdings Limited
 64th Fl., Hopewell Centre, 183 Queen's Rd. East, Wan Chai, Hong Kong
Phone: +852-2528-4975   **Fax:** +852-2865-6276
Web: www.hopewellholdings.com

Hopewell Holdings operates primarily in Asia, including China, Hong Kong, Indonesia, the Philippines, and Thailand.

2005 Sales

	% of total
Hong Kong	92
China & Macau	8
Total	**100**

PRODUCTS/OPERATIONS

2005 Sales

	% of total
Property letting, agency & management	43
Hotel investment & management	26
Restaurant operations & food catering	22
Infrastructure project investments	8
Other operations	1
Total	**100**

Selected Subsidiaries

HH Finance Limited (loan financing)
Hopewell Centre Management Limited (property management)
Hopewell China Development (Superhighway) Limited (98%, investment in superhighway project)
Hopewell Construction Company, Limited (construction, project management, and investments)
Hopewell Food Industries Limited (restaurant operations)
Hopewell Guangzhou-Zhuhai Superhighway Development Limited (investment in superhighway project)
Hopewell Housing Limited (property agents and investment holding)
Hopewell Property Management Company Limited (building and car park management)
Hopewell Shunde Roads Limited (investment in highway systems project)
International Trademart Company Limited (property investment and operation of trademart)
Kowloon Panda Hotel Limited (hotel owernship and operations)

COMPETITORS

ABB	Jardine Matheson
AES	Marriott
ALSTOM	McDermott
Bechtel	Peter Kiewit Sons'
Fluor	Siemens
Foster Wheeler	Sime Darby
GE	Swire Pacific
Hutchison Whampoa	

HISTORICAL FINANCIALS

Company Type: Public

Income Statement

FYE: June 30

	REVENUE ($ mil.)	NET INCOME ($ mil.)	NET PROFIT MARGIN	EMPLOYEES
6/05	87	214	245.1%	1,110
6/04	84	186	222.4%	1,057
6/03	103	79	77.3%	1,100
6/02	145	44	30.0%	1,123
6/01	224	39	17.5%	1,009
6/00	202	22	10.8%	1,100
6/99	174	18	10.5%	2,000
6/98	191	(363)	—	4,000
6/97	368	28	7.5%	5,318
6/96	306	99	32.5%	7,095
Annual Growth	(13.0%)	8.9%	—	(18.6%)

2005 Year-End Financials

Debt ratio: 0.3%
Return on equity: 10.7%
Cash ($ mil.): 328

Current ratio: 4.38
Long-term debt ($ mil.): 7

Net Income History

OTC: HOWWY

HSBC Holdings

HSBC would be a real alphabet soup if the company's name reflected its geographic diversity. HSBC Holdings is the UK's largest banking company; it is also active throughout the rest of Europe, North and South America, Asia, Australia, the Middle East, and Africa. All told, HSBC has more than 9,800 offices in nearly 80 countries, providing consumer and commercial banking services, credit cards, asset management, investment banking, private banking, securities trading, insurance, and leasing. US operations, which include HSBC USA, got a boost with the 2003 purchase of consumer lender Household International (now HSBC Finance).

In 2004 the company acquired The Bank of Bermuda, as well as Marks and Spencer Financial Services (aka M&S Money), one of the UK's leading credit card issuers. It bought US credit card company Metris the following year.

Founded in Hong Kong in 1865, the company is targeting Asia for growth. In 2005 the company joined forces with Global Payments to provide merchant processing services in that part of the world; HSBC owns some 44% of the joint venture. In addition, the company bought a 70% stake in investment bank Dar es Salaam, becoming one of the first foreign banks to operate in Iraq after Saddam Hussein banned them from operating there some 35 years ago. HSBC also made the largest-ever investment at the time by a foreign bank in a Chinese bank when it bought a 20% stake in Bank of Communications in 2004. HSBC purchased a stake in India's UTI Bank that year as well.

The company also owns all or parts of The Hongkong and Shanghai Banking Corporation, HSBC Bank Canada, HSBC France (formerly CCF), and Hong Kong's Hang Seng Bank. In Central and South America it operates primarily in Argentina, Brazil, and Mexico.

HISTORY

Scotsman Thomas Sutherland and other businessmen in 1865 opened the doors to Hongkong & Shanghai Bank, financing and promoting British imperial trade in opium, silk, and tea in East Asia. It soon established a London office and created an international branch network emphasizing China and East Asia. It claims to have been the first bank in Thailand (1888).

War repeatedly disrupted, but never demolished, the bank's operations. During WWII the headquarters were temporarily moved to London. (They moved back on a permanent basis in 1991.) The bank's chief prewar manager, Sir Vandeleur Grayborn, died in a Japanese POW camp. After the Communists took power in China in 1949, the bank gradually withdrew; by 1955 only its Shanghai office remained, and it was later closed. The bank played a key role in Hong Kong's postwar growth by financing industrialists who fled there from China.

In the late 1950s Hongkong & Shanghai Bank's acquisitions included the British Bank of the Middle East (founded 1889; now The Saudi British Bank) and Mercantile Bank (with offices in India and Southeast Asia). In 1965 the company bought 62% of Hang Seng, Hong Kong's #2 bank. It also added new subsidiaries, including Wayfoong (mortgage and small-business finance, 1960) and Wardley (investment banking, Hong Kong, 1972).

In the late 1970s and into the 1980s, China began opening to foreign business. The bank added operations in North America to capitalize on business between China and the US and Canada. Acquisitions included Marine Midland Bank (US, 1980), Hongkong Bank of Canada (1981), 51% of treasury securities dealer Carroll McEntee & McGinley (US, 1983), most of the assets and liabilities of the Bank of British Columbia (1986), and Lloyds Bank Canada (1990).

Following the 1984 agreement to return Hong Kong to China, Hongkong & Shanghai Bank began beefing up in the UK, buying London securities dealer James Capel & Co. (1986) and the UK's #3 bank, Midland plc (1992). In 1993 the company formed London-based HSBC Holdings and divested assets, most notably its interest in Hong Kong-based Cathay Pacific Airways.

HSBC then began expanding in Asia again, particularly in Malaysia, where its Hongkong Bank Malaysia became the country's first locally incorporated foreign bank. The company returned to China with offices in Beijing and Guangzhou. It also added new European branches.

Latin American banks acquired in 1997 were among the non-Asian operations that cushioned HSBC from the worst of 1998's economic crises. Nonetheless, The Hong Kong Monetary Authority took a stake in the bank to shore up the stock exchange and foil short-sellers.

In 1999 China's government made HSBC a loan for mainland expansion. That year the company was foiled in its attempt to buy South Korea's government-owned Seoulbank, but did buy the late Edmond Safra's Republic New York Corporation and his international bank holding company, Safra Republic Holdings (it negotiated a $450 million discount on the $10 billion deal

after a Japanese probe of Republic's securities division caused delays).

In 2000 the company unveiled several online initiatives, including Internet ventures with Cheung Kong (Holdings) and Merrill Lynch, and bought CCF (then called Crédit Commercial de France). However, HSBC's plans to buy a controlling stake in Bangkok Metropolitan Bank fell through before the year's end.

In 2001 HSBC agreed to pick up Barclays Bank's fund management operations in Greece. Later, in response to the slowing economy, it froze the salaries of 14,000 employees. Argentina's 2001 peso devaluation cost the company half a billion dollars in currency conversion losses alone. Total charges pertaining to Argentina equaled more than $1 billion that year.

EXECUTIVES

Group Chairman: Sir John R. H. Bond, age 64
Deputy Chairman: The Baroness Dunn, age 64
Deputy Chairman: Sir Brian Moffat, age 66
Group Chief Executive and Executive Director: Stephen K. Green, age 56
Group COO and Executive Director: Alan W. Jebson, age 55
Group Finance Director and Executive Director: Douglas J. Flint, age 49
Executive Director; CEO, HSBC Bank UK: Michael F. Geoghegan, age 52
Group Managing Director; Chairman and CEO, HSBC France: Charles-Henri Filippi, age 52
Group Managing Director and Co-Head, Corporate and Investment Banking and Markets: Stuart T. Gulliver, age 45
Group Managing Director; CEO, HSBC North America; Chairman and CEO, HSBC Finance: Siddharth N. (Bobby) Mehta, age 47
Group Managing Director; President and CEO, HSBC Bank Brasil — Banco Multiplo: Youssef A. Nasr, age 50
Group Company Secretary: R. G. Barber, age 54
Group Managing Director and Co-Head Corporate and Investment Banking and Markets: John J. Studzinski, age 48
Group General Manager, Legal and Compliance: R. E. T. Bennett, age 53
Group General Manager; President and CEO, HSBC USA and HSBC Bank USA: Martin J. G. Glynn, age 53
Group General Manager and Group Chief Accounting Officer: R. C. Picot, age 47
Group General Manager, Human Resources: J. C. S. Rankin, age 63
Group General Manager, Marketing: P. E. Stringham, age 55
Auditors: KPMG Audit Plc

LOCATIONS

HQ: HSBC Holdings plc
8 Canada Sq., London E14 5HQ, United Kingdom
Phone: +44-20-7991-8888   **Fax:** +44-20-7992-4880
US HQ: 452 5th Ave., New York, NY 10018
US Phone: 212-525-5000
Web: www.hsbc.com

PRODUCTS/OPERATIONS

2004 Sales

	$ mil.	% of total
Interest		
Debt securities	7,845	11
Other	42,358	60
Noninterest		
Fees & commissions	13,093	18
Dealing profits	2,566	4
Dividend income	601	1
Other	4,397	6
Total	**70,860**	**100**

Selected Subsidiaries

Asia/Pacific
Hang Seng Bank Limited (62%, Hong Kong)
The Hongkong and Shanghai Banking Corporation Limited (Hong Kong)
HSBC Asset Management (Taiwan) Ltd.
HSBC Bank Australia Limited
HSBC Bank Malaysia Berhad
HSBC Insurance (Asia) Limited (Hong Kong)

Europe
CCF S.A. (France)
HFC Bank Limited
HSBC Asset Finance (UK) Limited
HSBC Asset Management (Europe) Limited
HSBC Bank A.S. (Turkey)
HSBC Bank Malta p.l.c. (70%)
HSBC Bank plc
HSBC Guyerzeller Bank AG (Switzerland)
HSBC Insurance Brokers Limited
HSBC Investment Bank plc
HSBC Life (UK) Limited
HSBC Private Bank (Guernsey) Limited (Channel Islands)
HSBC Private Bank (Suisse) S.A. (Switzerland)
HSBC Private Bank (UK) Limited
HSBC Trinkaus & Burkhardt KGaA (73%, Germany)

Latin America
HSBC Bank Argentina S.A
HSBC Bank Brasil S.A. — Banco Múltiplo
HSBC La Buenos Aires Seguros SA (Argentina)
HSBC Mexico S.A.
HSBC Seguros (Brasil) S.A. (98%)
Máxima S.A. AFJP (60%, Argentina)

Middle East and Africa
British Arab Commercial Bank Limited (46%)
HSBC Bank Egypt S.A.E. (95%)
HSBC Bank Middle East Limited
The Saudi British Bank (40%, Saudi Arabia)

North America
The Bank of Bermuda Limited
HSBC Bank Canada
HSBC Bank USA
HSBC Finance Corporation
HSBC North America Holdings Inc.
HSBC Securities (USA) Inc
HSBC Technology & Services (USA) Inc.
HSBC USA Inc.

COMPETITORS

Bank of America	JPMorgan Chase
Bank of China	Lloyds TSB
Barclays	Mizuho Financial
CIBC	RBC Financial Group
Citigroup	RBS
Credit Suisse	Standard Chartered
Deutsche Bank	Sun Hung Kai
HBOS	UBS
Hutchison Whampoa	

HISTORICAL FINANCIALS

Company Type: Public

Income Statement

FYE: December 31

	ASSETS ($ mil.)	NET INCOME ($ mil.)	INCOME AS % OF ASSETS	EMPLOYEES
12/04	1,276,778	11,840	0.9%	253,000
12/03	1,034,216	8,774	0.8%	232,000
12/02	759,246	6,239	0.8%	192,000
12/01	695,877	5,406	0.8%	176,682
12/00	673,814	6,628	1.0%	169,858
12/99	569,139	5,408	1.0%	146,897
12/98	483,128	4,318	0.9%	144,521
12/97	472,431	5,534	1.2%	132,969
12/96	401,904	5,287	1.3%	109,298
12/95	351,466	3,815	1.1%	109,093
Annual Growth	15.4%	13.4%	—	9.8%

2004 Year-End Financials

Equity as % of assets: 6.8%	Dividends
Return on assets: 1.0%	Yield: 2.9%
Return on equity: 14.7%	Payout: 46.7%
Long-term debt ($ mil.): 135,638	Market value ($ mil.): 190,238
No. of shares (mil.): 2,234	Sales ($ mil.): 70,860

Stock History

NYSE: HBC

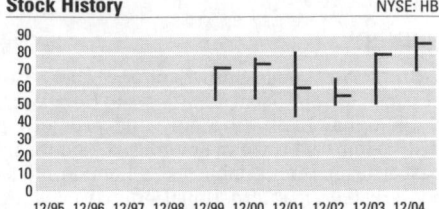

12/95 12/96 12/97 12/98 12/99 12/00 12/01 12/02 12/03 12/04

	STOCK PRICE ($) FY Close	P/E High/Low		PER SHARE ($) Earnings	Dividends	Book Value
12/04	85.14	17	13	5.35	2.50	38.77
12/03	78.82	19	12	4.15	3.01	33.86
12/02	54.98	20	15	3.30	2.75	27.64
12/01	59.71	138	75	0.58	3.21	24.57
12/00	73.60	20	14	3.75	1.98	24.58
12/99	71.38	22	16	3.25	0.57	19.75
Annual Growth	3.6%	—	—	10.5%	34.4%	14.4%

Hudson's Bay

Here's a company that's traveled a fur piece from its 17th-century roots. (The chain's coat of arms features two moose, four beavers, and a fox.) Hudson's Bay Company (HBC) is Canada's largest department store chain. Founded in 1670 as a fur trading enterprise, HBC is also Canada's oldest corporation. The company's Zellers chain is Canada's #2 discount department store (behind Wal-Mart Canada), with nearly 300 stores. HBC also runs nearly 100 The Bay department stores, more than 100 smaller Fields general merchandise and apparel stores in western Canada, 45 Home Outfitters superstores, and Hbc.com, an e-commerce site. HBC has rejected an unsolicited offer from Maple Leaf Heritage Investments to buy the company.

Led by US investor Jerry Zucker, Maple Leaf has offered to buy the outstanding shares of the company for about $855 million. (Zucker and his affiliates already own nearly 19% of the HBC's shares.) HBC's board said the offer was inadequate, but did not rule out the possibility of a takeover at a loftier price.

Mass merchandiser Zellers, which accounts for about 60% of company sales, is facing increasing pressure from discounters and specialty stores, such as Best Buy. Wal-Mart Canada operates nearly 250 discount stores throughout Canada, as well as six SAM'S CLUB outlets in Ontario. As a countermeasure, HBC has been renovating and enlarging its Zellers stores and enlisting hot designers, including Mossimo, to promote the image of an upscale discounter (à la Target), along with introducing smaller Zellers Select stores in smaller markets and emphasizing private labels in all of its stores. The company has signed a deal with Salton, whereby Westinghouse-branded products and a new line of home appliances are available across HBC's retail banners. Hilary Duff's line of merchandise ("Stuff by Duff"), which features fashion apparel and accessories as well as home accessories and cosmetics, made its debut in Zellers stores in spring 2004.

The company is considering selling its credit card portfolio with C$1.2 billion in receivables, representing 3.1 million active accounts. Earlier this year rival Sears Canada sold its credit card business for a hefty premium. Also, to cut costs, HBC has announced that it is laying off about 825 management and administrative staff.

HBC's the Bay traditional department stores focus on more-upscale fashion merchandise and home furnishings, and its Home Outfitters superstores (launched in 1999) emphasize bedding and linens. Fast-growing Home Outfitters opened eight locations in 2003 and four more stores in 2004.

HBC's retail reach stretches from Newfoundland to British Columbia.

HISTORY

In 1668 the British ketch *Nonsuch* reached the bay named for explorer Henry Hudson. The ship returned to Britain the following year laden with furs, attracting the attention of King Charles II, who in 1670 granted a royal trading charter to a party of 18 men. Hudson's Bay Company (HBC) built a series of fortifications and fought French warships for control of the bay in a seesaw battle that continued until 1713, when the Treaty of Utrecht placed the bay officially in British hands. From the company's base at York Factory, company explorers began to penetrate Canada's vast interior. In 1774 Samuel Hearne established the firm's first inland post on the Saskatchewan River.

During the late 18th century, the Montreal-based North West Company, a rival fur-trading concern, threatened HBC's dominance. After a period of violent clashes between the competing traders, the two competitors merged under the Hudson's Bay Company name in 1821, giving the enterprise control over 173 posts throughout 3 million sq. mi. of wilderness. It transferred possession of company-chartered land to the Canadian government in 1869.

By the turn of the century, HBC had transformed many posts into stores to serve growing Canadian cities. In 1929 the company formed Hudson's Bay Oil and Gas. It acquired the Henry Morgan department store chain in 1960 and five years later changed its store name to Bay. HBC moved its headquarters from London to Winnipeg in 1970 (and later to Toronto).

The company expanded its department store holdings in the late 1970s by purchasing Zellers, Fields, and Simpsons. Newspaper magnate Kenneth Thomson bought 75% of HBC in 1979 (the last of the family's interest was sold in 1997). Mired in debt during the 1980s from its prolific acquisitions, the company sold its oil and gas operations, its large fur houses, and 179 of its original stores in the far north.

During a steep recession in 1990, the company spun off its Markborough real estate subsidiary to shareholders and purchased the Towers Bonimart chain of discount department stores (which it converted to the Zellers format). HBC later converted six of its Simpsons high-fashion stores into the Bay stores, selling the rest to Sears for $37 million.

HBC in 1995 opened the first of its Zellers Plus larger stores with expanded merchandise (almost twice as large as its average format) to compete with Wal-Mart. Profits dropped almost 80% in fiscal 1996 because of a Wal-Mart price war and depressed Christmas sales. In 1997 Bill

Fields, former head of Blockbuster Entertainment, succeeded CEO George Kosich. Fields liquidated old inventory at Zellers, writing off more than $100 million. (The move, along with restructuring, created a loss for fiscal 1998.)

In 1998 the company bought Kmart Canada (112 discount stores) for $168 million. HBC then set about converting about 60 former Kmarts into Zellers stores; about 40 weaker stores were closed, and about a dozen were converted to specialty stores. Fields, who had touted the growth potential of the Kmart stores, resigned in 1999 and was replaced as president and CEO by George Heller, head of the Zellers chain. In 2000 the company launched its e-commerce site, hbc.com. The company also began opening Zellers Select stores, smaller concept stores that include grocery sections, and Home Outfitters, superstores carrying kitchen, bed, and bath décor. HBC opened 16 new Home Outfitters stores in 2001 and 2002; in 2003 eight locations were opened.

In November 2004 HBC launched Designer Depot targeted at the off-price market.

EXECUTIVES

Governor: L. Yves Fortier, age 69
President, CEO, and Director: George J. Heller, age 57, $1,250,540 pay
EVP and CFO: Michael S. (Mike) Rousseau, $484,080 pay
COO: Marc R. Chouinard, $685,780 pay (prior to promotion)
EVP, Office of the CEO: Thomas Haig, $625,270 pay (prior to promotion)
EVP, Hbc Managed Services: Peter A. Kenyon, $463,910 pay (prior to promotion)
SVP, Total Brand Management: Deborah A. (Debbie) Edwards
SVP, Human Resources: Robert M. (Bob) Kolida
SVP, Merchandising: Bruce Dinan
SVP, Real Estate and Development: Donald C. Rogers
VP and CIO: Gary B. Davenport
VP and Controller: Arthur N. (Art) Mitchell
VP, Audit Services: J. Gregory (Greg) Armstrong
VP, Corporate Communications: Robert R. (Rob) Moore
VP, Customer Relationship Management and Chief Privacy Officer: Robert J. (Rob) Shields
VP, Logistics: Michael J. (Mike) Thomas
VP, Human Resources Planning and Development: Gillian L. Platt
VP, Secretary, and General Counsel: James A. (Jim) Ingram
Treasurer: Kenneth C. Wong
Director, Corporate Communications: Hillary Stauth
Auditors: KPMG LLP

LOCATIONS

HQ: Hudson's Bay Company
401 Bay St., Ste. 500,
Toronto, Ontario M5H 2Y4, Canada
Phone: 416-861-6112   **Fax:** 416-861-4720
Web: www.hbc.com

2005 Sales

	% of total
Ontario	43
Western Canada	33
Quebec	17
Maritimes	7
Total	**100**

PRODUCTS/OPERATIONS

2005 Sales

	% of total
Zellers	61
the Bay	38
Other	1
Total	**100**

2005 Stores

	No.
Zellers	298
Fields	103
the Bay	98
Home Outfitters	47
Designer Depot	1
Total	**547**

Stores

the Bay (department stores)
Designer Depot (off-price apparel and home merchandise)
Fields (small general-merchandise stores)
Home Outfitters (household furnishings superstores)
Zellers (discount stores)

COMPETITORS

American Eagle Outfitters
Best Buy
The Brick Warehouse
Canadian Tire
Costco Wholesale Canada
Gap
Gendis
Le Château
Men's Wearhouse
North West Company
Reitmans
SAM'S CLUB
Sears Canada
Toys "R" Us
Wal-Mart Canada

HISTORICAL FINANCIALS

Company Type: Public

Income Statement

FYE: January 31

	REVENUE ($ mil.)	NET INCOME ($ mil.)	NET PROFIT MARGIN	EMPLOYEES
1/05	5,704	48	0.8%	62,394
1/04	5,562	52	0.9%	70,000
1/03	4,831	73	1.5%	70,678
1/02	4,686	46	1.0%	71,730
1/01	4,999	83	1.7%	71,700
1/00	5,046	66	1.3%	70,000
1/99	4,680	26	0.6%	65,000
1/98	4,435	(62)	—	61,500
1/97	4,457	27	0.6%	60,000
1/96	4,343	25	0.6%	60,900
Annual Growth	**3.1%**	**7.5%**	**—**	**0.3%**

2005 Year-End Financials

Debt ratio: 22.4%
Return on equity: 2.7%
Cash ($ mil.): 6
Current ratio: 2.08
Long-term debt ($ mil.): 397

Net Income History

Toronto: HBC

Hutchison Whampoa

Hutchison Whampoa has a hand in just about everything in Hong Kong. The company, one of Hong Kong's oldest *hongs* (trading companies), has extensive holdings in retailing and manufacturing (A.S. Watson & Co.), ports, energy (Hongkong Electric, Husky Energy), telecommunications (wireless phone, and paging services), and infrastructure (power plants, toll roads, and construction materials). In addition, Hutchison Whampoa owns hotels and a sizable portfolio of Hong Kong properties. Outside Hong Kong, the company has operations in China and elsewhere in the Asia/Pacific region, as well as in Europe and the Americas. Hutchison Whampoa is controlled by Li Ka-shing, one of the world's wealthiest men.

Hutchison Whampoa's retail and manufacturing subsidiary, A.S. Watson & Co. (ASW), accounts for about 45% of sales. Operations include supermarkets (Park'N Shop), health and beauty stores (Watson's Your Personal Store, Kruidvat), 70 Fortress electrical appliance stores in Hong Kong, soft drink and water bottling operations, and wine retailing (Watson's Wine Cellar). ASW recently acquired the French retail perfume chain Marionnaud Parfumeries and has made a bid to acquire the UK's Merchant Retail Group, operator of the Perfume Shop chain.

With about 220 berths in 39 ports, Hutchison Port Holdings (HPH) is the world's biggest container terminal operator. HPH operates in five of the eight busiest container ports in the world, including three key ports on Britain's east coast and ports on both ends of the Panama Canal. In addition to owning a controlling interest in Hongkong International Terminals, which handles traffic passing through Hong Kong's container port, HPH has large investments in terminal operations in southern China, where it is expanding its operations.

Hutchison Whampoa is a leading competitor in mobile telecommunications offering wireless service to some 8 million customers throughout Australia, Europe, and Hong Kong. Subsidiary company Hutchison Telecommunications International Limited (HTIL) focuses on mobile and fixed-line telecommunications services in emerging markets in Asia, Israel, and South America.

Hutchison Whampoa has strong connections to the Chinese government, thanks to its rags-to-riches chairman, Li, who has spent years building business relationships inside China. His Cheung Kong (Holdings) Limited owns 49.9% of Hutchison Whampoa. In turn, Hutchison Whampoa owns about 85% of Cheung Kong Infrastructure.

HISTORY

Hongkong and Whampoa Dock was the first registered company in Hong Kong. The enterprise was founded in 1861 when it bought dry docks in Whampoa (near present-day Guangzhou, China) after the kidnapping and disappearance of the docks' owner, John Couper, during the Second Opium War (1856-60). It bought docks in Hong Kong in 1865.

Founded in 1880 by John Hutchison, Hutchison International became a major Hong Kong consumer goods importer and wholesaler. It took control of Hongkong and Whampoa Dock and in A.S. Watson (drugstores, supermarkets, soft drinks) during an acquisition spree in the 1960s. The purchases entailed a complex web of deals that fell apart in the mid-1970s. To save Hutchison International, the Hongkong & Shanghai Bank took a large stake in the company and brought in Australian turnaround specialist Bill Wyllie. Wyllie slashed expenses, sold 103 companies in 1976, and bought the rest of Hongkong and Whampoa Dock in 1977. The company became Hutchison Whampoa that year.

In a surprise move, in 1979 Hongkong & Shanghai Bank sold its 23% stake in Hutchison to Cheung Kong Holdings: Cheung Kong founder Li Ka-shing, who began his career at age 14 by selling plastic flowers, became the first Chinese to control a British-style *hong*. Wyllie left in 1981.

In the 1980s Hutchison redeveloped its older dockyard sites, which had become prime real estate. The company's International Terminals unit grew with Hong Kong's container traffic into the world's largest privately owned container terminal operator. In the 1980s the firm diversified into energy (buying stakes in utility Hongkong Electric and Canada-based Husky Oil) and precious metals and mining. It also moved into telecommunications, buying Australian paging and UK mobile telephone units in 1989.

The following year the *hong* launched the AsiaSat I satellite in a venture with Cable & Wireless (C&W) and China International Trust & Investment. More acquisitions followed, including European mobile phone businesses and telecom equipment makers. In 1996 the firm reorganized its Hong Kong telecom operations into Hutchison Telecommunications and launched its European wireless operations as a new public company, Orange. In 1998 Hutchison Telecommunications made a move into the US when it bought a 20% stake in Western Wireless' digital PCS unit, VoiceStream.

In 1999 the company and C&W sold their stakes in AsiaSat. Hutchison Whampoa also traded its stake in Orange to Mannesmann, acquiring 10% of the German conglomerate, which was later acquired by Vodafone.

In 2001 Hutchison Whampoa sold its 18% stake in US-based mobile phone operator VoiceStream to Deutsche Telekom for $5.1 billion in cash and stocks and purchased a 15% stake in travel Web site priceline.com. The next year its A.S. Watson Group bought the Netherlands-based health-and-beauty retail chain Kruidvat Group, which operates about 1,900 stores in six European countries.

In 2004, Hutchison Whampoa sold the remaining 20% stake in its joint venture in China with household-products-giant Procter & Gamble to P&G for $1.8 billion. Also that year the company's fixed-line telecommunications group acquired Vanda Systems, and became a listed company on the Hong Kong Stock exchange under the new name Hutchison Global Communications Holdings (HGCH). In October the company combined its 52% stake in HGCH with its interests in the 2G cellular businesses under a single parent company Hutchison Telecommunications International Limited (HTIL) and took HTIL public on the Hong Kong and New York stock exchanges. In August Watson acquired a 40% stake in Germany health and beauty chain Rossmann, which operates more than 1,100 stores throughout Germany, Hungary, Poland, and the Czech Republic.

EXECUTIVES

Chairman: Li Ka-shing, age 76
Deputy Chairman and Executive Director: Victor T. K. Li, age 40
Group Managing Director and Executive Director: Canning K. N. Fok, age 54
Deputy Group Managing Director and Executive Director: Susan M. F. Chow Woo, age 51
Group Finance Director and Executive Director: Frank J. Sixt, age 53
Executive Director: Dominic K. M. Lai, age 51
Executive Director: George C. Magnus, age 69
Executive Director: Kam Hing Lam, age 58
Company Secretary: Edith Shih, age 52
General Manager, Human Resources: Mary Tung
Group Managing Director, Hutchison Port Holdings: John E. Meredith
Group Managing Director, A.S. Watson & Co.: Ian F. Wade, age 65
Managing Director, Fortress: Peter J. Dove
Auditors: PricewaterhouseCoopers

LOCATIONS

HQ: Hutchison Whampoa Limited
Hutchison House, 22nd Fl., 10 Harcourt Rd., Hong Kong
Phone: +852-2128-1188   **Fax:** +852-2128-1705
Web: www.hutchison-whampoa.com

Hutchison Whampoa operates in Hong Kong and China. It has other diversified holdings in more than 40 other countries, including Australia, Austria, the Bahamas, Canada, France, Germany, Ghana, India, Indonesia, Israel, Italy, Japan, Latvia, Macao, Myanmar, Panama, the Philippines, Singapore, Sri Lanka, Switzerland, Taiwan, Thailand, Turkey, the UK, and the US.

2004 Sales

	% of total
Europe	33
Hong Kong	26
Asia & Australia	17
Americas & other	14
China	10
Total	**100**

PRODUCTS/OPERATIONS

2004 Sales

	% of total
Retail & manufacturing	45
Ports & related services	16
Telecommunications, 3G, 2G & others	11
Energy	11
Infrastructure	8
Property & hotels	6
Finance & investments	3
Total	**100**

Selected Subsidiaries and Affiliates

Retail and Manufacturing
A. S. Watson & Co., Limited (Hong Kong)
A.S. Drogras (Latvia)
Dirk Rossmann GmbH (40%, Germany)
Fortess Limited (Hong Kong)
Kruidvat Retail B.V. (Netherlands)
Park'N Shop Limited (supermarkets, Hong Kong)
Savers Health and Beauty Limited (UK)
Superdrug Stores plc (UK)
TOM Group Limited (24%, Internet portal, Cayman Islands/Hong Kong)
Watson's Personal Care Stores (Taiwan) Co., Limited (Taiwan)

Ports and Related Services
Hongkong International Terminals Limited (87%, container terminal operating, Hong Kong)
Hongkong United Dockyards Limited (50%, ship retail and general engineering, Hong Kong)
Shanghai Container Terminals Limited (37%, container terminal operating, China)
Yantian International Container Terminals Limited (48%, container terminal operating, China)

Energy
Hongkong Electric Holdings Limited (33%, utility, Hong Kong)
Husky Energy Inc. (35%, oil & gas investment, Canada)
Powercor Australia Limited (42%, electricity distribution, Australia)

Telecommunications and E-commerce
Hutchison 3G UK Ltd. (65%, UK)
Hutchison Global Communications Holdings Limited (37%, fixed line communications, Bermuda/Hong Kong)
Hutchison Telecommunications (Australia) Limited (58%, holding company and telecommunications, Australia)
Hutchison Telecommunications (Hong Kong) Limited (70%, telecommunications, Hong Kong)

Infrastructure
Cheung Kong Infrastructure Holdings Limited (85%, holding company, Bermuda/Hong Kong)

Property and Hotels
Harbour Plaza Hotel Management (International) Limited (50%, hotel management, BVI/Hong Kong)
Hutchison Properties Limited (holding company, Hong Kong)

Finance and Investments
Hutchison Whampoa (Europe) Limited (consulting services, UK)

COMPETITORS

AT&T	Jardine Matheson
Boots Group	Orange
BT	Sime Darby
Cable & Wireless	SkyTel Communications
China Mobile (Hong Kong)	Sprint Nextel
China Unicom	Swire Pacific
Deutsche Telekom	TIM
France Telecom	Verizon
Hopewell Holdings	Wharf

HISTORICAL FINANCIALS

Company Type: Public

Income Statement

FYE: December 31

	REVENUE ($ mil.)	NET INCOME ($ mil.)	NET PROFIT MARGIN	EMPLOYEES
12/04	17,309	2,074	12.0%	182,000
12/03	13,514	1,852	13.7%	172,653
12/02	9,645	1,832	19.0%	117,843
12/01	7,879	1,550	19.7%	77,253
12/00	7,310	4,374	59.8%	49,570
12/99	7,135	15,102	211.7%	42,510
12/98	6,633	1,124	16.9%	39,860
12/97	5,755	1,635	28.4%	31,271
12/96	4,740	1,554	32.8%	27,733
12/95	4,530	1,237	27.3%	29,137
Annual Growth	**16.1%**	**5.9%**	**—**	**22.6%**

2004 Year-End Financials

Debt ratio: 97.7%
Return on equity: 6.3%
Cash ($ mil.): 9,490
Current ratio: 1.57
Long-term debt ($ mil.): 32,765

Net Income History

Pink Sheets: HUWHY

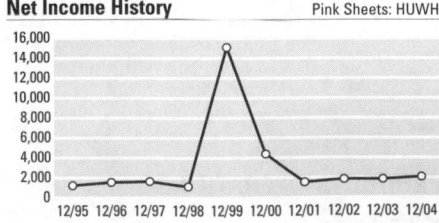

HVB Group

Other banks can set their sights on the world; Bayerische Hypo- und Vereinsbank (HVB Group for short) has its eyes on its neighbors. Germany's second-largest bank, after Deutsche Bank, HVB operates more than 2,000 branches in over 40 countries. In addition to offering lending and deposit services, it underwrites securities and provides investment services, capital management, and retail services for private clients. One of Europe's largest residential and commercial real estate lenders, the company has spun-off its commercial real estate financing business as Hypo Real Estate Group.

While Deutsche Bank aspires to worldwide dominance, HVB is content to be a central European superregional. Under its own brand and subsidiaries, the company mainly operates in Austria, Croatia, Germany, Poland, and Switzerland. HVB is growing throughout Central and Eastern Europe by acquisitions. However, the company has announced planned job cuts as it streamlines operations and merges branches in certain areas.

Munich Re owns almost a fifth of HVB Group. UniCredit, one of Italy's largest banks, has announced plans to acquire HVB (along with its Austrian and Polish subsidiaries) in an all-share deal valued at about $23.2 billion. The merger, which will give UniCredit a strong presence in Germany and Eastern Europe, will likely involve job cuts of up to 9,000 employees or about 7% of the combined banks' staff.

HISTORY

King Ludwig I formed Bayerische Hypotheken- und Wechsel-Bank (BHWB) in 1835 as Bavaria's national bank to provide real estate loans, offer insurance, and issue currency (until German unification in 1871). The bank had become Germany's largest mortgage lender by 1908.

Bayerische Vereinsbank was created by Bavarian investors in 1869 with the permission of Ludwig's more eccentric grandson Ludwig II. Formed as a commercial bank to stimulate the Bavarian economy, it began writing mortgage loans within two years.

By the end of WWI, both Vereinsbank and BHWB had formed agreements with other regional lenders to guard against larger banks. Due partly to these agreements, Vereinsbank slipped through the Great Depression relatively unscathed. As paper currency value sank daily, the bank began issuing gold-backed loans in 1924.

Germany's defeat in WWII was crucial to Vereinsbank and BHWB's ascent: As punishment for having financed Nazi rampages, national banks were broken up and regionals filled the void. By 1946 Vereinsbank and BHWB had emerged as each other's main competitors; they considered, but nixed, a merger.

Both banks expanded throughout West Germany and overseas in the 1950s. In 1958, however, the national banks regrouped, and within 10 years, Germany's former Big Three (Deutsche Bank, Dresdner Bank, and Commerzbank) were back on top. Vereinsbank and BHWB again flirted with merger in 1969, but Bavaria intervened, insisting on the inclusion of state bank Bayerische Staatsbank in any merger. Ultimately Vereinsbank bought only Staatsbank in 1971.

Over the next decade, both banks expanded. As the Soviet Union faltered in 1989, Vereinsbank formed the Bank of Moscow through a joint venture with Credit Lyonnais and other European banks. After reunification, BHWB made the most real estate loans in the former East (and was thus the most exposed to failed loans).

In 1994 BHWB formed Direkt Anlage Bank, Germany's first discount brokerage. In 1996 Vereinsbank formed online bank Advance Bank (sold to Dresdner after the HypoVereinsbank merger, when Direkt Anlage became the merged bank's online unit).

Throughout the 1990s, the Big Three overran the regional markets vital to BHWB and Vereinsbank; to stay alive, the banks finally merged in 1998, creating Europe's largest mortgage lender and Germany's first US-style superregional bank. HypoVereinsbank stayed regionally focused as Deutsche and Dresdner carved up foreign markets.

In 1999 HypoVereinsbank began talks with competitors about merging retail units; the bank decided to take its Direkt Anlage (now operating under the name DAB Bank AG) unit public that year. The following year the bank made plans to acquire Bank Austria to strengthen its presence in Eastern Europe and Austria (the deal was completed in 2001). Its Activest fund management unit began selling third-party funds, which made the business of UK asset manager subsidiary Foreign & Colonial redundant. Accordingly, HypoVereinsbank sold Foreign & Colonial to Eureko B.V., the pan-European insurance consortium.

In an effort to bolster flagging profits in mortgage lending, HypoVereinsbank announced plans to roll its real estate financing businesses together into a new bank by 2002. In 2001 the bank announced about 8,000 layoffs and the closure of up to 15% of its branches. The move underscores HypoVereinsbank's hopes to corral more customers into using its online and telephone banking services.

HypoVereinsbank also sold a 50% stake in mortgage-lender Westfälische Hypothekenbank to Düsseldorf-based WGZ Bank. HypoVereinsbank's remaining 25% share was sold to German insurer Signal Iduna. In a bid to become more universally recognized, the bank took on the name HVB Group.

A loss of nearly $1 billion in 2002 (caused in part by investment losses and Germany's languid economy) compelled the company to cancel its dividend for the first time since WWII. HVB overhauled its management and pared more than 10,000 positions, mainly in Germany and in its Polish subsidiaries, such as BPH-PBK Bank.

EXECUTIVES

Chairman, Supervisory Board: Albrecht Schmidt, age 67
Deputy Chairman, Supervisory Board: Hans-Jürgen Schinzler, age 65
Deputy Chairman, Supervisory Board: Peter König
CEO and Board Spokesman: Dieter Rampl, age 58
Managing Director, Austria and Central and Eastern Europe: Michael Mendel, age 48
Managing Director and CFO: Wolfgang Sprissler, age 60
Managing Director, Corporate Customers and Real Estate Business: Johann Berger, age 44
Managing Director and Chief Risk Officer: Michael Kemmer, age 48
Managing Director, Germany Private Customers: Christine Licci, age 41

First Executive, Corporate Customers and Professionals, Germany: Günther Berger
First Executive, Real Estate Finance and Sales: Jürgen Cancik
First Executive, Executive Office/Corporate Communication: Gunter Ernst
First Executive, Legal Department: Andreas Früh
First Executive and Chief Credit Risk Officer: Henning Giesecke
First Executive, Group IT and Deputy Chairman and COO, Austria and Central and Eastern Europe: Wolfgang Haller, age 54
First Executive, Human Resource Management: Heinz Laber
First Executive, Group Finance and Tax: Rolf Friedhofen
Auditors: KPMG Deutsche Treuhand-Gesellschaft AG

LOCATIONS

HQ: Bayerische Hypo- und Vereinsbank Aktiengesellschaft
Am Tucherpark 16, 80538 Munich, Germany
Phone: +49-89-378-0   **Fax:** +49-89-378-27784
US HQ: 150 E. 42nd St., New York, NY 10017
US Phone: 212-672-6000   **US Fax:** 212-672-5555
Web: www.hvbgroup.com

COMPETITORS

BayernLB
Citigroup
Commerzbank
DEPFA BANK
Deutsche Bank
Dresdner Bank
KfW
Landesbank Baden-Württemberg
WestLB

HISTORICAL FINANCIALS

Company Type: Public

Income Statement

FYE: December 31

	ASSETS ($ mil.)	NET INCOME ($ mil.)	INCOME AS % OF ASSETS	EMPLOYEES
12/04	637,545	(3,107)	—	57,806
12/03	601,812	(3,313)	—	60,214
12/02	724,402	(899)	—	65,926
12/01	645,013	857	0.1%	69,520
12/00	674,670	429	0.1%	72,867
12/99	506,748	362	0.1%	46,170
12/98	537,608	1,098	0.2%	36,900
12/97	244,890	472	0.2%	22,000
12/96	253,855	522	0.2%	21,825
12/95	243,401	418	0.2%	22,188
Annual Growth	11.3%	—	—	11.2%

2004 Year-End Financials

Equity as % of assets: 2.5%   Long-term debt ($ mil.): 149,443
Return on assets: —   Sales ($ mil.): 28,209
Return on equity: —

Net Income History

German: HVM

Hyundai Motor

Hyundai Motor has been selling cars in the US since 1986, but it only started selling its heavy trucks stateside in 1998. South Korea's #1 carmaker, Hyundai produces 14 models of cars and minivans, as well as trucks, buses, and other commercial vehicles. The company reestablished itself as Korea's leading carmaker in 1998 by acquiring a 51% stake in Kia Motors (since reduced to about 45%). Hyundai's exports include the Accent and Sonata, while its Korean models include the Atos subcompact. The company also manufactures machine tools for factory automation and material-handling equipment.

Although DaimlerChrysler had purchased a 10% stake in the company as part of a plan to boost DaimlerChrysler's Asian market presence, the Germany-based carmaker sold its stake in Hyundai to an undisclosed buyer in the late summer of 2004. Although the two companies have parted ways in terms of ownership structure, they intend to continue their cooperation. Projects include the development of a new four-cylinder engine and a joint purchasing plan. In another deal, DaimlerChrysler chose to exercise its option to purchase 50% of Hyundai's spun-off heavy-truck business.

To increase its presence in the US Hyundai completed construction of a new manufacturing plant, Hyundai Motor Manufacturing Alabama, in 2005. The new plant will build about 300,000 cars per year. Hyundai is also expanding in China. Since opening its first Chinese plant in 2002, Hyundai has doubled its production in that country. The company plans to have a 20% share of the Chinese market by 2010. To that end the automaker has signed a $1.24 billion deal to form a joint venture with Guangzhou Motor Group, giving Hyundai access to the commercial-vehicle market in China.

To keep pace with markets in Europe, Hyundai has chosen the Czech Republic for the site of a $1.2 billion manufacturing complex.

HISTORY

Hyundai Motor Company was established in 1967, and it initially began manufacturing cars and light trucks through a technology collaboration with Ford's UK operations. By the early 1970s Hyundai was ready to build cars under its own nameplate. The company debuted the subcompact Hyundai Pony in 1974 at Italy's annual Turin Motor Show.

The Pony was an instant domestic success and soon propelled Hyundai to the top spot among Korea's carmakers. During the mid-1970s the company began exporting the Pony to El Salvador and Guatemala.

By the 1980s Hyundai was ready to shift into high gear and begin high-volume production in anticipation of penetrating more overseas markets. The company began exporting to Canada in 1983.

Hyundai introduced the Hyundai Excel in 1985. That year the company established its US subsidiary, Hyundai Motor America. By 1986 Hyundai was exporting Excels for sale in the US. Sales of the Excel soared the next year, so Hyundai decided to build a factory in Bromont, Quebec.

But by the time the factory was finished in 1989, consumers were tiring of the aging compact car and the quality problems that came with it. Hyundai closed the plant after just four years of operation.

The company introduced its first sports car, the Scoupe, in 1990. The following year it developed the first Hyundai-designed engine, called the Alpha. Two years later the carmaker unveiled its second-generation proprietary engine, the Beta.

By 1998 Hyundai was beginning to feel the pinch of the Asian economic crisis as domestic demand dropped drastically. However, the decrease in Korean demand was largely offset by exports. That year Hyundai took a controlling stake in Korean competitor Kia Motors.

In hopes of increasing its share of the Asian automotive market, DaimlerChrysler took a 10% stake in Hyundai in 2000 (sold in 2004). The deal included the establishment of a joint venture to manufacture commercial vehicles, as well as an agreement among Hyundai, DaimlerChrysler, and Mitsubishi Motors to develop small cars for the global market.

In 2001 Hyundai decreased its stake in Kia Motors to about 46%.

The following year DaimlerChrysler announced it would exercise its option to take a 50% stake in Hyundai's heavy-truck business.

In 2004 Hyundai CEO Kim Dong-Jin was indicted in South Korea on charges that he violated campaign finance laws and engaged in managerial negligence. The charges stemmed from a general crackdown on campaign finance violations, during which more than a dozen members of South Korea's parliament were either indicted or detained. Later in 2004 Kim was convicted of the charges against him and sentenced to a suspended two-year jail term.

EXECUTIVES

Chairman and Co-CEO: Mong-Koo Chung
Vice Chairman and Co-CEO: Kim Dong-Jin
President, Manufacturing: Jeon Cheon-Soo
Auditors: Deloitte HanaAnjin LLC

LOCATIONS

HQ: Hyundai Motor Company
(Hyundai Jadongcha Chusik Hoesa)
231 Yangjae-dong, Seocho-gu,
Seoul 137-938, South Korea
Phone: +82-2-3464-1114
US HQ: 10550 Talbert Ave., Fountain Valley, CA 92728
US Phone: 714-965-3000   **US Fax:** 714-965-3001
Web: www.hyundai-motor.com

Hyundai Motor has manufacturing subsidiaries in China, Egypt, India, Indonesia, Iran, Malaysia, Russia, South Korea, the Sudan, Turkey, the US, and Venezuela, and sells its vehicles worldwide.

2004 Sales

	$ mil.	% of total
South Korea	29,228	58
North America	12,712	25
Europe	5,877	11
Asia	2,878	6
Total	**50,695**	**100**

PRODUCTS/OPERATIONS

Selected Models

Commercial vehicles
  Aero Town (medium bus)
  Cargo Truck (large truck)
  County (small bus)
  H 1 Truck (light commercial vehicle)
  H 120 Truck (medium truck)
  HD 65/HD72 (small truck)
  HD 250 (refrigerated van truck)
Passenger cars
  Accent (sedan)
  Atos Prime (subcompact)
  Centennial (luxury sedan)
  Elantra (sedan)
  Getz (compact sedan)
  Grandeur (sedan)
  H-I Van
  Matrix (compact SUV)
  Santa Fe (SUV)
  Sonata (sedan)
  Terracan (SUV)
  Tucson (SUV)
  Trajet (SUV)

COMPETITORS

DaimlerChrysler
Fiat
Ford
General Motors
GM Daewoo Auto
Honda
Ingersoll-Rand Industrial Technologies
Isuzu
Mazda
Nissan
Peugeot
Renault
Toyota
Volkswagen

HISTORICAL FINANCIALS

Company Type: Public

Income Statement

FYE: December 31

	REVENUE ($ mil.)	NET INCOME ($ mil.)	NET PROFIT MARGIN	EMPLOYEES
12/04	50,695	1,610	3.2%	—
12/03	38,995	1,486	3.8%	51,471
12/02	40,111	1,196	3.0%	49,855
12/01	30,108	870	2.9%	50,000
12/00	25,667	476	1.9%	52,000
12/99	21,401	480	2.2%	48,000
Annual Growth	**18.8%**	**27.4%**	**—**	**1.8%**

2004 Year-End Financials

Debt ratio: 59.0%
Return on equity: 14.1%
Cash ($ mil.): 8,783
Current ratio: 0.81
Long-term debt ($ mil.): 7,336

Net Income History

Exchange: Korea

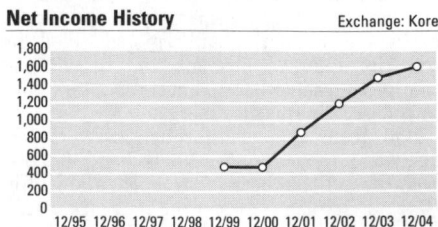

Ifi

What are the chances of untangling the Agnelli web of holdings? Pretty Ifi. Controlled by the wealthy Agnelli family through parent firm Giovanni Agnelli and C., the holding company IFI — Istituto Finanziario Industriale owns stakes in a variety of enterprises. These holdings include a more than 60% stake in sister company Ifil Investments (Ifil). Through Ifil, the company owns about 30% of automotive giant Fiat (which gives the Agnelli family effective control of the automaker). Ifil also holds interests in companies involved in professional sports, retail, publishing, insurance, paper making, tourism, and other businesses.

Carmaker Fiat also makes Maserati, Alfa Romeo, and Ferrari sports cars. Through Ifil, Ifi also owns Turin, Italy's top-ranked Juventus soccer club. In addition, Ifil has shares of companies involved in tourism (Alpitour) and manufacturing (Sequana Capital, formerly known as Worms & Cie). Ifil has sold its stake in Gruppo Rinascente, the department store chain.

Subsidiary EXOR Group extends Ifi's reach beyond Italy with international holdings in French wine (Domaines Codem), American packaging (17% of Graphic Packaging Corporation), and Asian telecommunications (7% of Distacom).

HISTORY

Istituto Finanziario Industriale (Ifi) was formed by Giovanni Agnelli in 1927 as a family "safe" for his stakes of various industrial businesses. Automaker Fiat immediately became and remains the centerpiece of Ifi's holdings.

Fiat benefited from Mussolini's protectionist policies in the 1930s, but Agnelli remained a liberal. During WWII, when Axis defeat appeared imminent, Agnelli slowed war production and put Italian resistance members on his payroll. At the end of the war, Fiat executives — unable to wait for the Marshall Plan — traveled to the US to seek reconstruction loans.

Upon Agnelli's death in 1945, ownership of Ifi passed to his Agnelli and Nasi family heirs. In 1958 Ifi gained control of Finanziaria di Partecipazioni (Ifil), another industrial holding company.

Ten years later Ifi formed Infint (renamed EXOR Group in 1994) to manage Ifi's foreign shares. Also in 1968 Ifi stock was offered to the public to fund company expansion. The Agnelli and Nasi families' shares decreased throughout the 1970s and 1980s as more capital was sought.

The 1970s saw Ifi dispose of non-core holdings, such as Società Assicuratrice Industriale, in order to cut debt.

Ifi and Ifil bought back shares of Fiat in the 1980s while Ifil began to invest more widely. Parent company Giovanni Agnelli e C. S.a.p.az. (G.A. e C.), controlled solely by the Agnelli and Nasi families, formed in 1987 and bought Ifi.

In 1997 Ifi and Ifil reacted to the privatization and competition rocking the once-static world of Italian financial holdings. The companies invested in Istituto Bancario San Paolo di Torino (now San Paolo IMI) and spun off cement maker Unicem.

In 1999 G.A. e C. and Ifi upped their stakes in EXOR Group; together they controlled about 85%. Two years later Ifi sold its stake in the Rockefeller Center to T. Speyer & Crown. In 2003 the junior Giovanni Agnelli died; Umberto Agnelli died in 2004.

EXECUTIVES

Chairman: Gianluigi Gabetti, age 77
Deputy Chairman: Pio Teodorani-Fabbri
General Manager: Virgilio Marrone, age 59
Secretary: Pierluigi Bernasconi
Auditors: Deloitte & Touche S.p.A.

LOCATIONS

HQ: IFI — Istituto Finanziario Industriale S.p.A.
  Corso Matteotti, 26, 10121 Turin, Italy
Phone: +39-011-509-0266   **Fax:** +39-011-535-600
Web: www.gruppoifi.com

IFI — Istituto Finanziario Industriale has holdings primarily in Italy, and to a lesser degree in France, Hong Kong, and the US.

PRODUCTS/OPERATIONS

Selected Holdings

EXOR Group (29%)
  Distacom (7%, telecommunications, Hong Kong)
  Domaines Codem (wine, France)
  Graphic Packaging Corporation (17%, packaging, US)
Ifil (62%)
  Alpitour (tourism)
  Fiat (30%, with Ifil's holding)
    CNH Global (84%, agriculture
      and construction equipment)
    COMAU (production systems)
    Ferrari e Maserati (56%, sports cars)
    Fiat Auto Holdings (90%)
    Itedi (publishing and communications)
    IVECO (commercial vehicles)
    Magneti Marelli Holding S.p.A. (auto components)
    Teksid (81%, metallurgical products)
  Juventus F.C. S.p.A. (62%)
  SanPaolo IMI (6%, bank)
  Sequana Capital (formerly Worms
    & Cie; 53%, paper, France)

COMPETITORS

Edison
Investor
Italmobiliare
Wendel Investissement

HISTORICAL FINANCIALS

Company Type: Public

Income Statement

FYE: December 31

	REVENUE ($ mil.)	NET INCOME ($ mil.)	NET PROFIT MARGIN	EMPLOYEES
12/04	70,762	160	0.2%	179,790
12/03	67,165	(163)	—	192,550
12/02	63,717	(842)	—	209,141
12/01	55,968	145	0.3%	198,764
12/00	59,613	205	0.3%	223,953
12/99	54,868	215	0.4%	244,385
Annual Growth	5.2%	(5.7%)	—	(6.0%)

2004 Year-End Financials

Debt ratio: 404.5%
Return on equity: 5.4%
Cash ($ mil.): 5,032
Current ratio: 1.40
Long-term debt ($ mil.): 12,520

Net Income History

Italian: IFP

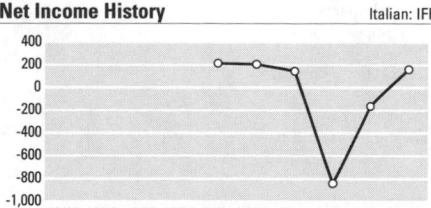

IKEA

How Swede it is. One of the world's top furniture retailers, IKEA International sells Scandinavian-style home furnishings and other housewares in some 220 stores in 33 countries. To cut transportation costs, IKEA uses flat packaging; customers assemble the products at home. The company designs its own furniture, which is made by about 1,500 suppliers in more than 50 countries. IKEA's stores feature playrooms for children and Swedish cuisine restaurants. It also sells by mail order and online. An acronym for founder Ingvar Kamprad and his boyhood home, Elmtaryd, Agunnaryd, IKEA began operating in Sweden in 1943. It is owned by Kamprad's Netherlands-based charitable foundation, Stichting Ingka.

If you're looking for fussy furniture in neutral tones, IKEA is not the place for you. Known for its use of bold colors and creative product names (a Ticka alarm clock, a Ringo stool), the company sells furniture and other household items, including dinnerware, pillows, lighting, and rugs. In a bid to get consumers to replace home furnishing — and visit IKEA — more frequently, the retailer began offering four collections of linens a year in 2005.

IKEA plans to open two stores in Japan in 2006. Overall in 2006 the company expects to open 19 stores. A new store is slated to open in Portland, Oregon in the spring of 2007; IKEA's second store in the Pacific Northwest.

IKEA operates about two dozen US stores, which account for 11% of the company's sales. Germany is IKEA's biggest market, accounting for nearly one-fifth of annual sales. The company mails about 160 million catalogs in 25 languages each year.

IKEA's sales have been growing thanks to expansion of its store network and price cuts; the retailer reduced prices by 3% in fiscal 2005.

IKEA's manufacturing arm, The Swedwood Group, makes wood-based furniture and components at 32 plants in nine countries.

Sweden's largest food exporter, IKEA is replacing its non-organic offerings with organic fare, including cheese, coffee, and jams.

HISTORY

At the age of 17, Ingvar Kamprad formed his own company in Sweden in 1943, peddling fish, vegetable seeds, and magazines by bicycle. He called the company IKEA, an acronym for his name and the village in which he grew up (Elmtaryd, Agunnaryd). Four years later he added the newly invented ballpoint pen to his product assortment and started a mail-order catalog.

In 1950 Kamprad added furniture and housewares to his mail-order products, and in 1953 he bought a furniture factory and opened a small showroom. The showroom was a hit with price-conscious Swedes and was replaced by the first official IKEA store in 1958. The first store outside Sweden was established in 1963 in Norway. Two years later the company opened its flagship store in Stockholm, a 150,000-sq.-ft. marvel whose round design was inspired by the Guggenheim Museum in New York. The store featured a nursery, a restaurant, a bank, and parking spaces for 1,000 cars. By 1969 two more stores were opened in Sweden and another in Denmark.

A fire badly damaged the Stockholm store in 1973, but the subsequent fire sale pulled in more shoppers than the store's grand opening. That year IKEA expanded beyond Scandinavia, opening stores in Switzerland and Germany. In 1976 it opened its first store outside Europe, in Canada, and during the late 1970s and early 1980s, it entered Australia, the Canary Islands, Hong Kong, Iceland, Kuwait, Saudi Arabia, and Singapore. To avoid questions of succession after his death, Kamprad in 1980 transferred ownership of the company to a charitable foundation. IKEA opened its first US store, in Philadelphia, in 1985. Anders Moberg was named president of IKEA in 1986. By 1991 there were seven outlets in the US and 95 total in 23 countries. IKEA began its push into Eastern Europe two years later, but at the same time struggled with economic downturns in its major markets, Germany and Scandinavia.

Kamprad's reluctant announcement that he had associated with pro-Nazi groups in the 1940s and 1950s brought a torrent of bad press. The revelation prompted IKEA to reconsider opening a store in Israel, believing the Israeli government would not sanction the investment. Instead, Jewish groups claimed the company was deliberately avoiding the country. IKEA agreed in 1995 to open an Israeli store and finally granted a license for a franchise to Blue Square — Israel Ltd. in 1997.

That year IKEA announced plans to build about 20 plants over five years in the Baltics, Bulgaria, and Romania, a move designed to reduce its dependence on contract manufacturers and nearly double its own manufacturing capacity. Also in 1997 it began offering prefab housing in Sweden with construction firm Skanska.

IKEA opened its largest store (400,000 sq. ft.) outside Europe in Chicago in 1998 and announced plans to open more stores in Russia, China, and Eastern Europe. In 1999 Anders Dahlvig was named group president, replacing Moberg, who left to take a position with retailer Home Depot. In 2000 the company opened its first store in Moscow, with plans for more Russian locations.

In 2001 IKEA stated plans to open 60 to 70 more store locations in Europe, North America, and Asia over the next five years. Since June 2002 IKEA has run its own freight trains between depots in Sweden and Germany, and the company plans to extend its rail services to Italy and Poland and to double its rail transport of goods to 40% by 2006. In December 2002 IKEA Netherlands received a letter with a bomb threat and temporarily shut down ten of its retail locations. Explosives were discovered in two stores in the Netherlands and detonated; two IKEA employees were minimally injured. Federal authorities confirmed that the motive behind the attacks was extortion.

In 2004 IKEA opened its first store in Portugal and stores in Russia outside the metro areas of Moscow and St. Petersburg. The Swedish home furnishings group opened 18 new stores in fiscal year 2005 (15 in Europe and three in North America).

EXECUTIVES

Group President: Anders Dahlvig
Group VP: Hans Gydell
Senior Adviser: Ingvar Kamprad
Global Design Chief: Lars Engman
President, IKEA North America: Pernille Spiers-Lopez, age 45
Managing Director, IKEA Food Service: Jan Kjellman
Regional Manager, Mid-Europe: Peter Høgsted
Creative Director, IKEA North America: Mats Nilsson

Property Director, UK: Scott Cordrey
Global Information Manager: Marianne Barner
Human Resources Manager: Lars Gejrot

LOCATIONS

HQ: IKEA International A/S
Box 640, SE 25 106 Helsingborg, Sweden
Phone: +46-42-267-100   **Fax:** +46-42-132-805
US HQ: 496 W. Germantown Pike,
Plymouth Meeting, PA 19462
US Phone: 610-834-0180   **US Fax:** 610-834-0872
Web: www.ikea.com

2005 Sales

	% of total
Europe	81
North America	16
Asia & Australia	3
Total	**100**

PRODUCTS/OPERATIONS

2005 Stores

	No.
Company-owned	196
Franchised	24
Total	**220**

Selected Products

Armchairs	Instruments for children
Bath accessories	Kitchen organizers
Bath suites	Kitchen units
Bean bags	Leather sofas
Bed linens	Lighting
Beds and bedroom suites	Mattresses
Bookcases	Mirrors
Boxes	Office chairs and suites
CD storage	Posters
Ceiling lamps	Rugs
Children's furniture	Sofas and sofa beds
Clocks	Spotlights
Coffee tables	Stools
Cookware	Table lamps
Cord management	Toy storage
Desk accessories	TV cabinets and stands
Dining tables and chairs	Utility storage
Dinnerware	Video storage
Entertainment units	Wall shelves and systems
Floor lamps	Wardrobe units
Frames	Window treatments

COMPETITORS

Bassett Furniture
Bed Bath & Beyond
Bombay Company
Euromarket Designs
Eurway
Gruppo Coin
GUS
Harvey Norman Holdings
Horten
Hulsta-Werke Huls
Jennifer Convertibles
John Lewis
Levitz Furniture
Linens 'n Things
METRO AG
MFI Furniture
Otto
Pier 1 Imports
Pier Import Europe
PPR
Restoration Hardware
Rinascente
Rooms To Go
Williams-Sonoma

HISTORICAL FINANCIALS

Company Type: Private

Income Statement

FYE: August 31

	REVENUE ($ mil.)	NET INCOME ($ mil.)	NET PROFIT MARGIN	EMPLOYEES
8/05	18,089	—	—	90,000
8/04	15,425	—	—	84,000
8/03	12,409	—	—	80,000
8/02	11,779	—	—	75,500
8/01	10,355	—	—	70,000
8/00	8,500	—	—	58,000
8/99	8,076	—	—	49,400
8/98	7,027	—	—	36,400
8/97	5,885	—	—	36,400
8/96	6,149	—	—	33,400
Annual Growth	**12.7%**	**—**	**—**	**11.6%**

Revenue History

Imperial Chemical Industries

Empire may not be such a popular word any longer, but Imperial Chemical Industries (ICI) is still among the chemical royalty. Its specialty products group consists of National Starch and Chemical (industrial adhesives, starch), Quest (fragrance and flavors), and Uniqema (natural and synthetic lubricants and personal care products). Its paint offerings include the Alba, Dulux, and Glidden brands. ICI's regional and industrial chemicals segment (subsidiaries in Argentina, India, and Pakistan) makes explosives, soda ash, rubber chemicals, sulfur-related products, and fibers. Quest sold its food ingredients business to the Kerry Group in 2004 for about $440 million.

ICI set out in 2003 to identify growth opportunities within its portfolio and direct investment accordingly. Thus came the sale of Quest's food ingredients business and National Starch's emulsion polymers unit to Celanese. Also the company has followed the rest of the world into Asia and China in particular, expanding ICI Paints sales and marketing operations throughout the region and opening two manufacturing plants for National Starch in 2004.

The company has broken out its businesses into two groups, those it is choosing to grow aggressively (North American paints, flavors and fragrances, and all of its Asian businesses) and those it is trying to make more efficient if not grow larger (specialty chemicals, paints in Europe and Latin America).

Quest has been looking to concentrate on its core flavors and fragrance businesses and, so, sold off the food ingredients product line to Ireland's Kerry Group. The deal was completed at the end of April 2004 and involves about 900 employees and nine manufacturing sites (which make emulsifiers, proteins, yeast, and enzymes).

HISTORY

Imperial Chemical Industries (ICI) began in 1926 when four British chemical companies (Nobel Industries; Brunner, Mond and Company; United Alkali; and British Dyestuffs) merged to compete with German cartel I. G. Farben. The most-famed ICI predecessor, Nobel Industries, was created as the British arm of Alfred Nobel's explosives empire. Nobel mixed nitroglycerin with porous clay to make dynamite. In 1886 he created the London-based Nobel Dynamite Trust to embrace British and German interests. After Nobel's death in 1896, the empire unraveled, and WWI severed the German and UK components of the Nobel firm. The British arm became Nobel Industries (1920).

In 1929 ICI and American chemical company DuPont signed a patents-and-process agreement to share research information. Around the same time it focused on research and between 1933 and 1935 created some 87 new products, including polyethylene.

After WWII the cartel club began to disband. The US government won antitrust sanctions against the DuPont-ICI alliance in 1952, and ICI faced new competition from the sundered components of I. G. Farben (Bayer, BASF, Hoechst). ICI added foreign operations in the 1960s, but fortunes declined, and in 1980 it posted losses and cut its dividend for the first time.

The company recruited turnaround artist John Harvey-Jones in 1982. He cut layers of decision making, reorganized along product lines, and added non-UK directors to the board. ICI also shifted production from bulk chemicals such as soda and chlorine to high-margin specialty chemicals such as pharmaceuticals and pesticides.

Harvey-Jones bought 100 companies between 1982 and his retirement in 1987. ICI expanded in the US market by purchasing Beatrice's chemical operations (1985) and Glidden paints (1986).

ICI sold its nylon business to DuPont in 1992 and spun off its pharmaceutical and agricultural operations as Zeneca the next year. It opened its first plant in China, a paint factory, in 1994 and named 30-year Unilever veteran Charles Miller Smith its new CEO in 1995.

In 1997 ICI bought Unilever's specialty chemicals unit in a deal worth about $8 billion. The same year it picked up Canada-based St. Clair Paint & Wallpaper. ICI then sold its polyester resin and intermediates operations (1997) and film business (1998) to Dupont for around $2 billion. In 1998 ICI paid $560 million for specialty chemicals maker Acheson Industries. ICI's attempts to reduce debt from the Unilever purchase stumbled when W. R. Grace & Co. terminated its deal to buy ICI's Crosfield silicas and catalysts business and DuPont and NL Industries backed out of the $1 billion purchase of ICI's titanium dioxide business.

Still saddled with debt, ICI sold a rash of companies in 1999: its utilities and services division to Enron for about $500 million; its polyurethanes and titanium-dioxide businesses and some petrochemicals businesses to US-based Huntsman for about $2.8 billion (though it kept a 30% stake, which it then sold back to Huntsman in 2003); its

industrial coatings and auto refinish businesses in the Americas and Europe, and Germany-based coatings business to PPG Industries for $684 million; and its acrylics division (raw materials such as methylacrylates and value-added products such as Lucite and Perspex) to Belgium-based Ineos Acrylics (which has since become Lucite International) for $833 million.

Continuing to divest in 2000, ICI sold paint distribution network Master Distribution to Lafarge SA. The next year ICI sold its giant plant in Runcorn, UK, to Ineos Chlor. Despite the money brought in from all the sell-offs, ICI was threatened with its debt rating being reduced to junk bond status. In response, the company raised about $1.15 billion in a share offering in order to reduce debt. It also sold its 30% stake in Huntsman ICI Chemicals back to Utah-based Huntsman for nearly $500 million, which it then used to pay down more of its debt in 2003.

EXECUTIVES

Chairman: Peter B. Ellwood, age 62
CEO: John D. G. McAdam, age 57
EVP, Mergers & Acquisitions, General Counsel, and Company Secretary: Andy Ransom
EVP, Uniqema: Leonard J. (Len) Berlik, age 57
EVP, Regional and International Business: David Gee, age 56
EVP, Human Resources: Rolf Deusinger, age 47
CFO: Alan J. Brown, age 48
Chairman and CEO, ICI Paints: David Hamill, age 47
Chairman and CEO, National Starch and Director: William H. Powell, age 59
Chairman and Chief Executive, Quest International: Charles F. Knott, age 50
SVP, Technology: Carmine P. Iovine
SVP, Technology: Graeme D. Armstrong, age 43
VP, Investor Relations and Corporate Communications: John Dawson
Chief Press Officer: John Edgar
Director, Corporate Communications: Regina Kilfoyle
Auditors: KPMG Audit Plc

LOCATIONS

HQ: Imperial Chemical Industries PLC
20 Manchester Sq.,
London W1U 3AN, United Kingdom
Phone: +44-20-7009-5000   **Fax:** +44-20-7009-5001
US HQ: 10 Finderne Ave., Bridgewater, NJ 08807-3300
US Phone: 908-685-5000   **US Fax:** 908-685-5005
Web: www.ici.com

Imperial Chemical Industries has more than 200 manufacturing facilities on six continents.

2004 Sales

	$ mil.	% of total
Americas		
US	3,186	30
Other countries	1,162	11
Europe		
UK	1,204	11
Other countries	2,418	22
Asia/Pacific	2,540	24
Other regions	228	2
Total	**10,738**	**100**

PRODUCTS/OPERATIONS

2004 Sales

	$ mil.	% of total
Paints	4,143	39
National Starch	3,585	33
Uniqema	1,206	11
Quest	1,120	10
Regional & Industrial	719	7
Adjustments	(35)	—
Total	**10,738**	**100**

International Businesses
Paints
 Packaging coatings (for food and drink cans)
 Paints (Devoe, Dulux, Inca, Glidden)
National Starch
 Adhesives
 Electronic and engineering materials
 Specialty starches
 Specialty synthetic polymers
Uniqema
 Natural and synthetic lubricants
 Personal care products
Quest (flavors and fragrance)
Regional and Industrial Chemicals
 ICI Argentina
  Sulfur-related chemicals
  Wine chemicals
 ICI India
  Catalysts
  Explosives
  Adhesives
  Rubber chemicals
 ICI Pakistan
  Fibers
  Soda ash

COMPETITORS

3M	H.B. Fuller
Air Products	Hercules
Akzo Nobel	Honeywell Specialty
BASF AG	Materials
Bayer	Huntsman
Ciba Specialty Chemicals	International Flavors
Clariant International	Lyondell Chemical
Degussa	Millennium Chemicals
Dow Chemical	Mitsubishi Chemical
Dow Corning	Norsk Hydro
DSM	Occidental Petroleum
DuPont	PPG
Eastman Chemical	Reliance Industries
Engelhard	Rhodia
E.ON	Rohm and Haas
Ferro	Royal Dutch/Shell Group
Firmenich	RPM
Formosa Plastics	Sherwin-Williams
Frutarom	TOTAL
GE Industrial	Wattyl
GEA Group	

HISTORICAL FINANCIALS

Company Type: Public

Income Statement

FYE: December 31

	REVENUE ($ mil.)	NET INCOME ($ mil.)	NET PROFIT MARGIN	EMPLOYEES
12/04	10,738	402	3.7%	33,300
12/03	10,431	36	0.3%	35,030
12/02	9,870	288	2.9%	36,660
12/01	9,356	176	1.9%	38,600
12/00	11,565	(340)	—	45,930
12/99	11,616	407	3.5%	53,500
12/98	15,093	320	2.1%	58,700
12/97	14,395	428	3.0%	69,500
12/96	18,016	471	2.6%	64,000
12/95	15,927	830	5.2%	64,800
Annual Growth	**(4.3%)**	**(7.7%)**	**—**	**(7.1%)**

2004 Year-End Financials

Debt ratio: 155.0%
Return on equity: 36.8%
Cash ($ mil.): 759
Current ratio: 1.32
Long-term debt ($ mil.): 2,142
No. of shares (mil.): 298
Dividends
 Yield: 2.8%
 Payout: 37.5%
Market value ($ mil.): 5,488

| | 12/95 | 12/96 | 12/97 | 12/98 | 12/99 | 12/00 | 12/01 | 12/02 | 12/03 | 12/04 |

	STOCK PRICE ($) FY Close	P/E High/Low		PER SHARE ($) Earnings	Dividends	Book Value
12/04	18.43	14	10	1.36	0.51	4.64
12/03	14.32	14	5	0.13	0.49	2.70
12/02	14.39	18	9	1.04	0.82	2.70
12/01	21.85	16	7	0.98	1.64	(2.26)
12/00	33.69	—	—	(1.89)	2.22	(1.77)
12/99	42.56	19	11	2.26	2.19	2.16
12/98	34.94	26	10	1.77	2.10	1.36
12/97	64.94	9	6	2.35	2.42	1.33
12/96	52.00	18	14	3.33	2.18	34.08
12/95	46.75	11	9	4.58	2.06	33.59
Annual Growth	(9.8%)	—	—	(12.6%)	(14.4%)	(19.7%)

Imperial Oil

Imperial Oil, Canada's largest oil company, holds sway over a vast empire of oil and gas resources. It has proved reserves of 1.1 billion barrels of oil and 704 billion cu. ft. of natural gas. Imperial is one of Canada's top natural gas producers, the #1 refiner and marketer of petroleum products, and a major supplier of petrochemicals. It sells petroleum products, including gasoline, heating oil, and diesel fuel, under the Esso name and other brand names. Most of the company's production comes from fields in Alberta and the Northwest Territories. Imperial also owns 25% of Syncrude Canada, which operates the world's largest oil sands development. Exxon Mobil owns about 70% of Imperial.

The oil company sells gasoline to motorists at 2,100 Esso service stations across Canada. At Cold Lake, Alberta, the company uses steam to recover very heavy crude and related products from oil sands deposits, through its participation in the Syncrude Project. Management is seeking to boost production from its plentiful oil sands holdings; its research laboratories in Ontario and Alberta are focused on developing technology for finding better ways to recover heavy oil.

Imperial's petroleum products and chemicals business operates four refineries and has an extensive network of wholesale outlets (in addition to its gas station chain) in every region of Canada. The company's chemicals segment operates a manufacturing plant in Sarnia, Ontario, and a number of distribution centers across Canada.

Imperial has reduced employment and closed service stations to stay competitive; it also is selling noncore assets and underperforming units (including refineries).

In 2002 Imperial worked out a deal to offer the popular Tim Hortons brand of soups and sandwiches at its Esso stations across Canada.

HISTORY

London, Ontario, boomed from the discovery of oil in the 1860s and 1870s, but when the market for Canadian kerosene became saturated in 1880, 16 refiners banded together to form the Imperial Oil Company.

The company refined sulfurous Canadian oil, nicknamed "skunk oil" for its powerful smell. Imperial faced tough competition from America's Standard Oil, which marketed kerosene made from lighter, less-odorous Pennsylvania crude. Guided by American expatriate Jacob Englehart, Imperial built a better refinery and hired a chemist to develop a process to clean sulfur from the crude.

By the mid-1890s Imperial had expanded from coast to Canadian coast. Cash-starved from its expansion, the company turned to old nemesis Standard Oil, which bought controlling interest in Imperial in 1898. That interest is today held by Exxon Mobil.

After the turn of the century, Imperial began producing gasoline to serve the new automobiles. The horseless carriages were spooking the workhorses at the warehouse where fuel was sold, so an Imperial manager in Vancouver opened the first Canadian service station in 1907. The company marketed its gas under the Esso banner borrowed from Standard Oil.

An Imperial crew discovered oil in 1920 at Norman Wells in the remote Northwest Territories. In 1924 a subsidiary sparked a new boom with a gas well discovery in the Turner Valley area northeast of Edmonton. But soon Imperial's luck ran as dry as the holes it was drilling; it came away empty from the next 133 consecutive wells. That string ended in 1947 when it struck oil in Alberta at the Leduc No. 1. To get the oil to market, Imperial invested in the Interprovincial Pipe Line from Alberta to Superior, Wisconsin.

In 1964 the company began research to extract bitumen from the oil sands in Cold Lake, Alberta. During the 1970s oil crisis, Imperial continued to search for oil in northern Canada. It found crude on land near the Beaufort Sea (1970) and in its icy waters (1972). The company formed its Esso Resources Canadian Ltd. subsidiary in 1978 to oversee natural resources production.

In 1989 Texaco (acquired by Chevron in 2001), still reeling from a court battle with Pennzoil, sold Texaco Canada to Imperial. To diminish debt and comply with regulators, Imperial agreed to sell some of Texaco Canada's refining and marketing assets in Atlantic Canada, its interests in Interhome Energy, and oil and gas properties in western Canada.

Imperial reorganized in 1992, centralizing several units, and in 1993 closed its refinery at Port Moody, British Columbia. It sold most of its fertilizer business in 1994; disposed of 339 unprofitable gas stations in 1995; and the next year closed down Canada's northernmost oil refinery at Norman Wells.

In 1997 Imperial announced an ambitious program to expand Syncrude's oil sands bitumen upgrading plant. In 1998 Exxon agreed to buy Mobil, which had substantial Canadian oil assets. In 1999 Canada pre-approved the potential merger of Imperial Oil and Mobil Canada. Later that year Exxon completed its purchase of Mobil to form Exxon Mobil.

In the face of public pressure for cleaner gasoline (Imperial had been implicated by government tests as Canada's "dirtiest" oil producer), Bob Peterson (who stepped down as CEO in 2002) told shareholders in 2000 that he did not agree with the theory of global warming. Activities at its Mackenzie Gas Project were halted in 2005 due to what Imperial termed as "insufficient progress."

EXECUTIVES

Chairman, President, and CEO:
Timothy J. (Tim) Hearn, age 61, $1,553,981 pay
SVP, Finance and Administration, Controller, and Director: Paul A. Smith, age 51, $474,704 pay
SVP, Resources: J.M. (Michael) Yeager, $447,833 pay (partial-year salary)
SVP, Resources Division and Director: Randy Broiles
VP and Treasurer: John F. Kyle, age 62, $441,301 pay
VP and General Counsel: Brian W. Livingston
Corporate Secretary: John Zych
Public Affairs: Hart Searle
Auditors: PricewaterhouseCoopers LLP

LOCATIONS

HQ: Imperial Oil Limited
111 St. Clair Ave. W.,
Toronto, Ontario M5W 1K3, Canada
Phone: 800-567-3776   **Fax:** 800-367-0585
Web: www.imperialoil.ca

Imperial Oil's exploration and development are conducted primarily in Alberta and the Northwest Territories. It owns two refineries in Ontario, and one each in Alberta and Nova Scotia. It also operates a chemical plant in Ontario.

PRODUCTS/OPERATIONS

2004 Sales

	$ mil.	% of total
Petroleum products	14,588	78
Natural resources	3,105	17
Chemicals	1,011	5
Adjustments	(29)	—
Total	**18,675**	**100**

COMPETITORS

Abraxas Petroleum	Lyondell Chemical
Ashland	Marathon Oil
Barnwell Industries	Murphy Oil
BHP Billiton	Occidental Petroleum
BP	PDVSA
Canadian Natural	PEMEX
ConocoPhillips	PETROBRAS
Devon Energy	Petro-Canada
Dominion Resources	Pioneer Natural Resources
DuPont	Royal Dutch/Shell Group
EnCana	Suncor
Eni	Sunoco
Hunting	Talisman Energy
Husky Energy	TOTAL
Koch	Unocal

HISTORICAL FINANCIALS

Company Type: Public

Income Statement   FYE: December 31

	REVENUE ($ mil.)	NET INCOME ($ mil.)	NET PROFIT MARGIN	EMPLOYEES
12/04	18,675	1,710	9.2%	6,100
12/03	14,823	1,306	8.8%	6,300
12/02	10,732	769	7.2%	6,460
12/01	10,776	781	7.2%	6,740
12/00	11,888	947	8.0%	6,704
12/99	7,091	402	5.7%	6,550
12/98	5,815	358	6.2%	6,689
12/97	7,463	593	7.9%	7,096
12/96	7,577	574	7.6%	7,483
12/95	6,810	377	5.5%	7,800
Annual Growth	11.9%	18.3%	—	(2.7%)

2004 Year-End Financials

Debt ratio: 5.8%
Return on equity: 35.1%
Cash ($ mil.): 1,066
Current ratio: 0.84
Long-term debt ($ mil.): 306
No. of shares (mil.): 349
Dividends
Yield: 0.8%
Payout: 10.5%
Market value ($ mil.): 20,743

Stock History

AMEX: IMO

	STOCK PRICE ($)	P/E		PER SHARE ($)		
	FY Close	High/Low		Earnings	Dividends	Book Value
12/04	59.38	13	9	4.78	0.50	15.08
12/03	44.42	13	8	3.51	0.59	12.37
12/02	28.70	16	12	2.03	0.54	8.74
12/01	27.88	15	11	1.99	0.74	7.34
12/00	26.30	12	8	2.27	0.78	7.23
12/99	21.63	26	16	0.93	0.74	7.11
12/98	16.06	26	17	0.81	0.50	6.26
12/97	21.29	17	11	1.28	0.54	6.89
12/96	15.65	14	11	1.09	0.36	6.98
12/95	12.03	20	16	0.65	0.43	7.44
Annual Growth	**19.4%**	—	—	**24.8%**	**1.7%**	**8.2%**

Imperial Tobacco Group

The UK's #1 cigarette maker (ahead of Gallaher Group), Imperial Tobacco Group has traded up to an even bigger throne. The company's purchase of German tobacco firm Reemtsma (Davidoff and West cigarettes) nearly doubled its size and made it the world's #4 tobacco company. Imperial's brands include Lambert & Butler, the UK's #1 cigarette, as well as Castella cigars, and Amphora and St Bruno pipe tobacco. Its Drum brand is the #1 hand-rolling tobacco worldwide, and Rizla is a top cigarette paper. Acquisitions in Australia and New Zealand have assured Imperial's presence in emerging markets.

Imperial Tobacco also looks to open new markets in China, where it recently signed a 10-year deal to produce and sell cigarettes. Imperial also is expanding to new markets in Africa. Despite global expansion, the UK still rings up nearly a majority of its sales. Imperial controls nearly 45% of the UK market.

Like rivals British American Tobacco and Gallaher, Imperial was spun off from a conglomerate eager to distance itself from increasingly problematic tobacco operations (it was part of Hanson until that group's 1996 four-way split).

In early 2005 Imperial restructured its European production, resulting in the closure of its operations in Dublin, Ireland and nearly 100 job cuts. At around the same time, the company braced itself for the first round of class-action lawsuits directed at Canadian tobacco companies, in which subsidiary Imperial Tobacco Canada was named.

Later the same year, the company announced further restructuring measures, which included moving production of about 10 billion cigarettes, distributed in Eastern Europe, from Germany to Poland; though production in Germany has been consolidated, it will not cease. Instead, that facility will move from Berlin to Hannover, and will feed the habits of the German smoking populace. It also announced the transfer of production from its Treforest, Wales, production facility to Wilrijk, Belgium. All told more than 350 jobs will be lost in the closures.

HISTORY

Imperial Tobacco Group was formed in 1901 to fight American Tobacco's invasion of the UK. American Tobacco had become the dominant US tobacco company partly by using a large cash reserve to undercut competitors. When it bought UK tobacco and cigarette factory Ogden's that year, 13 UK tobacco firms responded by registering as The Imperial Tobacco Company. The firms (including Wills, Lambert & Butler, and John Player & Sons) continued to make and sell their products separately.

As expected, American Tobacco cut prices, and Imperial fought back, acquiring the Salmon & Cluckstein tobacco shop chain and offering bonuses to retailers that sold its products. When Imperial threatened US expansion in 1902, American Tobacco surrendered: It gave Ogden's to Imperial and halted its Ireland and Great Britain business in exchange for Imperial's pledge to stay out of the US (except for buying tobacco leaf). The two formed the British American Tobacco Company (BAT) to sell both firms' cigarettes overseas. But when American Tobacco split into four companies in 1911 and sold its BAT interest, the agreement was modified to let Imperial sell some of its brands in the US.

By the 1950s Imperial controlled more than 80% of the UK tobacco market, but its share decreased during the 1960s due to competition from Gallaher Group (Benson & Hedges). Imperial diversified, buying companies such as Golden Wonder Crisps snack food (1961) and the Courage & Barclay brewery (1972).

In 1973 BAT and Imperial agreed that each firm would control its own brands in the UK and Continental Europe. Imperial sold the last of its stake in BAT in 1980. Conglomerate Hanson Trust paid $4.3 billion for Imperial in a 1986 hostile takeover. Hanson reduced Imperial's tobacco brands from more than 100 to five brand families (a move that decreased its UK market share to 33% by 1990). It also sold Imperial's drinks unit, including Courage and John Smith beer, to Elders IXL (now Foster's Brewing). Between 1986 and 1993 Hanson cut Imperial's tobacco operations from five factories and 7,500 employees to three factories and 2,600 employees; it also sold Imperial's restaurant and food operations.

As UK cigarette consumption dropped, Imperial began expanding overseas in 1994. By 1996 exports had risen to 15% of sales. That year Gareth Davis became CEO of Imperial.

Facing further declining UK cigarette sales and a government tax hike, Imperial bought the world's #1 cigarette paper brand, Rizla (1997), and Sara Lee's cut-tobacco unit, Douwe Egberts Van Nelle (1998), which it renamed Van Nelle Tabak. That acquisition added Drum hand-rolling tobacco and Amphora pipe tobacco to Imperial's brands. In 1999 the company added a bevy of Australian and New Zealand brands (Horizon, Brandon, Flagship, Peter Stuyvesant) from BAT.

In 2000 Imperial acquired paper maker EFKA (Germany, Canada) and tobacco maker Baelen (Belgium). That year Imperial tripled its cigarette vending operations by acquiring Mayfield Vending (27,000 UK locations).

Imperial expanded operations in Africa in 2001 with the acquisition of 75% of Tobaccor. It also began distributing the Marlboro brand in the UK.

The company bought 90% of Reemtsma in 2002; the deal at the time was valued at $5.1 billion.

In 2004, Imperial cut 940 jobs as it closed manufacturing plants in Hungary, Slovakia, and Slovenia. The company shifted production to Germany and Poland. More cuts arrived in 2005 with the closing of a plant in Dublin.

EXECUTIVES

Chairman: Derek C. Bonham, age 61
Vice Chairman: Iain Napier, age 55
CEO and Board Member: Gareth Davis, age 55, $1,666,300 pay
Finance Director: Robert (Bob) Dyrbus, age 51, $1,054,768 pay
Corporate Affairs Director and Board Member: Frank A. Rogerson, age 52, $231,616 pay
Manufacturing Director and Board Member: David Cresswell, age 60, $231,616 pay
Sales and Marketing Director and Board Member: Graham Blashill
Director of Finance and Planning: Alison Cooper, age 38
Group Human Resources Director: Kathryn Brown, age 49
Company Secretary: Matthew Phillips, age 34
Group Media Relations Manager: Alex Parson
Regional Director, Southern Central European Region: Zsolt Totos
Head, Corporate Communications: Jacqueline Smithson
Group Media Relations Executive: Simon Evans
Auditors: PricewaterhouseCoopers LLP

LOCATIONS

HQ: Imperial Tobacco Group PLC
Upton Rd., Bristol BS99 7UJ, United Kingdom
Phone: +44-117-963-6636   **Fax:** +44-117-966-7405
Web: www.imperial-tobacco.com

Imperial Tobacco Group operates about 32 factories in Africa, Canada, Europe, New Zealand, and the UK.

2004 Sales

	% of total
Europe	
UK	26
Germany	20
Other countries	21
Other regions	33
Total	**100**

PRODUCTS/OPERATIONS

Selected Products and Brands

Cigarettes
Bastos
Cabinet
Davidoff (flagship brand)
Drum (roll-your-own tobacco)
Embassy
Excellence
Golden Virginia (launched in the UK in 1877)
Horizon
John Player (Blue, Special)
Lambert & Butler (discount brand)
Prima
Regal
Richmond (discount brand)
Rizla (rolling paper)
Route 66 (American blend sold in France, Belgium, and Eastern Europe)
R1
Superkings
West (sold in more than 100 countries)

Cigars
  Cadena
  Castella
  Classic
  Panama
Rolling Paper and Tobacco
  Amphora
  Drum
  Rizla (rolling paper)
  St Bruno

COMPETITORS

Altadis
Altria
British American Tobacco
Gallaher
General Cigar
Gudang Garam
Japan Tobacco
JT International
Philip Morris International
Rothmans
Skandinavisk Tobakskompagni
Swedish Match
Swisher International
Tiedemanns
UST

HISTORICAL FINANCIALS

Company Type: Public

Income Statement

FYE: Saturday nearest September 30

	REVENUE ($ mil.)	NET INCOME ($ mil.)	NET PROFIT MARGIN	EMPLOYEES
9/04	5,495	806	14.7%	15,633
9/03	5,321	700	13.2%	16,804
9/02	3,478	426	12.2%	11,440
9/01	2,171	515	23.7%	6,360
9/00	1,917	476	24.8%	4,915
9/99	1,979	473	23.9%	4,306
9/98	1,611	392	24.4%	3,630
9/97	1,346	342	25.4%	3,296
9/96	1,219	542	44.5%	2,800
Annual Growth	20.7%	5.1%	—	24.0%

2004 Year-End Financials

Debt ratio: 2,716.8%
Return on equity: 474.1%
Cash ($ mil.): 475
Current ratio: 0.87
Long-term debt ($ mil.): 5,814
No. of shares (mil.): 365
Dividends
  Yield: 3.6%
  Payout: 70.7%
Market value ($ mil.): 15,984

Stock History

NYSE: ITY

	STOCK PRICE ($) FY Close	P/E High/Low	PER SHARE ($) Earnings	Dividends	Book Value
9/04	43.84	21 14	2.22	1.57	0.59
9/03	33.02	19 15	1.93	1.16	0.35
9/02	31.75	28 18	1.28	7.00	(0.39)
9/01	24.91	13 9	1.98	1.04	(6.34)
9/00	18.63	13 6	1.84	1.04	(7.28)
9/99	23.50	14 10	1.82	1.08	(9.33)
Annual Growth	13.3%	— —	4.1%	7.8%	—

InBev NV/SA

InBev NV/SA is way into and way back into selling beer. With origins that date back to 1366 it has a collection of more than 200 global beers brands. The company outranks all others as the world's largest brewer by volume thanks to an ambitious merger in 2004 with the world's #5 brewer, Brazil's Companhia de Bebidas das Américas (AmBev). InBev operates facilities in more than 30 countries, producing lagers, premium beers, and specialty brews that are sold in 140 countries. InBev's flagship brands include Beck's Brahma, Leffe, Skol, and Stella Artois.

InBev was created through the merger of Interbrew and AmBev, which now serves as InBev's headquarters in the Americas. The merger resulted in a series of transactions between Interbrew subsidiary Labatt and Mexico's FEMSA. By creating InBev, Interbrew gave up interest in distributing FEMSA beer brands in the US. In return, Interbrew retained full control of the US division of Labatt. InBev has merged Labatt U.S.A. with what was Beck's North America to create InBev USA.

In addition to expanding in Latin America through AmBev, InBev is looking to emerging markets for growth, particularly in the Asian sector. InBev owns the brewing operations of Malaysia's Lion Group and a controlling interest in the KK Group, both of which brew popular beers in China. It also owns a controlling interest in Chinese brewers Zhejiang Shiliang Brewery Company Ltd. and Hunan Debier Brewery Company Ltd. In South Korea, InBev has a majority stake in Oriental Brewery.

HISTORY

Monks at the Leffe Abbey in Belgium were brewing beer as early as 1240, and surviving records from 1366 mention Belgium's Den Horen brewery. Belgian master brewer Sebastien Artois (best known for his Stella Artois lager) took over Den Horen in 1717. In 1853 the Piedboeuf family founded a brewery at Liege and established the Jupiler lager. Albert Van Damme assumed management of that brewery in 1920.

Over the years, the Artois and Piedboeuf families took over or established operations both in and outside Belgium. Direct descendants (the clans de Spoelberch, Van Damme, and de Mevius) of the two families were still managing the companies in 1987 when they decided the key to survival in the fragmented European beer market was to merge.

Artois-Piedboeuf-Interbrew acquired the Hoegaarden brewery in Belgium in 1989. The company changed its name to Interbrew three years later, acquired another Belgian brewery (Belle-Vue), and bought stakes in breweries in Bulgaria, Croatia, and Hungary. In 1995 Dommelsche Bierbrouwerij bought Allied Breweries Nederland, an Allied Domecq subsidiary, and Interbrew acquired the Oranjeboom breweries in the Netherlands.

The company purchased John Labatt Ltd. for $2 billion in 1995. As a result of the deal, Interbrew gained control of Latrobe Brewing (Rolling Rock beer, US), 22% of Mexico's FEMSA Cerveza (increased to 30% in 1998), the Toronto Argonauts football team, 90% of the Toronto Blue Jays (it sold an 80% stake in the baseball team to cable firm Rogers Communications in 2000) and various broadcast properties.

Interbrew sold many noncore assets, including Lehigh Valley Dairies (US) and John Labatt Retail (pubs, UK), in 1996. Also that year the company established joint ventures in the Dominican Republic and the US (to import Mexican beers through FEMSA).

In 1998 Interbrew paid $250 million for 50% of the Doosan Group's Oriental Brewery, South Korea's second-largest brewer, and bought a majority stake in Russian brewer Rosar. The next year Interbrew combined its Russian operations with Sun Brewing, forming Russian brewer Sun-Interbrew. It then bought Korea's Jinro-Coors Brewery for about $378 million. Hugo Powell was later named CEO of Interbrew.

Interbrew bought Britain's third-largest brewer, Whitbread Beer Company, in 2000 for $590 million. Having gained a foothold in the UK market, the company then bought Bass Brewers from Bass PLC in 2000 for more than $3 billion. Interbrew went public on the Euronext (Brussels) exchange in 2000.

In 2001 Baron Paul De Keersmaeker retired as chairman and was replaced by Pierre Jean Everaert. That year the company took an 80% stake in Germany's tenth-largest brewer, Diebels. Interbrew also sold Carling, which controls about 18% of the UK beer market, to Coors for $1.7 billion, after being ordered to remedy unfair competition advantages related to the Bass Brewers purchase.

John Brock, former COO of Cadbury Schweppes, became CEO of Interbrew in 2003. That year it sold a minority stake of its Namibian Breweries in southern Africa to Diageo and Heineken.

In 2004 Interbrew purchased a 70% stake in Chinese brewer Zhejiang Shiliang, which gave Interbrew nearly a 50% market share in China's Zhejiang province. Later that year, Interbrew changed its name to InBev following its merger with Brazilian brewer AmBev.

Exiting the Slovenian market, InBev sold its stake in Pivovarna Union to Pivovarna Lasko in 2005. That year it acquired Russian premium brewer Tinkoff and sold its stake in soft-drink company Bremer Erfrischungsgetränke to Coca-Cola. It also sold its minority stake in Spanish brewer Damm.

EXECUTIVES

Chairman: Pierre Jean Everaert
CEO: John Franklin Brock, age 57
CFO: Felipe Dutra, age 40
SVP, External Growth: Gauthier de Biolley
VP, External Growth and Market Development: Simon Thorpe
VP, Export and Licenses Asia Pacific: Ben Cheng
VP, Investor Relations: Patrick Verelst
VP, Marketing North America: Miguel Patricio
VP, Marketing Global Brand: Devin Kelly
Zone President, Asia Pacific: Brent Willis, age 45
Zone President, Central and Eastern Europe: Stéfan Descheemaeker, age 45
Zone President, Latin America: Luiz Fernando Zeigler de Saint Edmond, age 39
Zone President, North America: Carlos Brito, age 45
Zone President Western Europe: Stewart Gilliland, age 48
President, Central Europe: Philipp Vandervoort
President, InBev France: Sabine Sagaert
President, Interbrew UK: Colin Pedrick, age 52
CTO: André Weckx, age 52
CIO and Chief Services Officer: Claudio Garcia, age 37
Chief Legal Officer: Sabine Chalmers
Chief People Officer: Peter Vrijsen, age 51
Director, Corporate Media Relations: Marianne Amssoms
Manager, Public Affairs and External Communications: Lian Verhoeven
Auditors: Klynveld Peat Marwick Goerdeler

LOCATIONS

HQ: InBev NV/SA
Brouwerijplein 1, 3000 Leuven, Belgium
Phone: +32-16-24-71-11   **Fax:** +32-16-24-74-07
US HQ: 101 Merritt 7, Norwalk, CT 06856-5075
US Phone: 203-750-6600   **US Fax:** 203-750-6699
Web: www.inbev.com

2004 Sales

	% of total
Western Europe	42
North America	22
Central & Eastern Europe	15
Central & South America	14
Asia/Pacific	7
Total	**100**

PRODUCTS/OPERATIONS

Selected Brands

Global flagship brands
  Beck's
  Brahma
  Stella Artois

Global specialty brands
  Cuvée
  Hoegaarden
  Leffe

Licensed brands
  Absolut Cut
  Budweiser
  Castelmaine
  Murphy's

Local brands
  Boddingtons
  Kokanee
  Labatt
  Liber
  Löwenbräu
  Rolling Rock
  Tennet's
  Zhujiang

Multicountry brands
  Bass
  Staropramen

COMPETITORS

Anchor Brewing	Heineken
Anheuser-Busch	Holsten-Brauerei
Asahi Breweries	Kirin
Asia Pacific Breweries	Miller Brewing
Big Rock Brewery	Molson Coors
Blaue Quellen Mineral	Pyramid Breweries
Boston Beer	Radeberger Gruppe
Brau und Brunnen	Redhook Ale
Carlsberg	SABMiller
CBR Brewing	San Miguel
Constellation Brands	Sapporo
Diageo	Scottish & Newcastle
FEMSA	Suntory Ltd.
Foster's	Tsingtao
Gambrinus	Vidrala
Grolsch	Yanjing
Grupo Modelo	Yuengling & Son

HISTORICAL FINANCIALS

Company Type: Public

Income Statement

FYE: December 31

	REVENUE ($ mil.)	NET INCOME ($ mil.)	NET PROFIT MARGIN	EMPLOYEES
12/04	11,687	981	8.4%	74,694
12/03	8,842	634	7.2%	50,000
12/02	7,328	490	6.7%	35,044
12/01	6,469	618	9.6%	37,617
12/00	7,690	(857)	—	34,203
12/99	4,532	232	5.1%	24,348
12/98	4,200	222	5.3%	16,727
12/97	2,886	144	5.0%	13,835
12/96*	3,016	127	4.2%	13,735
9/95	2,757	117	4.3%	13,237
Annual Growth	**17.4%**	**26.6%**	**—**	**21.2%**

*Fiscal year change

2004 Year-End Financials

Debt ratio: 31.9%   Current ratio: 0.67
Return on equity: 11.2%   Long-term debt ($ mil.): 3,709
Cash ($ mil.): 1,331

Net Income History

Euronext Brussels: INBS

1,000	
800	
600	
400	
200	
0	
-200	
-400	
-600	
-800	
-1,000	

9/95 12/96 12/97 12/98 12/99 12/00 12/01 12/02 12/03 12/04

Inco Limited

Inco turns nickel into gold. The company is the world's #2 producer of nickel (after Russian giant Norilsk Nickel), which is used primarily for manufacturing stainless steel and batteries. Inco also mines and processes copper, gold, cobalt, and platinum group metals. It makes nickel battery materials and nickel foams, flakes, and powders for use in catalysts, electronics, and paints. Sulphuric acid and liquid sulphur dioxide are produced as byproducts. The company's primary mining and processing operations are in Canada, Indonesia, and the UK. In 2005 Inco announced the acquisition of Canadian nickel and copper mining giant Falconbridge Limited. The merger will make Inco the world's largest nickel producer.

Inco has begun the development of its Voisey's Bay nickel and copper deposit in Labrador and Newfoundland, Canada, as well as its Goro Nickel project in New Caledonia.

The company has benefited from strong nickel prices and increasing demand in the metal from Asia, especially China. To leverage this, the company is making inroads into China through its joint venture in Inco Advanced Technology Materials (77% ownership) to produce nickel foam for use in rechargeable batteries. In 2005, Inco acquired a large stake in another nickel foam producer, Shenyang Golden Champower New Materials. Asia accounts for about 60% of the company's overall nickel sales.

Copper accounts for about 10% of Inco's sales. The company produces the metal at its operations in Ontario and sells the copper to customers in North America.

HISTORY

In 1883 a Canadian Pacific Railway blacksmith discovered copper and nickel deposits in the Sudbury Basin. Two companies — the Orford Nickel and Copper Company and the Canadian Copper Company — tried to exploit the ore but couldn't separate the copper from the nickel. Nickel was all but worthless at the time. In 1890 Orford, led by Robert Thompson, patented a process to separate the two metals just as the US Navy was beginning to use a nickel-steel alloy for armaments.

Enter financier J. P. Morgan, architect of U.S. Steel. With Morgan's help Orford and Canadian Copper combined with five smaller companies in 1902 to form New Jersey-based International Nickel Company. In 1916 the company formed a Canadian subsidiary, International Nickel Company of Canada.

Sales plummeted after WWI, and in a 1928 restructuring, the Canadian subsidiary became the parent company. In 1929 International Nickel gained control of the world's nickel output when it bought Mond Nickel, a British metals refiner. By the 1950s the company accounted for 85% of noncommunist production.

Oil crises and inflation decreased demand for metals and battered International Nickel during the 1970s and early 1980s. In 1974 the company bought ESB Ray-O-Vac, the world's largest battery maker (sold in the early 1980s). Two years later the company shortened its name to Inco Limited.

Inco suffered from lack of demand for its metals until 1986. Then-CEO Donald Phillips cut employees and boosted productivity at Inco's mines and refineries. Demand for stainless steel rose in the late 1980s; Inco's sales more than doubled from 1987 to 1989.

Metal prices declined again in the early 1990s in response to a North American recession as well as the entry of former Iron Curtain countries into the metals markets. With a worldwide surplus, Inco cut nickel production. The company also reorganized. In 1991 it merged its gold interests with Consolidated TVX Mining (in 1993 it sold its 62% interest in TVX). These actions, however, could not stave off a loss in 1992.

As the US economy recovered and new Asian markets developed, exploration activities revved up with new ore discoveries in 1994 and 1995. In 1995 Inco bought a 25% share of the copper, cobalt, and nickel rights to rich deposits at Voisey's Bay in Newfoundland and Labrador; the following year it bought the remaining rights along with their holder, mining company Diamond Fields (the total cost was $3.2 billion).

Inco also unloaded some of its nonmining businesses. The company spun off Doncasters (aircraft components) in 1997. About 4,700 miners went on strike that year, cutting the company's nickel production by more than half. As rising worldwide nickel production drove prices down in 1998, the company reduced its workforce by more than 1,400. It also sold Inco Alloys International to Special Metals.

In 1999 Inco entered into joint ventures with Dowa Mining of Japan to search for copper, zinc, silver, and gold in Indonesia and Turkey. That year the company shut down its Manitoba nickel production facility for several months over a contract dispute with labor. Inco also created Inco

Special Products and commissioned a $14 million nickel processing plant in Wales to increase its sales of value-added nickel products.

Inco started building a nickel-cobalt mining and refining facility on the French island of New Caledonia in 2000 (expecting to begin production in 2007). The company continued negotiations throughout 2001 with the governments of Canada, Labrador, and Newfoundland, and an agreement was reached in mid-2002. Inco eventually began construction and development of its Voisey's Bay nickel project in 2003.

EXECUTIVES

Chairman and CEO: Scott M. Hand, age 62, $2,520,133 pay
President, COO, and Director: Peter C. Jones, age 57, $1,561,007 pay
EVP and CFO: Farokh S. Hakimi, age 56, $488,074 pay
EVP and CFO: Robert D. J. (Bob) Davies, age 55
EVP and President, Canadian and UK Operations: Ronald C. (Ron) Aelick, age 56
EVP, General Counsel, and Secretary: Stuart F. Feiner, age 57, $959,127 pay
EVP, Marketing: Peter J. Goudie, age 56, $1,005,183 pay
VP and CIO: Subhash (Subi) Bhandari, age 60
VP and Comptroller: Ronald A. Lehtovaara, age 54
VP and Treasurer: Stephanie E. Anderson
VP, Business Development — Asia: John B. Jones, age 62
VP, Capital Projects and Engineering: Edward H. Bassett, age 58
VP, Environment and Health: William A. Napier, age 50
VP, Exploration: S. Nicholas Sheard, age 55
VP, Human Resources: Mark J. Daniel, age 58
VP, Inco Special Products: William B. Kipkie, age 59
VP, Public and Government Affairs: Bruce R. Drysdale
VP, Taxation: Gary G. Kaiway, age 56
President, Asia/Pacific: Logan W. Kruger, age 55, $884,917 pay
Auditors: PricewaterhouseCoopers LLP

LOCATIONS

HQ: Inco Limited
    145 King St. West, Ste. 1500, Toronto, Ontario
    M5H 4B7, Canada
Phone: 416-361-7511   **Fax:** 416-361-7781
US HQ: Park 80 West, Plaza 2, Saddle Brook, NJ 07663
US Phone: 201-368-4800   **US Fax:** 201-368-4858
Web: www.inco.com

Inco Limited's core subsidiaries operate mines and facilities in Canada, China, Indonesia, Japan, New Caledonia (in the southwest Pacific), South Korea, Taiwan, and the UK. The company also operates in the US and has exploration activities in Australia, Brazil, Canada, China, and Finland.

2004 Sales

	$ mil.	% of total
North America		
US	1,353	32
Canada	100	2
Asia		
Japan	618	14
China	583	14
Indonesia	158	4
UK	691	16
Other regions	775	18
Total	**4,278**	**100**

PRODUCTS/OPERATIONS

2004 Sales

	$ mil.	% of total
Primary nickel	3,503	82
Copper	364	9
Precious metals	246	6
Cobalt	71	1
Other	94	2
Total	**4,278**	**100**

Selected Products
Cobalt
Copper
Nickel (including intermediates)
Precious metals
    Gold
    Iridium
    Palladium
    Platinum
    Rhodium
    Ruthenium
    Silver
Special products (foams, flakes, powders, oxides, and nickel-coated graphite and carbon fibers)
Other
    Liquid sulfur dioxide
    Sulfuric acid

Selected Subsidiaries and Affiliates
I.E.L. Holdings (UK)
    Inco Europe Limited (UK)
International Nickel, Inc.
Inco S.A. (France)
Inco TNC Limited (67%, Japan)
Inco United States, Inc.
Goro Nickel S.A. (90%, France)
Monticello Capital (Barbados) Limited
    Inco Asia Limited (Barbados)
P.T. International Nickel Indonesia Tbk (61%, Indonesia)
Voisey's Bay Nickel Company Limited (Newfoundland and Labrador)

COMPETITORS

Anglo American
ASARCO
BHP Billiton
Eramet
Falconbridge
Newmont Mining
Nippon Mining
Norilsk Nickel
Outokumpu
Phelps Dodge
Rio Tinto
Southern Peru Copper
Special Metals
Stillwater Mining
Umicore
WMC Resources

HISTORICAL FINANCIALS

Company Type: Public

Income Statement

FYE: December 31

	REVENUE ($ mil.)	NET INCOME ($ mil.)	NET PROFIT MARGIN	EMPLOYEES
12/04	4,278	612	14.3%	10,973
12/03	2,474	137	5.5%	10,478
12/02	2,161	(1,481)	—	10,534
12/01	2,066	305	14.8%	10,258
12/00	2,917	400	13.7%	10,143
12/99	2,113	17	0.8%	10,198
12/98	1,766	(76)	—	11,007
12/97	2,367	75	3.2%	14,278
12/96	3,105	179	5.8%	16,308
12/95	3,471	227	6.5%	15,818
Annual Growth	**2.3%**	**11.6%**	**—**	**(4.0%)**

2004 Year-End Financials
Debt ratio: 34.2%
Return on equity: 14.6%
Cash ($ mil.): 1,076
Current ratio: 1.94
Long-term debt ($ mil.): 1,551
No. of shares (mil.): 188
Dividends
    Yield: 0.0%
    Payout: —
Market value ($ mil.): 6,920

Stock History

NYSE: N

12/95 12/96 12/97 12/98 12/99 12/00 12/01 12/02 12/03 12/04

	STOCK PRICE ($) FY Close	P/E High	P/E Low	PER SHARE ($) Earnings	PER SHARE ($) Dividends	PER SHARE ($) Book Value
12/04	36.78	14	9	2.99	0.00	24.13
12/03	39.82	71	31	0.58	0.00	20.66
12/02	21.22	—	—	(8.27)	0.00	20.77
12/01	16.94	14	7	1.49	0.00	29.06
12/00	16.76	13	7	1.97	0.00	26.30
12/99	23.50	—	—	(0.05)	0.00	25.50
12/98	10.44	—	—	(0.63)	0.10	26.24
12/97	17.00	151	68	0.25	0.40	26.93
12/96	31.88	34	26	1.09	0.40	27.12
12/95	33.25	21	13	1.82	0.40	16.95
Annual Growth	**1.1%**	—	—	**5.7%**	—	**4.0%**

Infosys Technologies

IT normally means information technology, but in the case of this company it could also stand for Indian technology. Infosys Technologies is one of India's leading technology consulting firms with operations in more than 15 countries. The company provides software development and engineering through a network of development centers in Asia and North America. It also provides data management, systems integration, project management, support, and maintenance services. In addition, its Progeon subsidiary offers business process outsourcing (BPO) services and US-based Infosys Consulting provides strategic consulting.

Infosys has rapidly expanded its presence in international markets, especially in North America which now accounts for about 65% of sales. In 2004 it launched Infosys Consulting to capture additional business in the US. The company has also added operations in China and Australia and continues to eye opportunities in Asia, Africa, and Latin America.

For India, Infosys has been a beacon of success as one of the country's fastest-growing and most admired businesses. Its main campus, called Infosys City, resembles many modern American technology facilities, sporting such features as a gymnasium, a sauna, a pool hall, a mini golf course, several tennis courts, and even its own power generators. Infosys was one of the first companies in India to offer employees stock options.

Leading the way has been chairman Narayana Murthy, who founded Infosys with six friends and $250 borrowed from their wives. Murthy is also a generous philanthropist who has made improving social welfare in India a major goal. Despite being one of India's wealthiest men (he owns almost 7% of Infosys), Murthy lives a modest life: his wife often drives him to the bus stop, where he boards a company bus to work.

HISTORY

After receiving a master's degree in electrical engineering from one of India's highly regarded Institutes of Technology (Kanpur) in the 1960s, Narayana Murthy left for France and a job developing software for the air traffic control system at Paris' Charles de Gaulle airport.

During college Murthy had developed the belief that communism was the answer to his country's problems with poverty and corruption, a stance that was fortified during his time spent with Paris leftists in the 1970s. But while hitchhiking back to India in 1974, Murthy's Marxist sympathies eroded quickly after he was jailed in Hungary for allegedly disclosing state secrets while talking with Austrian tourists on a train. Murthy became a socialist at heart but capitalist in practice, setting out on a mission to create wealth rather than redistribute poverty.

That mission officially began in 1981, when Murthy convinced six fellow software engineers to start their own company. Infosys was founded that year with $250 in capital (mostly borrowed from their wives) and no idea of what it would sell.

From the beginning Murthy looked for business outside of India, where he was able to sell multinational corporations such as Reebok and Nordstrom customizable, inexpensive software. But a lack of reputation and government regulations made business difficult for Infosys during the 1980s — it took nine months just to get the company's first telephone line, and three years to import new computers. Infosys opened its first US office in 1987.

Many of the government regulations that had kept India's economy stagnant were lifted when reform swept the country in 1991. But this also opened the door for companies such as IBM (which had been asked to leave in 1977) and Digital Equipment (later acquired by Compaq) to enter India and lure away its best engineers. While no Indian company had ever done this before, Murthy initiated a stock option plan and other perks to retain his employees. Infosys went public in 1993. Morgan Stanley swooped in to salvage the under-subscribed IPO in a move that would later reap millions when Infosys' stock began to soar.

In 1995 Infosys lost its biggest customer, General Electric, which had accounted for more than 20% of sales. Murthy took it as a lesson to never let one client or product drive more than 10% of a business. Infosys responded quickly by inking big deals with Xerox, Levi Strauss, and Nynex. By 2003, the company's biggest customer accounted for only about 6% of revenues.

The company grew rapidly in the mid-1990s by signing short-term pilot projects that it was able to leverage into more extensive contracts for managing mainframe upgrades, designing custom software, and implementing e-commerce systems.

In the late 1990s Infosys established offices in Canada, Japan, and the UK to better market its offshore development capabilities. The move paid off — by the end of fiscal 1999 sales had reached $121 million. That year Infosys became the first Indian company to list its shares on Nasdaq, an offering timed perfectly with the surge in demand for technology stocks. Infosys' market cap ballooned to more than $17 billion in 2000.

The company that year inked a long-term pact with Microsoft to dedicate more than 1,200 engineers to build e-commerce, financial services, and customer relationship management applications for the software giant.

Not immune to the slowing economy, Murthy saw his wealth drastically decrease in 2001; he lost more than $100 million due to Infosys' declining share value. In 2002 Murthy stepped down from the daily management of the company; co-founder Nandan Nilekan took over as CEO while Murthy, who remained chairman, adopted the new title chief mentor. That same year, Infosys launched a new subsidiary, Progeon, to provide business process outsourcing services.

EXECUTIVES

Chairman and Chief Mentor: N. R. Narayana Murthy, age 58, $27,337 pay
President, CEO, and Managing Director: Nandan M. Nilekani, age 50, $27,337 pay
Deputy Managing Director and COO; Head of Customer Service and Technology: S. (Kris) Gopalakrishnan, age 50, $27,337 pay
CFO, Head of Finance and Administration, and Director; Chairman, Progeon: T. V. Mohandas Pai, age 46, $39,588 pay
Director and Head of Education and Research, Information Systems, Quality and Productivity, and Communication Design Group: Krishnaswamy Dinesh, age 50, $27,337 pay
Director and Head of Strategic Groups and Co-Customer Delivery: Srinath Batni, age 50, $35,695 pay
Director and Head of Worldwide Customer Delivery: S. D. Shibulal, age 50, $189,331 pay
SVP Accounts and Administration: U. Ramadas Kamath, age 44
SVP Commercial and Facilities: H. R. Binod, age 42
SVP Finance: Girish G. Vaidya, age 54
SVP Finance and Company Secretary: V. Balakrishnan, age 40, $27,516 pay
SVP Global Alliances: John K. Conlon
SVP Human Resources Development: Hema Ravichandar, age 43
SVP Quality and Productivity: Satyendra Kumar, age 51
SVP Worldwide Sales: Basab Pradhan
SVP Engineering & IT Solutions: M. S. S. Prabhu, age 57, $37,790 pay
SVP Retail, Distribution & Consumer Products Group: U. B. Pravin Rao, age 43
VP Global Sales and Marketing: Merwin Fernandes, age 45
VP Talent Management: Bikramjit Maitra, age 50
Associate VP Human Resources Business Partner: Geetha Kannan, age 40
Auditors: KPMG LLP; Bharat S. Raut & Co.

LOCATIONS

HQ: Infosys Technologies Limited
Electronics City, Hosur Road, Bangalore, Karnataka 560 100, India
Phone: +91-80-2852-0261   **Fax:** +91-80-2852-0362
US HQ: 6607 Kaiser Dr., Fremont, CA 94555
US Phone: 510-742-3000   **US Fax:** 510-742-3090
Web: www.infosys.com

Infosys Technologies has operations in Australia, Belgium, Canada, China, France, Germany, India, Italy, Japan, Mauritius, the Netherlands, Sweden, Switzerland, the United Arab Emirates, the UK, and the US.

2005 Sales

	$ mil.	% of total
North America	1,038	65
Europe	355	22
India	30	2
Other regions	169	11
Total	**1,592**	**100**

PRODUCTS/OPERATIONS

2005 Sales

	$ mil.	% of total
Financial services	549	34
Telecommunications	295	19
Manufacturing	231	14
Retail	155	10
Other	362	23
Total	**1,592**	**100**

Selected Services

Custom application development
Information technology consulting
Maintenance and production support
Package evaluation and implementation
Software re-engineering
Other services
  Business process management
  Engineering
  Infrastructure management
  Management consulting
  Operations and business process consulting
  Systems integration
  Testing

COMPETITORS

Accenture	IBM Global Services
BearingPoint	iGate
Bull	Keane
Capgemini	LogicaCMG
Cognizant Tech Solutions	Ness Technologies
Computer Sciences Corp.	Oracle
Deloitte Consulting	Patni Computer Systems
Dimension Data	Perot Systems
EDS	SAP
Getronics	Satyam
HCL Technologies	Silverline Technologies
HP Technology	Tata Consultancy
Solutions Group	Wipro Technologies

HISTORICAL FINANCIALS

Company Type: Public

Income Statement

FYE: March 31

	REVENUE ($ mil.)	NET INCOME ($ mil.)	NET PROFIT MARGIN	EMPLOYEES
3/05	1,592	419	26.3%	36,800
3/04	1,063	270	25.4%	25,700
3/03	754	195	25.9%	15,940
3/02	545	165	30.2%	10,740
3/01	414	132	31.9%	9,830
3/00	203	61	30.1%	5,300
3/99	121	17	14.4%	3,766
3/98	68	12	18.2%	2,614
3/97	39	10	26.5%	1,705
3/96	26	6	23.8%	1,172
Annual Growth	**58.0%**	**59.7%**	**—**	**46.7%**

2005 Year-End Financials

Debt ratio: 0.0%
Return on equity: 38.0%
Cash ($ mil.): 410
Current ratio: 6.06
Long-term debt ($ mil.): 0
No. of shares (mil.): 271
Dividends
  Yield: 0.0%
  Payout: —
Market value ($ mil.): 19,949

	STOCK PRICE ($) FY Close	P/E High/Low	PER SHARE ($) Earnings	Dividends	Book Value
3/05	73.73	52 22	1.52	0.00	4.63
3/04	40.87	51 19	1.01	0.16	7.15
3/03	30.68	59 32	0.73	0.13	4.73
3/02	32.75	66 25	0.62	0.08	3.34
3/01	32.75	285 60	0.50	0.05	2.36
3/00	96.50	781 41	0.24	0.00	0.75
3/99	10.78	156 117	0.08	0.00	1.06
Annual Growth	37.8%	— —	63.4%	—	28.0%

ING Groep

Together ING stands — a hybrid of banking, insurance, and financial services. One of the world's largest insurers, ING Groep also offers banking and asset management. Its operations are focused on North America, Asia/Pacific, and its home country, but ING has businesses in more than 50 countries. Key products include life insurance; consumer banking and mortgage lending (through branches in the Netherlands and through ING Direct in Australia, Canada, France, Germany, Italy, Spain, the UK, and the US); and asset management, which offers products geared to individual and institutional investors. ING also offers such products as non-life insurance, corporate finance, employee benefits, and securities services.

ING has taken aim at becoming a financial services player in all four corners of the world. In addition to its Asian operations (which generated more than half of the company's new insurance business in 2003), ING has taken a majority stake in India's Vysya Bank and has set up joint banking ventures in Australia and China. It also is acquiring a 20% stake in the Bank of Beijing as part of a strategic alliance.

ING in 2004 realigned its management structure, dividing the company's operations into six business lines: Insurance Americas, Insurance Europe, Insurance Asia-Pacific, Wholesale Banking, Retail Banking, and ING Direct. ING boosted its North American insurance operations with the acquisition of Allianz's Canadian property and casualty operations.

The company struggled with investment banking arm ING Barings, which it bought after the Nick Leeson trading scandal but before the Asian and Russian economic crises. The unit was reorganized and streamlined for cost-savings purposes (as were other business areas, including banking and ING's Dutch operations), but ultimately was put on the block. The bulk of the Barings unit has been sold to MassMutual (Barings's investment management operations) and Northern Trust (its fund administration, trust, and custody operations).

Other pieces of Barings have been or are slated to be sold, including New York-based investment banking firm Furman Selz, sold to Dutch rival ABN AMRO; Asian equities operations, sold to Macquarie Bank; and the Baring Private Equity Partners unit, sold to its management.

ING in 2004 sold Sal. Oppenheim most of ING BHF-Bank; another portion of the bank business is being sold to HVB Group. The following year ING turned over to Scottish Re its US life reinsurance operations and sold subsidiary Life Insurance Company of Georgia to Jackson National Life.

Like many other major financial players, ING was stung by investments related to Enron and WorldCom (now MCI).

HISTORY

ING Groep's roots go back to 1845 when its earliest predecessor, the Netherlands Insurance Co., was founded. The firm began expanding geographically; in 1903 it added life insurance. In 1963 it merged with the century-old Nationale Life Insurance Bank to form Nationale-Nederland (NN). Over the next three decades, the company grew primarily through acquisitions in Europe, North America, and Australia. In 1986 NN became the first European life insurance company to be licensed in Japan.

Another predecessor, the Rijkspostspaarbank, was founded in 1881 to provide Dutch citizens with simple post office savings accounts. In 1918 the Postcheque-en Girondienst (giro) system was established to allow people to use vouchers drawn on their savings accounts to pay bills. This system became the main method of settling accounts (instead of bank checking accounts).

Rijkspostspaarbank and Postcheque merged in 1986 to become Postbank. Postbank merged in 1989 with the Nederlandse Middenstandsbank (founded 1927) to become NMB Postbank. The vast amounts of cash tied up in the post office savings and giro systems fueled NMB's business.

In 1991, as the Europe economic union became a reality, and barriers between banking and insurance began to fall, NN merged with NMB Postbank to form Internationale Nederland Groep (ING). ING began cutting costs, shedding redundant offices and unprofitable operations in both its segments. In the US, where insurance and banking were legally divided, the company "debanked" itself in order to keep its more lucrative insurance operations (but retained the right to provide banking services to those operations).

In the 1990s ING sought to increase its investment banking and finance operations. In 1995 it took over UK-based Barings Bank (personal banker to the Queen of England) after Nicholas Leeson, a trader in Barings' Singapore office, lost huge sums of money in derivatives trading. The acquisition gave the firm a higher profile but cost more than anticipated and left it embroiled in lingering legal actions.

In 1996 ING bought Poland's Bank Slaski (the company had first entered Poland in 1994). The next year it expanded its securities business by acquiring investment bank Furman Selz, doubled its US life insurance operations by purchasing Equitable of Iowa, and listed on the NYSE. In 1998 ING's acquisition strategy again involved Europe and North America: It bought Belgium's Banque Bruxelles Lambert and Canadian life insurer Guardian Insurance Co. (from Guardian Royal Exchange, now part of AXA UK).

In 1999 ING turned eastward, kicking off asset management operations in India and buying a minority stake in Korea's HC&B (formerly Housing & Commercial Bank). In 2000 the company bulked up its North American operations with the purchase of 40% of Savia SA, a Mexican insurance concern. It also bought US firm ReliaStar Financial in a $6 billion deal and Charterhouse Securities from CCF (then called Crédit Commercial de France).

Soon after, however, ING announced plans to unload ING Barings through sales and closures. ING also acquired US-based Aetna's financial services and international divisions. ING Barings axed 1,100 jobs in 2001, primarily in London.

EXECUTIVES

Chairman, Supervisory Board:
Cornelius A. J. (Cor) Herkströter, age 68
Vice Chairman, Supervisory Board:
Eric Bourdais de Charbonnière, age 66
CEO and Chairman, Executive Board: Michel Tilmant, age 53, $2,479,740 pay
CFO and Vice Chairman, Executive Board: Cees Maas, age 58, $1,414,483 pay
Executive Board, Insurance Americas:
Frederick S. (Fred) Hubbell, age 54, $2,315,675 pay
Executive Board, Insurance Asia Pacific and Central Europe: Alexander H. G. Rinnooy Kan, age 56, $1,320,732 pay
Executive Board, Retail Banking: Eli P. Leenaars, age 44, $877,753 pay (partial-year salary)
Executive Board Member, Wholesale Banking:
Eric Boyer de la Giroday, age 53, $1,194,167 pay
Executive Board, ING Direct: Hans K. Verkoren, age 58
Chairman, Management Committee, Netherlands, ING Europe: Diederik Laman Trip
Chairman, Management Committee, Southwest-Europe, ING Europe: Luc Vandewalle
Global Head of Pensions; CEO, ING Central Europe Insurance: Jan Nijssen, age 52
CEO, Private Banking Group; CEO, Retail Banking, Asia; CEO, ING Trust: Philippe Damas
Head of UK Region: Igno van Waesberghe
CEO, ING Asia/Pacific: Jacques Kemp
CEO, ING Chile: Tom Kliphuis, age 41
CEO, ING U.S. Financial Services:
Thomas J. (Tom) McInerney
Chief Investment Officer, ING Europe: Angelien Kemna
Operations/IT, ING Europe: Erik Dralans
Wholesale Operations, ING Europe: Harry van Tooren
Auditors: Ernst & Young Accountants

LOCATIONS

HQ: ING Groep N.V.
   ING House, Amstelveenseweg 500,
   1081 KL Amsterdam, The Netherlands
Phone: +31-20-541-5411   **Fax:** +31-20-541-5412
US HQ: INH Financial Holdings Corporation, 1325
   Avenue of the Americas, New York, NY 10019
US Phone: 646-424-6000   **US Fax:** 646-424-6018
Web: www.ing.com

ING Groep operates in more than 50 countries in Africa, Asia, Europe, North America, the Pacific Rim, and South America.

2004 Sales

	% of total
Americas	
North America	39
Latin America	4
Europe	
Netherlands	25
Belgium	7
Other countries	7
Asia/Pacific	
Asia	13
Australia	3
Other regions	2
Total	**100**

PRODUCTS/OPERATIONS

2004 Sales

	% of total
Premium income	64
Income from investments of the insurance operations	14
Interest from banking operations	13
Commissions	6
Other	3
Total	**100**

2004 Sales

	% of total
Insurance Americas	41
Insurance Europe	24
Insurance Asia Pacific	15
Wholesale Banking	9
Retail Banking	7
ING Direct	2
Other revenues	2
Total	**100**

Selected Products and Services

Personal Finance
  Checking accounts
  Individual insurance (life, health, property & casualty)
  Individual loans (lines of credit, mortgage loans)
  Private banking
  Savings and investment products
Corporate and Institutional Clients
  Cash management
  Corporate insurance (group benefits and pensions; general insurance)
  Corporate lending
  Debt capital markets
  Debt markets (fixed income products)
  Employee benefits
  Equities
  Equity capital markets and IPOs
  Equity derivatives
  Foreign exchange
  Institutional asset management
  Interest rate derivatives
  Leasing (equipment, automobiles)
  Mergers and acquisitions advisory
  Money market products
  Real estate (development, management, financing)
  Research
  Securities services
  Securitization
  Structured finance
  Structured products
  Trust services

COMPETITORS

ABN AMRO	Generali
AEGON	Goldman Sachs
AGF	HSBC Holdings
AIG	HVB Group
Allianz	KBC
Allstate	Legal & General Group
AXA	Lehman Brothers
Barclays	Lloyd's
Bear Stearns	Merrill Lynch
Chubb	MetLife
CIGNA	Prudential
Citigroup	Prudential plc
CNP Assurances	Royal & Sun
Credit Suisse	Alliance Insurance
Deutsche Bank	Swiss Life
Deutsche Bundesbank	UBS
Dexia	Union des
Fortis SA/NV	Assurances Fédérales
General Re	Zurich Financial Services

HISTORICAL FINANCIALS

Company Type: Public

Income Statement

FYE: December 31

	ASSETS ($ mil.)	NET INCOME ($ mil.)	INCOME AS % OF ASSETS	EMPLOYEES
12/04	1,173,356	8,084	0.7%	113,039
12/03	979,071	5,083	0.5%	115,218
12/02	752,403	4,726	0.6%	113,060
12/01	628,473	4,079	0.6%	112,000
12/00	612,332	11,287	1.8%	108,965
12/99	497,349	4,967	1.0%	86,040
12/98	460,563	3,113	0.7%	82,750
12/97	306,232	2,026	0.7%	64,162
12/96	279,985	1,922	0.7%	58,106
12/95	246,356	1,647	0.7%	52,144
Annual Growth	**18.9%**	**19.3%**	**—**	**9.0%**

2004 Year-End Financials

Equity as % of assets: 3.0%
Return on assets: 0.8%
Return on equity: 26.1%
Long-term debt ($ mil.): 158,361
No. of shares (mil.): 2,205
Dividends
  Yield: 4.0%
  Payout: 31.9%
Market value ($ mil.): 66,693
Sales ($ mil.): 115,324

Stock History

NYSE: ING

	STOCK PRICE ($) FY Close	P/E High/Low		PER SHARE ($) Earnings	Dividends	Book Value
12/04	30.25	8	5	3.79	1.21	16.68
12/03	23.41	9	4	2.51	1.06	13.73
12/02	16.84	11	5	2.44	0.90	10.75
12/01	25.45	20	10	2.09	1.06	10.76
12/00	40.06	7	4	5.91	0.85	13.24
12/99	30.50	14	9	2.55	1.17	18.29
12/98	31.09	24	11	1.63	0.32	16.41
12/97	21.16	20	15	1.30	0.00	12.32
Annual Growth	**5.2%**	**—**	**—**	**16.5%**	**—**	**4.4%**

Invensys plc

Having slimmed down and sold off many of its assets, Invensys is betting that its trimmer figure will help it stay in control. The company's five units now consist of Controls (for industrial refrigeration systems and appliances), Process Systems (automation technology for the energy and chemical industries), Rail Systems (signalling, communication, and control systems for railroads and subways), APV (valves for food, beverage, and dairy plants), and Eurotherm (monitoring systems). Invensys operates in more than 60 countries on all the major continents. Its customers include BP, China Light and Power, Bayer, Eli Lilly, Corus, Pilkington, and Bombardier.

Formed by the 1999 purchase of BTR by Siebe, Invensys has fallen on hard times of late. Faced with a faltering economy — and steadily declining sales and profits since its formation — Invensys has cut jobs and costs and divested much of

what constituted its business five years ago. Its annual sales in 2005 are just over a third of what they were in 1999.

Among the things to go: its energy storage, sensor systems, flow control, metering, and power supply businesses. Also, the company sold its US-based APV Baker Goldsboro division (bread and bun equipment) to Turkington Industries for a reported $10 million. Late in 2005 Invensys sold that power supply business, which comprises a majority-owned JV called Densei-Lambda, to TDK for $235 million.

HISTORY

Immigrant Austrian artillery officer Augustus Siebe founded Siebe in London in 1819. A life-long inventor, Siebe's creations included breech-loading rifles, carbon arc lamps, the world's first diving suit, and early ice-making machines.

From the 1890s to the early 1970s, Siebe made a name for itself in marine engineering and as a maker of breathing apparatuses, developing products such as submarine escape and diving equipment for Britain's Royal Navy. General Dynamics veteran Barrie Stephens took over management of the struggling Siebe in 1963. Stephens cut costs, restructured, terminated half the workforce, and in the late 1960s, started making acquisitions.

With its 1972 purchase of European safety equipment specialist James North & Sons, Siebe began transforming from a marine-based engineer to a controls and engineering company. It expanded into continental Europe and in 1982 moved into North America with the purchase of Tecalemit (garage equipment).

Included in the Tecalemit buy were two healthy electronic controls businesses, which Stephens tried, but failed, to sell. When Siebe acquired CompAir (compressed air) in 1985 (sold 2002), the deal included three pneumatic controls companies. Without trying, Siebe had established a controls presence. That segment was strengthened further in 1986 when it bought Robertshaw (appliance controls, US). The following year's additions of US concerns Ranco and Barber-Colman added automotive, industrial, and commercial building controls.

In 1990 Siebe hit the jackpot with the $650 million acquisition of Foxboro, which had developed a UNIX-based system capable of controlling entire oil refineries and automobile plants. With the Foxboro purchase, Siebe's control business began to seriously challenge Honeywell.

Mid-to-late-1990s acquisitions included AVP (food and drinks industry equipment), Wonderware (factory application software), Eurotherm (temperature controls), and Electronic Measurement (industrial power supply). To offset costs associated with these acquisitions, Siebe began restructuring in 1998 and sold its North Safety Products Business (personal safety and life support products) to Norcross Safety Products.

In 1999 Siebe acquired engineering rival BTR plc in a $6 billion deal that nearly tripled Siebe's size; the combined company changed its name to BTR Siebe and later to Invensys. Also that year the company sold more than a dozen businesses, including its automotive and aerospace operations. It also sold 90% of its Paper Technology Group to investment firm Apax Partners in a deal valued at about $800 million. Invensys' 1999 acquisitions included Best Power (uninterruptible power supplies), purchased from industrial products maker SPX for around $240 million.

Invensys formed a pact with Microsoft in early 2000 to develop standards for connecting home appliances to the Internet. Later that year the company gained control of Netherlands-based Baan Company, a near-bankrupt maker of software that allows manufacturers to manage their internal operations, in a $709 million deal.

Early in 2002 Invensys sold its energy storage business for $425 million. That May the company reorganized and sold its flow control business to US-based Flowserve Corporation for $535 million. Invensys also sold its Invensys Sensor Systems business to Honeywell for $415 million in cash. In late 2003 Invensys agreed to sell its metering business for about $650 million. The following year Invensys sold its Powerware subsidiary (uninterruptible power supplies and power management systems) to Eaton for $560 million.

EXECUTIVES

Chairman: Martin Jay, age 65
CEO and Director: Ulf Henriksson, age 42
CFO and Director: Adrian N. Hennah, age 46
SVP, Human Resources: Paula Larson
SVP and General Counsel: Victoria Hull
President, Invensys Process Systems: Mike Caliel
President, Invensys Controls: John H. Duerden, age 63
President, Invensys Rail Systems: Nigel W. R. Smith
President, APV: Haluk Durudogan
President, Eurotherm: Peter Tompkins
President, Invensys Process Systems, North America: Virginia Burnell
VP, Communications: Steve Devany
Secretary: John Clayton
Manager, Investor Relations: Nina Delangle
Auditors: Ernst & Young LLP

LOCATIONS

HQ: Invensys plc
Portland House, Stag Place,
London SW1E 5BF, United Kingdom
Phone: +44-20-7834-3848   **Fax:** +44-20-7834-3879
US HQ: 33 Commercial St., Foxborough, MA 02035
US Phone: 508-543-8750   **US Fax:** 508-543-2735
Web: www.invensys.com

Invensys has major subsidiaries in Australia, Brazil, Denmark, Japan, Luxembourg, the Netherlands, Spain, the UK, and the US.

2005 Sales

| | by Origin | | by Destination | |
	$ mil.	% of total	$ mil.	% of total
Europe				
UK	798	15	725	13
Other countries	1,443	26	1,454	26
North America	1,928	35	1,839	34
Asia/Pacific	829	15	885	16
South America	144	3	165	3
Africa/Middle East	124	2	198	4
Discontinued operations	225	4	225	4
Total	**5,491**	**100**	**5,491**	**100**

PRODUCTS/OPERATIONS

2005 Sales

	$ mil.	% of total
Controls	1,730	32
Process Systems	1,332	24
Rail Systems	774	14
APV	676	12
Eurotherm	229	4
Businesses for sale	524	10
Discontinued operations	226	4
Total	**5,491**	**100**

COMPETITORS

ABB	Honeywell International
Emerson Electric	Parker Hannifin
Endress + Hauser	Rockwell Automation
Finuchem	SICK
FWMurphy	Siemens
GE Energy	SPX
GE Fanuc	Texas Instruments
GE Infrastructure	Tomkins

HISTORICAL FINANCIALS

Company Type: Public

Income Statement

FYE: March 31

	REVENUE ($ mil.)	NET INCOME ($ mil.)	NET PROFIT MARGIN	EMPLOYEES
3/05	5,491	(889)	—	36,365
3/04	7,104	(599)	—	43,602
3/03	7,898	(2,270)	—	48,867
3/02	9,939	(1,239)	—	73,005
3/01	11,136	111	1.0%	89,922
3/00	14,380	(379)	—	96,260
3/99	15,185	(169)	—	129,504
3/98	6,153	519	8.4%	148,355
3/97	4,925	416	8.4%	—
Annual Growth	**1.4%**	**—**	**—**	**(18.2%)**

2005 Year-End Financials

Debt ratio: —
Return on equity: —
Cash ($ mil.): 1,225

Current ratio: 2.07
Long-term debt ($ mil.): 2,634

Net Income History

OTC: IVNSY

force, Isuzu offered voluntary retirement to about 3,700 workers.

The plan seems to be working. Fiscal 2005, the third and last year of the three-year plan, saw all of Isuzu's market segments return to profitability. The company's emphasis on becoming a worldwide player in commercial vehicles and engines is evident by the diminishing number of passenger models available in the US. The 5- and 7-passenger Ascender SUVs, and the i-350 and i-280 pickups are the only passenger models that Isuzu still sells in the US. The once popular Rodeo and Axiom SUVs have been discontinued with the last ones rolling off the assembly line in Lafayette, Illinois in July 2004.

HISTORY

After collaborating on car and truck production for 21 years, Tokyo Ishikawajima Shipbuilding and Engineering and Tokyo Gas and Electric Industrial formed Tokyo Motors, Inc., in 1937. The partners began producing the A truck (1918) and the A9 car (1922) under licenses from Wolseley (UK).

Tokyo Motors made its first truck under the Isuzu nameplate in 1938. It spun off Hino Heavy Industries in 1942. By 1943 the company was selling trucks powered by its own diesel engines, mostly to the Japanese military.

By 1948 the company was Japan's premier maker of diesel engines. It was renamed Isuzu (Japanese for "50 bells") in 1949. With generous public- and private-sector financing and truck orders from the US Army during the Korean War, Isuzu survived and refined its engine- and truck-making prowess. A pact with the Rootes Group (UK) enabled Isuzu to enter automaking. Beginning in 1953, Isuzu built Rootes' Hillman Minx in Japan.

Despite its strong reputation as a truck builder, Isuzu suffered financially, and by the late 1960s its bankers were shopping the company around to more stable competitors. GM, after witnessing rapid Japanese progress in US and Asian auto markets, bought about 34% of Isuzu in 1971. During the 1970s Isuzu launched the popular Gemini car and gained rapid entry to the US through GM, exporting such vehicles as the Chevy Luv truck and the Buick Opel.

As exports to GM waned, Isuzu set up its own dealer network in the US in 1981. That year GM CEO Roger Smith told a stunned Isuzu chairman Toshio Okamoto that Isuzu lacked the global scale GM was seeking. Smith asked Okamoto for help in buying a piece of Honda. After Honda declined and GM settled for 5% of Suzuki, Isuzu extended its GM ties, building the Geo Storm and establishing joint production facilities in the UK and Australia.

Despite a high-profile advertising campaign featuring Joe Isuzu, the company suffered in the 1980s in its efforts to gain any kind of significant share of the US passenger car market. Post-1985 yen appreciation hurt exports. Subaru-Isuzu Automotive, a joint venture with Fuji Heavy Industries, initiated production of Rodeos in Lafayette, Indiana, in 1989.

After Isuzu lost nearly $500 million in 1991 and 1992, it called on GM for help. GM responded by sending Donald Sullivan, a strategic business planning expert, to become Isuzu's #2 operations executive.

Isuzu signed a joint venture with Jiangxi Automobile Factory and ITOCHU in 1993 to build light-duty trucks in China. In 1994 Nissan and Isuzu agreed to cross-supply vehicles.

Isuzu Motors

After years of traveling the backroads to financial losses, Isuzu Motors is plotting a shortcut to profitability. In addition to producing its line of SUVs (including the Axiom and the Rodeo), Tokyo-based Isuzu is one of the world's top makers of light-, medium-, and heavy-duty trucks (N Series, F Series, and C&E Series, respectively). It also makes pickups, diesel engines, and buses. Isuzu introduced its latest SUV offering, the seven-passenger Ascender, in 2003. After a recapitalization scheme, General Motor's stake in the company was reduced from 49% to 12%.

In the summer of 2002 Isuzu announced a revised three-year business plan. To avoid bankruptcy, Isuzu asked its creditor banks to forgive 100 billion yen (about $750 million) in debt in exchange for stakes in the company. As part of the plan, GM wrote off its entire stake in Isuzu, and re-infused the ailing carmaker with $84 million. The deal resulted in a recapitalized Isuzu and reduced GM's stake to 12%. As part of the scheme GM boosted its stake in US-based joint venture DMAX Ltd., and took a stake in Isuzu's wholly owned Polish unit. To reduce its work-

Isuzu weathered a public relations storm in 1996 when *Consumer Reports* magazine claimed that the top-selling Trooper sport utility vehicle was prone to tip over at relatively low speeds. Isuzu dismissed the report as unscientific, and the National Highway Traffic Safety Administration sided with the automaker. In 1997 the company sued the magazine for defamation. (Isuzu lost the case in 2000.) Also in 1997 Isuzu agreed to develop GM's diesel engines and began constructing a plant in Poland to supply engines to GM's Germany-based subsidiary Opel AG.

The next year GM and Isuzu announced a joint venture to make diesel engines in the US. Also in 1998 Isuzu announced restructuring plans that included cutting 4,000 jobs and reducing the number of its domestic marketing subsidiaries. In 1999 the plant in Poland opened, and GM boosted its stake in Isuzu to 49%. Isuzu also agreed to form a joint venture with Toyota to manufacture buses.

Amid mounting losses and pressure from GM, Isuzu announced a management shake-up in 2001 that included naming GM chairman John Smith Jr. as special advisor and installing Randall Schwarz (GM truck group) as vice president. Days later Isuzu announced its "Isuzu V plan," its sweeping cost-savings scheme that included job cuts and the closure of one factory.

The Isuzu V plan was revised in 2002 when the company announced GM would write off its entire stake while infusing Isuzu with about $84 million. Near the close of 2002 Isuzu agreed to sell its 49% stake in carmaking joint venture Subaru-Isuzu Automotive Inc. to Fuji Heavy Industries (FHI). When the deal was completed in January 2003, FHI renamed the company Subaru of Indiana Automotive Inc.

EXECUTIVES

President and Representative Director: Yoshinori Ida
EVP and Representative Director: Basil N. Drossos
EVP and Director: Hiroshi Suzuki
EVP and Director: Shigeki Toma
Senior Executive Officer: Fujio Anzai
Senior Executive Officer: Shunichi Satomi
Senior Executive Officer: Akira Shinohara
Senior Executive Officer: Takashi Urata
Executive Officer: Masanori Katayama
Executive Officer: Shigeji Nakamori
Executive Officer: Yukio Narimatsu
Executive Officer: Masaru Odajima
Executive Officer: Shinichi Ohoka
Executive Officer: Takafumi Ozawa
Executive Officer: Hakaru Shibata
Executive Officer: Yasuaki Shimizu
Executive Officer: Ryozo Tsukioka
Executive Officer: Makoto Ushiyama
Executive Officer: Tsutomu Yamada
Auditors: Ernst & Young ShinNihon

LOCATIONS

HQ: Isuzu Motors Limited
(Isuzu Jidosha Kabushiki Kaisha)
26-1, Minami-oi 6-chome, Shinagawa-ku,
Tokyo 140-8722, Japan
Phone: +81-3-5471-1141   **Fax:** +81-3-5471-1043
US HQ: 13340 183rd Street, Cerritos, CA 90702-6007
US Phone: 562-229-5000   **US Fax:** 562-229-5463
Web: www.isuzu.co.jp

2005 Sales

	$ mil.	% of total
Japan	9,035	65
Asia	2,723	20
North America	1,822	13
Other regions	307	2
Total	**13,887**	**100**

PRODUCTS/OPERATIONS

Selected Vehicles and Brands

Buses
  Erga heavy-duty bus
  Erga Mio medium-duty bus
Commercial Vehicles
  Heavy-duty trucks (C&E Series)
  Light-duty trucks (N Series)
  Medium-duty trucks (F Series)
Pickups
  D-MAX pickup
  i-280 Extended Cab
  i-350 Crew Cab
Sport Utility Vehicles and Minivans
  Ascender
  Axiom
  MU-2
  Panther
  Rodeo

Selected Subsidiaries and Affiliates

American Isuzu Motors Inc. (US)
Anadolu Isuzu Otomotiv Sanayi Ve Ticaret AS (Turkey)
DMAX Ltd. (US)
Isuzu (China) Holding Co., Ltd.
Isuzu Commercial Truck of America, Inc.
Isuzu LINEX Corporation
Isuzu Motors Asia Ltd. (Singapore)
Isuzu Motors Europe Ltd. (UK)
Isuzu Motors Germany GmbH
Isuzu Motors Kinki Co., Ltd.
Isuzu Motors Polska Sp. zo. o. (Poland)
Isuzu Philippines Corporation
Isuzu Truck (UK) Ltd.
Isuzu-General Motors Australia Ltd.
IT Forging (Thailand) Co., Ltd.
Jidosha Buhin Kogyo Co., Ltd.
Kanagawa Isuzu Motors Co., Ltd.
P.T. Mesin Isuzu Indonesia
Qingling Motors Co., Ltd. (China)
Taiwan Isuzu Motors Co., Ltd.
TDF Corporation
Tokyo Isuzu Motors Ltd.
Tri Petch Isuzu Sales Co., Ltd. (Thailand)

COMPETITORS

BMW	Nissan
Caterpillar	Oshkosh Truck
Cummins	PACCAR
DaimlerChrysler	Penske
Fiat	Peugeot
Ford	Renault
General Motors	Scania
Honda	Suzuki Motor
Kubota	Toyota
Mazda	Volkswagen
Navistar	Volvo

HISTORICAL FINANCIALS

Company Type: Public

Income Statement

FYE: March 31

	REVENUE ($ mil.)	NET INCOME ($ mil.)	NET PROFIT MARGIN	EMPLOYEES
3/05	13,887	558	4.0%	19,600
3/04	13,540	518	3.8%	18,130
3/03	11,260	(1,204)	—	20,690
3/02	12,045	(324)	—	26,234
3/01	12,422	(529)	—	30,232
3/00	14,280	(988)	—	28,802
3/99	13,593	52	0.4%	28,508
3/98	13,524	45	0.3%	29,118
3/97	15,536	77	0.5%	—
3/96	15,681	350	2.2%	—
Annual Growth	**(1.3%)**	**5.3%**	**—**	**(5.5%)**

2005 Year-End Financials

Debt ratio: 187.8%   Current ratio: 1.05
Return on equity: 44.4% Long-term debt ($ mil.): 2,767
Cash ($ mil.): 1,296

Net Income History   OTC: ISUZF

ITOCHU

Trading giant ITOCHU is nothing to sneeze at. With more than 150 offices in about 80 countries, ITOCHU is a leading Japanese *sogo shosha* (general trading company), along with Mitsui and Mitsubishi. The company has seven major business groups: aerospace, electronics, and multimedia; chemicals, forest products, and general merchandise; energy, metals, and minerals; finance, realty, insurance, and logistics services; food; plant, automobile and industrial machinery; and textiles. ITOCHU's textile businesses account for about 25% of the company's revenue.

Divesting unprofitable operations, the company is focusing on expected moneymakers — multimedia, consumer and retail, financial services, and natural-resource development. It also is working to expand its presence in North America and in Asian nations other than Japan. Recently, it has begun a concerted effort to penetrate the Chinese market.

HISTORY

Chubei Itoh was only 18 when he organized his own wholesale linen business, C. Itoh & Co., in 1858. As Japan opened to foreign trade in the 1860s, the company prospered and was one of Osaka's largest textile wholesalers by the 1870s. C. Itoh established a trade office in San Francisco in 1889.

By 1919 C. Itoh had trading offices in New York, Calcutta, Manila, and four cities in China. Although it was not one of the *zaibatsu* (industrial groups) that flourished in Japan during the period between the world wars, C. Itoh benefited from the general increase in trade.

In 1941 C. Itoh was merged with two other trading companies, Marubeni and Kishimoto, into a new company, Sanko Kabushiki Kaisha. C. Itoh and Marubeni were separated in 1949. C. Itoh supplied UN troops with provisions during the Korean War; profits were used to diversify into petroleum, machinery, aircraft, and automobiles.

After the oil crisis of 1973 demonstrated Japan's vulnerability to oil import disruptions, C. Itoh actively participated in the development of petroleum production technology. To prevent the failure of Japan's 10th-largest trading company, Ataka, the Japanese government arranged a merger in 1977, making C. Itoh the third-largest *sogo shosha*.

The company established Japan Communications Satellite (JCSAT) with Mitsui and Hughes Communications in 1985. JCSAT launched its first two satellites in 1989 and 1990. The following year C. Itoh and Toshiba joined Time Warner in a limited partnership, Time Warner Entertainment Company, to produce and distribute movies and television programs and to operate cable TV systems in the US. C. Itoh, Time Warner, and Toshiba formed another joint venture to distribute Warner Bros. films and develop amusement parks in Japan.

C. Itoh changed its name to ITOCHU, a transliteration of its Japanese name, in 1992. After sales dropped the next year, ITOCHU began selling poorly performing subsidiaries, reducing its investment portfolio by more than one-third.

In 1996 the company formed an alliance with US oil company Atlantic Richfield to buy Coastal Corp.'s western US coal operations, and it took a stake in a massive project led by Amoco and British Petroleum to develop oil and gas deposits in the Caspian Sea. That year PerfecTV! (a joint venture with Sumitomo and other Japanese companies) began satellite broadcasting. Also in 1996 ITOCHU bought stakes in the Asia Broadcasting and Communications Network, a satellite communications company.

To help cover its losses from the Asian currency crisis, the company sold 40% of its stake in Time Warner in 1998; in 1999 ITOCHU sold its remaining stake. ITOCHU also sold low-performing real estate investments and laid plans to divest about one-third of its subsidiaries.

Two of ITOCHU's agricultural subsidiaries were liquidated in 2000. The company also sought out partnerships in order to offset costs incurred in new ventures: it joined with Japan's other top trading companies and Brazil's Petrobras to develop oil fields in South America. And in response to the rapid consolidation of Japan's steel industry, ITOCHU and Marubeni agreed to integrate their steel operations in 2001 to better compete.

In 2002 ITOCHU formed a partnership with Bally International to expand the European fashion brand's presence in Japan. In 2004 the company sold its interest in Utah-based Canyon Fuel Co. to Arch Coal, Inc. for $112 million, and dissolved its subsidiary, ITOCHU Coal International Inc. Also that year, the company formed a joint venture with Ishimori Shotaro Pro Inc. to establish Ishimori Entertainment, which produces movies, television programs, and publications based on Shotaro Ishimori titles, including the popular MASKED RIDER. In 2005 it established a fund with Turner Broadcasting to fund Japanese animation; and bought two US medical-device-distribution companies, Products for Surgery and Flanagan Instruments, marking ITOCHU's first step into this market.

EXECUTIVES

Chairman: Uichiro Niwa
President and CEO: Eizo Kobayashi
EVP; COO: Makoto Kato
EVP; Chief Administration Officer, CFO, and Chief Compliance Officer: Sumitaka Fujita
EVP; President, Energy, Metals, and Minerals: Akira Yokota
Senior Managing Director; Chief Corporate Planning Officer, CIO, and Chief Officer, International: Toshihito Tamba
Senior Managing Director; President, Food Company: Kouhei Watanabe
Managing Director; President, Aerospace, Electronics, and Multimedia Company: Shigeki Nishiyama
Managing Director, President, Chemicals, Forest Products, and General Merchandise Company: Hiroshi Kitamura
Managing Director; President, Finance, Realty, Insurance, and Logistics Services Company: Akira Kodera

Managing Director; President, Machinery Company: Jiro Takemori
Managing Director; President, Textile Company: Masahiro Okafuji
General Manager, China: Nobuo Kuwayama
General Manager, Human Resources Division: Masahiro Nakagawa
General Manager, Indochina: Tetsushi Ishizuka
General Manager, Legal: Kazutoshi Maeda
General Manager, Strategic Business Development: Toyoshige Yamada
Auditors: Deloitte Touche Tohmatsu

LOCATIONS

HQ: ITOCHU Corporation
(Itochu Shoji Kabushiki Kaisha)
5-1, Kita-Aoyama 2-chome, Minato-ku,
Tokyo 107-8077, Japan
Phone: +81-3-3497-2121   **Fax:** +81-3-3497-4141
US HQ: 335 Madison Ave., Bank of America Plaza, 22nd, 23rd, and 24th Fl., New York, NY 10017
US Phone: 212-818-8000   **US Fax:** 212-818-8543
Web: www.itochu.co.jp

2005 Transactions

	% of total
Asia	
Japan	75
Other countries	16
North America	5
Europe	2
Other regions	2
Total	**100**

PRODUCTS/OPERATIONS

2005 Sales

	% of total
Food	26
Textile	22
Aerospace, electronics & multimedia	20
Chemicals, forest products & general merchandise	12
Machinery	9
Energy, metals & minerals	7
Finance, realty, insurance & logistics	2
Other	2
Total	**100**

COMPETITORS

ADM
Altria
Balli
Dow Chemical
Exxon Mobil
Fluor
Hutchison Whampoa
Kanematsu
Klöckner
LG Group
Lockheed Martin
Marubeni
Matsushita
MAXXAM
Mitsubishi Corporation
Mitsui
Nestlé
Nippon Steel
Nippon Television
NTT
Samsung
Samsung America
SEPI
Sharp
Sojitz
Sumitomo
Tokyo Broadcasting System
TOMEN
TOTAL
Unilever

HISTORICAL FINANCIALS

Company Type: Public

Income Statement

FYE: March 31

	REVENUE ($ mil.)	NET INCOME ($ mil.)	NET PROFIT MARGIN	EMPLOYEES
3/05	5,865	723	12.3%	40,890
3/04	5,262	(302)	—	40,737
3/03	4,723	168	3.5%	39,109
3/02	4,364	228	5.2%	36,529
3/01	4,841	558	11.5%	38,867
3/00	5,804	(837)	—	40,683
3/99	5,388	(286)	—	—
3/98	4,484	(714)	—	—
Annual Growth	**3.9%**	**—**	**—**	**0.1%**

2005 Year-End Financials

Debt ratio: 343.0%   Current ratio: 1.19
Return on equity: 16.5%   Long-term debt ($ mil.): 16,279
Cash ($ mil.): 4

Net Income History

OTC: ITOCY

Ito-Yokado

From morning coffee-and-paper pit stops to late night runs for diapers and milk, Ito-Yokado Co. is eclectic, convenient, and its territory is wide-reaching. The firm operates about 1,300 department stores, restaurants, specialty shops, supermarkets, and superstores. The retailer's York Mart supermarket chain operates about 55 grocery stores in the Tokyo metro area. The company is also the Japanese franchisee for Oshman's sporting goods stores, and Robinson's department stores. In 2005 it was made a wholly owned subsidiary of holding company Seven & I Holdings.

Ito-Yokado runs about 330 Famil restaurants in Japan. The company's banking subsidiary, IYBank, maintains more than 7,800 ATMs (no branches).

Ito-Yokado has five superstores and a single convenience store in China and plans to begin selling fresh food, such as meat and vegetables, there via a joint venture with China's Beijing Wangfujing Department Store Group. The first outlet opened in Beijing in spring 2005.

Ito-Yokado has begun a new clothing line, L&B, and is expanding its other private-label clothing line, IY Basics (IYB). The company is upgrading its information technology capabilities to compete with US rivals, including Wal-Mart Stores.

Along with US retail giant Wal-Mart and Japan's AEON Co., Ito-Yokado is vying to sponsor the reorganization of debt-laden Japanese retailer The Daiei.

Until 2005 the company held about 73% of 7-Eleven, Inc., which franchises the 7-Eleven name worldwide though it recently sold its interest in 7-Eleven to 7-Eleven Japan. Later in the year, however, Ito-Yokado joined Seven-Eleven Japan and Denny's Japan to form a new holding company, Seven & I Holdings, which then purchased all shares of the Ito-Yokado (and therefore its subsidiaries) and made them wholly owned subsidiaries. In September, 2005, Seven & I began trading publicly on the Tokyo Stock Exchange.

HISTORY

After fighting in WWII, 21-year-old Masatoshi Ito joined his mother and brother in running a small family clothing shop (founded 1913) in Tokyo that grew into a department store. Ito took over the store when his brother died in 1956. Two years later the company was incorporated as Kabushiki Kaisha Yokado.

Ito visited the US in 1961, meeting with officials of National Cash Register (who wanted to sell cash registers to Japanese retailers still using abacuses) and retailers such as Sears and Safeway. Confident that US-style self-service retailing could work in Japan, Ito opened two hypermarkets (food, clothing, and household products) in Tokyo. By 1965, the year he changed the operation's name to Ito-Yokado Co., he had opened six more stores.

Famil, a chain of family-style restaurants, was launched in 1972, as were several Denny's restaurant franchises in Japan. Ito returned to the US that year to meet with Dallas-based Southland, owner of the 7-Eleven convenience store chain, and in 1974 he opened Japan's first 7-Eleven. The 7-Elevens quickly stole much of the market from the family-owned shops that dominated Japanese retailing. (The 7-Elevens were small enough to avoid triggering Japan's Large-Scale Retail Store Law, a law designed to protect small family stores by establishing rigid controls over store sizes and hours.) Ito co-opted his fallen competitors by recruiting them to become 7-Eleven franchisees. In 1975 Ito-Yokado established its York Mart subsidiary to open supermarkets in areas that could not support hypermarkets.

In the 1980s Ito acquired Japanese rights to Robinson's department stores (from the May Company) and Oshman's sporting goods stores. The company bought 58 7-Elevens in Hawaii in 1989 and the next year acquired 70% of the bankrupt Southland for $430 million.

Ito, along with several other heads of major corporations, was found in 1992 to have paid protection money to local mobsters, known as *sokaiya*, to prevent disruption of the company's annual meeting. Ito resigned, remaining a director and honorary chairman, and was replaced by Toshifumi Suzuki.

Earnings remained flat as sales rose slowly in the early 1990s, reflecting consumer uncertainty. In 1996 Ito-Yokado signed a joint venture agreement to develop superstores in China. The company opened its first store in Sichuan (1997), followed by a second superstore in Beijing (1998). With the Asian markets weak, and after years of cutting the store count in the US, Southland began expanding again in 1997.

Southland changed its name to 7-Eleven, Inc., in 1999. Seven-Eleven Japan Co. joined with SOFTBANK and two other companies in 1999 to form an online bookselling joint venture, e-Shopping! Books.

Seven-Eleven Japan Co. launched the Web site 7dream.com in 2000. In 2001 the company established an Internet bank accessible through Web kiosks in its retail stores. It launched a credit card company, IY Card Service, in October 2001. As part of a restructuring plan, the company sold its 88.4% stake in the Daikuma discount store chain to Yamada Denki in May 2002.

In August 2003 Seven-Eleven Japan broke the 10,000-store mark, becoming the first retailer in Japan to do so.

In April 2004, Ito-Yokado opened its first convenience store in Beijing, China.

EXECUTIVES

Chairman and CEO; Chairman of Seven-Eleven Japan; Chairman of 7-Eleven, Inc.: Toshifumi Suzuki, age 72
Vice Chairman; Chairman of York-Benimaru; Director of Denny's Japan; Director of 7-Eleven, Inc.: Nobutake Sato, age 67
President and COO: Sakae Isaka, age 63
Senior Managing Director and Director of China Division: Akihiko Hanawa, age 63
Senior Managing Director, Chief Administrative Officer, and CFO: Noritoshi Murata, age 61
Senior Managing Director, Development: Atsushi Kamei, age 61
Senior Managing Director, Sales: Akira Hinosawa, age 59
Managing Director and Director of Corporate Communications Department and Office of Social and Cultural Affairs: Sakue Mizukoshi, age 64
Managing Director and Chief of General Affairs Division: Minoru Inaoka, age 60
Managing Director and Chief of Housing Business Division: Yoshiaki Ota, age 59
Managing Director and Secretary: Katsuhiro Goto
Managing Executive Officer: Yoshiyuki Yamaguchi
Director of Information System Division: Yoji Okamura, age 56
Director of Finance Division: Shiro Ozeki
President IYBank: Takashi Anzai
Auditors: ChuoAoyama Audit Corporation

LOCATIONS

HQ: Ito-Yokado Co., Ltd.
8-8, Nibancho, Chiyoda-ku, Tokyo 102-8450, Japan
Phone: +81-3-6238-2111   **Fax:** +81-3-6238-3492
US HQ: 1 Union Sq., 600 University St., Ste. 1916, Seattle, WA 98101
US Phone: 206-667-8973   **US Fax:** 206-667-8971
Web: www.itoyokado.co.jp

2004 Sales

	% of total
Japan	64
US	33
Other	3
Total	**100**

PRODUCTS/OPERATIONS

2004 Sales

	% of total
Convenience stores	48
Superstores	47
Restaurants	4
Other countries	1
Total	**100**

2004 Stores

	No.
Seven-Eleven Japan	10,356
7-Eleven, Inc.	7,784
Denny's Japan	578
Famil restaurants	334
Ito-Yokado Superstore	177
York-Benimaru	104
York Mart	55
Mary Ann	52
Oshman's	4
Robinson's	3
Total	**19,447**

Principal Retail and Restaurant Operations

Convenience Stores
7-Eleven, Inc. (73%, US)
Seven-Eleven Japan Co., Ltd. (51%)

Superstores and Other Retail Operations
Ito-Yokado superstores
Mary Ann womenswear boutiques
Oshman's sporting goods stores (Japan)
Robinson's department stores (Japan)
York Benimaru supermarkets
York Mart supermarkets

Restaurants
Denny's Japan
Famil

Other
IY Bank
IY Card Service

COMPETITORS

AEON
Carrefour
Casey's General Stores
Daiei
Daimaru
FamilyMart
Isetan
Marui
Matsuzakaya
MYCAL
Seiyu
Takashimaya
Tokyu Department Store
Uny
Wal-Mart
Yamazaki Baking

HISTORICAL FINANCIALS

Company Type: Subsidiary

Income Statement

FYE: Last day in February

	REVENUE ($ mil.)	NET INCOME ($ mil.)	NET PROFIT MARGIN	EMPLOYEES
2/04	28,948	491	1.7%	47,947
2/03	28,436	179	0.6%	125,400
2/02	22,352	390	1.7%	106,911
2/01	26,440	417	1.6%	109,077
2/00	29,308	433	1.5%	116,636
2/99	27,225	555	2.0%	113,921
2/98	24,642	555	2.3%	39,245
2/97	24,949	614	2.5%	38,149
2/96	27,543	730	2.7%	36,932
2/95	29,771	737	2.5%	34,597
Annual Growth	**(0.3%)**	**(4.4%)**	**—**	**3.7%**

2004 Year-End Financials

Debt ratio: 22.4%   Current ratio: 1.57
Return on equity: 5.0%   Long-term debt ($ mil.): 2,340
Cash ($ mil.): 5,196

Net Income History

ITV plc

With operations in television broadcasting and production, pay and digital TV, and television leasing, ITV plc (formerly Granada) has the channels covered. The company owns 11 of the UK's Independent Television 1 (ITV1, a national broadcast network) stations. ITV plc also owns sister digital channels ITV2, ITV3, and ITV News and has stakes in pay-TV channels and Internet ventures. Its ITV Production division produces some 3,500 hours of programming for ITV and other broadcasters and maintains a library of 35,000 hours of television programs and 1,500 movie titles. In 2004 ITV licensees Granada and Carlton combined operations to form ITV plc.

The company's productions range from drama specials (Agatha Christie's *Marple*) to serialized soaps (*Coronation Street*), and from news to reality programs (*I'm A Celebrity. Get Me Out Of Here!*).

In 2000 the old Granada Group split its hospitality and media businesses into separate entities. To do that, the company acquired Compass Group and spun off its TV unit as Granada Media. (Granada Compass retained about 80% of the new media company.) However, the new firm didn't last very long. In early 2001 Granada Compass de-merged by transferring its hospitality and catering assets back into Compass Group (which is public again), absorbing Granada Media, and changing its name to Granada plc. The company jumped back on the merger train in 2004 when it purchased rival Carlton Communications and changed its name to ITV plc.

The company is planning to expand through boosting its production business, increasing its channel offerings, and building on non-advertising revenue. ITV in 2005 restructured its divisions to align with these goals; several boardroom changes were made at that time.

A strategy to boost the company's content-based offerings also came into focus in 2005, when ITV launched several Internet services and acquired Friends Reunited, a popular community-building Web site.

HISTORY

Granada (now ITV) traces its roots to the Edmonton Empire, a northern London theater built by Alexander Bernstein in 1906. After Bernstein died in 1922, his sons Cecil and Sidney set up a chain of movie theaters during the 1920s and incorporated their business as Granada Theatres Ltd. in 1934. Granada went public the next year. Between 1936 and 1938 it opened a cinema every three months.

In 1955 Granada was granted a TV broadcasting license for the north of England. Changing its name to Granada Group Ltd. in 1957, the company began diversifying in the late 1950s. Granada first got into the TV rental business and later started Granada Motorway Services. By 1967 Granada was operating more than 200 TV-rental showrooms nationwide and later expanded into North America. Sidney Bernstein resigned in 1979, and his nephew Alex took over as chairman.

During the 1980s the company's TV production arm gained international acclaim with shows like *Brideshead Revisited* (1981) and *The Jewel in the Crown* (1984). In 1986 it fended off a hostile bid from rival leisure company The Rank Organisation (now The Rank Group). By the end of the 1980s, Granada had disposed of its theater operations and invested in startup British Satellite Broadcasting (later British Sky Broadcasting) in 1990. Overextended and facing a recession, Granada sold its bingo businesses in 1991.

That year chief executive Derek Lewis resigned and Irish-born Gerry Robinson took over. The former chief of catering giant Compass Group, Robinson fired nearly all of the senior management during his first year. Under his acquisitive management, Granada bought the Sutcliffe Group, a major catering firm, from cruise operators P & O for $500 million in 1993 and the next year acquired London Weekend Television for $150 million.

Robinson replaced Bernstein as chairman in 1996, and Granada TV head Charles Allen was appointed as chief executive. Buying Forte for $6.1 billion that year added hotel operations and Little Chefs restaurants. In 1997 the company bought the 73% of Yorkshire Tyne Tees Television it did not already own in a deal valued at about $1.1 billion. The next year Granada's digital TV joint venture ON Digital (with Carlton Communications) began broadcasting. (The venture was later renamed ITV Digital and was shut down in 2002.)

In 1999 the company disposed of its stake in BSkyB and acquired fish and chips chain Harry Ramsden's. A proposed merger between rivals Carlton and United News & Media (now United Business Media) that year threatened Granada's dominance in UK television. In 2000 Granada proposed its own merger with either company, temporarily derailing the deal. (It was all moot anyway when Carlton and United canceled their deal after it raised too many competition concerns.) Later that year the company purchased hospitality firm Compass Group and spun off its media business as Granada Media, retaining about 83% of the new TV company.

In early 2001 Allen took on the title of chairman and Steve Morrison took over as chief executive. Shortly after completing the deal, in 2001 the fickle company de-merged by placing its hospitality assets back into Compass Group (which is a public firm again) and absorbing its stake in Granada Media. Granada Compass then changed its name to Granada plc. Morrison left as CEO in 2002.

In 2004 Granada bought rival Carlton Communications and renamed the combined company ITV plc. Also that year, ITV acquired BSkyB's 49.5% stake in Granada Sky Broadcasting, which had been formed as a Granada International and BSkyB joint venture in 1996.

EXECUTIVES

Chairman: Sir Peter A. Burt, age 61, $355,580 pay
Deputy Chairman: Sir George Russell, age 70
CEO and Director: Charles L. Allen, age 48, $2,519,470 pay
Commercial Director: Graham Parrot, age 53
Finance Director: Henry Staunton, age 57
Director of Television: Simon Shaps
Director of ITV Sales: Gary Digby
Director of Treasury: Charles van der Welle
Secretary: James Tibbitts
Commercial Director: Ian McCulloch
Managing Director, Sales: Graham Duff
Head of Investor Relations: Georgina Blackburn
Communications Director: Brigitte Trafford
Acting Head, ITV Worldwide: William Medlicott

Finance Director, Group Finance and Strategy: Neil Canetty-Clarke
Finance Director, ITV Broadcasting: Mike Green, age 44
Finance Director, ITV News Group: Mike Fegan
CEO, ITV Regions and News: Clive Jones, age 56
Director, ITV Consumer: Jeff Henry
Acting Head, ITV Production: John Whiston
Auditors: KPMG Audit Plc

LOCATIONS

HQ: ITV plc
    London Television Centre, Upper Ground,
    London SE1 9LT, United Kingdom
Phone: +44-20-7620-1620   **Fax:** +44-20-7261-3520
Web: www.itvplc.com

2004 Sales

	% of total
UK	98
Other countries	2
Total	**100**

COMPETITORS

BBC
BSkyB
Channel 4
Daily Mail and General Trust
Flextech
Liberty Media International
PTV
RTL Group
SMG
Telewest
Vivendi Universal

HISTORICAL FINANCIALS

Company Type: Public

Income Statement

FYE: December 31

	REVENUE ($ mil.)	NET INCOME ($ mil.)	NET PROFIT MARGIN	EMPLOYEES
12/04	3,955	268	6.8%	6,262
12/03*	5,245	(420)	—	4,316
9/02	2,228	(590)	—	4,696
9/01	3,602	(194)	—	30,797
9/00	7,968	180	2.3%	211,127
9/99	6,751	1,425	21.1%	191,407
9/98	6,845	946	13.8%	170,158
9/97	6,600	761	11.5%	—
9/96	5,964	460	7.7%	—
9/95	3,563	392	11.0%	—
Annual Growth	**1.2%**	**(4.1%)**	**—**	**(42.3%)**

*Fiscal year change

2004 Year-End Financials

Debt ratio: 24.9%
Return on equity: 5.4%
Cash ($ mil.): 1,121
Current ratio: 1.38
Long-term debt ($ mil.): 1,641

Net Income History

London: ITV

J Sainsbury

J Sainsbury is trying to get its trolley back on track. The UK's third-largest grocery retailer (after Tesco and ASDA) operates the long-struggling Sainsbury's Supermarkets chain — some 464 supermarkets in the UK (accounting for nearly 85% of sales). The supermarkets get about 40% of their sales from private-label products. In addition to supermarkets, the company operates 260 convenience stores under the Sainsbury's Local, Bells and Jacksons banners. Sainsbury also owns 55% of Sainsbury's Bank (in a joint venture with Scottish bank HBOS) and a property development company. Sainsbury sold its US business, Shaw's Supermarkets, to Albertson's in 2004. The Sainsbury family controls 38% of the company's shares.

Stiff competition from price-chopping rivals Tesco and Wal-Mart-owned ASDA has eroded Sainsbury's market share to about 16% of the UK grocery market. Also, the recent merger of Wm Morrison Supermarkets and Safeway plc has created another strong competitor. To fulfill regulatory requirements following the merger, Morrison sold 13 Safeway stores and its original Morrison store in North Yorkshire to Sainsbury in 2004 and has since agreed to sell nine more Safeway stores to Sainsbury.

The food retailer is also making a big push into the rapidly consolidating UK convenience store market. Acquisitions have pushed Sainsbury's convenience store count to more than 260 outlets throughout the UK.

Concentrating on its struggling grocery business, the company sold its 280-outlet UK-based Homebase home and garden supply superstores. In a drive to cut costs, Sainsbury is reported to be considering abandoning its London headquarters for cheaper digs elsewhere.

Facing the most severe financial crisis in its 135-year history, Sainsbury plans to add about 3,000 jobs in its stores, while eliminating an additional 750 jobs at its headquarters. The ailing grocery chain will also spend £400 million to lower prices, to better compete with its rivals and discounters. In a defensive move, Sainsbury has hired a team of investment bankers, led by Morgan Stanley, to advise the company on defending itself from unwanted takeover attempts.

HISTORY

Newlyweds John James and Mary Ann Sainsbury established a small dairy shop in their London home in 1869. Customers flocked to the clean and efficient store, a far cry from most cluttered and dirty London shops. They opened a second store in 1876. By 1914, 115 stores had been opened, and the couple's sons had entered the business.

During WWI the company's stores established grocery departments to meet demand for preserved products, such as meat and jams, which were sold under the Sainsbury's label. Mary Ann died in 1927 and John James the next year. Son John Benjamin, wholly devoted to the family business, took charge. (He is reported to have said on his deathbed, "Keep the stores well lit.") In the 1930s he engineered the company's first acquisition, the Thoroughgood stores.

Sales dropped by 50% during WWII, and some shops were destroyed by German bombing. Under third-generation leader Alan John Sainsbury, the company opened its first self-service store in 1950 in Croydon. The 75,000-sq.-ft. store opened in 1955 in Lewisham was considered to be the largest supermarket in Europe.

J Sainsbury went public in 1973. It established a joint venture with British Home Stores in 1975, forming the Savacentre hypermarkets (the company bought out its partner in 1989).

Sainsbury partnered with Grand Bazaar Innovation Bon Marche, of Belgium, in 1979 to establish Homebase, a do-it-yourself chain. (It bought the remaining 25% in 1996 and then sold the company in 2001, retaining only 18%.)

By 1983 most of Sainsbury's 229 stores were clustered in the south of England. A mature market and stiff competition forced the company to look elsewhere — both overseas and close to home. It began buying out US-based Shaw's Supermarkets in New England and in 1984 opened its first Scottish hypermarket. By 1987 the grocer owned 100% of Shaw's, which had 60 stores in Massachusetts, Maine, and New Hampshire.

In 1991 Sainsbury came under competitive pressure from Tesco and the Argyll Group (later renamed Safeway plc), which also began building superstores. It responded with an expansion drive of its own, including opening its first Scottish supermarket (in Glasgow) the next year.

In 1994 the company purchased a $325 million stake in Maryland-based Giant Food. Sainsbury bought home improvement retailer Texas Homecare from UK leisure concern Ladbroke in 1995 and integrated it into its Homebase unit. Royal Ahold bought Giant Food, including Sainsbury's 20% stake in 1998. David Sainsbury — a great-grandson of the founders — retired as chairman in 1998 to pursue politics, marking the first time a Sainsbury had not headed up the company in its more-than-a-century history.

As a cost-cutting effort in 1999, Sainsbury cut 2,200 jobs, more than half in management. It also launched its convenience store concept, called Sainsbury's Local. Also that year Sainsbury bought the 53-store Star Markets chain of Massachusetts, merging it into its Shaw's operations. In March 2000 Sir Peter Davis took over as CEO of Sainsbury's Supermarkets, replacing David Bremner.

In 2001 Sainsbury acquired 19 Grand Union stores in the US (17 of which were converted to the Shaw's banner), and opened 25 new stores in the UK. In Shaw's Supermarkets bought control of 18 stores in New England from bankrupt discounter Ames in 2002.

In 2004 Sainsbury acquired 54 Bells convenience stores. Justin King (formerly of Marks and Spencer) joined Sainsbury as its CEO that year, succeeding Sir Peter Davis who became chairman of the board. Sainsbury sold JS USA Holdings, which operated 203 Shaw's and Star Markets stores in New England, to US grocery chain Albertson's in a deal worth about $2.4 billion. Davis stepped down as chairman of Sainsbury on July 1, 2004, one year ahead of schedule and following a prolonged dispute with investors that culminated in a fight over his compensation.

Philip Hampton (former finance director of Lloyds TSB, BT Group, and BG Group) joined Sainsbury as its new chairman. In September the company agreed to pay ex-chairman Davis £2.6 million despite shareholder protests in July that forced the grocery retailer to withdraw a similar offer. At that time Lord Levene of Portsoken and Keith Butler-Wheelhouse, both non-executive directors of the company and members of the remuneration committee, resigned from the board.

EXECUTIVES

Chairman: Philip Hampton, age 51, $512,885 pay
CEO and Board Member: Justin King, age 44, $1,991,423 pay
CFO and Board Member: Darren Shapland, age 38
CEO, Sainsbury's Bank: Tim Pile, age 52
Managing Director, Convenience: James J. (Jim) McCarthy, age 49
Managing Director, Sainsbury's To You: Toby Anderson
Managing Director, Bells Stores and Jacksons Stores: Angus Oughtred
Company Secretary: Tim Fallowfield, age 41
Brand Communications Director: Helen Buck
Director, Supermarket Finance: Jonny Mason
Buying Director, Tu: Adrian Mountford
Change Director: Hamish Elvidge, age 51
Corporate Relations Director: Jan Shawe
Customer Services Director: Gwen Burr, age 42
General Merchandise Director: Penny Teale
Human Resources Director, Sainsbury's Supermarkets: Imelda Walsh, age 41
Information Technology Director: Angela Morrison
Retail Director: Ken McMeikan, age 39
Head of Group Legal Services: David Thurston
Head of Investor Relations: Lynda Ashton
Head of Media: Pip Wood
Head of Public Affairs: Erica Zimmer
Auditors: PricewaterhouseCoopers LLP

LOCATIONS

HQ: J Sainsbury plc
    33 Holborn, London EC1N 2HT, United Kingdom
Phone: +44-20-7695-6000   **Fax:** +44-20-7695-7610
Web: www.j-sainsbury.co.uk

PRODUCTS/OPERATIONS

2005 Sales

	% of total
Food retailing	97
Sainsbury's Bank	2
Discontinued operations	1
Total	**100**

2005 Stores

	No.
Sainsbury's Supermarkets	465
Jackson's	116
Sainsbury's Local	85
Bells Stores	55
Beaumont's	6
Total	**727**

Store Formats

Sainsbury's at Bells Stores (convenience stores)
Sainsbury's Central (convenience stores averaging 10,000 sq. ft. and 6,500 product lines)
Sainsbury's Local (convenience stores averaging 3,000 sq. ft. and 2,500 product lines)
Sainsbury's Supermarkets (full-service supermarkets averaging 20,000-30,000 sq. ft. and 17,000 product lines)
Superstores (full-service supermarkets averaging 30,000-50,000 sq. ft. and 26,000 product lines, plus amenities such as restaurants, dry cleaners, and gasoline stations)

Other Operations

Bells Stores Ltd. (food retailing)
Sainsbury's Bank plc (55%, financial services)
J Sainsbury Distribution Ltd (logistical services)

COMPETITORS

ALDI	METRO AG
ASDA	Musgrave Budgens-Londis
Big Food	Somerfield
Boots Group	T&S Stores
Co-operative Group	Tesco
First Quench	Wm Morrison
John Lewis	Supermarkets
Marks & Spencer	

HISTORICAL FINANCIALS

Company Type: Public

Income Statement

FYE: March 31

	REVENUE ($ mil.)	NET INCOME ($ mil.)	NET PROFIT MARGIN	EMPLOYEES
3/05	28,949	(98)	—	154,900
3/04	31,296	723	2.3%	180,200
3/03	27,433	715	2.6%	174,500
3/02	24,466	519	2.1%	174,700
3/01	24,423	371	1.5%	185,200
3/00*	25,900	556	2.1%	189,227
2/99	26,283	956	3.6%	178,000
2/98	23,874	802	3.4%	175,551
2/97	21,794	656	3.0%	165,992
2/96	20,670	747	3.6%	160,435
Annual Growth	3.8%	—	—	(0.4%)

*Fiscal year change

2005 Year-End Financials

Debt ratio: 39.6%
Return on equity: —
Cash ($ mil.): 1,264
Current ratio: 0.85
Long-term debt ($ mil.): 3,250

Net Income History

OTC: JSNSY

Japan Airlines

Japan Airlines Corporation (formerly Japan Airlines System Corporation) is going back to its roots. The holding company was created as a result of the merger of Japan's #1 airline, Japan Airlines (JAL), and Japan Air Systems (Japan's #3 airline) to boost domestic coverage. Combined, the airlines serve more than 170 cities in some 30 countries and operate more than 270 mostly jet aircraft. Both carriers continue to operate separately as Japan Airlines International (JAL International) and Japan Airlines Domestic (JAL Domestic), though they are combined in a single brand as JAL/Japan Airlines.

The group also carries air cargo, operates a low-fare domestic airline, provides maintenance and ground-support services, and owns the international chain of Nikko hotels.

Competition has been growing, with the deregulation wave making its way to Japan's shores. However, the merger of the two airlines gives the group a better grasp on domestic routes. The merger has also expanded the group's presence in China, a rapidly growing new market.

Although it's been courted by Oneworld (led by American Airlines and British Airways), Japan Airlines has long refused to join a global marketing alliance. Instead it has signed code-sharing agreements with about 20 carriers, including American, Air France, and Iberia. The airline signaled a turnaround in its policy, however, with the October 2005 announcement that it would join Oneworld and continue present code-sharing agreements. Japan Airlines will be the al-

liance's third largest member after American and British Airways.

Like other airlines, Japan Airlines is struggling to keep profits aloft over rising jet fuel prices. It has announced plans to discontinue low-profit international routes and cut nearly 6,000 jobs by 2007, among other measures, to compensate for the higher cost of fuel. Nonetheless, Japan Airlines has ordered about 60 planes worth $5.3 billion from Boeing.

Japan Airlines will merge Japan Airlines International with Japan Airlines Domestic in October 2006. Japan Airlines International will remain as the surviving entity, which will take its name. Japan Airlines will continue to be the group's holding company.

HISTORY

After WWII Japan was not allowed to form its own airline until the end of US occupation in 1951. That year a group of bankers led by Seijiro Yanagito founded Japanese Air Lines (JAL). JAL was essentially a revival of the prewar Nihon Koku Kabushiki Kaisha (Japan Air Transport Company), the national airline created by the Japanese government in 1928 and dissolved by the Allies in 1945. Since the Allied Peace Treaty forbade the airline to use Japanese flight crews, it leased both pilots and equipment from Northwest. In 1953 the airline was reorganized as Japan Airlines, with the government and the public owning equal shares.

Under Yanagito, who ran the airline until 1961, JAL expanded quickly, opening a transpacific route from Tokyo to San Francisco in 1954 and extending regional service to Hong Kong in 1955, Bangkok in 1956, and Singapore in 1958. A polar route from Tokyo to London and Paris gave the airline a foothold in Europe in 1961. Service to Moscow began in 1967, and that year JAL formed Southwest Airlines (now Japan TransOcean Air) to serve the islands of Japan.

In 1974 JAL suspended flights to Taipei, the mainstay of Chinese nationalists, in favor of new service to Beijing and Shanghai. Japan Asia Airways, a new subsidiary, resumed flights to Taipei the next year.

JAL ran into problems in the early 1980s: in 1982 a mentally unstable pilot crashed a plane into Tokyo Bay, killing 24; and in 1985 a JAL 747 crashed into a mountainside, killing all but four of the 524 on board. The worst single-plane accident in history, the disaster led to the resignation of most of JAL's top executives.

Facing a strong US currency in 1985, JAL signed an 11-year, $3 billion aircraft contract with Boeing, set at a fixed exchange rate of 184 yen per dollar. But the contract would haunt the airline in the 1990s, denying JAL the benefit of a weakened dollar that would fall below 100 yen.

The government sold its stake in JAL to the public in 1987. With air transport no longer nationalized, overseas routes were opened to the company's longtime domestic rival, All Nippon Airways (ANA).

In 1992 JAL reported its first loss ($100 million) since privatization, the result of high labor costs and the expansion of its fleet and facilities. With Japan sliding into recession, the company announced a five-year, $4.8 billion belt-tightening program.

Falling short of those cost-cutting goals, in 1993 JAL announced it would close half its North American offices, suspend recruitment, and freeze salaries. It also signed an agreement with ANA to share some aircraft maintenance costs.

Traffic increased in 1994, but JAL was forced to cut prices to meet lower competing fares.

In 1995 JAL hooked up with American Airlines to connect computer reservation systems and act as agents for each other's cargo businesses. But JAL's losses continued, and chairman Susumu Yamaji and president Akira Kondo resigned in 1998. That year the airline announced job cuts, restructured routes, and launched low-cost domestic carrier JAL Express.

JAL finally posted a profit again in 1999. It also added Alitalia and Iberia Airlines as code-sharing partners and reduced its stake in delivery giant DHL from 26% to 6%. JAL came under renewed pressure in 2000, when government deregulation of domestic fares sparked a price war.

The next year demand for international travel slumped in the wake of the September 11 terrorist attacks on the US. In response, JAL had to modify its route structure, which included reducing several flights and modifying its code-sharing agreement with American Airlines.

In 2002 JAL merged with Japan's #3 carrier Japan Air Systems and created a new holding company called Japan Airlines System to operate the two airlines. In 2004 the company was reorganized under the JAL/Japan Airlines brand, which includes Japan Airlines Domestic and Japan Airlines International.

EXECUTIVES

President and CEO: Toshiyuki Shinmachi
EVP and Assistant to the President: Katsuo Haneda
Senior Managing Director, SVP and General Manager, Corporate Safety and Corporate Planning, and SVP, Human Resources Planning, Corporate Compliance, and Public Relations: Hidekazu Nishizuka
Managing Director, SVP and Deputy General Manager, Corporate Safety and SVP, Environmental Affairs: Takenori Matsumoto
SVP, Public Relations: Nobuyoshi Sera
SVP and Deputy General Manager, Corporate Planning and SVP, Brand Management: Fumio Tsuchiya
SVP, Finance and Purchasing: Haruka Nishimatsu
SVP: Shunji Kono
SVP: Ken Moroi, age 77
SVP: Shinobu Shimizu, age 74
Senior Executive Officer and General Manager, Corporate Affairs and VP, Executive Secretariat Office: Sumio Yasunaga
Senior Executive Officer Marketing Strategy and Research, Corporate Planning, and Corporate Affairs, and VP Strategic Policy and Research: Hideyuki Kanenari
Executive Officer, Associated Business: Kimio Hiroike
Executive Officer, IT Strategy and Planning: Shunichi Saito
Auditors: Ernst & Young ShinNihon

LOCATIONS

HQ: Japan Airlines Corporation
(Nippon Koku Kabushiki Kaisha)
2-4-11, Higashi-shinagawa, Shinagawa-ku,
Tokyo 140-8605, Japan
Phone: +81-0120-25-5931
US HQ: 655 Fifth Ave., New York, NY 10022
Web: www.jal.co.jp

PRODUCTS/OPERATIONS

Selected Subsidiaries

Airport Ground Service Co., Ltd.
AXESS International Network Inc. (75%, computer reservation system)
JAL Express Co., Ltd. (domestic regional carrier)
JAL Logistics Inc. (cargo services)
JAL Royal Catering Co., Ltd. (51%, in-flight catering)
JALPAK Co., Ltd. (78%, package tours)
JALways Co., Ltd. (low-fare carrier)
Japan Asia Airways Co., Ltd. (regional services)

COMPETITORS

Accor	Garuda Indonesia
ACE Aviation	Hyatt
Air France	Kintetsu Corp.
All Nippon Airways	KLM
British Airways	Korean Air
Carlson	Lufthansa
Central Japan Railway	Northwest Airlines
China Airlines	Singapore Airlines
China Eastern Airlines	Skymark
Continental Airlines	Thai Airways
Delta Air	UAL
Dragonair	Virgin Atlantic Airways
East Japan Railway	West Japan Railway
Evergreen Marine	

HISTORICAL FINANCIALS

Company Type: Public

Income Statement

FYE: March 31

	REVENUE ($ mil.)	NET INCOME ($ mil.)	NET PROFIT MARGIN	EMPLOYEES
3/04	18,286	(839)	—	54,053
3/03	17,385	97	0.6%	54,885
3/02	12,095	(276)	—	46,075
3/01	13,740	331	2.4%	45,319
3/00	15,080	186	1.2%	18,535
3/99	13,051	223	1.7%	16,325
3/98	11,982	(477)	—	17,863
3/97	12,638	(117)	—	19,046
3/96	13,670	(86)	—	20,030
3/95	15,578	(169)	—	21,396
Annual Growth	1.8%	—	—	10.8%

2004 Year-End Financials

Debt ratio: 734.7%
Return on equity: —
Cash ($ mil.): 1,367

Current ratio: 0.93
Long-term debt ($ mil.): 11,077

Net Income History

Exchange: Tokyo

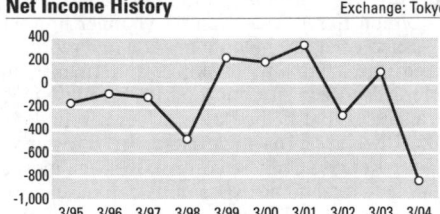

Japan Tobacco

Japan Tobacco has plenty to puff about. The company controls more than 70% of the cigarette market in a country where about half of the male population smokes. Japan Tobacco is the world's #3 tobacco company, after Altria and British American Tobacco. The company's JT International unit sells Camel, Salem, and Winston brands outside the US. Japan Tobacco also operates in the foods, pharmaceuticals, agribusiness, engineering, and real estate industries. A state-owned monopoly until 1985, the Japanese Finance Ministry now own half of the company.

In a country where the average smoker burns through a pack each day, Japan Tobacco makes nine of the nation's top 10 brands, including such favorites as Mild Seven, Caster, and Seven Stars. Two new brands, Icene Super Cooling Menthol and LUCIA Citrus Fresh Menthol are being touted

as producing less odor and smoke than conventional brands. Japan Tobacco has expanded into 70 markets worldwide through its JT International unit. The company also is expected to bid for a government-run tobacco firm in Turkey.

The company intends to close 13 of its 25 manufacturing plants and six of its 30 sales branches by March 2006 as part of an effort to increase profits. These reductions will slash as many as 4,000 jobs from company payrolls, as demand for cigarettes, partly depressed by higher taxes, continues to decline. Japan Tobacco is also using its own line of premium smokes to fill the gap left in the product line by the absence of Marlboro cigarettes. The company's deal with Philip Morris to sell Marlboro lapsed in 2005.

HISTORY

In 1898, roughly 325 years after tobacco was introduced in Japan, the nation's Ministry of Finance formed a bureau to monopolize its production to fund military and industrial expansion.

During WWII, Japan's tobacco leaf imports from North and South America grew scarce and led to cigarette rationing. In 1949 the government began operating the tobacco production bureau as a business: the Japan Tobacco and Salt Public Corporation (in 1905 the bureau also became responsible for a salt monopoly).

The company launched Hope, the first Japanese-made filter cigarette, in 1957, and it became the world's best seller a decade later. In 1972 it began printing mild packaging "warnings": "Be careful not to smoke excessively for your health."

Japan Tobacco and Salt began selling Marlboro cigarettes licensed from Philip Morris in 1973. The Mild Seven brand (its current bestseller) went on sale in 1977; it became the world's #1 cigarette in 1981 but dropped to #2 (behind Marlboro) in 1993.

When its tobacco monopoly ended in 1985, the government established the firm as Japan Tobacco (a government-owned joint stock company). As competition from foreign imports increased, the firm came up with new means of making yen. It formed Japan Tobacco International (cigarette exports mainly to the US and Southeast Asia), moved into agribusiness and real estate operations, and, in 1986, created JT Pharmaceutical. In 1987 cigarette import tariffs ended, and importers lowered prices to match the company's; its sales and market share subsequently declined. During the late 1980s it introduced HALF TIME beverages and its first low-tar cigarettes (Mild Seven Lights is now the world's #1 light cigarette).

In 1992 Japan Tobacco bought its first overseas production facility, Manchester Tobacco (closed in 2001). Former Ministry of Finance official Masaru Mizuno became CEO that year — and soon took up smoking. Also in 1992 the company and Agouron Pharmaceuticals agreed to jointly develop immune system drugs; in 1994 they added antiviral drugs. The government sold about 20% of the firm's stock to the public in 1994 and 13% in 1996. The firm began operating Burger King restaurants in Japan in 1996. Japan Tobacco bought Pillsbury Japan in 1998.

Japan Tobacco in 1999 paid nearly $8 billion for R.J. Reynolds International, the international tobacco unit of what was then RJR Nabisco. The company then renamed the unit, which has operations in 70 countries worldwide, JT International. It also bought the food products division of Asahi Chemical, Torii Pharmaceutical from

Asahi Breweries, and the Unimat vending machine company.

Slowing sales prompted Japan Tobacco to announce in 2000 that it would reduce its workforce by 6,100 by 2005. Company exec Katsuhiko Honda became CEO that year (Mizuno remained as chairman) and said he'd push the government to sell its stake. In February 2001 the company announced plans to sell parts of its OTC drugs and health care businesses to Nichiiko Pharmaceutical to concentrate on prescription drugs. It also intends to sell all 25 of its Burger King outlets. In May Mizuno stepped down as chairman and was replaced by Takashi Ogawa.

In December 2001 Japan's Ministry of Finance recommended that it cut its holdings in the company from 66% to 50%; it would also allow the company to sell additional shares, which could further dilute the government's stake to as little as 33%. In 2002 Japan Tobacco completed the sale of its 25 Burger King outlets and its OTC drug business.

In January 2004 the company unveiled six new brands: Mild Seven One Menthol Box, Bitter Valley, Fuji Renaissance, Fuji Renaissance 100's, Hi-Lite Menthol, and BB Slugger. An added brand, Hope Menthol, currently being tested in the marketplace, also will see expanded availability. Japan Tobacco's Canadian subsidiary filed for bankruptcy protection in August 2004 following a billion-dollar smuggling claim by the Canadian government. Canada said that the company owed $1.4 billion in Canadian back taxes for allegedly smuggling cigarettes in 1998 and 1999.

Japan Tobacco in 2005 ended its agreement with Philip Morris to make and sell Marlboro cigarettes.

EXECUTIVES

Chairman: Yoji Wakui
President, CEO, and Representative Director: Katsuhiko Honda, age 63
Executive Deputy President, Finance, Pharmaceutical, Food, Printing, and Vending Machinery: Masakazu Kakei
Executive Deputy President; Assistant to CEO in Compliance, Finance, Communications, General Administration, Legal, and Operational Review and Business Assurance; and Representative Director: Takao Hotta
Executive Deputy President; Chief Strategy Officer; Assistant to CEO in Human Resources; and Representative Director: Kazuei Obata
Executive Deputy President; President, Tobacco Business; Assistant to CEO in Vending Machinery; and Representative Director: Seigo Nishizawa
SEVP; Head, Central Pharmaceutical Research Institute; and Chief Scientific Officer, Pharmaceutical Business: Shigeo Ishiguro
SEVP; President, Food Business; and Director: Tetsuji Kanamori
SEVP; R&D, General Division, Tobacco Business: Ichiro Kumakura
SEVP; Deputy President, Tobacco Business: Mutsumi Makinoda
SEVP, Product Group, Tobacco Business: Yasumasa Matsunaga
SEVP, Sales Headquarters, Tobacco Business: Koji Nishihara
SEVP, Chief Legal Officer: Ryuichi Shimomura
SEVP, Chief General Affairs Officer: Ryoichi Yamada
SVP and Chief Human Resources Officer: Yoshiyuki Murai
SVP and Chief Communications Officer: Masakazu Shimizu
CEO, JTI-Macdonald: Michel Poirier
Auditors: Deloitte Touche Tohmatsu

LOCATIONS

HQ: Japan Tobacco Inc.
(Nihon Tabako Sangyo)
2-1, Toranomon 2-chome, Minato-ku,
Tokyo 105-8422, Japan
Phone: +81-3-3582-3111 **Fax:** +81-3-5572-1441
Web: www.jti.co.jp

Japan Tobacco operates 25 tobacco factories in Japan.

PRODUCTS/OPERATIONS

2005 Sales

	% of total
Tobacco	
Japan	60
Other countries	21
Foods	13
Pharmaceuticals	3
Other	3
Total	**100**

Selected Cigarette Brands

BB Slugger
Bitter Valley
Cabin and Cabin Mild
Camel (outside the US)
Caster and Caster Mild
Frontier
Fuji Renaissance
Hi-Lite Menthol
Hope Menthol
Icene Super Cooling Menthol
LUCIA Citrus Fresh Menthol
Mild Seven (regular, Lights, Super Lights)
Salem (outside the US)
Seven Stars
Winston (outside the US)

Selected Divisions and Operations

Agribusiness
Beverage business
Engineering
Food business
Pharmaceuticals
Real estate
Tobacco

COMPETITORS

Ajinomoto	Mitsubishi Chemical
Altadis	Nestlé
Asahi Breweries	Nisshin Seifun Group
British American Tobacco	Philip Morris International
Coca-Cola	Reemtsma
Gallaher	Suntory Ltd.
Imperial Tobacco	Unilever
Kraft Foods International	Vector

HISTORICAL FINANCIALS

Company Type: Public

Income Statement

FYE: March 31

	REVENUE ($ mil.)	NET INCOME ($ mil.)	NET PROFIT MARGIN	EMPLOYEES
3/05	43,371	582	1.3%	32,640
3/04	43,782	(72)	—	39,243
3/03	37,483	628	1.7%	38,628
3/02	34,259	278	0.8%	39,387
3/01	35,636	346	1.0%	40,237
3/00	41,431	481	1.2%	41,703
3/99	16,107	627	3.9%	—
3/98	13,030	436	3.3%	28,326
3/97	14,605	648	4.4%	22,160
3/96	16,116	634	3.9%	22,625
Annual Growth	**11.6%**	**(0.9%)**	**—**	**4.2%**

2005 Year-End Financials

Debt ratio: 12.3%   Current ratio: 2.03
Return on equity: 4.1%   Long-term debt ($ mil.): 1,720
Cash ($ mil.): 7,709

Net Income History   Exchange: Tokyo

Jardine Matheson

The British no longer govern Hong Kong, but don't tell Jardine Matheson Holdings (JMH), which governs the many interests of its affiliate Jardine Strategic Holdings; one of the oldest of the Hong Kong *hongs* (diversified trading companies) and one of the few still in British hands. JMH's subsidiaries include Jardine Pacific and Jardine Motors Group, Asian supermarket operator Dairy Farm, and Hongkong Land, which owns prime real estate in Hong Kong. Other businesses include financial services, hotels (Mandarin Oriental), construction, and shipping. Members of the Keswick family, descendants of the co-founder William Jardine, control JMH and Jardine Strategic through a complex ownership structure.

JMH owns about 80% of Jardine Strategic, while Jardine Strategic owns more than 50% of JMH. (The cross shareholding between the two companies is designed to repel takeovers. JMH created Jardine Strategic in 1986 in an anti-takeover transaction.)

JMH also has numerous investments in China and throughout Asia. The company has diversified geographically, but the Asia/Pacific region is where the money is — more than three-quarters of the company's revenues come from that part of the world. To maintain its footing in the region's uncertain economic times, JMH is working to control costs. The company is also moving to buy up additional shares in its affiliates, and focusing on building its businesses in Southeast Asian countries including Indonesia, Malaysia, and Singapore. Dairy Farm is growing rapidly in China and Hong Kong through supermarkets, convenience and health and beauty stores, and restaurants. Through Jardine Cycle & Carriage the group owns about 48% stake in carmaker Astra in Indonesia. Jardine Motors is expanding its Mercedes-Benz network in Southern China and developing its Hyundai passenger car business in Hong Kong. In the UK it is going upmarket.

Across the Pacific, Jardine Matheson is expanding its Mandarin Oriental hotel business with five new hotels under development and 21 in operation.

Managing Director Percy Weatherall plans to retire in 2006. Weatherall will be succeeded by Anthony Nightingale, currently chairman of Jardine Cycle & Carriage, Jardine Motors, Jardine Pacific, and MCL Land.

HISTORY

Scotsmen William Jardine and James Matheson met in Bombay in 1820. In 1832 they founded Jardine, Matheson in Canton, the only Chinese city then open to foreigners. The company started shipping tea from China to Europe and smuggling opium from India to China. In 1839 Chinese authorities tried to stop the drug trade, seizing 20,000 chests of opium, 7,000 of them Jardine's. Jardine persuaded Britain to send gunboats to China, precipitating the First Opium War. China lost the war and ceded Hong Kong to Britain in 1842.

Jardine moved to Hong Kong and resumed trading opium. The Second Opium War (1856-60) resulted in the opening of 11 more ports and the legalization of opium imports. Jardine flourished and later branched into the more legitimate fields of brewing, textiles, banking, insurance, and sugar. It formed Hongkong Land (HKL), a real estate company; introduced steamships to China; and built the country's first railroad line (1876). The company earned the sobriquet "the Princely *Hong*" because of its high-society officers with free-spending habits.

The Sino-Japanese War and WWII shut the company down. In 1945, with China gripped by civil war, Jardine reopened in Hong Kong. Attempts to re-establish operations in China ended in 1954 after the Communist takeover. The company went public in 1961 and was run during the 1960s by members of the Keswick family. Henry Keswick was succeeded by *Taipan* (big boss) David Newbigging in 1972.

The cost incurred in an acquisition program begun in the 1970s made Jardine a takeover target by 1980. Newbigging defended the company by erecting a bulwark of crossholdings of it and HKL stock. The resulting debt pushed Jardine to the brink of bankruptcy, forcing it to sell assets.

Simon Keswick — Henry's younger brother — succeeded Newbigging in 1984 and reorganized the company, making investments in Mercedes-Benz distributorships and fast-food franchises that helped turn Jardine around. As the UK and China negotiated the transfer of Hong Kong to Chinese control, Keswick moved Jardine's legal home to Bermuda. Jardine continued to be plagued by takeover attempts, however, particularly by Li Ka-shing, who was assisted by China's investment organization, CITIC. In a 1986 anti-takeover transaction, the company created Jardine Strategic Holdings to hold interests in HKL and its spin-offs. When the Chinese army put down student demonstrations in Beijing two years later, Keswick called the Chinese government "a thuggish, oppressive regime."

To increase its holdings outside of Hong Kong, Jardine bought 26% of Trafalgar House in 1993 but sold its stake in the troubled British conglomerate in 1996, which contributed to lower profits. Jardine delisted five of its companies from the Hong Kong stock exchange in 1994. Continuing to expand geographically, the company acquired 20% of India's Tata Industries and bought London's Hyde Park Hotel in 1996.

Hong Kong was returned to China in 1997, and in a display of public fence-mending, Chinese Vice Premier Zhu Rongji welcomed Jardine's participation in mainland ventures. But Jardine's stormy relationship with China continued even as Jardine's profits dropped during the Asian economic crisis. In 1999 China closed down Jardine's Beijing and Guangzhou brokerage offices (and banned the two chief China officers from the business for life), claiming that Jardine was engaging in unauthorized activities.

In 2000 Jardine sold its minority holdings in UK-based investment firm Robert Fleming Group. That year and again in 2001 the Keswicks — Simon and his brother Henry — turned back attempts by US-based Brandes Investment Partners, which owns about 10% of Jardine, to seize control of the company.

In 2002 Jardine increased its stake in Singapore-based Cycle & Carriage from 29% to more than 50%. Also that year, Dairy Farm sold its New Zealand business in June to focus on its Asian retail network. (Dairy Farm exited the Australian market in 2001.)

In 2004 Mandarin Oriental opened new hotels in New York and Washington, DC.

EXECUTIVES

Chairman, Jardine Matheson Holdings, Matheson & Co., and Jardine Strategic: Henry Keswick, age 64
Managing Director, Jardine Matheson Holdings, Dairy Farm, Hongkong Land, Jardine Strategic, and Mandarin Oriental; Chairman, Jardine Matheson Ltd.: Percy Weatherall
Chairman, Cycle & Carriage, Jardine Motors Group, Jardine Pacific, and MCL Land: Anthony J. L. Nightingale
Group General Counsel: Jonathan Gould
CFO; Finance Director, Jardine Matheson Limited: James Riley
Company Secretary: C.H. Wilken
Chairman, Dairy Farm, Hongkong Land, and Mandarin Oriental, and Director: Simon Keswick, age 61
Director; Deputy Chairman, Jardine Lloyd Thompson, and Director: C. G. Rodney Leach, age 70
Group Head of Human Resources, Jardine Matheson Limited: Ritchie Bent
Group Taxation Manager, Jardine Matheson Limited: Betty Chan
Group Treasurer, Jardine Matheson Limited: Simon Mawson
Group Financial Controller, Jardine Matheson Limited: P. M. Kam
Group Corporate Secretary; Director, Group Corporate Affairs, Jardine Matheson Limited: Neil M. McNamara
Group Legal Manager, Jardine Matheson Limited: Jonathan Collins
Group Audit Controller, Jardine Matheson Limited: Eric van der Hoeven
Auditors: PricewaterhouseCoopers LLP

LOCATIONS

HQ: Jardine Matheson Holdings Limited
    48th Fl., Jardine House, Hong Kong
Phone: +852-2843-8288   **Fax:** +852-2845-9005
Web: www.jardines.com

2004 Sales

	$ mil.	% of total
Southeast Asia	3,187	36
Hong Kong & China	3,142	35
UK	1,691	19
Northeast Asia	520	6
North America	289	3
Australasia	99	1
Continental Europe	42	—
Total	**8,970**	**100**

PRODUCTS/OPERATIONS

2004 Sales

	$ mil.	% of total
Dairy Farm	3,956	44
Jardine Motors Group	2,082	23
Jardine Cycle & Carriage	1,500	17
Jardine Pacific	1,093	12
Mandarin Oriental	337	4
Other activities	2	—
Total	**8,970**	**100**

Major Subsidiaries and Affiliates

Cycle & Carriage Ltd (47%, motor and property group, Singapore)
Dairy Farm International Holdings Ltd (62%; supermarkets and restaurants)
Hongkong Land Holdings Ltd (34%, real estate)
Jardine Lloyd Thompson plc (32%, insurance and brokerage, UK)
Jardine Motors Group Holdings Ltd. (auto distribution)
Jardine Pacific Holdings Ltd. (engineering and construction, property, restaurants, shipping and financial services, trading, and distribution)
Jardine Strategic Holdings Ltd. (79%, holding company)
Mandarin Oriental International Ltd. (59%, hotels)

COMPETITORS

Accor
Carrefour
Cheung Kong Holdings
China Resources Enterprise
Daiei
Hopewell Holdings
HSBC Holdings
Hutchison Whampoa
Hyatt
ITOCHU
Kumagai Gumi
Marriott
Marubeni
McDonald's
Royal Ahold
Samsung
Seiyu
Sime Darby
Swire Pacific

HISTORICAL FINANCIALS

Company Type: Public

Income Statement

FYE: December 31

	REVENUE ($ mil.)	NET INCOME ($ mil.)	NET PROFIT MARGIN	EMPLOYEES
12/04	8,970	947	10.6%	100,000
12/03	8,452	181	2.1%	105,000
12/02	7,398	352	4.8%	110,000
12/01	9,413	115	1.2%	130,000
12/00	10,362	931	9.0%	150,000
12/99	10,675	207	1.9%	150,000
12/98	11,230	117	1.0%	160,000
12/97	11,522	476	4.1%	175,000
12/96	11,605	536	4.6%	200,000
12/95	10,636	420	3.9%	200,000
Annual Growth	**(1.9%)**	**9.5%**	**—**	**(7.4%)**

2004 Year-End Financials

Debt ratio: 65.5%
Return on equity: 30.0%
Cash ($ mil.): 1,300
Current ratio: 1.30
Long-term debt ($ mil.): 2,382

Net Income History

Singapore: JARD

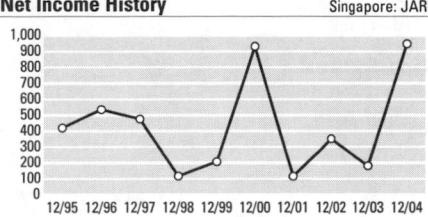

1,000
900
800
700
600
500
400
300
200
100
0

12/95 12/96 12/97 12/98 12/99 12/00 12/01 12/02 12/03 12/04

Kao Corporation

More than a century after Kao affixed a lunar logo to its name, Japanese consumers still think the company's products hang the moon. Kao (pronounced "cow") is Japan's #1 maker of personal care, laundry, and cleaning products. Its brands include Attack (laundry detergent), Bioré (skin care), Family Pure (dishwashing detergent), Feather (shampoo), Laurier (sanitary napkins), Merries (disposable diapers), and Prestige (cosmetics). The company also makes cooking oils and fatty chemicals, printer and copier toner products, and plastics used in products such as sneaker soles.

Although popular in Japan, Kao is striving to attain the international scope of rivals like Procter & Gamble (P&G) and Unilever. Subsidiaries Kao Professional Salon Services and Guhl Ikebana make hair care products in Europe, and its Kao Brands subsidiary makes skin care products, including Jergens brand items, in North America. To bring new products to market, Kao invests heavily in research and development.

Kao brought its fat-reducing Econa cooking oil to the US in early 2003. Introduced in Japan in 1999, Econa is marketed as Enova in the US through a joint venture with Archer Daniels Midland Co.

HISTORY

Tomiro Nagase founded the Kao Soap Company in 1887; shortly afterward, he began selling bars under the motto, "A Clean Nation Prospers." Kao's longtime rivalry with Procter & Gamble (P&G) was foreshadowed when it adopted a moon trademark in 1890 strikingly similar to the one chosen by P&G eight years earlier.

Kao moved into detergents in the 1940s. In the 1960s the company struck upon an idea that would vertically integrate it and set it apart from other consumer products manufacturers: It set up a network of wholesale distributors ("hansha") who sell only Kao products. The hansha system improved distribution time and cut costs by eliminating middlemen.

Yoshio Maruta, one of several chemical engineers to run Kao, took over as president in 1971. Maruta presented himself as more Buddhist scholar than corporate honcho; during his 19 years at the top, he gave the company a wider vision through his emphasis on creativity and his insistence on an active learning environment. To encourage sharing of ideas, the company used open conference rooms for meetings and anyone interested could attend and participate in any meeting.

Under Maruta, Kao launched a string of successful products in new areas in the 1980s. In 1982 the company introduced its Sofina cosmetics line, emphasizing the line's scientific basis in a break from traditional beauty products marketing. The next year its Super Merries diapers (with a new design that reduced diaper rash) trounced P&G's Pampers in Japan. Its popular Attack laundry detergent (the first concentrated laundry soap) led the market within six months of its 1987 debut.

Seeking a way to enter the US market, Kao bought the Andrew Jergens skin care company — based in Cincinnati, as is P&G — in 1988. (It also purchased a chemical company to supply the materials to make Jergens' products.) P&G and

Unilever braced themselves for the new competition, but Kao didn't deliver, releasing products like fizzy bath tablets that didn't sell well in a nation of shower-takers. In 1989 it bought a 75% interest in Goldwell, a German maker of hair care and beauty products sold through hair stylists. (By 1994 Kao owned all of Goldwell, which is now called Kao Professional Salon Services.)

In the mid-1980s Kao built a name for itself in the floppy disk market and became the top producer of 3 1/2-in. floppy disks in North America by 1990. However, competition crowded the field and drove the price of disks down. In 1997 the company stopped production of floppy disks in the US.

Chemical engineer Takuya Goto took over as president that year. Kao looked to other Asian markets and the US for potential consumers and found a willing audience in the US for its Bioré face strips. In 1998 Kao purchased Bausch & Lomb's skin care business, gaining the Curel and Soft Sense lotion brands.

In 2000 Kao established a joint venture with Novartis to make baby foods and over-the-counter drugs such as stomach medicines and other pain relief drugs. In 2001 Kao lost out on its offer for Clairol to P&G. Also in 2001 it formed a joint venture with Archer Daniels Midland to produce an anti-obesity diacylglycerol oil (used in margarine, cooking oil, salad dressing, and mayonnaise) and in 2002 began marketing it in the US under the brand name Enova. That year Kao dissolved its OTC-medicine-manufacturing joint venture with Novartis and renamed its Sofina cosmetics brand Prestige Cosmetics. Additionally in 2002 Kao acquired John Frieda Professional Hair Care through Andrew Jergens. (Andrew Jergens became Kao Brands in 2004.)

In 2004 Goto became chairman and Motoki Ozaki was promoted from president of the Global Fabric and Home Care division to president and CEO. The same year Kao broke off talks to purchase Kanebo.

EXECUTIVES

Chairman: Takuya Goto
President, CEO, and Director: Motoki Ozaki
SEVP, Corporate Functions and Director:
 Toshio Hoshino
EVP, Global Consumer Products and Director:
 Takahiko Kagawa
EVP, Global Procurement and Director: Akio Tsuruoka
EVP, Greater China and Director: Nobuatsu Higuchi
EVP, Global R&D and Director: Naotake Takaishi
**Executive Officer, Legal and Compliance — Global and
 Global Communications and Director:**
 Shunichi Nakagawa
Executive Officer, Global Accounting and Finance:
 Shinichi Mita
President and CEO, Kao Hanbai and Director:
 Toshio Takayama
**President, International Business — Consumer
 Products and Director:** Norihiko Takagi
**Executive Officer, Global Production and Engineering
 and Director:** Takuo Goto
**President, Global Feminine and Baby Care and
 Director:** Hiroshi Kanda
President, Chemical Company and Director:
 Toshihide Saito
VP, Global Production and Engineering:
 Yoshitaka Nakatani
VP, Global Marketing Service: Yoshiiku Hirai
VP, Global R&D: Toshiharu Numata
VP, Global R&D: Akio Kimura
Auditors: Deloitte Touche Tohmatsu

LOCATIONS

HQ: Kao Corporation
 14-10 Nihonbashi Kayabacho, 1-chome, Chuo-ku,
 Tokyo 103-8210, Japan
Phone: +81-3-3660-7111 **Fax:** +81-3-3660-8978
Web: www.kao.co.jp

Kao sells its products primarily in Asia but also in Australia, Europe, North America, and South Africa.

2005 Sales

	% of total
Asia & Oceania	
Japan	74
Other countries	8
Europe	9
North America	9
Total	**100**

PRODUCTS/OPERATIONS

2005 Sales

	% of total
Consumer products	74
Chemical products	18
Prestige cosmetics	8
Total	**100**

Selected Products

Fatty chemicals and edible oils (fatty acids, fatty
 alcohols, fatty amines, glycerin)
Hygiene and bath products (sanitary napkins, disposable
 diapers, bath additives)
Laundry and cleaning products (laundry detergents,
 laundry finishers, kitchen and other household
 detergents, fabric softeners)
Personal care products and cosmetics (soap, body
 cleansers, shampoos, conditioners, hair care
 products, cosmetics and skin care products,
 toothpastes, toothbrushes)

Selected Brand Names

Attack (laundry detergent)
Ban (deodorant)
Bioré (skin care)
Bub (shower gel)
Econa (cooking oil)
Emal (laundry detergent)
Family Pure (dishwashing detergent)
Guhl Ikebana (hair care)
Jergens (skin care)
Laurier (sanitary napkins)
Merries (disposable diapers)
Prestige (cosmetics)
Quickle Wiper (electrostatic duster)

COMPETITORS

Alticor
Colgate-Palmolive
Johnson & Johnson
Kanebo
Kimberly-Clark
Lion Corporation
Nisshin Oillio
Pfizer
Procter & Gamble
Revlon International
Shiseido
Unicharm
Unilever

HISTORICAL FINANCIALS

Company Type: Public

Income Statement

FYE: March 31

	REVENUE ($ mil.)	NET INCOME ($ mil.)	NET PROFIT MARGIN	EMPLOYEES
3/05	8,711	671	7.7%	19,143
3/04	8,544	619	7.2%	19,330
3/03	7,220	521	7.2%	19,807
3/02	6,325	454	7.2%	19,923
3/01	6,504	470	7.2%	19,068
3/00	8,027	494	6.2%	16,088
3/99	7,763	291	3.8%	15,900
3/98	6,818	184	2.7%	17,100
3/97	7,281	231	3.2%	18,700
3/96	7,791	229	2.9%	18,900
Annual Growth	1.2%	12.7%	—	0.1%

2005 Year-End Financials

Debt ratio: 0.3%
Return on equity: 16.3%
Cash ($ mil.): 710
Current ratio: 1.37
Long-term debt ($ mil.): 13

Net Income History

Exchange: Tokyo

Karstadt Quelle

Seems like unification has caught on in Germany. Karstadt Quelle is the product of a merger between Germany's biggest department store group, Karstadt, and #1 mail-order firm, Quelle. It operates about 180 department stores (Karstadt, Hertie, Wertheim, Alsterhaus, and KaDeWe) and about 300 specialty stores. Karstadt Quelle is a leader in travel services and has expanded into real estate and financial services. Schickedanz-Holding, owned by the Riedel and Herl families, has a stake of more than 50% in Karstadt Quelle. The company's 2004 plan to divest 77 of its Karstadt stores and to sell all of its specialty shops was rejected by trade union officials, whose concern is the nearly 30,000 jobs that may be lost.

Karstadt Quelle has reshaped itself for a new Germany. The group has reorganized into four principal business segments: retail stores, mail order, services, and real estate. The German retailer is attempting to raise capital, via a rights offering, to fund the restructuring, but is meeting opposition from shareholders. Karstadt Quelle is also shedding noncore assets to raise funds. To that end, the company has agreed to sell its 82% stake in Karstadt Coffee back to Starbucks Corporation. The business operates 37 Starbucks coffee shops in Germany. In early 2005 Karstadt also agreed to sell portions of its department store and logistics business to Deutsche Post for $261 million. A few weeks later, it also sold its shipping and mail-order delivery operations to Deutsche Post for about $257 million.

With a whopping 50% of the department store market, Karstadt Quelle is prevalent in Germany.

Under the Quelle and Neckermann brands, the company mails out 730 million catalogs per year all over Europe. Those are supplemented by nearly 180 specialty catalogs, which cover women's fashion, baby products, kitchenware, and children's clothing, among other things.

The service companies of Karstadt Quelle provide consulting, information, financial, and travel services. With airline operator Deutsche Lufthansa, Karstadt Quelle shares a 50/50 joint venture in Thomas Cook AG, making it the #3 travel services company in the world (behind American Express and Carlson Wagonlit) and the second-largest in Europe (after TUI).

In 2005 the Schickedanz family increased its share in the company from 38% to more than 50%, adding to speculation that the family has plans to split up the company and sell off separate parts of it in order to pay off debts to German private bank Sal Oppenheim.

In April 2005 CEO Christoph Achenbach resigned abruptly in the midst of the company's restructuring. Mr. Achenbach had served as CEO for only ten months. A month later, Thomas Middelhoff filled the spot and immediately announced plans to streamline the company's structure and speed up the refurbishment of its Karstadt department stores as well as boost catalog sales.

HISTORY

In 1881 Rudolph Karstadt opened a store in Mecklenburg, Germany, selling candy, apparel, and fabric. His store was one of Germany's first department stores; it offered separate departments for merchandise and offered low, fixed prices and cash-only sales. In 1885 Theodor Althoff took control of his mother's haberdashery, wool, and linen shop in Westfalen, Germany. He adopted the same business model as Karstadt.

Rudolph Karstadt AG was founded in 1920 and soon merged with Althoff's business. Six years later Karstadt founded EPA Einheitspreis, an American-style discount store. The company grew rapidly, reaching 89 outlets in 1929. But overexpansion and a worldwide depression hurt Karstadt, and it found itself in financial trouble by 1931. With the help of a bank consortium, the company restructured that year.

Karstadt operated 67 stores in 1939, but by the end of WWII, only 45 remained in West Germany and most were heavily damaged. (The company lost the remainder to East Germany and the Iron Curtain.) Postwar economic reform and reconstruction boosted personal incomes; as a result, Karstadt's sales rose too. In 1948 the retailer was accepted into "Interkontinentale Warenhausgruppe" (the "Intercontinental Department Store Group").

In 1971 Karstadt and mail-order firm Quelle founded travel firm TransEuropa-Reisen, which became KS-Touristik-Beteiligungs in 1972. (Karstadt sold its share in 1976.) In 1976 Karstadt became a major shareholder in Germany's third-largest mail-order company, Neckermann Versand, which was restructured into a public limited company. The next year Karstadt upped its stake to 51% of Neckermann Versand, and it controlled virtually all of the company by 1984. (Neckermann Versand travel subsidiary NUR Neckermann+Reisen became NUR Touristik in 1982.) Karstadt also founded Runners Point in 1984.

The company in 1988 opened a distribution center in Unna, Germany. When the wall came down, bringing trade barriers with it, Karstadt established cooperation agreements with 10 Centrum and four Magnet department stores in the former East Germany. The same sort of agreement was set up with GUM department store in Moscow in 1992.

Karstadt opened Optic Point Warenhandelsgesellschaft in 1993 and acquired Hertie Waren- und Kaufhaus in 1994, making it by far Germany's largest department store group. In 1995 the company extended its travel empire with the acquisition of 51% of business travel chain Euro Lloyd Reiseburo from Lufthansa. Euro Lloyd went online the next year.

Retail group Schickedanz bought 20% of Karstadt in 1997. A year later Karstadt formed travel group C&N Touristic with Lufthansa (regulations forced the companies to sell Euro Lloyd, which was picked up by Swiss-based Kuoni). Karstadt also transferred its NUR Touristik operations to C&N Touristic.

In 1999 the company purchased mail-order company Quelle from Schickedanz-Holding and became Karstadt Quelle, one of Europe's largest retailers. Amidst European travel industry consolidation in 2000, C&N Touristic bought Thomas Cook from rival Preussag AG (now TUI) and took on the Thomas Cook name. The move made it the second-largest travel company in Europe and #3 in the world.

In 2001 Karstadt Quelle's major restructuring plan included almost 4,000 job cuts.

In September 2002, the company reorganized into four subholding companies for each of its four business segments: retail stores, mail order, real estate, and services.

EXECUTIVES

CEO: Thomas Middelhoff, age 52
CFO and Head of Mail Order Division: Harald Pinger, age 45
Head and Director, Corporate Communications: Jörg Howe
Director, Corporate Communications: Thomas Diehl
Director, Foreign Offices, Logistics, Personnel, Environment and Corporate Policy, and Synergies: Helmut Merkel, age 55
Director, Human Resources: Matthias Bellmann, age 52
Director, Investor Relations: Detlef Neveling
Director, Logistics and IT, Neckermann Versand and Quelle AG: Ulrich Wiggers
Director, Marketing and Sales, Neckermann Versand and Quelle AG: Gebhard Stammler
Director, Sales and Marketing: Thomas Freude
Director, Specialty Mail Order, Neckermann Versand and Quelle AG: Leo Günther Kraftsik
Director, Technology and Consumer Durables, Neckermann Versand and Quelle AG: Michael Badke
Director, Textile, Neckermann Versand and Quelle AG: Helmut Klier
Group Secretary: Sylvia Ehlert
Director, Human Resources Management Board, Quelle: Georg Suso Sutter
Head of Public Relations: Stephanie Venus
Auditors: BDO Deutsche Warentreuhand AG

LOCATIONS

HQ: Karstadt Quelle AG
Theodor-Althoff-Strasse 2, D-45133 Essen, Germany
Phone: +49-20-17271   **Fax:** +49-20-1727-5216
Web: www.karstadtquelle.com

Karstadt Quelle has operations in Austria, Belgium, Eastern Europe, France, Germany, the Netherlands, Scandinavia, Spain, and Switzerland.

PRODUCTS/OPERATIONS

2004 Sales

	% of total
Mail order	50
Retail stores	38
Services	8
Real estate	4
Total	**100**

Selected Operations

Mail Order
  Neckermann
  Quelle
Department Stores
  Alsterhaus
  Hertie
  Karstadt
  KaDeWe
  Wertheim
Specialty Retail
  Runners Point and Golf House (sports)
  SinnLeffers and Wehmeyer (fashion)
  Schaulandt/Schürmann and WOM World of Music (multimedia)
  LeBuffet (restaurants)
Services
  INTELLIUM (information technology)
  KarstadtQuelle Bank (financial services)
  Quelle Versicherungen (insurance)
  Thomas Cook Tourism Group (50% joint venture)
Real Estate
  KARSTADT Immobilien

COMPETITORS

American Express	H&M
AVA AG	Lidl & Schwarz Stiftung
C&A	METRO AG
Carlson Wagonlit	Otto
Carrefour	TUI
Douglas Holding	Wal-Mart
Edeka Zentrale	

HISTORICAL FINANCIALS

Company Type: Public

Income Statement

FYE: December 31

	REVENUE ($ mil.)	NET INCOME ($ mil.)	NET PROFIT MARGIN	EMPLOYEES
12/04	18,342	(2,225)	—	92,546
12/03	19,167	135	0.7%	100,956
12/02	16,575	170	1.0%	104,536
12/01	14,232	208	1.5%	112,141
12/00	14,350	234	1.6%	113,120
12/99	14,948	73	0.5%	113,490
12/98	10,884	119	1.1%	89,399
12/97	13,272	92	0.7%	94,463
12/96	15,482	38	0.2%	99,991
12/95	16,756	76	0.5%	105,129
Annual Growth	**1.0%**	**—**	**—**	**(1.4%)**

2004 Year-End Financials

Debt ratio: 601.8%   Current ratio: 1.36
Return on equity: —   Long-term debt ($ mil.): 4,532
Cash ($ mil.): 677

Net Income History

German: KAR

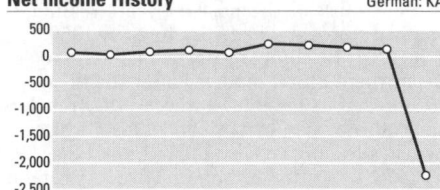

| | 12/95 | 12/96 | 12/97 | 12/98 | 12/99 | 12/00 | 12/01 | 12/02 | 12/03 | 12/04 |

Kingfisher plc

Home improvement is netting the big catch in retail these days, and Kingfisher is angling for it. Kingfisher operates a network of more than 550 home improvement stores in more than 10 countries, mostly in Europe, where it is the largest DIY retailer. The company's do-it-yourself (DIY) portfolio includes France's Castorama, which merged with Kingfisher's B&Q chain. Kingfisher's other DIY stores include Brico Dépôt in France and 50%-owned Koçtas in Turkey. Kingfisher sold its chain of about 700 Superdrug stores (even though it was the UK's #2 drugstore chain, behind Boots The Chemists) in 2001, and it spun off its Woolworths and other general merchandise stores in a public offering in August 2001.

Kingfisher also owns 21% of Hornbach Holding, the parent company of Germany's Hornbach-Baumarkt chain. Kingfisher operates 22 B&Qs in China (the Beijing B&Q is the world's biggest) and plans to operate 75 stores in that country by 2009 (it is additionally setting up a store in South Korea). In 2005 the company announced its intent to purchase its biggest competitor in Asia, OBI Asia, which would add 13 stores to its stable.

Russia, too, is on Kingfisher's expansion list. The company plans to enter Russia in the next two years with the goal of opening some 50 stores that will operate under the Castorama banner. To that end, Kingfisher has appointed a former IKEA executive, Peter Partma, as the country manager for Castorama Russia. Kingfisher also plans to increase its Polish store count to more than 60 by 2009.

In addition to the Web sites of its banners, Kingfisher reels in more business online through Screwfix Direct, which operates a Web site that offers next-day delivery of tools and other hardware products. Screwfix in 2005, however, came into legal troubles for employing illegal immigrants.

In 2005 The Home Depot announced that it was considering a buyout of the company, but added provisions including the requirement that the company sell off its loss-making French Castorama business. This, in combination with a recent investment by Warren Buffett, through Berkshire Hathaway insurance subsidiary Geico, has led to rumors that the company is seeking suitors.

HISTORY

The beginning of Kingfisher is directly tied to the former US Woolworth chain (now Foot Locker). With the success of F.W. Woolworth general merchandise stores in the US, founder Frank Woolworth expanded overseas, first to Canada, then in 1909 to Liverpool, England. By 1914 Woolworth's UK subsidiaries had 31 stores.

Growing quickly, the company went public in 1931, with its US parent retaining a 53% stake. It spent most of the postwar years rebuilding bombed stores and had 762 stores by 1950.

In 1967 the company opened its first Woolco Department Store, modeled after the US Woolco stores of its parent. However, other retailers had cut into sales, and by 1968 it lost its place as Britain's leading retailer to Marks and Spencer. In 1973 it opened Shoppers World, a catalog showroom. It made its first takeover in 1980, buying B&Q, a chain of 40 do-it-yourself stores.

An investment group acquired Woolworth in 1982 using the vehicle Paternoster Stores. (The US parent sold its stake in Woolworth.) The company, renamed Woolworth Holdings, closed unprofitable Woolworth stores and sold its Shoppers World stores in 1983 and its Ireland Woolworth stores in 1984. It also acquired Comet, a UK home electronics chain, and continued to expand B&Q.

Two years later all of its F.W. Woolworth stores were renamed Woolworths, and food and clothing lines were abandoned. Also in 1986 the company sold its Woolco stores and bought record and tape distributor Record Merchandisers (later renamed Entertainment UK). The next year Woolworth Holdings acquired Superdrug, a chain of 297 discount drugstores. Adding to its Superdrug chain, in 1988 the firm acquired and integrated two UK pharmacy chains: 110-store Tip Top Drugstores and 145-store Share Drug.

To reflect its growing diversity of businesses, the company was renamed Kingfisher in 1989. Also that year it bought drug retailer Medicare, with 86 stores. Expanding further into electronics, in 1993 Kingfisher acquired Darty, with 130 stores. Adding music retail to music distribution, that year the firm founded Music and Video Club (MVC).

In 1998 Kingfisher increased its presence in France by taking control of electronics chain BUT. It also merged its B&Q chain with the do-it-yourself stores of France's Castorama in 1998 and gained a 55% stake in the new group (though as part of the deal Kingfisher received only 50% of the group's voting rights).

Following the lead of rival Dixons, in 1999 Kingfisher launched its own free Internet access service in France called Libertysurf. Soon thereafter, Libertysurf acquired 70% of Objectif Net and its Web site, Nomade.fr.

Kingfisher sold its 35% stake in Libertysurf to Italian ISP Tiscali in 2001, and it sold its Superdrug chain to Kruidvat, a Dutch health and beauty group. Kingfisher demerged Woolworths Group the same year in a public offering. With Woolies went electronic entertainment companies EUK, MVC, VCI, and Streets Online. Also in 2001 Kingfisher bought 25% plus one share of the unlisted ordinary voting shares of Germany's Hornbach Holding, a family-owned group that owns 80% of one of Germany's leading DIY chains, Hornbach-Baumarkt.

In 2002 Kingfisher acquired the remainder of Castorama and bought 17.4% of Hornbach's listed non-voting preference shares (which with the 2001 purchase represents a 21.2% stake in Hornbach).

CEO Geoffrey Mulcahy stepped down in 2002 and was replaced by Gerry Murphy, formerly CEO for Carlton (now ITV plc), in 2003. Kingfisher sold its 20 retail parks for $1.1 billion to a consortium that includes real estate firms Pillar Property and Capital & Regional Properties the same year. Also in 2003 Kingfisher sold ProMarkt, with about 190 stores in Germany, to its former owners, Michael and Matthias Wegert.

To focus on DIY, Kingfisher floated its electrical businesses as a new company, Kesa Electricals, in 2003. Kesa Electricals includes Darty, France's leading electrical retailer with more than 180 stores, and Comet, with some 260 stores in the UK. Kingfisher sold two home improvement chains that year. Réno-Dépôt, which operates about 20 home-improvement stores in Canada, was sold to RONA. NOMI, with about 40 stores in Poland, was acquired by Enterprise Investors.

EXECUTIVES

Chairman: Sir Francis H. Mackay, age 61, $411,725 pay
Deputy Chairman: John Nelson, age 58, $79,195 pay
CEO: Gerry Murphy, age 50, $2,143,598 pay
Group Finance Director: Duncan Tatton-Brown, age 40, $806,256 pay
Group Human Resources Director: Tony Stanworth, age 54
CEO, B&Q: Ian Cheshire, age 46, $847,119 pay
CEO, Castorama France: Phillippe Tible, age 53
CEO, UK Trade: George Adams, age 48
Director, Communications: Ian Harding, age 40
Managing Director, Screwfix: John Allan
Secretary: Helen Jones, age 49
Head, External Communications: Nigel Cope
Head, Investor Relations: Loraine Woodhouse
Country Manager, Castorama Russia: Peter Partma, age 34
Assistant Company Secretary: Julie Wilson
Group Property Director: Terry Hartwell, age 48
Group Chief Information Officer: Paul Worthington, age 42
Group Strategy, Development and Planning Director: Régis Schultz, age 37
Chief Executive, Brico Dépôt: Patrick Langlade, age 57
Auditors: PricewaterhouseCoopers LLP

LOCATIONS

HQ: Kingfisher plc
3 Sheldon Square, Paddington,
London W2 6PX, United Kingdom
Phone: +44-20-7372-8008   **Fax:** +44-20-7644-1001
Web: www.kingfisher.co.uk

Kingfisher operates mostly in the UK, but also in China, France, Ireland, Italy, Poland, South Korea, Spain, Taiwan, and Turkey.

2005 Sales

	% of total
UK & Ireland	56
France	34
Other	10
Total	**100**

PRODUCTS/OPERATIONS

2005 Sales

	% of total
Home improvement	85
Electrical & furniture	15
Total	**100**

Selected Operations

B&Q (UK, Ireland, China, Taiwan)
B&Q Korea
Brico Dépôt (France)
Brico Stock (Spain)
Castorama (France, Poland, Italy)
Koçtas (50%, Turkey)
Screwfix Direct (UK)

COMPETITORS

BMB Buildbase
Focus
Grafton Group
Homebase
METRO AG
MPS
Saint-Gobain Building Distribution
Tengelmann
Travis Perkins
Wolseley

HISTORICAL FINANCIALS

Company Type: Public

Income Statement

FYE: January 31

	REVENUE ($ mil.)	NET INCOME ($ mil.)	NET PROFIT MARGIN	EMPLOYEES
1/05	14,447	885	6.1%	70,811
1/04	15,981	417	2.6%	81,096
1/03	17,735	281	1.6%	99,879
1/02	15,893	(352)	—	119,002
1/01	17,744	608	3.4%	134,061
1/00	17,484	677	3.9%	118,416
1/99	12,282	720	5.9%	78,133
1/98	10,458	631	6.0%	83,364
1/97	9,310	445	4.8%	77,254
1/96	7,958	347	4.4%	75,501
Annual Growth	6.8%	11.0%	—	(0.7%)

2005 Year-End Financials

Debt ratio: 15.7%
Return on equity: 10.2%
Cash ($ mil.): 288
Current ratio: 0.94
Long-term debt ($ mil.): 1,459

Net Income History

London: KGF

| | 1/96 | 1/97 | 1/98 | 1/99 | 1/00 | 1/01 | 1/02 | 1/03 | 1/04 | 1/05 |

Kirin Brewery

A mythical eastern unicorn called a *kirin* — a symbol of good fortune — brands the Kirin beer bottle. But Tokyo-based Kirin Brewery Company, one of Japan's — and the world's — largest brewers, may need more than luck in its battle with archrival Asahi Breweries, Japan's top brewer by a razor-thin margin. Kirin makes several leading brews in Japan, including Kirin Lager and Ichiban Shibori. Kirin Tanrei is Japan's leading happo-shu (low-malt) beer. Other beverages include canned coffee and tea, fruit juices, and soft drinks. Also active in floriculture and pharmaceuticals, Kirin is part of the Mitsubishi *keiretsu*.

Kirin also sells beer in Europe and owns more than 45% of Lion Nathan. The company also owns about 25% of China-based Dalian Daxue Brewery. In reciprocal deals with Anheuser-Busch, Kirin brews Budweiser beer in Japan while Anheuser-Busch makes Kirin brands in the US. Kirin has negotiated exclusive rights with Pernod Ricard and Diageo to distribute Chivas Regal in Japan.

In addition, Kirin Beverage offers Tropicana fruit juices. Facing declining beer sales, it has high hopes for its chuhai fruit-flavored cocktail drink. Kirin also is looking for growth from the "shochu" distilled liquor market with its Pure Blue brand and from selling Haizhu beer in China.

Kirin has a number of other businesses, including a joint venture with Danone and Mitsubishi to sell mineral water as well as flower growing and food processing operations. Its pharmaceuticals unit has developed two popular

blood treatments. Kirin plans to expand its medical sales force and more than double revenues from its pharmaceutical business by 2010. As part of that initiative, the company claims to have produced a cow immune to mad cow disease that will assist in the research of medicines for hepatitis, peneumonia, and rheumatism.

Other businesses include dairy, dietary supplements, tomato-based foods, and processed meats. Its US-based Gemini Science division develops pharmaceuticals. Kirin also owns 15% of Philippine food and beverage firm San Miguel Corporation.

HISTORY

American William Copeland went to Yokohama, Japan, in 1864 and five years later established the Spring Valley Brewery, the first in Japan, to provide beer for foreign nationals. Lacking funds to continue the brewery, Copeland closed it in 1884. The next year a group of foreign and Japanese businessmen reopened it as Japan Brewery. The business created the Kirin label in 1888 and was soon profitable.

The operation was run primarily by Americans and Europeans at first, but by 1907 Japanese workers had filled the ranks and adopted the Kirin Brewery Company name. Sales plummeted during WWII when the government limited brewing output. After the war, the US occupation forces inadvertently assisted Kirin when they split Dai Nippon Brewery (Kirin's main competitor) into two companies (Asahi and Sapporo Breweries) while leaving Kirin intact. The company became Japan's leading brewer during the 1950s.

During the 1970s it introduced several soft drinks and in 1972 branched into hard liquor through a joint venture with Seagram (Kirin-Seagram).

The firm bought several Coca-Cola bottling operations in New England and Japan in the 1980s. Kirin also entered the pharmaceuticals business, in part through a joint venture with US-based Amgen. In 1988 the brewer signed an agreement with Molson to produce Kirin beer for the North American market. In 1989 Kirin bought Napa Valley's Raymond Vineyards.

In 1991 Kirin formed a partnership to market Tropicana drinks in Japan. It also entered an alliance with Sankyo (Japan's #2 drug company) in 1991 to market Kirin's medication for anemia, which it had developed with Amgen.

Chairman Hideyo Motoyama resigned in 1993 after four company executives were arrested for allegedly paying a group of racketeers who had threatened to disrupt Kirin's annual meeting. Joint venture Kirin-Amgen won the rights to make thrombopoietin (TPO), a blood platelet growth stimulator in 1995.

Yasuhiro Satoh became president of Kirin in 1996. The brewer moved into China that year through an agreement with China Resources (Shenyang) Snowflake Brewery. To brew its beers in the US, the company formed Kirin Brewery of America, also in 1996.

In response to losing market share to Asahi, Kirin cut its workforce in 1998 and introduced Tanrei, a cheaper, low-malt beer that quickly captured half its market. Building on its presence in China, Kirin bought 45% of brewer Lion Nathan (based in Australia and New Zealand) for $742.5 million that year. It became a licensed brewer of Anheuser-Busch in 1999.

Like other Japanese brewers, Kirin struggled against dwindling demand for its most expensive brews in 2000. In 2002 Kirin bought 15% of

Philippine food and drink giant San Miguel for about $530 million as part of its plan to overcome slow growth domestically through expanded global interests. It also boosted ties with beverage giant Pernod Ricard by purchasing 32% of SIFA, a French food services firm, for an estimated $155 million. (The deal gave Kirin a 3% indirect interest in Pernod Ricard.) In 2002 Kirin also formed Flower Season Ltd., a joint venture with Dole Food Company to sell flowers to Japanese retailers. Also in 2002 Kirin launched its new Pure Blue brand of "shochu" distilled liquor.

Kirin said in 2003 it planned to sell Four Roses Kentucky Straight Bourbon in the US with the help of Southern Wine & Spirits of America. The brand had been sold exclusively as an export since 1959. Kirin purchased the Four Roses brand from Diageo.

EXECUTIVES

President: Koichiro Aramaki
Managing Executive Officer: Kazuyasu Kato
Managing Executive Officer: Akira Negami
Managing Executive Officer: Shozo Sawada
Managing Executive Officer: Takeshi Shigenaga
Managing Executive Officer: Kazuhiro Sato
Managing Executive Officer: Takeshi Shimazu
SVP, Pharmaceutical Division: Ken Yamazumi
VP, Pharmaceutical Research Laboratories: Junichi Koumegawa
President, Agribio Business Division: Yoshiyuki Matsushima
President, International Beer Division: Hitoshi Oshima
President, Nutrient Food and Feed Division: Yoshihiko Kitamura
President, Pharmaceutical Division: Katsuhiko Asano
General Manager, Corporate Communications Department: Hideo Mori
General Manager, Marketing Department, Sales and Marketing Division: Hitoshi Maeda
General Manager, Personnel Department: Tomohiro Mune
General Manager, Planning Department, Sales and Marketing Division: Kenichiro Kanegae
General Manager, Production and Quality Control Department: Koichi Matsuzawa
General Manager, Research and Development Department: Kazuo Yoshioka
Auditors: Asahi & Co.

LOCATIONS

HQ: Kirin Brewery Company, Limited
10-1 Shinkawa 2-chome, Chuo-ku,
Tokyo 104-8288, Japan
Phone: +81-3-5540-3411   **Fax:** +81-3-5540-3547
US HQ: 2400 Broadway, Ste. 240,
Santa Monica, CA 90404
US Phone: 310-829-2400   **US Fax:** 310-829-0424
Web: www.kirin.co.jp

Kirin Brewery Company owns 11 breweries, one hop center, a pharmaceutical plant, seven laboratories, and 10 regional sales offices in Japan. The company has subsidiaries and affiliates in Asia, Australia, Europe, and the US.

PRODUCTS/OPERATIONS

2004 Sales

	% of total
Alcoholic beverages	51
Soft drinks	30
Pharmaceuticals	5
Other	14
Total	**100**

Selected Products and Brands

Beverages
  Kirin
    Amino Supli
    Gogono-Kocha
    Ichiban Shibori
    Lager
    Tanrei
    Chu-Hi Hyoketsu
    Mugi Shochu Pure Blue
  Chivas Regal (licensed)
  Four Roses (licensed)
  Franzia (licensed)

Other
  Agribio (Kirin carnation, mum, and
    petunia; kalanchoe)
  Pharmaceuticals (ESPO glycoprotein, GRAN
    white-blood cell stimulant)
  Restaurants and Food (Giraffe, Kirin City, Koiwai Pure
    Butter, Makiba Milk, Tavola Baccano, Tsubu-Tsubu
    Yasai Ketchup)
  Yeast-related (Brewer's yeast, GBF, high-moleculated
    chitosan, Kirin Chlorella 5.5, mushroom-growing
    medium, RNA, yeast extract)

Selected Operations and Subsidiaries

Agribio (floriculture and potatoes)
  Flowergate Co., Ltd.
  Hiljo B.V.
  Qingdao International Seeds Co., Ltd.
  Southern Glasshouse Produce Ltd. (UK)
  Tokita Seed Co., Ltd.
  Twyford International, Inc.
  Verde Co., Ltd.
  Wintech, Inc.

Beer
  Heineken Japan Co., Ltd.
  KYC Co., Ltd.
  Lion Nathan Ltd. (45%, Australia and New Zealand)

Liquors and Wines
  Raymond Vineyard and Cellar, Inc. (US)

Pharmaceuticals
  Gemini Science, Inc.
  Kirin-Amgen, Inc.

Restaurants and Food
  Cafe Sebol Japon
  Kirin City Co., Ltd.
  Nagano Tomato Co., Ltd.
  Soft Drinks
  The Coca-Cola Bottling Company of Northern New
    England, Inc. (US)
  Kinki Coca-Cola Bottling Co., Ltd.

Yeast-related
  Cosmo Foods Co., Ltd.
  Marinenet Co., Ltd.
  Nihon Fine Foods Co., Ltd.

COMPETITORS

Allied Domecq	Molson Coors
Anheuser-Busch	Nippon Beet Sugar
Asahi Breweries	Novartis
Asia Pacific Breweries	Pabst
Carlsberg	Pepsi Bottling
Chugai	Red Bull
Diageo	SABMiller
FEMSA	San Miguel
Foster's	Sapporo
Gallo	Snow Brand Milk
Heineken	Suntory Ltd.
InBev	Taiwan Tobacco & Wine
ITOCHU	Takara
Kokubu & Co.	Tsingtao
LVMH	Yanjing
Mercian	YUM!
Miller Brewing	

HISTORICAL FINANCIALS

Company Type: Public

Income Statement

FYE: December 31

	REVENUE ($ mil.)	NET INCOME ($ mil.)	NET PROFIT MARGIN	EMPLOYEES
12/04	11,745	471	4.0%	22,160
12/03	10,882	302	2.8%	22,852
12/02	9,486	271	2.9%	23,070
12/01	8,341	175	2.1%	—
12/00	9,353	287	3.1%	—
12/99	8,860	325	3.7%	—
12/98	7,735	234	3.0%	—
12/97	6,649	195	2.9%	—
12/96	7,598	296	3.9%	—
12/95	8,652	389	4.5%	—
Annual Growth	3.5%	2.1%	—	(2.0%)

2004 Year-End Financials

Debt ratio: 27.8%
Return on equity: 6.0%
Cash ($ mil.): 1,761
Current ratio: 1.40
Long-term debt ($ mil.): 2,290

No. of shares (mil.): 966
Dividends
  Yield: 0.5%
  Payout: 10.4%
Market value ($ mil.): 9,563

Stock History

NASDAQ (SC): KNBWY

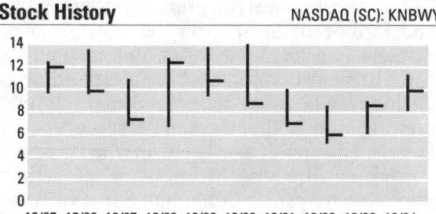

12/95 12/96 12/97 12/98 12/99 12/00 12/01 12/02 12/03 12/04

	STOCK PRICE ($) FY Close	P/E High/Low	Earnings	PER SHARE ($) Dividends	Book Value
12/04	9.90	23 17	0.48	0.05	8.53
12/03	8.59	29 20	0.31	0.10	7.77
12/02	6.01	31 20	0.27	0.09	6.52
12/01	7.00	59 40	0.17	0.10	0.60
12/00	8.78	50 31	0.28	0.11	0.65
12/99	10.78	43 30	0.32	0.10	0.69
12/98	12.38	58 31	0.22	0.05	0.62
12/97	7.34	57 36	0.19	0.05	0.55
12/96	9.85	48 35	0.28	0.09	0.61
12/95	11.95	33 26	0.37	0.13	0.67
Annual Growth	(2.1%)	— —	2.9%	(10.1%)	32.8%

KLM Royal Dutch Airlines

Venerable KLM Royal Dutch Airlines is the world's oldest international airline, and it's now part of Europe's largest. Through its partnerships (including a long-time codeshare agreement with Northwest), the airline provides passenger and cargo services to some 350 destinations in almost 75 countries. With its primary hub located in Amsterdam, the airline carries nearly 16 million passengers and about 490,000 tons of cargo annually. KLM operates a fleet of more than 210 aircraft, mostly Boeings. KLM also operates regional carrier KLM cityhopper. The company merged with European competitor Air France in 2004.

Part of KLM's woes had been rooted in its inability to find a European partner — until Air France came along.

In 2003 the two airlines agreed to merge to form a joint holding company in a deal that would create Europe's largest airline. The new holding company, Air France-KLM, is 44% owned by the French government and 17% controlled by Dutch interests including the Dutch government (about 6%). Employees and the public hold the remainder. Remaining shares of KLM have been traded for Air France stock, and KLM has been delisted.

The new deal did not come in time to prevent the airline from seeking to cut some 3,000 jobs (about 10% of its workforce) in 2003.

The airlines have continued to operate independently, even on competing routes, but they have been working on shifting routes and streamlining redundant systems. Also, they are positioning themselves against low-fare upstarts around the continent.

KLM, along with US carriers Northwest Airlines and Continental Airlines, has joined the SkyTeam marketing alliance of which Air France is already a leading member. The alliance serves some 500 destinations across 110 countries.

HISTORY

Flight lieutenant Albert Plesman founded Koninklijke Luchtvaart Maatschappij voor Nederland en Kolonien (Royal Airline Company for the Netherlands and Colonies) in The Hague in 1919. Queen Wilhelmina granted the honorary title of *koninklijke* (or royal), and Dutch businessmen financed the venture. Early passengers — who flew in an open cockpit with the pilot — were issued leather jackets, goggles, gloves, and parachutes.

Under Plesman's leadership KLM established service between Amsterdam and London, Copenhagen, Brussels, and Paris in the early 1920s. The airline initiated the longest air route in the world, from Amsterdam to Indonesia, in 1928 and extended its European network in the years before WWII. Hitler's occupation of Holland shut down KLM's European operations in 1940; the Germans imprisoned Plesman from 1940 to 1942, bombing or confiscating two-thirds of KLM's planes.

After the war Plesman quickly re-established commercial service, using 47 US military surplus airplanes, and in 1946 KLM became the first continental European airline to offer scheduled service from Europe to the US. Plesman died in 1953. KLM began trading on the NYSE in 1957.

KLM established NLM Dutch Airlines in 1966 (renamed cityhopper in 1976) to provide commuter flights within the Netherlands. The airline addressed overcapacity problems in the 1970s by converting the rear portions of its 747s to cargo space.

In 1988 KLM bought 40% of Dutch charter airline Transavia (increased to 80% in 1991) and began looking for partners to help it compete in key markets. It bought 10% of Covia Partnership, owner and operator of United Airlines' Apollo computer reservation system (1988), and invested in Wings Holdings, a company formed to buy Northwest Airlines (1989). In 1991 KLM bought 35% of Air Littoral, a French regional airline, and 40% of ALM Antillean Airlines.

Airline deregulation in Europe spawned numerous efforts to develop strategic relationships. A deal giving KLM and British Airways 20% each of Belgium's national airline, Sabena, fell apart in 1990, and KLM-British Airways merger talks collapsed in early 1992. In 1994, when Northwest recovered from four straight losses, KLM bought brewer Foster's 6% stake in the airline.

American Airlines and British Airways invited KLM in 1996 to join a proposed alliance, which would combine transatlantic flights and marketing. However, the plan would have required KLM to sell its Northwest stake. That year KLM executed a buyback of about 13% of KLM stock from the Dutch government; it also took a 25% stake in Kenya Airways.

In 1998 KLM sold back its 19% stake in Northwest Airlines for about $1.1 billion, while forming a strategic partnership with the carrier. The deal resolved a feud stemming from KLM's attempt to increase its Northwest stake to 25%.

Meanwhile, in 1997 KLM and Italian carrier Alitalia announced a partnership that would later evolve into the integration of their fleets. Although it remained an independent company, KLM contributed its fleet and personnel to the operation, as did Alitalia.

In 2000 KLM's low-fare European service, buzz, began service from its hub at London's Stansted airport. Also that year KLM terminated its passenger and cargo joint operations with Alitalia, citing problems with the operations of a new airport near Milan and a delay in the sale of the Italian government's stake in Alitalia.

The airline cut back its flights in the wake of the September 11, 2001, terrorist attacks on the US in anticipation of reduced demand for transatlantic service. Early in 2002, KLM began talks with Air France over forming an alliance. Those discussions soon turned to talks of a merger, and by late 2003 the two carriers began formulating their plan to form Europe's largest single carrier.

The European Commission initiated an investigation in potential anti-competition elements of the merger in 2004, potentially delaying the roll-out of Europe's new giant airline. To appease the Commission, the airlines had to give up crucial slots at some of Europe's busiest hubs. Their cooperation paid off, and the Commission approved the merger on the condition the airlines give up 94 slots per day to ensure a competitive environment.

Before it found its European partner, the Dutch carrier was relying on KLM cityhopper to cover smaller markets, and low-fare carrier buzz, based at London's Stansted airport, to give it a better foothold in Europe. However, the carrier was unable to turn a profit with buzz and chose instead to sell the low-fare carrier to Ryanair in 2003.

EXECUTIVES

Chairman of the Supervisory Board: Kees J. Storm, age 63
President and CEO: Leo M. van Wijk, age 59
Managing Director and COO: Peter F. Hartman, age 55
Managing Director and CFO: Frederic Gagey
Managing Director and Chief Human Resources Officer: Cees van Woudenberg, age 57
SVP Corporate Communications: Peter Elbers, age 41
Secretary: Barbara C.P. van Koppen
Auditors: KPMG Accountants N.V.

LOCATIONS

HQ: KLM Royal Dutch Airlines
(Koninklijke Luchtvaart Maatschappij N.V.)
Amsterdamseweg 55,
1182GP Amstelveen, The Netherlands
Phone: +31-20-649-9123   **Fax:** +31-20-649-2324
Web: www.klm.nl

PRODUCTS/OPERATIONS

Selected Subsidiaries and Affiliates

Kenya Airways Ltd. (26%)
KLM cityhopper bv (regional airline)
Martinair Holland nv (50%, international cargo and passenger airline)
Transavia Airlines bv (charters and scheduled holiday service)

COMPETITORS

ACE Aviation
All Nippon Airways
AMR Corp.
BAX Global
British Airways
Delta Air
Delta Air Transport
DHL
FedEx
Finnair
Iberia
Lufthansa
SAS
Singapore Airlines
UAL
UPS
US Airways
Virgin Atlantic Airways
Virgin Group

HISTORICAL FINANCIALS

Company Type: Subsidiary

Income Statement

FYE: March 31

	REVENUE ($ mil.)	NET INCOME ($ mil.)	NET PROFIT MARGIN	EMPLOYEES
3/05	8,317	118	1.4%	27,983
3/04	7,154	29	0.4%	31,182
3/03	7,066	(454)	—	33,038
3/02	5,688	(136)	—	33,265
3/01	6,100	67	1.1%	33,763
3/00	6,018	322	5.4%	30,159
3/99	5,718	223	3.9%	28,374
3/98	5,666	1,059	18.7%	26,811
3/97	5,516	126	2.3%	26,385
3/96	5,769	330	5.7%	25,003
Annual Growth	4.1%	(10.9%)	—	1.3%

2005 Year-End Financials

Debt ratio: 219.6%
Return on equity: 5.7%
Cash ($ mil.): 953
Current ratio: 0.94
Long-term debt ($ mil.): 5,028

Net Income History

Koç Holding

In Turkey, Koç (pronounced "coach") class equals first class. Led by its automotive businesses, Koç Holding is Turkey's top industrial conglomerate. The company's Tofas unit, a joint venture with Fiat, is Turkey's leading carmaker; Koç's joint venture with Ford Motor sells imported Ford models. Other businesses include supermarkets (Migros), large household appliances (Arçelik), and energy (distribution of liquefied petroleum gas). Subsidiaries engage in food production, construction, international trading, and hospitality and tourism. Koç also operates banking, securities brokerage, and insurance businesses. The Koç family, Turkey's wealthiest dynasty, controls the company.

Koç is looking far across the Bosphorus for growth. With a goal modeled on its success at home, Koç intends to enter every household in Europe with at least one product and one day take in 50% of its revenue from outside Turkey's borders.

HISTORY

In 1917, 16-year-old Vehbi Koç and his father opened a small grocery store in Ankara, Turkey. With the fall of the Ottoman Empire after WWI, Turkey's capital was moved to Ankara, which was then only a village. The Koçs recognized an opportunity and expanded into construction and building supplies, winning a contract to repair the roof of the Turkish parliament building. By age 26, Koç was a millionaire.

Ford Motor made Koç its Turkish agent in 1928. In 1931 Mobil Oil and Koç entered an exclusive agreement to search for oil in Turkey. The company incorporated in 1938 as Koç Ticaret Corporation, the first Turkish joint stock company with an employee stock-ownership program.

Despite Turkey's neutrality in WWII, the fighting disrupted Koç's business. The nation became isolationist after the war and restricted foreign concerns to selling through local agents; Koç benefited by importing foreign products.

General Electric and Koç entered a joint venture in 1946 to build Turkey's first lightbulb factory. In 1955 Koç set up Arçelik, the first Turkish producer of refrigerators, washing machines, and water heaters; Türk Demir Döküm, the first Turkish producer of radiators and, later, auto castings; and Turkay, the country's first private producer of matches. In 1959 Koç constructed Turkey's first truck assembly plant (Otosan).

Other firsts followed in the 1960s as the company leveraged its size and government influence to attract more ventures. These included a tire factory (with Uniroyal), a cable factory (with Siemens), production of electric motors and compressors (with GE), and the production of Anadol, the first car to be made entirely in Turkey (by Otosan, under license from Ford). In 1974 Koç expanded into retailing with the purchase of Migros, Turkey's largest chain of supermarkets.

The Turkish military imposed martial law in 1980 and restricted foreign exchange payments, forcing Koç to limit its operations. In 1986, a year after foreign companies were allowed to export products directly to Turkey, Koç and American Express started Koç-Amerikan Bank (which Koç bought out and renamed Koçbank in 1992). In the late 1980s Vehbi's only son, Rahmi, took over the company's leadership. Vehbi Koç died in 1996.

Auto sales fell sharply in 1996 as buyers awaited the country's entry into the European Union's customs union. In an effort to offset market risks, Koç forged a number of alliances in 1997. It participated in a British-Canadian-Turkish consortium that was building a large power plant in central Turkey.

Reflecting a greater willingness to open the company to foreign investors, Koç announced plans to offer $250 million in shares in a public offering in 1998, but it soon canceled the offering because of market volatility. A year later, the company completed an auto plant in Samarkand, Uzbekistan, to build Otoyol-Iveco buses and trucks.

Koç entered into a joint venture — Koç Finansal Hizmetler — with Unicredito Italiano in 2002 in an effort to further consolidate its financial holdings.

EXECUTIVES

Honorary Chairman: Rahmi M. Koç
Chairman: Mustafa V. Koç
Vice Chairman: Temel Atay
Vice Chairman: Suna Kiraç, age 64
CEO: F. Bülend Özaydinli
Auditing Group President: Ali Tark Uzun
Corporate Communications and Foreign Relations President: Hasan Bengü, age 56
Construction Group President: Bülent Bulgurlu
Energy Group President: Erol Memioǝlu, age 51
Financial Services Group President: Rüsdü Saraçoglu
Food/Retailing and Tourism Group President: Ömer Bozer
Information Technologies Group President: Ali Y. Koç, age 38
Other Automotive Companies Group President: Selçuk Gezdur
General Secretary: Tahsin Saltik
Human Resources Director: Neslihan Tözge
Governmental Affairs Coordinator: Ömer Tunç Koyuncu
Information Systems Coordinator: Alper Gögüs, age 45
Legal Affairs: Kemal Erol
Auditors: PricewaterhouseCoopers

LOCATIONS

HQ: Koç Holding A.S.
  Nakkastepe, Azizbey Sokak No. 1, Kuzguncuk,
  Kuzguncuk, 34674 Istanbul, Turkey
Phone: +90-216-531-00-00   **Fax:** +90-216-531-00-99
Web: www.koc.com.tr

Koç Holding has operations in Algeria, Austria, Azerbaijan, Bahrain, Bulgaria, China, France, Germany, Hong Kong, Iraq, Ireland, Italy, Kazakhstan, Macedonia, the Netherlands, Poland, Romania, Russia, Spain, Switzerland, the UK, the US, and Uzbekistan.

PRODUCTS/OPERATIONS

2004 Sales

	% of total
Automotive	26
Durable goods	26
Energy	20
Food & retailing	13
Financial	8
Other	7
Total	**100**

Core Businesses

Automotive
Construction and mining
Durable goods
Energy
Financial services
Food and retailing
International trade
New business development
Tourism and services

COMPETITORS

Caterpillar	Renault
Electrolux	Robert Bosch
Honda	Sabanci
International Power	Siemens
Opel	

HISTORICAL FINANCIALS

Company Type: Public

Income Statement

FYE: December 31

	REVENUE ($ mil.)	NET INCOME ($ mil.)	NET PROFIT MARGIN	EMPLOYEES
12/04	16,624	380	2.3%	59,513
12/03	11,152	275	2.5%	53,985
12/02	6,828	25	0.4%	50,019
12/01	4,901	(214)	—	39,866
12/00	6,580	101	1.5%	45,626
12/99	5,424	24	0.4%	35,531
12/98	5,794	169	2.9%	37,178
12/97	9,585	157	1.6%	39,931
12/96	9,192	438	4.8%	41,750
12/95	11,504	425	3.7%	36,280
Annual Growth	**4.2%**	**(1.2%)**	**—**	**5.7%**

2004 Year-End Financials

Debt ratio: 35.5%   Current ratio: 1.15
Return on equity: 14.0%   Long-term debt ($ mil.): 1,103
Cash ($ mil.): 1,506

Net Income History

Istanbul: KCHOL

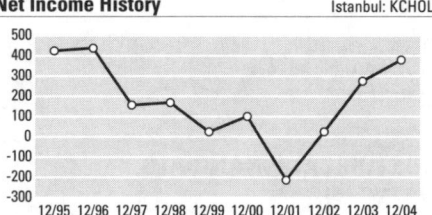

HISTORY

Komatsu's roots reach back to the Takeuchi Mining Company, founded in Japan in 1894. The company grew during WWI, and in 1917 it created an in-house ironworks to make machine tools and mining equipment. The ironworks was separated in 1921 to create Komatsu Manufacturing.

The firm grew into one of Japan's major makers of machine tools and pumps by adding new products to its line. Komatsu introduced its first metal press in 1924 and in 1931 made Japan's first crawler-type farm tractor. Komatsu began making high-grade casting and specialty steel materials in 1935.

During WWII Komatsu made munitions and bulldozers for the Japanese Navy. After the war it began making construction machinery and industrial vehicles as Japan rebuilt its infrastructure. The company began building diesel engines in 1948. Komatsu continued to expand during the 1950s. In 1952 it began producing motor graders, which became its first construction equipment to be exported (to Argentina) in 1955.

During the 1960s Komatsu entered joint ventures with US manufacturers, including Cummins Engine (1961), Bucyrus Erie (1963), and International Harvester (now Navistar, 1965). Komatsu established its first overseas subsidiary, Komatsu Europe, in Belgium in 1967 and introduced the world's first radio-controlled bulldozer.

The company changed its name to Komatsu Limited in 1970. International expansion continued as subsidiaries were established in the US, Brazil, and Germany (1970), Singapore (1971), and Panama (1972). Komatsu began making bulldozers in Mexico (1976) and opened an Australian subsidiary (1978).

In the 1980s Komatsu pushed further into the US market, going head-to-head with Caterpillar. A strong dollar helped Komatsu undercut Caterpillar's prices by as much as 30%. In 1986 the company opened its first US factory in Chattanooga, Tennessee. In 1988 it merged American construction equipment-making operations with those of Dresser Industries, creating Komatsu Dresser.

Komatsu partnered with semiconductor giant Applied Materials in 1993 and entered the LAN market the next year with a print server and two types of hubs. The company expanded its construction equipment operations outside Japan in the mid-1990s, when it formed a joint venture in Vietnam and opened plants in China. Demand for construction equipment in Japan plunged soon after.

In 1997 Komatsu set up a joint venture with India's Larsen & Toubro to make hydraulic excavators. A semiconductor industry downturn prompted Komatsu to close some of its US silicon wafer operations in 1998.

Komatsu Ltd.

Like a sumo wrestler, Komatsu can throw a lot of weight around. The diversified company is the world's #2 construction equipment maker, behind Caterpillar. Komatsu makes building and mining equipment ranging from bulldozers and wheel loaders to dump trucks and debris crushers. Komatsu also makes industrial machinery such as laser-cutting machines and sheet-metal presses. Its electronics division produces LCD manufacturing equipment and silicon wafers; a civil engineering and construction division makes prefabricated structures and offers contracting and real-estate sales and leasing services. Other products include generators, armored vehicles, diesel engines, and computer software.

Komatsu means "little pine tree" in Japanese.

Its largest segment, construction and mining equipment, generates more than 70% of the company's sales. Although the weak demand for construction equipment in Japan has improved somewhat, Komatsu has been consolidating, reducing inventory, and closing plants to cut costs. The company, which recorded its first loss in fiscal 1999, has since focused on its construction and mining equipment businesses in the US and Europe. The company is also expecting opera-

tions in China and the former Soviet Republics to grow.

Komatsu acquired KONE Corporation's Partek Forest AB and Partek Forest Holdings (collectively known as Partek Forest) in 2003; the new additions are now a part of Komatsu Forest AB.

In 2005 the company agreed to sell a 75% stake in its US subsidiary Advanced Silicon Materials to the Norwegian company Renewable Energy Corporation. Advanced Silicon makes polycrystalline silicon for use in semiconductors. The company makes nearly $140 million in annual sales.

Hammered by low demand for construction equipment in Japan (down nearly 80% over three years), Komatsu recorded its first loss in fiscal 1999 and closed plants. The company backed out of its joint venture with Applied Materials, selling its stake back to Applied Materials for $87 million in cash. Former GM manager Keith Sheldon was hired to overhaul the company's ailing global finances and prepare the company for stock listing on the New York Stock Exchange. In March 2000 the company sold its machine vision systems business to Cognex Corporation. Komatsu reached profitability in fiscal 2001 thanks to a new growth strategy focused on its construction and mining equipment businesses. Later the same year — as the economy swooned — Komatsu announced that it expected losses and was cutting about 2,200 jobs in Japan.

Komatsu's reorganization plans launched during the last quarter of 2001 carried over through 2002 and 2003. The company implemented its new growth strategy for the construction and mining equipment business, reduced fixed costs, and restructured its electronics business. In 2003 the company showed an increase of 5.2% in consolidated net sales over the previous year. That year the company decided to dissolve its Komatsu Metal Ltd. subsidiary.

EXECUTIVES

Chairman: Toshitaka Hagiwara, age 65
President, CEO, and Director: Masahiro Sakane, age 64
Senior Executive Officer; President, Construction and Mining Equipment Marketing Division, Regional Director of Japan, Asia and Pacific and China: Kunio Noji, age 59
Senior Executive Officer; President, Defense Systems Division: Shigeki Fujimori
Senior Executive Officer; President, Development Division and President, Engines and Hydraulics Business Division, Supervising Research and Development Operations: Kunihiko Komiyama, age 60
Senior Executive Officer; President, Production Division: Susumu Isoda
Senior Executive Officer; General Manager Corporate Planning, Supervising External Corporate Affairs, Structural Reorganization, Compliance, Safety and Environment, and Human Resources; and Director: Masahiro Yoneyama, age 59
Senior Executive Officer; Supervising CSR, General Affairs, Corporate Communications, and Investor Relations: Munenori Nakao
Senior Executive Officer; CFO: Kenji Kinoshita
Senior Executive Officer; General Manager, Corporate Planning; and Director: Yasuo Suzuki, age 57
Senior Executive Officer; President, Construction and Mining Equipment Marketing Division; and Director: Yoshinori Komamura, age 57
Executive Officer; President, Overseas Marketing, Construction and Mining Equipment Marketing Division: Taizo Kayata
Executive Officer; President, Research Division: Masao Fuchigami
Executive Officer; General Manager, Human Resources: Masakatsu Hioki
Chairman and CEO, Komatsu America: David W. (Dave) Grzelak
Auditors: KPMG AZSA & Co.

LOCATIONS

HQ: Komatsu Ltd.
  2-3-6 Akasaka, Minato-ku, Tokyo 107-8414, Japan
Phone: +81-3-5561-2687   **Fax:** +81-3-3505-9662
US HQ: 440 N. Fairway Dr., Vernon Hills, IL 60061-8112
US Phone: 847-970-4100   **US Fax:** 847-970-4183
Web: www.komatsu.com

Komatsu has subsidiaries and affiliates in Australia, Belgium, Brazil, Canada, China, Egypt, France, Germany, Ghana, Hong Kong, India, Indonesia, Iran, Italy, Kenya, Malaysia, Mexico, Mongolia, Myanmar, the Netherlands, Norway, Pakistan, the Philippines, Poland, Russia, Saudi Arabia, Singapore, South Africa, Spain, Taiwan, Thailand, Turkey, United Arab Emirates, the UK, the US, and Vietnam.

2005 Sales

	$ mil.	% of total
Asia		
Japan	4,913	36
China	526	4
Other	1,988	15
Americas	3,390	25
Europe	1,919	14
Middle East & Africa	791	6
Total	**13,527**	**100**

PRODUCTS/OPERATIONS

2005 Sales

	$ mil.	% of total
Construction & Mining Equipment	10,148	71
Industrial Machinery & Vehicles	3,111	22
Electronics	1,010	7
Adjustments	(742)	—
Total	**13,527**	**100**

Products and Services

Construction and Mining Equipment
  Articulated-type dump trucks
  Backhoe loaders
  Bulldozers
  Crawler carriers
  Hydraulic excavators
  Mini excavators
  Mini wheel loaders
  Motor graders
  Rigid-type dump trucks
  Shield Machines
  Skid steer loaders
  Small-diameter pipe jacking machines (Iron Moles)
  Tunnel-boring machines
  Vibratory rollers
  Wheel loaders
Industrial Machinery, Vehicles, and Other
  Crankshaft millers
  Defense systems (ammunition and armored personnel carriers)
  Fine plasma cutting machines
  Forging presses
  Forklift trucks
  Large presses
  Laser cutting machines
  Outdoor power equipment
  Packing and transport
  Prefabricated office structures
  Press brakes
  Recycling plants
  Shears
  Small and medium-sized presses
Electronics
  Excimer laser
  LAN peripheral equipment
  Mobile tracking and communication terminals
  Monosilane gas
  Network information terminals
  Semiconductor manufacturing-related thermoelectric devices
  Silicon wafers
  Thermoelectric modules
  Vehicle controllers

COMPETITORS

Barloworld	Metso Minerals
CAMECO Industries	Mitsubishi Heavy
Caterpillar	Industries
CLARK Material	Mitsubishi Materials
CNH Global	Mitsui
Comau	Nisshinbo
Cymer	RAG
Deere	Rasa
Deere-Hitachi	Shin-Etsu Handotai
Furukawa	Sumitomo
Harnischfeger Corporation	Terex
JLG Industries	Toyota
Kubota	Victor L. Phillips

HISTORICAL FINANCIALS

Company Type: Public

Income Statement

FYE: March 31

	REVENUE ($ mil.)	NET INCOME ($ mil.)	NET PROFIT MARGIN	EMPLOYEES
3/05	13,527	549	4.1%	33,008
3/04	11,438	255	2.2%	31,635
3/03	9,093	25	0.3%	30,666
3/02	7,810	(608)	—	30,760
3/01	8,679	55	0.6%	32,002
3/00	10,006	127	1.3%	28,522
3/99	8,913	(104)	—	31,785
3/98	8,297	145	1.7%	26,871
3/97	8,877	147	1.7%	27,007
3/96	9,317	133	1.4%	27,917
Annual Growth	**4.2%**	**17.0%**	**—**	**1.9%**

2005 Year-End Financials

Debt ratio: 45.6%   Current ratio: 1.27
Return on equity: 13.0%   Long-term debt ($ mil.): 2,024
Cash ($ mil.): 907

Net Income History

OTC: KMTUY

Koor Industries

Once a socialist vision, now a model of capitalism, Koor Industries is Israel's leading holding company. Koor's core businesses have been its holdings in agrochemicals (Makhteshim-Agan), defense electronics (Elisra Electronics Group), and telecommunications equipment (ECI Telecom, ECTel, and Telrad Networks). The company's venture capital arm has invested in enterprises including Chiaro Networks and Mysticom. Koor Industries also has operations in tourism, real estate, and trade. Claridge Israel, a unit of Canadian billionaire Charles Bronfman's investment firm, owns 30% of the group. The company was founded to provide employment for Jewish refugees during WWII.

Koor's general strategy for its agrochemical business is based upon timing the commercial release of the generic equivalent products that it develops to coincide with the expiration of patents for similar existing products.

While Koor's bread and butter is its chemical business, the company is attempting to build up its export-based businesses, which include its telecom equipment and defense electronics units. To this end, the company's investment arm has distributed venture capital primarily to communications-oriented hardware and software developers. The company invests in telecommunications businesses through its ECI Telecom, Telrad Networks, and ECTel holdings.

The company announced in early 2005 that it is selling its 32% stake in military communication systems manufacturer Tadiran Communications to shareholders of international defense electronics company Elbit Systems, but is acquiring 10% of Elbit. Koor Industries has completed the first stage of the transactions, acquiring more than 5% of Elbit from Federmann Enterprises for $52.2 million and selling nearly 14% of Tadiran to Elbit for $62.5 million. Elbit now holds about 20% of Taridran.

Koor also sold 39% of Telrad Networks to Fortissimo Capital and has agreed to sell part of its share in Makhteshim Agan, a top generic manufacturer of crop protection products.

HISTORY

Koor Industries is an offshoot of Solel Boneh, a construction company formed in 1924 in British Palestine by the Histadrut Labour Federation. Solel Boneh founded Koor in 1944 to build factories to provide employment for Jewish refugees arriving during WWII.

An Arab attack quickly followed Israel's creation in 1948. Israel prevailed, but the threat of future conflicts spurred development of its defense industry. In 1952 Koor teamed with a Finnish firm to create Soltam, an Israeli artillery manufacturer. The previous year, it had diversified into telecommunications equipment with Telrad.

Koor continued to expand and diversify through joint ventures, creating a steel company in 1954 and Alliance Tire & Rubber in 1955 (it bought full control of Alliance in 1983). Koor and the Israeli government founded Tadiran (defense electronics, 1962), and Koor acquired chemical maker Makhteshim (1963) and food processor Hamashbir Lata (1970). The Sinai campaign (1956), Six-Day War (1967), and Yom Kippur War (1973) continued to spur Israeli defense spending. However, with Histadrut's emphasis on socialist aims, Koor never became very profitable. Successful subsidiaries were offset by money-losers.

The company was hurt in the 1980s by a government program that cut subsidies and lowered trade barriers. Inflation damaged Koor's global competitiveness. With the help of junk bond guru Michael Milken, Koor raised $105 million in a 1986 debt issue. That year, however, Koor posted its first loss in 20 years, and losses widened in 1987. Benjamin Gaon became CEO in 1988 and began restructuring the heavily indebted company, which by then had about 130 units. He kept closing plants, but the company incurred a loss in 1988 and a record $369 million deficit in 1989. Gaon negotiated a new arrangement with creditors in 1991.

By 1992 Gaon's cost cutting had begun to pay off, and the company returned to profitability. Histadrut sold out in 1995, severing a link to Koor's socialist past. That year the company raised nearly $120 million in an international IPO, and Northern Telecom (now Nortel Networks) acquired 20% of Telrad (sold back to Koor in 2000).

Koor continued divesting assets to focus on its core businesses. ITT Sheraton International took a 50% stake in Koor Tourism in a 1996 alliance to manage hotels in Israel, and Henkel bought 50% of Koor's detergent operations. Discontinued operations included Beep-A-Call (wireless paging, 1995), Gamda Trade (food retail, 1996), and TAMI (food industry, 1997).

In 1995 Gaon sowed the seeds for his departure by selling a controlling stake in Koor to the Shamrock Group, a Disney family investment firm. Disagreements with Gaon over Koor's strategy led Shamrock to sell its stake in 1997 to Claridge Israel, an investment fund controlled by Canadian billionaire Charles Bronfman. Jonathan Kolber, then CEO of Claridge Israel, replaced Gaon in 1998.

Kolber made plans to increase exports and focus on Koor's telecom equipment, defense electronics, and agrochemicals segments, while scaling back in construction materials. In 1998 Koor bought a stake in Israel's ECI Telecom, which merged with Tadiran Telecom in 1999. Koor also dumped several non-core assets (including cable TV, energy, and software services units), raising more than $360 million. It then sold its 50% stake in cement group Mashav.

In 2000 Koor and Nortel Networks launched Nortel Networks Israel to deliver high-performance Internet products to carrier and enterprise customers. The restructuring of the Elisra Group (formerly the Elisra-Tadiran Group) was completed in 2001. The next year Koor sold a 30% stake in Elisra Electronics Systems to government-owned Israel Aircraft Industries.

The company reorganized the operations of ECI Telecom in part by divesting its wireless networking equipment unit in 2002 so that ECI could focus more closely on core wireline products. In 2003 Nortel took over Koor Industries' 28% stake in Nortel Networks Israel.

EXECUTIVES

Chairman: Charles R. Bronfman, age 74
Vice Chairman and CEO: Jonathan Kolber, age 43
President: Danny Biran
VP: Aaron Zuker
CFO: Ran Maidan
Managing Director, Koor Corporate Venture Capital: Jackie Goren, age 39
General Counsel and Corporate Secretary: Shlomo Heller, age 62
Director of Corporate Communications: Fiona Darmon
Auditors: Somekh Chaikin

LOCATIONS

HQ: Koor Industries Ltd.
    14 Hamelacha St., Park Afek,
    Rosh Ha'ayin 48091, Israel
Phone: +972-3-900-8333   **Fax:** +972-3-900-8334
Web: www.koor.com

2004 Sales

	% of total
Europe	34
South America	22
North America	17
Israel	15
Asia & Australia	9
Africa	3
Total	**100**

PRODUCTS/OPERATIONS

2004 Sales

	% of total
Agrochemicals	75
Defense electronics	13
Telecommunication	7
Other	5
Total	**100**

Selected Subsidiaries and Affiliates

Agrochemicals
    Makhteshim-Agan Industries Ltd. (34%)
Defense Electronics
    Elisra Electronics Systems (70%)
    BVR Systems (46%)
    Spectralink
    Tadiran Electronic Systems
Telecommunications Equipment
    ECI Telecom Ltd. (31%)
    Nortel Networks Israel (28%)
    Telrad Networks
Venture Capital Investments
    Koor Corporate Venture Capital
Other
    Knafaim-Arkia Holdings (28%,
        flight and tourism operator)
    Koor Trade
    Sheraton-Moriah Israel (hotels, 55%)

COMPETITORS

Alcatel
Ampal-American Israel
Clal Industries
DIRECTV
Dow AgroSciences
DuPont Agriculture & Nutrition
Elron
GE
Gilat Satellite
Harris Corp.
The Israel Corporation
Lucent
NEC
Oryx Technology
Philips Electronics
Raytheon
Rockwell Automation
Siemens
Toshiba

HISTORICAL FINANCIALS

Company Type: Public

Income Statement

	REVENUE ($ mil.)	NET INCOME ($ mil.)	NET PROFIT MARGIN	EMPLOYEES
				FYE: December 31
12/04	2,129	33	1.6%	6,559
12/03	1,763	11	0.6%	6,328
12/02	1,528	(165)	—	6,899
12/01	1,618	(575)	—	7,297
12/00	2,049	66	3.2%	8,680
12/99	2,571	132	5.1%	8,680
12/98	3,034	11	0.4%	15,035
12/97	3,565	138	3.9%	21,500
12/96	3,525	181	5.1%	21,000
12/95	3,256	156	4.8%	20,600
Annual Growth	**(4.6%)**	**(15.8%)**	**—**	**(11.9%)**

2004 Year-End Financials

Debt ratio: 168.0%	No. of shares (mil.): 79
Return on equity: 8.0%	Dividends
Cash ($ mil.): 142	Yield: 0.0%
Current ratio: 1.22	Payout: —
Long-term debt ($ mil.): 727	Market value ($ mil.): 836

	STOCK PRICE ($) FY Close	P/E High/Low		PER SHARE ($) Earnings	Dividends	Book Value
12/04	10.56	26	17	0.41	0.00	5.47
12/03	7.74	58	14	0.14	0.00	4.99
12/02	2.10	—	—	(2.18)	0.00	4.90
12/01	6.51	—	—	(7.56)	0.00	6.27
12/00	13.13	21	12	1.08	0.70	10.32
12/99	20.00	15	10	1.66	0.42	13.42
12/98	17.44	177	83	0.15	0.62	12.30
12/97	21.94	14	10	1.74	0.00	14.65
12/96	17.13	9	7	2.27	0.24	13.96
12/95	20.25	10	8	2.09	0.00	11.40
Annual Growth	(7.0%)	—	—	(16.6%)	—	(7.8%)

KPMG

Businesses all over the world count on KPMG for accounting. KPMG is the smallest, yet most geographically dispersed of accounting's Big Four, which also includes Deloitte Touche Tohmatsu, Ernst & Young, and PricewaterhouseCoopers. KPMG, a cooperative that operates as an umbrella organization for its member firms, has organized its structure into three operating regions: the Americas; Asia/Pacific; and Europe, Middle East, Africa. Member firms' offerings include audit, tax, and advisory services; KPMG focuses on clients in such industries as financial services, consumer products, government, health care, information, communications, and entertainment. KPMG has discontinued its KLegal International network.

After much regulatory pressure, KPMG separated its accounting and consulting operations; it sold a chunk of the consulting business to networking equipment maker Cisco Systems, then took it public and sold off its shares in 2002. The consulting unit, which in 2002 changed its name to BearingPoint, acquired KPMG's Austrian, German, and Swiss consulting businesses.

A run-in with the US government over questionable tax shelters characterized as abusive (costing the US more than $1 billion in tax revenues) led to a shakeup in the US firm's tax services unit in 2004 and the payment of a $456 million penalty in mid-2005. While KPMG appears to have headed off an indictment of the firm, eight former KPMG executives have been indicted and charged with conspiracy in connection with the tax shelters.

Lawsuits over KPMG's work for other former clients hit the accountancy's pocketbook. In 2003 KPMG agreed to pay $125 million to settle a dispute regarding work for Rite Aid. The next year, KPMG's Belgian and US units agreed to a $115 million settlement regarding now-defunct Lernout & Hauspie Speech Products.

HISTORY

Peat Marwick was founded in 1911, when William Peat, a London accountant, met James Marwick during an Atlantic crossing. University of Glasgow alumni Marwick and Roger Mitchell had formed Marwick, Mitchell & Company in New York in 1897. Peat and Marwick agreed to ally their firms temporarily, and in 1925 they merged as Peat, Marwick, Mitchell, & Copartners.

In 1947 William Black became senior partner, a position he held until 1965. He guided the firm's 1950 merger with Barrow, Wade, Guthrie, one of the US's oldest firms, and built its consulting practice. Peat Marwick restructured its international practice as PMM&Co. (International) in 1972 (renamed Peat Marwick International in 1978).

The next year several European accounting firms led by Klynveld Kraayenhoff (the Netherlands) and Deutsche Treuhand (Germany) began forming an international accounting federation. Needing an American member, the European firms encouraged the merger of two American firms founded around the turn of the century, Main Lafrentz and Hurdman Cranstoun. Main Hurdman & Cranstoun joined the Europeans to form Klynveld Main Goerdeler (KMG), named after two of the member firms and the chairman of Deutsche Treuhand, Reinhard Goerdeler. Other members were C. Jespersen (Denmark), Thorne Riddel (Canada), Thomson McLintok (UK), and Fides Revision (Switzerland).

Peat Marwick merged with KMG in 1987 to form Klynveld Peat Marwick Goerdeler (KPMG). KPMG lost 10% of its business as competing client companies departed. Professional staff departures followed in 1990 when, as part of a consolidation, the firm trimmed its partnership rolls.

In the 1990s the then-Big Six accounting firms all faced lawsuits arising from an evolving standard holding auditors responsible for the substance, rather than merely the form, of clients' accounts. KPMG was hit by suits stemming from its audits of defunct S&Ls and litigation relating to the bankruptcy of Orange County, California (settled for $75 million in 1998). Nevertheless KPMG kept growing; it expanded its consulting division with the acquisition of banking consultancy Barefoot, Marrinan & Associates in 1996.

In 1997, after Price Waterhouse and Coopers & Lybrand announced their merger, KPMG and Ernst & Young announced one of their own. But they called it quits the next year, fearing that regulatory approval of the deal would be too onerous.

The creation of PricewaterhouseCoopers (PwC) and increasing competition in the consulting sides of all of the Big Five brought a realignment of loyalties in their national practices. KPMG Consulting's Belgian group moved to PwC and its French group to Computer Sciences Corporation. Andersen nearly wooed away KPMG's Canadian consulting group, but the plan was foiled by the ever-sullen Andersen Consulting group (now Accenture) and by KPMG's promises of more money. Against this background, KPMG sold 20% of its consulting operations to Cisco Systems for $1 billion. In addition to the cash infusion, the deal allowed KPMG to provide installation and system management to Cisco's customers.

Even while KPMG worked on the IPO of its consulting group (which took place in 2001), it continued to rail against the SEC as it called for relationships between consulting and auditing organizations to be severed. In 2002 KPMG sold its British and Dutch consultancy units to France's Atos Origin.

In 2003 the SEC charged US member firm KPMG L.L.P. and four partners with fraud in relation to alleged profit inflation at former client Xerox in the late 1990s. (In April 2005 the accounting firm paid almost $22.5 million, including a $10 million civil penalty, to settle the charges.)

KPMG exited various businesses around the globe during fiscal 2004, including full-scope legal services and certain advisory services, to focus on higher-demand services.

EXECUTIVES

Chairman; Senior Partner, KPMG UK: Michael (Mike) Rake, age 57
CEO: Robert W. (Bob) Alspaugh, age 58
Chairman and CEO, KPMG LLP: Timothy P. Flynn, age 48
Chairman, Europe, Middle East, and Africa: Harald Wiedmann
Chairman, Asia Pacific: John Harrison
Vice Chairman: Ruth Anderson
Vice Chairman and Managing Partner, Global Markets: Alistair Johnston
Vice Chairman: Philip Wallace
Vice Chairman: Derek Zissman
CEO, Switzerland: Hubert Achermann
Senior Partner, Brazil: David Bunce
Managing Partner, Singapore: Bobby Chin
President, France: Jean-Luc Decornoy
Senior Partner, Mexico: Guillermo Garcia-Naranjo
Chairman and Senior Partner, South Africa: Tom Grieve
Senior Partner, Italy: Renato Guerini
National Chairman, Australia: Doug Jukes
Managing Partner, Ireland: Denis O'Connor
Chairman and CEO, Canada: Bill MacKinnon
Senior Partner, Denmark: Finn L. Meyer
Senior Partner, Sweden: Thomas Thiel
Chairman, Board of Management, Netherlands: Ben van der Veer
Senior Partner and CEO, Japan: Masanori Sato
COO: Colin Holland
General Counsel: Tom Wethered
Secretary: Needra Patel

LOCATIONS

HQ: KPMG International
Burgemeester Rijnderslaan 10,
1185 MC Amstelveen, The Netherlands
Phone: +31-20-656-7890   **Fax:** +31-20-656-7700
US HQ: 345 Park Ave., New York, NY 10154-0102
US Phone: 212-758-9700   **US Fax:** 212-758-9819
Web: www.kpmg.com

KPMG International has offices in nearly 150 countries.

2004 Sales

	$ mil.	% of total
Europe, Middle East, South Asia & Africa	6,840	51
Americas	4,930	37
Asia/Pacific	1,670	12
Total	**13,440**	**100**

PRODUCTS/OPERATIONS

2004 Sales

	$ mil.	% of total
Audit services	6,420	48
Advisory services	3,910	29
Tax services	3,110	23
Total	**13,440**	**100**

2004 Sales by Customer Type

	$ mil.	% of total
Financial services	3,810	28
Infrastructure, government & health care	2,960	22
Industrial markets	2,900	22
Information, communications & entertainment	2,080	15
Consumer markets	1,690	13
Total	**13,440**	**100**

Selected Services

Audit services
  Financial statement audit
  Internal audit services

Tax services
  Corporate & business tax
  Global tax
  Indirect tax
  Personal tax

Advisory services
  Audit support services
  Financial risk management
  Information risk management
  Process improvement
  Regulatory & compliance

COMPETITORS

Aon	H&R Block
Bain & Company	Hewitt Associates
Baker Tilly International	Marsh & McLennan
BDO International	McKinsey & Company
Booz Allen	PricewaterhouseCoopers
Deloitte	Towers Perrin
Ernst & Young	Watson Wyatt
Grant Thornton International	

HISTORICAL FINANCIALS

Company Type: Partnership

Income Statement

FYE: September 30

	REVENUE ($ mil.)	NET INCOME ($ mil.)	NET PROFIT MARGIN	EMPLOYEES
9/04	13,440	—	—	93,983
9/03	12,160	—	—	93,470
9/02	10,720	—	—	98,000
9/01	11,700	—	—	103,000
9/00	10,700	—	—	108,000
9/99	12,200	—	—	102,000
9/98	10,600	—	—	85,300
9/97	9,200	—	—	83,500
9/96	8,100	—	—	77,000
9/95	7,500	—	—	72,000
Annual Growth	**6.7%**	**—**	**—**	**3.0%**

Revenue History

KPN

Spawned from one of the Old World's state-owned postal and telephone monopolies — Dutch PTT — Koninklijke KPN (also known as Royal KPN) faces a new world of technology and competition. In the Netherlands, the company has 7.7 million fixed-line phone customers. Its mobile division, KPN Mobile, has more than 14.7 million subscribers in the Netherlands, Germany, and Belgium. Through its ownership of several European ISPs, KPN also provides Internet access to 1.5 million customers, and it offers business network services and data transport throughout Western Europe. The Dutch government has cut its stake in KPN to 8% and agreed to give up the "golden share" that has given it veto rights over major changes to KPN.

KPN remains the dominant telecom operator in the Netherlands, a position it stands to improve with its 2005 acquisition of wireless telecom operator Telfort. KPN also is extending its European data communications network, including the purchase of some assets from KPNQwest, its failed joint venture with US-based Qwest Communications that operated a pan-European data communications network with connections to North America.

KPN Mobile, in which Japanese wireless operator NTT DoCoMo has taken a 15% stake, has mobile phone operations in Belgium, Germany, and the Netherlands, and it is introducing NTT DoCoMo's i-mode mobile multimedia services to these markets. KPN also has acquired HubHop, a wireless Internet (Wi-Fi) services provider, and Freeler, a small ISP in the Netherlands. KPN has introduced a no-frills wireless service called simyo for customers in Germany.

Up-and-down economic conditions and the company's sizable debt (due largely to paying high prices for advanced wireless phone licenses) have led KPN to seek the sale of many of its international holdings, including its stakes in US-based Infonet, Ireland's eircom, Czech phone company Ceský Telecom, and Hungarian mobile phone operator Pannon GSM. It also sold KPN Belgium and its Belgian ISP, Planet Internet Belgium. The company also has said it will cut up to 8,000 jobs through the year 2010 and focus on broadband Internet business for growth.

KPN finds itself facing challenges in its Dutch market. Opta, the Dutch telecom regulator, dealt the company a blow by proposing that KPN's competitors must be given room to offer fixed-line subscriptions to customers, a revenue source dominated by KPN.

HISTORY

Koninklijke KPN is a descendant of the Dutch PTT — a traditional European state-owned postal, telegraph, and telephone monopoly. The PTT traces its roots to the 1700s, when the Dutch provinces began taking over postal operations from the cities. Under Napoleonic rule in 1799, mail delivery was organized under one national service.

In 1877 postal and telegraph services were assigned to the new ministry for water, commerce, and industry. The operation became an independent administration, called Postal Services and Telegraphy (P&T), in 1893.

The telephone made its Dutch debut in 1881 with Netherlands Bell Telephone, and several private operators and the P&T soon entered the business. After building its first local phone exchange in 1911, the P&T became the Staats Bedrijf der Posterijen, Telegraphie & Telephony (PTT) in 1928. In 1941 during the Nazi occupation, all independent phone operators were folded into the PTT.

After WWII, business began to boom for the PTT, which had fully automated its phone systems by 1962. Despite inflation and the government's practice of siphoning off PTT funds in the 1970s, the company stuck to a course of investment and new services. It launched a packet data network in 1982 and an analog mobile phone network in 1985.

Following years of debate, the PTT became an independent corporation called PTT Nederland NV in 1989, but the state was its only shareholder. Momentum had been building within Europe for liberalizing telecom services, and the door was opened to competition for some postal and telecom services. Fearing competition from the likes of British Telecom (now BT Group), PTT joined Sweden's Televerket (renamed Telia in 1993) to form Unisource, a global communications provider. Swisscom joined Unisource in 1993, and AT&T began working with the venture the next year.

Meanwhile, KPN launched a digital GSM (global system for mobile communications) mobile phone network in 1994, and Dutch mobile use began to take off. The company, now called Koninklijke PTT Nederland NV (or KPN; *Koninklijke* means "royal"), launched its long-awaited IPO that year; the state sold a 30% share. Also in 1995 the firm began offering Internet access.

KPN's mail delivery and logistics businesses were finally spun off in 1998 as TNT Post Group (KPN had bought express carrier TNT in 1996). The company began to focus squarely on telecom and adopted the name Royal KPN. AT&T abandoned the unsuccessful Unisource venture that year, and the others decided to sell its assets. Wireless subsidiary KPN Mobile was formed in 1999 and took a 77% interest in German GSM operator E-Plus (BellSouth bought the remaining 23%, then sold it to KPN in 2002).

KPN announced it would take KPN Mobile public in 2001 and entered merger talks with Belgacom, Belgium's leading telecom company, but the companies could not come to terms.

Also in 2001 KPN raised $4.6 billion in a public offering that reduced the Dutch government's stake in the company to 35%. The next year the company dissolved KPNQwest, its bankrupt joint venture formed in 1999 with US-based Qwest Communications, which operated a pan-European data communications network with connections to North America. The venture became another victim of the overdevelopment of broadband infrastructure and a general economic downturn in the telecom sector.

Also in 2002 KPN began searching for a buyer for its stake in the European wireless services joint venture with NTT DoCoMo and Hutchison Whampoa (formed in 2000). The next year the company sold its directory unit to private equity firm 3i Group and investment bank Veronis Suhler Stevenson Partners in a deal valued at $503 million. Also in 2003 the company sold its 16% stake in Ukrainian Mobile Communications for $55 million to Mobile Telesystems of Russia.

EXECUTIVES

Chairman of the Supervisory Board:
A. H. J. (Ton) Risseeuw, age 69
Vice Chairman of the Supervisory Board:
Dudley G. (D.G.) Eustace, age 69
Chairman of the Management Board and CEO:
A. J. (Ad) Scheepbouwer, age 61, $2,237,964 pay
Member of the Board of Management and CFO:
Marcel H. M. Smits, age 44, $231,023 pay (partial-year salary)
Member of the Management Board; Managing Director, Mobile Division: Guy J. M. Demuynck, age 54, $1,235,177 pay
CEO, BASE (Belgium): Stan P. Miller, age 46
Corporate Strategy Division: Eelco Blok
Head of Investor Relations: Jantiene T. Klein Roseboom
CEO, E-Plus (Germany): Uwe Bergheim, age 49
Operations Manager, Fixed Division: Cees P. Bosman
Business Developments and Strategy Manager, Fixed Division: J. Wildeboer
Finance Manager, Fixed Division: S. van Schilfgaarde
Consumer Market Manager, Fixed Division:
M. Buitelaar
Carrier Services Manager, Fixed Division:
J. F. E. Farwerck
Senior Investor Relations Officer:
Catrien H. van Buttingha Wichers
Auditors: PricewaterhouseCoopers Accountants N.V.

LOCATIONS

HQ: Koninklijke KPN N.V.
Maanplein 5, 2516 CK The Hague, The Netherlands
Phone: +31-70-343-43-43 **Fax:** +31-70-332-44-85
US HQ: 494 8th Ave., 23rd Fl., New York, NY 10001
US Phone: 212-560-9898 **US Fax:** 212-560-0770
Web: www.kpn.com

Koninklijke KPN N.V. operates primarily in Belgium, Germany, and the Netherlands.

PRODUCTS/OPERATIONS

2004 Sales

	% of total
Fixed Division	56
Mobile Division	41
Other	3
Total	**100**

Selected Subsidiaries and Affiliates

KPN EnterCom
  KPN EnterCom Solutions B.V. (voice and data business communications)
  Telecom Management B.V. (management of integrated business communications services)
KPN Mobile Holding B.V.
  KPN Mobile N.V. (85%, mobile telecommunications)
    BASE N.V./S.A.
    (mobile telecommunications, Belgium)
    E-Plus Mobilfunk GmbH & Co KG (mobile telecommunications, Germany)
    Hutchison 3G UK Holdings Ltd.
    (15%, mobile telecommunications)
    KPN International B.V.
    KPN Mobile The Netherlands B.V.
KPN Telecom B.V.
  Infonet Services Corporation (18%, data network operator, US)
  Proclare (10%)
KPN Telecommerce B.V.
  KPN Consumer Internet and Media Services B.V.
    Planet Media Group N.V.
    SNT Group N.V.
    XS4ALL Holding B.V.
KPN Vastgoed & Facilities B.V.
Volker Wessels Netwerk Bouw B.V. (45%)

COMPETITORS

Belgacom
BT
COLT Telecom
Deutsche Telekom
Energis
Equant
France Telecom
Magyar Telekom
MCI
TDC
Tele2
TeliaSonera
UGC Europe
VersaTel Telecom International
Vodafone
Vodafone Libertel

HISTORICAL FINANCIALS

Company Type: Public

Income Statement

FYE: December 31

	REVENUE ($ mil.)	NET INCOME ($ mil.)	NET PROFIT MARGIN	EMPLOYEES
12/04	16,393	2,047	12.5%	31,116
12/03	16,227	3,433	21.2%	32,736
12/02	13,427	(10,022)	—	38,118
12/01	11,461	(6,680)	—	49,121
12/00	12,725	1,765	13.9%	47,688
12/99	9,177	832	9.1%	38,550
12/98	9,377	802	8.5%	36,073
12/97	15,191	1,328	8.7%	34,257
12/96	12,246	1,413	11.5%	34,494
12/95	12,344	1,403	11.4%	35,004
Annual Growth	**3.2%**	**4.3%**	**—**	**(1.3%)**

2004 Year-End Financials

Debt ratio: 114.2%
Return on equity: 22.4%
Cash ($ mil.): 2,131
Current ratio: 0.87
Long-term debt ($ mil.): 10,555

No. of shares (mil.): 2,329
Dividends
Yield: 4.3%
Payout: 48.2%
Market value ($ mil.): 22,269

Stock History

NYSE: KPN

	STOCK PRICE ($) FY Close	P/E High	P/E Low	PER SHARE ($) Earnings	PER SHARE ($) Dividends	PER SHARE ($) Book Value
12/04	9.56	11	8	0.85	0.41	3.97
12/03	7.71	6	4	1.37	0.00	3.62
12/02	6.42	—	—	(4.14)	0.00	1.90
12/01	5.06	—	—	(5.24)	0.00	4.74
12/00	11.13	40	6	1.79	0.49	15.64
12/99	48.00	57	22	0.87	0.56	6.67
12/98	25.13	30	13	0.85	0.21	7.24
12/97	11.62	8	7	1.41	0.27	9.26
12/96	10.61	8	6	1.53	0.74	9.90
Annual Growth	**(1.3%)**	**—**	**—**	**(7.1%)**	**(7.1%)**	**(10.8%)**

Kubota

Kubota is an old hand when it comes to turning Japanese soil. The Osaka-based company, which dates to 1890, is Japan's top maker of tractors and farm equipment such as rice transplanters and combine harvesters. It also leads the nation in the production of iron ductile pipe used in water-supply systems. Kubota, a diversified enterprise, makes industrial castings (ductile tunnel segments), PVC pipe, building materials (siding, cement roofing, and prefabricated houses), waste-recycling plants, and agricultural and industrial engines. In addition, the company builds water- and sewage-treatment plants, and it makes vending machines for cigarettes and beverages.

Kubota utilizes what it calls a "medium-term management strategy" that focuses on goals in the near future in an attempt to overcome a dismal economy. The company, which has suffered from the Japanese economic downturn (more than 70% of its sales are in Japan), has reorganized its businesses, cut thousands of jobs, and reduced costs throughout the company in an effort to streamline its operations and return to profitability. Cost reduction and improved efficiency remain top goals for the company as it expects conditions to remain bleak.

That said, Kubota believes its overseas tractor business has good room for growth. The company is less optimistic about its environmental engineering businesses because Japan has reduced its public works expenditures.

HISTORY

The son of a poor farmer and coppersmith, Gonshiro Oode left home in 1885 at age 14 and moved to Osaka to find work. He began as an apprentice at the Kuro Casting Shop, where he learned about metal casting. He saved his money and in 1890 opened Oode Casting.

Oode's shop grew rapidly, thanks to the industrialization of the Japanese economy and the expansion of the iron and steel industries. One of Oode's customers, Toshiro Kubota, took a liking to the hardworking young man, and in 1897 Kubota adopted him. Oode changed his own name to Kubota and also changed the name of his company to Kubota Iron Works.

Kubota made a number of technological breakthroughs in the early 1900s, including a new method of producing cast-iron pipe (developed in 1900). The company became the first to make the pipe in Japan, and it continued to grow as the country modernized its infrastructure.

Kubota began making steam engines, machine tools, and agricultural engines in 1917, and it also began exporting products to countries in Southeast Asia. In 1930 Kubota restructured and incorporated. It continued to add product lines, including agricultural and industrial motors.

Although WWII brought massive destruction to Japan, the peacetime that followed created plenty of work for Kubota's farm equipment and pipe operations as the country rebuilt. By 1960 the company was Japan's largest maker of farm equipment, ductile iron pipe, and cement roofing materials. That year Kubota introduced the first small agricultural tractor in Japan.

Over the next three decades, Kubota expanded its products and its geographic reach. The company created subsidiaries in Taiwan (1961), the

US (1972), Iran (1973), France (1974), and Thailand (1977). It also made a major push into the US high-tech industry during the 1980s with the 44% purchase of supercomputer graphics company Ardent (1985). Two years later Kubota bought disk company Akashic Memories, and in 1989 it formed a joint venture with disk drive maker Maxtor to build optical storage products.

While loading up on high-tech operations, Kubota also expanded its lower-tech core businesses in the US. The company opened its first US manufacturing plant in 1989 in Georgia to make front-end loader attachments, and in 1990 it bought a 5% interest in Cummins Engine.

The next year Kubota took over the operations of struggling Stardent Computers; however, Kubota was unable to revive the graphic workstation business and dissolved its Kubota Graphics subsidiary in California in 1994.

In 1995 Kubota formed subsidiary Kubota Biotech to develop and sell biotechnological products such as biological insecticides. The next year Kubota launched a rice-cultivation machine for use in large fields.

Kubota gave its unprofitable computer hard disk business the boot in 1997 with the sale of Akashic Memories and the management buyout of subsidiary Maxoptix (computer memory storage drives). In 1998 the company formed a joint venture in China to make cast-steel products, and the following year it established a subsidiary there to make combine harvesters.

With its sales decreasing in response to Japan's economic slowdown, in 2000 Kubota implemented a three-year cost-cutting strategy. It began cutting its workforce by about 13% and jettisoning unprofitable businesses. The company's net sales increased in 2001, the result in part of its introduction of sub-compact tractors to the US the previous year. Kubota continued slimming down in 2002, exiting its Kubota Concrete (concrete piles) and Kubota House (pre-manufactured housing) businesses.

EXECUTIVES

President and Representative Director:
  Daisuke Hatakake, age 64
EVP and Representative Director: Akio Nishino, age 64
Executive Managing Director: Yoshihiro Fujio, age 61
Executive Managing Director: Moriya Hayashi, age 61
Executive Managing Director: Toshihiro Fukuda, age 60
Managing Director: Yasuo Masumoto, age 58
Managing Director: Yoshiharu Nishiguchi, age 58
Managing Director: Eisaku Shinohara, age 58
Managing Director: Nobuo Izawa, age 57
Director: Yoshihiko Tabata, age 59
Director: Kazunobu Ueta, age 58
Director: Takashi Shoji, age 58
Director: Tokuji Ohgi, age 58
Director: Morimitsu Katayama, age 57
Director: Nobuyuki Toshikuni, age 54
Director: Hirokazu Nara, age 57
Director: Masayoshi Kitaoka, age 56
Director and President, Kubota Tractor Corporation:
  Tetsuji (Mike) Tomita, age 55
Director: Masatoshi Kimata, age 54
Auditors: Deloitte Touche Tohmatsu

LOCATIONS

HQ: Kubota Corporation
  2-47, Shikitsuhigashi 1-chome, Naniwa-ku,
  Osaka 556-8601, Japan
Phone: +81-6-6648-2111   **Fax:** +81-6-6648-3862
US HQ: 2715 Ramsey Rd., Gainesville, GA 30501
US Phone: 770-532-0038   **US Fax:** 770-532-9057
Web: www.kubota.co.jp

Kubota has primary manufacturing facilities in Japan, and it has subsidiaries and affiliates in the Americas, Asia, Australia, Europe, and the Pacific Rim region.

2005 Sales

	$ mil.	% of total
Japan	7,967	72
North America	2,198	20
Other	884	8
Adjustments	(1,860)	—
Total	**9,189**	**100**

PRODUCTS/OPERATIONS

2005 Sales

	$ mil.	% of total
Internal Combustion Engine & Machinery	5,445	59
Pipes, Valves & Industrial Castings	1,595	18
Environmental Engineering	1,100	12
Other	1,049	11
Total	**9,189**	**100**

Selected Products

Internal Combustion Engine and Machinery
  Ancillary tools and implements for agriculture
  Implements and attachments for farm equipment
  Construction machinery
  Carriers
  Mini-excavators
  Welders
  Wheel loaders
  Engines
  Gasoline and diesel engines
    for farming and industrial purposes
  Farm facilities
  Cleaning and vending machines for rice
  Cooperative facilities for rice seedlings
  Dairy and stock raising facilities
  Farm facilities
  Gardening facilities
  Multipurpose warehouse
  Rice driers
  Rice mill plants
  Farm machinery
  Combine harvesters
  Harvesters
  Power tillers
  Reaper binders
  Rice transplanters
  Tillers
  Tractors
  Outdoor power equipment
  Lawn and garden equipment
Pipes, Valves, and Industrial Castings
  Castings
  Cargo oil pipes
  Cast steel products
  Castings for engines
  Castings for machinery
  Cast-iron soil pipes
  Ductile tunnel segments
  G-columns
  G-piles
  Reformer tubes
  Rolls for steel mills
  Suction roll shells for paper industry
  Pipes
  Ductile iron pipes
  Filament winding pipes
  Plastic valves
  Polyethylene pipes
  Polyvinyl chloride pipes and fittings
  Spiral welded steel pipes
Environmental Engineering
  Amusement fountains
  Solid waste treatment plants
  Water and sewage treatment plants

Other
  Air-conditioning equipment
  CAD systems
  Cement siding materials
  Colored cement roofing materials
  Condominiums
  Irrigation and water supply systems
  Photovoltaic shingles
  Pipe-laying work
  Scales
  Vending machines
  Weighing and measuring control systems
  Crushing plants
  Dioxins decomposition systems
  Grinding mills
  Industrial waste treatment plants
  Landfill leachate treatment facilities
  Nightsoil treatment plants
  Pumps
  Pyrolysis gasification and melting furnaces
  Refuse incineration and melting plants
  Repair and maintenance works for sewage treatment
    and refuse incineration plants
  Septic tanks
  Sewage sludge incineration and melting plants
  Sewage treatment plants
  Submerged membrane systems for night-soil
    and wastewater purification
  Waste pulverizing plants
  Waste recycling plants
  Water purification facilities
  Water treatment plants

COMPETITORS

AGCO
Caterpillar
CNH Global
Crane
Deere
Fiat
Fuji Electric
Ishikawajima-Harima
Isuzu
Komatsu
Lafarge
Marubeni-Komatsu
Nippon Steel
Sekisui House
Toro
Toyota

HISTORICAL FINANCIALS

Company Type: Public

Income Statement

FYE: March 31

	REVENUE ($ mil.)	NET INCOME ($ mil.)	NET PROFIT MARGIN	EMPLOYEES
3/05	9,189	1,102	12.0%	—
3/04	8,776	110	1.3%	22,198
3/03	7,718	(67)	—	22,834
3/02	7,339	72	1.0%	23,064
3/01	8,020	79	1.0%	25,369
3/00	9,314	155	1.7%	24,334
3/99	8,072	125	1.5%	24,900
3/98	7,799	165	2.1%	20,000
3/97	9,206	233	2.5%	18,500
3/96	10,110	243	2.4%	21,000
Annual Growth	(1.1%)	18.3%	—	0.7%

2005 Year-End Financials

Debt ratio: 24.4%
Return on equity: 26.9%
Cash ($ mil.): 697
Current ratio: 1.34
Long-term debt ($ mil.): 1,098
No. of shares (mil.): 260
Dividends
  Yield: 0.9%
  Payout: 6.2%
Market value ($ mil.): 6,988

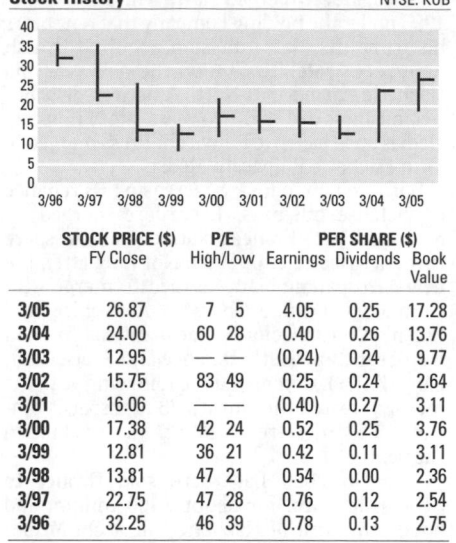

	STOCK PRICE ($) FY Close	P/E High/Low		PER SHARE ($) Earnings	Dividends	Book Value
3/05	26.87	7	5	4.05	0.25	17.28
3/04	24.00	60	28	0.40	0.26	13.76
3/03	12.95	—	—	(0.24)	0.24	9.77
3/02	15.75	83	49	0.25	0.24	2.64
3/01	16.06	—	—	(0.40)	0.27	3.11
3/00	17.38	42	24	0.52	0.25	3.76
3/99	12.81	36	21	0.42	0.11	3.11
3/98	13.81	47	21	0.54	0.00	2.36
3/97	22.75	47	28	0.76	0.12	2.54
3/96	32.25	46	39	0.78	0.13	2.75
Annual Growth	(2.0%)	—	—	20.1%	7.5%	22.6%

Kyocera

Don't confuse Kyocera's ceramics with teacups and pottery. The company, which began producing technical ceramics more than half a century ago, makes a wide range of components and fine ceramic products — including capacitors, fiber-optic connectors, and semiconductors — primarily for customers in the electronics industry. Besides its ceramics and other electronic components, the company makes various types of finished electronics products, including cell phones, office equipment such as photocopiers and fax machines, and digital and film cameras.

Kyocera was hit hard in the early 2000s by weak demand for electronics and telecommunications gear, as more than 80% of its business came from customers in the information technology and telecom markets. In response, the company has worked to diversify its customer base by developing products for new markets, such as components for the automotive industry.

Kyocera has also expanded its manufacturing operations in China and consolidated operations elsewhere to cut costs. The company has operations in the Americas, Asia, and Europe; Japan accounts for 40% of sales.

HISTORY

Born to a poor Japanese family in 1932, Kazuo Inamori never quite fit the mold. He went to work for Shofu Industries (ceramic insulators) in the mid-1950s, but quit three years later and started Kyoto Ceramic with seven colleagues in 1959. Their first product was a ceramic insulator for cathode-ray tubes. In the late 1960s the company developed the ceramic package for integrated circuits (ICs) that has made it a world-class supplier.

Kyoto Ceramic started manufacturing in the US in 1971. A few years later the company began to diversify its interests when it ventured into artificial gemstones (Crescent Vert, 1977) and dental implants (New Medical, 1978). In 1979

Inamori bought control of failing Cybernet Electronics (Japanese citizens-band radio maker), using it to move Kyoto Ceramic into the production of copiers and stereos.

The company merged five subsidiaries in 1982, forming Kyocera Corporation. The 1983 acquisition of Yashica moved it into the production of cameras and other optical equipment. That year Kyocera ran into trouble. At the time Nippon Telegraph and Telephone (NTT) was the only legal supplier of phones in Japan, and when Kyocera started marketing cordless phones without the required approval, the government forced it to recall the phones.

The government abolished NTT's monopoly in 1984, and Kyocera joined 24 other companies to form Daini-Denden ("second phone company") — now KDDI. In 1988 Inamori set up Kyocera regional offices in Asia, Europe, and the US. The company bought Elco (electronic connectors, US) in 1989 and AVX (multilayer ceramic capacitors, US) in 1990.

In order to diversify further, Kyocera entered into a series of alliances in the 1990s that included partnerships with Canon to produce video and electronic optical equipment, with Carl Zeiss (Germany) to make cameras and lenses, and with Cirrus Logic to make chips for a cordless phone project.

The company's Guangdong-based optical instrument joint venture began making cameras and lenses for the Chinese market in 1996. The next year Inamori went into partial retirement. In 1998 the company took over failed copier maker Mita Industrial, which had been a major buyer of Kyocera's electronic components.

In 1999 Kyocera acquired Golden Genesis (solar electric systems, US) and changed the company's name to Kyocera Solar, Inc. In the same year Kyocera's product line grew even more diverse as it entered the health food market and began selling mushroom products in Japan. Kyocera purchased the wireless phone business of QUALCOMM in early 2000.

Also in early in 2000 the company's acquisition of failed copier maker Mita Industrial (which changed its name to Kyocera Mita Corporation) was approved. The deal included the forgiveness (by Mita's creditors) of most of Mita's debt and a cash infusion in Kyocera Mita by Kyocera.

EXECUTIVES

Chairman Emeritus: Kazuo Inamori, age 73
Chairman, Kyocera Mita and Director: Koji Seki, age 67
Chairman and CEO: Yasuo Nishiguchi, age 62
Vice Chairman and CFO: Masahiro Umemura, age 62
President, COO, and Director: Makoto Kawamura
President, Kyocera Chemical and Director: Noboru Nakamura, age 61
President, Kyocera Communication Systems and Director: Naoyuki Morita, age 63
President, Kyocera ELCO and Director: Yuzo Yamamura, age 64
President, Kyocera International and Director: Rodney N. Lanthorne, age 60
President, Kyocera Kinseki and Director: Isao Kishimoto, age 61
President, Kyocera Optec and Director: Michihisa Yamamoto, age 63
President, Kyocera Tianjin Sales and Trading and Director: Hisao Hisaki, age 59
President and CEO, AVX Corporation and Director: John S. Gilbertson, age 61
Senior Managing Executive Officer: Isao Yukawa

Managing Executive Officer: Takashi Itoh
Managing Executive Officer: Tetsuo Kuba
Managing Executive Officer: Tatsumi Maeda
Managing Executive Officer: Osamu Nomoto
Managing Executive Officer: Hisashi Sakumi
Managing Executive Officer: Eiichi Toriyama
Managing Executive Officer: Tsutomu Yamori
Auditors: ChuoAoyama PricewaterhouseCoopers

LOCATIONS

HQ: Kyocera Corporation
6 Takeda Tobadono-cho, Fushimi-ku,
Kyoto 612-8501, Japan
Phone: +81-75-604-3500 **Fax:** +81-75-604-3501
US HQ: 8611 Balboa Ave., San Diego, CA 92123-1580
US Phone: 858-576-2600 **US Fax:** 858-569-9412
Web: www.kyocera.co.jp

Kyocera has operations in Australia, Brazil, China, the Czech Republic, France, Germany, Hong Kong, India, Indonesia, Israel, Italy, Japan, Malaysia, Mexico, the Netherlands, Singapore, South Korea, the UK, and the US.

2005 Sales

	% of total
Asia	
Japan	40
Other countries	17
US	21
Europe	15
Other countries	7
Total	**100**

PRODUCTS/OPERATIONS

2005 Sales

	% of total
Equipment Group	44
Fine Ceramics Group	24
Electronic Device Group	22
Other	10
Total	**100**

Selected Products

Electronic Equipment
  Information equipment
    Copy machines
    Facsimile machines
    Page printers (Ecosys)
  Optical instruments
    Compact zoom cameras
    Digital cameras
    SLR cameras and lenses
  Telecommunications equipment
    Cellular handsets
    Personal Handyphone System (PHS) products (base stations handsets)
    Wireless local loop systems
Fine Ceramics
  Applied Ceramic Products Group
    Cutting tools (Ceratip)
    Dental and orthopedic implants (Bioceram)
    Jewelry and applied ceramic products (Crescent Vert)
    Solar energy products
  Fine ceramic parts
    Ceramic substrates
    Fiber-optic network components
    OA equipment components
    Parts for semiconductor fabrication equipment
  Semiconductor parts
    Ceramic dual-in-line packages (Cerdips)
    Metalized products
    Multilayer packages
    Organic packages
Electronic Devices
  Capacitors
  High-frequency modules
  Thin-film products
  Timing devices (TCXOs, VCOs)

HISTORICAL FINANCIALS

Company Type: Public

Income Statement

FYE: March 31

	REVENUE ($ mil.)	NET INCOME ($ mil.)	NET PROFIT MARGIN	EMPLOYEES
3/05	11,034	429	3.9%	—
3/04	10,969	655	6.0%	57,870
3/03	9,066	349	3.8%	49,420
3/02	7,779	240	3.1%	44,235
3/01	10,199	1,742	17.1%	51,113
3/00	7,779	489	6.3%	—
3/99	6,007	239	4.0%	—
3/98	5,454	354	6.5%	—
3/97	5,764	368	6.4%	—
3/96	6,048	771	12.8%	—
Annual Growth	6.9%	(6.3%)	—	4.2%

2005 Year-End Financials

Debt ratio: 2.9%
Return on equity: 3.9%
Cash ($ mil.): 2,903
Current ratio: 2.60
Long-term debt ($ mil.): 314

No. of shares (mil.): 187
Dividends
  Yield: 0.4%
  Payout: 12.7%
Market value ($ mil.): 13,394

Stock History

NYSE: KYO

3/96 3/97 3/98 3/99 3/00 3/01 3/02 3/03 3/04 3/05

	STOCK PRICE ($) FY Close	P/E High/Low	PER SHARE ($) Earnings	PER SHARE ($) Dividends	PER SHARE ($) Book Value
3/05	71.44	40 30	2.29	0.29	58.57
3/04	83.94	24 13	3.51	0.22	59.17
3/03	49.29	41 24	1.87	0.49	45.98
3/02	70.00	79 40	1.27	0.48	41.19
3/01	92.50	20 8	9.19	0.55	42.62
3/00	166.00	109 20	2.58	0.50	41.00
3/99	52.63	47 32	1.26	0.22	34.26
3/98	53.63	46 23	1.86	0.45	15.21
3/97	56.88	40 27	1.96	0.27	15.31
3/96	67.25	22 15	4.10	0.24	16.68
Annual Growth	0.7%	— —	(6.3%)	2.1%	15.0%

Lagardère SCA

Lagardère is flying high with its mix of media and missiles. The company's primary holdings include publisher Hachette Filipacchi Médias (*Elle, Premier,* and *Car & Driver*) and a 15% stake in #3 aerospace firm European Aeronautic Defence and Space Company, which produces defense and weapon systems, military aircraft, satellites and space systems, and commercial aircraft. Lagardère's other media holdings include book publishing (Hachette Livre and Editis), Internet content (Lagardère Active), and satellite television (34%-owned CanalSatellite). The conglomerate's media operations account for about 65% of its revenue.

Eager to continue the growth of its media operations, Lagardère has been studying a number of possible acquisitions. The company bought the assets of Vivendi Universal Publishing (VUP), with the exception of the Houghton Mifflin educational subsidiary, from troubled media giant Vivendi Universal. To get past antitrust authorities, Lagardère sold 60% of VUP, which it renamed Editis, to Wendel Investissement. To fund further acquisitions, the firm also decreased its stake in T-Online International.

The company is also beginning to leverage its established print brands across other mediums such as television and the Internet through Lagardère Active. Lagardère has expanded its retailing business through its purchase of 16 French Virgin Megastores from Richard Branson's Virgin Group. Chairman Arnaud Lagardère owns about 5% of the company through Lagardère Capital & Management.

HISTORY

Jean-Luc Lagardère began his rise to industrial titan when he joined French aerospace contractor Dassault as an engineer in the 1950s. He was tapped to be president and CEO of military equipment manufacturer Mécanique Aviation TRAction (Matra) in 1963, where he pushed the firm to branch out into electronics, space systems, and automobiles during the 1970s. Lagardère turned his focus to the media world in 1981 when he joined with Filipacchi Médias to acquire control of venerable French publishing firm Hachette.

Started by schoolteacher Louis Hachette in 1826, the publishing firm first catered to the textbook market and later began producing general trade books and travel guides. It became involved in the newspaper business in the 1920s and launched fashion magazine *Elle* in 1945. A diversification strategy in the 1970s proved disastrous, however, leading to Lagardère's takeover.

The engineer-turned-entrepreneur launched international spinoffs of Hachette's magazines, including a successful US *Elle* in 1985 in partnership with media maven Rupert Murdoch. In the late 1980s Hachette invested in radio broadcasting, bought US magazine distributor Curtis Circulation, and acquired Spanish encyclopedia publisher Salvat. Meanwhile, Matra launched its Espace minivan in 1983 (marketed by Renault). In 1988 Hachette acquired encyclopedia publisher Grolier for $1.1 billion and later bought out Murdoch's share of *Elle*.

In 1990 Hachette bought a 25% stake in money-losing French TV network La Cinq. The station collapsed a year later, leaving Hachette with a $643 million write-off. To cover the huge

debt, Lagardère merged Matra with Hachette in 1993 under the holding company that now bears his name. Its Matra division acquired British Aerospace's satellite division the next year and Hachette expanded its North American distribution business in 1995. Two years later Filipacchi Médias and Hachette Filipacchi Press merged to form Hachette Filipacchi Médias.

With French industry decreasing its reliance on defense business, Lagardère merged its Matra unit with France's state-owned aerospace firm, Aerospatiale, in 1999. Not long after, the new Aerospatiale Matra agreed to merge with Germany's DaimlerChrysler Aerospace and Spain's Construcciones Aeronauticas to form European Aeronautic Defence and Space Company (EADS). Completed the following year, the merger created the world's #3 aerospace company. (Lagardère retained a minority stake in the venture.)

Later in 2000 Lagardère sold Grolier to Scholastic Corp. for about $400 million and bought the rest of Hachette Filipacchi Médias from its minority shareholders. The same year Jean-Luc Lagardère escaped a 1988 fraud charge when a judge ruled that the time limit for prosecution had expired. To begin leveraging its media assets, the company created multimedia unit Lagardère Active in 2001.

Jean-Luc Lagardère died in 2003 of a rare neurological disease. Also that year the company exited the automotive design business with the sale of its Matra subsidiary.

EXECUTIVES

Chairman; Chairman and CEO, Lagardère Media; and Chairman, EADS: Arnaud Lagardère, age 44
Deputy Chairman and COO: Philippe Camus, age 55
COO: Pierre Leroy
EVP Human Relations and Communications: Thierry Funck-Brentano
EVP and CFO: Dominique D'Hinnin
EVP, EADS International: Jean-Paul Gut, age 44
COO, Lagardère Media: Jean-Luc Allavena
VP Strategy and Development, Lagardère Media: Frèdèrique Bredin
Chairman and CEO, Hachette Distribution Services: Jean-Louis Nachury
Chairman and CEO, Hachette Filipacchi Médias: Gérald de Roquemaurel
Chairman and CEO, Hachette Livre: Arnaud Nourry
Co-CEO, EADS: Thomas Enders, age 46
CEO, Lagardère Newspapers: Ghislain Leleu
Co-CEO, EADS: Noel Forgeard
Auditors: Barbier Frinault & Autres; Mazars & Guérard; Alain Ghez

LOCATIONS

HQ: Lagardère SCA
  4 rue de Presbourg, 75016 Paris, France
Phone: +33-1-40-69-1600   **Fax:** +33-1-40-69-2131
US HQ: 1633 Broadway, 45th Fl., New York, NY 10019
US Phone: 212-767-6753   **US Fax:** 212-767-5635
Web: www.lagardere.fr

2004 Sales

	% of total
Europe	
France	31
Other EU countries	33
Other countries	4
North America	20
Asia/Pacific	7
Middle East	3
Other regions	2
Total	**100**

PRODUCTS/OPERATIONS

2004 Sales

	% of total
Lagardère Media	64
EADS	36
Total	**100**

Selected Operations

Lagardère Media
  Editis (book publishing)
  Hachette Distribution Services (newspaper and
    magazine distribution)
  Virgin Megastores (entertainment retail stores)
  Hachette Filipacchi Médias (magazine publishing)
  Hachette Livre (book publishing)
    Hodder Headline
Lagardère Active
  CanalSatellite (34%, satellite broadcasting)
  Lagardère Active Broadband
    (Internet and new media)
  Lagardère Active Broadcasting
    (99%, radio broadcasting)
  Lagardère Thématiques
High Technology
  European Aeronautic Defence
    and Space Company (15%)
    Aeronautics
    Airbus
    Defense and civil systems
    Military transport aircraft
    Space systems
Magazines
  Car & Driver
  Elle
  Entrevue
  Paris Match
  Premiere
Radio Stations
  Europe 1 Communication (news and talk radio)
  Europe 2 (pop music)
  RFM (oldies)

COMPETITORS

Advance Publications	Meredith
Axel Springer	Modern Times Group
BAE SYSTEMS	News Corp.
BAE Systems Inc.	Northrop Grumman
Bertelsmann	NRJ
Boeing	Pearson
Bombardier	PRIMEDIA
Dawson Holdings	Raytheon
Disney	Siemens
Emap	Textron
Hearst	Time Warner
Lockheed Martin	Viacom

HISTORICAL FINANCIALS

Company Type: Public

Income Statement

FYE: December 31

	REVENUE ($ mil.)	NET INCOME ($ mil.)	NET PROFIT MARGIN	EMPLOYEES
12/04	19,065	521	2.7%	46,947
12/03	16,404	419	2.6%	43,009
12/02	14,474	(305)	—	45,826
12/01	11,777	546	4.6%	46,337
12/00	12,173	547	4.5%	43,902
12/99	12,865	243	1.9%	49,285
12/98	1,967	50	2.5%	49,961
12/97	10,986	230	2.1%	46,230
12/96	10,778	198	1.8%	47,172
12/95	10,711	128	1.2%	43,622
Annual Growth	**6.6%**	**16.8%**	**—**	**0.8%**

2004 Year-End Financials

Debt ratio: 68.1%   Current ratio: 1.31
Return on equity: 10.0%   Long-term debt ($ mil.): 3,744
Cash ($ mil.): 2,435

Net Income History   Euronext Paris: MMB

Legal & General Group

Generally speaking, Legal & General Group is one of the UK's biggest life insurers. The holding company's subsidiaries provide groups and individuals with life, health, property, auto, and liability lines of insurance. The firm is a major provider of investment services, including fund management, unit trusts, and individual savings accounts, or ISAs. Legal & General also provides mortgage loans and has real estate (Legal & General Estate Agencies) and venture capital (Legal & General Ventures) operations. In the US, the company does business as Banner Life Insurance Company and William Penn Life Insurance Company of New York.

The company's primary market is the UK, where it has deals with UK-based Bradford & Bingley, Alliance & Leicester, and Barclays to expand its product offerings and boost its distribution channels.

Legal & General is known for conservative, prudent growth. Longer-living pensioners, as well as the general slump in the global equities market, have impacted the company's bottom line. Although Legal & General is focusing on its core domestic market, it has expanded in France, Germany, and the Netherlands. Legal & General's fund management unit is one of the UK's largest pension funds managers.

The company's venture capital arm, Legal & General Ventures, may be buying a number of hospitals from BUPA in a deal that could be worth about $187 million (£100 million).

Legal & General has agreed to sell its 90% stake in Gresham Insurance Company to Barclays, which already holds the other 10%.

HISTORY

The Legal in Legal & General's name comes from its founding mission — to provide life insurance to members of the legal profession. The company was started in 1836 by six lawyers as the Legal & General Life Assurance Society; its first customer, solicitor Thomas Smith, ill-manneredly died four years later after paying less than 200 pounds on a 1,000-pound policy.

Throughout that century and into the next, the company made loans to individuals and corporations; it also moved into real estate. After struggling under claims during WWI and the 1918 flu pandemic, it moved into fire and accident coverage in 1920. It opened membership to nonlawyers in 1929. The company took over the UK operations of the US firm Metropolitan Life (MetLife) in 1933.

In 1934 Legal & General bought Gresham Life Assurance and Gresham Fire and Accident, to gain a presence in Australia. During WWII the company was hit hard by German air attacks, both physically (it had to relocate away from London for a time) and at the bottom line.

The postwar years were a time of expansion as the company moved into South Africa and also broadened its operations at home. In 1949 it moved into marine insurance and in 1956 inaugurated life insurance in Australia.

The company began expanding its product offerings in the 1970s with managed pension funds and retail unit trusts. It established a direct sales force for life and pensions in 1977. The company also formed alliances with several European insurance companies and sold its Gresham life subsidiary. In 1979 it formed Legal & General Group Limited as a holding company for its now-separate insurance, international, and investment management operations.

In 1981 Legal & General bought US auto insurer GEICO's two-thirds interest in Government Employees Life Insurance Company, changing the subsidiary's name to Banner Life. Three years later it bought the Dutch operations of Unilife Assurance and created a subsidiary in the Netherlands. Despite all this activity, however, the company's performance during the 1980s was poor, and it brought in David Prosser (who became CEO in 1991) to goose its asset management operations.

In 1989 the company bought William Penn Life Insurance from Continental Corp. and opened its first real estate agency — just in time for the real estate market crash. Legal & General and other mortgage guarantee insurers were also squeezed by the resulting increase in mortgage default rates as homebuyers were caught between high interest rates and high unemployment.

The company formed a joint venture with Woolwich Building Society to provide Woolwich customers with insurance products in 1995. The next year it followed the insurance industry trend by establishing a bank of its own.

With each succeeding merger of its rivals, Legal & General became the target of rumors about its own fate. The company has remained adamantly independent, with Prosser claiming that Legal & General could instead benefit by picking up business left behind by the new entities.

In 1998 the British insurance industry was stung by scandalous revelations regarding improper pension sales in the late 1980s and early 1990s. Legal & General set aside about $1 billion to compensate victims; it also sold its Australian operations. In 1999 banking company National Westminster and Legal & General talked takeover, but the deal fell through (NatWest was eventually bought by Royal Bank of Scotland).

In 2001 Legal & General announced a deal with UK-based Barclays to provide the bank's customers with life insurance and pension products. In 2002 Legal & General extended its marketing agreement with UK financial services company Alliance & Leicester.

EXECUTIVES

Chairman: Rob J. Margetts, age 58, $520,074 pay
Vice Chairman: Sir David A. Walker, age 65,
  $167,579 pay
Group Chief Executive: David Prosser, age 61,
  $2,195,868 pay
Deputy CEO: Tim Breedon, age 46

Group Director, Retail Distribution: Kate Avery, age 44, $770,480 pay
Group Director, Finance: Andrew Palmer, age 51, $1,024,738 pay
Group Director, UK Operations: Robin Phipps, age 54, $1,097,934 pay
Group Director, Product and Corporate: John Pollock, age 46, $568,229 pay
Chief Executive Officer of Legal & General Investment Management (LGIM): Peter Chambers
Insurance Business Development Director: Peter Richmond
Marketing Director, General Insurance: Garry Skelton
Head of Legal: Geoffrey Timms
Head, Publicity and Press Relations: John Morgan, age 50
Company Secretary: David W. Binding
Systems Actuary: Anant Chavda
Auditors: PricewaterhouseCoopers LLP

LOCATIONS

HQ: Legal & General Group Plc
Temple Court, 11 Queen Victoria St.,
London EC4N 4TP, United Kingdom
Phone: +44-20-7528-6200   **Fax:** +44-20-7528-6222
US HQ: 1701 Research Blvd., Rockville, MD 20850
US Phone: 301-279-4800   **US Fax:** 301-294-6960
Web: www.landg.com

Legal & General Group operates primarily in the UK, but also in France, Germany, the Netherlands, and the US.

PRODUCTS/OPERATIONS

2004 Operating Profits

	% of total
Life & pensions	78
Institutional fund management	13
General insurance	4
Other	5
Total	**100**

COMPETITORS

AEGON	ING
AIG	Lincoln National (UK)
Alliance & Leicester	Lloyds TSB
Allianz	Prudential plc
AMVESCAP	Resolution
Aviva	Royal & Sun Alliance
AXA	Insurance
Guardian Royal	Standard Life
Exchange plc	United Assurance

HISTORICAL FINANCIALS

Company Type: Public

Income Statement

FYE: December 31

	ASSETS ($ mil.)	NET INCOME ($ mil.)	INCOME AS % OF ASSETS	EMPLOYEES
12/04	292,079	894	0.3%	8,807
12/03	222,126	718	0.3%	8,547
12/02	171,125	(289)	—	8,873
12/01	157,114	(277)	—	8,453
12/00	161,651	473	0.3%	7,900
12/99	165,216	949	0.6%	8,289
12/98	130,354	675	0.5%	7,899
12/97	97,434	811	0.8%	7,203
Annual Growth	**17.0%**	**1.4%**	**—**	**2.9%**

2004 Year-End Financials

Equity as % of assets: 2.2%   Long-term debt ($ mil.): 65,364
Return on assets: 0.3%   Sales ($ mil.): 68,099
Return on equity: 14.5%

Net Income History   Pink Sheets: LGGNY

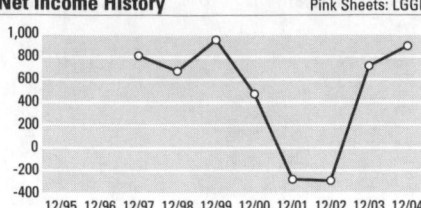

LEGO Holding

Toy blocks are the building blocks of success at LEGO. Since 1949 LEGO Holding (aka LEGO Group) has made more than 200 billion of its interlocking toys, keeping little hands and imaginations busy around the globe. In a nod to kids' high-tech skills, it offers LEGO kits to build PC-programmable robots (including Spybotics and Mindstorms), and its BIONICLE line features an evolving story line on the Internet and various merchandising opportunities. The group also owns LEGO retail outlets in the US and Europe. Because of a slump in toy sales and subsequent losses, the group has sold its theme parks and is closing factories and cutting its staff. Vice chairman Kjeld Kirk Kristiansen is LEGO's majority shareholder.

The word LEGO is derived from the Danish words for "play well," and children have been playing well with the company's familiar building blocks for years. In fact, LEGO toys were named the Toy of the Century by *Fortune* magazine in 1999. In an effort to incorporate its blocks into the business world, LEGO has introduced a tool called Serious Play, which is designed to assist business managers by combining creative play with corporate strategizing.

The company has been working to improve its disappointing sales performance in the past few years with other product additions such as the widely successful *Harry Potter* and *Bob the Builder* lines, as well as forming alliances with the NHL, the NBA, and NIKE. In July 2005 the group sold its LEGOLAND parks, which feature LEGO sculptures, rides, and exhibits, to the Blackstone Group.

In addition, the company is trying to divest its 44% stake in playground equipment manufacturer KOMPAN. As part of its reorganization strategy, LEGO plans to shift much of its production operations, which have been in Denmark, Switzerland, and the US, to low-costing countries in 2006. If the company's revenues do not improve, LEGO might consider selling itself, according to chairman Mads Øvlisen, instead of closing down.

LEGO also produces television shows, educational materials, and merchandise such as books, video games, and computer game software. In late 2003 LEGO and Miramax Film Corp. debuted (on DVD and video) *BIONICLE: Mask of Light* — a 3-D animated film based on the BIONICLE toy line. It has strengthened its licensing agreement with book publisher Scholastic, giving the company the rights to publish a wide variety of materials based on LEGO's intellectual properties.

HISTORY

Ole Kirk Christiansen opened a carpentry shop in 1916 in Denmark and in 1932 began making carved wooden toys. Two years later Ole held a contest among his employees to name the company, from which came LEGO (a combination of two Danish words, "leg" and "godt," meaning "play well"). A fire destroyed the LEGO factory in 1942, but the company quickly resumed manufacturing.

The availability of quality plastic following WWII prompted the company to add plastic toys to its line. The predecessor to the common LEGO block was invented in 1949; called Automatic Binding Bricks, they fit on top of each other but did not snap together.

After hearing criticism that no company made a comprehensive toy system, in 1954 Ole's son Godtfred assembled a list of 10 product criteria for LEGO's toys, including that they have lots of compatible components. Deciding that the Automatic Binding Bricks had the most potential, the firm launched the first LEGO playset in 1955. It introduced the "stud and tube" snap-together building block in 1958. LEGOs were soon one of the most popular toys in Europe. When a second fire in 1960 destroyed its warehouse for wooden toys, the company ceased production of wooden items in favor of plastics.

Luggage-maker Samsonite began manufacturing and distributing LEGOs in the US in 1961 under license. LEGO's first LEGOLAND park, built from 42 million LEGO blocks, opened in Billund, Denmark, in 1968. (A UK park followed in 1996, a California park in 1999, and one in Germany in 2002.) By 1973, after relatively lackluster US sales, Samsonite opted not to renew its license, and the LEGO Company set up a sales and production facility in Connecticut. US sales increased tenfold by 1975.

Aiming for the preteen market, the company introduced the more-complex LEGO Technic model sets in 1977 and the popular LEGOLAND Space playset two years later. However, LEGO hit a bump when its patent for the LEGO brick expired in 1981 and a slew of knockoffs flooded the market.

The first LEGO Imagination Center opened in Minneapolis in 1992, and the second followed in Walt Disney World five years later. Two years later Godtfred died; his son, Kjeld, who changed the spelling of Christiansen to Kristiansen, succeeded him.

In the 1990s growth of the video game industry far outpaced the growth of the construction toys market, and LEGO suffered. With profits shrinking, in 1998 the company reversed its tradition of avoiding commercial tie-ins; it snapped together an agreement to produce building kits and figures based on the popular *Star Wars* movies and Walt Disney's Winnie the Pooh. However, those events came too late to prevent LEGO from suffering its first loss since the 1930s. The company began cutting up to 10% of its workers in 1999.

To build up its interactive, electronic, and educational toy development, LEGO bought smart toys developer Zowie Intertainment in 2000, marking the first time the company purchased another toy maker. In 2001, LEGO inked a deal to create children's online games and activities for software giant Microsoft Corporation. After suffering its biggest annual loss since 1954, LEGO announced in 2001 it would cut 500 jobs and discontinue some noncore products.

In 2003 LEGO entered into the arts and crafts market with the introduction of CLIKITS: a fashion design system made up of a variety of kits allowing girls (ages six and up) to design room decor, picture frames, jewelry, and fashion and hair accessories.

In 2004 co-owner Kjeld Kirk Kristiansen resigned as the company's CEO, but remained on the board as vice chairman. Joergen Vig Knudstorp, SVP of corporate affairs, was named as his replacement. Later that year the company changed its name from LEGO Company to LEGO Group. It also created LEGO Holding A/S to be parent of both the Danish and Swiss operations of the group.

EXECUTIVES

Chairman: Mads Øvlisen, age 65
Vice Chairman: Kjeld Kirk Kristiansen
CEO: Jørgen Vig Knudstorp, age 35
SVP, Corporate Finance: Jesper Ovesen, age 46
SVP, Global Innovation and Marketing: Mads Nipper
SVP, Global Supply Chain: Lars Altemark
SVP, European and Emerging Markets: Henrik Poulsen
SVP, LEGO Americas/Pacific/Direct:
  Søren Torp Laursen
SVP, LEGOLAND Parks: Mads Ryder
COO, LEGO Americas: Stig Toftgaard
Head, Legal Services: Poul H. Nielsen
Head, Corporate Communications: Charlotte Simonsen
Director, Human Resources: Christian Iversen
Senior Producer, LEGO Virtual (Web Division):
  Leah Weston
Manager, Marketing, Bionicle: Lars Kaae
Brand Manager, CLIKITS: Joanna Gale
VP, LEGO Brand Retail, US: Matt Harker
Director, Global Marketing Communications, LEGO Systems, US: Lars Norman Andersen
Senior Manager, Strategic Alliances and Promotions, LEGO Systems, US: Heather Kashner
Auditors: PricewaterhouseCoopers

LOCATIONS

HQ: LEGO Holding A/S
  Aastvej 1, DK-7190 Billund, Denmark
Phone: +45-79-50-60-70   **Fax:** +45-75-33-27-25
US HQ: 555 Taylor Rd., Enfield, CT 06083
US Phone: 860-763-3211   **US Fax:** 860-763-6680
Web: www.lego.com

LEGO Holding operates in more than 30 countries worldwide.

PRODUCTS/OPERATIONS

Selected Products

Alpha Team
BIONICLE
CLIKITS (fashion design system for girls)
Discovery Kids
Dora the Explorer
Harry Potter
Knights Kindom
LEGO BABY toys
LEGO Belville toys (for girls)
LEGO *Bob the Builder*
LEGO City
LEGO Creator sets
LEGO Designer
LEGO Duplo
LEGO Factory
LEGO Mindstorms
LEGO Quatro
LEGO Racers
LEGO Star Wars
LEGO Technic
Orient Expedition
Spiderman 2
Spybotics
Trains
X-Pod

COMPETITORS

Apple Computer	Mega Bloks
Corgi International	Namco Bandai
Discovery Toys	Playmobil
Disney	SMOBY
Hasbro	Sony
Hershey Entertainment	StarParks
JAKKS Pacific	Toy Quest
K'NEX Industries	VTech Holdings
Mattel	

HISTORICAL FINANCIALS

Company Type: Private

Income Statement
FYE: December 31

	REVENUE ($ mil.)	NET INCOME ($ mil.)	NET PROFIT MARGIN	EMPLOYEES
12/04	1,229	(289)	—	7,294
12/03	1,213	(138)	—	8,298
12/02	1,612	60	3.7%	8,297
12/01	1,266	51	4.0%	7,247
12/00	1,194	(105)	—	7,669
12/99	1,327	37	2.8%	7,821
12/98	1,200	(30)	—	8,670
12/97	1,115	9	0.8%	9,867
12/96	1,267	79	6.2%	9,450
12/95	1,230	77	6.3%	9,660
Annual Growth	(0.0%)	—	—	(3.1%)

2004 Year-End Financials

Debt ratio: 90.0%
Return on equity: —
Cash ($ mil.): 57
Current ratio: 2.45
Long-term debt ($ mil.): 431

Net Income History

Lloyd's

After a lot of R&R (reconstruction and renewal), Lloyd's (aka Lloyd's of London) is back at work as the world's leading insurance exchange. Not an insurance company, it regulates about 60 syndicates with more than 40 managing agents, which are made up of corporate underwriters and wealthy individuals (called Names, their number has been dropping since the 1980s and is down to some 2,000) that transact insurance business worth billions in premiums each year. Also part of the picture are Lloyd's brokers, which bring business to the market. Lloyd's is a top conduit for aviation and marine insurance, as well as specialty insurance, such as policies covering art and jewelry or protecting against acts of terrorism.

Gross premiums written, for the entire Lloyd's market as a whole, total more than $24 billion (£14,000 billion). Reinsurance adds up to about 30% of that, with the next biggest chunks coming from third-party liability insurance (23%) and fire and other property damage (20%). Business

in the US accounts for about a third of premiums written, followed by the UK, with a quarter.

Despite its overhaul, Lloyd's tradition of specialty lines has hampered its ability to compete against global insurance firms offering more comprehensive service. Encouraged by Lloyd's to consolidate, some syndicates, infused with capital from corporate-owned managing agencies that enables them to completely underwrite a contract, are turning into full-service insurance companies. Corporate underwriters, such as ACE Limited and Berkshire Hathaway's General Re, now account for most of Lloyd's capital backing, where Names once dominated.

Lloyd's is catching up to its rivals, particularly bargain-rate insurers who entered the offshore markets in the early 1990s. Catastrophic losses in recent years have forced them to raise their prices, making the Lloyd's market competitive again. But Lloyd's corporation is taking cost-cutting steps such as outsourcing operations ranging from data processing and catering to facilities management.

In another attempt to renew itself, Lloyd's has unveiled plans to replace its current accounting system and stop accepting capital from traditional Names. The company is lobbying for changes in the regulatory practices of the Names, most significantly the shift to a franchise system. Lord Peter Levene, the former Mayor of London, has assumed the chairman's post. Despite Levene's inexperience in the insurance industry, critics feel his government experience is the change needed to jumpstart the Lloyd's market.

HISTORY

In 1688 Edward Lloyd opened Lloyd's Coffee House near London's docks. Maritime insurance brokers and underwriters met at Lloyd's, which offered a comfortable venue for exchanging shipping information. The loose association of brokers began publishing shipping newspaper *Lloyd's List* in 1734 (sold 1996).

The coffeehouse attracted people who used insurance as a cover for gambling — members who "insured" the gender of the transvestite Chevalier d'Eon began Lloyd's tradition of specialty insurance.

In 1871 Parliament enacted the Lloyd's Act, which formed Lloyd's Corporation to oversee the activities of the underwriting syndicates (made up of Names with unlimited personal liability). In the 1880s the market began covering nonmarine risks. By 1900 Lloyd's members wrote 50% of the world's nonlife insurance.

Prompt claims payment after the 1906 San Francisco earthquake boosted the market's image in the US. After WWI, Lloyd's members began writing automotive, credit, and aviation insurance.

In 1981 and 1982 a syndicate managed by Richard Outhwaite wrote contracts on the future liabilities of old insurance contracts with claims (many with environmental exposure) still pending.

That decade Lloyd's attracted new Names: the merely well-off — highly paid people without great wealth — who pledged assets often overvalued in the 1980s boom. Exercising little oversight, Lloyd's let syndicates close their books on pending claims by reinsuring them repeatedly through new syndicates financed by neophyte Names.

The boom's end coincided with a rise in US environmental claims covered by insurance contracts such as those written by Outhwaite. When

Names with reduced net worth balked at paying claims, Lloyd's faced disaster. From 1991 to 1994, the number of syndicates fell by half and premium rates increased. In 1993, with billions in claims and many Names refusing to pay or suing their syndicates for not disclosing the risks, Lloyd's imposed new underwriting and reporting rules, took control of most syndicates' back-office functions, and brought in capital by finally admitting corporate members (mostly foreign insurers).

Lloyd's reached a multibillion-pound settlement with most of its Names in 1996. It also required its active investors to help finance a new insurance company, Equitas, to cover old liabilities (billions in claims are still outstanding). In 1997 Lloyd's sought to increase the number of broker members. The next year, amid regulatory disagreements with Singapore's government and a faltering Asian economy, it called off plans to open an exchange branch there. In 1999 Lloyd's began cutting its operating costs. It also began bolstering its Central Fund with insurance rather than cash (providers include Swiss Re and The Chubb Corporation) and admitted the captive insurer of pharmaceuticals powerhouse SmithKline Beecham (now GlaxoSmithKline) into its marketplace.

In 2000, as litigation dragged on over whether a recalcitrant group of Names owed Lloyd's more than £50 million for claims, the corporation continued to trim costs by selling property. That year the US became Lloyd's single largest market for the first time in the company's 300-year history.

After the insurer was hit hard by the attacks on the World Trade Center, resulting in £3.1 billion in losses, another first occurred: It issued an annual report to publicly document the heavy deficits.

EXECUTIVES

Chairman: Lord Peter Levene, $1,074,820 pay
Deputy Chairman: John Coldman, age 57
Deputy Chairman: Bronislaw E. (Bronek) Masojada, age 43
CEO: Nicholas E. T. (Nick) Prettejohn, age 45, $1,361,823 pay
CIO: Chris Rawson
Director, Finance and Risk Management: Luke Savage, $283,152 pay (partial-year salary)
Director, Franchise Performance: Rolf Tolle, $1,354,119 pay
Director, Legal and Compliance and General Counsel: Sean McGovern
Director, Operations: Steve Quiddington
Director, Worldwide Markets: Julian James
President, Lloyd's America: Wendy Baker
Head, Change Management and Human Resources: Steven Haasz
Head, Strategy and Business Planning: Stuart Degg
Auditors: Ernst & Young LLP

LOCATIONS

HQ: Society of Lloyd's
1 Lime St., London EC3M 7HA, United Kingdom
Phone: +44-20-7327-1000   **Fax:** +44-20-7327-5599
US HQ: The Museum Office Bldg., 25 W. 53rd St., 14th Fl., New York, NY 10019
US Phone: 212-382-4060   **US Fax:** 212-382-4070
Web: www.lloyds.com

Lloyd's syndicates operate in about 190 countries.

COMPETITORS

AGF	General Re
AIG	ING
Allianz	Markel
Aon	Marsh & McLennan
Aviva	Millea Holdings
AXA	Munich Re
Chubb	Swiss Re
Citigroup	Zurich Financial Services

HISTORICAL FINANCIALS

Company Type: Insurance society

Income Statement

FYE: December 31

	REVENUE ($ mil.)	NET INCOME ($ mil.)	NET PROFIT MARGIN	EMPLOYEES
12/04	348	94	26.9%	587
12/03	238	(31)	—	582
12/02	207	(7)	—	589
12/01	208	85	41.0%	825
12/00	218	177	81.1%	1,176
12/99	266	124	46.8%	1,645
12/98	311	40	13.0%	1,833
12/97	327	57	17.6%	—
Annual Growth	0.9%	7.2%	—	(17.3%)

2004 Year-End Financials

Debt ratio: 0.0%
Return on equity: 52.0%
Cash ($ mil.): 127
Current ratio: 1.94
Long-term debt ($ mil.): 0

Net Income History

Lonmin Plc

At Lonmin, all that glitters is not gold — platinum is more precious to the company these days. The company is the world's #3 platinum producer (after Anglo Platinum and Impala Platinum), with an annual production of more than 900,000 ounces. Applications for platinum include catalytic converters for vehicles and jewelry. Its Lonmin Platinum, or Lonplats, unit mines platinum group metals (PGMs, including platinum, palladium, and rhodium) through two South African companies: Western Platinum and Eastern Platinum. In addition to its Australian PGM investments, Lonmin has exploration activities in North America, South Africa, and Tanzania. Prudential plc has a 12% stake in the company.

Lonmin has decided to concentrate primarily on its PGM operations and says it intends to up its platinum production to more than 1,100,000 ounces per year staring in 2010. To that end, the company has added smelter capacity and sunk new shafts in South Africa. The company has been selling off its non-platinum assets, including its gold assets in politically troubled Zimbabwe. It also divested its holdings in coal-mining, hotel, and insurance businesses. It

exited the gold business completely in 2004 when Lonmin sold its stake in Ashanti.

Looking to expand its operations in Africa, the company made a successful $190 million offer for Southern Platinum in 2005.

HISTORY

Founded in 1909 as the London & Rhodesian Mining & Land Company to acquire mining rights in Zambia and Zimbabwe, the company later expanded into real estate, ranching, and agriculture. In 1961 Roland "Tiny" Rowland traded his Rhodesian assets for a 48% interest in the company and managing directorship.

Rowland then bought the Beira oil pipeline (southern Rhodesia to Mozambique) in 1961, changed its name to Lonrho in 1963, and shut down the pipeline in 1965 when economic sanctions were imposed against Rhodesia after white settlers declared independence. Rowland also bought a major interest in the Ashanti gold fields of Ghana in 1968.

In 1973 a group of directors tried to oust Rowland, claiming he had bribed African leaders and violated Rhodesian sanctions. A British inquiry cleared him but found that he had made questionable payments. Lonrho bought Volkswagen and Audi distributors in the UK in 1975, Princess Hotels in 1979, and the *Observer* newspaper in 1981. His attempt to buy retailer House of Fraser (owner of Harrod's) was frustrated by the British Mergers and Monopolies Commission in 1985.

Back in Africa, where Tanzania had nationalized Lonrho's operations (1978), Rowland continued his politically incorrect dealings through the 1980s. He helped the Marxist government of Mozambique manage its agricultural resources and increased Lonrho's South African holdings despite sanctions against the government's policy of apartheid.

Weakened by debt and low commodity prices, Lonrho began shedding assets in the late 1980s. In 1992 Rowland sold a third of the Metropole Hotel chain to Libya and accepted a loan from Colonel Gadhafi. Lonrho's stock plummeted, attracting the attention of German financier Dieter Bock, who bought about 18% of the company.

Bock and Rowland were co-CEOs for about a year until Bock won control of the board. Rowland was forced out of management in 1994. Rowland, angered by Bock's plan to dismember the company, sold his 6% of the firm in 1995 but remained a frequent critic of its new management. In 1996 EU regulators rejected Bock's plan to spin off Lonrho's mining operations.

Bock resigned as CEO in 1996 and sold his 18% interest in Lonrho to South African titan Anglo American. Nicholas Morrell assumed the CEO position that year. Lonrho sold its Metropole Hotel chain to Stakis (UK) for $533 million that year, as well, and sold its Lonrho Sugar operations in 1997. Sir John Craven took the helm as chairman as the company continued to restructure. Anglo sold its 26% stake in Lonrho to JCI in 1997. The next year the deal was restructured so that Anglo kept a 7% stake in Lonrho. In 1998 Lonrho bought Tavistock (a JCI coal operation) and divested its Lonrho Africa division, Hondo Oil & Gas, and Princess Hotels.

The company changed its name to Lonmin in 1999 and made a failed attempt to increase its interests in the Ashanti gold mines. Having decided to focus on platinum production that year, Lonmin sold its Duiker and Tweefontein coal operations for $209 million to Switzerland-based commodity house Glencore International in

2000. The company sold its interests in its hotel and insurance businesses that year, as well. With restructuring completed, Nick Morrell stepped down as CEO to become director of Cardew & Co., a London PR firm, and Edward Haslam, a lifelong mining executive, took his place.

Lonmin was able to bounce back from a major smelting furnace fire in early 2003 by recommissioning a stand-by facility. The company also sold its 12% stake in the Munni Munni project that year. Lonmin, which owned a substantial stake in Ashanti Goldfields, received cash and a small stake (which it sold) in new company AngloGold Ashanti, upon the merger of Ashanti and AngloGold in 2004. Bradford Mills replaced Edward Haslam as CEO in 2004.

EXECUTIVES

Chairman: Sir John A. Craven, age 64, $359,760 pay
Deputy Chairman: J. Roger B. Phillimore, age 55
Chief Executive: Bradford A. (Brad) Mills, age 50, $963,741 pay
CFO: John N. Robinson, age 50, $899,605 pay
Chief Strategy Officer: Ian P. Farmer, age 42, $863,676 pay
President, Lonplats: Peter J. Ledger, age 55, $760,993 pay
VP, Business Development: Jack Jones
VP, Business Development — Technical: Geoff Fenner
VP, Exploration and Business Development: Chris Davies
VP, Finance: Amanda Bradshaw
VP, Human Capital: Lee Johnson
VP, Investor Relations: Alexandra Shorland-Ball
VP, Marketing: Fraser King
VP, SHEC, Platinum Operations: Ricus Grimbeek
General Manager, Information Services: Karel Van Zyl
General Manager, Investor Relations Manager and Assistant Secretary: Teresa Heritage
Company Secretary: Rob C. Bellhouse, age 38
Auditors: KPMG Audit Plc

LOCATIONS

HQ: Lonmin Plc
4 Grosvenor Place,
London SW1X 7YL, United Kingdom
Phone: +44-20-7201-6000   **Fax:** +44-20-7201-6100
Web: www.lonmin.com

Lonmin has mining and exploration activities in North America, Tanzania, and South Africa.

2005 Sales by Destination

	% of total
The Americas	33
Asia	31
Europe	19
South Africa	16
Zimbabwe	1
Total	**100**

PRODUCTS/OPERATIONS

Selected Mining and Refining Operations

Incwala Resources Ltd. (25%, PGMs, South Africa)
Lonmin Platinum (Lonplats, 82%)
  Eastern Platinum Ltd. (PGMs, South Africa)
  Western Metal Sales Limited
  Western Platinum Ltd. (PGMs, South Africa)

COMPETITORS

African Rainbow Minerals	Inco Limited
Anglo Platinum	Norilsk Nickel
Aquarius Platinum	North American Palladium
Barrick Gold	Placer Dome
BHP Billiton Plc	Rio Tinto
Gold Fields	Stillwater Mining
Impala Platinum	

HISTORICAL FINANCIALS

Company Type: Public

Income Statement

FYE: September 30

	REVENUE ($ mil.)	NET INCOME ($ mil.)	NET PROFIT MARGIN	EMPLOYEES
9/05	1,128	163	14.5%	22,402
9/04	1,030	195	18.9%	20,931
9/03	779	74	9.5%	20,668
9/02	697	185	26.5%	24,071
9/01	866	274	31.6%	26,829
9/00	891	215	24.1%	31,051
9/99	896	130	14.5%	32,027
9/98	1,705	66	3.9%	55,382
Annual Growth	**(5.7%)**	**13.7%**	**—**	**(12.1%)**

2005 Year-End Financials

Debt ratio: 62.8%
Return on equity: 21.0%
Cash ($ mil.): 11
Current ratio: 0.91
Long-term debt ($ mil.): 510

Net Income History

Pink Sheets: LNMIY

L'Oréal SA

L'Oréal's success is built on a strong foundation. The world's largest beauty products company, it creates makeup, perfume, and hair and skin care items. Its brands include L'Oréal and Maybelline (mass-market), Lancôme (upscale), and Redken and SoftSheen/Carson (retail and salon). L'Oréal, which is buying Dallas-based SkinCeuticals, also conducts cosmetology and dermatology research. With about half of its sales generated outside Europe, L'Oréal has focused on buying brands in those markets. Liliane Bettencourt, daughter of the firm's founder, and her family indirectly control L'Oréal. Nestlé owns a large stake. Chairman and CEO Lindsay Owen-Jones passes his CEO title to Jean-Paul Agon in April 2006.

The Bettencourts and Nestlé have been indirect owners of L'Oréal through the Gesparal holding company for some 30 years. In Spring 2004 L'Oréal shareholders considered a reorganization proposal that would dissolve the holding company and restructure L'Oréal. The proposal gave Liliane Bettencourt, then 82, and her family a direct 27.5% stake and 28.6% of the voting rights. Nestlé, which now indirectly owns about 49% of L'Oréal, gets a 26.4% direct share and 27.5% in voting rights. In early 2004 Ms. Bettencourt's inherited share of L'Oréal was valued at $12.7 billion. (She ranked 11th, with $18.8 billion, on Forbes magazine's 2004 billionaire list behind six Walton family members from Wal-Mart.) As part of the proposed agreement, the two major shareholders would not increase their holdings in L'Oréal as long as Ms. Bettencourt is alive, or for at least three years.

Another change, announced in early 2005, will shake up what has been in place at the company for nearly two decades. Lindsay Owen-Jones, who turned 59 in March and has logged a lengthy, impressive career at L'Oréal, has tapped Jean-Paul Agon to run the firm as its chief executive beginning April 2006.

L'Oréal's cosmetics, which generate nearly all of the company's revenue, generally fall under four divisions: Professional (salon hair care), Consumer (hair and skin care, makeup), Luxury (beauty products, fragrances), and Active Cosmetics (dermo-cosmetic products). L'Oréal is expanding its Active Cosmetics division (with existing brands Vichy, La Roche-Posay, and Inneov) by folding SkinCeuticals into the operation in 2005. The acquisition opens doors for L'Oréal in the dermatology arena, which caters to high-end spas and plastic surgeons.

Consumer brands such as GARNIER, L'Oréal, Maybelline, and Softsheen/Carson make up 54% of the company's cosmetic sales. However, well-known Luxury brands, including Lancôme, Ralph Lauren, and Giorgio Armani, continue to gain popularity.

Expanding aggressively into the Chinese market, L'Oréal acquired Chinese skin care brand Mininurse in late 2003 and purchased Yue-Sai, a mass-market Chinese makeup and skin care brand in 2004, and its Shanghai manufacturing plant from Coty.

L'Oréal funds more than 2,800 scientists on three continents who file about 500 patents a year. Of note is the company's creation of UV absorbing makeup and test models of human skin.

In early 2005 L'Oréal launched a line of men's grooming products.

HISTORY

Parisian Eugène Schueller, a chemist by trade, invented the first synthetic hair dye in 1907. Schueller quickly found a market for his products with local hairdressers and in 1909 established L'Oréal to pursue his growing hair products operation. The company's name came from its first hair color, Auréole (French for "aura of light").

L'Oréal expanded to include shampoos and soaps, all under the watchful direction of the energetic Schueller, who was known to taste hair creams to ensure that they were made up of the exact chemical composition that he required. In the 1920s the company began advertising on the radio (before its French competitors).

Demand for L'Oréal's products intensified after WWII. In 1953 the company formed licensee Cosmair to distribute its hair products to US beauty salons, and Cosmair soon offered L'Oréal's makeup and perfume as well. (Cosmair became L'Oréal USA in 2000.) When Schueller died in 1957, control of L'Oréal passed to right-hand man François Dalle. Dalle carried L'Oréal's hair care products into the consumer market and overseas and sold its soap units in 1961.

The company went public in 1963; Schueller's daughter, Liliane Bettencourt, retained a majority interest. Diversification came in 1965 with the acquisition of upscale French cosmetics maker Lancôme. L'Oréal entered the pharmaceuticals business in 1973 by purchasing Synthélabo. Bettencourt traded nearly half of her L'Oréal stock for a 3% stake in Swiss food producer Nestlé in 1974. L'Oréal purchased a minority stake in the publisher of French fashion magazine Marie Claire three years later.

During the 1980s L'Oréal vaulted from relative obscurity to become the world's #1 cosmetics company, largely through acquisitions. These included Warner Communications' cosmetics operations (Ralph Lauren and Gloria Vanderbilt brands, 1984), Helena Rubinstein (US beauty products, 1988), Laboratories Pharmaeutiques Goupil (1988), and its first major investment in Lanvin (1989). Englishman Lindsay Owen-Jones became CEO in 1988.

Chairman Jacques Correze died in 1991 during an investigation into his Nazi war activities. (He had served five years in prison.) In 1994 the company purchased control of Cosmair from Nestlé and Bettencourt. It acquired two generic drug companies in 1995: Lichtenstein Pharmazeutica in Germany and Irex in France. That year L'Oréal became the #2 US cosmetics maker (behind Procter & Gamble, maker of Cover Girl and Max Factor) by buying #3 Maybelline for $508 million.

L'Oréal then added subsidiaries in Japan and China (1996) and in Romania and Slovenia (1997). In 2000 L'Oréal acquired Carson, family-owned prestige cosmetics company Kiehl's Since 1851, and salon products maker Matrix Essentials (from Bristol-Myers Squibb).

In 2001 L'Oréal acquired CosMedic Concepts' 60 BioMedic products, which are distributed to dermatologists in 60 countries. Expanding its leadership in the professional hair salon products market, L'Oréal subsidiary L'Oréal USA acquired Artec Systems Group in 2002.

Looking to compete head-to-head in the domestic shampoo and conditioner market, in early 2003 L'Oréal introduced its Fructis line in the US via the biggest product launch in the company's history. (The brand has been sold in Europe for several years.)

EXECUTIVES

Chairman and CEO: Lindsay Owen-Jones, age 59
Vice Chairman: Jean-Pierre Meyers
EVP Administration and Finance: Christian Mulliez, age 44
EVP, Corporate Communications and External Affairs: Giorgio Galli
EVP, Human Resources: François Vachey
EVP, Production and Technology: Marcel Lafforgue
EVP, Research and Development: Jean-François Grollier
EVP, Strategic Business Development: Béatrice Dautresme
CEO, Lancôme International, Paris: Marc Dubrule
Managing Director, Africa: Alain Evrard
Managing Director, Luxury Products Division: Marc Menesguen, age 49
President, Consumer Products: Patrick Rabain
President, Luxury Products: Gilles Weil
President, Professional Products: Jean-Jacques Lebel
President and CEO, L'Oréal USA: Jean-Paul Agon, age 48
President and CEO, L'Oréal USA: Laurent Attal, age 47
President, Luxury Products and EVP Corporate Communications/External Relations: Luc Nadeau
President, Prestige and Collections International and Helena Rubenstein: Patricia Turck-Paquelier
Director of International Press Relations: Mike Rumsby
Director of Investor Relations: Caroline Millot
Auditors: Étienne Jacquemin

LOCATIONS

HQ: L'Oréal SA
41, rue Martre, 92117 Clichy, France
Phone: +33-1-47-56-70-00   **Fax:** +33-1-47-56-80-02
US HQ: 575 5th Ave., New York, NY 10017
US Phone: 212-818-1500   **US Fax:** 212-984-4538
Web: www.loreal.com

PRODUCTS/OPERATIONS

Selected Operations

Cosmetics
  Active Cosmetics
  La Roche-Posay
  Vichy

Consumer Products
  Gemey
  Laboratoires GARNIER
  L'Oréal
  Maybelline
  SoftSheen/Carson

Luxury Products
  Biotherm
  Cacharel (fragrances only)
  Giorgio Armani (fragrances only)
  Guy Laroche (fragrances only)
  Helena Rubinstein
  Kiehl's
  Lancôme
  Paloma Picasso (fragrances only)
  Ralph Lauren (fragrances only)
  Shu Uemura

Pharmaceuticals and Dermatology
  Innéov Firmness
  Tri-Luma
  RozexMetvix

Professional Products
  Artec
  Inne
  Kérastase
  L'Oréal Professionnel
  Matrix
  Redken

Selected Subsidiaries

Carson/Soft Sheen Products
Galderma
L'Oréal USA
The Laboratoires Inneov
Sanofi-Synthélabo

COMPETITORS

Alberto-Culver
Alticor
Avon
Bath & Body Works
BeautiControl Cosmetics
Body Shop
Chanel
Clarins
Diamond Products
Estée Lauder
Gillette
Hoffmann-La Roche
Intimate Brands
Johnson & Johnson
LVMH
Mary Kay
Merle Norman
Modern Organic Products
Novartis
Nu Skin
Perrigo
Procter & Gamble
Puig Beauty & Fashion
Revlon
Shiseido
Unilever
Yves Saint-Laurent Groupe

HISTORICAL FINANCIALS

Company Type: Public

Income Statement

FYE: December 31

	REVENUE ($ mil.)	NET INCOME ($ mil.)	NET PROFIT MARGIN	EMPLOYEES
12/04	19,824	4,946	24.9%	52,081
12/03	17,609	1,872	10.6%	50,500
12/02	14,975	1,526	10.2%	50,491
12/01	12,171	1,089	8.9%	49,150
12/00	11,931	968	8.1%	48,222
12/99	10,825	702	6.5%	42,164
12/98	13,417	839	6.3%	49,665
12/97	11,522	664	5.8%	47,242
12/96	11,532	668	5.8%	43,158
12/95	10,872	641	5.9%	39,929
Annual Growth	6.9%	25.5%	—	3.0%

2004 Year-End Financials

Debt ratio: 6.8%
Return on equity: 40.2%
Cash ($ mil.): 547
Current ratio: 1.33
Long-term debt ($ mil.): 975

Net Income History

OTC: LORLY

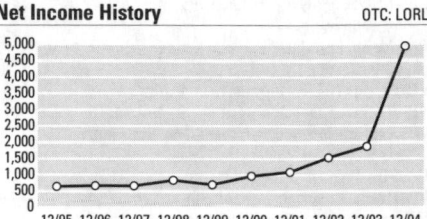

Lufthansa

Germany's Deutsche Lufthansa is Europe's #3 passenger airline (behind #1 British Airways and #2 Air France); it is also the world's #2 cargo airline behind FedEx. Including code-sharing agreements, Lufthansa serves about 330 destinations in more than 90 countries. It flies about 370 aircraft. With hubs in Frankfurt and Munich, the carrier is part of the Star Alliance that includes United Airlines, Air Canada, and All Nippon Airways. Lufthansa also has interests in travel-related businesses, including ground services, catering, and leisure travel services. Lufthansa owns about a 5% stake in Amadeus, one of the world's largest computerized airline reservation systems.

Lufthansa, along with Iberia, Air France, and Amadelux Investment (a joint venture between private equity firms Cinven and BC Partners) have formed WAM Acquisition Corp. for the purpose of taking Amadeus private. When the transaction is complete Lufthansa will hold an 11% stake in Amadeus.

European airline deregulation, rising fuel prices, and air traffic constraints have applied pressure to Lufthansa's bottom line, but the carrier has still managed to turn a profit. It's even expanding its catering, ground services, and information technology operations.

The company is also flying high on the wings of the Star Alliance, the global marketing and code-sharing alliance that includes such major carriers as UAL's United, Air Canada, and All Nippon Airways. Member airlines share revenues on some routes, operate joint ticketing offices, and offer joint frequent-flier programs.

Lufthansa is facing fierce competition from Air France, which has acquired Dutch carrier KLM, and British Airways, which is looking for another European partner and has begun courting Iberia. Lufthansa found a European partner in Swiss International Air Lines. The Swiss government, which owns 20% of the airline, has approved the $238 million deal. Once the merger is complete (maybe as late as 2007) Swiss International Air Lines will retain its name and Zurich will become an additional Lufthansa hub. The combined companies will carry about 60 million passengers per year — a close second to Air France and KLM (65 million). Lufthansa will set up a holding company to manage the combined operations of the two airlines, similar to the one established by Air France and KLM.

Lufthansa is looking to expand its fleet with new double-decker Airbus A380 jets, capable of holding as many as 800 passengers. Lufthansa hopes the new, modern jets will provide a more cost-effective solution for long-haul flights.

HISTORY

The Weimar government created Deutsche Luft Hansa (DLH) in 1926 by merging private German airlines Deutscher Aero Lloyd (founded 1919) and Junkers Luftverkehr (formed in 1921 by aircraft manufacturer Junkers Flugzeugwerke). DLH built what would become Europe's most comprehensive air route network by 1931. It served the USSR through Deruluft (formed 1921; dissolved 1941), an airline jointly owned by DLH and the Soviet government. In 1930 DLH and the Chinese government formed Eurasia Aviation Corporation to develop air transport in China.

DLH established the world's first transatlantic airmail service from Berlin to Buenos Aires in 1934 and went on to develop air transport throughout South America. The outbreak of WWII ended operations in Europe, and the Chinese government seized Eurasia Aviation in 1941. Klaus Bonhoeffer, head of DLH's legal department, led an unsuccessful coup against the Nazi leadership and was executed in 1945. Soon afterward all DLH operations ceased.

In 1954 the Allies allowed the recapitalization of Deutsche Lufthansa. The airline started with domestic routes, returned to London and Paris (1955), and then re-entered South America (1956). In 1958 it made its first nonstop flight between Germany and New York and initiated service to Tokyo and Cairo. Meanwhile, it started a charter airline with several partners in 1955. Lufthansa bought out its partners in 1959 and renamed the unit Condor two years later.

The carrier resumed service behind the Iron Curtain in 1966 with flights to Prague. The stable West German economy helped Lufthansa maintain profitability through most of the 1970s.

The reunification of Germany in 1990 ended Allied control over Berlin airspace, allowing Lufthansa, which had bought Pan Am's Berlin routes, to fly there under its own colors for the first time since the end of WWII. The company began seeking international partners in 1991, but that year European air travel suffered its first-ever slowdown, forcing Lufthansa into the red for the first time since 1973.

The company restructured in 1994 into a group of new business units: Lufthansa Technik, Lufthansa Cargo, and Lufthansa Systems. In 1995 the carrier began to face increased domestic competition from Deutsche BA, a British Airways affiliate.

The airline formed a code-sharing agreement with Air Canada in 1996. In 1997 the Star Alliance was formed, and Lufthansa signed a pact with Singapore Airlines. That year the German government sold its remaining 38% stake in Lufthansa. In 1998 Lufthansa and All Nippon Airways formed a code-sharing alliance, and Condor was combined with Karstadt's tour company NUR Touristic to form C&N Touristic. (After buying UK-based travel operator Thomas Cook in 2000, C&N Touristic changed its name to Thomas Cook in 2001.)

In a plan to gain more access to London's Heathrow Airport, Lufthansa took a 20% stake in British Midland, which was admitted into the Star Alliance in 2000 along with Mexicana Airlines. In 2001 the airline bought the 52% of Texas-based Sky Chefs it did not already own and formed a new unit, LSG Sky Chefs International, to hold its catering operations.

Lufthansa said goodbye to its 24% stake in delivery firm DHL when it sold its share to Deutsche Post in 2002. In 2004 the company sold its facilities management division, Lufthansa Gebäudemanagement (LGM), to German construction company HOCHTIEF.

In early 2005 Swiss International Air Lines agreed to be acquired by Lufthansa. As the first step in a lengthy and complicated transition process, Lufthansa created a Swiss holding entity named AirTrust through which all Swiss International shares were held. Lufthansa then took an initial 11% stake in the newly created company.

EXECUTIVES

Chairman of the Executive Board and CEO; CEO, Lufthansa German Airlines: Wolfgang Mayrhuber, age 58
Member of the Executive Board and CFO: Karl-Ludwig Kley, age 54
Member of the Executive Board and Chief Officer of Aviation Services and Human Resources: Stefan Lauer, age 50
Marketing and Sales, Lufthansa German Airlines: Thierry Antinori
Services and Human Resources, Lufthansa German Airlines: Carsten Spohr
Operations, Lufthansa German Airlines: Carl Sigel
Network Management, IT, and Purchases, Lufthansa German Airlines: Holger Hätty
Chairman, Logistics and Production, Lufthansa Cargo AG: Jean-Peter Jansen
Human Resources and Finance, Lufthansa Cargo AG: Stephan Gemkow
Marketing and Sales, Lufthansa Cargo AG: Andreas Otto
Product and Service, Lufthansa Technik AG: Thomas Stüger, age 49
Finance, Lufthansa Technik AG: Peter Jansen, age 51
Human Resources, Lufthansa Technik AG: Wolfgang Warburg, age 63
CEO, Finance, Human Resources, Information Management, and Corporate Functions, LSG Lufthansa Service Holding AG: Walter Gehl
Inflight Service Solutions, LSG Lufthansa Service Holding AG: Jochen Müller
Operations and Sales, LSG Lufthansa Service Holding AG: Thomas Nagel
Chairman and CEO, Thomas Cook AG: Wolfgang Beeser
Finance and Human Resources, Thomas Cook AG: Heinz-Ludger Heuberg
Chairman, Lufthansa Systems Group GmbH: Wolfgang Gohde
Chairman, Lufthansa Technik AG: August-Wilhelm Henningsen
Director Public Affairs, The Americas: Natalie A. Hartman
Auditors: PwC Deutsche Revision AG

LOCATIONS

HQ: Deutsche Lufthansa AG
Von-Gablenz-Strasse 2-6,
D-50679 Cologne 21, Germany
Phone: +49-69-696-0 **Fax:** +49-69-696-6818
US HQ: 1640 Hempstead Tpke., East Meadow, NY 11554
US Phone: 516-296-9200 **US Fax:** 516-296-9660
Web: www.lufthansa.com

Deutsche Lufthansa serves about 330 destinations in more than 90 countries. The company has hubs in Frankfurt and Munich, Germany.

2004 Sales

	% of total
Europe	70
Asia/Pacific	14
North America	11
Africa	2
Central & South America	2
Middle East	1
Total	**100**

PRODUCTS/OPERATIONS

2004 Sales

	% of total
Lufthansa Passenger Airline	63
Lufthansa Logistics	15
LSG Sky Chefs	11
Lufthansa Technik	10
Lufthansa Systems	1
Total	**100**

2004 Sales by Sector

	% of total
Passenger	82
Cargo	17
Mail	1
Total	**100**

2004 Sales

	% of total
Scheduled	97
Charter	3
Total	**100**

Selected Operations

Lufthansa Cargo AG (cargo services)
Lufthansa CityLine GmbH (passenger airline)
Lufthansa Commercial Holding GmbH (holding company)
Lufthansa Flight Training GmbH (LFT)
Lufthansa Systems GmbH (support services, information technology services)
Lufthansa Technik AG (technical services)
Thomas Cook AG (50%, leisure travel services)

COMPETITORS

Accor	FedEx
Aer Lingus	Finnair
Air France	Iberia
Air Inter	Japan Airlines
AMR Corp.	KLM
BAX Global	Liberty Travel
British Airways	Northwest Airlines
Carlson	Otto
CNF	Qantas
Continental Airlines	Sabre
Cuisine Solutions	Swire Pacific
Delta Air	TUI
Delta Air Transport	US Airways
Deutsche Bahn	Virgin Atlantic Airways
DHL	

HISTORICAL FINANCIALS

Company Type: Public

Income Statement

FYE: December 31

	REVENUE ($ mil.)	NET INCOME ($ mil.)	NET PROFIT MARGIN	EMPLOYEES
12/04	23,140	551	2.4%	90,673
12/03	20,029	(1,235)	—	93,246
12/02	17,788	751	4.2%	94,135
12/01	14,784	(561)	—	87,975
12/00	14,313	649	4.5%	69,523
12/99	12,885	635	4.9%	66,207
12/98	13,515	854	6.3%	54,867
12/97	12,917	466	3.6%	58,250
12/96	13,431	357	2.7%	57,999
12/95	13,841	1,020	7.4%	57,586
Annual Growth	5.9%	(6.6%)	—	5.2%

2004 Year-End Financials

Debt ratio: 77.7%
Return on equity: 12.6%
Cash ($ mil.): 5,167
Current ratio: 2.52
Long-term debt ($ mil.): 4,209

Net Income History

OTC: DLAKY

LUKOIL

Most Russians look to LUKOIL for their oil and gas needs. Russia's #1 integrated oil company produces, refines, and sells oil and oil products; it accounts for 19% of Russia's crude oil production. LUKOIL has proved reserves of 20 billion barrels of oil equivalent. The company has operations in 60 regions in Russia and 25 other countries and owns eight refineries and more than 4,700 gas stations. LUKOIL moved into the US retail market by buying Getty Petroleum Marketing. It owns about 2,000 gas stations in the US. That year the Russian government sold its remaining 7.6% stake in LUKOIL to ConocoPhillips, which announced plans to increase its stake to 20% by 2008. ConocoPhillips owns about 10%.

LUKOIL, Russia's second-largest company behind natural gas monopoly Gazprom, is trying to transform itself from a top-heavy, bureaucratic enterprise into a decentralized, entrepreneurial company with hopes of competing in free markets.

The company explores for oil and gas in Azerbaijan, Egypt, Iraq, Kazakhstan, and other areas in the Middle East and central Asia. It operates four refineries in Russia, one in the Ukraine, one in Bulgaria, and one in Romania, and owns a gas stations network in Russia, the Baltic States, Central and Eastern Europe, and the US. More than three-quarter's of LUKOIL's sales are outside of Russia.

With an appetite for expansion, the company is upping its production with refinery acquisitions, and is investing heavily in new oil patches, such as the Caspian Sea. LUKOIL has announced plans to acquire Finland-based Oy Teboil AB and Suomen Petrooli Oy, affiliated refined oil products companies, for an undisclosed amount. LUKOIL also acquired Nelson Resources, which has oil and gas interests in Western Kazakhstan, for about $2 billion.

HISTORY

LUKOIL was formed from the combination of three major state-owned oil and gas exploration companies — Langepasneftegaz, Uraineftegaz, and Kogalymneftegaz — that traced their origins to the discovery of oil in western Siberia in 1964. More than 25 years later, after the Soviet Union broke up, the oil and gas sector was one of the first industries marked for privatization.

In 1992 the government called for Langepasneftegaz, Uraineftegaz, and Kogalymneftegaz to merge, and LUKOIL was created the next year. (The LUK of LUKOIL comes from the initials of the three companies.) Russian president Boris Yeltsin appointed Siberian oil veteran Vagit Alekperov as the company's first president. The Russian government also formed several other large integrated oil companies, including Yukos, Surgutneftegaz, Sidanco, and Sibneft.

LUKOIL went public on the fledgling Russian Trading System in 1994. The next year the company absorbed nine other enterprises, including oil exploration companies Astrakhanneft, Kaliningradmorneftegaz, and Permneft. That year LUKOIL became the first Russian oil company to set up an exploration and production trading arm. In 1996 LUKOIL acquired a 41% stake in *Izvestia*, Russia's major independent newspaper.

Chevron and LUKOIL, with seven other oil and gas companies and three governments, agreed in 1996 to build a 1,500-kilometer pipeline to link the Kazakhstan oil fields to world markets.

In 1997 LUKOIL became the first Russian corporation to sell bonds to international investors, and the government sold 15% of its stake in the company. That year LUKOIL's 50%-owned Nexus Fuels unit opened its first gas stations located in the parking lots of US grocery stores (the partnership dissolved and Nexus went bankrupt in 2000).

LUKOIL began a partnership with Conoco (later ConocoPhillips) in 1998 to develop oil and natural gas reserves in Russia's northern territories. LUKOIL also acquired 51% of Romania's Petrorel refinery. In 1999 it acquired control of refineries in Bulgaria and Ukraine and in a petrochemical firm in Saratov. It also acquired oil company KomiTEK in one of Russia's largest mergers.

The government sold a 9% stake in LUKOIL to a Cyprus-based unit, Reforma Investments, held in part by LUKOIL's "boss of bosses," Vagit Alekperov (gained at the bargain price of $200 million). Critics cited the sale as Yeltsin's bid to gain Alekperov's political support.

The company announced the first major oil find in the Russian part of the Caspian Sea in 2000, and formed a joint venture (Caspian Oil Company) with fellow Russian energy giants Gazprom and Yukos to exploit resources in the Caspian. The next year LUKOIL acquired more than 1,300 gas stations on the East Coast of the US when it bought Getty Petroleum Marketing.

That year LUKOIL also acquired Bitech, a Canadian oil exploration and production firm with operations in the Republic of Komi in the Russian Federation. In 2002 the company sold its oil service business, a move that cut its overall workforce by some 20,000 and resulted in savings of $500 million annually.

EXECUTIVES

Chairman: Valery Grayfer
President and Director: Vagit Y. Alekperov
First VP Exploration and Production and Director: Ravil U. Maganov
First VP Economics and Finance: Sergei P. Kukura
First VP Refining, Marketing, and Distribution: Dmitri Tarasov
VP and Head of the Main Division of General Affairs, Corporate Security, and Communications: Anatoly A. Barkov
VP and Head of the Main Division of Oil and Gas Production and Infrastructure: Dzhevan K. Cheloyants
VP and Head of the Main Division of Strategic Development and Investment Analysis: Leonid A. Fedun
VP and Head of the Main Division of Treasury and Corporate Financing: Alexander K. Matytsyn
VP and Head of the Main Division of Capital Construction and Corporate Agencies: Serik Rakhmetov
VP and Head of the Main Division of Control and Internal Audit: Vagit S. Sharifov
VP and Head of the Main Division of Sales and Supplies: Yury Storozhev
Head of the Main Division of Legal Support: Ivan Masliaev
Head of the Main Division of Human Resources: Anatoly Moskalenko
Chief Accountant: Lyubov Khoba
Secretary of the Board of Directors and Head of the Board's Office: Evgueni Havkin
Auditors: ZAO KPMG

LOCATIONS

HQ: OAO LUKOIL
11 Sretenski Blvd., 101 000 Moscow, Russia
Phone: +7-095-928-9841   **Fax:** +7-095-916-0020
Web: www.lukoil.com

LUKOIL operates in 60 regions within Russia and in 25 other countries.

2004 Sales

	$ mil.	% of total
Russia		
European Russia	6,739	20
Western Siberia	698	2
Other countries	26,408	78
Total	**33,845**	**100**

PRODUCTS/OPERATIONS

2004 Sales

	$ mil.	% of total
Refining, marketing & distribution	30,807	91
Exploration & production	1,614	5
Chemicals	1,384	4
Other	40	—
Total	**33,845**	**100**

Selected Subsidiaries

Refining, Supplies, Marketing, and Transportation
Getty Petroleum Marketing
OAO LUKOIL Ukhtaneftepererabotka (refining)
LUKOIL Volgogradneftepererabotka (refining)
LUKOIL Volgogradnefteprodukt (marketing)
LUKOIL Vologdanefteprodukt (marketing)

Exploration and Production
OAO KomiTEK
LUKOIL Astrakhanmorneft
LUKOIL Kaliningradmorneft
LUKOIL Nizhnevolzhskneft
LUKOIL Permneft
LUKOIL Western Siberia
ZAO LUKOIL Perm

Other
LUKOIL International GmbH
OAO LUKOIL Arktic Tanker (shipping)
ZAO LUKOIL Neftekhim (petrochemicals)

COMPETITORS

Ashland	Rosneft
BP	Royal Dutch/Shell Group
Exxon Mobil	Sibneft
Imperial Oil	Surgutneftegas
Norsk Hydro	Tatneft
Occidental Petroleum	TOTAL
PDVSA	Unocal
PEMEX	Yukos
PETROBRAS	

HISTORICAL FINANCIALS

Company Type: Public

Income Statement				FYE: December 31
	REVENUE ($ mil.)	NET INCOME ($ mil.)	NET PROFIT MARGIN	EMPLOYEES
12/04	33,845	4,248	12.6%	—
12/03	22,299	3,701	16.6%	14,000
12/02	15,449	1,843	11.9%	130,000
12/01	13,562	2,109	15.6%	130,000
12/00	13,240	3,312	25.0%	120,000
12/99	9,752	1,120	11.5%	120,000
12/98	3,960	6	0.1%	90,000
12/97	9,003	303	3.4%	107,000
12/96	8,787	767	8.7%	94,236
12/95	6,711	546	8.1%	119,824
Annual Growth	19.7%	25.6%	—	(23.5%)

2004 Year-End Financials

Debt ratio: 12.5%
Return on equity: 22.2%
Cash ($ mil.): 1,406
Current ratio: 1.89
Long-term debt ($ mil.): 2,609

Net Income History

OTC: LUKOY

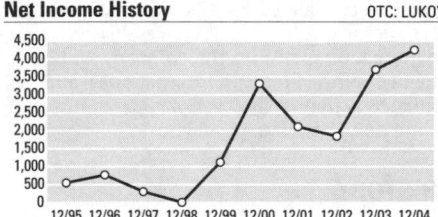

LVMH

LVMH Moët Hennessy Louis Vuitton is the world's largest luxury goods company, with brands that are bywords for the good life. LVMH makes wines and spirits (Dom Pérignon, Moët & Chandon, Veuve Clicquot, and Hennessy), perfumes (Christian Dior, Guerlain, and Givenchy), cosmetics (Bliss, Fresh, and BeneFit), fashion and leather goods (Donna Karan, Givenchy, Kenzo, and Louis Vuitton), and watches and jewelry (TAG Heuer, Ebel, Chaumet, and Fred). LVMH's retail division includes Sephora cosmetics stores, Le Bon Marché Paris department stores, and 61% of DFS Group (duty-free shops). Chairman Bernard Arnault and his family own 48% of LVMH.

The company has been focusing on controlling as much of its distribution as possible. LVMH has more than 1,500 retail outlets, including 280-plus Vuitton stores, some 150 DFS Group duty-free shops, Le Bon Marché, and hundreds of designer boutiques. Its Sephora self-serve cosmetics and fragrance chain boasts nearly 500 stores worldwide.

Competition in the UK from department stores and upscale retailers, though, has been more difficult than the firm had anticipated. LVMH exited the UK altogether in mid-2005 by closing all nine of its Sephora shops. In 2000 the company had launched its first store in Kent, with plans to open some 50 others within a few years.

Though the company denies rumors that it wants to unload DFS and Sephora, it has sold its teen-targeted Hard Candy and Urban Decay cosmetics brands. LVMH shed several of the less productive of its 50 brands in 2003, including auction house Phillips, de Pury & Luxemborg, and fashion brand Michael Kors; in 2004, Bliss spas was sold off, followed in 2005 by fashion design house Christian Lacroix SNC. The company nonetheless maintains one eye on growth. In 2005 LVMH was the winning bidder for whisky-maker Glenmorangie PLC, for which it paid £300 million.

In early 2004, LVMH won a landmark lawsuit against Morgan Stanley, alleging that the firm had used biased research in misstatements about the financial health of LVMH that caused damage to the company's image. The presiding Parisian court ordered Morgan Stanley to pay 100 million euros (about $38 million) in damages. Morgan Stanley appealed the ruling later that year.

In late February 2005 Japanese designer Kenzo Takada filed a lawsuit in Paris alleging that LVMH, which owns Kenzo SA, does not have the right to use the brand name in any language. Takada says he has had the right to use his first and last names since 1996. LVMH says that the designer was given the right to use his full name in Latin letters under certain circumstances.

HISTORY

Woodworker Louis Vuitton started his Paris career packing dresses for French Empress Eugenie. He later designed new types of luggage, and in 1854 he opened a store to sell his designs. In 1896 Vuitton introduced the LV monogram fabric that the company still uses. By 1900 Louis Vuitton had stores in the US and England, and by WWI Louis' son, Georges, had the world's largest retail store for travel goods.

Henry Racamier, a former steel executive who had married into the Vuitton family, took charge in 1977, repositioning the company's goods from esoteric status symbols to designer must-haves. Sales soared from $20 million to nearly $2.5 billion within a decade. Concerned about being a takeover target, Racamier merged Louis Vuitton in 1987 with Moët Hennessy (which made wines, spirits, and fragrances) and adopted the name LVMH Moët Hennessy Louis Vuitton.

Moët Hennessy had been formed through the 1971 merger of Moët et Chandon (the world's #1 champagne maker) and the Hennessy Cognac company (founded by Irish mercenary Richard Hennessy in 1765). Moët Hennessy acquired rights to Christian Dior fragrances in 1971.

Racamier tried to reverse the merger when disagreements with chairman Alain Chevalier arose. Racamier invited outside investor Bernard Arnault to increase his interest in the company. Arnault gained control of 43% of LVMH and became chairman in 1989. Chevalier stepped down, but Racamier fought for control for another 18 months and then set up Orcofi, a partner of cosmetics rival L'Oréal.

LVMH increased its fashion holdings with the purchases of the Givenchy Couture Group (1988), Christian Lacroix (1993), and Kenzo (1993). The company also acquired 55% of French media firm Desfosses International (1993), Celine fashions (1996), the Château d'Yquem winery (1996), and duty-free retailer DFS Group (1996). Next LVMH bought perfume chains Sephora (1997) and Marie-Jeanne Godard (1998). In 1998 LVMH integrated the Paris department store Le Bon Marché, which was controlled by Arnault.

LVMH accumulated a 34% stake in Italian luxury goods maker Gucci in early 1999 and planned to buy all of it. Fellow French conglomerate Pinault-Printemps-Redoute (PPR) later thwarted LVMH by purchasing 42% of Gucci.

Through its LV Capital unit, in 1999 LVMH began acquiring stakes in a host of luxury companies, including a joint venture with fashion company Prada to buy 51% of design house Fendi (LVMH bought Prada's 25.5% stake for $265 million in November 2001). It has since upped its Fendi stake to about 70%. LVMH later added the Ebel, Chaumet, and TAG Heuer brands to its new watch division.

In early 2000 LVMH bought Miami Cruiseline Services, which operates duty-free shops on cruise ships, auction house L'Etude Tajan, and 67% of Italian fashion house Emilio Pucci. The company later purchased 35% of French video game retailer Micromania and 51% of department store Samaritaine. In late 2000 LVMH acquired Gabrielle Studio, which owns all Donna Karan licenses. In 2001 the company bought Donna Karan International.

That year LVMH began marketing De Beers diamond jewelry in a 50-50 joint venture with the diamond powerhouse. Also that year it sold its stake in Gucci to PPR for $806.5 million.

In 2002 LVMH ceased trading on the Brussels and Nasdaq exchanges to concentrate on its Euronext investors. In October 2003 the company sold Canard-Duchene to the Alain Thienot Group. LVMH opened its biggest store — a four-story emporium on New York's Fifth Avenue — in February 2004. A few months later, the company added whisky-maker Glenmorangie PLC to its subsidiary roster. LVMH also made its debut in the South African market in October 2004, opening its first sub-Saharan boutique in Johannesburg.

EXECUTIVES

Chairman and CEO: Bernard Arnault
Vice Chairman: Antoine Bernheim, age 81
Group Managing Director: Antonio (Toni) Belloni
Adviser to the Chairman: Pierre Godé
Adviser to the Chairman, Group EVP of Synergies, and President, LVMH Italy: Concetta Lanciaux
Finance Director: Jean-Jacques Guiony
Development and Acquisitions, Managing Director, Groupe Arnault: Nicolas Bazire
Executive Committee, Fashion & Leather Goods: Yves Carcelle
Executive Committee, Perfumes & Cosmetics: Patrick Choël
Executive Committee, LV Capital: Daniel Piette, age 60
Executive Committee, Operations: Bernard Rolley
Executive Committee, Travel Retail: Edward (Ed) Brennan
Executive Committee, Watches and Jewelry: Philippe Pascal
Executive Committee, Wines and Spirits Group: Christophe Navarre
Executive Committee, Selective Retailing: Pierre Letzelter
CEO, LVMH (US): Bruce Ingram
CEO, Sephora Americas: David Suliteanu
President, Fendi North America: Gianluca Flore
President, Fendi USA: François Cress
President, Moët & Chandon: Frederic Cumenal
President, Perfumes and Cosmetics Group, US: Pamela Baxter

SVP, Olfactive Development, Perfumes:
  François Demachy
SVP, Public Relations and Communications, North America: Katherine Ross
SVP, Sales and Marketing, Dior US: Terry Darland
SVP, Human Resources, Perfumes and Cosmetics Division: Joanna Grillo
Auditors: Cogerco-Flipo; Ernst & Young Audit

LOCATIONS

HQ: LVMH Moët Hennessy Louis Vuitton SA
  22 avenue Montaigne, 75008 Paris, France
Phone: +33-1-44-13-22-22   **Fax:** +33-1-44-13-21-19
US HQ: 19 E. 57th St., New York, NY 10022
US Phone: 212-931-2000   **US Fax:** 212-931-2903
Web: www.lvmh.com

2004 Sales

	% of total
Europe	
France	8
Other countries	25
Asia	
Japan	16
Other countries	14
US	22
Other regions	15
Total	**100**

PRODUCTS/OPERATIONS

2004 Sales

	% of total
Fashion & leather goods	33
Selective retailing	26
Perfumes & cosmetics	19
Wines & spirits	18
Watches & jewelry	4
Total	**100**

Selected Brands and Operations

Fashion and leather goods
  Berluti
  Celine
  Christian Lacroix
  Donna Karan
  Emilio Pucci
  Fendi
  Gabrielle Studio (Donna Karan label)
  Givenchy
  Kenzo
  Loewe
  Louis Vuitton
  Marc Jacobs
  Thomas Pink

Retailing
  DFS Group
  La Samaritaine
  Le Bon Marché
  Miami Cruiseline Services (duty-free shops)
  Sephora

Fragrances and cosmetics
  Aqua di Parma
  BeneFit
  Bliss
  Fresh
  Guerlain
  Kenzo Parfums
  Make Up For Ever
  Marc Jacobs Fragrances
  Parfums Christian Dior
  Parfums Givenchy

Spirits and wines
10 Cane	Krug
Belvedere	Mercier
Canard-Duchêne	Moët & Chandon
Chandon Estates	MountAdam
Château d'Yquem	Newton
Dom Pérignon	Ruinart
Hennessy	Veuve Clicquot

Watches and jewelry
  Chaumet
  De Beers
  Ebel
  Fred
  Omas
  TAG Heuer
  Zenith
Media (Desfosses International Group)
  Investir
  La Tribune
  Radio Classique

COMPETITORS

Allied Domecq	Kirin
Armani	L'Oréal
Avon	MacAndrews & Forbes
Bacardi	Oscar de la Renta
Brown-Forman	Polo Ralph Lauren
Calvin Klein	PPR
Chanel	Prada
Douglas Holding	Puig Beauty & Fashion
Eckes	Rémy Cointreau
Escada	Richemont
Estée Lauder	Shiseido
Galeries Lafayette	Swatch
Gallo	Taittinger
Gianni Versace	Tiffany
GUS	Unilever
Hermès	Vera Wang
Hugo Boss	Yves Saint-Laurent Groupe
Inditex	

HISTORICAL FINANCIALS

Company Type: Public

Income Statement

FYE: December 31

	REVENUE ($ mil.)	NET INCOME ($ mil.)	NET PROFIT MARGIN	EMPLOYEES
12/04	17,218	1,378	8.0%	59,840
12/03	15,015	908	6.0%	56,386
12/02	13,304	583	4.4%	56,591
12/01	10,900	9	0.1%	53,795
12/00	10,909	680	6.2%	51,127
12/99	8,589	696	8.1%	41,235
12/98	8,126	313	3.9%	33,057
12/97	7,974	752	9.4%	32,348
12/96	6,007	711	11.8%	20,644
12/95	6,071	825	13.6%	19,517
Annual Growth	**12.3%**	**5.9%**	**—**	**13.3%**

2004 Year-End Financials

Debt ratio: 54.0%
Return on equity: 14.5%
Cash ($ mil.): 2,724
Current ratio: 1.40
Long-term debt ($ mil.): 5,505

Net Income History

Euronext Paris: MC

MAN

This venerable old MAN still shows considerable strength. MAN Aktiengesellschaft (founded in 1845) and its subsidiaries manufacture a variety of heavy equipment ranging from commercial vehicles to diesel engines for ships. MAN is one of Europe's largest truck makers as well as a leading supplier of equipment for newspaper printing presses and industrial compressors and turbines. The company also makes components for rocket launchers and space transport systems, and it provides trading and industrial services. Additionally, MAN is a top manufacturer of equipment used to process plastics and metals.

In an effort its operations to better compete within the EU market, the company has restructured its organization under two main divisions headings: Manufacturing (commercial vehicles, printing machines, diesel engines, Further Industrial Holdings, and turbomachines) and Services (industrial and financial services). It plans to expand its operations in China and Russia in the years ahead.

Although MAN's reach is global, Europe accounts for more than two-thirds of sales. The company's commercial vehicle division accounts for about 45% of its total revenue.

In 2005 MAN group sold off its MAN Wolffkran subsidiary to private investors. The subsidiary sells and rents tower cranes, a.k.a. cherry pickers, for the building industry; the sale was part of the company's effort to pare down its operations to what are considered to be its core divisions. It also restructured its financial services division to prepare it for expansion; the company will be renamed MAN Finance International and will finance activities in seven countries including Germany, Italy, France, and Spain.

HISTORY

MAN grew out of a company started by Carl August Reichenbach and Carl Buz, who leased an engineering plant in Augsburg, Germany, in 1844. Reichenbach, whose uncle had invented the flatbed printing press, began producing printing presses in 1845. On the same premises, Buz began manufacturing steam engines and industrial drive systems, and he soon added rotary printing presses, water turbines, pumps, and diesel engines. In 1898 the company took the name MAN (Maschinenfabrik Augsburg-Nurnberg) after merging with a German engineering company of the same name.

Another German heavy-industry company, Gutehoffnungshutte Aktienverein AG (GHH, with roots stretching to 1758), bought a majority interest in MAN in 1921. Through acquisitions and internal growth MAN emerged from the world wars as one of Germany's major heavy-industry companies, with added interests in commercial vehicles, shipbuilding, and plant construction. By 1955 MAN's commercial vehicles were a major division destined to dominate the company's sales; MAN moved the division's headquarters to Munich that year.

During the 1970s an overseas recession caused the sales of some operations to slump, although MAN's commercial vehicles and printing-equipment businesses held steady. When economic hardship reached Europe in the 1980s, MAN sought markets outside its home region, especially targeting Asia, the Middle East, and the US. Late in the decade the company dropped its less-profitable products (lifts, pumps, heavy cranes) and began licensing more of its technology and subcontracting out more work. MAN moved its corporate headquarters to Munich in 1985 and merged with GHH in 1986.

After a fast start in the 1990s, Europe's economy again faltered, taking a toll on the company's sales. MAN's profits slumped in fiscal 1994. It laid off about 10% of its workforce between 1993 and 1995. As the economy recovered, so did MAN, and by fiscal 1998, its stagnant profits had rebounded.

Early in 2000 MAN purchased truck makers ERF Holdings (UK) and STAR (Poland). Later that year MAN picked up Alstom's diesel engine business. MAN acquired the Neoplan bus making business of Gottlob Auwarter GmbH in 2001, as well as the turbomachinery business of Sulzer AG of Switzerland. After discovering accounting irregularities that year, the company suspended the CEO (John Bryant) and CFO (Klaus Wagner) of the newly acquired ERF. In 2002 the company began implementing its Truck Generation A (TG-A) technology into all of its commercial vehicles. In 2003, MAN sold its 51% stake in SMS AG.

EXECUTIVES

Chairman of the Supervisory Board: Volker Jung, age 66
Deputy Chairman of the Supervisory Board: Gerlinde Strauss-Wieczorek
Chairman of the Executive Board: Rudolf Rupprecht, age 65
Chairman: Håkan Samuelsson, age 53
Member of the Executive Board, Controlling: Philipp J. Zahn
Member of the Executive Board, Diesel Engines: Hans-Jürgen Schulte
Member of the Executive Board, Industrial Services; Chairman, Ferrostaal: Matthias Mitscherlich, age 56
Member of the Executive Board, Finances: Ferdinand Graf von Ballestrem, age 61
Member of the Executive Board, Printing Machines: Gerd Finkbeiner, age 47
Member of the Executive Board, Technology; Chairman, MAN Technologie: Wolfgang Brunn, age 61
Chairman, MAN B&W Diesel: Fritz Pape, age 63
Chairman, MAN Roland Druckmaschinen: Ingo Koch
Chairman, MAN Turbomaschinen: Jürgen Maus, age 60
Chairman, Schwäbische Hüttenwerke: Lothar Hauck
Press Speaker: Wieland Schmitz
Member of Executive Board, Controlling: Karlheinz Hornung, age 54
Investor Relations Director: Ulf Steinborn
Auditors: BDO Deutsche Warentreuhand AG

LOCATIONS

HQ: MAN Aktiengesellschaft
Ungererstrasse 69, D-80805 Munich, Germany
Phone: +49-89-36098-0   **Fax:** +49-89-36098-250
Web: www.man.de

MAN Aktiengesellschaft has manufacturing facilities in Austria, Germany, Poland, South Africa, Turkey, and the UK.

2004 Sales

	% of total
Germany	25
Americas	14
Asia	13
Africa	4
Australia & Oceania	2
Other European Union	35
Other Europe	7
Total	**100**

PRODUCTS/OPERATIONS

2004 Sales

	% of total
Commercial vehicles	47
Industrial services	22
Printing systems	12
Diesel engines	12
Turbomachines	4
Other	3
Total	**100**

Selected Subsidiaries and Products

Deggendorfer Werft und Eisenbau
  Autoclaves
  Condensers
  Dump barges
  Floating dredgers
  Gas coolers
  Heat exchangers
  Pilot reactors
  Pressure vessels
  Tube reactors
  Salt bath-cooled reactors
Ferrostaal
  Facility construction and contracting
  Industrial equipment and systems
  Steel trading and logistics
MAN B&W Diesel
  Diesel engines for locomotives, marine propulsion, and power plants
  Exhaust gas turbochargers
  Power turbines
MAN Nutzfarzeuge
  Buses and coaches
  Components
    Axles
    Cabs
    Cast parts
    Pressed parts
    Tools
    Transfer cases
  Diesel engines for automobiles, boats, and power generation
  Gas Motors
  Transport logistics and fleet management
  Trucks (6 to 50 tons gross weight)
MAN Roland Druckmaschinen
  Digital-based printing systems
  Sheet-fed offset printing presses
  Web-fed offset printing presses
MAN Technologie
  Space transport propulsion components and systems
MAN Turbomaschinen GHH BORSIG
  Industrial compressors
  Industrial turbines
Schwäbische Hüttenwerke
  Brake discs
  Castings
  Chilled cast iron rolls
  Industrial pumps
  Sintered parts

COMPETITORS

ALSTOM	ITT Industries
ArvinMeritor, Inc.	Kawasaki Heavy Industries
Baldwin Technology	Koenig & Bauer
Cummins	Mitsubishi Heavy
DaimlerChrysler	Industries
Dana	Navistar
DEUTZ	PACCAR
Federal-Mogul	Renault
Fiat	Scania
GE Energy	Sumitomo Heavy
GEA Group	Industries
Goss International	TUI
Hanjin Heavy Industries	Voith
& Construction	Volvo
Heidelberg	

HISTORICAL FINANCIALS

Company Type: Public

Income Statement

FYE: December 31

	REVENUE ($ mil.)	NET INCOME ($ mil.)	NET PROFIT MARGIN	EMPLOYEES
12/04	20,388	420	2.1%	61,259
12/03	18,854	285	1.5%	64,158
12/02	16,812	142	0.8%	75,054
12/01	14,439	134	0.9%	77,606
12/00*	7,085	151	2.1%	76,604
6/00	13,881	404	2.9%	71,239
6/99	13,687	355	2.6%	66,838
6/98	13,716	316	2.3%	64,054
6/97	12,251	184	1.5%	62,564
6/96	13,279	198	1.5%	57,826
Annual Growth	**4.9%**	**8.7%**	**—**	**0.6%**

*Fiscal year change

2004 Year-End Financials

Debt ratio: 12.4%
Return on equity: 11.3%
Cash ($ mil.): 824
Current ratio: 1.41
Long-term debt ($ mil.): 499

Net Income History

German: MAN

Marks and Spencer

The sun now sets on Marks and Spencer (M&S). The department stores sell mid-priced clothing, food, and household items under the company's famous private label, the "very British" St Michael brand (found on items ranging from tweed jackets to marmalade). One of the UK's largest sellers of clothing, it has sold off most overseas operations in order to salvage its 400 M&S stores in the UK. The company got rid of more than 220 Brooks Brothers clothing stores in the US and Asia (to Retail Brand Alliance, 2001) and its 18 M&S stores in France (to Galeries Lafayette, 2001). M&S owns stores in Ireand and Hong Kong, operates franchises in 30 countries, as well as the 25-store Kings Super Markets chain in the US.

In the UK, M&S (Marks & Sparks in Cockney rhyming slang) also sells prepared foods, such as its popular (and high-margin) ready-to-go meals. The company has about 130 Simply Food outlets around the UK, and it is rebranding more than two dozen of its existing food stores as Marks & Spencer Food over the next two years. M&S Food stores are larger than the Simply Food outlets and designate a small amount of floor space to general merchandise.

M&S has taken a number of steps to defend its UK apparel business, which has suffered from stiff competition over the past several years. It recently upgraded its women's Classic range and launched a petite line. The company has pared its menswear offering from eight brands to three (Autograph, Blue Harbour, and Collezione) Building on the success of its Per Una clothing line, M&S launched Per Una Due (designed by high-street legend George Davies), an edgy clothing line targeted at women in their late teens to early 30s. Overall, M&S has about a 10% share of the clothing market in the UK and is the leading lingerie retailer in Britain with more than 25% of the market.

In October 2005 Lord Burns, chairman of Abbey National and Glas Cymru (Welsh Water), joined Marks and Spencer as deputy chairman and has agreed to become its chairman in July 2006. He will succeed interim chairman Paul Myners, who took over from Luc Vandevelde when Vandevelde and chief executive Roger Holmes left the company in 2004.

HISTORY

Fleeing anti-Semitic persecution in Russian Poland, 19-year-old Michael Marks immigrated to England in 1882. Eventually settling in Leeds, Marks eked out a meager existence as a traveling peddler until he opened a small stall at the town market in 1884. Because he spoke little English, Marks laid out all of his merchandise and hung a sign that read, "Don't Ask the Price, It's a Penny," unaware at the time that self-service would eventually become the retailing standard. His methods were so successful that he had penny bazaars in five cities by 1890.

Finding himself unable to run the growing operation alone, Marks established an equal partnership with Englishman Tom Spencer, a cashier for a local distributor, forming Marks and Spencer in 1894. By the turn of the century, the company had 36 branches. Following the deaths of Spencer (1905) and Marks (1907), management of the company did not return to family hands until 1916, when Marks' 28-year-old son Simon became chairman.

Marks and Spencer broke with time-honored British retailing tradition in 1924 by eliminating wholesalers and establishing direct links with manufacturers. In 1926 the firm went public, and two years later it launched its now famous St Michael brand. The company turned its attention to pruning unprofitable departments to concentrate on goods that had a rapid turnover. In 1931 the Marks & Spencer stores (M&S) introduced a food department that sold produce and canned goods.

The company sustained severe losses during WWII, when bombing damaged approximately half of its stores. Marks and Spencer rebuilt, and in 1964 Simon's brother-in-law Israel Sieff became chairman. The firm expanded to North America a decade later by buying three Canadian chains: Peoples (general merchandise, sold 1992), D'Allaird's (women's clothing, sold 1996), and Walker's (clothing shops, converted to M&S). Sieff's son Marcus Sieff became chairman in 1972. It opened its first store in Paris in 1975.

Derek Rayner replaced Marcus Sieff as chairman in 1984, becoming the first chairman hired from outside the Marks family since 1916. Under Rayner, Marks and Spencer moved into financial services by launching a charge card in 1985. The company purchased US-based Kings Super Markets and Brooks Brothers (upscale clothing stores) in 1988. Rayner retired in 1991, and CEO Richard Greenbury became chairman. During the 1990s M&S opened new stores in Germany, Hong Kong, Hungary, Spain, and Turkey.

Greenbury, facing criticism that the company was too slow to expand and embrace new ideas, in 1999 was succeeded as CEO by handpicked heir Peter Salsbury. That year, continued poor sales led Marks and Spencer to cut 700 jobs and close its 38 M&S stores in Canada, and part ways with its clothing supplier of 30 years, William Baird. In early 2000 Marks and Spencer dodged a takeover attempt by investor Philip Green. Chairman Luc Vandevelde took over as CEO, in September, when Salsbury resigned.

In spring 2001 Marks and Spencer announced a recovery plan to salvage its struggling M&S chain by selling off many of its global operations, including its profitable US businesses (Brooks Brothers and Kings Super Markets). Unhappy with the company's direction and its departure from older values, Marks and Spencer board members Sir David Sieff (the last remaining founder member), Sir Ralph Robins, and Sir Michael Perry left the board in July 2001. Marks and Spencer sold Brooks Brothers to Retail Brand Alliance for $225 million (a loss from the $750 million the company paid for it in 1988).

In 2002 Vandevelde — who is credited with masterminding the M&S turnaround — announced he would give up his role as CEO and hand the reins to managing director Roger Holmes. Vandevelde became the company's part-time chairman in January 2003.

In May 2004 both Vandevelde and Holmes left M&S. Stuart Rose, formerly head of Arcadia, was named CEO; non-executive board member Paul Myners was named interim chairman of the company. In October M&S bought the Per Una brand from designer George Davies for about £126 million.

In 2005 M&S sold its Lifestore in Gateshead to Active Asset Investment Management for £43 million.

EXECUTIVES

Interim Chairman: Paul Myners, age 57, $375,740 pay
CEO and Director: Stuart A. Rose, age 56, $1,596,895 pay (partial-year salary)
CFO and Director: Ian Dyson, age 43
Group Secretary and Head of Corporate Governance: Graham Oakley, age 48
Executive Director, Marketing, e-Commerce, and Store Design and Development, and Director: Steven Sharp, age 55
Director of General Merchandise Planning: Andrew Moore, age 47
Director, Retail Operations: Anthony Thompson, age 40
Director, Communications: Flic Howard-Allen, age 44
Business Unit Director, Food: Guy Farrant, age 42
Director, Human Resources: Keith Cameron, age 57
Business Unit Director, Home: Steve Rowe, age 37
Director, Information Technology: Alastair Tipple, age 47
Director, Per Una: George Davies
Director, Property, Development, and Facilities Management Group: Chris Williams, age 48
Director, Supply Chain: Stuart McIver
Director, Lingerie and Beauty: Matthew (Matt) Hudson, age 36
Corporate Press Manager: Sue Sadler
Auditors: PricewaterhouseCoopers LLP

LOCATIONS

HQ: Marks and Spencer Group p.l.c.
Waterside House, 35 N. Wharf Rd., London W2 1NW, United Kingdom
Phone: +44-20-7935-4422 **Fax:** +44-20-7487-2679
Web: www.marksandspencer.com

2005 Sales

	% of total
UK	
Clothing	45
Food	41
Home	5
Other countries	9
Total	**100**

COMPETITORS

Arcadia	J Sainsbury
ASDA	John Lewis
Benetton	Kingfisher
Berwin & Berwin	Littlewoods
Burberry	Mothercare
Carrefour	New Look
Debenhams	NEXT
Fortnum & Mason	Pret A Manger
Gap	Primark
GUS	Somerfield
Harrods	Syms
Harvey Nichols	Tesco
House of Fraser	T.K. Maxx

HISTORICAL FINANCIALS

Company Type: Public

Income Statement

FYE: March 31

	REVENUE ($ mil.)	NET INCOME ($ mil.)	NET PROFIT MARGIN	EMPLOYEES
3/05	14,921	1,103	7.4%	70,550
3/04	15,157	1,008	6.7%	70,101
3/03	12,713	756	5.9%	67,133
3/02	11,598	218	1.9%	69,899
3/01	11,438	2	0.0%	76,491
3/00	13,046	412	3.2%	75,657
3/99	13,265	600	4.5%	75,492
3/98	13,820	1,390	10.1%	71,297
3/97	12,850	1,237	9.6%	68,208
3/96	11,000	996	9.0%	65,498
Annual Growth	3.4%	1.1%	—	0.8%

2005 Year-End Financials

Debt ratio: 421.3%
Return on equity: 42.6%
Cash ($ mil.): 525
Current ratio: 0.65
Long-term debt ($ mil.): 3,607

Net Income History

Pink Sheets: MAKSY.PK

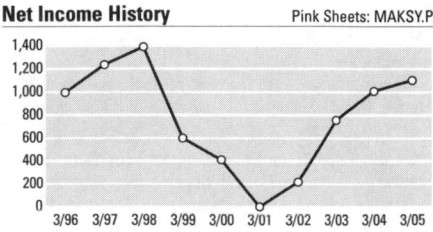

Matsushita

Matsushita Electric Industrial, one of the world's top consumer electronics makers, may have an unfamiliar name, but its brands are recognizable: Panasonic, Quasar, Technics, and JVC, to name a few. Its AVC Networks sector produces TVs, VCRs, CD and DVD players, PCs, cellular phones, and fax machines. Matsushita also sells components (batteries, electric motors, displays, semiconductors), home appliances (washing machines, vacuum cleaners), and factory automation equipment (industrial robots, welding equipment). The Matsushita group includes about 380 consolidated companies around the globe; its products are sold worldwide.

Matsushita (whose founder's name means "lucky man under the pine tree") also makes products sold around the world under the National and Victor brands. Its top revenue generator, the AVC Networks segment, accounts for about 45% of sales.

China is becoming a more important manufacturing center for Matsushita; the company is shifting its low-end product manufacturing to China (due primarily to lower production costs), with more expensive products being made in Japan and Southeast Asia. However, the company is planning to build a large manufacturing plant in China. The plant, which will produce home appliances, will primarily serve the Chinese market.

In early 2004 Matsushita acquired affiliate Matsushita Electric Works (MEW), a company in which it previously held a 32% share. MEW, which makes lighting, security systems, kitchen and bathroom fittings, was spun off from Matsushita in 1935. The acquisition makes Matsushita the largest Japanese electronic and electrical equipment manufacturer.

The company is merging its resources with other companies in order to launch new technologies, particularly in the consumer home electronics segment. It became a member of the Blu-ray Disc Founders (along with Sony and Samsung) to promote the Blu-ray optical disc format as the standard for next-generation optical storage media — succeeding the DVD format.

The fast-growing flat-screen television market has become a new focus for Matsushita, particularly its PDP (plasma display panel) and liquid crystal display (LCD) products.

The company is accelerating its chip-making operations, viewing semiconductors as a key ingredient in product innovation. Matsushita began construction on a new Japanese semiconductor plant in 2004, with chip production to begin in 2006.

HISTORY

Grade school dropout Konosuke Matsushita took $50 in 1918 and went into business making electric plugs (with his brother-in-law, Toshio Iue, founder of SANYO). His mission, to help people by making high-quality, low-priced conveniences while providing his employees with good working conditions, earned him the sobriquet, "god of business management." Matsushita Electric Industrial grew by developing inexpensive lamps, batteries, radios, and motors in the 1920s and 1930s.

During WWII the Japanese government ordered the firm to build wood-laminate products for the military. Postwar occupation forces prevented Matsushita from working at his firm for four years. Thanks to unions' efforts, he rejoined his namesake company shortly before it entered a joint venture with Dutch manufacturer Philips in 1952. The following year it moved into consumer goods, making televisions, refrigerators, and washing machines and later expanding into high-performance audio products. Matsushita bought a majority stake in Victor Company of Japan (JVC, originally established by RCA Victor) in 1954. Its 1959 New York subsidiary opening began Matsushita's drive overseas.

Sold under the National, Panasonic, and Technics names, the firm's products were usually not cutting-edge but were attractively priced. Under Masaharu Matsushita, the founder's son-in-law who became president in 1961, the company became Japan's largest home appliance maker, introducing air conditioners, microwave ovens, stereo components, and VCRs in the 1960s and 1970s. JVC developed the VHS format for VCRs, which beat out Sony's Betamax format.

Matsushita built much of its sales growth on new industrial and commercial customers in the 1980s. The company expanded its semiconductor, office and factory automation, auto electronics, audio-visual, housing, and air-conditioning product offerings that decade. Konosuke died in 1989.

The next year Matsushita joined the Japanese stampede for US acquisitions, buying Universal Studios' then-owner, MCA. In 1993 Yoichi Morishita was named president and the company acquired Philips' stake in the their joint venture. Two years later, when cultural incompatibility depressed MCA's performance, Matsushita sold 80% of the company (now Universal) to liquor mogul Seagram, resulting in a fiscal 1996 loss. That same year Matsushita pushed the technology envelope, introducing the first DVD player.

Declining sales forced the firm to rethink its strategy; it began a multiyear restructuring, including a buildup in parts of Asia with cheaper labor and job cuts.

A lagging market led Matsushita to close its North American semiconductor operations in late 1998. Also that year the company bought a stake in Mobile Broadcasting (a digital satellite broadcasting venture of nine companies) and introduced digital TVs.

In 2000 Yoichi Morishita became chairman and Kunio Nakamura took the reigns as president of Matsushita. The next December, following a year with a three-fold increase in expenditures on chip-making ($1.2 billion), the company began making chips for cell phones, digital cameras, and digital TVs.

In early 2002 Matsushita announced plans to turn around its financial slump by cutting 13,000 local jobs (through early retirement) and trimming directors' salaries. Also in 2002 Matsushita buddied up with Chinese home appliance manufacturer TCL Holdings; the move was intended to help Matsushita increase its presence in China's growing consumer electronic market.

The company launched a global brand consolidation strategy in 2003, rebranding all home appliance products in non-Japanese markets to Panasonic from National. It further expanded the Panasonic brand's reach in 2004 when it increased its stake (to 60%) in Indonesian manufacturing PT Panasonic Gobel, a joint venture between Matsushita and the Gobel family. The transaction allowed Matsushita to assume control of Panasonic sales in that country.

EXECUTIVES

Honorary Chairman: Masaharu Matsushita, age 93
Chairman: Yoichi Morishita, age 71
Vice Chairman: Masayuki Matsushita, age 60
President and Director: Kunio Nakamura, age 66
EVP Corporate Marketing and Corporate Sales Strategy and Director: Kazuo Toda, age 64
EVP and Director; President, Panasonic Automotive Systems Company: Takami Sano, age 60
Senior Managing Director, Technology, Device Technology, and Environmental Technology and Director; President, Semiconductor Company: Susumu Koike, age 60
Senior Managing Director, Storage Devices Business, Digital Network Strategic Planning Office, and Matsushita Fujisawa Manufacturing Center and Director; President, Panasonic AVC Networks Company: Fumio Ohtsubo, age 60
Senior Managing Director, Finance and Accounting and Director: Tetsuya Kawakami, age 63
Senior Managing Director, Home Appliances and Director; President, Matsushita Home Appliances Company: Yoshitaka Hayashi, age 59
Managing Director, Facility Management, Quality Assurance and Environmental Affairs and Director: Hidetsugu Otsuru, age 62
Managing Director, Planning and Director: Toshihiro Sakamoto, age 59
Managing Director, Corporate Communications and Director; Vice Chairman, Showroom Strategic Committee: Takahiro Mori
Managing Director, Personnel, General Affairs, and Social Relations and Director: Shinichi Fukushima, age 57
Director, Corporate Legal Affairs: Mikio Ito
Director; President, Panasonic System Solutions Company: Masaki Akiyama
Director; Deputy Chief, Overseas Operations and Director, Global Strategy Research Institute: Ikusaburo Kashima
Auditors: KPMG AZSA & Co.

LOCATIONS

HQ: Matsushita Electric Industrial Co., Ltd.
(Matsushita Denki Sangyo Kabushiki Kaisha)
1006 Oaza Kadoma, Kadoma,
Osaka 571-8501, Japan
Phone: +81-6-6908-1121   **Fax:** +81-6-6908-2351
US HQ: 1 Rockefeller Plaza, Ste. 1001,
New York, NY 10020-2002
US Phone: 212-698-1365   **US Fax:** 212-698-1369
Web: matsushita.co.jp

2005 Sales

	% of total
Japan	52
North and South America	15
Europe	13
Other regions (including Asia)	20
Total	**100**

PRODUCTS/OPERATIONS

2005 Sales

	% of total
AVC Networks	41
Video & audio equipment	17
Information & communications equipment	24
Home appliances	14
Components & devices	13
MEW & PanaHome	17
JVC	8
Other	7
Total	**100**

Selected Segments and Products

AVC Networks
  Audio equipment (home, broadcast)
  Camcorders
  CD and mini-disc players
  Computer drives (CD-ROM, DVD-ROM/RAM)
  Computers (PCs)
  Digital cameras
  DVD players and recorders
  Fax machines
  Memory cards
  Photocopiers
  Printers
  Telephones
  TVs (color, LCD, plasma display)
  VCRs
Home appliances
  Air conditioners and purifiers
  Dishwashers
  Dryers
  Fans
  Irons
  Microwave ovens
  Refrigerators
  Vacuum cleaners
  Water heaters
  Washing machines
Components and devices
  Batteries (dry, rechargeable)
  Displays (CRTs, LCDs, PDPs)
  Electric motors
  General components
    (capacitors, resistors, printed circuit boards)
  Magnetic recording heads
  Semiconductors
MEW and PanaHome
  Automation controls
  Beauty and personal care products
  Condominiums
  Detached housing
  Electronic and plastic materials
  Health-enhancing products
  Home amenity and security systems
  Home remodeling
  Interior furnishings
  Land lots for housing
  Lighting products
  Medical and nursing care facilities
  Modular kitchens
  Rental apartment housing
  Residential real estate
  Wiring devices
JVC (Victor Company of Japan)
  Camcorders
  Car audio equipment
  CD radio cassette recorders
  DVD players and recorders
  Karaoke systems
  Stereo equipment
  TVs
  VCRs
  Video projectors

Selected Brands

JVC	Quasar
National	Technics
Panasonic	Victor

COMPETITORS

Apple Computer	Konica Minolta
BSH Bosch und Siemens	LG Electronics
Hausgerte	Maytag
Canon	Motorola
Dell	NEC
Duracell	Nokia
Eastman Kodak	Olympus
Electrolux	Philips Electronics
Fujitsu Siemens	Samsung Electronics
Computers	Sharp
GE Consumer & Industrial	Sony
Haier Group	THOMSON
Hewlett-Packard	Tyco Electronics
IBM	Whirlpool
Intel	

HISTORICAL FINANCIALS

Company Type: Public

Income Statement

FYE: March 31

	REVENUE ($ mil.)	NET INCOME ($ mil.)	NET PROFIT MARGIN	EMPLOYEES
3/05	81,298	546	0.7%	334,752
3/04	71,921	405	0.6%	290,493
3/03	61,681	(162)	—	288,324
3/02	51,830	(3,248)	—	297,196
3/01	61,199	331	0.5%	292,790
3/00	71,118	971	1.4%	290,448
3/99	63,668	113	0.2%	282,000
3/98	59,259	703	1.2%	—
3/97	61,903	1,112	1.8%	—
3/96	64,102	(537)	—	—
Annual Growth	**2.7%**	**—**	**—**	**2.9%**

2005 Year-End Financials

Debt ratio: 13.5%
Return on equity: 1.6%
Cash ($ mil.): 10,914
Current ratio: 1.42
Long-term debt ($ mil.): 4,452

No. of shares (mil.): 2,258
Dividends
  Yield: 0.4%
  Payout: 25.0%
Market value ($ mil.): 33,243

Stock History

NYSE: MC

		STOCK PRICE ($) FY Close	P/E High/Low		PER SHARE ($) Earnings	Dividends	Book Value
3/05		14.72	67	52	0.24	0.06	14.64
3/04		15.42	92	43	0.17	0.11	14.32
3/03		8.53	—	—	(0.07)	0.08	11.23
3/02		12.35	—	—	(1.57)	0.10	11.78
3/01		18.45	332	178	0.09	0.12	7.23
3/00		30.30	67	39	0.45	0.12	1.64
3/99		19.34	390	256	0.05	0.05	1.43
3/98		15.99	68	44	0.31	0.00	1.34
3/97		15.63	38	29	0.49	0.05	1.41
3/96		16.50	—	—	(0.25)	0.06	1.53
Annual Growth		**(1.3%)**	**—**	**—**	**—**	**0.0%**	**28.5%**

Mazda Motor

Having outrun an ailing Mitsubishi, Mazda Motor Corporation is now Japan's fourth-largest automaker behind Toyota, Nissan, and Honda. Mazda makes cars, minivans, pickup trucks, and commercial vehicles. Models sold by Mazda in the US include sedans (Mazda 3, Mazda 6), minivans (MPV), sports cars (Miata, RX-8), and pickup trucks (B-Series). Mazda has added an SUV to its lineup with the introduction of the Tribute. Operating from two Japanese and 17 international manufacturing plants, Mazda sells some 286,000 vehicles annually in Japan, and more than 730,000 abroad. Ford Motor owns a controlling 33% of Mazda.

Mazda is profitable — a condition of which Ford is no doubt envious. The company has turned itself around in the last few years despite a weak North American market. In fact, Mazda sold more cars in Europe in 2005 than it did in North America — a fact that would have been hard to imagine just a few years ago.

To stay on track Mazda will introduce 16 new models by 2007. In the US, currently the company's toughest market, Mazda plans to offer new SUV crossover vehicles as the country's fascination with large SUVs wanes in response to higher fuel prices. In Europe Mazda plans to offer new models that feature diesel engines, a feature favored by European drivers. At home in Japan Mazda is bringing new minivans to market while revamping its dealer network.

In conjunction with its partner Ford, Mazda has made huge gains in China. In 2001 Mazda sold 6,000 cars. By 2004 Mazda was selling 96,000 cars. By 2006 Mazda wants to sell 103,000 cars. It plans to do this by introducing more models, building cars in China, and shoring up its Chinese dealer network.

HISTORY

Ingiro Matsuda founded cork producer Toyo Cork Kogyo in Hiroshima in 1920. The company changed its name to Toyo Kogyo in 1927 and began making machine tools. Impressed by Ford trucks used in 1923 earthquake-relief efforts, Matsuda had the company make a three-wheel motorcycle/truck hybrid in 1931.

The second Sino-Japanese War forced Toyo Kogyo to make rifles and cut back on its truck production. Although the company built a prototype passenger car in 1940, the outbreak of WWII refocused it on weapons. The August 1945 bombing of Hiroshima killed more than 400 Toyo Kogyo workers, but the company persevered, producing 10 trucks that December. By 1949 it was turning out 800 per month.

The company launched the first Mazda, a two-seat minicar, in 1960. The next year Toyo Kogyo licensed Audi's new rotary engine technology. After releasing a string of models, the company became Japan's #3 automaker in 1964. Toyo Kogyo introduced the first Mazda powered by a rotary engine, Cosmo/110S, in 1967, followed by the Familia in 1968.

The company grew rapidly and began exporting to the US in 1970. However, recession, high gas prices, and concern over the inefficiency of rotary engines halted growth in the mid-1970s. Sumitomo Bank bailed out Toyo Kogyo. The company shifted emphasis back to piston engines but managed to launch the rotary engine RX-7 in 1978.

Ford's need for small-car expertise and Sumitomo's desire for a large partner for its client led to Ford's purchase of 25% of Toyo Kogyo in 1979. The company's early 1980s GLC/323 and 626 models were sold as Fords in Asia, Latin America, and the Middle East.

Toyo Kogyo changed its name to Mazda Motor Corporation in 1984. ("Mazda" is loosely derived from Matsuda's name, but the carmaker has never discouraged an association with the Zoroastrian god of light, Ahura Mazda.) The company opened a US plant in 1985, but a strong yen, expensive increases in production capacity, and a growing number of models led to increased overhead, soaring debt, and shrinking margins. By 1988 Mazda had begun to focus on sporty niche cars; it launched the hot-selling Miata in 1989.

The company faced more problems with the early 1990s' recession. In 1992 Mazda introduced a new 626 model. That year Mazda also sold half its interest in its Flat Rock, Michigan, plant to

Ford. As the yen, development costs, and prices for its cars in the US all rose, sales in the US fell. In 1993 Mazda reorganized subsidiary Mazda of America by cutting staff.

Ford sank $481 million into Mazda in 1996, increasing its stake to 33%. That year the Ford-appointed former EVP of Mazda, Henry Wallace, became Mazda's president, making history as the first non-Japanese to head a major Japanese corporation. In 1997 Wallace resigned to become CFO of Ford's European operations, and former Ford executive James Miller replaced him. That year Mazda consolidated four US operations into Mazda North American Operations.

Restructuring continued in 1998 as Mazda consolidated some European operations and closed a plant in Thailand. In 1999 Mazda sold its credit division to Ford and its Naldec auto parts unit to Ford's Visteon unit. It announced plans to sell its stake in South Korean carmaker Kia Motors. Later in the year, another American, Ford's Mark Fields, took over as president.

In 2000 Mazda recalled 30,000 MPV minivans (year 2000) to fix a powertrain control module and asked owners of all year 2000 MPVs to bring in their vehicles for front-bumper reinforcement. Mazda also announced plans to close about 40% of its North American dealership outlets over the next three years.

In 2001 Mazda completed a program to assume direct control over distribution in some European markets including France, Italy, Spain, and the UK.

EXECUTIVES

Representative Director and Chairman:
Kazuhide Watanabe
President, CEO, and Representative Director:
Hisakazu Imaki
Senior Managing Executive Officer, CFO, and Representative Director: Gideon Wolthers
EVP and Assistant to the President In Charge of R&D, Purchasing, Quality Assurance, Marketing, Sales, and IT Solutions and Representative Director:
John G. Parker
Senior Managing Executive Officer, China Business and Director: Kiyoshi Ozaki
Senior Managing Executive Officer, IT Solutions, e-Business, Corporate Affairs, Risk Management; Assistant to the CFO and Director: Ryoichi Hasegawa
Senior Managing Executive Officer, Marketing, Sales, and Customer Service and Director: Daniel T. Morris
Senior Managing Executive Officer, Purchasing and Director: Mutsumi Fujiwara
Senior Managing Executive Officer, Secretariat, Personnel and Human Development, Internal Auditing and Mazda Hospital and Director: Takashi Yamanouchi
Managing Executive Officer, Corporate Communications and Liaison: Masazumi Wakayama
Managing Executive Officer, Domestic Marketing, Domestic Sales, and Domestic Customer Service:
Masao Furuta
Managing Executive Officer, Research and Development Quality: Nobuhiro Hayama
Managing Executive Officer, Research and Development: Seita Kanai
Managing Executive Officer; President and CEO, Mazda Motor of America (Mazda North American Operations): James J. (Jim) O'Sullivan
Executive Officer, Financial Services; General Manager, Financial Services Division: Keishi Egawa
Executive Officer; General Manager, Personnel and Human Development Division: Masaki Kanda
Auditors: KPMG AZSA & Co.

LOCATIONS

HQ: Mazda Motor Corporation
(Matsuda Jidosha Kabushiki Kaisha)
3-1, Shinchi, Fuchu-cho, Aki-gun,
Hiroshima 730-8670, Japan
Phone: +81-82-282-1111 **Fax:** +81-82-287-5190
US HQ: 10 Corporate Park, Ste. 200, Irvine, CA 92606
US Phone: 949-727-1990 **US Fax:** 949-752-2130
Web: www.mazda.co.jp

Mazda Motor Corporation has production facilities in 15 countries. Its sales and service network includes 1,660 dealers, sales, and service outlets in Japan and more than 5,000 in other countries.

2004 Sales

	$ mil.	% of total
Japan	18,128	52
North America	8,832	25
Europe	6,315	18
Other regions	1,754	5
Adjustments	(7,425)	—
Total	**27,604**	**100**

PRODUCTS/OPERATIONS

Selected Models
B-Series (pickup)
Mazda 3 (hatchback sedan)
Mazda 5 (minivan)
Mazda 6 (sport sedan)
MX-5 Miata (roadster)
MPV (van)
RX-8 (sports car)
Tribute (SUV)

Selected Subsidiaries and Affiliates
AutoAlliance International, Inc. (50%, US)
Malox Co., Ltd.
Mazda Australia Pty. Ltd.
Mazda Motor Logistics Europe NV (Belgium)
Mazda Motor of America, Inc. (93%, US)
Toyo Advanced Technologies Co., Ltd.

COMPETITORS

BMW	Kia Motors
DaimlerChrysler	Nissan
Fiat	Peugeot
Ford	Renault
Fuji Heavy Industries	Saab Automobile
General Motors	Suzuki Motor
Honda	Toyota
Isuzu	Volkswagen

HISTORICAL FINANCIALS
Company Type: Public

Income Statement
FYE: March 31

	REVENUE ($ mil.)	NET INCOME ($ mil.)	NET PROFIT MARGIN	EMPLOYEES
3/04	27,604	321	1.2%	35,627
3/03	19,730	201	1.0%	36,184
3/02	15,794	67	0.4%	37,824
3/01	15,957	(1,229)	—	39,601
3/00	20,487	248	1.2%	43,818
3/99	17,271	325	1.9%	31,851
3/98	15,341	(51)	—	31,665
3/97	15,301	(142)	—	32,919
3/96	17,182	(111)	—	33,705
3/95	25,467	(476)	—	35,361
Annual Growth	**0.9%**	**—**	**—**	**0.1%**

2004 Year-End Financials
Debt ratio: 145.3%   Current ratio: 0.87
Return on equity: 17.2%   Long-term debt ($ mil.): 3,062
Cash ($ mil.): 2,577

Net Income History   Exchange: Tokyo

(chart showing values from -1,400 to 400, years 3/95 to 3/04)

METRO AG

A ride on METRO could be a shopper's delight. The company, Germany's largest retailer, owns and operates about 2,400 wholesale stores, supermarkets, hypermarkets, department stores, and specialty retailers (home improvement, consumer electronics), mainly in Germany but also in 28 other countries, including India, Russia, and Ukraine. Its store banners include Metro Cash & Carry, Makro, and Galeria Kaufhof. METRO also runs restaurants in its department stores and hypermarkets and offers advertising and insurance to its retail chains. Nearly 60% of METRO is owned by founder Otto Beisheim, Franz Haniel & Cie, and the Schmidt-Ruthenbeck family.

The world's fourth-largest retailer, METRO would like to unseat #3, financially troubled Dutch grocer Royal Ahold. But due to the lackluster retail economy in its home country, the German retail giant's growth is being driven by its international operations. (Sales outside Germany have overtaken those in the company's home market for the first time.)

At home METRO is unloading about 120 of its Extra supermarkets in southern and eastern Germany (where its presence is small) to rival REWE, and is closing or converting nearly 20 others. The remaining 280 Extra stores are in northern and western Germany.

METRO is investing heavily in eastern Europe and Asia. The German retailer opened its first METRO Cash & Carry stores in Moscow and Moldavia in late 2004, is adding eight more in 2005, and has expanded into Serbia. Beyond Europe, the retailer has stores in China, India, Japan, Morocco, Russia, Turkey, Ukraine, and Vietnam, giving the retailer a presence in 29 countries worldwide. METRO plans to open 30 Metro Cash & Carry markets throughout China in 2005 and three in Beijing by 2006. (The first opened in August 2004.)

Nearly half of the firm's revenues (about 47%) are earned from its Metro Cash & Carry and Makro wholesale outlets, which sell food and other grocery and non-grocery items to businesses and institutional customers. More than 750 hypermarkets (Real) and supermarkets (Extra), located primarily in Germany, complete its food retailing operations. METRO also runs consumer electronics chains (Media Markt, Saturn), home improvement centers (nearly 340 Praktiker stores), and department stores (Galeria Kaufhof). METRO is seeking buyers for its Praktiker stores after the chain missed financial targets.

In mid-2005, METRO said it was exploring options for its ailing DIY home improvement chain Praktiker Bau- und Heimwerkermrkte, including sale of the unit or an IPO.

HISTORY

Otto Beisheim founded METRO SB-Grossmarkte in the German town of Mulheim in 1964. A wholesale business serving commercial customers, it operated under the name METRO Cash & Carry. Three years later Beisheim received backing from the owners of Franz Haniel & Cie (an industrial company founded in 1756) and members of the Schmidt-Ruthenbeck family (also in wholesaling). This allowed METRO to expand rapidly in Germany and, in 1968, into the Netherlands under the name Makro Cash & Carry via a partnership with Steenkolen Handelsvereeniging (SHV). During the 1970s the company expanded its wholesaling operations within Europe and moved into retailing.

METRO's foray into retailing was aided during the next decade by the acquisition of department store chain Kaufhof AG. By the 1980s the rise of specialty stores had many department stores on the defensive, and Kaufhof's owners sold it to METRO and its investment partner, Union Bank of Switzerland.

As METRO's ownership interest in Kaufhof rose above 50%, the chain began converting some of its stores from department stores into fashion and sporting goods sellers. Kaufhof began acquiring a stake in computer manufacturer and retailer Vobis in 1989. In 1993 METRO, now operating as METRO Holding AG, acquired a majority interest in supermarket company Asko Deutsche Kaufhaus, which owned the Praktiker building materials chain. The reclusive Beisheim retired from active management the following year.

To cut costs and prepare for expansion into Asia, in 1996 METRO Holding merged its German retail holdings — Kaufhof; Asko; another grocery operation, Deutsche SB Kauf; and its German cash-and-carry operations — into one holding company, METRO AG. The new subsidiary purchased 58 Wirichs home improvement centers in Germany that year to complement its Praktiker chain.

In 1998 METRO bought the 196-store Makro self-service wholesale chain from Dutch-based SHV. METRO also added to its German food operations by acquiring the 94-store German Allkauf hypermarket chain.

Hans-Joachim Korber became METRO's CEO in 1999. In 2000 the company transferred 290 hypermarkets and department stores in Germany, Greece, Hungary, Luxembourg, and Turkey to a joint venture company (51% owned by Westdeutsche Landesbank) to raise cash for the expansion and remodeling of its wholesale outlets.

In 2001 the first two Cash & Carry stores in Russia and one in Croatia opened. Overall in 2002 METRO opened 61 stores — 53 of which were Metro Cash & Carry outlets — including new stores in China, Bulgaria, and Russia (one each), and Vietnam (two outlets). In April 2003 the company opened its first store in St. Petersburg (its fourth in Russia). In July, a third Metro Cash and Carry store opened in Vietnam. The German retailer opened a global sourcing headquarters in Hong Kong in September that covers all markets outside the European Union.

As part of its international expansion plan, in October 2003 METRO opened the first of two cash and carry distribution centers in Bangalore, India. In December 2003, METRO sold its 49% stake in Divaco in a buyout led by Divaco's management. Divaco was originally founded together with financial investors as a joint venture with the objective of optimally divesting non-core METRO Group activities.

Gunther Hulse stepped down as chairman of METRO's supervisory board for personal reasons in June 2004. Hulse was succeeded by Theo Siegert, a member of the management board of Franz Haniel & Cie, a German wholesale drug distribution company. The German retailer added two new nations to its roster in 2004: Russia and Moldova.

EXECUTIVES

Chairman, Supervisory Board: Theo Siegert, age 57
Vice Chairman, Supervisory Board: Klaus Bruns
Chairman and CEO, Management Board:
  Hans-Joachim Krber, age 54
CFO: Thomas Unger
Director of Purchasing/Imports, Advertising, and Catering: Stefan Feuerstein
EVP, Human Resources and CIO: Zygmunt Meirdorf
Managing Director and Country Manager, India:
  Harsh Bahadur
General Director, Metro Cash and Carry, Russia:
  Andrea F. Martinelli
General Director, Metro Cash and Carry, Vietnam:
  James Scott
COO, Asia-Pacific: Heinrich Birr
COO, Eastern Europe and Russia: Franz Muller
Head of Quality Assurance: Hans-Jürgen Matern
Auditors: Fasselt-Mette & Partner GmbH

LOCATIONS

HQ: METRO AG
  Schlüterstrasse 1, 40235 Düsseldorf, Germany
Phone: +49-211-6886-0   **Fax:** +49-211-6886-2178
Web: www.metro.de

METRO AG operates approximately 2,400 stores in 29 countries, primarily in Europe, but also in China, India, Japan, Moldova, Morocco, Russia, Turkey, Ukraine, and Vietnam.

2004 Sales

	% of total
Germany	51
Other countries	49
Total	**100**

PRODUCTS/OPERATIONS

2004 Sales

	% of total
Cash & carry	47
Nonfood specialty	
(consumerelectronics & home improvement chains)	27
Food retail	19
Department stores	7
Total	**100**

Selected Operations

Retail
  Makro
  Metro Cash & Carry (wholesale stores)

Food
  Extra (supermarkets)
  Real (hypermarkets)

Nonfood Specialty Stores
  Media Markt (consumer electronics)
  Praktiker (home improvement)
  Saturn (consumer electronics)

Department Store
  Galeria Kaufhof

Other Operations

Dinea-Gastronomie (restaurants/catering)
METRO MGE Einkauf (purchasing)
METRO MGI Informatik (IT services)
METRO Real Estate Management (construction services)
METRO Werbegesellschaft (advertising)
METRO Online AG (Internet retailer)
MGB METRO Buying Group Hong Kong Ltd.
  (purchasing, Asia and Non-European Union countries)

COMPETITORS

ALDI
AVA AG
Carrefour
Casino Guichard
Edeka Zentrale
Karstadt
Lidl & Schwarz Stiftung
REWE-Zentral
Royal Ahold
Tengelmann
Vendex
Wal-Mart

HISTORICAL FINANCIALS

Company Type: Public

Income Statement

FYE: December 31

	REVENUE ($ mil.)	NET INCOME ($ mil.)	NET PROFIT MARGIN	EMPLOYEES
12/04	76,942	1,128	1.5%	261,438
12/03	67,272	623	0.9%	252,037
12/02	54,004	464	0.9%	235,283
12/01	43,867	296	0.7%	230,848
12/00	44,189	398	0.9%	234,351
12/99	44,114	367	0.8%	216,457
12/98	54,711	439	0.8%	181,300
12/97	31,717	309	1.0%	134,019
12/96	35,431	393	1.1%	130,019
Annual Growth	**10.2%**	**14.1%**	**—**	**9.1%**

2004 Year-End Financials

Debt ratio: 135.4%   Current ratio: 0.78
Return on equity: 19.3%   Long-term debt ($ mil.): 8,754
Cash ($ mil.): 2,905

Net Income History

German: MEO

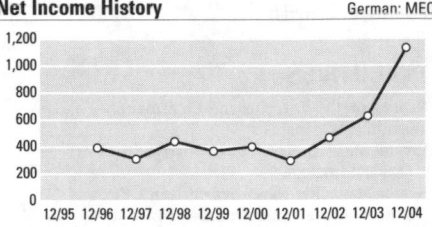

12/95 12/96 12/97 12/98 12/99 12/00 12/01 12/02 12/03 12/04

Michelin

The Michelin Man (whose name, by the way, is Bibendum) produces more than 190 million tires a year — pity the Michelin Woman. Compagnie Générale des Établissements Michelin sells about 36,000 products, including tires, wheels, and inner tubes used on passenger cars and trucks, aircraft, bicycles, and agricultural vehicles. Included in Michelin's stable of tires are brands recognized all over the world (BF Goodrich and Uniroyal), as well as more regional lines (Kleber in Europe and Warrior in China). Other company products include travel publications such as road maps and travel guides. A vertically integrated corporation, Michelin owns rubber plantations and factories around the globe.

Michelin is banking on Asia — a region that accounts for 30% of the global tire market. India's truck market has grown to half the size of Europe's, and China is poised to surpass Japan as the third-largest market for automobiles (behind the US and Europe). China also boasts a 28% share of the global truck market. Other emerging markets include Eastern Europe, South Korea, and Russia. Together, emerging markets account for 20% of Michelin's sales.

The company is also doing well in the developed markets of North America, Europe, and Japan by focusing on high-margin specialty tires such as high performance, winter, and 4x4 tires. In these markets Michelin has experienced double-digit growth — margins that outperform market norms.

Edouard Michelin, youngest son of patriarch François Michelin and the fourth generation of Michelins in the business, now leads Michelin. Edouard and his father, along with partner René Zingraff, control the company.

HISTORY

After toying with making rubber balls, Edouard Daubrée and Aristide Barbier formed a partnership in Clermont-Ferrand, France, in 1863 and entered the rubber business in earnest. Both men soon died, but Barbier in-law André Michelin, a successful businessman, took over the company in 1886. André recruited his brother, Edouard, a Parisian artist, to run the company, and in 1889 it was renamed Compagnie Générale des Établissements Michelin.

That year Edouard found that air-filled tires made bicycling more comfortable. But pneumatic tires were experimental and, because they were glued to the rims, required hours to change. In 1891 Edouard made a detachable bicycle tire that took only 15 minutes to change.

The Michelins promoted their tires by persuading cyclists to use them in long-distance races where punctures were likely. They demonstrated the applicability of such tires for cars in an auto race in 1895. In 1898 André commented that a stack of tires would look like a man if it had arms, a notion that led to the creation of Bibendum, the Michelin Man. André launched the *Michelin Guide* for auto tourists in 1900.

Expansion followed as Michelin opened a London office (1905) and began production in Italy (1906) and the US (in New Jersey in 1908). Innovations included detachable rims and spare tires (1906), tubeless tires (1930), treads (1934), and modern low-profile tires (1937). During the Depression, Michelin closed its US plant and accepted a stake in Citroën, later converted into a minority stake in Peugeot, in lieu of payment for tires.

Michelin patented radial tires in 1946. Expansion was largely confined to Europe in the 1950s but, thanks to radials, increased worldwide in the 1960s. Sears began selling Michelin radials in 1966. Radials took hold during the 1970s, and Michelin returned to manufacturing in the US, opening a plant in South Carolina in 1975.

Expanding aggressively (Michelin opened or bought a plant every nine months from 1960 to 1990), the company went into the red when economic conditions dipped in the early 1980s and in 1990 and 1991. The company's $1.5 billion purchase of Uniroyal Goodrich in 1990 contributed to the latter losses but improved Michelin's position in the US, the world's largest auto market.

In response to the losses, Michelin attacked its bloated infrastructure and reinvented itself along nine product lines (according to tire/vehicle type plus travel, suspension, and primary product manufacturing). It also consolidated facilities and cut about 30,000 jobs. The company continued to focus on R&D, bringing out new high-performance tires such as its "green" tire designed to help cars save fuel.

Michelin bought a majority interest in a Polish tire maker in 1995, and the next year it bought 90% of Taurus, a Hungarian firm that produces most of that country's rubber. Michelin joined German competitor Continental in 1996 to make private-label tires for independent distributors. The next year Michelin introduced a run-flat tire — capable of traveling 50 miles after a puncture — for the automotive aftermarket. The company acquired Icollantas, a Colombian tire group with two factories in Bogotá and Cali, in 1998.

After leading the company for more than 40 years, patriarch François Michelin stepped down in 1999, leaving his youngest son, Edouard, in charge. Almost immediately, Edouard announced a restructuring that would cut 7,500 jobs in Europe, including almost 2,000 in France. The company benefited somewhat from Firestone's recall woes in 2000, but Michelin still faced rising material costs and difficult market conditions.

The European Commission fined Michelin nearly $20 million in 2001, claiming the company engaged in anticompetitive behavior by abusing its dominant position in Europe. In 2003 Michelin and TRW Automotive created EnTire Solutions, a joint venture, to develop a tire pressure monitoring system. Michelin announced a licensing agreement in 2004 for Toyo Tire to make, sell, and promote PAX system tires (run-flat tires).

EXECUTIVES

Chairman of the Supervisory Board:
Eric Bourdais de Charbonnière, age 66
Co-Managing Partner and General Partner:
Edouard Michelin
Co-Managing Partner and General Partner:
René Zingraff
Member of the Group Executive Counsil, Asia:
Jean-Marc François
Member of the Group Executive Counsil, Europe:
Christian Tschann
Member of the Group Executive Counsil, Euromaster, Truck, TCI, Africa, and Middle East: Thierry Coudurier
Member of the Group Executive Counsil, Financial Affairs, Legal Services, and Plans and Results:
Michel Rollier
Member of the Group Executive Counsil, North America: Jim Micali
Member of the Group Executive Counsil, Passenger Car and Light Truck, Competition: Hervé Coyco
Member of the Group Executive Counsil, Personnel and Environment and Prevention: Jean Moreau
Member of the Group Executive Counsil, Tourist Services, ViaMichelin, Supply Chain, and IT Systems: Michel Caron
Member of the Group Executive Counsil, Agricultural, Aircraft, 2-Wheel, Earthmover, Wheels, Components, South America, Purchasing: Bernard Vasdeboncoeur
Member of the Group Executive Counsil, Technology Center and Industrial Performance: Didier Miraton
CEO, Euromaster: Eric Van Geel
Investor Relations: Eric Le Corre
Project Coordinator, North America: Doug Rogers
Auditors: PricewaterhouseCoopers Audit

LOCATIONS

HQ: Compagnie Générale des Établissements Michelin
23, place des Carmes-Déchaux,
63040 Clermont-Ferrand, France
Phone: +33-4-73-32-20-00   **Fax:** +33-45-66-15-53
US HQ: 1 Parkway South, Greenville, SC 29615
US Phone: 864-458-5000   **US Fax:** 864-458-6359
Web: www.michelin.com

Michelin has more than 70 manufacturing facilities in 19 countries, six rubber plantations in Brazil and Nigeria, and offices in more than 170 countries.

2004 Sales

	$ mil.	% of total
Europe	11,352	53
North America	7,118	33
Other regions	2,930	14
Total	**21,400**	**100**

PRODUCTS/OPERATIONS

2004 Sales

	$ mil.	% of total
Passenger car & light truck tires	10,268	45
Truck tires	5,757	26
Other	6,610	29
Adjustments	(1,235)	—
Total	**21,400**	**100**

Selected Products and Services

Agricultural tires
Aircraft tires
Earthmover tires
Passenger car and light-truck tires
Suspension systems
Travel publications
Truck tires
Two-wheel tires

Selected Brands

BF Goodrich
Encore
Euromaster
Kleber
Michelin
Taurus
Uniroyal

Selected Subsidiaries

Compagnie Financière Michelin (Switzerland)
Manufacture Française des Pneumatiques Michelin (60%)
Michelin Aircraft Tire Company (US)
Michelin Americas Research & Development Corporation (US)
Michelin Asia-Pacific Import-Export (HK) Limited (Hong Kong)
Michelin Corporation (US)
Michelin Investment Holding Company Limited (Bermuda)
Michelin North America, Inc. (US)
Michelin Gummi Compagni A/S (Denmark)

COMPETITORS

Avalon Travel Publishing	Kumho Tire
Bandag	Sime Darby
Bridgestone	Sumitomo Rubber
Continental AG	Toyo Tire & Rubber
Cooper Tire & Rubber	Vredestein
Fieldens	Watts Industrial Tyres
Goodyear	Yokohama Rubber

HISTORICAL FINANCIALS

Company Type: Public

Income Statement

FYE: December 31

	REVENUE ($ mil.)	NET INCOME ($ mil.)	NET PROFIT MARGIN	EMPLOYEES
12/04	21,400	703	3.3%	126,474
12/03	19,292	399	2.1%	127,210
12/02	16,398	609	3.7%	126,285
12/01	13,973	262	1.9%	127,467
12/00	14,887	376	2.5%	128,122
12/99	13,859	155	1.1%	130,434
12/98	15,289	669	4.4%	127,241
12/97	12,110	647	5.3%	123,254
12/96	13,615	553	4.1%	119,780
12/95	13,467	570	4.2%	115,000
Annual Growth	**5.3%**	**2.4%**	**—**	**1.1%**

2004 Year-End Financials

Debt ratio: 62.4% Current ratio: 1.67
Return on equity: 12.0% Long-term debt ($ mil.): 3,920
Cash ($ mil.): 2,258

Net Income History Euronext Paris: ML

12/95 12/96 12/97 12/98 12/99 12/00 12/01 12/02 12/03 12/04

Millea Holdings

Tokio Marine and Fire Insurance may have been old, but it showed it could learn new tricks. Japan's oldest and largest property/casualty insurance company, Tokio Marine merged with Nichido Fire and Marine to create Tokio Marine & Nichido Fire Insurance, which operates as a subsidiary of holding company Millea Holdings. The merger created the largest insurance sales network in Japan. Through Tokio Marine & Nichido and other subsidiaries, Millea Holdings provides marine, fire, property/casualty, personal accident, and auto insurance. The company also offers securities through a joint venture with online brokerage bigwig Charles Schwab. Millea Holdings is allied with the Mitsubishi industrial group.

The ailing Japanese economy has affected Millea, but it hopes to draw more customers by selling on the Internet (including overseas travel insurance) and offering express service for accidents. It has also expanded its lines to include such products as Lady Guard, insurance for women that covers the costs of damage caused by stalkers. Auto insurance, the company's main line of business, still accounts for more than half of sales.

Millea hopes to strengthen cross-selling, closely aligning its life insurance units (including Tokio Marine Life and Nichido Life). A proposed merger between Asahi Mutual and Millea was postponed.

HISTORY

After the US forced Japan to open to trade in 1854, Western marine insurers began operating there. In 1878 Japan's government organized backers for a Japanese marine insurance firm. Tokio Marine and Fire was founded the next year.

Tokio grew quickly, insuring trading companies like Mitsubishi and Mitsui; it soon had offices in London, Paris, and New York. Increased competition in the 1890s forced it to curtail its foreign operations and begin using brokers in most other countries.

Victory in the Russo-Japanese War of 1904-05 buoyed the country, but the economy slowed as it demobilized. Businesses responded by forming cooperative groups known as *zaibatsu*. Tokio Marine and Fire was allied with the Mitsubishi group.

Before WWI, Tokio expanded by adding fire, personal accident, theft, and auto insurance, and it continued to buy foreign sales brokers. Japan's insurance industry consolidated in the 1920s,

and the company bought up smaller competitors. The 1923 Tokyo earthquake hit the industry hard, but Tokio's new fire insurance operations had little exposure.

Most of Tokio Marine's foreign operations were seized during WWII. In 1944 Tokio merged with Mitsubishi Marine Insurance and Meiji Fire Insurance. Business grew in WWII, but wartime destruction left Tokio with nothing to insure and no money to pay claims.

After the war Tokio slowly recovered and resumed overseas operations. Although the US had dismantled the *zaibatsu* during occupation, Tokio Marine allied once again with Mitsubishi when Japan's government rebuilt most of the old groups as *keiretsu*.

During the 1950s and 1960s, the company grew its personal lines, adding homeowners coverage. Domestic business slowed during the 1970s and 1980s, and Tokio boosted operations overseas. It added commercial property/casualty insurer Houston General Insurance (a US company sold in 1997), Tokio Reinsurance, and interests in insurance and investment management firms.

In the 1980s the firm invested heavily in real estate through *jusen* (mortgage companies). Japan's overheated real estate market collapsed in the early 1990s, dumping masses of nonperforming assets on *jusen* and their investors (the country's major banks and insurers, including Tokio Marine).

Deregulation began in 1996, and economic recession soon followed. In 1998 Tokio Marine joined other members of the Mitsubishi group, including Bank of Tokyo-Mitsubishi and Meiji Life Insurance, to form investment banking, pension, and trust joint ventures. The firm also formed its own investment trust and allied with such foreign financial companies as BANK ONE and United Asset Management to develop new investment products. Brokerage Charles Schwab Tokio Marine Securities, a joint venture, was launched in 1999. That year Tokio consolidated its foreign reinsurance operations into Tokio Marine Global Re in Dublin, Ireland, and kicked off a business push that included reorganizing its agent force and planning for online sales.

Millea Holdings was created in 2002 as the holding company for the merger between Tokio Marine and Nichido Fire and Marine. The two were combined and renamed Tokio Marine & Nichido Fire Insurance, a subsidiary of Millea Holdings.

EXECUTIVES

President and Board Member: Kunio Ishihara, age 62
Senior Managing Director and Board Member: Yasuo Yaoita, age 58
Managing Director, Principal Financial Officer, and Board Member: Tomohiro Kotani, age 61
Managing Director, Tokio Marine & Nichido; Board Member: Toshiro Yagi, age 58
President, Tokio Marine & Nichido Life; Board Member: Sukeaki Ohta, age 62
EVP, Tokio Marine & Nichido; Board Member: Tomochika Iwashita, age 59
Senior Managing Director, Tokio Marine & Nichido; Board Member: Morio Ishii, age 58
Managing Director, Tokio Marine & Nichido; Board Member: Hiroshi Amemiya, age 55
CEO, Millea Asia: Takaaki Tamai
General Manager of Corporate Legal and Risk Management Department: Tetsuya Unno
Corporate Communications and Investor Relations: Mitsuru Muraki
Auditors: ChuoAoyama PricewaterhouseCoopers

LOCATIONS

HQ: Millea Holdings, Inc.
Tokyo Kaijo Nichido Building Shinkan 9F, 1-2-1 Marunouchi, Chiyoda-ku, Tokyo 100-0005, Japan
Phone: +81-3-6212-3333 **Fax:** +81-3-6212-3343
Web: www.millea.co.jp

Millea Holdings has operations in about 30 countries.

PRODUCTS/OPERATIONS

2005 Premiums

	% of total
Voluntary auto	44
Compulsory auto	16
Fire & allied lines	15
Personal accident	8
Marine — hull, cargo & transit	5
Other	12
Total	**100**

Selected Subsidiaries

First Insurance Company of Hawaii, Ltd.
Millea Asia Pte. Ltd. (Singapore)
The Tokio Marine and Fire Insurance Company (Hong Kong) Limited
The Tokio Marine and Fire Insurance Company (Singapore) Pte. Ltd
Tokio Marine Asset Management Company, Limited (97.5%)
Tokio Marine Brasil Seguradora S.A. (91%)
Tokio Marine Compa–ia de Seguros, S.A. de C.V.
Tokio Marine Europe Insurance Limited (UK)
Tokio Marine Financial Solutions Ltd. (Cayman Islands)
Tokio Marine Global Limited
Tokio Marine Global Re Limited (Ireland)
Tokio Marine Management, Inc.
Tokio Marine Management (Australasia) Pty. Ltd.
Tokio Marine Newa Insurance Co., Ltd.
Tokio Marine & Nichido Career Service Co., Ltd.
Tokio Marine & Nichido Financial Life Insurance Co., Ltd.
Tokio Marine & Nichido Fire Insurance Co., Ltd.
Tokio Marine & Nichido Life Insurance Co., Ltd.
Tokio Millennium Re (Bermuda)
Trans Pacific Insurance Company (US)

COMPETITORS

AEGON	The Hartford
AIG	HCC Insurance
Aioi	ING
Allianz	Kemper Insurance
Aviva	Mitsui Sumitomo
AXA	Insurance
CIGNA	Nippon Life Insurance
CNA Financial	Nipponkoa
General Re	Sompo Japan Insurance

HISTORICAL FINANCIALS

Company Type: Public

Income Statement

FYE: March 31

	ASSETS ($ mil.)	NET INCOME ($ mil.)	INCOME AS % OF ASSETS	EMPLOYEES
3/05	120,309	858	0.7%	18,910
3/04	116,916	986	0.8%	19,779
3/03	92,212	3,200	3.5%	21,235
3/02	63,581	1,208	1.9%	6,700
3/01	65,435	754	1.2%	6,588
3/00	76,146	794	1.0%	13,616
3/99	63,445	1,205	1.9%	13,751
3/98	58,629	1,147	2.0%	15,294
3/97	61,077	952	1.6%	14,029
3/96	73,235	806	1.1%	14,000
Annual Growth	5.7%	0.7%	—	3.4%

2005 Year-End Financials

Equity as % of assets: 26.6%
Return on assets: 0.7%
Return on equity: 2.7%
Long-term debt ($ mil.): 2,527
No. of shares (mil.): 344

Dividends
Yield: 0.0%
Payout: —
Market value ($ mil.): 24,940
Sales ($ mil.): 22,477

Stock History

NASDAQ: MLEA

	STOCK PRICE ($) FY Close	P/E High/Low		PER SHARE ($) Earnings	Dividends	Book Value
3/05	72.50	40	27	2.11	0.00	93.10
3/04	77.76	30	11	2.71	0.41	91.34
3/03	30.75	15	10	8.61	0.00	64.37
3/02	37.29	30	17	3.90	0.34	0.06
3/01	50.25	25	19	2.44	0.40	0.07
3/00	52.44	26	18	2.56	0.30	0.08
3/99	56.13	16	10	3.89	0.00	0.07
3/98	56.00	18	11	3.71	0.70	0.06
3/97	50.75	22	14	3.07	0.32	0.06
3/96	65.00	27	20	2.60	0.38	0.07
Annual Growth	1.2%	—	—	(2.3%)	—	121.1%

Mitsubishi

In Japanese *mitsubishi* means "three diamonds," but Mitsubishi Corporation claims six jewels. The *sogo shosha*, or trading company, operates through six main business groups: living essentials (agricultural products, food and beverages, textiles, and construction materials); metals (ferrous and nonferrous); machinery (power generation equipment, electrical systems, automobile parts); energy (liquefied natural gas, crude oil); chemicals (petrochemicals, fertilizers, plastics); and a new business initiatives unit, which provides software, logistics, telecommunications, and other services.

Mitsubishi Corporation is part of the Mitsubishi *keiretsu*, a network of affiliated companies that has no official status as a group, but within which there is some cross-ownership and considerable business activity. Other affiliates include Mitsubishi Heavy Industries, The Bank of Tokyo-Mitsubishi, Mitsubishi Electric, Mitsubishi Motors, and Nikon.

Along with the rest of the Mitsubishi companies, Mitsubishi Corporportion was hurt by Japan's persistent economic slump. The company restructured and reduced its workforce; it has divided the operations of its former information technology and electronics business between two other groups. It plans to focus on its energy and natural resources, independent power production, and food distribution businesses.

In February 2004 the company announced plans to form a food-distribution joint venture with five Japanese food wholesalers, comprising national wholesaler Meidi-ya and four regional companies. To be named Alliance Network, the joint venture will be one of Japan's largest food wholesalers. Mitsubishi will have a 51% stake in Alliance Network. Later in 2004 Mitsubishi it acquired the food, beverage additive and pharmaceutical active and excipient businesses of Ashland Distribution.

HISTORY

Yataro Iwasaki's close ties to the Japanese government (along with subsidies and monopoly rights) ensured the success of his shipping and trading company, Mitsubishi. Founded in 1870, Mitsubishi diversified into mining (1873), banking (1885), and shipbuilding (1887); it began to withdraw from shipping in the 1880s. During the next decade it invested in Japanese railroads and property.

In 1918 the Mitsubishi *zaibatsu* (conglomerate) spun off its central management arm, Mitsubishi Trading (the forerunner of Mitsubishi Corporation). By WWII the group was a huge amalgam of divisions and public companies. During the war it made warplanes, ships, explosives, and beer.

The *zaibatsu* were dissolved by US occupation forces, and Mitsubishi was split into 139 entities. After the occupation, the Japanese government encouraged many of the former business groups to reunite around the old *zaibatsu* banks. In 1954 Mitsubishi Trading became the leader of the Mitsubishi Group and established Mitsubishi International (US), which became a leading exporter of US goods.

The 1964 merger of three Mitsubishi companies created Mitsubishi Heavy Industries, a top Japanese maker of ships, aircraft, plants, and heavy machinery. Mitsubishi Kasei, separated from Asahi Glass and Mitsubishi Rayon by a US fiat, became Japan's #1 chemical concern. Mitsubishi Electric emerged as one of the country's leading electrical equipment and electronics manufacturers. In 1971 Chrysler invested in Mitsubishi Motors, which began making cars for the US automaker. That year Mitsubishi Trading was renamed Mitsubishi Corp.

Through the 1980s Japan seemed economically invincible. Then its "bubble economy" burst. The group fell behind in electronics and autos in the US, consumer demand dried up at home, and Mitsubishi Bank was left with a heavy burden of bad loans. Group members, which traditionally provided materials, supplies, and sales outlets for each other, began loosening old *keiretsu* ties during Japan's recession of the 1990s.

In 1993 Chrysler sold its stock in Mitsubishi Motors, and two years later the companies severed production ties. This loss and declining demand in the US for Mitsubishi cars hurt auto sales.

Mitsubishi Bank merged with Bank of Tokyo in 1996 to form the biggest bank in the world, The Bank of Tokyo-Mitsubishi (BTM). In 1997 several Mitsubishi companies admitted paying off a corporate racketeer, setting off a wave of executive resignations.

By 1999 BTM had tumbled from the top spot and was unable to keep the money freely flowing to fellow Mitsubishi members.

Hit hard by the Asian economic crisis, all the struggling Mitsubishi companies had to look outside of the *keiretsu* for help. In 1999 Mitsubishi Motors found a foreign partner, Volvo, for its truck making operations. Mitsubishi Oil merged with an outsider, Nippon Oil, to form Nippon Mitsubishi Oil (later renamed Nippon Oil). In 2000 DaimlerChrysler acquired a controlling stake in Mitsubishi Motors for $2.1 billion.

Executives at Mitsubishi Motors were charged in 2001 after they allegedly kept the lid on thousands of reported defects in Mitsubishi cars instead of issuing recalls. Stung by this and the after-effects of scandals from the previous decade, Mitsubishi unveiled a new corporate philosophy as part of a strategy to revive the group's reputation.

In 2003 Mitsubishi disbanded its information technology and electronics business unit. The unit's operations were divided between the new business and machinery groups. In 2004 the company formed an alliance with GE Yokogawa Medical Systems (GEYMS) to provide GEYMS with help in developing its presence in the Japanese diagnostic imaging market.

EXECUTIVES

Chairman: Mikio Sasaki, age 68
President, CEO, and Chief Innovation Officer, Internal Audit: Yorihiko Kojima
SEVP; Assistant to the President, Resources and Energy Officer, Chief Compliance Officer, CIO, and Member of the Board: Yukio Masuda
SEVP; Regional CEO, Kansai Block, General Manager, Kansai Branch, and Member of the Board: Yukio Ueno
SEVP; Chief Information Security Officer and Chief Regional Officer: Hidetoshi Kamezaki
SEVP; Group CEO, Chemicals, Regional Officer, China, and Member of the Board: Takeru Ishibashi
EVP; Regional CEO, North America, and President, Mitsubishi International: Motoatsu Sakurai
EVP; Group CEO, Living Essentials, and Member of the Board: Takeshi Inoue
EVP; Group CEO, Machinery: Masao Miyamoto
EVP; Group COO, Machinery Group: Hajime Katsumura
EVP; Group CEO, Energy Business Group: Hisanori Yoshimura
EVP; Chief Representative China, President Mitsubishi Corporation (China) Investment Co., General Manager Bejing Branch: Katsutoshi Takeda
EVP and CFO: Ichiro Mizuno
SVP and Treasurer: Hideshi Takeuchi
SVP and Controller: Ryoichi Ueda
SVP; Corporate Functional Officer, Human Resources, Administration Corporate Secretariat, and Legal: Tsuneo Iyobe
Auditors: Deloitte Touche Tohmatsu

LOCATIONS

HQ: Mitsubishi Corporation
(Mitsubishi Shoji Kabushiki Kaisha)
6-3, Marunouchi 2-chome, Chiyoda-ku,
Tokyo 100-8086, Japan
Phone: +81-3-3210-2121   **Fax:** +81-3-3210-8583
US HQ: 655 3rd Ave., New York, NY 10017
US Phone: 212-605-2000   **US Fax:** 212-605-2486
Web: www.mitsubishi.co.jp

In addition to its more than 200 sites in Japan, Mitsubishi Corporation has operations in 80 other countries and regions around the world.

2005 Sales

	% of total
Japan	83
US	5
Thailand	3
Other countries	9
Total	**100**

PRODUCTS/OPERATIONS

2005 Sales

	% of total
Living Essentials	26
Energy	25
Metals	20
Machinery	16
Chemicals	11
New business initiative	2
Total	**100**

Selected Products and Services

Living Essentials
Apparel
Canned foods
Ceramic materials
Cigarettes
Coffee beans, coffee and beverages
Confections and snacks
Contract food services
Dairy foods and processed foods
Fabrics
Feedstuffs
Fresh and frozen foods
Grains and agricultural products
Marine products
Meat and livestock
Mineral water
Oils and fats
Photosensitized materials
Pulp, paper and packaging materials
Soft drinks
Sweeteners
Textiles for industrial use
Textile raw materials
Tires
Wood, wood products and construction materials

Energy
Carbon materials and products
Crude oil
LNG
LPG
Orimulsion
Petroleum products

Metals
Bullion and metals futures
Fabricated steel structures
Metallurgical and thermal coal
Nonferrous metals
Nonferrous metal products
Nuclear fuel and components
Precious metals
Raw materials for steel
Semifinished products
Steel materials
Specialty steel

Machinery
Automobiles
Commercial aviation
Defense systems and equipment
Electronics products
Industrial, agricultural, construction and other
　general machinery
Plant and machinery for power generation, electricity,
　oil/gas/chemicals, steel/cement and
　environmental protection
Project development and construction
Satellite communications
Ships
Space systems
Transportation systems

Chemicals
Fertilizers
Fine and specialty chemicals
Inorganic chemicals
Petrochemicals
Plastics

New Business Initiative
Commerce services
Consumer services
Financial services
Information technology services
Logistics
Telecommunications systems and services

COMPETITORS

ITOCHU
Marubeni
Mitsui
Samsung
Sime Darby
Sumitomo
TOMEN

HISTORICAL FINANCIALS

Company Type: Public

Income Statement

FYE: March 31

	REVENUE ($ mil.)	NET INCOME ($ mil.)	NET PROFIT MARGIN	EMPLOYEES
3/05	38,548	1,696	4.4%	51,381
3/04	15,094	1,092	7.2%	49,219
3/03	12,273	520	4.2%	47,370
3/02	9,737	454	4.7%	44,034
3/01	4,779	729	15.3%	—
3/00	5,450	247	4.5%	—
Annual Growth	47.9%	47.1%	—	5.3%

2005 Year-End Financials

Debt ratio: 201.1%
Return on equity: 13.3%
Cash ($ mil.): 5,363

Current ratio: 1.26
Long-term debt ($ mil.): 28,124

Net Income History

OTC: MSBHY

Net income ($ mil.), 3/96 through 3/05: 3/00 ≈ 247, 3/01 ≈ 729, 3/02 ≈ 454, 3/03 ≈ 520, 3/04 ≈ 1,092, 3/05 ≈ 1,696 (scale 0–1,800).

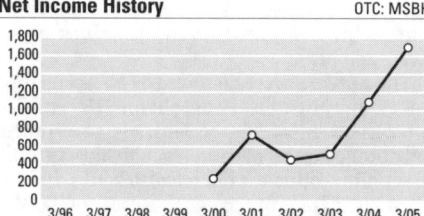

Mitsui & Co.

Part of a network of companies that was founded by a samurai centuries ago, Mitsui & Co. battles to make money. Mitsui & Co., a leading Japanese *sogo shosha* (general trading firm), has more than 700 subsidiaries in a wide range of industries. The company has reorganized its business units into seven main classifications: chemical; consumer products and services (retailing, foods, textiles, property development); energy (liquefied natural gas); logistics and financial markets; machinery, electronics and information (power plants, aircraft leasing, IT services); metal products and minerals (iron and steel, nonferrous metals); and overseas. The Master Trust Bank of Japan holds a 10% stake in Mitsui.

Mitsui & Co. is part of Mitsui Group, one of Japan's largest *keiretsu* (companies loosely connected through cross-ownership). The company's largest revenue generators are its trading activities in the energy (32% of sales) and chemical (17% of sales) sectors. The company plans to invest about $2.8 billion during 2005 and 2006 to expanded its iron ore and core interests in Australia, acquire new non-ferrous metal interests, and to expand its LNG and oil operations. Mitsui also plans to invest nearly $950 million to strengthen and develop its Consumer Service, Foods and Retail, Lifestyle, and Motor Vehicle related business units.

In an effort to expand its metal products and minerals segment, Mitsui has created a joint venture company with Posco, named Posco Terminal, which is responsible for the transportation, storage, and distribution of coal, iron ore, and ferroalloy. The company has also acquired a 15% stake in Valepar, a holding company of Brazilian-based iron ore producer Companhia Vale do Rio

Doce. In an effort to boost coal production, Mitsui plans to buy a stake in the Moranbah North coal mine in Australia

The company is working to build its biotechnology and IT businesses. It has created TM Cell Research, a 35% owned biotechnology joint venture created with Toyobo. Mitsui has also developed five nanotechnology research institutes in an effort to capture a stake of the market in Japan. Mitsui has moved into the German pesticide market by acquiring a majority stake in Spiess-Urania Chemical, a subsidiary of Norddeutsche Affinerie.

HISTORY

In the 17th century unemployed samurai (warrior nobleman) Sokubei Mitsui opened a sake and soy sauce brewery at the urging of his wife, Shuho. After parental encouragement, their youngest son, Hachirobei, went to Edo (now Tokyo) and opened a dry goods store in 1673. Breaking with Japanese retailing tradition, the store offered merchandise at fixed prices on a cash-and-carry basis.

Hachirobei in 1683 opened a currency exchange that evolved into Mitsui Bank. The bank became the Osaka government's official money changer in 1691 and was the first bank to offer money orders in Japan. Before his death in 1694, Hachirobei drafted a unique succession plan to hand down control of the company to every related family, not just the eldest son's side.

The shogun's government called upon Mitsui in the mid-1800s to help finance its war against rebels. The family hired Rizaemon Minomura, an outsider with influence in the government, to protect the company from increasing demands for money. Mitsui became the bank of the Meiji government after Minomura astutely switched support to the winning rebels. Government industrialization pushed Mitsui into textiles, paper goods, and machinery. Minomura emphasized foreign trade and banking, creating Mitsui Bussan (now Mitsui & Co.) and Mitsui Bank in 1876. In the late 1800s Mitsui Bussan profited from a Japanese military buildup, formed a shipping line to take on Mitsubishi's monopoly, and bought coal mines. The Mitsui family withdrew from Mitsui Bussan management in 1936, following attacks by right-wing terrorists who opposed its democratic leanings.

Mitsui prospered during the 1930s as Japan's military prepared for war. After the defeat, occupation forces disbanded Japan's *zaibatsu* industrial groups, slicing Mitsui into more than 200 separate entities. By 1950 more than two dozen leaders of the former Mitsui companies began gathering the Mitsui Group back together. Trading firm Mitsui & Co. was established in 1959. The oil crises of the 1970s stalled the oil-dependent Japanese economy, prompting Mitsui companies to expand operations overseas and move into industries such as technology and aluminum.

The mammoth Sakura Bank was formed in 1990 with the merger of Mitsui Bank and Taiyo Kobe Bank. Other major ventures were to follow: In 1992 Mitsui & Co. joined with Marathon and Royal Dutch/Shell and others to search for oil and gas off Russia's Sakhalin Island; and Mitsui & Co. and other Japanese traders were enlisted by Oman in 1993 for a $9 billion liquefied natural gas transport venture. As cable TV emerged in Japan, Mitsui & Co. teamed up the next year with National Media Corp. to launch a home-shopping network.

In anticipation of deregulation in Japan's financial markets, four Mitsui Group firms' pension funds — Sakura Bank, Mitsui Marine & Fire Insurance, Mitsui Mutual Life Insurance, and Mitsui Trust and Banking — were linked in 1998. The next year Sakura Bank set aside old loyalties and agreed to merge with Sumitomo Bank, the Sumitomo *keiretsu's* main bank; the deal closed in 2001. The group's Mitsui Trust and Banking merged with Chuo Trust and Banking to form Chuo Mitsui Trust and Banking, part of Mitsui Trust Holdings.

Mitsui & Co. was implicated in bid-rigging and bribery scandals in 2002, and the company's chairman and CEO resigned. In 2003, the company moved into the German pesticide market by acquiring an 80% stake in Spiess-Urania Chemical, a subsidiary of Norddeutsche Affinerie. Later that year, it entered the biotechnology market by creating TM Cell Research, a 35% owned joint venture created with Toyobo. The company also entered the telecommunications market by acquiring a 30% stake in Shineedotcom from Shin Corp.

In 2003 Mitsui turned its focus back to the expansion of its current operations. The company acquired a 15% stake in Valepar, a holding company of Brazilian-based iron ore producer Companhia Vale do Rio Doce. Mitsui and International Power completed the acquisition of the 1,200 MW gas-fired Saltend Power plant in the UK from Calpine Corporation. In 2005 Mitsui acquired a stake in Global in Gás Participações (Gaspart), a Brazil-based gas distribution company.

EXECUTIVES

Chairman: Nobuo Ohashi, age 67
President and CEO: Shoei Utsuda, age 62
EVP and CFO: Tasuku Kondo, age 63
EVP; Managing Director, Mitsui & Co. Europe: Yasuo Hayashi, age 63
EVP: Katsuo Momii, age 62
Senior Executive Managing Officer; COO, Business Process Re-Engineering Project Headquarters: Yushi Nagata, age 59
Senior Executive Managing Officer, Regional Managing Director, Asia; Executive Director: Gempachiro Aihara, age 62
Senior Executive Managing Officer: Tetsuya Matsuoka, age 60
Senior Executive Managing Officer: Masataka Suzuki, age 61
Senior Executive Managing Officer, Chief Compliance Officer; Chief Privacy Officer; Environmental Matters; Deputy Chief Operating Officer, Business Process Re-Engineering Project Headquarters; Executive Director: Yasunori Yokote, age 59
Senior Executive Managing Officer; Executive Director: Hiroshi Tada, age 60
Senior Executive Managing Officer, Chief Financial Officer, Deputy Chief Operating Officer, Business Process Re-Engineering Project Headquarters; Executive Director: Kazuya Imai, age 59
Executive Managing Officer, Chairman for the Americas and President and Chief Executive Officer of Mitsui & Co. (U.S.A.), Inc.: Motokazu Yoshida, age 57
Managing Officer; General Manager, Personnel Division: Kenichi Yamamoto, age 56
Auditors: Deloitte Touche Tohmatsu

LOCATIONS

HQ: Mitsui & Co., Ltd.
(Mitsui Bussan Kabushiki Kaisha)
2-1, Ohtemachi 1-chome, Chiyoda-ku,
Tokyo 100-0004, Japan
Phone: +81-3-3285-1111   **Fax:** +81-3-3285-9819
US HQ: 200 Park Ave., New York, NY 10166
US Phone: 212-878-4000   **US Fax:** 212-878-4800
Web: www.mitsui.co.jp

Mitsui & Co. operates through offices in 79 countries.

2005 Trading Transactions

	% of total
Asia	
Japan	57
China	5
US	8
UK	1
Other countries	29
Total	**100**

PRODUCTS/OPERATIONS

2005 Sales

	% of total
Energy	30
Chemicals	21
Foods	13
Iron & steel	11
Machinery	8
Non-ferrous metals	5
Electronics & information	4
Property & service business	4
General merchandise	3
Textiles	1
Total	**100**

Selected Business Units

Chemical
  Organic Chemicals business unit
  Plastics and Inorganic Chemicals business unit
Consumer Products and Services
  Consumer Service business unit
  Foods and Retail business unit
  Lifestyle business unit
Energy
Logistics and Financial Markets
  Financial Markets business unit
  Transportation Logistics business unit
Machinery, Electronics, and Information
  Information, Electronics, and Telecommunication business unit
  Machinery business unit
  Power, Transportation, and Plant Products business unit
Metal Products and Minerals
  Iron and Steel Products business unit
  Iron and Steel Raw Materials and Non-Ferrous Metals business unit

COMPETITORS

ITOCHU	Samsung
Kanematsu	Sojitz
Komatsu	Sumitomo
Marubeni	TOMEN
Mitsubishi Corporation	

HISTORICAL FINANCIALS

Company Type: Public

Income Statement

FYE: March 31

	REVENUE ($ mil.)	NET INCOME ($ mil.)	NET PROFIT MARGIN	EMPLOYEES
3/05	32,951	1,132	3.4%	38,210
3/04	28,657	658	2.3%	39,735
3/03	4,829	264	5.5%	37,734
3/02	4,166	416	10.0%	36,116
3/01	4,541	409	9.0%	10,337
3/00	5,222	346	6.6%	10,702
3/99	4,789	252	5.3%	—
3/98	4,460	248	5.6%	—
3/97	4,689	292	6.2%	—
3/96	5,025	284	5.7%	—
Annual Growth	**23.2%**	**16.6%**	**—**	**29.0%**

2005 Year-End Financials

Debt ratio: 258.7%   No. of shares (mil.): 79
Return on equity: 11.5%   Dividends
Cash ($ mil.): 7,400   Yield: 0.0%
Current ratio: 1.35   Payout: —
Long-term debt ($ mil.): 27,149   Market value ($ mil.): 14,575

Stock History

NASDAQ: MITSY

	STOCK PRICE ($) FY Close	P/E High/Low		Earnings	PER SHARE ($) Dividends	Book Value
3/05	184.24	15	10	13.40	0.00	132.65
3/04	181.50	22	11	8.00	0.73	1,226.59
3/03	98.04	46	28	3.17	1.32	92.40
3/02	122.50	31	18	4.94	1.95	86.90
3/01	98.00	33	20	4.87	1.46	83.63
3/00	164.50	40	30	4.14	1.44	80.24
3/99	132.13	46	26	2.97	0.68	71.98
3/98	125.75	67	34	2.89	0.00	66.76
3/97	146.00	56	41	3.40	0.57	68.37
3/96	181.00	54	45	3.34	0.66	71.52
Annual Growth	**0.2%**	**—**	**—**	**16.7%**	**—**	**7.1%**

Mittal Steel

Many metal makers lack the mettle of Mittal Steel. Mittal was forged late in 2004 when publicly traded Ispat International (of which the Mittal family owned 70%) purchased Antilles-based LNM Holdings (wholly owned by the Mittals) for roughly $13.3 billion. When the dust settled, the combined entity stood as the largest steel company in the world, with annual steel production of more than 50 million metric tons. The company manufactures flat rolled and long steel products utilizing direct-reduced iron, which is cheaper than using iron ore or scrap iron. Top customers include Ford Motor, General Motors, Maytag, and Whirlpool. CEO and founder Lakshmi Mittal and his family control nearly all of Mittal Steel.

Mittal Steel furthered its hold on the world steel market through its 2005 purchase of the US-based International Steel Group (ISG) for about $4.5 billion. The purchase made the company the largest steel producer in the US (ahead of U.S. Steel and Nucor), a market that had long been a targeted area for expansion for CEO Mittal. Once the deal closed, the company combined ISG's operations with those of Mittal subsidiary Ispat Inland to form a single North American entity, Mittal Steel USA. Lakshmi Mittal has also said that in the wake of the ISG deal he would like to see the entire firm reduce its staff by perhaps 45,000 — or 30% — through a gradual five-year reduction.

Mittal Steel, which operates through subsidiaries in Europe, Africa, and the Americas, has laid plans for Asian expansion as well. In 2005 it paid the Valin Group more than $300 million for a 37% stake — the largest for a non-Chinese company — in Hunan Valin Steel Tube & Wire. It then agreed to construct a $10 billion plant in India.

The expansion plans of Mittal (both the company and the CEO) fit with an overall consolidation trend in the global steel industry. As they take advantage of rising steel prices and benefits of scale, companies like Mittal Steel and its main rival, Arcelor, continue to snap up part or all of smaller players throughout the world. Lakshmi Mittal's own dealmaking has put him among the wealthiest people in the world.

In 2005 it also acquired a 93% stake in Ukrainian state-run steel company KryvorizhStal with the winning $4.84 billion bid in an auction held by the Ukrainian government.

The company has recently begun to broaden its portfolio outside the steel industry, dipping its toe into the energy business. In mid-2005 Mittal formed two joint ventures with India's government controlled Oil & Natural Gas Corporation: one to buy stakes in foreign oil and gas projects, the other involved in oil and gas trading and shipping. The ventures are said to be looking for business in places like Indonesia, Kazakhstan, Angola, and Trinidad and Tobago. Analysts point to China's growing interest in foreign energy businesses as the impetus for India's move.

HISTORY

Mittal Steel Company is the product of decades of steelmaking by India's Mittal family. In 1967 patriarch Mohan Mittal unsuccessfully tried to open a steel mill in Egypt. He and his four younger brothers then set up a steel company in India, but squabbles pushed Mohan to chart his own course, eventually giving rise to an empire that flourished under the Ispat name. Mohan's son Lakshmi began working part-time at the family steel mill while in school; he started full-time at 21, after graduating in 1971.

Mohan set up an operation in Indonesia in 1975 (Ispat Indo) and put Lakshmi in charge. The next year, fueled by ambitions and held back by government regulations in India, Lakshmi formed Ispat International in Jakarta, Indonesia, to focus on expansion through acquisitions. He spent the next decade strengthening the Indonesian operations and perfecting the minimill process using direct-reduced iron (DRI).

Ispat took advantage of the recessionary late 1980s and early 1990s by making a string of acquisitions. In 1988 it took over the management of Trinidad and Tobago's state steel companies (bought 1994; renamed Caribbean Ispat).

In 1992 Ispat bought Mexico's third-largest (albeit bankrupt) steel and DRI producer. Two years later it acquired Canada's Sidbec-Dosco steelmaker. Also that year Lakshmi took exclusive control of international operations, leaving his brothers Pramod and Vinod to control the Indian divisions.

The mid-1990s brought more acquisitions: In 1995 Ispat bought Germany's Hamburger Stahlwerks and a mill in Kazakhstan. The next year it purchased Ireland's only steelmaker, Irish Steel. Lakshmi moved to London in 1996 and purchased a home on Bishops Avenue, known as "millionaire's row." (Saudi Arabia's King Fahd was a neighbor.)

In 1997 the company completed a $776 million IPO — the steel industry's biggest, outside of privatizations. Ispat acquired Chicago-based Inland Steel in 1998 (now Ispat Inland), including the steel-finishing operations of I/N Tek (60% Inland-owned joint venture with Nippon Steel) and I/N Kote (50% Inland-owned joint venture with NSC).

In 1999 Ispat formed a joint venture with Mexican steelmaker Grupo Imsa to make flat-rolled steel to sell throughout most of the Americas. It also paid $96 million for France-based Usinor's Unimétal, Tréfileurope, and Société Métallurgique de Révigny subsidiaries, which specialize in carbon long products. That year the company's Ispat Inland subsidiary became the target of a US federal criminal grand jury investigation and a related civil lawsuit for allegedly defrauding the Louisiana Highway Department. (The case was settled for $30 million, with the cost split between Ispat Inland and Contech Construction Products Inc. of Ohio.)

In 2000 the company responded to a downturn in the steel industry by starting a Web-based joint venture with Commerce One to connect buyers and sellers in the worldwide metals market. It also offered to buy VSZ, Slovakia's #1 steelworks, but was outbid by U.S. Steel.

After struggling with heavy debt, high labor and energy costs, new environmental regulations, and EU steel quotas in 2001, Ispat closed down its subsidiary, Irish Ispat, which accounted for about 2% of the parent company's steel production. In 2002, the company's 51%-owned pipe making subsidiary, Productura Mexicana de Tuberia, sold almost all of its production assets.

Late in 2004 the Mittal family combined its steel holdings into one company when Ispat International (at the time 70%-owned by the family) purchased Antilles-based LNM Holdings (then privately held by the Mittals) for about $13.3 billion.

EXECUTIVES

Chairman and CEO: Lakshmi N. Mittal, age 55
President, CFO, and Director: Aditya Mittal, age 29
COO and Director: Malay Mukherjee, age 57
EVP, Finance and Corporate Controller:
Bhikam C. Agarwal
EVP, Finance and Corporate Treasurer:
Sudhir Maheshwari
CEO, Mittal Steel Europe: Roeland Baan
CEO, Mittal Steel USA: Louis (Lou) Schorsch
Director, Investor Relations: Julien Onillon
Manager, North American Investor Relations:
Thomas A. (Tom) McCue
Director, Continous Improvement: Bill Scotting
Director, Corporate Finance and Advisory:
Ondra Otradovec, age 34
Director, Finance: Thekkemadom N. Ramaswamy
Director, Human Resources: Inder Walia
Director, Internal Assurance: Arvind Chopra
Director, Marketing: Eric Tierie
Director, Marketing, Flat Products: Jean-Pierre Picard
Director, Materials and Information Technology:
Ashok Aranha
Director, Technical and Business Development:
Abdellatif Laasraoui
Secretary: Henk Scheffer
General Counsel: Simon Evans
General Manager, Corporate Communications:
Nicola Davidson
Auditors: Deloitte Accountants B.V.

LOCATIONS

HQ: Mittal Steel Company N.V.
Hofplein 20, 15th Fl.,
3032 Rotterdam, The Netherlands
Phone: +31-10-217-8800   **Fax:** +31-10-217-8850
US HQ: 3210 Watling St., East Chicago, IN 46312
US Phone: 219-399-1200   **US Fax:** 219-399-5544
Web: www.mittalsteel.com

Based in the Netherlands and run from its London headquarters, Mittal Steel has steelmaking operations in Algeria, Bosnia, Canada, the Czech Republic, France, Germany, Kazakhstan, Macedonia, Mexico, Poland, Romania, South Africa, Trinidad and Tobago, and the US.

2004 Sales and Operating Income

	Sales		Operating Income	
	$ mil.	% of total	$ mil.	% of total
Europe	9,905	41	1,965	32
Americas	6,560	27	1,583	26
Rest of the World	7,648	32	2,399	39
Others	—	—	199	3
Adjustments	(1,916)	—	—	—
Total	**22,197**	**100**	**6,146**	**100**

PRODUCTS/OPERATIONS

Selected Products

Direct reduced iron (DRI)
Flat steel
  Cold-rolled sheet and slab
  Hot-rolled sheet and slab
Long steel
  Bars
  Pipes
  Structural
  Wire (products and rod)

Selected Subsidiaries

Caribbean Ispat Limited (Trinidad and Tobago)
Consorcio Minero Benito Juárez Peña Colorada SA de CV
  (50%, mining and pelletizing, Mexico)
Delta Tube (40%, Canada)
Empire Iron Mining Partnership (20%, taconite pellets)
I/N Kote (50%, galvanizing)
I/N Tek (60%, cold rolling)
Ispat Hamburger Stahlwerke GmbH (Germany)
Ispat Inland Inc. (US)
Ispat Mexicana, SA de CV (Mexico)
Ispat Ruhrort (Germany)
Ispat Sidbec Inc. (Canada)
Ispat Stahlwerk Ruhrort GmbH (Germany)
Ispat Unimétal (France)
Ispat Walzdraht Hochfeld GmbH (Germany)
Mittal Steel South Africa (50.01%)
PCI Associates (50%, pulverized coal)
Servicios Siderúrgicos Integrados, SA de CV
  (50%; port operations, lime, industrial gases, and
  engineering; Mexico)
Sorevco (50%, galvanizing plant, Canada)

COMPETITORS

AK Steel Holding
  Corporation
Algoma Steel
Arcelor
BlueScope Steel
Chaparral Steel
Corus Group
Dofasco
Gerdau AmeriSteel
Highveld Steel and
  Vanadium
JFE Holdings

Nippon Steel
Nucor
Oregon Steel Mills
POSCO
Severstal North America
Shanghai Baosteel
Stelco
ThyssenKrupp
United States Steel
Vallourec
Worthington Industries

HISTORICAL FINANCIALS

Company Type: Public

Income Statement

FYE: December 31

	REVENUE ($ mil.)	NET INCOME ($ mil.)	NET PROFIT MARGIN	EMPLOYEES
12/04	22,197	4,701	21.2%	164,393
12/03	5,441	66	1.2%	14,811
12/02	4,889	49	1.0%	15,400
12/01	4,486	(312)	—	16,344
12/00	5,097	99	1.9%	17,800
12/99	4,680	85	1.8%	15,000
12/98	3,492	237	6.8%	15,000
12/97	2,190	289	13.2%	7,550
12/96	1,774	613	34.6%	5,839
12/95	1,828	556	30.4%	5,358
Annual Growth	32.0%	26.8%	—	46.3%

2004 Year-End Financials

Debt ratio: 28.0%
Return on equity: 156.8%
Cash ($ mil.): 2,495
Current ratio: 1.54
Long-term debt ($ mil.): 1,639

No. of shares (mil.): 643
Dividends
Yield: 0.0%
Payout: —
Market value ($ mil.): 24,843

Stock History

NYSE: MT

	STOCK PRICE ($) FY Close	P/E High/Low		PER SHARE ($) Earnings	Dividends	Book Value
12/04	38.65	6	1	7.31	0.00	9.09
12/03	8.87	17	4	0.53	0.00	1.22
12/02	2.20	8	3	0.40	0.00	1.03
12/01	1.75	—	—	(2.58)	0.00	2.66
12/00	2.25	22	2	0.82	0.15	7.37
12/99	16.13	23	10	0.71	0.15	6.72
12/98	7.75	16	2	1.93	0.15	6.31
12/97	21.63	12	7	2.46	0.00	23.39
Annual Growth	8.6%	—	—	16.8%	—	(12.6%)

Mizuho Financial

Mizuho means "golden ears of rice" in Japanese, but in the banking world it means the first bank with a trillion dollars in assets. Battling Mitsubishi UFJ Financial Group and Citigroup for the title of the largest financial services company in the world (it trails both in assets), Mizuho Financial Group is the parent of Mizuho Bank (retail banking), Mizuho Corporate Bank (commercial financial services), Mizuho Securities (investment and brokerage services), and Mizuho Trust & Banking. All told, the company has approximately 700 branches, sub-branches, and agencies across Japan. Mizuho Financial Group was formed by the 2002 merger of The Dai-Ichi Kangyo Bank, Fuji Bank, and Industrial Bank of Japan (IBJ).

The company turned a profit in fiscal year 2004 after absorbing heavy losses during its first years of operation, mainly due to bad loans which have been an industry-wide problem in Japan.

More than 85% of the company's revenue comes from its home market, but it also operates in the US, Europe, Oceania, and other parts of Asia. Mizuho is expanding into Hong Kong and mainland China to profit from Chinese growth and the export of Japanese production facilities from their home market. The bank also plans to expand its nascent securities, investment, trust, and asset management activities by making these services available at most of its bank branches.

Hoping to elevate investor confidence, Mizuho formed alliances with three US banks in mid 2005 and plans on applying for a listing on the New York Stock Exchange by June 2006.

HISTORY

Of the three banks that formed Mizuho Holdings, Industrial Bank of Japan (IBJ) is the youngest, founded in 1902. Fuji Bank started in 1880 and Dai-Ichi Kangyo's roots reach back to 1872.

By the late 1990s Japanese banks faced the challenges of a fossilized banking system, chained together by the *keiretsu* cross-shareholding system that hindered companies' agility in the marketplace. Other economic stresses included the Asian financial crisis, which left banks holding thousands of bad loans. In 1997 the Big Bang of banking reform was supposed to free lending institutions to restructure for greater competition, with presumably sounder business models. The industry's reliance on government-sponsored bailouts underscored the need for change.

IBJ, Dai-Ichi Kangyo Bank, and Fuji Bank (none of them excessively chummy within their respective *keiretsu*) saw an opportunity to consolidate, strengthen their business through combined forces, and streamline their operations by closing redundant branches, agencies, and divisions.

Mizuho Holdings was formed in 1999 and placed atop the three banks as their new parent company. While Mizuho's $1.3 trillion in assets made it the largest bank in the world at the time, its copious debts weren't to be ignored, either (though the bank waived the nearly $1 billion in debt of troubled retailer Sogo in 2001).

Also in 2001, other Japanese banks followed the lead of IBJ, Dai-Ichi Kangyo, and Fuji by joining with peers in the quest for size. Sumitomo Bank and Sakura Bank merged to form Sumitomo Mitsui Financial Group; and Sanwa Bank, Tokai Bank, and Toyo Trust and Banking combined to create UFJ Holdings.

Initially, the CEOs of the three banks that comprised Mizuho were tapped as co-CEOs of the company, but they resigned in 2002 after the banks' consolidation was marred by PR gaffes and computer glitches that caused customers to be double-billed, created a logjam of money transfers, and crashed thousands of ATMs. Terunobu Maeda was named the sole CEO of Mizuho later that year.

EXECUTIVES

President and CEO: Terunobu Maeda
Deputy President and Head of Internal Audit Group: Shunichi Asada
Managing Director, Head of Financial Control and Accounting Group, and CFO: Satoru Nishibori
Managing Director, Head of Strategic Planning Group and IT, Chief Strategic Officer, and CIO: Tetsuji Kosaki
Managing Executive Officer, Head of Risk Management Group, Head of Human Resources Group, Chief Risk Officer, Chief Compliance Officer, and Chief Human Resources Officer: Masayuki Saito
Executive Officer and General Manager, Corporate Communications: Yoshiaki Ohashi
Executive Officer and General Manager, Corporate Planning: Hiroshi Kiyama
Executive Officer and Managing Executive Officer, Mizuho Research Institute, Ltd.: Tetsuro Sugiura
Corporate Auditor: Yoshiaki Sugita
President and CEO, Mizuho Bank: Seiji Sugiyama
Deputy President, Mizuho Bank: Tsutomu Abe
Deputy President, Mizuho Bank: Saburo Nishiura
Managing Director, Mizuho Bank: Mitsuru Machida
President and CEO, Mizuho Trust & Banking: Teruhiko Ikeda
President and CEO, Mizuho Corporate Bank: Hiroshi Saito
Auditors: Shin Nihon & Co.

LOCATIONS

HQ: Mizuho Financial Group, Inc.
1-5-5, Otemachi, Chiyoda-ku,
Tokyo 100-0004, Japan
Phone: +81-3-5224-1111   **Fax:** +81-3-3215-4616
Web: www.mizuho-fg.co.jp

PRODUCTS/OPERATIONS

2005 Sales

	% of total
Interest	
Loans & bills discounted	31
Securities	9
Receivables under resale agreements	3
Other	3
Noninterest	
Fee & commission income	16
Other operating income	10
Trading income	5
Other income	23
Total	100

COMPETITORS

Bank of Yokohama	Shinsei Bank
Citigroup	Shizuoka Bank
Mitsubishi UFJ Financial Group	Sumitomo Mitsui
Mitsui Trust	Sumitomo Trust and Banking

HISTORICAL FINANCIALS

Company Type: Public

Income Statement

FYE: March 31

	ASSETS ($ mil.)	NET INCOME ($ mil.)	INCOME AS % OF ASSETS	EMPLOYEES
3/05	1,330,323	5,833	0.4%	22,827
3/04	1,303,942	3,853	0.3%	26,575
3/03	1,118,369	(19,835)	—	27,900
3/02	1,140,744	(7,358)	—	30,262
3/01	1,293,914	1,672	0.1%	32,068
Annual Growth	0.7%	36.7%	—	(8.1%)

2005 Year-End Financials

Equity as % of assets: 2.7%
Return on assets: 0.4%
Return on equity: 16.5%
Long-term debt ($ mil.): 59,401
Sales ($ mil.): 32,131

Net Income History Exchange: Tokyo

MOL

The downstream operations of MOL Magyar Olaj-és Gázipari Rt. (Hungarian Oil and Gas Company, or MOL) have moved it up to become Hungary's biggest company and one of Central Europe's top refiners. MOL's refineries produce about 88,500 barrels of oil equivalent per day, and it operates more than 760 gas stations in the Czech Republic, Hungary, Poland, Romania, Slovakia, Slovenia, and Ukraine. Other activities include transmission, storage, and wholesale trading of natural gas and related products, and exploration and production in Hungary, Russia, and areas of Central and Eastern Europe. Proved reserves stack up to about 269 million barrels of oil equivalent. The Hungarian government owns 23% of MOL.

In Hungary the company operates approximately 350 service stations, marketing under the brand MOL 2000. MOL has more than 400 stations in neighboring countries, where it plans to expand. The company has also acquired a 36% stake in Slovnaft, Slovakia's sole refiner, and holds a 23% stake in TVK, Hungary's largest petrochemical producer. With Russian companies moving into the region, MOL has been in talks with Polish energy company PKN ORLEN to form alliances. In 2005 MOL acquired the Romanian subsidiary of Royal Dutch Shell group of companies, including the purchase of 59 Shell filling stations which the company plans to modernize immediately. Royal Dutch Shell also sold MOL its Romania-based lubricants, aviation, and commercial businesses.

In addition to expanding its refining and marketing operations across Central Europe, the company has restructured its exploration and production activities to focus on the development of oil fields in Russia.

In 2003 MOL concluded a long term crude oil supply agreement with Russian oil giant YUKOS.

In 2004 the company agreed to sell its gas businesses to E.ON Ruhrgas for about $1 billion. The sale is thought to threaten competition within in the energy market inside the country and is being examined by Hungarian parliament.

HISTORY

The oil refining industry in Hungary dates to the 1880s, when refineries were opened in Fiume (1882) and Budapest (1883). By 1913 Hungary had 28 plants.

Following Hungary's defeat in WWI, the country's refining industry fell into decline, as new national boundaries placed most of its former oil refineries and oil-producing regions outside its borders. By 1921 Hungary had only six operational refineries.

British and American investors set up the European Gas and Electric Company (EUROGASCO) in the US in 1931 to acquire oil and gas concessions in Central Europe and build power plants. By 1937 EUROGASCO (controlled by Standard Oil of New Jersey) was producing oil. A year later Standard Oil set up the Hungarian-American Oil Industry Shareholding Co. (MAORT) to develop the fields, and in 1940 MAORT's production was meeting all of Hungary's oil needs.

During WWII, MAORT requisitioned all oil assets. The oil industry boomed as Hungary served as a major supplier for the German war machine. But by 1944, with German armies in retreat from the Eastern Front, much of Hungary's oil machinery and plants were dismantled. The remaining plants suffered heavy bombing from Allied forces or had equipment confiscated by Russian and Romanian troops.

After the war the Hungarian Soviet Crude Oil Co. began rebuilding Hungary's oil industry and started drilling on the Great Hungarian Plain in 1946. MAORT also ramped up production in the Trans-Danubian fields. In 1949, following charges of sabotage against MAORT managers, MAORT was nationalized and broken up into five national companies, which re-merged in 1952 with Hungarian Soviet Oil Co. (successor to Hungarian Soviet Crude Oil Co.).

In 1957 all operations of the Hungarian crude oil industry were consolidated under Crude Oil Trust, which took over the gas industry by 1960. That year the company was renamed National Crude Oil and Gas Trust (OKGT), and the focus of exploration soon shifted from Trans-Danubian fields to the Great Plain. By 1970 the Great Plain accounted for 67% of oil production and 96% of natural gas production.

Hungary began allowing foreign gasoline distributors to compete in domestic markets during the 1980s. Moving toward privatization, the Hungarian government founded MOL in 1991 as the successor to OKGT, which comprised nine oil and gas enterprises. In 1993 the socialist government sold 8% of MOL to the public. By 1998 the government had sold all but 25% of MOL.

During the 1990s the company also expanded in Central Europe. With Austria's OMV in 1994 it began building a 120-km pipeline linking Austria and Hungary, which gave it access to natural gas from Western Europe for the first time. MOL also opened up service stations in neighboring countries, beginning with one in Romania in 1996. By 2000 the company was operating about 80 stations in Romania, 18 in Slovakia, three in Ukraine, and two in Slovenia, in addition to its 330 stations in Hungary. MOL also acquired about 20% of chemical processor TVK in 1999 and upped the stake to nearly 33% by 2000. That year MOL also acquired 36% of Slovnaft, Slovakia's only oil refiner and its major retailer.

EXECUTIVES

Executive Chairman: Zsolt Hernádi, age 45
Vice Chairman: Sándor Csányi, age 52
Group CEO: György Mosonyi, age 56
Group CFO: József Molnár, age 49
Group Chief Strategy Officer:
  Michel-Marc Delcommune, age 57
Managing Director Exploration and Production Division: Zoltán Áldott, age 36
Managing Director Natural Gas Division:
  Sándor Fasimon, age 39
Managing Director Refining and Marketing Division:
  Ferenc Horváth, age 44
Managing Director Petrochemical Division:
  Vratko Kassovic, age 62
Chief Legal Counsel: Ilona Bánhegyi, age 35
Investor Relations Director: Rupert Foster
Human Resources Director: József Simola
Enterprise Relations: László Miklós
Corporate Communications: Szabolcs Ferencz
Internal Auditor: Zoltán Jancsurák
Security and Protection: Frigyes Bozsik

LOCATIONS

HQ: MOL Magyar Olaj-és Gázipari Rt.
  Október huszonharmadika u.18,
  H-1502 Budapest, Hungary
Phone: +36-1-209-0000   **Fax:** +36-1-464-1335
Web: www.mol.hu

MOL Magyar Olaj-és Gázipari explores and produces oil and gas in Hungary, Russia, and other areas of Central and Eastern Europe, and owns and operates service stations in Croatia, Hungary, Poland, Romania, Slovakia, Slovenia, and Ukraine. It has refineries at Százhalombatta, Tiszaujvaros, and Zalaegerszeg in Hungary.

PRODUCTS/OPERATIONS

2004 Sales

	% of total
Refining & marketing	60
Natural gas	27
Petrochemicals	10
Other	3
Total	**100**

Major Subsidiaries

Balatongáz Ltd (natural gas)
Dunafiksz Ltd. (repair of chemical processing equipment)
GEOINFORM Well-Drilling Information Provider Ltd. (well-logging and geological and drilling data processing)
Geophysical Service Providing Ltd (GES, geophysical measuring and computer-aided data processing services)
Kiskungáz Co. Ltd. (regional gas supplier)
Koolajtároló Rt. (Crude Oil Storage Company Limited)
KUNPETROL Ltd. (maintenance, construction, and installation of oil and gas technological systems)
MOL Austria Handels GmbH (wholesale trading and sale of energy products)
MOL INVEST Asset Management and Sales Company Limited
MOL Romania Petroleum Products Srl (service stations and the wholesale and retail trading of fuels)
MOL Slovensko spol. s.r.o. (service stations and the wholesale and retail trading of fuels, Slovakia)
MOL-Chem Trading and Service Providing Ltd. (trading and distribution of chemical materials, synthetic materials, and agrochemicals)
MOL-GÁZ Trading Ltd (natural gas trading)
MOLTRADE-Mineralimpex Trading Company Limited (wholesale and retail fuel trading)
MOLTRANS Tanker Road Haulage Ltd. (domestic transport of mineral oil products)
Nitrogénmuvek Rt. (Nitrogen Works Company Limited, fertilizer production)
OLAJTERV Main Contracting and Design Company Limited (contracting and design)
PETROLSZERVIZ Oil Industry Maintenance and Construction Ltd. (plant maintenance and installation)
Petroszolg Maintenance and Service Provider Ltd. (maintenance of chemical and oil industry systems)
ROTARY Drilling Company Limited (drilling and development of wells)
Slovnaft (oil processing, Slovakia)
SZEB-GÁZ Industrial, Trading and Service Providing Ltd (PB gas provider)
Terméktároló Rt. (Product Storage Company Limited, oil and gas storage)
TURUL Gas Construction and Asset Management Company Limited (gas pipeline construction)
ZAB Zemplén-Abaúj Gas Supply Company Limited (regional gas supplier)
ZSÁMBÉKGÁZ Gas Pipeline Sublet-Construction and Asset Management Company Limited (regional gas supplier)

COMPETITORS

BG Group	OMV
BP	PKN ORLEN
CEPSA	Repsol YPF
Eni	Royal Dutch/Shell Group
Hellenic Petroleum	TOTAL
Norsk Hydro	

HISTORICAL FINANCIALS

Company Type: Public

Income Statement

FYE: December 31

	REVENUE ($ mil.)	NET INCOME ($ mil.)	NET PROFIT MARGIN	EMPLOYEES
12/04	10,839	1,160	10.7%	15,465
12/03	7,318	479	6.5%	15,932
12/02	5,173	289	5.6%	15,268
12/01	4,029	5	0.1%	14,253
12/00	3,704	72	1.9%	16,552
Annual Growth	30.8%	100.4%	—	(1.7%)

2004 Year-End Financials

Debt ratio: 27.2%
Return on equity: 35.2%
Cash ($ mil.): 488

Current ratio: 1.04
Long-term debt ($ mil.): 1,108

Net Income History

Budapest: MOL

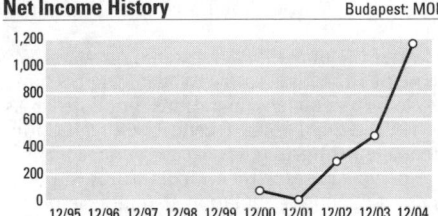

1,200 1,000 800 600 400 200 0
12/95 12/96 12/97 12/98 12/99 12/00 12/01 12/02 12/03 12/04

Munich Re

Some companies live with risk. Münchener Rückversicherungs-Gesellschaft Aktiengesellschaft (Munich Re), on the other hand, *thrives* with risk. Coverage includes fire, life, motor, liability, and other types on both facultative (individual risks) and treaty (groups of risks) bases. The firm owns about 90% of ERGO Versicherungsgruppe, putting it second only to Allianz in Germany's direct insurance market. Through American Re, Munich Re enjoys greater access to US markets. As the world's largest reinsurer, the company operates in some 160 countries.

Europe is its biggest market (about 75% of premiums) and the company plans expansion through acquisitions there.

As insurance clients seek less expensive ways to manage risk, reinsurance markets have stagnated. In response, Munich Re moved into direct insurance. Continuing its expansion, Munich Re has also entered the asset management game, forming MEAG Munich ERGO AssetManagement, a joint venture with ERGO.

Über-insurer Allianz AG owns about 15% of Munich Re, which in turn owns about 15% of Allianz. Other major shareholders include some of Germany's top banks: HypoVereinsbank and Dresdner Bank. Deutsche Bank has sold its stake in the company.

The company is hoping to continue the growth of its primary insurance segment (more than 80% of business comes from Germany), focusing on personal lines.

In 2005 Munich Re took a nearly 75% hit on its profit margin due to re-investment in its American Re subsidiary, whose internal reserves required a $1.6 billion injection for expected claims related to asbestos and environmental claims on policies mostly written between 1997 and 2002.

HISTORY

Investors Carl Thieme and Theodor Cramer-Klett founded Munich Re in 1880. Within a month Munich Re opened offices in Hamburg, Berlin, Vienna, and St. Petersburg, establishing treaties with German and Danish insurers. In 1888 Munich Re went public; two years later, it opened an office in London and helped finance the creation of Allianz, which would soon come to dominate the German insurance industry. In 1892 the firm opened a branch in the US (it incurred severe losses from the 1906 San Francisco earthquake).

WWI interrupted Munich Re's UK and US operations. The company recovered after 1918, only to be hobbled again by the Great Depression. In 1933 Munich Re executive Kurt Schmitt became minister of economic affairs for the Nazis. Objecting to the evolving policies of National Socialism, he left after a year, returning to Munich Re, where he became chief executive in 1938.

Hitler's ignition of WWII wasn't quite the boom Munich Re needed; its international business was again disrupted. After the war, the Allies further limited overseas operations. Because of his involvement with the Nazi government, Schmitt was replaced by Eberhard von Reininghaus in 1945. The division of Germany further hampered the company's recovery.

Jump-started by the Marshall Plan in 1950, the West German *Wirtschaftswunder* (economic miracle) kicked into high gear, as the devastated country rebuilt. Relaxation of occupation-era trading limits also helped as the company rebuilt its foreign business. By 1969, Munich Re's sales topped DM 2 billion. Amid the global oil crisis and a rash of terrorist acts in Germany, the firm reported its first-ever reinsurance loss in 1977.

German reunification in 1990 provided new markets for Munich Re, but advantages from new business in the East were wiped out by claims arising from that year's harsh winter.

In 1992 an investigation by the German Federal Cartel Office prompted a realignment in the insurance business — Allianz ceded its controlling interests in three life insurers (Hamburg-Mannheimer Versicherungs, Karlsruher Lebensversicherung, and Berlinische Lebensversicherung) to Munich Re, bringing it into direct insurance. Munich Re took over Deutsche Krankenversicherung (DKV) in 1996. Also that year Munich Re acquired American Re.

During the 1990s, reinsurance sales dwindled as competition increased, forcing lower premiums, and alternatives to insurance and reinsurance became more common. Munich Re looked to direct insurance, particularly individual property/casualty and life insurance, to compensate. In 1997 it merged Hamburg-Mannheimer and DKV with another insurer, Victoria AG, to form ERGO Versicherungsgruppe. Within a year, ERGO's insurance income accounted for half of all revenues.

Munich Re and ERGO launched asset management firm MEAG Munich ERGO Asset-Management in 1999. That year Munich Re experienced its worst year ever after natural disasters hit its reinsurance business hard. To recoup its losses, the next year the firm expanded both its reinsurance and primary insurance operations into key markets in Europe, North and South America, and Asia. Also in 2000, Munich Re bought CNA Financial's life reinsurance operations. Together with Swiss Re, the company launched Inreon, an online reinsurance exchange, in 2001.

As one of the companies hit hardest financially by the World Trade Center tragedy, Munich Re paid out some $2 billion in claims.

EXECUTIVES

Chairman, Supervisory Board: Hans-Jürgen Schinzler, age 65
Deputy Chairman, Supervisory Board: Herbert Bach
Chairman, Board of Management: Nikolaus von Bomhard, age 49
Member Board of Management, Accounting, Controlling, Taxes, and Investor Relations: Jörg Schneider, age 47
Member Board of Management, Corporate Underwriting/Global Clients: Stefan Heyd, age 60
Member Board of Management, Finance, General Services, Organisational Design and Development: Heiner Hasford, age 54
Member Board of Management, Life and Health and Human Resources: Detlef Schneidawind, age 61
Member Board of Management, Special and Financial Risks and Information Technology: Torsten Jeworrek, age 44
Member Board of Management, Asia, Australasia, and Africa: Karl Wittmann, age 60
Member Board of Management, Europe 1 and Corporate Communications: Christian Kluge, age 64
Member Board of Management, Europe 2 and Latin America: Georg Daschner, age 56
Member Board of Management, North America; Chairman and CEO, American Re: John P. Phelan, age 58
Company Spokesperson: Rainer Küppers
Media Relations: Ursula Jenne-Lindenberg
Auditors: KPMG Bayerische Treuhandgesellschaft AG

LOCATIONS

HQ: Münchener Rückversicherungs-Gesellschaft Aktiengesellschaft
Königinstrasse 107, D-80802 Munich, Germany
Phone: +49-89-38-91-0   **Fax:** +49-89-39-90-56
US HQ: American Re Corporation, 555 College Rd. East, Princeton, NJ 08543
US Phone: 609-243-4200   **US Fax:** 609-243-4257
Web: www.munichre.com

Munich Re operates in some 150 countries worldwide.

PRODUCTS/OPERATIONS

2004 Assets

	% of total
Cash	1
Real estate	4
Other securities	59
Receivables	4
Loans	10
Other	22
Total	**100**

2004 Sales

	% of total
Premiums	81
Investment income	17
Other	2
Total	**100**

Selected Subsidiaries

Asset Management
  MEAG MUNICH ERGO
Reinsurance
  American Re Corporation (US)
  American Re-Insurance Company (US)
  Great Lakes Reinsurance (UK) PLC
  Münchener Rück Italia S.p.A.
  Munich American Reassurance Company (US)
  Munich Reinsurance Company of
    Africa Limited (South Africa)
  Munich Reinsurance Company of
    Australasia Limited (Australia)
  Munich Reinsurance Company of Canada
  New Reinsurance Company (Switzerland)
Direct Insurance
  ERGO Versicherungsgruppe AG (92%)
  D.A.S. Deutscher Automobil Schutz Allgemeine
  Europäische Reiseversicherung AG
  Karlsruher Lebensversicherung AG (54%)
  Rechtsschutz-Versicherungs-AG (62%)
    D.A.S. Deutscher Automobil Schutz
      Versicherungs-AG (62%)
    DAS Legal Expenses Insurance Company Limited
      (62%, UK)
    D.A.S. Nederlandse Rechtsbijstand
      Verzekeringsmaatschappij N.V.
      (39%, The Netherlands)
  DKV Deutsche Krankenversicherung AG (63%)
  dkv International S.A. (63%, Belgium)
  Hamburg-Mannheimer Versicherungs-AG (63%)
    Hamburg-Mannheimer
      Sachversicherungs-AG (63%)
  VICTORIA Lebensversicherung AG (63%)
  VICTORIA Krankenversicherung AG (63%)
  VICTORIA MERIDIONAL Compañía Anónima de
    Seguros y Reaseguros, S.A. (61%, Spain)
  VICTORIA-Seguros de Vida, S.A. (62%, Portugal)
  VICTORIA-Seguros S.A. (62%, Portugal)
  VICTORIA-VOLKSBANKEN Versicherungs-AG
    (46%, Austria)

COMPETITORS

Allianz	General Reinsurance UK
AXA	Hannover Re
Bâloise-Holding	Nippon Life Insurance
Converium Reinsurance	RGA
Everest Re	Swiss Re
GE Insurance Solutions	Transatlantic Holdings
General Re	Winterthur

HISTORICAL FINANCIALS

Company Type: Public

Income Statement

FYE: December 31

	ASSETS ($ mil.)	NET INCOME ($ mil.)	INCOME AS % OF ASSETS	EMPLOYEES
12/04	292,975	2,500	0.9%	40,962
12/03	262,819	(545)	—	41,431
12/02	205,890	1,133	0.6%	41,396
12/01	178,979	221	0.1%	38,317
12/00	182,263	1,648	0.9%	27,489
12/99	181,139	1,141	0.6%	33,245
12/98	140,670	714	0.5%	23,948
12/97	90,370	332	0.4%	18,021
12/96	81,416	321	0.4%	16,343
12/95	84,746	199	0.2%	16,218
Annual Growth	14.8%	32.5%	—	10.8%

2004 Year-End Financials

Equity as % of assets: 9.4%   Long-term debt ($ mil.): 3,058
Return on assets: 0.9%   Sales ($ mil.): 64,419
Return on equity: 9.8%

Net Income History

German: MUV

12/95 12/96 12/97 12/98 12/99 12/00 12/01 12/02 12/03 12/04

National Australia Bank

National Australia Bank (NAB) is down under, up over, and all around. One of Australia's Big Four banks (the others are Westpac Banking, Australia and New Zealand Banking Group, and Commonwealth Bank of Australia), NAB offers retail banking (deposits, credit cards, and mortgages) and such business banking services as leasing, foreign exchange, and international trade finance. Other services include trust, insurance, and asset management. The company also owns Bank of New Zealand. NAB sold its Irish banks — National Irish Bank and Northern Bank — to Danske Bank. Its UK banks, Yorkshire Bank (England) and Clydesdale Bank (Scotland), are being retained.

NAB is streamlining its UK operations, trimming staff, closing branches, and simplifying its product range while revamping other branches and building the banks' online capabilities, with an emphasis on attracting small business and private banking clients.

This strategy dovetails with the company's reorganization along regional lines (Australia, Europe, and New Zealand) and the alignment of its banking and wealth management operations to better cross-sell financial products to customers.

HISTORY

Formed in 1858 in Melbourne, National Bank of Australasia (NBA) just missed the peak of the Victoria gold rush. The bank expanded across the territory and was one of the first to lend to farmers and ranchers using land deeds as security. In the late 1870s, drought imperiled Victoria. Seeking greener pastures, NBA entered New South Wales in 1885, then headed into Western Australia. Economic instability continued; in 1893 the bank experienced its first panic and was shuttered for eight weeks. NBA reopened only to close a quarter of its branches between 1893 and 1896.

During the Australian commonwealth's early years, Western Australia was the bank's salvation as the economies in Victoria and South Australia stagnated. NBA helped fund Australia's WWI efforts through public loans. A postwar consolidation wave in banking swept up NBA, which made acquisitions in 1918 and 1922.

Overdue farm and ranch loans weakened the bank during the Depression. As WWII raged, the Commonwealth Bank (established in 1912) took greater control of Australia's banks. With competition among banks primarily limited to branch growth, NBA acquired Queensland National Bank in 1948 and Ballarat Banking Co. in

1955. The bank diversified into consumer finance through acquisition. In the 1960s Australia experienced an economic boom as immigration and industrialization grew. The boom went bust in the 1970s as the world sunk into recession. Still under the Commonwealth Bank's tight control, the banks watched business that had once been theirs lost to building societies, merchant banks, and credit unions.

The 1980s brought banking deregulation. To vie with foreign banks entering Australia, NBA in 1981 merged with Commercial Banking Co. of Sydney and became the National Commercial Banking Corp. of Australia in 1982. (It took its present name in 1984.) Throughout the 1980s the bank diversified and moved into the US and Japan. It invested in property and made loans to foreign countries. All too quickly, though, property values sank and countries defaulted on loans.

To fight recession, NAB looked abroad for opportunities. In 1987 it bought Clydesdale Bank, Northern Bank, and National Irish Bank from Midland Bank Group (now part of HSBC Holdings). Three years later, NAB bought Yorkshire Bank, then turned the four banks around by linking them and tightening loan operations. In 1992 it bought the troubled Bank of New Zealand, again tightening loan operations. Three years later NAB claimed Michigan National in the US.

After the mid-1990s economic recovery, NAB bought HomeSide to try to adapt the US mortgage firm's efficient operations for all its banks.

NAB in 2000 bought Lend Lease's MLC fund management group. It also announced plans to launch a separate stock for its European businesses, fueling speculation it might be on the prowl to buy or merge with a large UK bank. The Australian Competition and Consumer Commission that year accused NAB of credit card transaction price-fixing; the bank faces a possible fine of nearly $6 million.

In 2001 NAB sold US-based Michigan National Bank to ABN AMRO and sold mortgage lender HomeSide International to Washington Mutual the following year. In fiscal year 2002, the bank cut some 2,000 jobs, mostly in back-office operations.

During fiscal year 2003 the company booked pre-tax losses of some $360 million due to unauthorized trading in the company's foreign currency options department. By the end of March 2004, chairman Charles Allen, chief executive Frank Cicutto, and the heads of global markets and foreign exchange had resigned. Three more executives and at least five traders were fired.

EXECUTIVES

Chairman: Michael A. Chaney, age 54
Managing Director and CEO: John M. Stewart, age 56, $2,232,515 pay
Group CFO: Michael J. Ullmer, age 53
CIO: Ian G. MacDonald, age 50, $578,700 pay
Group Chief Risk Officer: Michael Hamar, age 58
Deputy Group CFO: Gordon Lefevre, age 44
Group General Manager, Regulatory Affairs: Graeme Willis, age 53
Executive General Manager, Group Development: Cameron A. Clyne, age 36
Executive General Manager, Institutional Markets and Services: John Hooper, age 43
Executive General Manager, People and Culture: Elizabeth Hunter, age 40
Executive General Manager, Financial Services New Zealand; CEO, Bank of New Zealand: Peter L. Thodey, age 54, $566,220 pay
Executive Director, National Australia Group Europe: Gavin R. Slater, age 39
Company Secretary: Garry F. Nolan, age 57
Chief General Counsel: David M. Krasnostein, age 50

Head of Group Investor Relations: Callum Davidson
Head of Operational Integration: Kevin Turnbull
Group Manager, External Relations: Brandon Phillips
CEO, UK: Lynne M. Peacock, age 51
CEO, Australia: Ahmed Fahour, age 38, $95,199 pay
  (partial-year salary)
Manager, Investor Relations: Hany Messieh
Group Communications Adviser: Samantha Evans
Auditors: Ernst & Young

LOCATIONS

HQ: National Australia Bank Limited
  500 Bourke St., 24th Fl., Melbourne 3000, Australia
Phone: +61-3-8641-3500   **Fax:** +61-3-9208-5695
US HQ: 245 Park Ave., 28th Fl., New York, NY 10167
US Phone: 212-916-9500   **US Fax:** 212-983-1969
Web: www.nabgroup.com

2004 Sales

	$ mil.	% of total
Australia	15,325	69
Europe	4,195	19
New Zealand	1,923	9
Asia	429	2
US	183	1
Total	**22,055**	**100**

PRODUCTS/OPERATIONS

2004 Sales

	$ mil.	% of total
Interest		
Loans to customers	11,603	53
Marketable debt securities	1,226	5
Other	799	4
Life insurance		
Investment revenue	3,538	16
Premium & related revenue	734	3
Other		
Loan fees from banking	1,057	5
Fees & commissions	892	4
Money transfer fees	718	3
Trading income	420	2
Investment management fees	235	1
Other	833	4
Total	**22,055**	**100**

2004 Assets

	% of total
Cash & equivalents	12
Trading account	10
Securities	4
Investments relating to life insurance business	10
Loans & advances	60
Other	4
Total	**100**

Selected Subsidiaries

Bank of New Zealand
Clydesdale Bank PLC
MLC Limited
National Australia Financial Management Limited
Yorkshire Bank PLC.

COMPETITORS

Abbey National
Allied Irish Banks
Australia and New Zealand Banking
Bank of Ireland
Barclays
Commonwealth Bank of Australia
HBOS
HSBC Holdings
Lloyds TSB
Northern Rock
RBS
St.George Bank
Westpac Banking

HISTORICAL FINANCIALS

Company Type: Public

Income Statement

FYE: September 30

	ASSETS ($ mil.)	NET INCOME ($ mil.)	INCOME AS % OF ASSETS	EMPLOYEES
9/04	299,186	2,311	0.8%	43,517
9/03	270,320	2,690	1.0%	45,206
9/02	204,921	1,832	0.9%	46,642
9/01	184,774	1,027	0.6%	49,710
9/00	186,582	1,758	0.9%	47,000
9/99	165,813	1,841	1.1%	51,566
9/98	149,266	1,194	0.8%	46,300
9/97	146,428	1,610	1.1%	46,392
9/96	137,665	1,666	1.2%	47,178
9/95	108,028	1,446	1.3%	52,567
Annual Growth	**12.0%**	**5.3%**	**—**	**(2.1%)**

2004 Year-End Financials

Equity as % of assets: 6.1%
Return on assets: 0.8%
Return on equity: 13.8%
Long-term debt ($ mil.): 23,694
No. of shares (mil.): 310

Dividends
  Yield: 3.1%
  Payout: 41.9%
Market value ($ mil.): 30,395
Sales ($ mil.): 22,055

Stock History

NYSE: NAB

	STOCK PRICE ($) FY Close	P/E High/Low		PER SHARE ($) Earnings	Dividends	Book Value
9/04	98.00	17	13	7.13	2.99	60.74
9/03	104.33	14	10	8.28	4.72	55.18
9/02	90.68	19	12	5.50	3.71	41.01
9/01	63.81	31	20	3.01	3.46	50.84
9/00	69.38	15	11	5.54	3.54	38.25
9/99	73.81	16	10	5.93	3.44	40.72
9/98	59.94	20	14	4.09	3.15	31.44
9/97	77.13	15	10	5.50	3.43	30.78
9/96	52.88	9	7	5.69	3.27	33.48
9/95	44.38	9	7	5.18	2.93	29.16
Annual Growth	**9.2%**	**—**	**—**	**3.6%**	**0.2%**	**8.5%**

NEC Corporation

NEC has three arms and plenty of muscle. The company's IT Solutions business makes high-end computers (servers and supercomputers) and peripherals (monitors and projectors), and it wrestles with Fujitsu for the top spot among Japanese PC makers. Its Electron Devices division makes electronics ranging from transistors to display modules, and competes with Toshiba for the second spot among semiconductor makers (both companies trail Intel). The company sells broadband and wireless networking equipment through its Network Solutions group. NEC also runs one of Japan's largest Internet service providers (BIGLOBE).

Not wanting to be pigeonholed as a PC maker, centenarian NEC has followed industry suit and recast itself as a provider of Internet products and services. The company has restructured its operations numerous times in recent years.

NEC took its DRAM joint venture, Elpida Memory, public, thereby reducing its stake in the company and the volatile memory sector. NEC sold its plasma display business to Pioneer in 2004. Early in 2005 it dissolved its monitor joint venture with Mitsubishi and took full ownership of the unit (NEC Display Solutions).

HISTORY

A group of Japanese investors, led by Kunihiko Iwadare, formed Nippon Electric Company (NEC) in a joint venture with Western Electric (US) in 1899. Starting as an importer of telephone equipment, NEC soon became a maker and a major supplier to Japan's Communications Ministry. Western Electric sold its stake in NEC in 1925. The company became affiliated with the Sumitomo *keiretsu* (industrial group) in the 1930s and went public in 1949.

After Nippon Telegraph and Telephone (NTT) was formed in 1952, NEC became one of its four leading suppliers. The post-WWII need to repair Japan's telephone systems and the country's continuing economic recovery resulted in strong demand from NTT for NEC's products. In the 1950s and 1960s NTT business represented over 50% of sales, even though NEC had expanded overseas, diversified into home appliances, and formed a computer alliance with Honeywell (US). ITT (US), which had begun acquiring shares in the company decades earlier and owned as much as 59% of NEC, sold its stake in the 1960s.

In the 1970s Honeywell's lagging position in computers hurt NEC; the company recovered through in-house development efforts and a mainframe venture with Toshiba. In 1977 CEO Koji Kobayashi articulated his revolutionary vision of NEC's future as an integrator of computers and communications through semiconductor technology.

NEC invested heavily in R&D and expansion, becoming the world's largest semiconductor maker in 1985. Despite its proprietary operating system, NEC garnered over 50% of the Japanese computer market in the 1980s. NEC entered into a mainframe computer partnership with Honeywell and France's Groupe Bull in 1987.

By the early 1990s NEC had lost its status as world's largest semiconductor maker to Intel. NEC bought 20% of US computer maker Packard Bell in 1995. The following year NEC merged most of its PC business outside Japan with that company, creating Packard Bell NEC. Also in 1996 NEC created US subsidiary Holon Net Corp. to make hardware and software for Internet and intranet markets.

NEC took control of Packard Bell NEC in 1998, upping its stake to 53%. A sluggish Japanese economy and slumping memory prices contributed to NEC's drop in income for fiscal 1998. A defense contract scandal involving overbilling and improper hiring by an NEC unit forced the resignation of chairman Tadahiro Sekimoto and, later, president Hisashi Kaneko.

New president Koji Nishigaki, the first at NEC without an engineering background, led a sweeping reorganization to cut 10% of the company's workforce — 15,000 employees — over three years. He revamped NEC operations around Internet application hardware, software, and services. In 1998 NEC formed a rare pact with a Japanese rival, allying with Hitachi to consolidate memory chip operations. The restructuring of Packard Bell NEC (NEC by then owned 88%) helped cause a $1.3 billion loss for fiscal 1999, NEC's worst-ever drop. NEC folded up its Packard Bell NEC division later that year, imposing layoffs of about 80% of its staff, divesting it from the US retail market, and excising the historic Packard Bell brand name.

NEC restructured again in 2000, splitting into more autonomous units and streamlining its PC operations. That year the company launched an aggressive spending program in a move to lead the broadband mobile networking market. In early 2001 NEC ended a long-running dispute with Cray, investing $25 million in the company and granting distribution rights to its vector supercomputers in North America — a deal contingent upon Cray's dropping an antidumping suit that led to heavy import taxes being placed on NEC supercomputers sold in the US.

In 2002 NEC announced plans to spin off its semiconductor operations and form joint ventures for other divisions comprising its NEC Electron Devices business.

EXECUTIVES

Chairman: Hajime Sasaki, age 69
President: Akinobu Kanasugi, age 64
SEVP: Toshiro Kawamura
SEVP: Kaoru Yano
EVP: Kazuhiko Kobayashi
EVP: Shunichi Suzuki
SVP: Hirofumi Okuyama
SVP, Broadband Solutions Business Unit:
Saburo Takizawa
SVP: Yasuo Matoi
SVP, Domestic Sales Business Unit: Kazumasa Fujie
SVP, Infrastructure Solutions Business Unit and Mission Critical Systems Business Unit:
Masatoshi Aizawa
SVP, Mobile Business Unit: Tsutomu Nakamura
SVP, Computers Platform Business Unit:
Masahiko Yamamoto
SVP: Katsutoshi Nakada
SVP: Nobuhito Yagi
SVP, Software Business Unit: Koichi Ikumi
SVP, Industrial Solutions Business Unit:
Iwao Fuchigami
Auditors: Shin Nihon Ernst & Young

LOCATIONS

HQ: NEC Corporation
(Nippon Denki Kabushiki Kaisha)
7-1, Shiba 5-chome, Minato-ku,
Tokyo 108-8001, Japan
Phone: +81-3-3454-1111   **Fax:** +81-3-3798-1510
Web: www.nec.com

2005 Sales

	% of total
Japan	78
Other countries	22
Total	**100**

PRODUCTS/OPERATIONS

2005 Sales

	% of total
IT solutions	39
Network solutions	34
Electron devices	16
Other	11
Total	**100**

Selected Products

IT Solutions
 PCs
  Desktop
  Handheld
  Notebook
 Peripherals
  CD-ROMs
  Monitors
  Projectors
 Servers
 Supercomputers
Network Solutions
 Broadcasting equipment
 Control servers
 Fiber-optic devices
 Gateways
 Lasers
 Mobile networking and communications devices
 Multiplexers
 Network management applications
 Postal automation systems
 Routers and switches
 Satellite systems
Electron Devices
 Application-specific components
 Discrete devices
 Flat-panel displays
 Integrated circuits
 Memory
 Microprocessors
 Optoelectronics
 Radio-frequency and microwave devices

COMPETITORS

Acer	Microsoft
Alcatel	Mitsubishi Electric
AMD	Motorola
Apple Computer	Nokia
Canon	Nortel Networks
CASIO COMPUTER	Oki Electric
Cisco Systems	Philips Electronics
Dell	Ricoh
EDS	Samsung
Epson	Samsung Electronics
Ericsson	SANYO
Fujifilm	Sharp
Fujitsu	Siemens
Hewlett-Packard	Sony
Hitachi	STMicroelectronics
IBM	Sun Microsystems
Intel	Texas Instruments
Lucent	Toshiba
Matsushita	Unisys
Micron Technology	

HISTORICAL FINANCIALS

Company Type: Public

Income Statement

FYE: March 31

	REVENUE ($ mil.)	NET INCOME ($ mil.)	NET PROFIT MARGIN	EMPLOYEES
3/05	45,298	633	1.4%	147,800
3/04	47,022	394	0.8%	143,393
3/03	39,788	(208)	—	145,807
3/02	38,446	(2,352)	—	142,000
3/01	43,099	451	1.0%	150,000
3/00	48,461	101	0.2%	154,787
3/99	40,334	(1,339)	—	157,800
3/98	36,851	311	0.8%	152,450
3/97	39,907	739	1.9%	151,966
3/96	41,095	721	1.8%	152,719
Annual Growth	**1.1%**	**(1.4%)**	**—**	**(0.4%)**

2005 Year-End Financials

Debt ratio: 99.6%
Return on equity: 8.9%
Cash ($ mil.): 4,612
Current ratio: 1.25
Long-term debt ($ mil.): 7,382

No. of shares (mil.): 1,929
Dividends
 Yield: 0.0%
 Payout: —
Market value ($ mil.): 11,614

Stock History

NASDAQ: NIPNY

	STOCK PRICE ($) FY Close	P/E High/Low		Earnings	Dividends	Book Value
3/05	6.02	30	18	0.30	0.00	3.84
3/04	8.22	45	13	0.21	0.03	3.53
3/03	3.31	—	—	(0.13)	0.02	1.83
3/02	8.35	—	—	(1.42)	0.27	2.57
3/01	15.88	116	45	0.28	0.06	4.40
3/00	29.69	498	174	0.06	0.05	1.16
3/99	11.93	—	—	(0.84)	0.05	0.93
3/98	10.15	82	54	0.18	0.00	1.01
3/97	11.33	31	24	0.42	0.05	1.03
3/96	11.65	36	24	0.42	0.05	1.06
Annual Growth	**(7.1%)**	**—**	**—**	**(3.7%)**	**—**	**15.4%**

Nestlé S.A.

With instant coffee, baby formula, and bottled water in the mix, Nestlé's crunches more than just chocolate. The world's #1 food company in terms of sales, Nestlé is the world leader in coffee (Nescafé). It is also one of the world's largest bottled water (Perrier) and baby-food makers. Its 2001 purchase of Ralston Purina made it a top player in the pet food business. Ranging from kitty kibble to pasta, chocolate, and dairy products, its most well-known global brands include Buitoni, Friskies, Maggi, Nescafé, Nestea, and Nestlé. In addition to food products, Nestlé owns about 75% of Alcon Inc. (ophthalmic drugs, contact-lens solutions, and equipment for ocular surgery) and almost 27% of cosmetic giant L'Oréal.

The company has a joint venture with L'Oréal that makes nutritional supplements aimed at improving skin, hair, and nails; and another joint venture with Colgate-Palmolive, which develops and markets functional confectionery. Other joint ventures include Cereal Partners Worldwide, with General Mills.

Nestlé has long been an international company. Many of its brands are unique to particular countries, with products tailored to local tastes. Seeking to further strengthen its position in the worldwide ice cream market, in 2003 Nestlé acquired the ice cream and related products of the Mövenpick Group, a Swiss food company. The acquisition brought Nestlé licensing agreements with companies in Egypt, Finland, Germany, Norway, Sweden, and Saudi Arabia.

In line with its strategy to concentrate on value-added products, in 2004 Nestlé sold its cocoa processing facilities in Germany and the UK to Cargill. Also in 2004 the company acquired Finnish dairy company Valid's Valiojäätelö ice cream business. That year the company was ordered by the Brazilian government to sell its Chocolates Garoto on the grounds that ownership of Garoto presented unfair market competition. Nestlé is appealing the decision

Later in 2004 company CEO Peter Brabeck-Letmathe announced he was considering reducing the number of outside directorships that he holds because of increased demands as the leader of Nestlé. Brabeck-Letmathe sits on the boards of Alcon, Credit Suisse, Dreyer's Grand Ice Cream, L'Oréal, Roche Holdings, and "Winterthur" Swiss Insurance Company. And that same year, in a tangle with a French union over retirement benefits, Nestlé threatened to sell Perrier or produce its popular water from another source.

HISTORY

Henri Nestlé purchased a factory in Vevey, Switzerland, in 1843 that made products ranging from nut oils to rum. In 1867 he developed a powder made from cow's milk and wheat flour as a substitute for mother's milk. A year earlier Americans Charles and George Page had founded the Anglo-Swiss Condensed Milk Company in Cham, Switzerland, using Gail Borden's milk-canning technology.

In 1875 Nestlé sold his eponymous company, then doing business in 16 countries. When Anglo-Swiss launched a milk-based infant food in 1878, Nestlé's new owners responded by introducing a condensed-milk product. In 1905, a year after Nestlé began selling chocolate, the companies ended their rivalry by merging under the Nestlé name.

Hampered by limited milk supplies during WWI, the company expanded into regions less affected by the war, such as the US. In 1929 it acquired Cailler, the first company to mass-produce chocolate bars, and Swiss General, inventor of milk chocolate.

An investment in a Brazilian condensed-milk factory in the 1920s paid an unexpected dividend when Brazilian coffee growers suggested the company develop a water-soluble "coffee cube." Released in 1938, Nescafé instant coffee quickly became popular.

Other new products included Nestlé's Crunch bar (1938), Quik drink mix (1948), and Taster's Choice instant coffee (1966). Nestlé expanded during the 1970s with acquisitions such as Beringer Brothers wines (sold in 1995), Stouffer's, and Libby's.

Moving beyond foods in 1974, Nestlé acquired a 49% stake in Gesparal, a holding company that controls the French cosmetics company L'Oréal. It acquired pharmaceutical firm Alcon Laboratories three years later.

Helmut Maucher was named chairman and CEO in 1981. He began beefing up Nestlé's global presence. Boycotters had long accused Nestlé of harming children in developing countries through the unethical promotion of infant formula, and Maucher acknowledged the ongoing boycott by meeting with the critics and setting up a commission to police adherence to World Health Organization guidelines.

Nestlé bought Carnation in 1985. Maucher doubled the company's chocolate business in 1988 with the purchase of UK chocolate maker Rowntree (Kit Kat).

The company expanded in the 1990s with the purchases of Butterfinger and Baby Ruth candies, Source Perrier water, Alpo pet food, and Ortega Mexican foods. Company veteran Peter Brabeck-Letmathe succeeded Maucher as CEO in 1997. He cleaned out Nestlé's pantry by selling non-core businesses (Contadina tomato products, Libby's canned meat products) but restocked with San Pellegrino (mineral water) and Dalgety's Spillers (pet food) in 1998.

In 2001 Nestlé bought Ralston Purina for $10.3 billion, making it the world's largest pet food maker. To win FTC approval, the companies agreed to sell Meow Mix and Alley Cat dry cat food brands to Hartz Mountain.

In 2002 Nestlé acquired German ice-cream maker Schoeller Holding Group, as well as US food company, Chef America, maker of Hot Pockets and Lean Pockets. That same year Nestlé also spun off eyecare subsidiary, Alcon Laboratories, but retained about 75% ownership of it. In 2003, Nestlé merged its US ice cream business with Dreyer's, giving it 67% of Dreyer's.

In 2004 Nestlé sold its cocoa-processing facilities in Germany and the UK to Cargill. It also sold its German frozen food distributor Eastman that year; and Nestlé España bought Nestlé Portugal for about $682 million.

Later that same year, in a tangle with a French union over retirement benefits, Nestlé threatened to sell Perrier or produce its popular water from another source. However, the company reached a settlement with the union and the production of Perrier continued.

Long-time chairman Rainer Gut retired in 2005; Brabeck-Letmathe replaced him.

EXECUTIVES

Chairman and CEO: Peter Brabeck-Letmathe, age 61
CFO: Paul Polman
EVP, Asia, Oceania, Africa, and Middle East: Frits van Dijk, age 58
EVP, Europe: Lars Olofsson, age 53
EVP, Finance, Control, Legal, Tax, Purchasing, Export; and CFO: Wolfgang H. Reichenberger, age 52
EVP, Pharmaceutical and Cosmetic Products, Liaison with L'Oreal, Human Resources, and Corporate Affairs: Francisco Castañer, age 61
EVP, Stratgegic Business Units and Marketing: Ed Marra, age 53
EVP, Sales and Marketing, Nestlé Thailand: Suresh Narayanan
EVP, Technical, Production, Environment, and Research and Development: Werner J. Bauer, age 54
EVP, US, Canada, Latin America, and Caribbean: Paul Bulcke
EVP and Chairman and CEO, Nestlé Waters: Carlo Maria Donati, age 59
Deputy EVP, Corporate Business Development: Richard T. Laube, age 48
Deputy EVP, Nurtition: Luis Cantarell, age 53
General Secretary: Bernard Daniel
Investor Relations: Roddy Child-Villiers
Manager, Research and Development: Jeff Bogusz
Media Relations: François-Xavier Perroud
Auditors: KPMG Klynveld Peat Marwick Goerdeler SA

LOCATIONS

HQ: Nestlé S.A.
  Avenue Nestlé 55, CH-1800 Vevey, Vaud, Switzerland
Phone: +41-21-924-21-11   **Fax:** +41-21-924-48-00
US HQ: 800 N. Brand Blvd., Glendale, CA 91203
US Phone: 818-549-6000   **US Fax:** 818-549-6952
Web: www.nestle.com

Nestlé operates more than 500 factories in 83 countries.

2004 Sales

	% of total
Europe	33
The Americas	32
Asia, Oceania & Africa	17
Other regions	18
Total	**100**

PRODUCTS/OPERATIONS

2004 Sales

	% of total
Beverages	
Milk products, nutrition & ice cream	27
Beverages	25
Prepared dishes & cooking aids	18
Chocolate, confectionery & biscuits	12
Petcare	12
Pharmaceuticals	6
Total	**100**

Selected Products and Brands

Bouillons, soups, seasonings, pasta, and sauces
  Buitoni
  Maggi
  Thomy
  Winiary

Chilled Nestlé
  Chiquitin
  La Lechera
  LC1
  Molico
  Ski
  Sveltesse
  Yoco

Chocolate, confectionery, and biscuits
  Aero
  Baci
  Butterfinger
  Crunch
  Galak/Milkybar
  Kit Kat
  Nestlé
  Polo
  Smarties

Coffee
  Bonka
  Loumidis
  Nescafé
  Taster's Choice
  Zoégas

Foodservice and professional products
  Chef
  Davigel
  Minor's
  Santa Rica

Frozen foods (prepared dishes, pizzas)
  Buitoni
  Hot Pockets
  Lean Cuisine
  Maggi
  Stouffer's

Health-care nutrition
  Clinutren
  Modulen
  Nutren
  Peptamen

Ice cream
  Dreyer's
  Drumstick/Extrême
  Edy's
  Häagen Dazs
  La Cremeria
  Maxibon/Tandem
  Mega
  Mövenpick

Infant nutrition
  Beba
  Good Start
  Guigoz
  Lactogen
  Nan
  Neslac
  Nestogen

Other beverages
  Carnation
  Caro
  Libby's
  Milo
  Nesquik
  Nestea

Performance nutrition
  PowerBar
  Pria
Petcare
  Alpo
  Cat Chow
  Dog Chow
  Fancy Feast
  Gourmet
  Mon Petit
  Pro Plan
  Purina Friskies
  Purina ONE
  Tidy Cats
Refrigerated products (cold meat products, dough, pasta,
  pizzas, sauces)
  Buitoni
  Herta
  Nestlé
  Toll House
Shelf-stable products
  Carnation
  Coffee-Mate
  Klim
  La Lechera
  Milkmaid
  Molico
  Nespray
  Nido
  Ninho
  Svelty
Water
  Al Manhal
  Arrowhead
  Contrex
  Hépar
  Ice Mountain
  Levissima
  Nestlé Aquarel
  Ozarka
  Perrier
  Poland Spring
  S.Pellegrino
  San Bernardo
  Vittel
  Zephyrhills

COMPETITORS

Abbott Labs
Barilla
Bausch & Lomb
Brach's
Cadbury Schweppes
Campbell Soup
Colgate-Palmolive
ConAgra
Danone
Ferrara Pan Candy
General Mills
Goya
Heinz
Hershey
Kellogg
Kerry Group
Kraft Foods
Kraft Foods International
Kraft Foods North America
Lindt & Sprüngli
Mars
Novartis
Parmalat
PepsiCo
Procter & Gamble
Revlon
Russell Stover
Sara Lee
Suntory Ltd.
TCHIBO Holding
Thorntons
Unilever
Unilever NV
Unilever PLC
United Biscuits
World's Finest Chocolate

HISTORICAL FINANCIALS

Company Type: Public

Income Statement

FYE: December 31

	REVENUE ($ mil.)	NET INCOME ($ mil.)	NET PROFIT MARGIN	EMPLOYEES
12/04	76,660	5,935	7.7%	247,000
12/03	70,823	5,002	7.1%	253,000
12/02	64,258	5,451	8.5%	254,199
12/01	50,624	3,993	7.9%	229,765
12/00	50,522	3,576	7.1%	224,541
12/99	46,924	2,969	6.3%	230,929
12/98	52,031	3,112	6.0%	231,881
12/97	48,061	2,750	5.7%	225,808
12/96	44,835	2,521	5.6%	221,144
12/95	48,934	2,528	5.2%	220,172
Annual Growth	5.1%	9.9%	—	1.3%

2004 Year-End Financials

Debt ratio: 27.4%
Return on equity: 18.4%
Cash ($ mil.): 13,502

Current ratio: 1.21
Long-term debt ($ mil.): 9,481

Net Income History

OTC: NSRGY

Nikon

Paul Simon may still have a Nikon camera and still love to take a photograph, but Nikon's focus extends far wider than that. Though well-known for its cameras, lenses, and other consumer optical products, Nikon vies with national rival Canon and Netherlands-based ASML Holding to be the world's top producer of photolithography steppers — crucial equipment used to etch circuitry onto semiconductor wafers and LCD panels. The company makes a broad range of other products, including binoculars, eyewear, surveying instruments, microscopes, industrial equipment, and electronic imaging equipment. Nikon is part of the huge Mitsubishi *keiretsu*, a group of businesses linked by cross-ownership.

The range of Nikon's products offers a snapshot of the optical world. Its cameras have caught images from every manned space flight since Apollo 13. Its microscopes are used in schools and cell biology research laboratories, and its eye examination equipment and prescription glasses and sunglasses are fixtures in opticians' offices worldwide.

Nikon has adjusted operations in an effort to become more nimble in the face of a notoriously volatile chip market. It has reorganized into more-autonomous divisions, an arrangement under which the parent corporation serves as a holding company.

HISTORY

Lensmaker Nippon Kogaku KK formed in 1917 with the merger of three large Japanese optical glassmakers. Nippon Kogaku started selling binoculars in 1921; the company introduced its first microscope four years later.

In 1932 the company adopted the brand name Nikkor for its lenses, which were attached to other manufacturers' cameras. By WWII the company had diversified into cameras, microscopes, binoculars, surveying equipment, measuring instruments, and eyeglass lenses. During this time the Japanese government bought nearly all of the company's products. Nippon Kogaku began using the Nikon brand name on its cameras in 1946.

The company introduced its first commercially available pocket camera in the early 1950s, but few of Nikon's cameras made it out of Japan. The world would not begin to appreciate the quality of Nikon's products until photojournalists began using them in the Korean War.

Continuing a European expansion in the 1960s, the company opened subsidiaries in Switzerland (1961) and the Netherlands (1968). The company, in conjunction with undersea explorer Jacques Cousteau and a partner, introduced an underwater camera system in 1963. The 1970s were years of further development: The company introduced high-precision coordinate measuring instruments (1971) and sunglasses (1972), among other products. During the late 1970s Canon passed Minolta and Nikon as the world's top seller of cameras, setting off a battle that has seesawed ever since.

In 1980 the company developed its first stepper system for the semiconductor industry. By 1984 Nikon controlled 53% of the Japanese stepper market. Nippon Kogaku changed its name in 1988 to Nikon Corporation.

The company further broadened its geographic scope in the early 1990s, opening subsidiaries in South Korea (1990), Thailand (1990), Hungary (1991), Italy (1993), and Singapore (1995). When demand for chips dropped in the early 1990s, so did Nikon's sales: the company lost money in fiscal 1993 and fiscal 1994. It restructured its unprofitable camera division, cutting staff by a third to save cash.

In 1997 Shoichiro Yoshida, a Nikon designer since the 1950s who became a proponent of the company's stepper business, was named president, replacing Shigeo Ono, who became chairman. A slumping Asian market and declining prices for chips caused demand for steppers to fall and left the company with slack earnings for fiscal 1998 and 1999. Rebounds in the markets for digital cameras and semiconductor equipment led Nikon back into the black in 2000.

In 2001 the company expanded its semiconductor equipment offerings by entering the market for chemical mechanical polishing (CMP) equipment. In June of that year Ono retired as chairman; Yoshida replaced him.

EXECUTIVES

President, CEO, COO, and Director: Michio Kariya
EVP, CFO, and Director: Ichiro Terato
Senior Managing Director; President, Imaging Company; and Director: Makoto Kimura
Senior Managing Director; President, Core Technology Center; General Manager, Production Technology Headquarters; General Manager, Glass Division; and Director: Kyoichi Suwa

Managing Director; President, Corporate Strategy; General Manager, Information System Management; President, Business Administration; and Director: Mamoru Kajiwara

Managing Director; Divisional President, Office of Management Strategy; and Director: Norio Miyauchi

Managing Director; VP, Imaging Company; and Director: Naoki Tomino

Managing Director; President, Precision Equipment; and Director: Kazuo Ushida

Managing Director; VP, Precision Equipment Company; General Manager, Production Headquarters, Precision Equipment Company; and Director: Yoshimichi Kawai

President, Instruments Company and Director: Hidetoshi Mori

VP, Core Technology Center; General Manager, Optical Technology Headquarters, Core Technology Center; and Director: Yutaka Ichihara

VP, Core Technology Center and General Manager, Intellectual Property Headquarters, Core Technology Center: Takao Watanabe

VP, Corporate Strategy Center: Hideshi Hirai

VP, Precision Equipment Company: Masami Kumazawa

VP, Business Administration Center: Koji Morishita

President and CEO, Nikon Inc.: Toshiyuki Masai

Auditors: Deloitte Touche Tohmatsu

LOCATIONS

HQ: Nikon Corporation
Fuji Bldg., 2-3 Marunouchi 3-chome, Chiyoda-ku, Tokyo 100-8331, Japan

Phone: +81-3-3214-5311   Fax: +81-3-3216-1454
US HQ: 1300 Walt Whitman Rd., Melville, NY 11747
US Phone: 631-547-4200   US Fax: 631-547-0362
Web: www.nikon.com

Nikon has operations in Canada, China, the Czech Republic, France, Germany, Hong Kong, Hungary, Italy, Japan, Malaysia, the Netherlands, Poland, Singapore, South Korea, Sweden, Switzerland, Taiwan, Thailand, the UK, and the US.

2005 Sales

	% of total
Asia/Pacific	
Japan	25
Other countries	28
North America	25
Europe	22
Total	**100**

PRODUCTS/OPERATIONS

2005 Sales

	% of total
Imaging Products	55
Precision Equipment	33
Instruments	8
Other	4
Total	**100**

Selected Products

Imaging Products
  Camera lenses
  Compact cameras
  Digital cameras
  Film scanners
  Single-lens reflex (SLR) cameras

Precision Equipment
  Semiconductor and liquid crystal display (LCD) steppers

Instruments
  Biological and industrial microscopes
  Inspection equipment
  Measuring instruments
  Medical imaging systems
  Ophthalmic instruments

Other
  Binoculars
  Eyeglasses
  Sunglasses
  Surveying instruments
  Telescopes

COMPETITORS

ASML	Fujifilm
Canon	Olympus
Carl Zeiss	Pentax
Eastman Kodak	Ultratech
FSI International	

HISTORICAL FINANCIALS

Company Type: Public

Income Statement				FYE: March 31
	REVENUE ($ mil.)	NET INCOME ($ mil.)	NET PROFIT MARGIN	EMPLOYEES
3/05	5,937	225	3.8%	16,758
3/04	4,793	23	0.5%	13,636
3/03	3,913	(68)	—	13,184
3/02	3,641	(45)	—	14,328
3/01	3,831	166	4.3%	13,894
3/00	3,524	74	2.1%	11,946
3/99	2,567	(153)	—	—
3/98	2,797	63	2.2%	—
3/97	3,062	161	5.3%	—
3/96	3,103	173	5.6%	—
Annual Growth	**7.5%**	**2.9%**	**—**	**7.0%**

2005 Year-End Financials

Debt ratio: 76.6%
Return on equity: 13.0%
Cash ($ mil.): 200
Current ratio: 1.62
Long-term debt ($ mil.): 1,396

Net Income History

Exchange: Tokyo

Nintendo Co.

It's not a game, boy, it's serious business, and Nintendo knows it. One of the Big Three video game console makers, Nintendo makes the GameCube console, which battles with Microsoft's Xbox for second place in its industry (Sony's PlayStation 2 is the world's top game system). In the handheld console segment, however, Nintendo's Game Boy system remains the leader. In 2004 the company introduced a two-screen, videogame player called Nintendo DS (Nintendo Double Screen) and the smallest, lightest offering so far, the Game Boy Micro (which is the size of a cell phone and is the same platform as the company's Game Boy Advance SP) is slated for release in late 2005.

Nintendo is also the game software market leader and has sold over two billion games since 1985; hit series include *Pokemon, Super Mario Brothers,* and *The Legend of Zelda.*

Nintendo (which, loosely translated, means "leave luck to heaven") once ruled the golden age of the video game industry until more powerful machines introduced by SEGA (in 1989) and Sony (in 1994) pared down its kingdom (SEGA has since stopped making console systems). Microsoft

entered the gaming hardware market in 2001, leaving Nintendo with a shrinking piece of the pie.

The company plans to broaden its previous focus on kids and concentrate its efforts on its games, in contrast to competitors Sony and Microsoft, which are developing increasingly complex multimedia systems. The introduction of the Nintendo DS system is competitive move designed to counter the launch of Sony's PlayStation Portable. Before the end of 2005, the company will launch Nintendo Wi-Fi Connection, a free service that will allow DS system players to play other users simply by connecting to wireless network.

Nintendo also plans to introduce a new game console (dubbed "Revolution") which will most likely not be released until its competitors' new offerings, Microsoft's Xbox 360 and Sony's PlayStation 3, have hit the market. Unlike those two offerings, Revolution will be a game console first and foremost and not a digital entertainment hub.

Nintendo owns a majority stake in the Seattle Mariners baseball team, which it purchased for $125 million in 1992.

HISTORY

Nintendo Co. was founded in 1889 as the Marufuku Company to make and sell *hanafuda,* Japanese game cards. In 1907 the company began producing Western playing cards. It became the Nintendo Playing Card Company in 1951 and began making theme cards under a licensing agreement with Disney in 1959.

During the 1950s and 1960s, Hiroshi Yamauchi took the company public and diversified into new areas (including a "love hotel"). The company took its current name in 1963. Nintendo began making toys at the start of the 1970s and entered the budding field of video games toward the end of the decade by licensing Magnavox's Pong technology. Then it moved into arcade games. Nintendo established its US subsidiary, Nintendo of America, in 1980; its first hit was *Donkey Kong* ("silly monkey") and its next was *Super Mario Bros.* (named after Nintendo of America's warehouse landlord).

The company released Famicom, a technologically advanced home video game system, in Japan in 1983. With its high-quality sound and graphics, Famicom was a smash, selling 15.2 million consoles and more than 183 million game cartridges in Japan alone. Meanwhile, in 1983 and 1984, the US home game market crashed, sending pioneer Atari up in flames. Nintendo persevered, successfully launching Famicom in the US in 1986 as the Nintendo Entertainment System (NES).

To prevent a barrage of independently produced, low-quality software (which had contributed to Atari's demise), Nintendo established stringent licensing policies for its software developers. Licensees were required to have approval of every game design, buy the blank cartridges from the company, agree not to make the game for any of Nintendo's competitors, and pay Nintendo royalties for the honor of developing a game.

As the market became saturated, Nintendo sought new products, releasing Game Boy in 1989 and the Super Family Computer game system (Super NES in the US) in 1991. The company broke with tradition in 1994 by making design alliances with companies like Silicon Graphics. After creating a 32-bit product in 1995, Nintendo launched the much-touted N64 game system in 1996. It also teamed with Microsoft and Nomura Research Institute on a satellite-delivered Internet system for Japan. Price wars between the top contenders continued in the US and Japan.

In 1998 Nintendo released Pokemon, which involves trading and training virtual monsters (it had been popular in Japan since 1996), in the US. The company also launched the video game *The Legend of Zelda: Ocarina of Time*, which sold 2.5 million units in about six weeks. Nintendo issued 50 new games for 1998, compared to Sony's 131. Nintendo announced in 1999 that its next-generation game system, Dolphin (later renamed GameCube), would use IBM's PowerPC microprocessor and Matsushita's DVD players.

The company bought a 3% stake in convenience store operator LAWSON in early 2000 in hopes of using its online operations to sell video games. Nintendo also teamed with advertising agency Dentsu to form ND Cube, a joint company that develops game software for mobile phones and portable machines.

In September 2001 Nintendo launched its long-awaited GameCube console system (which retailed at $100 less than its console rivals, Sony's PlayStation 2 and Microsoft's XBox); the system debuted in North America in November. In addition, the company came out with Game Boy Advance, its newest handheld model with a bigger screen and faster chip.

Nintendo formed a business alliance with game software developer, Namco, in May 2002 for the development and sales of games for the GameCube platform. In October the European Union fined Nintendo $165 million for colluding with seven of its distributors to limit the cross-border flow of its products in a scam to raise prices.

In April 2003 the company cut its royalty rates (charged to outside game developers), in an effort to enhance its video game titles portfolio. Later in the year Nintendo bought a stake (about 3%) in game developer and toy maker Bandai, a move expected to solidify cooperation between the two companies in marketing game software.

EXECUTIVES

President: Satoru Iwata
Senior Managing Director; General Manager, Corporate Analysis and Administration Division: Yoshihiro Mori
Senior Managing Director; General Manager, Licensing Division: Shinji Hatano
Senior Managing Director; General Manager, Entertainment Analysis and Development Division: Shigeru Miyamoto
Senior Managing Director; General Manager, Integrated Research and Development Division: Genyo Takeda
Senior Managing Director; General Manager, Research and Engineering Division: Nobuo Nagai
Managing Director; General Manager, Finance and Information Systems Division: Masaharu Matsumoto
Managing Director; General Manager, General Affairs Division: Eiichi Suzuki
Director; General Manager, Tokyo Branch Office: Kazuo Kawahara
Director; President, Nintendo of America: Tatsumi Kimishima
Director; General Manager, Manufacturing Division: Takao Ohta
Director; General Manager, Personnel Department: Kaoru Takemura
Auditors: ChuoAoyama PricewaterhouseCoopers

LOCATIONS

HQ: Nintendo Co., Ltd.
11-1 Kamitoba hokotate-cho, Minami-ku, Kyoto 601-8501, Japan
Phone: +81-75-662-9600 **Fax:** +81-75-662-9620
US HQ: 4820 150th Ave. NE, Redmond, WA 98052
US Phone: 425-882-2040 **US Fax:** 425-882-3585
Web: www.nintendo.co.jp

Nintendo Co. has offices and plants in Japan and major subsidiaries in Australia, Canada, France, Germany, the Netherlands, Spain, and the US.

2005 Sales

	$ mil.	% of total
Americas	2,382	50
Japan	1,216	25
Europe	1,128	24
Other regions	62	1
Total	**4,788**	**100**

PRODUCTS/OPERATIONS

Game Consoles and Hardware

Game Boy
Game Boy Advance
Game Boy Player
GameCube
Nintendo DS
Super Nintendo Entertainment System (Super NES)
Wavebird

Selected Games

Donkey Kong series
Pokemon series
Star Wars Episode I Racer
Spider-Man series
Super Mario series
Yoshi series
Zelda series

COMPETITORS

Atari	Namco Bandai
Editis	Radica Games
Electronic Arts	SEGA
LucasArts	Sony
Microsoft	Take-Two
Midway Games	

HISTORICAL FINANCIALS

Company Type: Public

Income Statement

FYE: March 31

	REVENUE ($ mil.)	NET INCOME ($ mil.)	NET PROFIT MARGIN	EMPLOYEES
3/05	4,788	813	17.0%	—
3/04	4,869	314	6.5%	—
3/03	4,203	561	13.4%	2,977
3/02	4,183	803	19.2%	3,073
3/01	3,661	765	20.9%	2,937
3/00	5,279	531	10.1%	2,806
3/99	4,806	721	15.0%	2,463
3/98	4,015	629	15.7%	—
3/97	3,378	529	15.7%	—
3/96	3,302	558	16.9%	—
Annual Growth	**4.2%**	**4.3%**	**—**	**4.9%**

2005 Year-End Financials

Debt ratio: 0.1%
Return on equity: 9.6%
Cash ($ mil.): 7,371
Current ratio: 4.84
Long-term debt ($ mil.): 4

Net Income History Pink Sheets: NTDOY

Nippon Life Insurance

There's competition "nippon" at this company's heels. Nippon Life Insurance, also known as Nissay, is one of Japan's biggest life insurers (along with Dai-Ichi Mutual Life and Meiji Yasuda Life). A door-to-door sales corps peddles its plain-vanilla products, including individual and group life and annuity products, and the company has 11 million policyholders and 300,000 corporate customers. Deregulation has allowed the company to move into such areas as corporate lending. Other activities include real estate development and management and a variety of educational and philanthropic projects. The company's overseas activities traditionally focus on providing coverage to Japanese companies and citizens abroad.

As the Japanese economy struggles to recover, Nippon Life has grappled with declining individual sales as consumers cut back on expenditures. To attract customers, the company continues to broaden its sales channels, adding Internet and telephone sales and allowing customers to access loans directly through ATMs. The company has also started to target female customers more heavily as potential customers.

Since deregulation in the financial services industry has boosted competition, the company has expanded its offerings to include nursing/medical services and a 401(k)-like pension plan. Nippon Life has also partnered with such firms as Deutsche Bank and Putnam to offer investment trusts, investment advisory, and other services. Other business lines include property/casualty insurance (the company merged its Nissay General subsidiary with Dowa Fire & Marine) and information technology services for other insurers.

HISTORY

Nippon Life, known as Nissay, was a product of the modernization that began after US Commodore Perry opened Japan's ports to foreigners in 1854. Industry and trade were Japan's first focus, but financial infrastructure soon followed. The country's first insurer (Meiji Mutual) opened in 1881. In 1889 Osaka banker Sukesaburo Hirose founded Nippon Life as a stock company. It grew and opened branches in Tokyo (1890) and Kyushu (1895).

In the 20th century, the company developed a direct sales force and began lending directly to businesses. Lending remained the backbone of its asset strategy through most of the century. The insurance market in Japan grew quickly until the late 1920s but had already slowed by the eve of the Depression.

After WWII the company reorganized as a mutual and began mobilizing an army of women to build its sales of installment-premium, basic life policies. In 1962 the company began automating its systems and established operations in the US (1972) and UK (1981).

As interest rates rose in the wake of oil price hikes in the 1970s, the company began offering term life and annuities and slowly moved to diversify its asset holdings from mostly government bonds (whose yields declined as rates rose) to stocks. This movement accelerated in the 1980s, as the businesses that traditionally borrowed from Nippon Life turned directly to capital markets to raise money through debt issues. Seeking to replace its shrinking lending business, the company began investing in US real estate and businesses whose values rose in the mid-1980s. The company reached its zenith in 1987; it owned about 3% of all the stocks on the Tokyo Exchange, held more real estate than Mitsubishi's real estate units, and had bought 13% of US brokerage Shearson Lehman from American Express.

By the end of the year, thanks to the US stock market crash, the value of the Shearson investment had fallen 40%. But the company felt confident enough of its importance as the world's largest insurance company (by assets) to crow its intentions to strong-arm Japan's Ministry of Finance into letting it diversify into trust and securities operations.

Then its bubble burst. In 1989 real estate crashed, and the stock market lost more than half its value. Japan's economy failed to improve, and Nippon Life was left struggling with nonperforming loans and assets whose value had declined. The company suffered further from policy cancellations and from the Ministry of Finance's focus on buoying banks. In 1997 the ministry asked Nippon Life to convert its subordinated debt from Nippon Credit Bank (now Aozora Bank) to stock. That year Nippon Life formed an alliance with Marsh & McLennan's Putnam Investments subsidiary to help manage its assets; the relationship deepened in 1998 when they began developing investment trust products.

The next year Nippon Life faced a shareholder lawsuit over its involvement in the collapse of Nippon Credit Bank; the company claims the Ministry of Finance tricked it into bailing out the bank, even though it was beyond rescue. In 2001 the company merged its Nissay General subsidiary with Dowa Fire & Marine, creating nonlife insurer Nissay Dowa.

EXECUTIVES

Chairman: Ikuo Uno, age 70
Vice Chairman: Mitsuhiro Ishibashi, age 63
President: Kunie Okamoto, age 61
EVP: Shingo Okada, age 60
EVP: Eitaro Waki, age 60
Senior Managing Director: Mitsutoshi Kimura, age 63
Senior Managing Director: Takao Arai, age 57
Managing Director: Takashi Matsukubo, age 58
Managing Director: Takashi Minagawa, age 58
Managing Director: Tetsuro Taki, age 56
Managing Director: Sadao Kato, age 56
Managing Director: Keizo Tsutsui, age 57
Managing Director: Shunsuke Wada, age 57
Managing Director: Takeshi Asahara
Managing Director: Kiyoshi Ujihara
Managing Director: Chiaki Hamaguchi
Managing Director: Akito Kuwabara
Auditors: ChuoAoyama PricewaterhouseCoopers

LOCATIONS

HQ: Nippon Life Insurance Company
(Nippon Seimei Hoken Kabushiki Kaisha)
3-5-12, Imabashi, Chuo-ku, Osaka 541-8501, Japan
Phone: +81-6-6209-5525   **Fax:** +81-3-5510-7340
US HQ: Nippon Life Insurance Company of America,
512 5th Ave., New York, NY 10175
US Phone: 212-682-3000   **US Fax:** 212-682-3002
Web: www.nissay.co.jp

Nippon Life has operations in China, Germany, Japan, the Philippines, Singapore, Thailand, the UK, and the US.

PRODUCTS/OPERATIONS

2005 Sales

	% of total
Premiums	76
Investment income	20
Other	4
Total	**100**

Selected Subsidiaries and Affiliates

Nippon Life Insurance Company of America (97%, US)
Nippon Life Insurance Company of the Philippines, Inc. (50%)
Nissay Asset Management Corporation (90%)
Nissay Capital Co., Ltd.
Nissay Card Service Co., Ltd. (95%)
Nissay Computer Co., Ltd. (45%)
Nissay Dowa General Insurance Co., Ltd. (36%)
Nissay Guarantee Corporation (15%)
Nissay Information Technology Co., Ltd. (75%)
Nissay Leasing Co., Ltd. (51%)
Nissay-SVA Life Insurance Co., Ltd. (50%)
NLI Commercial Mortgage Fund, LLC (US)
NLI Properties Central, Inc. (US)
NLI Properties East, Inc. (US)
NLI Properties West, Inc. (US)

COMPETITORS

Aflac	Gibraltar Life Insurance
Allianz	ING
Asahi Mutual Life	Meiji Yasuda Life
AXA Life Insurance	Millea Holdings
Daido Life	Mitsui Life
Dai-ichi Mutual Life	Sumitomo Life
Fukoku Mutual	Taiyo Life

HISTORICAL FINANCIALS

Company Type: Mutual company

Income Statement

	ASSETS ($ mil.)	NET INCOME ($ mil.)	INCOME AS % OF ASSETS	FYE: March 31 EMPLOYEES
3/05	434,942	1,885	0.4%	67,116
3/04	430,631	1,880	0.4%	70,073
3/03	366,426	943	0.3%	72,784
3/02	343,097	2,100	0.6%	72,895
3/01	350,340	2,367	0.7%	60,000
3/00	411,477	3,594	0.9%	60,000
3/99	360,772	888	0.2%	—
3/98	317,199	1,954	0.6%	75,851
3/97	323,424	2,547	0.8%	86,695
3/96	363,895	3,023	0.8%	—
Annual Growth	**2.0%**	**(5.1%)**	**—**	**(3.1%)**

2005 Year-End Financials

Equity as % of assets: 7.2%
Return on assets: 0.4%
Return on equity: 6.2%
Long-term debt ($ mil.): 3,303
Sales ($ mil.): 60,477

Net Income History

Nippon Steel

When it comes to steel, Nippon Steel rates as Japan's heavy lifter. The company manufactures steel plates, sheets, pipes, and tubes, as well as specialty, processed, and fabricated steel products. Nippon Steel's annual crude steel output is roughly 30 million tons. The company's operations include engineering, construction, chemicals, nonferrous metals, ceramics, electronics, information and communications, and urban development. Nippon Steel also provides energy, finance, and insurance services. With sales and profits down because of a weak Japanese economy and antidumping petitions in the US, Nippon Steel plans to place more emphasis on its engineering and energy businesses.

The company has experienced steady growth in its overall business due to an increase in capital investments and exports primarily to East Asia and more specifically, China. Overseas demand in the automotive, industrial machinery, and shipbuilding sectors boosted the company's financial position. China's robust economy and demand for steel also contributed to Nippon's improved financial position.

The company plans to keep steel operations as its core business and has formed separate cooperative alliances with steel giants POSCO (South Korea) and Nippon Metal Industry (Japan). It also plans to expand its engineering and energy businesses.

The company has announced that it will form an alliance with Kobe Steel to cut costs by joining the procurement of raw materials and the use of storage facilities. Hoping to strengthen its environment-related operations overseas, Nippon Steel has plans with POSCO in such areas as plastic recycling, water treatment, and soil purification. Nippon Steel has been contracted by POSCO Engineering & Construction, (POSCO's engineering subsidiary), to provide gasified melting furnaces, which reduces dioxin emissions.

The company signed an agreement with Baosteel to produce steel sheets for cars made in China's burgeoning vehicle market.

HISTORY

As Japan prepared for war, the government in 1934 merged Yawata Works, its largest steel producer, and other Japanese steelmakers into one giant company — Japan Iron & Steel. During postwar occupation, Japan Iron & Steel was ordered to dissolve. Yawata Iron & Steel and Fuji Iron & Steel emerged from the dissolution, and with Western assistance the Japanese steel industry recovered from the war years. In the late 1960s Fuji Steel bought Tokai Iron & Steel (1967), and

Yawata Steel took over Yawata Steel Tube Company (1968).

Yawata and Fuji merged in 1970 and became Nippon Steel, the world's largest steelmaker. In the 1970s the Japanese steel industry was criticized in the US; American competitors complained that Japan was "dumping" low-cost exports. Meanwhile, Nippon Steel aggressively courted China.

The company diversified in the mid-1980s to wean itself from dependence on steel. It created a New Materials unit in 1984, retraining "redundant" steelworkers to make silicon wafers and forming an Electronics Division in 1986. Nippon Steel began joint ventures with IBM Japan (small computers and software), Hitachi (office workstations), and C. Itoh (information systems for small and midsize companies) in 1988 as increased steel demand for construction and cars in Japan's "bubble economy" took the company to new heights.

In an atmosphere of economic optimism, the company spent more than four times the expected expense to build an amusement park capable of competing with Tokyo Disneyland. The company plowed ahead, spending more than ¥15 billion on the park. Space World amusement park opened on the island of Kyushu in 1990. The company's bubble burst that year.

In response, Nippon Steel cut costs and intensified its diversification efforts by targeting electronics, information and telecommunications, new materials, and chemicals markets. Seeking to remake its steel operations, the company began a drastic, phased restructuring in 1993 that included a step most Japanese companies try to avoid — cutting personnel. A semiconductor division was organized that year as part of the company's diversification strategy.

Upgrading its steel operations, Nippon Steel and partner Mitsubishi in 1996 introduced the world's first mass-production method for making hot-rolled steel sheet directly from smelted stainless steel. Profits were hurt that year by a loss-making project in the information and communications segment and by a steep decline in computer memory-chip prices.

The company began operation of a Chinese steelmaking joint venture, Guangzhou Pacific Tinplate, in 1997. The next year its Singapore-based joint venture with Hitachi, Ltd., began mass-producing computer memory chips in hopes of stemming semiconductor losses. But falling prices convinced Nippon Steel to get out of the memory chip business and in 1999 it sold its semiconductor subsidiary to South Korea's United Microelectronics.

That year the US imposed antidumping duties on the company's steel products. The next year Nippon Steel agreed to form a strategic alliance with South Korea-based Pohang Iron and Steel (POSCO), at that time the world's #1 steel maker. The deal calls for the exploration of joint ventures, shared research, and joint procurement, as well as increased equity stakes in each other (at 2%-3%). Also in 2000 Nippon Steel agreed to provide Sumitomo Metal Industries and Nisshin Steel Co. with stainless steel products.

Early in 2001 Nippon Steel formed a cooperative alliance — focused on automotive sheet products — with French steel giant Usinor (now a part of Arcelor). At the end of the year, Nippon Steel decided to form an alliance with Kobe Steel to pare down costs and share in distribution and production facilities. In 2002 the company continued its series of comprehensive alliances by forming alliances with Japanese steelmaker Nippon Metal Industry to exchange its semi-finished stainless steel technologies and with POSCO to build environment-related businesses.

The company reported a huge loss of 51.69 billion for fiscal 2003 due to securities valuation losses and group restructuring charges. The steelmaker expects to recover profitability in the current fiscal year, however, through cutting costs and steel price increases. In 2004 Nippon Steel formed a joint venture with Baoshan Iron & Steel and Arcelor to manufacture high-grade automotive steel sheets and sold primarily to China.

EXECUTIVES

Chairman and Representative Director: Akira Chihara, age 70
President, CEO, and Representative Director: Akio Mimura, age 65
EVP and Representative Director: Takashi Hirao, age 60
EVP and Representative Director: Seiki Miyamoto
EVP and Representative Director: Yasushi Sawada, age 62
EVP and Representative Director: Jujiro Yagi, age 63
EVP and Representative Director: Toshio Yonezawa, age 63
Managing Director: Hideki Furuno, age 61
Managing Director: Nobuyoshi Fujiwara, age 60
Managing Director: Makoto Haya, age 60
Managing Director: Mitsuo Kitagawa, age 59
Managing Director: Shoji Muneoka, age 59
Managing Director: Kazuo Nagahiro, age 60
Managing Director: Koichi Nakamura, age 59
Managing Director: Toshio Ochiai, age 62
Managing Director: Naoki Okumura, age 60
Managing Director: Hideaki Sekizawa, age 60
Managing Director: Hiroshi Shima, age 58
Senior Corporate Auditor: Tetsuo Seki, age 67
Auditors: ChuoAoyama Audit Corporation

LOCATIONS

HQ: Nippon Steel Corporation
(Shin Nippon Seitetsu Kabushiki Kaisha)
6-3 Otemachi 2-chome, Chiyoda-ku,
Tokyo 100-8071, Japan
Phone: +81-3-3242-4111　　**Fax:** +81-3-3275-5607
US HQ: 10 E. 50th St., 29th Fl., New York, NY 10022
US Phone: 212-486-7150　　**US Fax:** 212-593-3049
Web: www.nsc.co.jp

Nippon Steel has operations in the Americas, Asia, Australia, and Europe. Its principal subsidiaries are in Australia, Brazil, China, Germany, Singapore, Thailand, the UK, and the US.

PRODUCTS/OPERATIONS

2005 Sales

	% of total
Steelmaking & steel fabrication	74
Chemicals & nonferrous materials	9
Engineering & construction	9
Systems solutions	4
Urban development	2
Other	2
Total	**100**

Selected Products and Services

Steelmaking and Steel Fabrication
　Fabricated and processed steels
　Pig iron and ingots
　Pipes and tubes
　Plates and sheets
　Sections
　Specialty sheets

Chemicals, Nonferrous Metals, and Ceramics
　Aluminum products
　Ammonium sulfate
　Cement
　Ceramic products
　Coal tar
　Coke
　Ferrite
　Metallic foils
　Semiconductor bonding wire
　Silicon wafers
　Slag products
　Titanium products
　Transformers

Engineering and Construction
　Building construction
　Civil engineering
　Marine construction
　Plant and machinery
　Technical cooperation

Urban Development
　Condominiums
　Theme parks

Electronics, Information/Communications, and LSIs
　Communications services
　Computers and equipment
　Data processing
　Systems development and integration

Other Operations
　Services
　　Energy services
　　Financial services
　　Insurance services
　Transportation
　　Loading and unloading
　　Marine and land transportation
　　Warehousing

COMPETITORS

Arcelor	Mitsubishi Corporation
Bechtel	News Corp.
BlueScope Steel	POSCO
Corus Group	Samsung
Fluor	ThyssenKrupp
Hitachi	TUI
Ito-Yokado	United States Steel
JFE Holdings	Vale do Rio Doce
Kobe Steel	Yamato Kogyo
Marubeni	

HISTORICAL FINANCIALS

Company Type: Public

Income Statement

FYE: March 31

	REVENUE ($ mil.)	NET INCOME ($ mil.)	NET PROFIT MARGIN	EMPLOYEES
3/05	31,514	2,051	6.5%	46,451
3/04	27,696	393	1.4%	46,233
3/03	22,940	(431)	—	49,400
3/02	19,461	(214)	—	50,463
3/01	21,772	210	1.0%	52,247
3/00	25,407	106	0.4%	40,000
3/99	23,167	96	0.4%	35,000
3/98	23,120	45	0.2%	35,500
3/97	24,729	28	0.1%	—
3/96	27,550	509	1.8%	—
Annual Growth	**1.5%**	**16.8%**	**—**	**3.9%**

2005 Year-End Financials

Debt ratio: 69.0%
Return on equity: 20.6%
Cash ($ mil.): 1,158

Current ratio: 0.86
Long-term debt ($ mil.): 7,629

Net Income History Exchange: Tokyo

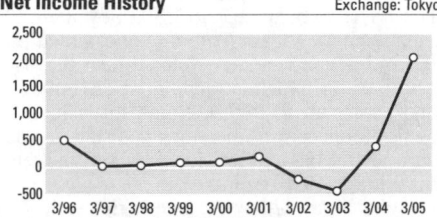

Nissan Motor

Nissan Motor, Japan's #2 auto manufacturer after Toyota and just ahead of Honda, is enjoying one of the car industry's most dramatic turnarounds in recent memory. Nissan's models include Maxima and Sentra cars, Altima and Infiniti upscale sedans, Frontier pickups, the 350Z sports car, and Xterra and Pathfinder SUVs. In 1999 French automaker Renault took a 37% stake in Nissan, and installed president and CEO Carlos Ghosn (nicknamed "Le Cost Killer" based on his talent for turning red ink black) who has since returned the company to profitability. Renault now owns almost 45% of Nissan.

Under the watchful eye of Ghosn, Nissan has gone from a doubtful future to a corporate success story in just a few years. The company announced its Nissan Revival Plan (NRP) in 1999. The plan called for the closing of inefficient factories, workforce reductions, curbing purchasing costs, sharing operations with Renault, and introducing new products. By 2001 Nissan was again making a profit — one year earlier than the NRP predicted. Not satisfied with this, Nissan then launched a three-year business scheme called Nissan 180. This plan aimed to: grow annual sales by 1 million units, generate an 8% operating profit margin, and eliminate automotive debt.

Nissan has made good on all these goals. In fact, the company's operating margin has exceeded 10% every year since the plan was initiated (making it the envy of most of the world's carmakers). Nissan not only managed to erase automotive debt, it now has cash reserves of about $1.65 billion.

Nissan has a number of new initiatives, including increasing its presence in emerging markets such as China, Russia, and India; further development of its light commercial vehicle business, and globalization of its engineering, production, and purchasing operations.

HISTORY

In 1911 US-trained Hashimoto Masujiro established Tokyo-based Kwaishinsha Motor Car Works to repair, import, and make cars. Kwaishinsha made its first car, sporting its DAT ("fast rabbit" in Japanese) logo, in 1913. Renamed DAT Motors in 1925 and suffering from a strong domestic preference for American cars, the company consolidated with ailing Jitsuyo Motors in 1926. DAT introduced the son of DAT in 1931 — the Datsun minicar ("son" means "damage or loss" in Japanese, hence the spelling change).

Tobata Casting (cast iron and auto parts) bought Datsun's production facilities in 1933. Tobata's Yoshisuke Aikawa believed there was a niche for small cars, and the car operations were spun off as Nissan Motors that year.

During WWII the Japanese government limited Nissan's production to trucks and airplane engines; Nissan survived postwar occupation, in part, due to business with the US Army. The company went public in 1951 and signed a licensing agreement the next year with Austin Motor (UK), which put it back in the car business. A 40% import tax allowed Nissan to compete in Japan even though it had higher costs than those of foreign carmakers.

Nissan entered the US market in 1958 with the model 211, using the Datsun name; it established Nissan Motor Corporation in Los Angeles in 1960. Exports rose as factory automation led to higher quality and lower costs. In the 1970s Nissan expanded exports of fuel-efficient cars such as the Datsun B210. The company became the leading US car importer in 1975.

The company's name change in the US from Datsun to Nissan during the 1980s confused customers and took six years to complete. In 1986 Nissan became the first major Japanese carmaker to build its products in Europe. It launched its high-end Infiniti line in the US in 1989.

Nissan and Japanese telecom firm DDI Corporation set up cellular phone operations in 1992. Japan's recession resulted in a $450 million loss the next year. The company cut costs in 1993 and sold $200 million in real-estate holdings in 1994.

Nissan suffered its fourth straight year of losses, posting an $834 million loss for 1996. Fiscal 1997 brought profits for Nissan — its first since 1992 — in part the result of cost-cutting moves, sales to countries with currencies stronger than the yen, and the launching of new models. In 1998 Nissan made plans to cut production in Japan by 15% over five years, and it received an $827 million loan from the government-owned Japan Development Bank to restructure its debt.

Suffering under an estimated $30 billion in debt in 1999, Nissan invited major carmakers to buy into the company. Renault took a 37% stake and a 15% stake (later increased to 23%) in affiliate Nissan Diesel Motor for $5.4 billion. The stake gave Renault veto power and enabled it to install its chief cost-cutter, Carlos Ghosn, as chief operating officer. Ghosn began plans to slash the number of suppliers, close five plants, and cut its workforce by 14% by 2002. Meanwhile, Nissan sold its interests in nine mobile-phone companies and its powder metallurgy business.

In 2000 Nissan sold its stake in Fuji Heavy Industries. That year Ghosn became president of Nissan; Nissan's former president, Yoshikazu Hanawa, remained as CEO and chairman. Nissan also announced that it was developing a full-sized truck for the US market and that it and Renault were combining their European sales and marketing operations. Late in the year the company announced plans to build a $930 million manufacturing plant in the US.

Ghosn was named CEO (in addition to president) in 2001. Later in 2001 Nissan announced it would take a 15% stake in Renault while the French carmaker would increase its stake in Nissan to 44%. These steps, along with the French government's decision to reduce its interest in Renault from 44% to 25%, are aimed at further strengthening the bond between the two companies. In 2002 Nissan and Renault completed their planned equity swap.

The following year Nissan rolled out the most dramatic new lineup of vehicles it had introduced in years. The company debuted the Murano urban SUV, the full-size Titan pickup, and the full-size Armada SUV.

In mid-2005 Nissan announced that it had selected its assembly plant in Tennessee for production of its first hybrid vehicle.

EXECUTIVES

Co-Chairman, President, CEO, Representative Board Member, and Member of the Executive Committee; President and CEO, Nissan North America: Carlos Ghosn, age 50
Co-Chairman, EVP, Administration for Affiliated Companies, External and Government Affairs, Intellectual Asset Management, Industrial Machinery, and Marine, Representative Board Member, and Member of the Executive Committee: Itaru Koeda, age 63
Vice Chairman, External and Government Affairs and Intellectual Asset Management Office: Takeshi Isayama
COO; Japan Operations, General Overseas Markets Operations, China Operations, Global Marketing and Sales, Global Aftersales and Conversion Business, Corporate Quality Assurance and Customer Service, Human Resources, and Treasuery, Representative Director and Member of the Executive Committee: Toshiyuki Shiga
EVP, Design, Corporate Planning, Product Planning, Market Intelligence, and LVC Bussiness, Board Member and Member of the Executive Committee: Carlos Tavares
SVP, Alliance Coordination Office, Security Office, Legal Department, Organization Development, Process Re-Engineering, and Secretary; CEO and COO, Global Motorsports: Bernard Rey
SVP, General Overseas Markets Marketing and Sales: Mark C. McNabb
SVP, Global Controller, and Member of the Executive Committee: Alain-Pierre Raynaud
SVP, Global Sales Management Department, Marketing and Sales Brand Management Office, Global Marketing Department, and Global Infiniti Support Department: Steven Wilhite
SVP, Human Resources Department and Diversity Development Office: Hitoshi Kawaguchi
Auditors: Shin Nihon & Co.

LOCATIONS

HQ: Nissan Motor Co., Ltd.
(Nissan Jidosha Kabushiki Kaisha)
17-1, Ginza 6-chome, Chuo-ku,
Tokyo 104-8023, Japan
Phone: +81-3-3543-5523   **Fax:** +81-3-5565-2228
US HQ: 18501 S. Figueroa St., Gardena, CA 90248
US Phone: 310-771-5631   **US Fax:** 310-516-7967
Web: www.nissan-global.com

Nissan Motor Co. has major manufacturing subsidiaries in China, France, Japan, Mexico, Spain, Taiwan, Thailand, the UK, and the US.

2005 Sales

	$ mil.	% of total
North America	34,827	43
Japan	23,894	30
Europe	11,720	15
Other regions	9,711	12
Total	**80,152**	**100**

PRODUCTS/OPERATIONS

2005 Sales

	$ mil.	% of total
Automobiles	76,428	95
Financing	3,724	5
Total	**80,152**	**100**

HISTORICAL FINANCIALS

Company Type: Public

Income Statement

FYE: March 31

	REVENUE ($ mil.)	NET INCOME ($ mil.)	NET PROFIT MARGIN	EMPLOYEES
3/05	80,152	4,788	6.0%	183,607
3/04	70,087	4,752	6.8%	123,748
3/03	56,905	4,126	7.3%	127,625
3/02	46,588	2,799	6.0%	125,099
3/01	49,110	2,670	5.4%	133,833
3/00	56,388	(6,456)	—	136,397
3/99	54,380	(229)	—	143,681
3/98	49,732	(106)	—	137,201
3/97	53,701	627	1.2%	135,331
3/96	56,973	(834)	—	139,856
Annual Growth	3.9%	—		3.1%

2005 Year-End Financials

Debt ratio: 79.6%
Return on equity: 22.7%
Cash ($ mil.): 2,708
Current ratio: 1.29
Long-term debt ($ mil.): 18,347

No. of shares (mil.): 2,190
Dividends
  Yield: 0.0%
  Payout: —
Market value ($ mil.): 44,824

Stock History

NASDAQ (SC): NSANY

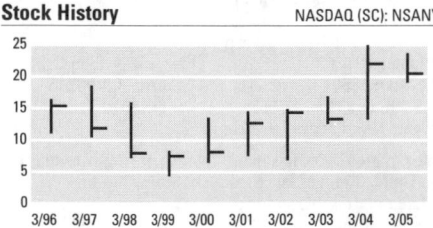

	STOCK PRICE ($) FY Close	P/E High/Low		PER SHARE ($) Earnings	Dividends	Book Value
3/05	20.47	10	8	2.32	0.00	10.52
3/04	22.01	11	6	2.28	0.29	8.68
3/03	13.31	9	7	1.96	0.20	6.75
3/02	14.36	11	5	1.40	0.11	5.40
3/01	12.69	11	6	1.34	0.00	3.89
3/00	8.13	—	—	(3.40)	0.00	4.47
3/99	7.50	—	—	(0.18)	0.00	8.25
3/98	7.94	—	—	(0.08)	0.00	7.73
3/97	11.88	74	43	0.25	0.11	8.70
3/96	15.38	—	—	(0.66)	0.12	10.19
Annual Growth	3.2%	—	—	—	—	0.4%

Nokia

Wireless wizard Nokia has cast a spell on the mobile phone market. The company is the world's #1 maker of cell phones (ahead of such rivals as Motorola, Siemens, and Samsung among others). Nokia is also aiming for the top of the nascent mobile Internet market. The company's products are divided primarily between four divisions: mobile phones (wireless voice and data devices for personal and business uses), multimedia (set-top boxes, home satellite systems, and mobile gaming devices), networks (wireless switching and transmission equipment used in carrier networks), and enterprise solutions (wireless systems for businesses). The company's BlueRun Ventures division invests in technology-related startups.

One of Europe's largest companies by market capitalization, Nokia has set its sights on becoming the leader in third generation (3G) wireless network equipment. The company has found itself the supplier to half of the world's commercial 3G networks. Contracts such as these have helped Nokia gain momentum in the race to the top of the wireless network infrastructure market led by Ericsson.

Nokia's historically robust mobile phone unit also has introduced new products across a range of market niches and managed to pick up market share in the process; the company commands nearly 40% of the global cell phone market. Nokia rolled out new business and consumer models with color screens worldwide as well as delivering a unit capable of English and Chinese text recognition to be sold by vendors in China. The company also introduced the N-Gage mobile gaming device.

HISTORY

Nokia got its start in 1865 when engineer Fredrik Idestam established a mill to manufacture pulp and paper on the Nokia River in Finland. Although Nokia flourished within Finland, the company was not well known to the rest of the world until it attempted to become a regional conglomerate in the early 1960s. French computer firm Machines Bull selected Nokia as its Finnish agent in 1962, and Nokia began researching radio transmission technology. In 1967, with the encouragement of Finland's government, Nokia merged with Finnish Rubber Works (a maker of tires and rubber footwear, formed in 1898) and Finnish Cable Works (a cable and electronics manufacturer formed in 1912) to form Nokia Corporation.

The oil crisis of 1973 created severe inflation and a large trade deficit for Finland. Nokia reassessed its heavy reliance on Soviet trade and shifted its focus to consumer and business electronics. Nokia's basic industries — paper, chemicals, electricity, and machinery — were modernized and expanded into robotics, fiber optics, and high-grade tissues.

The company acquired a 51% interest in the state-owned Finnish telecom company in 1981 and named it Telenokia. The next year Nokia designed and installed (in Finland) the first European digital telephone system. Also in 1982 Nokia acquired interests in Salora, Scandinavia's largest maker of color televisions, and Luxor, the Swedish state-owned electronics and computer firm.

Nokia acquired control of Sahkoliikkeiden, Finland's largest electrical wholesaler, in 1986. It then created the largest information technol-ogy (IT) group in Scandinavia, Nokia Data, by purchasing Ericsson's Data Division in 1988. Sales soared, but profits plunged because of stiff price competition in consumer electronics.

To raise cash, the company sold Nokia Data to IT services company ICL in 1991 and bought UK mobile phone maker Technophone, which had been #2 in Europe, after Nokia. Under the leadership of Jorma Ollila (appointed CEO in 1992 and chairman in 1999), Nokia intensified its focus on telecommunications and sold its non-core power (1994), televisions, and tire and cable machinery (1995) units.

It also began selling digital phones at the end of 1993. The company expected to sell 400,000; it shipped 20 million in 1995. The company rode the phones' success to a billion-dollar profit in 1997.

Nokia sold more than 40 million mobile phones in 1998 to surpass Motorola and became the world's #1 mobile phone company. Extending its push into Internet capability, Nokia that year bought several small companies that develop e-commerce and telephony technologies. In 1999 Nokia penned deals to put its wireless application protocol (WAP) software into Hewlett-Packard's and IBM's network servers.

The company, which also unveiled several WAP-enabled phones designed to access the Internet, widened its lead as the world's top seller of mobile phones, and made several acquisitions to strengthen its Internet protocol networks business.

Although Nokia was leaps and bounds ahead of its rivals with digital phones and dominated the European global system for mobile communications (GSM) market, it lagged in the US market, where many big carriers adopted QUALCOMM's CDMA standard. Nokia in 2000 began to cover the bases for the third generation by offering products to bridge the gap between generations.

In 2001 Nokia added Internet security appliances to its product line-up with the acquisition of Ramp Networks. Later that year, as part of an initiative to build up its line of network infrastructure products, the company bought US-based router maker Amber Networks. Nokia began working with other equipment makers and wireless service providers that year to develop a global standard for 3G phone software.

In an effort to jumpstart slowing handset sales as the cell phone market in the West and Japan flirted with saturation, Nokia in 2003 teamed with other phone makers and wireless service providers to develop a common global standard for 3G phone software. The effort was also backed by Motorola, Sony Ericsson, and Japan's NTT DoCoMo. After inking several new deals in Europe and Asia, Nokia was a supplier to half of the world's commercial 3G networks by the end of that year by the end of 2003.

The mobile phone unit introduced new products in 2003 across a range of market niches and the company rolled out new business and consumer models and introduced a unit capable of English and Chinese text recognition to be sold by vendors in China. The company also introduced the N-Gage mobile gaming device.

In 2004 the company expanded its focus beyond the traditional mobile phones and networks and reorganized its business units.

EXECUTIVES

Chairman and CEO: Jorma Ollila, age 55, $4,653,230 pay
Vice Chairman: Paul J. Collins, age 68
President and COO: Olli-Pekka Kallasvuo, age 52, $1,247,026 pay (prior to promotion)

EVP and General Manager, Networks:
Simon Beresford-Wylie, age 47
EVP; General Manager, Multimedia: Anssi Vanjoki,
age 49
EVP, Customer and Market Operations:
Robert Andersson, age 45
SVP and CFO: Richard A. Simonson, age 47
SVP and Chief Strategy Officer: Tero Ojanperä, age 39
SVP, CTO, and Head of Technology Platforms:
Pertti Korhonen, age 44
SVP, Core Networks, Networks: Juha Äkräs
SVP; General Manager, Enterprise Solutions:
Mary T. McDowell, age 41
SVP, Human Resources: Hallstein Moerk, age 52
SVP and Technology Advisor: Yrjö Neuvo, age 62
Head of Mobile Phones Business Group: Kai Öistämö,
age 41
**SVP, Global Sales and Marketing, Nokia Enterprise
Solutions:** Greg Shortell
VP, Investor Relations: Ulla James
VP, Communications: Arja Suominen
**VP, External Affairs, Nokia Corporate Communications,
Americas:** William Plummer
President, Nokia Inc.: Kari-Pekka (K-P) Wilska
Director, Investor Relations, US: Bill Seymour
Auditors: SVH Pricewaterhouse Coopers Oy

LOCATIONS

HQ: Nokia Corporation
Keilalahdentie 4, FIN-00045 Espoo, Finland
Phone: +358-7180-08000   **Fax:** +358-7180-38226
US HQ: 6000 Connection Dr., Irving, TX 75039
US Phone: 972-894-5000   **US Fax:** 972-894-5050
Web: www.nokia.com

Nokia sells its products in more than 130 countries.
The company has manufacturing plants in 10 countries
and research and development centers in 15 countries.

2004 Sales

	$ mil.	% of total
US	4,627	12
China	3,603	9
UK	3,063	8
Germany	2,343	6
Finland	475	1
Other countries	25,534	64
Total	**39,645**	**100**

PRODUCTS/OPERATIONS

2004 Sales

	$ mil.	% of total
Mobile phones	24,952	63
Networks	8,713	22
Multimedia	4,753	12
Enterprise solutions	1,188	3
Other	39	—
Total	**39,645**	**100**

Selected Operations

Mobile phones
Analog mobile cellular phones
Digital mobile cellular phones
Handheld telephone/personal organizers
Phone accessories (batteries, cases, chargers)
Networks
Base station site products
Corporate network products
Base stations
Messaging platforms
Wireless local-area network (LAN) systems
Wireless access systems
Fault-tolerant network routers
Fixed network switching systems
Internet protocol (IP) network switching systems
Microwave radios
Mobile radio systems
Network, messaging, and multimedia services and
software
Radio base station controllers
Radio network controllers
Wireless network nodes, gateways,
switches, and servers

Multimedia (services for advanced mobile devices)
Convergence products
Enhancements
Entertainment
Imaging
Enterprise solutions
Business-optimized mobile services

COMPETITORS

Alcatel	Pace Micro
Cisco Systems	Panasonic Mobile
ECI Telecom	Communications
Ericsson	Philips Electronics
Fujitsu	Pioneer
GE	QUALCOMM
Harris Corp.	Robert Bosch
Kyocera	SAFRAN
Lucent	Samsung
Marconi	Samsung Electronics
Microsoft	SANYO
Mitsubishi Electric	Scientific-Atlanta
Motorola	Siemens
NEC	Sony Ericsson Mobile
Nortel Networks	Tellabs
Oki Electric	Toshiba
Openwave Systems	

HISTORICAL FINANCIALS

Company Type: Public

Income Statement

FYE: December 31

	REVENUE ($ mil.)	NET INCOME ($ mil.)	NET PROFIT MARGIN	EMPLOYEES
12/04	39,645	4,344	11.0%	55,505
12/03	37,031	4,516	12.2%	51,359
12/02	31,526	3,551	11.3%	51,748
12/01	27,801	1,961	7.1%	53,849
12/00	28,608	3,709	13.0%	60,000
12/99	19,954	2,601	13.0%	51,177
12/98	15,553	2,043	13.1%	44,543
12/97	9,702	1,154	11.9%	36,647
12/96	8,446	745	8.8%	31,723
12/95	8,400	509	6.1%	31,948
Annual Growth	**18.8%**	**26.9%**	**—**	**6.3%**

2004 Year-End Financials

Debt ratio: 0.1%
Return on equity: 22.7%
Cash ($ mil.): 1,477
Current ratio: 2.45
Long-term debt ($ mil.): 26

No. of shares (mil.): 4,664
Dividends
Yield: 2.4%
Payout: 40.0%
Market value ($ mil.): 73,081

Stock History

NYSE: NOK

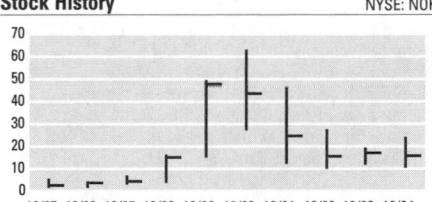

	STOCK PRICE ($) FY Close	P/E High/Low		PER SHARE ($) Earnings	Dividends	Book Value
12/04	15.67	25	11	0.95	0.38	4.14
12/03	17.00	20	13	0.94	0.30	3.97
12/02	15.50	36	14	0.75	0.24	3.13
12/01	24.53	111	31	0.41	0.25	2.30
12/00	43.50	81	36	0.77	0.20	2.17
12/99	47.77	89	28	0.55	0.12	1.60
12/98	15.05	37	10	0.44	0.00	1.23
12/97	4.34	25	13	0.26	0.00	0.83
12/96	3.60	2	1	2.31	0.04	0.71
12/95	2.44	54	22	0.12	0.00	0.66
Annual Growth	**23.0%**	**—**	**—**	**25.8%**	**—**	**22.7%**

Nomura Holdings

Nomura Holdings is the parent company of Nomura Securities, Japan's #1 brokerage house ahead of Daiwa Securities and Nikko Cordial. Nomura Securities offers a variety of retail and institutional brokerage, corporate and governmental underwriting, asset management, and mergers and acquisitions services. Its primary business is individual and corporate trading services in its home market. Increased competition and deregulation have caused sagging commissions, but the firm has countered by trying to bolster its M&A business. Nomura Securities International is the company's US trading and investment banking unit.

Rocked by recession in Asia and stung by bribery and racketeering scandals, Nomura buckled down, reorganized, and is slowly emerging from its gloom. Although primarily focused on domestic retail services, the company also offers fixed income and equity trading, investment banking, merchant banking, and asset management, with operations in more than 20 countries.

Deregulation of Japanese financial markets has created new competition, and the firm has watched commissions — traditionally its prime source of revenues — tumble. In response to decreased M&A activity and the anemic Japanese economy, Nomura made significant organizational changes. Its business now falls into three segments: Domestic Retail (retail brokerage); Global Wholesale (equity and fixed income trading, investment banking, and merchant banking); and Asset Management (trusts and investment advice). In addition to trying to boost its M&A-associated stock and securities transactions, the company has tried to become more involved in the management of its M&A clients.

HISTORY

Tokushichi Nomura started a currency exchange, Nomura Shoten, in Osaka in 1872 and began trading stock. His son, Tokushichi II, took over and in 1910 formed Nomura's first syndicate to underwrite part of a government bond issue. It established the Osaka Nomura Bank in 1918. The bond department became independent in 1925 and became Nomura Securities. The company opened a New York office in 1927, entering stock brokerage in 1938.

The firm rebuilt and expanded retail operations after WWII. It encouraged stock market investing by promoting "million ryo savings chests," small boxes in which people saved cash (ryo was an old form of currency); when savings reached 5,000 yen, savers could buy into investment trusts. Nomura distributed more than a million chests in 10 years.

Nomura followed clients overseas in the 1960s, helped underwrite a US issue of Sony stock and opened a London office. It became Japan's leading securities firm after a 1965 stock market crash decimated rival Yamaichi Securities. The firm grew rapidly in the 1970s, ushering investment capital in and out of Japan and competing with banks by issuing corporate debt securities.

As the Japanese economy soared in the 1980s, it opened Nomura Bank International in London (1986) and bought 20% of US mergers and acquisitions advisor Wasserstein Perella (1988, sold 2001).

Then the Japanese economic bubble burst. Nomura's stock toppled 70% from its 1987 peak and underwriting plummeted. In 1991 and 1992, amid revelations that Nomura and other brokerages had reimbursed favored clients' trading losses, the firm was accused of manipulating stock in companies owned by Japanese racketeers. Nomura's chairman and president — both named Tabuchi — resigned, admitting no wrongdoing.

The firm trimmed staff and offices and focused on its most efficient operations. From 1993 to 2000, it seesawed from red to black and back again.

Junichi Ujiie became president after the payoff scandal; he restructured operations to prepare for Japan's financial deregulation. Nomura invested in pub chain Inntrepreneur and William Hill, a UK betting chain. It also created an entertainment lending unit to lend against future royalties or syndication fees, and spun off a minority stake in its high-risk US real estate business, which ceased lending altogether the next year.

In 1998 Nomura was dealt a double blow when Asian economies collapsed and Russia defaulted on its debts; incurring substantial losses, the firm refocused on its domestic market and reduced overseas operations. That year it teamed with Industrial Bank of Japan for derivatives sales in the UK and pension plan consulting in Japan.

In 1999 Nomura bailed out its ailing property subsidiary Nomura Finance, crippled by the sinking Japanese real estate market. It also invested heavily in UK real estate and bought 40% of the Czech beer market with South African Breweries.

The next year the firm agreed to buy the business services arm of Welsh utilities firm Hyder; it also bought 114,000 flats in Germany with local government authorities, its first European deal outside the UK. Also in 2000 Nomura sold its assets in pachinko parlors and "love" hotels, Japanese cultural traditions with less-than sparkling reputations. British authorities that year fined Nomura traders in relation to charges of trying to rig Australia's stock market in 1996.

The company made two big deals in the UK in 2001, buying hotel chain Le Méridien and becoming the nation's largest pub owner via the purchase of some 1,000 locations from Bass. Also that year Nomura bought a stake in Thomas Weisel Partners to increase its participation in M&A action between US and Japanese firms. The following year, the company decided to sell the network of more than 4,100 pubs to a consortium of private investors for almost $3 billion.

Meanwhile, a dispute with the Czech Republic over the seizure of Investicni a Postovni Banka, a Czech bank in which Nomura acquired a 46% stake in 1998, resulted in both sides seeking billions of dollars in damages.

EXECUTIVES

Chairman: Junichi Ujiie, age 60
President and CEO: Nobuyuki Koga, age 55
Deputy President and Co-COO: Hiroshi Toda, age 54
Deputy President and Co-COO: Kazutoshi Inano, age 52
Head of Global Merchant Banking: Akira Maruyama
Head of Global Risk Management, Treasury, Controller, and Investor Relations: Masafumi Nakada
Head of Global Corporate Communications: Tetsu Ozaki
Head of Global Equity: Hiromasa Yamazaki
Head of Global Fixed Income: Shigesuke Kashiwagi
Head of Global Investment Banking: Takashi Yanagiya, age 54
Head of Global IT and Operations: Akihiko Nakamura
Head of Asset Finance: Atsuo Sakurai

Head of Asset Management: Takumi Shibata
Head of Domestic Retail: Kenichi Watanabe, age 53
Head of Global Markets: Yasuo Agemura
Regional Manager, Americas: Hideyuki Takahashi
Head of Global Research: Akihito Watanabe
Regional Manager, Europe: Yugo Ishida
Executive Managing Director, Nomura Asset Management Co.: Atsushi Yoshikawa
Regional Manager, Asia and Oceania Region: Noriyasu Yoshizawa
Auditors: Shin Nihon & Co.

LOCATIONS

HQ: Nomura Holdings, Inc.
   1-9-1, Nihonbashi, Chuo-ku, Tokyo 103-8645, Japan
Phone: +81-3-5255-1000   **Fax:** +81-3-5255-1064
US HQ: 2 World Financial Center, Bldg. B,
   New York, NY 10281-1198
US Phone: 212-667-9300   **US Fax:** 212-667-1058
Web: www.nomura.com

Nomura Holdings operates in more than 20 countries. Nomura Securities Co. has some 130 branch offices.

PRODUCTS/OPERATIONS

Selected Subsidiaries

Banque Nomura France
The Capital Company of America, LLC
Nomura Advisory Services (Malaysia) Sdn. Bhd.
Nomura Asia Holding N.V. (the Netherlands)
Nomura Asia Ltd. (Hong Kong)
Nomura Asset Capital Corp. (US)
Nomura Asset Management Co., Ltd.
Nomura Australia Ltd.
Nomura Bank (Deutschland) GmbH (Germany)
Nomura Bank International PLC (UK)
Nomura Bank (Luxembourg) S.A.
Nomura Bank (Switzerland) LTD.
Nomura Canada Inc.
Nomura Corporate Research and
   Asset Management Inc. (US)
Nomura Europe Finance NV (the Netherlands)
Nomura Europe Holdings PLC (UK)
Nomura Finance Co., Ltd.
Nomura Futures (Hong Kong) Ltd.
Nomura Futures (Singapore) Pte. Ltd.
Nomura Global Funding PLC (UK)
Nomura Holding America Inc. (US)
P.T. Nomura Indonesia
Nomura International (Hong Kong) Ltd.
Nomura International PLC (UK)
Nomura International Trust Co. (US)
Nomura Investment Banking
   (Middle East) E.C. (Bahrain)
Nomura Investor Relations Co., Ltd.
Nomura Italia S.I.M.p.A. (Italy)
Nomura Realty Advisors, Inc. (US)
Nomura Satellite Communications Co., Ltd.
Nomura Securities (Hong Kong) Ltd.
Nomura Securities Hungary Ltd.
Nomura Securities Philippines, Inc.
Nomura Securities (Singapore) Pte. Ltd.
Nomura Singapore Limited
The Nomura Trust & Banking Co., Ltd.

COMPETITORS

Bank of America	Deutsche Bank
Barclays	Goldman Sachs
Bear Stearns	HSBC Holdings
Boom Securities	Lehman Brothers
Charles Schwab	Merrill Lynch
Citigroup	Nikko Cordial
CSFB	UBS
Daiwa	UBS Financial Services

HISTORICAL FINANCIALS

Company Type: Public

Income Statement

FYE: March 31

	REVENUE ($ mil.)	NET INCOME ($ mil.)	NET PROFIT MARGIN	EMPLOYEES
3/05	10,504	884	8.4%	14,344
3/04	10,554	1,654	15.7%	13,987
3/03	7,122	1,016	14.3%	14,385
3/02	13,756	1,266	9.2%	14,500
3/01	10,286	1,438	14.0%	15,000
3/00	10,788	1,380	12.8%	15,581
3/99	5,525	(3,920)	—	13,770
3/98	7,582	323	4.3%	9,888
3/97	7,901	(736)	—	9,938
3/96	8,015	758	9.5%	10,306
Annual Growth	3.1%	1.7%		3.7%

2005 Year-End Financials

Debt ratio: 173.6%
Return on equity: 5.1%
Cash ($ mil.): —
Current ratio: —
Long-term debt ($ mil.): 30,248

No. of shares (mil.): 1,941
Dividends
Yield: 1.2%
Payout: 35.6%
Market value ($ mil.): 26,906

Stock History

NYSE: NMR

	STOCK PRICE ($) FY Close	P/E High/Low		PER SHARE ($) Earnings	Dividends	Book Value
3/05	13.86	41	27	0.45	0.16	8.98
3/04	18.24	22	11	0.85	0.00	8.83
3/03	10.33	435	255	0.52	0.00	7.08
3/02	13.24	23	14	0.64	0.00	6.15
Annual Growth	1.5%	—	—	(11.1%)	—	13.4%

Norsk Hydro

Norsk Hydro is at home in Norwegian waters. Norway's largest publicly traded industrial company, Norsk Hydro makes aluminum and energy operations. Aluminum is its largest business segment, accounting for just over half of sales. Its oil and energy operations boast 2 billion barrels of reserves and are focused on its home turf. The company also has a much smaller petrochemicals business. In 2004 Norsk Hydro spun off its agrochemical unit (now known as Yara International ASA) and then sold its remaining ownership to UBS Limited for about $570 million. The Norwegian government owns close to 45% of Norsk Hydro.

Norsk Hydro's aluminum unit produces aluminum and the raw materials to make aluminum extruded sections and sheets, which are sold to the building and automotive industries worldwide. The company also produces aluminum rolled products, automotive structures, and magnesium for the automotive, packaging, transportation, and building industries. It is the world's #3 aluminum company behind Alcoa and Alcan.

The energy segment explores primarily on the Norwegian continental shelf, but it also has operations off the coasts of Angola and Canada as well as in Russia, Libya, and the Gulf of Mexico. The company has refining operations and markets its products through a network of more than 1,800 stations in Sweden, Norway, Denmark, and the Baltics. (The non-Swedish service stations are operated through a joint venture with Texaco.) Norsk Hydro expects its oil and gas output to increase by around 8% annually through 2007.

The company has made a deal with Comalco, a subsidiary of Rio Tinto, to purchase alumina (the raw material to make aluminum) beginning with 300,000 tonnes in 2005 and increasing to 500,000 tonnes in 2006-2030. This deal is Norsk Hydro's largest ever alumina supply contract.

As can be seen with the Yara spin-off, Norsk Hydro has been making moves designed to allow it to concentrate on aluminum and energy.

Yet another, this time much larger, move in the direction of boosting its energy business was the 2005 acquisition of Spinnaker Exploration for about $2.45 billion. Spinnaker is an oil and gas production company that explores in the Gulf of Mexico and off the coast of West Africa.

HISTORY

Norwegian entrepreneurs Sam Eyde and Kristian Birkeland began Norsk Hydro-Elektrisk Kvaelstofaktieselskap (Norwegian Hydro-Electric Nitrogen Corp.) in 1905. The company used electricity generated from waterfalls to extract nitrogen from the air to produce fertilizer.

After WWII the Norwegian government seized German holdings in Norsk Hydro and took a 48% stake in the company. It grew to be the largest chemical firm in Scandinavia. In 1965, when Norway granted licenses for offshore petroleum exploration, the company formed partnerships with foreign companies. These included Phillips Petroleum, which spurred the North Sea boom in 1969 when its drilling rig Ocean Viking struck oil in the giant Ekofisk field, and Elf Aquitaine, which oversaw the Frigg discovery in 1971. The Norwegian state increased its share of Norsk Hydro to 51% in 1972.

The company also branched out with hydroelectric-powered aluminum processing at its Karmoy Works (1967) and with a fish-farming subsidiary, Mowi (1969). During much of the 1970s, it focused on oil and gas development, which added to the treasury and helped finance growth, often through acquisitions.

Norsk Hydro pushed into the European fertilizer market by buying Dutch company NSM in 1979; during the 1980s it acquired interests in fertilizer operations in France, Sweden, and the UK. In petrochemicals it expanded by buying two British PVC makers. Norsk Hydro-controlled Hydro Aluminum merged with ASV, another Norwegian aluminum company, in 1986, and the company consolidated its aluminum holdings two years later.

Hydro served as operator in the Oseberg field, which began production in 1988 and grew rapidly to become a major source of oil and gas. In 1990 it bought 330 Danish gasoline stations from UNO-X; in 1992 it purchased Mobil Oil's Norwegian marketing and distribution system. Two years later Norsk Hydro merged its oil and marketing operations in Norway and Denmark with Texaco's.

A weak world economy and increased competition limited its revenues in 1992 and 1993. The company countered slumping sales by selling noncore subsidiaries, including pharmaceutical unit Hydro Pharma (1992) and chocolate maker Freia Marabou (1993).

Norsk Hydro expanded further during the early 1990s, acquiring fertilizer plants in Germany, the UK, and the US, as well as W. R. Grace's ammonia plants in Trinidad and Tobago. The firm acquired Fisons' NPK fertilizer business in 1994. The company agreed to an asset swap with Petro-Canada in 1996, becoming a partner in oil and gas fields off the east coast of Canada. That year Norsk Hydro bought UNO-X's Swedish gas station operations.

The Norwegian government's stake in Norsk Hydro was reduced from 51% to about 45% in 1999 when the company and state-owned Statoil made a deal to take over Saga Petroleum, Norway's leading independent oil producer, to keep it out of foreign hands.

In light of major losses in 1999 by Hydro Agri, the company made plans in 2000 to close several European nitrogen fertilizer operations. However, it agreed to modernize and expand its Hydro Aluminum Sunndal facility, to make it the largest aluminum plant in Europe. That year the company also sold Saga UK (North Sea assets) to Conoco, and its fish-farming unit to Dutch company Nutreco.

In 2001 the company acquired a stake in Soquimich, an industrial minerals company in Chile, and majority control of Slovakian aluminum producer Slolvalco.

The new decade brought with it a new focus; the company began to make aluminum and oil and energy its primary business lines. Toward that end Norsk Hydro bought VAW Aluminum from E.On AG for $2.8 billion in a deal that enabled it to expand its product base in Europe and the US, especially to key customers in the automobile industry. It then sold its flexible packaging unit to Alcan for about $545 million in 2003. Furthering the same goal, the company announced in 2003 and then followed through on a spin-off of its agrochemical unit the following year. The resultant company is called Yara International.

EXECUTIVES

Chairman: Jan Reinås, age 59
Deputy Chairman: Borger A. Lenth, age 67
President and CEO: Eivind Reiten, age 52
EVP and CFO: John Ove Ottestad, age 56
EVP, Leadership and Culture: Hilde Aasheim, age 46
EVP, Aluminium: Jon-Harald Nilsen, age 53
EVP, Oil and Energy: Tore Torvund, age 53
SVP and General Counsel: Odd I. Biller, age 56
SVP, Investor Relations: Idar Eikrem, age 43
SVP, Communications: Cecilie Ditlev-Simonsen, age 43
SVP, Corporate Finance: Ida Helliesen, age 58
SVP, Corporate Internal Audit: Espen Uvholt, age 42
SVP, Operations: Torgeir Kydland, age 49
SVP, Projects: Morten Ruud, age 52
SVP, Corporate Portfolio Strategy: David W. Nunn
SVP, Exploration: Lars Christian Alsvik
SVP, Finance: Helge Vatn
SVP, Industrial Relations: Arild Andreassen, age 57
SVP, Markets: Hilde Myrberg
SVP, Oil Marketing: Bengt Göran Markeborn, age 60
VP, CCE Business Support: Tore Bjørsvik, age 43
VP, Corporate Financial Reporting and Performance: Anne Harris
VP, Human Resources: Lise Sollerud, age 46

LOCATIONS

HQ: Norsk Hydro ASA
    Bygdøy allé 2, N-0240 Oslo 2, Norway
Phone: +47-22-53-81-00   **Fax:** +47-22-53-27-25
US HQ: 15995 N. Barkers Landing Rd.,
    Houston, TX 77079-2467
US Phone: 281-504-1100   **US Fax:** 281-504-1101
Web: www.hydro.com

Norsk Hydro sells its products in Europe, including Norway, and in Asia, North America, and other regions. It has oil and gas exploration and production operations along the Norwegian continental shelf, as well as in Angola, Canada, Iran, Libya, Russia, and the UK.

2004 Sales

	$ mil.	% of total
Europe		
EU		
UK	4,735	19
Germany	3,206	12
Sweden	1,392	5
Italy	1,220	5
France	1,137	4
The Netherlands	1,102	4
Spain	1,022	4
Denmark	199	1
Other EU countries	2,153	8
Norway	4,145	16
Switzerland	928	4
Other countries	275	1
Americas		
US	1,716	7
Canada	860	3
Other countries	418	2
Asia	994	4
Australia & New Zealand	161	1
Africa	91	—
Total	25,754	100

PRODUCTS/OPERATIONS

2004 Sales

	$ mil.	% of total
Hydro Aluminium	13,169	51
Hydro Oil & Energy	11,020	43
Other	1,602	6
Adjustments	(37)	—
Total	25,754	100

Selected Operations

Hydro Aluminum
    Hydro Aluminum Automotive
    Hydro Aluminum Extrusion
    Hydro Aluminum Metal Products
    Hydro Aluminum Rolled Products and Wire Rod
    Hydro North America
    Hydro Primary Metals
Hydro Oil & Energy
    Hydro Energy
    Hydro Exploration and Development Norway
    Hydro Exploration and Production International
    Hydro Oil Marketing
    Hydro Operation and Production Norway
    Hydro Technology and Projects
Other
    Hydro Petrochemicals

HISTORICAL FINANCIALS

Company Type: Public

Income Statement

FYE: December 31

	REVENUE ($ mil.)	NET INCOME ($ mil.)	NET PROFIT MARGIN	EMPLOYEES
12/04	25,754	2,081	8.1%	34,600
12/03	25,836	1,649	6.4%	42,911
12/02	23,463	1,262	5.4%	50,000
12/01	17,099	883	5.2%	35,563
12/00	17,694	1,577	8.9%	38,166
12/99	12,804	427	3.3%	37,900
12/98	12,827	494	3.9%	40,000
12/97	13,069	707	5.4%	38,000
12/96	13,167	963	7.3%	35,400
12/95	12,606	1,128	8.9%	28,305
Annual Growth	8.3%	7.0%	—	2.3%

2004 Year-End Financials

Debt ratio: 22.7%	No. of shares (mil.): 251
Return on equity: 15.1%	Dividends
Cash ($ mil.): 2,380	Yield: 2.0%
Current ratio: 1.53	Payout: 19.7%
Long-term debt ($ mil.): 3,229	Market value ($ mil.): 19,746

Stock History

NYSE: NHY

12/95 12/96 12/97 12/98 12/99 12/00 12/01 12/02 12/03 12/04

	STOCK PRICE ($) FY Close	P/E High/Low		PER SHARE ($) Earnings	Dividends	Book Value
12/04	78.72	10	7	8.17	1.61	56.74
12/03	56.18	9	5	6.41	1.41	51.60
12/02	40.37	11	8	4.45	1.11	38.50
12/01	38.18	13	10	3.10	0.04	29.43
12/00	38.24	7	5	6.02	0.87	30.90
12/99	38.86	27	19	1.57	1.69	25.83
12/98	31.08	24	14	1.96	0.00	25.22
12/97	46.36	20	15	2.80	0.89	24.65
12/96	48.75	13	10	3.83	0.72	22.47
12/95	38.06	9	7	4.46	0.62	23.31
Annual Growth	8.4%	—	—	7.0%	11.2%	10.4%

Nortel Networks

Nortel Networks is one of telecom's North (American) stars. The company, which operates through its Nortel Networks Limited subsidiary, is one of the top global makers of telecom equipment in North America. It makes core network switching, wireless, and optical systems for customers worldwide. Nortel's wireline and enterprise network equipment includes systems for digital voice and data switching, routing, and call center communications. Wireless products include cellular base stations and controllers. The company makes such long-haul fiber optic products as multiplexers and optical switches. Clients include global communications carriers; regional, local, and wireless phone carriers; and corporations.

Nortel in 2004 terminated the employment of its CEO Frank Dunn — as well as CFO Douglas Beatty, controller Michael Gollogly, and several other top financial managers — amid an SEC investigation into accounting problems dating back several years. The company installed director Bill Owens as its new chief; Owens previously held the top spot at Teledesic LLC and was the president of SAIC prior to that. Late in 2005, GE and Motorola veteran Mike Zafirovski succeeded Owens.

In early 2005, the company released its 2003 financial statements, nearly a year late, following a massive accounting investigation that uncovered billions in overstated revenues for the years 1999 and 2000. The company also filed a lawsuit against Dunn, Beatty, and Gollogly in an unprecedented attempt to reclaim $10.4 million in bonuses paid to the three executives who, the company claims, were "unjustly enriched at the expense of Nortel."

To boost its efforts to expand operations in developing telecom markets, Nortel has acquired a stake in Indian communication software firm Sasken Communication Technologies, in a deal valued at $10 million. The company also bought IT services contract PEC Solutions in a deal valued at $448 million. Nortel plans to create a US subsidiary to be called Nortel PEC Solutions using the Fairfax, Virginia-based company.

HISTORY

Nortel Networks traces its lineage to 1880, when Bell Telephone Company of Canada was established in Montreal four years after the invention of the telephone. In 1882 the Northern Electric and Manufacturing Co. was founded to produce Bell Canada's mechanical equipment. Northern Electric pooled its resources with electrical wire maker Imperial Wire & Cable to form the Northern Electric Co. in 1914. AT&T's manufacturing subsidiary Western Electric owned 44% of the company.

During the 1930s the company created an electronics division and purchased a majority interest in Amalgamated Electric (1932). In the mid-1950s, the US Justice Department forced Western Electric to sell its interest in Northern Electric, and Bell Canada purchased most of the shares. In 1958 the company formed Northern Electric Laboratories to push research and development.

During the 1960s Northern Electric began supplying switching gear overseas. In 1971 the company merged its Northern Electric Laboratories with Bell Canada's R&D unit to form Bell Northern Research. (Northern Electric retained 70% ownership, while Bell Canada owned the remaining 30%.)

Northern Electric remained wholly owned by Bell Canada until 1973, when that company began reducing its stake. In 1976 Northern Electric changed its name to Northern Telecom and became the first equipment company to introduce a digital switch. When AT&T approved use of the switch in its equipment in 1981, Northern Telecom's growth took off.

Paul Stern became CEO in 1989 as the company thrived on its digital switch sales. The former IBM executive focused on cutting costs in lieu of technical advancement, and customer dissatisfaction built as the company failed to develop the software in its switching systems. Directors forced Stern out and replaced him with Jean Monty as CEO in 1992, just before Northern Telecom suffered a loss of nearly $900 million for 1993.

Monty acted quickly, calming customers, revamping the software, and selling underused divisions and factories. In 1996 the company acquired data networking maker Micom Communications. The next year Monty was succeeded by COO John Roth, who began to lead Nortel down a path to expansion.

In 1998 Northern Telecom bought Bell Canada's 30% stake in Bell Northern Research, which had been renamed Nortel Technology Limited. Also that year the company boosted its networking expertise through such acquisitions as Bay Networks. The Bay Networks deal, worth $6.7 billion, led to a loss that year and prompted the 1999 name change to Nortel Networks.

The change was pivotal for the company, transforming it from a staid seller of simple telephone systems to a fast-moving Internet supplier. That year Nortel acquired Shasta Networks (network management products for Internet service providers).

Nortel increased its purchasing pace in 2000 to boost fiber optics and software holdings. It bought optical equipment startups Qtera, CoreTek, and Xros. Bell Canada parent BCE distributed to its shareholders most of its 40% stake in Nortel in 2000.

In 2001 the company announced and then postponed plans to take its fiber-optic components business public. Amid an economic downturn Nortel laid off 30,000 employees and scaled back its digital subscriber line operations. Frank Carlucci (chairman since March 2000) stepped down that year. CFO Lynton Wilson took the chair and Roth stepped down as president and CEO in late 2001. Former CFO Frank Dunn was named CEO and Roth assumed the vice chairman role. Nortel decided that year to cut an additional 20,000 employees. It also sold its Clarify customer service software business (originally purchased for $2.1 billion) to Amdocs for $200 million.

In 2002 Nortel restructured its fiber optic business, cutting jobs and selling some of its optical components assets (advanced tunable lasers, transmitters, receivers, and amplifiers) to Bookham Technology.

In 2004, the company outsourced all of its manufacturing operations to Singapore-based Flextronics in a deal valued at more than $2 billion annually. Nortel fired Dunn as well as the company's CFO that year amid an accounting scandal; director Bill Owens assumed the top spot. Late in 2005, veteran high-tech executive Mike Zafirovski succeeded Owens.

EXECUTIVES

Chairman Emeritus: Lynton R. (Red) Wilson, age 64
Chairman: Harry J. Pearce, age 63
President, CEO, and Director: Mike S. Zafirovski, age 51
EVP and CFO: Peter W. Currie, age 54
SVP, Global Human Resources:
William J. (Bill) Donovan, age 48
SVP, Global Supply Chain and Quality: Joel Hackney
VP, Tax: John M. Doolittle, age 41
VP, Chief Architect, and Interim Chief Research Officer: Peter Carbone
VP, Audit: Robert J. Bartzokas, age 54, $500,000 pay (partial-year salary)
President, North America: Dion C. Joannou, age 39
CIO: Albert R. Hitchcock, age 40
Chief Marketing Officer:
Ralph Edward Clenton (Clent) Richardson, age 43
Senior Advisor: Pascal Debon, age 58, $590,000 pay (prior to title change)
Treasurer: Katharine Berghuis Stevenson, age 42
Controller: Paul W. Karr, age 49
Assistant General Counsel, Securities, and Corporate Secretary: Gordon Allan Davies, age 43
Corporate Communications, North America:
Tina Warren
Auditors: Deloitte & Touche LLP

LOCATIONS

HQ: Nortel Networks Corporation
8200 Dixie Rd., Ste. 100,
Brampton, Ontario L6T 5P6, Canada
Phone: 905-863-0000   **Fax:** 905-863-8408
US HQ: 2221 Lakeside Blvd.,
Richardson, TX 75082-4399
US Phone: 972-684-1000
Web: www.nortelnetworks.com

2004 Sales

	$ mil.	% of total
US	4,833	49
Europe, Middle East & Africa	2,580	26
Asia/Pacific	1,253	13
Central America & Latin America	594	6
Canada	568	6
Total	**9,828**	**100**

PRODUCTS/OPERATIONS

2004 Sales

	$ mil.	% of total
Wireless networks	4,839	49
Enterprise networks	2,354	24
Wireline networks	1,723	18
Optical networks	906	9
Other	6	—
Total	**9,828**	**100**

Selected Products

Wireless
Base station transceivers and controllers
Core networking equipment
Gateway support nodes
Home location registers
Mobile switching centers
Enterprise
Call center communications systems (Symposium)
Digital telephone switching systems
(Meridian, Norstar)
Interactive voice response systems (Directory Assistance, Periphonics)
Network management software (Preside, Optivity)

Wireline
Circuit to packet voice network systems
Voice and data communications systems for service providers and large enterprises (Succession)
Packet switching and routing
Data network access aggregation nodes (Shasta)
Data routers (Bay)
Data switching platforms for Internet-based virtual private networks (Contivity)
Ethernet data switches (Baystack, Business Policy)
Multi-service switches (Passport)
Voice and data communications systems for small to mid-sized businesses (Business Communications Manager)
Optical and long-haul
Dense wavelength division multiplexing equipment
Repeaters
Transmission terminals
Network management software (Preside)
Optical Ethernet (OPTera)
Optical networking components
Optical switching equipment
Synchronous optical transmission systems
SDH-based products (TN-X line)
SONET-based products (SDMS TransportNode)
SONET/SDH (OPTera Connect DX)

COMPETITORS

3Com	Harris Corp.
ADC Telecommunications	Hitachi
ADVA	Huawei Technologies
Agere Systems	JDS Uniphase
Alcatel	Juniper Networks
Allied Telesyn	Lucent
Amdocs	Marconi
Avaya	Motorola
BroadSoft	NEC
Ciena	Nokia
Cisco Systems	Panasonic Mobile
Corning	Communications
Enterasys	Redback Networks
Ericsson	Samsung
Extreme Networks	Siemens
Foundry Networks	Sonus Networks
Fujitsu	Sycamore Networks
Genesys Telecommunications	

HISTORICAL FINANCIALS

Company Type: Public

Income Statement

FYE: December 31

	REVENUE ($ mil.)	NET INCOME ($ mil.)	NET PROFIT MARGIN	EMPLOYEES
12/04	9,828	(51)	—	34,150
12/03	10,193	434	4.3%	35,160
12/02	10,560	(3,585)	—	36,960
12/01	17,511	(27,302)	—	53,600
12/00	30,275	(3,470)	—	94,500
12/99	22,217	(170)	—	76,700
12/98	17,575	(537)	—	75,052
12/97	15,449	829	5.4%	73,000
12/96	12,847	623	4.8%	68,000
12/95	10,672	473	4.4%	63,715
Annual Growth	**(0.9%)**	**—**	**—**	**(6.7%)**

2004 Year-End Financials

Debt ratio: 96.9%
Return on equity: —
Cash ($ mil.): 3,686
Current ratio: 1.61
Long-term debt ($ mil.): 3,862
No. of shares (mil.): 4,273
Dividends
  Yield: 0.0%
  Payout: —
Market value ($ mil.): 14,826

Stock History

NYSE: NT

	STOCK PRICE ($) FY Close	P/E High/Low		PER SHARE ($) Earnings	Dividends	Book Value
12/04	3.47	—	—	(0.01)	0.00	0.93
12/03	4.23	48	17	0.10	0.00	0.95
12/02	1.61	—	—	(0.93)	0.00	0.51
12/01	7.50	—	—	(8.56)	0.04	1.50
12/00	32.06	—	—	(1.17)	0.08	9.40
12/99	50.50	—	—	(0.08)	0.08	4.54
12/98	12.50	—	—	(0.25)	0.06	4.36
12/97	11.09	36	19	0.39	0.07	2.61
12/96	7.73	28	17	0.30	0.06	2.35
12/95	5.38	24	17	0.23	0.06	1.90
Annual Growth	**(4.8%)**	—	—	—	—	**(7.6%)**

Novartis AG

Although it's based in Switzerland, Novartis has been aggressive in attacking illnesses. The company's prescription drugs include treatments for nervous system and ophthalmic disorders, cardiovascular diseases, and cancer. Its Sandoz generics subsidiary produces finished dosage products as well as active pharmaceutical ingredients for other generics companies to manufacture. Novartis' consumer health unit includes such brands as Ex-Lax, Maalox, and Theraflu. Novartis is also the proud parent of the Gerber baby. CIBA Vision makes eye drops, contact lenses (Focus), and contact lens solutions. Its animal health unit offers parasite control products (Sentinel) and pharmaceuticals for pets and farm animals.

Recognizing the preference for generics by many US health plans and some US consumers, Novartis consolidated its 14 generic drug brands under the visible and respected Sandoz name. To expand those operations, in 2004 the druggernaut bought a Canadian maker of generic injectable drugs and a Danish generics maker to increase market share in key regional markets. In 2005, the firm acquired Hexal AG, one of Germany's top generics makers; it has received US regulatory approval for the acquisition of a controlling stake in Hexal's sister firm Eon Labs, a US generics manufacturer. The deal would make Sandoz the largest manufacturer of generic drugs in the world, ahead of powerhouse Teva Pharmaceuticals.

In a move to bolster its consumer offerings, the company has purchased the US and Canadian consumer products division of Bristol-Myers Squibb, which brings headache remedy Excedrin, cold and flu treatment Comtrex, and Keri moisturizers into the company's consumer products stable.

To compete head to head with Roche Holdings, the company has been busy beefing up its vaccine offerings. It is acquiring the remaining shares of struggling vaccine and biopharmaceuticals products maker Chiron that it doesn't already own, despite Chiron's board rebuffing the offer a month earlier. The buyout is valued at $5.1 billion.

Novartis also boasts a healthy drug pipeline with more than 50 candidates in late-stage development. Novartis is gleeful over Gleevec, a bioengineered drug that "turns off" a rare form of leukemia and cancerous gastrointestinal tumors by inhibiting tumor growth. The drug, approved by the FDA in near-record time, may be useful in treating other cancers. Novartis' pipeline includes other drugs that inhibit tumor growth. Based on the strength of this new technology, the company aims to become an oncology drug kingpin.

In one of the largest deals in European pharma, Novartis has acquired the rights to a prospective chronic obstructive pulmonary disease (COPD) treatment from UK drug concerns Arakis and Vectura Group, who will, as part of the licensing deal, reap as share of the revenues if the drug is approved for sale.

The FDA required Novartis in early 2005 to place a extra warnings on its epilepsy drug, Trileptal, warning consumers of serious skin reactions such as Stevens-Johnson syndrome and toxic epidermal nerolysis after receiving nearly 20 reports (including one fatality) of these reactions in patients taking the drug.

HISTORY

Johann Geigy began selling spices and natural dyes in Basel, Switzerland, in 1758. A century later the Geigy family began producing synthetic dyes. About that time Alexander Clavel also entered the synthetic dye trade in Basel, forming the Gesellschaft fur Chemische Industrie Basel (Ciba). Ciba was Switzerland's #1 chemical firm at century's end.

After WWI, Ciba, Geigy, and Sandoz (a Basel synthetic dye maker founded in 1886) formed the Basel AG cartel to compete with German rival I.G. Farben. Basel used its profits to diversify into pharmaceuticals and other chemicals and to gain a foothold in the US. In 1929 Basel merged with German and, later, French and British counterparts, but WWII shattered the so-called Quadrapartite Cartel in 1939, leaving only Basel AG intact.

Basel scientist Paul Muller won a Nobel Prize in 1948 for inventing DDT. Basel AG voluntarily dissolved itself back into its component parts in 1951.

Ciba, Geigy, and Sandoz continued to diversify. Finding new markets in agricultural chemicals, Geigy had passed Ciba in sales by 1967. That year Sandoz bought the Wander group of companies (dietetic products). Ciba and Geigy merged in 1970 and began a series of US acquisitions, including Funk Seeds in 1974. Sandoz bought Minneapolis-based Northrup, King & Co. (1976) and Dutch seed company Zaadunie (1980).

Ciba-Geigy and US biotech company Chiron started a joint venture in 1986 to produce and market genetically engineered vaccines (Ciba-Geigy acquired 50% of Chiron in 1994). Sandoz also bought shares in US biotechnology companies, including Genetic Therapy and SyStemix, in 1991. It bought Gerber (founded 1927) in 1994.

Ciba-Geigy and Sandoz rejoined to form Novartis in 1996. To win approval for the merger, Sandoz (whose Daniel Vasella became CEO of the new company) sold its corn herbicide and US animal health businesses. Novartis spun off its

specialty chemicals unit in 1997 and bought Merck's insecticide and fungicide operations.

In 1999 the company sold several units, including cracker maker Wasa, to focus the new division's operations. Chairman Alex Krauer, who had overseen the formation of Novartis, stepped down that year, leaving the post to Vasella.

To boost its market share, CIBA Vision bought colored contact lens maker Wesley Jessen VisionCare in 2000. Novartis spun off its crop protection and seed units, merging them with AstraZeneca's Agrochemicals unit to create Syngenta.

Novartis Ophthalmics split off from the CIBA Vision division to become a separate eye health care unit under the Pharmaceutical Division of Novartis in 2001. The firm's joint venture with BioTransplant successfully cloned genetically altered pigs whose organs would be more suitable for human transplants. Attempting to refine the company's focus on pharmaceuticals, Novartis made several acquisitions in 2002, including two animal vaccine companies, Grand Laboratories and Immtech Biologies, and generic manufacturer Lek Pharmaceuticals, while divesting its food and beverage division to Associated British Foods. The remaining assets, including sports nutrition, health, and weight loss products, were grouped under the Nutrition & Santé banner and are still up for sale.

EXECUTIVES

Chairman and CEO: Daniel L. Vasella, age 51, $2,650,500 pay
Vice Chairman: Helmut Sihler, age 74
Vice Chairman: Hans-Jörg Rudlof, age 64
CFO: Raymond Breu, age 60, $876,138 pay
CIO: Jim Barrington
CEO, Novartis Consumer Health: Paul Choffat, age 55, $1,209,659 pay
CEO, Novartis Pharma: Thomas Ebeling, age 46, $1,943,700 pay
CEO, CIBA Vision: Joseph T. Mallof, age 52
CEO, Sandoz: Andreas Rummelt, age 48
CEO, Novartis Pharma Schweiz: Theodor Sproll, age 47
President, Novartis Institutes for BioMedical Research: Mark C. Fishman, age 54, $862,425 pay
Head of OTC: Larry Allgaier, age 46
Head of Legal and General Affairs: Urs Bärlocher, age 62, $699,438 pay
Head of Human Resources: Juergen Brokatzky-Geiger, age 52
Head of Specialty Medicines and Oncology: David Epstein, age 43
Head of Corporate Research: Paul L. Herrling, age 58
Head of Public Affairs and Communications: Steven Kelmar, age 51
Corporate Secretary: Ingrid Duplain
General Counsel: Thomas Werlen
Auditors: PricewaterhouseCoopers AG

LOCATIONS

HQ: Novartis AG
Lichtstrasse 35, CH-4056 Basel, Switzerland
Phone: +41-61-324-1111   **Fax:** +41-61-324-8001
US HQ: 608 5th Ave., New York, NY 10020
US Phone: 212-307-1122   **US Fax:** 212-246-0185
Web: www.novartis.com

Novartis has operations in more than 140 countries.

2004 Sales

	$ mil.	% of total
Americas	13,285	47
Europe	10,289	36
Asia, Africa & Australia	4,673	17
Total	**28,247**	**100**

PRODUCTS/OPERATIONS

2004 Sales

	$ mil.	% of total
Pharmaceuticals		
Sandoz	3,045	11
OTC	1,975	7
Infant & Baby	1,441	5
CIBA Vision	1,412	5
Medical Nutrition	1,121	4
Animal Health	756	3
Other	8,747	31
Consumer Health	9,750	34
Total	**28,247**	**100**

Selected Products

Animal Health
Endex (liver fluke and gastrointestinal roundworm treatment for sheep and cattle)
Fasinex (liver fluke treatment for sheep and cattle)
Fortekor (treatment for canine heart failure)
Interceptor (canine heartworm prevention and intestinal worm treatment)
Program (canine and feline flea treatment)
Sentinel (canine heartworm and flea control)
Baby and Infant
Argos (baby care and wellness products)
Gerber (baby food, care, and wellness products)
Gerber Life (insurance)
Ninet (baby care and wellness products)
NUK (baby care products)
Branded Pharmaceuticals
Cibacen (hypertension drug)
Comtan (treatment for Parkinson's disease)
Diovan (hypertension drug)
Elidel (eczema treatment)
Estraderm (estrogen treatment)
Exelon (treatment of Alzheimer's disease)
Famvir (antiviral treatment for herpes)
Femara (advanced breast cancer treatment)
Focalin (attention deficit hyperactivity disorder treatment)
Foradil (asthma drug)
Gleevec (leukemia and gastrointestinal tumor treatment)
Lamisil (antifungal)
Leponex/Clozaril (schizophrenia drug)
Lescol (cholesterol drug)
Lotrel (hypertension drug)
Neoral (transplant rejection preventative; also treatment for rheumatoid arthritis and psoriasis)
Ritalin (attention deficit hyperactivity disorder)
Sandostatin LAR (acromegaly, cancer treatment)
Simulect (prophylaxis to prevent transplant rejection)
Starlix (type 2 diabetes treatment)
Tegretol (epilepsy, acute mania, and bipolar affective disorders drug)
Trileptal (epilepsy drug)
Visudyne (wet age-related macular degeneration drug)
Voltaren (antirheumatic)
Xolair (asthma drug)
Zaditen (allergic conjunctivitis drug)
Zelmac/Zelnorm (irritable bowel syndrome treatment)
Zometa (cancer treatment)
Consumer Health
Ex-Lax (laxative)
Gas-X (antacid)
Lamisil AT Cream (athlete's foot treatment)
Maalox (antacid)
Nicotinell (smoking cessation patch)
Theraflu (flu treatment)
Triaminic (cough and cold remedy)
Voltaren Emulgel (topical analgesic)
Generic Pharmaceuticals
Atenolol (hypertension drug)
Amoxicillin/clavulanic acid (antibiotic)
Citalopram (anti-depressant)
Enalapril (ACE inhibitor)
Lisinopril (ACE inhibitor)
Loratadine (allergy drug)
Metformin (diabetes drug)
Metoprolol (hypertension drug)
Omeprazole (ulcer and acid reflux drug)
Penicillin (antibiotic)
Ranitidine (ulcer drug)
Terazosin (hypertension drug)

CIBA Vision
  AOSept (contact lens cleaning system)
  DuraSoft (tinted contact lenses)
  Focus (contact lenses)
  Focus Dailies (disposable contact lenses)
  FreshLook (tinted contact lenses)
  SOLO-care (contact lens disinfecting solution)
  WildEyes (novelty contact lenses)
Medical Nutrition
  Boost (nutritional supplement drink)
  Impact (oral and enteral products)
  Nutrament (energy drink)
  Optifast (weight loss products)
  Resource (oral nutritional supplements)

COMPETITORS

Abbott Labs	Johnson & Johnson
Allergan	Merck
Altana	Milnot
AstraZeneca	Perrigo
Bausch & Lomb	Pfizer
Bayer	Roche
Bristol-Myers Squibb	Sanofi-Aventis
Eli Lilly	Schering
Essilor International	Schering-Plough
Genentech	Wyeth
GlaxoSmithKline	

HISTORICAL FINANCIALS

Company Type: Public

Income Statement

FYE: December 31

	REVENUE ($ mil.)	NET INCOME ($ mil.)	NET PROFIT MARGIN	EMPLOYEES
12/04	28,247	5,767	20.4%	81,392
12/03	24,864	5,016	20.2%	78,541
12/02	23,151	5,224	22.6%	72,877
12/01	19,335	4,239	21.9%	71,116
12/00	21,832	4,395	20.1%	68,000
12/99	20,418	4,188	20.5%	81,854
12/98	22,990	4,398	19.1%	82,449
12/97	21,408	3,578	16.7%	87,000
12/96	27,009	1,718	6.4%	116,178
12/95	31,138	3,652	11.7%	133,959
Annual Growth	(1.1%)	5.2%	—	(5.4%)

2004 Year-End Financials

Debt ratio: 8.1%	No. of shares (mil.): 2,427
Return on equity: 18.0%	Dividends
Cash ($ mil.): 6,083	Yield: 1.4%
Current ratio: 2.22	Payout: 29.5%
Long-term debt ($ mil.): 2,736	Market value ($ mil.): 122,651

Stock History

NYSE: NVS

12/95 12/96 12/97 12/98 12/99 12/00 12/01 12/02 12/03 12/04

	STOCK PRICE ($) FY Close	P/E High/Low	PER SHARE ($) Earnings	Dividends	Book Value
12/04	50.54	22 18	2.34	0.69	13.92
12/03	45.89	23 17	2.00	0.70	12.33
12/02	36.73	22 17	2.03	0.52	11.45
12/01	36.50	29 20	1.64	0.50	10.01
12/00	44.75	27 21	1.68	0.00	344.91
Annual Growth	3.1%	— —	8.6%	—	(55.2%)

Novo Nordisk

Novo Nordisk can tell diabetics where to stick it. The company is one of the world's leading producers of insulin. In addition, Novo Nordisk offers a line of diabetes education and training materials and services to doctors and patients under the name NovoCare. It also is involved in biopharmaceuticals, which include hemostasis management (for bleeding problems and hemophilia), growth hormone therapy, and hormone replacement therapy. Products include Activelle (hormone replacement), NovoSeven (hemostasis management), and Norditropin SimpleXx (liquid growth hormone).Through its Novo A/S subsidiary, Novo Nordisk Foundation owns nearly 26% of the shares and controls about 71% of the voting power in Novo Nordisk.

The company has been expanding its sales in key growth markets, primarily in the US, Brazil, and China. Its key market remains Europe, which generates 43% of its total sales. The US is the largest market for its NovoSeven product.

Novo Nordisk has bought out the remaining shares in its Brazilian subsidiary, Biobrás, and delisted the company. In addition, the company owns about 40% of ZymoGenetics, a Seattle-based biotechnology company.

The company is pursuing new drugs in its areas of core competency, including diabetes, hemophilia, and organ transplantation. Novo Nordisk holds research alliances with such companies as Abbott Laboratories, Boehringer Ingelheim, and Schering AG.

It has formed a partnership with US-based medical device manufacturer Medtronic to make prefilled insulin cartridges for Medtronic's insulin pumps.

HISTORY

Novo Nordisk was formed by the 1989 merger of Danish insulin producers Novo and Nordisk.

Soon after Canadian researchers extracted insulin from pancreas of cattle, Danish researcher August Krogh (winner of the 1920 Nobel Prize in physiology) and physician Marie Krogh, his wife, teamed up with H. C. Hagedorn, also a physician, to found Nordisk Insulinlaboratorium. One of their lab workers was an inventor named Harald Pedersen, and in 1923 Nordisk hired Pedersen's brother, Thorvald, to analyze chemicals. The relationship was unsuccessful, however, and the brothers left the company.

The Pedersens decided to produce insulin themselves and set up operations in their basement in 1924. Harald also designed a syringe that patients could use for their own insulin injections. Within a decade their firm, Novo Terapeutisk Laboratorium, was selling its product in 40 countries.

Meanwhile, Nordisk introduced a slow-acting insulin in 1936. NPH insulin, launched in the US in 1950, soon became the leading longer-acting insulin. Nordisk later became a major maker of human growth hormone.

During WWII Novo produced its first enzyme, trypsin, used to soften leather. It began producing penicillin in 1947 and during the 1950s developed Heparin, a trypsin-based drug used to treat blood clots. The company unveiled more industrial enzymes in the 1960s.

In 1981 Novo began selling its insulin in the US through a joint venture with E. R. Squibb (now part of Bristol-Myers Squibb). The next year Novo was the first to produce human insulin (actually a modified form of pig insulin), and in 1983 Nordisk introduced the Nordisk Infuser, a pump that constantly released small quantities of insulin. Two years later Novo debuted the NovoPen, a refillable injector that looked like a fountain pen.

Novo was the world's #2 insulin maker (and the world's largest maker of industrial enzymes) when it merged with #3, Nordisk, in 1989. By combining their research and market share, they were better able to complete globally with then-#1 Eli Lilly. After the merger, Novo Nordisk introduced the NovoLet, the world's first prefilled, disposable insulin syringe.

Novo Nordisk introduced drugs for depression (Seroxat, 1992), epilepsy (Gabitril, 1995), and hemophilia (NovoSeven, 1995). The company entered a joint marketing alliance with Johnson & Johnson subsidiary LifeScan, the world's #1 maker of blood glucose monitors, in 1995. It also began working with Rhône-Poulenc Rorer on estrogen replacement therapies.

Eli Lilly raised a new challenge in 1996 with the FDA approval of Humalog (the US's first new insulin product in 14 years), which is absorbed faster, giving users more flexibility in their injection schedule. (Novo Nordisk's own fast-acting insulin product, NovoLog, received FDA approval four years later.) A 1998 marketing pact with Schering-Plough signaled Novo Nordisk's desire to boost sales of its diabetes drugs in the US, where Eli Lilly has historically dominated.

In 2000 Novo Nordisk split its health care and enzymes businesses; the split left Novo Nordisk with all the health care operations, while a new company, Novozymes, was formed to carry out the enzyme business. In 2002 Novo Nordisk focused its operations even further by spinning off its US-based biotechnology firm, ZymoGenetics; it retained about 40% of its stake in the company.

The company divested its 29% stake in Ferrosan, a Danish consumer health care and medical devices company, in 2005.

EXECUTIVES

Chairman: Mads Øvlisen, age 65
Vice Chairman: Sten Scheibye, age 54
President and CEO: Lars Rebien Sørensen, age 51, $1,094,800 pay
EVP and CFO: Jesper Brandgaard, age 42, $563,500 pay
EVP and COO: Kåre Schultz, age 44, $499,100 pay
EVP, Quality, Regulatory, and Business Development: Lars A. Jørgensen, age 57, $586,560 pay
EVP and Chief Science Officer: Mads Krogsgaard Thomsen, age 44, $466,900 pay
EVP, People, Reputation, and Relations: Lise Kingo, age 44, $641,550 pay
Member, Senior Management Board, International Operations: Jesper Høiland
Member, Senior Management Board, International Marketing: Jakob Riis
Member, Senior Management Board, Legal Affairs: Ole Ramsby
Member, Senior Management Board, North America: Martin Soeters
Member, Senior Management Board, Regulatory Affairs: Peter Bonne Eriksen
Member, Senior Management Board, Global Development: Lars Guldbæk Karlsen
Executive Director, Corporate Branding and Communications: Lori Moore
SVP, Corporate People and Organization: Ginger Gregory
Director Investor Relations, North America: Christian Kanstrup
Auditors: PricewaterhouseCoopers

LOCATIONS

HQ: Novo Nordisk A/S
Novo Allé, 2880 Bagsværd, Denmark
Phone: +45-4444-8888   **Fax:** +45-4449-0555
US HQ: 100 College Rd. West, Princeton, NJ 08540
US Phone: 609-987-5800   **US Fax:** 609-921-8082
Web: www.novonordisk.com

Novo Nordisk has production facilities in Brazil, China, Denmark, France, Japan, South Africa, and the US.

2004 Sales

	% of total
Europe	43
North America	26
Japan & Oceania	15
Other regions	16
Total	**100**

PRODUCTS/OPERATIONS

2004 Sales

	% of total
Diabetes care	71
Hemostasis management	15
Human growth hormone	8
Hormone replacement therapy	5
Other	1
Total	**100**

Selected Products

Activelle (hormone therapy)
Estrofem (hormone therapy)
FlexPen (prefilled insulin injector)
InDuo (combination blood glucose monitor and insulin injection system)
InnoLet (insulin device for people with poor eyesight and reduced manual dexterity)
Innovo (electronic insulin doser)
Norditropin (recombinant human growth hormone)
Novofem (hormone therapy)
NovoFine (needles)
NovoLet (prefilled disposable syringe)
NovoPen (durable injection system)
NovoSeven (hemophilia treatment)
Vagifem (hormone therapy)

COMPETITORS

Abbott Labs	Medtronic MiniMed
Akzo Nobel	Merck
Amylin Pharmaceuticals	Novartis
Baxter	Pfizer
Bayer	Roche
Becton Dickinson	Sankyo Co
Bristol-Myers Squibb	Sanofi-Aventis
Eli Lilly	Schering-Plough
Forest Labs	Wyeth
GlaxoSmithKline	

HISTORICAL FINANCIALS

Company Type: Public

Income Statement

FYE: December 31

	REVENUE ($ mil.)	NET INCOME ($ mil.)	NET PROFIT MARGIN	EMPLOYEES
12/04	5,327	920	17.3%	20,285
12/03	4,501	824	18.3%	18,800
12/02	3,554	578	16.3%	18,005
12/01	2,839	461	16.2%	16,141
12/00	2,595	385	14.8%	13,752
12/99	2,833	326	11.5%	15,184
12/98	2,812	378	13.4%	14,857
12/97	2,481	324	13.1%	14,175
12/96	2,502	303	12.1%	13,395
12/95	2,474	282	11.4%	12,997
Annual Growth	**8.9%**	**14.0%**	**—**	**5.1%**

2004 Year-End Financials

Debt ratio: 4.5%
Return on equity: 20.1%
Cash ($ mil.): 630
Current ratio: 2.44
Long-term debt ($ mil.): 218
No. of shares (mil.): 332
Dividends
Yield: 1.4%
Payout: 27.2%
Market value ($ mil.): 18,020

Stock History

NYSE: NVO

	STOCK PRICE ($) FY Close	P/E High/Low		PER SHARE ($) Earnings	PER SHARE ($) Dividends	PER SHARE ($) Book Value
12/04	54.26	20	14	2.72	0.74	14.64
12/03	40.96	17	10	2.40	0.52	12.06
12/02	28.90	25	13	1.65	0.37	9.12
12/01	40.10	35	26	1.33	0.32	13.81
12/00	35.40	41	22	1.12	0.24	11.24
12/99	25.85	31	21	0.91	0.22	14.16
12/98	26.60	33	21	1.02	0.00	15.57
12/97	28.85	34	20	0.86	0.00	14.11
12/96	18.70	23	16	0.81	0.07	14.34
12/95	13.70	18	12	0.75	0.07	13.87
Annual Growth	**16.5%**	**—**	**—**	**15.4%**	**30.0%**	**0.6%**

NTT

Nippon Telegraph and Telephone (NTT) has executed an AT&T-style breakup into two local carriers and a long-distance provider — but unlike Ma Bell's gang, this family is sticking together. The world's #1 telecommunications firm, NTT is a holding company for regional local phone companies NTT East and NTT West, which enjoy *de facto* monopolies in their markets, and long-distance carrier NTT Communications, which faces growing competition. NTT also operates a leading ISP and it owns 63% of Japan's dominant cellular carrier, NTT DoCoMo. The firm has made international investments, too, throughout the Pacific Rim and the US. NTT remains 43%-owned by the state.

While the Japanese government has restructured this telecom Godzilla, the telecom market has worked other changes. Combined sales from data transport, Internet services, and mobile phone operations have eclipsed conventional wireline voice revenue; in contrast to the high-growth cellular market, NTT's number of fixed-line subscribers (about 30 million) is on the decline. Still, the company has announced plans to spend $47 billion in enhancing the fixed-line network. The effort includes replacing traditional phone lines with fiber-optic lines. The company also has announced a new business unit, NTT Resonant, that focuses on the development of video communications and broadband portal services.

NTT's international holdings include Hong Kong's HKNet, a 15% stake in Philippine Long Distance Telephone, and Australia-based Davnet Telecommunications (Davtel), which it has renamed NTT Australia. In the US, NTT owns Web-hosting company Verio.

HISTORY

In 1889 the Japanese Ministry of Communications began telephone service, operated as a monopoly after 1900. In 1952 the ministry formed Nippon Telegraph and Telephone Public Corporation (NTT). Regulated by the Ministry of Posts and Telecommunications, NTT was charged with rebuilding Japan's war-ravaged phone system. Another company, Kokusai Denshin Denwa (now KDD), was created in 1953 to handle international phone service.

Japanese authorities cast NTT in the image of AT&T but prohibited it from manufacturing to encourage competition among equipment suppliers. Nonetheless, NTT bought most equipment from favored Japanese vendors. By the late 1970s NTT was a large bureaucracy, perceived as inefficient and corrupt. NTT's president quipped that the only equipment the firm would buy overseas was telephone poles and mops, but in 1981 NTT was forced to allow US companies to bid. The phone firm spent heavily in the 1980s, installing a nationwide fiber-optic network and high-speed ISDN lines.

In 1985 Japan privatized NTT as a precursor to deregulation. At its IPO, NTT became the world's most valuable public company. NTT International was established to provide overseas telecom engineering, and NTT Data Communications Systems, Japan's largest systems integrator, was formed in 1988.

As Japan's stock market bubble burst in 1990, NTT chose AT&T, Motorola, and Ericsson to develop a digital mobile phone system and the next year formed NTT Mobile Communications Network (NTT DoCoMo) as its mobile carrier. Following the deregulation of Japan's cellular market, NTT launched its Personal Handyphone Service (PHS) in 1995.

The Japanese government unveiled a plan to break up NTT in 1996, a year before the World Trade Organization spearheaded a historic agreement to open international telecom markets. Meanwhile, the government forced NTT to allow rivals to connect to its new, all-digital systems. Overseas, NTT made its first significant investment in the US by buying a 12.5% stake in local carrier Teligent (later reduced).

In 1998 tiny Tokyo Telecommunications Net (a Tokyo Electric Power affiliate) offered discount phone rates, spurring NTT to do the same. NTT spun off DoCoMo in the world's largest IPO at the time.

NTT lost its 1999 bidding war with the UK's Cable and Wireless for International Digital Communications. That year NTT split into three carriers, two near-monopoly regional local phone providers — NTT East and NTT West — and a long-distance and international carrier called NTT Communications. Unlike AT&T's breakup in 1984, this split featured a holding company — the new NTT — that owns the three carriers. Criticized for continuing to promote last-generation ISDN as the key to high-speed Internet access, NTT in 1999 began to test higher-speed digital subscriber line (DSL) service and planned to cut 21,000 jobs at NTT West and NTT East over three years.

The company pressed forward with international investments, taking a 49% stake in HKNet of Hong Kong and a 49% stake in Davnet Telecommunications, a subsidiary of Australia's

Davnet Limited (both were later increased to 100%). In 2000 the Japanese government said it would sell another 6% of NTT. That year NTT paid $5.5 billion for the 90% of US Web-hosting firm Verio that it didn't already own.

But as a result of the economic downturn, NTT took a write-down of around $4.5 billion on its Verio acquisition in 2001 and shifted more than 25% of its workers to lower-paying positions.

EXECUTIVES

President, CEO, and Director: Norio Wada, age 65
SEVP, CFO, Director of Corporate Management Strategy Division, and Board Member: Satoshi Miura, age 61
SEVP, Technical Strategy and Resonant Promotion, and Director: Ryuji Yamada, age 57
SVP, Intellectual Property, Director of Department III, and Board Member: Yuji Inoue, age 57
SVP, Director of Department II, and Board Member: Shin Hashimoto, age 56
SVP, Director of Department IV, and Board Member: Hiroo Unoura, age 56
SVP, Director of Department IV, and Board Member: Ken Yagi, age 55
SVP, Corporate Management Strategy, and Director: Akira Arima, age 56
SVP, Director of Department I, and Board Member: Kiyoshi Kousaka, age 54
Chief Executive Counselor and Director: Haruki Matsuno, age 68
President, NTT East: Toyohiko Takabe, age 58
President, NTT West: Shunzo Morishita, age 60
President, NTT Communications: Hiromi Wasai, age 59
President and CEO, NTT DATA: Tomokazu Hamaguchi, age 61
President, NTT DoCoMo, Inc.: Masao Nakamura, age 61
Auditors: ChuoAoyama PricewaterhouseCoopers

LOCATIONS

HQ: Nippon Telegraph and Telephone Corporation (Nippon Denshin Denwa Kabushiki Kaisha) 3-1, Otemachi 2-chome, Chiyoda-ku, Tokyo 100-8116, Japan
Phone: +81-3-5205-5581   **Fax:** +81-3-5205-5589
US HQ: 101 Park Ave., 41st Fl., New York, NY 10178
US Phone: 212-661-0810   **US Fax:** 212-661-1078
Web: www.ntt.co.jp

Nippon Telegraph and Telephone operates principally in Japan. The company also operates or has investments in operations throughout the Pacific Rim — including in Australia, Hong Kong, Malaysia, the Philippines, Singapore, and Taiwan — as well as in Europe, Latin America, and the US.

PRODUCTS/OPERATIONS

2005 Sales

	$ mil.	% of total
Fixed voice services	33,440	33
Mobile voice services	30,057	30
IP, packet communications services	16,568	16
Systems integration	8,507	9
Sales of telecom equipment	6,431	6
Other services	5,987	6
Total	**100,990**	**100**

Selected Subsidiaries and Affiliates

Internet Initiative Japan Inc. (32%)
Nippon Telegraph and Telephone East Corporation (NTT East, regional telecommunications)
Nippon Telegraph and Telephone West Corporation (NTT West, regional telecommunications)
NTT Australia IP Pty Ltd (formerly Davnet Telecommunications Pty Ltd. (Davtel), Australia)

NTT Communications Corporation (long-distance and international telecommunications)
HKNet Company Limited (ISP, Hong Kong)
NTT DATA Corporation (54%, systems integration and network services)
NTT DoCoMo, Inc. (63%, mobile telecommunications)
NTT Resonant Inc. (development of video communications and broadband portal services)
Philippine Long Distance Telephone (PLDT, 15%)
Verio Inc. (corporate Internet services, US)

COMPETITORS

Asia Netcom	KDDI
AT&T	MCI
BT	Microsoft
BT Infonet	NEC
Cable & Wireless	SOFTBANK
Equant	Telstra
Fujitsu	Tokyo Electric
Internet Initiative Japan	Tokyo Telecommunication
Kansai Electric	Vodafone K.K.

HISTORICAL FINANCIALS

Company Type: Public

Income Statement

FYE: March 31

	REVENUE ($ mil.)	NET INCOME ($ mil.)	NET PROFIT MARGIN	EMPLOYEES
3/05	100,990	6,637	6.6%	201,486
3/04	105,672	6,132	5.8%	205,288
3/03	91,026	1,945	2.1%	207,363
3/02	86,734	(6,276)	—	213,062
3/01	92,098	4,340	4.7%	222,000
3/00	97,956	2,821	2.9%	224,000
3/99	80,411	4,582	5.7%	224,000
3/98	71,591	1,625	2.3%	226,000
3/97	71,143	2,028	2.9%	230,000
3/96	74,610	2,582	3.5%	231,000
Annual Growth	**3.4%**	**11.1%**	**—**	**(1.5%)**

2005 Year-End Financials

Debt ratio: 66.7%
Return on equity: 10.7%
Cash ($ mil.): 12,915
Current ratio: 1.23
Long-term debt ($ mil.): 42,164

No. of shares (mil.): 2,988
Dividends
Yield: 1.1%
Payout: 11.7%
Market value ($ mil.): 65,292

Stock History

NYSE: NTT

	STOCK PRICE ($) FY Close	P/E High/Low		PER SHARE ($) Earnings	Dividends	Book Value
3/05	21.85	14	9	2.14	0.25	21.17
3/04	28.34	15	9	1.93	0.20	19.35
3/03	16.98	35	24	0.61	0.20	14.74
3/02	19.35	—	—	(1.60)	0.21	13.67
3/01	32.28	57	21	1.37	0.23	17.02
3/00	78.81	104	53	0.89	0.39	17.92
3/99	48.75	35	22	1.44	0.09	15.35
3/98	42.31	103	67	0.51	0.00	13.01
3/97	35.88	63	53	0.64	0.10	13.53
3/96	37.00	46	36	1.01	0.11	15.40
Annual Growth	**(5.7%)**	**—**	**—**	**8.7%**	**9.6%**	**3.6%**

NTT DoCoMo

The Japanese yen for mobile phones means business for NTT DoCoMo. Formerly NTT Mobile Communications Network, the wireless spinoff of Nippon Telegraph and Telephone (NTT), the mobile phone carrier has more than 50 million subscribers to its digital network (a 56% market share). It is one of the world's largest mobile phone operators by subscribers, behind #1 Vodafone. More than 41 million customers subscribe to NTT DoCoMo's i-mode service, which provides Internet access from mobile phones. The company also offers maritime and in-flight phone services and sells handsets. NTT owns 63% of NTT DoCoMo.

DoCoMo (which means "anywhere") corners nearly 60% of the Japanese market for mobile phones through its eight majority-owned regional operating subsidiaries. It has announced plans to take full ownership of these units and consolidate them.

The company has scored big with the rollout of its popular i-mode service. It became the first company in the world to offer the third-generation (3G) mobile phone service with its 2001 debut in Tokyo.

DoCoMo is now building a presence in Europe. It has teamed up with Telecom Italia Mobile to introduce i-mode services in Italy. It also joined Hutchison Whampoa and Dutch phone company KPN in an alliance to bid on European next-generation mobile phone licenses and the company paid $4.5 billion for a 15% stake in KPN's wireless unit, KPN Mobile (the stake was reduced to 2.2% when DoCoMo declined to subscribe to additional shares offered the transferred back to parent KPN. DoCoMo continues its i-mode affiliation, however).

The company also has licensed its i-mode technology to the telecom unit of French construction group Bouygues, to Italy's Wind, and to Telefónica Móviles in Spain, and it has reorganized its European holdings under a single subsidiary, DoCoMo Europe Ltd. But failed expectations have led the company to sell its 20% stake in Hutchison 3G UK to Hutchison Whampoa in a deal valued at E120 million.

DoCoMo has staked its claim in the US, too, by paying $9.8 billion for a 16% stake in AT&T Wireless. However, AT&T Wireless was the subject of a takeover bidding war won by rival Cingular Wireless in a deal valued at $41 billion and DoCoMo sold its stake. DoCoMo is taking an active role in advancing new mobile communications technologies through the creation of a US-based venture investment firm, DoCoMo Capital. The company is planning new services for all its markets, through a joint venture with Sony focused on developing mobile phones equipped with Sony's smart-card technology. DoCoMo has, however, agreed to sell its 43% stake in DoCoMo AOL to America Online, and it has liquidated several subsidiaries, including an operating unit in Brazil.

After the number of paging service subscribers fell to less than 300,000 from a high of 6.5 million (in 1996), the company is ending the service in early 2007.

HISTORY

Formed in 1952 by the Japanese Ministry of Communications to rebuild Japan's war-ravaged phone system, Nippon Telegraph and Telephone (NTT) enjoyed a monopoly on phone services for more than four decades.

NTT first went into mobile communications with a maritime phone service in 1959, and in 1968 the company began offering paging services. Other telecommunications services followed: car phone service (1979), in-flight phone service (1986), and mobile phone service (1987).

In 1991 NTT established a subsidiary to adopt these wireless segments: It launched operations in 1992 as NTT Mobile Communications Network under the leadership of NTT executive Kouji Ohboshi. The firm quickly took on the DoCoMo nickname. The year closed with slightly more than a million analog mobile phone users in Japan — a market DoCoMo shared with upstart telecom companies DDI and IDO (later bought by DDI). Paging service was more popular, and DoCoMo won more than 3 million customers.

DoCoMo in 1993 launched digital mobile phone service based on a scheme called PDC (personal digital cellular) — a system incompatible with the digital standards that would take root in Europe and the US. Liberalization of the cellular phone market in 1994 triggered unexpected growth: Customers who previously had to lease mobile phones from the network operators could now buy them at retail stores. Further competition emerged in 1995 with the launch of personal handyphone services, or PHS (parent company NTT was among the companies providing PHS), but DoCoMo's subscriber count passed 3.5 million mobile phone users — about half the market.

DoCoMo's pager business peaked in 1996 before commencing a long-term decline; the mobile phone market, where DoCoMo had more than 8 million subscribers, overtook it. The company launched a satellite-based mobile phone system that year to serve customers beyond the range of cell sites, reaching ships and mountainous regions.

Financial crises rocked the Pacific Rim in 1997, and Japan's Fair Trade Commission rocked NTT by ordering it to cut its 95%-ownership of DoCoMo. Customers continued to flock to mobile phones despite economic turmoil, and DoCoMo passed the 15 million-subscriber mark. In 1998 DoCoMo gave hope to Japan's low-flying market when it left the nest: Its mammoth IPO raised more than $18 billion.

Meanwhile, DDI (now KDDI) had become the first Japanese carrier to launch a digital mobile phone network based on CDMA (code division multiple access) technology. Though DoCoMo still used PDC, it redoubled its efforts to help develop and standardize a next-generation, wideband version of CDMA.

In 1999 DoCoMo took over NTT's unprofitable PHS unit and rolled out a high-speed data service over the PHS network.

It also became the first company in the world to offer the third-generation (3G) mobile phone service with a 2001 debut in Tokyo of i-mode, which gave customers Internet access on a specialized handset. To promote such new data services, DoCoMo launched a joint venture in Japan with Microsoft (Mobimagic). That year it acquired a 19% stake in the telecom unit of Hong Kong's Hutchison Whampoa.

DoCoMo took the i-mode service international in 2001 when the company teamed up with Telecom Italia Mobile to introduce the 3G service in Europe. The next year DoCoMo became the largest shareholder in America Online Japan when it acquired a 42% stake.

EXECUTIVES

President, CEO, and Director: Masao Nakamura, age 61
SEVP, Managing Director, Global Business Division, and Director: Masayuki Hirata, age 58
SEVP, Managing Director, Network Division, and Director: Kunio Ishikawa, age 57
SEVP and Director: Seijiro Adachi, age 61
EVP, CTO, Managing Director, Research and Development Division, and Director: Takanori Utano, age 56
EVP, Managing Director, Products and Services Division, and Director: Kiyoyuki Tsujimura, age 55
EVP, Managing Director, Marketing Division, and Director: Takashi Sakamoto, age 56
EVP, Managing Director, Corporate Marketing Department, and Director: Shuro Hoshizawa, age 56
EVP, CFO, Managing Director, Accounts and Finance Department, and Director: Yoshiaki Ugaki, age 56
EVP and Deputy Managing Director, Corporate Marketing Division: Seiji Tanaka, age 63
SVP, Managing Director, Personnel Development Department, and Director: Harunari Futatsugi, age 54
SVP and Managing Director, Public Relations Department: Masatoshi Suzuki, age 54
SVP and Managing Director, Sales Promotion Department, Marketing Division: Toru Kobayashi
Auditors: KPMG AZSA & Co.

LOCATIONS

HQ: NTT DoCoMo, Inc.
Sanno Park Tower, 11-1 Nagatacho-2-chome, Chiyoda-ku, Tokyo 100-6150, Japan
Phone: +81-3-5156-1111   **Fax:** +81-3-5156-0271
Web: www.nttdocomo.com

PRODUCTS/OPERATIONS

2005 Sales

	$ mil.	% of total
Wireless services	40,072	89
Equipment sales	5,112	11
Total	**45,184**	**100**

Selected Services

Cellular
i-mode (wireless Internet access)
In-flight telephone
Mobile multimedia
Personal Handyphone System (PHS, wireless voice and data transmission service)
Satellite mobile communications
Third-generation (3G) wireless (W-CDMA)
World Call (direct international calling)

Regional Operating Subsidiaries

NTT DoCoMo Chugoku, Inc.
NTT DoCoMo Hokkaido, Inc.
NTT DoCoMo Hokuriku, Inc.
NTT DoCoMo Kansai, Inc.
NTT DoCoMo Kyushu, Inc.
NTT DoCoMo Shikoku, Inc.
NTT DoCoMo Tohoku, Inc.
NTT DoCoMo Tokai, Inc.

Selected Subsidiaries and Affiliates

DoCoMo Capital, Inc. (advanced mobile communications technologies venture investments, US)
DoCoMo Europe Ltd.
Far EasTone Telecommunications Co., Ltd. (5%, Taiwan)
KG Telecommunications Co. (Taiwan)
Hutchison Telephone Company Ltd. (24%, Hong Kong)

COMPETITORS

BT
China Mobile (Hong Kong)
Cingular Wireless
Deutsche Telekom
France Telecom
KDDI
Optus
Orange
SK Telecom
Telstra
Verizon Wireless
Vodafone
Vodafone K.K.

HISTORICAL FINANCIALS

Company Type: Public

Income Statement

	REVENUE ($ mil.)	NET INCOME ($ mil.)	NET PROFIT MARGIN	EMPLOYEES
3/05	45,184	6,972	15.4%	21,527
3/04	48,455	6,239	12.9%	21,241
3/03	40,731	1,800	4.4%	23,310
3/02	38,939	(876)	—	19,700
3/01	37,194	3,200	8.6%	18,015
3/00	35,246	2,390	6.8%	10,098
3/99	26,181	1,720	6.6%	9,342
3/98	19,735	907	4.6%	7,557
3/97	15,856	232	1.5%	6,901
3/96	11,535	199	1.7%	6,323
Annual Growth	16.4%	48.4%	—	14.6%

FYE: March 31

2005 Year-End Financials

Debt ratio: 20.4%
Return on equity: 19.4%
Cash ($ mil.): 7,181
Current ratio: 1.96
Long-term debt ($ mil.): 7,445
No. of shares (mil.): 4,627
Dividends
Yield: 0.5%
Payout: 6.1%
Market value ($ mil.): 77,506

Stock History

NYSE: DCM

	STOCK PRICE ($) FY Close	P/E High/Low		PER SHARE ($) Earnings	Dividends	Book Value
3/05	16.75	16	11	1.47	0.09	7.88
3/04	22.16	22	15	1.26	0.00	7.32
3/03	18.86	67	39	0.36	0.04	5.87
3/02	27.36	—	—	(0.17)	0.00	4.94
Annual Growth	(15.1%)	—	—	—	—	16.8%

Oki Electric

Oki Electric Industry is plugged into a variety of products. The company's core businesses include information systems, telecommunication systems, semiconductors, and printers. Its information products include facsimile machines offered through its Oki Data subsidiary, as well as automated teller machines, terminals, banking systems, and security systems. The company's electronics operations (represented by Oki Semiconductor in the US) produce integrated circuits, microprocessors, and audiovisual products. Oki's telecom products include network equipment, switching systems, and computer telephony integration systems.

The company generates about half of sales from its information systems segment and the company's electronics operations account for a little more than 20% of sales. In order to combat a slumping telecommunications market and worldwide downturn in information technology spending, Oki Electric has realigned its operations. Its restructuring efforts include a shift away from hardware sales to broader service offerings such as network design, installation, and maintenance.

Oki acquired the driver chip business for large TFT-LCDs from Texas Instruments Japan in early 2005. TFT-LCDs drive chips are used in notebook computers, monitors, and TVs.

HISTORY

Engineer Kibataro Oki founded Meikosha in Tokyo in 1881 to produce telephones (only five years after they were invented). Meikosha was soon producing telegraphs, bells, and medical equipment. Its main factory adopted the name Oki Electric Plant in 1889, and the marketing division began operating under the name Oki & Company in 1896.

In 1907, a year after the founder's death, the Oki groups were united as a limited partnership. Divided again in 1912, they were recombined in 1917 as Oki Electric Co. Oki continued to expand its product line to include automatic switching equipment (1926) and electric clocks (1929).

The manufacturer produced communications equipment for the Japanese military during WWII, but after the war it started working on the teleprinter and added consumer goods such as portable stoves. The company adopted its present name, Oki Electric Industry Company, in 1949.

Oki entered the semiconductor and computer industries in the 1950s, joining Fujitsu, Hitachi, Mitsubishi, Nippon Electric Co., and Toshiba as one of Japan's Big Six electronics makers by 1960. It then began developing overseas businesses, particularly in Latin America, where it built communications networks in Honduras (1962) and Bolivia (1966) and radio networks in Brazil (1971).

In 1970 Oki formed a computer software unit. The company was a major telecommunications equipment supplier for the Japanese government until the mid-1970s, when the government increased its purchases from other companies. Former Nippon Telegraph and Telephone executive Masao Miyake took over as president, initiating a dramatic reorganization into 15 business units.

Oki started building PCs in 1981. It consolidated its US operations as Oki America in 1984. A new financial crisis followed in the mid-1980s when the bottom fell out of the semiconductor market — Oki's earnings plummeted into the red in 1986. However, by the end of the decade Oki had become a major provider of automated teller machines (ATMs) and bank computer systems; growth in the Japanese financial industry sparked a ninefold increase in Oki's sales in 1989. In 1994 Oki established subsidiary Oki Data Corp. to handle printer and fax machine operations.

Plunging memory prices and higher taxes stymied Oki's recovery in fiscal 1998, so the company halted mass random-access memory (RAM) production and closed an assembly and testing facility. Oki shifted its semiconductor focus to large-scale integrated circuits, and placed more emphasis on its information systems segment, which had seen increasing sales.

Further battered by a weak Asian economy, Oki restructured in 1999. That year the company bought Toshiba's ATM operations. It also launched an access control system that uses a person's iris for identification and payment services.

In 2000 Oki announced plans to establish (along with NTT Data, NTT DoCoMo, Microsoft and others) Payment First Corporation, an Internet payment company.

Responding to poor market conditions, Oki announced in 2001 that it would reduce its workforce by about 10% over two years. The company also sold its automotive electronics division to Keihin Corporation.

EXECUTIVES

President, CEO, and Board Member: Katsumasa Shinozuka
EVP, CFO, Chief Compliance Officer, and Board Member: Kazuo Tanaka
EVP; Chairman, Systems Network Business Group; General Manager, China Business Promotion Division; Board Member: Yutaka Maeda
SVP and Board Member: Tadao Murase
SVP, CIO, and Board Member: Nobuhide Hara
SVP; Group Operating Officer, Systems Network Business Group; and Board Member: Takashi Hattori
SVP and Board Member: Naoki Sato
SVP, CTO, and Board Member: Harushige Sugimoto
Senior Operating Officer, Systems Network Business Group; Acting General Manager, Strategic Planning Office: Kazushige Matsui
General Manager, Marketing Promotion Division; Board Member: Hideichi Kawasaki
Group Operating Officer, Semiconductor Business Group: Hironori Kitabayashi
General Manager, Accounting and Control Division: Keiichi Fukumura
Auditors: Ernst & Young ShinNihon

LOCATIONS

HQ: Oki Electric Industry Company, Limited (Oki Denki Kogyo Kabushiki Kaisha)
7-12, Toranomon 1-chome,
Minato-ku, Tokyo 105-8460, Japan
Phone: +81-3-3501-3111   **Fax:** +81-3-3581-5522
US HQ: 785 N. Mary Ave., Sunnyvale, CA 94085-2909
US Phone: 408-720-1900   **US Fax:** 408-720-1918
Web: www.oki.com

2005 Sales

	% of total
Japan	71
Europe	9
North America	7
Other regions	13
Total	**100**

PRODUCTS/OPERATIONS

2005 Sales

	% of total
Information systems	49
Electronic devices	22
Telecommunications	20
Other	9
Total	**100**

Selected Products

Information Systems
  Automated teller machines
  Point-of-sale terminals
  Printers
  Terminals
  Video delivery software
Electronic Devices
  Large-scale integrated circuits
  Memory chips
  Microprocessors
  Optical components
  Telecommunications and voice synthesis circuits
Telecommunications Systems
  ATM (asynchronous transfer mode) switches
  Computer telephony integration
  ISDN terminals
  Key telephone systems
  Fiber-optic communications products
  Modems
  PBX systems
  Radio equipment
  Teleconferencing systems
  Video/audio encoders/decoders

COMPETITORS

Canon	Mitsubishi Electric
CASIO COMPUTER	NCR
Cisco Systems	NEC
Dell	NTT DATA
Diebold	Ricoh
Epson	Samsung
Fuji Xerox	SANYO
Fujitsu	Sharp
Hewlett-Packard	Siemens
Hitachi	Sony
IBM	Symbol Technologies
Konica Minolta	Toshiba
Kyocera	VeriFone
Lexmark	Wincor Nixdorf
Matsushita	Xerox
MICROS Systems	

HISTORICAL FINANCIALS

Company Type: Public

Income Statement

FYE: March 31

	REVENUE ($ mil.)	NET INCOME ($ mil.)	NET PROFIT MARGIN	EMPLOYEES
3/05	6,402	104	1.6%	20,410
3/04	6,193	13	0.2%	20,960
3/03	4,885	(55)	—	22,520
3/02	4,558	(257)	—	23,597
3/01	5,860	71	1.2%	25,626
3/00	6,348	11	0.2%	25,444
3/99	5,652	(398)	—	23,425
3/98	5,746	(61)	—	23,968
3/97	5,915	26	0.4%	21,355
3/96	6,977	230	3.3%	21,718
Annual Growth	**(1.0%)**	**(8.5%)**	**—**	**(0.7%)**

2005 Year-End Financials

Debt ratio: 96.0%
Return on equity: 9.4%
Cash ($ mil.): 459
Current ratio: 1.20
Long-term debt ($ mil.): 1,114

Net Income History

Exchange: Tokyo

OMV

Oil and chemicals group OMV is Austria's largest industrial company. It explores for natural gas and crude oil, refines crude oil, and imports, transports, and stores gas. A leading oil and gas company in Central and Eastern Europe, OMV has proved reserves of 410 million barrels of oil equivalent. With petroleum products marketed through OMV gas stations and direct distributors, OMV has a 14% retail market share in Central and Eastern Europe. The company also makes plastics (it owns geotextile producer Polyfelt) and chemicals (fertilizers and melamine). OMV's largest shareholders are Austrian state holding company ÖIAG (31.5%) and the International Petroleum Investment Company (IPIC) of Abu Dhabi (17.6%).

OMV has exploration activities in Austria as well as internationally (including Australia, Libya, Pakistan, and the UK).

The bulk of OMV's sales come from refining and marketing. It has two refineries and a total refining capacity of 380,000 barrels of oil equivalent per day. Petroleum products are marketed through more than 1,780 OMV filling stations and direct distributors. Its natural gas network, serving about 90% of Austria's natural gas demand, draws gas supplies from Russia, Norway, and Germany, as well as from domestic reserves.

Subsidiary Agrolinz Melamin is the Austrian leader in plant nutrients and the world's #2 producer of melamine (a synthetic resin used to manufacture flooring and furniture) behind DSM Chemicals North America. OMV also makes nonwoven geotextiles for engineering materials through its Polyfelt unit and owns 25% of Danish polyolefin producer Borealis.

Austria's gas market, now dominated by OMV, is slated for full competition, and OMV is among state-controlled companies set for full privatization. Meanwhile, the company's expansion eastwards into Romania is supporting its eventual goal: Russia.

HISTORY

Oil exploration began in Austria in the 1920s, largely as joint ventures with foreign firms such as Shell and Socony-Vacuum. Full-scale production did not get underway until 1938, when the Anschluss (the absorption of Austria by Germany) paved the way for Germany to exploit Austria's natural resources to fuel its growing war machine. In the division of spoils following WWII, Russia gained control of Austria's oil reserves.

The Russian-administered oil assets were transferred to the new Austrian government in 1955, which authorized the company Österreichische Mineralölverwaltung (ÖMG) in 1956 to control state oil assets. ÖMG, state-controlled by the Austrian Mineral Oil Administration, set about building a major refinery in 1960 and acquiring marketing companies Martha and ÖROP in 1965.

In 1968 ÖMG became the first Western company to sign a natural gas supply contract with Russia. In 1974 the company commissioned the Trans-Austria Gas Pipeline, which enabled the supply of natural gas to Italy. That year ÖMG changed its named to ÖMV Aktiengesellschaft (ÖMV became OMV in 1995 for international markets).

During the 1970s OMV expanded its crude supply arrangements, tapping supplies from Iran, Iraq, Libya, and other Middle Eastern countries. It moved into oil and gas exploration in the mid-1980s, forming OMV Libya (acquiring 25% of Occidental's Libyan production) and OMV UK.

With Austria moving toward increasing privatization, in 1987 about 15% of OMV's shares were sold to the public. The government sold a further 10% two years later. In 1989 OMV acquired PCD Polymere. With the aim of merging state-owned oil and chemical activities, OMV acquired Chemie Linz in 1990. The company also opened its first OMV-branded service station that year. In 1994 OMV reorganized itself as an integrated oil and gas group based in Central Europe, with international exploration and production activities, and with other operations in the chemical and petrochemical sectors.

In 1995 OMV acquired TOTAL-AUSTRIA, expanding its service stations by 59. The company introduced OMV lubricants to the Greek market in 1996. It also expanded its OMV service station network in Hungary to 66 stations after acquiring 31 Q8 (Kuwait) sites. In 1997 the Stroh Company's retail network in Austria was merged into OMV.

Expanding its retail network even further, OMV acquired BP's retail network in the Czech Republic, Slovakia, and Hungary in 1998. It also sold its stake in Chemie Linz and acquired a 25% stake in major European polyolefin producer Borealis, which in turn acquired PCD Polymere. In 1999 the company pushed its retail network into Bulgaria and Romania. That year OMV also acquired Australian company Cultus Petroleum.

OMV and Shell agreed to develop North Sea fields together in 2000. That year OMV also formed a joint venture with Italy's Edison International to explore in Vietnam and acquired more than 9% of Hungarian rival MOL. It upped that stake to 10% in 2001. The company also made a bid that year for 18% of Poland's largest refiner, PKN Orlen.

In 2002 OMV opened its first gas station in Serbia and Montenegro. It also increased its German gas station count from 79 to 151 with the purchase of 32 units from Royal Dutch/Shell Group and 40 stations from Martin GmbH & Co.

In 2003 the company acquired Preussag Energie's exploration and production assets for $320 million. That same year, the company moved into Bosnia-Herzegovina, opening nine gas stations.

During 2004 the company bought up 51% of Romania's Petrom, making it the top oil and gas producer in Central Europe. As part of the deal, OMV chose to divest itself of its quarter-chunk of Rompetrol.

EXECUTIVES

Chairman: Rainer Wieltsch
Chairman of the Executive Board and CEO:
Wolfgang Ruttenstorfer, age 55
Deputy Chairman of the Executive Board and VP Refining and Marketing and Petrochemicals:
Gerhard Roiss, age 53
CFO: David C. Davies, age 50
VP Exploration and Production; Managing Director, OMV Exploration and Production: Helmut Langanger, age 55
Investor Relations: Ana-Barbara Kuncic
Auditors: Deloitte Touche Tohmatsu WirtschaftsprüfungsgmbH

LOCATIONS

HQ: OMV Aktiengesellschaft
Otto-Wagner-Platz 5, A-1090 Vienna, Austria
Phone: +43-1-40-440-0   **Fax:** +43-1-40-440-20999
Web: www.omv.com

OMV has marketing operations across Central and Eastern Europe, including Austria, Bulgaria, the Czech Republic, Germany, Hungary, Romania, Serbia and Montenegro, Slovakia, and Switzerland. The company operates refineries in Schwechat, Austria, and Burghausen, Germany, and has chemicals and plastics plants in Austria, Italy, and Malaysia.

2004 Oil and Gas Production

	% of total
Austria	31
Libya	19
UK	12
Pakistan	13
South America	9
Tunisia	7
New Zealand	5
Australia	3
Qatar	1
Total	**100**

PRODUCTS/OPERATIONS

2004 Sales

	% of total
Refining & marketing	78
Exploration & production	9
Gas	7
Chemicals & plastics	4
Other	2
Total	**100**

Selected Subsidiaries

AMI Agrolinz Melamine International GmbH
AUSTRIA Mineralöl GmbH
OMV (ALBANIEN) offshore Exploration GmbH
OMV Erdgas GmbH
OMV OF LIBYA LIMITED (UK)
OMV (PAKISTAN) Exploration Gesellschaft m.b.H.
OMV (SUDAN) Exploration GmbH
OMV (U.K.) Limited
POLYFELT Gesellschaft m.b.H.
WÄRME-ENERGIE VORARLBERG Beratung- und Handels GmbH (80%)

COMPETITORS

BP
DSM
Eni
Exxon Mobil
Hellenic Petroleum
MOL
PKN ORLEN
Royal Dutch/Shell Group
Unipetrol

HISTORICAL FINANCIALS

Company Type: Public

Income Statement

	REVENUE ($ mil.)	NET INCOME ($ mil.)	NET PROFIT MARGIN	EMPLOYEES
12/04	18,237	876	4.8%	6,232
12/03	9,595	493	5.1%	6,137
12/02	7,420	338	4.6%	5,828
12/01	6,853	338	4.9%	5,659
12/00	7,019	304	4.3%	5,757
12/99	5,215	195	3.7%	5,953
12/98	5,508	198	3.6%	6,360
12/97	6,591	180	2.7%	7,934
Annual Growth	**15.6%**	**25.3%**	**—**	**(3.4%)**

FYE: December 31

2004 Year-End Financials

Debt ratio: 32.6%
Return on equity: 16.4%
Cash ($ mil.): 2,000
Current ratio: 1.95
Long-term debt ($ mil.): 2,392

Net Income History

Pink Sheets: OMVKY

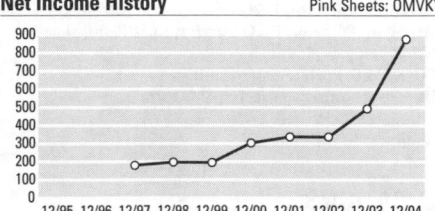

Otto GmbH

Otto GmbH & Co KG (formerly Otto Versand) has the mail-order business in the bag. The world's largest mail-order company sells merchandise in about 20 countries through more than 100 subsidiaries. Customers order from more than 600 print catalogs, as well as through CD-ROM catalogs and the Internet. The firm sells products from clothing to appliances to sporting goods. Otto also owns a majority stake in the Euromarket Designs (a.k.a. Crate & Barrel) housewares chain, and it owns travel agencies in Germany. The family of executive board chairman Michael Otto owns the majority of the company; in 2005 it sold off its longstanding controlling interest in US catalog company Spiegel (now Eddie Bauer Holdings).

The company controls Actebis Holding, a major computer distributor in Europe.

The Otto Group has grown largely through its acquisitions and diversification tactics (entering non-mail-order businesses). The firm does about 50% of its business in Germany, and customers there can get same-day delivery of many of Otto's wares.

HISTORY

East German refugee Werner Otto founded Otto Versand (German for "dispatch") in Hamburg, West Germany, in 1949. It distributed its first catalog in 1950; 300 hand-bound copies offered only shoes, but in 28 styles. Instead of being required to pay upon delivery, customers received bills with their orders; this was new for mail orders. By 1956 the firm employed 500 people; by 1958 the catalog had expanded to 200 pages, offering low-cost women's fashions and other products to 200,000 potential customers.

In 1963 Otto Versand began taking phone orders. Its catalog grew to 800 pages and one million copies by 1967. The following year it published the Post Shop Magazine, its first special-interest catalog, which targeted fashion-conscious youth. In 1969 Otto Versand formed Hanseatic Bank to offer customers monthly payment plans; three years later it formed the Hermes Express Package delivery service.

The firm began a shopping spree in the 1970s by investing in mail-order companies 3 Suisses International (France, 1974), Heinrich Heine (luxury clothes and household goods, West Germany, 1974) and Hanau (West Germany, 1979).

Werner's son Michael succeeded him as chairman in 1981, and in 1982 he led the acquisition of low-cost women's apparel firm Spiegel. Michael immediately revamped Spiegel into an upscale retailer. The ownership of Spiegel was restructured in 1984, but the Otto family remained in control of the US company.

Throughout the 1980s the firm continued investing in European companies (entering the UK in 1986 and Austria in 1988) and began Otto-Sumisho in Japan (a joint venture, 1986). Its combined catalog circulation reached 200 million in 1987.

Otto Versand launched 24-hour delivery service in 1990; that year it expanded to the Polish market by forming joint venture Otto-Epoka. In 1991 it began 24-hour phone sales and acquired a majority stake in Grattan (the UK's fourth-largest mail-order firm). Acquisitions continued during the early and mid-1990s, including Margareta (Hungary), Postalmarket (Italy's largest mail-order firm), and Otto-Burlingtons (joint venture between Germany and India).

Otto Versand acquired a majority stake in Reiseland's 60 travel agencies in 1993 and bought two UK collection agencies in 1994. In 1994 it became Germany's first mail-order firm to offer an interactive CD-ROM catalog.

The firm bought a majority stake in US housewares retailer Crate & Barrel in 1998 and bought German computer wholesaler Actebis Holding. It then formed Zara Deutschland, a joint venture in Germany (with Spain's Inditex), to sell clothing in a new chain of outlets. Otto Versand added to its travel business (about 140 locations) in 1998 with the purchase of 25 offices from American Express Germany. It closed Postalmarket that year because of problems with the Italian postal service.

In 1999 Otto Versand acquired the Freemans catalog business (nearly $900 million in 1998 sales) from the UK's Sears PLC. The deal nearly doubled the company's UK mail-order market share, from 8% to 15%. In late 1999 the firm formed a joint venture with Harrods to sell fancy English goods online.

In early 2000 Otto Versand set up a joint venture with America Online (now part of Time Warner) and Deutsche Bank 24 to offer online banking, Internet service, and PCs. In October 2001 the company entered into a joint venture with US Internet travel service provider Travelocity.com to form Travelocity Europe.

In 2003 Otto Versand changed its name to Otto GmbH & Co KG.

EXECUTIVES

Supervisory Board Chairman: Hans Jörg Hammer
Executive Board Chairman and Chief Executive Officer, Otto Group: Michael Otto, age 62
CEO: Gordon Segal, age 65
CFO: Juergen Schulte-Laggenbeck, age 39
COO: Peer Witten, age 59
General Manager, Marketing, Sales, E-Commerce OTTO: Rainer Hillebrand
General Manager, Human Resources and Planning and Controlling: Winfried Zimmermann
VP, Corporate Communications: Thomas Voigt
Chief Human Resources Officer: Alexander Birken
Chairman and CEO, 3 Suisses International: Pierre Zucchini
CEO, ACTEBIS Holding: Dirk Hauke, age 40
CEO, Baur Versand: Richard Krekeler, age 62
CEO, Hanseatic Bank: Torsten Brandes, age 50
CEO, Handelsgesellschaft Heinrich Heine: Werner Schulz, age 52
CEO, Hermes Logistik Group: Hanjo Schneider, age 40
CEO, KG EOS Holding: Hans-Werner Scherer, age 50
CEO, oHG Fegro/Selgros Gesellschaft für Großhandel: Rüdiger Strein, age 64
CEO, Otto Doosan Mail Order: Hyung-Suk Kwon, age 62
Chairman and CEO, Otto Sumisho: Hiroki Hachiya
CEO, SCHWAB VERSAND: Rolf Schäfer, age 58
Auditors: KPMG Deutsche Treuhand-Gesellschaft AG

LOCATIONS

HQ: Otto GmbH & Co KG
Wandsbeker Strasse 3-7, 2217 Hamburg, Germany
Phone: +49-40-64-61-0 **Fax:** +49-40-64-61-85-71
Web: www.ottogroup.com

2004 Sales

	% of total
Germany	51
Other countries	49
Total	**100**

PRODUCTS/OPERATIONS

2004 Sales

	% of total
Retail	69
Wholesale	23
Financial services	7
Other services	1
Total	**100**

Selected Subsidiaries

3 Suisses France
Actebis Holding
Crate & Barrel (majority stake)
Grattan
Handelsgesellshaft Heinrich Heine GmbH
Hanseatic Bank GmbH
Otto-Sumisho (51%)
Reiseland GmbH (100%)

COMPETITORS

Amazon.com	Lands' End
Bed Bath & Beyond	Lillian Vernon
Blair	Linens 'n Things
Direct Marketing	Littlewoods
Fast Retailing	L.L. Bean
Federated	METRO AG
GUS	Pier 1 Imports
Hammacher Schlemmer & Co.	PPR
	Provell
Hanover Direct	Schickedanz
J. C. Penney	Vendex
Karstadt	Williams-Sonoma

HISTORICAL FINANCIALS

Company Type: Private

Income Statement

FYE: Last day in February

	REVENUE ($ mil.)	NET INCOME ($ mil.)	NET PROFIT MARGIN	EMPLOYEES
2/04	17,879	136	0.8%	55,406
2/03	15,083	141	0.9%	65,854
2/02	12,461	125	1.0%	79,137
2/01	13,636	192	1.4%	75,962
2/00	12,741	266	2.1%	71,350
2/99	15,535	288	1.9%	50,055
2/98	13,364	201	1.5%	41,476
2/97	12,439	249	2.0%	46,500
2/96	16,876	—	—	41,221
2/95	13,176	—	—	39,817
Annual Growth	3.4%	(8.2%)	—	3.7%

2004 Year-End Financials

Debt ratio: 320.2%
Return on equity: 14.6%
Cash ($ mil.): 492
Current ratio: 1.18
Long-term debt ($ mil.): 1,904

Net Income History

P&O Steam Navigation

It's all hands on deck as The Peninsular and Oriental Steam Navigation Company (P&O) reorganizes to battle stiff competition. The Eurotunnel torpedoed P&O's cross-Channel ferry dominance, prompting it to merge ferry operations with rival Stena Line. Still, the company has other resources. Subsidiary P&O Ports is one of the world's leading port operators, with stakes in about two dozen container terminals and cargo-handling and other operations in more than 100 ports in 18 countries. P&O's cold logistics unit provides temperature-controlled warehousing and distribution services. P&O sold its 50% stake in one of the world's largest container shippers, P&O Nedlloyd to Royal P&O Nedlloyd (formerly Royal Nedlloyd).

P&O expects its port operations to benefit from the trend toward containerization of freight. The company plans to increase its cargo handling capacity at its existing terminals — notably at the Qingdao terminal in China — and to bid for new port concessions. At the same time, P&O is working to cut costs in its ferry operations.

The company has expanded its cold logistics business in the US, particularly in California and Texas, and it is working to integrate those acquisitions. It has sold off its contract logistics operations.

HISTORY

In 1815 Scotsman Arthur Anderson joined the London office of shipbroker Brodi Willcox. They formed a partnership in 1822 and built a business based on trade between Britain and the Iberian Peninsula. Their ships ran guns and transported troops for the royalists during the Portuguese and Spanish civil wars of the 1830s.

The two men teamed up with Irish shipowner Richard Bourne in 1835 to establish the Peninsular Steam Navigation Company, which offered regular trading service between London and ports in Spain, Portugal, and Gibraltar. Two years later Bourne won a contract to carry mail by sea between England and Spanish and Portuguese ports. The company extended its mail routes to the Mediterranean, and in 1840 a contract for monthly mail deliveries to Alexandria, Egypt, allowed it to raise enough money to incorporate as a limited liability company, the Peninsular and Oriental Steam Navigation Company.

The firm began offering cruises in the 1840s and continued to add mail routes, including Suez/Calcutta (1843), Hong Kong (1845), and Sydney (1852). P&O's mail and passenger steamships provided vital logistical support to the expansion of the British Empire.

Between 1914 and 1946 P&O acquired several other shipping firms, including the British India Steam Navigation Company and the New Zealand Shipping Company. The company operated nearly 500 ships in the 1920s.

During WWII, P&O lost 182 ships that were drafted as troop carriers and cargo vessels. After the war, as aircraft took away its passenger and mail income, P&O added cruise ships and various forms of cargo ships, from containers to tankers.

By the 1970s P&O was involved in nearly every kind of merchant shipping. In 1974 it further diversified with the purchase of Britain's #4 construction company (at that time), Bovis Construction. Jeffrey Sterling joined P&O as chairman in 1983.

Two years later the firm acquired its chairman's Sterling Guarantee Trust, which owned US commercial properties and London's Earls Court and Olympia exhibition halls. In the late 1980s and early 1990s, chairman Sterling kept the company on a course of expansion: P&O bought Sitmar Cruises in 1988, formed P&O Asia in 1992, and acquired interests in Chinese container terminals.

But P&O had hit the business doldrums. To put some wind in its sails, P&O and rival Royal Nedlloyd merged their container shipping lines into P&O Nedlloyd Container Line in 1996 and spun off faltering Bovis Homes (residential construction) the next year. In 1998 it combined its ferries with those of Stena Line in order to compete against the Eurotunnel. P&O's Grand Princess, the biggest cruise ship in the world at the time, also came into service that year.

In 1999 P&O began jettisoning noncore businesses. It sold Bovis Construction to real estate group Lend Lease; it also sold Earls Court and Olympia. The next year the company spun off its cruise line business as P&O Princess Cruises (expanded in 1999 with the acquisition of Germany's Aida). P&O had announced plans to add privately held Festival to its cruise line offerings before the spinoff, but a slump in the price of P&O's stock forced the company to call off the $400 million acquisition.

Also in 2000 P&O pulled the IPO of bulk shipping unit Associated Bulk Carriers (ABC), citing poor market conditions. Instead the company sold 50% of ABC to Eurotower Holdings and turned over the company's management to Zodiac Maritime Agencies. (P&O sold its remaining 50% stake in ABC to Eurotower Holdings in 2003.)

In 2002 P&O bought Stena Line's 40% stake in the companies' combined ferry business. It also sold its 50% interest in P&O Nedlloyd to Royal P&O Nedlloyd in 2004 (P&O has a 25% stake in Royal P&O Nedlloyd).

EXECUTIVES

Chief Executive; Executive Chairman, P&O Ports: Robert B. Woods, age 59, $718,272 pay
CFO: Nick Luff, age 37, $392,916 pay
Executive Director, Commercial and Legal Affairs and Company Secretary: R. Michael Gradon, age 46, $480,033 pay
Executive Director, Communications and Strategy: Peter Smith, age 53, $400,027 pay
Executive Director, P&O Ports: Robin Silvester
Managing Director, P&O Ferries: Russ Peters, age 56, $248,906 pay
COO, P&O Ports: Alistair Baillie
Human Resources Director, P&O Ports: Margaret Pickworth
Auditors: KPMG Audit Plc

LOCATIONS

HQ: The Peninsular and Oriental Steam Navigation Company
79 Pall Mall, London SW1Y 5EJ, United Kingdom
Phone: +44-20-7930-4343 **Fax:** +44-20-7930-8572
US HQ: 19840 Rancho Way, Dominguez Hills, CA 90221
US Phone: 310-632-6265 **US Fax:** 310-900-7050
Web: www.pogroup.com

2004 Sales

	$ mil.	% of total
Europe	2,418.6	52
Americas	1,187.3	26
Australasia	717.5	16
Asia	294.7	6
Total	**4,618.1**	**100**

PRODUCTS/OPERATIONS

2004 Sales

	$ mil.	% of total
Ferries	1,895.4	41
Ports	1,626.5	35
Property	700.2	15
Cold logistics	396.0	9
Total	**4,618.1**	**100**

Selected Subsidiaries and Affiliates

Ferries
Larne Harbour Ltd. (harbor operator, Ireland)
P&O European Ferries (Irish Sea) Ltd.
P&O European Ferries (Portsmouth) Ltd.
P&O Ferries Ltd.
P&O North Sea Ferries BV (Holland)
P&O North Sea Ferries Ltd. (England)
Three Quays International Ltd. (marine consultancy and project management services)

Ports
- Asian Terminals Inc. (84%, container terminals and stevedoring, Philippines)
- Container Terminals Australia Ltd. (90%)
- Nhava Sheva International Container Terminal Ltd. (95%, container terminals, India)
- Partrederiet International Offshore Services ANS (50%, offshore maritime services, Norway)
- P&O Maritime Services Pty. Ltd. (offshore services, ships agency, and chartering, Australia)
- P&O Polar Australia Pty. Ltd. (Antarctic research and resupply services)
- P&O Ports Ltd. (container terminals, stevedoring, and international port management, Australia)
- P&O Ports North America Inc. (stevedoring and passenger terminal services)
- Shekou Container Terminals Ltd. (25%, container terminals, China)
- Southampton Container Terminals Ltd. (51%, container terminals)
- Terminales Rio de la Plata SA (53%, container terminal and stevedoring, Argentina)
- Tilbury Container Services Ltd. (34%, container terminal operations)

Cold Logistics
- Pacific Cold Storage Inc. (US)
- P&O Cold Logistics Argentina SA (freezer, handling, and cold storage of consumables)
- P&O Cold Logistics Ltd. (freezing, handling, and cold storage of consumables, Australia)

COMPETITORS

A.P. Møller — Mærsk	Hanjin Shipping
Associated British Ports	Hutchison Whampoa
CMA CGM	Kuehne & Nagel
Compañía Sud Americana de Vapores	Mitsui O.S.K. Lines
	Neptune Orient
COSCO Group	NYK Line
Crowley Maritime	Orient Overseas
DFDS	Sea Containers
Eurotunnel	SSA Marine
Eurotunnel S.A.	Stolt-Nielsen
Evergreen Marine	Yang Ming

HISTORICAL FINANCIALS

Company Type: Public

Income Statement

FYE: December 31

	REVENUE ($ mil.)	NET INCOME ($ mil.)	NET PROFIT MARGIN	EMPLOYEES
12/04	4,618	(482)	—	22,038
12/03	4,073	89	2.2%	24,856
12/02	4,292	(288)	—	30,194
12/01	3,593	173	4.8%	26,891
12/00	5,888	102	1.7%	41,853
12/99	9,920	650	6.6%	62,674
12/98	9,806	451	4.6%	68,333
12/97	9,762	549	5.6%	69,533
12/96	12,047	426	3.5%	71,205
12/95	10,182	366	3.6%	66,924
Annual Growth	(8.4%)	—	—	(11.6%)

2004 Year-End Financials

Debt ratio: 100.4%
Return on equity: —
Cash ($ mil.): 98
Current ratio: 1.40
Long-term debt ($ mil.): 1,887

Net Income History

London: PO

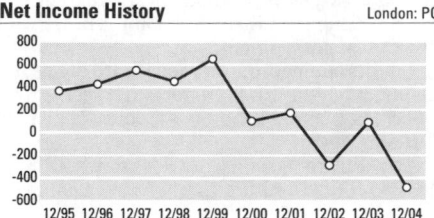

800									
600									
400									
200									
0									
-200									
-400									
-600									

12/95 12/96 12/97 12/98 12/99 12/00 12/01 12/02 12/03 12/04

Pearson plc

There's nothing fishy about information from Pearson, home of salmon-colored newspaper *The Financial Times*. The media giant provides financial information and business news with such titles as *The Financial Times* (known locally as the "Pink 'Un"), the 50%-owned *The Economist*, and its 60% stake in US-based Interactive Data Corporation. The company's Pearson Education unit is the world's top educational publisher through imprints Pearson Scott Foresman, Pearson Addison Wesley, and Pearson Prentice Hall. Pearson's Penguin Group (Penguin, Putnam, Viking) publishes trade books. The company sold its Recoletos Grupo de Comunicacion containing its Spanish media holdings in 2005.

In addition to printed works, the company is making strides with its Internet investments, including the *Financial Times* Web site (FT.com) and online educational services.

Under CEO Marjorie Scardino, Pearson has shed many of its non-media assets — which once included The Tussaud Group's wax museums — and is moving to strengthen its printed content brands. Its FT Group (business information holdings) ailed for several years with a shortage of advertising due to an economic turndown, but has seen improvements in recent years. The company has denied that it will sell off the FT unit amid rampant speculation.

Spain's Telefónica divested its 5% stake in the company in late 2004.

HISTORY

In 1844 Samuel Pearson became a partner in a small Yorkshire building firm. When he retired in 1879 his grandson Weetman took over, moving the company to London in 1884. The business enjoyed extraordinary success — building the first tunnel under New York's Hudson River and installing Mexico City's drainage system. By the 1890s the company (incorporated as S. Pearson & Son in 1897) was the world's #1 contractor.

In the 1920s the company bought newspapers and engaged in oil exploration. Weetman died in 1927, and so did the construction business. His heirs then bought into several unrelated businesses. Pearson bought control of *The Financial Times* newspaper in 1957, a deal that also brought it 50% of *The Economist* (*The Financial Times* had acquired half of *The Economist* in 1928). The company later added stakes in vintner Chateau Latour (1963, sold 1988) and publisher Longman (1968). The firm went public in 1969.

During the 1970s Pearson bought Penguin Books (1971) and Madame Tussaud's (1978). In 1989 it added Addison-Wesley (educational publisher, US) and Les Echos (financial newspaper publisher, France).

Concentrating on media interests, the company bought Thames Television in 1993 and Grundy Worldwide (game shows and soap operas) in 1995. It acquired HarperCollins Educational Publishing from News Corp. in 1996, as well as US publisher Putnam Berkley from MCA, gaining such authors as Tom Clancy and Amy Tan. By the mid-1990s, however, Pearson's holdings still lacked focus, and earnings were depressed. Marjorie Scardino, a Texan who had been CEO of The Economist Group since 1992, replaced Frank Barlow in 1997, becoming the first woman to lead a major UK company. She

rounded out Pearson's TV holdings with the purchase of All American Communications that year.

In 1998 Pearson bought Simon & Schuster's reference and educational publishing divisions from Viacom for $4.6 billion and sold Tussaud's amusement business. In 1999 Pearson shed $58 million in college textbooks and instructional programs to John Wiley & Sons.

As part of a long-term plan to build *The Financial Times* brand online, Pearson bought 60% of Data Broadcasting Corporation (now called Interactive Data Corporation) in 2000. It began to cross-promote the FT.com Web site with MarketWatch.com (Data Broadcast sold its 34% stake in the now-called MarketWatch to Pearson in 2001) as part of a $35 million marketing campaign. MarketWatch was later sold to Dow Jones & Company in 2005. Pearson bought troubled UK publisher Dorling Kindersley for nearly $500 million and later combined the firm with its Penguin unit. It also launched a German version of *The Financial Times* with Bertelsmann's Gruner + Jahr.

Later in 2000, Pearson combined its TV operations with CLT-Ufa, co-owned by German media company Bertelsmann and Audiofina, into a new publicly traded broadcasting firm called RTL Group. Pearson took a 22% stake in RTL. In addition, Pearson bought educational test processing firm National Computer Systems (later called NCS Pearson before being integrated into operations). In 2001 Pearson expanded its educational operations, announcing plans for a joint venture with Telefónica to distribute online educational content in Latin America. That year the company also formed a joint venture with an arm of Chinese state television to produce programming for a Chinese audience. In late 2001 Pearson sold its stake in RTL to Bertelsmann.

Pearson sold its 79% stake in Spanish media company Recoletos in 2005 to Retos Cartera. In 2005 the company acquired special needs publisher AGS Publishing from WRC Media.

EXECUTIVES

Chairman: Glen Moreno, age 62
Chief Executive: Dame Marjorie M. Scardino, age 58, $1,466,767 pay
CFO: Rona A. Fairhead, age 43, $851,614 pay
Director for People; Chairman, Financial Times Group: Sir David C. M. Bell, age 58, $844,502 pay
Director of Global Communications: Luke Swanson
Chairman and CEO, Pearson Education: Peter Jovanovich, age 55, $1,219,639 pay
Chairman and CEO, The Penguin Group: John C. Makinson, age 50, $1,025,848 pay
President and CEO, Pearson School Technology: Jack Lynch
CEO/Managing Director, Financial Times Group: Olivier Fleurot, age 52
VP Marketing, Pearson Digital Learning: Kelly Goodrich
Auditors: PricewaterhouseCoopers LLP

LOCATIONS

HQ: Pearson plc
80 Strand, London WC2R ORL, United Kingdom
Phone: +44-20-7010-2000   **Fax:** +44-20-7010-6060
US HQ: 1330 Avenue of the Americas, New York, NY 10019
US Phone: 212-641-2400   **US Fax:** 212-641-2500
Web: www.pearson.com

2004 Sales

	% of total
North America	67
Europe	
UK	15
Continental Europe	8
Asia/Pacific	7
Other regions	3
Total	**100**

PRODUCTS/OPERATIONS

2004 Sales

	% of total
School	30
Penguin	21
Higher Education	19
FT Group	16
Professional	14
Total	**100**

Pearson Education

Early Learning
Elementary education
  Pearson Learning Group
  Pearson Scott Foresman
Secondary education
  Globe Fearon
  Prentice Hall
Higher education
  Pearson Addison Wesley
  Pearson Allyn & Beacon
  Pearson Prentice Hall College
Pearson Educational Measurement

Financial Times Group

Business Day & Financial Mail (50%; South Africa)
The Economist Group (50%)
  CFO
  The Economist
  The Journal of Commerce
  Roll Call
The Financial Times
Financial Times Deutschland (with Gruner + Jahr)
FT asset Management
FT.com (financial news)
FTSE International (market indices, with London Stock
  Exchange)
Interactive Data Corp. (61%; US)
Les Echos (France)

Penguin Group

Avery
Berkley Books
Dorling Kindersley
Dutton
Frederick Warne
Hamish Hamilton
Ladybird
Michael Joseph
Penguin
Penguin Business
Penguin Classics
Penguin Reference
Plume
Puffin
Viking

COMPETITORS

1mage	New York Times
Compass Learning	News Corp.
Daily Mail and General	PLATO Learning
Trust	Prometric
Dow Jones	ProQuest
Editis	Random House
Educational Testing	Reed Elsevier Group
Service	Reuters
Gruner + Jahr	Scholastic
HarperCollins	Simon & Schuster
Houghton Mifflin	Thomson Corporation
John Harland	Time
John Wiley	Touchstone
Knowledge Universe	Applied Science
Laureate Education	Verlagsgruppe Georg von
Learning Tree	Holtzbrinck
McGraw-Hill	Washington Post
Moody's	Wolters Kluwer
New Horizons Worldwide	

HISTORICAL FINANCIALS

Company Type: Public

Income Statement

FYE: December 31

	REVENUE ($ mil.)	NET INCOME ($ mil.)	NET PROFIT MARGIN	EMPLOYEES
12/04	7,514	169	2.2%	33,389
12/03	7,219	98	1.4%	30,868
12/02	6,962	(179)	—	30,359
12/01	6,152	(569)	—	29,027
12/00	5,792	268	4.6%	24,688
12/99	5,384	485	9.0%	20,000
12/98	3,973	625	15.7%	18,400
12/97	3,783	63	1.7%	18,306
12/96	3,714	410	11.0%	17,383
12/95	2,836	404	14.3%	19,422
Annual Growth	**11.4%**	**(9.2%)**	**—**	**6.2%**

2004 Year-End Financials

Debt ratio: 65.9%	No. of shares (mil.): 803
Return on equity: 3.3%	Dividends
Cash ($ mil.): 1,175	Yield: 3.7%
Current ratio: 2.01	Payout: 214.3%
Long-term debt ($ mil.): 3,286	Market value ($ mil.): 9,768

Stock History

NYSE: PSO

STOCK PRICE ($) FY Close	P/E High/Low	PER SHARE ($) Earnings	Dividends	Book Value
12/04	12.16	64 51	0.21	0.45	6.21
12/03	11.21	99 59	0.12	0.41	6.56
12/02	9.35	— —	(0.22)	0.37	6.71
12/01	12.28	— —	(0.57)	0.35	6.53
12/00	23.56	85 62	0.36	0.00	7.58
Annual Growth	**(15.2%)**	**— —**	**(12.6%)**	**—**	**(4.9%)**

Pernod Ricard

Pernod Ricard, one of the world's largest spirits firms, feathers its nest with the help of Wild Turkey bourbon, but its global brand is its premium Scotch whisky Chivas Regal. The beverage firm also sells spirits ranging from anise drinks and liqueurs (Pernod, Ricard, Zoco) to clear spirits (Wyborova vodka, Havana Club Cuban rum, Beefeater and Seagram's gins). In addition, Pernod Ricard offers Jameson Irish whiskey, Martell cognac, and Jacob's Creek wine. The company in 2005 allied with Fortune Brands to buy UK competitor Allied Domecq (which had been #2 in spirits) and provide stiffer competition for #1 drinks company Diageo.

Pernod Ricard had already boosted its stable of brands with the 2000 purchase of nearly 40% of Seagram's spirits business, but by early 2005 was back in the shopping mood again. To help allay anti-competitive concerns, Pernod Ricard enlisted the help of Fortune Brands for its friendly bid for Allied Domecq. As part of the deal, Fortune Brands ended up with Pernod Ricard's Larios gin, as well as several brands from Allied Domecq (including Canadian Club whisky, Clos du Bois wine, Courvoisier cognac, Maker's Mark bourbon, and Sauza tequila).

Pernod Ricard paid about $14 billion for its former chief competitor Allied Domecq, whose holdings include Dunkin' Donuts and Baskin-Robbins ice cream in addition to its alcoholic beverages; Fortune Brands anted up about $5 billion for its part of the acquisition. Pernod Ricard in 2005 agreed to sell the Dunkin' Donuts and Baskin-Robbins lines to a consortium of buyers that included Bain Capital, Carlyle Group, and Thomas H. Lee Partners. Other investors also bid on the food companies.

Pernod Ricard also sold its Bushmills Irish whisky to competitor Diageo in 2005 as part of the juggling that took place in the Allied Domecq acquisition.

A rival bid from Constellation Brands (in cooperation with Blackstone, Brown-Forman, and Lion Capital) had threatened Pernod Ricard's acquisition of Allied Domecq, but Constellation Brands ultimately withdrew from the bidding group, clearing the path for Pernod Ricard.

Pernod Ricard's 2000 deal with Seagram's added Chivas and a number of other brands to the company's portfolio and improved its presence in Asia, Latin America, and North America.

To help fund the Seagram's acquisition, Pernod Ricard sold its soft-drink business (Pampryl fruit juice, Orangina soft drinks, Yoo-Hoo chocolate drink, and cider) in North America, Europe, and Australia to Cadbury Schweppes for $640 million.

The company claims that the US Patent and Trademark Office supports the position that Pernod Ricard is the rightful owner of the Havana Club trademark in the US. Bacardi challenges this claim. Pernod Ricard markets its Havana Club rum through a joint venture with the Cuban government.

Like its competitors, Pernod Ricard has begun selling ready-to-drink products. The company's offerings include Seagram's Coolers and Wild Turkey Coolers.

The Ricard family controls some 15% of Pernod Ricard's voting rights.

HISTORY

Henri-Louis Pernod inherited Pernod Fils, an absinthe distillery, from his father-in-law in 1805 and immediately moved it to Pontarlier, France, to avoid stiff French import taxes. Demand for absinthe, a potent liqueur, spread quickly, and by the 1870s the liqueur was the toast of Paris. It was even featured in the Impressionist paintings, and rumor has it that Vincent Van Gogh's psychosis might have been caused by it.

In the late 1800s serious competition for the absinthe market emerged from distiller Pernod Avignon, run by Jules Pernod (no relation to Henri-Louis). In 1906 Switzerland banned absinthe and France followed suit in 1915. In 1926 Henri-Louis joined with another anise distiller, Aristide Hemard, and formed Etablissements Hemard et Pernod Fils. Jules joined them in 1928. The resulting company was named Pernod.

Four years later the ban on pastis was lifted by the French government, and Paul Ricard, who made pastis illegally beforehand, began selling it openly. The licorice-flavored drink became a popular French drink. His company, Ricard, became a successful spirits maker and went public in 1962. Ricard acquired the Biscuit cognac brand in 1966.

Pernod and Ricard merged in 1975 to form Pernod Ricard. The company's operations included Campbell (scotch), SEGM (spirits exporter), and JFA Pampryl (fruit juice). In 1976 the group acquired CDC (Cinzano, Dubonnet). Two years later Patrick Ricard, son of Paul, became chairman and CEO.

Expanding through acquisitions in the 1980s, Pernod Ricard bought US-based Austin Nichols (Wild Turkey) from du Ligget Group in 1980 and acquired control of both Sias-MPA (fruit preparations) in 1982 and Compagnie Francaise des Produits Orangina (soft drinks) in 1984. The next year the firm added Ramazzotti (spirits, Italy) and IGM (distribution, Germany) to its mix, and in 1988 it bought Irish Distillers (whiskey), Yoo-Hoo Industries (US), and BWG (distribution, Ireland; sold in 2002). Australia's Orlando Wyndham Wines was added to the company's wine list in 1989 and merged with Pernod Ricard's Wyndham Estate winery the following year.

The group also acquired Spain's Larios gin, the Czech Republic's Becherovka liqueurs, and Italcanditi, a fruit preparations firm. Pernod Ricard added Mexican distillery Tequila Viuda de Romero (Real Hacienda tequila) to its liquor cabinet in January 2000.

Pernod Ricard later teamed up with liquor giant Diageo to bid on Seagram's spirits and wine business. Their collective bid of $8.2 billion (with Pernod Ricard paying $3.2 billion) was accepted in December 2000, with Pernod Ricard agreeing to acquire such brands as Chivas Regal, Glen Grant, and Glenlivet.

In 2001 the company sold its soft-drink business in Continental Europe, North America, and Australia to Cadbury Schweppes for about $640 million to help finance the Seagram's deal. After months of delay, the company finalized its deal to buy a part of Seagram's drinks business from Vivendi Universal after finally gaining FTC approval in December 2001. Six months later, Pernod Ricard and brand co-owner Diageo licensed Seagram's nonalcoholic mixers to The Coca-Cola Company. In 2002 Pernod Ricard sold Polish juice-making subsidiary Agros Fortuna.

EXECUTIVES

Chairman and CEO: Patrick Ricard, age 60, $2,678,888 pay
Deputy CEO and Director: Richard Burrows, age 59, $1,781,215 pay
Deputy CEO and Director: Pierre Pringuet, age 55, $1,781,215 pay
VP, Finance: Emmanuel Babeau, age 36
Adviser to General Management: Bernard Cazals
VP, Human Resources: Yves Flaissier
VP, Marketing: Jean-Paul Richard
Chairman and CEO, Martell Mumm Perrier-Jouët: Lionel Breton
Chairman and CEO, Pernod: Pierre Coppéré
CEO, Irish Distillers Group: Paul Duffy, age 39
Chairman and CEO, Orlando Wyndham: Laurent Lacassagne, age 41
Chairman and CEO, Chivas Brothers: Christian Porta, age 41
Chairman and CEO, Ricard: Philippe Savinel, age 47
Chairman and CEO, Pernod Ricard Europe: Thierry Billot
President and CEO, Pernod Ricard North America: Michel Bord
VP, Audit and Development: Gilles Bogaert
VP, Information Systems: Jean Chavinier
VP, Research Center: Patrice Desmarest
VP, Corporate Legal Affairs and General Counsel: Ian Fitzsimons
VP, Corporate Communications: Francisco de la Vega
VP, Investor Relations: Patrick de Borredon
Auditors: Deloitte Touche Tohmatsu; Mazars & Guérard

LOCATIONS

HQ: Pernod Ricard SA
12, place des États-Unis, 75116 Paris, France
Phone: +33-1-41-00-41-00   **Fax:** +33-1-41-00-41-41
US HQ: 777 Westchester Ave., White Plains, NY 10604
US Phone: 914-539-4500   **US Fax:** 914-539-4777
Web: www.pernod-ricard.com/fr

Pernod Ricard has operations in the Americas, Asia, and Europe.

2005 Sales

	% of total
Europe	
France	16
Other countries	40
Americas	21
Asia & other regions	23
Total	**100**

PRODUCTS/OPERATIONS

2005 Sales

	% of total
Wine & spirits	98
Other	2
Total	**100**

Selected Brands

Ballantine's
Beefeater
Chivas Regal
The Glenlivet
Havana Club
Jacob's Creek
Jameson
Kahlua
Malibu
Martell
Mumm
Perrier-Jouët
Ricard
Wyborowa

COMPETITORS

Bacardi	Highland Distillers
Blavod Extreme Spirits	Jim Beam Brands
Brown-Forman	Rémy Cointreau
Cabo Wabo	Sidney Frank Importing
Constellation Brands	Skyy
Diageo	Southcorp
Fortune Brands	Suntory Ltd.
Foster's Wine Estates	V&S
Americas	William Grant & Sons
Gallo	

HISTORICAL FINANCIALS

Company Type: Public

Income Statement

FYE: June 30

	REVENUE ($ mil.)	NET INCOME ($ mil.)	NET PROFIT MARGIN	EMPLOYEES
6/05*	6,329	777	12.3%	12,304
12/03	4,436	582	13.1%	12,254
12/02	5,068	433	8.5%	12,526
12/01	4,035	317	7.9%	13,090
12/00	4,126	184	4.4%	14,609
12/99	3,615	215	5.9%	14,000
12/98	3,662	236	6.4%	12,819
12/97	3,176	226	7.1%	12,057
12/96	3,213	227	7.1%	11,233
12/95	3,246	225	6.9%	11,150
Annual Growth	**7.7%**	**14.8%**	—	**1.1%**

*Fiscal year change

2005 Year-End Financials

Debt ratio: 32.6%
Return on equity: 21.7%
Cash ($ mil.): 154

Current ratio: 1.59
Long-term debt ($ mil.): 1,218

Net Income History

Exchange: Euronext Paris

| 12/95 | 12/96 | 12/97 | 12/98 | 12/99 | 12/00 | 12/01 | 12/02 | 12/03 | 6/05 |

PETROBRAS

PETRÓLEO BRASILEIRO (PETROBRAS) isn't brash, but it is Brazil's largest industrial company. It engages in exploration for oil and gas and in production, refining, purchasing, and transportation of oil and gas products. The company has proved reserves of 11.6 billion barrels of oil equivalent. It operates 16 refineries, more than 20,000 miles of pipeline, and more than 5,000 gas stations. Subsidiary Petrobras Distribuidora is Brazil's leading retailer of oil products and fuel alcohol. Petrobras Energía Participaciones is a leading Argentine oil company. Other units produce petrochemicals and natural gas. The Brazilian government owns 32% of PETROBRAS and 56% of its voting shares.

Petrobras Internacional, also known as Braspetro, conducts international exploration in Angola, Kazakhstan, Nigeria, the UK, the US, and Latin America.

Although most of PETROBRAS' wells are onshore, the bulk of its production comes from offshore operations; the company is recognized as a leader in offshore drilling technology and deepwater wells. To boost its natural gas operations, PETROBRAS is investing $2 billion to build a pipeline from gas fields in Bolivia to Brazil. The company also plans to triple production outside Brazil to 300,000 barrels per day by 2005 and is eyeing a major acquisition to boost its Gulf of Mexico assets.

HISTORY

"O petróleo é nosso!"

"The oil is ours!" proclaimed the Brazilian nationalists' slogan in 1953, and President Getúlio Vargas approved a bill creating a state-run monopoly on petroleum discovery, development, refining, and transport. The same year that PETRÓLEO BRASILEIRO (PETROBRAS) was created, a team led by American geologist Walter Link reported that the prospects of finding petroleum in Brazil were slim. The report outraged Brazilian nationalists, who saw it as a ploy for foreign exploitation. PETROBRAS proved it could find oil, but Brazil continued to import crude oil and petroleum products. By 1973 the company produced about 10% of the nation's needs.

When oil prices soared during the Arab embargo, the government, instead of encouraging exploration for domestic oil, pushed PETROBRAS into a program to promote alcohol fuels. The company was forced to raise gasoline prices to make the more costly gasohol attractive to consumers. During the 1979 oil crunch the price of gasohol was fixed at 65% of gasoline. But during the oil glut of the mid-1980s, PETROBRAS' cost of making gasohol was twice what it cost to buy gasoline — in other words, PETROBRAS lost money.

PETROBRAS soon began overseas exploration. In 1980 it found an oil field in Iraq, an important trading partner during the 1980s. The company also drilled in Angola and, through a 1987 agreement with Texaco, in the Gulf of Mexico.

In the mid-1980s PETROBRAS began production in the deepwater Campos basin off the coast of Rio de Janeiro state. Discoveries there in 1988, in the Marlim and Albacora fields, more than tripled its oil reserves. It plunged deep into the thick Amazon jungle in 1986 to explore for oil, and by 1990 Amazon wells were making a significant contribution to total production. That year, to ease dependence on imports, PETROBRAS launched a five-year, $16.9 billion plan to boost crude oil production. It also began selling its mining and trading assets.

Before the invasion of Kuwait, Brazil relied heavily on Iraq, trading weapons for oil. After the invasion spawned increases in crude prices, PETROBRAS raised pump prices but, yielding to the government's anti-inflation program, still did not raise them enough to cover costs. It lost $13 million a day.

The company sold 26% of Petrobras Distribuidora to the public in 1993 and privatized several of its petrochemical and fertilizer subsidiaries. A 1994 presidential order, bent on stabilizing Brazil's 40%-per-month inflation, cut the prices of oil products. In 1995 the government loosened its grip on the oil and gas industry and allowed foreign companies to enter the Brazilian market. In the wake of this reform, PETROBRAS teamed up with a Japanese consortium to build Brazil's largest oil refinery.

In 1997 PETROBRAS appealed a $4 billion judgment from a 1992 shareholder lawsuit; the suit alleged PETROBRAS had undervalued shares during the privatization of the loss-making Petroquisa affiliate. (The appeal was granted in 1999.)

As part of an effort to boost oil production, PETROBRAS also began to raise money abroad in 1999. The next year PETROBRAS and Spanish oil giant Repsol YPF agreed to swap oil and gas assets in Argentina and Brazil in a deal worth more than $1 billion.

In 2000 the company announced plans to change its corporate name to PETROBRAX, but fierce political and popular reaction forced the company to abort this plan in 2001. In an even greater public relations disaster that year, one of PETROBRAS' giant rigs sank off of Brazil and 10 workers were killed. In 2001 PETROBRAS announced that it was going to spend as much as $3 billion to buy an oil company in order to increase its production in the Gulf of Mexico.

In 2002 the company expressed an interest in buying Argentina's major oil company (YPF) from Spanish/Argentine energy giant Repsol YPF. That year PETROBRAS bought control (59%) of Argentine energy company Perez Companc in a deal valued at $1 billion. PETROBRAS also reported its first oil find in Argentina in 2002.

EXECUTIVES

Chairman: Dilma Vana Rousseff, age 57
President and CEO: José Sérgio Gabrielli de Azevedo, age 56
CFO and Director Investor Relations:
Almir Guilherme Barbassa
Director Exploration and Production:
Guilherme de Oliveira Estrella, age 63
Director Gas and Energy: Ildo L. Sauer, age 51
Director International: Nestor C. Cervero, age 54
Director Services: Renato de Souza Duque, age 50
Director Downstream: Paulo Roberto Costa, age 51
Auditors: Ernst & Young Auditores Independentes S/C

LOCATIONS

HQ: PETRÓLEO BRASILEIRO S.A. — PETROBRAS
Avenida República do Chile 65, sala 401 E,
20035-900 Rio de Janeiro, Brazil
Phone: +55-21-2534-1510   **Fax:** +55-21-2534-6055
US HQ: 750 Lexington Ave., 43rd Fl.,
New York, NY 10022
US Phone: 212-829-1517   **US Fax:** 212-832-5300
Web: www.petrobras.com.br

PETRÓLEO BRASILEIRO S.A. — PETROBRAS explores for oil and gas in Brazil, as well as in Angola, Argentina, Bolivia, Colombia, Cuba, Ecuador, Equatorial Guinea, Kazakhstan, Nigeria, Peru, Trinidad and Tobago, the UK, and the US.

PRODUCTS/OPERATIONS

Selected Subsidiaries

Downstream Participações S.A. (asset exchanges between Petrobras and Repsol-YPF)
Petrobras Comercializadora de Energia Ltda
Petrobras Distribuidora SA (BR; distribution and marketing of petroleum products, fuel alcohol, and natural gas)
Petrobras Energía Participaciones (59%; oil and gas, Argentina)
Petrobras Gás SA (Gaspetro, management of the Brazil-Bolivia pipeline and other natural gas assets)
Petrobras Internacional SA (Braspetro; overseas exploration and production, marketing, and services)
Petrobras International Finance Company PIFCO (oil imports)
Petrobras Negócios Eletrônicos S.A.
Petrobras Química SA (Petroquisa, petrochemicals)
Petrobras Transporte SA (Transpetro, oil and gas transportation and storage)

COMPETITORS

Ashland
BHP Billiton
BP
Chevron
Devon Energy
Eni
Exxon Mobil
Imperial Oil
Kerr-McGee
Koch
Lyondell Chemical
Marathon Oil
Norsk Hydro
Occidental Petroleum
PDVSA
PEMEX
Royal Dutch/Shell Group
Sunoco
TOTAL
Unocal

HISTORICAL FINANCIALS

Company Type: Public

Income Statement

FYE: December 31

	REVENUE ($ mil.)	NET INCOME ($ mil.)	NET PROFIT MARGIN	EMPLOYEES
12/04	37,452	6,190	16.5%	53,666
12/03	30,797	6,559	21.3%	48,798
12/02	22,612	2,311	10.2%	49,049
12/01	24,549	3,491	14.2%	38,483
12/00	26,955	5,342	19.8%	38,908
12/99	16,358	727	4.4%	35,891
12/98	14,914	1,150	7.7%	38,225
12/97	17,425	1,353	7.8%	41,200
12/96	17,483	644	3.7%	43,468
12/95	15,178	580	3.8%	46,226
Annual Growth	10.6%	30.1%	—	1.7%

2004 Year-End Financials

Debt ratio: 78.3%
Return on equity: 31.2%
Cash ($ mil.): 6,856
Current ratio: 1.46
Long-term debt ($ mil.): 17,613

No. of shares (mil.): 1,097
Dividends
Yield: 0.0%
Payout: —
Market value ($ mil.): 43,620

Stock History

NYSE: PBR

12/95 12/96 12/97 12/98 12/99 12/00 12/01 12/02 12/03 12/04

	STOCK PRICE ($) FY Close	P/E High/Low		Earnings	Dividends	Book Value
12/04	39.78	7	4	5.65	0.00	20.52
12/03	29.24	5	2	5.98	0.00	15.64
12/02	14.94	13	4	2.13	0.00	8.56
12/01	23.30	10	6	3.21	0.00	12.20
12/00	25.25	7	5	4.92	0.00	23.19
Annual Growth	12.0%	—	—	3.5%	—	(3.0%)

Petróleos de Venezuela S.A.

American motorists rely on Petróleos de Venezuela S.A. (PDVSA), one of the top exporters of oil to the US. The state-owned company has proved reserves of 77.2 billion barrels of oil — the most outside the Middle East — and 147.1 trillion cu. ft. of natural gas. PDVSA's exploration and production take place in Venezuela, but the company also has refining and marketing operations in the Caribbean, Europe, and the US. Subsidiary CITGO Petroleum supplies gasoline to 14,000 US retail outlets. PDVSA also makes Orimulsión, a coal alternative made from bitumen. Management protests of government policies in 2002 prompted disruption of production, two major strikes, and the temporary ouster of the country's president.

Outside Venezuela, PDVSA refines, markets, and transports petroleum products in Belgium, Germany, Sweden, the UK, the Caribbean, and the US. On the domestic front, PDVSA's BITOR subsidiary mines Venezuela's extensive bitumen reserves, turning the tarlike ooze into Orimulsión, a patented fuel marketed as an alternative to coal for electric generating plants.

In a move that requires foreign investment, PDVSA is expanding its production of petrochemicals, gas, and Orimulsión. However, investors will step carefully: Venezuelan President Hugo Chávez's tightening state control over the oil company's operations has led to management unrest and major political instability.

In 2003 the government threatened to split the company in two as a way to break the striking managers' hold on the company, and to restore full production. The strike led to a third of the workforce being laid off by February 2003.

HISTORY

Invited by dictator Juan Vicente Gómez, Royal Dutch/Shell looked for oil in Venezuela just before WWI. After the war US companies plunged in. Standard Oil of Indiana began Creole Petroleum in 1920 to explore in Venezuela, selling the company in 1928 to Standard of New Jersey.

When the Venezuelan government threatened to nationalize its oil industry in 1938, the foreign oil companies agreed to pay more taxes and royalties. But in 1945 Venezuela set a pattern for the rest of the world's oil-rich nations when it decreed it was a 50% partner in all oil operations. Venezuela was pivotal to OPEC's creation in 1960, and the next year the government created the Venezuelan Petroleum Corporation (CVP). CVP was granted the nation's unassigned petroleum reserves. By the early 1970s CVP produced about 2% of the nation's oil.

President Carlos Andrés Pérez nationalized oil holdings in 1975, paying only $1 billion for foreign-owned oil assets and creating Petróleos de Venezuela S.A. (PDVSA) to hold the properties. Venezuela formed stand-alone PDVSA subsidiaries: Shell operations became Maraven, Creole became Lagoven, and smaller companies combined into Corpoven. (All units were merged into PDVSA in 1998.)

Free of debt and buoyed by high crude prices in the late 1970s and early 1980s, PDVSA formed ventures (Ruhr Oel) with Germany's Veba Oel and Sweden's Nynas Petroleum. In the US,

PDVSA bought 50% of CITGO, the former refining and marketing arm of Cities Service Co., from Southland in 1986 (and the rest in 1990). PDVSA also bought a 50% stake in a Unocal refinery in 1989 to create joint venture UNO-VEN.

After the 1991 Gulf War, Venezuela increased its own production despite OPEC oil quotas. The next year PDVSA opened some marginal fields to foreign investment for the first time since the industry's 1975 nationalization.

Venezuelan President Rafael Caldera named Luis Giusti president of the company in 1994, and the next year Venezuela's oil industry was opened to foreign investment. In 1996 PDVSA began building a $1.5 billion plastics plant with Mobil (later Exxon Mobil). PDVSA and Unocal finally ended UNO-VEN the next year when UNO-VEN CEO David Tippeconnic took over as head of CITGO.

The rush for Venezuelan oil rights was on by 1997; one week's worth of bidding brought in $2 billion from top international oil companies. Meanwhile, PDVSA searched for facilities to refine the heavy crude, striking deals with Phillips Petroleum (later renamed ConocoPhillips) in 1997 and Amerada Hess in 1998.

PDVSA's profits took a hit in 1998 when oil prices fell to record lows. Concerns arose about the firm's direction that year after populist Hugo Chávez was elected as Venezuela's president. Chávez and his allies sought to retain state control over PDVSA's resources and to keep a closer check on foreign partners.

In 1999 PDVSA, suffering from a devastated domestic economy, decided to expand its downstream operations globally. As part of that plan, it formed a Houston-based crude and products marketing firm, PDVSA Trading.

Tightening his control of the company, in 2000 Chávez appointed army generals to head up both PDVSA (Gen. Guaicaipuro Lameda) and CITGO (Gen. Oswaldo Contreras Maza). The appointments followed a management shake-up and an oil workers' strike.

In 2001 PDVSA with other oil partners announced that it had secured $1.1 billion in funding to develop an extra-heavy crude production project in the Hamaca region of the Orinoco basin.

Tightening his control on the company, in 2002 Chávez replaced Lameda as PDVSA's top executive with banker Gaston Parra. However, growing management discontent with Chávez's board of directors led to a major strike and a serious disruption of the company's oil production.

The strike spread into other industries and led to violence and a revolt by some military leaders. Pedro Carmona, president of Venezuela's top business association, was appointed to lead a civilian junta in the run-up to national elections. But Chávez refused to step down, and within a few days loyalist troops brought him back to power. In a move to make peace with PDVSA managers, Chávez removed Parra and other controversial appointees from the company's board. He then announced that he would appoint Alí Rodríguez, the former oil minister and head of OPEC, to take over the reins at PDVSA. Venezuela's energy minister (Álvaro Silva Calderón) was appointed to complete Rodríguez's term as OPEC's top executive.

However, continued political turmoil led to another major strike in 2002.

Energy and mines minister Rafael Ramírez became PDVSA's new president in November 2004.

EXECUTIVES

President and CEO: Rafael Ramírez Carreño, age 41
CFO and VP, Finance and Planning:
  José Alejandro Rojas
VP: Luis Vierma, age 51
VP: Alejandro Granado, age 50
Managing Internal Director; President, CIED:
  Déster Rodríguez, age 43
Managing Internal Director and Director, PDVSA-CVP:
  Eulogio Delpino
Managing Internal Director and Executive Director, Commerce and Supply: Asdrúbal Chávez
Director: Iván Orellana, age 52
Auditors: KPMG Alcaraz Cabrera Vázquez

LOCATIONS

HQ: Petróleos de Venezuela S.A.
  Edificio Petróleos de Venezuela,
  Avenida Libertador, La Campiña, Apartado 169,
  Caracas 1010-A, Venezuela
Phone: +58-212-708-4111   **Fax:** +58-212-708-4661
US HQ: 1 Warren Place, 6100 S. Yale Ave.,
  Tulsa, OK 74136
US Phone: 918-495-4000   **US Fax:** 918-495-4511
Web: www.pdvsa.com.ve

Petróleos de Venezuela has exploration and production operations in Venezuela and conducts refining and marketing there and in Belgium, the Caribbean, Germany, Sweden, the UK, and the US.

PRODUCTS/OPERATIONS

Selected Subsidiaries and Affiliates

Bitúmenes Orinoco, SA (BITOR, bitumen and Orimulsión)
Carbozulia, SA (coal)
CIED
CITGO Petroleum Corp. (refining, marketing, and petrochemicals; US)
CVP
Deltaven
Intevep, SA (research and support)
Palmaven, SA (agricultural assistance and conservation projects)
PDV Marina
PDVSA Gas
PDVSA Petróleo
PDVSA Trading (crude oil and products marketing; US)
Pequiven, SA (petrochemicals)

COMPETITORS

BHP Billiton
BP
Chevron
ConocoPhillips
Devon Energy
Eni
Exxon Mobil
Imperial Oil
Kerr-McGee
Koch
Lyondell Chemical
Marathon Oil
NIOC
Norsk Hydro
Occidental Petroleum
PEMEX
PETROBRAS
Royal Dutch/Shell Group
Saudi Aramco
Sunoco
TOTAL

HISTORICAL FINANCIALS

Company Type: Government-owned

Income Statement

FYE: December 31

	REVENUE ($ mil.)	NET INCOME ($ mil.)	NET PROFIT MARGIN	EMPLOYEES
12/04	63,200	—	—	—
12/03	46,589	—	—	—
12/02	42,580	—	—	45,683
12/01	46,250	—	—	46,425
12/00	53,680	—	—	45,520
12/99	32,648	—	—	50,000
12/98	25,526	—	—	50,821
12/97	34,801	—	—	51,677
12/96	33,855	—	—	53,200
12/95	26,041	—	—	53,500
Annual Growth	10.4%	—	—	(2.2%)

Revenue History

Petróleos Mexicanos

Petróleos Mexicanos (PEMEX) not only fuels Mexico's automobile engines, the state-owned oil company also fuels the nation's economy, accounting for some one-third of the Mexican government's revenues and 7% of its export earnings. The integrated company's operations, spread throughout Mexico, range from exploration and production to refining and petrochemicals. PEMEX's P.M.I. Comercio Internacional subsidiary manages the company's trading operations outside the country. PEMEX has proved reserves of 16 billion barrels of oil and 14.8 trillion cu. ft. of natural gas.

PEMEX's refining operations convert crude oil into gasoline, jet fuel, diesel, fuel oil, asphalts and lubricants. In 2002 PEMEX-Refining produced 1.28 million barrels per day of refined products, up from 1.27 million barrels per day in 2001. PEMEX's Gas and Basic Petrochemicals unit processes natural gas and natural gas liquids, and ships and sells natural gas and liquefied petroleum gas throughout Mexico. It also produces several basic petrochemical feedstocks.

Long recognized as the tangible expression of Mexican nationalism, PEMEX has faced popular opposition in its bid to follow other Latin American state oil companies and privatize some operations. PEMEX is, however, working to become more responsive to market conditions and expand its international scope.

HISTORY

Histories of pre-colonial Mexico recount the nation's first oil business: Natives along the Tampico coast gathered asphalt from naturally occurring deposits and traded with the Aztecs.

As the 20th century began, Americans Edward Doheny and Charles Canfield struck oil near Tampico. Their success was eclipsed in 1910 by a nearby well drilled by British engineer Weetman Pearson, leader of the firm that became Pearson PLC.

President Porfirio Díaz had welcomed foreign ownership of Mexican resources, but revolution ousted Díaz, and the 1917 Constitution proclaimed that natural resources belonged to the nation. Without enforcing legislation, however, foreign oil companies continued business as usual until a 1925 act limited their concessions. During a bitter labor dispute in 1938, President Lázaro Cárdenas expropriated foreign oil holdings — the first nationalization of oil holdings by a non-Communist state. Subsequent legislation created Petróleos Mexicanos (PEMEX).

Without foreign capital and expertise, the new state-owned company struggled, and Mexico had to import petroleum in the early 1970s. But for many Mexicans, PEMEX remained a symbol of national identity and economic independence. That faith was rewarded in 1972 when a major oil discovery made PEMEX one of the world's top oil producers again. Ample domestic oil supplies and high world prices during the Iranian upheaval in the late 1970s fueled a boom and a government borrowing spree in Mexico. Between 1982 and 1985 PEMEX contributed more than 50% of government revenues.

When oil prices collapsed in 1985, Mexico cut investment in exploration, and production dropped. To decrease its reliance on oil, Mexico began lowering trade barriers and encouraging manufacturing, even allowing some foreign ownership of petrochemical processing.

Elected in 1988, President Carlos Salinas de Gortari began to reform PEMEX. Labor's grip on the company was loosened in 1989 when a union leader was arrested and jailed after a gun battle. In 1992, after a PEMEX pipeline explosion killed more than 200 people in Guadalajara, four of its executives and several local officials were sent to prison, amid public cries for company reform.

President Ernesto Zedillo appointed Adrián Lajous Vargas head of PEMEX in 1994. Under the professorial Lajous, PEMEX began to adopt modern business practices (such as trimming its bloated payroll), look for more reserves, and improve its refining capability. Lajous tried to sell some petrochemical assets in 1995, but had to modify the scheme the next year after massive public protests by the country's nationalists. Still, PEMEX began selling off natural gas production, distribution, and storage networks to private companies.

Though oil prices were dropping, in 1998 Mexico finally upped PEMEX's investment budget and PEMEX dramatically increased exploration and production. In spite of 2000's looming national election (elections traditionally had caused bureaucrats to keep a low profile to protect their jobs), Lajous again fanned the flames of the opposition: In 1998 he signed a major deal to sell Mexican crude to Exxon's Texas refinery, and in 1999 a four-year-old PEMEX/Shell joint venture announced it would expand its US refinery.

In 1999 Lajous resigned and was replaced by Rogelio Montemayor, a former governor. The next year Vicente Fox was elected as Mexico's new president, the country's first non-Institutional Revolutionary Party (PRI) leader in seven decades. He announced plans to replace PEMEX's politician-staffed board with professionals — Montemayor was among the casualties — and modernize the company, but he ruled out privatizing PEMEX as politically unfeasible.

Fox subsequently appointed Raúl Muñoz, formerly with Dupont Mexico, to lead PEMEX.

EXECUTIVES

Chairman: Fernando Elizondo Barragán, age 56
CEO: Luis Ramirez Corzo
Director Corporate Finance: José Juán Suárez Coppel
Managing Director, Finance and Treasury:
Octavio Ornelas Esquinca
Deputy Director of Programming and Budget:
Martha Alicia Olvera Rodríguez
Deputy Director of Financial Information Systems:
Victor Manuel Cámara Peón
Corporate Director of Operations:
José Antonio Ceballos Soberanis
Corporate Director of Administration:
Octavio Aguilar Valenzuela
General Counsel: Juan Carlos Soriano Rosas
Auditors: PricewaterhouseCoopers

LOCATIONS

HQ: Petróleos Mexicanos
Avenida Marina Nacional 329, Colonia Huasteca,
11311 México, D.F., Mexico
Phone: +52-55-5722-2500   **Fax:** +52-55-5531-6321
Web: www.pemex.com

PRODUCTS/OPERATIONS

2004 Drilling Activity

	Number
Wells Drilled	733
Wells Completed	727
Producing Wells (annual average)	5,286
Fields in Production	355
Drilling rigs	132
Kilometers Drilled	2,106
Average Depth by Well (in meters)	2,704
Discovered Fields	24
Oil and Gas (Barrels per Day)	833

2004 Crude Oil Production

	Barrels per Day
Marine region	2,829,000
Southern region	472,700
Northern region	81,200
Total	**3,382,900**

Major Subsidiaries

PEMEX Exploración y Producción (petroleum and natural gas exploration and production)
PEMEX Gas y Petroquímica Básica (natural gas, liquids from natural gas, and ethane processing)
PEMEX Petroquímica (petrochemical production)
PEMEX Refinación (refining and marketing)
P.M.I. Comercio Internacional (international trading)

COMPETITORS

Ashland	Marathon Oil
BHP Billiton	Norsk Hydro
BP	Occidental Petroleum
Chevron	PDVSA
Devon Energy	PETROBRAS
Eni	Royal Dutch/Shell Group
Exxon Mobil	Sunoco
Imperial Oil	TOTAL
Koch	Unocal

HISTORICAL FINANCIALS

Company Type: Government-owned

Income Statement

FYE: December 31

	REVENUE ($ mil.)	NET INCOME ($ mil.)	NET PROFIT MARGIN	EMPLOYEES
12/04	70,110	(2,278)	—	137,722
12/03	55,927	(3,619)	—	138,215
12/02	45,944	(2,910)	—	137,134
12/01	46,249	(3,519)	—	134,852
12/00	49,592	(2,084)	—	135,091
12/99	36,361	(1,921)	—	132,496
12/98	20,891	(1,108)	—	131,433
12/97	28,566	1,003	3.5%	121,220
12/96	29,403	2,091	7.1%	120,945
12/95	20,584	1,283	6.2%	119,928
Annual Growth	14.6%	—	—	1.5%

2004 Year-End Financials

Debt ratio: 1,217.2%
Return on equity: —
Cash ($ mil.): 7,583
Current ratio: 1.73
Long-term debt ($ mil.): 36,258

Net Income History

Peugeot

PSA Peugeot Citroën has regained its space under L'Arc de Triomphe, besting rival Renault to claim the top spot in the battle for auto sales in France. The best-selling auto brand in its home country, Peugeot is #2 behind Volkswagen in passenger car and commercial vehicle sales in Europe. Peugeot makes cars and light commercial vehicles under the Peugeot and Citroën brands. It also offers parts (Faurecia), transportation and logistics (Gefco), and financial services (Banque PSA Finance) for dealers and customers. Other products include motorbikes, scooters, and light-armored vehicles. The Peugeot family controls nearly 44% of the voting stock.

During the era of automotive industry consolidation, Peugeot preferred partnerships over mergers. This strategy includes an alliance with Toyota for the joint development of a small car for the European market, and a venture with BMW to develop engines for use in both companies' cars. Peugeot is even working with Ford Motor to produce diesel engines.

The company also focuses on efficiently building almost all of its vehicles on one of only a handful of basic platforms. This keeps the new models rolling out while keeping development and production costs under control.

Like every other car maker in the world, Peugeot is scrambling to get its share of the explosive growth in China. To that end the company plans to double its production capacity in China by 2006. Europe accounts for nearly 90% of sales.

HISTORY

In 1810 brothers Frédéric and Jean-Pierre Peugeot made a foundry out of the family textile mill in the Alsace region of France and invented the cold-roll process for producing spring steel. Bicycle production began in 1885 at the behest of avid cyclist Armand Peugeot, Jean-Pierre's grandson.

Armand turned to automobiles and built Peugeot's first car, a steam-powered three-wheeler, in 1889. A gas-fueled Peugeot tied for first place in the 1894 Paris-Rouen Trials, the earliest auto race on record. That year the budding carmaker built the first station wagon, followed in 1905 by the first compact, the 600-pound "Le Bébé."

Peugeot built factories in France, including one in Sochaux (1912) that remains the company's main plant. It made the first diesel passenger car in 1922. The 1929 introduction of the reliable 201 model was followed by innovations such as synchromesh gears in 1936. The company suffered heavy damage in WWII, but quickly bounced back and began expanding overseas after the war.

In 1954 CEO Roland Peugeot rebuffed a board proposal calling for global expansion that would place the company in competition with US automakers. By 1976 the French government had persuaded Peugeot to merge with Citroën.

André Citroën founded his company in 1915, and in 1919 it became the first in Europe to mass-produce cars. Citroën hit the skids during the Depression and in 1934 handed Michelin a large block of stock in lieu of payment for tires. Citroën never fully recovered, though by 1976 the company's line ranged from the 2CV minicar (discontinued 1990) to limousines.

In 1978 Peugeot bought Chrysler's aging European plants and withering nameplates, including Simca (France) and Rootes (UK). Peugeot changed the nameplates to Talbot but sales continued to slide. It lost nearly $1.2 billion from 1980 to 1984.

Jacques Calvet took over as CEO in 1984. He cut 30,000 jobs and spent heavily on modernization. Aided by the strong launch of the 205 superminicar, Peugeot returned to profitability in 1985, and by 1989 had halved its production break-even point. In the 1980s Peugeot inked production deals with Renault (industrial vehicles, motors, gearboxes) and Fiat (light trucks) and introduced a reasonably priced electric van in 1990.

Peugeot withdrew from the US in 1991 after five years of declining sales. A year later Renault and Peugeot developed electric cars and set up servicing centers throughout France. Citing an economic slump in 1993, Peugeot suffered its first loss ($239 million) since 1985. A French government incentive to replace cars over 10 years old boosted 1994 sales.

Peugeot and rival Renault together introduced a V6 engine in 1996. Jean-Martin Folz replaced Calvet as chairman and CEO in 1997; restructuring charges contributed to company losses that year. In 1998 the company began building Peugeots and Citroëns in the same plants and created its Faurecia unit when its ECIA subsidiary merged with car parts maker Bertrand Faure. In an effort to capitalize on the growing South American car market, the company purchased more than 80% of Argentina's Sevel, and built a plant in Brazil. In 1999 the company sold its flight systems supplier, SAMM, to TRW's Lucas Aerospace unit.

With demand for its cars falling steeply in South America due to the region's continuing economic crisis, Peugeot restructured its Brazil operations in 2000 and formed a new subsidiary, Citroën do Brasil.

In 2001 Peugeot announced that it was building a new engine plant in Brazil and agreed to produce a subcompact car for the European market with Toyota.

The following year Peugeot formed an alliance with BMW to develop and build a line of small diesel engines for use in vehicles made by both companies.

EXECUTIVES

Chairman of the Supervisory Board: Thierry Peugeot, age 48
Chairman of the Managing Board and Member of the Executive Committee: Jean-Martin Folz, age 58
EVP, Citroën Marque and Member of the Managing Board and Executive Committee: Claude Satinet
EVP, Employee Relations and Human Resources and and Member of the Managing Board and Executive Committee: Jean-Luc Vergne
EVP, Finance, Control, and Performance and Member of the Managing Board and Executive Committee: Yann Delabrière, age 55
EVP, Group Strategy and Products and and Member of the Managing Board and Executive Committee: Jean-Marc Nicolle
EVP, Innovation and Quality and Member of the Managing Board and Executive Committee: Robert Peugeot
EVP, Manufacturing and Components and and Member of the Managing Board and Executive Committee: Roland Vardanega
EVP, Peugeot Marque and Member of the Managing Board and Executive Committee: Frédéric Saint-Geours
EVP, Platforms, Technical Affairs, and Purchasing and Member of the Managing Board and Executive Committee: Gilles Michel
VP, Automotive Environment and Sustainable Development: Thérèse Martinet
VP, Corporate Communications: Liliane Lacourt
VP, Executive Development: Jean-Louis Grégoire
VP, Information Systems: Daniel Zamparini
VP, International Sales, Peugeot Marque: Bernd Schantz, age 56
VP, Legal Affairs: Jean-Claude Hanus, age 58
VP, Manufacturer Relations and Cooperation Agreements: Daniel Marteau
VP, Public Relations: Xavier Fels
VP, Research and Innovation: Pascal Hénault
Director, Communications, Peugeot Marque: Christian Peugeot, age 52
Head of Investor Relations: Valérie Magloire
Auditors: PricewaterhouseCoopers

LOCATIONS

HQ: PSA Peugeot Citroën S.A.
75, avenue de la Grande-Armée, 75116 Paris, France
Phone: +33-1-40-66-55-11   **Fax:** +33-1-40-66-54-14
US HQ: 150 Clove Rd., Little Falls, NJ 07424
US Phone: 973-812-4444   **US Fax:** 973-812-2280
Web: www.psa-peugeot-citroen.com

PSA Peugeot Citroën has manufacturing operations in Argentina, Brazil, China, the Czech Republic, France, Italy, Portugal, Spain, and the UK.

2004 Sales

	$ mil.	% of total
Europe		
Western Europe	64,369	83
Other countries	3,588	5
Latin America	1,940	2
Other regions	7,903	10
Total	**77,800**	**100**

2004 Sales

	$ mil.	% of total
Automobile	64,426	76
Automotive equipment	15,082	18
Transportation & logistics	4,072	5
Other	1,265	1
Adjustments	(7,045)	—
Total	**77,800**	**100**

COMPETITORS

BMW
Bridgestone
Caterpillar
DaimlerChrysler
Fiat
Ford
General Motors
Honda
Isuzu
Kia Motors
Mazda
Nissan
Renault
Renco
Saab Automobile
Suzuki Motor
Toyota
Volkswagen
Yamaha Motor

HISTORICAL FINANCIALS

Company Type: Public

Income Statement — FYE: December 31

	REVENUE ($ mil.)	NET INCOME ($ mil.)	NET PROFIT MARGIN	EMPLOYEES
12/04	77,800	3,469	4.5%	207,200
12/03	68,292	1,879	2.8%	199,910
12/02	57,233	1,771	3.1%	198,600
12/01	45,951	1,498	3.3%	192,500
12/00	41,601	1,235	3.0%	172,400
12/99	38,072	779	2.0%	165,800
12/98	39,394	565	1.4%	156,500
12/97	31,137	(461)	—	140,200
12/96	32,997	140	0.4%	139,100
12/95	33,459	347	1.0%	139,900
Annual Growth	**9.8%**	**29.2%**	**—**	**4.5%**

2004 Year-End Financials

Debt ratio: 26.6%
Return on equity: 21.5%
Cash ($ mil.): 12,077
Current ratio: 1.05
Long-term debt ($ mil.): 4,606

Net Income History — OTC: PEUGY

Philips Electronics

Royal Philips Electronics has its royal fingers in lots of different pies. The company makes consumer electronics, including TVs, VCRs, DVD players, phones, and fax machines. But it also makes light bulbs (#1 worldwide), electric shavers (#1) and other personal care appliances, picture tubes, semiconductors, and medical systems. Consumer electronics and appliances account for about a third of the company's sales. Philips has been dumping noncore businesses, such as its stake in music giant PolyGram, and acquiring and forming joint ventures in its core sectors (e.g., LG.Philips Displays, a CRT display joint venture with LG Electronics).

Philips' medical systems unit (with its Marconi acquisition) is now among the leaders in worldwide medical imaging and monitoring equipment (along with General Electric and Siemens). (Nearly a third of Philips' sales come from its medical systems group.) In 2004 Philips formed a joint venture with Société Générale, a Paris-based bank, to provide financial services to customers interested in purchasing medical equipment made by Philips.

In a joint venture with Neusoft Group (software and medical systems), Philips is building a medical-imaging equipment manufacturing plant in China.

In a transaction valued at $2 billion, Philips sold its computer monitor manufacturing operations and a portion of its flat screen TV business to Hong Kong-based TPV Technology, producer of CRT and LCD displays, making it the world's largest manufacturer of PC monitors. Philips also acquired a 30% stake in TPV Technology as part of the deal.

Philips is acquiring PC accessories maker (and Philips supplier) Gemini Industries; the move will help Philips expand its peripherals and accessories sales.

Philips is joining several other technology companies to develop software that will prevent music and films from being illegally copied. The alliance, named Coral, includes such companies as Hewlett-Packard, Samsung, and Sony. In October 2004 the company announced its own solution for tracking illegal copying activities with the launch of its RepliTrack software. The program embeds a unique watermark into DVDs that is transferred to all future copies of the recorded data.

HISTORY

Gerard Philips (later joined by brother Anton) founded Philips & Co. in the Dutch city of Eindhoven in 1891. Surviving an industry shakeout, Philips prospered as a result of Gerard's engineering and Anton's foreign sales efforts. The company had become Europe's #3 light bulb maker by 1900. It adopted the name Philips Gloeilampenfabrieken (light bulb factory) in 1912.

The Netherlands' neutrality during WWI allowed Philips to expand and integrate into glass manufacturing (1915) and X-ray and radio tubes (1918). The company set up its first foreign sales office in Belgium in 1919; it started building plants abroad in the 1930s to avoid trade barriers and tariffs.

During WWII Philips created US and British trusts to hold majority interests in North American Philips (NAP) and in Philips' British operations. Following the war, the company established hundreds of subsidiaries worldwide. It repurchased its British businesses in 1955; NAP operated independently until it was reacquired in 1987.

The company started marketing televisions and appliances in the 1950s. Philips introduced audiocassette, VCR, and laser disc technology in the 1960s but had limited success with computers and office equipment. Despite its development of new technologies, in the 1970s Philips was unable to maintain market share against an onslaught of inexpensive goods from Japan. Meanwhile, NAP acquired Magnavox (consumer electronics, US) in 1974. NAP also purchased GTE Television in 1981 and Westinghouse's lighting business in 1983. In 1986 it provided $60 million in seed money to start Taiwan Semiconductor Manufacturing with the Taiwanese government.

Philips' successful PolyGram unit (formed in 1972) went public in 1989 and bought record companies Island (UK) that year and A&M (US) the next. In 1991 the company changed its name to Royal Philips Electronics.

Ill-timed product introductions contributed to huge losses in the early 1990s. Philips cut some 60,000 jobs and sold money-losing businesses, including its computer business. Cor Boonstra, a former Sara Lee executive, was named chairman and president in 1996. The company sold its cellular communications business in 1996 to AT&T and merged its systems integration unit with BSO/Origin to form Origin B.V. Continuing to focus on core businesses, it sold its 75% stake in PolyGram to Seagram and bought US-based medical instruments maker ATL Ultrasound in 1998.

In 1999 Philips launched a hostile takeover of microchip maker VLSI Technology and, after negotiations, bought VLSI for nearly $1 billion. It also bought a 50% stake in LG LCD, a subsidiary of LG Group, for $1.6 billion; it was renamed LG.Philips LCD Co.

In 2000 the company formed TriMedia Technologies with Sony to create embedded processor core designs and software. Also that year, Philips divested its 24% stake ($3.8 billion) in semiconductor equipment maker ASML Holding. Philips bought 60% of top medical transcription service MedQuist, and agreed to buy Adac Laboratories (nuclear imaging technology).

In 2001 Boonstra retired and COO Gerard Kleisterlee became chairman and president. Also that year Philips completed its acquisition of the Healthcare Solutions Group of Agilent Technologies for $1.7 billion. Since 2001, Philips has cut more than 35,000 jobs; the reductions are the result of support staff job eliminations and the sale of noncore businesses (Communication, Security, and Imaging unit to Robert Bosch; contract manufacturing services to Jabil Circuit; health care products group to Platinum Equity Holdings).

In 2003 Fidelio Acquisition Company (an investor firm led by Philips, along with Sony Corporation of America) acquired InterTrust Technologies, a manufacturer of digital copy-protection software, for $450 million.

Frits Philips, son of founder Anton Philips and the last member of the Philips family to manage the company (he retired in 1977) and who helped develop audio cassettes and the compact disc, died in 2005 at the age of 100.

EXECUTIVES

President and CEO: Gerard Kleisterlee
CFO: Pierre-Jean Sivignon, age 48
EVP; CEO and President, Philips Consumer Electronics: Gottfried Dutiné, age 52
EVP, CTO, and Director: Ad Huijser, age 58
SVP and Chief Marketing Officer; CEO, Domestic Appliances and Personal Care: Andrea Ragnetti, age 44
SVP and Chief Procurement Officer: Barbara Kux, age 50
SVP and CIO: Daniel Hartert, age 46
SVP and Human Resources Management: Tjerk Hooghiemstra, age 48
SVP, Corporate Strategy and Asia Pacific Region: Jan P. Oosterveld, age 61
SVP, Secretary, and Chief Legal Officer: Arie Westerlaken, age 58
SVP; Sustainability and Quality: Arthur P. M. van der Poel, age 56
SVP; President and CEO, Philips Consumer Electronics: Rudy Provoost, age 45
SVP; President and CEO, Philips Lighting: Theo van Deursen, age 59
SVP; President and CEO, Medical Systems: Jouko Karvinen, age 47
SVP; President and CEO, Philips Semiconductors: Frans A. van Houten, age 45
VP, Corporate Communications: Ben Geerts
CEO, Philips Research: Rick Harwig
President, Philips Consumer Electronics, North America: Reinier Jens, age 46
Auditors: KPMG Accountants N.V.

LOCATIONS

HQ: Royal Philips Electronics N.V.
Breitner Center, Amstelplein 2,
1096 BC Amsterdam, The Netherlands
Phone: +31-20-59-77-777   **Fax:** +31-20-59-77-070
US HQ: 1251 Avenue of The Americas,
New York, NY 10020-1104
US Phone: 212-536-0500   **US Fax:** 212-536-0827
Web: www.philips.com

Royal Philips Electronics has about 135 manufacturing sites in 35 countries; it has sales and service operations in about 150 countries.

2004 Sales

	$ mil.	% of total
Europe & Africa	18,063.6	44
Asia/Pacific	10,867.9	26
North America	10,089.0	25
Latin America	2,049.5	5
Total	**41,070.0**	**100**

PRODUCTS/OPERATIONS

2004 Sales

	$ mil.	% of total
Consumer electronics	13,436.2	33
Medical systems	7,970.5	19
Semiconductors	7,401.5	18
Lighting	6,130.9	15
Domestic appliances & personal care	2,768.8	7
Other	3,362.1	8
Total	**41,070.0**	**100**

Selected Products

Consumer Electronics
  Audio
  Consumer communications
  Display
  Licenses
  Peripherals and accessories
  Video
Domestic Appliances and Personal Care
  Food and beverage
  Home environment care
  Oral health care
  Shaving and beauty

Lighting
  Automotive and special lighting
  Lamps
  Lighting electronics
  Luminaires
Medical Systems
  Asset management services
  Cardiac and monitoring systems
  Computed tomography
  Customer financing
  Dictation and speech recognition systems
  Document management services
  Magnetic resonance
  Medical IT
  Nuclear medicine
  Personal health care
  Ultrasound
  X-ray
Semiconductors
  Assembly and test
  Communications
  Consumer systems
  Foundries
  Mobile display systems
  Multi-market semiconductors
Miscellaneous
  Corporate investments
  Navigation technology
  Optical storage
  Shared services
  Technology and design

COMPETITORS

AMD	OSRAM
Fujitsu	Pioneer
GE	Samsung
Gillette	SANYO
Harman International	Sharp
Hitachi	Siemens
IBM Microelectronics	Siemens
Infineon Technologies	Sony
Intel	Spectrum Brands
LG Electronics	STMicroelectronics
Matsushita	Texas Instruments
Mitsubishi Electric	THOMSON
Motorola	Toshiba
Nokia	

HISTORICAL FINANCIALS

Company Type: Public

Income Statement

FYE: December 31

	REVENUE ($ mil.)	NET INCOME ($ mil.)	NET PROFIT MARGIN	EMPLOYEES
12/04	41,070	3,842	9.4%	161,586
12/03	36,505	873	2.4%	164,438
12/02	33,421	(3,367)	—	170,087
12/01	28,824	(2,321)	—	188,643
12/00	35,658	9,043	25.4%	219,429
12/99	31,748	1,816	5.7%	226,874
12/98	35,521	7,060	19.9%	233,686
12/97	37,737	2,829	7.5%	264,685
12/96	39,725	(339)	—	272,270
12/95	40,115	1,654	4.1%	263,554
Annual Growth	**0.3%**	**9.8%**	**—**	**(5.3%)**

2004 Year-End Financials

Debt ratio: 23.9%
Return on equity: 21.2%
Cash ($ mil.): 5,891
Current ratio: 1.45
Long-term debt ($ mil.): 4,812
No. of shares (mil.): 1,282
Dividends
  Yield: 0.0%
  Payout: —
Market value ($ mil.): 33,960

Pioneer

Pioneer takes you on a journey of sight and sound. A leading maker of consumer and commercial electronics, about 40% of its sales come from car electronics (stereos, speakers, navigation systems), which are sold to retailers and automobile manufacturers. Pioneer also makes video equipment (projection TVs, DVD players and DVD recorders, plasma displays) and audio products (stereo components, stereo systems). It also sells products to business customers (plasma displays, AV systems, factory automation systems) and, through Discovision Associates (US-based subsidiary), it generates revenue from licensing optical disc technologies. Pioneer has more than 30 manufacturing facilities worldwide.

Despite placing more emphasis on newer products, especially DVD players and plasma display TVs (products expected to have long-term growth potential), the company is still struggling with high production costs and falling retail prices. Pioneer acquired NEC's plasma display manufacturing business in September 2004; this turned out to be an ill-advised move, as prohibitively high production costs are driving the company to produce fewer product lines in the former NEC factory.

In connection with the failure of the push to increase its stake in the consumer electronics market and facing losses upwards of $200 million for the 2006 fiscal year, current president and CEO Kaneo Ito and chairman Kanya Matsumoto will step down and the end of 2005; executive vice president Tamihiko Sudo has been tapped to replace Ito.

Pioneer is also focusing efforts on its car navigation systems, a category which has grown to become a major revenue and profit source for the company.

The company — Pioneer Kabushiki Kaisha in Japanese — was the first to give us the laser disc (LD), car CD players, and car navigation devices that use a satellite-based global positioning system (GPS).

HISTORY

Nozomu Matsumoto, son of a Christian missionary, first heard high-fidelity speakers in 1932; nothing made in Japan compared in quality. In 1938 he founded Fukuin Shokai Denki Seisakusho (Gospel Electric Works) in Osaka to repair radios and speakers. It later began making these items. Matsumoto designed the company's trademark — a tuning fork overlaying the symbol for the ohm (a unit for measuring electrical resistance) — and chose the brand name Pioneer to reflect the company's spirit.

The firm introduced turntables and amplifiers in 1955 and hi-fi receivers in 1958. By the 1960s Pioneer Electronic was Japan's #1 audio equipment maker. It introduced the world's first stereo with speakers separate from the control unit in 1962 and the world's first car stereo in 1963. Subsidiaries opened in the US and Europe in 1966.

Convinced that laser disc (LD) technology was the wave of the future, Pioneer started work on a LD video player in 1972. Pioneer was listed on the NYSE four years later. It partnered with Discovision Associates (DVA, a partnership between IBM and Music Corporation of America) in 1977 to form Universal Pioneer Corporation (UPC). Home LD players appeared in the US in 1980 and in Japan in 1981. But consumers wanted machines that could record, not just play, and demand for LDs remained sluggish.

Matsumoto's eldest son, Seiya, became president in 1982. Two years later Pioneer introduced the world's first car CD system; it also created a LD/CD player, perhaps hoping customers would react better to LD products if they were combined with other features. Pioneer branched into office automation, introducing the Write-Once Read-Many (WORM) optical memory disk in 1985. In 1989 it bought DVA, by then a leading optical-disk research firm with more than 1,400 patents. Also that year it formed Pioneer Trimble with US-based Trimble Navigation to develop a computerized car navigation system.

Pioneer sold record company joint venture Warner-Pioneer to partner Warner — now Time Warner — in 1989, but it took another stab at the US entertainment business the next year when it bought 10% of theatrical filmmaker Carolco Pictures (*Basic Instinct*). But like many high-profile Japanese investments in the US, Carolco turned sour: It filed for Chapter 11 bankruptcy protection in 1995, leading Pioneer to write off its investment.

With sales not meeting expectations, in 1996 Pioneer replaced Seiya as president with his in-law Kaneo Ito (former head of Pioneer's Europe sales network); Seiya became chairman and his brother Kanya was made vice chairman. The company reentered the entertainment business with the 1996 launch of Pioneer Music Group. In 1997 Pioneer restructured itself into three separate operating units: Home Entertainment, Mobile Entertainment, and Business Systems; it added a Display Products unit the following year.

In 1999 the company opted for a simpler moniker, removing the word "electronic" from its name. Chairman Seiya died that year and was replaced by brother Kanya. With price wars and slow sales in its software business eroding profits, Pioneer announced in 1999 a three-year plan to cut more than 2,500 jobs. In 2000 Pioneer started making TV set-top boxes for digital cable. In 2001 Pioneer established two production subsidiaries in China to generate DVD pickups (the lens that converts the laser reflection into digital info), DVD-R/RW drives, and car electronics products.

Pioneer decided to exit the software and music business, opting to focus on hardware; in 2003 it sold subsidiaries Pioneer LDC and Pioneer Entertainment (USA) to Japanese advertising agency Dentsu.

EXECUTIVES

Chairman: Kanya Matsumoto, age 75
President, CEO, and Representative Director: Kaneo Ito, age 69
Senior Managing Director, Japanese Domestic Subsidiaries and Representative Director: Akira Niijima, age 61
EVP, Corporate Strategy Planning, Corporate Management, and Export Management and Representative Director: Tamihiko Sudo, age 58
Senior Managing Director and Representative Director; President, AV Business Company, General Manager, Tokorozawa Plant, and Head, Procurement Group: Hajime Ishizuka, age 58
Managing Director; EVP, Plasma Display Business Company: Tadahiro Yamaguchi, age 59
Managing Director; General Manager, Environmental Preservation Group: Satoshi Matsumoto, age 51
Senior Managing Director; General Manager, Research and Development Group and Corporate Research and Development Laboratories: Osamu Yamada, age 61
Managing Director; General Manager, Procurement Group: Koichi Shimizu, age 61
Senior Managing Executive Officer; President, Plasma Display Business Company: Masaru Saotome, age 61
Senior Managing Executive Officer; General Manager, International Business Group: Kazunori Yamamoto, age 63
Senior Executive Officer; President, Solutions Business: Kiyoshi Uchida, age 54
Senior Executive Officer; General Manager, Intellectual Property Division, Research and Development Group: Seiichiro Kurihara, age 62
Senior Executive Officer; General Manager, Corporate Branding and Communications Division: Masao Kawabata, age 57
Senior Executive Officer; General Manager, Finance and Accounting Division: Hideki Okayasu, age 55
Executive Officer; General Manager, Personnel Division: Osamu Takada, age 57
Executive Officer; President, Pioneer North America: Tsutomu (Tom) Haga, age 57
Auditors: Deloitte Touche Tohmatsu

LOCATIONS

HQ: Pioneer Corporation
4-1, Meguro 1-chome, Meguro-ku,
Tokyo 153-8654, Japan
Phone: +81-3-3495-6774　　**Fax:** +81-3-3495-4301
US HQ: 2265 E. 220th St., Long Beach, CA 90810
US Phone: 310-952-2000　　**US Fax:** 310-952-2199
Web: www.pioneer.co.jp

2005 Sales

	% of total
Japan	49
North America	15
Europe	12
Other regions	24
Total	**100**

PRODUCTS/OPERATIONS

2005 Sales

	% of total
Car electronics	39
Home electronics	38
Patent licensing	2
Other	21
Total	**100**

Selected Products

Home Electronics Products
　Digital broadcast set-top boxes
　DVD players
　DVD recorders
　DVD-ROM drives
　Equipment for cable-TV systems
　Plasma displays
　Projection TVs
　Recordable DVD drives
　Stereo components
　Stereo systems
　Telephones

Car Electronics Products
　Car AV systems
　Car navigation systems
　Car speakers
　Car stereos

Patent Licensing (related to optical disc technologies)
Other Products (business-use electronics)

COMPETITORS

Bose
Clarion
Harman International
Kenwood
LG Electronics
Matsushita
Philips Electronics
Robert Bosch
SANYO
Scientific-Atlanta
Sony
THOMSON
Victor Company of Japan

HISTORICAL FINANCIALS

Company Type: Public

Income Statement

FYE: March 31

	REVENUE ($ mil.)	NET INCOME ($ mil.)	NET PROFIT MARGIN	EMPLOYEES
3/05	6,857	(82)	—	39,362
3/04	6,612	234	3.5%	36,360
3/03	5,936	134	2.3%	34,656
3/02	5,029	61	1.2%	31,220
3/01	5,053	148	2.9%	28,871
3/00	5,627	123	2.2%	27,414
3/99	4,701	10	0.2%	23,647
3/98	4,241	47	1.1%	20,470
3/97	4,456	20	0.5%	19,962
3/96	4,779	(94)	—	19,378
Annual Growth	**4.1%**	**—**		**8.2%**

2005 Year-End Financials

Debt ratio: 24.4%
Return on equity: —
Cash ($ mil.): 1,091
Current ratio: 1.70
Long-term debt ($ mil.): 759
No. of shares (mil.): 174
Dividends
　Yield: 0.6%
　Payout: —
Market value ($ mil.): 3,134

	STOCK PRICE ($)	P/E		PER SHARE ($)		
	FY Close	High/Low	Earnings	Dividends	Book Value
3/05	17.97	— —	(0.47)	0.11	17.80
3/04	29.36	23 14	1.33	0.20	17.90
3/03	20.75	29 20	0.75	0.12	15.12
3/02	18.90	102 49	0.34	0.12	14.49
3/01	25.75	55 25	0.82	0.11	15.13
3/00	29.19	50 23	0.69	0.08	16.41
3/99	18.63	425 298	0.05	0.04	14.42
3/98	16.19	105 58	0.26	0.00	13.93
3/97	16.75	217 145	0.11	0.02	14.07
3/96	21.00	— —	(0.52)	0.12	15.55
Annual Growth	(1.7%)	— —	—	(1.0%)	1.5%

Pirelli & C.

Pirelli products travel the freeway, but may be exiting the information superhighway. After one reorganization Pirelli had four core businesses: tires, energy cables, real estate, and telecommunication cables, but the company has sold off the cable businesses in an effort to direct resources back towards its tire business. Pirelli makes tires for cars, industrial and commercial vehicles, motorcycles, and farm machinery, and the company has revved more than a few motors with its famous calendars. Its real estate sector invests in real estate companies and provides financing services. Italian holding company Camfin owns about a quarter of Pirelli.

Other members of the company's controlling shareholder pact include Banca Intesa, Capitalia, Edizione Holding (parent company of the Benetton Group), and Mediobanca.

Pirelli's two cable divisions sold in 2005 included energy (low-, medium-, and high-voltage power cables and building wire products) and telecommunications (cable assemblies and hardware and fiber-optics). The company sold the divisions to Goldman Sachs in a deal worth about $1.6 billion (E1.3 billion) including debt, and they are now known as Prysmian Cables & Systems. Pirelli still has some tech-related operations, through Pirelli Broadband Solutions and Pirelli Labs.

Although demand for Pirelli-brand tires has dropped in South America (particularly Brazil), the company expects the trend to change. The company plans to attempt to gain market share in the US by promoting its high performance tires, and also has plans to expand its market-share in eastern Europe and Asia. To this end Pirelli has formed a joint venture in China and is exploring its options in India.

In a bid to capitalize on the company's cache, Pirelli has launched a line of clothing, footwear, and accessories under the PZero brand. The items are produced under license by clothing firm IN.CO.M SpA and sold in the US and at more than 1,000 other locations around the world.

HISTORY

After fighting for Italian unification with Garibaldi in the 1860s, Giovanni Battista Pirelli observed that France, not Italy, was providing rubber tubes for an Italian ship salvage attempt. The young patriot reacted by founding Pirelli & Co. in Milan, Italy, in 1872 to manufacture rubber products. In 1879 Pirelli began making insulated cables for the rapidly growing telegraph industry, and by 1890 he was making bicycle tires. Pirelli introduced his first air-filled automobile tire in 1899.

Foreign expansion began when Pirelli opened cable factories in Spain (1902), the UK (1914), and Argentina (1917). The company set up Societe Internationale Pirelli (SIP) in Switzerland in 1937 and consolidated all non-Italian operations within it. After WWII the group expanded along with the growth in worldwide auto sales. Pirelli began production in Turkey and Greece in 1962, and six years later it set up cable plants in Peru.

Pirelli's first radial tires (early 1970s) backfired when they wore out too quickly. In 1971 the company swapped stock with tire maker Dunlop (UK). Although the firms engaged in joint research and development (R&D), they never consolidated production.

Pirelli S.p.A., the Italian operating company, and SIP became holding companies in 1982 by transferring their operating units into jointly owned Pirelli Societe Generale (Switzerland). That year Pirelli started producing fiber-optic cables.

Heavy spending on R&D and new equipment bolstered the newly unified tire business, and the 1986 purchase of Metzeler Kautscuk (Germany) made Pirelli one of the world's largest motorcycle tire manufacturers.

Pirelli S.p.A. became an operating company in 1988 when it bought SIP's Pirelli Societe Generale holdings. It launched a hostile bid for Firestone through Pirelli Tyre, but was outbid by Bridgestone. Pirelli settled for the much smaller Armstrong Tire. In 1989 Pirelli sold nearly 24% of Pirelli Tyre to the public.

In 1990 Pirelli proposed an unusually complex and convoluted merger with Continental AG (Germany) designed to leave Pirelli in control. Continental declined, but negotiations continued throughout 1991 until Continental terminated the talks after learning of Pirelli's deteriorating financial condition.

Pirelli became a top power-cable maker with operations in more than 20 countries in 1998 by acquiring Germany-based Siemens' power cable unit in a $277 million deal.

In 1999 Pirelli agreed to ally with Cooper Tire and Rubber, including an arrangement whereby Cooper would distribute and sell Pirelli tires for passenger cars and light trucks in the US, Canada, and Mexico. In return, Pirelli agreed to sell Cooper tires in South America. Additionally, Pirelli Cables Australia acquired Metal Manufacturers Ltd's energy cable business to strengthen its market share down under.

In 1999 Pirelli unveiled a compact, computerized manufacturing system designed to cut the cost of tire production about 25%, while raising tire quality. In 2000 Pirelli sold its terrestrial optical systems business to Cisco Systems for about $2.15 billion; Cisco agreed to invest $100 million in Pirelli's optical components and undersea cable transmissions divisions. Also in 2000 the company sold its fiber-optic telecommunications business to Corning for about $3.6 billion.

In 2001 the company separated energy cables and systems from its telecom business to focus on new growth and reached an alliance agreement with Alloptic to develop network fiber-optic solutions for commercial and home markets. In a surprise July announcement, Pirelli announced that it and the Benetton family had agreed to buy the 23% controlling stake in Olivetti — controlled by Roberto Colaninno, the CEO of both Olivetti and Telecom Italia. Pirelli sold its enameled wire holdings in late 2002 to Investitori Associati, an Italy-based investment group. After merging its operating company (Pirelli SpA) and holding company (Pirelli & C. SapA) in 2003, the company changed its name to Pirelli & C. SpA. The following year Pirelli sold its interest in Afcab, a South Africa-based cable manufacturer.

EXECUTIVES

Honorary Chairman: Leopoldo Pirelli
Chairman: Marco Tronchetti Provera, age 57
Deputy Chairman: Alberto Pirelli
Deputy Chairman: Carlo Alessandro Puri Negri
Managing Director; General Manager, Finance and Administration; Board Member: Carlo Orazio Buora, age 59
General Manager, Administration and Control: Claudio De Conto
General Manager, Finance: Luciano Gobbi
General Manager, Tires Sector: Francesco Gori
CIO: Dario Scagliotti
President and CEO, Pirelli, North America: Kevin Riddett
CEO, Pirelli Labs Optical Innovation: Giorgio Grasso
VP and General Manager, Pirelli Canada: Anthony (Tony) Ensor
Director, PZero: Antonio Gallo
Secretary: Carlo Montagna
Head, Investor Relations: Alberto Borgia
Corporate Communications: Ivan Dompé
Investor Relations: Massimiliano Cominelli
VP, Advertising, Public Relations and Motorsports, Pirelli Tire North America: Peter Tyson
Creative Director, PZero: Gigi Vezzola
Auditors: PricewaterhouseCoopers SpA

LOCATIONS

HQ: Pirelli & C. SpA
V.le Sarca, 222, 20126 Milan, Italy
Phone: +39-02-64421   **Fax:** +39-02-6442-4686
US HQ: 100 Pirelli Dr., Rome, GA 30162-7000
US Phone: 706-235-3786   **US Fax:** 706-368-5832
Web: www.pirelli.com

Pirelli has cable and tire manufacturing facilities around the globe.

2004 Sales

	% of total
Europe	
Italy	21
Other countries	44
Central & South America	14
Australia, Africa & Asia	11
North America	10
Total	**100**

2004 Sales

	% of total
Tires	46
Energy cables & systems	40
Real estate	8
Telecom cables & systems	6
Total	**100**

Selected Products

Tires
  Automobile (passenger car, SUV, and truck)
  Motorcycle

Real Estate
  Investment funds
  Real estate companies

COMPETITORS

Ansell
Bandag
Bridgestone
Continental AG
Falken Tire
Fieldens
Goodyear
Kumho Tire
Marangoni
Michelin
Sime Darby
Sumitomo Rubber
Watts Industrial Tyres

HISTORICAL FINANCIALS

Company Type: Public

Income Statement

FYE: December 31

	REVENUE ($ mil.)	NET INCOME ($ mil.)	NET PROFIT MARGIN	EMPLOYEES
12/04	9,704	374	3.9%	37,154
12/03	8,374	5	0.1%	36,337
12/02	6,615	(640)	—	36,079
12/01	6,652	73	1.1%	39,127
12/00	7,040	3,420	48.6%	41,914
12/99	6,619	307	4.6%	40,103
12/98	6,580	324	4.9%	36,226
12/97	6,395	261	4.1%	36,211
12/96	6,746	255	3.8%	36,534
12/95	6,862	162	2.4%	38,106
Annual Growth	3.9%	9.7%	—	(0.3%)

2004 Year-End Financials

Debt ratio: 47.3%
Return on equity: 8.0%
Cash ($ mil.): 752
Current ratio: 1.29
Long-term debt ($ mil.): 2,412

Net Income History

Italian: PC

```
3,500
3,000
2,500
2,000
1,500
1,000
 500
   0
-500
-1,000
     12/95 12/96 12/97 12/98 12/99 12/00 12/01 12/02 12/03 12/04
```

PKN ORLEN

Crudely moving into the private market, Polski Koncern Naftowy ORLEN (PKN) is the largest refiner and distributor of oil in Poland. Two former state monopolies, Petrochemia Plock (Poland's largest refinery) and Centrala Produktow Naftowych (Poland's #1 petroleum distributor), merged in 1999 to create PKN. The company also owns stakes in two other refineries (its total capacity is 600,000 barrels per day) and has some 1,900 retail sites, about a third of Poland's gas stations. PKN owns a 75% stake in chemical maker Anwil and has holdings in several other Polish companies. Outside Poland, the company has nearly 500 gas stations in Germany, and controls Czech refiner and retailer Unipetrol.

The company also manufactures liquefied propane-butane gas (LPG) for use at industrial plants and for heating public buildings. Other PKN products include polyvinylchloride plastics used in foils, containers, bottles, cable insulation, and auto parts; nitric fertilizers; asphalts for construction of roads, airports, and sports facilities; and basic industrial and engine oils.

Its Eko subsidiary burns hazardous waste, while its ORLEN Transport division handles the distribution of fuel to its gas stations. Its Solino holdings (70%) produces salt and brine, and uses salt caverns for underground storage of petroleum and fuels.

HISTORY

The merger between Petrochemia Plock, Poland's largest refiner and petrochemicals maker, and CPN (Centrala Produktow Naftowych), the nation's largest motor fuel distributor, created Polski Koncern Naftowy (PKN) in 1999.

Poland's oil industry stretches back to the late 1800s, when five refineries were built in the nation's southern region. The Polish Oil Monopoly was formed in 1944 to oversee the country's oil distribution operations; it assumed the CPN name a year later.

While the rest of the world increasingly turned to oil as an energy source after WWII, Poland continued to rely on coal, and its oil industry grew slowly. CPN was split up into 17 regional branches in 1955. The branches controlled local operations, and the head office in Warsaw handled pricing and purchasing.

In the late 1950s the Soviet Union began building the Friendship pipeline to deliver crude oil to East Germany and Poland. The Polish government responded by forming Petrochemia to develop a refinery next to the pipeline in the city of Plock.

The Petrochemia refinery began producing refined products in 1964; four years later it began processing crude oil to make fuels, lubricants, and bitumen. The refinery also began making products such as detergents and plastics from processed refinery gases and other hydrocarbons. It added petrochemicals in 1970.

Because of the oil industry's slow growth in Poland, the country managed to avoid some of the impact of the 1970s energy crisis. (Even as late as 1995, oil accounted for only 17% of Poland's energy consumption.) But it was forced to pay higher prices for Russian crude. In 1975 the government decided to expand its refining operations and created a second major refiner, Rafineria Gdanska, to focus on motor oils.

Locked behind the Iron Curtain, Poland was not able to build its oil operations until the early 1990s. In 1992 Petrochemia began expanding its refinery facilities to reach a production capacity of 820,000 barrels per day within 10 years.

After Communism's demise, the Polish government began planning the privatization of its oil operations. After several plans were adopted and discarded in the early 1990s, the government finally decided in 1996 to split CPN up among the nation's refineries. Holding company Nafta Polska was formed that year to own 75% stakes in Poland's refineries and in CPN and carry out the privatization process.

In 1997 CPN was stripped of its fuel depots and rail transport operations, which were placed under the Nafta Polska umbrella. Displeased with the plan to carve up CPN, the distributor's management rallied against the government's plan. The Polish government gave in and went back to the drawing board.

A successful plan was formed in 1998: to merge Petrochemia and CPN. The companies were combined in 1999, and 30% of the new PKN was floated on the Warsaw and London stock exchanges. The next year the government spun off an additional 42% stake. The company also added ORLEN to its name (combining the Polish words for eagle and energy).

Also in 2000 the government began preparing to float Refineria Gdanska. PKN hoped to get a piece of its regional rival, but the state left PKN out of the bidding to encourage competition.

To meet German antitrust regulations for its merger with Veba Oel, in late 2002 BP sold some 494 gas stations in Germany to PKN.

In 2004 PKN purchased 63% of Unipetrol; the European Commission's Competition Directorate granted approval of the purchase in mid-2005.

EXECUTIVES

Chairman: Jacek Bartkiewicz, age 50
President and CEO: Igor A. Chalupec, age 39
VP and COO: Janusz Wisniewski, age 46
CFO: Pawel Szymanski, age 32
VP and Head of Retail & Wholesale Operations:
Wojciech Heydel, age 44
VP and Chief Human Resources Officer:
Andrzej Ernest Macenowicz, age 58
VP and Head of Cost Management & IT:
Jan Maciejewicz, age 49
VP and Chief Investment Officer:
Cezary Smorszczewski, age 40
Head of Management Systems & Group Restructuring:
Dariusz Witkowski
Auditors: Ernst & Young

LOCATIONS

HQ: Polski Koncern Naftowy ORLEN SA
  ul. Chemików 7, 09-411 Plock, Poland
Phone: +48-24-365-00-00   **Fax:** +48-24-365-40-40
Web: www.orlen.pl

Polski Koncern Naftowy ORLEN has a major refinery in Plock, Poland; stakes in two refineries in southern Poland; and a network of gas stations in Poland and Germany.

2004 Sales

	% of total
Poland	65
Germany	28
Other countries	7
Total	**100**

PRODUCTS/OPERATIONS

2004 Sales

	% of total
Refining & marketing	81
Petrochemicals	15
Other	4
Total	**100**

Selected Subsidiaries

Inowroclawskie Kopalnie Soli "Solino"
  (70%, salt production)
Petrolot Sp. z o.o. (51%, distribution of aviation fuels)
Petroprofit Sp. z o.o. (85%; distribution of fuels, radiator
  fluids, and plastics)
Rafineria Nafty Jedlicze SA (75%, refining)
Rafineria Trzebinia SA (77%, refining)
Zaklady Azotowe Anwil SA
  (75%, chemical manufacturing)

COMPETITORS

BP
Exxon Mobil
LUKOIL
MOL
OMV
Royal Dutch/Shell Group
Statoil

HISTORICAL FINANCIALS

Company Type: Public

Income Statement

FYE: December 31

	REVENUE ($ mil.)	NET INCOME ($ mil.)	NET PROFIT MARGIN	EMPLOYEES
12/04	10,193	799	7.8%	14,296
12/03	6,499	263	4.0%	15,133
12/02	4,398	110	2.5%	17,818
12/01	4,278	94	2.2%	17,582
12/00	4,498	218	4.8%	13,342
12/99	3,206	228	7.1%	14,169
12/98	3,202	225	7.0%	—
Annual Growth	21.3%	23.6%	—	0.2%

2004 Year-End Financials

Debt ratio: 15.0%
Return on equity: 24.9%
Cash ($ mil.): 236
Current ratio: 2.05
Long-term debt ($ mil.): 586

Net Income History

Warsaw: PKNA

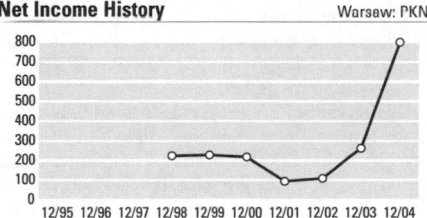

Placer Dome

When an Ontario prospector slipped and fell in 1909, he dislodged a clump of moss to reveal a dome-shaped rock sparkling with gold. Thus began the chain of events that led to the creation of Placer Dome, the world's sixth-largest gold mining company. Placer Dome produces more than 3.5 million ounces of gold (about 75% of sales) a year and has 60 million ounces in proven and probable reserves. It also produces about 410 million pounds of copper annually as well as silver as a byproduct of its gold mining. Placer Dome has interests in more than 15 mines in Australia, the Americas, Papua New Guinea, South Africa, and Tanzania. In 2005 Canadian mining giant Barrick Gold made a $9.2 billion offer for the company.

Even as Placer Dome wraps up operations at played-out mines in Australia and Papua New Guinea acquisitions are helping the company grow. In early 2003 it won a protracted battle for Australia's AurionGold, increasing its total annual production by about a million ounces. Placer Dome paid a pricey $1 billion for the Getchell Gold mine in Nevada in 1999 only to see gold prices languish; higher gold prices have allowed the company to start production in 2005. Placer Dome has sold a 25% stake in the Getchell mine to Newmont Mining.

In 2005 the company announced it would delay its Cerro Casale mine in Chile in favor of the Pueblo Viejo mine in the Dominican Republic. Pueblo Viejo is expected to produce 800,000 ounces of gold annually.

Much of the company's gold (about 70%) comes from its mines in Australia, Papua New Guinea, and the US. A majority of Placer Dome's copper is produced in Chile.

HISTORY

Placer Dome was formed by the 1987 amalgamation of three Canadian mining firms: Dome Mines Ltd. (the famed gold-studded dome of rock that gave the company its name was found in 1909; the business incorporated the next year), Placer Development Ltd. (1926), and Campbell Red Lake Mines (1944). The merger formed North America's largest gold-mining firm. When Australian mining companies moved to take over Placer and Dome in the 1980s, Placer engineered the merger.

Upon consolidation, Placer Dome began acquiring new operations using gold loans, in which the company borrowed gold from its lenders' reserves to make acquisitions and then repaid the loans in gold obtained from its mining operations. It bought Consolidated TVX Mining Corp. in the late 1980s. The company increased its interest in Nevada's Cortez Gold Mine joint venture in 1991 and bought half of Chile's Compañía Minera Zaldívar in 1992. That year Placer Dome's sales topped $1 billion for the first time.

In 1993 mining veteran John Willson became president and CEO and melded the company into an organization focused on regional operations. He also narrowed Placer Dome's primary focus to mining gold.

The company began production at two new mines in 1996, the Musselwhite in northern Ontario and the Pipeline in Nevada. That year a major spill of 4 million tons of tailings at Placer Dome's 40%-owned Marcopper mine in the Philippines led to a $43 million charge (the company sold its stake in Marcopper in 1997; in 2001 it agreed to fund further clean-up). In addition, Placer Dome began protracted battles, one to acquire Papua New Guinea-based Highlands Gold, the other to operate the Las Cristinas mine in Venezuela.

The Highlands Gold acquisition evolved into a hostile takeover bid. In Venezuela, Crystallex International Corporation disputed Placer Dome's claim to Las Cristinas, believed to be one of the richest gold deposits in South America. Placer Dome eventually won the court battle. Also in 1997 both the Pipeline and Musselwhite mines in North America began producing their first gold. That year Placer Dome completed its takeover of Highlands Gold, including a 50% stake in Papua New Guinea's Porgera mine.

Weak gold prices and writedowns for mining interests led to a big loss for Placer Dome in 1997. The company continued, nevertheless, to add mining properties. In 1998 it bought 51% of the Aldebaran copper-gold property in Chile, as well as the Can Can mine (also in Chile) with joint-venture partner PVX Gold. The next year Placer Dome bought a 50% share in the undeveloped South Deep gold deposit in South Africa (Western Areas Ltd. owns the rest) and Getchell Gold (two mines in central Nevada) for about $1 billion. Low metal prices caused Placer Dome to put operations at its Las Cristinas mine on hold (it was later sold). Later in 1999 gold prices increased on the promise from 15 European central banks to limit the sale of gold reserves.

In 2000 Willson retired, and Jay Taylor, an EVP and 20-year company veteran, replaced him as president and CEO. That year's loss, caused in part by charges related to the company's lowering of long-term gold price assumptions and adjustments to asset values, was laid at the door of lowered gold prices. In 2001 the company won a bid for the Pueblo Viejo mine in the Dominican Republic. It later put development at its Getchell mine on hold and took a $292 million write-off; production at Getchell was restarted in 2002.

In early 2003 Placer Dome expanded in Australia with the purchase of AurionGold. The company also bought East African Gold Mines, giving the company operations in Tanzania. Taylor retired in 2004 and Peter Tomsett was promoted to the position of president and CEO.

EXECUTIVES

Chairman: Robert M. Franklin, age 58
President, CEO, and Director: Peter W. Tomsett, age 47, $831,995 pay
EVP and CFO: Lindsay Hall, age 49
EVP, Project Development and Corporate Relations: William M. (Bill) Hayes, $524,399 pay
EVP, Operations: Evert van den Brand
EVP, Organization Development: Philip A. (Phil) Davis
EVP, Secretary, and General Counsel: J. Donald Rose, $377,320 pay
EVP, Strategic Development: Geoffrey A. (Geoff) Handley, $508,602 pay
SVP, AMS Project Development: Peter W. Harris
SVP, Projects — Technical Development: George N. Paspalas
VP, Controller and Interim CFO: Bruce B. Nicol
VP, Design and Construction: Martyn A. Creaney
VP, Evaluations, Strategic Development Group: Alfred Hills
VP, Research and Technology: Marilyn P. A. Hames
VP, Safety and Sustainability: Keith D. Ferguson
VP, Treasurer: Tony S. Giardini
VP, Associate General Counsel, and Assistant Secretary: Geoffrey Gold
Auditors: Ernst & Young LLP

LOCATIONS

HQ: Placer Dome Inc.
Ste. 1600, 1055 Dunsmuir St.,
Vancouver, British Columbia V7X 1P1, Canada
Phone: 604-682-7082   **Fax:** 604-682-7092
Web: www.placerdome.com

Placer Dome operates mines in Australia, Canada, Chile, Papua New Guinea, South Africa, Tanzania, and the US.

2004 Sales by Origin

	$ mil.	% of total
Australia	499	25
Chile	449	22
Papua New Guinea	333	17
US	316	16
Canada	241	12
South Africa	87	4
Tanzania	83	4
Metal hedging & other	(120)	—
Total	**1,888**	**100**

PRODUCTS/OPERATIONS

2004 Sales

	$ mil.	% of total
Gold	1,393	74
Copper	491	26
Other	4	—
Total	**1,888**	**100**

Selected Properties

Australia
  Granny Smith Mine
  Henty Mine
  Kalgoorlie West
  Kanowna Belle
  Osborne Mine (copper)
Canada
  Campbell Mine
  Musselwhite Mine (68%)
  Porcupine Mine (51%)
Chile
  La Coipa (50%)
  Zaldívar Mine (copper)
Papua New Guinea
  Porgera Mine (75%, joint venture with DRDGOLD)
South Africa
  South Deep Mine (50%)
Tanzania
  North Mara
US
  Bald Mountain Mine
  Cortez Mine (60%, joint venture with Kennecott
    Explorations)
  Golden Sunlight Mine
  Turquoise Ridge (75%)

COMPETITORS

AngloGold Ashanti
Apollo Gold
Barrick Gold
Cambior
Codelco
Freeport-McMoRan
Gold Fields
Goldcorp
Grupo México
Harmony Gold
Kinross Gold
Lihir Gold
Metaleurop
Newmont Mining
Peñoles
Phelps Dodge
Rio Tinto
Teck Cominco
Umicore
Vale do Rio Doce
WMC Resources

HISTORICAL FINANCIALS

Company Type: Public

Income Statement

FYE: December 31

	REVENUE ($ mil.)	NET INCOME ($ mil.)	NET PROFIT MARGIN	EMPLOYEES
12/04	1,888	284	15.0%	17,400
12/03	1,763	229	13.0%	12,500
12/02	1,209	116	9.6%	11,950
12/01	1,223	(133)	—	11,100
12/00	1,413	(92)	—	12,000
12/99	1,162	35	3.0%	12,000
12/98	1,279	105	8.2%	7,300
12/97	1,209	(249)	—	8,400
12/96	1,157	(65)	—	8,300
12/95	1,029	74	7.2%	8,000
Annual Growth	**7.0%**	**16.1%**	**—**	**9.0%**

2004 Year-End Financials

Debt ratio: 35.1%
Return on equity: 10.2%
Cash ($ mil.): 1,017
Current ratio: 3.61
Long-term debt ($ mil.): 1,109

No. of shares (mil.): 436
Dividends
  Yield: 0.5%
  Payout: 14.9%
Market value ($ mil.): 8,230

Stock History

NYSE: PDG

	STOCK PRICE ($) FY Close	P/E High/Low		PER SHARE ($) Earnings	Dividends	Book Value
12/04	18.86	36	20	0.67	0.10	7.25
12/03	17.91	31	15	0.56	0.10	5.83
12/02	11.50	42	23	0.33	0.10	5.28
12/01	10.91	—	—	(0.41)	0.10	4.09
12/00	9.63	—	—	(0.28)	0.10	4.62
12/99	10.75	159	84	0.11	0.10	5.00
12/98	11.50	50	22	0.36	0.10	6.79
12/97	12.69	—	—	(1.06)	0.30	6.52
12/96	21.75	—	—	(0.27)	0.30	7.24
12/95	24.13	95	59	0.31	0.30	6.45
Annual Growth	**(2.7%)**	**—**	**—**	**8.9%**	**(11.5%)**	**1.3%**

Porsche

Perhaps second only to Harley-Davidson as the premier cure for a mid-life crisis, Porsche is still going strong a century after its founder began designing autos. Porsche's lineup includes four model lines: the Boxster, the 911 models, the Cayenne SUV, and the Carrera GT. Can't afford a new Cayenne? Porsche also offers watches, luggage, and tennis rackets bearing its name. In addition, Porsche offers consulting services to other companies involved in auto and furniture manufacturing, mechanical and electronic engineering, and construction. Descendants of the founding family control Porsche.

While other carmakers toil over cash incentives, 0% financing gimmicks, market share, and strategies for the Chinese market, Porsche has

quietly transformed itself from serious money-loser into one of the most profitable car companies in the world. The company has nearly quadrupled its annual unit sales in just under a decade, all without the costs and risks of constantly rolling out new products. The most recent debuts have been the Boxster and the Cayenne, both of which have been hugely successful. The company plans to stick with the winning formula of long product life cycles, and growing unit sales year over year.

Porsche has acquired nearly 20% of Volkswagen (VW) in a deal initially valued at $3.6 billion. The deal makes Porsche the largest shareholder of VW.

HISTORY

Ferdinand Porsche was 25 when a battery-powered car with a motor he had designed was unveiled at the Paris Exposition in 1900. Six years later, Porsche was hired by Daimler Motor. During his rise to chief engineer at Daimler, he designed the famous Mercedes-Benz S-series.

Frustrated by the conservative nature of his employer, Porsche quit and opened an engine-design company bearing his name in 1931. The next year Josef Stalin offered to make Porsche the head of the Soviet Union's auto industry. Porsche turned Stalin down.

In 1933 Hitler announced his intention to build a widely affordable "volkswagen" (people's car). Soon Porsche was designing the vehicle that would become the Volkswagen Beetle. During WWII Porsche continued work on the Volkswagen project and also provided advice on increasing Germany's factory production. After the war, Ferdinand and his son Ferry were imprisoned for two years in France for allegedly abusing French laborers. Father and son were compelled to work on the Renault line of automobiles. After his release, Ferdinand reportedly burst into tears and exclaimed, "My Beetle!" when he saw his Volkswagen cars populating the streets in Germany.

By 1948 Ferdinand and Ferry had developed a Porsche sports-car prototype based on the Volkswagen. It was named the 356 because it was the 356th project undertaken at the Porsche design office. In 1950 the first Porsche 356 rolled off the assembly line in Stuttgart. Ferdinand Porsche lived just long enough to see his sports cars become highly sought by the rich and famous. He died in 1951.

In 1952 Ferry designed the Porsche emblem, which combined the Porsche name and the Stuttgart and Wurttemberg coats of arms. Porsches won hundreds of races during the 1950s, and the car's popularity grew. (James Dean was driving his brand-new Porsche when he was killed in 1955.)

By the 1960s Ferry Porsche decided to build an entirely new Porsche model that didn't rely so heavily on the Beetle's design. The company unveiled the Type 911 Porsche in 1964 and discontinued the 356 the next year. In 1973 the company went public under the Porsche AG name.

The company flourished in the 1980s, due largely to its cars' popularity in the US. By 1986 Porsche was producing almost 50,000 cars a year, with about 60% of them destined for the US market. Models introduced in the late 1980s included the 912, the 924, and the 928.

Porsche's fortunes crashed in the early 1990s, when the company faced tough competition and a recession priced many consumers out of the sports-car market. In 1992 the company sold only

23,060 cars — 4,100 of those in the US. That year Wendelin Wiedeking, an engineering and manufacturing expert, was brought in as CEO. He cut costs, in part, by convincing most workers to reduce the number of hours they worked each day and eliminating overtime. Wiedeking also updated the 911 and initiated development of the Boxster.

Introduced in 1996, the $40,000 Boxster was an instant hit — its first year of production sold out in advance. In 1998 the company initiated plans to produce a luxury SUV in partnership with Volkswagen. Porsche launched the Boxster S, featuring a 250-hp engine, in 1999. The next year Porsche announced that its Cayenne SUV — which shares a platform with Volkswagen's SUV — would hit the market in 2003.

Early in 2002 Porsche announced its next product launch — the Carrera GT. Production of the Carrera GT began the following year.

EXECUTIVES

Chairman of the Supervisory Board: Helmut Sihler, age 74
Deputy Chairman of the Supervisory Board: Hans Baur
Member of the Executive Board, Finance and Controlling: Holger P. Härter
Member of the Executive Board, Production and Logistics: Michael Macht
Member of the Executive Board, Research and Development: Wolfgang Dürheimer, age 47
Member of the Executive Board, Sales and Marketing: Hans Riedel
Member of the Executive Board, Human Resources and Labor Relations: Harro Harmel
President and CEO, Porsche Cars North America: Peter Schwarzenbauer
Managing Director, Porsche France: Detlev van Platen
Managing Director, Porsche Italia: Loris Casadei
Managing Director, Porsche Cars Great Britain: Andrew Goss
Managing Director, Porsche Germany: Bernhard Maier
Managing Director, Porsche Iberica: Joachim Lamla
Auditors: Ernst & Young

LOCATIONS

HQ: Dr. Ing. h.c. F. Porsche AG
Porscheplatz 1, D-70435 Stuttgart, Germany
Phone: +49-711-911-0   **Fax:** +49-711-911-5777
US HQ: 980 Hammond Dr., Ste. 1000, Atlanta, GA 30328
US Phone: 770-290-3500   **US Fax:** 770-290-3706
Web: www.porsche.com

Porsche operates main production facilities in Zuffenhausen, Germany, and in Finland.

2004 Sales

	$ mil.	% of total
Europe		
Germany	2,760	36
Other countries	1,676	22
North America	2,620	34
Other regions	589	8
Total	**7,645**	**100**

PRODUCTS/OPERATIONS

2004 Sales

	$ mil.	% of total
Vehicles	6,976	91
Financial services	669	9
Total	**7,645**	**100**

2004 Sales

	Units	% of total
Cayenne	39,913	52
911	23,704	31
Boxster	12,988	17
Carrera GT	222	—
Total	**76,827**	**100**

Selected Vehicles

Boxster	911 Carrera S
Boxster S	911 GT2
Carrera GT	911 GT3
Cayenne	911 Targa
Cayenne S	911 Turbo
Cayenne Turbo	911 Turbo Cabriolet
911 Carrera	911 Turbo S
911 Carrera 4S	911 Turbo S Cabriolet
911 Carrera Cabriolet	

COMPETITORS

BMW	Nissan
DaimlerChrysler	Peugeot
Fiat	Renault
Ford	Saab Automobile
General Motors	Saleen
Honda	Volkswagen
Mazda	

HISTORICAL FINANCIALS

Company Type: Public

Income Statement

FYE: July 31

	REVENUE ($ mil.)	NET INCOME ($ mil.)	NET PROFIT MARGIN	EMPLOYEES
7/04	7,645	293	3.8%	11,668
7/03	6,331	374	5.9%	10,699
7/02	4,776	509	10.7%	10,143
7/01	3,883	236	6.1%	9,752
7/00	3,440	194	5.6%	9,320
7/99	3,363	204	6.1%	8,712
7/98	2,767	156	5.6%	8,151
7/97	2,233	75	3.4%	7,959
7/96	1,912	32	1.7%	7,107
7/95	1,880	1	0.1%	6,847
Annual Growth	**16.9%**	**81.1%**	**—**	**6.1%**

2004 Year-End Financials

Debt ratio: 27.5%
Return on equity: 12.3%
Cash ($ mil.): 3,356
Current ratio: 4.37
Long-term debt ($ mil.): 767

Net Income History

OTC: PSEPF

POSCO

POSCO steeled itself against unfavorable market conditions in its neck of the woods, but things are looking up. The company makes hot- and cold-rolled steel products (plate steel, stainless steel, electrical steel, and wire rods), which it sells to the auto and shipbuilding industries. It produces about 31 million tons of steel a year and ships it worldwide. Subsidiaries include POSCO Engineering & Construction (which builds steel plants, steel-related infrastructure, and energy facilities) and POSDATA (systems integration). The South Korean government has privatized its remaining stake in POSCO, ending the company's 30-year steelmaking monopoly in that country.

Unfortunately for POSCO, South Korea has little native iron ore, and the company has had to look for iron elsewhere. The company purchases its iron ore and coal from Australia, Brazil, Canada, China, India, and Russia. To that end, POSCO has developed about 18 joint ventures, including six in China and others in Australia, Brazil, Canada, Indonesia, Myanmar, South Africa, Thailand, the US, and Venezuela. The company said it would cut steel production by 300,000 tons in 2005 due to low demand.

India sits predominantly in POSCO's expansion sights, as the company announced plans in March 2005 to join BHP Billiton in setting up a steelworks in the country capable of an annual capacity of more than 10 million tons. In June the company agreed to launch what could be the largest foreign investment ever in India — a $12 billion steel plant in the eastern state of Orissa. Work is expected to begin in 2007.

China is also on the radar: POSCO submitted plans to the Chinese government for another 10-million-metric-ton plant.

In May 2005 the company announced it would purchase 50% of Korea Independent Energy Corp., the country's largest private-power producer. In October, POSCO listed on the Tokyo Stock Exchange.

POSCO's hot-rolled products segment accounted for close to 40% of sales. Hot-rolled products are used in the construction of automobile chassis, buildings and bridges, industrial pipes and tanks, and railway rolling stocks. The company's cold-rolled segment resulted in just over 30% of sales. Its cold-rolled products such as cold-rolled coils and galvanized cold-rolled products are used in the automotive industry to manufacture car body panels and other uses like household goods, electrical appliances, and engineering and metal parts.

POSCO has also formed an alliance with long-time rival Nippon Steel and plans to establish agreements with other steelmakers in China and Europe. The company also intends to diversify into the energy distribution business, bioscience, and other emerging high-tech areas.

HISTORY

After the Korean War, South Korea, the US, and its allies wanted to rebuild South Korea's infrastructure as quickly as possible. Steel was given a high priority, and before long about 15 companies were making various steel products. Quality was a problem, though, as the companies used dated production processes.

With the backing of South Korean president Chung Hee Park, momentum for a large steel plant grew in the late 1960s. In 1967 the South Korean government and Korean International Steel Associates (KISA) — a consortium of seven Western steelmakers — signed an agreement that called for the completion of an integrated mill by 1972. Pohang Iron & Steel Co. (POSCO), the operating company, was incorporated in 1968. Efforts to raise the necessary capital failed, however, and KISA was dissolved in 1969.

Undaunted, the South Koreans turned to the Japanese, who arranged loans covering most of the mill's costs and the early phases of planning and construction. The Japanese also transferred the technology needed to run such a plant. Slow and deliberate planning resulted in a plant far away from Seoul (part of a plan to locate industries throughout the country) and a design that lent itself to future expansion. The first stage, including a blast furnace and two steel converters, was completed in 1973. By the time the fourth stage of construction began in 1979, the South Koreans had gained enough confidence to take over many of the tasks. When the last stage was completed in 1981, the plant had an annual capacity of 8.5 million tons.

To ensure steel of acceptable quality, POSCO focused first on plain high-carbon steel for general construction, rather than on specialized (and difficult to produce) varieties. The company gradually broadened its specialized offerings.

In 1985 POSCO began construction on a second integrated steel plant located in Kwangyang. That plant was also built in four stages; its annual production capacity, when it was completed in 1992, was 11.4 million tons. By 1987 POSCO was exporting almost 3 million tons of steel a year and using its knowledge to assist in plant construction projects in other countries.

By the mid-1990s POSCO was exporting 6 million tons of steel annually. The South Korean government sold a 5% stake in POSCO to the public in 1998 and vowed to open up the primary steelmaking industry to competition. However, facing a severe downturn in steel demand that year because of sluggishness in Asian and domestic markets, the company canceled two projects in China and suspended two in Indonesia. In 1999 POSCO merged its two subsidiaries, Pohang Coated Steel and Pohang Steel Industries, to create Pohang Steel Co. The South Korean government continued selling off its 13% stake in 1999.

In 2000 POSCO sold its 51% stake in telecommunications company Shinsegi Telecom to SK Telecom in exchange for cash and a 6.5% stake in SK Telecom. It also formed a strategic alliance — exploration of joint ventures, shared research, and joint procurement — with Nippon Steel, the world's #1 steel maker. The deal also calls for each to take increased equity stakes (2% or 3%) in the other. After about 30 years of government control, the South Korean government sold its remaining shares of POSCO in 2001.

In June 2002 Chairman Yoo was indicted for influencing POSCO subsidiaries and contractors to buy inflated shares of Tiger Pools International (South Korea's sole sports lottery business) for Kim Hong-Gul, the third son of South Korean President Kim Dae-Jung. That same year Pohang Iron & Steel Co. officially changed its company name to POSCO to try and strengthen brand recognition.

In 2003 Yoo resigned ahead of the company's shareholder meeting amid his possible involvement in illegal stock transactions.

EXECUTIVES

Chairman and CEO: Lee Ku-Taek, age 58
President: Kang Chang-Oh, age 61
CFO: Lee Dong-Hee
SEVP: Choi Kwang-Woong, age 59
SEVP, Corporate Communications and Secretary: Yoon Seok-Man, age 54
SEVP, General Superintendent, Pohang Works: Ryoo Kyeong-Ryul, age 55
SEVP, POSCO China President: Kim Dong-Jin, age 57
SEVP, Stainless Steel Division Manager, Stainless Steel Raw Materials Procurement Department: Lee Youn, age 56
EVP, Cold Rolled Steel Sales, Automotive Flat Panel Sales Dept., and Coated Steel Sales: Choi Jong-Doo, age 57
EVP, Corporate Strategic Planning: Cho Soung-Sik, age 53
EVP, General Administration, Human Resources and Labor and Welfare: Choi Jong-Tae, age 54
EVP, General Superintendent, Gwangyang Works: Chung Joon-Yang, age 55

EVP, General Superintendent, Technology Research Center: Hur Nam-Suk, age 53
EVP, Legal Affairs: Kim Sang-Ho, age 50
SVP, Coal Procurement, Iron Ore Procurement, Steel Raw Material Procurement, and Stainless Steel Raw Material Procurement: Kwon Young-Tae, age 53
SVP, Corporate Communications: Kim Sang-Young
SVP, Corporate Ethics and Audit: Park Han-Yong, age 53
SVP, Marketing Strategy, Market Development, Sales, and Production Planning: Oh Chang-Kwan, age 51
VP, Human Resources, Labor, and Welfare: Kim Tae-Man
Auditors: Samil Pricewaterhousecoopers

LOCATIONS

HQ: POSCO
POSCO Center, 892 Daechi-4-dong, Kangnam-ku, Seoul, South Korea
Phone: +82-2-3457-0114   **Fax:** +82-54-220-6000
US HQ: 2 Executive Dr., Ste. 805, Fort Lee, NJ 07024
US Phone: 201-585-3060   **US Fax:** 201-585-6001
Web: www.posco.co.kr

POSCO operates subsidiary companies in Australia, Brazil, Canada, China, Germany, Hong Kong, Indonesia, Japan, Myanmar, Russia, Singapore, South Africa, South Korea, Thailand, Turkey, the UK, the US, and Vietnam.

2004 Sales

	$ mil.	% of total
Asia		
South Korea	16,168	70
China	3,203	14
Japan	1,124	5
Other countries	1,214	5
North America	512	2
Other regions	937	4
Total	**23,158**	**100**

PRODUCTS/OPERATIONS

2004 Production

	Metric tons	% of total
Hot-rolled	10,966	34
Cold-rolled	10,242	32
Plates	3,385	11
Wire rods	2,503	8
Stainless steel	2,069	7
Silicon steel sheets	705	2
Other	1,926	6
Total	**31,796**	**100**

Selected Subsidiaries and Affiliates

Changwon Specialty Steel Co., Ltd. (99%, specialty steel)
Dalian POSCO-CFM Coated Steel Co., Ltd. (59%, coated-steel manufacturing, China)
Davey Distington Ltd. (54%, engineering)
IBC Corporation (58%, rent)
Pohang Steel America Corp. (99.9%, steel trading, US)
Pohang Steel Australia Pty., Ltd. (95%, ore mining)
Pohang Steel Canada Ltd. (95%, coal mining)
Pohang Steel Industries Co., Ltd. (coated steel)
POSCO Asia Co., Ltd. (57%, steel trading, Hong Kong)
POSCON Co., Ltd. (97%, electric control devices)
POSDATA Co., Ltd. (computer system development)
POSCO Machinery & Engineering Co., Ltd. (steel work maintenance)
POSCO Research Institute (99.8%, economic research and consulting)
POSCO Venezuela Compañía Anónima (POSVEN, 59%, steel manufacturing)
POSCO Engineering & Construction Co., Ltd. (97%)
POSCO International Osaka Inc. (95%, Japan)
POSEC-Europe, Ltd. (97%, engineering, UK)
POSEC-HAWAII Inc. (97%, construction and rent, US)
POS-Energy Co., Ltd. (99.9%)
POSLILAMA Steel Structure Co., Ltd. (68%, Vietnam)
POSMETAL Co., Ltd. (48%, steel processing, Japan)
POS-NPC (manufacturing, storage, and transportation of steel)
POS-THAI Steel Service Center Co., Ltd. (39%, steel sales)
POS-Tianjin Coil Center Co., Ltd. (67%, steel sales)

PT. Posnesia Stainless Steel Industry (70%, stainless steel sales, Thailand)
Seung Kwang Co., Ltd. (94%, athletic facilities)
Shanghai POSEC Real Estate Development Co., Ltd. (97%, rent, China)
SHUNDE Pohang Coated Steel Co., Ltd. (80%, China)
VSC-POSCO Steel Corp. (40%, Vietnam)
Zhangjiagang Pohang Stainless Steel Co., Ltd. (80%, China)
Zhangjiagang POSCO Coated Steel Co., Ltd. (90%, China)

COMPETITORS

Arcelor	Nippon Steel
Bechtel	Nucor
Corus Group	Samsung
Fluor	Shanghai Baosteel
Hitachi	ThyssenKrupp
JFE Holdings	Toyota Tsusho
Kobe Steel	United States Steel
Marubeni	

HISTORICAL FINANCIALS

Company Type: Public

Income Statement

FYE: December 31

	REVENUE ($ mil.)	NET INCOME ($ mil.)	NET PROFIT MARGIN	EMPLOYEES
12/04	23,158	3,685	15.9%	27,919
12/03	14,925	1,675	11.2%	27,415
12/02	12,101	918	7.6%	27,100
12/01	9,989	644	6.4%	25,000
12/00	10,873	1,289	11.9%	26,261
12/99	11,181	1,368	12.2%	27,949
12/98	11,288	790	7.0%	28,500
12/97	6,795	430	6.3%	29,161
12/96	11,381	698	6.1%	—
12/95	11,140	1,222	11.0%	—
Annual Growth	**8.5%**	**13.0%**	**—**	**(0.6%)**

2004 Year-End Financials

Debt ratio: 12.8%
Return on equity: 27.9%
Cash ($ mil.): 470
Current ratio: 2.10
Long-term debt ($ mil.): 1,981

No. of shares (mil.): 322
Dividends
  Yield: 0.0%
  Payout: —
Market value ($ mil.): 14,339

Stock History

NYSE: PKX

	STOCK PRICE ($) FY Close	P/E High	P/E Low	PER SHARE ($) Earnings	PER SHARE ($) Dividends	PER SHARE ($) Book Value
12/04	44.53	4	2	11.40	0.00	48.23
12/03	33.97	7	4	5.14	0.00	30.55
12/02	24.73	11	7	2.80	0.48	29.12
12/01	23.00	13	7	1.97	0.47	23.75
12/00	15.56	12	4	3.78	0.39	19.22
12/99	35.00	12	4	3.57	0.00	20.73
12/98	16.88	12	5	2.10	0.00	17.99
12/97	17.44	30	12	1.15	0.00	11.56
12/96	20.25	15	10	1.88	0.25	20.66
12/95	21.88	11	6	3.25	0.04	20.78
Annual Growth	**8.2%**	**—**	**—**	**15.0%**	**—**	**9.8%**

PPR SA

PPR (formerly Pinault-Printemps-Redoute) might have its roots in timber, but its branches are now firmly in the retail arena. PPR has axed its timber and building materials business, electrical equipment supplier Rexel, and its consumer credit unit to focus on its retail businesses, which include department stores (Printemps), catalogs (Redcats), and luxury goods (Gucci and Yves Saint Laurent). PPR has become the world's third-largest luxury group via its majority stake in Italian luxury goods company Gucci Group, and several perfume lines. Some 55% of PPR's sales are generated outside France. Founder François Pinault's investment firm, Artémis, owns 42% of PPR. The company changed its name to PPR in 2005.

PPR has transformed itself from a conglomerate to a focused luxury retail group. The "New PPR," as the company likes to call itself, also has new leadership: François-Henri Pinault, the son of the company's founder, joined the company as its new CEO in March 2005, replacing longtime chief Serge Weinberg.

PPR's retail and luxury goods divisions already account for more than two-thirds of sales. The retail group includes the world's #3 catalog merchant, Redcats, with distribution in the US and Europe. The division also operates three large retail chains: Conforama, France's #1 appliance retailer; Printemps, Paris' #1 department store; and Fnac books and music stores. Fnac operates more than 110 stores (45 outside of France) in eight countries.

To fund its transformation, the company sold Guilbert and Pinault Bois & Matériaux (lumber and building supplies), to shore up its balance sheet to fund its offer for the rest of Gucci. (The two men credited with the turnaround at Gucci — Domenico De Sole, the CEO, and Tom Ford, its creative director — as well as many other Gucci senior executives left the company at the end of April 2004. Ford was succeeded by four "unknown" designers. Months later (in October 2004), Giacomo Santucci, Gucci Brand's president and managing director, was abruptly terminated. PPR closed an offer to buy out minority shareholders in Gucci and now owns 99% of Gucci's shares.

Self-made billionaire and founder François Pinault has a cache of prestigious businesses, including auction house Christie's.

HISTORY

Sixteen-year-old François Pinault left school in 1952 to join the family timber business. He took over the firm when his father died in 1963; that year the company was renamed Pinault Group. Pinault diversified the company into wood importing and retailing, eventually building a flourishing enterprise. In 1973 Pinault began to show his talent for the art of the deal. Sensing the demand for timber was peaking, he sold 80% of the business, buying it back two years later at an 85% discount.

During the 1970s Pinault bought struggling timber businesses and turned them around. (He was helped, in part, by a policy of the French government that subsidized purchases of failing companies in order to preserve jobs.) Pinault purchased bankrupt wood panel manufacturer Isoroy in 1986 for a token fee. In 1987 he bought ailing paper company Chapelle Darblay, selling it three years later at a 40% profit. By 1988, when it filed to go public on the Paris exchange, Pinault Group was a vertically integrated timber manufacturing, trading, and distribution company.

Pinault began to diversify outside the timber industry in the 1990s. It acquired electrical equipment distributor CFAO (Compagnie Française de l'Afrique Occidentale) in 1990, the Conforama furniture chain in 1991, and Au Printemps (owner of Printemps stores and 54% of catalog company Redoute) in 1992. The firm then became the Pinault-Printemps Group. The purchase of Au Printemps left the company heavily in debt, and it sold some of its noncore assets during the early 1990s.

In 1993 the group reorganized into four divisions: retail, business-to-business, financial services, and international trade. That year Pinault-Printemps bought a majority stake in Groupelec and merged it with electrical equipment subsidiary CDME, forming Rexel. In 1994 the company completed its acquisition of Redoute. After renaming itself Pinault-Printemps-Redoute (PPR), it bought a majority stake in French book and music retailer Fnac (buying the rest in 1995). In 1995 Rexel head Serge Weinberg took over the company after CEO Pierre Blayau ran afoul of Pinault over strategy. PPR added West African pharmaceuticals distributor SCOA in 1996.

Expanding globally, Redcats (Redoute's new name) launched the Vertbaudet (children's wear) and Cyrillus (sportswear) catalogs in the UK in 1997. In 1998 PPR bought a majority stake in Guilbert, the European leader in office supplies and furniture, and a 44% stake in Brylane (renamed Redcats USA in 2004), the US's #4 mail-order company. PPR also opened a new store format in France called Made in Sport (sporting goods). In addition, it began offering phone cards through subsidiary Kertel.

PPR bought the remainder of Brylane in 1999 and also launched a new division to oversee the online efforts of its various businesses. Later that year, PPR sparked a string of legal battles between it and LVMH when it purchased 42% of luxury goods maker Gucci. (The move thwarted LVMH's efforts to take over Gucci by diluting LVMH's stake in the firm.) In early 2000 PPR bought France's largest computer retailer, Surcouf.

In 2001 a Dutch court granted a request by LVMH and ordered an investigation into the legality of the alliance of PPR and Gucci. In a deal to end years of litigation, PPR purchased LVMH's stake in Gucci for $806.5 million in October 2001, increasing its ownership to 53.2%.

The company sold Yves Saint Laurent's haute couture division to French dressmaking company SLPB Prestige Services in 2002. Guilbert's mail-order business was sold to US office supplies retailer Staples that year for $815 million. (The rest of Guilbert was later sold to Office Depot in 2003.) In 2003, PPR's timber wholesale business, Pinault Bois & Matériaux, was sold to the UK's Wolseley plc. Also in 2003, PPR increased its stake in Gucci to 67.6%.

In March 2005 François-Henri Pinault, the son of the company's founder, joined the company as its new CEO, succeeding Serge Weinberg. During his 10 years at the helm, Weinberg oversaw the transformation of the company from a business-to-business concern to a focused luxury retail group. At the annual general meeting in May shareholders approved the offical name change to PPR from Pinault-Printemps-Redoute.

EXECUTIVES

Chairman and CEO: François-Henri Pinault, age 44
EVP, Finance: Ross McInnes, age 51
Chief Corporate Officer: Patrice Marteau, age 57
SVP, Human Resources: Alain Luchez, age 52
VP, Strategy and Business Development:
Philippe Klocanas
Chairman and CEO, CFAO: Alain Viry
Chairman and CEO, Conforama: Christophe Cuvillier, age 42
Chairman and CEO, FNAC: Denis Olivennes, age 42
Chairman and CEO, France-Printemps:
Laurence Danon, age 49
Chairman, President, and CEO, Gucci Group:
Robert Polet, age 48
Chairman and CEO, Redcats: Thierry Falque-Pierrotin, age 42
Director, Communications: Laurent Claquin, age 24
Director, Financial Communications: Marc Willaume, age 42
Director, Media Relations: Lorie Lichtlen
General Manager, Fnac.com: Franck Leprou
Head of Corporate Social Responsibility:
Estelle Kistner-L'Hour, age 36
Auditors: Deloitte Touche Tohmatsu; KPMG Audit

LOCATIONS

HQ: PPR SA
10, Avenue Hoche, 75381 Paris, France
Phone: +33-1-45-64-61-00   **Fax:** +33-1-44-90-62-25
Web: www.pprgroup.com/pprgroup__Changelang-en.html

2004 Sales

	% of total
Europe	
France	44
Other countries	25
Americas	18
Africa	6
Asia	4
Oceania	3
Total	**100**

PRODUCTS/OPERATIONS

2004 Sales

	% of total
Retail	60
Rexel	27
Luxury goods	13
Total	**100**

Operations

Luxury Goods
  Gucci Group N.V. (99.23%, leather goods and apparel)
Retail
  CFAO (distribution of automobiles, motorcycles,
    pharmaceuticals, and consumer goods in
    Africa and French territories)
  Conforama (furniture and appliances; Croatia,
    France, Italy, Luxembourg, Portugal, Spain,
    and Switzerland)
  Fnac (electronics, books, music; Belgium, Brazil,
    France, Italy, Monaco, Portugal, Spain, Switzerland,
    and Taiwan)
  Printemps (department stores in France)
  Redcats (catalogs, including Brylane, Daxon,
    Ellos, and Redoute)

COMPETITORS

C&A	METRO AG
Carrefour	Otto
Casino Guichard	Pier Import Europe
Galeries Lafayette	Virgin Group
IKEA	Vivarte
LVMH	

HISTORICAL FINANCIALS

Company Type: Public

Income Statement

FYE: December 31

	REVENUE ($ mil.)	NET INCOME ($ mil.)	NET PROFIT MARGIN	EMPLOYEES
12/04	33,026	1,283	3.9%	95,397
12/03	30,578	809	2.6%	102,381
12/02	28,692	1,666	5.8%	113,453
12/01	24,624	667	2.7%	115,935
12/00	23,308	722	3.1%	110,862
12/99	19,042	630	3.3%	89,178
12/98	19,272	593	3.1%	81,073
12/97	14,866	476	3.2%	64,135
12/96	15,363	395	2.6%	57,241
12/95	15,848	309	1.9%	59,299
Annual Growth	8.5%	17.1%	—	5.4%

2004 Year-End Financials

Debt ratio: 73.8%
Return on equity: 13.4%
Cash ($ mil.): 933

Current ratio: 1.21
Long-term debt ($ mil.): 7,742

Net Income History

Euronext Paris: PP

1,800 / 1,600 / 1,400 / 1,200 / 1,000 / 800 / 600 / 400 / 200 / 0

12/95 12/96 12/97 12/98 12/99 12/00 12/01 12/02 12/03 12/04

Pricewaterhouse-Coopers

Not merely the firm with the longest one-word name, PricewaterhouseCoopers (PwC) is also one of the world's largest accounting firms, formed when Price Waterhouse merged with Coopers & Lybrand in 1998, passing then-leader Andersen. The accountancy has some 775 offices in 148 countries around the world, providing clients with services in three lines of business: Assurance (including financial and regulatory reporting), Tax, and Advisory. The umbrella entity for the PwC worldwide organization (officially PricewaterhouseCoopers International) is one of accounting's Big Four, along with Deloitte Touche Tohmatsu, Ernst & Young, and KPMG. PwC serves some of the world's largest businesses, as well as smaller firms.

PwC puts its heft to good use: Non-North American clients make up nearly two-thirds of the firm's sales. Its bottom line, though, changed significantly in 2002, when PwC sold its consulting arm to IBM. A separation had been under consideration for years in light of SEC concerns about conflicts of interest when firms perform auditing and consulting for the same clients. The collapse of Enron and concomitant downfall of Enron's auditor and PwC's erstwhile peer Andersen undoubtedly hastened plans to spin off PwC's consultancy via an IPO, which was scrapped in favor of the IBM deal.

Expansion in developing economies, including China and South America, as well as new

regulatory and financial reporting rules as a result of the adoption of International Financial Reporting Standards and the implementation of Sarbanes-Oxley requirements have been good for the firm's business.

Like the other members of the (now) Big Four, PwC picked up business and talent as scandal-felled Andersen was winding down its operations in 2002. The former Andersen organization in China and Hong Kong joined PwC, accounting for about 70% of the approximately 3,500 Andersen alumni that came aboard.

In 2003 former client AMERCO (parent of U-Haul) sued PwC for $2.5 billion, claiming negligence and fraud in relation to a series of events that led to AMERCO restating its results.

HISTORY

In 1850 Samuel Price founded an accounting firm in London and in 1865 took on partner Edwin Waterhouse. The firm and the industry grew rapidly, thanks to the growth of stock exchanges that required uniform financial statements from listees. By the late 1800s Price Waterhouse (PW) had become the world's best-known accounting firm.

US offices were opened in the 1890s, and in 1902 United States Steel chose the firm as its auditor. PW benefited from tough audit requirements instituted after the 1929 stock market crash. In 1935 the firm was given the prestigious job of handling Academy Awards balloting. It started a management consulting service in 1946. But PW's dominance slipped in the 1960s, as it gained a reputation as the most traditional and formal of the major firms.

Coopers & Lybrand, the product of a 1957 transatlantic merger, wrote the book on auditing. Lybrand, Ross Bros. & Montgomery was formed in 1898 by William Lybrand, Edward Ross, Adam Ross, and Robert Montgomery. In 1912 Montgomery wrote *Montgomery's Auditing,* which became the bible of accounting.

Cooper Brothers was founded in 1854 in London by William Cooper, eldest son of a Quaker banker. In 1957 Lybrand joined up to form Coopers & Lybrand. During the 1960s the firm expanded into employee benefits and internal control consulting, building its technology capabilities in the 1970s as it studied ways to automate the audit process.

Coopers & Lybrand lost market share as mergers reduced the Big Eight accounting firms to the Big Six. After the savings and loan debacle of the 1980s, investors and the government wanted accounting firms held liable not only for the form of audited financial statements but for their veracity. In 1992 the firm paid $95 million to settle claims of defrauded investors in MiniScribe, a failed disk-drive maker. Other hefty payments followed, including a $108 million settlement relating to the late Robert Maxwell's defunct media empire.

In 1998 Price Waterhouse and Coopers & Lybrand combined PW's strength in the media, entertainment, and utility industries, and Coopers & Lybrand's focus on telecommunications and mining. But the merger brought some expensive legal baggage involving Coopers & Lybrand's performance of audits related to a bid-rigging scheme involving former Arizona governor Fife Symington.

Further growth plans fell through in 1999 when merger talks between PwC and Grant Thornton International failed. The year 2000

began on a sour note: An SEC conflict-of-interest probe turned up more than 8,000 alleged violations, most involving PwC partners owning stock in their firm's audit clients.

As the SEC grew ever more shrill in its denunciation of the potential conflicts of interest arising from auditing companies that the firm hoped to recruit or retain as consulting clients, PwC saw the writing on the wall and in 2000 began making plans to split the two operations. As part of this move, the company downsized and reorganized many of its operations.

The following year PwC paid $55 million to shareholders of MicroStrategy Inc., who charged that the audit firm defrauded them by approving the client firm's inflated earnings and revenues figures.

The separation of PwC's auditing and consulting functions finally became a reality in 2002, when IBM bought the consulting business. (The acquisition took the place of a planned spinoff.)

In 2005 in the US PwC was ranked among the Top 10 companies for working mothers by *Working Mother* magazine.

EXECUTIVES

Global CEO and Global Board Member:
Samuel A. DiPiazza Jr., age 54
Global Managing Partner, Advisory and Tax:
Eugene (Gene) Donnelly
Global Managing Partner, Assurance:
Robert (Rob) Ward
Global Managing Partner, Markets & Operations:
Paul Boorman
Global Co-Leader, People: Richard L. Baird
Global Managing Partner, Markets: Willem L.J. Bröcker
Global Managing Partner, Risk and Quality:
Michael O. (Mike) Gagnon
Global General Counsel; Acting US General Counsel:
Lawrence W. Keeshan
Global Leader, Industries: Alec N. Jones
Global Leader, Regulatory and Public Policy:
Richard R. Kilgust
Senior Partner and CEO, Australia:
Anthony P.D. Harrington
CEO and Senior Partner of PricewaterhouseCoopers LLP, Canada: Christie J. B. Clark
Territory/Regional Leader, Central and Eastern Europe:
John K. Heywood
Chairman, Asia 7 Leadership Team; Executive Chairman, PricewaterhouseCoopers Singapore:
Gautam Banerjee
Senior Partner, Continental Europe: Wolfgang Wagner
Senior Partner, South and Central America:
Luis E. Frisoni Jr.
Chairman, UK: Kieran C. Poynter
Chairman and Senior Partner US: Dennis M. Nally
Global Leader, Entertainment and Media Practice:
R. Wayne Jackson
Global Leader, Transaction Services: Colin McKay, age 48
Global Strategy Leader: Edgargo Pappacena
Senior Managing Director, Global Public Relations:
Peter Horowitz
Global Co-Leader, Human Capital:
Marie-Jeanne Chèvremont-Lorenzini
Head of Media Relations, UK: Alison Sharpe
Director of Communications, Europe: Mike Davies
Director, Marketing and Communications, Asia Pacific:
Cynara Tan
Global Public Relations, Consumer and Industrial Products: Kristina Blissett
Global Public Relations, Financial Services:
Stephanie Peters
Global Public Relations, Technology, InfoComm, and Entertainment and Media: Fiona Scholes
Managing Partner, Global Operations:
Amyas C.E. Morse, age 55

LOCATIONS

HQ: PricewaterhouseCoopers International Limited
1177 Avenue of the Americas, New York, NY 10036
Phone: 646-471-4000   **Fax:** 646-471-3188
Web: www.pwcglobal.com

PricewaterhouseCoopers has more than 770 offices in 148 countries.

2005 Sales

	$ mil.	% of total
Europe	8,583	45
North America & Caribbean	7,047	37
Asia	1,753	10
Australasia & Pacific Islands	806	4
Middle East & Africa	441	2
South & Central America	368	2
Total	**18,998**	**100**

PRODUCTS/OPERATIONS

2005 Sales by Industry

	% of total
Industrial Products	18
Healthcare & Professional Services	15
Banking & Capital Markets	11
Retail & Consumer	10
Investment Management	9
Technology	9
Energy, Utilities & Mining	8
Insurance	6
Entertainment & Media	5
Infocomm	4
Automotive	3
Pharmaceuticals	2
Total	**100**

2005 Sales

	% of total
Assurance	57
Tax	24
Advisory	19
Total	**100**

Selected Products and Services

Audit and Assurance Services
  Actuarial services
    Audit support
    Financial modeling
    IFRS implementation
    Insolvencies and run-off solutions
    M&A and capital structuring
    Operational improvement
    Retirement, benefits, and actuarial
    Risk and capital management
  Assurance on capital market transactions
  Financial accounting
  IFRS readiness and conversions
  Independent controls and process assurance
  Internal audit
  Non-financial performance and reporting
  Regulatory compliance
  Sarbanes-Oxley readiness
  Statutory audit
  Web assurance solutions
Advisory Services
  Crisis management
    Business recovery services
    Dispute analysis and investigation
  Performance improvement
  Transaction services
    Corporate finance
    Valuation and strategy
Tax and Human Resource Services
  Customs and duties
  Finance and treasury
  Global compliance services
  Global VAT solutions
  Global visa solutions
  Human resource services
  International assignment solutions
  Mergers and acquisitions
  Transfer pricing

COMPETITORS

Bain & Company	H&R Block
Baker Tilly International	Hewitt Associates
BDO International	KPMG
Booz Allen	Marsh & McLennan
Boston Consulting	McKinsey & Company
Deloitte	Towers Perrin
Ernst & Young	Watson Wyatt
Grant Thornton International	

HISTORICAL FINANCIALS

Company Type: Partnership

Income Statement

FYE: June 30

	REVENUE ($ mil.)	NET INCOME ($ mil.)	NET PROFIT MARGIN	EMPLOYEES
6/05	18,998	—	—	130,203
6/04	16,283	—	—	122,471
6/03	14,683	—	—	122,820
6/02	13,800	—	—	124,563
6/01	24,000	—	—	160,000
6/00	21,500	—	—	150,000
6/99	15,300	—	—	155,000
6/98	15,000	—	—	140,000
6/97	5,630	—	—	60,000
6/96	5,020	—	—	56,000
Annual Growth	**15.9%**	**—**	**—**	**9.8%**

Revenue History

Prudential plc

The Man from the Pru no longer surfs the sidewalk, he surfs the Internet. The company is known for its iconic Man from the Pru agent, now relegated to memory after being supplanted by other sales channels. Prudential is one of the UK's largest insurers; it also has significant operations in Asia and the US. In addition to insurance, Prudential's UK businesses include its banking division; products include pensions, investment bonds, and personal loans. In Asia, the company sells life insurance, savings, and investment products through its Prudential Corporation Asia unit. In the US, Prudential owns Jackson National Life, which offers annuities and life insurance. Other businesses include fund manager M&G.

The company's publicly listed Egg subsidiary offers telephone and Internet banking services, as well as mortgages and VISA credit cards, and is expanding into online brokerage. In an attempt to boost capital, Prudential spent the first half of 2004 negotiating to sell Egg, but announced in August that it would retain its stake in the online bank. It later said it would acquire the minority stake it did not yet own in the company.

Overhauling its UK operations, Prudential abolished its direct sales force (some 2,000 people) and is concentrating on sales by phone and through the Internet. It began divesting non-core assets to concentrate on life insurance, group pensions, and with-profit bonds. The consolidation drive also saw Prudential dropping its Scottish Amicable products, which were re-branded under the Prudential name.

How do you say Pru in Mandarin? The company is well into an expansion strategy in the world's largest marketplace. It is the first European life insurer to gain licenses to operate in seven cities in China through its CITIC Prudential joint venture with China's CITIC Group.

HISTORY

Actually, prudence almost killed Prudential before it ever got started. Founded in 1848 as Prudential Mutual Assurance Investment and Loan Association, the firm initially insured middle-class customers. The Dickensian conditions of the working poor made them too risky for insurers. Unfortunately the company found few takers of the right sort, and by 1852 Prudential was in peril.

Two events saved Prudential: The House of Commons pressed for insurance coverage for all classes, and Prudential's own agents pushed for change. The company expanded into industrial insurance, a modest coverage for the working poor. In 1864, to quell criticism of the insurance industry, Prudential brought in independent auditors to confirm its soundness. This soon became a marketing tool and business took off. The Pru, as it came to be known, became the leading industrial insurer by the 1880s. It covered half the country's population by 1905. The firm's salesmen were known for making personal visits to customers (the "Man from the Pru" became a ubiquitous icon in the 1940s and was revived in 1997).

During the two world wars Prudential boosted its reputation by honoring the policies of war victims when it could have legally denied them. Between wars the company added fire and accident insurance in Europe.

In 1969 it bought Mercantile and General Reinsurance Company from Swiss Re.

In 1982, under the direction of CEO Brian Corby, the Pru reorganized product lines and in 1985 entered the real estate business. In 1986 it entered the US market by buying US-based Jackson National Life. The 1980s were volatile for insurance companies, especially in the wake of Britain's financial deregulation in 1986.

Prudential, which had considered selling Mercantile and General Reinsurance in the early 1990s, sold the reinsurer back to Swiss Re in 1996. It also formed Prudential Bank and created an Asian emerging-market investment fund that year.

In 1997 Prudential bought Scottish Amicable. Insurance regulators reprimanded the company for mis-selling financial products that year.

In 1998 Jackson National bought a California savings and loan, enabling it to sell investment products in the US. Also that year the Pru sold its Australian and New Zealand businesses, and Prudential Bank launched its pioneering Internet bank Egg. In 1999 Prudential bought investment manager M & G Group and to reduce costs it announced plans to cut more than 5,000 jobs in the subsequent three years.

The company changed its name to Prudential plc and began talks with the Prudential Insurance Company of America to resolve confusion of their similar names as they expand into new markets. The Pru in 1999 joined forces with the Bank of China to offer pension and asset management in Hong Kong.

In 2000 the company announced plans to sell a chunk of its institutional fund management business as well as its traditional balanced pension business to Deutsche Bank. Also that year the company spun off 20% of Egg and agreed to start an insurance joint venture in China with state-owned investment vehicle CITIC Group.

Entering the Japanese life insurance market, Prudential bought Orico Life in 2001. Prudential's hopes of capturing the lucrative annuities market by acquiring American General were dashed in 2001; American General instead embraced American International Group, leaving the Pru with a $600 million break-up fee.

To consolidate operations in 2001, the firm sold its general insurance business to Swiss insurer Winterthur (a subsidiary of Credit Suisse) and dropped its Scottish Amicable products, which were rebranded under the Prudential name.

EXECUTIVES

Chairman: Sir David C. Clementi, age 56, $837,897 pay
Group Chief Executive and Board Member:
Mark Tucker, age 47
Group Finance Director and Board Member:
Philip Broadley, age 44, $1,444,650 pay
Chief Executive, The M&G Group, and Board Member:
Michael McLintock, age 43, $3,305,359 pay
Chief Executive, Prudential Corporation Asia, and Board Member: Mark Norbom, age 47, $1,675,794 pay
Chief Executive, Prudential UK and European Insurance Operations, and Board Member:
Mark Wood, age 51, $1,770,178 pay
President and CEO, Jackson National Life, and Board Member: Clark P. Manning Jr., age 46, $2,825,736 pay
Chief Executive, Prudential UK and European Insurance Operations, and Board Member:
Nicholas E. T. (Nick) Prettejohn, age 45
Group Human Resources Director: Jane Kibbey
Group Communications Director: Rebecca Burrows
Group Legal Services Director and Secretary:
Peter Maynard
Group Corporate Relations Director: Geraldine Davies
Head of Business Development Services:
Pamela (Pam) Aurbach
EVP, Information Technology: J. George Napoles
EVP, Corporate Development: Jim Sopha
Group Chief Executive, Egg plc: Paul Gratton, age 45
Vice Chairman and COO, Jackson National Life:
Mike Wells
EVP and Chief Distribution Officer, Jackson National Life: Clifford J. Jack
Auditors: KPMG Audit Plc

LOCATIONS

HQ: Prudential plc
Laurence Pountney Hill,
London EC4R 0HH, United Kingdom
Phone: +44-20-7220-7588   **Fax:** +44-20-7548-3699
US HQ: Jackson National Life, 1 Corporate Way,
Lansing, MI 48951
US Phone: 517-381-5500   **US Fax:** 517-706-5517
Web: www.prudential.co.uk

2004 New Business Gross Premiums

	% of total
Asia	54
UK & Europe	33
US	13
Total	**100**

PRODUCTS/OPERATIONS

2004 Gross Premiums Written

	% of total
UK & Europe insurance operations	56
Jackson National Life	29
Asian operations	15
Total	**100**

Selected Subsidiaries and Affiliates

Egg plc (79%)
Egg Banking plc
Jackson National Life Insurance Company (US)
M&G Investment Management Limited
PCA Life Assurance Company Limited (99%, Taiwan)
Prudential Annuities Limited
Prudential Assurance Company Singapore (Pte) Limited
Prudential Retirement Income Limited
The Prudential Assurance Company Limited

COMPETITORS

Abbey National	Lincoln Financial Group
AEGON	Lloyds TSB
AIG	MetLife
Allianz	Millea Holdings
Aviva	Mitsui Sumitomo
AXA	Insurance
Barclays	Nationwide Financial
Canada Life	New York Life
Cathay Life Insurance	Nippon Life Insurance
Citigroup	Prudential
FMR	RBS
Friends Provident	Royal & Sun Alliance
The Hartford	Insurance
HBOS	Schroders
HSBC Holdings	Sompo Japan Insurance
ING	Standard Life
INVESCO UK	State Farm
Jupiter Unit	Woolwich
Trust Managers	Zurich Financial Services
Legal & General Group	

HISTORICAL FINANCIALS

Company Type: Public

Income Statement

FYE: December 31

	ASSETS ($ mil.)	NET INCOME ($ mil.)	INCOME AS % OF ASSETS	EMPLOYEES
12/04	334,628	821	0.2%	21,500
12/03	288,422	371	0.1%	21,012
12/02	245,207	724	0.3%	21,930
12/01	228,287	566	0.2%	23,047
12/00	231,681	1,029	0.4%	21,942
12/99	243,514	876	0.4%	22,372
12/98	196,742	1,460	0.7%	22,200
12/97	178,525	1,381	0.8%	22,100
12/96	134,445	2,412	1.8%	22,187
12/95	116,109	1,175	1.0%	23,064
Annual Growth	**12.5%**	**(3.9%)**	**—**	**(0.8%)**

2004 Year-End Financials

Equity as % of assets: 2.5%
Return on assets: 0.3%
Return on equity: 11.7%
Long-term debt ($ mil.): 206,544
No. of shares (mil.): 1,188
Dividends
Yield: 6.2%
Payout: 140.3%
Market value ($ mil.): 20,662
Sales ($ mil.): 59,685

Stock History

NYSE: PUK

12/95 12/96 12/97 12/98 12/99 12/00 12/01 12/02 12/03 12/04

	STOCK PRICE ($) FY Close	P/E High/Low	PER SHARE ($) Earnings	Dividends	Book Value
12/04	17.40	27 19	0.77	1.08	6.91
12/03	17.05	46 24	0.37	0.77	5.82
12/02	13.87	33 14	0.73	0.84	5.91
12/01	23.43	58 27	0.57	0.80	5.77
12/00	31.88	135 102	0.24	0.27	6.07
Annual Growth	**(14.0%)**	**— —**	**33.8%**	**41.4%**	**3.3%**

Publicis Groupe

Advertising is *la joie de vivre* for Publicis. One of the world's largest advertising and media services conglomerates, the company provides a wide range of corporate communication and media services, including creative advertising, media and campaign planning, marketing, and public relations. Its flagship advertising networks include Leo Burnett Worldwide, Publicis Worldwide, and Saatchi & Saatchi; Publicis' Starcom MediaVest and ZenithOptimedia units are among the world's largest media planning enterprises. The company serves such clients as Allied Domecq, Coca-Cola, Hewlett-Packard, Procter & Gamble through offices in about 110 countries.

Publicis is the leading provider of advertising and marketing services in Europe and ranks behind only Omnicom, WPP Group, and Interpublic in worldwide revenue. Its media services operations rank #2 behind WPP Group's MindShare and Mediaedge:cia in total worldwide billings. In addition, its Specialized Agencies and Marketing Services division provides marketing and communications services through a number of agencies, including Arc Worldwide (relationship marketing); Burrell Communications (multicultural advertising); and Manning, Selvage & Lee (public relations).

The company has been working to consolidate many of its operating units following a string of acquisitions, including its $3 billion purchase of Bcom3 in 2002. In the US it folded Publicis Sanchez & Levitan into Bromley Communications to form America's top Hispanic ad agency, while it combined several marketing firms (including Frankel and Semaphore Partners) to form Arc Worldwide. Publicis' acquisition of Bcom3 cemented its worldwide standing and gave the company a large foothold in the US, adding Leo Burnett and Starcom MediaVest to its holdings.

Elisabeth Badinter, daughter of late founder Marcel Bleustein-Blanchet, controls more than 15% of Publicis (through her stake in Somarel). Japanese advertising giant Dentsu, as a result of its investment in Bcom3, has 15% voting control of the company.

HISTORY

In 1926 Marcel Bleustein, then 19 years old, started France's first advertising agency, which he called Publicis (a takeoff on "publicity" and "six"). He launched his own radio station, Radio Cite, after the French government banned all advertising on state-run stations, and by 1939 he had expanded into film distribution and movie theaters. With the outbreak of WWII, Bleustein fled to London to serve with the Free French Forces.

Having adopted the name Bleustein-Blanchet, he returned to France following the liberation and revived his advertising business. In 1958 he bought the former Hotel Astoria on the Champs-Elysées and opened the first Le Drugstore. The original structure burned in a 1972 fire, and legend has it that Bleustein-Blanchet tapped Maurice Lévy to lead the company after he found Lévy salvaging records amid the ruins.

To expand its business, Publicis formed an alliance — Chicago-based Foote, Cone & Belding Communications (FCB) — in 1988. The partnership soured five years later, however, when Publicis acquired France's Groupe FCA. (FCB claimed the acquisition was a breach of contract and countered by establishing a new holding company for itself, True North Communications.) Bleustein-Blanchet died in 1996, and his daughter, Elisabeth Badinter, was named chair of the supervisory board.

In 1997 Publicis and True North divided their joint network, Publicis Communications, with True North getting the European offices and Publicis getting Africa, Asia, and Argentina. Later that year Publicis attempted a $700 million hostile bid for the 81.5% of True North it didn't already own to stop True North's acquisition of Bozell, Jacobs, Kenyon & Eckhardt. The bid failed, and Publicis' stake in True North was reduced to 11%. (True North was later acquired by Interpublic Group in 2001.)

The company gained new ground in the US through its acquisitions of Hal Riney & Partners and Evans Group in 1998. That year Lévy helped sooth a bitter feud among the descendants of Marcel Bleustein: Elisabeth Badinter had battled with her sister Michele Bleustein-Blanchet over Bleustein-Blanchet's desire to sell her stake in Publicis' holding company. Lévy's solution allowed Bleustein-Blanchet to sell her shares and left Badinter with control of the company.

Continuing its US expansion, in 1999 Publicis bought a 49% stake in Burrell Communications Group (one of the largest African-American-owned ad agencies in the US).

In 2000 the company bought advertising outfit Fallon McElligott (now Fallon Worldwide), marketing firm Frankel & Co., and media buyer DeWitt Media (which was merged into Optimedia). Publicis capped off the year by acquiring Saatchi & Saatchi for about $1.9 billion. Along with the deal, it inherited Saatchi's 50% of media buying unit Zenith Media (jointly owned by Cordiant Communications). In 2001 it merged Optimedia and Zenith, with Publicis owning 75% of the new business.

2002 was a big year for Publicis and the ad industry in general; the decision to acquire Bcom3 catapulted the company into the really big leagues and created a distinct size difference between the top four advertising conglomerates and everyone else.

EXECUTIVES

Chairperson, Supervisory Board: Elisabeth Badinter, age 61
Chairman, Management Board, and CEO: Maurice Lévy, age 63, $4,364,900 pay
General Secretary and Director, Management Board: Claudine Bienaimé, age 65, $368,280 pay
CFO: Jean-Michel Etienne
EVP: Jean-Yves Naouri
VP Internal Audit & Business Improvement: Jean-Marie Pillois
Chairman, Beacon Communications: Masahiro Akashi
Chairman, Fallon Worldwide: Patrick (Pat) Fallon
Chairman, Public Relations and Corporate Communications Group: Louis (Lou) Capozzi
Chairman, Publicis Groupe Media: Jack Klues, age 50
Chairman, Saatchi & Saatchi Worldwide and Director, Supervisory Board: Robert L. Seelert, age 63
Chairman and CEO, Leo Burnett Worldwide; CEO, Leo Burnett USA: Thomas (Tom) Bernardin, age 50
Chairman and CEO, Médias & Régies Europe and Director, Supervisory Board: Simon Badinter, age 37
Chairman and CEO, Publicis USA: Susan M. Gianinno, age 54
Chairman and Worldwide Creative Director, Bartle Bogle Hegarty: John Hegarty
President and CEO, Specialized Agencies and Marketing Services: John Farrell
CEO, Bartle Bogle Hegarty: Nigel Bogel
CEO, Saatchi & Saatchi Worldwide and Director, Management Board: Kevin J. Roberts, age 56, $7,497,368 pay
CEO, Starcom MediaVest Group: Renetta McCann, age 46
CEO, ZenithOptimedia: Steve King
CEO and Chief Creative Officer, The Kaplan Thaler Group: Linda Kaplan Thaler, age 54
EVP, Publicis Worldwide and Director, Management Board: Bertrand Siguier, age 64, $751,968 pay
Director of Investor Relations: Pierre Bénaich
Corporate Communications: Eve Magnant
Auditors: Ernst & Young Audit; Mazars & Guérard

LOCATIONS

HQ: Publicis Groupe S.A.
133, avenue des Champs-Elysées, 75008 Paris, France
Phone: +33-1-44-43-70-00   **Fax:** +33-1-44-43-75-25
US HQ: 950 6th Ave., New York, NY 10001
US Phone: 212-279-5550   **US Fax:** 212-279-5560
Web: www.publicis.fr

Publicis has about 180 offices in more than 100 countries.

2004 Sales

	$ mil.	% of total
North America	2,212	43
Europe	2,139	41
Asia/Pacific	513	10
Latin America	214	4
Other regions	103	2
Total	**5,181**	**100**

PRODUCTS/OPERATIONS

2004 Sales

	% of total
Advertising	55
Media	23
Specialized marketing	22
Total	**100**

Selected Operations and Agencies

Advertising
Beacon Communications (66%, Japan)
Fallon Worldwide (US)
Kaplan Thaler Group (US)
Leo Burnett Worldwide (US)
Publicis Worldwide
Saatchi & Saatchi Worldwide (US)

Media Services
Médias & Régies Europe
Starcom MediaVest Group (US)
ZenithOptimedia (UK)
Specialized Agencies and Marketing Services Group (SAMS)
Arc Worldwide (relationship marketing and promotional campaigns)
Bromley Communications (49%, US, multicultural advertising)
Lápiz (multicultural marketing, US)
Manning, Selvage & Lee (public relations, US)
Medicus Group (health care marketing, US)
Nelson Communications (health care marketing, US)
Publicis Dialog (sales promotion and direct marketing)
Rowland Companies (public relations, US)

COMPETITORS

Aegis Group
Dentsu
Hakuhodo
Havas
Interpublic Group
Omnicom
WPP Group

HISTORICAL FINANCIALS

Company Type: Public

Income Statement

FYE: December 31

	REVENUE ($ mil.)	NET INCOME ($ mil.)	NET PROFIT MARGIN	EMPLOYEES
12/04	5,181	284	5.5%	36,000
12/03	4,857	189	3.9%	35,166
12/02	3,073	154	5.0%	35,681
12/01	2,169	135	6.2%	20,592
12/00	1,667	119	7.1%	16,000
12/99	1,052	96	9.1%	10,362
12/98	993	55	5.6%	8,709
12/97	725	39	5.3%	7,363
12/96	716	35	4.9%	6,038
12/95	744	6	0.9%	6,000
Annual Growth	**24.1%**	**52.4%**	**—**	**22.0%**

2004 Year-End Financials

Debt ratio: 198.3%
Return on equity: 27.0%
Cash ($ mil.): 1,528
Current ratio: 1.04
Long-term debt ($ mil.): 2,366
No. of shares (mil.): 182
Dividends
Yield: 0.0%
Payout: —
Market value ($ mil.): 5,972

Stock History

NYSE: PUB

	STOCK PRICE ($) FY Close	P/E High/Low	PER SHARE ($) Earnings	Dividends	Book Value
12/04	32.73	29 19	1.31	0.00	6.54
12/03	32.42	35 16	0.94	0.26	5.01
12/02	20.96	34 16	1.02	0.22	8.60
12/01	26.00	38 15	0.96	0.17	1.87
12/00	33.63	35 24	1.08	0.00	2.05
Annual Growth	**(0.7%)**	**— —**	**4.9%**	**—**	**33.7%**

Qantas Airways

Some Australians go on walkabout; others fly about on Qantas Airways, Australia's #1 airline and a leader in international flights to and from the country. Qantas flies to more than 80 destinations in about 40 countries and to some 20 cities in Australia. It additionally operates a regional airline. Qantas' fleet includes about 200 aircraft. That will expand now that the company has ordered 12 Airbus A380-800s, the world's biggest passenger jet. Qantas is also part of the global marketing alliance Oneworld, which is led by code-sharing partners British Airways and American Airlines, among others. Other Qantas operations include catering and tourism.

Qantas' Australian regional airline Qantas-Link flies more than 40 planes to about 50 domestic destinations.

Qantas has an extensive code-sharing agreement with British Airways; they coordinate their scheduling, sales, and marketing and share facilities such as airport lounges.

To try to curb continued losses, the airline established a low-fare carrier called JetStar, for which Qantas has purchased 23 new Airbus jets to add to its previous total of 14 Boeing 717s.

The carrier also operates a low-fare airline based out of Singapore, JetStar Asia, that was merged with another low-cost Singapore-based airline, Valuair, into a holding-company structure in 2005. Qantas has a 44% stake in the holding company.

Qantas is additionally looking at ways to spread its wings out for a greater global presence, which could include expanded codeshare agreements. Complementing ties to British Airways, it signed an agreement with Air France in 2004.

Overall, Qantas is facing more competition in the crowded skies and is reviewing operations for greater productivity.

HISTORY

Ex-WWI pilots Wilmot Hudson Fysh and Paul McGinness and stockman Fergus McMaster founded Queensland and Northern Territory Aerial Services (Qantas) in 1920 to provide an air link between Darwin in the Northern Territory and the railheads in Queensland. In 1922 Qantas began carrying airmail over a 577-mile route between Charleville and Cloncurry, and by 1930 it covered northeastern Australia with air routes. Qantas moved its headquarters to Sydney in 1938.

Qantas and Imperial Airways (predecessor of British Airways, or BA) formed Qantas Empire Airways in 1934 to fly the last leg of a London-to-Australia mail route (Singapore to Brisbane). Qantas bought the British share of Qantas Empire in 1947 (when Qantas made its first Sydney-London flight) and was subsequently nationalized.

By 1950 the airline served most major cities in the Pacific Rim. Qantas inaugurated a route to Johannesburg (1952) and opened the Southern Cross route, previously operated by British Commonwealth Pacific Airlines, to San Francisco and Vancouver via Honolulu (1953).

In 1958 Qantas offered the first complete round-the-world service. (Pan Am had started a similar service in 1957 but was barred by the US government from crossing North America.) It bought 29% of Malayan Airways in 1959 and added several European destinations in the 1960s, including Frankfurt (1966) and Amsterdam (1967). Founder Fysh retired as chairman in 1966, and the airline took its present name in 1967.

Tourism in Australia boomed in the 1970s. Competition from foreign (especially US) airlines initially hurt Qantas, contributing to a $4 million loss in 1971 (its second since 1924). But in 1973 annual boardings jumped 28%. Qantas' Aussie passengers flew some 4,217 miles per journey — the longest average trip of any airline.

In 1987 Qantas bought a stake in Fiji's Air Pacific. Later acquisitions included Australia-Asia Airlines (1989) and 20% of Air New Zealand (1990; sold 1997). Qantas enjoyed record profits in 1989, but a strike by domestic pilots paralyzed Australia's tourist industry that year, hurting Qantas in 1990.

The Australian airline industry was deregulated in the early 1990s, and Qantas formed regional carrier Airlink in 1991. The next year it merged with Australia Airlines, and in 1993 the Australian government sold BA a 25% stake in Qantas. Still, the airlines' 1994 attempt to set prices and services together was rejected by Australian authorities.

Because Australian privatizations had deluged the stock exchange with issues, Qantas delayed its IPO until 1995. Also that year Qantas and BA got approval for a joint service agreement that allowed them to operate some facilities together.

The carrier began code-sharing with American Airlines in 1995; three years later Qantas joined the Oneworld global marketing alliance, led by American and BA. In 1998 and 1999 Qantas and BA began combining their operations in Hong Kong, Indonesia, Malaysia, Singapore, and Thailand. The airline expanded its code-sharing with affiliate Air Pacific in 2000, even as it braced for competition at home from Virgin Atlantic's new Australian low-fare carrier.

Unable to gain regulatory approval, Qantas dropped its bidding war with rival Ansett to acquire regional carrier Hazelton Airlines in 2001. That year Qantas agreed to acquire Impulse Airlines, an ailing Australian low-fare carrier. The company also entered negotiations with Air New Zealand to buy Ansett, but Qantas decided against a purchase of its troubled Australian rival. Air New Zealand subsequently shut down Ansett's operations.

On Sept. 11, 2001, two Qantas employees were killed when a plane on which they were traveling crashed into the north tower of the World Trade Center. The next year Qantas began negotiations to acquire a stake in Air New Zealand. Qantas' offer to acquire a 23% stake in the airline was rejected in 2003 by regulators in Australia and New Zealand. The airlines planned to appeal the decision the following year, but were once again denied. In July 2005 Qantas formed a new holding company, of which Qantas owns more than 44%, to own and operate Jetstar Asia and Valuair, which was previously owned by a group of Singapore executives. The next month, as part of an ongoing review of operations amid rising fuel costs and other challenges, Qantas laid off some 200 senior managers.

EXECUTIVES

Chairman: Margaret A. Jackson, $256,724 pay
CEO: Geoff Dixon, $2,342,466 pay
CFO: Peter Gregg, $1,324,012 pay
Executive General Manager Airports and Catering: Grant Fenn
Executive General Manager Associated Businesses and Head of Freight: Denis Adams, $805,000 pay
Executive General Manager Engineering Technical Operations and Maintenance Services: David Cox
Executive General Manager Alliances: Paul Edwards
Executive General Manager People: Kevin Brown
Executive General Manager Qantas: John Borghetti, $977,014 pay
Executive General Manager Qantas Business Services and Chief Information Officer: Fiona Balfour
Executive General Manager Regional Airlines: Narendra Kumar
Head of Sustainable Future Program: Curtis Davies
Executive General Manager Jetstar Airways: Alan Joyce
Head of Corporate Communications: Michael Sharp
Head of Flight Operations and Chief Pilot: Chris Manning
Head of Government and International Relations: David Hawes
VP Sales and Marketing, The Americas: Howard Goldberg
General Counsel and Company Secretary: Brett Johnson
Head of Corporate Communication: Belinda de Rome
Executive General Manager Australian Airlines: Andrea Staines
Auditors: KPMG

LOCATIONS

HQ: Qantas Airways Limited
Qantas Centre, Level 9, Bldg. A, 203 Coward St., Mascot, New South Wales 2020, Australia
Phone: +61-2-9691-3636   **Fax:** +61-2-9691-3339
US HQ: 300 Continental Blvd., Ste. 350, El Segundo, CA 90245
US Fax: 310-535-1057
Web: www.qantas.com.au

PRODUCTS/OPERATIONS

2005 Sales

	% of total
Passenger	84
Tours & travel	6
Contract work	4
Other	6
Total	**100**

Selected Partners

Air Pacific
Alaska Airlines
American Airlines
Asiana
British Airways (BA)
EVA Air
Finnair
Japan Airlines
Vietnam Airlines

COMPETITORS

Air New Zealand
All Nippon Airways
Cathay Pacific
Continental Airlines
Delta Air
DHL
FedEx
KLM
Lufthansa
Northwest Airlines
SAS
Singapore Airlines
UAL
UPS
Virgin Atlantic Airways

HISTORICAL FINANCIALS

Company Type: Public

Income Statement

FYE: June 30

	REVENUE ($ mil.)	NET INCOME ($ mil.)	NET PROFIT MARGIN	EMPLOYEES
6/05	9,632	580	6.0%	38,000
6/04	7,832	448	5.7%	33,862
6/03	7,585	229	3.0%	34,872
6/02	6,380	241	3.8%	33,044
6/01	5,196	212	4.1%	31,632
6/00	5,437	309	5.7%	29,217
6/99	5,585	279	5.0%	23,411
6/98	5,005	188	3.7%	30,000
6/97	5,850	189	3.2%	30,080
6/96	5,982	194	3.2%	29,627
Annual Growth	**5.4%**	**12.9%**	**—**	**2.8%**

2005 Year-End Financials

Debt ratio: 81.4%
Return on equity: 13.0%
Cash ($ mil.): 151

Current ratio: 0.80
Long-term debt ($ mil.): 3,986

Net Income History

Australian: QAN

Quebecor

Getting the word out through print, broadcast, and cable is all in a day's work at Quebecor Inc. Subsidiary Quebecor World is one of the world's top commercial printers, primarily producing advertising inserts, books, catalogs, direct mail, directories, and magazines. The company's Quebecor Media group owns book stores, cable TV companies, magazines, music stores, newspapers, publishing houses, and broadcast stations. Its Sun Media newspaper unit produces daily newspapers as well as more than 180 regional papers and magazines. Its Vidéotron Itée subsidiary is one of Canada's largest cable companies. Its TVA Group subsidiary owns the dominant French-language TV network in Quebec.

Through 150 printing plants in more than 15 countries, Quebecor makes advertising inserts, books, and magazines, as well as catalogs for North American retailers.

Quebecor also has operations in book publishing (Éditions CEC, among others) and music retail (Archambault superstores). In the Internet realm, the company operates Web portal canoe.com as well as several other Web sites. The company has also made a foray into radio with several station acquisitions.

In 2004 the company's TVA media group extended its reach into the English television market through the purchase of station Toronto 1 from CHUM Limited. TVA owns 75% of the station and Quebecor's newspaper division Sun Media holds the remaining quarter. Quebecor hopes to turn a profit on the station, which has

heretofore lost money and suffered low ratings, by 2008.

While the company's media businesses have been booming, its printing business has been struggling. Citing a downturn in its customer base, the company's Quebecor World unit announced in mid-2005 that it would look for a buyer for its North American commercial printing business.

The founding Péladeau family controls 64% of the company.

HISTORY

In 1950 law student Pierre Péladeau borrowed $1,500 from his mother so he could buy a small Montreal newspaper called *Le Journal de Rosemont*. This became the base for Péladeau's publishing empire. Within a few years he had established five other weekly newspapers and his first printing firm.

Péladeau seized the opportunity presented to him in 1964 by a strike at the major Montreal paper *La Presse*. He assembled a team from his various weeklies and, according to company legend, had the tabloid *Le Journal* on the streets within three days.

Quebecor went public in 1972 and expanded beyond Quebec, branching out into a variety of communication concerns. But by the late 1980s, the company had refocused on its core printing businesses.

Quebecor purchased printing plants in New Jersey and Michigan in 1985. Péladeau teamed with Robert Maxwell in 1987 to form Mircor to buy a stake in forestry concern Donohue. The company took a major step into the international arena when it bought the printing group BCE PubliTech in 1988, making the company the #1 commercial printer in Canada.

In 1990 Maxwell sold his US printing plants (with state-of-the-art printing presses) to Péladeau, who formed Quebecor Printing (USA) around the new assets. Maxwell subsequently bought a 26% stake in the new company for $100 million.

Maxwell died mysteriously in 1991 followed by revelations of deceptive finances and shady business dealings by the Maxwell empire. This allowed Péladeau to buy back all of Maxwell's shares in Quebecor at bargain-basement prices.

In the 1990s Quebecor continued expanding, buying a bookbinding and publishing company in Mexico (Gráficas Monte Alban, 1991), three US printing plants (1993), France's largest commercial printer (Group Jean Didier, 1995), and a UK printer (1995). Quebecor Printing went public in 1995, which reduced the parent company's interest to less than 50%. Quebecor also set up its multimedia unit and expanded it by acquiring 50% of Sierra Creative Communications and 25% of multimedia software publisher Micro-Intel (1996).

A Quebecor-controlled consortium in 1997 acquired Télévision Quatre Saisons, which operates three Canadian TV stations and the Quatre Saisons TV network license. (The company sold the network and related stations in 2001.) Péladeau died from heart failure that year.

In 1999 Quebecor bought Sun Media, which made the company the #2 Canadian newspaper publisher. It later sold a 30% stake in Sun Media to a group of private investors for $260 million. In 1999 Quebecor Printing acquired World Color Press. Also that year Pierre Karl Péladeau, the founder's second son, took over as president and CEO. Péladeau family members have filed a flood

of lawsuits against one another and the executor of Pierre Péladeau's estate in a battle for control of family assets, including the company.

Quebecor sold its controlling stake in market pulp, lumber, and newsprint producer Donohue to rival Abitibi-Consolidated in 2000. Also that year the company restructured into two operating units: Quebecor Printing (changing its name to Quebecor World) and Quebecor Media. Later in 2000 Quebecor and Caisse de Dépôt et Placement du Québec (Quebec's public-pension agency) won a bidding war with Rogers Communications for the acquisition of Le Groupe Vidéotron, Canada's #3 cable TV operator, with an offer of $3.6 billion. Le Groupe Vidéotron's broadcasting company TVA Group was part of the deal, but was not finalized until 2001 after Quebecor completed the sale of its TQS network, which had been required by regulators.

In 2001 the company bought the 30% of Sun Media that it didn't already own. That year it also bulked up its Latin American holdings with the purchase of Grupo Serla, a school book text printer in Mexico, and 75% of Grafica Melhoramentos, a Brazilian book publisher. That year Quebecor also agreed to buy the European printing facilities of Hachette Filipacchi Médias. In 2002 the company merged its Publicor and TVA Publishing operations under the TVA Publishing name.

EXECUTIVES

Chairman: Jean Neveu
EVP and Vice Chairman: Érik Péladeau
President, CEO, and Director: Pierre Karl Péladeau
EVP Corporate Affairs: Luc Lavoie
EVP and CFO: Jacques Mallette
VP and Corporate Controller: Denis Sabourin
VP and Treasurer: Marc D'Souza
VP Human Resources: Julie Tremblay
VP Internal Audit: Roger Martel
VP Legal Affairs and Secretary: Louis Saint-Arnaud
VP Taxation: Michel Éthier
Chairman, Quebecor Media: Serge Gouin, age 62
President and CEO, Vidéotron Itée: Robert Depatie
President and CEO, Nurun: Jacques-Hervé Roubert
President and CEO, TVA Group: Pierre Dion
President, Quebecor World Latin America: Guy Trahan
Special Advisor, Quebecor World: David S. Boles
VP Advertising Convergence, Quebecor Media:
  Jean-Francois Richard
Manager Corporate Services and Assistant Corporate Secretary: Claudine Tremblay
Director: Robert Dutton
Auditors: KPMG LLP

LOCATIONS

HQ: Quebecor Inc.
  612 Saint-Jacques St.,
  Montreal, Quebec H3C 4M8, Canada
Phone: 514-954-0101   **Fax:** 514-380-6097
Web: www.quebecor.com

Quebecor has operations in Argentina, Austria, Belgium, Brazil, Canada, Chile, Colombia, Finland, France, India, Mexico, Peru, Spain, Sweden, Switzerland, the UK, and the US.

2004 Sales

	$ mil.	% of total
US	4,824.6	53
Canada	2,671.6	29
Europe	1,411.9	16
Latin America	207.2	2
Total	**9,115.3**	**100**

PRODUCTS/OPERATIONS

2004 Sales

	$ mil.	% of total
Printing	7,135.0	78
Newspapers	737.1	8
Cable television	723.4	7
Broadcasting	297.2	3
Leisure & entertainment	200.6	2
Business telecommunications	65.2	1
Web integration/technology	43.1	1
Internet/portals	28.6	—
Head office	1.5	—
Adjustments	(116.4)	—
Total	**9,115.3**	**100**

Selected Operations

Quebecor Media Inc.
   Archambault Group Inc. (music and book stores,
      music recording and distribution)
   Books Segment (general literature and textbook
      publishing and distribution)
   Netgraphe Inc. (portals and e-commerce sites)
   Nurun Inc. (Web development and
      e-commerce consulting)
   Sun Media Corporation (newspaper publishing)
   TVA Group Inc. (broadcasting)
      TVA Publishing (magazine publishing)
   Vidéotron ltée (cable operator)
      Le SuperClub Vidéotron ltée (video rental chain)
Quebecor World Inc.
   Distribution
   Premedia
   Printing (advertising inserts, books, catalogs,
      direct mail, magazines)

Selected Publications

The Calgary Sun (daily newspaper)
Cool! (magazine)
Décoration Chez-Soi (magazine)
The Edmonton Sun (daily newspaper)
Femmes (magazine)
Filles d'aujourd'hui (magazine)
Le Journal de Montréal (daily newspaper)
Le Journal de Québec (daily newspaper)
Les idées de ma maison (magazine)
The London Free Press (daily newspaper)
The Ottawa Sun (daily newspaper)
The Toronto Sun (daily newspaper)
The Winnipeg Sun (daily newspaper)

COMPETITORS

Banta
BCE
Bell Globemedia
Cadmus Communications
Cancom
CanWest Global Communications
CBC
COGECO Inc.
Courier
Dai Nippon Printing
Hachette Filipacchi Médias
Hollinger
Quad/Graphics
Rogers Cable
Rogers Communications
R.R. Donnelley
Seven Worldwide
Shaw Communications
Toppan Printing
Torstar

HISTORICAL FINANCIALS

Company Type: Public

Income Statement

FYE: December 31

	REVENUE ($ mil.)	NET INCOME ($ mil.)	NET PROFIT MARGIN	EMPLOYEES
12/04	9,115	93	1.0%	47,400
12/03	8,668	51	0.6%	49,000
12/02	7,619	58	0.8%	50,000
12/01	7,312	(152)	—	54,000
12/00	7,282	724	9.9%	57,000
12/99	7,490	333	4.4%	60,000
12/98	5,486	112	2.0%	39,000
12/97	4,898	100	2.0%	37,000
12/96	4,562	107	2.3%	33,700
12/95	4,070	137	3.4%	28,900
Annual Growth	**9.4%**	**(4.2%)**	**—**	**5.7%**

2004 Year-End Financials

Debt ratio: 396.0%
Return on equity: 8.2%
Cash ($ mil.): 220
Current ratio: 0.95
Long-term debt ($ mil.): 4,745

Net Income History

Toronto: QBR.A

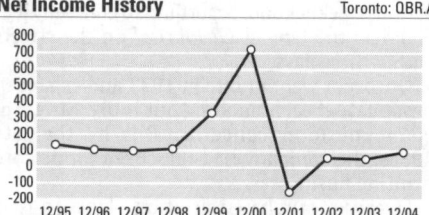

RALLYE S.A.

Retail giant Rallye musters its businesses around not just the French flag, but around flags worldwide. Rallye's Casino Guichard-Perrachon subsidiary operates about 8,600 hypermarkets, supermarkets, and convenience stores in Europe (mostly France), Asia, and Latin America. Rallye has merged two subsidiaries into Groupe Go Sport: Go Sport (France's #2 sporting goods retailer) and Courir (France's #1 sports and leisure footwear retailer). Rallye has sold its unprofitable footwear retail subsidiary and only significant US holding, The Athlete's Foot Group, to the chain's management. Finatis, through The Euris Group (founded by Rallye Chairman Jean-Charles Naouri) owns more than 75% of Rallye.

Rallye's Casino subsidiary is a leading supermarket chain in France and operates in about 20 countries worldwide. Store banners include Casino, Franprix, Géant, and Leader Price. Casino is the #1 convenience store operator in France with stores under the Eco Service, Petit Casino, Spar, and Vival names. Casino has grown by purchasing stakes in supermarket, hypermarket, and convenience store companies with international locations. It plans to continue this global expansion.

While Rallye exited the footwear retail business in the US with its sale of The Athlete's Foot, the company plans to continue to expand Groupe Go Sport in Europe.

Rallye has increased its e-commerce activities through its majority stake of Cdiscount.com, a French online retailer of CDs, videos, and more.

HISTORY

Rallye has its roots in Casino Guichard-Perrachon, which was formed after Geoffroy Guichard took over his father-in-law's general store in 1892.

In the early 1920s the company, which would later become a Rallye holding, opened factories to produce items that included food and soap. In 1924 Rallye was formed as a food retailer. Also that year a food distribution group that would become an important acquisition for Rallye in the 1990s, Genty, was founded (renamed Genty Cathiard in 1959).

By WWII Casino had 215 branches. During the war Casino's troubles included 70 stores leveled and 450 damaged in bomb attacks.

The firm launched its first supermarket (Grenoble) in 1960 and its first cafeteria in 1967. It expanded to Géant hypermarkets (Marseille) in 1970 and formed Casino USA in 1976.

Rallye entered sporting goods in 1981 through the purchase of France's 11-unit Athletic Attic chain and the acquisition of a minority stake of US sports footwear and apparel retailer The Athlete's Foot Group. Rallye then acquired majority control of Athlete's Foot in 1984.

Rallye's sales reached $4.4 billion in 1989. The next year it acquired the food distribution group Genty Cathiard, which included retail units Go Sport (sporting goods) and Courir (sports footwear). The acquisition moved Rallye from #8 to #5 in French supermarket groups.

By 1991 Rallye operated 51 hypermarkets and 227 supermarkets. That year Euris, headed by Jean-Charles Naouri, bought a stake in Rallye, which had heavy debt after borrowing funds to acquire Genty Cathiard. Rallye traded its food retail operations (close to 300 hypermarkets and supermarkets) with food giant Casino in exchange for a 29.5% stake in Casino in 1992.

Rallye merged with subsidiary Genty Cathiard in 1993, when the company went public. Also in 1993 Rallye began a major restructuring for Go Sport that lasted until 1996.

French supermarket chain Promodès made a hostile takeover attempt on Casino and Rallye in 1997, which would have made Promodès France's largest retailer. Rallye (which still had 29% of Casino and about 36% of voting rights) made a friendly counter bid; Promodès backed out and Rallye took control of Casino. By 1998 The Athlete's Foot Group had grown to more than 260 US outlets (company-owned) and more than 400 franchises (about 180 in the US).

Franchises were also located in 38 countries, including Australia, Canada, France, and Hong Kong. Go Sport operated 80 outlets in France and six in Belgium, and there were more than 100 Courir stores (France) by the beginning of 1998. Rallye spun off 22% of Courir in 1999.

Casino expanded its international markets in 1999 by acquiring stakes in food retailing companies in countries that included Brazil, Colombia, Thailand, and Venezuela. Go Sport grew in 1999 by launching new stores in France, Belgium, and Poland — a new market.

In 2000 Casino bought a 51% stake in French online CD retailer Cdiscount.com. Although Rallye as a whole nearly doubled its net profit in 2000, Athlete's Foot suffered a loss of almost $29 million that year and began a three-year restructuring plan that includes the closure of 84 unprofitable stores. However, 100 new Athlete's Foot franchises opened in 2001, including the first stores in Mexico and Hungary.

In June 2002, Casino acquired a 39% stake in Laurus, a leading retailer in the Netherlands.

In December 2003, Rallye sold its interest in The Athlete's Foot (TAF) to the chain's managers in a management-led buyout for an undisclosed sum. Accounting for less than 1% of Rallye's sales, TAF had closed nearly 100 branches since 2001 but was still unprofitable.

François de Montaudouin resigned as managing director or Rallye in January 2004 and was succeeded by Chairman Jean-Charles Naouri.

EXECUTIVES

Chairman, President, and CEO: Jean-Charles Naouri, age 56
Vice Chairman: André Crestey, age 66
Deputy Managing Director: Didier Carlier, age 53
CFO: Jean-Marie Grisard, age 62
Auditors: Barbier Frinault & Autres; KPMG Audit

LOCATIONS

HQ: RALLYE S.A.
83, rue du Faubourg-Saint-Honoré, 75008 Paris, France
Phone: +33-1-44-71-13-62 **Fax:** +33-1-44-71-13-60
Web: www.rallye.fr

2004 Sales

	% of total
Europe	
France	81
Other countries	3
North America	7
Asia	5
South America	3
Indian Ocean	1
Total	**100**

PRODUCTS/OPERATIONS

2004 Sales

	% of total
Food & general retailing	95
Sporting goods retailing	3
Other	2
Total	**100**

Selected Subsidiaries

Casino Guichard-Perrachon (51%)
Groupe Go Sport (69%)

COMPETITORS

ALDI
Auchan
Carrefour
E.Leclerc
Galeries Lafayette
Guyenne et Gascogne
Intersport International Cooperation
ITM Entreprises
METRO AG
PPR
Primisteres Reynoird
Royal Ahold
Tesco
Wal-Mart

HISTORICAL FINANCIALS

Company Type: Public

Income Statement

FYE: December 31

	REVENUE ($ mil.)	NET INCOME ($ mil.)	NET PROFIT MARGIN	EMPLOYEES
12/04	32,511	75	0.2%	124,223
12/03	29,834	535	1.8%	124,143
12/02	24,820	384	1.5%	122,040
12/01	20,252	303	1.5%	113,444
12/00	18,777	282	1.5%	107,805
12/99	16,489	216	1.3%	89,981
12/98	14,918	49	0.3%	78,912
12/97	652	81	12.5%	5,464
12/96	660	26	3.9%	4,872
12/95	635	16	2.5%	4,644
Annual Growth	**54.9%**	**18.6%**	**—**	**44.1%**

2004 Year-End Financials

Debt ratio: 946.0%
Return on equity: 7.3%
Cash ($ mil.): 4,196
Current ratio: 0.96
Long-term debt ($ mil.): 10,039

Net Income History

Euronext Paris: RAL

Rank Group

Leisure is highly rated by this company. The Rank Group owns a diverse portfolio of hospitality, leisure, and media businesses around the world. The company has UK gaming holdings, including more than 120 Mecca Bingo clubs and some 30 Grosvenor Casinos. It also offers online gaming and sports betting through a number of Web sites, primarily Blue Square. In addition to its gaming businesses, The Rank Group owns the Hard Rock Cafe franchise of restaurants, live entertainment venues, and hotels. The rest of the company's business is focused on services provided by its Deluxe Media Services subsidiary, one of the world's leading film processing and postproduction firms.

While Rank has received criticism in the past for its wide-ranging, and seemingly incongruent, holdings, the company's diversity has saved it from at least some of the ravages of the current economy. Its Hard Rock division has been hit by the slump in tourism while its UK gaming businesses, especially those located in the London area, have continued to remain popular. Meanwhile, the film services business at Deluxe has achieved success owing to the recent slate of blockbusters passing through its labs, including *Star Wars: Episode III*, *Spider-Man 2*, and *Die Another Day*. However, after Rank's media business contributed a $228 million loss to its parent's balance sheet in 2004, the company decided to sell the unit and focus on its gaming and leisure businesses.

Rank expanded its gaming business in 2003 when it acquired online betting site Blue Square

for about $100 million. That same year the company formed a joint venture with resort operator Sol Meliá to develop new luxury Hard Rock hotels. The effort, backed by $1 billion from Becker Ventures, comes after a boardroom row that ended in the abrupt departure of Hard Rock chief Peter Beaudrault.

In 2004 Rank sold its Rank Leisure Machine Services and Rank Seasonal Amusements businesses, which included 35,000 gaming machines, to Gamestec Leisure Limited for £30 million.

Citing the rising cost of compliance with US stock regulations, Rank Group in 2005 terminated its listing in that country.

HISTORY

The Rank Group grew out of a sense of strong conviction. Joseph Arthur Rank was a devout Methodist who saw films as a way to spread the message of his religion. Leaving the successful family milling business, he started a production company in 1934 called British National Films. Later Rank acquired General Film Distributors, Pinewood Studios, and the Odeon theater chain. By 1941, Rank's entertainment holdings were so vast that many saw him as a monopolist. But after WWII the British film business deteriorated as American films flooded into the country. Television and an emerging leisure industry also took their toll in the 1950s.

With the holding company recast as The Rank Organisation in 1955, J. Arthur Rank and his managing director, John Davis, set about searching for alternative businesses. Rank formed a joint venture with the Haloid Company (now Xerox) in 1956 to market photocopying equipment. Later called Rank Xerox, the joint venture eventually dwarfed the profits of Rank's other operating units. Davis became chairman in 1962 (Rank died in 1972) and invested in a diverse but underperforming group of businesses, including bingo parlors, hotels, and dance halls. The pitiful results of his efforts were exposed in the late 1970s as Rank Xerox's earnings receded under growing competition in the copier market. Investors forced Davis to step down in 1977.

Michael Gifford was installed as chief executive in 1983 and immediately began cutting overhead and dumping businesses, which increased profits. Rank joined with MCA to create the Universal Studios Florida theme park (now part of Universal Parks & Resorts) in 1988 and acquired Mecca Leisure Group's bingo parlors, casinos, hotels, and clubs in 1990. It also bought the rights to a number of Hard Rock Cafes (originally established in London in 1971).

Rank named former ICI chief Sir Denys Henderson as its new chairman in 1994, and two years later Andrew Teare became Rank's new CEO. Teare led Rank's buyout of Hard Rock cofounder Peter Morton that year and installed former schoolteacher Jim Berk as Hard Rock's CEO. Teare also restructured Rank into four divisions (Film and Entertainment Services, Hard Rock, Holidays, and Leisure) and changed its name to The Rank Group. The company sold its Rank Xerox stake back to Xerox for about $1.5 billion in 1997. After reporting more disappointing results, however, Teare left the company the next year. Mike Smith, former head of Ladbroke's (now Hilton Group) betting and gaming division, came in as CEO in 1999. Peter Beaudrault replaced Berk at Hard Rock that year.

Smith's restructuring efforts led to the sale of Rank's nightclub business to Northern Leisure in 1999. The Odeon theater chain went to UK buyout specialist Cinven for $450 million and Pinewood Studios was sold for about $100 million in 2000. Rank later sold its 50% stake in Universal Studios Orlando to Blackstone Capital Partners for $275 million, while its UK holiday resorts went to Bourne Leisure for $1 billion. In 2001 Henderson stepped down as chairman; former Avis Europe chairman Alun Cathcart was tapped as his replacement.

Early in 2003 Beaudrault left his post at Hard Rock as the theme restaurant chain posted declining sales. He was replaced by Hamish Dodds the following year.

EXECUTIVES

Chairman: W. Alun Cathcart, age 62, $337,085 pay
Chief Executive and Director: Mike Smith, age 58, $1,398,421 pay
President and CEO, Hard Rock Cafe International: Hamish Dodds
President, Deluxe Film Worldwide: Cyril Drabinsky, age 47
President, Deluxe Media Services: Tom Vale, age 42
Managing Director, Blue Square: Martin Belsham, age 44
Managing Director, Gaming Division; and Director: David Boden, age 48
Group Finance Director; and Director: Peter R. Gill
Group Human Resources Director: Christine Ra
Company Secretary: Pamela Coles
Director of Investor Relations: Peter Reynolds
Auditors: PricewaterhouseCoopers LLP

LOCATIONS

HQ: The Rank Group Plc
6 Connaught Place, London W2 2EZ,
United Kingdom
Phone: +44-20-7706-1111   **Fax:** +44-20-7262-9886
Web: www.rank.com

2004 Sales

	$ mil.	% of total
UK	2,236.0	60
North America	1,179.0	31
Other regions	348.1	9
Adjustments	(38)	—
Total	**3,725.1**	**100**

PRODUCTS/OPERATIONS

2004 Sales

	$ mil.	% of total
Gaming	1,805.9	48
Deluxe	1,448.2	38
Hard Rock	446.9	12
US Holidays	62.0	2
Adjustments	(37.9)	—
Total	**3,725.1**	**100**

Selected Operations

Deluxe Film and Media Services
  Distribution and fulfillment
  DVD manufacturing (Electric Switch)
  Film processing (Deluxe Film Laboratories)
  Post-production facilities and services
  Video duplication (Deluxe Video Services)
Gaming
  Blue Square (Internet and phone gambling)
  Grosvenor Casinos (Belgium and UK)
  Mecca Bingo (Spain and UK)
Hard Rock
  Hard Rock Cafes
  Hotels & Casinos
    Hard Rock Casino (London)
    Hard Rock Casino (Manchester)
    Hard Rock Hotel (Bali, Indonesia)
    Hard Rock Hotel (Orlando, Florida)
    Hard Rock Hotel (Pattaya, Thailand)
    Hard Rock Hotel & Casino (Las Vegas)

Other
  Universal Studios Escape Hotels,
    Orlando, Florida (25%)
    Hard Rock Hotel
    Portofino Bay Hotel
    Royal Pacific Resort Hotel
  Universal Studios Japan (10%, theme park)
  US Holidays (timeshare restart, campgrounds, and a hotel)

COMPETITORS

Ascent Media	Lucas Digital
Camelot	Macrovision
Cinram	MGM MIRAGE
Clear Channel	Planet Hollywood
Entertainment	Roularta
DOCdata	Stanley Leisure
Harrah's Entertainment	Technicolor Inc.
Hilton Group	Trump Resorts
HOB Entertainment	William Hill
LaserPacific Media	Zomax

HISTORICAL FINANCIALS

Company Type: Public

Income Statement

FYE: December 31

	REVENUE ($ mil.)	NET INCOME ($ mil.)	NET PROFIT MARGIN	EMPLOYEES
12/04	3,725	(171)	—	25,159
12/03	3,435	181	5.3%	24,003
12/02	2,360	220	9.3%	21,862
12/01	1,991	184	9.2%	20,955
12/00	2,682	(479)	—	37,057
12/99	3,298	110	3.3%	43,081
12/98	3,414	(181)	—	45,600
12/97	3,323	319	9.6%	43,698
12/96	3,569	(58)	—	43,478
12/95	4,054	814	20.1%	—
Annual Growth	**(0.9%)**	**—**		**(6.6%)**

2004 Year-End Financials

Debt ratio: 166.7%
Return on equity: —
Cash ($ mil.): 143
Current ratio: 1.77
Long-term debt ($ mil.): 1,297
No. of shares (mil.): 312
Dividends
  Yield: 4.9%
  Payout: 7.8%
Market value ($ mil.): 3,248

Stock History

London: RNK

12/95 12/96 12/97 12/98 12/99 12/00 12/01 12/02 12/03 12/04

	STOCK PRICE ($) FY Close	P/E High/Low		Earnings	PER SHARE ($) Dividends	Book Value
12/04	10.41	2	1	6.53	0.51	2.49
12/03	10.23	16	10	0.49	0.46	3.15
12/02	8.15	15	11	0.63	0.42	4.06
12/01	6.65	14	8	0.52	0.39	2.88
12/00	4.75	—	—	(1.47)	0.36	2.81
12/99	6.13	14	8	0.27	0.60	4.95
12/98	7.50	—	—	(0.44)	0.52	5.65
12/97	11.25	44	31	0.35	0.69	5.99
12/96	15.00	—	—	(0.23)	0.62	7.35
12/95	14.63	8	6	1.90	0.30	7.57
Annual Growth	**(3.7%)**	**—**	**—**	**14.7%**	**6.1%**	**(11.6%)**

Reckitt Benckiser

With a cart full of products, Reckitt Benckiser (rhymes with "freezer") is cleaning up. It's one of the largest household cleaning products makers worldwide. The firm's brands include air fresheners (Airwick), household cleaners (Lysol, Easy-Off), laundry products (Woolite), furniture polishes (Old English), and dishwashing detergents (Electrasol). It also makes over-the-counter pharmaceuticals such as analgesics, antiseptics, flu remedies, and gastrointestinal medications, and offers products for hair removal, denture cleaning, and pest control (d-Con). Reckitt Benckiser also makes French's mustard. It has agreed to acquire Boots Healthcare International, the consumer health care division of Boots Group.

The deal is valued at $3.4 billion and will add Nurofen (analgesic), Strepsils (cold remedies), and Clearasil (anti-acne) to Reckitt Benckiser's stable of non-prescription products.

The company, which was created by the merger of UK-based Reckitt & Colman and The Netherlands' Benckiser, sells products in 180 countries worldwide. Reckitt Benckiser has divested about 75 minor brands, allowing the firm to focus on its key brands in the areas of fabric care, surface care, dishwashing products, health and personal care, and home care.

In late 2002 the company lost a bid for Pfizer's Schick-Wilkinson Sword shaving products (the world's second-largest razor maker behind Gillette) to Energizer Holdings.

Reckitt, admitting that launching entirely new brands in the fast-moving consumer goods niche is risky and expensive, had been looking for acquisition opportunities. The company approached SSL International (the maker of Durex condoms and Dr. Scholl footcare products) in mid-2003 but talks weren't productive.

HISTORY

Reckitt & Colman's roots can be traced to Jeremiah Colman, who bought a flour mill near Norwich, England, in 1804. In 1823 his nephew James joined the company, and their business was incorporated as J. and J. Colman. Jeremiah died in 1851 and James' son, also named Jeremiah, became a partner, taking over the operations when his father died in 1854. The company moved to Carrow that year.

Colman worked to make the Carrow facilities as self-sufficient and waste-free as possible. The factory had its own foundry, print shop, paper mill (to make containers), and fire brigade. By-products from the milling process were sold to farmers for cattle feed and fertilizer. The company continued to expand, adding wheat flour and using the leftover starch from milling operations to make laundry bluing.

In 1903 the mill acquired Keen, Robinson & Co., a manufacturer of spices. J. and J. Colman got a lock on British mustard sales in 1912 when it acquired its only major competitor, Joseph Farrow & Company. A year later it joined another rival, starch maker Reckitt & Sons, in a joint venture in South America. The joint venture between Colman and Reckitt was a success, and in 1921 they pooled their overseas operations.

The two companies created Reckitt & Colman Ltd. in 1938 to manage their operations, although each company maintained a separate listing on the London Stock Exchange. In 1954 they formally merged into a single entity.

Reckitt & Colman formed its US subsidiary in 1977, and during the 1980s it made a number of acquisitions (Airwick air fresheners, Gold Seal bath products) to expand its presence in the US.

In 1990 the firm picked up such brands as Black Flag (insecticide), Woolite (fabric care), and Easy-Off (oven cleaner) when it bought Boyle-Midway from American Home Products.

The company gained the Lysol brand in 1994 when it bought L&F Household from Eastman Kodak. To help finance the $1.6 billion deal, Reckitt & Colman sold its flagship Colman Mustard unit to Unilever. Its French's operations in the US (mustard, Worcestershire sauce) were its only remaining food business.

Michael Colman, the last active family member, stepped down as chairman in 1995. In 1996 it sold its US personal products unit.

In 1998 Reckitt & Colman bought certain cleaning products brands, including Spray'n Wash and Glass Plus, from S.C. Johnson & Son for about $160 million. CEO Vernon Sankey resigned in 1999, and Michael Turrell became the acting chief executive.

Johann A. Benckiser founded Benckiser in 1823 in the Netherlands to make industrial chemicals. The company launched Calgon Water Softener in 1956 and released Calgonit automatic dishwashing detergent in 1964. From 1982 to 1992 a number of acquisitions expanded the company's market in Central Europe and North America. By 1999 Benckiser's products were sold in 45 countries, including Eastern Europe, Asia, and the Middle East.

After the merger in December 1999, Alan Dalby, former chairman of Reckitt & Colman, was named chairman of Reckitt Benckiser (he retired in 2001). Bart Becht, previously CEO of Benckiser, was named CEO of the new company. In 2000 Reckitt Benckiser announced plans to unload 75 brands to focus on more growth-oriented brands.

As part of an effort to expand its presence in the Asia/Pacific region, Reckitt Benckiser bought Korean household products maker Oxy Co. (Oxy Clean fabric treatment) in 2001.

In 2002 the company won FDA approval to market Subutex and Suboxone in the US. Both are drugs for the treatment of opiate dependence. They are available in 24 other countries.

EXECUTIVES

Chairman: Adrian D. P. Bellamy, age 63
Vice Chairman: Peter Harf
CEO and Director: Bart Becht, age 47, $4,215,401 pay
CFO and Director: Colin Day, age 50, $1,331,237 pay
President, Food Products: Elliott Penner
EVP, Category Development: Elio Leoni-Sceti, age 38
EVP, Developing Markets: Freddy Caspers, age 42
EVP, Europe: Erhard Schoewel
EVP, North America and Australia; Regional Director, North American Household: Javed Ahmed, age 45
EVP, Supply: Alain Le Goff, age 51
SVP, Human Resources: Frank Ruether, age 51
SVP, Information Services: Tony Gallagher, age 48
SVP, Investor Relations and Corporate Communications: Tom Corran
Brand Manager, Cattlemen's: Zoe Susice
Investor Relations Manager: Mark Wilson
Company Secretary: Elizabeth (Liz) Richardson
Financial Dynamics: Tim Spratt
Auditors: PricewaterhouseCoopers

LOCATIONS

HQ: Reckitt Benckiser plc
103-105 Bath Rd.,
Slough SL1 3UH, United Kingdom
Phone: +44-1753-217-800   **Fax:** +44-1753-217-899
US HQ: 399 Interpace Pkwy., Morris Corporate Ctr. IV, Parsippany, NJ 07054
US Phone: 973-404-2600   **US Fax:** 973-404-5700
Web: www.reckittbenckiser.com

2004 Sales

	% of total
Europe	53
North America and Australia	30
Developing markets	17
Total	**100**

PRODUCTS/OPERATIONS

2004 Sales

	% of total
Household & health & personal care	95
Food	5
Total	**100**

Selected Brands

Fabric care
  Ava
  Calgon
  Cherie
  Colon
  Dosia
  Napisan
  Oxy Clean
  Resolve
  Spray'n Wash
  Vanish
Surface care
  Brasso
  Dettox
  Easy Off
  Harpic
  Lime-A-Way
  Lysol
  Old English
  Home Care

Air care
  Airwick
  d-Con
  Haze
  Mortein
  Pest Control
  Wizard
Health and personal care
  Dettol
  Disprin
  Gaviscon
  Immac
  Kukident
  Lemsip
  Steradent
  Veet
Dishwashing
  Calgonit
  Electrasol
  Finish
  Jet-Dry

COMPETITORS

Alticor
Blyth
Boots Group
Chattem
Church & Dwight
Clorox
Colgate-Palmolive
Henkel
Johnson & Johnson
Procter & Gamble
S.C. Johnson
Unilever

HISTORICAL FINANCIALS

Company Type: Public

Income Statement

FYE: December 31

	REVENUE ($ mil.)	NET INCOME ($ mil.)	NET PROFIT MARGIN	EMPLOYEES
12/04	7,456	1,129	15.1%	19,900
12/03	6,601	869	13.2%	20,400
12/02	5,663	654	11.6%	22,300
12/01	4,990	517	10.4%	22,400
12/00	4,780	469	9.8%	18,900
12/99	4,937	(59)	—	20,200
12/98	5,128	410	8.0%	21,400
12/97	3,624	356	9.8%	16,500
12/96	3,933	558	14.2%	17,425
12/95	3,573	504	14.1%	18,739
Annual Growth	8.5%	9.4%	—	0.7%

2004 Year-End Financials

Debt ratio: 7.0%
Return on equity: 38.6%
Cash ($ mil.): 98
Current ratio: 1.13
Long-term debt ($ mil.): 227

Net Income History

London: RB

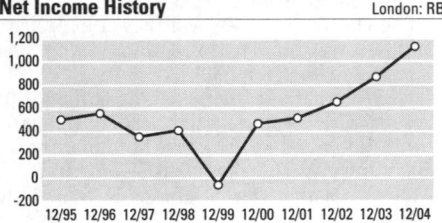

Reed Elsevier

Finding legal, business, scientific, or educational information is a cinch thanks to Reed Elsevier Group plc. Its Reed Business unit publishes business-to-business titles worldwide. Reed Elsevier's legal publishing operations fall under the LexisNexis banner, offering online, CD-ROM, and hard copy legal, corporate, and government information. Reed Elsevier Group also publishes scientific and medical information; its educational materials are published through units including Harcourt Education. Reed Elsevier PLC and Reed Elsevier NV each own 50% of Reed Elsevier Group.

The company also operates event organizer Reed Exhibition Companies.

No slouch in scientific publishing, Reed Elsevier Group issues thousands of scientific and medical journals and millions of research articles through Elsevier Science and ScienceDirect, its online scientific information service. Its Reed Educational & Professional Publishing unit produces the company's educational materials, an area Reed Elsevier Group rapidly expanded through its $4.5 billion acquisition of US-based Harcourt General (now called Harcourt Education) in 2001. To gain antitrust clearance for the deal Reed Elsevier Group sold Harcourt's higher education, corporate training, and assessment businesses to Canada's Thomson Corporation.

In 2004 Reed Elsevier through its LexisNexis unit acquired Seisint, a risk management information provider, for $775 million. The next year it purchased the medical publishing business of MediMedia for nearly $340 million.

HISTORY

Newsprint manufacturer Albert E. Reed & Co. was named after its founder in 1894. It went public in 1903. For the next 50 years, Reed grew by buying UK pulp and paper mills. Reed began making packaging materials in the 1930s and added building products in 1954. The company expanded into New Zealand (1955), Australia (1960), and Norway (1962).

Chairman Sir Don Ryder radically altered the company in the 1960s and 1970s, leading Reed into other paper-related products and into the wallpaper, paint, and interior-decorating and do-it-yourself markets. Reed bought International Publishing, Mirror Group Newspapers, and 29% of Cahners Publishing in 1970 (buying the remaining 71% in 1977). By 1978 Ryder's strategy proved flawed. Coordinating so many companies was difficult, and, strapped for cash, Reed dumped most of its Australian businesses.

The company sold the Mirror Group to Robert Maxwell in 1984 and divested the remainder of its nonpaper and nonpublishing companies by 1987 to focus on publishing. It bought Octopus Publishing (1987), the UK's TV Times (1989), News Corp.'s Travel Information Group (1989), and Martindale-Hubbell (1990).

Reed International merged its operations with those of Elsevier, the world's leading scholarly journal publisher, in 1993. Five Rotterdam booksellers and publishers founded Elsevier in 1880. It took its name from a famous Dutch family publishing company, which had operated from the late 16th century to the early 18th century.

Elsevier entered the scientific publishing market in the 1930s, and following WWII diversified into trade journals and consumer manuals. The company made its first US acquisition, Congressional Information Service, in 1979. The company fended off a takeover bid by Maxwell in 1988 by planning a merger with UK publisher Pearson; Maxwell was thwarted, the merger ultimately failed, and Elsevier later sold its Pearson stock. Elsevier bought Maxwell's Pergamon Press in 1991.

Reed and Elsevier were both listed on the NYSE in 1994. Reed Elsevier built its US presence that year with its purchase of Mead's LexisNexis online service. The company acquired Tolley, a UK tax and legal publisher, and a 50% interest in Shepard's, a US legal citation service in 1996. Reed Elsevier sold IPC Magazines (now IPC Media) for $1.4 billion in 1998 to an investment group led by venture capitalists Cinven. Later that year the company bought Matthew Bender and the remaining 50% of Shepard's from Times Mirror.

Crispin Davis, the former head of Aegis Group, became CEO in 1999. The firm reorganized Cahners that year, laying off several hundred employees and consolidating magazine operations. It also boosted its scientific publishing profile by unveiling Web-based scientific information service ScienceDirect. Reed Elsevier purchased educational publisher Harcourt General in 2001 to boost its market share in the US. The company had to sell some of Harcourt's businesses (including the higher education and corporate training operations) to Thomson Corporation in order to ease antitrust concerns.

In 2002 the company's US Cahners Business Information unit changed its name to Reed Business Information US. That year the company also changed its name to Reed Elsevier Group plc.

EXECUTIVES

Chairman: Jan H. M. Hommen, age 62
Executive Director and CEO: Sir Crispin Davis, age 55
Executive Director and CFO: Mark Armour, age 50
Executive Director; CEO, Harcourt Education: Patrick J. (Pat) Tierney, age 59
Executive Director; CEO, LexisNexis Group and Director: Andrew Prozes, age 59
CEO, Elsevier: Erik Engstrom, age 42
Executive Director; CEO, Reed Business Group and Director: Gerard van de Aast, age 47
CEO, Reed Business Information US: Tad Smith, age 40
President and CEO, Holt, Rinehart and Winston: Allen Wheatcroft
Director, Corporate Relations and Communications: Catherine May
Deputy Director, Corporate Relations: Patrick Kerr
Auditors: Deloitte & Touche

LOCATIONS

HQ: Reed Elsevier Group plc
  1-3 Strand, London WC2N 5JR, United Kingdom
Phone: +44-20-7930-7077   **Fax:** +44-20-7166-5799
US HQ: 125 Park Ave., 23rd Fl., New York, NY 10017
US Phone: 212-309-5498   **US Fax:** 212-309-5480
Web: www.reedelsevier.com

Reed Elsevier has offices in Asia, Australia, Canada, Europe, India, Latin America, New Zealand, South Africa, the UK, and the US.

PRODUCTS/OPERATIONS

2004 Sales

	% of total
Elsevier	28
LexisNexis	27
Reed Business	27
Harcourt Education	18
Total	**100**

Selected Operations

Business publishing
  Reed Business

Education publishing and testing
  Harcourt Education
  Harcourt Educational Assessment
  Reed Educational & Professional Publishing

Legal publishing
  LexisNexis

Scientific and medical publishing
  Elsevier
  Elsevier Health Sciences
  ScienceDirect (Web site)

COMPETITORS

Advance Publications
American Lawyer Media
Bertelsmann
Cadmus Communications
Dow Jones
Editis
Informa
John Wiley
McGraw-Hill
MediaLive International
Pearson
Penton Media
PRIMEDIA
Reuters
Thomson Corporation
Time Warner
United Business Media
Verlagsgruppe Georg von Holtzbrinck
VNU
Wolters Kluwer

HISTORICAL FINANCIALS

Company Type: Joint venture

Income Statement

FYE: December 31

	REVENUE ($ mil.)	NET INCOME ($ mil.)	NET PROFIT MARGIN	EMPLOYEES
12/04	9,269	584	6.3%	35,100
12/03	8,756	594	6.8%	35,600
12/02	8,052	290	3.6%	36,800
12/01	6,617	183	2.8%	34,600
12/00	5,625	49	0.9%	28,900
12/99	5,480	(102)	—	27,700
12/98	5,293	1,281	24.2%	26,100
12/97	5,637	343	6.1%	27,600
12/96	5,744	1,028	17.9%	25,800
12/95	5,247	794	15.1%	30,400
Annual Growth	**6.5%**	**(3.4%)**	**—**	**1.6%**

2004 Year-End Financials

Debt ratio: 528.1%
Return on equity: 13.4%
Cash ($ mil.): 433
Current ratio: 0.63
Long-term debt ($ mil.): 23,059

Net Income History

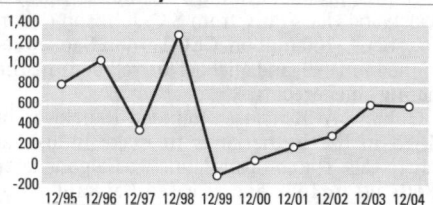

Renault S.A.

In Renault's road race against rival Peugeot Citroën to be France's dominant automaker, second place will have to deux. Renault S.A. manufactures a range of small to midsize cars (including Clio, Megane, Espace, Twingo, and Scenic) and light commercial vehicles (Kangoo Express, Traffic, and Master). Like General Motors, Ford, and DaimlerChrysler, Renault is investing heavily in Asia, specifically in Japan. Renault has taken a 44% stake in Japan's #3 automaker, Nissan Motor. In 2003 the French government reduced its stake in Renault from 26% to just under 16%.

With the Nissan deal and by taking a 93% stake in Automobile Dacia (Romania's leading automaker), Renault made it clear that it doesn't intend to be left in the international slow lane. The company also has purchased a 70% stake in South Korea-based Samsung Motors' automobile business. Renault sold its Renault V.I. subsidiary and its Mack Trucks unit to Volvo in return for a 20% stake in the Swedish truckmaker. To firm up ties between the two companies, Nissan has taken a 15% stake in Renault, and Renault has increased its share of Nissan from 37% to 44%. The plan also reduced the French government's stake in Renault to 26% from 44% through a public offering. The French Government then further reduced its stake through an offering to institutional investors, employees, and former employees.

Understandably impressed by Nissan's miraculous turnaround (led by Carlos Ghosn), Renault's board named Ghosn CEO of the French automaker in 2005. Loathe to mess with success, Renault has also kept Ghosn behind the wheel at Nissan.

HISTORY

In the Paris suburb of Billancourt in 1898, 21-year-old Louis Renault assembled a motorized vehicle with a transmission box of his own design. Louis and his brothers, Marcel and Fernand, established Renault Freres and produced the world's first sedan in 1899. Marcel died in a racing accident (1903) and Fernand left the business (1908), leaving Louis in sole possession of the company. He renamed it La Société Louis Renault in 1908.

In 1914 a fleet of 600 Paris taxis shuttled French troops to fight the Germans in the Battle of the Marne. Renault also built light tanks and airplane engines. Between world wars Renault expanded into trucks, tractors, and aircraft engines. Renault sustained heavy damage in WWII, but Louis Renault operated the remaining Paris facilities for the Germans during their occupation of France. After the liberation of Paris, he was accused of collaboration and died in prison while awaiting trial in 1944. The de Gaulle government nationalized Renault in 1945 and gave the company its present name.

Worldwide economic growth aided Renault's postwar comeback. The company achieved its greatest success in high-volume, low-cost cars such as the 4 CV in the late 1940s and 1950s, the Renault 4 in the 1960s and 1970s, and the Renault 5 in the 1970s and 1980s.

In 1979 Renault acquired 46% of American Motors Corporation (AMC). In the early 1980s AMC fared poorly, and Renault suffered from a worldwide slump in auto sales, an aging product line, and stiff competition from Japanese carmakers. Decreasing sales, an unwieldy bureaucracy, and above-average wages contributed to a $1.5 billion loss in 1984.

Georges Besse took over Renault in 1985, and trimmed employment by 20,000. When Besse was assassinated by terrorists in 1986, Raymond Levy assumed his role and continued his policies, laying off 30,000 more workers and selling AMC to Chrysler (1987).

Renault and Volvo agreed to extensive cross-ownership and cooperation in 1990. In 1994 Renault swapped its 25% stake in Volvo's car division for the latter's 45% stake in Renault's troubled truck unit. (Volvo sold its remaining 11% stake in 1997.)

The French government reduced its share of the firm from 80% to 52% in 1995 and to 44% the following year. In 1997 it shut down a Belgian plant that employed more than 3,000 workers and fired a similar number of employees in France. Renault paid a $13 million civil penalty to the EPA in 1998 to settle allegations that its Mack unit cheated on its diesel engine emissions tests.

Renault and Fiat struck several deals in 1999. They combined their bus-making operations under the name Irisbus and their foundry operations into jointly owned Teksid. Renault sold a 51% stake in Renault Automation to Fiat's Comau robotics unit. Also that year Renault bought a 51% stake in Romanian automaker, Automobile Dacia SA, and paid $5.4 billion for a 37% stake in Nissan and a 15% (later increased to 23%) stake in truck affiliate Nissan Diesel Motor.

Early in 2000 the company announced that it would spend around $100 million to build an SUV factory in Brazil and announced plans to trim almost $3 billion in costs between 2001 and 2003. The same year Renault agreed to buy a 70% stake in Samsung Motors' automobile business for around $550 million. It also sold its Mack truck unit to AB Volvo in exchange for a 15% stake in the Swedish truck maker. Renault plans to buy another 5% of Volvo on the open market. Renault and Nissan also announced plans to save about $1 billion by combining their European sales and marketing operations.

Later in 2001 Renault announced plans to further strengthen ties with Nissan. The plan would increase Renault's stake in Nissan to 44% while granting Nissan a 15% stake in Renault. The French Finance Ministry also announced that it would reduce the French government's stake in Renault from 44% to 25% through a future public offering. The two deals were completed in 2002.

Early in 2005 Renault sold its 18% stake in Nissan Diesel Motor Co., Ltd. to J.P. Morgan Securities, Ltd., who, in turn, sold the shares on the open market.

EXECUTIVES

Chairman: Louis Schweitzer, age 63
President, CEO, and Director: Carlos Ghosn, age 50
EVP and CFO: Thierry Moulonguet, age 53
EVP: Patrick Pelata, age 49
EVP, Group Human Resources and Corporate Secretary General: Michel de Virville, age 60
EVP, Manufacturing: Michel Gornet, age 58
EVP, Quality and Engineering (Vehicle and Powertrain): Jean-Louis Ricaud, age 52
EVP, Sales and Marketing: Patrick Blain, age 53
SVP, Advanced Vehicle Engineering and Research: Jacques Lacambre
SVP and CIO: Jean-Pierre Corniou
SVP and Corporate Controller: Jean-Baptiste Duzan
SVP, Chairman's Office: Philippe Klein
SVP, Corporate Communications: Patrick Bessy
SVP, Corporate Design: Patrick le Quément
SVP, Finance: Alain Dassas
SVP, Light Commercial Vehicles: Bruno Morange
SVP, Market Area France: Jacques Chauvet
SVP, Public Affairs: Luc-Alexandre Ménard
SVP, Strategy and Marketing: Benoit Marzloff
SVP, Vehicle Engineering Development: Michel Faivre-Duboz
Auditors: Ernst & Young Audit; Deloitte & Associés

LOCATIONS

HQ: Renault S.A.
13-15 quai Le Gallo,
92513 Boulogne-Billancourt, France
Phone: +33-1-76-84-50-50   **Fax:** +33-1-41-04-51-49
Web: www.renault.com

Renault has manufacturing operations in Argentina, Brazil, Chile, France, Mexico, Portugal, Romania, Slovakia, South Korea, Spain, Turkey, and the UK.

2004 Sales

	$ mil.	% of total
Europe		
France	19,280	35
Other EU countries	25,552	46
Other countries	3,785	7
Asia/Pacific	3,570	6
Americas	2,343	4
Africa	1,005	2
Total	**55,535**	**100**

PRODUCTS/OPERATIONS

2004 Sales

	$ mil.	% of total
Automobiles	52,712	95
Sales financing	2,823	5
Total	**55,535**	**100**

Selected Products

Automobiles
Clio
Clio Saloon
Clio Sport
Clio V6
Espace
Kangoo 4X4
Laguna
Megane Cabriolet
Megane Coupe
Megane Hatch
Megane Sport Hatch
Scenic
Vel Satis
Light Commercial Vehicles
Master
New Kangoo Express
Trafic

COMPETITORS

BMW	Mazda
CNH Global	Peugeot
DaimlerChrysler	Peugeot Motors
Fiat	of America, Inc.
Ford	Saab Automobile
General Motors	Suzuki Motor
Honda	Tata Group
Isuzu	Toyota
Kia Motors	Volkswagen

HISTORICAL FINANCIALS

Company Type: Public

Income Statement

FYE: December 31

	REVENUE ($ mil.)	NET INCOME ($ mil.)	NET PROFIT MARGIN	EMPLOYEES
12/04	55,535	4,844	8.7%	130,573
12/03	47,101	3,113	6.6%	130,740
12/02	38,084	2,050	5.4%	132,351
12/01	32,200	931	2.9%	140,417
12/00	37,829	1,017	2.7%	166,114
12/99	37,851	538	1.4%	159,608
12/98	43,396	1,560	3.6%	138,321
12/97	34,659	905	2.6%	141,315
12/96	35,177	(1,003)	—	140,905
12/95	37,495	436	1.2%	139,950
Annual Growth	**4.5%**	**30.7%**	**—**	**(0.8%)**

2004 Year-End Financials

Debt ratio: 28.9%
Return on equity: 24.9%
Cash ($ mil.): 10,626
Current ratio: 1.04
Long-term debt ($ mil.): 6,329

Net Income History

Euronext Paris: RNO

Repsol YPF

The sun shines on Repsol YPF, Spain's largest oil company. A fully integrated oil and gas company, it has proved reserves of 4.9 billion barrels of oil equivalent, mostly in Latin America, the Middle East, and North Africa. The company owns 99% of YPF, Argentina's #1 oil company, and has operations in more than 30 countries. Repsol YPF operates five refineries in Spain and four in Latin American and produces chemicals, plastics, and polymers. It sells gas under the brands Campsa, Petronor, and Repsol at more than 3,600 service stations in Spain and has about 3,000 stations in Latin America. It is one of Spain's largest sellers of liquefied petroleum gas. Spanish bank La Caixa owns more than 14% of Repsol YPF.

The company acquired its current name and expanded its reserves significantly with the 1999 purchase of YPF, Argentina's leading oil company. To comply with its agreement with Argentina's government to divest 11% of the company's refining and marketing assets in Argentina, Repsol YPF shed 700 of its stations and a refinery in a $1 billion asset swap with Brazil's Petrobras.

Through 31%-owned affiliate Gas Natural, the company owns about 41% of Spanish natural gas supplier Enagas. Also with Gas Natural, Repsol will form a liquefied natural gas joint venture that will have a marketing capacity of 12 million metric tons and a fleet of more than 10 carriers.

Repsol is also bidding for Royal Dutch/Shell's liquefied petroleum gas operations. And with Chevron the company will form a joint venture to develop oil operations in the Orinoco belt of Venezuela.

Altogether Repsol plans to invest more than €21 billion (more than $26 billion) over the next couple of years in its operations, particularly in exploration and production, including its Spanish refineries, which will receive an investment of about €4 billion (more than $4 billion).

HISTORY

Repsol YPF, officially created as Repsol in 1987, is actually the result of efforts that began as early as the 1920s to organize Spain's fragmented energy industry.

Following an era of dependency on foreign investment prior to and during Francisco Franco's dictatorship (1939-75), Spain began reorganizing its energy industry. In 1979 it set up the Instituto Nacional de Hidrocarburos, which in 1981 incorporated all public-sector firms involved in gas and oil under one government agency.

Repsol was formed six years later to provide central management to a Spanish oil company that could compete in the unified European market. The government chose the name Repsol, after a well-known brand of Spanish lubricant products. The firm was charged with pursuing a global strategy to bring together all levels of the industry.

In 1989 Repsol offered 26% of the firm on the Madrid and New York stock exchanges, raising over $1 billion. That year Repsol increased its marine fleet with the purchase of the Naviera Vizcaina shipping company and bought Carless Refining & Marketing, a UK business with a chain of 500 service stations operating mainly under the Anglo brand. Although Spain was opening its doors to foreign investment, the Spanish government maintained control over the country's energy industry, including a tightly

guarded distribution network under state-controlled Campsa. Campsa oversaw a marketing/logistics system of pipelines, storage terminals, and sales outlets.

The European Community demanded that Spain open its markets to other EC members, forcing Campsa in 1991 to divide its 3,800 gasoline stations among its four major shareholders: Cepsa (Spain's largest private refiner), Petromed, Ertoil, and Repsol. Repsol gained 66% of the logistical network and use of the Campsa brand name.

Repsol and Spanish bank La Caixa merged their interests in natural gas in 1992 to create Gas Natural, a new gas distributor. That year the Spanish government began reducing its majority holding, and by 1996 its stake had dwindled to 10%. (It sold its remaining stock in 1997.)

Expanding its South American operations, Repsol acquired control of Argentinian oil company Astra CAPSA and a Peruvian oil refinery in 1996. That year Repsol purchased a 30% stake in the Tin Fouye Tabankort field in Algeria.

In 1999 Repsol paid $2 billion for a 15% stake in giant oil company YPF, which was auctioned off by Argentina's government. After acquiring another 83% of YPF for $13.2 billion, Repsol changed its name to Repsol YPF. To help pay down debt incurred in the acquisition, Repsol YPF sold its UK North Sea oil and gas operations to US independent Kerr-McGee for $555 million in 2000. That year the company (as part of its commitment to Argentina's government after acquiring YPF) agreed to swap some of its Argentine refining and marketing assets for Brazilian oil and gas operations owned by Petrobras.

In 2002 Repsol YPF sold oil and gas assets in Indonesia to CNOOC for about $585 million.

In 2004 former chairman of Spain's top gas supplier Gas Natural S.A., Antonio Brufau, replaced Alfonso Cortina de Alcocer as chairman of Repsol.

EXECUTIVES

Chairman and CEO: Antonio Brufau Niubó
Vice Chairman: Ricardo Fornesa Ribó
CFO: Luis Mañas Antón
EVP Upstream: Miguel Ángel Remón Gil
Executive Director of Argentina, Brazil, and Bolivia: Enrique Locutura Rupérez
Executive Director of Downstream: Pedro Fernández Frial
Executive Director of Upstream: Nemesio Fernández-Cuesta Luca de Tena
Group Managing Director of Communication and Head of the Chairman's Office: Jaume Giró Ribas
Group Managing Director of Finance and Corporate Services: Fernando Ramírez Mazarredo
Group Managing Director of Human Resources: Jesus Fernández de la Vega
Managing Director of Refining and Marketing in Europe: Jorge Segrelles García
Executive Director of Management and Development Control: Miguel Martinez San Martin
Managing Director of Refining and Marketing Latin America: Pascual Olmos Navarro
Managing Director of RYTTSA: Alfonso Ballestero Aguilar
Director of Chemicals: Juan Pedro Maza Sabalete
Director of External Relations: Antonio Gomis Sáez
Director of Legal Affairs: Rafael Piqueras Bautista
Director of LPG: Manuel Guerrero Pemán
Director of Planning and Control: Pedro Fernández Frial
Secretary and Director: Luis Suárez de Lezo Mantilla
Auditors: Deloitte SL

LOCATIONS

HQ: Repsol YPF, S.A.
   Paseo de la Castellana, 278, 28046 Madrid, Spain
Phone: +34-91-348-80-00   **Fax:** +34-91-348-28-21
Web: www.repsol-ypf.com

Repsol YPF has operations in more than 30 countries in Africa, Asia, the Caribbean, Europe, Latin America, and the Middle East.

2004 Sales

	% of total
Spain	67
Argentina	15
Other Latin American countries	13
Other countries	5
Total	**100**

PRODUCTS/OPERATIONS

2004 Sales

	% of total
Refining & marketing	74
Exploration & production	16
Chemicals	6
Gas & electricity	4
Total	**100**

COMPETITORS

Anadarko Petroleum	Murphy Oil
Apco Argentina	Noble Energy
BHP Billiton	Norsk Hydro
BP	Occidental Petroleum
Devon Energy	PDVSA
Endesa	PEMEX
Eni	PETROBRAS
Exxon Mobil	Petrobras Energía
IBERDROLA	Pioneer Natural Resources
Imperial Oil	Royal Dutch/Shell Group
Kerr-McGee	TOTAL
Koch	Unión Fenosa
Marathon Oil	Unocal

HISTORICAL FINANCIALS

Company Type: Public

Income Statement				FYE: December 31
	REVENUE ($ mil.)	NET INCOME ($ mil.)	NET PROFIT MARGIN	EMPLOYEES
12/04	56,472	2,641	4.7%	33,337
12/03	46,775	2,540	5.4%	31,121
12/02	38,325	2,050	5.3%	30,110
12/01	38,908	914	2.3%	35,452
12/00	43,080	2,287	5.3%	37,387
12/99	26,537	1,020	3.8%	29,262
12/98	21,740	1,025	4.7%	23,762
12/97	21,057	827	3.9%	21,440
12/96	21,344	918	4.3%	19,560
12/95	20,962	970	4.6%	18,878
Annual Growth	**11.6%**	**11.8%**	**—**	**6.5%**

2004 Year-End Financials

Debt ratio: 41.3%
Return on equity: 14.3%
Cash ($ mil.): 485
Current ratio: 1.29
Long-term debt ($ mil.): 8,144

No. of shares (mil.): 1,221
Dividends
   Yield: 1.9%
   Payout: 22.6%
Market value ($ mil.): 31,865

	STOCK PRICE ($) FY Close	P/E High/Low		PER SHARE ($) Earnings	Dividends	Book Value
12/04	26.10	12	9	2.17	0.49	16.14
12/03	19.55	9	6	2.09	0.33	14.04
12/02	13.08	9	6	1.68	0.18	11.69
12/01	14.53	26	17	0.75	0.44	10.61
12/00	16.13	12	8	1.91	0.41	11.68
12/99	23.25	22	14	1.10	0.48	10.64
12/98	18.19	17	12	1.13	0.44	7.85
12/97	14.17	16	13	0.92	0.44	6.73
12/96	12.70	13	10	1.00	0.40	7.25
12/95	10.95	11	9	1.00	0.28	6.02
Annual Growth	10.1%	—	—	9.0%	6.4%	11.6%

Reuters Group

Reuters Group helps you stay informed on the business of business and just about everything else. One of the world's leading providers of news and information, the company provides global access to financial data, news feeds, and corporate information though its operations in more than 90 countries. It culls information from more than 250 stock exchanges and gathers information on more than 40,000 companies worldwide. With nearly 200 news bureaus, Reuters ranks as the world's largest international news agency, publishing stories in almost 20 languages. It also has a 50% stake in news and information joint venture Factiva with Dow Jones.

While probably best known for its international news reporting, the company gets just 5% of its revenue from its media operations. Financial data and software tools for traders and sales people, meanwhile, makes up more than 40% of Reuters' business. Almost three-quarters of the company's business comes through subscriptions or other recurring revenue streams.

Reuters has been struggling to get through a difficult recovery period after a near collapse of its business in 2001. Under the leadership of CEO Tom Glocer, the company has slashed headcount and closed down several operations in order to get costs under control. It has also sold off many operations, including two consulting and advisory businesses (TowerGroup and Yankee Group), most of its stake in TIBCO Software, and its Radianz network services business. In 2005 Reuters sold its 62% stake in Instinet to NASDAQ for $1.1 billion. However, the company did acquire Moneyline Telerate, a leading supplier of money market information, for about $145 million in 2005.

To complete its turnaround, though, Reuters is hoping to move beyond its core institutional and enterprise customers and become more of a consumer-oriented business. In 2004 it relaunched its reuters.com Web site as an advertising-supported news and information portal serving a general audience, and the following year the company brought in former MSNBC executive Dean Wright to take charge of its consumer products operation. The company has also started to reduce the amount of news it sells to customers such as Yahoo! and MSN and it is exploring ways to distribute content through subscriptions directly to consumers on mobile devices. Reuters marked another momentous change in 2005 when it left London's Fleet Street, historically the city's home for journalists, and moved into a new headquarters at Canary Wharf.

As a public company with a vested interest in maintaining the objectivity of its news and information, Reuters is ultimately controlled by the Founders Share Company, an organization established in 1984 that is overseen by representatives of four major news organizations.

HISTORY

In 1849 German news correspondent Paul Julius Reuter seized the chance to scoop his competitors by using carrier pigeons to bridge the telegraph gap between Aachen, Germany, and Brussels. He moved to London in 1851 and began telegraphing stock quotes between Paris and London. In 1865 Reuter's Telegram Co. was organized as a limited company.

Reuter ceded management to his son Herbert in 1878 and died in 1899. Herbert made the disastrous decision to establish Reuter's Bank in 1913. Two years later, under the strain of WWI anti-German sentiment and the death of his wife, Herbert committed suicide. Successor Roderick Jones changed the company's name to Reuters Ltd. and took it private in 1916 to avoid a hostile takeover. Reuters advanced into new technology by using radios and teleprinters in the 1920s. By 1925 The Press Association owned a majority of the company; it ousted Jones in 1941, displeased with his relationship to the British government. In an attempt to uphold Reuters' independence, The Reuters Trust was created that year.

Reuters established international bureaus during the 1940s and 1950s, but its owners' focus on the bottom line limited the scale of expansion. The company partnered with Ultronic Systems Corporation in 1964 to launch Stockmaster, a financial data transmission system. Nine years later Reuters introduced its Monitor electronic marketplace to track the foreign exchange market. Monitor Dealing, introduced in 1981, enabled dealers to trade currencies online.

The company went public in 1984 as Reuters Holdings PLC, and with the new capital, it accelerated acquisitions. It bought Visnews (now Reuters Television, 1985), Instinet (1986), TIBCO (1994), and Quotron (1994). The company also acquired a new CEO during this time when Peter Job, a journalist who joined Reuters in 1963, was named to the top spot in 1991. In 1994 the company launched Reuters Television for financial markets. The following year it agreed to make its information available on the Internet via IBM's infoMarket service.

With competition from the Internet nipping at its heels, Reuters restructured in 1998 to refocus along product lines (which led to the creation of holding company Reuters Group PLC). In 1999 Reuters and Dow Jones & Company launched a joint venture combining their online news databases.

In 2000 Reuters and telecommunications firm Equant launched Radianz, a joint venture to offer secure business-to-business Internet and telecommunications service. It also purchased The Yankee Group from fellow financial information provider Primark.

Job retired as CEO in 2001 and was replaced by Tom Glocer, the second American and first non-journalist (he's a lawyer) to hold the position. During his first week on the job, Glocer announced that the company would cut about 1,800 jobs by the end of 2002. As part of that initiative, the company closed its financial television services, cutting 45 jobs in the process.

Also in 2001 Reuters took Instinet public (retaining about a 60% stake) and bought several US-focused operations from the bankrupt Bridge Information Systems. In 2002 the company purchased foreign exchange transaction technology specialist AVT Technologies in order to form the Reuters Automated Dealing Technologies business unit for delivering Reuters automated dealing and limit order management offerings.

The company also sold The Yankee Group to private investors. The following year Reuters sold Radianz to UK-telecommunications giant BT Group after acquiring Equant's stake in the joint venture. Later in 2005 Reuters moved into a new headquarters building at Canary Wharf, leaving its Fleet Street offices after 66 years. Late that year the company sold its stake in Instinet to Nasdaq for $1.1 billion.

EXECUTIVES

Chairman: Niall FitzGerald, age 60, $313,971 pay
CEO and Director: Thomas H. (Tom) Glocer, age 45, $3,915,964 pay
CFO and Director: David J. Grigson, age 50, $1,537,108 pay
President, Business Divisions, and Director: Devin N. Wenig, age 38, $1,267,440 pay
Managing Director, Global Sales and Focus Group Accounts: Christopher Hagman, age 46
Global Head of Asset Management and Research: Julie Holland
Global Head of Corporate Affairs: Simon Walker, age 51
Global Head of Corporate Strategy: Susan Taylor-Martin, age 41
Global Head of Human Resources: Christian (Chris) Verougstraete, age 54
Global Head of Operations and Technology: Michael (Mike) Sayers, age 51
Global Head of Public Relations: Stephen Naru
Editor-in-Chief: Geert Linnebank, age 48
General Counsel and Secretary: Rosemary Martin, age 45
CIO: David Lister, age 45
Chief Marketing Officer: Alexander (Alex) Hungate, age 38
President and CEO, Factiva: Clare Hart
CEO, Lipper: Michael Peace
CEO, Reuters America: Phillip (Phil) Lynch
EVP Sales and Training, Reuters America: Michael Steinharter
Global Managing Editor and Head of Editorial Operations: David Schlesinger, age 43
Managing Editor and Head of Editorial Operations, Americas: Betty Wong
Head of Investor Relations: Miriam McKay
Public Relations Director: Yvonne Diaz
Auditors: PricewaterhouseCoopers LLP

LOCATIONS

HQ: Reuters Group PLC
The Reuters Building, Canary Wharf,
London E14 5EP, United Kingdom
Phone: +44-20-7250-1122   **Fax:** +44-20-7542-4064
US HQ: 3 Times Square, New York, NY 10036
US Phone: 646-223-4000   **US Fax:** 646-223-4001
Web: www.reuters.com

Reuters Group has operations in more than 90 countries.

2004 Sales

	$ mil.	% of total
Europe, Middle East & Africa	2,694	49
The Americas	2,061	37
Asia/Pacific	776	14
Total	**5,531**	**100**

PRODUCTS/OPERATIONS

2004 Sales

	$ mil.	% of total
Reuters		
Sales & trading	2,262	41
Enterprise	922	17
Recoveries	615	11
Asset management & research	451	8
Media	276	5
Instinet Group	1,016	18
Adjustments	(11)	—
Total	**5,531**	**100**

Selected Products

Multex 360 (research and analysis for
  portfolio managers and analysts)
Reuters 3000 Xtra (desktop information system)
Reuters DataScope (data management system)
Reuters Dealing 3000 (workstation for
  foreign exchange markets)
Reuters Messaging (instant messaging for
  traders and investors)

Selected Subsidiaries and Joint Ventures

Dow Jones Reuters Business Interactive
  (50%, Factiva online financial news database)
Lipper Analytical Services
  (mutual fund and global fund data)
Moneyline Telerate (money market information
  provider)
Multex.com (financial information provider)
TIBCO (8%, systems integration and software
  development)

COMPETITORS

Agence France-Presse	Misys
Algorithmics	Moneyline Telerate
Associated Press	Morningstar
Bloomberg	NASD
CSK	NYSE
D&B	Quick Corp.
Dow Jones	S&P
FactSet	SunGard
Financial Times	Telekurs
GL Trade	Thomson Corporation
IBM	TIBCO Software
Interactive Data	UPI
LexisNexis	Value Line

HISTORICAL FINANCIALS

Company Type: Public

Income Statement

FYE: December 31

	REVENUE ($ mil.)	NET INCOME ($ mil.)	NET PROFIT MARGIN	EMPLOYEES
12/04	5,531	673	12.2%	15,500
12/03	5,702	77	1.4%	16,744
12/02	5,761	(651)	—	17,414
12/01	5,657	67	1.2%	19,429
12/00	5,371	795	14.8%	18,082
12/99	5,049	687	13.6%	16,546
12/98	5,032	637	12.7%	16,938
12/97	4,760	644	13.5%	16,119
12/96	4,990	841	16.8%	15,478
12/95	4,198	643	15.3%	14,348
Annual Growth	**3.1%**	**0.5%**	**—**	**0.9%**

2004 Year-End Financials

Debt ratio: 79.9%
Return on equity: 103.5%
Cash ($ mil.): 159
Current ratio: 1.37
Long-term debt ($ mil.): 631
No. of shares (mil.): 239
Dividends
  Yield: 2.6%
  Payout: 39.7%
Market value ($ mil.): 10,276

Stock History

NASDAQ: RTRSY

12/95 12/96 12/97 12/98 12/99 12/00 12/01 12/02 12/03 12/04

	STOCK PRICE ($) FY Close	P/E High/Low		PER SHARE ($) Earnings	Dividends	Book Value
12/04	42.95	18	9	2.82	1.12	3.30
12/03	25.35	85	28	0.32	1.02	2.14
12/02	17.20	—	—	(2.80)	0.98	3.35
12/01	59.99	373	160	0.28	2.74	6.77
12/00	98.50	47	22	3.35	1.52	6.92
12/99	80.81	35	17	2.88	1.57	4.10
12/98	63.38	28	16	2.65	1.21	2.61
12/97	66.25	32	23	2.40	1.48	9.72
12/96	76.50	25	18	3.12	1.04	7.67
12/95	55.13	25	16	2.40	0.99	5.26
Annual Growth	**(2.7%)**	**—**	**—**	**1.8%**	**1.4%**	**(5.0%)**

Ricoh

Ricoh may be best known for its imaging equipment, but the company is more than just another copycat. One of the world's leading manufacturers of copiers and supplies, Ricoh also makes fax machines, scanners, and printers. Other products from the company, which has more than 400 subsidiaries and affiliates worldwide, include digital cameras, personal computers, servers, semiconductors, printed circuit boards, and optical data storage drives. Among Ricoh's US-based subsidiaries are office equipment specialists Ricoh Corporation, Lanier Worldwide and Savin.

Ricoh continues to expand its networked imaging and connectivity products, which include laser printers, copiers, and document management software and systems. The company has also moved beyond its core office products into related services, including systems customization, integration, consulting, and facilities management. The company's copiers and supplies account for about 40% of its sales. In 2004 Ricoh augmented its printer business by acquiring Hitachi Printing Solutions.

HISTORY

Ricoh began in 1936 as the Riken Kankoshi Company making photographic paper. With founder Kiyoshi Ichimura at the helm, the company soon became the leader in Japan's sensitized-paper market. It changed its name to Riken Optical Company in 1938 and started making cameras. Two years later it produced its first camera under the Ricoh brand.

By 1954 Ricoh cameras were Japan's #1 sellers and were also popular abroad. The next year the company entered the office machine market with its compact mimeograph machine. Ricoh followed that in 1960 with an offset duplicator.

Ricoh built its business in the 1960s with a range of office machines, including reproduction and data processing equipment and retrieval systems. The company began establishing operations overseas, including US subsidiary Ricoh Industries U.S.A. in 1962. The US unit started marketing cameras but found greener pastures in the copier industry, where Ricoh's products were sold under the Pitney Bowes and Savin brand names. The company changed its name to Ricoh Company in 1963. Two years later Ricoh entered the emerging field of office computers and introduced an electrostatic copier. In 1968 Ichimura died, and Mikio Tatebayashi took over as president for the next eight years.

During the 1970s Ricoh debuted the first high-speed fax machine and began consolidating its network outside Japan. In 1973 Ricoh established a second US subsidiary — Ricoh Electronics — to assemble copier supplies and parts, becoming the first Japanese company to produce copiers in the US. It released a plain-paper copier in 1975, followed the next year by a daisy wheel printer and its first word processor. Tatebayashi died in 1976 and was replaced by Takeshi Ouye as president. Subsidiary Rapicom was established in 1978 in Japan to develop fax products.

Throughout the 1970s Savin and Pitney Bowes continued to brand and sell Ricoh-made products in the US, but in the early 1980s Ricoh started marketing products under its own name. It introduced a PC and its first laser printer in 1983. By the next year Ricoh had 7% of the US copier market. Other products introduced in the 1980s included a color copier, minicomputers developed with AT&T, and (in Japan) a digital copier that could also be used as an input/output station for electronic filing systems. Ricoh's overseas sales continued to grow in the late 1980s and for a while exceeded its domestic sales. In 1983 Ouye turned over leadership of the company to Hiroshi Hamada.

Ricoh founded Tailien Optical (Shenzhen) Co. Ltd. in 1992 to make compact camera parts. As the 1990s progressed, the company increasingly pushed products based on digital technologies.

Ricoh won licensing fees from Samsung Electronics in a 1995 dispute over fax machine patents. Seeking to boost international sales, it bought marketing firms Savin in the US and Gestetner Holdings (later renamed NRG Group) in Europe that year. The next year Hamada became chairman and CEO, and Masamitsu Sakurai took over as president.

The company's push during the mid-1990s to increase overseas sales paid off. Amid an Asian economic crisis, Ricoh's overall sales remained relatively stable, while sales of its copiers outside Japan increased 20% and 9% for 1998 and 1999, respectively.

In 2000 the company reorganized its US operations and consolidated its European distribution centers. Early the following year Ricoh boosted its push into the US market with its acquisition of office equipment supplier Lanier Worldwide for about $250 million. Despite shaky world economic conditions, in fiscal 2002 Ricoh saw growth in sales and profits, with strong overseas sales making up for slightly lowered revenues from Japan.

EXECUTIVES

President, CEO, and COO: Masamitsu Sakurai, age 63
Deputy President: Tatsuo Hirakawa
Executive Managing Director: Koichi Endo
Executive Managing Director: Masayuki Matsumoto
Executive Managing Director: Katsumi (Kirk) Yoshida
Managing Director: Kazunori Azuma
Managing Director: Makoto Hashimoto
Managing Director: Yuji Inoue
Managing Director: Shiroh Kondoh
Managing Director: Zenji Miura
Managing Director: Takashi Nakamura
Managing Director: Kiyoshi Sakai
Managing Director: Kazuo Togashi
EVP; Chairman and CEO, Ricoh Corporation:
  Susumu (Sam) Ichioka
EVP: Kenji Hatanaka
EVP: Etsuo Kobayashi
EVP: Hideko Kunii
EVP: Hiroshi Kobayashi
EVP: Haruo Nakamura
EVP: Terumoto Nonaka
EVP: Tadatoshi Sakamaki
EVP: Hiroshi Tategami
Auditors: KPMG AZSA & Co.

LOCATIONS

HQ: Ricoh Company, Ltd.
  15-5, Minami-Aoyama 1-chome, Minato-ku,
  Tokyo 107-8544, Japan
Phone: +81-3-3479-3111   **Fax:** +81-3-3403-1578
US HQ: 5 Dedrick Place, West Caldwell, NJ 07006
US Phone: 973-882-2000   **US Fax:** 973-882-2506
Web: www.ricoh.com

Ricoh Company has more than 400 subsidiaries and affiliates worldwide. The company has manufacturing plants in China, France, Hong Kong, Japan, South Korea, Taiwan, the UK, and the US.

2005 Sales

	% of total
Japan	54
Europe	22
The Americas	18
Other regions	6
Total	**100**

PRODUCTS/OPERATIONS

2005 Sales

	% of total
Office equipment	
Imaging	40
Network input/output	37
Network system	11
Other	12
Total	**100**

Selected Products

Imaging Solutions
  Diazo copiers
  Digital duplicators
  Digital monochrome and color copiers
  Fax machines
  Imaging supplies and consumables
  Wide-format copiers
Network Input/Output Systems
  Printing systems
    Laser printers
    Multifunction printer/fax/copier/scanner devices
  Other input/output systems
    CD and DVD recordable and rewritable
      discs and drives
    Scanners
Network System Solutions
  Document management software
  Networking and applications software
  Network systems
  Personal computers
  Servers
  Services and support

Other
  Digital cameras and other photographic equipment
  Measurement equipment
  Printed circuit boards
  Semiconductors

COMPETITORS

3M	Imagistics
Brother Industries	Konica Minolta
Canon	Kyocera Mita
CASIO COMPUTER	Lexmark
Danka	Matsushita
Eastman Kodak	NEC
Epson	Nikon
Fuji Xerox	Oki Data
Fujifilm	Oki Electric
Hewlett-Packard	SANYO
Hitachi	Sharp
IBM	Toshiba
IKON	Xerox

HISTORICAL FINANCIALS

Company Type: Public

Income Statement

FYE: March 31

	REVENUE ($ mil.)	NET INCOME ($ mil.)	NET PROFIT MARGIN	EMPLOYEES
3/05	16,868	773	4.6%	75,097
3/04	16,852	869	5.2%	73,137
3/03	14,505	605	4.2%	74,600
3/02	12,608	465	3.7%	74,209
3/01	12,177	421	3.5%	74,200
3/00	13,716	397	2.9%	67,300
3/99	11,972	257	2.1%	65,000
3/98	10,546	226	2.1%	63,600
3/97	10,631	234	2.2%	60,200
3/96	10,377	204	2.0%	50,000
Annual Growth	**5.5%**	**16.0%**	**—**	**4.6%**

2005 Year-End Financials

Debt ratio: 26.3%   Current ratio: 1.53
Return on equity: 9.9%   Long-term debt ($ mil.): 2,107
Cash ($ mil.): 1,737

Net Income History

OTC: RICOY

Robert Bosch

Robert Bosch is one of the world's top makers of automobile components. Bosch's automotive offerings include antilock braking and fuel-injection systems, auto electronics, starters, and alternators. The company also makes industrial machinery and hand tools and owns 50% of Bosch-Siemens Hausgerate, a European appliance maker. Bosch's Blaupunkt unit is a major manufacturer of car audio equipment. Subsidiary Bosch Rexroth makes electric, hydraulic, and pneumatic machinery for applications ranging from automotive to mining. The Robert

Bosch Stiftung, a charitable organization, owns 92% of the company; the Bosch family owns 7%.

Bosch is enjoying healthy growth in the Americas, Asia, and Eastern Europe. To maintain momentum, the company plans to invest in these markets even more.

However, Robert Bosch faces competitors that move manufacturing operations to low wage regions, and encroach into Bosch's traditional geographic markets. Moving jobs out of Germany is extremely unpopular, so Bosch is struggling with keeping domestic jobs while remaining competitive.

HISTORY

Self-taught electrical engineer Robert Bosch opened a Stuttgart workshop in 1886 and the following year produced the world's first alternator for a stationary engine. In 1897 his company built the first automobile alternator. Later electrical automotive product launches included spark plugs (1902), starters (1912), and regulators (1913). Bosch believed in treating employees well and shortened their workday to eight hours (extraordinary for 1906).

US operations begun in 1909 were confiscated during WWI as part of a trade embargo against Germany. Bosch survived the German depression of the 1920s, introduced power tools (1928) and appliances (1933), and bought Blaupunkt (car radios, 1933). Industrial and military demand for the company's products continued from the 1930s until WWII. Bosch died in 1942 and left 90% of his company to charity.

Bosch suffered severe damage in WWII, and its US operations were again confiscated. It rebuilt after the war and enjoyed growing demand for its appliances and automotive products as postwar incomes increased worldwide. In 1963 Hans Merkle took the helm. Believing fuel efficiency and pollution control would be important issues in the future, Bosch invested heavily to develop automotive components that would raise gas mileage and lower emissions. The company made the world's first electronic fuel-injection (EFI) system in 1967. That year Bosch and Siemens (West Germany) formed Bosch-Siemens Hausgerate to make home appliances.

The oil crisis of the 1970s increased awareness of fuel efficiency and benefited sales of EFI systems. Buying a plant in Charleston, South Carolina, Bosch re-entered the US in 1974 to make fuel-injection systems. It introduced the first antilock braking system in 1978.

A 1984 strike against Bosch in Germany disrupted automobile production throughout Europe. In the late 1980s the company developed technology for multiplexing (employing one wire to replace many by using semiconductor controllers) in automobiles, established it as an industry standard, and licensed it to chip makers Intel (US), Philips (the Netherlands), and Motorola (US). Throughout the 1980s and into the 1990s, Bosch acquired various telecommunications companies.

In 1993 Bosch's sales dropped for the first time since 1967. In response, the company cut its workforce. In 1996 Bosch bought Emerson's half of joint venture S-B Power Tool Co., which makes Bosch, Dremel, and Skil brand tools. Further consolidating its position as a world leader in braking systems, Bosch also purchased AlliedSignal's struggling light-vehicle braking unit. The company sold its private mobile radio business to Motorola in 1997 and, to speed its business for mobile phones, bought Dancall Telecom (a maker of mobile-phone handsets) from UK-based Amstrad.

In 1998 the company's Bosch-Siemens Hausgerate joint venture opened a plant in the US and bought Masco's Thermador unit (cooktops, ovens, and ranges). In 1999 Bosch sold its US-based telecom unit to a joint venture of Motorola and Cisco Systems. The next year UK-based General Electric Company (now Marconi) bought the German operations of Bosch's telecom unit.

Early in 2000 the company sold its mobile-phone business to Siemens AG. That year the company's joint venture with Siemens bought Rexroth AG (Atecs Mannesmann AG's automation and packaging technology group) for about $9.2 billion. The new division was named Bosch Rexroth AG. In 2001 Bosch bought out Siemens' stake in Bosch Rexroth and consolidated its operations as a wholly owned subsidiary.

EXECUTIVES

Chairman, Supervisory Council: Herman Scholl
Deputy Chairman, Supervisory Council: Walter Bauer
Chairman, Management Board: Franz Fehrenbach, age 56
Deputy Chairman, Management Board: Seigfried Dais
Director, Management Board: Wolfgang Chur
Director, Management Board: Rudolf Colm
Director, Management Board: Wolfgang Drees
Director, Management Board: Gerhard Kümmel
Director, Management Board: Kurt W. Liedtke
Director, Management Board: Wolfgang Malchow
Director, Management Board: Peter Marks
Director, Management Board; Chairman of Automotive Technology Business Sector: Bernd Bohr
President, Thermotechnology: Joachim Berner
President, Automotive Electronics: Volkmar Denner
President, Diesel Systems: Ulrich Dohle
President, Security Systems: Uwe Glock
President, Bosch Rexroth: Manfred Grundke, age 50
President, Packaging Technology: Friedbert Klefenz
President, Automotive Aftermarket: Eugen Konrad
President, Power Tools: Uwe Raschke
President, Car Multimedia: Wolf-Henning Scheider
President, Gasoline Systems: Peter Tyroller
President, Energy and Body Systems: Rainer Lohse
President, Chassis Systems Modulation: Werner Struth
President, Chassis Systems Actuation and Foundation: Andreas Wiegert
Auditors: PwC Deutsche Revision AG

LOCATIONS

HQ: Robert Bosch GmbH
Postfach 106050, D-70049 Stuttgart, Germany
Phone: +49-711-811-0   **Fax:** +49-711-811-6630
US HQ: 2800 S. 25th Ave., Broadview, IL 60155
US Phone: 708-865-5200   **US Fax:** 708-865-6430
Web: www.bosch.com

2004 Sales

	$ mil.	% of total
Europe	37,307	68
The Americas	9,746	18
Asia	6,632	12
Africa & Australia	885	2
Total	**54,570**	**100**

PRODUCTS/OPERATIONS

2004 Sales

	$ mil.	% of total
Automotive technology	34,473	63
Consumer goods & building technology	12,950	24
Industrial technology	7,147	13
Total	**54,570**	**100**

Selected Divisions and Products

Automotive Technology
  Automotive aftermarket
  Automotive electronics
  Car multimedia
  Chassis systems
  Diesel systems
  Energy and body systems
  Gasoline systems
Consumer Goods and Building Technology
  Household appliances
  Power tools
  Security systems
  Thermotechnology (gas-fired hot water heating systems)
Industrial Technology
  Bosch Rexroth
  Metals technology
  Packaging technology

COMPETITORS

American Standard	Key Safety Systems
Black & Decker	Lucent
BorgWarner	Magna Donnelly
DaimlerChrysler	Maytag
Dana	Motorola
DIRECTV	Nokia
Eaton	Pioneer
Electrolux	Prestolite Electric
Emerson Electric	Senior
Federal-Mogul	Siemens
Fiat	Snap-on
Ford	Stanley Works
GE	Tenneco
General Motors	Textron
Honeywell International	ThyssenKrupp
Ingersoll-Rand	Valeo
ITT Industries	Whirlpool
Johnson Controls	Yamaha

HISTORICAL FINANCIALS

Company Type: Private

Income Statement

FYE: December 31

	REVENUE ($ mil.)	NET INCOME ($ mil.)	NET PROFIT MARGIN	EMPLOYEES
12/04	54,570	2,285	4.2%	242,348
12/03	45,635	1,381	3.0%	232,000
12/02	36,659	681	1.9%	224,341
12/01	30,143	576	1.9%	220,999
12/00	30,058	1,300	4.3%	196,880
12/99	28,103	463	1.6%	194,889
12/98	30,029	507	1.7%	188,017
12/97	26,143	926	3.5%	180,639
12/96	26,490	322	1.2%	176,481
12/95	24,930	383	1.5%	156,771
Annual Growth	**9.1%**	**22.0%**	**—**	**5.0%**

2004 Year-End Financials

Debt ratio: 23.5%   Current ratio: 4.96
Return on equity: 14.5%   Long-term debt ($ mil.): 4,073
Cash ($ mil.): 4,298

Net Income History

Roche Holding

Roche is on a roll. The company operates two segments: pharmaceuticals and diagnostics. Roche's prescription drugs include cancer therapies Rituxan and Herceptin, antibiotic Rocephin, obesity treatment Xenical, AIDS drug Invirase, acne medication Accutane, and Tamiflu, which is used to prevent and treat influenza. The company markets many of its bestsellers with affiliates Genentech and Chugai Pharmaceutical. Roche's diagnostics arm offers advanced DNA tests, diabetes monitoring supplies, and point-of-care diagnostics used in a variety of health care settings. Descendants of the founding Hoffmann and Oeri families own half of the company. Fellow druggernaut Novartis owns 33% of the company.

To narrow its focus on pharmaceuticals and diagnostics, Roche sold its consumer health business, which included vitamins, the analgesic Aleve, and antacid Rennie, to Bayer HealthCare in 2005. The company had two years before sold its fine chemicals business to DSM. In 2000 Roche spun off Givaudan, a leader in fragrances and flavors, and BASILEA Pharmaceutica, its biotech division focused on infectious disease and skin disorder drugs.

Roche owns almost 60% of Genentech, one of the world's largest biotech companies, and has a 51% stake in Japan's Chugai Pharmaceutical. Roche includes the sales of these two holdings in its own financial results, helping give muscle to its bottom line. Genentech accounts for 14% of sales, and Chugai contributes 10%.

The bulk of Roche's research and development efforts are aimed at cancer, diabetes, central nervous system disorders, and autoimmune conditions. The company maintains several development alliances with other companies to beef up its pipeline.

In response to the fears of a pandemic of Avian Influenza Virus, Roche is ramping up its production of its antiviral drug Tamiflu and will produce over 300 million doses by 2007. The company is also in talks with a number of generic drug manufacturers and Asian governments to increase inventories through outsourced manufacturing.

HISTORY

Fritz Hoffmann-La Roche, backed by family wealth, began making pharmaceuticals in a lab in Basel, Switzerland, in 1894. At the time, drug compounds were mixed at pharmacies and lacked uniformity. Hoffmann was not a chemist, but saw the potential for mass-produced, standardized, branded drugs.

By WWI, Hoffman had become successful, selling Thiocal (cough medicine), Digalen (digitalis extract), and other products on four continents. During the war, the Bolsheviks seized the firm's St. Petersburg, Russia, facility, and its Warsaw plant was almost destroyed. Devastated, Hoffmann sold company shares outside the family in 1919 and died in 1920.

As WWII loomed, Roche divided its holdings between F. Hoffman-La Roche and Sapac, which held many of Roche's foreign operations. US operations became more important during the war. Roche synthesized vitamins C, A, and E (eventually becoming the world's top vitamin maker) and built plants and research centers worldwide.

Roche continued to develop such successful products as tranquilizers Librium (1960) and

Valium (1963), the world's best-selling prescription drug prior to anti-ulcer successors Tagamet (SmithKline Beecham, now part of GlaxoSmithKline) and Prilosec (AstraZeneca). Roche made its first fragrance and flavor buy, Givaudan, in 1963.

In the 1970s, after several governments accused it of price-gouging on Librium and Valium, Roche agreed to price restraints. The company was fined for vitamin price-fixing in 1976. It was also rapped that year for its slow response to an Italian factory dioxin leak that killed thousands of animals and forced hundreds of families to evacuate.

Roche became one of the first drugmakers to sell another's products when it agreed to sell Glaxo's Zantac ulcer treatment in the US in 1982. The move let Roche maintain its large US sales force at the time when Valium went off patent, decimating the company's drug sales.

Roche acquired a product pipeline when it bought a majority stake in genetic engineering firm Genentech in 1990. In 1994 it bought the struggling Syntex, solidifying its position in North America. The company gained Aleve and other products in 1996 when it bought out its joint venture with Procter & Gamble and also acquired Cincinnati-based flavors and fragrances firm Tastemaker.

In its biggest acquisition ever, Roche bought Corange in 1998 for $10.2 billion; its subsidiary Boehringer Mannheim was renamed Roche Molecular Biochemicals. In 1999 Roche announced it had located the gene that causes osteoarthritis. The company began to market anti-obesity pharmaceutical Xenical in the US that year, despite reports of some unpleasant side effects.

Also in 1999 Roche agreed to a record-setting fine to end a US Justice Department investigation into Roche's role in an alleged vitamin price-fixing cartel; in 2000 it agreed to pay out again (to 22 states) to settle a lawsuit regarding the cartel. A related European Union probe the following year also found Roche guilty and levied heavy fines against the firm. In 1999 and 2000 Roche squeezed cash out of its high-flying biotech progeny; it bought the 33% of Genentech it didn't own in 1999, then raised a total of almost $8 billion by reselling 42% of the firm in three offerings in 1999 and 2000.

Influenza drug Tamiflu failed to win European Union approval in 2000, but breast cancer drug Herceptin was OK'd there. Also that year the company spun off its fragrances and flavors unit Givaudan SA, and two long-time Roche leaders, chairman Fritz Gerber and CFO Henri Meier, retired; both remained on Roche's board for a brief time thereafter.

In 2001 rival Swiss pharmaceuticals firm Novartis bought a 20% stake in Roche from financier Martin Ebner's BZ Gruppe Holding. Roche sold its vitamins and fine chemicals business in 2003 to narrow its focus.

EXECUTIVES

Chairman and CEO: Franz B. Humer, age 59, $6,211,005 pay
Vice Chairman: Bruno Gehrig, age 58
Vice Chairman: Rolf Hänggi, age 61
CFO: Erich Hunziker, age 52, $2,005,545 pay
Medical Director: Salvatore Badalamenti

Head of Corporate Services and Human Resources and Secretary: Gottlieb A. Keller, age 50, $733,311 pay
Head of Diabetes Care: Staffan Ek, age 60
Head of Global Corporate Communications: Rolf D. Schläpfer, age 49
Head of Global Pharma Development: Eduard E. Holdener, age 60
Head of Global Research: Jonathan K. C. Knowles, age 57, $1,435,688 pay
Head of Pharma Partnering: Peter Hug, age 47
Head of Roche Group Media Office: Daniel Piller
Head of Science Communications: Katja Prowald
Head of the Chairman's Office: Pierre Jaccoud, age 50
Head of the Roche Center for Medical Genomics: Klaus Lindpaintner
CEO, Roche Pharmaceuticals: William M. Burns, age 57, $1,552,800 pay (prior to title change)
CEO, Roche Diagnostics: Heino von Prondzynski, age 55, $1,436,340 pay (prior to title change)
President and CEO, Roche North American Pharmaceuticals Operations and Hoffmann-La Roche: George B. Abercrombie
Compliance Officer: Andreas Greuter
Auditors: KPMG Klynveld Peat Marwick Goerdeler SA

LOCATIONS

HQ: Roche Holding Ltd
Grenzacherstrasse 124, CH-4070 Basel, Switzerland
Phone: +41-61-688-1111 **Fax:** +41-61-691-9391
US HQ: 340 Kingsland St., Nutley, NJ 07110-1199
US Phone: 973-235-5000 **US Fax:** 973-235-7605
Web: www.roche.com

Roche sells its products in more than 150 countries.

2004 Sales

	% of total
Europe	
European Union	34
Switzerland	2
Other countries	3
North America	35
Asia	
Japan	12
Other countries	5
Latin America	6
Africa, Australia & Oceania	3
Total	**100**

PRODUCTS/OPERATIONS

2004 Sales

	% of total
Pharmaceuticals	
Roche Pharmaceuticals	45
Genentech	14
Chugai Pharmaceutical	10
Roche Diagnostics	25
Consumer Health	6
Total	**100**

COMPETITORS

Abbott Labs
Amgen
AstraZeneca
Bristol-Myers Squibb
Chiron
Dade Behring
Diagnostic Products
Eli Lilly
GlaxoSmithKline
Johnson & Johnson
Merck
Novartis
Pfizer
Sanofi-Aventis
Schering-Plough
Wyeth

HISTORICAL FINANCIALS

Company Type: Public

Income Statement

FYE: December 31

	REVENUE ($ mil.)	NET INCOME ($ mil.)	NET PROFIT MARGIN	EMPLOYEES
12/04	27,630	5,867	21.2%	64,703
12/03	25,132	2,471	9.8%	65,357
12/02	21,423	(2,902)	—	69,659
12/01	15,638	2,210	14.1%	63,717
12/00	17,791	5,366	30.2%	64,758
12/99	17,326	3,623	20.9%	67,695
12/98	17,885	3,185	17.8%	66,707
12/97	12,885	2,937	22.8%	51,643
12/96	11,834	2,890	24.4%	48,972
12/95	12,754	2,921	22.9%	50,497
Annual Growth	**9.0%**	**8.1%**	**—**	**2.8%**

2004 Year-End Financials

Debt ratio: 24.6%
Return on equity: 26.7%
Cash ($ mil.): 2,302
Current ratio: 2.97
Long-term debt ($ mil.): 6,138

Net Income History

OTC: RHHVF

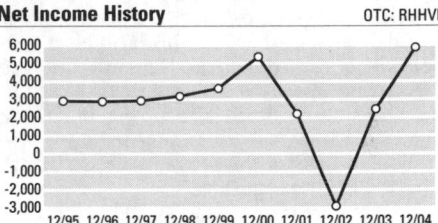

Rogers Communications

Canada is tuned in to Rogers Communications. As the nation's #1 cable TV operator, it has some 2.3 million subscribers throughout eastern Canada. The company's Rogers Wireless subsidiary is one of Canada's largest mobile phone outfits (the unit bought Microcell Communications in a deal worth roughly $1.3 billion in 2004). The Rogers Media unit owns 43 radio and two TV stations, and produces 70 consumer magazines and trade publications. In 2005, Rogers Communications entered the traditional phone market with the purchase of Call-Net Enterprises (now named Rogers Telecom Holdings), owner of Sprint Canada (also, now known as Rogers Telecom). CEO Ted Rogers controls about 91% of the firm's voting power. Microsoft has a minority stake.

The company formerly operated in British Columbia, but this Mr. Rogers moved neighborhoods when it swapped its western cable systems for Shaw Communications' eastern cable operations. Rogers is looking to become a one-stop communications shop for many of its neighbors.

Rogers' cable unit provides Internet access to more than 936,000 customers and in 2004 the company began offering co-branded Internet services with Yahoo! The cable networks are being upgraded for telephony services, and the company is poised to become a major player in that area now that it owns the former Sprint Canada. Rogers also offers a video-on-demand service, Rogers on Demand, which is able to reach almost 2 million homes. The company has introduced personal video recorders and launched high-definition TV channels.

In addition to magazines and its radio and television stations, Rogers Media also owns a regional sports network (Rogers Sportsnet), a home shopping network (The Shopping Channel), 50% of production and distribution firm Dome Productions. and numerous Internet holdings.

HISTORY

Edward Rogers, at age 21, transmitted Canada's first radio signal across the Atlantic in 1921. He invented the first alternating current (AC) radio tube in 1925, which revolutionized the home-receiver industry.

Son of a wealthy businessman, Rogers founded Rogers Majestic in Toronto in the mid-1920s to make his radio tubes. He also established several radio stations, including CFRB ("Canada's First Rogers Batteryless"), which later commanded the country's largest audience.

In 1931 Rogers won the first experimental license to broadcast TV, but his businesses were sold when he died in 1939. His son Ted Rogers Jr. was only five at the time, but even as a youngster he showed business acumen, buying up shares of Standard Broadcasting. In his twenties he bought CHFI, a Toronto radio station that pioneered FM broadcasting.

Rogers moved into cable TV and in 1967 was awarded licenses for Toronto, Brampton, and Leamington. Rogers Cable TV expanded when it bought Canadian Cablevision (1979) and Premier Cablevision (1980). With the takeover of UA-Columbia Cablevision in 1981, Rogers became Canada's largest cable operator.

The firm also began pushing cellular phone service through subsidiary Rogers Cantel in 1985. (The carrier won a license for nationwide coverage in 1992.) In 1986 all of Rogers' holdings were combined to form Rogers Communications.

Rogers acquired a stake in telecom company Unitel in 1989. When it received permission to sell long-distance in 1992, Unitel geared up to take on monopoly Bell Canada. However, the venture wasn't successful, and Rogers walked away from its 32% stake in 1995.

Meanwhile, in 1994 Rogers acquired rival cable TV and publishing firm Maclean-Hunter. The next year it acquired Shaw Communications' Vancouver cable system and began providing Internet access. After selling its 62% stake in Toronto Sun Publishing to management in 1996, Rogers extended its Internet content operations, including a partnership with Intuit to develop a financial Web site. (The company shuttered or reorganized many of its Internet operations in 2001.)

Expenses related to cable network upgrades and Cantel's development created operating losses for several years. To raise cash, in 1998 Rogers sold subsidiary Rogers Telecom to local phone startup MetroNet Communications and sold its home-security unit to Protection One. That year it turned its first profit in the 1990s.

In 1999 Microsoft paid $400 million for a 9% stake in the company; Rogers agreed to use Microsoft set-top box software and offer Microsoft's Web services to its customers. Also in 1999 AT&T and British Telecommunications (now BT Group) together bought a 33% stake in Cantel; Rogers' stake fell to 51%.

The next year Rogers agreed to buy Quebec cable operator Videotron. But media firm Quebecor, backed by pension fund manager Caisse, weighed in with a rival bid, and Rogers collected a breakup fee of about $160 million when Videotron terminated the companies' deal. Soon thereafter, the company announced the creation of Rogers Telecom (reusing the name), a unit set up to enter the telephone market.

Also in 2000 Rogers purchased an 80% stake in the Toronto Blue Jays baseball team for $112 million (it later acquired the remaining 20%). The next year Rogers gained another 75,000 cable subscribers with the acquisition of Cable Atlantic.

In 2001, AT&T Wireless bought out British Telecom's stake in Rogers Wireless, raising their ownership to a third. The same year, Rogers Communications offered to buy up the remaining shares of Rogers Wireless held by the public, but shareholders rejected the deal.

When, in 2004, Rogers Communications raised $250 million in capital, after having tried for up to $500 million, speculation abounded that the company would once again try to purchase AT&T Wireless' stake in Rogers Wireless, which later proved true. Rogers Communications has since bought all of the company that it didn't alread own in early 2005. Later that year the firm made another major purchase, this time the $264 million acquisition of Call-Net Enterprises, owner of Sprint Canada. (After the deal, Rogers rechristened Call-Net as Rogers Telecom Holdings, and changed the name of Sprint Canada to Rogers Telecom.)

EXECUTIVES

Chairman; Deputy Chairman, Rogers Wireless and Rogers Communications: H. Garfield (Gar) Emerson, age 64
Vice Chairman; VP, Rogers Cable: Philip B. (Phil) Lind, age 61
President and CEO; Chairman, Rogers Wireless and Rogers Cable; Vice Chairman, Rogers Media, and President and CEO, Rogers Telecommunications: Edward S. (Ted) Rogers, age 71, $2,835,581 pay
EVP: William W. (Bill) Linton
SVP Media; President and CEO, Rogers Media: Anthony P. (Tony) Viner, $1,334,231 pay
VP Business Development: Alexander R. Brock
VP Business Economics: David J. Watt
VP Business Performance: Richard Wong
VP and Chief Information Architect: Robert Terdeman
VP Communications: Jan L. Innes
VP Controller: Sarah Burcher
VP Convergence: Thomas A. Turner Jr.
VP Corporate Development: Bruce D. Day, age 49
VP Finance and CFO; VP Rogers Cable: Alan D. Horn, $1,538,048 pay
VP Human Resources: Donald B. (Don) Burt
VP Investor Relations: Bruce M. Mann
VP, General Counsel, and Secretary, Rogers Communications, Rogers Cable, and Rogers Wireless: David P. Miller, $815,573 pay
President and COO, Communications Division; and Director: Nadir H. Mohamed, $1,945,507 pay (prior to promotion)
Auditors: KPMG LLP

LOCATIONS

HQ: Rogers Communications Inc.
   333 Bloor St. East, 10th Fl.,
   Toronto, Ontario M4W 1G9, Canada
Phone: 416-935-7777   **Fax:** 416-935-3597
Web: www.rogers.com

PRODUCTS/OPERATIONS

2004 Sales

	$ mil.	% of total
Wireless	2,311.1	48
Cable	1,615.4	35
Media	747.0	16
Blue Jays	51.3	1
Adjustments	(50.9)	—
Total	**4,673.9**	**100**

Selected Operations

Cable
   Cable television
   Broadband Internet access
Media
   Radio
   TV broadcasting
   Televised shopping
   Publishing
Telephone
   Dial-up Internet access
   Local access
   Long-distance
   Teleconferencing
Wireless Communications
   Cellular service
   Data service
   Digital PCS
   Paging

Selected Subsidiaries

Rogers Cable Inc.
   Rogers Cable Communications Inc.
Rogers Media Inc.
   Blue Jays Holdco Inc.
   Rogers Broadcasting Ltd.
   Rogers Publishing Ltd.
Rogers Telecom Holdings
   Rogers Telecom
Rogers Wireless Communications Inc.
   Rogers Wireless Inc.
   Rogers Wireless Alberta Inc.
   Fido Inc.

COMPETITORS

Aliant
Alliance Atlantis Communications
Astral Media
Axia NetMedia
BCE
Bell Globemedia
Cancom
CanWest Global Communications
CBC
CHUM
Cogeco Cable
COGECO Inc.
Corus Entertainment
Fundy Communications
MTS Allstream
Persona
Quebecor
Shaw Communications
Sprint Nextel
Teleglobe
Telemedia
Tele-Metropole
TELUS
Transcontinental

HISTORICAL FINANCIALS

Company Type: Public

Income Statement

FYE: December 31

	REVENUE ($ mil.)	NET INCOME ($ mil.)	NET PROFIT MARGIN	EMPLOYEES
12/04	4,674	(11)	—	18,057
12/03	3,763	100	2.7%	15,027
12/02	2,747	198	7.2%	14,900
12/01	2,458	(273)	—	13,500
12/00	2,337	94	4.0%	12,700
12/99	2,148	581	27.0%	11,612
12/98	1,834	410	22.4%	10,010
12/97	1,885	(377)	—	10,300
12/96	1,812	(203)	—	16,425
12/95	1,975	(208)	—	14,000
Annual Growth	10.0%	—	—	2.9%

2004 Year-End Financials

Debt ratio: 323.1%
Return on equity: —
Cash ($ mil.): 203
Current ratio: 0.52
Long-term debt ($ mil.): 6,194

No. of shares (mil.): 275
Dividends
Yield: 0.3%
Payout: —
Market value ($ mil.): 7,197

Stock History

NYSE: RG

	STOCK PRICE ($) FY Close	P/E High/Low	PER SHARE ($) Earnings	Dividends	Book Value
12/04	26.15	— —	(0.23)	0.08	8.71
12/03	16.50	65 32	0.26	0.04	5.88
12/02	9.38	33 10	0.53	0.00	4.15
12/01	16.80	— —	(1.51)	0.00	7.23
12/00	17.00	119 50	0.29	0.03	7.89
12/99	24.75	10 3	2.55	0.00	5.05
12/98	8.88	5 2	1.89	0.00	(0.15)
12/97	4.88	— —	(2.22)	0.00	(2.03)
12/96	7.13	— —	(1.26)	0.00	0.19
Annual Growth	17.6%	— —	—	—	25.7%

Rolls-Royce

Rolls-Royce plc doesn't make luxury cars — BMW owns those operations — but it *can* provide serious horsepower. The company is the second-largest aircraft engine maker in the world, behind General Electric's GE Aircraft Engines division. Rolls-Royce's aerospace business makes commercial and military gas turbine engines for military, airline, and corporate aircraft customers worldwide. In the US, the company makes engines for regional and corporate jets, helicopters, and turboprop aircraft. Rolls-Royce also constructs and installs power generation systems and is one of the world's largest makers of marine propulsion systems.

Rolls-Royce's 1999 purchase of Vickers made it a world leader among makers of marine propulsion systems. That diversification may help since repercussions from the terrorist attacks of September 11 have hurt Rolls-Royce's civil aerospace operations. Previously, civil aerospace sales typically accounted for a bit over half of the company's sales; that figure dropped and stood at 48% of sales in 2003, but rebounded to 51% of sales as aircraft sales picked up in 2004. That year Rolls-Royce was also selected as one of two engine suppliers (the other was GE) for Boeing's upcoming 787 Dreamliner. Rolls-Royce engines were also used in the first flight of Airbus' A380 in 2005.

When engine deliveries dropped early in the decade, the company focused on increasing sales in the spare parts and aftermarket services arena. Rolls-Royce also sold off some non-core operations, including its Vickers Defence Systems unit. Sales of jet engines to Allied military forces still account for a large part of Rolls-Royce's business, however.

Rolls-Royce has used joint ventures to increase its global presence — more than 80% of its business is done outside the UK. Rolls-Royce shares its name with the luxury auto, but the two parted ways when the British government split them in 1971. German carmaker BMW owns 10% of Rolls-Royce.

HISTORY

In 1906 automobile and aviation enthusiast Charles Rolls and engineer Henry Royce unveiled the Silver Ghost, an automobile that earned Rolls-Royce a reputation as maker of the best car in the world.

A year after Rolls' 1910 death in a biplane crash, Royce suffered a breakdown. From his home Royce continued to design Rolls-Royce engines such as the Eagle, its first aircraft engine, in 1914, and other engines used to power airplanes during WWI — but management of the company fell to Claude Johnson, who remained chief executive until 1926.

Although the company returned to primarily making cars after WWI, its engines were used in several history-making flights and, in 1931, set world speed records for land, sea, and air. Rolls-Royce bought the Bentley Motor Company that year. In 1933 it introduced the Merlin engine, which powered the Spitfire, Hurricane, and Mustang fighters of WWII. Rolls-Royce began designing a jet engine in 1938 and over the years it pioneered the turboprop engine, turbofan, and vertical takeoff engine.

Realizing that it had to break into the lucrative US airliner market to stay alive, Rolls-Royce bought its main British competitor, Bristol-Siddley Engines in 1966. With Bristol-Siddley came its contract to build the engine for the Anglo-French Concorde in 1976 and a US presence.

Lockheed ordered the company's RB211 engine for its TriStar in 1968, but Rolls-Royce underestimated the project's technical and financial challenges and entered bankruptcy in 1971. The British government stepped in and nationalized the aerospace division and sold the auto group. The RB211 entered service on the TriStar in 1972 and on the Boeing 747 in 1977.

Rolls-Royce was reprivatized in 1987. In a diversification effort two years later, the company bought mining, marine, and power plant specialist Northern Engineering Industries. In the early 1990s the aerospace market was hurt by military spending cutbacks and a recession; the company cut over 18,000 jobs.

A joint venture with BMW launched the BR710 engine for Gulfstream and Canadair's long-range business jets in 1990. The company bought Allison Engine in 1995.

Rolls-Royce sold Parsons Power Generation Systems to Siemens in 1997. Also that year it won a contract to supply Trent 892 engines for Boeing 777 jets being built for American Airlines in a deal worth $1 billion.

In 1998 the British government approved a repayable investment of about $335 million in the company to develop a new model of Trent aircraft engines. Narrowing its focus, the company sold its power transmission and distribution business to Austria-based VA Technologie.

Rolls-Royce pumped up its gas and oil equipment business in 1999 by buying the rotating compression equipment unit of Cooper Cameron, and it became one of the world leaders in marine propulsion by acquiring Vickers. The company then bought the aero and industrial engine repair service of First Aviation Services and took full control of its aircraft-engine joint venture with BMW; in return BMW received a 10% stake in Rolls.

In 2000 subsidiary Rolls-Royce Energy Systems India Private was awarded its first order: producing a Bergen gas engine for Garden Silk Mills for powering a textile plant in India. That year Rolls-Royce won a contract to supply engines for Israel's El Al airline's Boeing 777s. Late in 2000 it was reported that the company would cut about 5,000 jobs over three years.

Early in 2001 Rolls-Royce sold most of its Vickers Turbine Components business. In October the company cut about 11% of its workforce in response to the worldwide crisis in the commercial jet business.

In 2002 the company announced that it had inked a 10-year, $2 billion deal to supply engines to Gulfstream Aerospace. That year Rolls-Royce sold its Vickers Defence Systems unit, which made tanks and armored vehicles, to Alvis Plc. In 2003 Sir Ralph Robins, who had been executive chairman for more than a decade, retired from his post. Early in 2004 Rolls-Royce and GE Aircraft Engines were picked to supply engines for Boeing's upcoming 787 Dreamliner. Rolls-Royce was also selected to supply engines for Airbus' upcoming behemoth A380.

EXECUTIVES

Non-Executive Chairman: Simon M. Robertson, age 64
Chief Executive: Sir John E. V. Rose, age 52, $2,053,329 pay
COO: John P. Cheffins, age 57, $1,225,063 pay
Finance Director: Andrew B. Shilston, age 49, $1,155,720 pay
Director, Engineering and Technology: Michael G. (Mike) Howse, age 62, $918,797 pay
Director, Human Resources: John R. Rivers, age 56
Director, Procurement: Chris J. Hole, age 57
President and CEO, Rolls-Royce North America: James M. Guyette, age 60, $1,013,181 pay
President, Civil Aerospace: Mike Terrett, age 47
President, Corporate & Regional Aircraft, Rolls-Royce North America Inc.: Ian C. Aitken
President, Defence Aerospace: Colin H. Green, age 57, $1,042,075 pay
President, Energy: E. Thomas (Tom) Curley, age 48
President, Helicopters, Rolls-Royce North America: Stuart Mullan, age 40
President, Marine: Saul Lanyado

Company Secretary and Director of Government Relations: Charles E. Blundell, age 53
Chairman, Rolls-Royce Deutschland: Axel Arendt, age 56
COO, Rolls Royce Corporation: Steven F. (Steve) Dwyer
Director, Gas Turbine Operations: Mike Lloyd
Managing Director, Airlines: Charles Cuddington, age 54
Director, Services: Miles A. Cowdry
Auditors: KPMG Audit Plc

LOCATIONS

HQ: Rolls-Royce plc
65 Buckingham Gate,
London SW1E 6AT, United Kingdom
Phone: +44-20-7222-9020   **Fax:** +44-20-7227-9178
US HQ: 14850 Conference Center Dr.,
Chantilly, VA 20151
US Phone: 703-834-1700   **US Fax:** 703-709-6087
Web: www.rolls-royce.com

Rolls-Royce has operations in about 15 countries and sells its products around the world.

2004 Sales

	$ mil.	% of total
North America		
US	3,744.5	33
Canada	394.9	4
Europe		
UK	1,762.5	15
Other countries	1,837.6	16
Asia	2,484.8	22
Africa	377.5	3
Australasia	163.7	1
Other regions	674.2	6
Total	**11,439.7**	**100**

PRODUCTS/OPERATIONS

2004 Sales

	$ mil.	% of total
Civil Aerospace	5,855.6	51
Defence	2,646.6	23
Marine	1854.9	16
Energy	941.9	9
Financial Services	140.7	1
Total	**11,439.7**	**100**

Selected Products and Services

Aircraft engines
Diesel engines
Engine support services
Gas turbine systems
Industrial power plants
Marine equipment
Nuclear submarine propulsion systems
Overhaul and repair services
Ship engines
Shiplift systems

COMPETITORS

AAR	Hitachi
ABB Inc.	Honeywell International
Bechtel	Ishikawajima-Harima
Cummins	Kawasaki Heavy Industries
DaimlerChrysler	Marubeni
Emerson Electric	McDermott
Fiat	Peter Kiewit Sons'
Fluor	Pratt & Whitney
GE Aircraft Engines	SAFRAN
GE Aircraft Engines UK	Siemens
GE Honda Aero Engines	Textron
Halliburton	Volvo

HISTORICAL FINANCIALS

Company Type: Public

Income Statement

FYE: December 31

	REVENUE ($ mil.)	NET INCOME ($ mil.)	NET PROFIT MARGIN	EMPLOYEES
12/04	11,440	393	3.4%	35,200
12/03	10,036	206	2.1%	36,100
12/02	9,283	85	0.9%	39,200
12/01	9,182	154	1.7%	43,300
12/00	8,753	124	1.4%	46,600
12/99	7,669	459	6.0%	40,900
12/98	7,458	428	5.7%	42,000
12/97	7,149	370	5.2%	42,600
12/96	7,290	(80)	—	42,600
Annual Growth	**5.8%**	**—**	**—**	**(2.4%)**

2004 Year-End Financials

Debt ratio: 59.1%
Return on equity: 9.5%
Cash ($ mil.): 1,460
Current ratio: 1.79
Long-term debt ($ mil.): 2,627

Net Income History

OTC: RYCEY

Royal Ahold

A tattered prince of global food retailing, Royal Ahold owns, services, or has interests in about 4,000 supermarkets, hypermarkets, discount stores, and specialty stores in Europe and the Americas. The company is the world's third-largest grocery retailer (behind Wal-Mart and Carrefour), as well as a leading supermarket operator in the US (mainly on the East Coast under names such as Giant Food, Stop & Shop, and Tops Markets), and also owns food distributor U.S. Foodservice. Royal Ahold runs Albert Heijn, the #1 food retailer in the Netherlands and Schuitema, a Dutch retailer and food distributor (73%-owned). Other interests include online food retailer Peapod and a 60% stake in Scandinavian food seller ICA AB.

In the Netherlands, the company owns or franchises the Albert Heijn supermarket chain (about 700 stores), as well as nearly 500 Gall & Gall liquor stores, and some 425 Etos health and beauty care stores. Its other European holdings include ICA AB, with about 2,800 outlets.

Often working with local partners, Royal Ahold has developed grocery chains in Indonesia, Malaysia, and Thailand. But a massive accounting scandal, most of it at U.S. Foodservice, and economic weakness in Latin America are causing the global food retailer to retrench by selling its Asian and Latin American holdings — among others — to reduce debt and focus on more-stable markets.

With its restructuring almost complete, Royal Ahold is setting its sights on markets closer to home in Central Europe. To that end,

the company recently acquired 56 Julius Meinl supermarkets in the Czech Republic.

In addition to Bruno's and BI-LO grocery chains in the southeastern US, Royal Ahold has sold its chain of 198 Wilson Farms and Sugarcreek convenience stores in the US. Meanwhile, Dutch shareholders filed suit against Royal Ahold in 2004, demanding that the company nullify and restate its accounts from 1998 to 2002. In response to pressure from investors, Royal Ahold has restructured its supervisory board and adopted measures to increase shareholder's rights. However, unforgiving shareholders on both sides of the Atlantic are demanding an independent investigation into alleged financial mismanagement at the company.

Jim Miller, ex-CEO of U.S. Foodservice, filed a lawsuit against his former employer in February 2004 for failing to pay severance and retirement benefits and $10 million in damages. Four former senior executives of U.S. Foodservice have been charged with fraud for artificially inflating the company's earnings by some $800 million from 2000 to 2002. Miller has not been charged.

HISTORY

Albert Heijn and his wife took over his father's grocery store in Ootzaan, Netherlands, in 1887. By the end of WWI, the company had 50 Albert Heijn grocery stores in Holland, and at WWII's end it had almost 250 stores. In 1948 the company went public.

It opened its first self-service store in 1952 and its first supermarket in 1955. Growing into the #1 grocer in the Netherlands, Albert Heijn opened liquor and cosmetic stores in 1973. (It changed its name to Ahold that year to better reflect its range of businesses.) Ahold expanded outside the Netherlands in 1976 when it founded supermarket chain Cadadia in Spain (sold 1985).

Ahold entered the US in 1977 by purchasing BI-LO and furthered its expansion in 1981 by adding Pennsylvania-based Giant Food Stores. In 1987, in honor of its 100th anniversary, Ahold was granted the title Koninklijke (Dutch for "royal"). In 1988 it bought a majority stake in Dutch food wholesaler Schuitema.

The company added New York-based Tops Markets in 1991. That year Royal Ahold founded food retailer and distributor Euronova (now called Ahold Czech Republic), and in 1992 it acquired 49% of Portuguese food retailer Jerónimo Martins Retail. In 1993 Cees van der Hoeven was promoted to chief executive and Royal Ahold was listed on the NYSE.

Other acquisitions included New England grocery giant The Stop & Shop Companies in 1996. That year saw the beginning of several Asian joint ventures that gave Royal Ahold stores in Singapore, Malaysia, and Thailand. Royal Ahold's moves in 1999 included the acquisition of several Spanish supermarket chains, the purchase of Dutch institutional food wholesaler Gastronoom, and the acquisition of 50% of Sweden's top food seller, ICA AB.

In 2000 Royal Ahold acquired Spanish food retailer Kampio, #2 and #4 foodservice distributors U.S. Foodservice and PYA/Monarch. The retailer in 2001 purchased Alliant Exchange, parent of Alliant Foodservice, which distributes food to more than 100,000 customers, and Bruno's Supermarkets, which operates more than 180 stores in the Southeast.

Royal Ahold reported its first net loss in nearly 30 years in the second quarter of 2002. In 2003

CEO Cees van der Hoeven and CFO Michiel Meurs resigned following an announcement that the grocery giant would restate its financial results by at least $500 million because of accounting irregularities at U.S. Foodservice. (Van der Hoeven is facing charges by Dutch prosecutors in connection with the scandal at U.S. Foodservice.) Chairman Henny de Ruiter became acting CEO. In May 2003 IKEA veteran Anders Moberg became acting CEO; de Ruiter remained chairman. Soon after, Ahold said it would restate earnings downward by $880 million (much more than the original $500 million projection) because of the accounting scandal at U.S. Foodservice. Adding to its woes, in July the public prosecutor in Amsterdam launched a criminal investigation into possible falsification of accounts by the company.

In October 2003 Royal Ahold published its long-awaited 2002 results revealing a $1.27 billion loss, which the retailer attributed to special charges related to overstated profits at U.S. Foodservice. At a shareholders meeting in 2004, Ahold placed the blame for the accounting scandal, which nearly bankrupted the company in 2003, squarely on the shoulders of Jim Miller, the former CEO of U.S. Foodservice. In September, Ahold reached a settlement with the Dutch Public Prosecutor in which the company agreed to pay €8 million. In return, the Dutch prosecutor will not undertake proceedings against Royal Ahold.

In November the company settled a US class action lawsuit by paying $1.1 billion to shareholders who purchased stock between July 3, 1999 and February 23, 2003; just before the 2003 accounting scandal broke. Concurrently, the company reached an agreement to settle litigation with the Dutch Shareholders' Association.

EXECUTIVES

Chairman: René Dahan, age 64
Vice Chairman: Jan H. M. Hommen, age 62
President and CEO: Anders C. Moberg, age 55, $1,231,351 pay (partial-year salary)
CFO: John Rishton, age 47
SVP, Chief Accounting Officer and Interim CFO: Joost L.M. Sliepenbeek, age 42
EVP, Chief Corporate Governance Counsel: Peter Wakkie, age 57, $128,030 pay (partial-year salary)
SVP, Chief Business Controlling Officer: Brian W. Hotarek, age 59
SVP, Chief Business Support Officer: Arthur J. (A. J.) Brouwer, age 44
SVP, Chief Human Resources Officer: James G. (Jim) Lawler, age 46
SVP, Chief Treasury and Tax Officer: Kimberly Ross, age 40
Corporate Secretary: Norbert L. J. (Nol) Berger, age 52
SVP, Finance and Fiscal Affairs: André Buitenhuis, age 58
SVP, Legal Affairs and General Counsel: A. H. P. M. (Ton) van Tielraden, age 50
SVP, Corporate Communications: Kerry Underhill, age 46
President and CEO, Giant Food Stores/Tops Markets: Anthony (Tony) Schiano
President and CEO, U.S. Foodservice: Lawrence S. (Larry) Benjamin, age 50
Director, Corporate Communications: Walter Samuels
Director, Human Resources: Jeroen Burger
Director, Public Relations: Nick Gale
Director, Investor Relations: Henk Wurfbain
Auditors: Deloitte & Touche AB

LOCATIONS

HQ: Royal Ahold N.V.
(Koninklijke Ahold N.V.)
Albert Heijnweg 1,
1507 EH Zaandam, The Netherlands
Phone: +31-75-659-9111   **Fax:** +31-75-659-8350
US HQ: 1385 Hancock St., Quincy Center Plaza, Quincy, MA 02169
US Phone: 781-380-8000   **US Fax:** 617-770-8190
Web: www.ahold.com

Royal Ahold operates or has interest in supermarkets and specialty stores in Europe (Baltic republics, Belgium, the Czech Republic, Denmark, the Netherlands, Norway, Poland, Portugal, Slovakia, and Sweden), Latin America (Argentina, El Salvador, Guatemala, and Honduras), and the US.

2004 Sales

	% of total
US	72
Europe	27
Other regions	1
Total	**100**

2004 Stores

	No.
Europe	2,541
US	1,499
Other regions	32
Total	**4,072**

PRODUCTS/OPERATIONS

2004 Sales

	% of total
Retail	69
Foodservice	31
Total	**100**

Selected Operations

Retail
  Central and South America
    CARHCO (33%; discount supermarkets; Costa Rica, Honduras, Nicaragua)
    Disco S.A. (supermarkets, Argentina)
    La Fragua (83%; supermarkets; Guatemala, El Salvador, Honduras)
  Europe
    Albert (supermarkets, Czech Republic)
    Albert Heijn (supermarkets)
    Etos (health and beauty stores)
    Feira Nova (hypermarkets, Portugal)
    Gall & Gall (liquor stores)
    Hypernova (hypermarkets, Czech Republic and Poland)
    ICA AB (60%, supermarkets, Scandinavia)
    Jerónimo Martins (49%, supermarkets and hypermarkets, Portugal)
    Max (supermarkets, Poland)
    Pingo Doce (supermarkets, Portugal)
    Prima (mini-hypermarkets, Czech Republic)
    Schuitema (73%, wholesale supplier)
    Sesam (supermarkets, Poland)
  US
    Giant-Carlisle (supermarkets)
    Giant-Landover (supermarkets)
    Stop & Shop (supermarkets)
    Tops (supermarkets)
Foodservice
  PYA/Monarch (US)
  U.S. Foodservice
Other
  Ahold Real Estate (real estate development; The Netherlands, US)
  Peapod (online grocery shopping, US)
  Statoil (50%, gasoline stations, Scandinavia)

COMPETITORS

A&P	Kroger
Albertson's	Laurus
ALDI	Lidl & Schwarz Stiftung
Auchan	Meijer
Carrefour	METRO AG
Casino Guichard	NorgesGruppen
Delhaize	Red Apple Group
Eroski	Safeway
Golub	Shaw's
Hannaford Bros.	SYSCO
IGA	Tengelmann
ITM Entreprises	Tesco
Kooperativa Förbundet	Wal-Mart

HISTORICAL FINANCIALS
Company Type: Public

Income Statement
FYE: Sunday nearest December 31

	REVENUE ($ mil.)	NET INCOME ($ mil.)	NET PROFIT MARGIN	EMPLOYEES
12/04	70,439	(591)	—	206,441
12/03	70,489	(1)	—	257,140
12/02	65,836	(1,269)	—	341,909
12/01	59,354	993	1.7%	404,453
12/00	49,449	1,052	2.1%	377,000
12/99	33,811	758	2.2%	309,000
12/98	30,946	639	2.1%	235,248
12/97	24,961	461	1.8%	218,446
12/96	20,891	362	1.7%	191,267
12/95	18,431	284	1.5%	139,839
Annual Growth	**16.1%**	**—**	**—**	**4.4%**

2004 Year-End Financials

Debt ratio: 157.2%
Return on equity: —
Cash ($ mil.): 4,430
Current ratio: 1.19
Long-term debt ($ mil.): 9,795
No. of shares (mil.): 1,554
Dividends
Yield: 0.0%
Payout: —
Market value ($ mil.): 12,077

Stock History
NYSE: AHO

	STOCK PRICE ($) FY Close	P/E High/Low		PER SHARE ($) Earnings	Dividends	Book Value
12/04	7.77	—	—	(0.42)	0.00	4.01
12/03	7.76	—	—	(0.05)	0.70	3.93
12/02	12.73	—	—	(1.41)	0.66	2.94
12/01	29.39	30	23	1.10	0.60	5.70
12/00	32.50	23	15	1.39	0.49	2.89
12/99	29.94	37	22	1.14	0.37	3.31
12/98	37.00	34	23	1.09	0.00	2.89
12/97	26.13	37	23	0.87	0.00	2.92
12/96	20.56	26	16	0.82	0.26	2.73
12/95	13.69	18	13	0.78	0.00	3.74
Annual Growth	**(6.1%)**	**—**	**—**	**—**	**—**	**0.8%**

Royal Bank
of Canada

Royal Bank of Canada sits enthroned as Canada's banking monarch. Also known as RBC Financial Group — and Canada's largest financial institution — the bank operates in three segments: a Canadian consumer unit, which includes banking, investments, and insurance; an international consumer unit (banking and investments in the US and abroad); and a global wholesale unit (capital markets and corporate and commercial banking). In addition to more than 1,300 domestic locations, the bank has about 40 offices in the Caribbean and more in some 30 countries. Its US operations include RBC Centura Banks, which operates in the Southeast, and brokerage firm RBC Dain Rauscher.

Other subsidiaries include investment bank RBC Dominion Securities (aka RBC Capital Markets), Canadian discount brokerage RBC Action Direct, and RBC Insurance.

RBC Centura has been purchasing community banks and other small financial services in the South and plans to add more branches in Georgia, Florida, and the Carolinas. However, the company is re-evaluating many of its other US operations. It sold Houston-based home lender RBC Mortgage to New Century Financial in 2005.

Beyond North America, RBC provides foreign exchange services and import/export services for multinational clients. The bank has set out to become a leader in wealth management, acquiring and adding services to attract high-net-worth clients (and the fees it can charge them for handling their assets). To that end, it acquired private bank Abacus Financial Services Group, which has five offices in the UK and another in Amsterdam. RBC has paired with Belgium-based bank Dexia to form a joint venture called RBC Dexia Investor Services, which will provide investment administration services to institutional clients.

HISTORY

Royal Bank of Canada (RBC) has looked south of the border ever since its 1864 creation as Merchants Bank in Halifax, Nova Scotia, a port city bustling with trade spawned by the US Civil War. After incorporating in 1869 as Merchants Bank of Halifax, the bank added branches in eastern Canada. Merchants opened a branch in Bermuda in 1882. Gold strikes in Canada and Alaska in the late 1890s pushed it into western Canada.

Merchants opened offices in New York and Cuba in 1899 and changed its name to Royal Bank of Canada in 1901. RBC moved into new Montreal headquarters in 1907 and grew by purchasing such banks as Union Bank of Canada (1925). In 1928 it moved into the 42-story Royal Bank Building, then the tallest in the British Empire.

The bank faltered during the Depression but recovered during WWII. After the war RBC financed the expanding minerals and oil and gas industries. When Castro took power in Cuba, RBC tried to operate its branches under communist rule but sold out to Banco Nacional de Cuba in 1960.

RBC opened offices in the UK in 1979 and in West Germany, Puerto Rico, and the Bahamas in 1980. As Canada's banking rules relaxed, RBC bought Dominion Securities in 1987. The US

Federal Reserve approved RBC's brokerage arm for participation in stock underwriting in 1991.

In 1992 the bank faced a $650 million loss after backing the Reichmann family's Olympia & York property development company, which failed under the weight of its UK projects. The next year an ever-diversifying RBC bought Royal Trustco, Canada's #2 trust company, and Voyageur Travel Insurance, its largest retail travel insurer. A management shakeup in late 1994 ended with bank president John Cleghorn taking control of the company.

In 1995 RBC listed on the New York Stock Exchange and the next year joined with Heller Financial (an affiliate of Japan's Fuji Bank) to finance trade between Canada and Mexico. It began offering PC home banking in 1996 and Internet banking in 1997. That year RBC became one of the world's largest securities-custody service providers with its acquisition of The Bank of Nova Scotia's institutional and pension custody operations.

The company and Bank of Montreal agreed to merge in 1998, but Canadian regulators, fearing the concentration of banking power seen in the US, rejected the merger. In response, the bank trimmed its workforce and orchestrated a sale-leaseback of its property portfolio (1999).

In the late 1990s RBC grew its online presence by purchasing the Internet banking operations of Security First Network Bank (now Security First Technologies, 1998), the online trading division of Bull & Bear Group (1999), and 20% of AOL Canada (1999). It also bought several trust and fiduciary services businesses from Ernst & Young.

In 2000 it acquired US mortgager Prism Financial (now RBC Mortgage) and the Canadian retail credit card business of BANK ONE. RBC also sold its commercial credit portfolio to U.S. Bancorp and bought the insurance subsidiaries of South Carolina-based Liberty Corporation to boost its US operations. The company agreed to pay a substantial fine after institutional asset management subsidiary RT Capital Management came under scrutiny from the Ontario Securities Commission for alleged involvement in illegal pension-fund stock manipulation. RBC ended up selling RT Capital to UBS AG the following year.

Also in 2001 RBC made another US purchase: North Carolina's Centura Banks (now RBC Centura Banks). It sold Bull & Bear Securities to JB Oxford Holdings of Los Angeles.

EXECUTIVES

Chairman: David P. O'Brien, age 63
President, CEO, and Director: Gordon M. Nixon, age 47, $2,227,935 pay
COO: Barbara G. Stymiest
Group Head, US and International: Peter Armenio, $1,078,694 pay
Group Head, Implementation Office and Human Resources: Elisabetta Bigsby
Group Head, Global Technology and Operations; Chairman and CEO, Royal Trust Corporation of Canada: Martin J. (Marty) Lippert, $1,579,077 pay
Group Head, Personal and Business Clients, Canada; Chairman and CEO, RBC Insurance: W. James (Jim) Westlake
Group Head, Global Capital Markets; President and CEO, RBC Capital Markets: Charles M. (Chuck) Winograd, $2,929,948 pay
EVP and CFO: Janice R. Fukakusa, $276,785 pay
EVP and Chief Risk Officer: Morten Friis
EVP and General Counsel: David Allgood
EVP, Corporate Treasury and Treasurer: James B. (Jim) Archer-Shee
EVP, Government and Community Affairs: Charles S. (Charlie) Coffey
EVP; President and CEO, Royal Mutual Funds: Anne Lockie
EVP, Corporate Treasury: Ian MacKay
EVP, RBC Global Services: José Placido
SVP, Investor Relations: Nabanita Merchant
VP and Secretary: Carol J. McNamara
VP and Chief Economist: Craig Wright
Head of Strategy and Development; CEO, RBC Capital Partners: Alan Hibben
Auditors: Deloitte & Touche LLP

LOCATIONS

HQ: Royal Bank of Canada
  200 Bay St., Toronto, Ontario M5J 2J5, Canada
Phone: 416-974-5151   **Fax:** 416-955-7800
US HQ: 1 Liberty Plaza, New York, NY 10006
US Phone: 212-428-6200   **US Fax:** 212-428-2329
Web: www.rbc.com

PRODUCTS/OPERATIONS

2004 Sales

	% of total
Interest	
Loans	40
Securities	14
Other	3
Noninterest	
Insurance premiums, investment & fee income	9
Trading revenues	6
Investment management & custodial fees	5
Securities brokerage commissions	5
Deposit & payment service charges	4
Underwriting & other advisory fees	4
Mutual fund revenues	3
Other	7
Total	**100**

2004 Assets

	% of total
Cash & equivalents	2
Trading account securities	20
Other securities	9
Assets purchased under reverse repurchase agreements	8
Residential mortgages	19
Personal loans	8
Credit card loans	1
Business & government loans	14
Derivative-related amounts	9
Other	10
Total	**100**

Selected Subsidiaries

RBC Alternative Assets, L.P. (US)
RBC Capital Investment Holdings (USA) Inc.
RBC Capital Partners Limited
RBC Capital Trust
RBC Capital Trust II
RBC Centura Banks, Inc. (US)
RBC Dominion Securities Limited
RBC Finance B.V. (The Netherlands)
  Royal Bank of Canada Holdings (UK) Limited
  RBC Holdings (Channel Islands) Limited (UK)
  Royal Bank of Canada (Suisse) (Switzerland)
RBC Global Services Australia Pty Limited
RBC Investment Management (Asia) Limited
  (Hong Kong)
RBC Technology Ventures Inc.
RBCF L.P. (US)
Royal Bank Holding Inc.
  Connor Clark Ltd.
  Investment Holdings (Cayman) Limited
  R.B.C. Holdings (Bahamas) Limited
  RBC Action Direct Inc.
  RBC Asset Management Inc.
  RBC Capital Markets Arbitrage, LLC (US)
  RBC Capital Markets Arbitrage, SA (Luxembourg)
  RBC Holdings (USA) Inc.
  RBC Insurance Holdings Inc.
  Royal Bank of Canada (Asia) Limited (Singapore)
Royal Bank of Canada Financial Corporation
Royal Mutual Funds Inc.
The Royal Trust Company
Royal Trust Corporation of Canada

Bank of America
Barclays
BB&T
BCE
Bear Stearns
BMO Financial Group
CIBC
Citigroup
Citigroup Global Markets
Deutsche Bank
First Citizens BancShares
FMR
Goldman Sachs
HSBC Holdings
JPMorgan Chase
Laurentian Bank
Mellon Financial
Merrill Lynch
National Bank of Canada
Nomura Securities
Scotiabank
TD Bank
UBS
UBS Financial Services

HISTORICAL FINANCIALS

Company Type: Public

Income Statement

FYE: October 31

	ASSETS ($ mil.)	NET INCOME ($ mil.)	INCOME AS % OF ASSETS	EMPLOYEES
10/04	352,027	2,311	0.7%	57,795
10/03	305,620	2,279	0.7%	60,812
10/02	242,006	1,773	0.7%	59,549
10/01	226,370	1,519	0.7%	57,568
10/00	193,076	1,450	0.8%	49,232
10/99	185,761	1,173	0.6%	60,168
10/98	177,783	1,182	0.7%	60,035
10/97	173,814	1,192	0.7%	50,719
10/96	163,011	1,069	0.7%	54,700
10/95	137,206	943	0.7%	49,011
Annual Growth	11.0%	10.5%	—	1.8%

2004 Year-End Financials

Equity as % of assets: 4.0%
Return on assets: 0.7%
Return on equity: 16.8%
Long-term debt ($ mil.): 6,657
No. of shares (mil.): 640

Dividends
Yield: 2.1%
Payout: 31.7%
Market value ($ mil.): 33,287
Sales ($ mil.): 20,672

Stock History

NYSE: RY

10/95 10/96 10/97 10/98 10/99 10/00 10/01 10/02 10/03 10/04

	STOCK PRICE ($) FY Close	P/E High/Low		PER SHARE ($) Earnings	Dividends	Book Value
10/04	52.02	15	12	3.47	1.10	23.33
10/03	48.18	15	10	3.33	1.12	21.24
10/02	35.27	15	11	2.52	0.94	18.13
10/01	29.50	16	12	2.24	0.89	16.98
10/00	31.63	15	9	2.23	1.08	14.49
10/99	21.59	17	12	1.69	0.61	13.65
10/98	23.00	19	11	1.72	0.59	12.48
10/97	26.84	16	9	1.75	0.54	11.96
10/96	16.50	11	7	1.53	0.25	12.44
10/95	11.25	9	8	1.31	0.00	10.74
Annual Growth	18.5%	—	—	11.4%	—	9.0%

Royal Bank of Scotland

It only seems like some banks print their own money — Royal Bank of Scotland (RBS) really does. In fact, it has been producing its own banknotes for nearly three centuries. Operating as Royal Bank of Scotland, NatWest, and Ulster Bank, the company has approximately 2,300 locations that offer such services as deposit accounts, credit cards, and mortgages to commercial and personal clients in Scotland, England, Wales, and Ireland. RBS also sells insurance and investment products over the telephone through its Direct Line subsidiary, and provides private banking through The Coutts Group. In the US it owns Citizens Financial and RBS Lynk (formerly Lynk Systems).

Citizens Financial is one of the largest foreign-owned banks in the US, with more than 1,500 branches in the Northeast, where it operates as Citizens Bank, and the Midwest, where it operates as Charter One. RBS bought Lynk Systems, an Atlanta-based payment processing firm, for some $525 million in cash in 2004.

RBS has organized its business into eight divisions: Corporate Banking and Financial Markets, Retail Banking (Royal Bank and NatWest), Retail Direct, Manufacturing (operations support for the customer-facing businesses), Wealth Management, RBS Insurance (including Churchill Insurance), Ulster Bank, and Citizens Financial.

Some of the divisions are busy growing through acquisitions. In 2004 Ulster Bank bought First Active and Citizens Financial bought Cleveland-based Charter One Financial. Its leasing arm, Lombard, owns one of the UK's largest car dealerships, Dixon Motors.

In 2004 RBS paid about $360 million for the credit card business of Connecticut-based People's Bank, a deal that beefed up the bank's presence in the US credit card market. RBS is also establishing a presence in China by buying a stake in, and forming a strategic partnership with, Bank of China, one of the country's largest banks.

If you have overdraft protection for your checking account, you can thank RBS, which invented the service in 1728.

HISTORY

Royal Bank of Scotland was founded in 1727, but its roots go back to the Darien Company, a merchant expedition that was established to set up a Scottish trading colony in Panama. The Darien expedition ended disastrously in 1699. In 1707 England voted to compensate Scottish creditors for the colony's failure (in part because England had promised support, then reneged, contributing to the collapse), and a small industry sprang up around paying creditors and loaning them money. In 1727 the Equivalent Company, the combined entity of these organizations, was granted a banking charter and became Royal Bank of Scotland.

In 1826 the Parliament voted to take away Scottish banks' right to issue banknotes for less than five pounds, which would have required banks to use gold or silver. Few banks had such reserves, and the move sparked an outcry. Novelist Sir Walter Scott's *The Letters of Malachi Malagrowther*, which defended the Scottish one-pound note, helped shoot down the proposal.

RBS expanded throughout Scotland over the next 50 years. It opened a London branch in 1874; it didn't establish a branch outside London until it bought Williams Deacon's Bank, which had a branch network in North England. RBS continued to use the Williams Deacon's name, as it did with Glyn, Mills & Co., which it purchased in 1939.

In 1968 RBS took on its modern persona as a public company when it merged with National Commercial Bank. The company moved overseas during the 1970s, establishing offices in Hong Kong and major US cities.

RBS spent the next 20 years trying to achieve another merger of the same scale as National Commercial. In 1981 the bank was wooed by Standard Chartered Bank and Hongkong and Shanghai Bank (now part of HSBC Holdings), but British regulators denied both suitors.

The bank moved into telephone operations in 1985, when it set up Direct Line for selling car insurance. In 1988 RBS bought New England bank Citizens Financial. In 1989 the company entered into an alliance with Banco Santander (now Santander Central Hispano), Spain's largest banking group. The alliance created a cross-pollination of ideas and strategies that boosted both banks' operations. The first fruit of the alliance came in 1991 with the launch of Interbank On-line Systems (IBOS), which connected several European banks and allowed for instantaneous money transfers.

In the 1990s RBS was linked with a variety of partners. It even made a bid for the much larger bank Barclays, in a move regarded as cheeky, but was rebuffed. In 1997 it announced a joint venture with Richard Branson's Virgin Group called Virgin Direct to offer personal banking. The company also bought Angel Trains Contract, a rolling stock leasing company, and established a transatlantic banking transfer system (similar to IBOS) with US bank CoreStates (now owned by First Union).

In 1999 RBS opened a branch in Frankfurt as a base for European activities. The next year Citizens Financial bought UST Corp., making it the #2 bank in New England next to FleetBoston.

The next year RBS acquired NatWest after a prolonged takeover battle with rival Bank of Scotland (now part of HBOS plc). The bank sold Gartmore Investment Management, its fund management unit, to Nationwide Mutual Insurance Company. Royal Bank also sold the assets of NatWest's Equity Partners unit and launched NatWest Private Banking to target wealthy investors.

EXECUTIVES

Chairman: Sir George R. Mathewson, age 64, $1,044,000 pay
Executive Chairman, Retail Markets: Gordon Pell, age 55, $2,382,087 pay (prior to promotion)
Deputy Chairman: Sir Thomas F.W. (Tom) McKillop, age 61
Group Chief Executive and Executive Director: Sir Fred A. Goodwin, age 47, $4,796,238 pay
Group Finance Director and Executive Director: Frederick I. (Fred) Watt, age 45, $2,436,643 pay
Executive Director; Chairman and CEO, Citizens Financial Group: Lawrence K. (Larry) Fish, age 60
Chief Executive, Corporate Banking and Financial Markets: Johnny Cameron
Chief Executive, Manufacturing: Mark Fisher
Chief Executive, RBS Insurance: Annette Court
Chief Executive, Retail Banking: Benny Higgins
Chief Executive, Retail Direct: Chris Sullivan
Chief Executive, Ulster Bank Group: Cormac McCarthy

Group Secretary and General Counsel:
Miller R. McLean, age 55
Group Director, Communications: Howard Moody
Group Director, Human Resources: Neil Roden
Head of Group Communications: Carolyn McAdam
Head of Group Media Relations: Andrew Wilson
Head of Group Secretariat: Hew Campbell
Head of Investor Relations: Richard O'Connor
CEO, RBS National Bank: Dennis Jones
Auditors: Deloitte & Touche LLP

LOCATIONS

HQ: The Royal Bank of Scotland Group plc
42 St Andrew Square,
Edinburgh EH2 2YE, United Kingdom
Phone: +44-131-556-8555   **Fax:** +44-131-557-6140
US HQ: 1 Citizens Plaza, Providence, RI 02903
US Phone: 401-456-7000   **US Fax:** 401-456-7819
Web: www.rbs.com

The Royal Bank of Scotland Group has operations in
Australia, France, Germany, Greece, Hong Kong,
Ireland, Italy, Japan, Singapore, the UK, and the US.

PRODUCTS/OPERATIONS

2004 Sales

	$ mil.	% of total
Interest receivable	32,159.8	51
Noninterest		
Fees & commissions	12,778.4	20
General insurance	10,318.7	17
Dealing profits	3,829.3	6
Other	3,725.3	6
Total	**62,811.5**	**100**

2004 Assets

	% of total
Loans & advances to banks	10
Loans & advances to customers	60
Debt securities	16
Fixed assets	6
Other	8
Total	**100**

Selected Subsidiaries

Citizens Financial Group, Inc (banking, US)
Churchill Insurance Group PLC
Coutts & Co (private banking)
Coutts Bank Ltd (private banking, Switzerland)
Direct Line Insurance plc
Greenwich Capital Markets, Inc. (broker dealer, US)
Lombard North Central PLC (banking, credit finance,
and leasing)
National Westminster Home Loans Limited (home
mortgage finance)
National Westminster Bank Plc
RBS Life Holdings Limited (life assurance)
The Royal Bank of Scotland International Limited
(Channel Islands)
The Royal Bank of Scotland plc
Ulster Bank Limited

COMPETITORS

Abbey National	Irish Life
Alliance & Leicester	JPMorgan Chase
Allied Irish Banks	Lloyds TSB
Bank of America	London Scottish Bank
Bank of Ireland	MBNA
Barclays	PNC Financial
Citigroup	Standard Chartered
HBOS	Standard Life
HSBC Holdings	Virgin Group
ING Direct UK	Woolwich

HISTORICAL FINANCIALS

Company Type: Public

Income Statement

FYE: December 31

	ASSETS ($ mil.)	NET INCOME ($ mil.)	INCOME AS % OF ASSETS	EMPLOYEES
12/04	1,123,874	8,691	0.8%	126,100
12/03	809,433	7,181	0.9%	120,000
12/02	660,807	4,930	0.7%	111,800
12/01*	535,103	3,842	0.7%	105,700
9/00	468,134	3,173	0.7%	19,620
9/99	146,233	1,409	1.0%	32,620
9/98	135,298	1,180	0.9%	29,645
9/97	117,135	823	0.7%	26,699
Annual Growth	**38.1%**	**40.0%**	**—**	**24.8%**

*Fiscal year change

2004 Year-End Financials

Equity as % of assets: 4.7%   Long-term debt ($ mil.): 131,585
Return on assets: 0.9%   Sales ($ mil.): 62,812
Return on equity: 17.7%

Net Income History

London: RBS

Royal Dutch/Shell

Royal Dutch/Shell sits on an oil and gas throne
that is only slightly lower than those of BP and
Exxon Mobil. The oil and gas group has proved
reserves of 14.4 billion barrels of oil equivalent.
The Group, a subsidiary of Shell Petroleum (once
Royal Dutch Shell), generates sales mainly from
oil products, but it also makes chemicals, transports natural gas, trades gas and electricity, and
develops renewable energy sources. It operates
more than 46,000 gas stations worldwide. In
2004 the company reported that it had overestimated its reserves by 24%. The bad news resulted
in the ouster of the group's chairman and CFO
and the merger of Royal Dutch Petroleum and
The "Shell" Transport and Trading Company.

Spain-based Repsol has teamed up with a
UK-based investment firm to offer a reported
$3 billion for Royal Dutch/Shell's liquefied petro-
leum operations.

The Anglo-Dutch entity has restructured to
stay competitive. Gone are the decentralized
committees that ruled the company's once
Byzantine bureaucracy; they have been replaced
by divisional chiefs who report to the CEO. However, the 2004 revelations of overestimated oil reserves had shareholders calling for even greater
transparency and simplicity in the group's organizational structure. The group plans to merge
its two holding companies, Royal Dutch Petroleum and "Shell" Transport and Trading, to form
a new company named Royal Dutch Shell PLC.

The new company will be based in London with
physical headquarters in the Netherlands.

Most of the oil giant's crude is produced in
Nigeria, Oman, the UK, and the US. Royal
Dutch/Shell owns or has interests in about 50 refineries worldwide. The company has announced,
however, that it will invest some $12 billion (in
addition to the $2.6 billion already spent) in off-
shore projects near Dubai. Dutch/Shell has also
pledged to infuse $600 million into its joint ven-
ture with PetroChina for the development of develop wells and to cover day-to-day operating
expenses. The ownership of the Gorgon LNG
project in Western Australia has been restructured so that Royal Dutch/Shell owns 25%,
Chevron 50%, and ExxonMobil 25%.

HISTORY

In 1870 Marcus Samuel inherited an interest
in his father's London trading company, which
imported seashells from the Far East. He expanded the business and, after securing a contract for Russian oil, began selling kerosene in
the Far East.

Standard Oil underpriced competitors to defend its Asian markets. Samuel secretly prepared
his response and in 1892 unveiled the first of a
fleet of tankers. Rejecting Standard's acquisition
overtures, Samuel created "Shell" Transport and
Trading in 1897.

Meanwhile, a Dutchman, Aeilko Zijlker, struck
oil in Sumatra and formed Royal Dutch Petroleum in 1890 to exploit the oil field. Young Henri
Deterding joined the firm in 1896 and established a sales force in the Far East.

Deterding became Royal Dutch's head in 1900
amid the battle for the Asian market. In 1903 Deterding, Samuel, and the Rothschilds created
Asiatic Petroleum, a marketing alliance. With
Shell's non-Asian business eroding, Deterding
engineered a merger between Royal Dutch and
Shell in 1907. Royal Dutch shareholders got 60%
control; "Shell" Transport and Trading, 40%.

After the 1911 Standard Oil breakup, Deterding entered the US, building refineries and buying producers. Shell products were available in
every state by 1929. Royal Dutch/Shell joined
the 1928 "As Is" cartel that fixed prices for most
of two decades.

The post-WWII Royal Dutch/Shell profited
from worldwide growth in oil consumption. It
acquired 100% of Shell Oil, its US arm, in 1985,
but shareholders sued, maintaining Shell Oil's
assets had been undervalued in the deal. They
were awarded $110 million in 1990.

After the 1990-91 Persian Gulf crisis, Shell sold
a major California refinery to Unocal (1991) and
its US coal mining unit to Zeigler Coal (1992).

Management's slow response to two 1995 con-
troversies — environmentalists' outrage over
the planned sinking of an oil platform and
human rights activists' criticism of Royal
Dutch/Shell's role in Nigeria — spurred a major
shakeup. It began moving away from its decentralized structure and adopted a new policy of
corporate openness.

In 1996 Royal Dutch/Shell and Exxon formed
a worldwide petroleum additives venture. Shell
Oil joined Texaco in 1998 to form Equilon Enterprises, combining US refining and marketing
operations in the West and Midwest. Similarly,
Shell Oil, Texaco, and Saudi Arabia's Aramco
combined downstream operations on the US's
East and Gulf coasts as Motiva Enterprises.

In 1999 Royal Dutch/Shell and the UK's BG plc
acquired a controlling stake in Comgas, a unit of

Companhia Energética de São Paulo and the largest natural gas distributor in Brazil, for about $1 billion.

In 2000 the company sold its coal business to UK-based mining giant Anglo American for more than $850 million. To gain a foothold in the US power marketing scene, Royal Dutch/Shell formed a joint venture with construction giant Bechtel (called InterGen). The next year the company agreed to combine its German refining and marketing operations with those of RWE-DEA. Royal Dutch/Shell tried to expand its US natural gas reserves in 2001 by making a $2 billion hostile bid for Barrett Resources, but the effort was withdrawn after Barrett agreed to be acquired by Williams for $2.5 billion.

In 2002, in connection with Chevron's acquisition of Texaco, Royal Dutch/Shell acquired ChevronTexaco's (now Chevron) stakes in the underperforming US marketing joint ventures Equilon and Motiva. That year the company, through its US Shell Oil unit, acquired Pennzoil-Quaker State for $1.8 billion. Also that year Royal Dutch/Shell acquired Enterprise Oil for $5 billion, plus debt. In addition, it purchased RWE's 50% stake in German refining and marketing joint venture Shell & DEA Oil (for $1.35 billion).

In 2004 the Group signed a $200 million exploration deal with Libya, signaling its return to that country after a more than decade-long absence. Plans to build a $7 billion LNG plant in Qatar were announced in early 2005. In the same year the company's Shell Chemicals subsidiary announced plans sell its 50% stake in Basell, one of the world's largest polyolefin makers. The company became part of Royal Dutch Shell after the merger Royal Dutch Petroleum and The "Shell" Transport and Trading Company.

EXECUTIVES

Managing Director: Jeroen van der Veer, age 58, $1,312,528 pay (prior to merger)
Group Managing Director: Malcom Brinded, age 52
Executive Director, Oil Products and Chemicals: Rob J. Routs, age 59, $474,620 pay (prior to merger)
Executive Director, Gas and Power: Linda Z. Cook, age 47
Group Managing Director and CFO: Peter Voser, age 47
Group Chief Information Officer: Michael J. Rose, age 52
Group Director, Human Resources: John D. Hofmeister
Group Director, International Directorate: Hugh Mitchell
Group Director, Legal: Beat Hess, age 54
Group Director, Strategic Planning, Sustainable Development, and External Affairs: Adrian Loader
Chairman Shell Nigeria and CEO Shell EP Africa: Chris Finlayson, age 48
President and CEO Shell Canada: Clive Mather
CEO, Shell Renewables; President, Shell Hydrogen: Graeme Sweeney
Chief Executive, Renewables: Karen de Segundo, age 59
Chief Executive, Shell Hydrogen: Jeremy B. Bentham
Chief Executive, Shell Consumer: Charles Harrison
CEO, Shell EP Americas: Raoul Restucci
President, Shell Trading: Mike Warwick
Group Research Advisor: Peter Kwant
Auditors: KPMG Accountants N.V.; PricewaterhouseCoopers LLP

LOCATIONS

HQ: Royal Dutch/Shell Group of Companies
Carel van Bylandtlaan 30,
2596 HR The Hague, The Netherlands
Phone: +31-70-377-9111   **Fax:** +31-70-377-3115
US HQ: 1 Shell Plaza, 910 Louisiana St.,
Houston, TX 77002
US Phone: 713-241-6161   **US Fax:** 713-241-6946
Web: www.shell.com

Royal Dutch/Shell operates in more than 145 countries. It has major oil and gas interests in Argentina, Australia, Bangladesh, Brunei, Canada, China, Colombia, Denmark, Egypt, Gabon, Germany, Kazakhstan, Malaysia, the Netherlands, New Zealand, Norway, Oman, Pakistan, Peru, the Philippines, Russia, Syria, the UK, the United Arab Emirates, the US, and Venezuela.

2004 Sales

	$ mil.	% of total
Eastern Hemisphere		
Europe	94,904	36
Other regions	49,482	18
Western Hemisphere		
US	102,877	39
Other countries	17,927	7
Total	**265,190**	**100**

PRODUCTS/OPERATIONS

2004 Sales

	$ mil.	% of total
Oil products	207,006	78
Chemicals	26,877	10
Exploration & production	20,643	8
Gas & power	9,604	4
Corporate & other	1,060	—
Total	**265,190**	**100**

COMPETITORS

7-Eleven	Kerr-McGee
Amerada Hess	Koch
Ashland	Lyondell Chemical
BHP Billiton	Marathon Oil
BP	Norsk Hydro
Celanese AG	Occidental Petroleum
Chevron	PDVSA
Dow Chemical	PEMEX
DuPont	PETROBRAS
Eastman Chemical	PetroKazakhstan
Eni	Repsol YPF
Exxon Mobil	Sinopec Shanghai
Forum Energy	Petrochemical
Huntsman	Sunoco
Imperial Chemical	TOTAL
Industries	Unocal
Imperial Oil	

HISTORICAL FINANCIALS

Company Type: Subsidiary

Income Statement

FYE: December 31

	REVENUE ($ mil.)	NET INCOME ($ mil.)	NET PROFIT MARGIN	EMPLOYEES
12/04	265,190	18,183	6.9%	112,000
12/03	201,728	12,496	6.2%	119,000
12/02	179,431	9,419	5.2%	111,000
12/01	135,211	10,852	8.0%	91,000
12/00	149,146	12,719	8.5%	90,000
12/99	105,366	8,584	8.1%	96,000
12/98	93,692	350	0.4%	102,000
12/97	128,115	7,753	6.1%	105,000
12/96	128,313	8,886	6.9%	104,000
12/95	109,872	6,919	6.3%	106,000
Annual Growth	**10.3%**	**11.3%**	**—**	**0.6%**

2004 Year-End Financials

Debt ratio: 10.2%   Current ratio: 1.02
Return on equity: 23.1%   Long-term debt ($ mil.): 8,600
Cash ($ mil.): 8,459

Net Income History

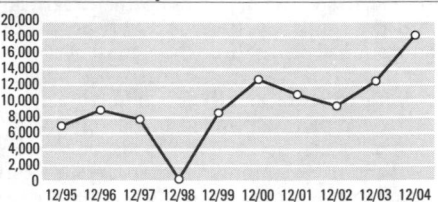

12/95 12/96 12/97 12/98 12/99 12/00 12/01 12/02 12/03 12/04

RWE

RWE doesn't stand for Runs With Electricity, but it could. Through its subsidiaries, the energy conglomerate provides electricity, gas, water, and environmental services to more than 120 million residential and business customers, primarily in Europe and North America. RWE is one of Germany's top two electricity suppliers (along with E.ON); it also owns two major UK-based utilities: #3 global water provider RWE Thames Water and domestic electricity and gas supplier RWE npower (formerly RWE Innogy). RWE owns oil and gas exploration and production company RWE-DEA; other businesses include companies engaged in gas transportation and storage, power generation, energy trading, and coal mining.

Rumors of the company's decision to sell RWE Thames Water (which would include the US-based American Water Works) have begun to surface due to the fact that the unit has failed to grow as expected.

Overall, the company serves 21 million electricity customers, 10 million gas customers, 70 million water customers, and 20 million waste disposal customers. Its core markets are Germany, central Eastern Europe, the UK, and the US.

As Germany's old industrial controls continue to tumble like Berlin's famous wall in the face of European Union-wide deregulation, RWE is doing its best to cope with the chaos of a new order by restructuring its regional energy businesses. The company's former German utility unit, RWE Energie, lost its regional monopoly status because of deregulation, and RWE has responded by splitting its domestic power generation, distribution, and supply operations into new units. It has also reorganized its corporate structure into seven core operating divisions.

HISTORY

Founded at the end of the 19th century, RWE mirrored the industrialization of Germany in its growth. It was formed as Rheinisch-Westfalisches Elektrizitatswerk in 1898 by Erich Zweigert, the mayor of Essen, and Hugo Stinnes, an industrialist from Mulheim, to provide electricity to Essen and surrounding areas. The company began supplying power in 1900.

Stinnes persuaded other cities — Gelsenkirchen and Mulheim — to buy shares in RWE in 1905. In 1908 RWE and rival Vereinigte Elektrizitatswerk Westfalen (VEW) agreed to divide up the territories that each would supply.

Germany's coal shortages, caused by WWI, prompted RWE to expand its coal operations, and it bought Rheinische Aktiengesellschaft für Braunkohlenbergbau, a coal producer, in 1932. RWE also built a power line network, completed in 1930, to connect populous northern Germany with the south. By 1939, as WWII began, the company had plants throughout most of western Germany. However, the war destroyed much of its infrastructure, and RWE had to rebuild.

The company continued to rely on coal for most of its fuel needs in the 1950s, but in 1961 RWE and Bayern Atomkraft sponsored the construction of a demonstration nuclear reactor, the first of several such projects, at Gundremmingen. The Gundremmingen plant was shut down in 1977, and to replace it RWE built two 1,300-MW reactors that began operation in 1984.

RWE began to diversify, and in 1988 it acquired Texaco's German petroleum and petrochemical unit, which became RWE-DEA. By 1990 RWE's operations also included waste management and construction. RWE reorganized, creating RWE Aktiengesellschaft as a holding company for group operations.

RWE-DEA acquired the US's Vista Chemical in 1991, and RWE's Rheinbraun mining unit bought a 50% stake in Consolidation Coal from DuPont. (The mining venture went public in 1999 as CONSOL Energy.) RWE led a consortium that acquired major stakes in three Hungarian power companies in 1995.

Hoping to play a role in Germany's telecommunications market, RWE teamed with VEBA in 1997 to form the o.tel.o joint venture, and RWE and VEBA gained control of large German mobile phone operator E-Plus. The nation's telecom market was deregulated in 1998, but Mannesmann and former monopoly Deutsche Telekom proved to be formidable competitors. In 1999 RWE and VEBA sold o.tel.o's fixed-line business (along with the o.tel.o brand name) and cable-TV unit Tele Columbus. The next year the companies sold their joint stake in E-Plus.

Faced with deregulating German electricity markets, RWE Energie had begun restructuring as soon as the market opened up in 1998. It agreed to buy fellow German power company VEW in a $20 billion deal that closed in 2000. RWE also joined with insurance giant Allianz and France's Vivendi in a successful bid for a 49.9% stake in state-owned water distributor Berliner Wasserbetriebe (Vivendi later spurned an RWE offer to buy its energy businesses).

After taking advantage of deregulating markets in Germany, RWE moved to pick up other European utilities: It acquired UK-based Thames Water (later renamed RWE Thames Water) in 2000 and bought a majority stake in Dutch gas supplier Intergas the next year. In 2002 the company issued an exchange offer to acquire UK electricity supplier Innogy (later renamed RWE npower) for a total of about $4.4 billion in cash and $3 billion in assumed debt. It also completed a $3.7 billion purchase of Czech Republic gas supplier Transgas.

In a move to further streamline operations, RWE sold its 50% stake in refinery and service station subsidiary Shell & DEA Oil to Deutsche Shell and Shell Petroleum. To do battle in an increasingly competitive utility industry, RWE is acquiring stakes in other European utilities. RWE has also acquired North American utility American Water Works, which was combined with the US operations of RWE Thames Water, for $4.6 billion in cash and $4 billion in assumed debt.

EXECUTIVES

Chairman: Thomas R. Fischer, age 58
Deputy Chairman: Frank Bsirske
President and CEO; Chairman, RWE Energy and RWE Thames Water: Harry J. M. Roels, age 57
EVP and CFO: Klaus Sturany, age 59
EVP Human Resources and Law: Jan Zilius, age 59
EVP; President and CEO, RWE Energy:
Berthold Bonekamp
CEO, RWE Dea Aktiengesellschaft: Georg Schöning, age 54
CEO, RWE Thames Water: William J. (Bill) Alexander, age 58
CEO, RWE npower: Andrew J. (Andy) Duff, age 46
Head of Investor Relations: Ingo Alphéus
Head of Press Department: Bill McAndrews
Auditors: PwC Deutsche Revision AG

LOCATIONS

HQ: RWE Aktiengesellschaft
Opernplatz 1, 45128 Essen, Germany
Phone: +49-201-12-00   **Fax:** +49-201-12-15199
Web: www.rwe.com

RWE operates in Europe and the Americas.

2004 Sales

	% of total
Europe	
Germany	56
Other countries	38
Americas	6
Total	**100**

PRODUCTS/OPERATIONS

2004 Sales

	% of total
RWE Energy	73
RWE npower	18
RWE Power	9
Total	**100**

Selected Divisions and Subsidiaries

RWE Energy (domestic and continental European downstream energy operations)
  RWE Aqua (water distribution)
  RWE Net AG (electricity transmission and distribution system operations)
  RWE Solutions AG (industrial services)
RWE npower (formerly RWE Innogy, electricity and gas supply, UK)
RWE Power (upstream energy operations)
  RWE-DEA AG (oil and gas exploration, production, and storage)
  RWE Rheinbraun AG (coal mining and coal-fired power generation)

COMPETITORS

BASF AG
Bewag
BP
Cegedel
Centrica
Electricité de France
EnBW
Endesa
Enel
E.ON
E.ON UK
European Minerals
Exxon Mobil
Royal Dutch/Shell Group
Severn Trent
SUEZ
UES of Russia
United Utilities
Vattenfall
Veolia Environnement

HISTORICAL FINANCIALS

Company Type: Public

Income Statement

FYE: December 31

	REVENUE ($ mil.)	NET INCOME ($ mil.)	NET PROFIT MARGIN	EMPLOYEES
12/04	55,919	2,915	5.2%	97,777
12/03	53,686	1,196	2.2%	127,028
12/02	45,579	1,101	2.4%	131,765
12/01*	26,592	550	2.1%	155,634
6/01	48,182	1,073	2.2%	163,720
6/00	45,618	1,154	2.5%	155,697
6/99	41,772	1,186	2.8%	155,576
6/98	40,226	1,223	3.0%	145,467
6/97	35,109	748	2.1%	136,115
6/96	35,887	784	2.2%	132,658
Annual Growth	**5.1%**	**15.7%**	**—**	**(3.3%)**

*Fiscal year change

2004 Year-End Financials

Debt ratio: 232.9%   Current ratio: 2.12
Return on equity: 26.5%   Long-term debt ($ mil.): 30,674
Cash ($ mil.): 2,081

Net Income History

Pink Sheets: RWEOY

SABMiller plc

It's Miller time at South African Breweries. SAB's 2002 purchase of Miller Brewing earned it a new name, SABMiller plc, and made it the world's third-largest brewer, behind InBev and Anheuser-Busch. The company, which has operations in more than 40 countries, dominates South African brewing with 98% of the market on the strength of Africa's best-selling beer, Castle Lager. It brews other regional brands, including Hansa Pilsener. SABMiller also makes wines, spirits, and fruit drinks as well as bottling Coca-Cola products. Miller's former parent Altria Group owns nearly 25% of SABMiller.

Apartheid kept SABMiller from investing overseas in the 1980s; so it grew by purchasing a diverse range of businesses at home. After sanctions were lifted in the early 1990s, the company bulked up on foreign breweries. It now has major operations in Africa, China, India, Central Europe, and Central America.

In 2005 SABMiller acquired almost 97% of Bavaria S.A., the second largest brewer in South America. Bavaria's brands include Águila, Atlas, Cristal, and Pilsener.

HISTORY

British sailor Frederick Mead purchased the Castle Brewery in Johannesburg in 1892, about 15 years after gold was discovered in South Africa. Mead took his brewing operation public as South African Breweries (SAB) in 1895. The company launched its flagship Castle Lager three years later and survived the Anglo-Boer War (1899-1902) as South Africa's fastest-growing non-industrial firm. Mead died in 1915.

The brewer acquired the Grand Hotel in Cape Town in 1921 and a stake in Schweppes (carbonated drinks) in 1925. In the late 1940s SAB began an extensive expansion program involving its breweries, small hotels, and pubs. In 1951 it acquired the Hotel Victoria in Johannesburg. An increase in beer taxes during the 1950s led SAB to start producing liquors. With beer demand slackening, South Africa's three largest brewers — SAB, Ohlsson's, and United Breweries — merged in 1956. The new company, which took the SAB name, controlled about 90% of the beer market. Beer taxes continued to pressure sales, and in 1960 SAB acquired control of Stellenbosch Farmers' Winery to extend its product range. In 1962 the restriction prohibiting alcohol consumption by blacks was lifted, opening an enormous market. SAB continued to extend its range of beer brands during the 1960s by adding licenses to brew Amstel and Carling Black Label.

Further diversifying, SAB formed Barsab (an investment venture with Thomas Barlow & Sons) in 1966. The company launched its hotel division, Southern Sun Hotels, three years later by merging its hotels with those owned by the Sol Kerzner family. The Barsab venture was dissolved in 1973, leaving SAB with furniture and footwear businesses. The following year it acquired the South African bottling business of Pepsi (converted to Coca-Cola in 1977). The company added the beer interests of the Rembrandt Group and a 49% stake in Appletiser, a fruit drinks company, in 1979. (It gained control of it in 1982.)

SAB moved into apparel retailing with its purchase of the Scotts Stores (1981) and Edgars (1982). After forming a joint venture with Ceres Fruit Juices (1986), SAB made a number of investments in South Africa, including Lion Match Company (1987), Da Gama Textiles (1989), and Plate Glass (1992).

In the 1990s, the company expanded internationally. It acquired stakes in breweries in Hungary (1993), Tanzania and China (1994), and Poland and Romania (1996). Graham Mackay (now CEO) became managing director in 1996.

Before moving its main listing to the London Stock Exchange in 1999, SAB sold its Amalgamated Retail unit (furniture, appliances), Lion Match Company, and a large stake in Edgars. It then bought controlling interests in Czech brewers Pilsner Urquell and Radegast to become the largest brewer in Central Europe and sold its 68% interest in Plate Glass to Dibelco (a D' Ieteren and Copeba joint venture). Bevcon (a consortium of three South African companies) sold its 27% interest in SAB in 1999.

The continuing woes of the South African economy in 2000 fueled SAB's desire to continue expanding its international base. In 2001 SAB announced its China Resources Breweries Ltd joint venture in the Sichuan province of China. It also became the first international brewer with a presence in Central America, spending more than $500 million on breweries in Honduras and El Salvador.

In 2002 SAB bought Miller Brewing from Philip Morris (now Altria Group) for $5.6 billion, making it the world's second-largest brewer at the time. SAB then changed its name to SABMiller plc. SABMiller moved into Western Europe in 2003 with the $270 million purchase of Italian brewer Birra Peroni.

Similar to rival Anheuser-Busch, SABMiller is particularly interested in growing its base in China, which has the world's largest market for alcohol. SABMiller has invested heavily in China Resources Breweries. It had hoped to purchase control of the Harbin Brewery Group but was spurned by Anheuser-Busch, which successfully outbid SABMiller for control of the brewery in 2004. Several months later, SABMiller and China Resources Breweries purchased the Chinese brewing assets of Lion Nathan Limited.

EXECUTIVES

Chairman: Meyer Kahn, age 65
CEO and Director: Ernest A. (Graham) Mackay, age 55, $2,761,690 pay
CFO and Director: Malcolm I. Wyman, age 58, $1,474,780 pay
VP, Investor Relations: Gary Leibowitz
Director, Marketing: Mark Sherrington, age 49
Managing Director, Miller Brands (UK): Gary Whitlie
President and CEO, Miller Brewing Company: Norman J. Adami, age 50
Managing Director, SABMiller Africa and Asia: André C. Parker, age 53
Managing Director, SABMiller Europe: Alan Clark, age 45
Managing Director, The South African Breweries Ltd.: Tony van Kralingen, age 47
Group Company Secretary: Andrew Tonkinson, age 60
Director, Corporate Affairs: Sue Clark, age 41
Director, Human Resources: Johann Nel, age 48
Director, International Brands: Tim Dewey, age 45
Director, Sales Miller Brands UK: Nick Miller
Head of Corporate Media: Ciaran Baker
Head of Media Relations: Nigel Fairbrass
Head of Strategy and Planning: Gail Lumsden
Communications Executive: Briony Gilbert
Auditors: PricewaterhouseCoopers LLP

LOCATIONS

HQ: SABMiller plc
1 Stanhope Gate, London W1K1AF, United Kingdom
Phone: +44-20-7659-0100   **Fax:** +44-20-7659-0111
Web: www.sabmiller.com

SABMiller has operations in more than 40 countries worldwide.

PRODUCTS/OPERATIONS

Selected Brands
Beer
  Africa
    Amstel (license)
    Carling Black Label
    Castle (Draught, Lager, Lite, Milk Stout)
    Fusion
    Hansa Pilsener
    Lion Lager (license)
    Redd's
    Rhino
    Vita Malt
    X-Cape
  Asia
    Haywards
    Knock Out
    Royal Challenge
    Snow
  Europe
    Dog In The Fog   Peroni
    Dorada   Redd's
    Dreher   Saris
    Frisco   Timisoreana
    Gambrinus   Tyskie
    Holsten   Wührer
    Keller   Zolotaya
    Miller   ubr

North America
  Hamm's
  Henry Weinhard's
  Leinenkugel's
  Miller
  Milwaukee's Best
  Miller Genuine Draft
  Miller High Life
  Olde English
  Port Royal
  Suprema
Soft Drinks
  Appletiser
  Coca-Cola (license)
  Grapetiser
Wines and Spirits
  Distell

COMPETITORS

AmBev
Anheuser-Busch
Asahi Breweries
Asia Pacific Breweries
Brau Union
Carlsberg
Constellation Brands
Diageo
Foster's
Grolsch
Heineken
InBev
Kirin
Lion Nathan
Molson Coors
PepsiCo
Suntory Ltd.
Tsingtao
Yanjing

HISTORICAL FINANCIALS

Company Type: Public

Income Statement

FYE: March 31

	REVENUE ($ mil.)	NET INCOME ($ mil.)	NET PROFIT MARGIN	EMPLOYEES
3/05	12,901	1,141	8.8%	40,892
3/04	11,366	645	5.7%	39,571
3/03	8,295	296	3.6%	42,402
3/02	3,185	250	7.9%	33,230
3/01	3,304	328	9.9%	31,327
3/00	4,135	456	11.0%	34,365
3/99	4,683	305	6.5%	49,099
3/98	6,436	240	3.7%	81,000
3/97	6,542	479	7.3%	105,000
3/96	6,301	435	6.9%	106,900
Annual Growth	8.3%	11.3%	—	(10.1%)

2005 Year-End Financials

Debt ratio: 33.0%   Current ratio: 0.83
Return on equity: 16.5%   Long-term debt ($ mil.): 2,526
Cash ($ mil.): 454

Net Income History

Pink Sheets: SBMRY

Saint-Gobain

Compagnie de Saint-Gobain is in a glass by itself. The materials mega-group controls more than 1,000 companies with operations in three sectors. Its Housing Products businesses (nearly half of sales) make and distribute building materials (roofing, mortars, wall siding) and pipe. The group's Glass Products operations make containers, flat glass, and insulation and reinforcements. Its High-Performance Materials unit includes ceramics, plastics, and abrasives businesses. Saint-Gobain is a world leader in many of its business segments. The operation dates to the 1660s, when it provided glass for Versailles; today it makes 30 billion glass containers a year and provides insulation for 20% of all US homes.

Saint-Gobain has been acquiring companies like its life depended on it, and believes that Eastern Europe, Asia, and Latin America are areas ripe for growth.

Saint-Gobain acquired dozens of companies in 2004. New distribution division acquisitions included some 30 companies in France, Germany, and the UK — in addition to the acquisition of Sweden-based building products distribution company Dahl International. Saint-Gobain also acquired 11 distribution sector companies in emerging countries. Non-distribution acquisitions included flat glass operations in China, construction products companies in China and the Czech Republic, and performance materials investments in China, Russia, and Romania.

In August 2005, the company made a hostile $6.5 billion bid for UK drywall/plasterboard maker BPB plc after friendly overtures were rejected. BPB, which operates about 90 factories, rejected Saint-Gobain's initial offer as too low. Late in 2005 Saint-Gobain agreed to acquire the company in a sweetened $6.68 billion deal. Saint-Gobain expects more than $100 million in savings over the first two years following the deal.

HISTORY

Originally called Dunoyer, Saint-Gobain (named after the factory location) was founded in 1665 by order of the Sun King, Louis XIV, who needed mirrors to adorn his palaces. Because Venice had the monopoly on glass, Louis lured Venetian artisans to Paris. Some were poisoned by Italian assassins, but enough remained to teach Parisians their secrets. Saint-Gobain glass decorates the Palace of Versailles' Hall of Mirrors.

With its decreed glass monopoly in France, the company grew steadily until the French Revolution interrupted its prosperity. By the early 1800s, however, Saint-Gobain was shining again. It set up a sales office in New York in 1830 and its first foreign subsidiary in Germany in 1857. Under chemist Joseph Gay-Lussac's direction, Saint-Gobain began dabbling in chemicals in the mid-1800s.

Expanding to Italy (1889) and Spain (1904), the firm was Europe's leading glassmaker by 1913. Saint-Gobain pioneered the production of tempered security glass in the 1920s; it diversified into glass fiber in the 1930s.

Pilkington, a UK competitor, developed a glassmaking method in 1959 that obviated the need for polishing and therefore slashed production costs. Saint-Gobain refit its factories to use the Pilkington method to keep its 50% EC market share. In 1968 the shareholding Suez Group forced Saint-Gobain to merge with Pont-à-Mousson (now Saint-Gobain Canalisation), then the world's leading iron pipe maker. The merger led to a much-needed restructuring that included selling Saint-Gobain's chemical interests.

The company acquired a majority interest in US building-material maker CertainTeed in 1976. In 1982 it was forced to divest some of its interests when it was nationalized by France's new socialist government. Despite nationalization the company grew steadily during the 1980s, investing in Compagnie Générale des Eaux, the world's largest drinking-water distributor.

In 1986, after a change in France's political climate, Saint-Gobain became the first company to be reprivatized. Three years later it purchased Générale Française de Céramique (clay tile) and controlling interest in Vetri (glass containers), Italy.

Saint-Gobain bought Norton (the world's leader in abrasives) and UK glassmaker Solaglas in 1990. With the 1991 purchases of German glassmakers GIAG and Oberland, Saint-Gobain became the world's #1 glass manufacturer within a year.

After the recession of the early 1990s, Saint-Gobain sold its paper and packaging interests to Jefferson Smurfit in 1994, raising more than $1 billion for acquisitions. With Ball Corporation, it formed a glass container joint venture, Ball-Foster Glass, in 1995; the next year it bought Ball's stake. Acquisitions in 1997 included industrial ceramics firms in Germany and France and UK abrasives maker Unicorn International. In 1998 Saint-Gobain bought Bird Corp. (roofing materials, US) and CALMAR (plastic pump sprayers, US). The next year it bought US-based Furon, which was absorbed into a new unit, Saint-Gobain Performance Plastics.

In 2000 Saint-Gobain acquired Meyer International (a UK building materials supplier), Raab Karcher (a German building materials distributor), and US-based polymer specialist Chemfab. The following year Saint-Gobain bolstered its ceiling systems operations with the acquisition of the Maars Group's metal ceiling-grid business. In 2002 Saint-Gobain acquired the 25% of France-based Lapeyre SA (doors, windows, cabinetry) stock it didn't own.

The company's most notable deal of 2004 was the €686 million acquisition of Swedish plumbing products distributor Dahl International. Early in 2005 Saint-Gobain raised its stake in Hankuk Glass Industries, a Korean glass maker with sales of more than $250 million, from 46% to more than 80%.

EXECUTIVES

Chairman and CEO: Jean-Louis Beffa, age 64, $1,230,096 pay
COO: Pierre-André de Chalendar, age 47
CFO: Benoît Bazin
SVP: Jean-Claude Breffort
SVP: Phillippe Crouzet
SVP: Jean-François Phelizon
SVP and President, Construction Products Division: Claude Imauven
SVP and President, Ceramics and Plastics Division: Roberto Caliari
SVP and President, Packaging Division: Jérôme Fessard
SVP and President, Flat Glass Division: Jacques Aschenbroich
VP, Construction Products Division, North America: Peter R. Dachowski
VP, External Relations: Nicole Grisoni-Bachelier
President, Abrasives Division: Américo Denes
President, Reinforcements Division: Jean-Philippe Buisson
Auditors: KPMG Audit; PricewaterhouseCoopers Audit

LOCATIONS

HQ: Compagnie de Saint-Gobain
Les Miroirs, 18 Avenue d'Alsace,
92096 La Défense, France
Phone: +33-1-47-62-30-00   **Fax:** +33-1-47-78-45-03
US HQ: 750 E. Swedesford Rd.,
Valley Forge, PA 19482-0101
US Phone: 610-341-7000   **US Fax:** 610-341-7797
Web: www.saint-gobain.com

Saint-Gobain has more than 1,000 subsidiaries in some 45 countries worldwide.

2004 Sales

	$ mil.	% of total
Europe		
France	14,624.5	32
Other countries	18,738.6	41
North America	7,792.2	17
Other regions	4,856.7	10
Adjustments	(2,329.9)	—
Total	**43,682.1**	**100**

PRODUCTS/OPERATIONS

2004 Sales

	$ mil.	% of total
Building distribution	18,536.2	42
Construction products		
Building materials	3,337.4	8
Insulation	2,575.7	6
Pipe	1,712.1	4
High-performance materials		
Ceramics, plastics & abrasives	4,653.1	10
Reinforcements	1,617.1	4
Flat glass	5,978.3	14
Packaging	5,262.7	12
Other	9.5	—
Total	**43,682.1**	**100**

Selected Segments and Products

Housing Products
　Building materials distribution
　　Industrial carpentry
　　Materials for new construction and renovation
　Building materials
　　Composite materials and mortars
　　Concrete products
　　PVC Siding
　　Roofing products
　Pipe
　　Ductile cast iron pipe
　　Pipe systems

Glass
　Flat glass (clear, colored, and layered)
　　Automotive glass
　　Construction materials glass
　　Specialty glass
　Containers
　　Bottles and jars
　　Flasks
　　Plastic pumps and dispensers
　Insulation and reinforcements
　　Glass threads
　　Glass wool
　　Insulating foam
　　Processing (glass, carbon, polyester glass grids and fabrics)
　　Rock wool

High-Performance Materials
　Abrasives
　　Coated abrasives
　　Grinding wheels
　　Superabrasives
　　Thin grinding wheels
　Ceramics and plastics
　　High-performance ceramics
　　Industrial ceramics
　　Specialty ceramics

HISTORICAL FINANCIALS

Company Type: Public

Income Statement

FYE: December 31

	REVENUE ($ mil.)	NET INCOME ($ mil.)	NET PROFIT MARGIN	EMPLOYEES
12/04	43,682	1,477	3.4%	181,228
12/03	37,141	1,304	3.5%	172,811
12/02	31,730	1,090	3.4%	172,357
12/01	26,920	1,005	3.7%	173,329
12/00	27,132	1,428	5.3%	171,125
12/99	23,113	1,235	5.3%	164,698
12/98	20,797	1,280	6.2%	117,287
12/97	17,850	938	5.3%	107,968
12/96	17,464	826	4.7%	111,701
12/95	14,323	858	6.0%	89,852
Annual Growth	**13.2%**	**6.2%**	**—**	**8.1%**

2004 Year-End Financials

Debt ratio: 46.7%
Return on equity: 10.0%
Cash ($ mil.): 2,028
Current ratio: 1.37
Long-term debt ($ mil.): 7,360

Net Income History

Euronext Paris: SGO

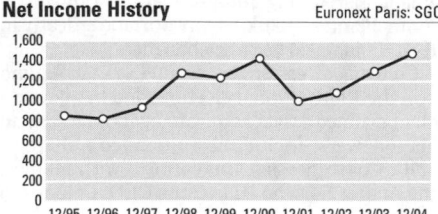

Samsung Group

Samsung Group has reason to sing. The *chaebol* (industrial group) has surpassed its former archrival, the erstwhile Hyundai Group, to become the #1 business group in South Korea. Samsung's flagship unit is Samsung Electronics, which is the world's top maker of dynamic random-access memory (DRAM) and other memory chips, as well as a global heavyweight in all sorts of electronic gear including LCD panels, DVD players, and cellular phones. Other affiliated companies include credit-card unit Samsung Card, Samsung General Chemicals, Samsung Life Insurance, Samsung Securities, and trading arm Samsung Corporation.

Forced into action by the Korean economic crisis of the late 1990s, Samsung has whittled away at its debt and shed noncore operations. While the group's holdings have fallen from 61 affiliates to about 35, it still spans many diverse business niches, including advertising, textile production, amusement parks, hotels, and professional baseball.

Lee Kun-Hee, son of Samsung's founder, has dissolved much of the central management structure, including his post as the group's chairman, in his revamp of the group. In April 2005 he announced he would step down as director of eight Samsung affiliates, including the holding company, but remain chairman of Samsung Electronics. However, in response to the Korean government's aims to restrict the voting rights of *chaebols* (family-controlled conglomerates), Samsung Group filed suit against the government in June 2005 over the legitimacy of current antitrust actions.

News surfaced in July 2005 that Samsung Group had attempted to acquire Kia Motors in 1997. Conversations between a Samsung official and the former head of a daily newspaper were allegedly intercepted and recorded by the country's National Intelligence Service. The group apologized over the conversation, which also allegedly centered on illegal political donations during the 1997 presidential election. Prosecutors exploring the allegations have considered calling Lee in for questioning.

The Korean National Assembly's finance and economy committee summoned Lee to question him over unpaid debts left by the group's bankrupt Samsung Motors in 2005 (Lee subsequently didn't appear). Korean President Roh Moo-Hyun simultaneously blasted Lee and the group, saying it sought to sidestep corporate governance reform. Led by main creditor Seoul Guarantee Insurance, 15 creditors planned to push ahead with a lawsuit over the unpaid debts — potentially the country's biggest lawsuit in financial terms.

Two executives — Her Tae-hak, former chief of Samsung Everland, and Park Ro-bin, current Samsung Everland president — were sentenced to prison in October 2005 on charges of helping chairman Lee transfer wealth to his son in illicit bond deals a decade earlier. The same month, the Korean Supreme Court ordered Lee and nine former and current Samsung Electronics executives to pay $18.7 million (19 billion won) for instigating heavy losses to the company.

HISTORY

In 1936 Japan-educated Lee Byung-Chull began operating a rice mill in Korea, then under Japanese rule. By 1938 Lee had begun trading in dried fish and had incorporated as Samsung (Korean for "three stars"). WWII left Korea fairly unscathed, and by war's end Samsung had transportation and real-estate adjuncts.

The Korean War, however, destroyed nearly all of Samsung's assets. Left with a brewery and an import business for UN personnel, Lee reconstructed Samsung in Korea. He formed the highly profitable Cheil Sugar Company, then the country's only sugar refiner, in 1953. Textile, banking, and insurance ventures followed.

A 1961 political coup brought Park Chung Hee to power in Korea. Lee, wealthy and tied to the former government, was accused of illegal profiteering. A 1966 smuggling case involving one of Lee's sons led to another scandal, but charges were dropped when Lee gave the government an immense fertilizer plant. Despite the political change, Samsung still grew, diversifying into paper products, department stores, and publishing.

In 1969, with help from SANYO, Lee established Samsung Electronics, which benefited from the government's export drive and low wage rates. By disassembling Western-designed electronics, Samsung Electronics figured out how to produce inexpensive black-and-white TVs and, later, color TVs, VCRs, and microwave ovens. It manufactured these products under private labels for corporations including General Electric and Sears. In concert with the government's industrialization push, the *chaebol* also began making ships (1974), petrochemicals (1977), and aircraft engines (1977). By the 1980s Samsung was exporting electronics under its own name.

When Lee died in 1987, his son Lee Kun-Hee assumed control. After years of importing technology and spending freely on R&D, in 1990 Samsung became a world leader in chip production. Encouraged by the government, Samsung agreed to cooperate with fellow *chaebol* Goldstar (now LG Group) to obtain foreign technology to develop liquid crystal displays. In 1994 Lee, a longtime car lover, announced plans to form Samsung Motors.

In 1996 Lee was caught in a corruption scandal and got a two-year suspended sentence for bribery. The next year Asian financial markets crashed. Nonetheless, Samsung bought the remaining 50.1% of struggling PC maker AST (it had bought a 49.9% share in 1996) but exited the US consumer PC market. Even as the bottom fell out of the Korean auto market, Samsung Motors began delivering its first cars in 1998. To lessen its debt, the group sold Samsung Heavy Industries' construction-equipment business to Sweden's Volvo and sold Samsung Electronics' power-device unit to Fairchild Semiconductor. Also in 1998 the Korean government fined several *chaebol*, including Samsung, a collective $93 million for illegally funneling money to weaker subsidiaries.

Samsung sold the ailing AST to Beny Alagem, former head of Packard Bell NEC, in 1999. The following year Samsung sold a 70% stake in the struggling Samsung Motors to France-based Renault.

The early 2000s saw the group surge as its flagship unit Samsung Electronics racked up big wins in microchips, cell phones, high-end televisions, and other gee-whiz gear.

EXECUTIVES

Chairman, Samsung Electronics: Lee Kun-Hee, age 63
Vice Chairman and CEO, Samsung Advanced Institute of Technology: Lee Yun-Woo, age 59
Vice Chairman and CEO, Samsung Electronics: Yun Jong-Yong, age 61
Vice Chairman, Corporate Restructuring Headquarters: Lee Hak-Soo
EVP, Samsung Human Resources Development Center: Sookeun Kim
President and CEO, Cheil Communications: Bai Dong-Man
President and CEO, Cheil Industries; President and CEO, Samsung BP Chemicals: Ahn Bok-Hyun
President and CEO, S1 Corporation: Lee Woo-Hee
President and CEO, Samsung Card: Yoo Suk-Ryul
President and CEO, Samsung Corning: Song Yong-Ro
President and CEO, Samsung Corning Precision Glass: Suk-Jai Lee
President and CEO, Samsung Corporation: Pae Chong-Yeul
President and CEO, Samsung Fine Chemicals: Lee Yong-Soon
President and CEO, Samsung Fire and Marine Insurance: Lee Soo-Chang
President and CEO, Samsung Petrochemical: Her Tae-Hak
President and CEO, Samsung SDI: Kim Soon-Taek
President and CEO, Samsung SDS: Kim In
President and CEO, Samsung Techwin: Lee Joong-Koo
President and CEO, Samsung TOTAL Petrochemicals: Ko Hong-Sik

LOCATIONS

HQ: Samsung Group
250, 2-ga, Taepyung-ro, Jung-gu,
Seoul 100-742, South Korea
Phone: +82-2-727-7114   **Fax:** +82-2-727-7985
US HQ: 105 Challenger Rd., Ridgefield Park, NJ 07660
US Phone: 201-229-4000   **US Fax:** 201-229-4110
Web: www.samsung.com

Samsung Group has operations in more than 50 countries around the world.

PRODUCTS/OPERATIONS

Selected Operations

Chemicals
Samsung Fine Chemicals Co., Ltd.
Samsung General Chemicals Co., Ltd.
Samsung Petrochemical Co., Ltd.

Electronics
Samsung Corning Co., Ltd. (TV picture-tube glass)
Samsung Electro-Mechanics Co., Ltd. (electronic components)
Samsung Electronics Co., Ltd. (semiconductors, consumer electronics)
Samsung SDI Co. Ltd.
Samsung SDS Co., Ltd. (systems integration, telecommunications)

Financial and Insurance
Samsung Capital Co., Ltd.
Samsung Card Co., Ltd. (loans, cash advances, financing)
Samsung Fire & Marine Insurance Co., Ltd.
Samsung Life Insurance Co., Ltd.
Samsung Life Investment Trust Management Co., Ltd.
Samsung Securities Co., Ltd.
Samsung Venture Investment Co., Ltd.

Other
Cheil Communications, Inc. (advertising)
Cheil Industries Inc. (textiles)
S1 Corporation (security systems)
Samsung Advanced Institute of Technology
Samsung Corporation (general trading)
Samsung Engineering Co., Ltd.
Samsung Everland Inc. (amusement parks)
Samsung Heavy Industries Co., Ltd. (machinery, vehicles)
Samsung Lions (pro baseball team)
Samsung Techwin Co., Ltd. (fine machinery including semiconductor equipment)
The Shilla Hotels & Resorts Co., Ltd.

COMPETITORS

Daewoo International	Micron Technology
DuPont	Millea Holdings
Ericsson	Motorola
Fujitsu	NEC
Hitachi	Nokia
Hyundai Corporation	Northrop Grumman
IBM	Philips Electronics
ITOCHU	SANYO
Kyobo Life Insurance	Sharp
LG Group	SK Group
Marconi	Sony
Marubeni	Ssangyong
Matsushita	Toshiba
Matsushita Electric Works	

HISTORICAL FINANCIALS

Company Type: Group

Income Statement

FYE: December 31

	REVENUE ($ mil.)	NET INCOME ($ mil.)	NET PROFIT MARGIN	EMPLOYEES
12/04	133,135	12,954	9.7%	222,000
12/03	101,459	5,632	5.6%	195,000
12/02	121,735	9,229	7.6%	175,000
12/01	98,700	4,500	4.6%	175,000
12/00	119,500	7,300	6.1%	174,000
12/99	93,500	2,200	2.4%	161,000
12/98	72,000	201	0.3%	193,000
12/97	57,199	173	0.3%	267,000
12/96	94,654	164	0.2%	256,000
12/95	87,000	3,802	4.4%	233,000
Annual Growth	**4.8%**	**14.6%**	**—**	**(0.5%)**

2004 Year-End Financials

Debt ratio: —
Return on equity: 20.1%
Cash ($ mil.): —
Current ratio: —
Long-term debt ($ mil.): —

Net Income History

San Miguel

Filipinos filling out their grocery lists often turn to San Miguel — they don't have much other choice. San Miguel Corporation (SMC) is the largest beverage and food firm in the Philippines, selling more than 200 product lines made in more than 100 area factories. The company brews and distributes beer, including San Miguel Pale Pilsen and Red Horse, and controls more than 90% of the Philippine beer market. It enjoys similar dominance of the soft-drink market, thanks to its 65% stake in bottler Coca-Cola Philippines (The Coca-Cola Company owns the remaining 35%) and its 2001 purchase of the Cosmos Bottling Corporation. Wrapping things up is San Miguel's can, bottle, and container business.

SMC's food and agribusiness subsidiaries make a variety of meat products, animal feeds,

coconut products, and dairy goods, while its packaging operations produce glass containers, aluminum cans, corrugated cartons, metal caps, and crowns. It also manages real estate.

The company says it plans to expand into Australia, China, Indonesia, Malaysia, Taiwan, Thailand, and Vietnam. SMC snapped up a majority stake in Singapore-based ice-cream producer King's Creameries in February 2005, and a month later announced its interest in acquiring New Zealand Dairy Foods Ltd. The company obtained full control of National Foods ($1.45 billion/A$1.9 billion) in June 2005. The company had been locked in a tight bidding race for the Australian dairy company with Fonterra Cooperative Group (Fonterra removed its offer only days after San Miguel's increased bid in April).

Chairman Eduardo Cojuangco says he owns less than 10% of the company; however, others report he owns as much as 20% of SMC and controls the voting rights of another 27% through the United Coconut Planters Bank. These shares are under government sequestration (but still controlled by Cojuangco); some Filipino government officials contend the shares were gained through corrupt use of a levy imposed on farmers during the presidential administration of Ferdinand Marcos.

HISTORY

Don Enrique Barretto y de Ycaza opened La Fabrica de Cerveza de San Miguel, a brewery, in Manila in 1890. By 1900 the European-styled beers of San Miguel were outselling imported brands five to one. The company became a corporation in 1913. By WWI the brewery was selling beer in Hong Kong, Shanghai, and Guam.

Andres Soriano y Roxas joined San Miguel in 1918 and in the 1920s established the Royal Soft Drinks Plant (1922), the Magnolia Ice Cream Plant (1925), and the first non-US national Coca-Cola bottling and distribution franchise (1927). After WWII, the company added additional facilities and factories as it modernized and expanded.

In the 1960s the firm changed its name to San Miguel Corporation (SMC). After the death of Andres in 1964, his son Andres Soriano Jr. became president. He decentralized operations into product segments. SMC continued to diversify in the 1970s.

A family feud erupted in 1983 when members of the controlling Soriano and Zobel families engaged in a proxy battle. Realizing he couldn't win the proxy fight, Enrique Zobel sold all of his shares (about 20% of SMC) to Eduardo Cojuangco, a Ferdinand Marcos ally and president of United Coconut Planters Bank. Upon Soriano's death in 1984, Cojuangco became chairman.

Cojuangco's estranged cousin Corazon Aquino won the 1986 national election, and her government claimed assets associated with Marcos and his followers, including Cojuangco's share of SMC. Cojuangco left the country with Marcos, and Andres Soriano III became CEO. Cojuangco returned to the Philippines in 1989 to reclaim his share of the company. In mid-1998, immediately following Cojuangco-backed Joseph Estrada's election as president of the Philippines, Andres Soriano III stepped down, and Cojuangco returned to SMC's helm.

SMC sold Coca-Cola Bottlers Philippines to Sydney-based Coca-Cola Amatil (CCA) in 1995 in exchange for a 25% stake in CCA. Four years later SMC flirted with plans to sell its interest in CCA, and then went on a buying binge. SMC and a company it majority owns, La Tondeña Distillers, jointly bought Filipino juice maker Sugarland. SMC then bought Australian brewer J. Boag & Son in June 2000.

Estrada announced the government's plan to sell a 27% stake in SMC, but those plans were altered dramatically after Estrada's ouster in early 2001. His successor, President Gloria Arroyo, said the government would seize 47% of the company's shares controlled by United Coconut Planters Bank (27%) and Cojuangco (20%).

Meanwhile, company expansion continued. San Miguel agreed to buy the Philippines' largest processed-meat maker, Pure Foods. The company bought 65% of bottler Coca-Coca Philippines from CCA in July, giving up its stake in CCA as part of the deal. In August 2001, SMC then acquired 83% of rival RFM's Cosmos Bottling, the Philippines' #2 soft drink company, further consolidating its domestic beverage dominance. In September the company transferred its 49% stake in Sugarland to La Tondeña Distillers, which then became the sole owner of the juice maker.

In 2002 Japanese brewer Kirin paid $530 million for 15% of San Miguel. Following an announced expansion plan into Asia, San Miguel purchased a Thailand industrial complex for $20 million in September 2003 and Thai Amarit Brewery Ltd. in April 2004.

EXECUTIVES

Chairman and CEO: Eduardo M. Cojuangco Jr.
Vice Chairman, President, and COO: Ramon S. Ang
CFO and Treasurer: Ferdinand K. Constantino
SVP, Corporate Human Resources: David S. Santos
SVP, Corporate Marketing: M.L. Menlou B. Bibonia
SVP, Corporate Planning and Development:
Maria Belen C. Buensuceso
SVP, Corporate Quality Management:
Alberto A. Manlapit
SVP, Corporate Technical Services:
Lubin B. Nepomuceno
SVP, Group Audit: Veneranda M. Tomas
President, Coca-Cola Bottlers Philippines:
Roberto N. Huang
President, Ginebra San Miguel: Danilo C. Navarro
President, San Miguel Beer Division:
Faustino F. Galang
President Director, P.T. Delta — Djakarta:
Manuel M. Moreno
CEO, Berri, Limited: Alison Watkins
VP, Corporate Export Sales and Business Development:
Antonio V. Enriquez II
VP, Corporate Export Sales and Business Development:
Lorenzo C. Manabat
VP, Corporate Finance: Mercy Marie L. Amador
VP, Corporate Human Resources: Eliezer O. Capacio
VP, Corporate Sales: Roberto T. Ongsiako
VP, Corporate Sales: Pablo P. Pacquing
VP, Ginebra San Miguel: Sylvia P. Quirino
Corporate Secretary and General Counsel:
Francis H. Jardeleza
Auditors: SyCip Gorres Velayo & Co.

LOCATIONS

HQ: San Miguel Corporation
40 San Miguel Ave., Mandaluyong,
Metro Manila 1550, Philippines
Phone: +63-2-632-3000   **Fax:** +63-2-632-3099
Web: www.sanmiguel.com.ph

San Miguel Corporation has manufacturing plants in China, Hong Kong, Indonesia, the Philippines, Vietnam, and other countries in Southeast Asia. The company's beers are sold in some 20 countries in the Americas, Asia, and Australia.

2004 Sales

	% of total
Philippines	87
China	4
Australia	4
Indonesia	2
Vietnam	1
Other countries	2
Total	**100**

PRODUCTS/OPERATIONS

2004 Sales

	% of total
Beverage	64
Food	33
Packaging	3
Total	**100**

Selected Products and Brands

Beverages
  Beer (Multinational)
    Ander Bir (licensed)
    Blue Ice
    Cerveza Negra
    Gold Eagle
    Miller Genuine Draft (licensed)
    Red Horse
    San Miguel Light
    San Miguel (Draft Beer, Pale Pilsen, Super Dry)
  Beer (Regional)
    China (Blue Star, Double Happiness Beer, Dragon Beer, Guang's Draft, Kirin, Pineapple Beer, Valor)
    Hong Kong (Bruck, Eagle High, Knight, Lowenbrau — licensed, San Miguel Dark)
    Indonesia (Anker Stout — licensed, Carlsberg — licensed)
    Vietnam (Bock)
  Bottled water
    Distilled drinking water (FIRST, Wilkins)
    Mineral water (VIVA!)
  Juice drinks
    Cordial lime juice
    Magnolia (Fruit Drinks, FunChum, Junior Juice, Ice Tea)
    Zip juice
  Nonalcoholic malt beverages
    Cali (Shandy, 10, Ice)
    Guang's Pineapple Shandy (China)
    San Miguel NAB
    Shanta Super Shandy (Indonesia)
  Wines and spirits
    Gin (Ginebra San Miguel, Oxford London Dry Gin — licensed)
    Rum (Añejo, Tondeña, San Miguel)
Food and Agribusiness
  Dairy
    Dari Creme
    Star
  Meat (beef, chicken, pork)
    Longanisa
    Magnolia
    Moby
    Valiente
Real Estate
  Bel Adea
  Buenavista Homes
  Country Mile Homes
  The Enterprise Center
  Greenwoods
  HOC Realty Inc.
  HQ Business Centers
  The Legacy
  Lexington
  Maravilla
  Primavera Hills
  San Miguel Properties Corp.
  Villa de Calamba
  Wedge Woods

COMPETITORS

Amcor	Diageo
Anheuser-Busch	Foster's
Asahi Breweries	Heineken
Asia Brewery	InBev
Bacardi USA	International Paper
Benguet	Kirin
Cadbury Schweppes	Lion Nathan
Cargill	Mercian
Carlsberg	Nestlé
CBR Brewing	PepsiCo
ConAgra	Tsingtao
Danone	Tyson Foods

HISTORICAL FINANCIALS

Company Type: Public

Income Statement

FYE: December 31

	REVENUE ($ mil.)	NET INCOME ($ mil.)	NET PROFIT MARGIN	EMPLOYEES
12/04	3,106	144	4.6%	26,427
12/03	2,666	132	5.0%	26,420
12/02	2,536	124	4.9%	27,259
12/01	2,353	125	5.3%	26,697
12/00	1,771	137	7.7%	14,864
12/99	1,881	150	8.0%	14,511
12/98	1,911	629	32.9%	15,923
12/97	1,699	75	4.4%	18,444
12/96	3,232	232	7.2%	28,544
12/95	3,027	223	7.4%	31,485
Annual Growth	0.3%	(4.8%)	—	(1.9%)

2004 Year-End Financials

Debt ratio: 24.7%   Current ratio: 1.61
Return on equity: 7.5%   Long-term debt ($ mil.): 479
Cash ($ mil.): 479

Net Income History

OTC: SMGBY

700	
600	
500	
400	
300	
200	
100	
0	
	12/95 12/96 12/97 12/98 12/99 12/00 12/01 12/02 12/03 12/04

Sanofi-Aventis

Sanofi-Aventis helps docs treat its sneezy patients without making them sleepy, grumpy, or dopey. The company's allergy drug Allegra promises relief from symptoms without the side effects typical of allergy medicines. The company specializes in cardiovascular, central nervous system, oncology, and internal medicine formulations; its other top sellers include Lovenox (deep vein thrombosis), Plavix (thrombosis), Avapro (hypertension), and Ambien (insomnia). The company was formed by the 2004 merger between two French drugmakers, Sanofi-Synthélabo and Aventis; the deal formed the world's third largest pharmaceutical company, behind only Pfizer and GlaxoSmithKline.

Sanofi-Aventis is also major player in the human vaccine market and benefitted from Chiron's inability to deliver flu shots in late 2004. Sales of Sanofi-Aventis' own flu vaccine were a a quarter higher in 2004, rising 70% in the fourth quarter of the year from 2003.

The company has built a 100-drug pipeline, with nearly half of the candidates in clinical trials and also has about 20 new vaccines in development. Sanofi-Aventis also partners with smaller firms, such as Immuno-Designed Molecules, to increase its potential products while keeping costs down.

In Europe, Sanofi-Aventis is focusing on its generic drug business. The company also makes over-the-counter analgesic products for the European market.

Since the merger, Sanofi-Aventis has focused on expanding its presence in the US market.

HISTORY

The Sanofi group got its start in 1973 when French oil conglomerate Elf Aquitaine merged several health care, cosmetics, and animal nutrition companies into one subsidiary. In 1977 Sanofi set up a Japanese subsidiary, through which it developed joint ventures with Japan's Meiji Seika Kaisha and Taisha Pharmaceutical firms. In 1979 Elf spun off Sanofi, although it retained ownership of more than half of the company. Almost from its founding Sanofi grew through acquisitions and alliances. During the 1980s, it used a massive war chest to buy stakes and set up joint ventures, such as one with American Home Products (now Wyeth) in 1982.

The company bought *couturier et parfumier* Nina Ricci in 1988; such well-known fragrances as L'Air du Temps put it among the industry's top perfume houses. But Sanofi overreached the next two years and was outbid by American Home Products for AH Robins (the drug firm bankrupted by lawsuits over deaths from its Dalkon Shield IUD) and by Rhône-Poulenc (now part of Aventis) for Rorer. A chastened Sanofi and Kodak subsidiary Sterling Drug in 1991 entered into an alliance that didn't involve an exchange of cash.

In 1993 Sanofi made a splash when it bought the perfume business of fashion designer Yves Saint-Laurent. The next year it bought out much of the pharmaceutical joint venture with Kodak. Sanofi began divesting such noncore businesses as veterinarian and biotech operations in 1995. After suffering a loss in its perfume and beauty division in 1996, it sold Nina Ricci. The rest of its beauty division was sold in 1999 in preparation for the Synthélabo merger.

Synthélabo was founded in 1970 when drug firms Laboratoires Dausse and Laboratoires Robert et Carriere merged. In 1973 it became a 53%-owned subsidiary of L'Oréal. In 1980 drug firm Metabio-Jouillie became a part of Synthélabo, making it the #3 drug company in France. In 1983 Synthélabo and US drugmaker Searle created Lorex to market the French firm's products in the UK. (Synthélabo bought Searle's interest 10 years later.)

Throughout the 1980s Synthélabo acquired, merged, and formed joint ventures, including some in Japan with Mitsubishi Chemical, Fujisawa Pharmaceutical (1985), and Tanabe Seiyaku (1987). The company continued its acquisitive ways in the 1990s, buying several French rivals.

Synthélabo openly admitted its quest for a large international presence in 1996, announcing it wanted 80% of its sales to come from such foreign markets as Asia and the US. That year the company entered an alliance with Genset to research cancer-causing genes; it also signed on with SmithKline Beecham (now GlaxoSmithKline) and Human Genome Sciences to fund genetic research. Synthélabo's Hungarian subsidiary began planning to make drugs for the first time, rather than just selling its parent's products as in the past.

The next year Synthélabo bought Pharmacia & Upjohn's German generic drug subsidiary Sanorania Pharma. As Synthélabo and Sanofi merged in 1999, the new company's concentration on pharmaceuticals dictated several changes, including the sale of the company's interests in joint venture Pasteur Sanofi Diagnostics, as well as its beauty division, home to such well-known perfume lines as Yves Saint Laurent. It also sold its veterinary and animal feed division to what is now BNP Paribas.

Sanofi-Synthélabo made good on its plans to target the US in 2000, expanding its sales force there. But the merger wasn't without its problems: Former Synthélabo CEO Hervé Guérin was ousted as vice-chairman and COO of Sanofi-Synthélabo after he and Chairman Jean-François Dehecq butted heads. In 2002 the company boosted its pipeline by entering into an alliance with Immuno-Designed Molecules, a biotechnology firm focusing on cancer drugs. Also that year the FDA approved the firm's colorectal cancer drug, Eloxatin, in record time.

EXECUTIVES

Chairman and CEO: Jean-François Dehecq, age 65, $5,837,920 pay
Vice Chairman: Jürgen Dormann, age 65
SEVP, Scientific and Medical Operations: Gérard Le Fur, age 54, $2,560,000 pay
SVP and Advisor to the Chairman: Jean-Pierre Kerjouan, age 65
SVP, Audit and Internal Control Assessment: Marie-Hélène Laimay
SVP, Business Development: Olivier Jacquesson, age 55
SVP, Commercial Operations, USA: Pascal Soriot, age 45
SVP, Communications: Nicole Cranois, age 56
SVP, Corporate Affairs: Philippe Peyre, age 53
SVP, Corporate Human Resources: Jean-Claude Armbruster, age 59
SVP, Finance: Jean-Claude Leroy, age 53
SVP, Global Marketing: Pierre Chancel
SVP, Industrial Affairs: Gilles Lhernould, age 49
SVP, Legal Affairs and General Counsel: Dirk Oldenburg, age 48
SVP, Pharmaceutical Operations, USA: Timothy G. Rothwell, age 53
VP, Media and Public Relations: Jean-Marc Podvin
President, Sanofi Pasteur Canada: Mark Lievonen
President, Sanofi Pasteur International: Jacques Cholat
Head of Advertising Operations: Richard Sherwood
EVP, Sanofi Pasteur North America: Wayne F. Pisano
Auditors: Befec-Price Waterhouse; Ernst & Young Audit

LOCATIONS

HQ: Sanofi-Aventis
174 avenue de France, 75013 Paris, France
Phone: +33-1-53-77-40-00   **Fax:** +33-1-53-77-42-96
US HQ: 300-400 Somerset Corporate Blvd., SC4-310A, Bridgewater, NJ 08807-0912
US Phone: 908-243-6000   **US Fax:** 908-243-6483
Web: www.sanofi-aventis.com

Sanofi-Aventis has about 75 manufacturing plants worldwide, located in Brazil, France, Germany, Hungary, India, Italy, Japan, Mexico, Morocco, Singapore, the UK, and the US.

2004 Sales

	$ mil.	% of total
Europe	9,957	49
US	6,310	31
Other regions	4,110	20
Total	**20,377**	**100**

PRODUCTS/OPERATIONS

2004 Sales

	$ mil.	% of total
Pharmaceuticals		
Lovenox	2,579	7
Plavix	2,294	7
Allegra	2,034	6
Taxotere	1,945	6
Stilnox	1,928	6
Eloxatine	1,653	5
Delix/Tritace	1,317	4
Lantus	1,142	3
Aprovel	1,070	3
Copaxone	1,005	3
Amaryl	927	3
Actonel	413	1
Depakine	410	1
Nasacort	389	1
Xatral	381	1
Other	12,744	37
Human vaccines		
Influenza	710	2
Pediatric combination	455	1
Polio	249	1
Adult booster	236	1
Travel	199	—
Meningitis	117	—
Other	234	1
Adjustments	(14,054)	—
Total	**20,377**	**100**

Selected Pharmaceutical Products

Actonel (osteoporosis)
Allegra/Telfast (allergies)
Amaryl (diabetes)
Ambien (sleep disorders)
Aprovel/Avapro (hypertension)
Arava (rheumatoid arthritis)
Copaxone (multiple sclerosis)
Cordarone (anti-arrhythmic)
Corotrope (acute congestive heart failure)
Delix/Tritace (cardiovascular conditions)
Depakine (anti-epileptic)
Dogmatil (psychosomatic disorders)
Eloxatin (colorectal cancer)
Fasturtec/Elitek (hyperuricemia)
Insuman (insulin for diabetes mellitus)
Kerlone (hypertension)
Ketek (antibiotic)
Lantus (long-acting insulin)
Lovenox/Clexane (cardiovascular conditions)
Nasacort (nasal congestion relief)
Plavix (atherothrombosis)
Solian (schizophrenia)
Stilnox (hypnotic for insomnia)
Targocid (anti-infective)
Tavanic (anti-infective)
Taxotere (breast and ovarian cancer)
Ticlid (thrombosis)
Tildiem (angina and hypertension)

COMPETITORS

Abbott Labs
Amgen
AstraZeneca
Bayer
Bristol-Myers Squibb
Chiron
Eli Lilly
GE Healthcare Bio-Sciences
GlaxoSmithKline
Johnson & Johnson
Merck
Novartis
Novo Nordisk
Pfizer
Schering
Wyeth

HISTORICAL FINANCIALS

Company Type: Public

Income Statement

FYE: December 31

	REVENUE ($ mil.)	NET INCOME ($ mil.)	NET PROFIT MARGIN	EMPLOYEES
12/04	20,377	(4,890)	—	96,439
12/03	10,118	2,610	25.8%	33,086
12/02	7,823	1,847	23.6%	32,436
12/01	5,747	1,404	24.4%	30,514
12/00	5,615	928	16.5%	29,200
12/99	5,388	629	11.7%	29,312
12/98	4,596	377	8.2%	29,621
12/97	4,288	321	7.5%	28,645
12/96	4,556	336	7.4%	28,207
12/95	4,692	321	6.8%	27,306
Annual Growth	17.7%	—	—	15.1%

2004 Year-End Financials

Debt ratio: 24.3%
Return on equity: —
Cash ($ mil.): 2,075
Current ratio: 0.96
Long-term debt ($ mil.): 11,701

No. of shares (mil.): 2,823
Dividends
Yield: 1.5%
Payout: —
Market value ($ mil.): 113,053

Stock History

NYSE: SNY

12/95 12/96 12/97 12/98 12/99 12/00 12/01 12/02 12/03 12/04

	STOCK PRICE ($) FY Close	P/E High/Low	PER SHARE ($) Earnings	Dividends	Book Value
12/04	40.05	— —	(2.65)	0.61	17.07
12/03	37.75	20 12	1.85	0.46	5.42
12/02	30.40	26 20	1.27	0.00	4.33
Annual Growth	14.8%	— —	—	—	98.6%

SANYO Electric

"Sanyo" means "three oceans" in Japanese, and when it comes to consumer and commercial electronics, SANYO covers the waterfront. The electronics powerhouse has more than 170 subsidiaries worldwide. From electric bicycles to semiconductors, SANYO manufactures products both innovative and prosaic. Its companies make a variety of electrical devices and appliances, including industrial and commercial equipment (refrigerated supermarket cases), audio and video equipment (DVD players, TVs, digital cameras), semiconductors, communications equipment (cellular phones, computers), batteries, and home appliances (microwave ovens, air conditioners).

Japan accounts for almost 70% of the company's sales. SANYO is focused on developing environment-friendly products such as solar cells, rechargeable batteries, and CFC-free refrigerators and air-conditioning units. The company also is placing particular emphasis on developing multimedia products, such as digital cameras and liquid-crystal displays (LCDs).

To remain competitive in the explosive high-tech environment, SANYO is forming alliances with leading technology developers, including a five-member consortium to address 3-D technology (ITOCHU, NTT DATA, Sharp, and Sony) and an initiative with Samsung (home-use air conditioners). SANYO also embarked on a joint venture with International Rectifier. In 2004 Seiko Epson and SANYO merged its LCD businesses. The new company, called Sanyo Epson Imaging Devices, began operations in October 2004. A month later Sanyo Epson announced plans to shift its focus to making TFD (thin-film diode) panels. As a result of this decision, the company moved part of its LCD panel manufacturing operations to China.

In 2004 the company began manufacturing car audio and navigation systems through a new Chinese subsidiary. It also started selling LCD televisions at Wal-Mart stores in the US; the products are manufactured in a Mexican plant.

Sanyo entered the European mobile phone market in 2004 by supplying wireless handsets to London-based Orange SA. The company also joined forces with Robert Bosch, a German manufacturer of car parts, to create rechargeable batteries for cars that run on both gasoline and battery power. Sanyo Electric has a similar agreement with DaimlerChrysler.

In further efforts to cut costs, the company announced plans in mid-2005 to cut 15% of its staff worldwide and close or sell 20% of its factory space in Japan.

HISTORY

Toshio Iue, SANYO's first CEO, had the "three oceans" (Pacific, Atlantic, and Indian) in mind — he wanted to turn the company into an international enterprise. SANYO was formed after WWII when the Allies broke Matsushita Electric into two companies. Toshio, brother-in-law to Matsushita founder Konosuke Matsushita, took charge of SANYO, which then made bicycle lamps.

By 1949 the company was producing radios, and in the 1950s it diversified into refrigerators, fans, and washing machines. In 1953 a Japanese household appliances rush began, and SANYO led washing machine sales. By the end of the decade, the company was Japan's leading exporter of transistor radios.

To raise money, in 1959 SANYO created Tokyo SANYO Electric, in which it took a 20% stake. The company established its first factory abroad, in Hong Kong, in 1961 and created Cadnica, a durable rechargeable battery.

The 1970s oil crisis drew SANYO into alternative energy development, and the company continued its energy research when the crisis had passed. In 1973 SANYO joined forces with Emerson Electric (US) to bail out Emerson's Fisher electronics subsidiary. (SANYO bought Fisher in 1978.) SANYO began shifting its focus from appliances to high-tech products in the mid-1970s. It started making color TVs in the US in 1976. Although sales slowed when SANYO initially opted to develop VCRs using the ill-fated Betamax format, they rose tremendously in the 1970s, from $71 million in 1972 to $855 million in 1978.

SANYO and Tokyo SANYO Electric merged in 1986. A high yen forced the company to move much of its manufacturing outside Japan; that year it made more products abroad than any other Japanese company. By then the country's leading TV maker, SANYO formed a joint venture with Sears to manufacture TVs. SANYO also developed the world's first CFC-free refrigeration

system, a version of which was installed in New York's Guggenheim Museum.

In 1993 SANYO set a world record for solar-energy conversion efficiency. The company strengthened its electronic components and solar businesses two years later by establishing SANYO Electronic Components and SANYO Solar Industries. In 1997 SANYO introduced the highest-output home-use solar cells, capable of producing 160 watts of electricity.

In 1998 the company formed a pact with IBM to make semiconductors using Big Blue's energy-saving copper-circuit technology. The next year SANYO allied with Philips to develop semiconductors and related products.

Also in 1999 SANYO teamed up with Eastman Kodak to develop flat-panel displays based on next-generation organic electroluminescent technology. The company announced several product developments, including an advanced battery for hybrid-fuel vehicles and an air-conditioning and refrigeration compressor that uses carbon dioxide instead of Freon.

Amid charges of knowingly selling defective solar cell systems, president Sadao Kondo resigned in 2000. He was replaced by Yukinori Kuwano. In 2001 SANYO acquired Toshiba's nickel metal hydride battery business, solidifying its position as one of the world's leading battery manufacturers.

In 2002 the company formed an alliance with China's largest consumer electronics maker, Haier Group, whereby SANYO sells its products through Haier's outlets and service centers and, in turn, selected Haier goods are sold in Japan.

SANYO's three-year initiative (launched 2001) resulted in the sale of the troubled vending-machine manufacturing operations (2002). The initiative also led to the restructuring of the company's Home Appliances business, including shifting production of home-use air conditioners to China.

That year SANYO and Eastman Kodak agreed to jointly fund production of full-color organic light-emitting diode (OLED) displays; OLED displays feature full-motion images viewable from very wide angles. Also in 2003 SANYO turned wholly owned SANYO Electric Software Co. into a 50/50 joint venture with NTT DATA.

EXECUTIVES

Chairman and CEO: Tomoyo Nonaka, age 50
Vice Chairman: Sadao Kondo
President, COO, and Director: Toshimasa Iue
Executive Officer and Director: Satoshi Inoue
Executive Officer and Director: Osamu Kajikawa
Executive Officer: Yasusuke Tanaka
Executive Officer: Hiroshi Ono
Executive Officer and Group Executive, Commercial Solutions Group: Akira Kan
Executive Officer and Group Executive, Power Solutions Group; President, Mobile Energy Company: Mitsuru Honma
Executive Officer and Group Executive, Business Planning & Business Group; General Manager, Business Development Headquarters; General Manager, International Mangement Headquarters: Shinichi Miki
Senior Officer: Teruo Tabata
Senior Officer: Toshiaki Iue
Senior Officer: Takenori Ugari
Senior Officer; President, Clean Energy Company, Commercial Solutions Group: Tadao Shimada
Senior Officer; President, AV Company, Home Electronics Group: Yoshio Iwasa
Senior Officer: Yoshihiro Nishiguchi
Auditors: ChuoAoyama PricewaterhouseCoopers

LOCATIONS

HQ: SANYO Electric Co., Ltd.
(San'yo Denki Kabushiki Kaisha)
5-5 Keihan-Hondori, 2-chome,
Moriguchi, Osaka 570-8677, Japan
Phone: +81-6-6991-1181   **Fax:** +81-6-6991-2086
US HQ: 2055 Sanyo Ave., San Diego, CA 92154
US Phone: 619-661-1134   **US Fax:** 619-661-6795
Web: www.sanyo.co.jp

SANYO Electric has more than 170 subsidiaries worldwide, and operates manufacturing facilities in more than 20 countries (located primarily in Asia, as well as in North America and Europe).

2005 Sales

	% of total
Japan	51
Rest of Asia	26
North America	13
Europe	7
Other countries	3
Total	**100**

PRODUCTS/OPERATIONS

2005 Sales

	% of total
Consumer	49
Component	38
Commercial	9
Other	4
Total	**100**

Selected Products

A/V Information and Communications Equipment
  Automotive stereo components
  CD-R/RW systems
  Cellular phones
  Color TVs
  Digital cameras
  Digital memory players
  DVD players
  DVD-ROM systems
  Fax machines
  High-definition plasma TVs
  Liquid crystal display (LCD) projectors
  Medical computer systems
  Optical pickups
  Personal Handyphone System (PHS)
    (phones and base stations)
  Portable navigation systems
  VCRs
  Video cameras
Electronic Devices
  CCD
  Electronic components
  Laser diodes
  LCDs
  LEDs
  MOS-LSIs
  Thick-film integrated circuits (ICs)
  Transistors and diodes
Batteries
  Alkaline batteries
  Lithium batteries
  Manganese batteries
  Nickel-cadmium rechargeable batteries
  Nickel-metal-hydride rechargeable batteries
  Solar cells
  Solar-cell power systems

Home Appliances
  Air conditioners
  Automatic tablet-wrapping machines
  Clothes dryers
  Compressors for freezers, refrigerators,
    and air conditioners
  Dehumidifiers
  Dishwashers and dryers
  Electric and kerosene heating equipment
  Electronic and electric products for bicycles
  Freezers
  Home-use pumps
  Massage loungers
  Medical sterilizing equipment
  Medical-use refrigerators
  Microwave ovens
  Motor-assisted bicycles
  Refrigerators
  Small kitchen appliances (toasters, rice cookers,
    electromagnetic cookers)
  Ultralow-temperature freezers
  Vacuum cleaners
  Washing machines
  Waste disposers
Industrial and Commercial Equipment
  Absorption chillers and heaters
  Automatic chip mounters
  Beverage dispensers
  Commercial freezers and refrigerators
  Gas-engine heat-pump air conditioners
  Golf cart systems
  Ice makers
  Package air conditioners
  Prefabricated freezers
  Refrigerated/freezer/supermarket showcases
  Water coolers

COMPETITORS

AMD	Maytag
Apple Computer	Mitsubishi Electric
Canon	Motorola
CASIO COMPUTER	National Semiconductor
Daewoo Electronics	NEC
Dell	Nokia
Electrolux	Oki Electric
Energizer Holdings	Philips Electronics
Epson	Pioneer
Fujitsu	Pitney Bowes
GE	Ricoh
Gillette	Samsung Electronics
Hewlett-Packard	Sharp
Hitachi	Siemens
IBM	Sony
Intel	THOMSON
Kyocera	Toshiba
LG Electronics	United Technologies
Matsushita	Whirlpool

HISTORICAL FINANCIALS

Company Type: Public

Income Statement

FYE: March 31

	REVENUE ($ mil.)	NET INCOME ($ mil.)	NET PROFIT MARGIN	EMPLOYEES
3/05	24,174	(1,603)	—	96,023
3/04	24,528	126	0.5%	82,337
3/03	18,949	(607)	—	79,025
3/02	15,881	13	0.1%	80,500
3/01	18,073	340	1.9%	86,009
3/00	19,002	205	1.1%	83,519
3/99	15,687	(216)	—	77,071
3/98	14,581	93	0.6%	67,887
3/97	14,889	143	1.0%	67,827
3/96	4,949	(35)	—	56,612
Annual Growth	**19.3%**	**—**	**—**	**6.0%**

2005 Year-End Financials

Debt ratio: 235.8%
Return on equity: —
Cash ($ mil.): 1,159
Current ratio: 1.09
Long-term debt ($ mil.): 6,353
No. of shares (mil.): 371
Dividends
  Yield: 1.5%
  Payout: —
Market value ($ mil.): 5,716

Stock History   NASDAQ (SC): SANYY

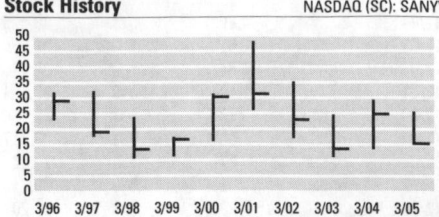

	STOCK PRICE ($) FY Close	P/E High/Low		PER SHARE ($) Earnings	Dividends	Book Value
3/05	15.41	— —		(4.32)	0.23	7.26
3/04	24.75	85	41	0.34	0.26	12.64
3/03	13.69	— —		(1.63)	0.25	10.81
3/02	22.99	580	292	0.06	0.00	12.10
3/01	31.25	54	30	0.89	0.25	14.06
3/00	30.25	57	30	0.54	0.22	16.77
3/99	16.63	— —		(0.56)	0.11	15.22
3/98	13.50	98	46	0.24	0.19	14.57
3/97	19.13	86	49	0.37	0.06	160.36
3/96	29.13	— —		(0.09)	0.12	19.58
Annual Growth	**(6.8%)**	**— —**		**—**	**7.5%**	**(10.4%)**

SAP

SAP's plans to dominate the software world are more than a little enterprising. The company is the leading provider of enterprise resource planning (ERP) software used to integrate back-office functions such as distribution, accounting, human resources, and manufacturing. More than 27,000 companies in over 120 countries use its software. SAP continues to shift its huge customer base to its mySAP products, which are Web-based software platforms used for a variety of enterprise functions. SAP has leveraged its prominent position in the ERP market to expand into related fields, including supply chain and customer relationship management (CRM).

SAP has methodically transitioned towards incorporating Web-based capabilities into its product lines. While the company's huge installed base of customers provides a steady stream of recurring licensing and service revenue, SAP has come under pressure from investors to pursue new areas of growth. With its legacy ERP software industry maturing, the company has intensified its efforts in the CRM software arena, battling head to head with CRM leader Siebel Systems, as well as with Oracle and Microsoft.

Following Oracle's acquisition of ERP rival PeopleSoft, SAP acquired PeopleSoft support firm TomorrowNow, in an effort to lure customers away from Oracle. Early in 2005 SAP agreed to acquire retail software specialist Retek, but it was eventually outbid by Oracle. Later in the year SAP acquired point-of-sale software provider Triversity. It has agreed to acquire KhiMetrics, a developer of pricing and forecasting software for the retail market.

Partially in response to Microsoft's expanding presence in the enterprise software market, SAP has also released a scaled-down version of its software designed specifically for small and mid-sized businesses, as well as new software development tools and services for its strategic partners in Europe. The company has also announced plans to expand its ERP business in fledgling, unsaturated markets in Latin America and Asia (with a particular emphasis on China).

SAP has also introduced its NetWeaver technology and application platform, which is designed to increase the interoperability between enterprise data and SAP's software products.

Three of SAP's founders — Hasso Plattner, Dietmar Hopp, and Klaus Tschira — control about 32% of the company.

HISTORY

Former IBM software engineers Hasso Plattner, Hans-Werner Hector, Dietmar Hopp, Claus Wellenreuther, and Klaus Tschira started SAP in 1972 when the project they were working on for was moved to another unit.

While rival software firms made many products to automate the various parts of a company's operations, these engineers decided to make a single system that would tie a corporation together. In 1973 they launched an instantaneous accounting transaction processing program called R/1. By 1979 they had adapted the program to create R/2, mainframe software that linked external databases and communication systems.

The company went public in 1988. That year Plattner began a project to create software for the computer network market. In 1992, as sales of its R/2 mainframe software lagged, SAP introduced its R/3 software.

In 1996 Hector decided to sell holdings amounting to about 10% of SAP's stock, a move that possibly undermined hostile-takeover barriers; he left the company after a dispute with Hopp.

In 1998 SAP listed its stock on the NYSE; long-time executive Henning Kagermann was named co-chairman along with Plattner. In 1999 the company expanded on the Internet, unveiling a Web-based exchange (mySAP.com) supporting online transactions and other services. The company's long-standing resistance to employee stock options weakened in 2000 when SAP approved an option program to offset the loss of more than 200 key US managers in an 18-month period.

Later that year SAP launched a US subsidiary (SAP Markets) and increased its minority stake in software maker Commerce One.

In 2001 SAP acquired enterprise portal software provider Top Tier Software, renaming it SAP Portals. It also invested additional money in Commerce One, raising its ownership stake to about 20%.

The company reabsorbed its SAP Portals and SAP Markets subsidiaries in 2002, integrating their offerings into its mySAP product family.

In 2003 Plattner stepped down, leaving Kagermann in sole control of the chairman and CEO positions.

The next year SAP announced it was acquiring the public stake in SAP SI as part of a plan to fold that company into its services operations.

EXECUTIVES

Chairman and CEO: Henning Kagermann, age 57
Executive Board, Finance and Administration: Werner Brandt, age 51
Executive Board, Global Sales, Field Services, and Marketing: Leo Apotheker, age 52
Executive Board, Global Service and Support: Gerhard Oswald, age 51
Executive Board, Human Resources and SAP Labs: Claus E. Heinrich, age 49
Executive Board, Research and Innovation: Peter Zencke, age 55
Executive Board, Software and Solution Development, Business Solution Groups, Product and Industry Marketing: Shai Agassi, age 36
Extended Management Board: Leslie Hayman
Extended Management Board, Global Marketing: Martin Homlish
Extended Management Board, SAP NetWeaver Development: Klaus Kreplin
Extended Management Board, Strategic Research and Development: Peter J. Kirschbauer
EVP; General Manager, Suite Optimization and Program Office: Doug Merritt
EVP, Platform Ecosystem Development: George Paolini
SVP, Global Communications: Anne M. McCarthy
President and CEO, SAP America: William R. (Bill) McDermott, age 44
Auditors: KPMG Deutsche Treuhand-Gesellschaft AG

LOCATIONS

HQ: SAP Aktiengesellschaft
   Neurottstrasse 16, 69190 Walldorf, Germany
Phone: +49-6227-74-7474   **Fax:** +49-6227-75-7575
US HQ: 3999 West Chester Pike,
   Newtown Square, PA 19073
US Phone: 610-661-1000   **US Fax:** 610-355-3106
Web: www.sap.com

2004 Sales

	% of total
Europe, Middle East & Africa	
Germany	24
Other countries	33
Americas	
US	25
Other countries	7
Asia/Pacific	
Japan	5
Other countries	6
Total	**100**

PRODUCTS/OPERATIONS

2004 Sales

	% of total
Services	
Maintenance	38
Consulting	26
Training	4
Software	31
Other	1
Total	**100**

2004 Software Sales

	% of total
Enterprise resource planning	42
Customer relationship management	21
Supply chain management	21
Product lifecycle management	7
Supplier relationship management	6
Other	3
Total	**100**

2004 Sales by Industry Sector

	% of total
Discrete	24
Service	22
Process	20
Consumer	18
Public	9
Financial	7
Total	**100**

COMPETITORS

Epicor Software
i2 Technologies
IBM
Intentia
Lawson Software
Manugistics Group
MAPICS
Microsoft
Oracle
Siebel Systems
SSA Global

HISTORICAL FINANCIALS

Company Type: Public

Income Statement

FYE: December 31

	REVENUE ($ mil.)	NET INCOME ($ mil.)	NET PROFIT MARGIN	EMPLOYEES
12/04	10,179	1,775	17.4%	32,802
12/03	8,831	1,354	15.3%	30,251
12/02	7,786	534	6.9%	29,374
12/01	6,534	517	7.9%	28,878
12/00	5,881	596	10.1%	24,480
12/99	5,146	605	11.8%	21,699
12/98	5,073	629	12.4%	17,323
12/97	3,346	515	15.4%	12,856
12/96	2,415	367	15.2%	9,202
12/95	1,875	281	15.0%	6,857
Annual Growth	**20.7%**	**22.8%**	**—**	**19.0%**

2004 Year-End Financials

Debt ratio: 0.2%
Return on equity: 32.6%
Cash ($ mil.): 4,330
Current ratio: 7.80
Long-term debt ($ mil.): 10
No. of shares (mil.): 1,264
Dividends
   Yield: 0.0%
   Payout: —
Market value ($ mil.): 55,882

Stock History

NYSE: SAP

	STOCK PRICE ($) FY Close	P/E High/Low		PER SHARE ($) Earnings	Dividends	Book Value
12/04	44.21	32	25	1.42	0.00	4.92
12/03	41.56	38	17	1.09	0.13	3.75
12/02	19.50	91	23	0.43	0.13	2.42
12/01	31.93	120	52	0.41	0.00	2.21
12/00	33.69	90	32	0.95	0.00	1.85
12/99	52.06	57	25	0.96	0.00	6.15
12/98	36.06	120	59	0.50	0.00	5.36
Annual Growth	**3.5%**	**—**	**—**	**19.0%**	**—**	**(1.4%)**

SAS AB

Danes, Norwegians, and Swedes travel the world via SAS. It is the Nordic region's largest listed airline group, providing daily departures to 146 destinations in the region. SAS airlines fly to and from Scandinavia and the rest of Europe and to and from North America and Asia. The company's Rezidor SAS Hospitality subsidiary operates about 190 hotels in more than 40 countries. The former Scandinavian Airlines System, a consortium made up of three companies controlled by the governments of Denmark, Norway, and Sweden, respectively, was restructured into a single, publicly traded company, SAS AB, in 2001. The Swedish government owns 21% of the new SAS, and the governments of Denmark and Norway each own 14%.

SAS is a founding member of the Star Alliance, whose members include Air Canada, All Nippon Airway, Lufthansa, Thai Airways, United Airlines, and VARIG of Brazil. The marketing alliance allows the carriers to pool frequent-flyer programs and share booking and airport facilities. Many of the members have signed code-sharing deals with one another. SAS serves more than 770 destinations worldwide through its Star Alliance partners. It has three alliance members within its group: Scandinavian Airlines, Spanair, and Blue1 (formerly Air Botnia). The SAS group also owns Widerøe, airBaltic, and Estonian Air. Widerøe is Norway's leading regional carrier, and Spanair is Spain's second-largest airline. Fast-growing Blue1 is based in Finland.

The company has split its Scandinavian Airlines businesses into four separate airlines. Three of the units operate in Denmark (Scandinavian Airlines Danmark), Norway (SAS Braathens), and Sweden (Scandinavian Airlines Sverige), and there is an additional airline to handle international flights (Scandinavian Airlines International). Together these airlines transport almost 24 million passengers yearly.

The airline has been struggling to keep costs down, and it has been exploring the usual ways to quickly eliminate high costs, including reducing jobs from its workforce. The increase in fuel prices has also exacerbated the airline's financial condition. And despite its cost-cutting efforts, SAS has failed to stop losses in the face of stiff competition and record jet fuel prices.

To reduce costs, the company has decided to focus on its core business. As part of that strategy, the company in 2005 agreed to sell its European Aeronautical Group, which has operations in Sweden and the UK, to Canada-based flight operations manager Navtech.

HISTORY

The national airlines of Sweden (ABA), Norway (DNL), and Denmark (DDL) first met in 1938 to negotiate joint service to New York. The plan was delayed by WWII but kept alive in Sweden, where banker Marcus Wallenberg founded Svensk Interkontinental Luftrafik (SILA), a private airline that in 1943 replaced ABA as Sweden's international carrier. With SILA's financial backing, the yet-to-be-formed Scandinavian Airlines System (SAS) obtained the necessary landing concessions to open a Stockholm-New York air route in 1945. SAS was formed in 1946.

After opening service to South America (1946), Southeast Asia (1949), and Africa (1953), SAS inaugurated the world's first commercial polar route in 1954. It formed charter airline Scanair in 1961 and Danish domestic carrier Danair, through a joint venture, in 1971.

Deregulation of US airlines (1978) signaled the demise of nationally protected airlines. SAS seemed ill-equipped to adapt and reported its first loss in 18 years in 1980. Jan Carlzon, former head of Swedish airline Linjeflyg, became SAS's president in 1981. By targeting businessmen as the airline's most stable market and substituting an economy-rate business class for first-class service on European flights, Carlzon turned SAS's losses into profits by the end of 1982.

The company bought about 25% of Airlines of Britain Holdings in 1988, gaining a foothold at London's Heathrow Airport. Another purchase that year brought SAS nearly 10% of Continental Airlines Holdings. In 1989 the airline signed agreements that provided route coordination and hub-sharing with Swissair, Finnair, LanChile, and Canadian Airlines International.

SAS tried in the early 1990s to merge with KLM, Swissair, and Austrian Airlines to create a new international carrier, but that effort failed in 1993, leading to the replacement of Carlzon. New CEO Jan Stenberg consolidated the group, shed noncore businesses, and cut 15,000 jobs. By late 1994 SAS had sold SAS Service Partner (catering, its largest nonairline unit), Diners Club Nordic, and most of the SAS Leisure Group. By spinning off its 42% stake in LanChile and creating a new Latvian airline with Baltic International, SAS focused its air routes in Scandinavia, Western Europe, and the Baltic region.

The SAS trading subsidiary was folded into the airline unit in 1994. Through its hotel unit, SAS allied itself with Radisson Hotels to expand its presence in Europe, the Middle East, and Asia. In 1997 the company joined UAL's United Airlines, Lufthansa, VARIG, and others to form the Star Alliance. In 1998 SAS acquired Finland's Air Botnia.

New code-sharing agreements in 1999 included deals with Singapore Airlines and Icelandair. SAS agreed to sell half its 40% stake in British Midland to Lufthansa, paving the way for British Midland to join the Star Alliance.

SAS boosted its cargo services in 2000 when it partnered with giants Lufthansa Cargo and Singapore Airlines to harmonize their cargo handling and information technology services.

The SAS consortium was restructured into a single publicly traded company, SAS AB, in 2001. That year SAS and Danish carrier Maersk Air were fined by the European Commission for agreeing not to compete on certain Scandinavian routes. SAS EVP Vagn Sørensen accepted responsibility for the illegal agreement and resigned. A month later SAS's board of directors also resigned, and a new board was elected at an extraordinary shareholders' meeting held later that year. At that time Jørgen Lindegaard took over the CEO position.

Also in 2001 a Scandinavian Airlines flight crashed while attempting to take off from Milan's Linate airport, killing all 110 on board. The following year SAS joined with Deutsche Lufthansa and Singapore Airlines to form WOW, a global cargo alliance.

EXECUTIVES

Chairman: Egil Myklebust, age 63
Vice Chairman: Jacob Wallenberg, age 49
President and CEO: Jørgen Lindegaard, age 56
Deputy CEO: Gunnar Reitan
EVP and CFO: Gunilla Berg, age 44
EVP, Corporate Administration and Support: Bernhard Rikardsen
EVP, Airline Support and Airline-Related Businesses: John S. Dueholm
President and CEO Denmark, Scandinavian Airlines: Susanne Larsen
CEO, SAS Braathens (Scandinavian Airlines Norway): Petter Jansen
President and CEO Sweden, Scandinavian Airlines: Anders Ehrling
President and CEO Intercontinental, Scandinavian Airlines: Lars Lindgren
President and CEO, SAS Cargo: Kenneth Marx, age 40
President and CEO, Spanair: Enrique Melia
President and CEO, Blue1: Sveneric Persson
President and CEO, Technical Services: Ørnulf Myrvoll, age 54
President and CEO, Flight Academy: Olof Bärve
General Counsel and Secretary: Mats Lönnkvist
Auditors: Deloitte & Touche AB

LOCATIONS

HQ: SAS AB
Frösundaviks Allé 1, Solna,
S-195 87 Stockholm, Sweden
Phone: +46-8-797-00-00   **Fax:** +46-8-797-16-03
Web: www.sasgroup.net

PRODUCTS/OPERATIONS

2004 Sales

	% of total
Scandinavian Airlines	52
Airline support	21
Subsidiary & affiliate airlines	17
Hotels	6
Airline-related businesses	4
Total	**100**

Selected Subsidiaries and Affiliates

Blue1 (Finnish airline)
Air Greenland A/S (38%)
airBaltic Corporation A/S (47%, Latvian airline)
AS Estonian Air (Estonian airline)
British Midland PLC (20%, UK airline)
Cimber Air A/S (26%, Danish airline)
Commercial Aviation Leasing Ltd. (49%)
Rezidor SAS Hospitality A/S (hotels)
Spanair S.A. (95%, Spanish airline)
Widerøe (Norwegian airline)

COMPETITORS

Accor
Aer Lingus
Air France
Air Portugal
Alitalia
AMR Corp.
A.P. Møller — Mærsk
British Airways
Cathay Pacific
Continental Airlines
Delta Air
Delta Air Transport
Finnair
Hilton Group
Hyatt
Iberia
ITV
KLM
Marriott
Ryanair
Starwood Hotels & Resorts
Virgin Atlantic Airways

HISTORICAL FINANCIALS

Company Type: Public

Income Statement

FYE: December 31

	REVENUE ($ mil.)	NET INCOME ($ mil.)	NET PROFIT MARGIN	EMPLOYEES
12/04	8,781	(283)	—	32,481
12/03	7,970	(195)	—	34,544
12/02	7,423	(15)	—	35,506
12/01	4,866	(101)	—	30,972
12/00	5,049	227	4.5%	30,939
12/99	4,869	198	4.1%	28,863
12/98	5,054	349	6.9%	27,071
12/97	4,919	282	5.7%	25,057
12/96	5,166	261	5.0%	23,607
12/95	5,318	355	6.7%	22,731
Annual Growth	5.7%	—	—	4.0%

2004 Year-End Financials

Debt ratio: 187.8%   Current ratio: 0.92
Return on equity: —   Long-term debt ($ mil.): 3,169
Cash ($ mil.): 188

Net Income History

Stockholm: SAS

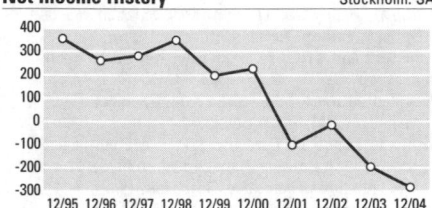

400
300
200
100
0
-100
-200
-300

12/95 12/96 12/97 12/98 12/99 12/00 12/01 12/02 12/03 12/04

Schneider Electric

Schneider Electric is one of the world's largest manufacturers of equipment for electrical distribution and industrial control and automation. The company helps power generators distribute electricity; designs automation systems for the automobile and water-treatment industries; builds infrastructure for airports, road and rail networks, and port facilities; and manages electric power in residential, industrial, and commercial buildings. Schneider's brands include Merlin Gerin and Square D (electrical distribution products), as well as Telemecanique (automation and control).

Other Schneider operations include MGE UPS Systems (power supplies), Kavlico (sensors and transducers), TAC (building automation and security controls), and Dinel (optoelectronic sensors and amplifiers). Schneider sells its products to the construction, electric power, industrial, and infrastructure markets.

Schneider acquired electronic sensor specialist BEI Technologies for about $562 million in 2005.

HISTORY

Schneider Electric's predecessor was founded in 1782 to make industrial equipment. After the upheavals of the French Revolution and the Napoleonic Wars, the company came under the control of brothers Adolphe and Eugene Schneider in 1836. Within two years they had built the first French locomotive (the country's first rail line had opened in 1832).

Schneider became one of France's most important heavy-industry companies, branching into a variety of machinery and steel operations. The country's industrial development continued to trail that of Britain and Germany, however, due to recurrent political strife, including the revolutions of 1848 and the Franco-Prussian War. France also possessed fewer coal and iron deposits.

During WWI Schneider was a key part of France's war effort. It entered the electrical contracting business in 1929 and fought off nationalization attempts in the mid-1930s.

The blitzkrieg of 1939 brought much of France under Nazi occupation, and the Schneider factories that were not destroyed were commandeered by the Germans. The company rebuilt after the war, aided by the French government. It was restructured as a holding company, and its operating units were split into three subsidiaries: civil and electrical engineering, industrial manufacturing, and construction. Charles Schneider, the last family member to lead the company, died in 1950.

In 1963 Schneider concluded an alliance with the Empain Group of Belgium, and by 1969, three years after Schneider went public, the two companies merged to become Empain-Schneider. It was a period when the company made numerous noncore acquisitions, entering such fields as ski equipment, fashion, publishing, and travel.

Schneider began reorganizing in 1980. The effort entered its final phase in 1993 with a major recapitalization that saw the merger of its former parent company, Société Parisienne d'Entreprises et de Participations, with Schneider SA and the issue of new stock to existing stockholders. The company also streamlined operations. Merlin Gerin (acquired 1975) and Télémécanique (1988) became Schneider Electric in Europe, and their North American operations were merged into Square D after its acquisition in 1991.

Schneider's 1994 takeover of two Belgian subsidiaries led Belgium's government to charge CEO Didier Pineau-Valencienne with fraud in the valuation of the stock. (A Belgian newsmagazine reported in 1997 that the government turned down an offer to settle out of court.)

In 1996 Schneider established the Schneider Electric (China) Investment Co. in Beijing, China's first totally French-owned firm. The next year the company sold Spie Batignolles, its electrical contracting subsidiary. Cost-cutting measures and strong sales in France and North America combined to boost the company's 1998 income.

In 1999 Schneider agreed to pay $1.1 billion for Lexel, a joint venture owned by Finland's Ahlstrom and Denmark's NKT Holding, to broaden its electrical equipment offerings for the household. That year the company changed its name to Schneider Electric and its main subsidiary's name to Schneider Electric Industries. Looking to add more machinery makers to its list of customers, the company acquired France-based Crouzet Automatismes as well as Switzerland-based Positec in 2000.

Although Schneider announced in early 2001 that it would buy Legrand (a deal valued at about $6.4 billion), EU regulators blocked the acquisition in October. As part of the UN's "Oil for Food" program, Schneider received an order from Iraq in 2002 for nearly 16,000 circuit breakers to be used in that country's power grid. In early 2003 the company's North American division and US-based Leviton Manufacturing inked a joint technology agreement to develop prototype voice-data-image products.

In 2004 Schneider acquired the Kavlico sensor business of Solectron for nearly $200 million. Also in 2004 Schneider acquired US-based Andover Controls (building automation and security controls) from Balfour Beatty for about $400 million. Schneider continued its acquisition spree with the purchase of France-based optoelectronics maker Dinel later that year.

EXECUTIVES

Chairman and CEO, Schneider Electric and Schneider Electric Industries: Henri Lachmann, age 67
COO: Jean-Pascal Tricoire, age 42
EVP, Asia and Pacific Operating Division: Russell Stocker, age 41
EVP, Customers and Market: Michel Crochon, age 54
EVP, European Operating Division: Christian Wiest, age 55
EVP, Finance and Control and Legal Affairs: Pierre B. Bouchut, age 49
EVP, Globalization and Industry: Hal Grant, age 45
EVP, Human Resources and Communication: Jean-François Pilliard, age 56
EVP, International and Iberian Operating Division: Julio Rodriguez
EVP, North American Operating Division: David D. Petratis, age 48
EVP, Product and Technology: Alain Marbach, age 43
EVP, Strategic Deployment: Eric Pilaud, age 48
Secretary: Philippe Bougon
Press Contact: Véronique Moine
Investor Relations and Financial Communications: Alexandre Brunet
Auditors: Barbier Frinault & Autres; Ernst & Young

LOCATIONS

HQ: Schneider Electric SA
43-45 boulevard Franklin-Roosevelt,
F-92500 Rueil-Malmaison, France
Phone: +33-1-41-29-70-00   **Fax:** +33-1-41-29-71-00
US HQ: 1415 S. Roselle Rd., Palatine, IL 60067
US Phone: 847-397-2600   **US Fax:** 847-397-8814
Web: www.schneider-electric.com

Schneider Electric has about 150 manufacturing and marketing facilities in 130 countries.

2004 Sales

	% of total
Europe	52
North America	24
Asia/Pacific	17
Other regions	7
Total	**100**

PRODUCTS/OPERATIONS

2004 Sales

	% of total
Electrical distribution	63
Automation & control	26
Other	11
Total	**100**

Selected Operations and Products

BEI Technologies (sensors, motors, actuators, encoders, motion control products)
Dinel (optoelectronic amplifiers and sensors)
Kavlico (sensors)
Merlin Gerin (circuit breakers, panelboards, and remote installation management equipment)
Square D (electrical distribution and industrial control equipment, US)
TAC (building automation and security products)
Télemécanique (industrial automation products and systems)

COMPETITORS

ABB	Fluor
Alcatel	GE
ALSTOM	Johnson Controls
Beghelli	Legris
Eaton	Mitsubishi Electric
Electricité de France	Siemens
EMCOR	Siemens Energy
Emerson Electric	& Automation
Endress + Hauser	Technology Research
Finmeccanica	Transtector

HISTORICAL FINANCIALS

Company Type: Public

Income Statement

FYE: December 31

	REVENUE ($ mil.)	NET INCOME ($ mil.)	NET PROFIT MARGIN	EMPLOYEES
12/04	14,138	770	5.4%	85,000
12/03	11,022	543	4.9%	74,276
12/02	9,496	442	4.7%	74,814
12/01	8,706	(874)	—	66,144
12/00	9,129	589	6.4%	72,144
12/99	8,437	484	5.7%	67,510
12/98	8,899	477	5.4%	60,780
12/97	7,901	366	4.6%	61,499
12/96	11,779	252	2.1%	63,000
12/95	12,104	166	1.4%	92,700
Annual Growth	1.7%	18.6%	—	(1.0%)

2004 Year-End Financials

Debt ratio: 17.1%
Return on equity: 7.7%
Cash ($ mil.): 1,450

Current ratio: 1.88
Long-term debt ($ mil.): 1,765

Net Income History

Euronext Paris: SU

Scottish Power

With more power in England than Bonnie Prince Charlie, Scottish Power is a hero in the UK's deregulated energy market. One of the largest multi-utilities in the country, the company supplies electricity and natural gas to 5.1 million customers and generates 5,400 MW of capacity (primarily fossil-fueled) through its UK Division, which also markets and trades energy. Scottish Power's Infrastructure Division operates the company's regulated domestic power transmission and distribution assets. Across the Atlantic, Scottish Power is selling PacifiCorp, which generates and distributes electricity to 1.6 million customers in the western US, to to MidAmerican Energy Holdings.

The company has made itself a target for a takeover since divesting noncore assets, including its water utility, telecommunications, and appliance retailing businesses. Subsidiary PPM Energy, formerly a part of PacifiCorp, markets and trades energy, operates renewable energy projects, and provides related services in the US.

Scottish Power is focused on growing its renewable generation portfolio in the UK and the US. It is also working to improve its traditional generation and infrastructure assets, as well as to expand its retail supply customer base in the UK.

HISTORY

The UK power industry was nationalized in 1947, and two regional state-controlled boards were charged with generating, transmitting, and distributing electricity in Scotland. The two monopolies were the North of Scotland Hydro-Electric Board (formed 1943) and the South of Scotland Electricity Board (SSEB, formed 1955). In keeping with the deregulation trend that swept the UK in the 1980s, Scottish Power was formed in 1989 to assume the non-nuclear operations of SSEB, and Hydro-Electric (now part of Scottish and Southern) took the northern board's assets. Scottish Power had to prepare for competition, which began in a limited form in 1990.

Scottish Power's initial assets included six coal, gas, and hydropower plants that served southern Scotland, including Glasgow and much of the Scottish industrial base, and England's Northumberland county. The company, which went public in 1991, also inherited 73 retail outlets that sold consumer electronic and electrical goods. It expanded this retail business across the UK in the 1990s.

The company teamed with SeaWest of the US and Japan's Toman in the early 1990s to set up Europe's largest wind farm, in Wales. It set up other wind-energy plants in Northern Ireland, Scotland, and England; by the mid-1990s Scottish Power was the largest wind-farm operator in the UK.

In 1993 the company moved into telecommunications. Running fiber-optic lines alongside its high-voltage power lines between Glasgow and Edinburgh, the company's Scottish Telecom unit (established 1994) provided high-speed voice and data services to several major businesses.

With opportunities for growth limited by the relatively small population base in southern Scotland, the company sought to expand through geographic and business diversification. In 1995 it became the first UK power firm to buy a rival when it acquired Manweb, a regional electricity company that served northwestern England and North Wales. The next year the company became the first British electricity firm to buy a water company when it acquired Southern Water, a water supply and wastewater services firm based on England's South Coast. Scottish Power disposed of many of Southern Water's noncore businesses in 1997.

In 1998 Scottish Power boosted its telecom business with the purchase of Demon Internet, then the UK's largest independent ISP. That year, after merger talks with two US electric utilities failed, Scottish Power agreed to acquire PacifiCorp, a major utility in the US Pacific Northwest. The deal was completed in 1999.

With the BBC, Scottish Telecom launched a free Internet service, Freebeeb.net, in 1999. That year Scottish Telecom's name was changed to Thus, and the company floated a 49.9% stake in the unit. Scottish Power also announced a restructuring plan that would cut jobs and divest noncore businesses. In 2000 it announced plans to join the Royal Bank of Scotland in offering bundled services, including banking, utilities, and telecommunications. The company also divested PacifiCorp's Powercor Australia unit.

In 2001 Scottish Power agreed to sell its retail appliance business to Powerhouse Retail. It also restructured into three business units: UK power generation and supply, infrastructure (asset management and water supply), and US operations (PacifiCorp). Later that year the company announced plans to spin off its remaining stake in Thus; the transaction was completed in 2002.

Scottish Power also sold its Southern Water unit to First Aqua, a private investment firm backed by the Royal Bank of Scotland, for $2.9 billion in 2002.

EXECUTIVES

Chairman: Charles Miller Smith, age 65, $502,095 pay
Chief Executive and Board Member; Chairman, PacifiCorp: Ian M. Russell, age 52, $1,186,770 pay
Executive Director, Finance and Strategy: Simon Lowth, age 43, $454,833 pay (prior to promotion)
Executive Director; President and CEO, PacifiCorp: Judith A. (Judi) Johansen, age 46, $377,210 pay
Secretary and Group Director, Commercial and Legal: James Stanley, age 50
EVP, PacifiCorp Operations: Ronnie Mercer, age 61
President and CEO, Energy Networks: David Rutherford, age 41
Group Company Secretary: Andrew Mitchell, age 53
President, Energy Retail: Willie MacDiarmid
President and CEO, PPM Energy: Terry F. Hudgens, age 50
President, Energy Wholesale: John Campbell
VP, Investor Relations: Bob Hess
Group Energy Risk Director: Robert A. Klein, age 57
Group Media Relations Manager: Colin McSeveny
Public Relations Executive: Jane Holmes
Group Director, Human Resources and Communications: Stephen Dunn
Auditors: PricewaterhouseCoopers LLP

LOCATIONS

HQ: Scottish Power plc
1 Atlantic Quay, Glasgow G2 8SP, United Kingdom
Phone: +44-141-248-8200   **Fax:** +44-141-248-8300
US HQ: 825 NE Multnomah St., Portland, OR 97232
US Phone: 503-813-5000   **US Fax:** 503-813-7247
Web: www.scottishpower.plc.uk

Scottish Power primarily operates in the UK and the US.

PRODUCTS/OPERATIONS

2005 Sales

	$ mil.	% of total
UK		
UK Division	6,964.1	54
Infrastructure Division	718.3	6
US		
PacifiCorp	4,311.6	33
PPM Energy	948.9	7
Total	**12,942.9**	**100**

Selected Subsidiaries

Infrastructure Division
Scottish Power UK plc
SP Power Systems Limited (PowerSystems, network management and maintenance)
SP Distribution Limited (operates as SP Transmission & Distribution, regulated distribution assets)
SP Manweb plc (operates as SP Transmission & Distribution, regulated distribution assets)
SP Transmission Limited (operates as SP Transmission & Distribution, regulated transmission assets)

PacifiCorp (electricity generation and distribution, US)
PPM Energy, Inc. (formerly PacifiCorp Power Marketing, wholesale power generation and marketing, US)
UK Division
  ScottishPower Energy Retail Limited (retail electricity and gas supply)
  ScottishPower Energy Management Limited (formerly ScottishPower Energy Trading, wholesale electricity and gas marketing and trading)
  ScottishPower Energy Management (Agency) Limited (formerly ScottishPower Energy Trading (Agency), wholesale electricity and gas marketing and trading)
  ScottishPower Generation Limited (power production)
  SP Dataserve Limited (data management, metering, and billing)

COMPETITORS

British Energy	PG&E
Centrica	Portland General Electric
EDF Energy	Premier Power
Edison International	Puget Energy
Electricity Supply Board	Questar
E.ON UK	Scottish and Southern
Green Energy (UK)	Energy
International Power	United Utilities
MidAmerican Energy	Viridian Group
National Grid	Western Power
National Grid Gas	Distribution
npower	

HISTORICAL FINANCIALS

Company Type: Public

Income Statement

FYE: March 31

	REVENUE ($ mil.)	NET INCOME ($ mil.)	NET PROFIT MARGIN	EMPLOYEES
3/05	12,943	(582)	—	16,142
3/04	10,684	991	9.3%	14,821
3/03	8,293	763	9.2%	13,825
3/02	9,000	(1,407)	—	16,162
3/01	9,000	436	4.8%	21,981
3/00	6,557	1,502	22.9%	24,114
3/99	5,225	810	15.5%	16,032
3/98	5,229	284	5.4%	15,099
3/97	4,821	690	14.3%	15,018
3/96	3,465	452	13.0%	11,359
Annual Growth	**15.8%**	**—**	**—**	**4.0%**

2005 Year-End Financials

Debt ratio: 134.1%
Return on equity: —
Cash ($ mil.): 3,303
Current ratio: 1.40
Long-term debt ($ mil.): 10,094

No. of shares (mil.): 466
Dividends
  Yield: 4.9%
  Payout: —
Market value ($ mil.): 14,550

Stock History

NYSE: SPI

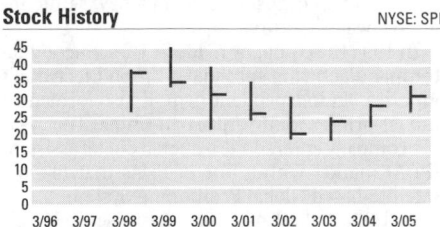

	STOCK PRICE ($) FY Close	P/E High/Low		PER SHARE ($) Earnings	Dividends	Book Value
3/05	31.20	—	—	(1.27)	1.54	16.14
3/04	28.42	13	11	2.13	1.43	18.60
3/03	23.99	15	11	1.66	1.87	15.80
3/02	20.45	—	—	(3.06)	1.63	14.68
3/01	26.22	30	21	0.95	1.70	18.18
3/00	31.69	9	5	4.32	2.83	21.95
3/99	35.19	17	13	2.71	1.73	10.46
3/98	37.94	14	10	0.96	0.00	9.54
Annual Growth	**(2.8%)**	**—**	**—**	**—**	**—**	**7.8%**

Securitas AB

Securitas profits from the lack of caritas in human nature. The world's #2 security services company (behind Group 4 Securicor) provides security guards, alarm systems, and cash transportation services to banks, retailers, large corporations, small businesses, and residential customers in more than 30 countries, mainly in Europe and North America. Securitas' purchase of US security firms Pinkerton's and Burns International Services, now included in its Security Services USA division, has given it a dominant position in the US security-guard services market. The company, founded in 1934, is 25%-owned by Swedish firm Säkl.

Securitas operates through five divisions: Security Services USA, Security Services Europe, Security Systems, Direct, and Cash Handling Services. The company's Security Services divisions account for nearly 75% of sales. The three other divisions account for the rest. The company holds an 11% share of the security market in Europe and 10% of the market in the US.

Securitas' Cash Handling division, which includes subsidiary Loomis, Fargo & Co., handles monetary flows — overseeing cash transport, cash-processing services, ATMs, and night deposit boxes. The company has expanded its cash-handling operations in the US through the acquisitions of Respond USA and Armored Motor Services of America. It has also expanded its cash-handling operations in France through the acquisition of certain assets of Valiance Cash Handling.

Securitas is conquering a fragmented industry replete with individual investigators and mom-and-pop security firms. In an effort to strengthen its position in the western US, Securitas has acquired Lincoln Security, a security guard service provider based in California. Through its Security Services Europe division, the company has acquired Spanish-based Ebro Vigilancia & Seguridad and Netherlands-based VNV. It has also acquired UK security alarm firm Bell Group. Due to week economic conditions in the US, the company has integrated its Security Service division, combining all brands under one roof.

HISTORY

Securitas established its first outpost in 1934, in Helsingborg, Sweden, when Erik Philip-Sörensen bought Hälsingborgs Nattvakt and renamed it Securitas. Erik was following in the footsteps of his father, who in 1901 had established a small Danish guard company as part of the ISS Group of security companies. Securitas was housed within ISS as well.

Sörensen spent the next two decades establishing and acquiring more Swedish firms and adding them to the Securitas family. He also added to his own family two sons, Sven and Jörgen, who would figure into Securitas' future. Jörgen began establishing new branches in Belgium and the UK in the late 1950s. The companies were combined into one company, Group 4, in 1968.

In 1974, two years after the Securitas name was finally branded onto all of the firm's security companies, the elder Sörensen retired. Sven and Jörgen bid against ISS for control of the company and won. Seven years later they divided the company equally: Sven took half of the Securitas operations in Sweden, and Jörgen assumed control of the international businesses (which became

Group 4 Securitas). In 1983 Sven sold Securitas. Jörgen bought back some of the Swedish operations, but by 1985 the rest of the company had ended up in the hands of Swedish investment firm Investment AB Latour (now chaired by Gustaf Douglas, also vice chairman of Securitas).

The new owners trimmed away all companies that weren't directly related to guard services and alarm systems. Securitas then began an acquisition rampage in 1988 with the purchase of Swedish lock manufacturer Assa. Not content with the lovely lakes and mountains of Sweden, Securitas bought companies in Denmark, Norway, and Portugal and set up new operations in Hungary.

Securitas went public in 1991 and soon bought US lock maker Arrow; it also began cutting a wider swath through Europe. With its 1992 purchase of security firm Protectas, Securitas gained operations in Austria, France, Germany, and Switzerland; it bought more firms in Spain in 1992 and in Finland the next year. To streamline further, Securitas merged its lock manufacturing operations with those of Finland's Metra, creating Assa-Abloy. It spun off the new company in 1994 but retained a 45% stake. Securitas made more acquisition raids in Estonia, Poland, and the UK in 1996.

In 1997 Securitas created Securitas Direct to handle its domestic and small-scale alarms business; the division quickly became active throughout Scandinavia, as well as in France, Spain, and Switzerland. That year the company made more acquisitions in France and Sweden. In 1998 Securitas made two significant purchases: Raab Karcher Sicherheit, the market leader in industrial guarding services in Germany, and Proteg, France's security market leader (Securitas sold Proteg's fire protection divisions to Williams PLC in 1999).

The grand-daddy of acquisitions was still to come. In early 1999 Securitas bought 150-year-old US security firm Pinkerton's in a bid to create the largest security firm in the world. Securitas took over Pinkerton's operations in the Czech Republic, Germany, Portugal, and the UK. The next year Securitas made several US acquisitions, including the purchase of Burns International Services for $650 million.

Securitas' takeover of US companies didn't stop with Pinkerton's and Burns. In 2001 the company became the second-largest cash-handling services provider in the US when it bought the remaining 51% of Loomis, Fargo & Co. (Securitas had previously acquired 49% of Loomis as part of the Burns deal).

Securitas continued expanding in 2002, but this time the company focused outside the US, buying security companies in the Netherlands and Canada. In 2003 it returned its focus to the US by acquiring Lincoln Security, a security-guard service provider operating in California, Nevada, and Oregon. It also acquired Armored Motor Services of America. Later that year Securitas expanded its Security Services Europe offerings through the acquisition of Spanish-based Ebro Vigilancia & Seguridad and Netherlands-based VNV.

In 2004 Securitas completed its acquisition of UK alarm service company Bell Group.

The following year the company sold its cash-handling services activities in the Czech Republic, Poland, and Hungary to Brink's.

EXECUTIVES

Chairman: Melker Schörling
Vice Chairman: Gustaf Douglas
President, CEO, and Director: Thomas Berglund
EVP and CFO: Håkan Winberg
SVP Investor Relations: Henrik Brehmer
Chairman and Chief Executive, Bell Group:
  Patrick B. Curran
Divisional President, Cash Handling Services;
  President and CEO, Loomis, Fargo & Co.: Clas Thelin
Divisional President, Direct: Dick Seger
Divisional President, Security Services Europe:
  Tore K. Nilsen
Divisional President, Security Services USA:
  Santiago Galaz
Divisional President, Security Systems: Juan Vallejo
EVP, Cash Handling Services: Johan Eriksson
Managing Director, Cash in Transit, Securitas UK:
  Nick Shotton
Managing Director, Cash Management, Securitas UK:
  Frank Williams
Managing Director, Micro-Route, Securitas UK:
  Anne Lewis
Auditors: PricewaterhouseCoopers AB

LOCATIONS

HQ: Securitas AB
  Lindhagensplan 70, SE-102 28 Stockholm, Sweden
Phone: +46-8-657-74-00   **Fax:** +46-8-657-70-72
US HQ: 2 Campus Dr., Parsippany, NJ 07054
US Phone: 973-397-2681   **US Fax:** 973-397-2681
Web: www.securitasgroup.com

Securitas has operations in Argentina, Austria, Belgium, Canada, the Czech Republic, Denmark, Estonia, Finland, France, Germany, Hungary, Ireland, Mexico, the Netherlands, Norway, Poland, Portugal, Spain, Sweden, Switzerland, the UK, and the US.

2004 Sales

	$ mil.	% of total
Europe		
Nordic Region	1,341	15
Other countries	4,035	45
US	3,459	38
Other regions	190	2
Total	**9,025**	**100**

PRODUCTS/OPERATIONS

2004 Sales

	$ mil.	% of total
Security Services Europe	3,630	40
Security Services USA	2,849	31
Cash Handling Services	1,524	17
Security Systems	728	8
Direct	397	4
Adjustments	(103)	—
Total	**9,025**	**100**

COMPETITORS

Allied-Barton Security
Chubb
Command Security
Group 4 Securicor
Initial Security
Prosegur
TransNational Security
Tyco Fire and Security
Wackenhut

HISTORICAL FINANCIALS

Company Type: Public

Income Statement

FYE: December 31

	REVENUE ($ mil.)	NET INCOME ($ mil.)	NET PROFIT MARGIN	EMPLOYEES
12/04	9,025	222	2.5%	206,153
12/03	8,121	171	2.1%	210,700
12/02	7,508	170	2.3%	203,070
12/01	5,710	112	2.0%	207,799
12/00	4,334	90	2.1%	202,794
12/99	3,008	94	3.1%	115,946
12/98	1,692	64	3.8%	66,420
12/97	1,360	56	4.1%	40,567
12/96	1,332	56	4.2%	36,689
12/95	1,098	52	4.7%	26,799
Annual Growth	**26.4%**	**17.5%**	**—**	**25.4%**

2004 Year-End Financials

Debt ratio: 93.9%
Return on equity: 14.0%
Cash ($ mil.): 140

Current ratio: 1.03
Long-term debt ($ mil.): 1,533

Net Income History

Stockholm: SECUB

Seiko Epson Corporation

Seiko Epson looked at its watch and saw that times have changed. Also referred to just as Epson, the company is a manufacturing arm of Seiko Group, the internationally known watchmaker. More important than its timekeeping operations are its information-related products such as desktop and portable computers; electronic devices and components, including semiconductors; and a variety of other products, such as lenses, motors, and magnets. A top printer manufacturer, Seiko Epson produces dot matrix, ink jet, laser, and thermal printers, as well as printer components; the company wants to dominate the home photo printing business. Heirs of Seiko's founder, Kitaro Hattori, control the company.

Although watches and precision products constitute the company's smallest segment (about 5% of sales), Seiko Epson has no plans to wind down its most dated business. The skills gleaned from watchmaking, including miniaturization and precision timing, have given rise to the company's other, more profitable lines, including LCDs, semiconductor products, and other parts for mobile phones.

Seiko Epson has combined its liquid crystal display (LCD) manufacturing operations with those of Sanyo Electric to form Sanyo Epson Imaging Devices Corporation.

HISTORY

In 1881, 21-year-old Kitaro Hattori, who had begun working in the jewelry trade at age 13, opened a Tokyo watch shop and called it K. Hattori & Co. In 1892 Hattori started a factory in Seikosha to manufacture wall clocks and, later, watches and alarm clocks. K. Hattori & Co. went public in 1917. In 1924 it began using the Seiko brand on its timepieces. Kitaro's son Ganzo formed Daini Seikosha Co., precursor of Seiko Instruments, in 1937.

The company formed Daiwa Kogyo Ltd., a maker of mechanical watches, in 1942; it would later become Seiko Epson. Developments included self-winding watches (1955) and transistorized table clocks (1959).

A big break came for the company in 1964, when it developed crystal chronometers and printing timers for the Tokyo Olympics' official timekeepers. It was the first time a precision timepiece and a printer had been combined. Based on that technology, in 1968 Seiko Epson debuted the EP-101, the first commercially successful miniature printer (used primarily with calculators).

During the late 1960s Seiko Epson entered the semiconductor field when it began developing LSIs (large-scale integrated circuits) for its watches. The company introduced the world's first quartz watch in 1969 and the first quartz digital watch in 1973. It soon expanded into liquid crystal display (LCD) technology. It formed its US affiliate, Epson America, in 1975. With the advent of the PC in the 1970s, Seiko Epson also began working on computer printers. It released its first dot matrix model in 1978. The next year the company introduced the Alba and Pulsar watch brands.

The company's European headquarters, in the Netherlands, opened in 1980. Seiko Epson debuted the first laptop computer, the HX-20, in 1982; a high-quality daisy wheel printer and LCD color TV in 1983; and an ink jet printer in 1984. In 1985 it began making contact lenses. Reijiro Hattori, grandson of the company's founder, took the helm in the late 1980s.

In 1990 Seiko baptized the Scubamaster, a computerized diver's watch featuring a dive table. The next year it introduced a wristwatch/pager. That year it added color printers to its line. Seiko Epson unveiled digital cameras for use with PCs and Macs in 1996. The next year Lattice Semiconductor invested $150 million with Seiko Epson to build a new semiconductor wafer factory.

In 1998 the company made its US semiconductor manufacturing subsidiary, Epson Electronics America, an independent firm. It also formed an ink jet printer joint venture in China. That year the company entered the personal digital assistant (PDA) market with a line of PDAs that use the satellite-based Global Positioning System.

In 1999 Seiko Epson acquired Pacific Metals Co.'s metal powder operations, a complement to metal injection molding subsidiary Injex.

With profit margins from its printers shrinking, in 2000 the company announced plans to consolidate its printer operations in China, Indonesia, and Singapore, and to expand its LCD products line. The following year Seiko Epson agreed to form a joint venture with IBM to produce logic chips for cell phones, handheld computers, and other devices.

EXECUTIVES

Chairman and CEO: Saburo Kusama
Vice Chairman: Yasuo Hattori
EVP, CFO, and Board Member: Toshio Kimura
President, COO, and Board Member: Seiji Hanaoka
EVP, CIO, and Board Member: Norio Niwa
Senior Managing Director and Board Member:
  Masayuki Morozumi
Managing Director and Board Member: Masao Akahane
Managing Director and Board Member:
  Yasumasa Otsuki
Managing Director and Board Member: Torao Yajima
Managing Director and Board Member: Kenji Kubota
Managing Director and Board Member:
  Hiroshi Komatsu
**Chief Executive, Imaging and Information Products
  Operations Division; Board Member:** Seiichi Hirano
**Chief Executive, Visual Instruments Operations
  Division; Board Member:** Kenji Uchida
Chief Executive, TFT Operations Division:
  Hideaki Iwano
President, Sanyo Epson Imaging Devices Corporation:
  Shuji Aruga
Auditors: ChuoAoyama PricewaterhouseCoopers

LOCATIONS

HQ: Seiko Epson Corporation
  3-3-5 Owa, Suwa, Nagano 392-8502, Japan
Phone: +81-266-52-3131   **Fax:** +81-266-53-4844
US HQ: 3840 Kilroy Airport Way, Long Beach, CA 90806
US Phone: 562-981-3840   **US Fax:** 562-290-5220
Web: www.epson.com

Seiko Epson has operations in Japan, as well as
manufacturing and sales operations in Australia, China,
France, Germany, Hong Kong, Indonesia, Italy, South
Korea, Malaysia, the Netherlands, the Philippines,
Singapore, Spain, Taiwan, the UK, and the US.

PRODUCTS/OPERATIONS

2005 Sales

	% of total
Information equipment	61
Electronic devices	31
Precision products	5
Other	3
Total	**100**

Selected Products

Information equipment
  Computers
  LCD projection TVs
  Printers
  Scanners

Electronic devices
  Crystal devices
  LCDs
  Semiconductors

Precision products
  Optical devices
  Watches

COMPETITORS

Acer	LSI Logic
Bausch & Lomb	Matsushita
Canon	NEC
CASIO COMPUTER	Océ
Citizen Watch	Oki Electric
Dell	Ricoh
Fujitsu	Samsung
Hewlett-Packard	SANYO
Hitachi	Sharp
IBM	Sony
Intel	Swatch
Kyocera	Toshiba
Lexmark	Xerox

HISTORICAL FINANCIALS

Company Type: Public

Income Statement

FYE: March 31

	REVENUE ($ mil.)	NET INCOME ($ mil.)	NET PROFIT MARGIN	EMPLOYEES
3/05	13,759	518	3.8%	85,647
3/04	13,378	360	2.7%	84,899
3/03	11,035	104	0.9%	73,797
3/02	9,606	(139)	—	68,786
3/01	10,615	293	2.8%	69,743
3/00	11,225	278	2.5%	42,500
3/99	8,874	268	3.0%	41,500
3/98	6,125	—	—	44,000
3/97	5,032	—	—	31,000
3/96	5,603	—	—	
Annual Growth	**10.5%**	**11.6%**	**—**	**13.5%**

2005 Year-End Financials

Debt ratio: 55.0%   Current ratio: 1.48
Return on equity: 12.4% Long-term debt ($ mil.): 2,417
Cash ($ mil.): 2,184

Net Income History

Exchange: Tokyo

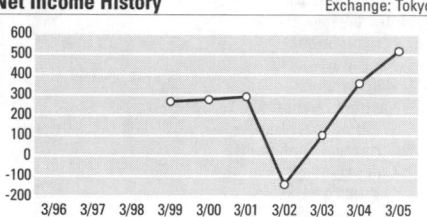

Sharp

Sharp's business is pointed at the electronics
market. Best known for its consumer electronics, the company is a leading maker of electronic
components and computer hardware and peripherals. Its flagship components business includes
liquid crystal displays (LCDs, used in everything
from airplane cockpits to PCs to pinball machines), flash memory, integrated circuits, and
laser diodes used in optical data drives. Sharp
also makes PCs, printers, and cell phones; consumer audio and video products, such as CD and
DVD players and video cameras; and a variety of
appliances, such as air conditioners, refrigerators, and vacuum cleaners.

Sharp has targeted such products as LCD televisions, next generation handsets, and home networking gear for growth. On the components side,
the company sees demand for advanced LCDs increasing as new handheld devices come into the
mainstream. Sharp has shifted the focus of its television business from traditional tube TVs to flat-
panel LCDs. In 2005 it acquired Fujitsu's LCD
subsidiary, Fujitsu Display Technology.

HISTORY

Tokuji Hayakawa got started in manufacturing
in 1912 when he established Hayakawa Electric
Industry to make a type of belt buckle he had designed. Three years later he invented the first
mechanical pencil, named the Ever-Sharp,

which was a commercial success. After an earthquake leveled much of Tokyo in 1923, including
Hayakawa's business, he moved to Osaka and
sold the rights to his pencil to finance a new factory. He introduced Japan's first crystal radio
sets in 1925 and four years later debuted a vacuum tube radio.

Following WWII, Hayakawa Electric developed
an experimental TV, which it began mass-
producing in 1953. The company was ready with
color TVs when Japan initiated color broadcasts
in 1960. Hayakawa Electric grew tremendously
during the 1960s, introducing microwave ovens
(1962), solar cells (1963), the first electronic all-
transistor-diode calculator (1964), and the first
gallium arsenide LED (1969). The firm opened
a US office in 1962.

In 1970 the company began to make its own
microchips and changed its name to Sharp Corporation, a nod to the name of its first product.
It began mass production of LCDs in 1973. Sharp
later introduced the first electronic calculator
with an LCD (1973), solar-powered calculators
(1976), and a credit card-sized calculator (1979).

The company began producing VCRs in the
early 1980s, and in 1984 Sharp introduced its
first color copier. That year the firm introduced
a fax machine and began concentrating its marketing efforts on small businesses (while its competitors were scrambling for large corporate
accounts). Haruo Tsuji became president in
1986. He restructured the company and concentrated research on LCDs. Sharp blitzed the market with a new line of creative products in the
late 1980s, including a high-definition LCD color
TV (1987) and a notebook-sized PC (1988).

Sharp introduced a cordless pocket telephone
in 1992 that operated continuously for over five
hours, as well as a low-cost high-definition television (HDTV). That year the company announced strategic alliances with Apple to build
the Newton personal digital assistant (which
flopped) and with the Shanghai Radio and Television to make air conditioners, fax machines,
copiers, and printers (Shanghai Sharp Electronics began production in 1994). During the mid-
1990s Sharp's ViewCam camcorder and Zaurus
personal digital assistant were both big sellers.

In 1996 Sharp formed partnerships with Alcatel, Advanced Micro Devices, Fujitsu, Intel, and
Nanjing Panda Electronics (China's second-
largest TV maker). More joint ventures followed
in 1997, including a partnership with Sony to develop flat-panel displays.

Katsuhiko Machida became president in 1998
as the company attempted to pump younger
blood into its veins; Tsuji became company adviser. That year the company restructured
around three business areas: home appliances
and consumer electronics, information and communications, and components. Restructuring
in its LCD operations reduced profits by 80% in
1999. The company rebounded the next year, but
a downturn in the global economy and competitive pricing in the LCD business again put
Sharp's profits under pressure in 2001. The
company reduced its workforce and simplified its
organizational structure, reorganizing its operations from 42 divisions into just 24.

EXECUTIVES

President: Katsuhiko Machida
SEVP; Chief General Administration Officer:
Hiroshi Saji
**Senior Executive Director; Group General Manager,
Human Resources Group:** Akihiko Kumagai
**Senior Executive Director; Group General Manager,
International Business Group:** Toshishige Hamano
**Senior Executive Director; Group General Manager,
Domestic Sales and Marketing Group:**
Masaaki Ohtsuka
**Senior Executive Director and Chief Environmental
Protection Officer:** Akira Mitarai
**Senior Executive Director; Group General Manager,
Sales and Marketing Group, Electronic Components
and Devices:** Shigeo Nakabu
Senior Executive Director and CTO: Kenji Ohta
**Executive Director; Group General Manager, Digital
Document Systems Group:** Yoshiaki Ibuchi
**Senior Executive Director, Information and
Communication Systems Group:** Masafumi Matsumoto
**Director; General Manager, Management Planning
Board:** Takashi Nakagawa
**Director; Group General Manager, Appliance Systems
Group:** Itsuro Kato
**Director; Group Deputy General Manager, Sales and
Marketing Group, Electronic Components and
Devices:** Yoshiki Sano
Executive Director, LCD Business: Mikio Katayama
**Director; Group General Manager, Audio-Visual
Systems Group; Assistant Group General Manager,
AVC Liquid Crystal Display Group:** Takashi Okuda
**Director; Group General Manager, Corporate
Accounting and Control Group:** Tetsuo Ohnishi
**Executive Director; Group General Manager, Tokyo
Branch:** Toshio Adachi
**Director; Group Deputy General Manager, International
Business Group; Chairman and President, Sharp
Electronics:** Toshihiko Fujimoto
**Director; Group General Manager, One-of-a-Kind
Products Planning Group:** Takuji Okawara
**Director; Group General Manager, Solar Systems
Group:** Takashi Tomita
Director; Group General Manager, Integrated Circuits:
Takashi Nukii
**Director; Group General Manager, Corporate Research
and Development:** Toru Chiba
**Director; Group General Manager, AVC Liquid Crystal
Display:** Shigeaki Mizushima
**Director; Group General Manager, Domestic Marketing
Communication Products:** Kohichi Takamori
**Director; Group General Manager, Communication
Systems:** Yoshisuke Hasegawa
Auditors: KPMG AZSA & Co.

LOCATIONS

HQ: Sharp Corporation
22-22 Nagaike-cho, Abeno-ku,
Osaka 545-8522, Japan
Phone: +81-6-6621-1221   **Fax:** +81-6-6627-1759
US HQ: Sharp Plaza, Mahwah, NJ 07430-2135
US Phone: 201-529-8200   **US Fax:** 201-529-8425
Web: www.sharp.co.jp

2005 Sales

	% of total
Asia	
Japan	52
Other countries	8
Europe	16
The Americas	15
Other regions	9
Total	**100**

PRODUCTS/OPERATIONS

2005 Sales

	% of total
Consumer/Information products	
Audio-Visual & communication equipment	38
Home appliances	8
Information equipment	16
Electronic components	
LCDs	22
ICs	6
Other	10
Total	**100**

Selected Products

Consumer/information products
  Audio-Visual and communication equipment
    Audio amplifiers
    Compact disc players
    Digital cameras
    DVD players
    High-definition televisions
    Liquid crystal display DVD televisions
    Liquid crystal display televisions
    Liquid crystal display video projectors
    Mobile phones
    Video cameras
  Home appliances
    Air conditioners
    Microwave ovens
    Refrigerators
    Vacuum cleaners
    Washing machines
  Information equipment
    Calculators
    Digital copiers
    Fax machines
    Mobile business tools
    Personal computers
    Printers
Electronic components
  Flash memory
  Integrated circuits
  Laser diodes and other optoelectronic devices
  Radio-frequency components
  Satellite broadcasting components
  Solar cells and other photovoltaic devices

COMPETITORS

AMD
Canon
CASIO COMPUTER
Dell
Eastman Kodak
Electrolux
Epson
Ericsson
Fuji Xerox
Fujifilm
Fujitsu
GE
Hewlett-Packard
Hitachi
IBM
Intel
Konica Minolta
Kyocera
LG Electronics
Matsushita
Motorola
NEC
Oki Electric
Philips Electronics
Pioneer
Ricoh
Samsung Electronics
SANYO
Siemens
Sony
Toshiba
Xerox

HISTORICAL FINANCIALS

Company Type: Public

Income Statement

FYE: March 31

	REVENUE ($ mil.)	NET INCOME ($ mil.)	NET PROFIT MARGIN	EMPLOYEES
3/05	23,616	715	3.0%	46,751
3/04	21,367	575	2.7%	46,164
3/03	16,715	272	1.6%	46,633
3/02	13,599	85	0.6%	46,518
3/01	15,934	305	1.9%	49,101
3/00	17,580	267	1.5%	49,748
3/99	14,655	39	0.3%	57,521
3/98	13,456	186	1.4%	47,981
3/97	14,464	392	2.7%	46,900
3/96	15,391	432	2.8%	44,789
Annual Growth	**4.9%**	**5.8%**	**—**	**0.5%**

2005 Year-End Financials

Debt ratio: 16.0%   Current ratio: 1.12
Return on equity: 7.8%   Long-term debt ($ mil.): 1,496
Cash ($ mil.): 2,746

Net Income History

OTC: SHCAY

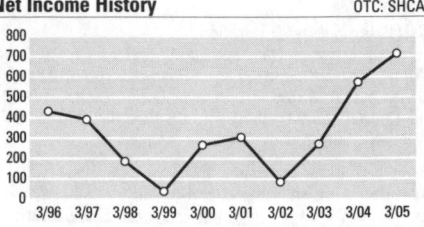

Shiseido

If your face is a canvas, Shiseido wants to be the paint. Shiseido, Japan's largest cosmetics firm, produces makeup and skin care products for men and women. It also makes toiletries, sun care products, fragrances, professional salon hair care products, pharmaceuticals, and fine chemicals. Upscale brands include Shiseido and Clé de Peau Beauté. Mid- and mass-market brands include Ayura and Aquair. Other interests include specialty fragrance, hair, and skin care salons. About three-quarters of Shiseido's sales come from Japan. Shinzo Maeda, general manager of corporate planning, became president and CEO in mid-2005. Morio Ikeda took the title of chairman.

Faced with growing competition in the Japanese cosmetics industry, Shiseido has been touching up business for its chain stores by using information from point-of-sale terminals and consultants' personal display assistants. It's also continuing to grow overseas. Shiseido opened its first store in Shanghai and opened more stores in China in March 2005.

In 2004 Shiseido also reorganized its operations in China, including the appointment of a senior officer, to boost its business there. Worldwide, the company has reorganized its business into five divisions: Global Cosmetics, Regional Cosmetics, Professional, Toiletries, and Diversified.

Shiseido plans to close two of its six primary plants in Japan (specifically, Tokyo and Kyoto) by June 2006. It's also closing its Shiseido Beautech and Haramachi Paper divisions in September 2005.

As Shinzo Maeda replaced Morio Ikeda as chief executive in mid-2005, he made plans to continue Shiseido's makeover begun by Ikeda in 2001. Maeda also anticipates growth amid increased competition.

Shiseido Malaysia Sdn. Bhd., a joint venture, was formed in early 2005 through a partnership with Warisan TC Holdings Berhad. Since 1977 a division of Warisan, Tung Pao Sdn. Bhd., has distributed Shiseido brands in Malaysia.

The firm has an Institute of Beauty Sciences which researches the relationship between "cosmetic behavior" and psychology.

HISTORY

Yushin Fukuhara, former head pharmacist for the Japanese admiralty, established Japan's first modern drugstore, Shiseido Pharmacy, in 1872. Attracted by the store's Western-style products and format, the customers were the nobility and the rich. Shiseido manufactured Japan's first toothpaste in 1888 and introduced its first cosmetics product (Eudermine, a skin lotion) in 1897. Fukuhara opened the country's first soda fountain in 1902.

Yushin's son, Shinzo, created Shiseido's first extensive makeup lines, introducing flesh-toned face powder in 1906 and a fragrance line in 1918. Under Shinzo's influence, cosmetics replaced drugs as Shiseido's mainstay.

Shiseido began franchise operations in 1923 and business boomed. The firm went public that year; in 1927 Shinzo became president. During WWII the company couldn't make cosmetics, only medicines, and many of Shiseido's factories were destroyed. This led to near-bankruptcy in 1945, but Shiseido rebounded the next year, thanks to nail enamel.

In 1951 it introduced its de Luxe high-end cosmetics line, and by 1956 it had become the #1 Japanese cosmetics firm. With a 1962 move into Hong Kong, Shiseido began overseas operations. It steadily expanded its international business by setting up subsidiaries across the world (including one in New York City in 1965).

In the 1970s Shiseido failed at marketing its products in the US, and at home its market share was slipping. Seen as being out of touch with the young, it was also hampered by strict product development laws that caused delays in getting products to market. In the mid-1980s it developed a successful US marketing strategy that included selling exclusive product lines in high-end department stores such as Macy's; it also made several acquisitions, including Zotos (hair products, US, 1988).

The firm's first prescription-only drug, an ophthalmological treatment used in certain types of cataract surgery and cornea transplants, was launched in 1993. In 1996 it announced a biological compound that retards skin aging by preventing oxidization. The company bought the Helene Curtis salon hair care business in the US and Canada from Unilever that year. In 1997 Shiseido bought Helene Curtis Japan salon hair operations and a New Jersey factory, which more than doubled its North American production.

Also in 1997 Akira Gemma (a Shiseido veteran of nearly four decades) became CEO, and the company expanded to Croatia, the Czech Republic, Hungary, and Vietnam. It bought the professional salon products business of the US's Lamaur Corporation in 1998.

Shiseido opened a New York City flagship store in 1998 and began selling cosmetics in Russia in 1999. It also began selling soap, shampoo, and baby powder in 1999 under the wildly popular Hello Kitty name, licensed from Japanese media firm Sanrio. Late that year Shiseido introduced Clé de Peau Beauté to international markets as its top-of-the-line beauty brand.

Looking to expand its foreign brands portfolio, in June 2000 Shiseido bought the Sea Breeze line of facial products from Bristol-Myers Squibb; it also acquired 75% of French cosmetics firm and aromatherapy specialists Laboratoires Decléor. In September the company announced an agreement with Intimate Brands (owner of Victoria's Secret and Bath & Body Works) to develop a new prestige beauty products line.

In June 2001 Morio Ikeda took over for Gemma as president and CEO; Gemma was named chairman.

In 2002 Shiseido, together with Limited Brands, introduced a new retail beauty company called aura science. One of 10 outlets planned to open in major US cities, the first aura science store was opened in Columbus, Ohio, in April of that year.

In the fall of 2003 the introduction of two new fragrances under the brand name FCUK (French Connection United Kingdom) by Shiseido's Zirh International subsidiary was met with vocal protest from some consumers. Shiseido reorganized its operations in China in 2004.

EXECUTIVES

Chairman: Morio Ikeda
President, CEO, and Director: Shinzo Maeda, age 57
VP: Seiji Nishimori
VP and Corporate Senior Executive Officer: Shigeo Shimizu
Corporate Executive Officer, R&D Strategy, Product Development, and Patents: Yoshimaru Kumano
Chief Officer, Cosmetics Business; President and CEO, Shiseido Sales: Toshimitsu Kobayashi
Chairman and CEO, Shiseido Cosmetics America Ltd.: Tosio Negami
Chief Officer, International Business: Masaaki Komatsu
President and CEO, FT Shiseido: Tadashi Noguchi
SVP, Shiseido Europe SA: Shuichi Tanaka
General Manager, Internal Audit: Yasuhiko Harada
General Manager, Personnel: Kazutoshi Satake
General Manager, Production Strategic, Planning: Toshiro Nagaya
General Manager, Technical: Kiyoshi Nakamura
Senior Corporate Auditor: Kazunari Moriya
Auditors: ChuoAoyama PricewaterhouseCoopers

LOCATIONS

HQ: Shiseido Company, Limited
5-5, Ginza 7-chome, Chuo-ku,
Tokyo 104-0061, Japan
Phone: +81-3-3572-5111　　**Fax:** +81-3-3289-1235
US HQ: 900 3rd Ave., New York, NY 10022
US Phone: 212-805-2300　　**US Fax:** 212-688-0109
Web: www.shiseido.co.jp

2004 Sales

	% of total
Japan	74
Europe	12
Americas	7
Asia & Oceania	7
Total	**100**

PRODUCTS/OPERATIONS

2004 Sales

	% of total
Cosmetics	78
Toiletries	11
Other	11
Total	**100**

Selected Brands and Operations

Mass Market
　Aquair
　SuperMild
Middle Market
　Aspril
　Ayura
　Uno
Prestige
　Aupres
　Carita
　Shiseido
High Prestige
　Clé de Peau Beauté
Other Operations
　Chromatography products (chemical analysis equipment)
　Fine chemicals (photochromic titanium dioxide pigment)
　Laboratoires Decléor (French cosmetics and aromatherapy products)
　Shiseido Pharmaceutical Co., Ltd.
　Zotos International, Inc. (research and development facilities)

COMPETITORS

Alberto-Culver	Kao
Alticor	L'Oréal
Avon	Mary Kay
Bath & Body Works	Procter & Gamble
Beiersdorf	Revlon
Body Shop	Revlon International
Chanel	Corporation
Colgate-Palmolive	Shu Uemura
Estée Lauder	Unilever
Henkel	Wella
Inter Parfums	Yves Saint-Laurent Groupe

HISTORICAL FINANCIALS

Company Type: Public

Income Statement

FYE: March 31

	REVENUE ($ mil.)	NET INCOME ($ mil.)	NET PROFIT MARGIN	EMPLOYEES
3/04	5,909	261	4.4%	24,839
3/03	5,184	204	3.9%	25,202
3/02	4,448	(172)	—	25,021
3/01	4,711	357	7.6%	24,959
3/00	5,655	145	2.6%	24,495
3/99	5,073	87	1.7%	23,688
3/98	4,666	127	2.7%	22,718
3/97	4,754	155	3.3%	22,045
3/96	5,229	163	3.1%	22,305
3/95	6,243	132	2.1%	23,355
Annual Growth	**(0.6%)**	**7.9%**	**—**	**0.7%**

2004 Year-End Financials

Debt ratio: 4.9%　　　　　Current ratio: 1.50
Return on equity: 8.0%　　Long-term debt ($ mil.): 175
Cash ($ mil.): 583

Net Income History

OTC: SSDOY

HOOVER'S HANDBOOK OF WORLD BUSINESS 2006

Siemens AG

Thinking globally and acting locally is more than semantics for Siemens. The company is Europe's largest electronics and electrical engineering firm and has operations worldwide in the industrial automation and control, information and communications, lighting, medical, power transmission, and transportation sectors. Siemens is a leading global manufacturer of telecom network equipment, which it provides through its Siemens Communications Group. The company is also active in the semiconductor sector through a minority stake in chip maker Infineon Technologies. Siemens Communications sold its mobile phone unit to Taiwan's BenQ in 2005.

The company has navigated through a three-year restructuring to focus its core business areas, making over 35,000 layoffs and selling off some of its affiliated companies.

Nearly 60% of Siemens' business is done in Europe, but the company makes more sales in the US than any other single country outside of Germany. As part of its focus on North America, Siemens has gained a listing on the New York Stock Exchange and reorganized its US operations as Siemens Corporation.

Siemens has acquired medical-imaging equipment maker CTI Molecular Imaging in a deal valued at about $1 billion. It also bolstered its financial services division, especially in the medical equipment financing sector, with the acquisition of UK-based financial services firm Broadcastle.

Siemens also acquired Flender Holding, a German supplier of gear systems, from a unit of Citigroup in a deal valued at $1.5 billion. Siemens in 2004 bought the equipment, treatment, and technology components of US Filter for more than $990 million in cash as part of its expansion into the US. The purchase, the company's largest since the 2001 acquisition of Efficient Networks, was intended to strengthen the its presence in the industrial water treatment and supply equipment market and to help it better compete with General Electric.

HISTORY

In 1847 electrical engineer Werner von Siemens and craftsman Johann Halske formed Siemens & Halske. The firm's first major project linked Berlin and Frankfurt with the first long-distance telegraph system in Europe (1848). In 1870 it completed a 6,600-mile telegraph line from London to Calcutta, India, and in 1874 it made the first transatlantic cable, linking Ireland to the US.

The company's history of firsts includes Europe's first electric power transmission system (1876), the world's first electrified railway (1879), and one of the first elevators (1880). In 1896 it patented the world's first X-ray tube and completed the first European subway, in Budapest, Hungary.

By the next century it had formed lightbulb cartel Osram with German rivals AEG and Auer (1919) and created a venture with Furukawa Electric called Fuji Electric (1923). It developed radios and traffic lights in the 1920s and began producing electron microscopes in 1939.

Siemens & Halske played a critical role in Germany's war effort in WWII and suffered heavy losses. During the 1950s it recovered by developing data processing equipment, silicates for semiconductors, and the first implantable pacemaker. It moved into the nuclear industry in 1959 when its first reactor went into service at Munich-Garching. In 1966 the company reincorporated as Siemens AG. It formed joint ventures with Bosch (BSH Bosch und Siemens Hausergäte, appliances, 1967) and AEG (Kraftwerk Union, nuclear power, 1969), among others. AEG dropped out of Kraftwerk Union (now Siemens Power Generation) in 1977.

In 1981 Karlheinz Kaske became the first CEO from outside the von Siemens family. Under his lead the firm entered joint ventures with Philips, Intel, and Advanced Micro Devices. In 1988 and 1989 it made several buys, including Bendix Electronics (US), and was a willing buyer when IBM wanted to unload Rolm (then the #1 maker of PBXs). It had acquired all of Rolm's businesses by 1992. That year Heinrich von Pierer replaced Kaske as CEO.

The 1990s saw more consolidation: Siemens and German computer maker Nixdorf combined computer businesses to form Siemens Nixdorf Informationssysteme (SNI, 1990); the firm acquired Sylvania's North American lamp business from GTE and merged it with the Osram companies in North America to form Osram Sylvania (1993).

The Asian economic crisis combined with other factors to make 1998 the worst year in the company's 150-year history. That year Siemens sold its defense electronics operations to British Aerospace (now BAE SYSTEMS) and Daimler-Benz (now DaimlerChrysler) and bought CBS's power generation business (formerly Westinghouse Electric).

In 1999 Siemens held an IPO for its passive components and electron tubes unit. It spun off its semiconductor operations into Infineon Technologies, but kept a 71% stake after Infineon's IPO in 2000. Siemens also sold its electromechanical components unit to Tyco International and its fiber-optic cable and hardware businesses to Corning.

In 2000 BSH paid $9.2 billion for the engineering and automotive parts unit Atecs Mannesmann. Also that year Siemens boosted its IT Service unit in the US by purchasing information services company ENTEX, and it agreed to merge its nuclear business with Framatome's.

Siemens shares began trading on the New York Stock Exchange in 2001. The company bought Dallas-based Efficient Networks for $1.5 billion that year. The slump in the telecommunications industry hurt Siemens that year, and the company cut 9,700 jobs.

Late in 2001 Siemens cut its stake in Infineon Technologies to less than 50%, and in 2002 it announced an additional 6,500 jobs to be cut from its telecom unit. The company continued to trim its information and communications holdings with the July 2002 sale of Unisphere Networks to Juniper Networks. Later that year, the company sold seven noncore subsidiaries (including Mannesmann Plastics Machinery, Stabilus, Demag Cranes & Components, and Gottwald Port Technology) to buyout firm Kohlberg Kravis Roberts for $1.7 billion.

In early 2005, CEO von Pierer was named chairman and stepped down as chief executive. Klaus Kleinfeld, CEO of US subsidiary Siemens Corporation, was named to the top spot at Siemens AG.

EXECUTIVES

President and CEO: Klaus Kleinfeld, age 48
EVP: Prof Edward G. Krubasik, age 61
EVP and CFO: Heinz-Joachim Neubürger, age 52
EVP, Power Generation: Uriel J. Sharef, age 61
EVP, Automation and Drives, Industrial Solutions and Services, and Asia and Australia: Klaus Wucherer, age 61
EVP: Johannes Feldmayer, age 49
EVP; Group President, Information and Communication Networks: Thomas Ganswindt, age 45
EVP; Group President, Information and Communication Mobile: Rudolf (Rudi) Lamprecht, age 57
SVP; Group President, Siemens Medical Solutions: Erich R. Reinhardt, age 59
SVP, Corporate Technology: Claus Weyrich, age 61, $2,032,888 pay
Chief Economist: Bernd Stecher
Labor Director: Jürgen Radomski, age 64
Head of Mobile Phones Division: Thorsten Heins, age 47
President and CEO, Siemens Financial Services: Herbert Lohneiss
Head of Corporate Strategies: Joe Kaeser
Director, Global Procurement and Logistics: Erich Hautz
Director, Corporate Communications: Eberhard Posner
Auditors: KPMG Deutsche Treuhand-Gesellschaft AG

LOCATIONS

HQ: Siemens AG
   Wittelsbacherplatz 2, D-80333 Munich, Germany
Phone: +49-89-636-00   **Fax:** +49-89-636-52-000
US HQ: Citicorp Center, 153 East 53rd St.,
   New York, NY 10022-4611
US Phone: 212-258-4000   **US Fax:** 212-767-0580
Web: www.siemens.com

2005 Sales (by location of customer)

	% of total
Europe	
Germany	21
Other countries	32
Americas	
US	20
Other countries	6
Asia/Pacific	13
Africa, Middle East & C.I.S.	8
Total	**100**

2005 Sales (by location of companies)

	% of total
Europe	
Germany	33
Other countries	31
Americas	
US	20
Other countries	5
Asia/Pacific	9
Africa, Middle East & C.I.S.	2
Total	**100**

PRODUCTS/OPERATIONS

2005 Sales

	$ mil.	% of total
Communications	14,747	16
Automation & Drives	11,047	12
Siemens VDO Automotive	10,785	12
Power Generation	9,046	10
Medical Solutions	8,558	9
Industrial Solutions & Services	6,048	7
Siemens Business Services	6,030	7
Siemens Building Technologies	4,955	6
OSRAM	4,826	5
Power Transmission & Distribution	4,770	5
Transportation Systems	4,702	5
Logistics & Assembly Systems	1,652	2
Other revenues	3,504	4
Total	**90,670**	**100**

COMPETITORS

ABB	Lucent
Agilent Technologies	Marconi
Alcatel	Matsushita
Bull	Mitsubishi Electric
Capgemini	Motorola
Cisco Systems	NEC
Cooper Industries	Nokia
Ericsson	Nortel Networks
GE	Oki Electric
Harris Corp.	Philips Electronics
Hitachi	Samsung
Honeywell ACS	SANYO
IBM	Schneider
Intel	Sharp
Jacobs Sverdrup	Tellabs
Johnson Controls	Texas Instruments
Koor Industries	Toshiba

HISTORICAL FINANCIALS

Company Type: Public

Income Statement

FYE: September 30

	REVENUE ($ mil.)	NET INCOME ($ mil.)	NET PROFIT MARGIN	EMPLOYEES
9/05	90,670	2,702	3.0%	461,000
9/04	93,455	4,233	4.5%	424,000
9/03	86,467	2,848	3.3%	411,000
9/02	82,865	2,561	3.1%	426,000
9/01	86,208	2,069	2.4%	450,000
9/00	68,387	7,820	11.4%	430,200
9/99	73,049	1,987	2.7%	443,000
9/98	70,323	548	0.8%	416,000
9/97	60,718	1,481	2.4%	386,000
9/96	61,796	1,960	3.2%	379,000
Annual Growth	4.4%	3.6%	—	2.2%

2005 Year-End Financials

Debt ratio: 31.1%
Return on equity: 8.2%
Cash ($ mil.): 9,760
Current ratio: 1.17
Long-term debt ($ mil.): 10,138

No. of shares (mil.): 891
Dividends
  Yield: 2.1%
  Payout: 56.2%
Market value ($ mil.): 68,907

Stock History

NYSE: SI

	STOCK PRICE ($) FY Close	P/E High/Low	PER SHARE ($) Earnings	Dividends	Book Value
9/05	77.33	29 25	2.90	1.63	36.57
9/04	73.70	19 13	4.55	1.29	37.47
9/03	59.41	21 10	3.21	1.00	31.01
9/02	33.61	24 11	2.88	0.00	26.06
9/01	38.40	34 14	2.34	0.00	26.56
Annual Growth	19.1%	— —	5.5%	—	8.3%

Sime Darby

Malaysia's oldest and largest conglomerate, Sime Darby started in rubber and stretched out. Its core business activities include the distribution of autos (BMW, Ford, Land Rover) and heavy equipment (Caterpillar); tire manufacturing; oil palm and rubber plantations; production of edible oils; residential and commercial property development; and the construction and operation of power plants. The general trading arm distributes products such as advanced composite materials, auto parts, and sealants. It also has stakes in hotels, hypermarkets, and medical facilities. Germany-based tire manufacturer Continental AG has acquired a 30% stake in Sime Darby's tire operations with an option to purchase a larger share.

Amid continued economic weakness in many of the Asian nations in which it does business, Sime Darby has worked to control costs and to limit acquisitions to companies that operate in its core business areas. It has also sought to expand in Australia, with its most recent acquisition in September 2005 of car dealer PPT Investment.

In 2005 the group also revealed its plan to expand its Indonesian plantation operations and auto assembly business. It opened talks to purchase up to 65,000 hectares of palm oil plantation land on Borneo island. On the auto front, Sime Darby announced it would assemble the Hyundai Getz, a compact car, at a Malaysian plant within the year.

HISTORY

William Sime, a 37-year-old Scottish adventurer, convinced Henry Darby, a wealthy 50-year-old English banker, that money could be made in rubber, a product that had just been introduced to Malaya from Brazil. Together they established Sime, Darby & Co., Ltd., in 1910 to manage about 500 acres of rubber estates in the jungles of Malacca, Malaya. To overcome local hostility to their venture, the pair maintained close links with the Chinese business community.

Riding a rubber boom, Sime, Darby became a managing agent for other plantations before moving into general trading. In 1915 it set up a branch office in Singapore and formed a London office for marketing. To clear jungle and meet growing demand for rubber, in 1929 Sime, Darby bought Sarawak Trading, which held a franchise for Caterpillar earth-moving equipment. In 1936 Sime, Darby moved its headquarters to Singapore.

In 1958 Sime Darby Holdings Ltd. was incorporated in England as successor to Sime, Darby & Co., Ltd. When demand for rubber softened in the 1960s, it was one of the first plantations to diversify into palm oil and cocoa production. It acquired the Seafield Estate and Consolidated Plantations in the 1970s, becoming a dominant force in Malaysian plantations while it started processing crops into finished products. Success of the switch to oil palms allowed the conglomerate's autocratic British CEO, Denis Pinder, to gobble up numerous firms. In 1973 allegations appeared in newspapers about improprieties at "Slime Darby." Pinder ended up in Changi prison on misdemeanor charges. The mysterious death of Sime Darby's outside auditor, found stabbed in his bathtub, was ruled a suicide.

After Pinder's successor upset Malaysians by investing in unsuccessful European ventures,

Pernas (the Malaysian government trading corporation) bought Sime Darby shares on the London Stock Exchange and demanded an Asian majority be placed on the board. Outmaneuvered, the British lost control of Sime Darby in 1976. The only man acceptable as chairman to both Asian and British board members was Tun Tan Siew Sin, a former Malaysian finance minister and son of Tun Tan Cheng Lock, one of Malaysia's founding fathers. The firm, reincorporated in Malaysia as Sime Darby Berhad in 1978, moved its head office to Kuala Lumpur in 1979.

Sime Darby acquired the tire-making operations of B.F. Goodrich Philippines in 1981 and the Apple Computer franchise for southeast Asia in 1982. It bought an interest in United Estates, a Malaysian property development firm, two years later. In 1989 Sime Darby bought Dur-A-Vend, a UK condom wholesaler marketing a product called Jiffy with the slogan "Do it in a Jiffy." Sime Darby moved into tourism in 1991, acquiring Sandestin Resorts in Florida.

Expanding its financial portfolio in 1996, Sime Darby acquired control of United Malayan Banking (breaking it up into Sime Bank and SimeSecurities). The next year it consolidated its travel-related holdings into its Sime Wings unit. Hurt by regional financial turmoil, Sime Darby in 1999 sold Sime Bank and SimeSecurities to Malaysian financier Tan Sri Rashid Hussain.

In 1999 it divested Sandestin Resorts, LEC Refrigeration, and its 7% stake in British chemical firm Elements. Despite its streamlining, the firm could not resist picking up power generation assets as the power industry restructured. In 2000 it increased its stake in Port Dickson Power to 60%. Sime Darby also sold its insurance operations that year.

In 2003 Sime Darby sold a 30% stake in its tire business to Continental AG. Continental has an option to purchase an additional 21% in the future.

EXECUTIVES

Chairman: Tan Sri Dato' Seri Ahmad Sarji bin Abdul Hamid, age 66
Deputy Chairman: Tunku Tan Sri Dato' Seri Ahmad bin Tunku Yahaya, age 75
Group Chief Executive: Dato' Ahmad Zubair Ahmad Zubir Bin Haji Murshid, age 47
Group Finance Director: Martin G. Manen, age 49
Managing Director, Consolidated Plantations Berhad and Divisional Director, Plantations Division: YBhg Datuk Syed Tamin Syed Mohamed
Managing Director, DMIB Berhad and Sime Tyres International, and Divisional Director, Tyre Manufacturing: Tuan Haji Ahmad Zubir bin Haji Murshid
Managing Director, Hastings Deering (Australia) Limited and Divisional Director, Heavy Equipment Distribution: James C. Sheed
Managing Director, Sime Darby China Limited: Tan Wan Hong
Managing Director, Sime Darby Motor Holdings Limited and Divisional Director, Motor Distribution Operations: Marc A. Singleton
Managing Director, Sime Engineering Services Berhad and Divisional Director, Engineering Services: Tuan Haji Mohamed Ja'far bin Abdul Carrim
Managing Director, Sime UEP Properties Berhad and Divisional Director, Property Development: YBhg Dato' Mohamed bin Haji Said
Managing Director, Tractors Malaysia Holdings Berhad and Divisional Director, Heavy Equipment Distribution: Azhar Bin Abdul Hamid

Divisional Director, Allied Products and Services:
Yip Jon Khiam
Divisional Director, Power Division: Encik Mohamed
Nor bin Abdul Hamid
Group Secretary and Tax Controller: Nancy P. Y. Yeoh
Joint Group Secretary and Senior Legal Advisor:
Puan Saleha binti M Ramly
Auditors: PricewaterhouseCoopers

LOCATIONS

HQ: Sime Darby Berhad
Wisma Sime Darby, 21st Fl., Jalan Raja Laut,
50350 Kuala Lumpur, Malaysia
Phone: +60-3-2691-4122   **Fax:** +60-3-2698-7398
Web: www.simenet.com

2004 Sales

	$ mil.	% of total
Malaysia	1,286.3	33
Hong Kong	877.2	22
Australia	667.0	17
Singapore	488.6	12
China	140.2	4
Other countries	463.3	12
Total	**3,922.6**	**100**

PRODUCTS/OPERATIONS

2004 Sales

	$ mil.	% of total
Motor vehicle distribution	1,404.8	36
Heavy equipment distribution	907.0	23
Plantations	415.1	10
Energy	207.1	5
Property	194.0	5
General trading, services & other	825.1	21
Adjustments	(30.5)	—
Total	**3,922.6**	**100**

COMPETITORS

Ansell	Hutchison Whampoa
Bridgestone	Jardine Matheson
Cummins	Joy Global
DaimlerChrysler	Komatsu
General Motors	Marubeni
Goodyear	Michelin
Hopewell Holdings	Swire Pacific
HSBC Holdings	

HISTORICAL FINANCIALS

Company Type: Public

Income Statement

FYE: June 30

	REVENUE ($ mil.)	NET INCOME ($ mil.)	NET PROFIT MARGIN	EMPLOYEES
6/04	3,923	242	6.2%	24,405
6/03	3,612	213	5.9%	27,484
6/02	3,164	202	6.4%	26,384
6/01	3,147	162	5.2%	26,000
6/00	2,888	203	7.0%	27,000
6/99	2,608	216	8.3%	29,000
6/98	2,924	(131)	—	36,000
6/97	4,349	323	7.4%	37,000
6/96	4,321	278	6.4%	32,000
6/95	3,854	216	5.6%	32,000
Annual Growth	**0.2%**	**1.2%**	**—**	**(3.0%)**

2004 Year-End Financials

Debt ratio: 20.6%
Return on equity: 11.2%
Cash ($ mil.): 754

Current ratio: 2.20
Long-term debt ($ mil.): 456

Singapore Airlines

With its wine selection, fine cuisine, and sarong-clad flight attendants, Singapore Airlines (SIA) has tried to cultivate a reputation for superior service. The carrier boasts a fleet of about 90 aircraft (one of the youngest among international carriers) and flies to more than 60 cities in 33 countries. It also belongs to the Star Alliance airline marketing network, which includes United Airlines, Lufthansa, and SAS. SIA units include regional carrier SilkAir, a pilot school, and repair and maintenance facilities. In addition, it owns a 49% stake in the UK's Virgin Atlantic Airways. The Singapore government owns 57% of SIA through Temasek Holdings.

The company's Singapore Airport Terminal Services (SATS) subsidiary provides catering, security, and cargo handling to other airlines, and it owns stakes in similar ventures outside Singapore. SIA sold minority stakes in SATS and in maintenance and repair unit SIA Engineering. Other SIA operations include cargo carrier SIA Cargo and property investment. It also owns a 49% interest in Virgin Atlantic.

With regional nightmares including a SARS outbreak and a tsunami disaster behind it, Singapore Airlines has caught a tailwind and is again posting profits. The company has outsourced some technology and finance operations and has struck better deals with its labor unions.

The company has also expanded into India and Amsterdam and increased services in Australia and the US.

HISTORY

Singapore Airlines (SIA) was formed as Malayan Airways in 1937 but did not begin scheduled service until 1947, when the Mansfield & Co. shipping line used it to link Singapore with other Malayan cities. The airline added service to Vietnam, Sumatra, and Java by 1951 and opened routes to Borneo, Brunei, Burma, and Thailand by 1958.

Meanwhile, British Overseas Airways Corporation (BOAC, predecessor of British Airways) bought 10% of Malayan in 1948 and raised its stake to 30% in 1959. Australia's Qantas Airways also took a 30% stake in Malayan that year. In 1963 the governments of Singapore, Malaya, Sarawak, and Sabah merged to form Malaysia, inspiring Malayan to change its name to Malaysian Airways. Singapore seceded from the federation in 1965 but joined Malaysia to buy control of the airline from BOAC and Qantas in 1966, changing the name to Malaysia-Singapore Airlines.

The carrier extended service to Bombay, Melbourne, Rome, and London in 1971 and then to Osaka, Athens, Zurich, and Frankfurt in 1972. That year managerial disagreements led Malaysia and Singapore to dissolve the company to form two separate national airlines: The domestic network went to the Malaysian Airline System, and international routes went to SIA. Joe Pillay of Singapore's ministry of finance became SIA's first chairman. The government owned 82%, and employees held 17%.

SIA initiated such now well-known amenities as free drinks, hot towels, and headsets in 1972, thereby gaining a reputation for outstanding service. By 1974 it served 25 cities worldwide. It added flights to Auckland and Paris in 1976, Tehran and Copenhagen in 1977, and San Francisco, its first US destination, in 1978.

In 1985 the government reduced its stake in SIA to 63%. The company joined Cathay Pacific and Thai International in 1988 to form Abacus, a computer reservation system for Asia/Pacific carriers.

The next year SIA bought stakes in Delta Air Lines and Swissair; the three created a route network reaching 82 countries. The Singapore airline also snagged a 40% stake in Royal Air Cambodge from the Cambodian government in 1993. In 1995 SIA ordered 77 Boeing 777s for delivery between 1997 and 2004.

The US and Singapore governments signed an "open skies" agreement in 1997 (the first between the US and an Asian nation), allowing unlimited flights between the two countries, but SIA canceled its alliance with Delta and Swissair in favor of one with Germany's Lufthansa.

A December 1997 crash of a new SilkAir 737 killed all 104 people on board; investigators speculated that the crash was an act of suicide by the pilot. (Two years later SIA agreed to pay each family settlements of up to $195,000.) The Asian crisis added to the airline's woes, but SIA was able to cut costs when the government reduced contributions to the national pension plan and the Singapore airport lowered landing fees.

In 1999 SIA implemented code-sharing with SAS, and soon SIA announced it would join SAS in the global Star Alliance marketing network. After failed attempts to buy into South African Airways and Australia Ansett, SIA bought a 49% stake in UK carrier Virgin Atlantic for some $960 million, acquired 25% of Air New Zealand (reduced to 7% in 2001), and joined the Star Alliance in 2000. Also that year 82 passengers died when Singapore Airlines flight SQ006 crashed into debris on an out-of-service runway.

SIA spun off its cargo operations, SIA Cargo, in 2001. Later in the year SIA Cargo formed an alliance with Lufthansa Cargo, SAS, and Deutsche Post.

In the airline industry downturn that followed the September 11, 2001, attacks on the US, SIA was forced to tighten its belt. By the next year, however, nearly all of the service that the carrier had suspended had been restored. The airline was forced to cut jobs, including more than 180 pilots and some 415 ground crew, in 2003 because of decreased demand for air travel as well as global fears of SARS, a mysterious virus with the highest reported incidents coming from Asian countries. SIA also had to cut back nearly 360 flights per week.

The carrier sold its remaining stake in Air New Zealand in 2004.

EXECUTIVES

Chairman: Koh Boon Hwee, age 54
CEO and Director: Chew Choon Seng
EVP Marketing and the Regions: Huang Cheng Eng
SEVP Operations and Services: Bey Soo Khiang
SVP Corporate Services: Teoh Tee Hooi
SVP Engineering: Mervyn Sirisena
SVP Europe: Theong Tjhoen Onn
SVP Finance: Goh Choon Phong
SVP Flight Operations: Raymond Ng
SVP Human Resources: Loh Meng See
SVP North Asia: Ng Kian Wah
SVP Planning: Mak Swee Wah
SVP Product and Services: Yap Kim Wah
SVP Southeast Asia, Korea, and Japan: Teh Ping Choon
SVP West Africa and Africa: Tan Chik Quee
VP Marketing USA: Ken Bright
Regional VP Americas: Subhas Menon
Chief Executive SilkAir: Mike Barclay
Auditors: Ernst & Young

LOCATIONS

HQ: Singapore Airlines Limited
Airline House, 25 Airline Rd., 819829, Singapore
Phone: +65-6541-4885   **Fax:** +65-6542-3002
US HQ: 5670 Wilshire Blvd., Ste. 1800,
Los Angeles, CA 90036
US Phone: 323-934-8833   **US Fax:** 323-934-4482
Web: www.singaporeair.com

2005 Sales

	% of total
East Asia	46
Europe	17
Southwest Pacific	13
Americas	8
West Asia & Africa	7
Non-scheduled services & other operations	9
Total	**100**

PRODUCTS/OPERATIONS

2005 Sales

	% of total
Airline operations	86
Airport terminal services	7
Engineering services	6
Other	1
Total	**100**

Selected Subsidiaries and Affiliates

SIA Engineering Company Limited (87%, engine maintenance and repair)
SIA Properties (Pte) Ltd. (building services)
SilkAir (Singapore) Private Limited (regional airline)
Singapore Airlines Cargo Private Limited
Singapore Airport Terminal Services Limited (87%)
   SATS Airport Services Pte. Ltd.
   SATS Catering Pte. Ltd.
   SATS Security Services Private Ltd.
Singapore Aviation and General Insurance Company (Pte) Limited
Singapore Flying College Pte. Ltd.
Virgin Atlantic Limited (49%, holding company for Virgin Atlantic Airways, UK)

COMPETITORS

AMR Corp.
British Airways
Cathay Pacific
China Airlines
China Eastern Airlines
China Southern Airlines
Continental Airlines
Delta Air
Japan Airlines
KLM
Korean Air
Malaysian Airlines
Northwest Airlines
Qantas

HISTORICAL FINANCIALS

Company Type: Public

Income Income Statement

FYE: March 31

	REVENUE ($ mil.)	NET INCOME ($ mil.)	NET PROFIT MARGIN	EMPLOYEES
3/05	7,271	841	11.6%	28,146
3/04	5,796	504	8.7%	29,734
3/03	5,934	601	10.1%	30,243
3/02	5,123	343	6.7%	29,316
3/01	5,510	858	15.6%	28,336
3/00	5,182	678	13.1%	27,513
3/99	4,506	597	13.3%	27,906
3/98	4,786	641	13.4%	27,516
3/97	4,998	714	14.3%	27,241
3/96	4,893	728	14.9%	26,326
Annual Growth	**4.5%**	**1.6%**	**—**	**0.7%**

2005 Year-End Financials

Debt ratio: 18.8%   Current ratio: 1.27
Return on equity: 11.7%   Long-term debt ($ mil.): 1,412
Cash ($ mil.): 1,719

Net Income History

Singapore: SIAL

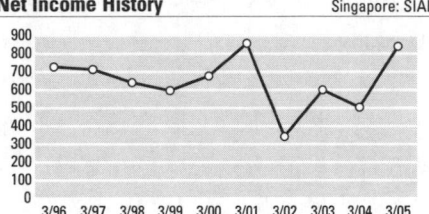

Sinopec Shanghai Petrochemical

China's own entry into the world of giant chemical companies, Sinopec Shanghai Petrochemical Company, is one of that country's largest producers of ethylene, a crucial ingredient in the manufacture of synthetic fibers, resins, and plastics. It also makes petroleum-based fuels and oils and other intermediate petrochemicals such as benzene. The company, which operates primarily within China (most of its revenues are from Eastern China), has joint ventures with UK company BP, US firm Dow Chemical, and Japan's ITOCHU Corporation. China Petroleum & Chemical (Sinopec), which is controlled by the Chinese government, owns about 55% of Shanghai Petrochemical.

The rising tide has certainly raised Shanghai Petrochemical's ship. The general economic recovery in 2003 and 2004 engendered high prices for its petroleum products and high sales volumes for its products across the board. The results were sales increases of 33%.

Throughout the first half of the decade more and more foreign chemical companies have gained entrance into the Chinese petrochemical market, increasing competition for Shanghai Petrochemical. Thus far the company isn't overly concerned about the trend, as the opening of the market has substantially increased its customer base and demand for its products.

In anticipation of China's admission to the World Trade Organization, Shanghai Petrochemical Company began to overhaul its production facilities. The upgrades have enabled the company to process 10 million tons of crude oil per year, along with 1 million tons of ethylene and other synthetic fiber materials. The current quality of Chinese ethylene is generally inferior to that produced in developed countries. The upgrades have allowed the company to produce world-class polyethylene and polypropylene, which it can use domestically and sell on the world market.

HISTORY

The Mao-inspired Cultural Revolution of the 1960s restored the aging leader's political grip, but it also caused immense economic disruptions in China, including a virtual shutdown of foreign trade. In the early 1970s party reformists led by Zhou Enlai and Deng Xiaoping advocated improved contact with the outside world and the restoration of foreign trade, giving the Chinese economy access to much-needed technology. In 1972, the year President Nixon's visit to China restored Sino-US ties, China began contracting for plant and equipment imports, especially in the petrochemical areas of chemical fertilizers for agriculture and artificial fibers for industrial use. That year Shanghai Petrochemical Company was founded as China's first large petrochemical enterprise, using imported equipment and technology.

Under Sinopec's control, Shanghai Petrochemical fit squarely into the government's Four Modernizations policy (agriculture, industry, technology, and defense). Other factors in the firm's growth were the booming economies of the coastal cities in the east and south, made possible by economic liberalization policies that encouraged foreign investment. The Guangdong province in the south led the way as Hong Kong enterprise migrated there in the 1980s in search of lower wages and overhead. The expansion of industrial output there and in other provinces resulted in greatly increased demand for petrochemicals.

Emboldened by growth and further reforms in the oil industry, Sinopec restructured Shanghai Petrochemical in 1993 and listed it on the Hong Kong and New York stock markets. (It was the first Chinese company listed on the New York Stock Exchange.) The company formed a joint venture with US-based agribusiness giant Continental Grain in 1995 to build a liquid petroleum gas plant and teamed up with British Petroleum (now BP) to build an acrylonitrile plant. The company entered a joint venture with Union Carbide (purchased by Dow Chemical) in 1996 to build a polymer emulsion plant in China. Shanghai Petrochemical increased its market share for acrylics with its 1997 purchase of the Zhejiang Acrylic Fibre Plant, then a producer of about 40% of China's total acrylic-fiber output. Annual production grew to 130,000 tons by 1999.

Three broad-reaching events have hammered the company's profits: the Asian economic crisis, the decrease of Sinopec's subsidy on crude oil, and a global oversupply of petrochemicals. In 1997 Shanghai Petrochemical's product-mix adjustments, combined with cost cutting, offset some of the increased crude costs and lower prices. The company announced in 1998 that the Chinese government planned to crack down on the smuggling of foreign petrochemicals and help the domestic market. The firm remains vulnerable to policy changes, however. Additionally, consolidation of the Chinese petrochemical industry could translate into lost jobs. The company continued to modernize its facilities and increase its capacity in 2000 when it moved to upgrade operations in order to become a world-class production base for petrochemicals and derivatives.

EXECUTIVES

Chairman: Lu Yiping, age 59
Vice Chairman and President: Rong Guangdao, age 49
Vice Chairman: Du Chongjun, age 50
CFO and Director: Han Zhihao, age 53
VP: Tang Chengjian, age 49
VP and Director: Wu Haijun, age 42
VP: Zhang Jianping, age 42
VP: Yin Jihai, age 47
VP: Shi Wei, age 45
VP: Zhang Zhiliang, age 51
Executive Director: Gao Jinping, age 38
Company Secretary: Zhang Jingming, age 47
Auditors: KPMG

LOCATIONS

HQ: Sinopec Shanghai Petrochemical Company Limited (Sinopec Shanghai Shiyou Huagong Gufen Youxien Gongsi)
48 Jinyi Rd., Jinshan District, Shanghai 200540, China
Phone: +86-21-5794-194   **Fax:** +86-21-5794-2267
Web: www.spc.com.cn

Sinopec Shanghai Petrochemical Company operates primarily in China.

PRODUCTS/OPERATIONS

2004 Sales

	% of total
Intermediate petrochemicals	29
Petroleum products	27
Resins & plastics	23
Synthetic fibers	9
Other	12
Total	**100**

Selected Products

Intermediate	Resins and Plastics
Petrochemicals	LDPE film and pellets
Benzene	Polyester chips
Butadiene	PP pellets
Ethylene	PVA
Ethylene glycol	
Ethylene oxide	Synthetic Fibers
	Acrylic staple
Petroleum Products	Acrylic top
Diesel	Polyester filament-POY
Gasoline	Polyester staple
Jet oil	PP fiber
Residual oil	PVA fiber

COMPETITORS

BASF AG
DuPont
ExxonMobil Chemical
Formosa Plastics
Huntsman
ICI American
Jilin Chemical
Marubeni
Shell Chemicals
Sinopec Beijing Yanhua Petrochemical

HISTORICAL FINANCIALS

Company Type: Public

Income Statement

FYE: December 31

	REVENUE ($ mil.)	NET INCOME ($ mil.)	NET PROFIT MARGIN	EMPLOYEES
12/04	4,671	480	10.3%	—
12/03	3,496	169	4.8%	31,008
12/02	2,624	111	4.2%	31,489
12/01	2,370	14	0.6%	32,081
12/00	2,406	104	4.3%	33,911
12/99	1,696	73	4.3%	35,826
12/98	1,294	29	2.2%	38,000
12/97	1,429	88	6.1%	38,000
12/96	1,434	122	8.5%	38,000
12/95	1,423	256	18.0%	38,000
Annual Growth	**14.1%**	**7.2%**	**—**	**(2.5%)**

2004 Year-End Financials

Debt ratio: 10.9%
Return on equity: 23.8%
Cash ($ mil.): 204
Current ratio: 1.16
Long-term debt ($ mil.): 243
No. of shares (mil.): 72
Dividends
Yield: 0.0%
Payout: —
Market value ($ mil.): 2,686

Stock History

NYSE: SHI

	STOCK PRICE ($) FY Close	P/E High/Low		PER SHARE ($) Earnings	Dividends	Book Value
12/04	37.30	8	4	6.67	0.00	30.90
12/03	46.26	20	6	2.36	0.60	25.20
12/02	14.95	11	6	1.50	0.00	23.46
12/01	9.03	90	37	0.19	0.73	22.12
12/00	9.63	13	6	1.45	0.60	22.65
12/99	15.06	25	7	1.01	0.36	21.22
12/98	8.50	44	13	0.40	0.00	20.80
12/97	15.56	38	12	1.20	0.00	20.82
12/96	29.38	19	13	1.80	1.56	19.68
12/95	28.50	9	6	3.90	2.54	17.55
Annual Growth	**3.0%**	**—**	**—**	**6.1%**	**—**	**6.5%**

SNCF

France's state-owned railway company, Société Nationale des Chemins de Fer Français (SNCF), is still blazing a trail as the nation's primary provider of local and long-distance passenger and freight service. Passenger transportation accounts for a majority of the company's sales. SNCF's Eurostar joint venture shuttles passengers between Paris and London via the Channel Tunnel, and Thalys links Paris with other European capitals. SNCF's high-speed TGV passenger trains travel at up to 250 mph. In addition, the company carries about 50 billion ton-km of freight annually. SNCF owns stakes in dozens of other passenger and freight transportation companies.

Holdings managed by the rail company's main investment arm, SNCF-Participations, include stakes in Keolis, a French bus operator that also

has operations in Canada and Germany; Geodis, one of France's largest transport and logistics groups; and Seafrance, a ferry operator.

To be a major player in Europe's increasingly deregulated road and rail transport network, SNCF is forging cross-border alliances: Transnational ventures have included working with Deutsche Bahn to design a European high-speed rail system, operating a bus and rail joint venture with UK-based Go-Ahead Group, and joining the UK's FirstGroup in bidding for a UK rail franchise.

HISTORY

France's first railway line, opened in 1827, was used to haul coal from Saint-Etienne to the port of Andrezieux. Four years later the first steam locomotives and passenger service were introduced between Saint-Etienne and Lyon. Paris opened its first rail line in 1837. Although the early railway companies were under private ownership, the state controlled the network of rail lines through licensing. Under Napoleon III's Second Empire (1852-1870), the government encouraged an expansion of railway lines that linked Paris to every major town and city in France. By 1870 the main routes of France's modern railway system had been laid; in 1914 the network system had grown to nearly 40,000 km.

After the devastation of WWI, railway companies invested heavily in rebuilding. Burdened by debt, the rail network was forced to seek government intervention for its survival. In 1938 the government set up Société Nationale des Chemins de Fer Français to unify the five largest railway systems: Compagnie de l'Est, Compagnie du Midi, Compagnie du Nord, Compagnie du Paris-Lyon-Méditerranée, and Compagnie du Paris-Orléans.

Although WWII destroyed the French railway system for a second time, the massive rebuilding enabled postwar French governments to adopt modern innovations. In 1950 SNCF began a systemwide electrification of its tracks; a decade later 7,600 km of its major lines were powered by electricity.

SNCF also pioneered the development of fast trains. Following an overhaul of SNCF in the early 1970s, the company continued to develop high-speed trains to stay competitive with airlines. In 1981 the company's TGV (*train à grande vitesse*) hit a record speed of 380 kph (236 mph). TGVs entered commercial service that year. By 1987 some 43 cities were connected to Paris by TGVs.

To add to its European logistics and freight services, SNCF acquired 20% of Spanish trucking firm TRANSFESA in 1993. In 1995 it launched Eurostar, a London-Paris service using the newly opened Channel Tunnel. Partners in the joint venture were Belgian National Railroads (Société Nationale des Chemins de Fer Belges) and European Passenger Services, the British Rail unit later spun off as Eurostar (UK). That year SNCF saw its operations disrupted by a nationwide rail strike that lasted three weeks. In 1995 SNCF also created road transport and logistics group Géodis, which it privatized a year later.

Diversifying further, SNCF also entered telecommunications in 1996 and set up a communications network to lease spare capacity. That year the company's chairman resigned following charges of corruption related to his tenure at an oil company. SNCF, also plagued by debts and strikes, decided to get back on track. It began restructuring and appointed former Aerospatiale chief Louis Gallois to head the company. In 1997 it shifted most of its debt load to Réseau Ferré de

France, which was created to manage France's rail infrastructure.

In 1999 SNCF acquired Via-GTI, France's largest privately owned public transport company, which was in a joint venture with UK transport group Go-Ahead to operate the Thameslink train franchise. That year SNCF acquired Swiss rolling stock group Ermewa; it also sold its hotel interests to Accor but formed an alliance with the hotelier to offer discount lodging.

SNCF and German railway Deutsche Bahn agreed in 2000 to collaborate on developing a new generation of high-speed trains.

SNCF's rail operations were hampered by labor unrest in 2003, capped by a strike in May and June of that year. The company responded by cutting costs.

EXECUTIVES

Chairman: Louis Gallois, age 61
CEO: Guillaume Pepy, age 47
Chief Financial and Information Officer:
  Jean-Pierre Menanteau
Deputy Managing Director, Operations: Jacques Couvert
Deputy Managing Director, Freight: Marc Véron
Director, Communications: Bernard Emsellem
Director, Human Resources: Pierre Izard
Director, Strategy: Elisabeth Borne
Director, Voyages France Europe: Mireille Faugère
Chairman, SNCF-Participations: Claire Dreyfus-Cloarec
Secretary General: Paul Mingasson
Auditors: Ernst & Young Audit; Mazars & Guérard

LOCATIONS

HQ: Société Nationale des Chemins de Fer Français
  34 rue du Commandant Mouchotte,
  75699 Paris, France
Phone: +33-1-53-25-60-00   **Fax:** +33-1-53-25-61-08
Web: www.sncf.fr

COMPETITORS

Air France
Arriva
British Airways
FirstGroup
National Express Group
P&O
Stagecoach
Veolia Environnement
Virgin Group

HISTORICAL FINANCIALS

Company Type: Government-owned

Income Statement

FYE: December 31

	REVENUE ($ mil.)	NET INCOME ($ mil.)	NET PROFIT MARGIN	EMPLOYEES
12/04	30,089	441	1.5%	229,877
12/03	28,271	14	0.0%	243,944
12/02	23,243	66	0.3%	242,163
12/01	17,830	(124)	—	220,700
12/00	18,680	167	0.9%	216,605
12/99	16,413	52	0.3%	210,911
12/98	21,619	(96)	—	210,437
12/97	20,496	(110)	—	210,437
12/96	15,442	—	—	209,746
12/95	13,785	—	—	215,787
Annual Growth	9.1%	—	—	0.7%

2004 Year-End Financials

Debt ratio: 422.1%   Current ratio: 0.54
Return on equity: 10.9%   Long-term debt ($ mil.): 18,541
Cash ($ mil.): 2,367

Net Income History

Sodexho Alliance has a lot of mouths to feed. The company is the world's #2 contract foodservice provider (after Compass Group), with operations in more than 75 countries. Its clients include corporations, colleges, hospitals, and public institutions. Besides foodservice, Sodexho Alliance also provides facilities management (grounds keeping, laundry), service vouchers, remote site management (including offshore rigs), and river pleasure cruises. In 2001 Sodexho Alliance bought Sodexho Marriott Services (one of the largest foodservice companies in the US) to serve as its North American subsidiary and renamed the firm Sodexho, Inc. Chairman Pierre Bellon and his family own about 40% of the company.

The company's client list spans the globe, and includes France's Peugeot and Total Fina, Sweden's Ericsson, the UK's Unilever, and Germany's Ministry of Foreign Affairs. Foodservice operations account for some 98% of the company's business. Sodexho Alliance is the largest such operator in North America through Sodexho, Inc.

Through its Sodexho Pass subsidiary, the company's service vouchers (passes, coupons, and smart cards for food, transportation, medical care, and employee and social benefits) are used in Europe and Latin America. It operates a fleet of boats for river and harbor dinner cruises in cities such as Boston, Chicago, London, New York, Paris, Philadelphia, Seattle, and Washington, DC. In 2002 the company announced it had detected accounting and management errors in its UK operations, causing the value of its stock to fall by nearly one-third.

Sodexho's North American operation, which generates about 40% of its total sales, grew during the last period of 2004 in a couple of units (education and health care), but was stalled or declining in units supplying business, defense, and industry.

HISTORY

The Bellon family had been luxury ship hospitality specialists since the turn of the century, 60 years before Pierre Bellon founded Sodexho in 1966. By 1971 Bellon had his first contract outside France to provide food service to a Brussels hospital. Sodexho continued to expand its services into the late 1970s, entering remote site management in Africa and the Middle East in 1975 and starting its service vouchers segment in Belgium and Germany in 1978.

Sodexho jumped the pond in 1980, expanding its businesses into North and South America. The company went public on the Paris Bourse exchange in 1983. Two years later it bought Seiler, a Boston vending machine company-turned-restaurateur. Sodexho then bought San Francisco's Food Dimensions in 1987. After beefing up its American operations with four other US acquisitions, the company merged Food Dimensions and Seiler in 1989. Sodexho's US river cruise company, Spirit Cruises — an echo of the Bellon family's original calling — was also included in the merger. The merged US companies were renamed Sodexho USA in 1993.

The 1990s proved an era of growth and acquisitions for Sodexho. The company expanded into Japan, Africa, Russia, and five Eastern European countries in 1993. The company acquired a 20% stake in Corrections Corporation of America the following year and virtually doubled its size with the acquisition of the UK's Gardner Merchant in 1995. The largest catering company in that region, Gardner Merchant had holdings that spanned Australia, the Far East, northern Europe, the UK, and the US — generally markets where Sodexho did not have a strong presence. That year the company also acquired Partena, a Swedish security and care company, from Volvo's Fortos.

Gardner Merchant's US business was officially merged with Sodexho USA in 1996 to make it the #4 foodservice company in the US. Also that year Sodexho acquired Brazilian service voucher company Cardapio. After a year of legal wrangling, Sodexho also lost a fight for control of Accor's Eurest France to rival caterer Compass Group and sold off its minority interest. The next year Sodexho acquired 49% of Universal Ogden Services, renamed Universal Services, an American remote site manager. To signify its efforts to maintain the individuality of the companies it acquires, Sodexho changed its name to Sodexho Alliance in 1997.

Marriott International merged its foodservice branch with Sodexho's North American foodservice operations in 1998. With a 48% stake, Sodexho Alliance became the largest shareholder; former Marriott International stockholders took the rest, with the Marriott family controlling 9%. Before the merger, Sodexho USA was less than one-fourth the size of Marriott International's foodservice division. Sodexho acquired GR Servicios Hoteleros in 1999, thereby becoming the largest caterer in Spain. The following year it agreed to merge its remote site management operations with Universal Services and rename it Universal Sodexho.

In 2001 its initial $900 million bid to buy the 52% of Sodexho Marriott Services it didn't already own was rebuffed by its subsidiary's shareholders. Sodexho Alliance made a better offer (about $1.1 billion) and finally reached an agreement to purchase the rest of Sodexho Marriott Services. The deal was completed later that year and Sodexho Marriott Services changed its name to Sodexho, Inc. Also that year the company agreed to pay some $470 million for French rival Sogeres and US-based food management firm Wood Dining.

In 2002 the company replaced its UK management team because of poor performance there. Founder and chairman Bellon announced in 2004 that he intended to pass the title of CEO to group president and COO Michel Landel on September 1, 2005.

Admitting no wrongdoing, Sodexho settled an $80 million race-bias lawsuit just before it was to go to trial in 2005. The suit, brought by

Sodexho Alliance

the African-American employees of its American subsidiary, Sodexho, Inc., charged that African-Americans were routinely passed over for promotions and were segregated within the company. In addition to paying the monetary award, Sodexho agreed to increase company diversity through promotion incentives, monitoring, and training.

In 2005 Bellon, 75, stepped down as company CEO but remained chairman. The CEO position was filled by Sodexho veteran Landel.

EXECUTIVES

Chairman: Pierre Bellon, age 75, $354,062 pay
Vice Chairman: Remí Baudin, age 75
CEO: Michel Landel, age 54
CEO, Continental Europe and South America: Jacques Petry
COO, Sodexho Group: Patrice Douce, age 63
Group SVP and CFO: Siân Herbert-Jones, age 45
Group SVP and Chief Human Resources Officer: Elisabeth Carpentier, age 51
Group SVP, Corporate Communications and Sustainable Development: Clodine Pincemin, age 53
Group SVP, Procurement: Philippe Lauthier, age 48
Group SVP, Strategic Planning: Vincent Hillenmeyer, age 39
President and CEO, Sodexho North America: Richard (Dick) Macedonia, age 62
CEO, UK and Ireland: Philip Jansen
President, Sodexho/Spirit Cruises: Lorna Donatone
CFO, UK and Ireland: Debbie White
Chief Information Security Officer, Sodexho North America: Joe Ford
Investor Relations: Jean-Jacques Vironda
Media Relations: Jérôme Chambin
Auditors: PricewaterhouseCoopers

LOCATIONS

HQ: Sodexho Alliance, SA
3, avenue Newton,
78180 Montigny-le-Bretonneux, France
Phone: +33-1-30-85-75-00   **Fax:** +33-1-30-43-09-58
US HQ: 9801 Washingtonian Blvd., Ste. 1234,
Gaithersburg, MD 20878
US Phone: 301-987-4431   **US Fax:** 301-987-4444
Web: sodexho.com

Sodexho Alliance has operations in more than 75 countries.

2004 Sales

	% of total
North America	44
Continental Europe	34
UK/Ireland	12
Other regions	10
Total	**100**

PRODUCTS/OPERATIONS

2004 Sales

	% of total
Food & Management Services	98
Service Vouchers & Cards	2
Total	**100**

COMPETITORS

Accor
ARAMARK
Compass Group
Delaware North
HDS Services
HMSHost
Host America

HISTORICAL FINANCIALS

Company Type: Public

Income Statement

FYE: August 31

	REVENUE ($ mil.)	NET INCOME ($ mil.)	NET PROFIT MARGIN	EMPLOYEES
8/04	13,993	223	1.6%	312,975
8/03	12,837	178	1.4%	308,385
8/02	12,378	198	1.6%	315,141
8/01	10,891	126	1.2%	313,469
8/00	9,490	165	1.7%	285,986
8/99	9,521	139	1.5%	269,973
8/98	6,933	123	1.8%	250,000
8/97	4,843	88	1.8%	152,000
8/96	4,922	135	2.7%	141,118
8/95	3,635	56	1.5%	115,669
Annual Growth	**16.2%**	**16.5%**	**—**	**11.7%**

2004 Year-End Financials

Debt ratio: 97.1%
Return on equity: 8.7%
Cash ($ mil.): 615
Current ratio: 1.03
Long-term debt ($ mil.): 2,591
No. of shares (mil.): 159
Dividends
  Yield: 2.9%
  Payout: 55.0%
Market value ($ mil.): 4,198

Stock History

NYSE: SDX

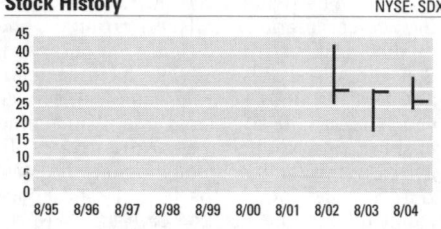

	STOCK PRICE ($) FY Close	P/E High/Low		PER SHARE ($) Earnings	Dividends	Book Value
8/04	26.40	24	18	1.40	0.77	16.78
8/03	29.15	27	17	1.10	0.65	15.53
8/02	29.50	35	22	1.20	0.00	14.80
Annual Growth	**(5.4%)**	**—**	**—**	**8.0%**	**—**	**6.5%**

SOFTBANK

With more than 165 subsidiaries, SOFTBANK's investment strategy is anything but soft. Full-throttle investing by founder, president, and CEO Masayoshi Son has molded SOFTBANK through aggressive investments in a variety of Internet ventures. Under Son's leadership (he is hailed by many as the Bill Gates of Japan), the holding company has extended its investment reach across e-commerce, financial services, Internet infrastructure, information technology-related distribution services, publishing and marketing, and technology services. SOFTBANK is shedding less profitable holdings to fund its high-speed Internet access business in Asia and its acquisition of Japan Telecom. Son owns more than 31% of the company.

With stakes in more than 100 Internet-related companies, the debt-heavy SOFTBANK is looking to prune some of its less profitable holdings (including Medialive International). SOFTBANK expanded into banking when it joined a consortium that purchased Japan's failed Nippon Credit Bank (later renamed Aozora). A stock market darling during the "Internet bubble" of the late 1990s, SOFTBANK has seen its stock price and bottom line take a beating.

The bedrock of the company's Internet holdings is its less than 10% stake in Yahoo!, but SOFTBANK's Internet investments also include stakes in ventures such as E*TRADE and Morningstar (however, SOFTBANK sold its entire 20% stake during Morningstar's IPO). It has ceased new investments in Latin America and Europe and is looking to sell off some of its assets.

In an attempt to create a larger domestic market for its e-commerce and Internet companies, SOFTBANK has moved into the broadband Internet connection market, providing asymmetric digital subscriber line (ADSL) services. The firm is also taking on Japanese telecom giant NTT and plans to offer a discounted land-line telephone service.

It acquired the Fukuoka Daiei Hawks, a professional baseball team, in 2005.

HISTORY

Ethnic Korean Masayoshi Son grew up in Japan using the name Yasumoto to conform with the Japanese policy of assimilation. In the early 1970s, the 16-year-old came to the US and began using his Korean name. Son entered the University of California at Berkeley and, while there, invented the prototype for the Sharp Wizard handheld organizer.

Bankrolled by the nearly $1 million that Sharp paid him for his patent, Son returned to Japan and founded software distributor SOFTBANK in 1981. The company got its first big break when it inked a distribution agreement with Joshin Denki, one of Japan's largest consumer electronics retailers, that year. Son used this agreement to gain exclusive distribution rights for much of the software he distributed.

SOFTBANK went public in 1994. That year, as part of an evolving plan to control digital data delivery, Son bought the trade show division of Ziff-Davis Publishing, augmenting it in 1995 with the purchase of COMDEX, the trade show operations of the Interface Group. The next year SOFTBANK bought the rest of Ziff-Davis. It also bought 80% of Kingston Technology (sold 1999) and a stake in Yahoo! — which laid the cornerstone for its Internet empire.

SOFTBANK accelerated its Internet investment pace in 1997, taking stakes in dozens of Web companies. That year it filed suit against Yell Publishing, a Japanese firm that published a book accusing SOFTBANK of issuing phony financial statements, among other improprieties.

In 1998 the firm moved into financial services, entering a joint venture with E*TRADE to offer online stock trading in Japan. SOFTBANK also took Ziff-Davis public (it retained a majority stake).

Internal changes marked 1999 when SOFTBANK merged with MAC, Son's private asset management company, and transformed itself into a holding company focused on Internet-related companies. It teamed with the National Association of Securities Dealers to create a Japanese version of the Nasdaq stock market (launched in 2000; closed in 2002). SOFTBANK also partnered with Microsoft and Tokyo Electric Power to launch SpeedNet, a Japanese Internet service provider.

In 2000 the nearly decimated Ziff-Davis announced it would transform its online arm, ZDNet, from a tracking stock into a stand-alone company and adopt the ZDNet name; later CNET Networks bought both companies instead. That year SOFTBANK formed venture capital funds focusing on areas such as Latin America, Japan, Europe, the UK, and emerging markets.

The company reorganized in 2000 and placed most of its non-Japan-based holdings under a new unit called SOFTBANK Global Ventures. Sharpening its focus on Internet investments, SOFTBANK sold its stake in antivirus software maker Trend Micro. Branching into banking, SOFTBANK headed a consortium that paid $932 million for Japan's failed Nippon Credit Bank. SOFTBANK's share of the bank (renamed Aozora) stood at nearly 49%. The firm's stock price tumbled in 2000, and it considered taking several holding companies public.

In 2001 Cisco bought a nearly 2% stake in SOFTBANK in exchange for the firm's 12% stake in the hardware company's Japanese unit. The company also sold its SOFTBANK Forums Japan, an Internet trade show company, to Medialive International. In 2002 Nasdaq Japan announced its plans to close, after two loss-making years. SOFTBANK owned 43%.

EXECUTIVES

President and CEO: Masayoshi Son, age 48
Director and President, SOFTBANK Holdings: Ronald D. Fisher, age 57
Director and President and CEO, JAPAN TELECOM CO., LTD.: Hideki Kurashige
Director and President and CEO, Yahoo Japan Corporation: Masahiro Inoue, age 48
Director: Kazuhiko Kasai
Director: Ken Miyauchi
Director: Jun Murai
Corporate Auditor: Mitsuo Sano
Director: Tadashi Yanai, age 56
Auditors: ChuoAoyama PricewaterhouseCoopers

LOCATIONS

HQ: SOFTBANK CORP.
1-9-1 Higashi Shinbashi, Minato-ku, Tokyo 105-7303, Japan
Phone: +81-3-5642-8000   **Fax:** +81-3-5543-0431
US HQ: 300 Delaware Ave., Wilmington, DE 19801
US Phone: 302-576-2713
Web: www.softbank.co.jp

PRODUCTS/OPERATIONS

2005 Sales

	% of total
e-Commerce	29
Broadband infrastructure	23
Fixed-line telecommunications	19
Internet culture	12
e-Finance	9
Technology services	3
Media & marketing	2
Broadmedia	2
Other	1
Total	**100**

Selected Holdings

Club iT Corporation
cyber communications inc.
M.P. Technologies, Inc.
Morningstar Japan K.K.
SOFTBANK INVESTMENT CORPORATION
SOFTBANK TECHNOLOGY CORP.
Vector Inc.
Yahoo Japan Corporation
Yahoo! Inc.

COMPETITORS

3i Group	Internet Capital
Accel Partners	Internet Initiative Japan
Alloy Ventures	Kleiner Perkins
Benchmark Capital	Safeguard Scientifics
CSK	Sequoia Capital
Fujitsu	Shikoku Electric
Hummer Winblad	Trinity Ventures

HISTORICAL FINANCIALS

Company Type: Public

Income Statement

FYE: March 31

	REVENUE ($ mil.)	NET INCOME ($ mil.)	NET PROFIT MARGIN	EMPLOYEES
3/05	7,083	(557)	—	—
3/04	4,898	(1,014)	—	6,662
3/03	3,395	(834)	—	6,170
3/02	3,056	(669)	—	5,706
3/01	2,891	290	10.0%	5,006
3/00	4,011	80	2.0%	7,636
3/99	4,434	315	7.1%	6,865
3/98	3,858	77	2.0%	7,743
3/97	2,906	73	2.5%	5,600
3/96	1,595	54	3.4%	4,375
Annual Growth	**18.0%**	—	—	**5.4%**

2005 Year-End Financials

Debt ratio: 342.1%
Return on equity: —
Cash ($ mil.): 2,678
Current ratio: 0.88
Long-term debt ($ mil.): 5,663

Net Income History

Exchange: Tokyo

400	
200	
0	
-200	
-400	
-600	
-800	
-1,000	
-1,200	
	3/96 3/97 3/98 3/99 3/00 3/01 3/02 3/03 3/04 3/05

Sojitz

Trading in all kinds of places is Sojitz Corporation. Formerly called Sojitz Holdings, the company's 400-plus subsidiaries trade in a wide array of businesses, ranging from steel and automobile parts to apparel, making it one of the largest trading houses in Japan. Sojitz's other major businesses include aerospace, foods, oil and gas, chemicals and plastics, retail property development, and construction materials. Asia and North America (through its Sojitz Corporation of America unit) are major contributors to its overseas trading operations. Sojitz was formed by a merger of two Japanese trading powerhouses, Nissho Iwai and Nichimen Corporation.

As part of its cost restructuring to reduce debt, Sojitz has been on a tear to sell off its low performing business divisions and additional real estate holdings. The company has reorganized into five business units: machinery and aerospace, energy and mineral resources, chemicals and plastics, real estate development and forest products, and consumer lifestyles. It has also formed a subsidiary in China to enter key industries, including automotive, ball bearing, textiles, and plastics.

HISTORY

The Nissho and Iwai companies got their acts together as Nissho Iwai in 1968, but each company dates back to the middle of the 19th century. In 1863, Bunsuke Iwai opened a shop in Osaka to sell imported goods such as glass, oil products, silk, and wine. The Meiji government, which came to power in 1868, encouraged modernization and industrialization, a climate in which Iwai's business flourished. In 1877 Iwajiro Suzuki established a similar trading concern, Suzuki & Co., that eventually became Nissho.

After cotton spinning machines were introduced in Japan in the 1890s, both Iwai and Suzuki imported cotton. Iwai began to trade directly with British trader William Duff & Son (an innovation in Japan, where the middleman, or *shokan*, played the paramount role in international trade). Iwai became the primary agent for Yawata Steel Works in 1901 and was incorporated in 1912. Meanwhile, Suzuki, solely engaged in the import trade, emerged as one of the top sugar brokers in the world and established an office in London.

To protect itself from foreign competition, Iwai established a number of companies to produce goods in Japan, including Nippon Steel Plate (1914) and Tokuyama Soda (1918). Stagnation after WWI forced Suzuki to restructure. In 1928 the company sold many of its assets to trading giant Mitsui and reorganized the rest under a new name, Nissho Co.

Both Iwai and Nissho subsequently grew as they helped fuel Japan's military expansion in Asia in the 1930s. But Japan's defeat in WWII devastated the companies. When the occupation forces broke up Mitsui and other larger trading conglomerates, both companies took advantage of the situation to move into new business areas. In 1949 Nissho established Nissho Chemical Industry, Nissho Fuel, and Nijko Shoji (a trading concern). It also opened its US operations, Nissho American Corp., in 1952.

Poor management by the Iwai family led the company into financial trouble in the 1960s and prompted the Japanese government to instruct the profitable Nissho to merge with Iwai in 1968.

In 1979 Nissho Iwai was accused of funneling kickbacks from US aircraft makers to Japanese politicians. The scandal led to arrests, the resignation of the company's chairman, and the suicide of another executive. Nissho Iwai exited the aircraft marketing business in 1980.

Despite Japan's recession in the 1990s, Nissho Iwai managed to make some significant investments. In 1991 the company teamed up with the Russian government to develop a Siberian oil refinery. A year later Nissho acquired a stake in courier DHL International, and in 1995 it set up a unit to process steel plates in Vietnam.

However, in the late 1990s rough economic conditions caught up with the firm. It dissolved its NI Finance unit (domestic financing) in 1998 after its disastrous performance. The large trading firm, or *sogo shosha*, also began a major restructuring effort to get back on track.

In 1999 Nissho Iwai sold its headquarters, its 5% stake in DHL International, and its stake in a Japanese ISP, Nifty. CEO Masatake Kusamichi resigned. He was replaced by Shiro Yasutake, who took charge of the firm's restructuring. In 2000, the company's ITX Corp. acquired five IT-related affiliates of Nichimen Corp.

As part of the group's streamlining efforts, in 2001 Nissho Iwai spun off its nonferrous marketing unit (Alconix) and agreed to merge the group's LNG operations with Sumitomo's LNG business. The next year Hidetoshi Nishimura replaced Yasutake as CEO.

In 2003 Nissho Iwai merged with the smaller Nichimen Corp. to form Nissho Iwai-Nichimen Holdings. Hidetoshi Nishimura, president and CEO of Nissho Iwai, and Toru Hambayashi, president of Nichimen, became co-CEOs of the new holding company. In 2004 the company changed its name from Nissho Iwai-Nichimen Holdings to Sojitz Holdings Corporation.

As part of its ongoing reorganization in 2005, the company renamed itself again when it merged the holding company into Sojitz Corporation.

EXECUTIVES

President and CEO: Akio Dobashi
EVP: Yutaka Kase
EVP: Masaki Hashikawa
Senior Managing Executive Officer, New Business Development: Yasuyuki Fujishima
Senior Managing Executive Officer, Risk Management: Katsuhiko Kobayashi
Managing Executive Officer: Keisuke Ishihara
Managing Executive Officer, CFO: Yoji Sato
Director: Shigeo Muraoka
Director: Yoshihiko Miyauchi
President and CEO, Europe and Africa: Yasushi Hoshika
President, Energy and Mineral Resources: Hiroyuki Tanabe
President and CEO, Asia: Hiroshi Kanematsu
President, Machinery and Aerospace: Kazunori Teraoka
President, Americas: Jun Matsumoto
CIO: Shinichi Taniguchi
President, Chemicals and Plastics: Joji Suzuki
President, China: Yoshimi Ota
President, Consumer Lifestyle Business: Taichi Yonemura
President, Real Estate Development and Forest Products: Masao Ichishi
Auditors: KPMG AZSA & Co.; Ernst & Young ShinNihon

LOCATIONS

HQ: Sojitz Corporation
1-20 Akasaka 6-chome, Minato-ku,
Tokyo 107-8655, Japan
Phone: +81-3-5446-3600   **Fax:** +81-3-5446-1542
US HQ: 1211 Avenue of the Americas, 44th Fl.,
New York, NY 10036
US Phone: 212-704-6500   **US Fax:** 212-704-6947
Web: www.sojitz.com

2005 Sales

	% of total
Japan	76
Asia & Oceania	13
North America	7
Europe	3
Other	1
Total	**100**

PRODUCTS/OPERATIONS

2005 Sales

	% of total
Energy & Mineral Resources	23
Machinery & Aerospace	19
Chemicals & Plastics	13
Foods	9
Forest Products & Building Materials	6
General Commodities & Consumer Business	5
Construction & Urban Development	4
Textiles	3
Overseas subsidiaries	16
Other	2
Total	**100**

COMPETITORS

Chori	Mitsui
ITOCHU	Sekisui House
Kanematsu	Sumitomo
Marubeni	TOMEN
Mitsubishi Corporation	Toyota Tsusho

HISTORICAL FINANCIALS

Company Type: Public

Income Statement

FYE: March 31

	REVENUE ($ mil.)	NET INCOME ($ mil.)	NET PROFIT MARGIN	EMPLOYEES
3/05	2,271	(3,835)	—	16,419
3/04	2,357	(318)	—	14,600
Annual Growth	(3.7%)	—	—	12.5%

2005 Year-End Financials

Debt ratio: 111.7%
Return on equity: —
Cash ($ mil.): 3,805
Current ratio: 0.81
Long-term debt ($ mil.): 2,910

Net Income History

Exchange: Tokyo

Sony

All eyes are on Sony — or, more likely, on its high-profit PlayStation home video game systems. PlayStation 2 dominates the game console market with about 70% of global sales (Nintendo's GameCube and Microsoft's Xbox control about 15% each). Sony, one of the world's top consumer electronics firms, also makes a host of other products, including PCs, digital cameras, Walkman stereos, and semiconductors; these products account for more than 60% of the company's sales. Sony's entertainment assets include recorded music and video (Epic and Columbia), motion pictures (Sony Pictures Entertainment, Sony Pictures Classics), DVDs (Sony Pictures Home Entertainment), and TV programming (Columbia TriStar).

In addition Sony sells mobile phones via Sony Ericsson, its joint venture with Ericsson. Sony also owns an 8% stake in music club Columbia House.

Though the PlayStation still dominates the game machine scene, sales of other electronics (DVD recorders, TVs, and computers) and music have seen a drop. Weak consumer demand, price wars, and increased competition from Apple Computer's iPod, which has clobbered Sony's CD and mini disk Walkman products, and Samsung's consumer electronics lines, have cut into Sony's TV sales (its biggest market). To boost sagging sales, Sony is emphasizing high-definition products for consumers and broadcasters, integrated mobile video, music, and gaming products, and semiconductors (aimed at improving product innovation).

Sony went through a major management shake-up in 2005, bringing Sir Howard Stringer on board as chairman and CEO in June. Stringer, who served as head of the company's US and electronics divisions, is the first non-Japanese CEO to head the company. Nobuyuki Idea stepped down as chairman and CEO and serves as a corporate advisor for the company.

Stringer's reorganization plans call for cutting 10,000 jobs, shuttering 11 manufacturing plants, and reducing the company's electronics product lines by 20%. The company plans to spin off Sony Communication Network, the subsidary that operates So-Net Internet service (which has nearly 3 million subscribers), in an IPO scheduled for late December 2005.

In an effort to combat losses in a weakening music industry, Sony merged its music division with BMG; the new company (Sony BMG Music Entertainment) is now the #2 player (after Universal Music). Sony led a consortium of companies (including cable company Comcast and several investment firms) that bought movie studio MGM in early 2005; the acquisition allows Sony to license and distribute MGM's sizeable film library (4,000 films and over 10,000 television episodes). The deal also provides for the creation of film co-productions, cable channels, and video-on-demand services that will generate additional revenue for Sony.

HISTORY

Akio Morita, Masaru Ibuka, and Tamon Maeda (Ibuka's father-in-law) started Tokyo Telecommunications Engineering in 1946 with funding from Morita's father's sake business. The company produced the first Japanese tape recorder in 1950. Three years later Morita paid Western Electric (US) $25,000 for transistor technology licenses, which sparked a consumer electronics revolution in Japan. His firm launched one of the first transistor radios in 1955, followed by the first Sony-trademarked product, a pocket-sized radio, in 1957. The next year the company changed its name to Sony (from "sonus," Latin for "sound," and "sonny," meaning "little man"). It beat the competition to newly emerging markets for transistor TVs (1959) and solid-state videotape recorders (1961).

Sony launched the first home video recorder (1964) and solid-state condenser microphone (1965). Its 1968 introduction of the Trinitron color TV tube began another decade of explosive growth. Sony bet wrong on its Betamax VCR (1976), which lost to rival Matsushita's VHS as the industry standard. However, 1979 brought another success, the Walkman personal stereo.

Pressured by adverse currency rates and competition worldwide, Sony used its technology to diversify beyond consumer electronics and began to move production to other countries. In the 1980s it introduced Japan's first 32-bit workstation and became a major producer of computer chips and floppy disk drives. The purchases of CBS Records in 1988 ($2 billion) and Columbia Pictures in 1989 (a $4.9 billion deal, which included TriStar Pictures) made Sony a major force in the rapidly growing entertainment industry.

The firm manufactured Apple's PowerBook, but its portable CD player, Data Discman, was successful only in Japan (1991). In the early 1990s Sony joined Nintendo to create a new kind of game console, combining Sony's CD-ROM drive with the graphic capabilities of a workstation. Although Nintendo pulled out in 1992, Sony released PlayStation in Japan (1994) and in the US (1995) to great success. Two years later, in a joint venture with Intel, it developed a line of PC desktop systems. In 1998 Sony shipped its first digital, high-definition TV to the US.

In 1999 Nobuyuki Idei became CEO, and the company introduced a Walkman with the capability to download music from the Internet. Sony introduced its 128-bit PlayStation 2, which plays DVD movies and connects to the Internet, in 2000. In 2002 an investment group led by Onex Corporation acquired its Loews Theatres unit (which filed for bankruptcy in February 2001). In the course of the fiscal year ending March 2002, Sony laid off about 13,700 employees, primarily in its electronics and music businesses.

In 2003 Sony adopted a US-style corporate governance model (made possible by a revision in Japan's Commercial Code) and acquired CIS Corp., a Japanese information system consulting firm. In an effort to cut costs through manufacturing consolidation, Sony closed its audio equipment plant in Indonesia that year.

The company's PSP (PlayStation Portable), a Walkman-like device with DVD-quality video, launched in Japan in late 2004. The marketing hype surrounding the device's US launch led to long lines at Sony stores when it was released stateside in early 2005. The PSP generated $150 million in sales for Sony the first week it was in stores.

To manage its financial units (Sony Life Insurance Company, Sony Assurance, and Sony Bank), it created Sony Financial Holdings in 2004. The company announced in 2005 that Idei would be succeeded by foreigner Howard Stringer, who had been in charge of Sony's entertainment unit.

EXECUTIVES

Chairman and CEO: Sir Howard Stringer, age 63
President and Director; President, Display Device Development Group: Ryoji Chubachi, age 58
Executive Deputy President and Director; President, TV Business Group: Katsumi Ihara, age 55
Executive Deputy President and Director; COO, Game Business Group, Home Electronics Network Company, and Semiconductor Solutions Network Company: Ken Kutaragi
Executive Deputy President and Sony Group China Representative: Shizuo Takashino, age 62
EVP and Corporate Executive in Charge of Electronics Marketing; Senior General Manager, Global Marketing Division; President and COO, Sony Electronics: Hideki (Dick) Komiyama
EVP and CFO: Nobuyuki Oneda, age 60
EVP and General Counsel: Nicole Seligman, age 49
EVP, Corporate Laboratories: Katsuaki Tsurushima, age 63
EVP, Electronics Marketing: Fujio Nishida, age 57
EVP, Technology Strategy; President, Technology Development Group: Keiji Kimura, age 53
SVP, Corporate Communications and External Relations: Naofumi Hara
SVP, Investor Relations: Takao Yuhara, age 59
SVP, Group Human Resources: Kunitaka Fujita
Chairman and CEO, Sony Music Entertainment: Andrew R. (Andy) Lack, age 58
Chairman and CEO, Sony Pictures Entertainment: Michael M. Lynton, age 45
Chief Marketing Officer: Andrew House
Auditors: PricewaterhouseCoopers

LOCATIONS

HQ: Sony Corporation
7-35, Kitashinagawa, 6-chome, Shinagawa-ku, Tokyo 141-0001, Japan
Phone: +81-3-5448-2111   **Fax:** +81-3-5448-2244
US HQ: 550 Madison Ave., New York, NY 10022-3211
US Phone: 212-833-6800   **US Fax:** 212-833-6956
Web: www.sony.net

Sony's primary manufacturing plants are located in Japan, as well as in China, Malaysia, Mexico, Spain, the UK, and the US; it sells its products worldwide.

2005 Sales

	$ mil.	% of total
Japan	19,634	29
United States	18,479	28
Europe	15,070	23
Other areas	13,729	20
Total	**66,912**	**100**

PRODUCTS/OPERATIONS

2005 Sales

	$ mil.	% of total
Electronics	44,515	67
Pictures	6,824	10
Games	6,534	10
Financial services	5,001	7
Music	2,016	3
Other	1,699	3
Adjustments	323	—
Total	**66,912**	**100**

2005 Electronics Sales

	$ mil.	% of total
Video	9,624	22
Televisions	8,902	20
Information & communications	7,239	16
Components	5,762	13
Audio	5,319	12
Semiconductors	2,302	5
Other	5,379	12
Adjustments	(12)	—
Total	**44,515**	**100**

Selected Products

Electronics
  Audio
    Car audio
    Car navigation systems
    Home audio
    Portable audio
  Video
    Digital cameras
    DVD and video players
    Set-top boxes
    Video cameras
  Information and communication
    PCs
    PDAs
    Professional-use audio and video equipment
    Printers
  Semiconductors
    CCDs
    LCDs
  TVs and monitors
    Computer displays
    LCD TVs
    Projection TVs
    Plasma TVs
Financial Services
  Insurance policy underwriting (life insurance)
  Internet banking
  Leasing and credit financing
  Non-life insurance products (auto and medical)
Games (hardware and software)
  PlayStation Portable (PSP)
  PlayStation 2
Music
  CDs and CD-ROMs
  DVDs and DVD-ROMs
  MDs
  Recorded music and music videos
  Super Audio CDs

Pictures
  Digital production
  Home entertainment acquisition and distribution
  Motion picture production, acquisition, and distribution
  Online distribution and broadband services
  Studio facilities
  Television broadcasting
  Television production, acquisition, and distribution

COMPETITORS

Apple Computer	Microsoft
Bertelsmann	Motorola
Dell	Nintendo
Disney	Nokia
Eastman Kodak	Philips Electronics
Fujitsu	Pioneer
Hewlett-Packard	Samsung
IBM	SANYO
Intel	Sharp
Kyocera	THOMSON
LG Electronics	Universal Studios
Matsushita	Victor Company of Japan

HISTORICAL FINANCIALS

Company Type: Public

Income Statement

FYE: March 31

	REVENUE ($ mil.)	NET INCOME ($ mil.)	NET PROFIT MARGIN	EMPLOYEES
3/05	66,912	1,531	2.3%	151,400
3/04	72,081	851	1.2%	162,000
3/03	63,264	978	1.5%	161,100
3/02	57,117	115	0.2%	168,000
3/01	58,518	134	0.2%	181,800
3/00	63,082	1,149	1.8%	189,700
3/99	57,109	1,505	2.6%	177,000
3/98	51,178	1,682	3.3%	173,000
3/97	45,670	1,125	2.5%	163,000
3/96	43,326	512	1.2%	151,000
Annual Growth	**4.9%**	**12.9%**	**—**	**0.0%**

2005 Year-End Financials

Debt ratio: 23.7%
Return on equity: 6.2%
Cash ($ mil.): 7,269
Current ratio: 1.27
Long-term debt ($ mil.): 6,335
No. of shares (mil.): 996
Dividends
  Yield: 0.6%
  Payout: 15.5%
Market value ($ mil.): 39,864

Stock History

NYSE: SNE

	STOCK PRICE ($) FY Close	P/E High/Low		PER SHARE ($) Earnings	Dividends	Book Value
3/05	40.02	29	21	1.48	0.23	26.89
3/04	41.81	48	26	0.87	0.21	24.68
3/03	35.13	60	35	1.00	0.20	20.86
3/02	51.70	1,072	410	0.13	0.20	19.36
3/01	72.25	143	66	0.15	0.35	20.14
3/00	140.06	127	36	1.24	0.20	22.70
3/99	45.66	31	18	1.65	0.10	18.70
3/98	42.53	28	19	1.83	0.00	16.90
3/97	34.56	30	24	1.25	0.10	15.32
3/96	30.38	53	36	0.63	0.12	14.74
Annual Growth	**3.1%**	**—**	**—**	**10.0%**	**7.5%**	**6.9%**

Statoil ASA

Statoil (formerly Den norske stats oljeselskap) is Norway's oil and gas exploration, production, transport, refining, and marketing giant. Statoil operates in 29 countries, focusing its upstream activities on the Norwegian continental shelf, the North Sea, the Caspian Sea, Western Africa, and Venezuela. It has proved reserves of nearly 4.3 billion barrels of oil equivalent. Statoil has a retail network of more than 2,000 gas stations under its own brand, as well as the 1-2-3 network of automated outlets, in nine north European countries. Statoil sold its 50% stake in petrochemicals venture Borealis in 2005. The Norwegian government, which has been divesting shares in Statoil, still owns nearly 71% of the group.

The company manages the state's direct financial interest (known as SDFI) in oil and gas partnerships active on the Norwegian continental shelf. It also owns the world's largest offshore gas platform, the Aasgard B off Norway's west coast. In addition, Statoil supplies electricity in Norway and Sweden.

Statoil is not only Norway's largest oil and gas group, it is also one of the largest international exploration and production companies. However, to focus on its core areas, Statoil has divested its US exploration and production operations, although the US is still a major market for the company's exports: Statoil ships about 500,000 barrels of oil per day to the US and Canada. It is also a major exporter to Asia. However, the company has agreed to acquire the Gulf of Mexico interests of Canada-based EnCana Corp. for about $2 billion. The assets include a 25% working interest in a Tahiti discovery operated by Chevron, as well as interests in five other discoveries now under appraisal.

Statoil has a production target for 2007 of 1.4 million barrels of oil equivalent per day, and it plans to obtain most of its production from the Norwegian continental shelf (1.1 million boe per day). The group has submitted a plan to develop and operate the Tyrihans field in the Norwegian Sea to Norway's Ministry of Petroleum and Energy. Statoil has a nearly 47% stake in the field.

HISTORY

To exert greater control over exploration and production of the Norwegian continental shelf (NCS), the government of Norway set up Den norske stats oljeselskap (Statoil) in 1972.

A decade earlier three geologists had visited Norway on behalf of Phillips Petroleum (later renamed ConocoPhillips) to apply for sole rights to explore on the NCS. The government initially refused drilling rights to foreign companies, and in 1963 Norway claimed sovereignty over the NCS. Two years later the government began allowing exploration. Phillips' major discovery in the Ekofisk field in 1969 prompted Norway to set up its own oil company. After Statoil's formation in 1972, the company garnered funds to expand through taxation of multinationals, production limits, leasing contracts, and other measures.

In 1974 a giant discovery was made in the North Sea's Statfjord field, and Statoil was given a 50% stake. A year later Statoil began exploring for oil and gas, exporting oil, and commissioning its first subsea oil pipeline, the Norpipe, which extended to the UK. In 1986 Statoil's gas pipeline system, the Statpipe, began transporting gas from the North Sea to the mainland.

Moving into retailing, Statoil acquired Esso's service stations and other downstream operations in Sweden and Denmark in 1985 and 1986. The next year, cost overruns stemming from the extension of Statoil's Mongstad oil refinery led to the ousting of the company's first president, Arve Johnsen, and many of his deputies. Harald Norvik was appointed CEO in 1988.

In 1990 Statoil and BP teamed up to develop international operations, and in 1992 Statoil acquired BP's service stations in Ireland. Statoil and Neste Chemicals (later part of Industri Kapital) formed the Borealis petrochemicals group in 1994.

The company in 1995 acquired Aran Energy, moving into exploration offshore Ireland and the UK. Statoil brought its field projects in China and Azerbaijan onstream in 1997. That year Statoil spun off its shipping operations as Navion, partly owned by Norway's Rasmussen group. It also contracted with Kvaerner to build a giant offshore gas platform for Aasgard field in the Norwegian Sea.

The Aasgard field project resulted in cost overruns in 1999, again leading to a Statoil board shakeup and CEO resignation. Norvik, who had advocated partial privatization of Statoil, was replaced by Olav Fjell, former head of Norway's Postbanken (who resigned in 2003). That year Statoil helped Norsk Hydro take over rival Saga in return for some of Saga's assets.

As part of a major restructuring in 2000, Statoil sold most assets of US unit Statoil Energy. Political opposition that year postponed Statoil's plans for partial privatization, but the government proceeded with an IPO in 2001, raising about $3 billion.

In 2002 Statoil sold its oil and gas assets in the Danish North Sea to Dong, the Danish state oil company, for about $120 million. That year the company also acquired the Polish unit of Sweden's Preem Petroleum, which owned 79 gas stations in Poland.

In 2003 Statoil sold its Navion unit to shipping group Teekay, for about $800 million. That year it also acquired two Algerian natural gas projects from BP for $740 million. A bribery scandal involving an Iranian oil contract forced the resignation of the chairman, CEO, and another top executive in 2003.

EXECUTIVES

Chairman: Jannik Lindbæk, age 66
Deputy Chair: Kaci Kullmann Five, age 53
President and CEO: Helge Lund, age 42
EVP and CFO: Eldar Sætre, age 49
EVP Communication: Reidar Gjærum, age 44
EVP Exploration and Production Norway: Terje Overvik, age 53
EVP Health, Safety, and Environment (HSE): Nina Udnes Tronstad, age 46
EVP Natural Gas: Rune Bjørnson, age 45
EVP International Exploration and Production: Peter Mellbye, age 56
EVP Manufacturing and Marketing: Jon A. Jacobsen, age 47
EVP Technology and Projects: Margareth Øvrum, age 47
EVP Human Resources: Jens R. Jenssen, age 52
SVP Corporate Audit: Svein Andersen
SVP Legal Affairs: Jacob S. Middelthon
SVP Corporate Services: Randi G. Olsen
SVP Investor Relations: Mari Thjømøe
VP Public Affairs: Wenche Skorge
Head of Research and Technology Development: Morten Loktu, age 45
Investor Relations, US: Geir Bjørnstad
Auditors: Ernst & Young AS

LOCATIONS

HQ: Statoil ASA
Forusbeen 50, N-4035 Stavanger, Norway
Phone: +47-51-99-00-00   **Fax:** +47-51-99-00-50
US HQ: 225 High Ridge Rd., Stamford, CT 06905
US Phone: 203-978-6900   **US Fax:** 203-978-6952
Web: www.statoil.com

Statoil has offices in 29 countries worldwide.

PRODUCTS/OPERATIONS

2004 Sales

	% of total
Manufacturing & marketing	70
Exploration & production	
Norway	19
International	2
Natural gas & other operations	9
Total	**100**

COMPETITORS

BP
Exxon Mobil
Norsk Hydro
OMV
Royal Dutch/Shell Group
TOTAL

HISTORICAL FINANCIALS

Company Type: Public

Income Statement

FYE: December 31

	REVENUE ($ mil.)	NET INCOME ($ mil.)	NET PROFIT MARGIN	EMPLOYEES
12/04	50,332	4,129	8.2%	23,899
12/03	37,378	2,490	6.7%	19,326
12/02	34,874	2,426	7.0%	17,115
12/01	25,720	1,919	7.5%	16,686
12/00	25,925	1,822	7.0%	16,800
12/99	17,415	423	2.4%	18,000
12/98	14,131	36	0.3%	18,133
12/97	16,915	585	3.5%	16,777
12/96	16,775	828	4.9%	15,171
Annual Growth	**14.7%**	**22.2%**	**—**	**5.8%**

2004 Year-End Financials

Debt ratio: 37.0%
Return on equity: 33.5%
Cash ($ mil.): 833
Current ratio: 1.06
Long-term debt ($ mil.): 5,213

No. of shares (mil.): 2,166
Dividends
  Yield: 2.7%
  Payout: 22.5%
Market value ($ mil.): 34,398

Stock History

NYSE: STO

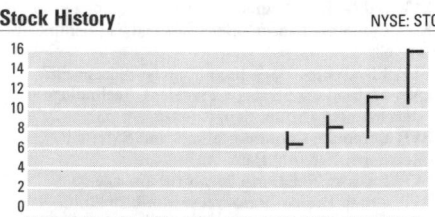

12/95 12/96 12/97 12/98 12/99 12/00 12/01 12/02 12/03 12/04

	STOCK PRICE ($) FY Close	P/E High/Low		PER SHARE ($) Earnings	Dividends	Book Value
12/04	15.88	8	6	1.91	0.43	6.50
12/03	11.30	10	6	1.15	0.40	4.87
12/02	8.27	8	6	1.12	0.33	3.79
12/01	6.55	8	7	0.92	0.00	2.66
Annual Growth	**34.3%**	**—**	**—**	**27.6%**	**—**	**34.7%**

ST

The list of European chip makers starts with ST. STMicroelectronics (ST) is one of the world's largest and most respected semiconductor companies; it is the #1 Europe-based chip maker (ahead of Infineon) and vies with Texas Instruments to be the top maker of analog chips. ST makes many types of discrete devices (such as transistors and diodes) and integrated circuits (ICs), including microcontrollers, memory chips, and application-specific and custom ICs. It sells to manufacturers in the telecommunications, computer, consumer electronics, industrial, and automotive markets. (ST chips are in half of all cars on the road.) Top clients include Nokia, Robert Bosch, Schlumberger, Scientific-Atlanta, and Sony.

ST focuses on intensive product development, especially in close concert with key long-term strategic allies such as Nokia, Seagate Technology, and Alcatel. It has joined big memory chip maker Hynix in a venture to build a multi-billion-dollar chip factory in China. The company has also expanded its product range through a series of small, complementary acquisitions. Its product breadth lends to its expertise in SOC (system-on-a-chip) ICs, which integrate disparate functions onto a single device.

The company, which employs a highly decentralized organizational structure that reflects its global reach, has also won many awards for its commitments to manufacturing quality, environmental responsibility, and employee satisfaction. Its top-flight management has been credited with helping ST to avoid the dismal losses and big layoffs experienced by many chipmakers during the brutal industry downturn of 2001-2003.

Through a complex structure of holding companies, French-government-controlled companies AREVA Group and France Telecom together own about 15% of ST. Italian state-run firm Cassa Depositi e Prestiti (CDP) owns about 10%.

HISTORY

SGS-THOMSON was formed through the 1987 merger of SGS Microelettronica, a state-owned Italian chip maker, and the nonmilitary electronics arm of Thomson-CSF (now Thales). Included in the deal were two US operations: SGS Semiconductor in Phoenix and Texas-based Thomson Components-Mostek (acquired by Thomson in 1986 from United Technologies).

Microelettronica was part of Finmeccanica, formed in 1948 as the engineering subsidiary of the (now liquidated) Italian state industrial holding company IRI.

Thomson SA got its start shortly before the turn of the century, when a group of French businessmen acquired patents from General Electric predecessor Thomson-Houston Electric and created Compagnie Française Thomson-Houston to produce power generation equipment.

Both Thomson and Microelettronica were struggling at the time of their merger. Pasquale Pistorio, a Motorola veteran who became head of SGS in 1980, was named president of the new company. To jump-start the organization, he closed and sold factories, trimmed management, and shifted jobs to the Mediterranean and Asia.

SGS-THOMSON lost $300 million in its first two years of operation, made a small profit in 1989, then stumbled again as recession spread across Europe. To secure the company's market presence, Pistorio began making acquisitions and forging alliances with major chip buyers such as Alcatel, Hewlett-Packard, and Sony. By 1993 SGS-THOMSON had become the world's #1 maker of erasable programmable read-only memories (EPROMs). Profits soared to $160 million, and the company bought Tag Semiconductors, a maker of low-cost chips, from US conglomerate Raytheon. SGS-THOMSON went public in 1994.

Thomson sold off its stake in the company in 1997 and SGS-THOMSON changed its name to STMicroelectronics (ST) in 1998. The company formed development deals with Philips Electronics (for advanced chip manufacturing processes) in 1997 and with Mitsubishi (for flash memory chips) in 1998.

In 1999 ST bought Adaptec's Peripheral Technology Solutions group, which makes chips for disk drives; Vision Group, a developer of image sensors; and Arithmos, a maker of ICs for digital displays.

In 2000 ST acquired the Canada-based semiconductor fabrication operations of Nortel Networks for about $100 million. The deal included a six-year supply agreement worth at least $2 billion. The following year, though, ST announced that a sluggish chip industry would lead it to close the former Nortel fab as part of an overall reduction in its capital spending; ST later closed a fab in California as well.

Early in 2002 the company announced that it planned to sell its small PC graphics chip business. Later that year ST bought Alcatel Microelectronics from French telecom giant Alcatel for about $345 million. In a related transaction, ST resold Alcatel's mixed-signal chip business to AMI Semiconductor (the operating unit of AMIS Holdings).

Pistorio retired early in 2005; company veteran Carlo Bozotti was designated as his successor. That year ST decided to exit the DSL chip business, a market it entered when it acquired Alcatel Microelectronics.

EXECUTIVES

Chairman: Gérald Arbola, age 56
Vice Chairman: Bruno Steve, age 63
President and CEO: Carlo Bozotti, age 52
COO: Alain Dutheil, age 60
EVP and CFO: Carlo Ferro, age 44
EVP and General Manager, Advanced System Technology and Chief Strategic Officer: Andrea Cuomo, age 51
EVP and General Manager, Home, Personal, Communication Groups: Philippe Geyres, age 53
EVP, European Region and External Technological Coordination: Enrico Villa, age 63
EVP, Front-End Technology and Manufacturing: Laurent Bosson, age 62
VP and CEO, Asia/Pacific Region: Jean-Claude Marquet, age 63
VP and Director, Total Quality and Environmental Management: Georges Auguste, age 56
VP and Treasurer: Piero Mosconi, age 65
VP, Corporate Communications: Carlo E. Ottaviani, age 61
VP, Human Resources: Patrice Chastagner, age 58
VP, Investor Relations: Stanley March
Director, US Media Relations: Michael Markowitz
Auditors: PricewaterhouseCoopers N.V.

LOCATIONS

HQ: STMicroelectronics N.V.
39 Chemin du Champ des Filles, Plan-Les-Ouates, 1228 Geneva, Switzerland
Phone: +41-22-929-29-29 **Fax:** +41-22-929-29-00
US HQ: 1310 Electronics Dr., Carrollton, TX 75006-5039
US Phone: 972-466-6000 **US Fax:** 972-466-8387
Web: www.st.com

STMicroelectronics has operations in more than 30 countries.

2004 Sales

	$ mil.	% of total
Asia/Pacific		
Japan	403	5
Other countries	3,710	42
Europe	2,363	27
North America	1,211	14
Other regions	1,073	12
Total	**8,760**	**100**

PRODUCTS/OPERATIONS

2004 Sales

	$ mil.	% of total
Telecommunications, Peripherals & Automotive	3,485	40
Memory	1,974	23
Consumer & Microcontrollers	1,619	18
Discrete & Standard ICs	1,614	18
Other	68	1
Total	**8,760**	**100**

Selected Products

Telecommunications, Peripherals, and Automotive
Telecommunications
Wireless telecommunications
Baseband devices
Multimedia processors
Radio-frequency signal semiconductors
Wireline telecommunications
Datacom ICs (packet switching, Ethernet)
Line cards (subscriber line interface circuits, or SLICs)
Modem ICs and boards
Telephone set ICs (speech circuits, line interfaces)
Peripherals and automotive
Audio and automotive
Audio power amplifiers, audio processors, and graphic equalizer ICs
Air bag controls
Alternator regulators
Antiskid braking system ICs
Car radio components (including satellite radio receivers)
Chipsets
Ignition circuits
Injection circuits
Microcontrollers
Multiplex wiring kits
Smart valves for motor control
Data storage
Disk drive actuators, controllers, host interfaces, and micromachinery
Industrial and power supplies
Battery chargers for portable electronic systems
Industrial automation system ICs
Lamp ballasts
Power ICs for motor controllers and read/write amplifiers
Printers
Head drivers, motor drivers, and pen chips for ink jet printers and color copiers

Memory
Electrically erasable programmable read-only
memories (EEPROMs)
Erasable programmable read-only
memories (EPROMs)
Flash memory
Nonvolatile random-access memories (NVRAMs)
Smart card ICs
Consumer and Microcontrollers
Consumer electronics
DVD (decoder/host processor chips)
Imaging and display (modules and sensors for
flat-panel displays, monitors, and video cameras)
Set-top box (decoders and integrated
tuner/demodulator/error correction chips)
TV (application-specific microcontrollers)
Microcontrollers (8- and 16-bit)
Discrete and Standard ICs
Discrete power devices
Protection devices (used to protect electronics from
power surges)
Rectifiers
Thyristors
Power transistors
Bipolar transistors
Power metal oxide semiconductor field-effect
transistors (MOSFETs)
Radio-frequency (RF) products (used in avionics,
telecom, and television broadcasting equipment)
Standard linear and logic ICs
Logic devices
Clocks
Gates
Registers
Standard linear ICs
Amplifiers
Comparators
Decoders
Filters
Modulators

COMPETITORS

Agere Systems	LSI Logic
AMD	Maxim Integrated
Analog Devices	Products
Atmel	National Semiconductor
Avago Technologies	NEC Electronics
Broadcom	ON Semiconductor
Cypress Semiconductor	Philips Semiconductors
Fairchild Semiconductor	QUALCOMM
Freescale Semiconductor	Renesas
Fujitsu	Samsung Electronics
IBM Microelectronics	Sharp
Infineon Technologies	Texas Instruments
Intel	Toshiba
International Rectifier	

HISTORICAL FINANCIALS

Company Type: Public

Income Statement

FYE: December 31

	REVENUE ($ mil.)	NET INCOME ($ mil.)	NET PROFIT MARGIN	EMPLOYEES
12/04	8,760	601	6.9%	49,500
12/03	7,238	253	3.5%	45,700
12/02	6,318	429	6.8%	43,170
12/01	6,357	257	4.0%	40,300
12/00	7,813	1,452	18.6%	43,650
12/99	5,056	547	10.8%	34,500
12/98	4,248	411	9.7%	29,182
12/97	4,019	407	10.1%	28,728
12/96	4,122	626	15.2%	25,468
12/95	3,554	527	14.8%	25,523
Annual Growth	10.5%	1.5%	—	7.6%

2004 Year-End Financials

Debt ratio: 19.4%
Return on equity: 7.0%
Cash ($ mil.): 1,950
Current ratio: 2.24
Long-term debt ($ mil.): 1,767

No. of shares (mil.): 892
Dividends
  Yield: 0.6%
  Payout: 18.5%
Market value ($ mil.): 17,232

Stock History

NYSE: STM

12/95 12/96 12/97 12/98 12/99 12/00 12/01 12/02 12/03 12/04

	STOCK PRICE ($) FY Close	P/E High/Low		PER SHARE ($) Earnings	Dividends	Book Value
12/04	19.32	46	25	0.65	0.12	10.21
12/03	27.01	106	62	0.27	0.00	9.11
12/02	19.51	75	23	0.48	0.04	7.88
12/01	31.67	168	62	0.29	0.00	6.83
12/00	42.81	47	25	1.58	0.00	6.88
12/99	50.43	83	22	0.62	0.00	5.24
12/98	13.00	32	12	0.48	0.00	4.77
12/97	10.17	34	17	0.49	0.00	3.96
12/96	11.66	16	6	0.75	0.00	3.91
12/95	6.70	14	6	0.67	0.00	3.21
Annual Growth	12.5%	—	—	(0.3%)	—	13.7%

Stora Enso Oyj

Forest products company Stora Enso Oyj's roots reach back more than 700 years. Stora Enso is the #1 producer of newsprint and sawn softwood timber in Europe and is a global leader in the production of a wide range of paper and wood products such as magazine paper, newsprint, fine papers, packaging boards, and sawn timber. The company also manufactures graphic products, office papers, and wallpaper base. Its publication paper products segment comprises more than 30% of Stora Enso's total sales, while the European market is the company's strongest, bringing in 85% of total sales. The Finnish State and Sweden's Knut and Alice Wallenberg Foundation each control about 24% of Stora Enso.

Stora Enso owns and operates facilities in more than 40 countries worldwide, with Stora Enso North America exemplifying one of the company's strongest subsidiaries. Stora Enso has identified China as a growth area. Current projects in the region include further development of eucalyptus plantations and expansion of the product range and capacity of its Suzhou Mill operations.

Stora Enso continues to focus on its core paper (magazine, newsprint, fine) and timber businesses (packaging boards, lumber) while divesting periphery businesses such as specialty paper, off-site energy generation, and packaging paper. With plans to strengthen its operations in Europe, Stora Enso acquired Netherlands-based Scaldia Paper from International Paper in 2004. Stora Enso has also agreed to buy German paper wholesaler Schneidersoehne Group for $588 million (€450 million).

In Finland, which accounts for more than a third of Stora Enso's production, labor disputes shut down all of the company's paper mills in that country in 2005, overshadowing reported sales and profit improvements. The labor disputes stemmed from disagreements over plant shutdowns for midsummer and Christmas holidays, as well as outsourcing. Strikes by workers have been followed by lockouts (one lasting more than a month) by employers, which has crippled the country's paper industry and is expected to affect the chemical and transportation sectors as well. Stora Enso has announced plans to eliminate about 2,000 jobs, close five plants in Europe and the US, and sell another six mills in Europe, as part of a nearly $400 million restructuring program.

HISTORY

Stora Kopparbergs Bergslag's ancestors were mining Kopperberg Mountain in Sweden as long ago as 1288. The mountain housed a copper mine that Swedish nobles and German merchants managed as a cooperative. By the 17th century King Karl IX instituted German mining methods to increase production. Copper became Sweden's largest export, accounting for 60% of the country's gross national product.

Copper production slowed after two cave-ins in 1655 and 1687, and exploitation of the region's timber and iron ore resources began. By the early 1800s the company was producing pig and bar iron. In 1862 all of the company's activities were combined to form Stora Kopparbergs Bergslag. The role of copper became less important as the company consolidated its iron works and ventured into forest products. The firm reorganized as a limited liability company in 1888.

By 1915 Stora Kopparbergs had firmly established pulp and paper mills, as well as iron and steel works concentrated along the Dalalven River Basin. The company's activities revolved around these facilities for the next 60 years.

During the 1960s Stora Kopparbergs was hurt by low bulk commodity prices and increased competition. The company, feeling the crunch of the oil crisis, sold its holdings in steel and mining between 1976 and 1978. With its purchase of Billerud (forestry), the company became Sweden's largest industrial concern in 1984. Stora Kopparbergs shortened its name to Stora, meaning "great" or "large" in Swedish, to commemorate the event.

Stora went on a shopping spree in the late 1980s and early 1990s to compete with its giant US rivals. At home it bought Papyrus and Swedish Match; abroad it acquired Feldmuhle Nobel of Germany and France's Les Paperteies de la Chapelle-Darblay. In 1998 Stora established operations in China through a joint venture. The company also merged with Finnish forest products company Enso Gutzeit Oyj to form Stora Enso Oyj that year.

Hans Gutzeit founded a sawmill in 1872 on the Finnish island of Kotka. Gutzeit bought Utra Wood Co. to eliminate competition and was incorporated in Finland as Aktiebolaget W. Gutzeit & Co. in 1896. The company constructed a pulp mill to use waste wood from the Kotka sawmill, and in 1912 it purchased rival sawmill Enso Trasliperi Aktiebolaget to increase its access to hydropower.

In 1917 the Russian Revolution marked the disappearance of a major market, and Finland's declaration of independence from Norway halted production. Gutzeit's Norwegian shareholders sold the company to the new Finnish state in 1919. In 1924 the company was renamed Enso-Gutzeit.

Enso-Gutzeit went from 400,000 hectares (99 acres) of forestlands in 1913 to 523,000 hectares (129 acres) in 1939. Russia attacked Finland that year, and in the armistice, Finland ceded land on which Enso-Gutzeit had many of its operations. However, postwar devastation in the former Russia created Soviet demand for the company's building products.

In the 1950s and 1960s the company added a paper mill, a box factory, bleaching plants, and pulp mills. It entered Canada through a 50% stake (obtaining full ownership in 1979) in Eurocan Pulp & Paper in 1970.

Enso-Gutzeit took part in a 1980s Finnish consolidation trend by buying rival A. Ahlstrom Oy's pulp and paper mills. The company merged with Veitsiluoto in 1996 to form Enso Oy. Two years later Enso Oy merged with Stora to form Stora Enso.

Stora Enso bought US-based Consolidated Papers (now Stora Enso North America) for $4.9 billion in 2000. The acquisition moved Stora Enso past International Paper as the world's #1 paper and board producer. The next year Stora Enso dissolved its pulp division by reallocating the mills to divisions that use pulp in their operations. In 2002 the company sold 300,000 acres of forestland, primarily in Wisconsin and Michigan, to paper maker Plum Creek Timber Company for about $140 million.

In 2004 Stora Enso acquired Netherlands-based Scaldia Paper from International Paper as it moved to strengthen its presence in Europe.

EXECUTIVES

Chairman: Claes Dahlbäck, age 58
Vice Chairman: Ilkka Niemi, age 59
CEO: Jukka Härmälä, age 59
SEVP, Finance, Accounting, Legal Affairs, and Investor Relations and CFO: Hannu Ryöppönen, age 53
SEVP, Corporate Support and Energy; Country Manager, Sweden: Yngve Stade, age 58
SEVP, Market Services: Jussi Huttunen, age 51
SEVP, Corporate Strategy and Emerging Markets: Arno Pelkonen, age 51
SEVP, Information Technology, Human Resources, and Business Excellence; Country Manager, Sweden: Christer Ågren, age 51
SEVP, Stora Enso Fine Paper: Pekka Laaksonen, age 49
SEVP, Publication Paper: Bernd Rettig, age 49
SEVP, Stora Enso North America: Lars Bengtsson, age 60
SEVP, Stora Enso Packaging Boards; Country Manager, Finland: Kai Korhonen, age 54
EVP, Corporate Communications: Kari Vainio, age 59
SVP, Investor Relations: Keith B. Russell, age 47
SVP, Legal Affairs: Jyrki Kurkinen, age 57
SVP, Stora Enso North America: John F. Bergin, age 62
EVP, Corporate Human Resources and Business Excellence: Per Ericson
VP, Investor Relations, North America: Scott Deitz
Auditors: SVH Pricewaterhouse Coopers Oy

LOCATIONS

HQ: Stora Enso Oyj
Kanavaranta 1, PO Box 309,
FIN-00101 Helsinki, Finland
Phone: +358-20-46-131   **Fax:** +358-20-46-214-71
US HQ: 231 1st Ave. North,
Wisconsin Rapids, WI 54495-8050
US Phone: 715-422-3111   **US Fax:** 715-422-3469
Web: www.storaenso.com

Stora Enso Oyj has operations in Asia, Europe, and North America.

2004 Sales

	% of total
Europe	85
US	11
Canada	2
China	1
Other regions	1
Total	**100**

PRODUCTS/OPERATIONS

2004 Sales

	% of total
Publication paper	34
Fine paper	23
Packaging boards	21
Wood products	12
Other	10
Total	**100**

Selected Products

Book paper
Business forms
Cartonboards
Coreboards and tubes
Corrugated boxes
Digital papers
Directory paper
Document papers
Envelope papers
Fluff pulp
Food service boards
Graphic board
Graphic paper
Kraft papers
Laminated papers
Liquid packaging boards
Magazine paper
Newsprint
Paper-grade pulp
Sawn boards
Scholastic paper

COMPETITORS

Abitibi-Consolidated
International Paper
Myllykoski Paper
NewPage Corporation
Norske Skog
OfficeMax
Smurfit-Stone Container
UPM-Kymmene
Weyerhaeuser

HISTORICAL FINANCIALS

Company Type: Public

Income Statement

FYE: December 31

	REVENUE ($ mil.)	NET INCOME ($ mil.)	NET PROFIT MARGIN	EMPLOYEES
12/04	16,791	1,002	6.0%	43,779
12/03	15,303	173	1.1%	44,264
12/02	13,426	(233)	—	42,461
12/01	13,386	918	6.9%	42,932
12/00	12,259	1,352	11.0%	41,785
12/99	10,734	759	7.1%	40,226
12/98	12,240	223	1.8%	40,987
12/97	5,371	106	2.0%	19,870
12/96	5,575	224	4.0%	19,094
12/95	6,424	398	6.2%	19,298
Annual Growth	11.3%	10.8%	—	9.5%

2004 Year-End Financials

Debt ratio: 41.3%
Return on equity: 9.6%
Cash ($ mil.): 372
Current ratio: 1.59
Long-term debt ($ mil.): 4,508
No. of shares (mil.): 820
Dividends
　Yield: 3.7%
　Payout: 47.1%
Market value ($ mil.): 12,479

Stock History

NYSE: SEO

	STOCK PRICE ($) FY Close	P/E High/Low		Earnings	PER SHARE ($) Dividends	Book Value
12/04	15.21	13	10	1.21	0.57	13.29
12/03	13.56	70	46	0.20	0.48	11.93
12/02	10.46	—	—	(0.26)	0.40	9.52
12/01	12.26	13	9	1.02	0.00	9.82
12/00	11.75	7	4	1.66	0.00	8.86
Annual Growth	6.7%	—	—	(7.6%)	—	10.7%

SUEZ S.A.

Having dredged up success from the Suez Canal to the sewers, SUEZ is channeling its efforts into utility operations around the world. The company operates in more than 130 countries and provides electricity, natural gas, water, and waste management services. Its SUEZ-TRACTEBEL unit is a leading global independent power producer and Belgium's top utility holding company. SUEZ's Ondeo unit is one of the top two global water companies, along with the water unit of Veolia Environnement (formerly Vivendi Environnement). The company has made a bid to acquire the 49.9% of Electrabel (a Belgium-based power utility) it does not already own.

The company has merged its Tractebel unit with Belgium holding company Société Générale de Belgique (SGB) to create SUEZ-TRACTEBEL, which owns approximately 55,000 MW of electric generating capacity, procures and transports natural gas, and distributes and trades energy worldwide. Similarly, its SITA unit, once one of Europe's top waste management firms, has been rolled into SUEZ Environmental. SUEZ's Ondeo unit provides water and wastewater services to about 125 million people. Suez has restructured its operations by combining its Ondeo, SITA, and Degrémont (water treatment plant construction) units under the SUEZ Environnement banner.

SUEZ is divesting noncore assets, including interests in manufacturing, construction, and financial services companies, to reduce debt. The company has sold subsidiary Nalco (formerly Ondeo Nalco) to a consortium of US equity firms (Blackstone Group, Apollo Management, and Goldman Sachs) in a $4.4 billion deal, and it has sold a 75% stake in its UK water utility, Northumbrian Water, to a group of institutional investors and the remaining 25% to the Ontario Teachers' Pension Plan. SUEZ is also selling its remaining communications assets and has reduced its stake in television channel M6 from 37% to 5%, and sold its 50% stake in cable operator NOOS in 2004.

The company had attempted to sell its stake in the waste and water utility to Aguas Provinciales, an Argentina-based water utility, but the two companies could not come to terms on the sale, so the deal was withdrawn.

The energy conglomerate was formed by the 1997 merger of Compagnie de Suez (builder of the Suez Canal) and water treatment and engineering giant Lyonnaise des Eaux.

HISTORY

The first canal in Egypt was dug in the 13th century BC, but it was Napoleon who revived the idea of a shorter trade route to India: a canal through Egypt linking the Gulf of Suez with the Mediterranean. Former French diplomat and engineer Ferdinand de Lesseps formed Compagnie Universelle du Canal Maritime de Suez in 1858 to build and eventually operate the canal, which opened 11 years later. Egypt's modernization had pushed it into debt and increased its ties to the British government, which, by 1875, had acquired a 44% stake in the company.

For more than 80 years the Suez Canal was a foreign enclave, protected by the British Army since 1936. After Egypt's puppet government fell, and as Gamal Abd Al-Nasser assumed power in 1956, British troops exited the Canal Zone, which Egypt quickly nationalized. Israel, Britain, and France attacked, but the United Nations arranged a truce and foreign forces withdrew, leaving the Suez in Egypt's control.

With no canal to operate, Universelle du Canal Maritime de Suez became Compagnie Financière de Suez in 1958. A year later it created a bank (which became Banque Indosuez in 1974).

In 1967 Financière de Suez became the largest shareholder in Société Lyonnaise des Eaux et de L'Eclairage, a leading French water company. Formed in 1880, Lyonnaise des Eaux had stakes in water (Northumbrian Water) and energy (Elyo). After France's energy firms were nationalized in 1946, Lyonnaise des Eaux dipped deeper into the water industry by acquiring Degrémont (now Ondeo-Degrémont) in 1972. It also purchased stakes in waste management (SITA, 1970) and heating systems (Cofreth, 1975).

In the 1980s Lyonnaise des Eaux expanded in Spain, the UK, and the US, and diversified into cable TV (1986) and broadcast TV (1987). It merged with construction firm Dumez in 1990.

Meanwhile, Financière de Suez became a financial power when it won a controlling stake in Société Générale de Belgique (SGB) in 1988 and bought Groupe Victoire in 1989. But the two buys left the firm (renamed Compagnie de Suez in 1990) deeply in debt.

Losing money, Compagnie de Suez disposed of Victoire (1994) and then the valuable Banque Indosuez (1996). In 1996 the company bought a controlling stake in Belgium's top utility, Tractebel (now SUEZ-TRACTEBEL). Compagnie de Suez and Lyonnaise des Eaux merged in 1997 to create Suez Lyonnaise des Eaux. The following year Suez Lyonnaise acquired the rest of SGB and bought the European and Asian operations of waste management giant Browning-Ferris Industries; it also began divesting noncore operations.

Suez Lyonnaise in 1999 expanded its core businesses, primarily in the US. The company bought Calgon (water treatment, US) and Nalco Chemical (water treatment chemicals, US), then merged Calgon into Nalco to form Ondeo Nalco. (The company's name was changed back to Nalco when it was divested in 2003.)

In 2000 Suez Lyonnaise bought United Water Resources (now United Water) and acquired the rest of SITA. Through its Elyo subsidiary, Suez Lyonnaise bought out minority shareholders in US-based Trigen Energy. The company also merged its construction unit, Groupe GTM, with French construction rival VINCI; Suez Lyonnaise then sold the VINCI shares that it received from the transaction.

The next year the company shortened its name to Suez (later modified to SUEZ) as part of a global rebranding effort. It also united its water services operations under the ONDEO brand. In 2002 SUEZ made Tractebel a wholly owned subsidiary by purchasing the remaining publicly held shares. Also in 2002, SUEZ sold minority stakes in communications equipment manufacturer Sagem (now SAFRAN), steelmaker Arcelor, and motorway operator Autopistas Concesionaria Española (ACESA).

SUEZ divested most of its 11% stake in Belgian insurance firm Fortis for nearly $2 billion in 2003. It also sold its 79% stake in cable company Coditel that year. In 2003 the company merged Tractebel and SGB (Tractebel's former holding company) to form SUEZ-TRACTEBEL.

EXECUTIVES

Chairman and CEO; Chairman, SUEZ-TRACTEBEL and SUEZ Environnement: Gérard Mestrallet, age 56
Vice Chairman: Baron Albert Frère, age 79
Vice Chairman: Jean Gandois, age 75
SEVP and COO; CEO, SUEZ-TRACTEBEL and Electrabel: Jean-Pierre Hansen, age 57
SEVP Finance and CFO: Gérard Lamarche, age 43
SEVP Business Strategy and Development: Patrick Buffet
SEVP International Affairs and Institutional Relations: Yves-Thibault de Silguy
EVP Communications: Valérie Bernis
EVP Electricity and Gas Europe; Chairman, Distrigas: Willy Bosmans, age 58
EVP Electricity and Gas International; CEO, Tractebel Electricity and Gas International: Dirk Beeuwsaert
EVP Environment; CEO, Suez Environnement: Jean-Louis Chaussade
EVP Energy and Industrial Services and Operational Assistance; CEO, Fabricom: Jérôme Tolot, age 50
EVP Human Resources; Vice Chairman, Electrabel: Emmanuel van Innis, age 58
EVP, Finance and Control, SUEZ Energy International: Pierre Chareyre
SEVP, SUEZ Energy North America: Michel Sirat, age 43
SVP Financial Communications: Arnaud Erbin
VP, Press Department: Anne Liontas
General Secretary: Yves de Gaulle, age 54
Investor Relations Contact: Bertrand Haas
Auditors: Barbier Frinault & Autres; Deloitte Touche Tohmatsu — Audit

LOCATIONS

HQ: SUEZ S.A.
16, rue de la Ville l'Evêque, 75008 Paris, France
Phone: +33-1-40-06-64-00   **Fax:** +33-1-40-06-67-33
Web: www.suez.fr

2004 Sales

	% of total
Europe	
Belgium	32
France	23
UK	3
Other EU countries	18
Other European countries	4
North America	9
Asia, Middle East & Oceania	5
South America	5
Africa	1
Total	**100**

PRODUCTS/OPERATIONS

2004 Sales

	% of total
Energy	72
Environment	28
Total	**100**

Selected Operations

Energy
SUEZ-TRACTEBEL (formerly Tractebel)
Distrigas (64%)
Electrabel (50.1%)
Elyo
Fluxys (64%)
Grupo Fabricom
Tractebel Electricity and Gas International
Tractebel Engineering
Environment (SUEZ Environnement)
Ondeo
Eurawasser (Germany)
Lyonnaise des Eaux France
Sociedad General de Aguas de Barcelona (Agbar, 26%, Spain)
United Water Inc. (formerly United Water Resources, US)
Ondeo Degrémont
Ondeo Industrial Solutions
SITA

COMPETITORS

Aqua America	France Telecom
AWG	Gaz de France
Bouygues	ITec Environmental
Brambles	National Grid
CANAL+	RWE
Centrica	SABESP
Covanta	Séché Environnement
Dragados	Severn Trent
Electricité de France	United Utilities
Electricité de Strasbourg	USFilter Water &
EnBW	Wastewater Systems
Enel	Vattenfall
Eni	Veolia Environnement
E.ON	Waste Management

HISTORICAL FINANCIALS

Company Type: Public

Income Statement

FYE: December 31

	REVENUE ($ mil.)	NET INCOME ($ mil.)	NET PROFIT MARGIN	EMPLOYEES
12/04	55,186	2,444	4.4%	160,700
12/03	49,813	(2,722)	—	172,300
12/02	48,408	(906)	—	198,750
12/01	37,755	1,860	4.9%	188,050
12/00	32,602	1,808	5.5%	173,200
12/99	31,682	2,719	8.6%	222,000
12/98	36,595	2,402	6.6%	210,100
12/97	31,743	669	2.1%	175,000
12/96	17,509	258	1.5%	116,290
12/95	20,089	185	0.9%	118,770
Annual Growth	11.9%	33.2%	—	3.4%

2004 Year-End Financials

Debt ratio: 253.4%
Return on equity: 25.2%
Cash ($ mil.): 7,065
Current ratio: 1.53
Long-term debt ($ mil.): 27,189

No. of shares (mil.): 1,008
Dividends
Yield: 2.4%
Payout: 26.2%
Market value ($ mil.): 26,961

	STOCK PRICE ($) FY Close	P/E High/Low		PER SHARE ($) Earnings	Dividends	Book Value
12/04	26.75	11	7	2.44	0.64	10.65
12/03	20.21	—	—	(2.74)	0.81	8.60
12/02	17.67	—	—	(0.91)	0.64	11.03
12/01	31.53	19	15	1.85	0.00	12.96
Annual Growth	(5.3%)	—	—	9.7%	—	(6.3%)

Suzuki Motor

Suzuki Motor Corporation is Japan's #1 minicar producer as well as its #3 motorcycle manufacturer (behind Honda and Yamaha). Suzuki's US cars and SUVs include the Aerio, Forenza, Verona, and the Grand Vitara; motorcycles include the Katana, V-Strom, Hayabusa, and Boulevard. Suzuki's nonvehicle products include generators, outboard marine engines, and prefabricated housing. The company operates in more than 190 countries. Suzuki has partnered to make cars with General Motors and has agreed to develop motorcycles and ATVs with fellow Japanese motorcycle manufacturer Kawasaki.

General Motors has invested in several Asian auto companies (including Isuzu Motors and Subaru maker Fuji Heavy Industries) to gain a better foothold in that market. GM took a 20% stake in Suzuki in a deal that gave the latter $600 million and strengthened cooperation in the development of small cars.

GM Daewoo Auto & Technology (formerly Daewoo Motor) GM, Suzuki, and Shanghai Automotive Industry Corp. together control 67% of GM Daewoo. The deal is anticipated to give GM and Suzuki a better footing in the Asian market.

HISTORY

In 1909 Michio Suzuki started Suzuki Loom Works in Hamamatsu, Japan. The company went public in 1920 and continued producing weaving equipment until the onset of WWII, when it began to make war-related products.

Suzuki began developing inexpensive motor vehicles in 1947, and in 1952 it introduced a 36cc engine to motorize bicycles. The company changed its name to Suzuki Motor and launched its first motorcycle in 1954. Suzuki's entry into the minicar market came in 1955 with the Suzulight, followed by the Suzumoped (1958), a delivery van (1959), and the Suzulight Carry FB small truck (1961).

Suzuki's triumph in the 1962 50cc-class Isle of Man TT motorcycle race started a string of racing successes that brought international prominence to the Suzuki name. The company established its first overseas plant in Thailand in 1967.

In the 1970s Suzuki met market demand for motorcycles with large engines. Meanwhile, a mid-1970s recession and falling demand for low-powered cars in Japan led the minicar industry there to produce two-thirds fewer minicars in 1974 than in 1970. Suzuki responded by pushing overseas, beginning auto exports, and expanding foreign distribution. In 1975 it started producing motorcycles in Taiwan, Thailand, and Indonesia.

Suzuki boosted capacity internationally throughout the 1980s through joint ventures. Motorcycle sales in Japan peaked in 1982, then tapered off, but enjoyed a modest rebound in the late 1980s. In 1988 the company agreed to handle distribution of Peugeot cars in Japan.

Suzuki and General Motors began their long-standing relationship in 1981 when GM bought a small stake in Suzuki. The company began producing Swift subcompacts in 1983 and sold them through GM as the Chevy Sprint and, later, the Geo Metro. In 1986 Suzuki and GM of Canada jointly formed CAMI Automotive to produce vehicles, including Sprints, Metros, and Geo Trackers (Suzuki Sidekicks), in Ontario; production began in 1989.

Although sales via GM increased through 1990, US efforts with the Suzuki nameplate faltered shortly after Suzuki formed its US subsidiary in Brea, California, in 1986. A 1988 *Consumer Reports* claim that the company's Samurai SUV was prone to rolling over devastated US sales. The next year Suzuki's top US executives quit, apparently questioning the company's commitment to the US market.

Suzuki established Magyar Suzuki, a joint venture with Hungarian automaker Autokonszern Rt., C. Itoh & Co., and International Finance Corporation in 1991 to begin producing the Swift sedan in Hungary. The company expanded a licensing agreement with a Chinese government partner in 1993, becoming the first Japanese company to take an equity stake in a Chinese carmaking venture. The next year Suzuki introduced the Alto van, Japan's cheapest car, at just over $5,000, and the Wagon R miniwagon, which quickly became one of Japan's top-selling vehicles.

In a case that was later overturned, a woman was awarded $90 million from Suzuki after being paralyzed in a Samurai rollover in 1990. The company sued Consumers Union, publisher of *Consumer Reports,* in 1996, charging it had intended to fix the results in the 1988 Samurai testing.

GM raised its 3% stake in Suzuki to 10% in 1998. The company teamed up with GM and Fuji Heavy Industries (Subaru) in 2000 to develop compact cars for the European market. It was also announced that GM would spend about $600 million to double its stake in Suzuki to 20%. In 2001 Suzuki announced that it had agreed to cooperate with Kawasaki in the development of new motorcycles, scooters, and ATVs.

The following year Suzuki agreed to take control of Maruti Udyog Ltd., the state-owned India-based car manufacturer, in an $80 million rights issue deal.

EXECUTIVES

Chairman and CEO: Osamu Suzuki
President and COO: Hiroshi Tsuda
Senior Managing Director: Takahira Kiriyama
Senior Managing Director: Shinzo Nakanishi
Senior Managing Director: Takashi Nakayama
Senior Managing Director: Shunichi Wakuda
Managing Director: Takao Hirosawa
Managing Director: Sadayuki Inobe
Managing Director: Akio Kosugi
Managing Director: Akihiro Sakamoto
Managing Director: Kazuo Suzuki
Managing Director: Takeo Shigemoto
Auditors: Seimei Audit Corporation

LOCATIONS

HQ: Suzuki Motor Corporation
300 Takatsuka, Hamamatsu,
Shizuoka 432-8611, Japan
Phone: +81-53-440-2061 **Fax:** +81-53-440-2776
US HQ: 3251 E. Imperial Hwy., Brea, CA 92821-6795
US Phone: 714-996-7040 **US Fax:** 714-524-8499
Web: www.globalsuzuki.com

Suzuki Motor Corporation operates major subsidiaries in Australia, Austria, Cambodia, Canada, Colombia, France, Germany, Hungary, India, Indonesia, Italy, Myanmar, New Zealand, Pakistan, the Philippines, Poland, Spain, Thailand, the UK, and the US. It distributes its products in more than 190 countries.

2004 Sales

	$ mil.	% of total
Asia		
Japan	9,996	48
Other countries	4,269	21
North America	2,788	13
Europe	3,533	17
Other regions	230	1
Total	**20,816**	**100**

PRODUCTS/OPERATIONS

2004 Sales

	$ mil.	% of total
Automobiles	16,327	78
Motorcycles	3,946	19
Other products	543	3
Total	**20,816**	**100**

Selected Products

Cars, Minicars, and SUVs
  Aerio Sedan
  Forenza
  Grand Vitara
  Reno
  Verona
  Wagon R
  XL-7

Motorcycles
  Boulevard C90
  Boulevard M95
  DR650SE
  DR-Z250
  DR-Z400E
  DR-Z400S
  DR-Z125L
  GSX-R600
  GSX-R750
  GSX-R1000
  GZ250
  Hayabusa 1300
  Katana 600
  Katana 750
  RM85
  RM125
  RM250
  SV650
  V-Strom 650

All Terrain Vehicles
  Eiger 400 4X4
  Eiger 400 Automatic 4X4
  Ozark 250
  QuadSport Z400
  Twin Peaks 700 4X4
  Vinson 500 4X4

Other Products
  Electro-scooters
  General-purpose engines
  Generators
  Motorized wheelchairs
  Outboard motors
  Prefabricated houses

Selected Overseas Subsidiares and Affiliates

American Suzuki Motor Corp.
Cambodia Suzuki Motor Co. Ltd.
Magyar Suzuki Corp. (Hungary)
Maruti Udyog Ltd. (India)
Pak Suzuki Motor Co., Ltd. (Pakistan)
Suzuki Motorcycles Pakistan Ltd.
Thai Suzuki Motor Company., Ltd. (Thailand)

COMPETITORS

Bajaj Auto
BMW
Bombardier
Brunswick
DaimlerChrysler
Dover
Ek Chor China Motorcycle
Fiat
Ford
General Motors
Harley-Davidson
Honda
Hyundai
Invacare
Isuzu
Kawasaki Heavy Industries
Kohler
Mazda
Nissan
Peugeot Motors of America, Inc.
Piaggio
Remy
Renault
Saab Automobile
Toyota
Triumph Motorcycles
Volkswagen
Volvo
Yamaha Motor

HISTORICAL FINANCIALS

Company Type: Public

Income Statement

FYE: March 31

	REVENUE ($ mil.)	NET INCOME ($ mil.)	NET PROFIT MARGIN	EMPLOYEES
3/04	20,816	415	2.0%	13,700
3/03	16,816	259	1.5%	13,920
3/02	12,577	169	1.3%	14,260
3/01	12,668	160	1.3%	14,460
3/00	14,418	255	1.8%	14,800
3/99	12,223	205	1.7%	14,760
3/98	11,188	227	2.0%	14,610
3/97	12,136	271	2.2%	13,873
3/96	12,877	248	1.9%	14,650
3/95	14,539	232	1.6%	13,455
Annual Growth	4.1%	6.7%	—	0.2%

2004 Year-End Financials

Debt ratio: 5.6%
Return on equity: 6.9%
Cash ($ mil.): 1,605
Current ratio: 1.31
Long-term debt ($ mil.): 367

Net Income History

OTC: SZKMF

Swatch Group

Swatch is worth watching. The Swatch Group (formerly Société Suisse de Microélectronique & d'Horlogerie) is the world's second-largest watchmaker (after Citizen Watch). Its watches range from low-priced, collectible Swatch and Flik Flak to premium-priced Longines, Blancpain, and Omega brands. Swatch watches are sold at some 15,000 retailers worldwide, plus at more than 500 Swatch stores, about 1,000 shop-in-shops, and some 140 kiosks. Its Dress Your Body subsidiary makes jewelry. Chairman Nicolas Hayek's family controls nearly 37% of The Swatch Group.

The Swatch Group holds 25% of the world's watch market.

The company, which has more than 100 subsidiaries and affiliated units, also makes watch components and private-label watches. In addition, it makes semiconductors, quartz oscillators, and industrial lasers, among other items, for industries such as telecommunications and medical electronics. The company's EM-Microelectronic subsidiary is the leading producer of radio frequency identification (RFID) technology that is taking hold in the retail industry. Swatch also provides timing and scoring services at major sporting events such as the Olympic Games.

In 2004 Swatch unveiled the Paparazzi, a watch it made in collaboration with MSN Direct (a division of Microsoft) which can link to updated international news, weather forecasts, and lottery results. All that, and it tells the time.

HISTORY

The Swatch Group was first established when watchmakers ASUAG and SSIH were merged in 1983. ASUAG was founded in 1931 in Switzerland to make watches. By the late 1970s ASUAG had acquired some 100 family-owned companies, many of which were operating independently and inefficiently. When it merged with SSIH, ASUAG owned the Longines and Rado brands and made watch components.

Watchmaker SSIH was formed in 1930 with the merger of brands Tissot and Omega (which traced its history to 1848). SSIH and other Swiss watchmakers were struggling by the late 1970s. The market was flooded with cheaper watches made in Japan and Hong Kong that used quartz technology (a technology invented — but ignored — by the Swiss). SSIH had licensed out its prestigious Omega brand to other manufacturers in various countries, hurting that brand's reputation.

With both ASUAG and SSIH on the verge of bankruptcy, Swiss banks named Nicolas Hayek (then the CEO of consulting firm Hayek Engineering) to advise the companies on their futures. He recommended that ASUAG and SSIH merge and then mass-produce a low-cost watch and sell it globally at a set price. The two companies merged in 1983, forming SMH (Société Suisse de Microélectronique & d'Horlogerie); its headquarters were ASUAG's in Biel, Switzerland.

SMH had sales of about $1.1 billion with losses of some $124 million in 1983. That year it introduced the Swatch watch amid some resistance and objections that the watch would ruin the Swiss image of makers of high-quality, premium-priced watches. But Swatch watches became fashion statements and pop-culture icons in the 1980s

and Hayek, who spearheaded the turnaround, became a Swiss business hero. Hayek and a group of investors bought a controlling 51% stake of SMH, and he became CEO in 1985.

In 1992 the company bought Blancpain (luxury watches) and Frederic Piguet (luxury watch components). By 1993 SMH had expanded into semiconductor chips, pagers, and telephones. The next year it formed a joint venture (19%-owned by SMH) called Micro Compact Car (MCC) with Daimler-Benz to make a battery- and gasoline-powered Swatchmobile.

Because of difficulty in translating its name into other languages, the company changed its name in 1998 to The Swatch Group. That year it also sold its 19% stake in MCC to Daimler-Benz. In 1999 Swatch bought Groupe Horloger Breguet, a manufacturer of mechanical timepieces since 1775, and Swiss watch case maker Favre & Perret. In 2000 the growing company pocketed German luxury watchmaker Glashütter, among others. Acquisitions in 2001 included two Greek companies, Aliki Perri and Alikonia. Swatch bought Swiss watch dial maker Rubattel & Weyermann in 2002. Later that year Hayek retired as CEO, but remained chairman; his son Nicolas became CEO.

EXECUTIVES

Chairman: H. C. Nicolas G. Hayek Sr.
Vice Chairman: Peter Gross
President of Executive Group Management Board: G. Nicolas (Nick) Hayek Jr.
President, ck watch & jewelry, Léon Hatot, Dress Your Body; Swatch Group Japan and South Korea: Arlett Emch
President, Swatch Group France, Les Boutiques, Italy, Span, and Flik Flak: Florence Ollivier-Lamarque
President, EM Microelectronic-Marin, Micro Crystal, Lasag, Oscilloquarts, Omega Electronics, Renata, and Sokymat: Mougahed Darwish
SVP and CFO: Edgar Geiser
General Manager, Blancpain, Swatch Group Middle East: Marc A. Hayek
SVP, Human Resources and General Counsel: Hanspeter Rentsch
General Manager, Rado, Hamilton, Swatch Group Belgium and Netherlands: Roland Streule
President, Hamilton Ltd.: Matthias Breschan
General Manager, Frédéric Piguet, Valdar, and Universo: Edmond Capt
General Manager, Asulab and Nivarox-FAR: Rudolf Dinger
President, Jaquet Droz SA, Eastern Europe and Russia: Manuel Emch
General Manager, Swatch Group USA and Canada: Yann Gamard
Corporate Treasurer: Thomas Dürr
Head of Public Relations: Beatrice Howald
Auditors: PricewaterhouseCoopers Ltd.

LOCATIONS

HQ: The Swatch Group Ltd.
Seevorstadt 6, CH-2501 Biel, Bern, Switzerland
Phone: +41-32-343-68-11 **Fax:** +41-32-343-69-11
US HQ: 1200 Harbor Blvd., Weehawken, NJ 07086
US Phone: 201-271-1400 **US Fax:** 201-558-5042
Web: www.swatchgroup.com

The Swatch Group sells its products worldwide. It has more than 150 manufacturing facilities, plus other operations in 50 countries throughout the world.

2004 Sales

	% of total
Europe	51
Asia	35
America	11
Oceania	2
Africa	1
Total	**100**

PRODUCTS/OPERATIONS

2004 Sales

	% of total
Watches	76
Watch production	12
Electronic systems	12
Total	**100**

Selected Products and Brands

Watches
  Basic Range
    Flik Flak
    Swatch
  High Range
    Longines
    Rado
  Middle Range
    Calvin Klein
    Certina
    Hamilton
    Mido
    Pierre Balmain
    Tissot
  Prestige
    Blancpain
    Breguet
    Glashütte Original/Union
    Jaquet-Droz
    Léon Hatot
    Omega
    Paparazzi
  Private Label
    Endura
Jewelry
  Dress Your Body
Retailing
  Les Boutiques

Selected Electronic Systems Operations

Asulab (research and development of watches and components and microtechnical products)
EM Microelectronic-Marin (semiconductors, LCDs)
Lasag (industrial lasers)
Micro Crystal (watch crystals, miniature oven oscillators, crystals for telecommunications, medical electronics, aerospace, automotive, and computer industries)
Microcomponents SA (precision micromechanical parts and components for automotive, electrical appliance, and watchmaking industries; miniaturized stepping motors)
Oscilloquartz (quartz crystal oscillators for telecommunications)
Renata (batteries for cellular phones, hearing aids, and other electronics)
SMH Immeubles SA (real estate)
Swiss Timing Ltd. (timing and scoring for major sporting events)

COMPETITORS

Benetton
Bulgari
CASIO COMPUTER
Citizen Watch
E. Gluck
Fossil
Guess
Hermès
Loews
LVMH
Movado Group
Richemont
Rolex
Seiko
Tiffany
Timex

HISTORICAL FINANCIALS

Company Type: Public

Income Statement

FYE: December 31

	REVENUE ($ mil.)	NET INCOME ($ mil.)	NET PROFIT MARGIN	EMPLOYEES
12/04	3,517	452	12.9%	20,949
12/03	3,095	396	12.8%	20,700
12/02	2,835	356	12.6%	20,327
12/01	2,420	301	12.4%	19,665
12/00	2,563	404	15.8%	17,719
12/99	2,279	282	12.4%	17,751
12/98	2,311	260	11.2%	18,000
12/97	2,032	225	11.1%	17,729
12/96	2,024	209	10.3%	16,459
12/95	2,220	237	10.7%	17,082
Annual Growth	**5.2%**	**7.5%**	**—**	**2.3%**

2004 Year-End Financials

Debt ratio: 9.3%
Return on equity: 12.9%
Cash ($ mil.): 1,215

Current ratio: 4.72
Long-term debt ($ mil.): 349

Net Income History

Pink Sheets: SWGAF

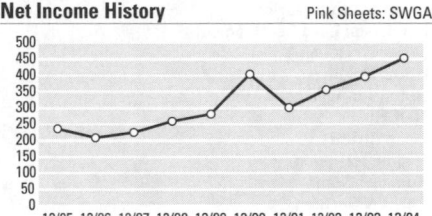

Swire Pacific

Swire Pacific has interests in airlines, beverages, and manufacturing, but the *hong* (general trading company) bases its prosperity on property in Hong Kong, where it holds some prime commercial real estate. The company's airline holdings include stakes in Cathay Pacific Airways and regional Chinese carrier Dragonair. Swire Pacific has extensive interests in apparel, sugar, and other manufacturing operations and is a major Coca-Cola bottler in southern China. Joint ventures include a paint factory and sporting goods stores. The firm is controlled by its founding family through UK-based John Swire & Sons, which owns more than 65% of Swire Pacific.

Sportswear seller Swire Resources — which operates more than 100 GigaSports and Marathon Sports stores in Hong Kong and China — plans to have some 300 stores open by mid-2007.

Despite regional economic turmoil, Swire Pacific is committed to building new office space in Hong Kong and to investing in Cathay Pacific. Not wanting to be shut out when the UK gave up control of Hong Kong, Swire Pacific over the years has assiduously allied itself with Chinese interests through joint ventures in Hong Kong and Taiwan and on the mainland.

HISTORY

John Swire began a Liverpool trading company in 1816. By the time he died in 1847 John Swire & Sons derived much of its revenues from the US cotton trade. One of Swire's sons, John Samuel Swire, refocused the company on Chinese tea and textiles during the US Civil War. Unhappy with his representatives in Asia, Swire went to Shanghai and in 1866 partnered with customer Richard Butterfield. Butterfield & Swire (B&S) took *Taikoo* ("great and ancient") as a Chinese name. Butterfield soon left, but his name lived on with the company until 1974.

By 1868 B&S had offices in New York and Yokohama, Japan; it added a Hong Kong office two years later. The firm created China Navigation Company in 1872 to transport goods on the Yangtze River; the shipping line served all the major Pacific Rim ports by the late 1880s. Hong Kong-based Taikoo Sugar Refinery began operations in 1884.

The third John Swire took over B&S in 1898 and built the Taikoo Dockyard in Hong Kong. The company's Chinese operations were eventually devastated by the Japanese attack on China in 1937, World War II, and the Communist takeover in 1949. However, the company rebuilt in Hong Kong, and in 1948 it bought control of Cathay Pacific, a Hong Kong airline with six DC-3s.

In the 1950s and 1960s the Swire family expanded the airline and established airport and aircraft service companies. Swire Pacific, the holding company for most of the family's Hong Kong interests, went public in 1959. It won the Coca-Cola bottling franchise for Hong Kong in 1965. The fifth generation of Swires, John and Adrian, took command of parent company John Swire & Sons in 1968 (Adrian became chairman in 1987). The Taikoo Dockyard merged its business with Hongkong & Whampoa Dockyard in 1972.

The 1984 agreement to return Hong Kong to Chinese control in 1997 plunged the colony into uncertainty. Capital flight and free-falling real estate values gave Swire an opportunity to pick up properties at bargain prices.

Meanwhile, Cathay Pacific had become a major Pacific carrier. In 1987 Swire sold about 12% of the airline to CITIC, China's state-owned overseas investment company. (CITIC later increased its share.) Three years later Swire bought 35% of Hong Kong's Dragonair, also partly owned by CITIC, and gave it Cathay Pacific's Shanghai and Beijing routes.

In the 1990s Swire's financial results and property values fluctuated along with confidence about the consequences of China's takeover. In 1997 Swire expanded its Chinese operations, acquiring the rights to distribute Volvo cars in China and Hong Kong. As Asian financial markets collapsed, Swire sold its insurance-underwriting businesses to focus on core operations. Adrian Swire stepped down that year, relinquishing the John Swire & Sons chairmanship to a nonfamily member, Edward Scott.

To expand its dwindling undeveloped property base, a Swire-led consortium bought reclaimed waterfront on Hong Kong Island in 1998. Reflecting a rebounding economy, in 1999 Swire sold more than 274,000 sq. ft. of Hong Kong office space to Time Warner and Cable & Wireless HKT.

In 2000 Swire sold health care and medical products trading unit Swire Loxley to CITIC Pacific. The next year Swire Properties announced plans to build a major retail, office, and hotel project in Guangzhou in a joint venture with the Guangzhou Daily Group.

That year Swire sold its 49% stake in Carlsberg Brewery Hong Kong Ltd., in order to focus on its growing regional soft drinks operations. The company sold its 49% stake in Schneider Swire Ltd. to joint venture partner Schneider Electric Industries in 2002.

EXECUTIVES

Chairman, Swire Pacific, Cathay Pacific Airways, and Hong Kong Aircraft Engineering: David M. Turnbull, age 49
Finance Director: M. Cubbon, age 47
Executive Director; Chairman, Taiwan Operations: Davy C. Y. Ho, age 57
Executive Director: Christopher D. Pratt, age 48
Property Director; Chairman, Swire Properties: Keith G. Kerr, age 52
Chairman, John Swire & Sons: James W. J. Hughes-Hallett, age 55
Managing Director, Beverages Division: John R. Slosar, age 48
Company Secretary: Margaret Yu, age 59
Auditors: PricewaterhouseCoopers

LOCATIONS

HQ: Swire Pacific Limited
35th Fl., 2 Pacific Place, 88 Queensway,, Hong Kong
Phone: +852-2840-8098   **Fax:** +852-2526-9365
Web: www.swirepacific.com

2004 Sales

	% of total
Hong Kong	41
Other Asian countries	25
North America	27
Shipping	7
Total	**100**

PRODUCTS/OPERATIONS

2004 Sales

	% of total
Property investment & trading	40
Beverages	27
Trading & industrial	26
Marine services	7
Total	**100**

Selected Subsidiaries

Aviation
  Abacus Distribution Systems (25%, reservation systems)
  AHK Air Hong Kong Limited (28%, cargo airline)
  Airline Stores Property Limited (46%, investment)
  Cathay Pacific Airways Limited (46%)
  Hong Kong Aircraft Engineering Co Ltd (45%)
  Hong Kong Dragon Airlines Limited (16%)
  Hong Kong Air Cargo Terminals Limited (25%, cargo handling service)
  Swire Aviation Limited (67%, investment holding)
  Troon Limited (46%, Bermuda, financial services)
  Vogue Laundry Service Limited (46%)

Beverages
  Swire Beverages Holdings Limited
  Swire Coca-Cola Beverages Hefei Limited (60%, China)
  Swire Coca-Cola HK Limited (88%)
  Tai Tung Foods Company Limited (80%, Taiwan)
  Xian BC Coca-Cola Beverages Limited (75%, China)

Marine Services
  Expro Swire Production (50%)
  Hongkong Salvage & Towage
  HUD General Engineering Services Limited (50%)
  Modern Terminals Limited (18%)
  Pacific Manning Company Pty Limited (ship personnel management)
  Swire Pacific Offshore Limited (Bermuda, management services)
  Swire Pacific Ship Management Limited (ship personnel management)
  Swire Supply Vessels Corporation (ship owning and operating)

Properties
  Aldrich Bay East Limited (investment)
  Cathay Limited (investment)
  Festival Walk Holdings Limited (50%, investment)
  Redhill Properties Limited (investment)
  Swire Brickell Key Hotel, Limited (75%, US, investment)
  Swire Carbonell Limited Partnership (US, trading)
  Swire Properties Limited (holding company)
  Swire Properties Management Limited

Trading and Industrial
  Beldare Motors Limited
  ICI Swire Paints (China) Limited (36%)
  Intermarket Agencies (Far East) Limited (70%, sports and casual apparel)
  Swire Duro Limited (marble fabrication)
  Swire Pacific Cold Storage Company Limited (Vietnam)
  Swire Resources (sports shoes and apparel)
  Taikoo Motors Offshore Limited
  Taikoo Sugar Limited (branded food products)
  Waylung Waste Services Limited

COMPETITORS

AMR Corp.
China Southern Airlines
Henderson Land Development
Hopewell Holdings
HSBC Holdings
Hutchison Whampoa
ITOCHU
Japan Airlines
Jardine Matheson
Kumagai Gumi
Marks & Spencer
Northwest Airlines
PepsiCo
Qantas
Sime Darby
Singapore Airlines
UAL
WBL Corporation
Wing Tai

HISTORICAL FINANCIALS

Company Type: Public

Income Statement

FYE: December 31

	REVENUE ($ mil.)	NET INCOME ($ mil.)	NET PROFIT MARGIN	EMPLOYEES
12/04	2,357	842	35.7%	60,400
12/03	2,263	634	28.0%	56,700
12/02	1,951	693	35.5%	58,000
12/01	1,948	528	27.1%	55,000
12/00	1,929	499	25.8%	60,000
12/99	2,170	571	26.3%	60,000
12/98	2,182	228	10.4%	58,000
12/97	3,163	862	27.2%	60,000
12/96	4,847	990	20.4%	56,000
12/95	6,939	835	12.0%	37,000
Annual Growth	**(11.3%)**	**0.1%**	**—**	**5.6%**

2004 Year-End Financials

Debt ratio: 3.0%
Return on equity: 8.4%
Cash ($ mil.): 193
Current ratio: 0.63
Long-term debt ($ mil.): 333

Net Income History

OTC: SWRAY

Tata Group

Founded as a textile trader more than a century ago, the Tata Group now includes enough businesses to blanket India. The nation's largest industrial conglomerate, Tata runs more than 90 companies in seven main business sectors: chemicals, communications and IT, consumer products, energy, engineering, materials, and services. Two of its largest operations are steel-making, through Tata Steel (Tisco), and vehicle manufacturing, through Tata Engineering. Tata is restructuring its vast empire to reduce hierarchy, focus on profitable operations, and increase efficiency. The group is managed through holding company Tata Sons, which controls the Tata brand.

Although a recessionary economy has hurt India's heavy industries, Tata has offset downturns with operations such as IT unit Tata Consultancy Services (TCS), which the group spun off in 2004 while still retaining ownership of 80% of it. The group is working to expand its telecommunications businesses.

In early 2005 the Group bought Singapore's National Steel, which boosted Tata's capacity by 2 million tons and greatly enhances its position in the Asia/Pacific region.

The Tata family's ownership stakes in group companies are managed through Tata Sons, the group's principal investment holding company, of which the family owns about 3%. Much of the rest is held by charitable trusts established by the Tata family; more than 60% of Tata Sons' profits are channeled into philanthropic trusts. Tata Sons generally holds only minority stakes in the group's companies but maintains control with the support of other investors, including state-owned financial institutions.

HISTORY

Jamsetji Tata, a Parsi (Zoroastrian) from Bombay, started a textile trading company in 1868. He began in textile manufacturing, then embarked on a mission to industrialize India. Before his death in 1904 Tata had built the Taj Mahal Hotel in Bombay and set in motion plans to create a hydroelectric power plant, a forum for technical education and research in India, and a steel mill to supply rapidly expanding railroads.

Jamsetji's son Dorabji carried on. Dorabji found a jungle site for the steel mill, renamed the area Jamshedpur after his father, and in 1907 established Tata Iron and Steel Company (Tisco). Three years later Tata Hydro-Electric Power went on line. By 1911 Jamsetji's plans were realized when the Indian Institute of Science opened.

The British chairman of the Railway Board promised "to eat every pound of steel rail" Tata made. Tata shipped 1,500 miles of rail to British troops in Mesopotamia during WWI.

Six years after Dorabji's death in 1932, J. R. D. Tata, the son of Dorabji's cousin, took over the family empire. India's first licensed pilot, J. R. D. had started Tata Airlines, later nationalized as Air India. He started Tata Chemicals in 1939. After WWII and Indian independence, the government built a state-owned steel industry but allowed Tata's mills to operate through a grandfather clause. Inefficient government operations led to high fixed prices for steel, and Tata profited.

Tata Engineering & Locomotive Co. (Telco), founded in 1945 to make steam locomotives, entered truck production in 1954 by collaborating with Daimler-Benz (now DaimlerChrysler). With help from Swiss firm Volkart Brothers, the company also started the Voltas manufacturing conglomerate. In 1962 Tata joined James Finlay of Scotland to create Tata-Finlay, now Tata Tea.

For a long time India's socialist government and unwieldy bureaucracy hampered Tata. The group was reluctant to pay bribes for licenses to enter new fields, and red tape and trade restrictions discouraged expansion abroad. A 1970 antitrust law ended the "managing agency" system, in which Tata Sons had held interests in subsidiaries and Tata Industries managed them for a fee; the subsidiaries became independently managed.

J. R. D. retired as chairman in 1991, and his nephew Ratan Tata took control of the company. In 1994 Tata formed a major alliance with Daimler-Benz to assemble cars. A Tata IBM joint venture in 1997 launched the first computer operating system in Hindi, India's national language (Tata sold its IBM stake in 1999).

Not every new venture flew. In 1998 Tata dropped a proposal to start an Indian airline that hadn't won government approval after three years. In 2000 Tata Tea bought UK tea bag maker Tetley, an acquisition that made Tata the world's largest tea producer. In 2001 Tata made plans to sell its pharmaceuticals unit (Rallis India) and float 10% of its information technology unit (TCS). That year Tata joined Singapore Airlines in bidding for a 40% stake in Air India being offered by the Indian government. Later in the year, however, Singapore Airlines withdrew and the deal fell through.

In 2002 Tata acquired a 25% stake in telecom giant Videsh Sanchar Nigam Ltd. (VSNL), from the Indian government. Tata said it would combine its Tata Teleservices unit with VSNL. In 2003 Tata International formed an alliance with Turbo Genset Company Limited (UK) to develop and distribute generational products and solutions used in the power generation industry. Tata Coffee signed an agreement with Starbucks to supply it with premium coffee beans starting in 2004.

EXECUTIVES

Chairman: Ratan N. Tata, age 67
Executive Office Member and Finance Director: Ishaat Hussain, age 58
Executive Office Member: R. Gopalakrishnan
Executive Office Member and Managing Director, Tata Industries: Kishor Chaukar, age 57
Executive Office Member: Arunkumar R. (Arun) Gandhi
Executive Office Member: Alan Rosling
CEO, Tata Consultancy Services: S. Ramadorai, age 61
EVP, Human Resources: Satish Pradhan
Managing Director, Tata Steel: B. Muthuraman
President, Tata Indicom Enterprise Business Unit: Ajay Pandey
CEO and SVP, Indian Hotels International Division: Rajiv Gujral
Managing Director, Tata Chemicals: Prasad Menon, age 57
Managing Director, Tata Power: Firdose Ardeshir Vandrevala, age 54
Managing Director, Tata Services: Tehmuras Rustom Doongaji
Managing Director, Tata Tea: Percy Siganporia
Managing Director, Tata Honeywell: Vinayak Deshpande, age 45
Managing Director, Tata Teleservices: S. Ramakrishnan
CEO, Tata Quality Management Services: Jehangir Ardeshir
COO, Fertiliser Business, Tata Chemicals: Kapil Mehan
SVP Finance and Secretary, Tata Sons: Farokh N. Subedar
Chief Corporate Communications, Tata Steel: Sanjay Singh

LOCATIONS

HQ: Tata Group
Tata Sons Limited, Bombay House, 24, Homi Mody St., Mumbai 400 001, India
Phone: +91-22-5665-8282   **Fax:** +91-22-5665-8160
US HQ: 1700 N. Moore St., Ste. 1005, Arlington, VA 22209
US Phone: 703-243-9787
Web: www.tata.com

PRODUCTS/OPERATIONS

2005 Sales

	% of total
Engineering	31
Materials	21
Communications & information systems	19
Services	10
Energy	8
Consumer goods	6
Chemicals	5
Total	**100**

Selected Operations

Communications and IT
  Control systems
    Nelco
    Tata Honeywell
  Information Technology
    Nelito Systems
    Tata Consultancy Services (TCS) (80%)
      Tata Infotech
    Tata Elxsi
    Tata Interactive Systems
    Tata Technologies
  Telecommunications
    Tata Cellular
    Tata Internet Services
    Tata Telecom
    Tata Teleservices
    VSNL
Engineering
  Automotive
    Tata Auto Component Systems
    Tata Cummins
    Tata Engineering
    Telco Construction Equipment Co.
    Tata Holset
  Engineering products
    TAL Manufacturing Solutions
    TRF
    Voltas
  Engineering services
    Stewarts and Lloyds of India
    Tata Construction and Projects
    Tata Korf Engineering Services
    Tata Projects
    TCE Consulting Engineers
Materials
  Composites
    Tata Advanced Materials
  Metals
    Tata Steel (Tisco)
    Tata Metaliks
    Tata Refractories
    Tata Ryerson
    Tata Sponge Iron
    Tata SSL
    Tinplate Company of India
Energy
  Tata BP Solar India
  Tata Electric Companies
Consumer Products
  Tata Ceramics
  Tata Coffee Limited
  Tata McGraw Hill Publishing Company
  Tata Tea
  Tata Tetley
  Titan Industries
  Trent

Services
  Hotels and property development
    Indian Hotels Company (Taj Group)
    Information Technology Park
    Tata Housing Development Company
  Financial services
    Tata-AIG General Insurance
    Tata-AIG Life Insurance
    Tata-AIG Risk Management
    Tata Investment Corporation
    Tata TD Waterhouse Asset Management
  International operations
    Tata International
  Other services
    Tata Economic Consultancy Services
    Tata Services
    Tata Strategic Management Group
Chemicals
  Rallis India
  Tata Chemicals
  Tata Pigments

COMPETITORS

Accor
Birla
Caterpillar
Essar Group
Fluor
Ford
Four Seasons Hotels
GE
General Motors
Hilton
Hindustan Lever
Hyatt
Indian Oil
Infosys
James Finlay
Nippon Steel
Procter & Gamble
Reliance Industries
Ritz-Carlton
RPG
Steel Authority of India
Suzuki Motor
Toyota
Wipro

HISTORICAL FINANCIALS

Company Type: Group

Income Statement

FYE: March 31

	REVENUE ($ mil.)	NET INCOME ($ mil.)	NET PROFIT MARGIN	EMPLOYEES
3/05	17,878	—	—	215,873
3/04	13,921	—	—	220,219
3/03	10,943	—	—	210,443
3/02	9,816	—	—	218,443
3/01	8,585	—	—	225,318
3/00	7,959	—	—	250,000
3/99	7,541	—	—	255,000
3/98	8,407	—	—	262,000
Annual Growth	11.4%	—	—	(2.7%)

Revenue History

Tate & Lyle PLC

Consumers get a rush from the business of Tate & Lyle — a sugar rush, that is. With operations on four continents, it is one of the world's largest producers of white and raw sugar, including leading brands Tate & Lyle (UK), Redpath (Canada), and Alcântara (Portugal). With headquarters in London, Tate & Lyle also makes sugar by-products such as molasses (used in animal feed and citric acid, glutamate, and starches used in foodstuffs and packaging. The company is also the world's supplier of sucralose, the low-calorie sweetener sold under the name SPLENDA.

With demand for SPLENDA at an all time high (it is used in more than 4,000 foods, beverages, and pharmaceuticals worldwide), Tate & Lyle is increasing its production and rationing its distribution. Some of the company's patents on Splenda will start to expire in 2006, which puts it at risk of having to compete with possible generic versions of the products. The company, however, maintains that it is difficult to manufacture sucralose on a large scale and only it is equipped to do so.

In addition to sugar products, the company uses grains, wheat, and corn to make citric acids (used in foods and beverages), starches (used in foodstuffs and packaging), and sweeteners (corn syrup, fructose, and others used in beverages, baked goods, and pharmaceuticals).

Archer Daniels Midland sold its 6% share of Tate & Lyle in 2005. British bank Barclays owns about 11%.

HISTORY

Henry Tate founded Henry Tate & Sons in 1869 and the next year began building a sugar refinery in Liverpool. Tate was noted for his philanthropy, and in 1896 he provided the money to found the Tate Gallery. When he died three years later, he left the business to his sons. In 1903 William Henry Tate took the company public, although only 17 investors, primarily family members, put up money for the company.

Abram Lyle founded his sugar company in 1881 when he bought Odam's and Plaistow Wharves, on the River Thames, to build a sugar refinery. While Tate focused on sugar cubes, Lyle concentrated on a sugary concoction called Golden Syrup.

WWI saw an interruption in raw beet sugar imports from Germany and Austria, and in 1918 the two companies began discussing a merger. Although they combined, creating Tate & Lyle in 1921, they kept separate sales organizations into the 1940s. Seeking new sources of sugar, Tate & Lyle began investing abroad. In 1937 it created the West Indies Sugar Company and built a processing plant in Jamaica.

Although WWII brought sugar rationing (1940) and both of Tate & Lyle's London factories were severely damaged by bombs, there was great demand for the company's inexpensive syrup. Following the war, a movement to nationalize Tate & Lyle failed. In the 1950s Tate & Lyle expanded, buying Rhodesian Sugar Refineries (1953, now ZSR) and Canada & Dominion Sugar Company (1959, later Redpath Industries). It added United Molasses in 1965.

Tate & Lyle acquired the only other independent British cane refiner, Manbre and Garton, in 1976. That year it entered the US market when it bought Refined Sugars. The company added

Portuguese sugar refiner Alcântara in 1983; US beet refiner Great Western Sugar Company in 1985; and Staley Continental (now A E Staley Manufacturing), a major producer of high-fructose corn syrup, in 1988. It sold Staley's food service business to SYSCO that year and bought Amstar Sugar Corporation (which became Domino Sugar). Tate & Lyle launched Sucralose, a low-calorie sweetener, in 1991 in cooperation with Johnson & Johnson. The company began investing millions in emerging markets in 1990 through acquisitions and joint ventures, including Mexico's Occidente in 1995. Although operations in Ukraine and Bulgaria were abandoned the next year, Tate & Lyle continued with new ventures in Vietnam and India.

Larry Pillard became CEO in 1996. Sucralose was approved for use in the US in 1998. The company reported disappointing profits that year due in part to low sugar prices in the US. Also in 1998 Tate & Lyle purchased the food ingredients division of Bayer Group's Haarmann & Reimer unit, renaming it Tate & Lyle Citric Acid. The deal made Tate & Lyle the only global producer of citric acid.

In 1999 Tate & Lyle sold its 61% share of Industrias de Maiz SA (Argentina). In 2000 it sold Bundaberg, its Australian sugar company, to Société Financière de Sucres and its US grain unit to J. D. Heiskell & Company. In 2001 Tate & Lyle sold off the Domino brand to a group of investors led by Flo-Sun, Inc., chairman Alfonso Fanjul and his brother, J. Pepe Fanjul. During the same year, the company sold its 51% stake in Zambia Sugar to Illova Sugar and its 15% stake in East Asia Properties to East Asia Sugar Investment Ltd. It also exited the sugar business in China with the sale of Well Pure to a group of Chinese investors.

As part of its strategy to jettison noncore or underperforming businesses, in 2002 Tate & Lyle sold its French monosodium glutamate production unit, Orsan S.A., to Ajinomoto. That year it announced plans for ingredients based on xanthan gum and related biological products made from carbohydrate feedstock.

The next year the company sold United Molasses Co. and UM Canada to Westway Holdings. That year Tate & Lyle formed a joint venture with Igene Biotechnology to develop fermented astaxanthin, a pigment used in aquaculture (specifically, to make farmed fish more red in color).

In 2004 Tate & Lyle became the sole manufacturer of SPLENDA brand of sucralose, when it renegotiated its alliance with McNeil Nutritionals regarding the product. Under the agreement, Tate produces SPLENDA and is responsible for its worldwide sales to food manufacturers; and McNeil is responsible for retail and foodservice sales. Due to customer demand, Tate & Lyle expanded sucralose production to include a plant in Singapore.

Later that same year Tate & Lyle formed a joint venture with DuPont to make an ingredient made from renewable sources such as corn to replace petrochemicals in the manufacture of clothing, plastics, and textiles. Equally owned by both companies, the company is called DuPont Tate & Lyle BioProducts, LLC. Tate & Lyle also bought South African food ingredients company Dolcré in 2004.

Continuing to add to its holdings the company acquired two companies: US specialty-food-ingredients company Continental Custom Ingredients (CCI) and Italy's Cesalpinia group of companies (Cesalpinia Foods).

EXECUTIVES

Non-Executive Chairman: Sir David Lees, age 68, $495,977 pay
CEO: Iain Ferguson, age 49, $2,216,866 pay
COO: Stanley Musesengwa, age 52, $1,429,691 pay
SVP, Industrial Ingredients: Peter Boynton
VP, Global Applications and Technical Services: Michael (Mike) Augustine
VP, Global Marketing: Greg Morency
VP, Global Research and Development: Robert Schanefelt
VP, Global Research and Development Engineering and Biochemicals: Jeff Lievense
Group President, Manufacturing & Technology: Loren Luppes
Group Director, Finance: Simon Gifford, age 58, $1,429,691 pay
President, North American Cereal Sweeteners & Starches; President, AE Staley: D. Lynn Grider
President, Sugar Americas: Silvio Allamandi
Group Director, Human Resources: Corry Wille
Managing Director, Food & Industrial Ingredients: Deiderick Ried
Director, Corporate Development: Stuart Strathdee, age 53, $894,261 pay
Director, Marketing Americas: Harvey Chimoff
Manager, Communications: Victoria Betteridge
Manager, Public Relations: Ferne Hudson
Manager, Research Technical Resource: Joni Simms
General Counsel and Secretary: Robert (Rob) Gibber, age 42
Head, Investor Relations: Mark Robinson
Auditors: PricewaterhouseCoopers LLP

LOCATIONS

HQ: Tate & Lyle PLC
Sugar Quay, Lower Thames St.,
London EC3R 6DQ, United Kingdom
Phone: +44-20-7626-6525   **Fax:** +44-20-7623-5213
US HQ: 2200 E. El Dorado St., Decatur, IL 62525
US Phone: 217-423-4411   **US Fax:** 217-421-3167
Web: www.tate-lyle.co.uk

Tate & Lyle has 61 manufacturing and production sites in 28 countries, mainly in the Americas, Europe, and Southeast Asia.

PRODUCTS/OPERATIONS

Selected Brands
Alcântara (Portugal)
Amylum (Europe)
Rebalance (Europe)
Redpath (Canada)
SPLENDA (worldwide)
Tate & Lyle (UK)

Selected Products
Animal feed (molasses)
Corn sweeteners (dextrose, fructose, glucose, high fructose corn syrup, maltodextrin)
Fermentation products (amino acid, citric acid, ethanol, monosodium glutamate, polyols, potable alcohol)
Starches and starch derivatives
Sugar (beet, cane, raw, white)

Selected Subsidiaries and Affiliates
A. E. Staley Manufacturing Co. (corn sweeteners and starches, US)
Alcântara Refinarias — Açucares, SA (sugar refining, Portugal)
Amylum UK Limited (corn sweeteners and starches)
DuPont Tate & Lyle BioProducts, LLC (industrial ingredients)
Hansa Melasse — Handelsgesellschaft mbH (molasses, Germany)
Melitalia SpA (molasses, Italy)
Mexama, SA de CV (citric acid, Mexico)
Nordisk Melasse A/S (molasses, Denmark)
Orsan Guangzhou Gourmet Powder Company Limited (glutamate producer, China)
United Molasses (Ireland) Ltd. (molasses)

COMPETITORS

ADM	Greencore
Ag Processing	Imperial Sugar
American Crystal Sugar	Merisant Worldwide
Associated British Foods	NutraSweet
C&H Sugar	Onex
Cargill	Penford
Connell Company	PPB
Corn Products	Südzucker
International	Sterling Sugars
CSM	Tereos
Cumberland Packing	Tongaat-Hulett
Danisco	U.S. Sugar
Florida Crystals	

HISTORICAL FINANCIALS

Company Type: Public

Income Statement

FYE: March 31

	REVENUE ($ mil.)	NET INCOME ($ mil.)	NET PROFIT MARGIN	EMPLOYEES
3/05	6,279	263	4.2%	11,200
3/04	5,782	281	4.9%	11,500
3/03	4,985	208	4.2%	9,500
3/02	5,623	168	3.0%	8,503
3/01	5,872	(382)	—	17,465
3/00*	8,987	293	3.3%	20,085
9/98	6,992	211	3.0%	21,494
9/97	7,504	164	2.2%	21,435
9/96	8,063	272	3.4%	21,281
Annual Growth	(3.1%)	(0.4%)	—	(7.7%)

*Fiscal year change

2005 Year-End Financials

Debt ratio: 76.9%
Return on equity: 14.1%
Cash ($ mil.): 667
Current ratio: 2.32
Long-term debt ($ mil.): 1,471

Net Income History

OTC: TATYY

300	
200	
100	
0	
-100	
-200	
-300	
-400	

9/95 9/96 9/97 9/98 3/00 3/01 3/02 3/03 3/04 3/05

Tatung Co.

This company can make sure you stay connected, stay cool, and cook a perfect bowl of rice. Tatung manufactures computer products (PCs, servers, monitors, workstations), appliances (air conditioners, refrigerators, rice cookers), industrial goods (cable and wire, transformers, motors), and medical devices (blood pressure monitors, electrical massage devices, thermometers). The company also offers product development, prototyping, and logistics services. The family-run company maintains a close relationship with Tatung University and Tatung Senior High School, institutions endowed by Tatung's founder, Shan-Chih Lin.

Tatung has subsidiaries in more than a dozen countries. Taiwan-based subsidiaries include Tatung OTIS Elevator (a joint venture with US-based elevator maker Otis Elevator), Chunghwa Picture Tubes (cathode-ray tube and LCD products), San Chih Semiconductor (silicon wafers), and Taiwan Telecommunication Industry (video-conferencing and phone products). Its US operations include Tatung Company of America (displays and appliances) and Tatung Science and Technology (SPARC workstations and servers).

HISTORY

Shan-Chih Lin founded a construction company, the Shan-Chih Business Association, in 1918. Projects during its 30-year lifespan included the Taiwanese government's Building of the Executive Yuan, which houses the country's ministry offices.

The company entered heavy industry in 1946 when it began repairing railway cars. It diversified into electric products in 1949 with fans, which it started exporting five years later. In 1950 the company changed its name to Tatung ("great harmony").

Because he believed strongly in the importance of education, when Lin retired in 1942, he donated 80% of his assets to the Hsieh-Chih Association for the Development of Industry, which went on to administer scholarships, awards, the Tatung Institute of Technology, and the Hsieh-Chih Industrial Publishing Company. The philanthropist's bequest established the Tatung Schools-Company, made up of the Institute of Technology and Tatung High School. This education-industry cooperative provides hands-on training in Tatung factories and offices. The Institute of Technology was founded in 1956.

During the 1960s Tatung expanded further into home appliances and electronics, adding refrigerators (1961), air conditioners (1964), and televisions (1964) to its product line. Taiwan Telecommunication was formed in 1966.

Lin died in 1971. In 1972 Lin's grandson, Lin Weishan (W. S.) was named president; he began expanding Tatung's operations overseas. Tatung established US subsidiary Tatung Co. of America that year, initially to make electric fans. In 1973 Tatung formed a joint venture with Japanese computer maker Fujitsu. Tatung would go on that decade to establish offices in Japan (1975) and Korea (1979).

The company's joint venture with US company Otis Elevator was formed in 1983. Tatung continued to expand overseas during the 1980s, establishing subsidiaries in the UK (1981) and Germany (1985). During that period the company continued to move production overseas, shipping the finished goods back to Taiwan as imports.

Tatung's profits slipped in the early 1990s as Taiwan's economy slowed, but the company rebounded, signing a deal with Packard Bell (folded into NEC) in 1991 to supply the computer marketer with 100,000 PCs a month. In 1994 the company formed an alliance with telecommunications company QUALCOMM to develop cellular phone systems for Taiwan.

The following year Tatung subsidiary Chunghwa Picture Tubes began making large picture tubes for Toshiba. Tatung started making computer motherboards in 1996.

To keep pace with Internet use, the company in 1997 introduced an Internet access set-top box. Sales were down that fiscal year, a result of the Asian economic crisis and falling cathode-ray tube prices. In 1998 Tatung unveiled a DVD player and PC Cinema, a PC which combined TV, computer, and telephone functions with Internet access.

In 1999 Chunghwa Picture Tubes opened Taiwan's first factory to build thin-film transistor LCDs. The subsidiary's chairman was indicted later that year for allegedly investing foreign capital to manipulate parent Tatung's stock. In 2000 Tatung spun off its information and communications department as a separate company, Tatung System Technologies.

Tatung jumped on the mobile computing bandwagon in 2001, introducing a tablet PC. Bucking the downsizing trend in the electronics industry, the company expanded its production capacity in China and Europe the next year.

EXECUTIVES

Chairman: Lin Tingsheng
President: Lin Weishan
EVP: W. T. Lin
Marketing Director: Greg Hwang
Production Director: H. H. Lin
Managing Director, Tatung (UK) Ltd.: C. T. Lin
President, Tatung Science and Technology: Kam Chan
European Manager, Tatung Server Europe: Andre Hu
UK Sales Manager, Tatung Server: Mark Burnett
Sales Manager: Shawn Chang

LOCATIONS

HQ: Tatung Co.
22 Chungshan North Rd., Sec. 3, Taipei, Taiwan
Phone: +886-22-592-5252 **Fax:** +886-22-592-1813
US HQ: 2850 El Presidio St., Long Beach, CA 90810
US Phone: 310-637-2105 **US Fax:** 310-637-8484
Web: www.tatung.com.tw

Tatung has operations in Canada, China, Hong Kong, Indonesia, Japan, Malaysia, Mexico, the Netherlands, Singapore, South Korea, Taiwan, Thailand, the UK, and the US.

PRODUCTS/OPERATIONS

Selected Products

Computers and Communications
  Monitors
  PCs
  Peripherals
  Servers
  Silicon wafers
  Workstations

Consumer Products
  Air conditioners and dehumidifiers
  Appliances
    Compressors
    Microwave ovens
    Refrigerators
    Rice cookers
  Office furniture and office furniture systems
  Televisions and video displays

Industrial Equipment
  Copper rods
  Cyclos
  Elevators
  Industrial castings
  Motors
  Switch gears
  Transformers
  Varnishes and varnish thinners
  Wire and cable (including communications and power cable)

COMPETITORS

Acer
CASIO COMPUTER
Dell
Dover
Electrolux
Emerson Electric
Fuji Electric
Fujitsu
GE
Hewlett-Packard
Hitachi
IBM
Kyocera
Lennox
Lenovo
LG Group
Marconi
Marubeni
Matsushita
Maytag
Mitsumi Electric
NEC
Oki Electric
Philips Electronics
Pioneer
Samsung
SANYO
Sharp
Siemens
Sony
Sumitomo Electric
Sun Microsystems
Taiwan Semiconductor
Toshiba
United Microelectronics
United Technologies
Whirlpool
Yamaha
Zenith

HISTORICAL FINANCIALS

Company Type: Public

Income Statement

FYE: December 31

	REVENUE ($ mil.)	NET INCOME ($ mil.)	NET PROFIT MARGIN	EMPLOYEES
12/02	4,327	(146)	—	35,000
12/01	3,891	(247)	—	20,000
12/00	4,133	107	2.6%	20,671
12/99	4,471	148	3.3%	35,000
12/98	2,921	(14)	—	
12/97	2,160	123	5.7%	19,570
12/96	3,040	270	8.9%	20,671
12/95	3,104	242	7.8%	19,491
12/94	2,466	205	8.3%	17,869
12/93	2,041	132	6.4%	26,000
Annual Growth	8.7%	—	—	3.4%

2002 Year-End Financials

Debt ratio: —
Return on equity: —
Cash ($ mil.): 707
Current ratio: 1.12
Long-term debt ($ mil.): 1,061

Net Income History

Exchange: Taiwan

TDK

While TDK may be best known for blank audiotapes and CDs, the company actually records most of its sales from the sale of manufactured electronic materials and components. The company, which pioneered the use of the magnetic substance ferrite in the 1930s, is a major supplier of such products as ferrite magnets, transformer and inductor cores, and multilayer chip capacitors. Other components include voltage-controlled oscillators, noise reduction filters, and magnetic recording heads used inside computer disk drives. The company also offers a range of recordable media including CDs and DVDs.

In 2005 TDK sold its semiconductor business in order to focus on other product lines. Also that year, the company acquired the Lambda power supply systems business of Invensys.

HISTORY

Kanzo Saito, who had previously raised rabbits for their fur, took out a patent in 1935 on ferrite, a type of ceramic made mainly from iron oxide that held promise for electronics applications. (Japan's Yogoru Kato is credited with inventing the material.) Saito founded Tokyo Denkikagaku Kogyo K.K. (TDK) to pioneer the mass production of ferrite and output rose quickly as developers found countless new uses for the substance. Saito handed over the presidency of the company in 1946 to Teiichi Yamazaki, who expanded TDK's portfolio into products such as magnetic recording tape (1952).

The company's global thrust began when it opened a Los Angeles office in 1959. Two years later it was listing shares on the Tokyo Stock Exchange. TDK branched into cassette tapes in 1966 and electromagnetic wave absorbers in 1968, the year the company opened its first overseas manufacturing center in Taiwan.

During the 1970s TDK launched operations in Australia, Europe, and South America. It began listing its shares on the New York Stock Exchange in 1982. That year the company also introduced a solar battery. In 1983 TDK officially changed its name to TDK Corporation.

In 1987 Hiroshi Sato was appointed president of the company. TDK bought integrated circuit maker Silicon Systems in 1989 (sold in 1996 to Texas Instruments) as Sato began to modernize the company's offerings and organization. With a conservative management style, he'd often wait to see how other companies fared in new markets before committing TDK, prompting the industry to label him the "gambler who follows someone else." During his tenure, Sato gave the company solid footholds in niches such as optical disks, high-density heads, and cellular phone components.

To reverse falling profits in 1992, Sato made plans to eliminate managers by playing on the Japanese sense of honor — he asked them to accept pay cuts and work on standby at home until their retirement, expecting that they would simply resign. Sato was forced to scuttle the plan amid international outcries and depleted morale.

The company revamped its organization in 1994 around four operating divisions. That year it began producing high-end magnetic heads in China, but poor demand and a weakened yen hurt sales and profits. Meanwhile, TDK had become the global leader in magnetic tape manufacturing.

The company bought UK-based communications equipment maker Grey Cell Systems in 1997, thereby gaining a European presence in the data transmission market. In 1998 Sato and Yamazaki retired and Hajime Sawabe was tapped as CEO. After a sluggish Japanese economy caused earnings to decline in 1999, TDK restructured its product lines again the next year and acquired California-based Headway Technologies, a maker of giant magnetoresistive heads used in computer disk drives.

TDK, like other high tech firms, suffered the ravages of the deep slump in the electronics market during the early 2000s. Sales of components fell off as manufacturers reacted to weak demand for PCs, mobile phones, and other electronics gear.

Competitive pricing in the CD-R market led to losses for TDK's recording media business in 2001, prompting the company to close many of its manufacturing plants and outsource its blank tape and CD manufacturing. Meanwhile, price pressures from competitors in China and Taiwan, especially in the recordable media sector, added to TDK's woes and contributed to losses in 2002.

The company late in 2003 sold subsidiary TDK Mediactive, which makes video games for PCs and game consoles, to Take-Two Interactive.

EXECUTIVES

President and CEO: Hajime Sawabe, age 63
EVP and General Manager, Circuit Devices Business: Kiyoshi Ito, age 61
EVP and General Manager, Data Storage and Thin Film Technology Components Business: Takehiro Kamigama, age 47
SVP and General Manager, China Business Development: Hirokazu Nakanishi, age 61
SVP and General Manager, Administration Group and Environment: Jiro Iwasaki, age 59
SVP and General Manager, Electronic Components Sales and Marketing: Shinji Yoko, age 57
SVP and General Manager, Intellectual Properties Center, Materials Research Center, and Information Technology Research Center: Takeshi Nomura, age 53
Corporate Officer and General Manager, Corporate Communications, Administration Group: Michinori Katayama, age 58
Corporate Officer and General Manager, Corporate Research and Development Center: Kenryo Namba, age 58
Corporate Officer; General Manager, Finance and Accounting Department; and CFO: Seiji Enami, age 58
President, TDK U.S.A. Corporation: Francis J. Sweeney
Auditors: KPMG

LOCATIONS

HQ: TDK Corporation
1-13-1 Nihonbashi, Chuo-ku,
Tokyo 103-8272, Japan
Phone: +81-3-5201-7102   **Fax:** +81-3-5201-7114
US HQ: 901 Franklin Ave., Garden City, NY 11530
US Phone: 516-535-2600   **US Fax:** 516-294-8318
Web: www.tdk.co.jp

TDK has operations in Australia, Brazil, China, France, Germany, Hong Kong, Hungary, Italy, Luxembourg, Malaysia, the Philippines, Poland, Singapore, South Korea, Sweden, Taiwan, Thailand, the UK, and the US.

2005 Sales

	$ mil.	% of total
Japan	1,490.5	24
Europe	664.4	11
North America	550.0	9
Other regions	3,443.3	56
Total	**6,148.2**	**100**

PRODUCTS/OPERATIONS

2005 Sales

	$ mil.	% of total
Electronics		
Recording devices	2,192.3	36
Electronic materials	1,633.7	26
Electronic devices	1,087.7	18
Semiconductors & others	181.8	3
Recording media & systems	1,052.7	17
Total	**6,148.2**	**100**

Selected Products

Data Storage
 Magnetic heads (hard disk drives)
 Thermal printing heads
Electronic Components
 Anechoic chambers
 Capacitors
 Converters
 Cores and magnets
  Ferrite
  Metal
  Rubber and plastic
 Electrodes
 Ferrite electromagnetic wave absorbers
 Inductors and coils
 Noise filters
 Optical isolators
 Oscillators
 Power supplies
 PTC/NTC thermistors
 Sensors
 Transformers
 Uninterrupted Power Supply (UPS)
 Varistors
Recording Media and Systems
 Audio tape
 Computer-aided instruction software
 Magnetic tape (computers)
 MiniDiscs
 PC cards and peripherals
 Removable media
  CD-R/RW
  DVD-R/DVD-RAM
 Video tape
Other
 Factory automation systems
 MPEG-4 based streaming server software
 Organic EL displays
 Solar cells

COMPETITORS

AVX
EPCOS
Fujifilm
Fujitsu
Hitachi
Imation
Kyocera
Matsushita
Murata Manufacturing
Philips Electronics
Pioneer
Samsung
Solectron
Sony
Toshiba
Vishay Intertechnology
Yamaha

HISTORICAL FINANCIALS

Company Type: Public

Income Statement   FYE: March 31

	REVENUE ($ mil.)	NET INCOME ($ mil.)	NET PROFIT MARGIN	EMPLOYEES
3/05	6,148	311	5.1%	37,115
3/04	6,216	397	6.4%	36,804
3/03	5,074	100	2.0%	31,705
3/02	4,324	(194)	—	32,249
3/01	5,564	355	6.4%	37,251
3/00	6,363	479	7.5%	34,321
3/99	5,589	380	6.8%	31,305
3/98	5,278	442	8.4%	29,747
3/97	5,006	486	9.7%	28,055
3/96	5,108	261	5.1%	29,070
Annual Growth	**2.1%**	**2.0%**	**—**	**2.8%**

2005 Year-End Financials

Debt ratio: 0.0%	No. of shares (mil.): 132
Return on equity: 5.5%	Dividends
Cash ($ mil.): 2,351	Yield: 0.4%
Current ratio: 3.90	Payout: 12.3%
Long-term debt ($ mil.): 1	Market value ($ mil.): 9,073

Stock History   NYSE: TDK

	STOCK PRICE ($) FY Close	P/E High/Low	Earnings	Dividends	Book Value
3/05	68.61	34 26	2.35	0.29	45.16
3/04	75.77	26 11	3.00	0.42	41.05
3/03	38.32	76 44	0.75	0.36	34.80
3/02	53.50	— —	(1.46)	0.49	33.05
3/01	65.90	59 20	2.67	0.56	38.66
3/00	131.50	40 21	3.59	0.52	39.91
3/99	80.75	32 20	2.85	0.18	33.02
3/98	76.75	29 21	3.32	0.45	29.63
3/97	67.25	19 14	3.65	0.23	28.71
3/96	51.88	28 21	1.97	0.23	28.84
Annual Growth	**3.2%**	**— —**	**2.0%**	**2.6%**	**5.1%**

Telecom Italia

Former state monopoly Telecom Italia is facing up to increasing competition. Italy's #1 fixed-line operator and #1 wireless provider (through Telecom Italia Mobile, or TIM), the company also holds stakes in telecom operations outside Italy, especially mobile phone carriers mainly in Europe and Central and South America. It operates a leading ISP (Tin.it) but has sold its nearly 62% stake in directories unit SEAT Pagine Gialle to an investor group in a deal valued at $3.55 billion. The company then created a new media division: Telecom Italia Media. Telecom Italia also provides information technology. Former rival Olivetti controlled 55% of Telecom Italia before a complex merger and reorganization.

As are all telecommunications companies, Telecom Italia is embracing convergence as the future of the industry. Evidence of the company's commitment to this strategy is its 2005 reorganization that eliminated the separate wireline and wireless division in favor of a "one company" strategy of integrated management. The effort should help to simplify a complicated management structure and reduce debt at the same time.

The company is selling its fixed-line assets outside Italy. It also has sold its 81% stake in Greek wireless carrier Hellas Telecommunications, to US-based private equity firms Texas Pacific Group and Apax Partners in a deal valued at $1.4 billion. It also has sold its stakes in Spanish joint venture Auna and satellite unit Telespazio (to Finmeccanica) and has sold 60% its holdings in IT services and consulting company Finsiel to Italian outsourcing firm Gruppo COS (it is selling its remaining 20% to Grupo COS in late 2005).

The company is increasing its ownership in Brasil Telecom by acquiring the stake held by Brazil's Opportunity investment bank in a deal valued at $441 million. The agreement settles a long-standing dispute over control of the wireless carrier, Brazil's third-largest telecom company.

Telecom Italia has acquired the Ebisnews unit from e.Biscom for an undisclosed amount. It later bought TMNews, which distributes Associated Press news and other content to media and corporate subscribers.

HISTORY

After gaining political power in Italy, Benito Mussolini began a program of nationalization, focusing first on three major banks and their equity portfolios. Included were three local phone companies that became the core of Societa Finanziaria Telefonica (STET), created in 1933 to handle Italy's phone services under the state's industrial holding company, Istituto per La Ricostruzione Industriale (IRI).

Germany and Italy grew closer in the years leading up to WWII, and Italian equipment makers entered a venture with Siemens to make phone equipment. STET came through the war with most of its infrastructure intact and a monopoly on phone service in Italy. Siemens' properties, along with those of other equipment makers, were taken over by another company, TETI, which was nationalized and put under STET's control in 1958. This expanded STET's monopoly to include equipment manufacturing.

Italy's industries were increasingly nationalized under IRI. Companies within the IRI family forged alliances with each other and with independent companies, which frequently were absorbed into STET.

STET's scope expanded during the 1960s and 1970s to include satellite and data communications, but its monopoly was undermined by new technologies such as faxes, PCs, and teleconferencing. In the technology race among equipment makers, STET fell behind. And in a satellite communications era, STET's status as a necessary long-distance carrier was threatened. Despite these pressures, change did not come easily to STET. State monopolies maintained popular support, not only on nationalistic grounds but also because of labor's strong anticompetitive stance.

Anticipating privatization, however, IRI reorganized STET in 1994 and poured new capital into the company. STET's five telecom companies were merged into one, Telecom Italia. Its mobile phone business was spun off as Telecom Italia Mobile (TIM) in 1995.

To end political feuding, the government abruptly replaced the heads of STET and Telecom

Italia in 1997. Telecom Italia was merged with STET, which took the Telecom Italia name and was privatized that year. Berardino Libonati became chairman, and Franco Bernabe, formerly CEO of oil company ENI, took the helm as CEO. The company had begun taking stakes in foreign telecom companies, including Mobilkom Austria, Spanish broadcaster Retevision, and — as European Union competition began in 1998 — Telekom Austria.

Erstwhile rival Olivetti launched a hostile takeover bid for Telecom Italia in 1999. Though Telecom Italia tried to fend off the smaller firm with various maneuvers, including a proposed merger with Deutsche Telekom, Olivetti gained 55% of Telecom Italia. Olivetti CEO Roberto Colaninno took over as chairman and CEO.

That year Telecom Italia sold 50% of Stream, its pay-TV unit, to an investor group led by News Corp. And in a venture with Lockheed Martin and TRW, Telecom Italia planned to develop a $3.5 billion global broadband satellite system called Astrolink.

In 2001 Colaninno and several other Telecom Italia officials were named as suspects in an investigation of whether the company had violated accounting, conflict-of-interest, and share-manipulation laws. Colaninno was replaced when tire maker Pirelli and Edizione Holding, the parent company of the Benetton Group, acquired a 23% stake in Olivetti.

Telecom Italia teamed up with Rupert Murdoch's News Corp. to develop the Stream pay TV joint venture, renamed Sky Italia. The venture gained a kick-start when the two companies teamed to buy Italian pay-TV business Telepiu from Vivendi Universal in a cash and debt assumption deal that was valued at $871 million. Telecom Italia then sold a 30% stake in the venture to News Corp. It retained a 20% share with News Corp. controlling 80%.

Once the subsidiary, Telecom Italia became the parent company after the 2003 merger with former parent Olivetti. The reorganization simplified a corporate structure that was at best confusing. Because Telecom Italia accounted for more than 95% of the revenues of Olivetti, the reorganization also kept the focus on the core business. The merger was met with favor among market watchers and some shareholders although a group of international investors opposed the restructuring.

EXECUTIVES

Chairman: Marco Tronchetti Provera, age 57, $5,389,829 pay
Deputy Chairman: Gilberto Benetton, age 64
CEO and Director: Carlo Orazio Buora, age 59
Operations CEO and Director: Riccardo Ruggiero, age 45
Head of Finance, Administration, and Control; Head of Internet and Media Business Unit; Managing Director, Telecom Italia Media: Enrico Parazzini, age 61
Head of Human Resources and Organization: Gustavo Emanuele Bracco, age 57
Head of Purchasing: Germanio Spreafico, age 53
Head of Mobile Business Unit and Director; Managing Director, Telecom Italia Mobile: Marco De Benedetti, age 43
Head of Communication and Image: Gian Carlo Rocco di Torrepadula
Head of Corporate and Legal Affairs: Aldo Cappuccio, age 56
Head of Telecom Italia Latin America: Paolo Dal Pino, age 43
Head of Internal Audit: Armando Focaroli, age 60
Head of Public and Economic Affairs: Riccardo Perissich, age 63

Head of International Affairs: Giampaolo Zambeletti
Head of International and Legal Affairs: Nicola Verdicchio
Head of Investor Relations: Valeria Leone
General Counsel: Francesco Chiappetta, age 45
Chairman and CEO, Olivetti Tecnost S.p.A.: Giovanni Ferrario, age 57
Auditors: Reconta Ernst & Young S.p.A.

LOCATIONS

HQ: Telecom Italia S.p.A.
Corso d'Italia 41, 00198 Rome, Italy
Phone: +39-06-36-881   **Fax:** +39-06-36-882-965
Web: www.telecomitalia.it

2004 Sales

	$ mil.	% of total
Europe		
Italy	33,334	79
Other countries	3,506	8
Central & South America	4,224	10
North America	727	2
Australia, Africa & Asia	523	1
Total	**42,314**	**100**

PRODUCTS/OPERATIONS

2004 Sales

	$ mil.	% of total
Wireline	23,441	49
Mobile	17,210	36
South America	1,435	3
Information technology (IT)		
IT Group	1,287	3
IT Market	973	2
Olivetti Tecnost	802	2
Internet & Media	796	2
Other revenues	1,576	3
Adjustments	(5,207)	—
Total	**42,314**	**100**

Selected Subsidiaries and Affiliates

Telecommunications
  Atesia S.p.A. (telemarketing)
  Avea Iletisim Hizmetleri A.S. (40%, Turkey)
  BBNed N.V. (96%, telecommunications services, The Netherlands)
  Corporación Digitel C.A. (Venezuela)
  HanseNet Telekommunikation GmbH (broadband network operator, Germany)
  Latin America Nautilus S.A. (70%, installation and maintenance of submarine cable systems)
  Loquendo S.p.A.
  MED-1 Submarine Cables Ltd. (23%, construction and maintenance of submarine cable systems)
  Mediterranean Nautilus S.A. (63%, installation and maintenance of submarine cable systems)
  Path.net S.p.A. (99.9%, networking systems and telecommunications)
  Telecom Italia Deutschland GmbH
  Telecom Italia Wireline
  Telecontact Center S.p.A.
  Telemedia International Italia S.p.A. (TMI, acquisition of telecommunications companies)
  Telecom Italia Sparkle Group (development of international services for heavy users such as fixed-line operators, ISPs, and international companies)
    Intelcom San Marina S.p.A.
    Pan European Backbone
    Telecom Italia of North America Inc.
    Telecom Italia Sparkle S.p.A.
  TIM Brasil Serviços e Participações S.A.(Brazil)
  Blah! S.A. (formerly TIMNet.com, Brazil)
  CRC Ltda.
  Starcell S.A.
  TIM Brasil Serviços e Participações Group
  TIM Celular S.A. (Brazil)
  Maxitel S.A.
  TIM Participações S.A. (24%)
  TIM Sul S.A.
  TIM Nordeste Telecomunicações S.A.
  TIM Hellas Telecommunications S.A. (81%, Greece)
  TIM International N.V. (formerly STET Mobile Holding N.V., The Netherlands)

South America
  Entel Bolivia Group
  Telecom Argentina Group
  Telecom Italia America Latina
  Telecom Italia South America
Information Technology
  IT Group (IT activities of the Telecom Italia Group)
    EPIClink S.p.A.
    IT Teleom Group
      IT Telecom S.p.A.
      Teco Soft Argentina S.A.
      Telesoft Russia ZAO
    IT Market (IT business activities)
      Eustema S.p.A.
      Webegg Group
        Software Factory S.p.A.
        Teleap S.p.A.
        Webegg S.p.A. (30%)
Olivetti Tecnost Group
  Cell-Tel S.p.A.
  Innovis S.p.A.
  Olivetti I-Jet S.p.A.
  Olivetti Tecnost International B.V.
  Olivetti Tecnost S.p.A.
  Wirelab S.p.A.
Internet and Media
  Buffetti Group (office products)
  Giallo Professional Publishing S.p.A. (GPP, publishing and advertising)
  Holding Media e Communicazione Group (TV)
  Matrix (Internet services)
  Telecom Italia Media S.p.A. (media and Internet services)
  Tin.it (Internet services)
  TM News

COMPETITORS

BT	Imagistics
Cable & Wireless	MCI
Canon	Ricoh
Danka	SFR Cegetel
Deutsche Telekom	Swisscom
FastWeb	Telefónica
France Telecom	Tiscali
Hewlett-Packard	Vodafone Omnitel
Hutchison Whampoa	Wind Telecomunicazioni
IBM	Xerox

HISTORICAL FINANCIALS

Company Type: Public

Income Statement

FYE: December 31

	REVENUE ($ mil.)	NET INCOME ($ mil.)	NET PROFIT MARGIN	EMPLOYEES
12/04	42,314	1,058	2.5%	91,365
12/03	38,785	1,499	3.9%	93,187
12/02	31,929	(338)	—	106,620
12/01*	27,468	(1,843)	—	116,020
12/99	25,989	1,666	6.4%	120,973
12/98	29,302	2,317	7.9%	122,300
12/97	24,203	1,475	6.1%	127,451
12/96	24,153	1,033	4.3%	126,381
12/95	23,588	921	3.9%	132,548
12/94	20,822	719	3.5%	139,346
Annual Growth	8.2%	4.4%	—	(4.6%)

*Irregular reporting interval

2004 Year-End Financials

Debt ratio: 242.7%
Return on equity: 5.2%
Cash ($ mil.): 11,601
Current ratio: 1.50
Long-term debt ($ mil.): 49,872

No. of shares (mil.): 1,612
Dividends
  Yield: 3.1%
  Payout: 233.3%
Market value ($ mil.): 65,874

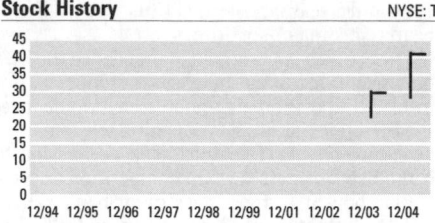

	STOCK PRICE ($) FY Close	P/E High/Low		PER SHARE ($) Earnings	Dividends	Book Value
12/04	40.87	76	53	0.54	1.26	12.75
12/03	29.70	34	26	0.88	0.00	12.57
Annual Growth	37.6%	—	—	(38.6%)	—	1.5%

Telefonica CTC Chile

Once a telecom dictator, Compañía de Telecomunicaciones de Chile is now battling to keep its top ranking in a highly competitive market. Known as Telefónica CTC Chile, the former state monopoly provides local phone access and long-distance services through subsidiaries Telefónica Mundo 188 and Globus (formerly VTR Larga Distancia). It also provides data transmission, directory services, and public phones. It has sold its 35% stake in Sonda, Chile's largest information systems provider. It also is selling its mobile communications subsidiary, Telefónica Móvil, the largest wireless provider in Chile, to Telefónica Móviles in a deal valued at $1 billion. Spain's Telefónica controls about 40% of the company.

Telefónica CTC Chile controls almost 90% of the local phone access market and handles more than a third of the long-distance market.

Having one of the world's first all-digital networks, CTC is well equipped to handle Chile's telecom needs, though competition is fierce. There is a lot of room for growth in Chile, where the lack of phone lines has aided the wireless market: Telefónica CTC Chile's mobile subsidiary has more than 1 million cellular customers.

Restructuring in the face of the telecom slump, the company in 2002 cut 900 jobs and reorganized into three main business units: consumer and small business customers, major business, and mobile services. It also sold a 25% stake in Sonda to Sonda founder Andres Navarro in a deal valued at $37.5 million. The deal also gave Navarro an option to acquire the remaining 35% stake held by CTC.

HISTORY

Telecommunications in Chile began in 1880, four years after Alexander Graham Bell's invention of the telephone, with the establishment of Compañía de Teléfonos de Edison in Valparaiso.

The International Telephone and Telegraph Corporation (ITT) bought the company's 26,205 phones in 1927. Three years later the Compañía de Teléfonos de Chile S.A. (CTC) was formed to acquire local phone companies. CTC became ITT's largest phone company in South America by gaining a 50-year concession that controlled 92% of Chile's phones. CTC became very valuable to ITT; by 1962 it provided about 12% of ITT's total profits. CTC was ITT's last phone property in South America to escape nationalization. In 1970 ITT CEO Harold Geneen, fearing that the election of Marxist Salvador Allende as president would lead to CTC's nationalization, met clandestinely with CIA officials to discuss how to prevent Allende's inauguration.

Allende won the election. The Chilean government assumed management control of CTC in 1971 but to delay having to compensate ITT, did not formally expropriate CTC. During sensitive negotiations over compensation, internal ITT memos that discussed the anti-Allende plans came to light. Allende offered a mere $12 million for CTC, about $141 million less than CTC was worth.

Allende was killed in a 1973 coup led by General Augusto Pinochet, who was to run Chile under a cruel military dictatorship for the next 17 years. Pinochet agreed to pay ITT's price for CTC, and in 1974 the Corporación de Fomento de la Producción (CORFO, or Corporation for the Promotion of Production) bought the 80% of the company that had been owned by ITT.

CORFO sold 30% of its CTC shares to Bond Corporation Chile in 1988. A subsidiary of Telefónica de España (today Telefónica), the Spanish telephone monopoly, bought Bond Chile stock in 1990 and changed Bond Chile's name to Telefónica Internacional Chile. Later that year CTC became the first South American company to be listed on the NYSE.

In 1994 Chile became the first Latin American country to allow all comers to offer fixed-line phone service. Although deregulation increased competition and slashed long-distance prices in 1994, other regulatory changes expanded CTC's protected local calling areas. CTC increased local call prices as much as 70%. That year CTC acquired 80% of Intercom, Chile's largest cable TV company.

The company changed its name to Compañía de Telecomunicaciones de Chile S.A. in 1995 and won the right to expand service to all regions of Chile. In 1996 CTC merged its cable operations with those of Metropolis to form Metropolis-Intercom, a cable TV company with over 40% of the market; it also merged its cellular operations with those of VTR-Celular, forming Startel, to achieve national coverage. That year CTC joined a Telefónica-led consortium that won a 35% stake in telecom company Companhia Riograndense de Telecomunicações in Brazil's first privatization auction.

In 1998, the year Pinochet retired, CTC received government approval to acquire VTR Larga Distancia, Chile's #4 long-distance carrier, despite regulatory concerns over the possible stifling of competition. A year later CTC sold its Internet division to Telefónica (as part of that company's Terra Networks subsidiary) and acquired 60% of Sonda, Chile's largest information systems provider. It also began using the brand name Telefónica CTC Chile. The next year the company announced the sale of its cable TV assets. In 2001 CTC created a new subsidiary to explore opportunities with fixed wireless local loop technology.

EXECUTIVES

Chairman: Bruno Philippi, age 61, $128,621 pay
Deputy Chairman: Narcís S. Serra, age 61, $57,736 pay
CEO: José Moles Valenzuela
Corporate Manager, Operations, and CTO:
Franco Faccilongo, age 49
Corporate Manager, CFO, and General Manager, t-gestiona: Julio Covarrubias, age 47
Corporate Manager, Small and Medium Business and Professionals: Luis F. de Godoy, age 41
Corporate Manager, Residential Communications:
Rafael Zamora, age 39
General Counsel and Secretary: Cristián Aninat, age 49
Corporate Manager, Regulation: Humberto Soto, age 46
Corporate Manager, Strategy and Business Development: Nicolás Domínguez, age 35
Corporate Manager, Management Control:
Diego Martínez-Caro, age 35
Corporate Manager, Internal Auditing: Jesús García, age 38
Corporate Manager, Human Resources:
Mauricio Malbrán, age 50
General Manager, Telefónica Empresas: Ricardo Majluf, age 58
Head of Investor Relations: Sofía Chellew
Auditors: Deloitte & Touche

LOCATIONS

HQ: Compañía de Telecomunicaciones de Chile S.A.
Avenida Providencia 111, Piso 2, Santiago, Chile
Phone: +56-2-691-2020   **Fax:** +56-2-691-7881
Web: www.ctc.cl

PRODUCTS/OPERATIONS

2004 Sales

	% of total
Fixed-line telecommunications	
Basic services	60
Long-distance	9
Wireless communications	19
Corporate communications	12
Total	**100**

Selected Services

Data transmission
Directory advertising
Domestic and international long distance
Equipment sales
Fixed wireless communications
Interconnections
Line installations and connections
Local phone service
Public telephones
Radio trunking

Selected Subsidiaries and Affiliates

Compañía de Telecomunicaciones de Chile — Equipos y Servicios de Telecomunicaciones S.A. (99.9%; equipment maintenance, line installation and services, and public phones)
Compañía de Teléfonos de Chile — Transmisiones Regionales S.A. (188 Telefónica Mundo, 99%, long-distance services)
Globus 120 S.A. (99.9%, long-distance services)
Tecnonáutica S.A. (Internet products and services)
Telefónica Empresas CTC Chile S.A. (99.9%, corporate telecommunications services)
Telefónica Gestión de Servicios Compartidos Chile S.A. (T-Gestiona, 99.9%, professional services)
Telefónica Móvil S.A. (Telefónica Móvil, 99.9%, wireless communications)

COMPETITORS

Chilesat Corp
Entel
TELECOM (Colombia)
TIM

HISTORICAL FINANCIALS

Company Type: Public

Income Statement

FYE: December 31

	REVENUE ($ mil.)	NET INCOME ($ mil.)	NET PROFIT MARGIN	EMPLOYEES
12/04	1,260	559	44.3%	3,774
12/03	1,369	17	1.2%	6,817
12/02	1,198	(25)	—	4,571
12/01	1,352	6	0.5%	7,720
12/00	1,479	(199)	—	9,250
12/99	1,604	(115)	—	9,933
12/98	1,602	237	14.8%	8,985
12/97	1,439	312	21.6%	8,802
12/96	1,274	354	27.8%	8,982
12/95	1,037	268	25.9%	9,170
Annual Growth	2.2%	8.5%	—	(9.4%)

2004 Year-End Financials

Debt ratio: 47.5%
Return on equity: 28.4%
Cash ($ mil.): 14
Current ratio: 1.21
Long-term debt ($ mil.): 839

No. of shares (mil.): 239
Dividends
  Yield: 0.0%
  Payout: —
Market value ($ mil.): 2,690

Stock History

NYSE: CTC

12/95 12/96 12/97 12/98 12/99 12/00 12/01 12/02 12/03 12/04

	STOCK PRICE ($) FY Close	P/E High/Low		PER SHARE ($) Earnings	Dividends	Book Value
12/04	11.24	13	7	1.30	0.00	7.38
12/03	14.95	231	124	0.07	0.10	9.08
12/02	9.59	—	—	(0.02)	0.00	7.46
12/01	13.46	397	215	0.04	0.00	8.01
12/00	13.19	—	—	(0.83)	0.00	8.94
12/99	18.25	—	—	(0.48)	0.00	9.21
12/98	20.69	30	12	1.00	0.00	10.68
12/97	29.88	27	16	1.40	0.00	9.57
12/96	23.76	15	11	1.65	0.59	8.98
12/95	19.47	13	7	1.64	0.41	7.93
Annual Growth	(5.9%)	—	—	(2.5%)	—	(0.8%)

Telefónica, S.A.

Spain's onetime phone monopoly, Telefónica, is still the telecommunications *jefé* among Spanish- and Portuguese-speaking populations worldwide. The company operates about 44 million fixed lines, including 19 million in Spain. Its wireless unit, Telefónica Móviles, has nearly 20 million subscribers in Spain among more than 54 million overall. Telefónica also owns the Terra Networks Internet portal, and the company provides ADSL broadband access to more than 1 million subscribers. Other operations include call centers and directory publishing. J.P. Morgan Chase and Banco Bilbao Vizcaya Argentaria (owning about 7% and 6%, respectively) are Telefónica's largest shareholders.

Spain's dominant phone company is like a latter-day conquistador. The company's most re-

cent victory is an agreement to acquire UK-based mobile phone operator O2. The deal, valued at more than $31 billion, gives Telefónica a strong presence in the UK, including Ireland, and in Germany. The Spanish operator does not yet have operations in those regions and has sought to expand in Europe.

Telefónica also is seeking fortune in Latin America where it has made acquisitions and formed partnerships to extend its holdings in both wire-line and wireless operations. Through its Telefónica Móviles unit, the company has agreed to acquire the assets of BellSouth Latin America Group, which has holdings in 10 South and Central American countries, in a deal valued at more than $5.8 billion. If completed, the deal would make Telefónica the region's largest telecom operator. Telefónica is also building an undersea fiber-optic cable to connect the US and Latin America.

At home Telefónica de España, the company's domestic operations, provides phone and data transmission services. Other operations include call centers, directory publishing, and public telephony. Telefónica also provides pay TV to about 700,000 subscribers in Spain, as well as 350,000 in Peru. In addition, the company has agreed to acquire a 51% stake in Ceský Telecom from the Czech government with the intention of taking full ownership in the company.

Although it's a leading telecom provider in some Latin American markets, such as Brazilian and Mexican mobile telecommunications, Telefónica has fallen victim to volatile currency and political issues in others. In addition, the company is facing increased competition at home, prompting Telefónica de España to cut nearly a third of its workforce by 2008. The company also is straightening out its media holdings by selling its Antena 3 broadcast TV station. It also has sold its Via Digital pay-TV service to rival Sogecable and the company is seeking to buy the stake in Terra Networks it doesn't already own.

HISTORY

When a 1923 military coup brought General Miguel Primo de Rivera to power in Spain, the government-run phone system was in shambles. More than half of the country's 90,000 lines did not work. With little cash in the government coffers, Primo de Rivera sought foreign assistance.

Supported by National City Bank (now Citigroup), US-based ITT bought three private Spanish phone companies, later combining them to form Compañía Telefónica Nacional de España. The ITT unit gained the state phone concession in 1924, and the government agreed not to reclaim the system for 20 years. But when Franco came to power in 1939, he froze Telefónica's assets. ITT tried to sell the company to German buyers in 1941 but backed out when the US State Department objected. The Spanish government nationalized Telefónica in 1945, keeping 41% of its shares.

Long-distance service was introduced in 1960, satellite communications in 1967, and international service in 1971. Still, when Spain entered the European Union (EU) in 1986, Telefónica was unprepared for the increase in demand for services, and complaints rose.

The firm purchased a minority stake in Compañía de Teléfonos de Chile in 1990, and a Telefónica-led consortium won a bid to manage the southern half of ENTEL, Argentina's former state phone system. The company acquired a majority stake in Peru's telecom monopoly in

1994 and a year later joined Unisource, a European telecom consortium.

The Spanish government at first defied the EU's directive to break up its telecom monopoly. But in 1994 the government announced it would meet the EU's 1998 deadline for opening telecom markets; in exchange Telefónica won permission to begin new businesses when competition arrived.

Flamboyant former investment banker Juan Villalonga took over as chairman in 1996. The boyhood friend of Spain's prime minister began expanding Telefónica's presence in Latin America with several acquisitions in 1997. They included 35% of Brazil's Companhia Riograndense de Telecomunicações (CRT); a large stake in Multicanal, Argentina's #1 cable company (sold in 1998 to Grupo Clarin); and 35% of satellite TV service Vía Digital.

The Spanish government had finished divesting its interest in the company in 1997 (retaining a golden share), and competition came to Spain the next year. The company revamped its corporate structure, cut 10,000 jobs, and became Telefónica S.A. It also won fixed-line phone company Telesp and a cellular company in Brazil's auction of the former national phone company, Telebras.

In 1999 Telefónica sold to the public part of its Internet unit, Terra Networks (formerly Telefónica Interactiva). The next year it took near-total ownership of four of its Latin American units: Telefónica de Argentina, Telefónica del Perú, Telesp, and Tele Sudeste Celular (it later sold its stake in CRT to meet regulatory approval) and separated the mobile and data operations to reorganize by business units.

To expand its multimedia offerings, Telefónica bought Netherlands-based independent TV producer Endemol for $5.3 billion in 2000 and formed Telefónica Media. After dropping out of the UK wireless license auction, the company teamed up with Finland's Sonera (later acquired by Telia) to win a license in the German auction. But when merger talks with Dutch telecom carrier Royal KPN broke down, Villalonga resigned over disagreements on the direction of the company.

In 2001 Telefónica combined its Brazilian mobile telephone holdings with those of Portugal Telecom to form market leader Brasilcel. Telefónica then spent $2.7 billion in Mexico in 2001 and 2002 to buy four wireless operators and a 65%-stake in a fifth (Pegaso PCS) to achieve #2 in that market.

EXECUTIVES

Chairman and CEO: César Alierta Izuel, age 60
Vice Chairman: Isidro Fainé Casas, age 62
CFO and General Manager of Finance and Shared Resources: Santiago Fernández Valbuena, age 46
General Manager, Development, Planning, and Regulation, and Director: Luis Lada Díaz, age 56
General Manager, Corporate Communication: Luis Abril Pérez, age 57
General Manager, Auditing and Management Resources: Calixto Ríos Pérez, age 60
General Director, Human Resources: Óscar Maraver Sánchez-Valdepeñas
General Director, Sponsorships and External Relations: Francisco de Bergia González, age 55
General Manager, Commercial Development and Subsidiaries: Guillermo Fernández-Vidal, age 58
General Manager, Corporate Development: Angel Vilá Boix
General Manager, Resources; CEO, Atento: Alberto M. Horcajo Aguirre
General Manager, Institutional Relations and the Telefónica Foundation: Javier Nadal Ariño, age 55
General Manager, Planning and Management Control: Alfonso Alonso Durán

LOCATIONS

HQ: Telefónica, S.A.
Gran Vía 28, 28013 Madrid, Spain
Phone: +34-91-584-0306   **Fax:** +34-91-584-9347
Web: www.telefonica.com

In addition to Spain, Telefónica's areas of operation include more than 40 countries in Africa, Asia, Europe, Latin America, and North America.

2004 Sales

	$ mil.	% of total
Spain	25,367	60
Latin American	14,797	35
Other regions	2,114	5
Total	**42,278**	**100**

PRODUCTS/OPERATIONS

2004 Sales

	$ mil.	% of total
Telefónica Móviles	14,748	35
Telefónica de España	14,355	34
Telefónica Latinoamérica	9,132	22
Telefónica Contenidos	1,673	4
Terra Networks	558	1
Other revenues	1,812	4
Total	**42,278**	**100**

Selected Subsidiaries and Affiliates

Atento N.V. (data center operations and customer relation management, The Netherlands)
Portugal Telecom, SGPS, S.A. (7%, telecommunications services)
Telefónica de Contenidos, S.A.U. (formerly Admira Media Group; content, entertainment, and media production and distribution services)
   Corporación Admira Media, S.A.
   Endemol Entertainment Holding N.V. (99%, television production, The Netherlands)
   Pearson plc (5%, publishing, UK)
   Sogecable, S.A. (24%, satellite and cable TV)
Telefónica Empresas (integrated corporate communications)
   Emergia Holding N.V. (submarine fiber-optic cable operations)
   Telefónica Data Group (data transmissions)
Telefónica Latinoamérica
   Telefónica Internacional, S.A. fixed-line telecommunications holdings in Latin America)
   Cia. Anónima N. de Teléfonos de Venezuela, C.A. (CANTV, 7%, fixed-line telecommunications)
   Telefónica CTC Chile (45%, fixed-line telecommunications and pay TV)
   Telefónica de Argentina, S.A. (98%, fixed-line telecommunications)
   Telefónica del Perú, S.A.A. (98%, fixed-line telecommunications and pay TV)
   Telesp Participações, S.A. (88%, fixed-line telecommunications, Brazil)
Telefónica Móviles, S.A. (93%, wireless telecommunications services)
   Brasilcel N.V. (46%, joint venture)
   Celular CRT Participações, S.A. (49%, wireless telecommunications, Brazil)
   Tele Leste Celular Participações, S.A. (Bahia Celular, 19%, cellular services, Brazil)
   Tele Sudeste Celular Participações, S.A. (Rio Celular, 84%, cellular service, Brazil)
   Telesp Celular Participações, S.A. (65%, cellular service, Brazil)
   Médi Telecom (30%, wireless telecommunications, Morocco)
   NewComm Wireless Puerto Rico (49.9%)
   Telefónica Centroamérica Guatemala (92%, wireless telecommunications)
   Telefónica Móviles El Salvador (84%, wireless telecommunications)
   Telefónica Móviles México, S.A. de C.V. (92%, wireless telecommunications)

Telefónica Sociedad Operadora de Servicios de Telecomunicaciones en España, S.A. (Telefónica de España, fixed-line telecommunications services, Spain)
Telefónica Publicidad e Información, S.A. (TPI-Paginas Amarillas, 60%, directory publishing and advertising)
Terra Networks Group (Internet portal operations)

COMPETITORS

Cableuropa
France Telecom
Jazztel
MCI
Portugal Telecom
Retevisión Móvil
Spantel
Telecom Italia
Teleconnect
Telmex
Uni2
Vodafone
Vodafone España

HISTORICAL FINANCIALS

Company Type: Public

Income Statement

FYE: December 31

	REVENUE ($ mil.)	NET INCOME ($ mil.)	NET PROFIT MARGIN	EMPLOYEES
12/04	42,278	3,898	9.2%	173,554
12/03	36,564	2,770	7.6%	148,288
12/02	30,656	(5,857)	—	152,845
12/01	28,424	1,875	6.6%	161,527
12/00	27,941	2,353	8.4%	148,707
12/99	23,168	1,821	7.9%	118,778
12/98	20,476	1,533	7.5%	101,809
12/97	15,601	1,255	8.0%	92,022
12/96	15,288	1,222	8.0%	92,148
12/95	14,297	1,094	7.7%	69,570
Annual Growth	**12.8%**	**15.2%**	**—**	**10.7%**

2004 Year-End Financials

Debt ratio: 93.4%
Return on equity: 18.1%
Cash ($ mil.): 1,158
Current ratio: 0.60
Long-term debt ($ mil.): 20,519

No. of shares (mil.): 1,717
Dividends
   Yield: 1.3%
   Payout: 31.1%
Market value ($ mil.): 93,331

Stock History

NYSE: TEF

	STOCK PRICE ($) FY Close	P/E High/Low		Earnings	PER SHARE ($) Dividends	Book Value
12/04	54.35	23	17	2.35	0.73	12.80
12/03	42.51	27	15	1.60	0.83	12.27
12/02	24.55	—	—	(3.43)	0.00	10.60
12/01	35.56	47	23	1.11	0.00	13.66
12/00	42.61	61	30	1.33	0.00	14.93
12/99	67.16	48	24	1.43	0.00	11.45
12/98	37.61	35	19	1.24	0.00	12.88
12/97	24.79	26	18	1.00	0.30	11.43
12/96	18.85	18	11	1.06	0.37	12.36
12/95	11.40	12	9	0.96	0.32	11.04
Annual Growth	**19.0%**	**—**	**—**	**10.5%**	**9.6%**	**1.7%**

Televisa

With its television, radio, and publishing interests, Grupo Televisa is *número uno* in the Latin media world. The firm is Mexico's #1 TV broadcaster with four networks and almost 260 affiliated stations (about 225 are wholly or partially company-owned). It also has a 51% stake in cable joint venture Cablevisión and a 60% stake in Innova, which operates the SKY direct-to-home satellite system (of which Televisa owns 30%). The company's publishing unit, Editorial Televisa, is a leading producer of Spanish-language magazines. Televisa also owns three soccer teams, a sports stadium, and 50% of 17 Mexican radio stations. Through a trust, chairman and CEO Emilio Azcárraga Jean owns 49% of Televisa.

The company's dominance in the Mexican television market was evidenced by the successful launch of Mexico's first reality TV program, *Big Brother* (produced by Televisa's new television partnership with Europe's Endemol), as well as strong ratings for the 2002 World Cup. It also floated about half of Cablevisión to the public and entered the live entertainment business through the purchase of 40% of OCESA Entretenimiento. Televisa has announced plans to acquire Editora Cinco, a Colombia-based magazine publisher that sells about 70 titles across Latin America and the US.

Televisa has cut some costs by selling its music recording operations to US-based Hispanic broadcaster Univision Communications (in which Televisa has a 15% stake), and 50% stake in its radio operations to Grupo Prisa.

HISTORY

Credited with launching the Golden Age of Mexican cinema in the 1940s via his Churrubusco Studios, Emilio Azcárraga Vidaurreta was a radio pioneer who also owned one of Mexico's first TV channels. He joined fellow TV channel owners Rómulo O'Farrill (a newspaper publisher) and Guillermo Camarena (an inventor) to form one network, Telesistema Mexicana, in 1954. When Azcárraga Vidaurreta died in 1972, his son Emilio Azcárraga Milmo took the reins of the company, dubbed it Grupo Televisa, and began his long stint as chairman. His aggressive style earned him the nickname "El Tigre" (The Tiger).

Azcárraga Milmo saw Mexican television as an escape for the nation's middle and lower classes. He nurtured stars for soap operas (called *telenovelas*) and variety shows and insisted upon the actors' loyalty in return. Grupo Televisa started producing feature films for markets in Mexico and abroad in 1978. It also ran cable TV and music recording businesses and a regional TV network that it bought in 1982. The company used its news programs to support Mexico's Institutional Revolutionary Party (PRI).

A 1990 attempt to start a sports newspaper in the US (*The National*) met with failure (it closed after a year, leaving the company with heavy debts). Azcárraga Milmo bought out the other principal investors in 1990 and reorganized Televisa into a holding company, taking it public in 1991. The company launched its Skytel paging service in Mexico in 1992 and bought a minority stake in US-based Univision. The Mexican government privatized the Televisión Azteca network in 1993, giving Televisa its first taste of competition in the TV broadcast market.

Televisa joined Brazil's Organizações Globo and TCI (now AT&T Broadband) in 1995 to develop direct-to-home (DTH) satellite television. (News Corp. joined the venture, now called SKY, in 1997.) The company also pared its staff by 12% and divested some of its lesser operations, including the sale of 49% of its cable TV businesses to telephone giant Teléfonos de México (Telmex).

A month before his death in 1997, Azcárraga Milmo installed his 29-year-old son, Emilio Azcárraga Jean, as president and CEO of the company. The company sold half of its stake in Univision the next year and slashed more jobs. Holding company Grupo Televicentro sold a 9% stake in Televisa in 2000 and used the proceeds to pay off debt. It also sold its newspaper, *Ovaciones*, in 2000. Later that year Televisa consolidated its ownership of publishing unit Editorial Televisa.

A plan to merge its radio stations with those of Grupo Acir was foiled when Mexican competition authorities ruled against it. But the next year the company was able to strike a deal to sell 50% of its radio station subsidiary to Grupo Prisa. Also that year the company eliminated 730 jobs in response to falling advertising revenue. It again increased its stake in Univision from 6% to 15%. The company agreed to form a television production company in a joint venture with Endemol in 2001.

In 2002 Televisa sold its Fonovisa Records regional music label to Univision for $210 million.

EXECUTIVES

Chairman, President, and CEO: Emilio Azcárraga Jean, age 37
Vice Chairwoman: María A. Aramburuzabala Larregui, age 42
CFO: Salvi Folch Viadero, age 38
EVP: Bernardo Gómez Martínez, age 38
EVP: Alfonso de Angoitia, age 43
VP and Controller: Jorge Lutteroth Echegoyen, age 52
VP, Administration: Rafael Carabias Príncipe, age 60
VP, Internal Auditing: Juan F. Calvillo Armendáriz, age 63
VP, Legal, Corporate General Counsel, and Secretary: Juan Sebastian Mijares, age 46
VP, Newscasts: Leopoldo G. González Blanco, age 46
VP, Operations, Technical Service, and Television Production: Maximiliano Arteaga Carlebach, age 62
VP, Production: Jorge E. Murguía Orozco, age 55
VP, Sales and Marketing: Alejandro Quintero Iñíguez, age 55
VP, Tax: José A. Lara del Olmo, age 35
VP, Television: José A. Bastón Patiño, age 37
CEO, Cablevision: Jean Paul Broc Haro, age 43
CEO, Editorial Televisa: Eduardo Michelsen Delgado, age 34
CEO, Innova: Alexandre M. Penna da Silva, age 50
CEO, Sistema Radiopolis: Raúl Rodríguez Gonzáles, age 46
Director of Investor Relations: Michel Boyance
Auditors: PricewaterhouseCoopers

LOCATIONS

HQ: Grupo Televisa, S.A.
Avenida Vasco de Quiroga, No. 2000,
Colonia Santa Fe, Delegación Álvaro Obregón,
01210 México, D.F., Mexico
Phone: +52-55-5261-2445   **Fax:** +52-55-5261-2494
Web: www.televisa.com

Grupo Televisa owns about 225 television stations and 17 radio stations in Mexico.

PRODUCTS/OPERATIONS

2004 Sales

	% of total
Television broadcasting	57
Sky Mexico	12
Publishing	7
Programming exports	6
Publishing distribution	5
Cable television	4
Pay television networks	3
Radio	1
Other	5
Total	**100**

Selected Operations

Paging Systems
    Skytel (51%)
Publishing and Internet
    EsMas.com (Internet service provider and portal)
    Magazines
        Conozca Mas (science and culture)
        Eres (teen interests)
        Furia Musical (music magazine)
        Tele Guía (television program guide)
        TV y Novelas (weekly entertainment magazine)
        Vanidades (women's magazine)
Radio and Television
    Cable Television
        Cablevisión (51%)
    Direct-To-Home Satellite
        Innova (60%)
            SKY (30%, Latin America and Caribbean basin)
    Radio
        Sistema Radiópolis (50%, 17 stations throughout Mexico)
    Television Broadcasting
        Channel 2
        Channel 4
        Channel 5
        Channel 9
        Univision Communications (10%, US)
Sports and Entertainment
    Azteca Stadium (Mexico City)
    OCESA Entretenimiento (40%, Mexican live-entertainment promoter)
    Soccer Teams
        America
        Necaxa
        Real San Luis
    Vivelo (50%, US Hispanic live-entertainment promoter)

COMPETITORS

Bertelsmann	Satmex
CIE	Telemundo
Cisneros Group	Time Warner
MVS	TV Azteca
Radio Centro	

HISTORICAL FINANCIALS

Company Type: Public

Income Statement

FYE: December 31

	REVENUE ($ mil.)	NET INCOME ($ mil.)	NET PROFIT MARGIN	EMPLOYEES
12/04	2,631	387	14.7%	14,100
12/03	2,099	320	15.3%	12,300
12/02	2,075	71	3.4%	12,600
12/01	2,147	147	6.8%	13,700
12/00	2,164	(82)	—	20,000
12/99	1,892	112	5.9%	19,900
12/98	1,699	77	4.5%	15,400
12/97	1,756	740	42.1%	19,900
12/96	1,460	(76)	—	20,700
12/95	1,147	122	10.7%	20,700
Annual Growth	**9.7%**	**13.7%**	**—**	**(4.2%)**

2004 Year-End Financials

Debt ratio: 73.1%
Return on equity: 16.0%
Cash ($ mil.): 35
Current ratio: 1.44
Long-term debt ($ mil.): 1,819
No. of shares (mil.): 123
Dividends
    Yield: 3.6%
    Payout: 82.0%
Market value ($ mil.): 7,465

Stock History

NYSE: TV

	STOCK PRICE ($) FY Close	P/E High/Low		PER SHARE ($) Earnings	Dividends	Book Value
12/04	60.50	24	15	2.66	2.18	20.17
12/03	39.86	20	10	2.19	0.36	5.38
12/02	27.93	122	52	0.46	0.00	4.39
12/01	43.18	55	27	0.98	0.00	4.38
12/00	44.94	—	—	(0.56)	0.00	3.80
12/99	68.25	328	83	0.22	0.00	46.12
12/98	24.69	270	93	0.16	0.00	43.05
12/97	38.69	25	14	1.59	0.00	41.42
12/96	25.63	—	—	(0.16)	0.00	25.52
12/95	22.50	108	40	0.30	0.07	25.56
Annual Growth	**11.6%**	**—**	**—**	**27.4%**	**46.5%**	**(2.6%)**

TeliaSonera

An expert at cold calling, TeliaSonera (formerly Telia) offers telecom services primarily in the chilly Nordic and Baltic regions. The company has become the leading telecom company in these regions, with more than 8 million fixed lines and about 15 million mobile phone subscribers. It also has more than 2 million Internet customers. Facing growing competition since Sweden deregulated its telecom industry in 1993, TeliaSonera has responded by traveling abroad. Its network facilities reach the European continent, the Americas, and Asia. It is expanding in growth markets such as Russia and Eurasia. The Kingdom of Sweden owns 45% of TeliaSonera; the Republic of Finland owns nearly 14%.

The company is organized into five business areas: mobile, international carrier, networks, Internet services, and equity holdings. It also is expanding into other countries with carrier services, using its fiber-optic network to reach the European continent and the US. The company's Internet protocol (IP) backbone connects Europe, the Americas, and Asia; TeliaSonera has investments in telecom ventures in nearly 30 countries, but the company has said it considers its international operations as financial assets rather than core business elements.

Although in 2005 TeliaSonera agreed to pay $3.1 billion to the Çukurova Group to buy another 27% of Turkish telecom Turkcell, which would have increased its stake to more than 63%, the company was outbid by Russian holding company Alfa Group. TeliaSonera has filed for breach of contract with Cukurova.

At home in Sweden and Finland, where it is the largest mobile operator, the group is building out its GSM networks, along with technology upgrades to quadruple the speed for mobile data services and increase its coverage to more than 90% of the land area. Most of TeliaSonera's growth is driven by its mobile phone services. It provides wireless phone services in Denmark, Finland, Norway, and Sweden. It also has mobile subsidiaries in the GSM markets of Azerbaijan, Georgia, Kazakhstan, and Moldovla. It has mobile and broadband operations through its 2004 acquisition of Omnitel. In addition, it has a stake in Russian mobile operator MegaFon.

TeliaSonera is pulling its wireless customers online using SMS (short messaging service) and WAP (wireless application protocol) technologies, and it has teamed up with Microsoft to offer e-mail access via mobile phones. TeliaSonera is the leading ISP in the Baltic and Nordic regions. Other TeliaSonera activities include directory publishing and telecom equipment sales, and the carrier also sells wholesale capacity on its networks to other carriers.

Following the merger that created Telia-Sonera, the company said it would eliminate as many as 1,500 jobs.

HISTORY

Telia's wires go back to 1853 when the Swedish government created Kongl. Elektriska Telegraf-Verket to operate a telegraph line linking Stockholm and Uppsala. The next year it opened a line that reached the main European continent; the company became Telegrafverket in 1860.

Just a year after the telephone was invented in 1876, the firm installed its first phone line. The 1880s saw private phone companies sprout up in Sweden's larger cities, and by 1900 Telegrafverket had installed some 62,000 telephones. Even though Sweden was open to telecom competition, the company became a de facto monopoly in 1918 when it bought the country's largest exchange, Stockholms Allmanna Telefon. In 1921 Telegrafverket began laying its first long-distance cable.

Telegrafverket began automating its phone systems in the 1930s. After WWII, the company entered a major growth period: More than 110,000 new telephone users were connected in 1947 alone. Also in the mid-1940s, Telegrafverket launched one of the world's first mobile phone networks (closed radio).

Renamed Televerket, the firm continued to grow rapidly in the 1960s and 1970s and introduced data communications services in 1965. It teamed up with equipment maker Ericsson in 1970 to form Ellemtel, an R&D concern that developed the first all-digital public switching system. (Ellemtel ceased operations in 1999.) Televerket began moving into satellite services in 1970, when INTELSAT installed an earth station in the Nordic region. In the early 1980s it rolled out several new services, including cable TV, cellular, and international packet switching.

Meanwhile, the company began losing its monopoly status in the 1980s and lost its government funding in 1984. Fearing competition from giants such as AT&T and British Telecom (now BT Group), the company in 1991 joined the Netherlands' Royal KPN to form Unisource, a global telecommunications provider; Swisscom joined the group two years later. Sweden's telecom deregulation was completed in 1993, and the firm became Telia. That year it ventured into the Baltic states.

AT&T teamed up with Unisource in 1994 to provide services to multinationals. In 1995 Telia began providing Internet access and announced it was installing an overlay Internet protocol (IP) backbone. Moving into the Americas in 1997, Telia led a consortium that secured rights to offer cellular service in Brazil.

Unisource never took off, and, after AT&T jumped ship in 1998, Telia and its partners began divesting the venture's assets. After Telia's proposed merger with Norway's Telenor fell through in 1999, the company began tweaking its strategy to become a strong global player. But conditions within the telecom industry forced the company to revamp its international carrier strategy, cut 400 jobs within the unit, and trim its operations.

In 2000 the Swedish government floated 30% of Telia. A restructuring in 2001 created five new business areas. Telia did acquire Norwegian mobile phone operator NetCom ASA and in 2002 it bought the UK operations of bankrupt Canadian network operator 360networks and acquired defunct KPNQwest's network in France.

Also in 2002 Telia acquired Nordic region competitor Sonera and the two companies were combined to form TeliaSonera. As a condition of the merger, the group was required to sell Telia Mobile Finland that year as well.

In 2004 the group acquired the Danish operations of Orange, the wireless unit of France Telecom. The acquisition improved TeliaSonera's market position in Denmark, moving it from fourth- to third-largest mobile operator.

TeliaSonera Sweden launched live TV broadcasts on its mobile phones in 2005, in collaboration with TV4 News and entertainment channels The Voice TV and Start.

EXECUTIVES

Chairman: Tom von Weymarn, age 61
Vice Chairman: Carl Bennet, age 54
President and CEO: Anders Igel, age 54, $837,274 pay
EVP and CFO: Kim J. Ignatius, age 49
Group VP, Corporate Communications: Michael Kongstad, age 45
Group VP, Corporate Human Resources: Rune Nyberg, age 56
Group VP, Corporate Legal Affairs, and General Counsel: Jan Henrik Ahrnell, age 46
Group VP, Corporate Networks and Technology: Lars-Gunnar Johansson, age 61
President, TeliaSonera Norway, Denmark, and the Baltic Countries: Kenneth Karlberg, age 51
Head, Large Corporate Segment: Esa Korvenmaa
President, TeliaSonera Finland: Juho Lipsanen, age 44
President, TeliaSonera Sweden: Marie Ehrling, age 50
Head of Corporate Marketing, Products, and Services: Terje Christoffersen, age 53
Media Relations: Marianne Laurell
Media Relations: Charlotte Zuger
Auditors: PricewaterhouseCoopers AB

LOCATIONS

HQ: TeliaSonera AB
Sturegatan 1, SE-106 63 Stockholm, Sweden
Phone: +46-8-504-550-00   **Fax:** +46-8-504-550-01
US HQ: 2201 Cooperative Way, Ste. 302, Herndon, VA 20171
US Phone: 703-546-4000   **US Fax:** 703-546-4125
Web: www.teliasonera.com

2004 Sales

	% of total
Nordic region	
Sweden	49
Finland	22
Norway	8
Denmark	4
Baltic region	7
Eurasia region	5
International carrier services	5
Total	**100**

PRODUCTS/OPERATIONS

Selected Subsidiaries and Affiliates

AB Lietuvos Telekomas (60%, fixed-line telecommunications, Lithuania)
AS Eesti Telekom (49%, fixed-line telecommunications, Estonia)
 EMT (formerly AS Eesti Mobiltelefon, 49%, mobile telecommunications, Estonia)
FinturHoldings B.V. (74%, mobile telecommunicationsholdings, The Netherlands)
 Azercell (51%, mobile telecommunications, Azerbaijan)
 Geocell (83%, mobile telecommunications, Georgia)
 KCell (51%, mobile telecommunications, Kazakhstan)
 Moldcell (mobile telecommunications, Moldova)
Latvijas Mobilais Telefons SIA (60%, mobile telecommunications, Latvia)
NetCom AS (telecommunications services, Norway)
OAO MegaFon (44%, mobile telecommunications, Russia)
Sonera Carrier Networks Oy (Finland)
Sonera Mobile Networks Oy (Finland)
Svenska UMTS-nät AB (50%, mobile telecommunications, UMTS joint venture with Tele2)
Telia Communications AB
TeliaSonera Finland Oyj
TeliaSonera Holding (holding company for noncore investments)
 Auria Group (home electronics retail outlets)
 Infonet Serices Corporation (20%, data communications services, US)
 Telefos AB (49%, holding company)
 Swedia Networks AB (telecom construction services)
 Validation AB (testing and integration services)
 Unite AB (security services)
TeliaSonera International Carrier AB (Internet protocol-based data transport)
TeliaSonera International Carrier Inc. (US)
TeliaSonera International Carrier UK Ltd.
TeliaSonera Sverige AB (IT services)
Tilts Communications A/S
 Lattelekom SIA (49%, fixed-line telecommunications, Latvia)
Turkcell Iletisim Hizmetleri A.S. (37%, mobile telecommunications, Turkey)
UAB Omnitel (mobile telecommunications, Lithuania)

COMPETITORS

BT	Level 3 Communications
Cable & Wireless	MCI
COLT Telecom	Sprint Nextel
Deutsche Telekom	TDC
Elisa	TDC Song
Equant	Tele2
France Telecom	Telenor
Global Crossing	UGC Europe
KPN	Vodafone

HISTORICAL FINANCIALS

Company Type: Public

Income Statement

FYE: December 31

	REVENUE ($ mil.)	NET INCOME ($ mil.)	NET PROFIT MARGIN	EMPLOYEES
12/04	12,389	1,960	15.8%	29,082
12/03	11,457	1,262	11.0%	26,694
12/02	6,858	(930)	—	29,173
12/01	5,411	177	3.3%	17,149
12/00	5,742	1,092	19.0%	29,868
12/99	6,114	495	8.1%	30,643
12/98	6,324	554	8.8%	31,320
12/97	5,868	346	5.9%	30,500
12/96	6,474	338	5.2%	34,192
12/95	6,167	336	5.4%	33,065
Annual Growth	**8.1%**	**21.7%**	**—**	**(1.4%)**

2004 Year-End Financials

Debt ratio: 10.6%
Return on equity: 11.5%
Cash ($ mil.): 838
Current ratio: 1.14
Long-term debt ($ mil.): 1,957

Net Income History Pink Sheets: TLSNF

2,000									
1,500									
1,000									
500									
0									
-500									
-1,000									
	12/95	12/96	12/97	12/98	12/99	12/00	12/01	12/02	12/03	12/04

Telmex

Teléfonos de México (Telmex) is no longer a monopoly, but it's still Mexico's #1 fixed-line telecom operator with more than 17 million access lines in service and over 70% of the market. Telmex has spun off its Telcel subsidiary (Mexico's leading wireless carrier) and most of its international investments to form América Móvil, which in turn owns a stake in Latin American wireless joint venture Telecom Americas. Telmex also owns a stake in Spanish-language portal T1msn, a partnership with Microsoft, and has acquired bankrupt AT&T Latin America and Brazil's Embratel. Carso Global Telecom, a holding company controlled by Mexican billionaire Carlos Slim Helú, owns a controlling 43% stake in Telmex.

After a decade of facing competition, Telmex continues to control about two-thirds of Mexico's long-distance market and more than 90% of the local phone traffic. But competitors — and the US government — have sought an end to what they claim are monopolistic practices by the telecom giant.

Telmex reached an agreement with rivals backed by AT&T Corp and MCI (formerly WorldCom) that would end a dispute over access to the Mexican telecommunications market. The wrangling had led the US to file a complaint against Mexico before the World Trade Organization.

The company's acquisition of AT&T Latin America, in a cash and debt deal valued at $207 million, expands Telmex's operations in Argentina, Brazil, Chile, Colombia, and Peru. Telmex executives said it would invest $50 million in the bankrupt company's network technology and use the assets to expand business with corporate clients in the region. The company also has acquired 40% of long-distance carrier Chilesat, and said it would acquire the rest. It also has taken control of Embratel by buying the stake formerly held by MCI in a deal valued at $400 million. In a separate deal, the company sold its stake in MCI to Verizon Communications in a cash deal valued at $1.1 billion. Telmex also has acquired a 37% stake in Net Serviços de Comunicação, the #1 cable TV operator in Brazil.

Long-time chairman Carlos Slim Helú stepped down in 2004, appointed with the title of honorary lifetime chairman of the board of directors. He was replaced as chairman by his son, Carlos Slim Domit. US-based AT&T Inc. (formerly known as SBC Communications) owns a nearly 8% stake in Telmex.

HISTORY

Mexican Telephone and Telegraph, backed by investors allied with AT&T Corp., received a government concession to operate in Mexico City in 1903. Two years later a Swedish consortium led by equipment maker Ericsson also won a concession, and it became Empresa de Teléfonos Ericsson in 1909.

In 1915 Mexican Telephone and Telegraph was nationalized. The company languished after WWI, but the Ericsson enterprise thrived. In 1925 International Telephone and Telegraph (ITT), led by telecom pioneer Sosthenes Behn, won the concession to operate Mexican Telephone and Telegraph. ITT expanded operations nationwide and linked to AT&T's system in the US. In 1932 ITT won control of Ericsson.

Teléfonos de México (Telmex) was created after WWII to buy the ITT and Ericsson subsidiaries in Mexico. Private investors bought Telmex in 1953, but it remained under close state regulation until the government bought 51% of the voting shares in 1972. Phone service grew slowly, and the government continually raised the long-distance tax until it accounted for half of Telmex's revenues. By the 1980s the government was using Telmex funds for unrelated programs.

The 1985 earthquakes heavily damaged Telmex's facilities, and it was forced to modernize and expand in the rebuilding stage. To improve the inefficient enterprise, President Carlos Salinas announced in 1989 that Telmex would be privatized. The following year a consortium that included Grupo Carso, SBC Communications (now known as AT&T Inc.), and France Telecom won voting control of Telmex. (France Telecom sold its stake in 2000.)

Telmex bought a 49% stake in Empresas Cablevision's Mexican cable business in 1995, and the next year it teamed with Sprint to offer business telecom services in the US and Mexico. After long-distance competition began in 1997, Telmex surrendered about a quarter of its market share. Many customers, angered over years of unexplained hang-ups and incorrect billings, switched providers. Also that year Telmex and Sprint formed another venture to resell long-distance service to Mexican Americans. However, the venture had to gain approval from the FCC, and regulators insisted that Telmex lower the high termination fees charged to US long-distance providers. Telmex agreed to do so, and the venture won approval in 1998. Telmex also invested in former US ISP Prodigy in 1998.

Meanwhile, Telmex maintained a de facto monopoly over local service until 1999 when MAXCOM, backed by Grupo Radio Centro, entered the market. Telmex gained strength in other communications arenas, receiving additional radio spectrum for mobile and PCS wireless services, joining SBC to buy Cellular Communications of Puerto Rico, and buying Miami-based Topp Telecom (prepaid cellular service) and Dallas-based CommSouth (prepaid local service). It bought out Sprint's share of their joint venture and took a 1% stake ($100 million) in Williams Communications Group (now WilTel Communications), the US-based fiber-optic firm. It also began managing Guatemalan phone company TELGUA and the next year acquired a controlling stake.

Also in 2000 Telmex and Microsoft introduced Spanish-language Internet portal T1msn (T1msn acquired the Spanish-language portal Yupi in 2001). Telmex also formed a joint venture with Bell Canada International and SBC to expand operations in South America.

EXECUTIVES

Honorary Chairman: Carlos Slim Helú, age 65
Chairman: Carlos Slim Domit, age 38
Vice Chairman: Juan Antonio Pérez Simón, age 64
Vice Chairman and CEO: Jaime Chico Pardo, age 55
CFO: Adolfo Cerezo Pérez
Secretary and General Counsel:
Sergio F. Medina Noriega
Director, Commercial — Corporate Market:
Isidoro Ambe Attar
Director, Commercial — Retail Markets:
Patricio (Patrick) Slim Domit
Director, Human Resources: Jaime Pérez Gómez
Director, Investments and Strategic Development:
Andrés R. Vazquez del Mercado Benshimol
Director, Regulation and Legal:
Javier Mondragón Alarcón
Director, Strategic Alliances, Communication, and Institutional Relations: Arturo Elías Ayub
Director, Support to Operations: Héctor Slim Seade
Director, Systems and Telecommunications Operators:
Oscar Von Hauske Solís
Director, Technical and Long-distance:
Eduardo Gómez Chibli
Dean of Inttelmex: Javier Elguea Solís
Auditors: Mancera, S.C.

LOCATIONS

HQ: Teléfonos de México, S.A. de C.V.
Parqué Vía 198, oficina 701, Colonia Cuauhtémoc, 06599 México, D.F., Mexico
Phone: +52-55-5703-3990 **Fax:** +52-55-5545-5550
Web: www.telmex.com.mx

Teléfonos de México (Telmex) has operations in Brazil, Guatemala, Mexico, Puerto Rico, and the US.

PRODUCTS/OPERATIONS

2004 Sales

	$ mil.	% of total
Local service	5,108	41
Long-distance		
Domestic	2,242	18
International	997	8
Interconnections	1,744	14
Corporate networks	1,121	9
Internet	747	6
Other revenues	498	4
Total	**12,457**	**100**

Selected Services

Calling cards
Internet access
Local fixed-line access
National and international fixed-line long-distance
Network engineering
Pay phones
Telephone directories
Wireless data networking

Selected Subsidiaries

Anuncios en Directorios, S.A. de C.V. (Seccion Amarilla (ADSA), directory publishing)
Consorcio Red Uno, S.A. de C.V. (corporate telecommunications services)
Embratel Participações S.A. (telecommunications services, Brazil)
Net Serviços de Comunicação, S.A. (37%, cable TV operator, Brazil)
Teléfonos del Noroeste, S.A. de C.V. (Telnor, fixed-line telecom services in the states of Baja California and Sonora)
Telmex USA, LLC (reseller of long-distance, US)
Telvista, Inc. (formerly The Telvista Company, 45%, telemarketing services, US and Mexico)
TM & MS, LLC (50%, Internet portal joint venture with Microsoft)
Uninet, S.A. de C.V. (data network support)

HISTORICAL FINANCIALS

Company Type: Public

Income Statement

FYE: December 31

	REVENUE ($ mil.)	NET INCOME ($ mil.)	NET PROFIT MARGIN	EMPLOYEES
12/04	12,458	2,498	20.1%	76,683
12/03	10,408	2,000	19.2%	62,103
12/02	10,944	1,897	17.3%	63,775
12/01	12,140	2,570	21.2%	67,550
12/00	10,670	2,757	25.8%	66,928
12/99	10,182	2,656	26.1%	72,321
12/98	7,903	1,657	21.0%	54,425
12/97	7,529	1,593	21.2%	54,758
12/96	6,714	1,478	22.0%	62,317
12/95	5,428	1,209	22.3%	62,777
Annual Growth	9.7%	8.4%	—	2.2%

2004 Year-End Financials

Debt ratio: 81.9%
Return on equity: 32.2%
Cash ($ mil.): 1,840
Current ratio: 1.24
Long-term debt ($ mil.): 6,897
No. of shares (mil.): 1,183
Dividends
Yield: 3.1%
Payout: 28.6%
Market value ($ mil.): 22,670

Stock History

NYSE: TMX

12/95 12/96 12/97 12/98 12/99 12/00 12/01 12/02 12/03 12/04

	STOCK PRICE ($) FY Close	P/E High/Low		PER SHARE ($) Earnings	Dividends	Book Value
12/04	19.16	9	7	2.06	0.59	7.12
12/03	16.52	11	9	1.56	0.58	5.86
12/02	15.99	296	189	0.07	0.57	4.64
12/01	17.51	11	7	1.78	0.52	4.22
12/00	13.27	13	7	1.78	0.48	3.68
12/99	16.54	10	3	1.72	0.30	8.60
12/98	7.16	8	5	1.05	0.31	6.92
12/97	8.24	9	5	0.95	0.11	6.74
12/96	4.85	7	5	0.81	0.23	6.40
12/95	4.69	10	5	0.63	0.23	5.32
Annual Growth	16.9%	—	—	14.1%	11.0%	3.3%

Telstra

With Telstra's telecommunications services, Matilda can stay connected, even while waltzing all around. As Australia's #1 carrier, this former monopoly provides traditional fixed-line phone services to more than 10 million residential and small business lines. Telstra also has more than 8 million mobile phone customers and it is the country's leading ISP (BigPond). Dancing in the international stage, Telstra has teamed up with PCCW to form a pan-Asian Internet protocol backbone network (REACH). The company may spin off or sell its Sensis directory services unit. The Australian government plans to sell its 50.1% stake in Telstra, valued at about $20 billion. The sale could be one of the world's largest.

Telstra operates a digital GSM (global system for mobile communications) network and a second digital network based on CDMA (code division multiple access) technology for wireless communications. Online, the carrier provides Internet access to more than 1.5 million subscribers and has developed remote access via satellite. The firm also owns 50% of pay TV operator Foxtel and it acquired Australia-based Trading Post Group in a deal valued at nearly $484 million that bolstered the company's advertising and publishing operations. Telstra also bought technology services provider Kaz Group in a deal valued at $252 million.

The company's Telstra International unit oversees Telstra's operations in Australasia. Telstra International has telecom facilities in Hong Kong, Singapore, and in New Zealand (through TelstraClear). Its 50-50 joint venture with PCCW, known as REACH, is Asia's largest international carrier of voice, private line, and Internet protocol data services; it attained nominal profits but was forced to seek a debt restructuring deal.

Telstra had halted its Asian expansion efforts to improve investor relations, but it's back exploring its options. The company has announced plans to buy competitor New World Mobile Holdings, merge its Hong Kong operations with theirs, and possibly take the merged entity public. Telstra also has sales and service operations in Europe and in the US, where it has opened offices in Chicago, Dallas, and Los Angeles.

Telstra provides wholesale services to some 50 licensed operators. With competition in every arena, it has focused on the Internet and mobile phone markets. To trim costs in the face of rising competition, Telstra has announced 10,000 job cuts (nearly 20% of its workforce) since 2000.

HISTORY

When Australia gained independence in 1901, telecommunications were assigned to the new state-owned Postmaster-General's Department (PMG). Engineer H. P. Brown, who had managed the UK's telegraph and telephone system, became head of PMG in 1923. He set up research labs that year, oversaw the first overseas call to London in 1930, and streamlined operations until his reign ended in 1939.

During WWII Australia quickly expanded its communications infrastructure to assist the Allied Front in the South Pacific. Following the war, the government formed the Overseas Telecommunications Commission (OTC) in 1946 to handle international operations independent of PMG.

Even as new technology connected the continent and boosted the productivity of PMG, its postal operations steadily recorded losses in the postwar era. In 1974 a Royal Commission recommended that postal and telecom services be split. Australian Telecommunications Commission (Telecom Australia) was launched in 1975 (OTC retained overseas services); it turned a profit in its first year.

Looking to connect residents in the outback, the firm signed Japan's Nippon Electric (now NEC) in 1981 to set up a digital radio transmission system; by the next decade it connected some 50,000 outback users. Also in 1981 Telecom Australia took a 25% stake in government-owned satellite operator AUSSAT and launched nationwide paging and mobile phone service in Melbourne and Sydney.

Renamed Australian Telecommunications in 1989, the carrier got its first whiff of competition as others were allowed to provide phone equipment. Two years later Optus Communications began competing with Telecom Australia; for the privilege it was forced to buy the unsuccessful AUSSAT. Long-distance competition began in 1991, and mobile phone competition began in 1992. In response, Telecom Australia merged with OTC to become the Australian and Overseas Telecommunications Corporation (AOTC). AT&T's Frank Blount became CEO to lead the transition.

AOTC became Telstra Corporation in 1993 and launched a digital wireless GSM-based network. It joined with Rupert Murdoch's News Corp. to form pay TV operator Foxtel in 1995.

That year Telstra teamed with Microsoft to create ISP On Australia. Microsoft dropped out in 1996, but Telstra kept the service (Big Pond) and its portal (renamed Telstra.com in 1999). The government fully deregulated telecommunications and sold a third of Telstra to the public in 1997.

Kerry Packer's Publishing and Broadcasting bought a 25% stake in Foxtel in 1998. The next year Telstra posted an Australian record-setting profit, former Optus CEO Ziggy Switkowski succeeded Blount, and the government floated an additional 17% stake.

Telstra combined its New Zealand operations with those of cable TV operator Austar United to form Telstra Saturn in 1999. Two years later it bought Clear Communications, the New Zealand unit of BT Group (formerly British Telecommunications), in a deal worth about $182 million and merged it with Telstra Saturn to form TelstraClear.

In 2004 former chairman Bob Mansfield resigned his post after conflicts with the board of directors over the proposed acquisition of publisher John Fairfax Holdings. Mansfield supported the acquisition. Late the same year CEO Ziggy Switkowski was sacked by the board after holding the position for six years, during which time the company's share price dropped considerably. The company hired former Orange SA CEO Sol Trujillo in his place.

EXECUTIVES

Chairman: Donald G. (Don) McGauchie, age 55
CEO and Board Member: Solomon D. (Sol) Trujillo, age 53
COO: Greg Winn
CFO and Group Managing Director, Finance and Administration: John Stanhope, $792,596 pay
Group Managing Director, Infrastructure Services: Michael Rocca, $877,546 pay
Group Managing Director, Public Policy and Communications: Phil Burgess
Group Managing Director, Strategic Marketing: William J. Stewart
Group Managing Director, Telstra Business and Government: David Thodey, $893,308 pay
Group Managing Director, Telstra Consumer and Marketing; President, International: David Moffatt, age 40, $1,051,985 pay
Group Managing Director, Telstra Country Wide: Douglas C. (Doug) Campbell, $953,394 pay
Group Managing Director, Telstra Media Services and CEO, Sensis: Bruce J. Akhurst, $1,105,137 pay
Group Managing Director, Telstra Wholesale: Deena Shiff, $435,937 pay (partial-year salary)
Managing Director, Corporate Development: John Allerton
Managing Director, Voice and Convergence, Telstra Technology Innovation and Products Group: Rosemary Howard
General Manager, Investor Relations: David Anderson
SVP, Sales and Global Accounts, Telstra Incorporated: Andrew Morawski
Company Secretary: Douglas Gration
Auditors: Ernst & Young; Auditor General of Melbourne

LOCATIONS

HQ: Telstra Corporation Limited
242 Exhibition St., Melbourne 3000, Australia
Phone: +61-3-9634-6400   **Fax:** +61-3-9634-1189
Web: telstra.com.au

2005 Sales

	% of total
Australia	92
Hong Kong	4
New Zealand	3
Other countries	1
Total	**100**

PRODUCTS/OPERATIONS

2005 Sales

	% of total
Country Wide	26
Business & Government	24
Consumer & Marketing	23
Wholesale	13
International	6
Other	8
Total	**100**

Selected Operating Divisions

Infrastructure Services (operations, delivery, and maintenance of fixed-line, mobile, IP, and data networks)
Sensis (advertising, directories, and information services)
Technology Innovation and Products (information technology services)
Telstra Asia (management of Asian operations)
Telstra Big Pond (consumer Internet services)
Telstra Consumer and Marketing (fixed-line, mobile, data, and pay TV services for metropolitan consumer and small business customers)
Telstra Country Wide (rural and remote telecom services)
Telstra Business and Government (telecom services for midsized and large enterprise clients and government agencies)
Telstra Media (Foxtel investment)
Telstra Wholesale (carrier services)

Selected Services

Advertising and directory services
Audio, video, and Internet conferencing
Broadband ISP
Cable TV
Data transmission
E-mail
Enhanced fax products and services
Freecall (toll-free 1-800 phone service)
Information technology (IT) services
Internet access
Mobile phone service
Prepaid telephony
Satellite transmission

COMPETITORS

Asia Netcom	Pacific Internet
Hutchison Whampoa	PowerTel
MCI	Telecom Corporation
NTT	of New Zealand
Optus	Vodafone

HISTORICAL FINANCIALS

Company Type: Public

Income Statement

FYE: June 30

	REVENUE ($ mil.)	NET INCOME ($ mil.)	NET PROFIT MARGIN	EMPLOYEES
6/05	16,829	3,377	20.1%	46,336
6/04	14,410	2,862	19.9%	41,941
6/03	13,732	2,274	16.6%	42,064
6/02	11,310	2,050	18.1%	44,977
6/01	9,641	2,070	21.5%	48,317
6/00	11,267	2,161	19.2%	53,055
6/99	11,616	2,305	19.8%	52,840
6/98	10,441	1,865	17.9%	57,234
6/97	11,935	1,207	10.1%	66,109
6/96	12,009	1,817	15.1%	76,522
Annual Growth	**3.8%**	**7.1%**	**—**	**(5.4%)**

2005 Year-End Financials

Debt ratio: 79.4%
Return on equity: 30.7%
Cash ($ mil.): 1,169
Current ratio: 0.97
Long-term debt ($ mil.): 8,973
No. of shares (mil.): 2,489
Dividends
Yield: 6.4%
Payout: 91.9%
Market value ($ mil.): 48,155

Stock History

NYSE: TLS

	STOCK PRICE ($) FY Close	P/E High/Low		PER SHARE ($) Earnings	Dividends	Book Value
6/05	19.35	16	12	1.35	1.24	4.54
6/04	17.68	18	13	1.13	0.41	4.23
6/03	14.85	17	13	0.90	0.76	4.01
6/02	13.30	19	15	0.80	0.58	3.07
6/01	13.89	28	17	0.80	0.49	2.62
6/00	20.69	30	19	0.85	0.00	2.69
Annual Growth	**(1.3%)**	**—**	**—**	**9.7%**	**—**	**11.0%**

Tengelmann

American shoppers know the Tengelmann Group best through its majority-owned A&P (Great Atlantic & Pacific Tea Company) supermarkets. More than 400 A&P-owned stores in the US make up only part of Tengelmann, one of Europe's leading food retailers (along with German rivals ALDI Group, METRO AG and REWE-Zentral). The group has more than 7,500 supermarkets, drugstores, and general stores in 15 countries (mostly in Europe) under such names as Tengelmann and Kaiser's (supermarkets and drugstores) in Germany, Obi (do-it-yourself supply stores), Plus (a discount food chain), and KiK (apparel and general merchandise stores). The sons of chairman and former CEO Erivan Haub now run the company. Germany accounts for 51% of the company's sales.

The youngest son, Christian, runs the group's troubled A&P business, and the eldest, Karl-Erivan, leads Tengelmann's European operations.

While Tengelmann is expanding its Plus and Obi chains in Europe, the company has closed or sold at least 600 of its Tengelmann and Kaiser's supermarkets, lessening its dependence on food retailing. The German retailer sold the last of its Kd chemist's shops to beauty retail chain Dirk Rossmann in 2005.

The Kaiser's and Tengelmann supermarket chains offer home delivery service in Berlin and Munich.

The company's Gubi manufacturing business operates meat processing plants, a bakery, and plant nursery to supply its retail chains. Another Tengelmann operation, Ligneus, makes interior fixtures for hotels and restaurants.

With the sale of its A&P Canada operation in 2005 and continued losses in the US, Tengelmann has chosen to concentrate on expanding its businesses in Europe, especially Southern and Eastern Europe. To that end, it has abandoned plans to expand its Obi DIY chain in China, where previously it had hoped to open as many as 100 stores. The international divisions of the company's Plus, Obi, and textile discounter KiK chains are growing rapidly.

HISTORY

William and Louise (Scholl) Schmitz founded Wilh. Schmitz Scholl in Mulheim, Germany, in 1867, importing goods and processing coffee. In 1893 the Schmitz's sons opened their first retail store, selling groceries, sweets, coffee, tea, and cocoa. The family called the store Tengelmann, after employee Emil Tengelmann, to avoid the social stigma then attached to grocers in Germany.

The company rebuilt after WWII left many of its stores in ruins. The man who would guide the company through much of its growth was still a youngster at this time. In 1952 Erivan Haub, the great-grandson of William and Louise Schmitz, was 20 when he was sent to the US for three years to learn the ropes at supermarkets in California and Illinois. He saw that US grocery stores, unlike most in Germany, let consumers serve themselves. Haub passed this practice along to his relatives, and Tengelmann Group opened its first self-serve stores in Germany soon afterward. Haub developed a fondness for the US during this trip that has not faded: His children were born in America to give them citizenship; St. Joseph's University in Philadelphia named its business school after Haub to recognize the family's contributions.

Haub took over as head of the company in 1969 after his uncle's death. First on his shopping list was acquisitions. He bought Kaiser's Kaffee-Geschaft, a troubled German supermarket chain, two years later, then converted some of the stores into the discount Plus format. Tengelmann came to the rescue in 1979 when it agreed to buy more than half of the troubled US supermarket chain Great Atlantic & Pacific Tea Company (A&P). Haub turned the grocer around by focusing on acquisitions and revamping older store formats.

International expansion marked the tone of Tengelmann in the 1990s. Using its Plus discount chain as a vehicle, Tengelmann branched out into East Germany and other countries once part of the communist bloc, such as Hungary and Poland. Germany, with its stiff competition and strict laws limiting acquisitions and requiring shops to close early on weeknights, paled in comparison as a growth opportunity to the hungry environments in the East.

Tengelmann enraged Holocaust survivors in 1991 when it proposed building a Kaiser's supermarket on part of the Ravensbrueck Nazi concentration camp site, where approximately 92,000 women and children were killed. The company canceled its plans after worldwide protests, although the local community, in need of jobs, had supported the idea.

Heavy competition among German retailers hammered profits in 1995. Haub announced plans to cut costs and restructure the company. The changes included modifying the Plus store format from discounter to neighborhood convenience store; Haub continued to back new deep-discount chain Ledi. Tengelmann entered a partnership in 1998 with the Pam group of Venice, merging its Italian supermarkets with Pam's. It also bought 165 German Tip discount stores from competitor Metro. The youngest Haub son, Christian, was promoted to CEO of A&P in 1998. He is also chairman of A&P's board of directors.

In the midst of a restructuring, in 2000 the company announced its would sell or close at least 600 of the poorly performing Tengelmann and Kaiser's stores. Meanwhile, it is extending its Obi do-it-yourself stores into Latvia, Slovakia, and Finland.

In 2002 Tengelmann restructured its troubled A&P operations, which posted a $72 million loss for the fiscal year ending in February 2002. After 33 years as the sole managing partner of the Tengelmann Group, Erivan Haub turned the management of the company over to his sons Karl-Erivan and Christian in 2002.

After 97 years in the chocolate business, Tengelmann sold its chocolate subsidiary Wissoll to German confectionery group Van Netten GmbH in 2003.

Tengelmann entered the Russian market in 2004 with the opening of two Obi stores in Moscow.

2005 was a year marked by retrenchment in several markets for Tengelmann. The Kd Kaiser's drugstore chain was sold to Dirk Rossmann in May. In July the company withdrew from its partnership with the Haier Group to open Obi stores in China. In August the company sold its profitable A&P Canada division to METRO INC. It also disposed of its 22 Interfruct Cash & Carry stores in Hungary and Slovenia.

EXECUTIVES

Chairman: Erivan Haub
Chairman of Holding Management Board; CEO, Europe: Karl-Erivan W. Haub
Chairman, President, and CEO, A&P: Christian W. E. Haub
CFO: Jens-Jürgen Böckel, age 62
CEO and Managing Partner, KiK: Stefan Heinig
CEO, Kaiser's Tengelmann AG: Bernd Ahlers
CEO, Obi: Sergio Giroldi
Head of Public Relations Department: Sieglinde Schuchardt

LOCATIONS

HQ: Tengelmann Warenhandelsgesellschaft KG
Wissollstraße 5-43,
45478 Mülheim an der Ruhr, Germany
Phone: +49-208-5806-7601   **Fax:** +49-208-5806-7605
Web: www.tengelmann.de

Tengelmann has stores in Austria, Bosnia and Herzegovina, the Czech Republic, Germany, Hungary, Italy, Poland, Portugal, Russia, Slovakia, Slovenia, Spain, Switzerland, and the US.

2005 Stores

	No.
Europe	
Germany	5,388
Other countries	1,426
North America	689
Total	**7,503**

2005 Sales

	% of total
Germany	51
Other countries	49
Total	**100**

PRODUCTS/OPERATIONS

2005 Stores

	No.
Plus	3,826
KiK	1,751
Kaiser's Tengelmann	718
A&P	689
Obi	497
Interfruct Cash & Carry	22
Total	**7,503**

Selected Store Operations

The Great Atlantic & Pacific Tea Company (56%, A&P grocery store chain)
Kaiser's (grocery and drugstore chain)
KiK (discount clothing and textile stores)
Obi (do-it-yourself supply, hardware, and appliance retailer)
Plus (grocery and goods discount store chain)
Tengelmann (grocery store chain)

COMPETITORS

ALDI	Lidl & Schwarz Stiftung
A.S. Watson	METRO AG
AVA AG	Praktiker
Carrefour	REWE-Zentral
Casino Guichard	Royal Ahold
Delhaize	Schlecker
Edeka Zentrale	SPAR Handels
Home Depot	Tesco
ITM Entreprises	Vendex
Kingfisher	Wal-Mart

HISTORICAL FINANCIALS

Company Type: Private

Income Statement

FYE: April 30

	REVENUE ($ mil.)	NET INCOME ($ mil.)	NET PROFIT MARGIN	EMPLOYEES
4/05	33,840	—	—	183,050
4/04	32,104	—	—	184,046
4/03*	29,511	—	—	183,638
6/02	28,227	—	—	183,396
6/01	22,626	—	—	186,000
6/00	30,800	—	—	200,000
6/99	28,820	—	—	200,000
6/98	29,430	—	—	200,000
6/97	30,005	—	—	200,000
6/96	33,000	—	—	200,000
Annual Growth	**0.3%**	**—**	**—**	**(1.0%)**

*Fiscal year change

Revenue History

Tesco PLC

Tesco is proof of the good a little dressing-up can do. The company runs more than 2,350 supermarkets, hypermarkets, and convenience stores in the UK (where it is the #1 food retailer), Ireland, Central Europe, and Asia. Built on the "pile it high and sell it cheap" philosophy of founder Sir Jack Cohen, Tesco abandoned its discount format, with its down-market image, for a variety of dressier mid-market formats. Its operations include convenience and gasoline retailing (Tesco Express), small urban stores (Tesco Metro), hypermarkets (Tesco Extra), and financial services through Tesco Personal Finance. A global leader in online grocery sales, it owns a 35% stake in US grocery chain Safeway's GroceryWorks.

Unlike its online competition, Tesco.com — founded in 1995 — is profitable (with a 65% share of the UK Internet grocery market) and has expanded beyond its homeland to South Korea as well as the US. The Internet grocery service covers 98% of the UK and delivers some 150,000 orders every week. In addition to groceries, Tesco.com's legal advice store offers do-it-yourself wills, leases, and even separation/divorce kits (£7.49).

Tesco's rapid growth in both the grocery and nonfood sectors has given the retail giant a 12% share of the entire UK retail market and a whopping 30.2% share of grocery sales in its home country. More than half of its selling space is outside the UK. Tesco is present in a dozen markets across Asia and Europe.

To strengthen its presence in the convenience store market, Tesco bought T&S Stores in 2003 and is still converting many of T&S's 800-plus One Stop shops to its Tesco Express banner. The acquisition gave Tesco about 5% of the convenience store market in Britain.

Since 1993 the company has grown significantly outside the UK: It has about 200 stores (including hypermarkets) in Poland, the Czech Republic, Slovakia, and Hungary. Tesco's acquisition of C Two-Network (C2), a small Japanese convenience store operator, marked its entry into the world's second-largest consumer market, and pits the British food giant against Wal-Mart Stores, which owns a controlling stake in Seiyu.

In China Tesco acquired in 2004 a 50% stake in Ting Hsin International's Hymall business. Hymall operates 31 hypermarkets in Shanghai and in northeastern China. The company also plans to open 15 to 20 new stores in Malaysia where it currently operates eight outlets. It also operates Homeplus hypermarkets in South Korea.

Although food has been the cornerstone of Tesco's operations, the company is actively expanding its nonfood offerings (about 6.5% of sales), including clothing, gasoline, music, travel, financial services (through a joint venture with the Royal Bank of Scotland), and even residential phone service under the "Tesco Telecom" banner.

HISTORY

With WWI behind him, in 1919 Jack Cohen invested his serviceman's gratuity in a grocery stall in London's East End. He introduced his first private-label product, Tesco Tea, in 1924 — the name was the combination of the initials of his tea supplier (T. E. Stockwell) and the first two letters of Cohen's last name. By the late 1920s Cohen had several stalls, and in 1929 he opened his first store, under the Tesco name, in Edgeware, London.

Cohen founded Tesco Stores Limited in 1932. During the rest of the decade, the company added more than 100 stores, mainly in London. Cohen visited the US in 1935, studying its self-service supermarkets, and returned to England with a plan of using a similar "pile it high and sell it cheap" format. Delayed by WWII, Tesco opened its first American-styled store in 1947 and went public that year as Tesco Stores Holdings. By 1950 the company ran 20 self-service stores.

Tesco grew primarily through acquisitions during the 1950s and 1960s, adding about 600 stores. By the early 1970s, however, competition and a recession battered Tesco. Managing director Ian MacLaurin initiated radical changes, including abandoning trading stamps and, to shed its down-market image, refurbishing stores with a more upscale decor. A price-slashing initiative in 1977 dramatically increased Tesco's market share within a year. Because cheap brands were best-sellers, Tesco began creating its own private-label brands. The company also started closing unprofitable stores while opening superstores, some with gas stations.

In 1979, the year Sir Jack Cohen died, Tesco entered Ireland by buying Three Guys (abandoning the effort in 1986). In 1983 the company became Tesco, and two years later it named MacLaurin as chairman. By 1991 Tesco was the UK's largest independent gasoline retailer.

Looking for new opportunities, in 1992 Tesco introduced small urban stores called Tesco Metro and the next year began expanding outside England, acquiring stores in France and Scotland. In 1994 it acquired an initial 51% stake in Global, a 43-store grocery chain in Hungary. That year it also opened Tesco Express (combination convenience stores and gas stations).

Tesco acquired 31 Stavia stores in Poland in 1995; a year later it added 13 Kmart stores in the Czech Republic and Slovakia. Tesco returned to Ireland in 1997 by acquiring 109 Associated British Food stores. It also launched its financial services division that year and named John Gardiner as chairman (replacing the retiring MacLaurin) and Terry Leahy as CEO. In 1998 the retailer purchased 75% of food retailer Lotus, with 13 stores in Thailand. The following year Tesco partnered with Samsung to develop Homeplus hypermarkets in South Korea.

By 2000, Tesco's profitable online shopping business was one of the world's most successful, and the company made it a separate subsidiary, Tesco.com. To build on that success, Tesco bought a 35% stake in GroceryWorks, a subsidiary of the US Safeway grocery chain, in 2001.

Tesco became the market leader in the fragmented Polish food retailing arena by acquiring German hypermarket operator HIT in 2002. In 2003 Tesco completed the acquisition of the British convenience store chain T&S Stores for £519 million. Also that year Tesco acquired Kipa, a small hypermarket operator in Turkey.

In 2004, David Reid became non-executive chairman, replacing Gardiner, who retired from Tesco. In 2005, Tesco transferred some 770 back office jobs from the UK to Bangalore, India, where it opened a software development and accounting office. In mid-2005 Tesco opened its first new Kipa store in Turkey since it acquired the Turkish chain in 2003.

EXECUTIVES

Non-Executive Chairman: David E. Reid, age 58, $1,034,018 pay
Chief Executive and Board Member: Terry P. Leahy, age 49, $2,115,995 pay
Commercial and Trading Director and Board Member: Richard W. P. Brasher, age 43
International and Information Technology Director and Board Member: Philip A. Clarke, age 44, $1,252,715 pay
Finance and Strategy Director and Board Member: Andrew T. Higginson, age 47, $1,254,633 pay
Finance Services Director: Martin Brown
Marketing, E-Commerce, Property and Republic of Ireland Director and Board Member: Tim J. R. Mason, age 47, $1,183,653 pay
Retail and Logistics Director, and Board Member: David T. Potts, age 47, $1,187,490 pay
Category Director, Produce: Peter Durose
Group Corporate and Legal Affairs Director and Secretary: Lucy Neville-Rolfe, age 52
Human Resources Director, Tesco Stores Ltd.: Clare M. Chapman, age 42
Information Technology Director, UK: Colin Cobain
International Corporate Affairs Director: Peter Bracher
Investor Relations Director: Steve Webb, age 43
Personnel Director: David Fairhurst
Manager, Press Office: Jonathan (Jon) Church
Auditors: PricewaterhouseCoopers LLP

LOCATIONS

HQ: Tesco PLC
Tesco House, Delamare Rd., Cheshunt, Hertfordshire EN8 9SL, United Kingdom
Phone: +44-1992-632-222   **Fax:** +44-1992-630-794
Web: www.tesco.com

Tesco has 2,350-plus stores in China, the Czech Republic, Hungary, Ireland, Japan, Malaysia, Poland, Slovakia, South Korea, Thailand, Turkey, and the UK.

2005 Sales

	% of total
Europe	
UK	80
Other countries	11
Asia	9
Total	**100**

2005 Stores

	No.
Europe	
UK	1,780
Ireland	82
Poland	78
Hungary	69
Slovakia	30
Czech Republic	25
Turkey	5
Asia	
Thailand	107
Japan	103
China	31
South Korea	31
Malaysia	6
Taiwan	5
Total	**2,352**

PRODUCTS/OPERATIONS

Selected Subsidiaries and Joint Ventures

Ek-Chai Distribution System Co. Ltd. (99%, Lotus stores, Thailand)
Global T.H. (99%, Kaposvar and Tesco stores, Hungary)
Samsung Tesco. Co. Limited (81%, Homeplus stores, South Korea)
Shopping Centres Limited (50%, property investment)
Tesco Home Shopping Limited (60%, mail order)
Tesco Ireland Limited (Tesco stores)
Tesco Kipa (hypermarkets, Turkey)
Tesco Personal Finance Group Limited (credit cards, savings accounts, loans, online banking, insurance)
Tesco Polska Sp. Z o.o. (Czestochowa stores, Poland)
Tesco Stores CR a.s. (Tesco stores, the Czech Republic)
Tesco Stores SR a.s. (Tesco stores, Slovakia)
Tesco.com (online sales)

COMPETITORS

ALDI
ASDA
Big Food
Boots Group
BP
Carphone Warehouse
Carrefour
Co-operative Group
Dunnes Stores
Exxon Mobil
First Quench
Gap
J Sainsbury
John Lewis
Marks & Spencer
Matalan
METRO AG
Musgrave Budgens-Londis
NEXT
Primark
Royal Ahold
Royal Dutch/Shell Group
Somerfield
SPAR Handels
T.K. Maxx
Wm Morrison Supermarkets
Woolworths Group

HISTORICAL FINANCIALS

Company Type: Public

Income Statement

FYE: Last Saturday in February

	REVENUE ($ mil.)	NET INCOME ($ mil.)	NET PROFIT MARGIN	EMPLOYEES
2/05	65,176	2,621	4.0%	335,750
2/04	57,564	2,055	3.6%	310,411
2/03	41,615	1,495	3.6%	270,800
2/02	33,575	1,178	3.5%	247,374
2/01	30,277	1,107	3.7%	225,388
2/00	29,666	1,064	3.6%	215,216
2/99	27,451	970	3.5%	198,342
2/98	29,273	832	2.8%	185,580
2/97	24,379	846	3.5%	153,198
Annual Growth	13.1%	15.2%	—	10.3%

2005 Year-End Financials

Debt ratio: 50.0%
Return on equity: 16.3%
Cash ($ mil.): 1,535

Current ratio: 0.57
Long-term debt ($ mil.): 8,692

Net Income History

OTC: TSCDY.PK

Thomson Corporation

Niche information is The Thomson Corporation's niche. The company provides specialized information (such as legal and financial data) online and through CD-ROMs, computer software, and print products. Thomson has divested almost all of its traditional media assets in favor of electronic products. It sold most of its 130 daily and non-daily newspapers, as well as its 20% stake in Canadian media giant Bell Globemedia, a firm it founded with telecommunications company BCE. It bought several Harcourt General businesses (after Harcourt was sold to Reed Elsevier Group) and also owns business information firm Dialog. The Thomson family, through their Woodbridge investment company, owns about 63% of Thomson.

Thomson's makeover into an electronic-based information provider has been successful for the company. It is dramatically increasing Internet-related and other electronic sales (now accounting for 66% of its revenues) and the purchases of rival information provider Primark (for about $1 billion), investor research firm Carson Group, and NewsEdge (which it folded into the Dialog business) were part of that strategy. The deals also cemented Thomson's presence in North America and helped it expand into Europe and Asia. Even though it initially benefited from its participation in the creation of Bell Globemedia, Thomson decided the venture didn't fit well into its stable of assets and it sold its stake in the businesses in 2003.

The company has leveraged its growing educational and Internet properties by investing with a consortium of several schools worldwide to launch online university Universitas 21 Global. The university targets Asian and Latin American markets and focuses on awarding business and information technology degrees.

Thomson sold sell its dental, veterinary, and medical economics publishing units to Advanstar Communications for $135 million. In 2004 the company acquired The Institute of Canadian Bankers, providers of educational programs for banking and financial services professionals.

All told, the company made 57 acquisitions in 2004 for a total of $1.5 billion.

HISTORY

Having failed at farming and auto parts distribution, Roy Thomson left Toronto for the hinterlands of Ontario and started a radio station in 1930. He purchased the *Timmons Press,* a gold-mining town newspaper, in 1934. Thomson bought other town papers, venturing outside Ontario in 1949 and into the US in 1952.

The Thomson Newspaper empire grew rapidly during the 1950s. In 1953 Thomson moved to the UK, where he bought the *Scotsman* (Edinburgh). When commercial TV broadcasting began in the UK, Thomson started Scottish Television (1957) and merged it with the UK's Kemsley Newspapers, publisher of the *Sunday Times,* to create the International Thomson Organization in 1959.

International Thomson bought the *Times* of London (1967) and entered the travel business. The next year J. Paul Getty invited International Thomson into a North Sea oil drilling venture. The consortium struck oil in 1973, just as the OPEC oil embargo took hold. Oil accounted for the bulk of International Thomson's profits by 1976, when Thomson died. His son, Kenneth, took over as chairman. In 1978 a public holding company was created to house International Thomson's operations.

Using oil earnings to expand and diversify its publishing interests, the company sold the *Times* in 1981 and began shopping for specialty publishers with subscription-based revenues, which would be less vulnerable to recession. Purchases included American Banker and Bond Buyer (financial publications, 1983), Gale Research (library reference materials, 1985), and several online information providers. The company then completed the sale of its oil and gas holdings.

Thomson Newspapers and International Thomson merged to become The Thomson Corporation in 1989, and in 1991 it bought Maxwell's Macmillan Professional and Business Reference Publishing. The company grouped its newspapers in regional clusters.

The firm bought law and textbook publisher West Publishing in 1996. Continuing its selective divestment of newspapers, the company sold 43 daily papers in the US and Canada in 1996.

In 1998 Thomson veteran Richard Harrington became CEO. Also that year Thomson bought tax return software maker Computer Language Research as well as a pair of tax and law publishing units from UK's Pearson. It also bought Knight Ridder's Technimetrics financial information unit and spun off its travel group business.

In 2000 Thomson announced it would sell its newspapers to focus on the Internet. The company bought Sylvan Learning Systems' Prometric division, which provides computer-based testing services, and Wave Technologies Interna-

tional, a provider of multimedia instructional products. Thomson also bought the online data services division of Dialog, and it acquired rival financial data provider Primark for $1 billion.

Thomson joined forces in 2001 with Canadian telecommunications giant BCE to create media firm Bell Globemedia, with Internet, newspapers, and broadcasting assets worth about $2.7 billion. (It sold its interest in the company two years later.) Also that year it bought the higher education and corporate training businesses of Harcourt General from Reed Elsevier Group plc (formerly Reed Elsevier plc) and acquired business content provider NewsEdge.

Thomson started trading on the New York Stock Exchange in mid-2002. Later that year it beefed up its Internet education group with the purchase of certain e-learning assets from McGraw-Hill. In 2003 the company purchased Elite Information Group, a maker of law firm practice software, for more than $100 million.

EXECUTIVES

Chairman: David K. R. Thomson, age 47
Deputy Chairman: W. Geoffrey Beattie, age 45
President, CEO, and Director:
Richard J. (Dick) Harrington, age 58, $2,771,503 pay
EVP, CFO, and Director: Robert D. (Bob) Daleo, age 55, $1,631,526 pay
EVP and Director: David H. (Dave) Shaffer, age 62, $2,260,570 pay (prior to title change)
EVP Human Resources: Robert Bogart
EVP; President and CEO, Thomson Learning:
Ronald H. Schlosser, age 53, $1,341,740 pay
EVP; President and CEO, Thomson Legal & Regulatory: Brian H. Hall, age 54, $2,280,038 pay
EVP; President and CEO, Thomson Scientific and Healthcare: Robert C. Cullen
President and CEO, Academic and Reference Group:
James C. (Jim) Smith
President and CEO, Thomson Financial:
Sharon Rowlands
President, Thomson Financial Global Sales, Marketing, and Service: Louis Eccleston
SVP Finance: David J. Hulland
SVP Human Resources: John J. Raffaeli Jr.
SVP Technology: Joe Rhyne
SVP and General Counsel: Deirdre Stanley, age 37
SVP and Treasurer: Stephane Bello, age 40
VP Communications: Janey M. Loyd
VP Investor Relations: Frank J. Golden, age 46
Secretary: David W. Binet
Auditors: PricewaterhouseCoopers LLP

LOCATIONS

HQ: The Thomson Corporation
Toronto-Dominion Bank Tower,
66 Wellington Street West,
Toronto, Ontario M5K 1A1, Canada
Phone: 416-360-8700   **Fax:** 416-360-8812
US HQ: Metro Center, 1 Station Place,
Stamford, CT 06902
US Phone: 203-539-8000   **US Fax:** 203-539-7734
Web: www.thomson.com

2004 Sales

	$ mil.	% of total
US	6,390	79
Europe	1,045	13
Asia/Pacific	329	4
Canada	261	3
Other countries	73	1
Total	**8,098**	**100**

PRODUCTS/OPERATIONS

2004 Sales

	$ mil.	% of total
Legal & regulatory	3,393	42
Learning	2,174	27
Financial	1,738	21
Scientific & health care	836	10
Adjustments	(43)	—
Total	**8,098**	**100**

Selected Operations

Thomson Financial
AutEx (global securities market tracking)
BASELINE (financial information and software for portfolio managers)
CCBN (investor relations information services)
Datastream International (current and historical economic and financial information, UK)
First Call (real-time broker research)
TradeWeb (online fixed income securities trading)
Vestek Systems, Inc. (investment information services and applications software)

Thomson Learning
NETg (information technology training)
Prometric (computer based testing)
Thomson Gale (academic and business reference material)
Universitas 21 Global (online university)
Wadsworth (higher education textbooks)

Thomson Legal & Regulatory
Australian Digest
Checkpoint (online tax research library)
FindLaw (Web portal of legal resources)
Foundation Press (law school publications)
Thomson CompuMark (trademark information)
Thomson Elite (law firm management software)
Thomson West (online and print legal book publishing)

Thomson News & Business
Dialog (business information and news service)
Dialog DataStar
Dialog NewsEdge
Dialog NewsRoom
Dialog Profound
Dialog TradStat

Thomson Scientific & Healthcare
Derwent World Patents Index (patent and scientific data)
ISI Web of Science (global research online)
MICROMEDIX (drug information)
Physician's Desk Reference

COMPETITORS

Addison-Wesley
American Lawyer Media
Berkshire Hathaway
Bloomberg
Comtex
D&B
Dow Jones
Encyclopædia Britannica
IHS
infoUSA
John Wiley
Kaplan
LexisNexis
McGraw-Hill
Pearson
ProQuest
Reed Elsevier Group
Reuters
Scholastic Library Publishing
Solucient
United Business Media
Wolters Kluwer
W.W. Norton

HISTORICAL FINANCIALS

Company Type: Public

Income Statement

FYE: December 31

	REVENUE ($ mil.)	NET INCOME ($ mil.)	NET PROFIT MARGIN	EMPLOYEES
12/04	8,098	1,011	12.5%	39,550
12/03	7,606	867	11.4%	39,000
12/02	7,756	615	7.9%	42,000
12/01	7,237	776	10.7%	44,000
12/00	6,514	1,223	18.8%	39,330
12/99	5,752	532	9.2%	32,500
12/98	6,269	3,665	58.5%	48,000
12/97	8,753	578	6.6%	48,400
12/96	7,719	581	7.5%	47,800
12/95	7,262	793	10.9%	48,600
Annual Growth	**1.2%**	**2.7%**	**—**	**(2.3%)**

2004 Year-End Financials

Debt ratio: 40.3%
Return on equity: 10.6%
Cash ($ mil.): 405
Current ratio: 0.94
Long-term debt ($ mil.): 4,013
No. of shares (mil.): 655
Dividends
  Yield: 2.2%
  Payout: 49.4%
Market value ($ mil.): 23,120

Stock History

NYSE: TOC

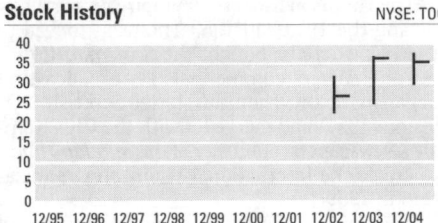

	STOCK PRICE ($) FY Close	P/E High/Low	Earnings	PER SHARE ($) Dividends	Book Value
12/04	35.29	24 19	1.54	0.76	15.21
12/03	36.25	27 19	1.34	0.93	14.05
12/02	26.73	34 24	0.93	0.53	13.75
Annual Growth	**14.9%**	**— —**	**28.7%**	**19.7%**	**5.2%**

ThyssenKrupp

How do you say "giant engineering and steel company" in German? Try "ThyssenKrupp." The company is one of the world's largest steel producers and getting larger. ThyssenKrupp operates worldwide in three business areas: steel, capital goods, and services. The steel unit concentrates on carbon steel and stainless steel, while the capital goods unit consists of three segments: elevators, automotive (parts, sub-assemblies, and modules), and technologies (machine tools, large-diameter bearings, and industrial doors). The services sector provides tailor-made materials, environmental services, mechanical engineering, and scaffolding services. In 2004 ThyssenKrupp sold its residential real estate unit for $2.8 billion.

ThyssenKrupp is a product of the 1999 merger of Thyssen AG, (pronounced "TISS-in") and Fried. Krupp AG Hoesch-Krupp. Although its combined interests range from elevators to shipbuilding, the company relies heavily on the cyclical steel market; hence, ThyssenKrupp has put on hold its plans to spin off the steel unit.

The company's steel unit is investing nearly $800 million throughout its global operations. ThyssenKrupp's largest investment has gone toward its tinplate manufacturing business, which supplies the food and beverage industries. To take full advantage of China's fast-paced economy, ThyssenKrupp's Shanghai stainless steel venture with Shanghai Baosteel is multiplying its cold strip mill production capacity by five in 2006. It also submitted a bid for Dofasco, a move that trumped Arcelor's initial bid for Canada's largest steel company. ThyssenKrupp's $4.1 billion bid, coming in late 2005, was accepted by Dofasco's board; the move is designed to strengthen the company's position in the North American auto market.

The Krupp Foundation owns 20% of the company.

HISTORY

Formed separately in the 1800s, both Thyssen and Krupp flourished in their early years under family control. Friedrich Krupp opened his steel factory in 1811. He died in 1826 and left the nearly bankrupt factory in the hands of his 14-year-old son Alfred, who turned the business around. At the first World's Fair in 1851, Alfred unveiled a steel cannon far superior to earlier bronze models.

Twenty years later, August Thyssen founded a puddling and rolling mill near Mulheim. He bought small factories and mines, and by WWI, he ran Germany's largest iron and steel company. During the world wars the resources of both companies were turned toward war efforts.

Post-WWII years were tough for both companies. Thyssen was split up by the Allies, and when it began production again in 1953, it consisted of one steel plant. In the Krupp camp, Alfred's great-grandson Alfried was convicted in 1948 of using slave labor during WWII. Released from prison in 1951, Alfried rebuilt Krupp. After near ruin following WWII, both companies emerged and enjoyed a resurgence, along with the German economy, in which they prospered and expanded during the 1950s.

By the 1980s Thyssen's businesses included ships, locomotives, offshore oil rigs, specialty steel, and metals trading and distribution. Krupp continued to grow, and in 1992 it took over engineering and steelmaking concern Hoesch AG. (Eberhard Hoesch had begun making railroad tracks in the 1820s. The company grew and expanded into infrastructure and building products.)

The new Fried. Krupp AG Hoesch-Krupp bought Italian specialty steelmaker Acciai Speciali Terni, chemical plant builder Uhde, and South African shipper J.H. Bachmann. Its automotive division formed a joint venture in Brazil and added production sites in China, Mexico, Romania, and the US.

In 1997 Thyssen expanded in North America with its $675 million acquisition of Giddings & Lewis (machine tools, US) and the purchase of Copper & Brass Sales (metals processing and distributing).

Krupp attempted a hostile takeover of Thyssen in 1997. The takeover failed, but the companies soon agreed to merge their steel operations to form Thyssen Krupp Stahl. Bigger plans were in the works, and in 1998 the two companies agreed to merge. That year Thyssen sold its Plusnet fixed-line phone business to Esprit Telecom Group.

In 1999 Krupp's automotive division (Krupp Hoesch Automotive) bought Cummins' Atlas

Crankshaft subsidiary. Thyssen also bought US-based Dover's elevator business for $1.1 billion. Krupp and Thyssen completed their merger in 1999. The company planned to spin off its steel operations, but held off due to its success in 2000. ThyssenKrupp did, however, sell its Krupp Kunststofftechnik unit (plastic molding machines) for about $183 million. To speed corporate decision-making, the company made plans to scrap its dual-management structure in 2001.

Early in 2001 ThyssenKrupp agreed to buy 51% of Fiat unit Magneti Marelli's suspension-systems and shock-absorbers business. It also has the option of buying the remainder after 2004. In 2002 the company formed alliances with NKK and Kawasaki Steel to share its steel sheet making technologies while expanding its business with Japanese automotive makers in Europe. ThyssenKrupp's joint venture with Chinese steelmaker ANSC Angang New Steel, known as TAGAL, began producing galvanized coil of which about 80% will be used in China's burgeoning automotive industry.

In 2004 ThyssenKrupp sold its residential real estate unit for around $2.8 billion to a consortium of real estate funds operated by Morgan Stanley and Corpus-Immobiliengruppe.

EXECUTIVES

Chairman, Supervisory Board: Gerhard Cromme, age 62, $207,060 pay
Chairman, Executive Board: Prof Ekkehard D. Schulz, age 64, $2,704,721 pay
Vice Chairman, Executive Board; Chairman, Executive Board, ThyssenKrupp Steel AG: Ulrich Middelmann, age 60, $2,049,031 pay
Member, Executive Board; Chairman, Executive Board, ThyssenKrupp Technologies: Olaf Berlien, age 43, $1,639,225 pay
Member, Executive Board; Chairman, Executive Board, ThyssenKrupp Services: Edwin Eichler, $1,639,225 pay
Member, Executive Board, CFO, and Controller: A. Stefan Kirsten, $1,639,225 pay
Executive Board Member and Labor Director; Executive Board Member and Labor Director, ThyssenKrupp Steel: Ralph Labonte, age 52, $1,330,000 pay
Member, Executive Board; Chairman, Executive Board, ThyssenKrupp Automotive: Wolfram Mörsdorf, age 57, $3,130,550 pay (partial-year salary)
Chairman, Executive Board, ThyssenKrupp Stainless, Executive Board Member, ThyssenKrupp Steel: Jürgen H. Fechter, age 43
Member, Executive Board, ThyssenKrupp Technologies: Prof Heinrich Igelbüscher, age 62
Corporate Communications, Strategy, and Executive Affairs: Jürgen Claassen
Director Central Bureau/Public Relations, ThyssenKrupp Automotive: Viktor Braun
Auditors: KPMG Deutsche Treuhand-Gesellschaft AG

LOCATIONS

HQ: ThyssenKrupp AG
August-Thyssen-Strasse 1,
40211 Düsseldorf, Germany
Phone: +49-211-824-0   **Fax:** +49-211-824-36000
Web: www.thyssenkrupp.com

ThyssenKrupp operates worldwide; it has current operations centered in Europe and North America.

2004 Sales

	$ mil.	% of total
EU		
Germany	16,720	35
Other countries	13,628	28
US	8,770	18
Other regions	9,371	19
Total	**48,489**	**100**

PRODUCTS/OPERATIONS

2004

	$ mil.	% of total
Steel	16,885	33
Services	14,651	28
Automotive	9,012	17
Technologies	6,276	12
Elevator	4,398	9
Real Estate	415	1
Corporate	34	—
Adjustments	(3,182)	—
Total	**48,489**	**100**

COMPETITORS

Acerinox	MAN
Allegheny Technologies	Marubeni
Arcelor	Mittal Steel Company
Bechtel	Nippon Steel
BlueScope Steel	Otis Elevator
Cargill	POSCO
Corus Group	Robert Bosch
Dana	RWE
Descours & Cabaud	Schindler Holding
GEA Group	Siderar
Ingersoll-Rand	Siemens
Ingersoll-Rand Industrial	Sumitomo Metal
Technologies	Industries
ITOCHU	Tenneco
JFE Holdings	Tower Automotive
Kobe Steel	United States Steel
Magna International	United Technologies

HISTORICAL FINANCIALS

Company Type: Public

Income Statement

FYE: September 30

	REVENUE ($ mil.)	NET INCOME ($ mil.)	NET PROFIT MARGIN	EMPLOYEES
9/04	48,489	1,114	2.3%	187,678
9/03	41,897	594	1.4%	190,102
9/02	36,001	212	0.6%	191,254
9/01	34,572	605	1.7%	193,516
9/00	32,710	463	1.4%	193,316
9/99	31,734	284	0.9%	184,770
9/98	26,013	1,309	5.0%	116,174
9/97	23,058	1,233	5.3%	127,873
9/96	25,327	229	0.9%	122,659
9/95	27,407	543	2.0%	126,987
Annual Growth	**6.5%**	**8.3%**	**—**	**4.4%**

2004 Year-End Financials

Debt ratio: 55.4%
Return on equity: 11.7%
Cash ($ mil.): 1,716
Current ratio: 1.31
Long-term debt ($ mil.): 5,687

Net Income History

German: TKA

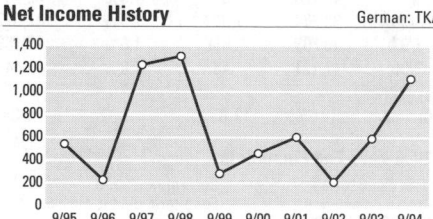

Tokyo Electric Power

Japan Inc. would grind to a halt without Tokyo Electric Power Company (TEPCO), which supplies power to nearly 28 million customers in Tokyo, Yokohama, and the rest of the Kanto region. One of the world's largest electric utilities, TEPCO has a generating capacity of approximately 63,000 MW, primarily produced by thermal, nuclear, and hydroelectric power sources. Through interests in telecom businesses, the company offers telephony and Internet services; it also has international consulting and power generation operations. Other businesses include construction, real estate, and transportation companies.

Although public confidence has been shaken by a rash of accidents within Japan's nuclear industry, the company promotes the use of nuclear power as an earth-friendly energy source. TEPCO currently operates three power plants. However, the company has struggled to restore its credibility after the Japanese government shut down TEPCO's 17 nuclear reactors due to safety concerns, prompted by the company's admittance of falsifying safety data to cover up faults at several of its nuclear facilities in 2002.

TEPCO is diversifying its operations in the face of further deregulation. In 2005 the company's liberalization of the retail electric power market has resulted in about 60% of TEPCO's revenues coming from retail sales. The company also owns a majority stake in telecommunications firm POWEREDCOM, which offers data communications services through TEPCO and other Japanese utilities' fiber-optic networks; TEPCO increased its stake in POWEREDCOM to 84% in 2004. POWEREDCOM has absorbed local and long-distance phone company Tokyo Telecommunication Network (TTNet), in which TEPCO held a 39% stake.

HISTORY

The Tokyo Electric Power Company (TEPCO) descended from Tokyo Electric Light, which was formed in 1883. In 1887 the company switched on Japan's first power plant, a 25-KW fossil fuel generator. Fossil fuels were the main source of electricity in Japan until 1912, when long-distance transmission techniques became more efficient, making hydroelectric power cheaper.

In 1938 Japan nationalized electric utilities, despite strong objections from Yasuzaemon Matsunaga, a leader in Japan's utility industry and former president of the Japan Electric Association. After WWII Matsunaga championed public ownership of Japan's power companies, which helped in 1951 to establish the current system of 10 regional companies, each with a service monopoly. Tokyo Electric Power was the largest. That year it was listed on the Tokyo Stock Exchange and was regulated by the Ministry of International Trade and Industry. (The ministry has regulated electric utilities since 1965.)

Fossil fuel plants made a comeback in Japan in the postwar era because they could be built more economically than hydroelectric plants. When the OPEC oil embargo of the 1970s demonstrated Japan's dependence on foreign oil, TEPCO increased its use of liquefied natural gas (LNG) and nuclear energy sources. (It brought its first nuke online in 1971.) In 1977 it formed the Energy Conservation Center to promote conservation and related legislation.

To further reduce its oil dependence TEPCO joined other US and Japanese firms in building a coal gasification plant in California's Mojave Desert in 1982. Two years later TEPCO announced it would begin building its first coal-burning generator since the oil crisis. It established Tokyo Telecommunication Network (TTNet), a partnership to provide telecommunications services, in 1986 and TEPCO Cable TV in 1989.

As part of its interest in alternative energy systems, TEPCO established a global environment department in 1990 to conduct R&D on energy and the environment. Its environmental program has included reforestation and fuel cell research.

Liberalization in 1995 allowed Japan's electric utilities to buy power from independent power producers; TEPCO quickly lined up 10 suppliers. The company proceeded with energy experimentation in 1996, trying a 6,000-KW sodium-sulfur battery at a Yokohama transformer station. The next year the company announced that it would become the first electric utility to sell liquefied natural gas as part of its energy mix, and finished building the world's largest nuclear plant.

To gain experience in deregulating markets, TEPCO invested in US power generating company Orion Power in 1999. (It agreed to sell its 5% stake to Reliant Energy in 2001.) At home the firm joined Microsoft and SOFTBANK to form SpeedNet, which provides Internet access over TTNet's network. In 2000 TEPCO got its first taste of deregulation when large customers (accounting for about a third of the market) began choosing their electricity suppliers. Also in 2000 TEPCO joined a group of nine Japanese electric companies to create POWEREDCOM.

In 2001 TEPCO joined up with Sumitomo and Electricité de France to build Vietnam's first independent power plant.

EXECUTIVES

Chairman: Shigemi Tamura
President: Tsunehisa Katsumata
EVP, General Accounting, Planning, and International: Katsutoshi Chikudate
EVP: Hisao Naito
EVP: Yoshihisa Morimoto
EVP: Takashi Hayashi
EVP: Susumu Shirakawa
EVP: Takuya Hattori
Managing Director: Yuichi Hayase
Managing Director: Katsumi Mizutani
Managing Director: Masataka Shimizu
Managing Director: Ichiro Takekuro
Managing Director: Norio Tsuzumi
Managing Director: Takashi Fujimoto
Managing Director: Akio Nakamura
Managing Director: Shigeru Kimura
Auditors: Ernst & Young ShinNihon

LOCATIONS

HQ: The Tokyo Electric Power Company, Incorporated (Tokyo Denryoku Kabushiki Kaisha)
1-3, Uchisaiwai-cho 1-chome, Chiyoda-ku, Tokyo 100-8560, Japan
Phone: +81-3-4216-1111   **Fax:** +81-3-4216-2539
US HQ: 1901 L St. NW, Ste. 720, Washington, DC 20036
US Phone: 202-457-0790   **US Fax:** 202-457-0810
Web: www.tepco.co.jp

The Tokyo Electric Power Company provides electricity in Japan's Kanto region, which includes Tokyo and Yokohama. It also has independent power projects, consulting operations, and/or other investments in Asia, Australia, Europe, the Middle East, North America, and South America.

PRODUCTS/OPERATIONS

2005 Sales

	% of total
Electricity	89
Information & telecommunications	3
Other	8
Total	**100**

Selected Subsidiaries and Affiliates

AT TOKYO Corporation (52%, information software and services)
POWEREDCOM, Incorporated (84%, telecommunications)
TEPCO CABLE TELEVISION Inc. (85%, cable television)
TEPCO SYSTEMS CORPORATION (information software and services)
Toden Kogyo Co., Ltd. (facilities construction and maintenance)
Toden Real Estate Co., Inc. (property management)
TOKYO DENSETSU SERVICE CO., LTD. (facilities construction and maintenance)
Tokyo Electric Power Environmental Engineering Company, Incorporated (facilities construction and maintenance)
Tokyo Electric Power Services Company, Limited (facilities construction and maintenance)

COMPETITORS

Chubu Electric Power
Chugoku Electric Power
Hokkaido Electric Power
Hokuriku Electric Power
Internet Initiative Japan
Jinpan International
Kansai Electric
KDDI
Korea Electric Power
Kyushu Electric Power
NTT
Osaka Gas
Shikoku Electric
Tohoku Electric Power
Tokyo Gas

HISTORICAL FINANCIALS

Company Type: Public

Income Statement

FYE: March 31

	REVENUE ($ mil.)	NET INCOME ($ mil.)	NET PROFIT MARGIN	EMPLOYEES
3/05	44,609	2,103	4.7%	53,380
3/04	45,946	1,416	3.1%	51,694
3/03	41,045	1,379	3.4%	52,322
3/02	39,358	1,521	3.9%	40,725
3/01	41,622	1,646	4.0%	42,000
3/00	48,258	829	1.7%	43,000
3/99	42,720	818	1.9%	42,700
3/98	39,664	1,017	2.6%	42,672
3/97	40,703	659	1.6%	43,166
3/96	47,121	483	1.0%	43,448
Annual Growth	**(0.6%)**	**17.8%**	**—**	**2.3%**

2005 Year-End Financials

Debt ratio: 285.8%
Return on equity: 9.2%
Cash ($ mil.): 1,302
Current ratio: 0.39
Long-term debt ($ mil.): 66,496

Net Income History

Pink Sheets: TKECF

Tokyo Electron

Let me tell you about TEL. Tokyo Electron Limited (TEL) is the world's #2 manufacturer of semiconductor production equipment — well behind #1 Applied Materials, but well ahead of other contenders. TEL's chip making systems include chemical vapor deposition, thermal processing, etching, cleaning, and probing equipment. The company also makes flat-panel display (FPD) production equipment, and distributes other companies' chip making equipment, computer systems, networking products, and software in Japan. Subsidiary Tokyo Electron Device distributes chips, boards, and software made by companies including Advanced Micro Devices, Agilent, Motorola, and Microsoft.

Chip production equipment accounts for nearly three-quarters of TEL's sales, and customers outside Japan account for nearly two-thirds of sales.

Like its customers and competitors, TEL suffered through a dismal time during the chip industry slump of 2001-2003. To counter these conditions, and to give itself more flexibility for future market ups and downs, TEL restructured its operations. Among other measures, it merged production plants, closed field offices, and let go many of its contract workers. It has also sold its physical vapor deposition (PVD) product line to Metron Technology (now Nortem), which sold its assets to Applied Materials in late 2004.

HISTORY

Frustrated by the unreliable semiconductor production equipment their employer, Nissho Trading Co. (now Nissho Iwai-Nichimen), was importing from the US, Tokuo Kubo and Toshio Kodada quit their jobs at Nissho in 1963 and founded Tokyo Electron Laboratories (TEL). Tokyo Broadcasting System provided some initial backing.

At first about half of the company's sales came from importing US semiconductor equipment. The other half came from exporting Japanese electronics such as car radios. In 1968 TEL and US-based diffusion furnace maker Thermco Systems (later acquired by Allegheny International) formed TEL-Thermco Engineering Co. TEL followed with other joint ventures, paying royalties to manufacture other companies' products in Japan.

The company's US unit, TEL America (now Tokyo Electron America), was established in 1972. In 1978 Tokyo Electron Laboratories was renamed Tokyo Electron Limited (also TEL).

TEL went public in 1980. In 1981 the company formed a joint venture with GenRad (later acquired by Teradyne) to make test systems in the US. In 1988 TEL acquired Thermco's stake in their joint venture.

The company began a major international expansion in 1993, setting up shop in South Korea. In the following years it expanded into Germany, Italy, the UK, and Taiwan. In 1996 TEL managing director Tetsuro Higashi was named president. (He is now chairman.)

In 1997 TEL delivered the first of its 300mm wafer production equipment. The next year the company acquired the semiconductor equipment division (now part of Tokyo Electron Arizona) of Sony's Material Research Corp. Also in

1998 TEL formed Tokyo Electron EE Limited to refurbish and upgrade semiconductor manufacturing equipment.

The company formed its French subsidiary in 1999. That year TEL and AlliedSignal (now Honeywell International) formed a joint venture to develop chip making equipment. Also in 1999 rival Tegal won a permanent injunction against TEL to stop US sales of some of TEL's wafer etching equipment; legal wrangling over patent issues continued between the two companies through 2000.

In 2000 TEL acquired US-based Supercritical Systems, a maker of semiconductor cleaning devices. The next year the company bought Timbre Technologies, a US-based maker of metrology tools used in chip production.

In 2002 the company expanded its reach into China — which many industry watchers project as the next great market for the chip industry — when it opened a support office there.

EXECUTIVES

Chairman and CEO: Tetsuro (Terry) Higashi
Vice Chairman: Tetsuo (Tom) Tsuneishi
President and COO: Kiyoshi (Ken) Sato
SVP, Technology and Development: Masao Kubodera
SVP, FPD and General Manager, FPD Division:
Mitsuru Onozato
SVP, Business Development and Account Management and General Manager, Business Development and Account Management, Japan: Makoto Mizokuchi
SVP, Corporate Strategic Planning: Hiroki Takebuchi
SVP, Technology: Ben Tsai
VP; General Manager, Computer Network Division:
Katsuyuki Amano
VP; General Manager, Administration: Yoshiteru Harada
VP; General Manager, Technology and Development Center/Development Planning: Shigetsutoshi Hosaka
VP; General Manager, Clean Track: Hikaru Ito
VP; General Manager, Etch Systems: Takashi Ito
VP; General Manager, Marketing: Yoichi Ishikawa
VP; General Manager, Business Development and Account Management, Korea: Yasuyuki Kuriki
VP; General Manager, Manufacturing and IT:
Satoshi Nakashima
VP; General Manager, Test Systems: Syunro Nagasawa
VP; General Manager, Human Resources and Finance:
Yutaka Nanasawa
Chairman and CEO, Tokyo Electron America:
Barry R. Rapozo
Auditors: Masatoshi Yoshino, Eiji Miyashita,
Fumihiko Sugiura

LOCATIONS

HQ: Tokyo Electron Limited
TBS Broadcast Center, 3-6 Akasaka 5-chome,
Minato-ku, Tokyo 107-8481, Japan
Phone: +81-3-5561-7000   **Fax:** +81-3-5561-7400
US HQ: 2400 Grove Blvd., Austin, TX 78741-1000
US Phone: 512-424-1000   **US Fax:** 512-424-1001
Web: www.tel.com

Tokyo Electron Limited has operations in China, France, Germany, Ireland, Israel, Italy, Japan, the Netherlands, South Korea, Taiwan, the UK, and the US.

2005 Sales

	% of total
Asia	
Japan	37
Taiwan	22
South Korea	13
China & Southeast Asia	13
US	10
Europe	5
Total	**100**

PRODUCTS/OPERATIONS

2005 Sales

	% of total
Industrial electronic equipment	
Semiconductor production	72
FPD production	12
Computer network equipment	2
Electronic equipment	14
Total	**100**

Selected Products

Production Equipment
  Liquid crystal displays
    Coater/developers
    Plasma etcher/ashers
  Semiconductors
    Carrierless cleaners
    Coater/developers
    Metal chemical vapor deposition (CVD) systems
    Oxidation/diffusion furnaces and LP-CVD systems
    Plasma etchers
    Scrubbers
    Spin-on dielectric coaters
    Wafer probers
    Wafer-level burn-in and test systems
Distributed Products
  Data management software
  Film metrology tools
  Lithography process management software
  Semiconductor manufacturing yield
    management software
  Semiconductors and board-level products
  Storage area network (SAN) equipment
  Wafer inspection systems

COMPETITORS

Amtech Systems	Genus
Applied Materials	Hitachi
ASM International	Lam Research
Aviza Technology	Novellus
Dainippon Screen	Semitool
Electroglas	Tegal
FSI International	ULVAC
Future Electronics	Veeco Instruments

HISTORICAL FINANCIALS

Company Type: Public

Income Statement

FYE: March 31

	REVENUE ($ mil.)	NET INCOME ($ mil.)	NET PROFIT MARGIN	EMPLOYEES
3/05	5,911	573	9.7%	8,864
3/04	5,014	79	1.6%	8,870
3/03	3,843	(347)	—	10,053
3/02	3,150	(150)	—	10,171
3/01	5,730	491	8.6%	10,236
3/00	4,177	188	4.5%	8,946
3/99	2,603	16	0.6%	8,576
3/98	3,424	226	6.6%	8,242
3/97	3,496	242	6.9%	6,988
3/96	3,752	229	6.1%	6,148
Annual Growth	**5.2%**	**10.7%**	**—**	**4.1%**

2005 Year-End Financials

Debt ratio: 19.0%   Current ratio: 2.40
Return on equity: 20.1%   Long-term debt ($ mil.): 586
Cash ($ mil.): 1,073

Net Income History

Exchange: Tokyo

Tomkins plc

Not so long ago, whether you wanted to pack some heat or merely pack some lunch, multinational conglomerate Tomkins had a subsidiary that could make your day. But the company has sold its food manufacturing operations and subsidiary Smith & Wesson in order to reshape itself as a global engineering group. Tomkins companies make and distribute automotive products, industrial power systems, plumbing components, windows, doors, valves, and other construction products. In the US, Tomkins' brand divisions include Gates (automotive belts and hoses) and Trico (wiper blades), and Stant (automotive caps, seals, and gaskets).

Tomkins fortines improved in 2004 despite the weakness of the US dollar relative to the pound and euro, and high raw materials costs. The company plans to stay competitive by focusing on core products and keeping an eye out for acquisitions that offer a complimentary and profitable fit.

Meanwhile, Tomkins is well positioned to take advantage of the explosive growth of the automotive industry in China. The company already leads the Chinese market for transmission belts, and with its local manufacturing partner is building an additional plant to meet demand.

HISTORY

Tomkins was founded in 1925 as the F. H. Tomkins Buckle Company, a maker of buckles and fasteners. Tomkins continued to develop within this niche market for the next six decades. In 1983 Gregory Hutchings acquired a 23% stake in the company. Hutchings, who at age 24 had started his own construction business, had won a reputation as a go-getter when he caught the eye of Lords Hanson and White; he was hired by the Hanson Group in 1980 as its chief acquisition scout. In 1984 Hutchings became Tomkins' CEO and set about acquiring manufacturing companies in the UK and the US.

The company acquired Ferraris Piston Service (auto components) and Hayters (a garden tool manufacturer) that year, followed by Pegler-Hattersley (plumbing fixtures) in 1986, Smith & Wesson (guns) in 1987, and Murray Ohio (lawn mowers and bicycles) the next year. In 1992 the company acquired Rank Hovis McDougall, a leading UK baker and food manufacturer.

Tomkins made only eight major purchases between 1983 and 1993, as Hutchings worked to put his acquisitions on a sound financial footing, upgrading plants and equipment and giving each company the autonomy to become efficient.

In 1994 Tomkins bought Outdoor Products and Dynamark Plastics from Noma Industries of Canada: Outdoor Products complemented the Murray Ohio operations, and injection molder Dynamark Plastics fit into Tomkins' industrial products portfolio.

Two years later the company acquired Gates, a US maker of belts and hoses, with operations in 15 countries; the move gave Tomkins access to new markets in Latin America and Southeast Asia. That year Tomkins acquired the hose operations of Nationwide Rubber Enterprises, making Gates the leading manufacturer of curved hose in Australia. In 1997 Tomkins acquired US firm Stant Corp., a leading maker of windshield wipers, fuel tank caps, and other auto accessories, to further complement Gates' product lines.

Besides acquisitions, Tomkins regularly disposed of companies that no longer fit its strategic plan. It sold Inchbrook Printers in 1996 and Ferraris Piston Service, the first business purchased by Tomkins under Hutchings' leadership, in 1997. In a symbolic break with its past, Tomkins sold F. H. Tomkins Buckle in 1998.

That year Tomkins made another automotive equipment acquisition when it bought US-based Schrader-Bridgeport; it also bought Martine Spécialités, a supplier of frozen patisserie products. In 1999 the company acquired ACD Tridon, a Canadian manufacturer of automotive parts.

In 2000 Smith & Wesson settled more than a dozen lawsuits with US cities attempting to collect damages for handgun violence cases. Breaking rank with other handgun makers, the company agreed to install child-safety locks on its guns and ensure that gun sellers conduct background checks.

Tomkins moved to exit the food manufacturing business in 2000, selling Red Wing and agreeing to sell the European operations of Ranks Hovis McDougall. Hutchings resigned that year in the midst of an investigation of his spending practices (including his use of corporate jets and the presence of Hutchings' wife and housekeeper on the company payroll), and chairman David Newlands took over. That year the company sold its bicycle, snowblower, and mowing machinery businesses (Hayter and Murray). In 2001 Tomkins sold Smith & Wesson to US-based Saf-T-Hammer, a manufacturer of gun safety equipment, for $15 million.

In 2002 Tomkins sold its Gates Consumer and Industrial (GCI) division to the Rutland Fund for about $35 million in cash. GCI's products include carpet padding and accessories, diving suits, and commercial rubber compounds. Also that year Jim Nicol took over as CEO. The following year Tomkins sold its Milliken Valve Company, Inc. subsidiary to the Henry Pratt Company for $7.3 million in cash.

EXECUTIVES

Non-Executive Chairman: David B. Newlands, age 58, $633,720 pay
CEO and Director: Jim Nicol, age 50, $5,470,408 pay
CFO and Director: Ken Lever, age 51, $2,430,865 pay
EVP: David Carroll, age 48
EVP, Human Resources: Malcolm T. Swain, age 51
VP, Corporate Development: John Zimmerman, age 42
President, Air Systems Components Division: Terry J. O'Halloran
President, Dexter Axle Company: W.M. Jones, age 55
President, The Gates Rubber Company: Richard Bell, age 57
Secretary: N.C. Porter, age 53
General Counsel: G.S. Pappayliou, age 51
Auditors: Deloitte & Touche

LOCATIONS

HQ: Tomkins plc
East Putney House, 84 Upper Richmond Rd., London SW15 2ST, United Kingdom
Phone: +44-20-8871-4544 **Fax:** +44-20-8877-9700
Web: www.tomkins.co.uk

2004 Sales

	% of total
North America	74
Europe	15
Asia	7
Other regions	4
Total	**100**

PRODUCTS/OPERATIONS

2004 Sales

	$ mil.	% of total
Industrial & automotive	3,706	65
Engineered & construction products	1,197	21
Air systems components	811	14
Total	**5,714**	**100**

Subsidiaries and Affiliates

Industrial and Automotive
  Gates Corporation (automotive belts, hoses, pulleys; US)
  Schrader Bridgeport (automotive electronics, tire valves and gauges; US)
  Schrader Electronics Ltd. (remote tire pressure measuring systems, US)
  Stackpole Limited (belts, pulleys, tensioners, engine modules, and electromechanical drive systems; Canada)
  Standard-Thomson Corporation (automotive thermostats, US)
  Stant Manufacturing Inc. (gas caps, closure caps; US)
  Trico Products Corporation (wiper systems, signal flashers; US)
Engineered and Construction Products
  Aquatic Industries (whirlpool baths, US)
  Dearborn Mid-West Conveyor Company (heavy-duty conveyor systems, US)
  Dexter Axle (axles and wheels for trailers, US)
  Lasco Bathware (fiberglass and acrylic baths and whirlpools, US)
  Lasco Fittings (PVC pipe fittings, US)
  Mayfran International (conveying systems and filtration equipment, US)
  Philips Products (aluminum and vinyl windows, vinyl-clad steel doors, ventilation devices; US)
Air Systems Components
  Hart & Cooley (heating, ventilation, and air-conditioning components; US)
  Ruskin Air Management Ltd (air handling products and louvers, US)
  Ruskin Company (air, fire, and smoke dampers; louvers and fiberglass products; US)

COMPETITORS

Applied Industrial Technologies	Goodyear
Bridgestone	Tenneco
Continental AG	United Technologies

HISTORICAL FINANCIALS

Company Type: Public

Income Statement

FYE: December 31

	REVENUE ($ mil.)	NET INCOME ($ mil.)	NET PROFIT MARGIN	EMPLOYEES
12/04	5,714	331	5.8%	36,720
12/03	5,618	306	5.5%	39,328
12/02*	3,380	190	5.6%	39,596
4/02	4,916	273	5.6%	40,670
4/01	5,875	96	1.6%	52,755
4/00	8,722	164	1.9%	70,039
4/99	8,600	491	5.7%	66,927
4/98	8,442	545	6.5%	65,300
4/97	7,451	459	6.2%	54,496
4/96	5,431	338	6.2%	46,096
Annual Growth	**0.6%**	**(0.2%)**	**—**	**(2.5%)**

*Fiscal year change

2004 Year-End Financials

Debt ratio: 91.6%
Return on equity: 41.7%
Cash ($ mil.): 355
Current ratio: 2.28
Long-term debt ($ mil.): 787
No. of shares (mil.): 193
Dividends
  Yield: 4.5%
  Payout: 49.7%
Market value ($ mil.): 3,829

Stock History

NYSE: TK3

	STOCK PRICE ($) FY Close	P/E High/Low		PER SHARE ($) Earnings	Dividends	Book Value
12/04	19.79	12	10	1.81	0.90	7.79
12/03	19.15	15	8	1.32	0.62	6.86
12/02*	15.30	15	7	1.09	0.76	8.36
4/02	12.22	21	14	0.76	0.50	8.67
4/01	8.81	13	7	0.20	1.16	7.70
4/00	12.19	11	6	0.47	1.41	4.45
4/99	17.63	17	9	1.42	0.94	3.99
4/98	23.06	18	11	1.52	0.94	5.71
4/97	18.00	15	11	1.34	0.73	7.81
4/96	17.00	16	12	1.14	0.59	5.57
Annual Growth	**1.7%**	**—**	**—**	**5.3%**	**4.8%**	**3.8%**

*Fiscal year change

Tommy Hilfiger

From the blacktop to the greens, designer Tommy Hilfiger has it covered. His namesake casual wear is worn by rap, rock, teen, and sports stars and fans, and, these days, many of them are women. Tommy designs, sources, makes, and markets men's and women's sportswear and denim wear, as well as athletic wear, children's wear, swimwear, and accessories. He also hosted *The Cut* on CBS. Through extensive licensing deals (almost 40 product lines), Tommy also offers products such as fragrances, belts, bedding, home furnishings, and cosmetics. The company's clean-cut clothing is sold in major department and specialty stores as well as some 165 Tommy Hilfiger shops and outlets. Chairman Joel Horowitz retired in October.

Upon the exit of Horowitz, it's speculated that Tommy Hilfiger Corporation (THC) is considering selling itself and could fetch between $1.8 billion and $2.2 billion. Jones Apparel, Liz Claiborne, and Perry Ellis, as well as Wal-Mart, are considering acquiring the company.

Disparaged by some as a triumph of merchandising rather than design, Hilfigerwear features traditional styles often decorated with nothing more than the company's red, white, and blue logo. THC licenses its name and logo to such companies as Hartmarx, Jockey, Jones Apparel, Movado, and Stride Rite for everything from handbags and watches to shoes.

THC has introduced H Hilfiger, a more upscale apparel line targeted at 30- to 45-year-old men and women, though the brand did not catch on as quickly as the company had anticipated. In an effort to further expand its upscale image, THC purchased ownership of the trademarks and related licenses and fashion lines of notable Chanel designer Karl Lagerfeld.

With Lagerfeld's name among Hilfiger's brand portfolio and double-digit growth within its European business, the company began streamlining its own operations close to home. The goal of the restructuring is to speed product time to market and eliminate inefficiencies. It also allows THC to pave the way for a Lagerfeld launch in 2006. A solution was to shed some 200 salaried positions, create division heads, and close its young men's division. THC is also re-evaluating the health of its H Hilfiger line after a disappointing debut and the loss of its designer, Ginny Hilfiger (Tommy's younger sister), who left the company in late 2004 to spend more time with her family.

Strategically, Tommy Hilfiger's reality TV series, *The Cut*, debuted in June 2005 and indirectly provided the designer and his company with a unique vehicle for boosting its brand. For the show Hilfiger shepherded 16 contestants, who performed style assignments and were judged by Hilfiger and a committee in hopes of making "the cut" and returning for another round. The winning contestant, Christopher Cortez, began working at THC in September 2005 to design a collection under the Tommy Hilfiger label.

HISTORY

Teenage clotheshorse Tommy Hilfiger once bought trendy clothes in New York City then resold them from the trunk of his car in his hometown of Elmira, New York. In 1969, while a senior in high school, he opened a boutique. By the mid-1970s Hilfiger had seven stores in upstate New York operating under The People's Place name. Hilfiger designed items for the shops, but the chain went bankrupt during the recession of the late 1970s. He briefly designed jeans for Jordache in the early 1980s.

Hilfiger launched an independent menswear collection in 1984 as a licensee of Murjani International, headed by Mohan Murjani (who also backed Gloria Vanderbilt). The line received a good bit of notoriety from a 1985 ad campaign that called Hilfiger one of "the four great American designers for men" along with Ralph Lauren, Perry Ellis, and Calvin Klein.

Eventually outgrowing Murjani, in 1989 Hilfiger partnered with Joel Horowitz, Lawrence Stroll, and Hong Kong-based manufacturer Silas Chou, part of one of Hong Kong's most established textile and apparel families. Hilfiger retained control of design. Their company, Tommy Hilfiger, went public in 1992.

Sales were helped even more when rapper Snoop Doggy Dog hosted *Saturday Night Live* in 1994 wearing a rugby shirt emblazoned with a Tommy Hilfiger logo. Much of the sales increase was credited to fans of the artist (and other Hilfiger-clad musicians) who loyally outfitted themselves head-to-toe in Tommy Hilfiger. Horowitz, Hilfiger COO, moved up to the CEO spot that year. In 1995 the company licensed sister company Pepe Jeans USA to make and distribute its jeans and womenswear in the US. The women's clothing line debuted the next year, as did a line of men's athletic shoes through licensee Stride Rite.

In 1997 Tommy Hilfiger opened its first flagship store in Beverly Hills, California, and a small store in London. The following year the company added licensing agreements for women's hosiery and home furnishings; it also began offering men's dress shoes and women's shoes through Stride Rite. In addition, in 1998 the company purchased its Canadian distributor and Pepe Jeans USA, which held the license for womenswear and jeans. The deal gave Hilfiger, chairman Chou, Horowitz, and director Stroll (who together controlled the affiliates) nearly 20% in

Tommy Hilfiger. Stroll was also named co-chairman that year.

Discounter Wal-Mart Stores agreed in 1999 to pay $6.4 million to settle a claim it was selling counterfeit Tommy Hilfiger merchandise. In early 2000, after the stock had lost two-thirds of its value in six months, the company scrapped plans for its upscale women's label and began considering acquisitions to bolster its share price. It later closed its London flagship store. In 2001 Tommy Hilfiger closed its remaining flagship store in Beverly Hills. To penetrate selected markets not served by its department store distribution, the company announced plans in mid-2001 to open around 35 new stores by the middle of 2002.

Tommy Hilfiger bought its European licensee, T.H. International, in 2001 for $200 million. In 2002 namesake founder Tommy Hilfiger was named chairman (later honorary chairman), replacing longtime founding chairman Silas Chou.

Efforts to combat counterfeiting and trademark infringements received their first payoff in 2003, when Hilfiger prevailed in a suit against budget store chain Goody's Family Clothing.

In mid-2005 THC's Tommy Hilfiger Licensing Inc., however, began licensing the development, manufacture, and distribution of branded swimwear to RAJ Manufacturing, located in Tustin, California.

EXECUTIVES

Principal Designer and Honorary Chairman: Thomas J. (Tommy) Hilfiger, age 53, $18,344,000 pay
President and Director: David F. Dyer, age 56, $3,333,333 pay
COO; Group President, Tommy Hilfiger USA: Bob Rosenblatt
EVP and General Counsel: James (Jamie) Gallagher
EVP Human Resources: Theo Killion
SVP, CFO, and Treasurer: Joseph (Joe) Scirocco, age 47, $899,800 pay
SVP and Corporate Controller: Quentin Walsh
Group President, US Wholesale: Lynn Shanahan
President, Childrenswear Division: Christopher (Chris) Nakatani, age 41
President, Men's Underwear: Michael Spillane, age 44
President, Worldwide Production: JoAnne Bies
President, Men's Sportswear: Allan Zwerner
President, New Business Development and the H Line: Ann Ancierno
President, Retail: Gary Sheinbalm
President, Women's and Special Sizes: Patricia Stensrud
President and CEO, Tommy Hilfiger Canada: Howard J. Starr
CEO, Tommy Hilfiger Europe: Fred Gehring
President, Tommy Hilfiger Corporate Foundation: Guy Vickers
Director, Corporate Communications: Heidi Kang
Lead Counsel: Mary Jo White
Investor Relations: Valerie Martinez
Auditors: PricewaterhouseCoopers LLP

LOCATIONS

HQ: Tommy Hilfiger Corporation
9/F Novel Industrial Bldg. 850-870 Lai Chi Kok Rd., Cheung Sha Wan, Kowloon, Hong Kong
Phone: +852-2216-0668   **Fax:** +852-2312-1368
US HQ: 25 W. 39th St., New York, NY 10018
US Phone: 212-840-8888   **US Fax:** 212-548-1818
Web: www.tommy.com

Tommy Hilfiger's products are sold in Asia, Europe, and North and South America.

2005 Stores

	No.
US	117
Europe	26
Canada	24
Total	**167**

PRODUCTS/OPERATIONS

2005 Sales

	$ mil.	% of total
Wholesale	1,204.7	66
Retail	500.6	27
Licensing	119.9	7
Other	1.3	—
Adjustments	(45.8)	—
Total	**1,780.8**	**100**

Selected Licensing Partners

Aramis, Inc. (fragrances)
Bestform Intimates (women's intimate apparel)
FAO Schwartz (dolls)
Hartmarx (men's suits)
Jantzen (women's swimwear)
Jockey International (men's underwear)
Lantis Eyewear Corporation (sunglasses)
Mountain High Hosiery (socks and women's hosiery)
Movado Group, Inc. (watches)
Oxford Industries (men's dress shirts and golfwear)
Revman Industries, Inc. (linens, bedding, and bath products)
Russell-Newman, Inc. (robes and sleepwear)
Strellson AG (men's tailored clothing, Europe)
Swank (men's accessories)
The Stride Rite Corporation (footwear)
Victoria & Co. Ltd. (jewelry)

COMPETITORS

Abercrombie & Fitch	Levi Strauss
American Eagle Outfitters	Limited Brands
Armani	Liz Claiborne
Benetton	L.L. Bean
Calvin Klein	Nautica Enterprises
Diesel	NIKE
Donna Karan	Oxford Industries
Eddie Bauer Holdings	Perry Ellis International
Fruit of the Loom	Perry Ellis Menswear
FUBU	Phat
Gap	Phillips-Van Heusen
Gucci	Polo Ralph Lauren
Guess	Quiksilver
Haggar	Reebok
Hugo Boss	Sara Lee Branded
J. Crew	Viewpoint
Kenneth Cole	Warnaco Group

HISTORICAL FINANCIALS

Company Type: Public

Income Statement

FYE: March 31

	REVENUE ($ mil.)	NET INCOME ($ mil.)	NET PROFIT MARGIN	EMPLOYEES
3/05	1,781	86	4.8%	—
3/04	1,876	132	7.0%	5,400
3/03	1,888	(514)	—	5,400
3/02	1,877	135	7.2%	4,900
3/01	1,881	131	7.0%	4,100
3/00	1,977	172	8.7%	2,600
3/99	1,637	174	10.6%	3,000
3/98	847	113	13.4%	1,820
3/97	662	86	13.1%	1,570
3/96	478	62	12.9%	—
Annual Growth	**15.7%**	**3.8%**	**—**	**19.3%**

2005 Year-End Financials

Debt ratio: 26.0%
Return on equity: 6.7%
Cash ($ mil.): 481
Current ratio: 3.18
Long-term debt ($ mil.): 344

No. of shares (mil.): 92
Dividends
Yield: 0.0%
Payout: —
Market value ($ mil.): 1,075

Stock History

NYSE: TOM

	STOCK PRICE ($) FY Close	P/E High/Low		PER SHARE ($) Earnings	Dividends	Book Value
3/05	11.70	20	9	0.93	0.00	14.42
3/04	17.00	12	5	1.45	0.00	13.43
3/03	7.23	—	—	(5.68)	0.00	11.52
3/02	14.35	11	6	1.49	0.00	16.67
3/01	12.85	12	4	1.43	0.00	15.16
3/00	14.50	23	6	1.80	0.00	13.47
3/99	34.44	21	9	1.86	0.00	11.58
3/98	30.03	21	11	1.50	0.00	6.91
3/97	26.13	27	18	1.14	0.00	5.34
3/96	22.94	29	12	0.83	0.00	4.08
Annual Growth	(7.2%)	—	—	1.3%	—	15.0%

Toronto-Dominion Bank

The Toronto-Dominion Bank wants to score financial TDs at home and abroad. Also known as TD Bank or TD Financial Group, Canada's third-largest bank provides retail banking services under the TD Canada Trust banner, including deposits, loans, credit cards, mortgages, and investment management. The company also offers financial and advisory services to businesses. Other operations include TD Insurance, TD Asset Management (mutual funds), and TD Securities (investment banking, equities, and foreign exchange). Toronto-Dominion bought a majority stake in US-based Banknorth (now TD Banknorth) in early 2005. It is selling the US operations of online discount brokerage subsidiary TD Waterhouse to Ameritrade.

Frustrated by limited growth opportunities within Canada, Toronto-Dominion decided to venture south of the border with its purchase of Banknorth. Toronto-Dominion paid about $4.8 billion in cash and stock for a 51% stake, with the option to raise its position to two-thirds. Toronto-Dominion hopes to use the acquisition as a springboard for further southward expansion, such as the possible purchase of a mortgage lender. Additionally, the company will own about a third of the combined Ameritrade/TD Waterhouse USA, which will be called TD Ameritrade once the deal is complete.

Back home, Toronto-Dominion is looking for new ways to increase earnings outside of its core business of retail banking, a mature market in Canada with limited growth potential and several large competitors.

However, the company's plans to hitch a ride on the Wal-Mart gravy train have been derailed. Arrangements to open bank branches in some US-based Wal-Mart stores were squelched by regulators enforcing the banking and commerce barrier. Toronto-Dominion also announced it will close all of its existing branches (more than 100 in all) inside Canadian Wal-Marts by 2006 as part of a broader restructuring.

HISTORY

The Bank of Toronto was established in 1855 by flour traders who wanted their own banking facilities. Its growth encouraged another group of businessmen to found the Dominion Bank in 1869. Dominion emphasized commercial banking and invested heavily in railways and construction.

As the new nation expanded westward, both banks established branch networks. They helped fund Canada's primary industries — dairy, mining, oil, pulp, and textiles. True to its pioneering spirit, a Bank of Toronto official claimed to be the first to have set up a branch office with the help of aviation (in Manitoba in the 1920s).

The demand for agricultural products and commodities dropped after WWI, but production continued full throttle, creating a world grain glut that helped trigger the stock market crash of 1929. Both the Bank of Toronto and Dominion Bank contracted during the 1930s. After growing during and subsequent to WWII, The Bank of Toronto and Dominion Bank decided to increase their capital base, merging into a 450-branch bank in 1955.

In the 1970s TD opened offices in Bangkok, Beirut, and Frankfurt, among other cities abroad. During the 1980s it was active in making loans to less-developed countries. After the deregulation of the Canadian securities industry in 1987, CEO Richard Thomson reduced international lending and began focusing on brokerage activities. The strategy paid off when several Latin American countries fell behind on their loans in the late 1980s.

As the North American economy slowed in the early 1990s, TD's nonperforming loans increased and, with it, its loan loss reserves. The bank still made acquisitions, including Central Guaranty Trust (1993) and Lancaster Financial Holdings (1995, investment banking). It worked to build its financial services, expanding its range of service offerings and geographic coverage and buying New York-based Waterhouse Investor Services (1996); 97% of Australia-based Pont Securities (1997); and California-based Kennedy, Cabot & Co. (1997). In 1998 the bank sold its payroll services to Ceridian, and its Waterhouse Securities unit bought US discount brokerage Jack White & Co.

That year the government nixed TD's merger with Canadian Imperial on the same day it voided the Royal Bank of Canada/Bank of Montreal deal. The banks believed the consolidation necessary to stave off foreign banks' encroachment into Canada, but the government had domestic anti-competition concerns: Though Canada has one-tenth the population of the US, its five top banks all ranked in the top 15 in North America.

In 1999 TD bought Trimark Financial's retail trust banking business and spun off part of Waterhouse Investor Services (now TD Waterhouse Group). That year the bank ramped up its focus on Internet banking; the company's Web site sells competitors' products, as well as TD's.

Not giving up on acquisition-fueled growth, in 2000 the company bought CT Financial Services (now Canada Trust) from British American Tobacco. As a condition for government approval, TD had to sell its MasterCard credit portfolio (sold to Citibank Canada) and a dozen southern Ontario branches (to Bank of Montreal). TD is also shopping for a US bank and has teamed up with Commerce One to launch TDMarketSite, a business-to-business Web site.

TD suffered its first-ever annual loss during fiscal year 2002. Write-downs on loans to telecommunications, technology, and energy firms contributed mightily to the dismal results.

EXECUTIVES

Chairman: John M. Thompson, age 62
President, CEO, and Director: W. Edmund (Ed) Clark, age 57, $3,620,661 pay
Vice Chair and Group Head, Wholesale Banking; Chairman and CEO, TD Securities: Robert E. (Bob) Dorrance, age 49, $2,714,658 pay (prior to title change)
Vice Chair and Chief Risk Officer: Bharat B. Masrani
Vice Chair; President, TD Canada Trust: Andrea S. Rosen, $1,190,559 pay
Vice Chair and Group Head, US Personal and Commercial Banking; Chairman, President, and CEO, TD Banknorth: William J. (Bill) Ryan, age 61
Vice Chair, Corporate Operations: Fredric J. Tomczyk, $1,109,659 pay
EVP; Vice Chair, Sales and Marketing, TD Waterhouse USA: T. Christian Armstrong
EVP and Group Head, Business Banking and Insurance; Co-Chair, TD Canada Trust: Bernard T. (Bernie) Dorval, age 51
EVP, TD UK Brokerage: Michael A. Foulkes
EVP and Group Head, Personal Banking; Co-Chair, TD Canada Trust: Timothy D. (Tim) Hockey, age 41
EVP and Group Head, Wealth Management; Chairman and CEO, TD Waterhouse: William H. (Bill) Hatanaka
EVP and CFO: Colleen M. Johnston
EVP; President, TD Securities: Michael W. (Mike) MacBain
EVP and Chief Investment Officer: Robert F. MacLellan
EVP, Corporate Development: Daniel A. Marinangeli, $680,415 pay (prior to title change)
EVP and General Counsel: Christopher A. Montague
SVP, Human Resources: Theresa L. Currie
SVP, Marketing: Dominic J. Mercuri
SVP, Corporate and Public Affairs: Kerry A. Peacock
President and CEO, TD Waterhouse USA: Timothy P. (Tim) Pinnington, age 40
Auditors: Ernst & Young LLP; PricewaterhouseCoopers LLP

LOCATIONS

HQ: The Toronto-Dominion Bank
Toronto-Dominion Centre,
King St. West and Bay St.,
Toronto, Ontario M5K 1A2, Canada
Phone: 416-982-8222   **Fax:** 416-982-5671
US HQ: 31 W. 52nd St., New York, NY 10019
US Phone: 212-827-7000   **US Fax:** 212-827-7428
Web: www.td.com

PRODUCTS/OPERATIONS

2004 Sales

	$ mil.	% of total
Interest		
Loans	5,707	44
Securities	2,295	18
Dividends	705	5
Deposits with banks	424	3
Noninterest		
Investment & securities services	1,883	14
Service charges	552	4
Insurance	486	4
Loan securitizations	320	3
Credit fees	281	2
Net investment securities gains	158	1
Card services	141	1
Other	184	1
Total	**13,136**	**100**

2004 Assets

	$ mil.	% of total
Cash & equivalents	7,413	3
Trading securities	54,866	21
Securities purchased under resale agreements	17,952	7
Investment securities	25,744	10
Residential mortgages	42,175	17
Consumer installment & other personal loans	40,072	16
Business & government loans	18,261	7
Trading derivatives' market revaluation	27,638	11
Other	20,983	8
Total	**255,104**	**100**

COMPETITORS

Ameritrade	FMR
BMO Financial Group	Laurentian Bank
Caisses Desjardins	MLIM
Charles Schwab	Morgan Stanley
CIBC	National Bank of Canada
CSFB (USA)	RBC Financial Group
E*TRADE Financial	Scotiabank
Edward Jones	

HISTORICAL FINANCIALS

Company Type: Public

Income Statement

FYE: October 31

	ASSETS ($ mil.)	NET INCOME ($ mil.)	INCOME AS % OF ASSETS	EMPLOYEES
10/04	255,104	1,895	0.7%	42,843
10/03	207,419	816	0.4%	41,934
10/02	178,502	(49)	—	51,000
10/01	181,367	871	0.5%	51,000
10/00	173,879	673	0.4%	44,798
10/99	145,739	2,026	1.4%	30,636
10/98	117,808	726	0.6%	29,236
10/97	116,351	773	0.7%	28,001
10/96	93,919	683	0.7%	26,815
10/95	80,930	591	0.7%	25,413
Annual Growth	**13.6%**	**13.8%**	**—**	**6.0%**

2004 Year-End Financials

Equity as % of assets: 4.1%
Return on assets: 0.8%
Return on equity: 19.8%
Long-term debt ($ mil.): 4,629
No. of shares (mil.): 656
Dividends
Yield: 1.7%
Payout: 24.5%
Market value ($ mil.): 26,354
Sales ($ mil.): 13,136

Stock History

NYSE: TD

10/95 10/96 10/97 10/98 10/99 10/00 10/01 10/02 10/03 10/04

	STOCK PRICE ($) FY Close	P/E High/Low		PER SHARE ($) Earnings	Dividends	Book Value
10/04	40.18	14	11	2.78	0.68	17.48
10/03	33.29	29	15	1.15	0.76	15.15
10/02	19.13	—	—	(0.16)	0.71	12.97
10/01	22.51	23	17	1.30	1.09	13.44
10/00	27.56	31	22	1.02	0.92	13.02
10/99	23.06	9	4	3.33	0.48	12.64
10/98	15.00	22	10	1.18	0.45	9.30
10/97	18.25	15	9	1.26	0.41	8.73
10/96	11.69	11	9	1.11	0.09	8.25
Annual Growth	**16.7%**	**—**	**—**	**12.8%**	**—**	**9.9%**

Toshiba

Toshiba products play an active role, be it in computing, controlling, powering, or communicating — transporting, cooking, playing, or even elevating. The company's portfolio includes personal and professional computers (notebook PCs, servers), telecommunications and medical equipment (mobile phones, X-ray machines), industrial machinery (power plant reactors, elevators), consumer appliances (microwaves, DVD players), electronic components (electron tubes, batteries), and semiconductors. Its portfolio also includes air traffic control and railway transportation systems.

Toshiba's ongoing restructuring efforts have resulted in cost-cutting measures and a shift in emphasis to more profitable segments such as consumer electronics and components. Toshiba has pulled out of the commodity DRAM (dynamic random-access memory) business, and is instead focused on specialty memory products. The company has cut costs in its PC operations by increasing its outsourcing agreements with contract manufacturers in Taiwan and mainland China. Toshiba sells about 80% of its products in Asia.

Toshiba has used partnerships (often with competitors) to fuel product development. It merged its LCD operations with those of Matsushita, forming Toshiba Matsushita Display Technology. The company formed an alliance with rival Fujitsu that will focus on system-on-chip (SOC) operations, leaving the door open for wider semiconductor product integration in the future. Toshiba has partnered with Canon to develop surface conduction electron emitter display (SED) panels, which it views as the successor to LCD televisions. It also joined with Sony and IBM to develop new microprocessors.

HISTORY

Two Japanese electrical equipment manufacturers came together in 1939 to create Toshiba. Tanaka Seizo-sha, Japan's first telegraph equipment manufacturer, was founded in 1875 by Hisashige Tanaka, the so-called Edison of Japan. In the 1890s the company started making heavier electrical equipment such as transformers and electric motors, adopting the name Shibaura Seisakusho Works in 1893. Seisakusho went on to pioneer the production of hydroelectric generators (1894) and X-ray tubes (1915) in Japan.

The other half of Toshiba, Hakunetsusha & Company, was founded by Ichisuke Fujioka and Shoichi Miyoshi as Japan's first incandescent lamp maker (1890). Renamed Tokyo Electric Company (1899), the company developed the coiled filament lightbulb (1921), Japan's first radio receiver and cathode-ray tube (1924), and the internally frosted glass lightbulb (1925). In 1939 it merged with Shibaura Seisakusho to form Tokyo Shibaura Electric Company (Toshiba).

Toshiba was the first company in Japan to make fluorescent lamps (1940), radar systems (1942), broadcasting equipment (1952), and digital computers (1954). Production of black-and-white televisions began in 1949. Even so, through the 1970s the company was considered an also-ran, trailing other Japanese business groups, known as *keiretsu*, partly because of its bureaucratic management style.

Electrical engineer Shoichi Saba became president in 1980. Saba invested heavily in Toshiba's information and communications units. The company became the world's first to produce a powerful one-megabit DRAM chip (1985). That year it unveiled its first laptop PC. Meanwhile, Saba (named chairman 1986) pushed Toshiba into joint ventures to exchange technology with companies such as Siemens and Motorola.

But in 1987 Toshiba incurred the wrath of the US government. A subsidiary sold submarine sound-deadening equipment to the USSR, resulting in threats of US sanctions and a precipitous decline in its stock price and in US sales. Saba and president Sugichiro Watari resigned.

Toshiba in 1992 bought a $500 million stake in Time Warner (the stake was reduced in 1998). In 1996 the company appointed marketing and multimedia specialist Taizo Nishimuro as president, breaking its tradition of filling the position with an engineer from its heavy electrical operations.

In 1997 Toshiba and IBM formed joint venture Dominion Semiconductor to develop memory chips. (IBM sold its stake to Toshiba in 1999.) The next year the company looked to boost earnings by cutting its workforce and allying with other manufacturers such as GE and Fujitsu in development deals. But continued semiconductor price declines, and sluggish demand in Japan, caused the company to record its first annual loss in more than two decades.

Nishimuro made plans to cut 5,000 jobs, and streamlined Toshiba's 15 divisions to eight in-house companies. Toshiba in 1999 agreed to take a $1 billion charge to settle a class-action lawsuit alleging some manufacturers supplied potentially corrupt disk drives in its portable computers — even though no Toshiba customer complaints were filed.

In 2000 Nishimuro stepped down as CEO. SVP and Information and Industrial Systems and Services subsidiary president Tadashi Okamura assumed the post. Nishimuro filled the vacant chairman's seat. Toshiba announced another restructuring effort in 2001, which included plans to reduce its workforce, shift manufacturing to overseas plants, and withdraw from unprofitable businesses. The following year it sold its DRAM manufacturing plant, Dominion Semiconductor, to Micron Technology.

EXECUTIVES

President and CEO: Atsutoshi Nishida
Chairman: Tadashi Okamura
SEVP: Shigeo Koguchi
SEVP: Takeshi Nakagawa
SEVP: Sadazumi Ryu
SEVP: Yoshiaki Sato
EVP: Makoto Azuma
EVP: Tsuyoshi Kimura
EVP: Yuji Kiyokawa
EVP: Masao Niwano
EVP: Toshitake Takagi
EVP: Toshio Yonezawa
SVP: Yoshihide Fujii
SVP: Tsutomu Miyamoto
SVP: Masashi Muromachi
SVP: Masao Namiki
SVP: Yoshihiro Nitta
SVP: Hisatsugu Nonaka
Auditors: Ernst & Young

LOCATIONS

HQ: Toshiba Corporation
1-1, Shibaura 1-chome, Minato-ku,
Tokyo 105-8001, Japan
Phone: +81-3-3457-4511   **Fax:** +81-3-3455-1631
US HQ: 1251 Avenue of the Americas, 41st Fl.,
New York, NY 10020
US Phone: 212-596-0600   **US Fax:** 212-593-3875
Web: www.toshiba.co.jp

2005 Sales

	% of total
Asia	
Japan	64
Other countries	17
North America	10
Europe	8
Other regions	1
Total	**100**

PRODUCTS/OPERATIONS

2005 Sales

	% of total
Digital products	35
Social infrastructure	28
Electronic devices	21
Home appliances	10
Other	6
Total	**100**

Selected Products

Digital products
Digital Media Network Company
Digital cameras
Digital tuners
DVD players and recorders
Hard disk drives
Industrial and surveillance cameras
Optical disk drives
Projectors
Televisions
Mobile Communications Company
Mobile phones
Personal Computer & Network Company
Handheld computers
Notebook computers
Servers

Social infrastructure
Industrial and Power Systems & Services Company
Boiling water reactor plants
Building energy management systems
Control and measurement system devices
Industrial computers
Nuclear fuel reprocessing plants
Power generating equipment (hydroelectric,
thermal, geothermal)
Railway station service systems
Superconducting magnets
Transportation management systems
Water supply and sewage monitoring systems
Social Network & Infrastructure Systems Company
Air traffic control and navigation aid systems
Automatic letter processing systems
Banknote processing machines
Broadcasting systems
Face recognition security systems
Electronic devices
Semiconductor Company
LSI systems
Memory
Microprocessors
Home appliances
Air conditioners
Batteries
Lighting
Microwaves
Refrigerators
Washing machines

COMPETITORS

Acer	Lenovo
Alcatel	Lucent
Apple Computer	Matsushita
Canon	Mitsubishi Electric
CASIO COMPUTER	Motorola
Dell	NEC
Electrolux	Nokia
Emerson Electric	Oki Electric
Ericsson	Philips Electronics
Fujifilm	Pioneer
Fujitsu	Ricoh
Fujitsu Siemens	Samsung
Gateway	Samsung Electronics
GE	SANYO
Hewlett-Packard	Seiko
Hitachi	Sharp
IBM	Siemens
Ingersoll-Rand	Sony
Intel	Spansion
Kyocera	Sun Microsystems

HISTORICAL FINANCIALS

Company Type: Public

Income Statement

FYE: March 31

	REVENUE ($ mil.)	NET INCOME ($ mil.)	NET PROFIT MARGIN	EMPLOYEES
3/05	54,264	428	0.8%	165,000
3/04	52,816	273	0.5%	166,651
3/03	47,192	154	0.3%	165,776
3/02	40,666	(1,915)	—	176,398
3/01	47,111	761	1.6%	188,042
3/00	54,493	(265)	—	198,000
3/99	44,504	(117)	—	198,000
3/98	41,020	55	0.1%	186,000
3/97	44,605	542	1.2%	186,000
3/96	48,410	843	1.7%	186,000
Annual Growth	**1.3%**	**(7.2%)**	**—**	**(1.3%)**

2005 Year-End Financials

Debt ratio: 83.8%
Return on equity: 5.8%
Cash ($ mil.): 2,743
Current ratio: 1.09
Long-term debt ($ mil.): 6,354

Net Income History — Pink Sheets: TOSBF

TOTAL S.A.

TOTAL, one of the world's largest integrated oil companies, explores for, develops, and produces crude oil and natural gas; refines and markets oil; and trades and transports both crude and finished products. Operating in more than 100 countries, the company has reserves of 11.1 billion barrels of oil equivalent. It operates 28 refineries and more than 16,000 Total, Elf, or Fina-branded gas stations, mostly in Europe and Africa. The company is also a major producer of chemicals. TOTAL FINA was formed in 1999 when France's TOTAL bought Belgium-based PetroFina. It became TOTAL FINA ELF in 2000 with the acquisition of French rival Elf Aquitaine. The company renamed itself as TOTAL S.A. in 2003.

TOTAL gas stations operate under the Premier, FINA, and Elf brands. Its chemical units produce monomers, polymers, and specialty chemicals such as adhesives, inks, paints, resins, and rubbers. TOTAL also owns 13% of drug maker Sanofi-Aventis (formerly Sanofi-Synthélabo) gained in the Elf acquisition, but has indicated that ownership in the drug company is not in the company's long-range plans.

HISTORY

A French consortium formed the Compagnie Française des Pétroles (CFP) in 1924 to develop an oil industry for the country. Lacking reserves within its borders, France had a 24% stake in the Turkish Petroleum Company (TPC), acquired from Germany in 1920 as part of the spoils from WWI. When oil was discovered in Iraq in 1927, the TPC partners (CFP; Anglo-Persian Oil, later BP; Royal Dutch/Shell; and a consortium of five US oil companies) became major players in the oil game.

In 1929 France acquired a 25% stake in CFP (raised to 35% in 1931) but ensured the company's independence from government control. CFP began establishing refining and transporting capabilities, and by the start of WWII it was a vertically integrated petroleum company.

With France's occupation by Germany during WWII, CFP was effectively blocked from further expansion, and its stake in Iraq Petroleum (formerly the TPC) was held by its partners until the end of the war. In 1948, over French protests, the US partners ended the "Red Line" agreement, a pact that limited members' competition in that Middle Eastern region.

After WWII, CFP diversified its sources for crude, opening a supply in 1947 from the Venezuelan company Pantepec and making several major discoveries in colonial Algeria in 1956. It also began supplying crude to Japan, South Korea, and

Taiwan in the 1950s. To market its products in North Africa and France and other European areas, it introduced the brand name TOTAL in 1954. It began making petrochemicals in 1956.

Algeria in 1971 became North Africa's first major oil-producing country to nationalize its petroleum industry. This was not as dire a blow to CFP as it could have been; by that time the company got only about 20% of its supplies from Algeria. Exploration had paid off, with discoveries in Indonesia in the 1960s and, in the early 1970s, the North Sea.

CFP joined Elf Aquitaine in 1980 to buy Rhône-Poulenc's petrochemical segment. Ten years later it purchased state-owned Orkem's coating business (inks, resins, paints, and adhesives).

In 1985 the company had adopted its brand name as part of its new name, TOTAL Compagnie Française des Pétroles, shortened in 1991 to TOTAL. The firm was listed on the NYSE that year. The French government began reducing its stake in TOTAL in 1992 (ultimately to less than 1%). The company expanded reserves with stakes in fields in Argentina, the Caspian Sea, and Colombia.

In 1995, the year Thierry Desmarest became CEO, TOTAL contracted to develop two large oil and gas fields in Iran, despite US pressure not to do business there. The next year TOTAL led a consortium (including Russia's Gazprom and Malaysia's Petronas) in a $2 billion investment in Iran's gas sector, just days after selling its 55% stake in its North American arm, Total Petroleum, to Ultramar Diamond Shamrock — insulating TOTAL from the threat of US sanctions.

TOTAL bought Belgium's Petrofina, an integrated oil and gas company, for $11 billion in 1999 and became TOTAL FINA. Within days the new TOTAL FINA launched a $43 billion hostile bid for rival Elf Aquitaine. Elf made a counterbid, but TOTAL FINA wound up acquiring 95% of Elf in 2000 for $48.7 billion and became TOTAL FINA ELF. The new company gained control of the remainder of Elf later that year.

In 2001 the company, in collaboration with Pertamina and Unocal Indonesia, agreed to invest $500 million to boost its production of liquefied gas in Indonesia by 14%. That year the company also acquired generating assets in Argentina from AES for $370 million. Also that year an explosion in a TOTAL FINA ELF subsidiary's petrochemical and fertilizer plant in southern France killed 29 people and injured 2,500. In 2003 a number of former Elf executives and state officials were named in a corruption scandal that implicated the former French oil giant in influence peddling and bribery in the early 1990s.

EXECUTIVES

Chairman and CEO: Thierry Desmarest, age 60
EVP and CFO: Robert Castaigne, age 58
EVP; President Gas and Power: Yves-Louis Darricarrère
EVP; President, Exploration and Production: Chrisophe de Margerie
EVP; President, Refining and Marketing: Jean-Paul Vettier
EVP; President, Strategy and Risk Assessment: Bruno Weymuller, age 56
SVP Executive Career Management: Michel Bonnet
SVP Human Resources and Corporate Communications: Jean-Jacques Guilbaud
SVP; President Trading and Shipping: François Groh
SVP Performance Products, Arkema: Philippe Goebel, age 52
SVP Administration, Refining and Marketing Division: Pierre Klein
SVP Marketing Europe, Refining and Marketing Division: Eric De Menten
SVP Marketing France, Refining and Marketing Division: André Tricoire
SVP North America; ATOFINA General Representative in the US, Organic Peroxides and Additives: Jean-Pierre Seeuws, age 59
SVP Overseas, Refining and Marketing Division: Alain Champeaux
SVP; President TOTAL Petrochemicals: Jean-Bernard Lartigue
SVP Refining, Refining and Marketing Division: Jean-Claude Company
EVP and COO, TOTAL Holdings USA, Inc.: Otto Takken, age 52
VP Investor Relations: Ladislas Paszkiewicz
Auditors: Ernst & Young Audit; KPMG Audit

LOCATIONS

HQ: TOTAL S.A.
2 place de la Coupole, La Défense 6, 92400 Courbevoie, France
Phone: +33-1-47-44-58-53   **Fax:** +33-1-47-44-58-24
US HQ: 444 Madison Ave, 42nd Fl., New York, NY 10022
US Phone: 212-922-3065   **US Fax:** 212-922-3074
Web: www.total.com

TOTAL has operations in more than 100 countries.

2004 Sales

	$ mil.	% of total
Europe		
France	31,734	19
Other countries	56,694	34
North America	24,361	14
Africa	7,487	5
Asia & other regions	45,933	28
Total	**166,209**	**100**

PRODUCTS/OPERATIONS

2004 Sales

	$ mil.	% of total
Downstream	109,235	66
Upstream	29,794	18
Chemicals	27,149	16
Corporate	31	—
Total	**166,209**	**100**

COMPETITORS

Akzo Nobel
Anglo American
Ashland
BASF AG
BHP Billiton
BP
Chevron
ConocoPhillips
Devon Energy
DuPont
Eni
Exxon Mobil
Imperial Oil
Kerr-McGee
Lyondell Chemical
MOL
Norsk Hydro
Occidental Petroleum
Pakistan State Oil
PDVSA
PEMEX
PETROBRAS
PPG
Royal Dutch/Shell Group
Statoil
Unocal

HISTORICAL FINANCIALS

Company Type: Public

Income Statement

FYE: December 31

	REVENUE ($ mil.)	NET INCOME ($ mil.)	NET PROFIT MARGIN	EMPLOYEES
12/04	166,209	13,020	7.8%	111,401
12/03	131,568	8,832	6.7%	110,783
12/02	107,698	6,240	5.8%	121,469
12/01	93,870	6,826	7.3%	122,025
12/00	107,890	6,502	6.0%	123,303
12/99	42,566	1,534	3.6%	127,252
12/98	28,507	1,038	3.6%	57,166
12/97	31,720	1,263	4.0%	54,391
12/96	34,062	1,089	3.2%	57,555
12/95	27,696	458	1.7%	53,000
Annual Growth	**22.0%**	**45.0%**	**—**	**8.6%**

2004 Year-End Financials

Debt ratio: 31.1%
Return on equity: 32.3%
Cash ($ mil.): 5,198
Current ratio: 1.20
Long-term debt ($ mil.): 13,186
No. of shares (mil.): 1,270
Dividends
Yield: 4.1%
Payout: 42.9%
Market value ($ mil.): 139,500

Stock History

NYSE: TOT

	STOCK PRICE ($) FY Close	P/E High/Low		PER SHARE ($) Earnings	Dividends	Book Value
12/04	109.84	10	8	10.57	4.53	33.34
12/03	92.51	13	9	6.95	2.22	30.69
12/02	71.50	18	13	4.68	1.67	24.57
12/01	70.24	16	12	4.92	1.46	21.82
12/00	72.69	18	13	4.60	1.13	21.68
12/99	69.25	33	23	2.18	0.88	20.45
12/98	49.75	32	22	2.12	0.00	25.27
12/97	55.75	23	15	2.58	0.00	23.14
12/96	40.25	18	14	2.27	0.64	24.13
12/95	34.00	35	26	0.98	0.61	23.34
Annual Growth	**13.9%**	**—**	**—**	**30.2%**	**25.0%**	**4.0%**

Toyota Motor

Toyota Motor Corporation, Japan's #1 carmaker, has a driving ambition to become greener. The company makes a hybrid-powered (gas and electric) sedan — the Prius — that is already being snapped up in US and European markets. Its gas-powered cars, pickups, minivans, and SUVs include such models as the Camry, Celica, Corolla, 4Runner, Echo, Land Cruiser, Sienna, the luxury Lexus line, the new Scion brand, and a full-sized pickup truck, the V-8 Tundra. Toyota also makes forklifts and manufactured housing, and offers consumer financial services. Once a darkhorse in the global automotive game, Toyota has begun to close the gap between itself and rivals like General Motors, Ford, and DaimlerChrysler.

While most of its North American and European competitors are contracting their operations due to falling demand and overcapacity, Toyota is growing to meet increased global demand.

The company has an expressed plan of gaining a global 10% share of the automotive market by the early 2010s. To do this, Toyota feels it must build the cars where, or very near where, they will be bought. To this end Toyota has opened new vehicle plants in the Czech Republic in 2005, and is scheduled to open its 11th US plant in San Antonio, Texas in 2006.

The greatest focus of Toyota's overseas strategy is currently in China, a country that is expected to become the second-largest car market (behind the US) by 2010. By that year Toyota wants to have a 10% market share in China. Like its competitors, Toyota is beefing up its Chinese operations by joining forces with local automotive players. With its Chinese partner China FAW Group Corporation, Toyota builds Land Cruisers and Corollas in China. Through another agreement with Guangzhou Automobile Group, Toyota began jointly developing engines in 2005.

While growing its worldwide production base, Toyota has committed itself to leading the charge toward the development of more efficient, environmentally friendly vehicles, primarily powered by hybrid gasoline-electric technology. Toyota's global production of hybrids in 2005 totaled 151,000 units, or two-and-one-half times production levels of the previous fiscal year.

HISTORY

In 1926 Sakichi Toyoda founded Toyoda Automatic Loom Works. In 1930 he sold the rights to the loom he invented and gave the proceeds to his son Kiichiro Toyoda to begin an automotive business. Kiichiro opened an auto shop within the loom works in 1933. When protectionist legislation (1936) improved prospects for Japanese automakers, Kiichiro split off the car department, took it public (1937), and changed its name to Toyota.

During WWII the company made military trucks, but financial problems after the war caused Toyota to reorganize in 1950. Its postwar commitment to R&D paid off with the launch of the four-wheel-drive Land Cruiser (1951); full-sized Crown (1955); and the small Corona (1957).

Toyota Motor Sales, U.S.A., debuted the Toyopet Crown in the US in 1957, but it proved underpowered for the US market. Toyota had better luck with the Corona in 1965 and with the Corolla (which became the best-selling car of all time) in 1968. By 1970 Toyota was the world's fourth-largest carmaker.

Toyota expanded rapidly in the US. During the 1970s the oil crisis caused demand for fuel-efficient cars, and Toyota was there to grab market share from US makers. In 1975 Toyota displaced Volkswagen as the US's #1 auto importer. Toyota began auto production in the US in 1984 through NUMMI, its joint venture with GM. The Lexus line was launched in the US in 1989.

Because of the European Community's restrictions on Japanese auto imports until the year 2000, Toyota's European expansion slowed. Toyota responded in 1992 by agreeing to distribute cars in Japan for Volkswagen and also by establishing an engine plant (later moved to full auto production) in the UK.

The sport utility vehicle (SUV) mania of the 1990s spurred Toyota's introduction of luxury minivans and light trucks. Hiroshi Okuda, a 40-year veteran with Toyota and the first person from outside the Toyoda family to run the firm, succeeded Tatsuro Toyoda as president in 1995. The next year Toyota consolidated its North American production units into Cincinnati-based Toyota Motor Manufacturing North America.

In 1997 Toyota introduced the Prius, a hybrid electric- and gas-powered car. The next year Toyota boosted its stake in affiliate Daihatsu (minivehicles) to about 51% and started Toyota Mapmaster (51%-owned), to make map databases for car navigation systems.

Okuda became chairman in 1999, replacing Shoichiro Toyoda, and Fujio Cho became president. Also that year Toyota agreed to form a joint venture with Isuzu to manufacture buses, and it announced plans to invest $800 million to boost US auto production by 16% (200,000 vehicles) to about 1.45 million.

In 2000 Toyota launched the WiLL Vi, a sedan aimed at young people. It announced that it was building an online replacement parts marketplace with i2 Technology and that it was forming a financial services company (Toyota Financial Service) and a brokerage firm (Toyota Financial Services Securities Corp.). Toyota also made plans to buy a 5% stake in Yamaha (the world's #2 motorcycle maker) and raised its stake in truck maker Hino Motors from about 20% to almost 34%. International developments included Toyota's agreement with the Chinese government to produce passenger cars for sale in China. The cars are to be built by Tianjin Toyota Motor Corp., a joint venture between Chinese carmaker Tianjin Automobile Xiali and Toyota.

Early in 2001 Toyota opened a new plant in France. Later that year the company formed an agreement with PSA Peugeot Citroën to begin joint car production in Europe by 2005. Toyota also increased its stake in Hino Motors to 50%.

With partners Toyoda Gosei, Ltd. and Horie Metal Co., Ltd., Toyota formed a joint venture in 2002 to manufacture resin fuel tank systems.

In 2004 Toyota announced that it would establish 14 Lexus dealerships in China; the dealers were all open by mid-2005. Later in 2004 Toyota forged a joint venture agreement with Guangzhou Automobile Group Co., Ltd. to build engines in China.

In 2005 Toyota bought just under 9% of General Motors' 20% stake in Fuji Heavy Industries — the Japanese maker of Subaru passenger vehicles.

EXECUTIVES

Honorary Chairman and Member of the Board: Shoichiro Toyoda, age 80
Chairman: Hiroshi Okuda, age 72
Vice Chairman: Fujio Cho, age 68
Vice Chairman: Katsuhiro Nakagawa, age 63
President and Member of the Board: Katsuaki Watanabe, age 63
EVP and Member of the Board: Mitsuo Kinoshita, age 60
EVP, Product Development and Vehicle Engineering and Member of the Board: Kazuo Okamoto, age 61
EVP and Member of the Board: Akio Toyoda, age 49
EVP, Powertrains and Quality and Member of the Board: Masatami Takimoto, age 59
EVP and Member of the Board: Takeshi Uchiyamada, age 58
EVP and Member of the Board: Yoshimi Inaba, age 59
EVP and Member of the Board: Tokuichi Uranishi, age 63
EVP and Member of the Board: Kyoji Sasazu, age 61
Senior Managing Director, Finance and Accounting Group and Member of the Board: Takeshi Suzuki, age 57
Senior Managing Director; President and CEO, Toyota Motor Sales, U.S.A., Inc. and Member of the Board: Yukitoshi (Yuki) Funo, age 58
Managing Officer; President and CEO, Toyota Motor Manufacuring North America: Seiichi Sudo
General Manager, Public Affairs Division: Masayuki Nakai
Auditors: PricewaterhouseCoopers Audit

LOCATIONS

HQ: Toyota Motor Corporation
(Toyota Jidosha Kabushiki Kaisha)
1, Toyota-cho, Toyota, Aichi 471-8571, Japan
Phone: +81-565-28-2121   **Fax:** +81-565-23-5800
US HQ: 9 W. 57th St., Ste. 4900, New York, NY 10019
US Phone: 212-223-0303   **US Fax:** 212-759-7670
Web: www.toyota.co.jp

Toyota Motor operates more than 60 manufacturing facilities in 26 countries throughout the world.

2005 Sales

	$ mil.	% of total
Japan	68,983	40
North America	57,618	33
Europe	21,468	13
Other regions	24,680	14
Total	**172,749**	**100**

2005 Unit Sales

	No. (thou.)	% of total
Japan	2,381	32
North America	2,271	31
Europe	979	13
Other regions	1,777	24
Total	**7,408**	**100**

PRODUCTS/OPERATIONS

2005 Sales

	$ mil.	% of total
Automotive	159,358	91
Financial services	7,275	4
Other	9,594	5
Adjustments	(3,478)	—
Total	**172,749**	**100**

Selected Products

Selected Automobile Models
4Runner (SUV)
Avalon (full-sized sedan)
Camry (midsized sedan)
Camry Solara (midsized coupe)
Corolla (compact sedan)
Highlander (SUV)
Highlander Hybrid
Land Cruiser (SUV)
Lexus (luxury sedan)
Matrix (compact sport wagon)
Prius (gas/electric hybrid compact sedan)
RAV4 (SUV)
Scion (tC, xA,xB)
Sequoia (SUV)
Sienna (minivan)
Tacoma (pickup truck)
Tundra (pickup truck)

Other Products
Factory automation equipment
Forklifts and other industrial vehicles
Housing products

Selected Investments

Crest Homes (98%, prefabricated homes)
Daihatsu Motor (51%, motor vehicles)
Hino Motors Ltd. (50%, trucks)
Life Creation Co., Ltd. (40%, camping facilities)
Tacti Corporation (80%, retail auto parts)
Toyota Epoch Life Co., Ltd.
(95%, off-road driving instruction)
Toyota Mizunami Development Co., Ltd.
(38%, golf course operator)

HISTORICAL FINANCIALS

Company Type: Public

Income Statement

FYE: March 31

	REVENUE ($ mil.)	NET INCOME ($ mil.)	NET PROFIT MARGIN	EMPLOYEES
3/05	172,749	10,907	6.3%	265,753
3/04	163,637	10,995	6.7%	264,410
3/03	128,965	6,247	4.8%	264,096
3/02	107,443	4,177	3.9%	246,702
3/01	106,030	5,447	5.1%	215,648
3/00	119,656	4,540	3.8%	214,631
3/99	105,832	3,747	3.5%	183,879
3/98	88,473	3,442	3.9%	159,035
3/97	98,741	3,112	3.2%	150,736
3/96	101,120	2,424	2.4%	146,855
Annual Growth	6.1%	18.2%	—	6.8%

2005 Year-End Financials

Debt ratio: 55.4%
Return on equity: 13.5%
Cash ($ mil.): 13,816
Current ratio: 1.15
Long-term debt ($ mil.): 46,698

No. of shares (mil.): 1,634
Dividends
Yield: 0.6%
Payout: 6.9%
Market value ($ mil.): 121,540

Stock History

NYSE: TM

	STOCK PRICE ($) FY Close	P/E High/Low		PER SHARE ($) Earnings	Dividends	Book Value
3/05	74.38	13	10	6.62	0.46	51.54
3/04	74.50	12	6	6.48	0.36	44.85
3/03	44.95	16	13	3.52	0.51	34.33
3/02	58.15	31	20	2.28	0.38	29.87
3/01	70.75	37	20	2.92	0.45	31.00
3/00	104.00	43	22	2.42	0.34	34.73
3/99	57.25	30	21	1.98	0.37	29.37
3/98	52.75	36	28	1.80	0.16	23.98
3/97	50.50	36	27	1.62	0.33	24.15
3/96	44.50	36	29	1.24	0.27	26.74
Annual Growth	5.9%	—	—	20.5%	6.1%	7.6%

TUI AG

Once a steel and mining conglomerate, TUI (formerly Preussag) now makes a living on the road. Its tourism business, which is the largest in Europe, serves about 18 million customers and accounts for almost 75% of the company's sales. TUI operates more than 3,500 travel agencies, more than 285 hotels, and about 80 tour operators, as well as more than 100 aircraft through six airlines. TUI's service division provides various support services for travelers, including airport reception, medical support, and departure assistance. The firm is also a significant logistics and shipping concern through Hapag-Lloyd, which has more than 40 container ships. State-owned Westdeutsche Landesbank owns about a third of TUI.

To reposition itself as a tourism company, TUI sold its operations in such areas as building engineering, metals trading, and real estate. In early 2004 TUI announced a divestment program which would have involved the public flotation of Hapag-Lloyd, all while Hapag-Lloyd was unloading all non-shipping and tourism business including VTG-Lehnkering and the sale of its two-thirds stake in French building company Algeco. TUI later abandoned the plan to spin off Hapag-Lloyd, but the disposition of the other Hapag-Lloyd assets was still a good move and has simplified TUI's operations (tourism now accounts for almost 75% of total revenues). It plans to expand its logistics business even further with the planned purchase of Canadian shipping firm CP Ships for almost $2 billion.

Also in 2004 TUI acquired the 49% stake, previously held by Kuoni Reisen Holding AG, in its Swiss joint venture TUI Suisse (the third-largest travel company in Switzerland). It also entered the Russian travel market by forming a joint venture, TUI Mostravel Russia, with Russian tour operator Mostravel. TUI holds a 34% stake in the joint venture with the option of increasing its share to 51% by 2006.

TUI Travel Solutions GmbH sold 50% of its stake in TQ3 Travel Solutions to Navigant International in 2004, thereby turning TQ3 into a global joint venture company. It continues to operate globally under the TQ3 Travel Solutions brand, while in the US and Canada it is branded TQ3Navigant.

HISTORY

TUI was founded in Berlin in 1923 as Preussische Bergwerks-und Hutten-Aktiengesellschaft (Prussian Mine and Foundry Company) to operate former state-owned mining companies, saltworks, and smelters. Despite outmoded equipment and a war-shattered economy, the company prospered. So in 1929 the Prussian parliament combined Preussag with Hibernia and Preussischen Elektrizitats to form the state-run VEBA group, hoping to stimulate foreign investment. It didn't.

WWII left Preussag a shell of its former self. In 1952, as restrictions on steel production were lifted and industry rebounded, Preussag relocated to Hanover. After taking steps to reestablish itself, Preussag made a public offering in 1959; VEBA kept about 22%.

A worldwide steel glut that lasted through the 1960s forced Preussag to diversify. Acquisitions included railroad tank car and transport agent VTG and shipbuilding and chemical companies. The company also formed oil exploration unit Preussag Energie in 1968. In 1969 VEBA finally sold its remaining stake in Preussag to Westdeusche Landesbank (WestLB).

When the 1970s oil crisis drove up steel costs, Preussag began international ventures to counter falling revenues at home. But the 1980s brought PR disasters. The European Commission fined Preussag and five other zinc producers for antitrust violations in 1984.

In 1989 Preussag reorganized into a holding company with four independent units: coal, oil, natural gas, and plant construction. But it was about to take a sharp business turn. Michael Frenzel, who had managed WestLB's industry holdings, became CEO in 1994 in the midst of another steel recession. Frenzel was determined to shift Preussag away from its rusting past and toward services and technology. In 1997 it acquired container shipping and travel firm Hapag-Lloyd, which had a 30% stake in Touristik Union International (TUI). By the end of 1998 it was Europe's top tourism group after buying the rest of TUI, First Reisebuero Management, and a 25% stake in the UK's Thomas Cook (raised to 50.1% in 1999).

As part of its restructuring, Preussag traded its plant engineering units and half of its shipbuilding unit (HDW) to Babcock Borsig for a 33% stake in that company in 1999. Preussag then made plans to transfer another 25% of HDW to Sweden's Celsius in a deal (along with Babcock Borsig) to merge Celsius' Kockums submarine shipyards with HDW. That year Hapag-Lloyd and TUI were merged into Hapag Touristik Union (renamed TUI Group in 2000); VTG merged with Lehnkering, a 126-year-old freight forwarding group, becoming VTG-Lehnkering.

The group also acquired a stake in French package tour leader Nouvelles Frontières and sold a metals trading unit, W. & O. Bergmann, to Enron. By 2002 the company had sold off most of its non-tourism operations, changed its name to TUI, and restructured its business to focus primarily on tourism.

In 2004 TUI sold a division of its VTG-Lehnkering logistics operation to investors for an undisclosed amount. In March 2004 TUI Travel Solutions GmbH sold 50% of its stake in TQ3 Travel Solutions to Navigant International.

EXECUTIVES

Chairman: Michael Frenzel, age 58
Executive Director, Finance: Rainer Feuerhake, age 61
Executive Director, Human Resources and Legal Affairs: Peter Engelen, age 49
Executive Director, Platforms: Sebastian Ebel
Head of the Group Controlling Department and Board Member: Olaf Seifert
Director, Logistics/Holdings: Helmut Stodieck, age 66
Director, Central Europe Sector: Volker Böettcher
Director, Source Market North; CEO, TUI Northern Europe: Peter Rothwell
Director, Source Market West; President, Nouvelles Frontieres: Eric Debry
Auditors: PwC Deutsche Revision AG

LOCATIONS

HQ: TUI AG
Karl-Wiechert-Allee 4, D-30625 Hanover, Germany
Phone: +49-511-566-00   **Fax:** +49-511-566-1098
Web: www.tui.com

PRODUCTS/OPERATIONS

2004 Sales

	% of total
Tourism	73
Logistics	19
Other	8
Total	**100**

2004 Tourism Division Sales

	% of total
Central Europe	40
Northern Europe	36
Western Europe	19
Destinations	4
Other tourism	1
Total	**100**

2004 Logistics Division Sales

	% of total
Shipping	77
Logistics	23
Total	**100**

COMPETITORS

Accor	Kuoni Travel
American Express	Mitsui O.S.K. Lines
A.P. Møller — Mærsk	MyTravel
Brambles	Neptune Orient
BTI Canada	REWE-Zentral
Carlson	Royal Caribbean Cruises
Carnival	Stinnes
Club Med	Thomas Cook AG
First Choice	

HISTORICAL FINANCIALS

Company Type: Public

Income Statement

FYE: December 31

	REVENUE ($ mil.)	NET INCOME ($ mil.)	NET PROFIT MARGIN	EMPLOYEES
12/04	24,615	666	2.7%	57,716
12/03	24,119	345	1.4%	64,257
12/02	22,710	34	0.1%	70,299
12/01*	21,080	307	1.5%	69,550
9/00	19,212	291	1.5%	79,959
9/99	18,739	368	2.0%	57,673
9/98	21,003	322	1.5%	66,563
9/97	15,083	205	1.4%	62,601
9/96	16,401	164	1.0%	66,226
9/95	18,461	260	1.4%	65,227
Annual Growth	**3.2%**	**11.0%**	**—**	**(1.4%)**

*Fiscal year change

2004 Year-End Financials

Debt ratio: 120.9%
Return on equity: 18.4%
Cash ($ mil.): 656
Current ratio: 0.56
Long-term debt ($ mil.): 4,540

Net Income History

German: TUI

9/95	9/96	9/97	9/98	9/99	9/00	12/01	12/02	12/03	12/04

UBS AG

One of the largest investment managers in the world, UBS has offices in some 50 nations — primarily in Europe and North America — that provide financial services through four major segments. Its Wealth Management & Business Banking, UBS Wealth Management USA, and Global Asset Management divisions serve institutional investors and high-net-worth individuals by offering mutual funds, asset management, corporate finance, and estate planning. UBS Investment Bank provides securities underwriting, mergers acquisitions advice, fixed-income products, and foreign exchange. The company also provides traditional banking services in its home country of Switzerland.

UBS is looking to catapult itself higher into the echelons of global finance. In late 2004 bought SoundView (now UBS Capital Markets), the capital markets and specialist business of US company Charles Schwab, for $265 million in cash. UBS integrated the operations into the equities business of its investment bank, making the unit one of the top market makers of Nasdaq stock.

Continuing to target the mass affluent around the planet, UBS also acquired the South American wealth management operations of Dresdner Bank and the North American wealth management business of Julius Baer in 2004. It sold some of its private banking business in Switzerland to Julius Baer the following year.

UBS is making a bold move into China, buying stakes in Bank of China and midsized brokerage Beijing Securities.

HISTORY

Businessmen in Winterthur, Switzerland, formed the Bank of Winterthur in 1862 to serve trading interests, finance railroads, and operate a warehouse. In 1912 the bank merged with the Bank of Toggenburg (formed in 1863) to create Schweizerische Bankgesellschaft — Union Bank of Switzerland (UBS).

It expanded in Switzerland, buying smaller banks and adding branches. After growing in the post-WWI era, it was hit hard by the Depression. UBS benefited from Switzerland's neutrality in WWII, gaining deposits from both Jews and Nazis. In 1946 the bank opened an office in New York. Expansion in Switzerland continued after the war with the purchase of Eidgenossische Bank of Zurich.

UBS continued its acquisitions in the 1950s; by 1962 it had 81 branches. Other purchases included Interhandel, a cash-rich Swiss financial concern (1967), and four savings banks (1968). In 1967 it opened a full-service office in London, and during the 1970s established several securities underwriting subsidiaries abroad.

International financial markets became supercharged in the 1980s, and UBS resolved to catch up with its domestic peers in international operations. As London prepared for financial deregulation in 1986, UBS bought brokerage house Phillips & Drew.

The firm's UK brokerage business was hit hard by the 1987 US stock market crash; over the next two years losses continued, prompting an overhaul of the London operations. Then its US operations were jarred by the collapse of the junk bond market in 1990. The next year UBS set up offices in Paris, Singapore, and Hong Kong and

took over Chase Manhattan's (now J.P. Morgan Chase) New York money management unit.

Meanwhile, the firm continued to expand within Switzerland, buying five more banks to boost market share and fill in gaps in its branch network. These buys left UBS with overlapping operations and a bloated infrastructure when recession hit. Falling real estate values left the bank with a heavy load of nonperforming loans.

In 1994 profits plummeted. Stockholder Martin Ebner, dissatisfied with the performance of president Robert Studer, tried to gain control of UBS; failing that, he sought to have Studer charged with criminal fraud. In 1996 he almost thwarted Studer's election to the chairmanship.

UBS launched a multiyear reorganization in 1994 by consolidating its consumer credit operations. The next year it joined with Swiss Life/Rentenanstalt to offer insurance products through its bank network.

In 1996, after rebuffing Credit Suisse Group's merger bid, UBS began an even more draconian reorganization, cutting domestic branches and writing down billions of francs in bad loans, leading to UBS' first loss ever (with another the next year). In 1998 the company merged with Swiss Bank Corp. then cut 23% of its staff. Later that year the bank lost $1.6 billion in the stumbling Long-Term Capital Management hedge fund, prompting chairman Mathis Cabiallavetta to resign.

As UBS struggled to swallow Swiss Bank in 1999, it retreated somewhat from riskier markets, began selling some $2 billion in real estate, and sold its 25% stake in Swiss Life/Rentenanstalt. Looking to bulk up, the firm that year bought Bank of America's European and Asian private banking operations and Allegis Realty Investors, a US real estate investment management firm.

In 2000 UBS reorganized yet again and bought US broker Paine Webber (now UBS Paine Webber). UBS's integration of Paine Webber continued into the next year. Also in 2001 chairman Marcel Ospel was criticized for UBS's handling of Swissair's cash crisis, which resulted in the air fleet's grounding.

EXECUTIVES

Chairman: Marcel Ospel, age 55
Vice Chairman: Peter Böckli, age 69
Executive Vice Chairman: Stephan Haeringer, age 59
Executive Vice Chairman and Group Chief Credit Officer: Marco Suter
President and CEO: Peter A. Wuffli, age 48
Deputy CEO; Chairman and CEO, UBS Investment Bank: John P. Costas, age 48
Chairman and CEO, UBS Global Asset Management: John A. Fraser, age 54
Chairman and CEO, UBS Wealth Management and Business Banking: Marcel Rohner, age 41
Chairman and CEO, UBS Wealth Management USA: Mark B. Sutton, age 51
CFO: Clive Standish, age 52
Group Chief Communication Officer: Mark Branson
Group Treasurer: Rolf Enderli
Group Head of Human Resources: Thomas Hammer
Group General Counsel: Peter Kurer, age 56
Group Controller: Hugo Schaub
Group Chief Risk Officer: Walter H. Stürzinger, age 50
CTO: Scott G. Abbey
Corporate Secretary: Luzius Cameron
Vice Chairman, Wealth Management: Carlo Grigioni
Vice Chairman, Business Banking: Eugen Haltiner
President, Dillon Read Capital Management: Michael (Mike) Hutchins
President and COO, UBS Wealth Management USA: Robert H. (Bob) Silver
Auditors: Ernst & Young Ltd.

LOCATIONS

HQ: UBS AG
   Bahnhofstrasse 45, CH-8098 Zurich, Switzerland
Phone: +41-44-234-4111   **Fax:** +41-44-234-3415
US HQ: 1285 Avenue of the Americas, 2nd Fl.,
   New York, NY 10019
US Phone: 212-713-2000   **US Fax:** 212-713-1381
Web: www.ubs.com

PRODUCTS/OPERATIONS

2004 Assets

	% of total
Cash & equivalents	15
Reverse repurchase agreements	21
Trading portfolio	31
Positive replacement values	16
Loans	13
Other	4
Total	**100**

2004 Sales

	% of total
Interest	58
Net fee & commission income	28
Net trading income	7
Other	7
Total	**100**

COMPETITORS

Bank of America
Barclays
CIBC
Citigroup
Coutts Group
Credit Suisse
Deutsche Bank
HSBC Holdings
JPMorgan Chase
Mitsubishi UFJ Financial Group
Mizuho Financial
RBC Financial Group
Sal. Oppenheim Jr. & Cie.
UniCredit

HISTORICAL FINANCIALS

Company Type: Public

Income Statement
FYE: December 31

	ASSETS ($ mil.)	NET INCOME ($ mil.)	INCOME AS % OF ASSETS	EMPLOYEES
12/04	1,520,191	7,088	0.5%	67,424
12/03	1,117,809	5,150	0.5%	65,929
12/02	855,248	2,560	0.3%	69,061
12/01	756,365	3,001	0.4%	69,985
12/00	673,847	4,828	0.7%	71,000
12/99	616,330	3,956	0.6%	49,058
12/98	684,673	2,197	0.3%	48,011
12/97	396,564	(89)	—	27,611
12/96	324,091	(258)	—	29,153
12/95	335,081	1,458	0.4%	29,071
Annual Growth	**18.3%**	**19.2%**	—	**9.8%**

2004 Year-End Financials

Equity as % of assets: 2.0%
Return on assets: 0.5%
Return on equity: 23.9%
Long-term debt ($ mil.): 103,253
No. of shares (mil.): 1,023
Dividends
   Yield: 2.4%
   Payout: 30.5%
Market value ($ mil.): 85,796
Sales ($ mil.): 59,878

Stock History

NYSE: UBS

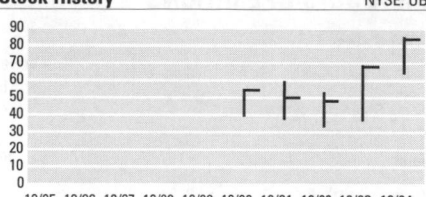

12/95 12/96 12/97 12/98 12/99 12/00 12/01 12/02 12/03 12/04

	STOCK PRICE ($) FY Close	P/E High	P/E Low	PER SHARE ($) Earnings	PER SHARE ($) Dividends	PER SHARE ($) Book Value
12/04	83.84	13	10	6.55	2.00	29.95
12/03	67.99	15	8	4.52	1.46	26.67
12/02	48.12	25	16	2.08	0.00	24.36
12/01	50.00	25	16	2.37	0.30	20.50
12/00	54.41	14	10	3.93	0.86	21.72
Annual Growth	**11.4%**	—	—	**13.6%**	**23.5%**	**8.4%**

Unilever

One is a lonely number, unless you're Unilever. One of the largest producers of some 400 packaged consumer goods, Unilever operates in nearly all countries in Asia, Africa, North America, the Middle East, Western Europe, and Latin America. The company's brand names for fragrances, frozen foods, soap, and tea include Calvin Klein, Birds Eye, Dove, and Lipton. Unilever is part of the Unilever Group owned by the Netherlands-based Unilever N.V. and UK-based Unilever PLC. Unilever has two global divisions, Home & Personal Care and Food. The company is selling its Unilever Cosmetics International unit to Coty in 2005 for about $800 million.

Unilever foods account for more than half of the firm's sales. Brands range from the widely recognized, such as Hellmann's mayonnaise, to locally marketed products, such as Italy's Findus frozen foods. The Unilever line of home and personal care products include deodorants (Axe, Degree), hair care products (Suave, ThermaSilk), prestige fragrances (Calvin Klein), and skincare (Lever 2000, Pond's). Its other familiar goods include Q-Tips, Vaseline, and laundry and cleaning products such as all, Wisk, and Surf.

The early 2005 announcement that The Procter & Gamble Company (P&G) would acquire The Gillette Company — making P&G the largest consumer products maker in the world, ahead of Unilever — put pressure on the company to quickly fine-tune its restructuring.

A couple weeks later, amid reports of a flat year for growth, Unilever announced sweeping changes in its leadership organization and that it would abandon its dual chairman/CEO structure that has been in place for decades. Antony Burgmans became chairman and Patrick Cescau took the title of CEO.

Unilever is focusing on supporting a smaller number of global brands and selling underperforming businesses. It is also is supporting its core by extending some of its traditional brands into new markets. For example, the company set aside $100 million to introduce a new line of Dove hair care products in North America. The launch of Dove shampoo in Europe, Latin America, and South East Asia reportedly has boosted sale of Dove products worldwide by 25%.

HISTORY

After sharpening his sales skills in the family wholesale grocery business, Englishman William Lever formed a new company in 1885 with his brother James. Lever Brothers introduced Sunlight, the world's first packaged, branded laundry soap. Sunlight was a success in Britain, and within 15 years Lever Brothers was selling soap worldwide. Between 1906 and 1915 the company grew mostly through acquisitions. Needing vegetable oil to make soap, the company established plantations and trading companies worldwide. During WWI Lever began using its vegetable oil to make margarine.

Rival Dutch butter makers Jurgens and Van den Berghs were pioneers in margarine production. In 1927 they created the Margarine Union, a cartel that owned the European market. The Margarine Union and Lever Brothers merged in 1930, but for tax reasons formed two separate entities: Unilever PLC in London and Unilever N.V. in Rotterdam, the Netherlands.

Despite the Depression and WWII, Unilever expanded, acquiring US companies Thomas J. Lipton (1937) and Pepsodent (1944). Unilever benefited from the postwar boom in Europe, the increasing use of margarine, new detergent technologies, and the growing use of personal care products.

Although product development fueled some growth, acquisitions (at one time running at the rate of one per week) played a major role in shaping Unilever. These included Birds Eye Foods in the UK (1957) and, in the US, Good Humor (1961), Lawry's Foods (1979), Ragu (1986), Chesebrough-Ponds (1987), Calvin Klein Cosmetics (1989, now Unilever Cosmetics International), Faberge/Elizabeth Arden (1989), and Breyers ice cream (1993).

In 1995 Unilever began cutting its global workforce by 7,500. The following year it bought hair care and deodorant maker Helene Curtis. Unilever shed its specialty chemicals operations in 1997. In 1998 the company sold its Plant Breeding International Cambridge (PBIC) business to Monsanto.

Unilever bought US weight-management firm Slim-Fast Foods in 2000 for $2.3 billion and ice-cream maker Ben & Jerry's. As part of its previously announced brand-reduction strategy, Unilever also that year sold its European bakery supplies business to CSM. Later that same year, the company bought Bestfoods for $24 billion, which would result in putting Bestfoods' US baking business (Entenmann's, Oroweat bread) up for sale. George Weston's offer of $1.77 billion won the bidding war for Bestfoods' US baking business. Unilever also owns the rights to the game show Wheel of Fortune.

In 2001 Unilever sold its Elizabeth Arden fragrance and skin care business to French Fragrances. Also in 2001, it sold its North American seafood businesses (the Gorton's brand in the US and BlueWater in Canada) to seafood conglomerate Nippon Suisan Kaisha.

In 2002 Unilever sold 19 of its North American food brands (including Mazola corn oil, Argo and Kingsford cornstarches, Karo corn syrup, and Henri's salad dressings) to a subsidiary of Associated British Foods plc.

Unilever sold its French frozen-products company Fridedoc to home-vending company Toupargel in 2003. It also sold its Brut brand of male personal care products, including fragrance, antiperspirant, and deodorant products, to Helen of Troy. The agreement gives Helen of Troy ownership of the brand in the Americas, Canada, Mexico, Puerto Rico, and elsewhere in Latin America; Unilever retains ownership in Europe, Africa, Australia, Asia, and the Middle East.

Also in 2003 Church & Dwight agreed to purchase Unilever's oral care brands in the US and Canada. Products included in the deal are Mentadent toothpaste and toothbrushes, Pepsodent and Aim toothpaste, and exclusive licensing rights to Close-Up toothpaste.

Unilever sold the rest of its Mazola brand, an operation in Mexico, to the Mexican subsidiary of Associated British Foods in early 2004, along with its Capullo cooking oil and Inca brand butter. ABF had acquired the US Mazola brand in 2002.

In early 2005, in line with its strategy to spin off stale brands, Unilever also sold its Crisp 'n Dry and Cookeen units, which produce oil and cooking fat, to Princes. Unilever retains ownership of the Flora sunflower oil and Olivio vegetable and olive oil spread.

EXECUTIVES

Chairman: Antony Burgmans, age 58, $2,692,050 pay (prior to promotion)
Vice Chairman, Unilever N.V and Unilever PLC, and Director: Bertrand P. Collomb, age 62
Group Chief Executive: Patrick J. Cescau, age 56, $2,096,100 pay (prior to promotion)
CFO: Rudy Markham, age 59, $1,724,487 pay (prior to promotion)
President and CEO, Unilever Cosmetics International: Fergus Balfour, age 51
President, Americas and President, Slim Fast Worldwide: John Rice, age 53
President, Europe: Kees van der Graaf, age 54
President, Global Foods: M. S. (Vindi) Banga, age 50
President, Global Foodsolutions: Diego Bevilacqua, age 51
President, Home and Personal Care and Director of the Boards: Ralph Kugler, age 49
President, Marketing Foods Division: Anthonie Stal, age 50
President and COO, Unilever Bestfoods North America: David Landers
Chief Human Resources Officer: Sandy Ogg, age 51
Joint Secretary and General Counsel: Stephen G. Williams, age 57
Director, Public Relations, Unilever United States: Nancy L. Goldfarb
Corporate Communications: Paul Wood
Investor Relations: Leigh Ferst
Auditors: PricewaterhouseCoopers

LOCATIONS

HQ: Unilever PLC
Unilever House, Blackfriars,
London EC4P 4BQ, United Kingdom
Phone: +44-20-7822-5252   **Fax:** +44-20-7822-6191
HQ: Unilever N.V.
Weena 455, 3000 DK Rotterdam, The Netherlands
Phone: +31-10-217-4000   **Fax:** +31-10-217-4798
US HQ: 700 Sylvan Ave., Englewood Cliffs, NJ 07632
US Phone: 201-894-7760   **US Fax:** 201-871-8257
Web: www.unilever.com

2004 Sales

	% of total
Europe	43
North America	22
Asia/Pacific	16
Latin America	11
Africa & Middle East	8
Total	**100**

PRODUCTS/OPERATIONS

2004 Sales

	% of total
Foods	56
Home & personal care	43
Other operations	1
Total	**100**

Selected Brands

Culinary (Calvé, Colmans, Hellman's, Knorr, Lipton Cup-a-Soup, Ragu, Skippy)
Carb Options (low carb Ragu, Wish-Bone, Skippy, Lipton, and Lawry's)
Deodorants (Axe, Brut, Degree, Dove, Rexona)
Fragrances (Brut, Calvin Klein, House of Cerruti, House of Valentino, Lagerfeld)
Frozen foods (Birds Eye, Findus)
Hair care (Organics, Suave, SunSilk, ThermaSilk)
Household care (Cif, Domestos)
Ice cream (Ben & Jerry's, Breyers, Good-Humor, Klondike, Magnum, Popsicle, Solero)
Laundry (all, Ala, Comfort, Omo, Snuggle, Surf, Wisk)
Personal wash (Dove, Lever 2000, Lux, Pond's, Q-tips, Vaseline)
Professional cleaning (DiverseyLever)
Salad dressing (Wish-Bone)
Spreads and cooking products (Becel, Country Crock, I Can't Believe It's Not Butter!, Promise, Rama)
Tea-based beverages (Lipton)
Weight management (Slim-Fast)

COMPETITORS

Alberto-Culver	Johnson & Johnson
Alticor	Kao
Atkins Nutritionals	Kraft Foods
Avon	L'Oréal
Beiersdorf	LVMH
Campbell Soup	Mars
Church & Dwight	McBride
Clorox	MedPointe
Coca-Cola	Nestlé
Colgate-Palmolive	PepsiCo
ConAgra	Procter & Gamble
Dairy Farmers of America	Reckitt Benckiser
Danone	Revlon
Del Monte Foods	Sara Lee Household
Dial	S.C. Johnson
Estée Lauder	Shiseido
General Mills	Tata Group
Gillette	Uniq
Inter Parfums	

HISTORICAL FINANCIALS

Company Type: Joint venture

Income Statement

FYE: December 31

	REVENUE ($ mil.)	NET INCOME ($ mil.)	NET PROFIT MARGIN	EMPLOYEES
12/04	54,413	2,541	4.7%	223,000
12/03	53,674	3,472	6.5%	234,000
12/02	50,698	2,236	4.4%	247,000
12/01	45,914	1,638	3.6%	279,000
12/00	44,813	1,041	2.3%	261,000
12/99	43,636	3,165	7.3%	255,000
12/98	47,532	3,432	7.2%	265,000
12/97	46,693	5,568	11.9%	270,000
12/96	50,403	2,420	4.8%	306,000
12/95	48,881	2,285	4.7%	308,000
Annual Growth	**1.2%**	**1.2%**	**—**	**(3.5%)**

2004 Year-End Financials

Debt ratio: 127.6%
Return on equity: 34.8%
Cash ($ mil.): 2,150
Current ratio: 0.83
Long-term debt ($ mil.): 9,337

Net Income History

Veolia Environnement

Veolia Environnement holds water — as well as waste management, energy, and transportation — operations. The company's Veolia Water unit, which provides water and wastewater services to more than 110 million people, is the world's largest water company, ahead of Suez. Subsidiary Onyx, one of the world's leading waste management companies, treats more than 50 million tons of waste per year. Majority-owned energy unit Dalkia operates global cogeneration facilities and heating and cooling systems, and Connex is a top European provider of bus, light-rail, and rail transport.

Veolia Environnement has been selling off its noncore businesses. In 2004 the company sold the assets of its former USFilter unit, a leading water-treatment equipment manufacturer, as well as its US-based Culligan water-treatment business. Also divested was Veolia Environnement's stake in Spanish construction group Fomento de Construcciones y Contratas (FCC).

Today's Veolia Environnement consists of the water, waste, energy, and transport businesses of the former Vivendi group. The group spun off Veolia Environnement (then called Vivendi Environnement), sold a minority stake to the public, and renamed itself Vivendi Universal in 2000. To raise cash, Vivendi Universal reduced its stake in the environmental services company from 63% to about 20% in 2002. Vivendi Universal sold a 15% stake in Veolia Environnement in 2004, leaving Vivendi Universal with a 5% stake in its former subsidiary.

The former Vivendi Environnement changed its name to Veolia Environnement in 2003 to signify the break with Vivendi Universal. The name Veolia is derived from Aeolus, the keeper of the winds in Greek mythology.

HISTORY

What is now Veolia Environnement originated in 1853 as Compagnie Générale des Eaux in Paris. The company irrigated farmlands and subsequently supplied water. By 1860 Paris had granted the company a 50-year contract to provide the city's water. In 1880 it moved beyond France to provide water in Venice, Italy. Operations in Turkey (Istanbul) and Portugal (Oporto) followed.

Compagnie Générale des Eaux extended its water network in 1924, and by WWII it supplied half of all urban households in France. After the war the company expanded into household waste collection (1953) and operation of household waste incineration and compost plants (1967). Wastewater treatment activities began in 1972.

In the next decade Compagnie Générale des Eaux dove into diversification. It increased its holding in energy-conversion systems operator Compagnie Générale de Chauffe to 100% (making it France's leading energy company) in 1980. That year it merged its wastewater treatment subsidiaries to create Omnium de Traitement et de Valorisation (OTV). Its waste operations were further augmented through the takeover of Compagnie Générale d'Entreprises Automobiles (CGEA), a transport and waste management firm. The company also ventured into telecommunications, pay-TV, and construction (it gained a controlling stake in builder SGE in 1988 but disposed of its interest in the firm, later known as VINCI, in 2000).

CGEA bid for and won control of several former British Rail lines in 1996 when the UK's railway system was privatized. Operating under the name Connex, the company began to run trains throughout southeastern England, the UK's largest commuting area.

In 1998 CGEA changed its name to Vivendi. The group (which came to include mobile phone provider Cegetel and a stake in the Havas media company) transferred the Compagnie Générale des Eaux name to its water business. Vivendi also organized its Compagnie Générale de Chauffe and Sithe subsidiaries into a single energy division, named Dalkia. In 1999 Sithe Energies bought 23 thermal power plants from US utility GPU (later FirstEnergy) and became the leading independent power producer in the northeastern US.

Vivendi continued its charge into the US that year. The group acquired waste services company Superior Services (then the US's fourth-biggest solid waste company). Its purchase of USFilter transformed Vivendi into the world's largest water company and marked the biggest acquisition of a US firm by a French company.

The ever-evolving Vivendi transformed into a global media company and renamed itself Vivendi Universal in 2000. It bought Seagram and French pay-TV provider CANAL+ and spun off its water, waste management, transportation, and energy operations (Vivendi Environnement) after turning down German utility RWE's $28 million offer to buy the business.

Vivendi Environnement's waste operations grew after snapping up operations in Brazil, Hong Kong, and Mexico from Waste Management. In 2001 the company merged its Dalkia energy operations with the energy services operations of Electricité de France (EDF).

In 2002 Vivendi Universal reduced its stake in Vivendi Environnement from 63% to about 20%; the following year Vivendi Environnement changed its name to Veolia Environnement.

EXECUTIVES

Chairman and CEO: Henri Proglio, age 55, $1,912,376 pay
SEVP, Deputy Managing Director, and CFO: Jérôme Contamine, age 47
EVP, Human Resources: Eric Marie de Ficquelmont, age 50
EVP and Head, Energy Services Division: Olivier Barbaroux, age 49
EVP and Head, Transportation Division: Stéphane Richard, age 43
EVP and Head, Waste Management Division: Denis Gasquet, age 51
EVP and Head, Water Division: Antoine Frérot, age 46
Investor Relations: Nathalie Pinon
US Investor Relations: Brian Sullivan
Auditors: Barbier Frinault & Cie; RSM Salustro Reydel

LOCATIONS

HQ: Veolia Environnement SA
36-38, avenue Kléber, 75116 Paris, France
Phone: +33-1-71-75-00-00 **Fax:** +33-1-71-75-10-45
US HQ: 14950 Heathrow Forest, Ste. 200, Houston, TX 77032
US Phone: 281-985-5479 **US Fax:** 713-302-1059
Web: www.veoliaenvironnement.com

2004 Sales

	$ mil.	% of total
Europe		
France	18,204.6	55
UK	2,077.0	6
Germany	1,768.2	5
Other countries	5,679.9	17
US	2,478.2	7
Other regions	3,214.6	10
Total	**33,422.5**	**100**

PRODUCTS/OPERATIONS

2004 Sales

	$ mil.	% of total
Water	13,281.6	40
Waste management	8,425.6	25
Energy services	6,821.1	20
Transportation	4,894.2	15
Total	**33,422.5**	**100**

Selected Operations

Water
  Compagnie Générale des Eaux
    Veolia Water S.A.
Waste Management
  CGEA Onyx
  Onyx Environmental Group Plc (UK)
  Onyx North America Corp.
  Renosol
  Société d'Assainissement Rationnel et de Pompage (SARP)
  SARP Industries
Energy
  Dalkia (66%)
Transport
  CGEA Connex
  Connex Transport Ltd (formerly Connex Rail Ltd, UK)

COMPETITORS

Alpheus
American States Water
AWG
Bouygues
Electricité de France
Electricité de Strasbourg
Elyo
Kelda
Northumbrian Water Group
Pennon
RWE Thames Water
SABESP
Scottish Power
Severn Trent
Shanks
SNCF
Stagecoach
SUEZ
SUEZ Environnement
ThermoEnergy
United Utilities
USFilter Water & Wastewater Systems
Vattenfall
Waste Management
Waste Recycling
Welsh Water

HISTORICAL FINANCIALS

Company Type: Public

Income Statement

FYE: December 31

	REVENUE ($ mil.)	NET INCOME ($ mil.)	NET PROFIT MARGIN	EMPLOYEES
12/04	33,423	170	0.5%	251,584
12/03	35,960	(2,583)	—	309,563
12/02	31,592	356	1.1%	302,283
12/01	25,647	(1,982)	—	295,286
12/00	24,858	579	2.3%	215,376
12/99	41,914	1,441	3.4%	275,000
12/98	37,034	1,308	3.5%	235,610
12/97	29,729	959	3.2%	193,300
Annual Growth	**1.7%**	**(21.9%)**	**—**	**3.8%**

2004 Year-End Financials

Debt ratio: 303.1%
Return on equity: 3.6%
Cash ($ mil.): 4,924
Current ratio: 1.02
Long-term debt ($ mil.): 14,632
No. of shares (mil.): 406
Dividends
  Yield: 1.8%
  Payout: 157.1%
Market value ($ mil.): 14,814

Stock History

NYSE: VE

	STOCK PRICE ($) FY Close	P/E High/Low	Earnings	Dividends	Book Value
12/04	36.45	87 60	0.42	0.66	11.88
12/03	27.00	— —	(6.45)	0.59	11.09
12/02	23.31	35 18	0.98	1.37	16.41
12/01	34.25	— —	(5.80)	0.00	14.60
Annual Growth	**2.1%**	**— —**	**—**	**—**	**(6.7%)**

VINCI

Veni, vidi, vici . . . VINCI. VINCI has come, seen, and conquered a number of European markets. Formerly Société Générale d'Enterprises (SGE), the company, through its VINCI Construction unit, has become one of the world's largest contractors. It is engaged in building, civil engineering, and maintenance. VINCI Energies unit is a French leader in electrical engineering and information technology. Eurovia (the major operating unit of the VINCI Roads division) is a top European roadworks and urban redevelopment company. VINCI Concessions, one of the world's largest concessions companies, builds and operates car parks, toll roads, and airports.

Although VINCI has subsidiaries in more than 100 countries, its home base of France accounts for more than 60% of the company's sales by region.

By business activity, VINCI's core construction operations still generate more than 40% of total sales. VINCI Construction unit's lead contractor is subsidiary Campenon Bernard, builder of Paris' 80,000-seat Stade de France. Subsidiary Sogea performs general contracting and engineering. The group, whose major projects include restoring the Strasbourg cathedral and the fountains of Place de la Concorde in Paris, has agreed to manage the restoration of the Château de Versailles Hall of Mirrors and contribute its technical expertise to the project.

The group's VINCI Energies (formerly GTIE, or Générale de Travaux et d'Installation Électrique) division is a top electrical engineering group in France, as well as a major European player in information and communication technologies. The unit also focuses on power supply infrastructure and public lighting systems.

In addition to being one of Europe's top roadworks and urban redevelopment companies, Eurovia is a leader in the road construction materials, demolition, and waste recycling markets. The company operates in 17 countries, including Chile, Canada, and the US. In the US it owns two southeastern highway contractors, Orlando, Florida-based Hubbard Construction and Charlotte, North Carolina-based Blythe Construction. Eurovia has won a contract to replace cobblestones at the Place de L'Etoile in Paris, near the Arc de Triomphe. The cobblestones have not been replaced since 1947.

Another unit that ranks among the world's leading companies in its industry is VINCI Concessions. With construction rivals Eiffage and Bouygues it runs toll road operator Cofiroute, and it has a 23% stake in European toll road operator ASF.

VINCI Park, which resulted from the merger of Sogeparc and Parc GTM, manages parking facilities in about a dozen countries.

HISTORY

VINCI's origins lie with French conglomerate Vivendi (now Vivendi Universal), which was founded in 1853 as Compagnie Générale des Eaux. Its mission was to irrigate French farmland and supply water to towns. The company won contracts to serve Lyons (1853), Nantes (1854), Paris (1860), and Venice (1880). Générale des Eaux moved into construction in 1972, building an office tower (and later hotels and houses) in Paris. The company also entered communications in the 1980s.

In 1988 Générale des Eaux acquired control of construction and civil engineering giant Société Générale d'Entreprises. SGE subsidiaries included Campenon Bernard SGE (part of Générale des Eaux since 1981), Sogea, Freyssinet, Cochery Bourdin Chaussé, Saunier Duval, Tunzini, Lefort Francheteau, and Wanner. SGE traces its construction roots to 1910. It became a subsidiary of Générale d'Electricité in 1966. Glassmaker Saint-Gobain acquired control of SGE in 1984. Under Générale des Eaux, SGE enhanced its European profile through acquisitions, including British builder Norwest Holst (1989), German road builder VBU (1991), and German pipe and duct maker MLTU (1992).

Générale des Eaux acquired publisher Havas in 1998 and took the name Vivendi — representing vivacity and mobility. Its purchase of US Filter in 1999 made Vivendi the world's largest water company. Vivendi's SGE unit (renamed VINCI) agreed to acquire the construction arm of rival conglomerate Suez's GTM unit in 2000.

Groupe GTM traces its roots to Société Lyonnaise des Eaux et de L'Eclairage, a leading French water utility. Formed in 1880, Lyonnaise des Eaux built up its French and international operations to include water distribution, as well as gas and electricity production and distribution. A century later the company had diversified into such businesses as heating (Cofreth), waste management (Sita), and communications, acquiring a stake in Lyonnaise Communications (now Lyonnaise Câble) in 1986.

In 1990 Lyonnaise des Eaux acquired construction firm Dumez, whose subsidiary GTM-Entrepose was France's largest car park manager. Four years later Dumez-GTM was formed to consolidate the construction and civil engineering businesses of Dumez and GTM-Entrepose. In 1997 Lyonnaise des Eaux and Compagnie de Suez merged to create a leading provider of private infrastructure services, Suez Lyonnaise des Eaux (which shortened its name to Suez in 2001). Compagnie Universal du Canal Maritime de Suez, the builder of the Suez Canal, was founded in 1858 and became Financière de Suez in 1958. In 1967 Financière de Suez acquired control of Lyonnaise des Eaux.

SGE changed its name to VINCI in 2000. That year, as part of their strategy to rationalize operations and focus on core businesses, Vivendi and Suez agreed to a friendly takeover of GTM by VINCI. Suez emerged as the combined company's largest shareholder, but by the following year both Suez and Vivendi Universal had exited most of VINCI's capital, leaving no core stockholder.

To better control its car park management operations, the company in 2001 created VINCI Park to operate as an umbrella of its VINCI Concessions unit. It expanded its concessions holdings even more in 2002 by hooking up with construction group Eiffage to grab a 17% stake in Europe's second-largest toll road operator, ASF, which was floated that year by the French government.

In 2003 the group won the contract to manage the restoration of the historic Hall of Mirrors. It also won the concession contract to operate, along with joint venture partner Keolis, the International Airport of Grenoble.

EXECUTIVES

Chairman and CEO: Antoine Zacharias, age 65
Vice Chairman: Bernard Huvelin, age 68
Co-COO; Chairman and CEO, VINCI Energies: Xavier Huillard
Co-COO; Chairman and CEO, Eurovia (VINCI Roads): Roger Martin
Chairman and CEO, VINCI Construction: Philippe Ratynski
VP and CFO: Christian Labeyrie
VP Corporate Communications, Human Resources, and Synergies: Pierre Coppey
VP Business Development: Jean-Luc Pommier
Chairman and CEO, GTM Construction: Robert Hosselet
Chairman and CEO, Freyssinet: Bruno Dupety
Chairman, Sogea Construction: Jean Rossi
Chairman, VINCI Construction Filiales Internationales: Richard Francioli, age 45
Chairman and CEO, Cofiroute: Henri Stouff
Chairman and CEO, VINCI Airports Services: Jean-Pierre Marchand-Arpoumé
Chairman and CEO, VINCI Park: Denis Grand
Chairman and CEO, VINCI plc: John Stanion
Auditors: Deloitte Touche Tohmatsu — Audit; RSM Salustro Reydel

LOCATIONS

HQ: VINCI
1 cours Ferdinand-de-Lesseps,
92851 Rueil-Malmaison, France
Phone: +33-1-47-16-35-00   **Fax:** +33-1-47-51-91-02
Web: www.groupe-vinci.com

VINCI has operations in more than 100 countries.

2004 Sales

	% of total
Europe	
France	62
Germany	8
UK	8
Central & Eastern Europe	6
Other regions	8
North America	4
Other regions	4
Total	**100**

PRODUCTS/OPERATIONS

2004 Sales

	% of total
Construction	42
Roads	30
Energy	17
Concessions & services	10
Other operations	1
Total	**100**

Selected Subsidiaries

VINCI Construction
  Campenon Bernard Construction
  Compagnie d 'Entreprises CFE (45%, Belgium)
  Dumez-GTM
  Freyssinet
  GTM Construction
  Janin Atlas (Canada)
  Les Travaux du Midi
  VINCI Bautec (Germany)
  VINCI plc (formerly Norwest Holst Group PLC, UK)
  SKE SSI (US)
  Sogea Construction
VINCI Roads
  Blythe (US)
  Eurovia
  Hubbard (USA)
  Ringway Ltd. (91%, UK)
  SSZ (92%, Czech Republic)
VINCI Energies (Energy and Information)
  Emil Lundgren (Sweden)
  Saga Enterprises
  Santerne Exploitation
VINCI Concessions
  Autopista del Bosque (83%, Chile)
  Cofiroute Participations (65%)
  Gestipark (50%, Canada)
  Société Concessionnaire de l 'Aéroport de Pochentong (70%, Cambodia)
  Sogeparc France
  VINCI Airports US
  VINCI Park

COMPETITORS

AMEC
Autostrade
Avionic Services International
Bechtel
Bilfinger Berger
Bouygues
Bovis Lend Lease
EIFFAGE
FCC
Halliburton
HOCHTIEF
Louis Berger
Schneider
Skanska
WS Atkins

HISTORICAL FINANCIALS

Company Type: Public

Income Statement

FYE: December 31

	REVENUE ($ mil.)	NET INCOME ($ mil.)	NET PROFIT MARGIN	EMPLOYEES
12/04	26,626	998	3.7%	128,000
12/03	22,733	680	3.0%	127,513
12/02	19,331	501	2.6%	140,000
12/01	16,115	402	2.5%	129,000
12/00	13,881	282	2.0%	120,000
12/99	9,479	147	1.6%	70,699
12/98	9,349	108	1.2%	64,451
12/97	8,913	51	0.6%	68,251
12/96	8,282	(72)	—	57,289
12/95	9,218	(190)	—	60,898
Annual Growth	12.5%	—	—	8.6%

2004 Year-End Financials

Debt ratio: 207.1%
Return on equity: 25.0%
Cash ($ mil.): 1,133

Current ratio: 1.26
Long-term debt ($ mil.): 8,893

Net Income History

Euronext Paris: DG

Virgin Group

Led by adventurous founder, chairman, and owner Sir Richard Branson, Virgin Group gets around. The group's travel operations, led by 51%-owned Virgin Atlantic Airways, are among its biggest breadwinners. Virgin Atlantic is complemented by its pan-European and Australian low-fare cousins, Virgin Express and Virgin Blue. Virgin Group also operates two UK rail franchises and sells tour packages. The group's Virgin Megastores sell music, videos, and computer games. Other Virgin Group operations include balloon flights, beverages, bridal stores, cosmetics, financial services, health clubs, Internet services, mobile phone services, publishing, and a record label.

Branson has made Virgin Group's name one of the most recognizable brands in the world by plastering it on everything from airplanes to cola. But with the airline industry slumping, Virgin Group is looking for new growth opportunities, and the company believes it may have found one in the US mobile phone market.

In addition, Branson has announced plans to raise cash by selling stakes in several group companies to the public by 2010. Australian airline Virgin Blue and Virgin Mobile have already gone public and next in line is Virgin Group's 50% stake in the US arm of Virgin Mobile (Sprint owns the other 50%).

Virgin acquired the share it did not already own in online ticket seller Thetrainline.com, a joint venture with Stagecoach, in 2004. The company plans to merge Thetrainline.com's operations with Qjump, the online ticketing agent

for ScotRail. The new company will maintain the Trainline name. Virgin acquired the 41% stake for 4 million GBP.

The group's latest venture, another airline called Virgin America, plans to take to the skies in 2005. Another low-fare affair, Virgin America will operate out of San Francisco using a leased fleet of more than 100 Airbus jets.

The group is also looking at expanding into the Indian airline services market. Branson has initiated talks to acquire stakes in several unspecified Indian airlines as part of an effort to establish the Virgin brand in that country.

HISTORY

Always one to revel in competition, Richard Branson got his start in the business world at the age of 17, dropping out of boarding school to pursue his magazine, *Student,* in 1968. Two years later he was on to a new challenge when he started Virgin — a mail-order record company named for his lack of experience at such things. After a postal strike the next year put a damper on that enterprise, Branson opened the first Virgin record store. Continued success led to a recording studio and record label that went on to sign several popular British rock bands in the 1970s, including the Sex Pistols, Genesis, and the Rolling Stones.

With his entertainment businesses flourishing in the early 1980s, Branson sought a new adventure and found it in the airline industry, another business he knew very little about. Virgin Atlantic Airways took off in 1984 with one plane and one transatlantic route. Growing steadily, Virgin Atlantic became one of the world's most profitable airlines in the 1980s. The company added Virgin Holidays (tours) to its travel group in 1985.

Branson collected all his businesses (except the travel operations) into a new company called Virgin Group and took it public in 1986. Despite the company's continued growth and profits, the market slashed its value after the crash of 1987, and a frustrated Branson bought it all back the following year. Virgin sold its smaller UK record stores in 1988 to focus on the development of its Megastores concept. It also entered the hotel business that year.

Virgin started Britain's first national commercial rock radio station in 1992. Branson sold the Virgin Music Group (a decision he still regrets) to THORN EMI that year for about $1 billion. He used the proceeds to build Virgin Atlantic. By the early 1990s the airline had added to its fleet and had new routes, including flights to Asia. It also took on British Airways and won a libel suit in 1993.

The company debuted Virgin Cola in 1994 and bought 25% of the Our Price record store chain with WH Smith (it purchased the rest in 1998). Virgin acquired MGM Cinemas (the UK's largest theater operator) and introduced its financial services business in 1995. Meanwhile it added dozens of new Megastores around the world in the mid-1990s. Virgin got back into the recording business in 1996 when it launched the V2 record label. It also bought low-fare Euro Belgian Airlines (renamed Virgin Express).

Virgin looked to keep itself on the right track in 1997 when it got into the rail business. Realizing that the right track might be the Internet, Branson has pushed the group towards the age of e-commerce and online services with Virgin.com. Mobile phone sales (at its existing retail locations) entered the company's cornucopia in 1999. In late 1999 Virgin agreed to sell

its cinema chain to Vivendi (now Vivendi Universal), raising funds for other online and retail ventures. It launched a major Australian airline (Virgin Blue) in 2000.

That year Branson's bid to wrest the operation of UK's national lottery from current contract holder Camelot Group came up short. The National Lottery Commission extended Camelot's contract for seven years. Later in 2000 the company sold 49% of Virgin Atlantic to Singapore Airlines.

In 2001 Virgin agreed to sell Virgin Sun (package holidays) to rival travel firm First Choice Holidays. Also that year the company sold its 16 French Megastores, as well as some international rights to the Virgin brand, to France's Lagardère.

Virgin Mobile in 2002 began offering prepaid wireless service in the US in conjunction with Sprint PCS.

EXECUTIVES

Chairman: Sir Richard Branson, age 55
Chief Executive: Stephen Murphy
Director Financial Control: Susannah Parden
Group Brand Marketing Director: Ashley Stockwell
IT Services Director: Gareth Lewis
General Counsel: Helena Samaha
Auditors: KPMG

LOCATIONS

HQ: Virgin Group Ltd.
120 Campden Hill Rd., London W8 7AR,
United Kingdom
Phone: +44-20-7229-1282 **Fax:** +44-20-7727-8200
Web: www.virgin.com

Virgin Group has operations in Africa, Asia, Australia, Europe, and North America.

PRODUCTS/OPERATIONS

Major Operations

Virgin Active (45%, health clubs)
Virgin Arcadia Productions (video production)
Virgin Airship & Balloon company (hot air balloon)
Virgin Atlantic Airways (51%, international airline)
Virgin Balloon Flights (passenger balloons)
Virgin Biz Net (Online services for small businesses)
Virgin Blue (Australian low-fare airline)
Virgin Books (book publishing)
Virgin Bride (bridal emporium)
Virgin Cars (car purchasing Web site)
Virgin Cola (beverage brands)
Virgin Cosmetics (more than 500 products for men and women available in the UK)
Virgin Direct (financial services)
Virgin Energy (25%, utility bill payment program)
Virgin Express (pan-European low-fare airline)
Virgin Holidays (UK-based tour operator)
Virgin Limobike (motorcycle passenger service)
Virgin Limousines (Northern California limo service)
Virgin Megastores (retail music, movies, and computer games)
Virgin Mobile (mobile phone services)
Virgin Money (financial information)
Virgin Net (online entertainment, sports and leisure service)
Virgin One (banking services)
Virgin Student (online community)
Virgin Trains (passenger trains)
Virgin Travelstore (online travel agency)
Virgin Vouchers (voucher program)
V2 Music (record label)
V.SHOP (entertainment stores)

COMPETITORS

Accor	MyTravel
Air France	News Corp.
AMR Corp.	Pearson
Bertelsmann	PepsiCo
British Airways	Rank
Coca-Cola	Sony
Disney	Starwood Hotels & Resorts
EMI Group	Time Warner
HMV	Tower Records
Japan Airlines	UAL
KLM	Viacom
Lufthansa	Vivendi Universal
Marriott	

HISTORICAL FINANCIALS

Company Type: Private

Income Statement

FYE: January 31

	ESTIMATED REVENUE ($ mil.)	NET INCOME ($ mil.)	NET PROFIT MARGIN	EMPLOYEES
1/04	8,100	—	—	35,000
1/03	7,000	—	—	36,000
1/02	6,500	—	—	34,000
1/01	6,000	—	—	32,000
1/00	5,200	—	—	30,000
1/99	4,941	—	—	25,000
1/98	5,000	—	—	24,000
1/97*	4,003	—	—	20,000
10/96	3,254	—	—	10,000
10/95	2,800	—	—	10,000
Annual Growth	12.5%	—	—	14.9%

*Fiscal year change

Revenue History

Vivendi Universal

Vivendi Universal (VU) has seen its Hollywood aspirations fade to black, but the company remains a world leader in media and telecommunications. It sold many of its US-based entertainment assets in the 2004 deal that created NBC Universal. VU's current assets include Canal+ Group, one of Europe's largest pay-TV services. Its 92%-owned subsidiary Universal Music Group is a leading recording company and music publishing house. Vivendi Universal Games is a 99%-owned subsidiary that develops, publishes, and distributes interactive entertainment. Telecom holdings include the 56%-owned Groupe SFR Cegetel, which includes France's #2 wireless carrier (SFR) and fixed-line operator Cegetel. France's Groupe SFR Cegetel, which VU co-owns with UK-based wireless phone giant Vodafone Group, is its largest division.

VU's rise from a water utility into the #2 media group in the world (after US-based Time Warner) was, to a large degree, the work of former CEO Jean-Marie Messier, who gained a reputation as perhaps the most powerful businessman in France. But the empire had been built on expensive acquisitions, especially the US media assets, and Messier's meteoric rise ended when VU's board of directors, fearing he could not change the company's fortunes, forced his resignation.

Jean-René Fourtou, formerly vice chairman of drug maker Aventis, replaced Messier and after two-and-a-half years has cut VU's debt from €35 billion to about €3 billion.

A prominent deal in Fourtou's debt reduction plan, VU's 86%-owned Vivendi Universal Entertainment (VUE) unit, with the exception of Universal Music Group, was sold to GE, the parent company to NBC TV network, creating NBC Universal. VU received $3.8 billion in cash and retains a 19% stake in NBC Universal in the deal that included Universal Studios, cable TV channels, and theme parks.

Because French authorities wanted the CANAL+ pay-TV channel to remain independent, VU has transferred the majority of its CANAL+ Group operations to CANAL Plus SA, a publicly traded entity. VU retains a 49% stake.

HISTORY

Authorized by an imperial decree, Compagnie Générale des Eaux was founded in 1853 by investors such as the Rothschild family and Napoleon III's half-brother to irrigate French farmland and supply water to towns. It won contracts to serve Lyons (1853), Nantes (1854), Paris (1860), and Venice (1880).

After WWI Générale des Eaux created water engineering firm Société Auxiliaire de Distribution d'Eau (Sade, 1918) and extended its water distribution network to several areas of France. By 1953 the company had added trash collection to its services. In the 1960s it began managing district heating networks and waste incineration/composting plants. The company moved into construction in 1972. By the time Guy Dejouany became chairman in 1976, water distribution accounted for less than half of the company's sales.

Dejouany began an expansion drive. In 1980 Générale des Eaux became France's #1 private energy management firm when it bought Générale de Chauffe. Also that year it expanded its wastewater and waste management businesses and moved into transportation, buying Compagnie Générale d'Entreprises Automobiles (CGEA). The company also entered communications in the 1980s: it took a 15% stake in pay-TV provider CANAL+ (1983) and it created mobile phone unit Société Francaise de Radiotelephonie (SFR, 1987).

Générale des Eaux's took its water services global in the 1990s. Dejouany stepped down in 1996, and was succeeded by Jean-Marie Messier, who immediately dumped some businesses. In 1997 the company launched telecom provider Cegetel and increased its stake in publisher Havas to 30%. In 1998 the firm bought the rest of Havas, increased its ownership in CANAL+, and took the name Vivendi to represent "vivacity" and "mobility."

Its purchase of USFilter in 1999 made Vivendi the world's largest water company; it also bought US waste management company Superior Services. The company sold sold its hotel and restaurant businesses to Accor, the French hotels group.

In 2000 Vivendi brought its environmental services businesses together under the Vivendi Environnement umbrella and sold a minority stake in the new company to the public.

Later that year, in a $34 billion deal that set the state for Vivendi's transformation into a global conglomerate, the company bought Seagram and the portion of CANAL+ that it didn't already own. The combined company became Vivendi Universal (VU). VU also sold Seagram's liquor business for $8.1 billion to Diageo and Pernod Ricard, which split up the various Seagram's brands between them.

In 2001 the company struck the biggest deal in its short history by agreeing to buy the entertainment assets of USA Networks. The deal closed the following year and VU combined Universal Studios with the USA business — which included film and TV production and cable channels — into a new company called Vivendi Universal Entertainment.

But in 2002 VU posted a roughly $25 billion loss, the largest one-year loss in French corporate history, and Messier's reputation took on some tarnish. He was forced to resign after the board of directors, following months of squabbling, withdrew support for his leadership. He was replaced by Jean-René Fourtou, the vice chairman of drug maker Aventis (now Sanofi-Aventis).

Adding insult to injury, the US SEC accused Messier and other executives, including finance director Guillaume Hannezo, with accounting irregularities. Messier was fined $1 million, barred from being an officer or director of a public US company for 10 years, and denied a $25 million "golden parachute" deal. He was later fined €1 million by France's market regulators for inaccurate financial reporting. VU shareholders also filed a lawsuit against the former managers demanding that they pay $54 million towards a US civil fine and legal costs.

In 2002 VU completely exited the publishing business by selling Vivendi Universal Publishing (now named Editis) to Lagardère for $1.2 billion, and Houghton Mifflin to Thomas H. Lee and Bain Capital for $1.6 billion. In 2003, the company's water utility changed its name to Veolia Environnement to further distance itself from its tarnished former parent.

EXECUTIVES

Chairman and CEO: Jean-René Fourtou, age 66
COO: Jean-Bernard Lévy, age 49
SEVP and CFO: Jacques Espinasse, age 61
SEVP Divestitures, Mergers, and Acquisitions: Robert de Metz, age 52
SEVP Human Resources; Advisor to Chairman; Chairman, Vivendi Universal Games: René Pénisson, age 62
EVP Divestitures, Mergers, and Acquisitions: Régis Turrini, age 45
EVP and General Counsel: Jean-François Dubos, age 59
EVP Corporate Communications: Michel Bourgeois, age 54
EVP Investor Relations: Daniel Scolan
EVP Marketing Strategy and Customer Relationship: Bruno Delecour, age 51
SVP Internal Audit and Special Projects: Vincent Vallejo, age 43
Deputy CFO: Sandrine Dufour, age 37

Chairman, CANAL+ Group; Chairman and CEO, Canal
Plus SA: Bertrand Méheut
Chairman and CEO, Universal Music Group:
Douglas (Doug) Morris
Chairman and CEO, Universal Music International:
Jorgen Larsen
Chairman and CEO, Veolia Environnement:
Henri Proglio, age 55
President and Director General, Groupe SFR Cegetel:
Frank Esser, age 47
President and COO, Universal Music Group:
Zach Horowitz
Vice Chairman and CFO, Universal Music Group:
Marinus N. (Nick) Henny
CEO, Vivendi Universal Games: Bruce Hack
Auditors: RSM Salustro Reydel

LOCATIONS

HQ: Vivendi Universal S.A.
  42 avenue de Friedland, 75380 Paris, France
Phone: +33-1-71-71-10-00   Fax: +33-1-71-71-10-01
US HQ: 800 Third Ave., New York, NY 10022
US Phone: 212-572-7000   US Fax: 212-753-9301
Web: www.vivendiuniversal.com

2004 Sales

	$ mil.	% of total
Europe		
France	16,357	56
Other countries	3,724	13
US	5,017	17
Other countries	3,928	14
Total	**29,026**	**100**

PRODUCTS/OPERATIONS

2004 Sales

	$ mil.	% of total
Media		
Universal Music Group	6,763	23
CANAL+ Group	4,849	17
Vivendi Universal Entertainment	3,152	11
Vivendi Universal Games	643	2
Telecom		
Groupe SFR Cegetel	11,266	39
Maroc Telecom	2,204	7
Other	149	1
Total	**29,026**	**100**

Selected Subsidiaries and Affiliates

Media
  CANAL+ Group
    CANAL+ SA (49%, pay TV operations)
    NBC Universal (19%, media holdings, US)
    Sogecable, S.A. (10%, TV broadcaster, Spain)
  Universal Music Group (92%, music production and
    distribution, US)
  Vivendi Universal Games (99%, interactive
    entertainment software)
Telecom
  Groupe SFR Cegetel (56%, telecom services)
  Maroc Telecom (51%, telecom services, Morocco)
Other
  Veolia Environnement (5%, environmental services)

COMPETITORS

Bertelsmann
Eidos
EMI Group
France Telecom
ITV
Terra Networks
Time Warner
Virgin Group

HISTORICAL FINANCIALS

Company Type: Public

Income Statement

FYE: December 31

	REVENUE ($ mil.)	NET INCOME ($ mil.)	NET PROFIT MARGIN	EMPLOYEES
12/04	29,026	1,021	3.5%	37,906
12/03	32,036	(1,437)	—	55,451
12/02	61,075	(24,473)	—	61,815
12/01	51,125	(12,119)	—	381,504
12/00	40,138	2,165	5.4%	290,000
12/99	43,774	1,438	3.3%	275,000
12/98	37,034	1,308	3.5%	234,800
12/97	27,858	899	3.2%	193,300
12/96	31,623	373	1.2%	217,300
12/95	32,713	(751)	—	221,157
Annual Growth	**(1.3%)**	**—**	**—**	**(17.8%)**

2004 Year-End Financials

Debt ratio: 33.4%
Return on equity: 6.1%
Cash ($ mil.): 4,278
Current ratio: 0.78
Long-term debt ($ mil.): 6,162
No. of shares (mil.): 1,073
Dividends
Yield: 0.0%
Payout: —
Market value ($ mil.): 34,399

Stock History

NYSE: V

12/95 12/96 12/97 12/98 12/99 12/00 12/01 12/02 12/03 12/04

	STOCK PRICE ($) FY Close	P/E High/Low	Earnings	Dividends	Book Value
12/04	32.07	38 27	0.85	0.00	17.20
12/03	24.28	— —	(1.35)	0.00	13.99
12/02	16.07	— —	(22.51)	0.89	13.78
12/01	53.79	— —	(0.12)	0.90	30.16
12/00	65.31	25 19	3.20	0.00	49.39
Annual Growth	**(16.3%)**	**— —**	**(28.2%)**	**—**	**(23.2%)**

VNU N.V.

VNU keeps tabs on what people are buying and
what they are watching. The #1 market research
firm in the world provides a wealth of information on consumer habits and business trends to
customers around the globe. Its largest subsidiary units include top retail sales tracker
ACNielsen and media measurement giant Nielsen
Media Research. It also owns stakes in Web traffic measurement firm NetRatings (65%) and de-
mographics researcher Scarborough Research
(50%). In addition, the company publishes well
known trade magazines such as *ADWEEK, Billboard,* and *The Hollywood Reporter* though its
VNU Business Media division.

Formerly known more for its publishing operations, VNU jumped to the top of the market research business through its acquisition of the
Nielsen family of companies in 2000 and 2001.
The deals also gave the company a very large
foothold in the US market, which accounts for
more than half of its revenue.

VNU planned to boost its US presence even
further with its 2005 announcement that it
would buy market research firm IMS Health.
However, the deal drew some opposition from
big shareholders at VNU and was later scrapped.
When announcing the termination of the deal,
VNU chief Rob van den Bergh also said he would
step down as head of the company as soon as a
successor was found.

The condition of the global economy, however,
continues to put the squeeze on profits, but the
company feels that its business-to-business sectors will remain relatively safe from the effects of
a recession.

Having completed its major acquisitions, the
company has been focused on realigning its business units and fostering organic growth within
those units. VNU sold its business and telephone
directory publishing unit in 2004 for about
$2.8 billion to investment firms Apax Partners
and Cinven. The directories business had accounted for about 15% of VNU's revenue. The following year the company contributed the
international operations of Nielsen Media Research to form a 50-50 joint venture with the
AGB Group (part of the Kantar Group). Called
AGB Nielsen Media Research, the firm monitors
television ratings in 30 countries. VNU has also
announced plans to merge its French business
publishing operations with those of tech information provider International Data Group to
form a new joint venture in which each firm will
own 50%.

HISTORY

VNU was formed in 1964 through the merger
of Dutch mass-market consumer publishing
companies Cebema ('sHertogenbosch) and De
Spaarnestad (Haarlem). The newly formed company acquired regional newspaper publisher Het
Nieuwsblad van het Zuiden and book publisher
Het Spectrum in 1967. The next year it acquired
magazine publisher NRM and Smeets, one of the
largest offset printers in Europe. The company's
buying spree pumped up sales and profits but
also created an unwieldy organization. During
the early 1970s VNU hired US management con-
sultant McKinsey & Company to help streamline
its operations.

Acquisitions continued through the 1970s, including trade journal publisher Intermediair
(1973) and Belgian bookbinder Reliure Indus-
trielle de Barchon (1974). In the late 1970s the
company began moving into professional publishing, and in 1980 VNU acquired the publishing
units of Computing Publications and Business
and Career Publications. In 1985 Joep Brentjens
was appointed chairman of VNU. That year the
company began to focus on expanding into the US
and bought financial information provider Disclosure. It later acquired New Jersey-based Hayden
Publishing (1986, sold in 1989). Back at home,
VNU became the #1 regional newspaper publisher
in The Netherlands when it bought Audet in 1988.
The next year the company made its first foray
into television, buying stakes in Belgian station
VTM and Dutch TV station RTL 4. (Both investments were sold in 1998.)

In 1990 the company entered the eastern Eu-
ropean market with *Moscow Magazine.* As part
of a plan to focus on publishing, VNU sold its
printing operations to Koninklijke De Boer
Boekhoven in 1993. The next year it acquired
US-based BPI Communications (*Billboard, AD-
WEEK*) and Bill Communications (*Beverage
World*). VNU sold Disclosure in 1995 and bought

SRDS, a business information provider, as part of its strategy to increase its US market share of business information services (professional newsletters, magazines, directories, trade shows).

In 1997 VNU acquired Czech consumer magazine publisher Kwety Ceske and a 50% stake in RCV Entertainment (later boosted to full-ownership), a Netherlands-based film, video, and TV program distributor. The company paid $2.1 billion for a directories unit of ITT the next year. After acquiring venerable *Editor & Publisher Magazine* in 1999, VNU made its biggest US investment when it agreed to buy TV ratings firm Nielsen Media Research for $2.5 billion (completed in 2000).

Rob van den Bergh, a 20-year company veteran, was appointed chairman of VNU in 2000. That year the company entered into a joint venture with Germany's Gatrixx to create localized financial portals in Europe and bought Netherlands-based Internet portal Startpagina (starting page). It also sold its VNU Dagbladen newspaper publishing division. Later in 2000 VNU acquired trade show unit Miller Freeman from United News & Media (now United Business Media).

At the beginning of 2001 VNU took another major step with its $2.3 billion acquisition of US market research firm ACNielsen. It also announced plans to get out of the consumer magazine and educational publishing business. Later that year it sold its consumer titles to Finland-based SanomaWSOY for about $1.1 billion (one of the largest acquisitions ever by a Finnish company) and its educational publishing business to a management group.

VNU continued its business realignment in 2004, selling its business and telephone directories unit to investment firms Apax Partners and Cinven for about $2.8 billion.

EXECUTIVES

Chairman, Supervisory Board: Aad G. Jacobs, age 69
Vice Chairman, Supervisory Board: Frank L. Meysman, age 52
Chairman and CEO, Executive Board:
R. F. (Rob) van den Bergh, age 54, $1,528,500 pay
President and CEO, Nielsen Media Research; EVP, VNU Media Measurement & Information: Susan D. Whiting
Executive Director and CFO: Rob A. Ruijter, age 53
SVP Tax: Bart Kuper, age 41
Chairman and CEO, Nielsen Media Research International: Robert L. McCann Jr.
President and CEO, Media Solutions:
Christopher (Chris) Lehman
President and CEO, NetRatings: William R. (Bill) Pulver, age 45
President and CEO, Nielsen Entertainment:
Andrew Wing
President and CEO, VNU Advisory Services:
Steven A. Wilson
President and CEO, VNU Business Media; President, Nielsen Entertainment: Michael (Mike) Marchesano
President and CEO, VNU Business Media Europe:
Ruud H. Bakker
EVP, VNU Marketing Information; President and CEO, ACNielsen: Steven M. (Steve) Schmidt
SVP and Chief Communications Officer: Will Thoretz
VP and Secretary: Harris Black
VP Investor Relations, US: Peter M. Wortel
Chief Legal Officer: Earl H. Doppelt
Corporate Development; COO, VNU USA:
Thomas A. (Thom) Mastrelli, age 57
Human Resources/Management Development:
Greg Anderson
Auditors: Ernst & Young Accountants

LOCATIONS

HQ: VNU N.V.
Ceylonpoort 5-25,
2037 AA Haarlem, The Netherlands
Phone: +31-23-546-34-63   **Fax:** +31-23-546-39-38
US HQ: 770 Broadway, New York, NY 10003-9595
US Phone: 646-654-5000   **US Fax:** 646-654-5001
Web: www.vnu.com

2004 Sales

	% of total
The Americas	54
Europe, Middle East & Africa	38
Asia/Pacific	8
Total	**100**

PRODUCTS/OPERATIONS

2004 Sales

	% of total
Marketing Information	54
Media Measurement & Information	28
Business Information	18
Total	**100**

Selected Operations

Marketing information
   ACNielsen
      Solucient (35%, US)
   VNU Advisory Services
      Claritas (US)
      Spectra (US)
Media measurement and information
   AGB Nielsen Media Research (50%, Italy)
   NetRatings (65%, US)
   Nielsen Entertainment (Nielsen EDI, US)
   Nielsen Media Research (US)
   Scarborough Research (50%, US)
   SRDS (Standard Rate and Data Service, US)
Business information
   VNU Business Publications USA
      ADWEEK
      Airplay Monitor
      American Artist
      Amusement Business
      Beverage World
      Billboard
      BRANDWEEK
      Editor & Publisher
      The Hollywood Reporter
      MEDIAWEEK
      Restaurant Business
      SHOOT
   VNU Business Media Europe
   VNU Expositions
   VNU eMedia & Information Marketing

COMPETITORS

Aegis Group
Bertelsmann
Catalina Marketing
Cegedim
Crain Communications
Financial Times
GfK
Havas
IMS Health
Information Resources
International Data Group
Interpublic Group
Ipsos
Kantar Group
McGraw-Hill
Omnicom
Publicis
Reed Elsevier Group
Taylor Nelson
Thomson Corporation
United Business Media
Wolters Kluwer

HISTORICAL FINANCIALS

Company Type: Public

Income Statement

FYE: December 31

	REVENUE ($ mil.)	NET INCOME ($ mil.)	NET PROFIT MARGIN	EMPLOYEES
12/04	5,157	222	4.3%	39,366
12/03	4,872	163	3.3%	38,100
12/02	4,481	178	4.0%	37,590
12/01	4,274	708	16.6%	36,796
12/00	3,187	752	23.6%	18,720
12/99	2,829	247	8.7%	14,591
12/98	2,848	294	10.3%	12,059
12/97	1,935	207	10.7%	12,123
12/96	1,949	186	9.5%	10,462
12/95	1,897	268	14.1%	9,285
Annual Growth	**11.8%**	**(2.0%)**	**—**	**17.4%**

2004 Year-End Financials

Debt ratio: 66.8%   Current ratio: 2.51
Return on equity: 4.2%   Long-term debt ($ mil.): 3,607
Cash ($ mil.): 2,954

Net Income History

Pink Sheets: VNUVY

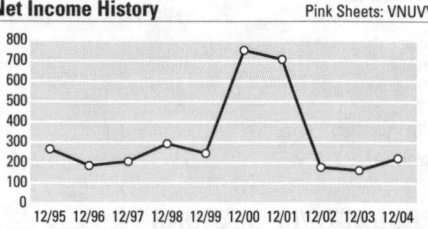

| | 12/95 | 12/96 | 12/97 | 12/98 | 12/99 | 12/00 | 12/01 | 12/02 | 12/03 | 12/04 |

Vodafone Group

Customers have voted with their phones to make Vodafone Group the world's #2 wireless phone services provider (by subscribers) — with more than 133 million (trailing only China Mobile (Hong Kong)). Vodafone Group has grown rapidly through acquisitions and has advanced toward its goal of creating a pan-European wireless network. The company, formerly known as Vodafone AirTouch, owns stakes in wireless carriers around the globe. Vodafone companies are leading mobile phone operators in the US (45%-owned Verizon Wireless), Germany (D2), and the UK (Vodafone). The company is uniting its far-flung affiliates under the Vodafone brand.

The Vodafone Group owns stakes in operating affiliates in Europe, the Americas, the Asia/Pacific region, the Middle East, and Africa.

Besides leading the mobile carrier market in the UK, the company has teamed up with BT Group to supply the UK incumbent carrier with mobile network services. Vodafone Group's other acquisitions include Germany's Mannesmann, which had controlled the #1 network in Germany (D2) and the #2 network in Italy (Omnitel). Vodafone also owns stakes in wireless carriers in several other European countries, including France, the Netherlands, and Spain. The company also has acquired a 79% stake in Romanian mobile operator MobiFon and all of Oskar Mobil, the Czech Republic wireless carrier, from Telesystem International Wireless in a cash deal valued at $3.5 billion that increases Vodafone Group's holding to 99% of MobiFon. Vodafone is also assuming $950 million in debt with the transaction. Vodafone has agreed to acquire Telsim, the number two mobile service operator in Turkey, for about $4.6 billion.

On the other side of the Atlantic, Vodafone Group has combined its US wireless operations (acquired when the company bought AirTouch in 1999) with those of Bell Atlantic and GTE to form Verizon Wireless, the #1 US wireless provider. Verizon Wireless is 45%-owned by Vodafone Group and 55%-owned by Verizon Communications (formed when Bell Atlantic bought GTE). In 2004 Vodafone Group lost out in a bidding war with Cingular Wireless over the acquisition of AT&T Wireless.

Vodafone Group also has expanded its wireless data offerings and it took full ownership in the Vizzavi Internet portal, buying out France's Vivendi Universal, its original 50% partner.

Vodafone Group has announced plans to consolidate its holdings both in Asia and Europe, including an agreement to sell Japan Telecom's fixed-line assets and the acquisition of outstanding stakes in wireless subsidiaries in Japan, Sweden, Portugal, and the Netherlands. It has sold its 74% stake in Mexico's Grupo Iusacell, held jointly with Verizon Communications, to Movilccess in a deal valued at $7.4 million. It also is selling its 21% stake in Indian regional operator RPG Cellular Services and its operations in Sweden (Europolitan Vodafone).

Vodafone Group also has teamed up with US-based software giant Microsoft to develop mobile Web services and standards.

HISTORY

Vodafone was formed in 1983 as a joint venture between Racal Electronics (a UK electronics firm) and Millicom (a US telecom company), and was granted one of two mobile phone licenses in the UK. It launched service in 1985 as a Racal subsidiary. Vodafone and Cellnet, the other licensee, were swamped with demand. In 1988 Racal offered 20% of Vodafone to the public; three years later the rest of the firm was spun off to become Vodafone Group.

Vodafone moved beyond the UK in the 1990s. By 1993 it had interests in mobile phone networks in Australia, Greece, Hong Kong, Malta, and Scandinavia.

For a time Vodafone and Cellnet, a joint venture of British Telecom (now BT Group) and Securicor, enjoyed a duopoly in the UK. Regulators elected not to impose price controls, and the pounds rolled in. But in 1993 a new wireless provider, One 2 One, launched a digital network in London. Vodafone countered that year with its own GSM (global system for mobile communications) digital network.

With increasing competition at home, Vodafone continued to expand in 1994. It launched or bought stakes in operations in Fiji, Germany, South Africa, and Uganda. Digital service took on a larger role in Vodafone's UK business, and by 1997 some 85% of new subscribers were opting for digital GSM. In 1998 Vodafone sold its French service provider, Vodafone SA, and bought digital cellular carrier BellSouth New Zealand. It also expanded into Egypt by buying a minority stake in Misrfone, marking the largest British investment in Egypt since the Suez Canal.

In 1999 Vodafone prevailed in a brief bidding war with Bell Atlantic (now Verizon) to buy AirTouch Communications for about $60 billion. Vodafone's Chris Gent took over as CEO of the new company, Vodafone AirTouch. The prize for Vodafone: entry into the lucrative US market,

plus the opportunity to consolidate minority interests in European wireless carriers.

Vodafone AirTouch moved to significantly boost its European footprint in 1999 by launching a $131 billion hostile takeover bid for Germany's Mannesmann. The company acquired Mannesmann for about $180 billion in stock in 2000 and agreed to sell the conglomerate's engineering operations and its UK mobile phone unit, Orange. (France Telecom bought Orange for $37.5 billion later that year.) Vodafone AirTouch also announced plans for an IPO for Italian fixed-line carrier Infostrada, acquired in the Mannesmann deal, but the company instead agreed to sell Infostrada to Italian utility giant Enel. (The deal closed in 2001.)

Also in 2000 Vodafone AirTouch expanded its presence in the US, buying CommNet Cellular for $1.4 billion, then combining its US wireless operations with those of Bell Atlantic and GTE to form Verizon Wireless.

That year the company dropped AirTouch from its name and became Vodafone Group once again. It also continued its expansion push, investing in China Mobile (Hong Kong) and agreeing to buy Irish mobile phone operator Eircell (now Vodafone Ireland) in a deal that was completed in 2001. Also in 2001 Vodafone expanded its stakes in Japan Telecom Holdings (now Vodafone Holdings K.K.) and its J-Phone mobile phone operations (now Vodafone K.K.) by buying out rival BT Group; it also bought BT's remaining interest in Spain's Airtel.

In 2003 the company agreed to buy UK-based Project Telecom in a deal valued at about $250 million. It also reached an agreement to buy Singlepoint, the fast-growing UK independent service provider, from Caudwell Holdings, in a deal valued at $650 million.

EXECUTIVES

Chairman: Lord Ian MacLaurin, age 68, $911,170 pay
Deputy Chairman: Paul M. Hazen, age 63, $244,231 pay
CEO and Director: Arun Sarin, age 50, $2,207,473 pay
Deputy CEO and Director: Sir Julian Horn-Smith, age 56, $1,822,339 pay (prior to promotion)
Group CFO and Director: Andrew N. (Andy) Halford, age 46
Chief Marketing Officer and Director: Peter R. Bamford, age 51, $1,448,478 pay
Group Corporate Affairs Director: Simon Lewis, age 46
CTO and Director: Thomas Geitner, age 50, $1,275,637 pay
Group Human Resources Director: J. Brian Clark, age 56
Group General Counsel and Company Secretary: Stephen R. Scott, age 51
Group Strategy and Business Integration Director: Alan Harper, age 48
Group Treasurer; CFO, Vodafone Group Services Limited: Gerry Bacon
Chief Executive, Americas Region: Gavin Darby, age 49
Director of Corporate Responsibility: Charlotte Grezo
Director of Global Terminals and Consumer Marketing: Guy Laurence
Head of Group Media Relations: Bobby Leach
Group Investor Relations Director: Charles Butterworth
Senior Corporate Media Relations Manager: Jon Earl
Global Resourcing and People Development Director, Vodafone Group Services Limited: Pauline Best
Auditors: Deloitte & Touche LLP

LOCATIONS

HQ: Vodafone Group Plc
  Vodafone House, The Connection, Newbury,
  West Berkshire RG14 2FN, United Kingdom
Phone: +44-1635-33-251   **Fax:** +44-1635-45-713
Web: www.vodafone.com

2005 Sales

	$ mil.	% of total
Mobile telecommunications		
Europe		
Germany	10,437	16
Italy	10,433	16
UK	9,483	15
Other Europe, Middle East & Africa	16,029	25
Asia/Pacific	16,114	25
Other operations		
Germany	2,009	3
Total	**64,505**	**100**

PRODUCTS/OPERATIONS

Selected Subsidiaries and Affiliates

Belgacom Mobile S.A. (Proximus, 25%, wireless network operator, Belgium)
Cellco Partnership (Verizon Wireless, 45%, wireless network operator, US)
China Mobile (Hong Kong) Limited (3%, wireless network operator, China)
Europolitan Vodafone AB (Vodafone Sweden, wireless network operator, Sweden)
Groupe SFR Cegetel (29%, telecommunications services and holding company, France)
  Société Française du Radiotéléphone S.A. (SFR, 44%, wireless network operator, France)
Polkomtel S.A. (Plus GSM, 20%, wireless network operator, Poland)
Safaricom Limited (35%, wireless network operator, Kenya)
Swisscom Mobile A.G. (25%, wireless network operator, Switzerland)
Vodacom Group (Pty) Limited (35%, holding company, South Africa)
Vodafone AG (formerly Mannesmann AG, holding company, Germany)
  Arcor AG & Co KG (74%, fixed-line operator, Germany)
Vodafone Albania Sh. A. (99.9%, wireless network operator)
Vodafone Americas Inc. (holding company, US)
Vodafone D2 GmbH (formerly Mobilfunk GmbH, wireless network operator, Germany)
Vodafone Egypt Telecommunications SAE (formerly Misrfone Telecommunications Company SAE, 67%, wireless network operator)
Vodafone España, S.A. (formerly Airtel Móvil S.A., wireless network operator, Spain)
Vodafone Europe B.V. (holding company, The Netherlands)
Vodafone Fiji Limited (49%, wireless network operator)
Vodafone Group Services Limited (global products and services provider)
Vodafone Holding GmbH (formerly Vodafone AG, holding company, Germany)
Vodafone Holdings Europe S.L. (holding company, Spain)
Vodafone K.K. (formerly J-PHONE Co., Ltd. (98%, wireless network operator holding company, Japan)
Vodafone Hungary Mobile Telecommunications Limited, (formerly V.R.A.M. Telecommunications Company Limited, wireless network operator, Hungary)
Vodafone International Holdings B.V. (holding company, The Netherlands)
Vodafone Investments Luxembourg S. a. r.l. (holding company)
Vodafone Ireland Limited (formerly Eircell, wireless network operator)
Vodafone Libertel N.V. (wireless network operator, The Netherlands)
Vodafone Limited (wireless network operator, UK)
Vodafone Malta Limited (wireless network operator)
Vodafone Network Pty Limited (wireless network operator, Australia)
Vodafone New Zealand Limited (wireless network operator)
Vodafone Omnitel N.V. (formerly Omnitel Pronto Italia, 77%, wireless network operator, Italy)
Vodafone-Panafon Hellenic Telecommunications Company S.A. (99.8%, telecommunications and wireless network operator, Greece)
Vodafone Portugal-Comunicações Pessoais, S.A. (formerly Telecel Comunicações Pessoais, wireless network operator, Portugal)

HISTORICAL FINANCIALS

Company Type: Public

Income Statement

FYE: March 31

	REVENUE ($ mil.)	NET INCOME ($ mil.)	NET PROFIT MARGIN	EMPLOYEES
3/05	64,505	(14,249)	—	57,378
3/04	61,849	(16,615)	—	60,109
3/03	48,005	(15,518)	—	66,667
3/02	32,561	(23,026)	—	70,800
3/01	21,267	(13,838)	—	56,800
3/00	12,545	776	6.2%	29,465
3/99	5,415	1,026	18.9%	12,642
3/98	4,130	700	16.9%	9,640
3/97	2,868	597	20.8%	6,051
3/96	2,140	473	22.1%	4,728
Annual Growth	46.0%	—	—	32.0%

2005 Year-End Financials

Debt ratio: 11.7%
Return on equity: —
Cash ($ mil.): 5,386
Current ratio: 0.79
Long-term debt ($ mil.): 21,947

No. of shares (mil.): 6,838
Dividends
Yield: 1.3%
Payout: —
Market value ($ mil.): 181,620

Stock History

NYSE: VOD

	3/96	3/97	3/98	3/99	3/00	3/01	3/02	3/03	3/04	3/05

	STOCK PRICE ($) FY Close	P/E High/Low		PER SHARE ($) Earnings	Dividends	Book Value
3/05	26.56	—	—	(2.15)	0.35	27.45
3/04	23.90	—	—	(2.44)	0.31	30.22
3/03	18.22	—	—	(2.28)	0.26	29.83
3/02	18.43	—	—	(3.40)	0.22	27.38
3/01	27.15	—	—	(2.25)	0.22	31.70
3/00	55.56	230 121		0.28	0.23	36.59
3/99	37.55	60 28		0.66	0.13	0.85
3/98	20.78	45 19		0.46	0.10	0.31
3/97	8.83	25 17		0.39	0.17	0.82
3/96	7.50	29 19		0.31	0.13	1.02
Annual Growth	15.1%	— —		—	11.6%	44.2%

Volkswagen AG

With cars named for Scottish sports and cutesy insects, Volkswagen (VW) leads the Continent as Europe's #1 carmaker. Along with Golf and the New Beetle, VW's annual production of 5 million cars, trucks, and vans include such models as Passat, Touareg, Phaeton, and Fox. VW also owns a garage full of luxury carmakers — AUDI, Lamborghini, Bentley, and Bugatti. Other makes include SEAT (family cars, Spain) and SKODA (family cars, the Czech Republic). VW operates plants in Africa, the Americas, the Asia/Pacific region, and Europe. It also holds 34% of the voting rights in Swedish truck maker Scania. VW's other interests include consumer financing and Europcar (car rental).

Volkswagen has announced it is in crisis. The company has admitted it suffers from a triple threat of high costs, products with inflated sticker prices, and flagging quality. To turn the company around former DaimlerChrysler master hatchetman Wolfgang Bernhard (now head of the VW brand group) plans to squeeze $8.4 billion in savings from VW's operations by 2010. The plan also calls for the introduction of as many as 10 new, low-price models.

The bureaucracy amongst VW's management, labor leaders, and the company's leading shareholder, the state of Lower Saxony, has left the company essentially handcuffed in its attempts at reforms. However, the mid-2005 news of a corporate scandal involving kickbacks and sexual dalliances has had the sobering effect of forcing VW to face its dysfunction head on.

Increased focus on the problems is key, as the problems are myriad. VW is starting to rethink the efficacy of the generally accepted German practice of having a strong labor presence on supervisory boards. As with many other German companies, VW's attempts to manufacture competitively priced products are at odds with the labor contingent's demands for high wages.

VW's global markets are also suffering. Sales in the US are falling through the floor while its new models are selling sluggishly in Europe. Meanwhile its once dominant position in China is seriously threatened by General Motors. VW realizes exports out of Europe are key to its survival and nimble competitors like Nissan and Toyota are eating up market share at a disturbing pace — and doing so at profit margins that are even more disturbing. Toyota and Nissan earn a profit margin of more than $2,000 per car; VW earns $1 per car.

To win, VW has to cut wage costs, trim jobs, and cut way back on its current overcapacity of 30%. These cuts are going to be extremely painful and difficult to achieve given the power of German organized labor. VW is considering the sale of some non-core operations. Candidates for divestment include its Europcar car rental business and gedas AG, an automotive technology consulting firm.

The German state of Lower Saxony controls about 14% of Volkswagen (or 18% of the voting rights). Fellow German automaker Porsche has taken about a 19% stake in VW.

HISTORY

Since the early 1920s auto engineer Ferdinand Porsche (whose son later founded the Porsche car company) had wanted to make a small car for the masses. He found no backers until he met Adolf Hitler in 1934. Hitler formed the Gesellschaft zur Vorbereitung des Volkswagens (Company for the Development of People's Cars) in 1937 and built a factory in Wolfsburg, Germany. No cars were delivered during WWII, as the firm produced military vehicles using the slave labor of Jews and Russian prisoners of war.

Following WWII British occupation forces oversaw the rebuilding of the bomb-damaged plant and initial production of the odd-looking "people's car" (1945). The British appointed Heinz Nordhoff to manage Volkswagen (1948) and then turned the company over to the German government (1949).

In the 1950s VW launched the Microbus and built foreign plants. Although US sales began slowly, by the end of the decade acceptance of the little car had increased. Advertising that coined the name "Beetle" helped carve VW's niche in the US.

VW sold stock to the German public in 1960. In 1966 it purchased Auto Union (AUDI) from Daimler-Benz. The Beetle became a counterculture symbol in the 1960s, and US sales took off. By the time of Nordhoff's death in 1968, the Beetle had become the best-selling car in history.

In the 1970s the Beetle was discontinued in every country except Mexico. VW lost heavily during the model-changeover period.

VW agreed to several deals in the 1980s, including a car venture in China (1984), the purchase of 75% of SEAT (1986; it bought the rest in 1990), and the merger of its suddenly faltering Brazilian unit with Ford's ailing Argentine operations to form Autolatina (1987). In 1990 the company began building China's largest auto plant and acquired a 70% stake in Czech auto company Skoda. After suffering a $1.1 billion loss, the firm put Ferdinand Piech in the driver's seat in 1993. Under his leadership the company cut costs and boosted sales by resuscitating the SEAT and Skoda brands and launching a bigger, more luxurious Passat sedan in 1997.

VW acquired Rolls-Royce Motor Cars, Vickers' Cosworth auto engines subsidiary, Italian sportscar maker Bugatti, and Italy's Automobili Lamborghini — all in 1998. Although less luxurious than VW's other pursuits, the New Beetle helped boost US sales that year. Also in 1998 VW established a $12 million fund to compensate the surviving 2,000 concentration-camp inmates forced to work as slave labor during WWII. However, the company was hit with a class-action lawsuit filed on behalf of Holocaust survivors anyway.

In 1999 chairman Ferdinand Piech announced an end to VW's acquisition binge, saying that growth would be driven from within; VW announced it would pour $31.5 billion into modernizing its factories through 2004. VW hoped to tap the market in China after getting approval in 1999 to sell a newly developed minicar there.

Volkswagen expanded into heavy commercial vehicles in 2000 by purchasing a 34% stake in Swedish truck maker Scania. That year it also bought the 30% of Skoda that it didn't already own. Anticipating China's entry into the World Trade Organization, Volkswagen announced in 2001 that it would invest $1.7 billion in China and the Asia/Pacific region over the next five years.

In April 2002 former BMW head Bernd Pischetsrieder succeeded Piech as CEO. The following year the final classic Beetle rolled off the VW assembly line in Mexico. The final Beetle concluded a 70-year run of constant production. Also in 2003, BMW took control of the Rolls-Royce brand from Volkswagen.

EXECUTIVES

Chairman of the Supervisory Board: Ferdinand K. Piëch, age 67
Deputy Chairman of the Supervisory Board: Jürgen Peters, age 60
Chairman of the Board of Management: Bernd Pischetsrieder
Member of the Board of Management; Chairman of the Board of Management, AUDI AG: Martin Winterkorn
Member of the Board of Management, Finance and Controlling: Hans Dieter Pötsch, age 53
Member of the Board of Management, Labor and Human Resources: Horst Günter Neumann
Member of the Board of Management, Procurement: Francisco Javier Garcia Sanz
Director, Design: Murat Günak
Chairman, Automobili Lamborghini: Werner Mischke
Member of the Board of Management, Volkswagen Brand Group (VW, Skoda, Bentley, and Bugatti): Wolfgang Bernhard
Chairman, Volkswagen Financial Services: Burkhard Breiing
Chairman of the Executive Committee, SEAT: Andreas Schleef
CEO, gedas AG: Axel Knobe, age 54
CEO, VW China: Winfried Vahland
Auditors: PwC Deutsche Revision AG

LOCATIONS

HQ: Volkswagen AG
   Brieffach 1848-2, 38436 Wolfsburg, Germany
Phone: +49-53-61-90   **Fax:** +49-53-61-92-82-82
US HQ: 3800 Hamlin Rd., Auburn Hills, MI 48326
US Phone: 248-340-5000
Web: www.volkswagen.de

Volkswagen AG operates 43 production facilities worldwide.

2004 Sales

	$ mil.	% of total
Europe		
Germany	33,424	28
Other countries	54,226	45
North America	18,152	15
Asia/Oceania	8,000	6
South America	5,386	4
Africa	2,158	2
Total	**121,346**	**100**

PRODUCTS/OPERATIONS

2004 Sales

	$ mil.	% of total
Automotive	110,192	91
Financial services	11,154	9
Total	**121,346**	**100**

Selected Makes and Models

AUDI
   A3
   A4
   A6
   A8
   allroad quattro
   S4
   TT Coupe
   TT Roadster
Bentley
   Bentley Arnage R
   Bentley Arnage RL
   Bentley Arnage T
   Bentley Continental Flying Spur
   Bentley Continental GT
Bugatti
   EB 110
   Veyron 16.4
Lamborghini
   Gallardo
   Murcièlago

SEAT
   Alhambra
   Altea
   Cordoba
   Ibiza
   Leon
   Toledo
Skoda
   Fabia
   Octavia
   Superb
Volkswagen Passenger Vehicles
   Bora
   Golf
   Lupo
   Multivan
   New Beetle
   Passat
   Phaeton
   Polo
   Sharan
   Touareg
   Touran

COMPETITORS

BMW
DaimlerChrysler
Fiat
Ford
Fuji Heavy Industries
General Motors
Honda
Isuzu
Mazda
Nissan
Peugeot
Porsche
Renault
Saab Automobile
Suzuki Motor
Toyota

HISTORICAL FINANCIALS

Company Type: Public

Income Statement

FYE: December 31

	REVENUE ($ mil.)	NET INCOME ($ mil.)	NET PROFIT MARGIN	EMPLOYEES
12/04	121,346	923	0.8%	342,502
12/03	109,394	1,374	1.3%	336,843
12/02	91,130	2,708	3.0%	324,892
12/01	78,429	2,582	3.3%	322,070
12/00	80,553	1,941	2.4%	324,402
12/99	75,697	850	1.1%	306,275
12/98	80,089	1,338	1.7%	297,916
12/97	63,191	759	1.2%	279,892
12/96	64,459	424	0.7%	260,811
12/95	61,287	246	0.4%	259,342
Annual Growth	**7.9%**	**15.8%**	**—**	**3.1%**

2004 Year-End Financials

Debt ratio: 134.9%
Return on equity: 2.9%
Cash ($ mil.): 13,941
Current ratio: 1.14
Long-term debt ($ mil.): 43,918

Net Income History

German: VOW

Volvo

Despite the fact that the name "Volvo" conjures up more visions of soccer moms than of burly truck drivers, AB Volvo has parked its car business. The company is now a leading maker of trucks, buses, and construction equipment as well as marine (Volvo Penta); aircraft (Volvo Aero); and industrial engines. The company's most widely known business — auto making — has been sold to US-based carmaker Ford Motor Company. The sale enabled Volvo to focus on its remaining units, particularly trucks. Its other interests include full control of the famous Mack Trucks brand in North America and Renault Trucks in Europe.

Volvo is enjoying the benefits of a global cyclical upswing in worldwide demand for commercial vehicles — particularly heavy-duty trucks. The company's construction equipment and aerospace components businesses also enjoyed record sales in 2004, and Volvo's bus business returned to profitability.

Volvo managed its recent growth with minimal expenses for increased capacity even as some of the company's businesses saw production increases of up to 20%. These skills will come in handy in the near future. Volvo expects European demand for heavy-duty trucks to continue its upward trend in response to rapid growth in Eastern Europe, and the North American market is expected to grow as aging fleets are updated.

HISTORY

Swedish ball bearing maker SKF formed Volvo (Latin for "I roll") as a subsidiary in 1915. The new unit began building cars in 1926, trucks in 1928, and bus chassis in 1932 in Gothenburg. Sweden's winters and icy roads made the company keenly attentive to engineering and safety. Volvo bought an engine maker in 1931. In 1935 it became an independent company led by Assar Gabrielsson and Gustaf Larson.

Sweden's neutrality during WWII allowed Volvo to grow and move into component manufacturing and tractor production. Output in 1949 exceeded 100,000 units, 80% of which were sold in Sweden. The purchase of Bolinder-Munktell (farm machinery, diesel engines; Sweden; 1950) enhanced Volvo's position in the Swedish tractor market. Volvo introduced turbocharged diesel truck engines and windshield defrosters and washers in the 1950s. By 1956 car production had outstripped truck and bus output.

Aware that it was too small to compete in global markets, Volvo diversified (energy, industrial products, food, finance, and trading). Volvo increased its market share by purchasing several trucking and construction equipment companies that included White Motors' truck unit (US, 1981) and Leyland Bus (UK, 1986). In the 1980s Volvo acquired drug and biotechnology concern Pharmacia (now Pfizer) and Custos (investments, Sweden). The company consolidated its food and drug units with state-controlled holding company Procordia in 1990.

At that time, however, Volvo was facing stagnant sales. It embarked on the largest industrial undertaking in Swedish history, spending more than $2 billion to modernize plants and develop a series of high-performance family sedans, which it introduced in 1991. Still, high costs and persistent recession in Europe kept the company in the red during the early 1990s.

Adding to its troubles, there was public outcry against a planned merger with French automaker Renault. The plan was abandoned in 1993, and the company sold its drug and consumer product interests (which had landed back in Volvo's lap when the government divested Procordia in 1993). These sales brought Volvo back into the black.

In 1997 Volvo sold its 11% stake in Renault left over from the abandoned merger. The next year the company strengthened its line of excavators and its Far Eastern presence by buying Samsung Heavy Industries' construction equipment unit. Volvo also bought Mexico's bus maker Mexicana de Autobuses and GM's share in Volvo GM Heavy Truck (now Volvo Trucks North America).

Anticipating a lower demand for cars, Volvo closed an assembly plant in Canada in 1998, and in 1999 Volvo acquired a 13% stake (later upped to 25%) in rival truck maker Scania. To pay for its new focus on making heavy trucks, Volvo sold its auto brand and manufacturing operations in Sweden, Belgium, and the Netherlands to Ford Motor Company for $6.45 billion in 1999. Volvo then agreed to take a 20% stake in the truck and construction equipment operations of Japan's Mitsubishi Motors.

In 2000 Volvo boosted its stake in Scania to 46%, but its hope of acquiring a majority interest died when the EU rejected the $7.53 billion deal. Volvo then turned to France's Renault, and bought the company's Mack truck unit in exchange for a 15% stake in Volvo. Later in the year Volvo entered into talks with Volkswagen AG concerning the possible sale of Volvo's stake in Scania. The EU later thwarted the proposed deal, citing anti-competitive issues.

DaimlerChrysler bought out Volvo's 3.3% stake in Mitsubishi in 2001. Volvo's Renault Trucks subsidiary inked a technology transfer deal in 2002 with Chinese truckmaker Dong Feng Motors. The agreement clears the road for Dong Feng to equip its heavy- and medium-duty trucks with Renault engines. In 2003 Volvo became the first Western truck manufacturer to produce vehicles under its own name in Russia. The following year Volvo opened a new truck factory in China with its partner China National Heavy Truck Corporation; the factory can produce up to 1,200 trucks per year. Also in 2004 Volvo Construction Equipment (Volvo CE) sold its line of compact motor graders to Champion LLC, a company headed up by Gary Abernathy, a former manager at Volvo CE. Volvo acquired the remaining 50% of bus manufacturer Prévost Car from Henlys Group in late 2004.

EXECUTIVES

Chairman: Finn Johnsson, age 59
President and Director; CEO, Volvo Group:
 Leif Johansson, age 53
Deputy CEO and EVP: Jorma Halonen, age 57
Deputy CEO and EVP: Lennart Jeansson, age 64
SVP and CFO: Par Ostberg
SVP: Michel Gigou, age 59
SVP: Karl-Erling Trogen, age 59
SVP: Per Löjdquist, age 55
SVP, Secretary, and Director; General Counsel, Volvo Group: Eva Persson, age 52
SVP, Strategic Planning and Business Development: Ricard Fritz
SVP, Volvo Parts, Volvo Logistics; Chairman, Volvo Financial Services; Chairman, Volvo IT:
 Stefan Johnsson, age 46
President and CEO, Mack Trucks: Paul L. Vikner
President, Volvo Trucks North America: Peter Karlsten

VP, Investor Relations: Christer Johansson
Investor Relations, North America: John Hartwell
Head, Media Relations: Mårten Wikforss
Corporate Communications, North America:
 Marjorie A. Meyers
Auditors: PricewaterhouseCoopers AB

LOCATIONS

HQ: AB Volvo
 S-405 08 Gothenburg, Sweden
Phone: +46-31-660000　　**Fax:** +46-31-54-57-72
US HQ: 570 Lexington Ave., 20th Fl.,
 New York, NY 10022
US Phone: 212-418-7400　　**US Fax:** 212-418-7435
Web: www.volvo.com

2004 Sales

	$ mil.	% of total
Europe		
Western Europe	16,332	51
Eastern Europe	1,673	5
North America	8,179	26
Asia	3,143	10
South America	1,110	4
Other regions	1,376	4
Total	**31,813**	**100**

PRODUCTS/OPERATIONS

2004 Sales

	$ mil.	% of total
Trucks	20,696	65
Construction equipment	4,337	14
Buses	1,924	6
Financial services	1,451	5
Volvo Penta	1,370	4
Volvo Aero	1,047	3
Other	988	3
Total	**31,813**	**100**

Selected Products and Brand Names

Trucks
 Mack
 Renault
 Volvo
Construction Equipment
 Articulated haulers
 Backhoe loaders
 Excavators
 Wheel loaders
Buses
 City buses
 Coaches
 Intercity buses
Financial Services
 Customer financing
 Insurance
Volvo Penta
 Marine engines (luxury and work boats)
 Industrial engines (forklifts and construction equipment)
Volvo Aero
 Aircraft engines
 Industrial gas turbines
 Space propulsion

COMPETITORS

Cummins	Mitsubishi Motors
Cummins Westport	Navistar
DaimlerChrysler	Nissan
Deere	Nissan Diesel
Fiat	Oshkosh Truck
Freightliner	PACCAR
Fuji Heavy Industries	Penske
General Motors	Rolls-Royce
Hino Motors	Scania
Honda	Suzuki Motor
International Truck and	Terex
Engine Corporation	Toyota
Isuzu	Yamaha Motor
MAN	

HISTORICAL FINANCIALS

Company Type: Public

Income Statement

FYE: December 31

	REVENUE ($ mil.)	NET INCOME ($ mil.)	NET PROFIT MARGIN	EMPLOYEES
12/04	31,813	1,414	4.4%	78,196
12/03	25,477	41	0.2%	75,740
12/02	21,469	161	0.7%	71,160
12/01	18,057	(140)	—	70,921
12/00	13,800	500	3.6%	54,270
12/99	14,665	3,780	25.8%	53,600
12/98	26,276	1,066	4.1%	79,820
12/97	23,229	1,310	5.6%	79,050
12/96	22,676	1,813	8.0%	70,330
12/95	25,641	1,385	5.4%	79,050
Annual Growth	**2.4%**	**0.2%**	**—**	**(0.1%)**

2004 Year-End Financials

Debt ratio: 58.2%
Return on equity: 13.8%
Cash ($ mil.): 1,329
Current ratio: 1.52
Long-term debt ($ mil.): 6,110
No. of shares (mil.): 442
Dividends
 Yield: 6.4%
 Payout: 75.4%
Market value ($ mil.): 17,480

Stock History

NASDAQ: VOLVY

12/95 12/96 12/97 12/98 12/99 12/00 12/01 12/02 12/03 12/04

	STOCK PRICE ($) FY Close	P/E High/Low		Earnings	Dividends	Book Value
12/04	39.59	12	9	3.38	2.55	23.77
12/03	30.62	308	160	0.10	0.67	24.00
12/02	16.55	55	35	0.38	0.78	21.52
12/01	16.40	—	—	(0.33)	0.78	19.38
12/00	16.50	23	12	1.19	0.80	23.59
12/99	25.25	4	3	8.80	0.61	25.95
12/98	23.31	15	8	2.42	0.00	19.02
12/97	27.00	11	7	2.90	0.00	17.31
12/96	21.75	6	5	3.91	0.60	18.14
12/95	20.59	8	5	3.02	0.46	16.51
Annual Growth	**7.5%**	**—**	**—**	**1.3%**	**21.0%**	**4.1%**

Wal-Mart de México

Just call it Wal-Mex. Formerly known as Cifra, Wal-Mart de México is the numero uno retailer in Mexico, with 700-plus stores or restaurants. These include Bodega discount stores and Superama supermarkets and hypermarkets; Suburbia apparel stores; and Vips, El Porton, and Ragazzi restaurants. It also runs about 150 Wal-Mart Supercenters and SAM'S CLUB warehouses, which generate about 55% of the company's sales. Its stores are located in 73 cities throughout Mexico, although more than half are in and around Mexico City. Wal-Mart Stores first grabbed a stake in the company when it combined its Mexican stores (a joint venture with

Cifra) with Cifra's stores. Wal-Mart Stores owns about 62% of Wal-Mart de México.

Wal-Mart has shaken up Mexico's grocery and department store sectors since entering the country in the 1990s. Now the country's largest supermarket operator and private employer, Wal-Mart de México operates more stores than any of its parent company's other international divisions and contributes more than 25% of its international sales.

But success has sparked a backlash; Mexican antitrust regulators launched an investigation into Wal-Mex's purchasing practices in May 2002, and the retailer has quit the country's supermarket and department store trade group because of the group's opposition to comparative advertising. Three of Mexico's largest supermarket chains — Grupo Gigante, Soriana, and Comerci — have formed purchasing and other alliances to better compete with Wal-Mex, which accounts for about 40% of Mexico's retail market. Nevertheless, the country's top mass merchandiser spent about $635 million to open about 90 stores and restaurants in 2005, including about 40 Bodega Aurrera stores in rural areas. Wal-Mex is opening stores in Monterrey, the country's most affluent city, and throughout northern Mexico, where its Texas rival H. E. Butt Grocery is well established.

Wal-Mex has agreed to acquire the Mexican assets of French retailer Carrefour. Carrefour, which operates 28 hypermarkets in Mexico, is restructuring its operations and leaving the Mexican market.

In its bid to become the ultimate supplier to small business, SAM'S CLUBs in Mexico have begun selling fully-stocked convenience store stands to independent entrepreneurs. The "Mi Tiendita" (Spanish for "My Little Store") package includes shelving, some 200 products, a cash register, and even training for would-be convenience store operators. Wal-Mex is also testing a new smaller format, called MercaMas, designed for poorer neighborhoods on the fringes of big cities.

HISTORY

Spanish-born Jerónimo Arango Arias studied art and literature at several American universities without graduating. In his 20s he wandered around Spain, Mexico, and the US. He struck upon an idea after seeing a crowd waiting in line at the E. J. Korvette discount department store in New York City. Jerónimo called his two brothers, Plácido and Manuel, and convinced them to join him in a new business venture.

Borrowing about $250,000 from their father, a Spanish immigrant to Mexico successful in textiles, the three brothers opened their first Aurrerá Bolivar discount store in downtown Mexico City in 1958. Offering goods and clothing well below manufacturers' list prices, the store was an immediate hit with consumers but encountered hostility from competing Mexico City retailers. When local retailers threatened to boycott the Arangos' suppliers, the company turned to suppliers in Guadalajara and Monterrey.

In 1965 the Arango brothers formed a joint venture with Jewel Cos. of Chicago to open new Aurrerá stores. Jewel bought a 49% interest in the business a year later. Plácido and Manuel left the business with their portion of the money, but Jerónimo stayed as head of the company, taking it public in 1976.

By 1981 almost a third of Jewel's earnings came from its operations in Mexico. But the next year the peso crashed, obliterating its earnings there. American Stores took over Jewel in 1984,

and Jerónimo bought back Jewel's stake in the company (which was renamed Cifra that year).

With the Mexican economy staggering from the peso devaluation, weak oil markets, and a huge debt crisis, Jerónimo was taking a major risk. Although no new stores were opened, none were closed. Employees were expected to work longer, and those who left were not replaced. With Mexico's middle class hit hard, Jerónimo emphasized the Bodega Aurrerá no-frill warehouses, which discounted all kinds of nonperishable merchandise, from canned chili to VCRs.

Cifra and Wal-Mart Stores formed a joint venture in 1991 to open Club Aurrerá membership clubs similar to Sam's Club outlets. The two companies expanded the venture the next year to include the development of Sam's Club and Wal-Mart Supercenters in Mexico.

Devaluation struck again late in 1994, and the resulting contraction of credit and rise in prices hit Mexican consumers hard, and Cifra's 1995 sales declined 15%. But again it kept on as many employees as possible, transferring them to new stores that had been in development. Despite the hard times, Cifra opened 27 new stores (including 15 restaurants).

Wal-Mart consolidated its joint venture into Cifra in 1997 in exchange for about 34% of that company; Wal-Mart later raised its stake to 51%. The cost-conscious companies combined the joint venture stores and Cifra's separate stores under one umbrella. Cifra opened 11 stores and eight restaurants that year.

In early 2000 Cifra was renamed Wal-Mart de México. Shortly thereafter, Wal-Mart upped its stake in Wal-Mart de México to about 61%.

In 2002 Eduardo Castro-Wright was promoted from COO to CEO of Wal-Mart de México, succeeding Cesareo Fernandez who retained the chairman's title.

In 2003 Mexico's Federal Competition Commission closed an investigation of Wal-Mex's purchasing practices citing a lack of evidence that the retailer violated competition laws. In 2004 Mexico's largest retailer grew bigger, adding 17 restaurants, 23 Aurrerá stores, eight SAM'S CLUBS, six supercenters, and four Superama stores.

In January 2005 Fernandez stepped down as chairman and was succeeded by Ernesto Vega. CEO Eduardo Castro-Wright left Wal-Mex in February to become executive vice president and COO of the Wal-Mart Stores Division in the US. He was succeeded by Eduardo Solorzano, formerly COO of Wal-Mex.

EXECUTIVES

Chairman: Ernesto Vega
President and CEO: Eduardo Solorzano, age 47
EVP and CFO, Director: Rafael Matute
EVP, Human Resources: José Angel Gallegos
EVP, Real Estate: Xavier del Río
VP, Self-service: Scot Rank
VP, Internal Audit: Eduardo Juárez
VP, Logistics and Distribution: Joaquin Gonzalez
VP, Corporate Affairs: Raul Argüelles
VP, Purchasing (Food): Francisco Casado
VP, Purchasing (General Merchandise and Clothing): David Dager
VP, Bodega Aurrera: Jose Luis Torres
VP, Sam's Club: Simona Visztova
VP, Suburbia: Alejandro Bustos
VP, Superama: Mario Sanchez
VP, Vips: Gian Carlo Nucci
VP, Wal-Mart Supercenter: Miguel Baltazar
Secretary: Jose Luis Rodriguez
Director, Finance: Federico Casillas
Manager, Investor Relations: Mariana Rodríguez
Auditors: Mancera, S.C.

LOCATIONS

HQ: Wal-Mart de México, S.A. de C.V.
Blvd. Manuel Avila Camacho 647, Delegación Miguel Hidalgo, 11220 México, D.F., Mexico
Phone: +52-55-5283-0100   **Fax:** +52-55-5387-9240
Web: www.walmartmexico.com.mx

Wal-Mart de México operates nearly 700 stores and restaurants in 73 cities throughout Mexico.

PRODUCTS/OPERATIONS

2004 Stores

	No.
Restaurants	284
Bodega	162
Wal-Mart Supercenters	89
SAM'S CLUB	61
Suburbia	50
Superama	48
Total	**694**

2004 Sales

	% of total
Bodega	30
SAM'S CLUB	29
Wal-Mart Supercenters	27
Superama	6
Suburbia	5
Restaurants	3
Total	**100**

Selected Stores

Bodega (large, limited assortment discount warehouses)
El Portón (restaurants)
Ragazzi (Italian-style restaurants)
Sam's Club (membership-only warehouse outlets)
Suburbia (apparel stores)
Superama (supermarkets)
Vips (restaurants)
Wal-Mart Supercenters (discount hypermarkets)

COMPETITORS

Chedraui
Comerci
Costco Wholesale
El Puerto de Liverpool
Gigante
Grupo Carso
H-E-B
Safeway
Sanborns
Soriana

HISTORICAL FINANCIALS

Company Type: Public

Income Statement   FYE: December 31

	REVENUE ($ mil.)	NET INCOME ($ mil.)	NET PROFIT MARGIN	EMPLOYEES
12/04	12,549	700	5.6%	109,057
12/03	10,729	486	4.5%	99,881
12/02	10,097	472	4.7%	92,708
12/01	9,642	457	4.7%	84,607
12/00	7,661	370	4.8%	74,790
12/99	6,406	374	5.8%	70,700
12/98	6,009	281	4.7%	61,145
12/97	4,086	432	10.6%	57,649
12/96	2,947	257	8.7%	49,510
12/95	2,623	202	7.7%	47,129
Annual Growth	19.0%	14.8%	—	9.8%

2004 Year-End Financials

Debt ratio: 0.0%   Current ratio: 1.32
Return on equity: 17.7%   Long-term debt ($ mil.): 0
Cash ($ mil.): 1,058

Net Income History OTC: WMMVY

OTC: WMMVY

Waterford Wedgwood

Waterford Wedgwood is (gently) toasting its position as the world's premier maker of luxury crystal and fine china. The company's Waterford Crystal Group produces handcrafted crystal stemware, lamps, and giftware under the Waterford and Stuart brands. The Wedgwood Group makes fine bone china giftware and tableware under the Wedgwood brand. The company owns German ceramics makers Rosenthal. In 2004 it sold its US premium cookware maker, All-Clad, to SEB to reduce debt. Chairman Tony O'Reilly and his brother-in-law, deputy chairman Peter Goulandris, increased their control of the company in 2005 to about 51% of the company.

Not every company has a great-great-great-great-grandson of its founder sitting on the board of directors. And although Waterford Wedgwood has just that in Alan Wedgwood, it's former Heinz ketchup king Tony O'Reilly who has given the firm its luster.

O'Reilly helped turn the company around after years of losses in the late 1980s and early 1990s. He outsourced product lines to cheaper manufacturers and licensed the company's popular brands to makers of products such as linens and writing instruments. Most of Waterford Wedgwood's sales are through department stores and specialty retailers. In October 2004 Waterford Wedgwood unveiled a $72 million plan to acquire rival UK ceramics maker Royal Doulton, of which the firm already owned more than 20%. Waterford also bought the remaining 10% stake it did not already own in Rosenthal.

In response to the worldwide economic downturn and diminished interest in luxury goods, Waterford Wedgwood laid off nearly 15% of its workforce in 2002, and in 2003 shut down two of its British factories and moved production to China (eliminating more than 1,000 jobs).

In August 2004 New York State Attorney General Eliot Spitzer alleged that The May Department Stores and Federated Department Stores conspired to pressure Waterford Wedgwood into backing out as the planned anchors of Bed Bath & Beyond's new tableware division. Though the four companies admitted no wrongdoing in the antitrust case, they paid a total of $2.9 million in civil penalties.

In late 2004 the company announced it asked 1,400 employees at its two Irish crystal-cutting plants to take pay cuts and work fewer hours to offset sluggish sales.

In 2005 the company was buoyed by the announcement of Waterford Wedgwood's restructuring plan, which included closure of its Waterford Crystal plant in Dungarvan, Ireland and its Rosenthal division in Germany. In total approximately 1,800 jobs were lost in the process.

Later in 2005 Waterford Wedgwood was delisted from the Nasdaq stock exchange because it was trading at such a low price and level for an extended period of time.

HISTORY

Waterford Wedgwood traces its roots back to two companies more than 200 years old. Josiah Wedgwood, an 18th-century English artisan, got his start as a potter bridging the gap between wooden bowls for the common people and fine porcelain for the rich. He developed a method of making ordinary clay look like porcelain and later developed fine ceramic ware incorporating neoclassical figures applied in a white cameo relief on a colored background — which became the signature product of Josiah Wedgwood and Sons.

Wedgwood operated as a family business for the next 176 years and may have indirectly contributed to Darwin's theory of evolution. Charles Darwin married into the Wedgwood clan and thus gained the financial security to pursue his scientific research on a full-time basis. Wedgwood did not have a non-family director on its board until 1945.

Around the same time that Wedgwood was gaining recognition in England, Quakers George and William Penrose founded a crystal glassmaking business in 1783 in the Irish port city of Waterford. The two companies shared a reputation for quality and for exquisite craftsmanship. However, they both experienced the vagaries of fashion and financial difficulties.

Waterford went bankrupt in 1851 and remained inactive until its revival, aided by WWII refugees. With this new base of skilled artisans from Central Europe, it started operations again in 1947. The company quickly re-established the Waterford reputation. Profits rose steadily in the 1970s and early 1980s, with the US emerging as Waterford's primary market. In addition to consumer products, Waterford glassware has been used for the Boston Marathon Trophy and to hold the late President Reagan's jelly beans.

In 1986 Waterford borrowed heavily to acquire Wedgwood for $360 million, a move designed to allow both companies to cut costs by sharing marketing operations and by streamlining production. Waterford Wedgwood was still struggling in 1990 when Tony O'Reilly (the Irish-born then chairman of US-based H.J. Heinz) and Morgan Stanley bought a 30% stake worth $125 million. That year the company launched its first new brand of crystal in 200 years, Marquis by Waterford. The line was a success, and by 1993 Waterford Wedgwood had returned to profitability.

The company acquired Stuart & Sons, the leading UK maker of premium crystal, in 1995 and introduced a best-seller, its Cornucopia fine bone china pattern. In 1997, in a departure from tradition, the company introduced a line of china under the Waterford name.

In 1998 Waterford Wedgwood increased its stake in German luxury ceramics maker Rosenthal to nearly 85%, making it the world's #1 producer of fine porcelain, and cut 1,500 jobs to reduce costs. In 1999 the company bought a 15% stake in ceramics maker Royal Doulton.

In 2002 Waterford Wedgwood acquired Ashling Corporation, a maker of luxury linens. The same year Waterford Wedgwood laid off nearly 15% of its workforce amid a worldwide economic downturn and diminished interest in luxury goods.

In 2003 Waterford Wedgwood acquired the Spring premium cookware business (Switzerland) and Cashs, a catalog and mail-order business (Ireland). Also that year the company cut more than 1,000 jobs by closing two British factories and moving production to China. In addition, Waterford Wedgwood upped its stake in Royal Doulton to nearly 22%. The next year Wedgwood sold its US premium cookware maker, All-Clad, to SEB for $250 million.

EXECUTIVES

Chairman: Sir Anthony O'Reilly, age 68
Deputy Chairman; Chairman, Waterford Wedgwood UK: Peter John Goulandris, age 56
CEO: Peter B. Cameron, age 57
Company Secretary and Acting CFO: Patrick J. Dowling, age 58
Creative Director: Georgina Godley
Director; CEO, Waterford; CEO, Waterford Crystal Limited: John Foley, age 52
Director; CEO, Rosenthal AG: Ottmar C. Küsel, age 53
CEO, Wedgwood: Moira Gavin, age 48
Director; CEO, Wedgwood: Anthony (Tony) O'Reilly Jr., age 37
Managing Director, Wedgwood Europe: Nick Robinson
Director of Public Relations: Abigail Hearne
Financial Spokesman: Michael Dennehy
Auditors: PricewaterhouseCoopers

LOCATIONS

HQ: Waterford Wedgwood plc
1-2 Upper Hatch St., Dublin 2, Ireland
Phone: +353-147-81855   **Fax:** +353-147-84863
US HQ: 1330 Campus Pkwy., Wall, NJ 07719
US Phone: 732-938-5800   **US Fax:** 732-378-2120
Web: www.waterfordwedgwood.com

2004 Sales

	% of total
North America	51
Europe	36
Asia/Pacific	10
Other regions	3
Total	**100**

PRODUCTS/OPERATIONS

2004 Sales

	% of total
Ceramics	43
Crystal	32
Premium cookware	13
Other	12
Total	**100**

Selected Operations

Rosenthal
  Hutschenreuther
  Rosenthal Studio-Line
  Thomas — The Trend Factory
Waterford Crystal
  Marquis by Waterford Crystal
  Stuart Crystal
  Waterford
Wedgwood
  Coalport
  Franciscan
  Johnson Brothers
  Masons Ironstone

HISTORICAL FINANCIALS

Company Type: Public

Income Statement

FYE: March 31

	REVENUE ($ mil.)	NET INCOME ($ mil.)	NET PROFIT MARGIN	EMPLOYEES
3/04	1,024	(61)	—	8,059
3/03*	1,037	2	0.2%	9,120
12/01	902	(40)	—	9,743
12/00	1,021	64	6.3%	9,671
12/99	888	58	6.5%	9,116
12/98	856	19	2.2%	—
12/97	596	9	1.5%	—
12/96	623	48	7.7%	—
12/95	551	39	7.0%	—
12/94	509	32	6.3%	—
Annual Growth	8.1%	—	—	(3.0%)

*Fiscal year change

2004 Year-End Financials

Debt ratio: 217.6%
Return on equity: —
Cash ($ mil.): 64
Current ratio: 2.79
Long-term debt ($ mil.): 520

No. of shares (mil.): 100
Dividends
  Yield: 8.4%
  Payout: —
Market value ($ mil.): 308

Stock History

London: WTFU

	STOCK PRICE ($) FY Close	P/E High/Low		PER SHARE ($) Earnings	Dividends	Book Value
3/04	3.09	—	—	(0.69)	0.26	2.40
3/03*	3.04	20	7	0.02	0.28	2.81
12/01	8.01	—	—	(0.54)	0.29	2.82
12/00	10.50	14	10	0.86	0.26	3.72
12/99	9.75	15	9	0.79	0.26	3.23
12/98	9.00	22	11	0.26	0.07	2.94
12/97	12.63	21	17	0.12	0.00	3.09
12/96	12.13	20	14	0.66	0.27	3.90
12/95	9.25	18	15	0.54	0.14	3.28
12/94	9.25	49	32	0.20	0.00	2.92
Annual Growth	(11.5%)	—	—	—	—	(2.2%)

*Fiscal year change

Whitbread PLC

Whitbread wins the award for being one of the UK's leading hospitality and leisure groups. The company, which sponsors a prestigious UK book award, has operations ranging from restaurants to hotels to fitness clubs. Its restaurant division includes a 50% stake in about 600 Pizza Hut (UK) locations, in partnership with YUM! Brands. It also operates about 600 pub restaurants (primarily operating under the Brewers Fayre and Beefeater names), about 350 Costa coffee outlets, and about 45 T.G.I Friday's locations. Whitbread's hospitality operations include about 460 Premier Travel Inn budget hotels The company also runs nearly 60 David Lloyd Leisure clubs in the UK and Ireland.

Whitbread has been assiduously whittling its operation to get down to its core businesses. Formerly one of the largest brewers and pub operators in the UK, the company sold its beer businesses in 2000 to focus on hospitality and restaurants.

In 2004 the company doubled its budget hotel business with the acquisition of more than 130 Premier Lodge hotels, which it combined with its Travel Inn operations to create Premier Travel Inns. The company in 2004 began an exit from the full-service hotel business via the sale of its Marriott locations. About a dozen Courtyard by Marriott units were sold to Kew Green Hotels Group; another 45 are being sold into a joint venture between Whitbread and Marriott International and will be operated by Marriott.

On the pub restaurant front, Whitbread has been concentrating on its Brewers Fayre and Beefeater nameplates, converting other locations to these brands. Its Costa coffee business, the leading coffee chain in the UK, is branching out through co-located shops in retail locations (including WH Smith, Virgin Megastores, and Madame Tussaud's); the company also announced a franchising agreement to open about 300 Costa Coffee units in India over a span of several years.

Despite a challenging economy, the company has been pressing ahead with expansion in its restaurant business, opening some 160 locations during fiscal 2005. It is also expanding its David Lloyd Leisure operations internationally, with locations planned for Belgium, the Netherlands, and Spain.

Disposals of non-core holdings have included the company's nearly 25% stake in Britvic, which was sold in a public offering in 2005, and nearly 60 Maredo steakhouses in Germany, which are being sold to a group of investors that includes a private equity unit of financial services powerhouse Fortis.

Leading all of these developments is chief executive (and former hotels head) Alan Parker, who succeeded longtime chief executive David Thomas.

HISTORY

Samuel Whitbread became a brewer's apprentice in 1734 and learned his lessons well; in 1742 he began brewing beer at his own brewery. By 1750 he had built a new brewery and began producing porter in bulk. Whitbread had a head for business as well as beer, acquiring other breweries and investing in new brewing techniques to increase the quality of his beers. The company prospered despite an unlucky venture into poli-

tics by Samuel II; he opposed the war with Napoleon and committed suicide after Waterloo.

In the 1880s beer drinking declined, and Whitbread began buying up sinking pubs. But by WWI, the company started to concentrate on bottled beer sales in order to reduce its dependence on the tied pubs.

In 1944 W. H. Whitbread became chairman (the first Whitbread since founder Samuel) and took advantage of the aftermath of WWII to snap up less-robust rivals. The company first absorbed smaller breweries into its production and distribution operations but later made a living from taking over breweries and keeping their tied houses. The company went public in 1948 and had 10,000 pubs by 1970.

In the 1970s beer consumption fell yet again, and Whitbread started streamlining operations. It closed its original brewery in 1976. The company also began its shift from beer to other businesses, including acquiring a Pizza Hut franchise. It sold its wines and spirits business at the end of the 1980s.

The company continued to remake itself the next decade under the leadership of CEO Peter Jarvis. As more Britons began to eat out instead of going to the local pub for entertainment, Whitbread shifted with them, buying and developing restaurant concepts including its Beefeater Restaurant and Pub and family-friendly Brewers Fayre (complete with Charlie Chalk Fun Factories for kids). In 1995 Whitbread went shopping, buying David Lloyd Leisure and 16 Marriott hotels (even as it divested 400 underperforming pubs). The company later sold its Australian and Canadian Keg steak houses in 1995 and 1996, respectively, and expanded its Pizza Hut chain.

Whitbread bought Busy Bees day care centers and put them under its David Lloyd Leisure unit in 1997. That year Jarvis stepped down and was succeeded by David Thomas. A renewed focus on its core business that year also prompted the company to dispose of all pubs that served beer not brewed by Whitbread.

In 1998 Whitbread and Allied Domecq agreed to merge their retail beer and wine stores into a new company called First Quench. It also sold one of its five breweries, put another brewery on the market, and in the wake of the declining popularity of old-fashioned pubs, sold 253 of its pubs and 40 of its Beefeaters Restaurant & Pubs.

Whitbread's attempt to buy more than 3,500 UK pubs and restaurants from Allied Domecq for $3.8 billion failed in 1999. (Rival Punch Taverns had the winning bid.) Later that year the company sold off 75 pubs to Alehouse Company. In early 2000 the company bought Swallow Group, a hotel and pub operator, with plans to convert the Swallow locations to the Marriott brand. That same year Whitbread sold its brewery business to Interbrew (now InBev).

Whitbread unloaded all 3,000 of its pubs in 2001, selling them to Deutsche Bank's Morgan Grenfell equity fund for $2.3 billion. (The equity fund later formed The Laurel Pub Company.)

Whitbread acquired the Dutch chain Cannons Health & Fitness in 2003, adding to its health club holdings.

In 2004 the company acquired Premier Lodge, the UK's #3 budget-hotel chain, from Texas Pacific Group's Spirit Group Holdings Ltd — making Travel Inn the top budget-hotel chain in Britain. Whitbread merged the chain with its Travel Inn hotels to form Premier Travel Inn.

EXECUTIVES

Chairman: Anthony J. (Tony) Habgood, age 58
Group Finance Director:
Christopher C. B. (Chris) Rogers, age 45
Chief Executive and Director: Alan Parker, age 58,
$1,023,066 pay
Group Human Resources Director: Angie Risley, age 46,
$435,715 pay
Managing Director, Premier Travel Inn:
Patrick Dempsey, age 45
Chief Executive, Pizza Hut (UK): John Derkach, age 45
Managing Director, TGI Friday's: Tim Hammond, age 44
Managing Director, Costa: Mark Phillips
Managing Director, David Lloyd Leisure: Mike Tye,
age 50
Managing Director, Pub Restaurants: Phil Urban
Company Secretary and Legal Affairs Director:
Simon Barratt
Communications Director: Anna Glover
Group Development Director: Desmond Taljaard, age 43
Group IT Director: Ben Wishart
**Commercial Director, Marriott Hotels, Whitbread Hotel
Company:** Tony Dangerfield
Finance Director, David Lloyd Leisure: Eric Dodd,
age 34
**Information Technology Director, Whitbread
Restaurants:** Ann Fraser
Director of Communications, Hotels: Abigail Langan
Public Relations Manager: Mark Webb
Auditors: Ernst & Young LLP

LOCATIONS

HQ: Whitbread PLC
Whitbread House, Park Street West,
Luton LU1 3BG, United Kingdom
Phone: +44-15 8242-4200   **Fax:** +44-15-8284-4451
Web: www.whitbread.co.uk

2005 Sales

	% of total
UK	96
Other countries	4
Total	**100**

PRODUCTS/OPERATIONS

2005 Sales

	% of total
Restaurants	
Pub restaurants	28
High street restaurants	23
Hotels	
Marriott brands	19
Premier Travel Inn	15
Health & fitness clubs	10
Other	5
Total	**100**

COMPETITORS

Bannatyne Fitness
Best Western
Compass Group
De Vere Group
Domino's Pizza UK
Enterprise Inns
Esporta
First Leisure
Four Seasons Hotels
Greene King
Hilton International
Hyatt
InterContinental Hotels
J D Wetherspoon
Mitchells & Butlers
Papa John's
PizzaExpress
Punch Taverns
Restaurant Group
Spirit Group
Starwood Hotels & Resorts
Thistle Hotels
Wolverhampton & Dudley

HISTORICAL FINANCIALS

Company Type: Public

Income Statement

FYE: February 28

	REVENUE ($ mil.)	NET INCOME ($ mil.)	NET PROFIT MARGIN	EMPLOYEES
2/05	3,516	339	9.6%	53,483
2/04	3,341	307	9.2%	52,437
2/03	2,835	241	8.5%	55,315
2/02	2,859	(75)	—	61,470
2/01	3,743	285	7.6%	79,209
2/00	4,658	284	6.1%	73,058
2/99	4,745	398	8.4%	76,100
2/98	5,266	492	9.3%	81,375
2/97	4,925	402	8.2%	80,074
2/96	4,211	341	8.1%	70,594
Annual Growth	**(2.0%)**	**(0.1%)**	**—**	**(3.0%)**

2005 Year-End Financials

Debt ratio: 55.3%   Current ratio: 0.57
Return on equity: 8.3%   Long-term debt ($ mil.): 2,339
Cash ($ mil.): 103

Net Income History

London: WTB

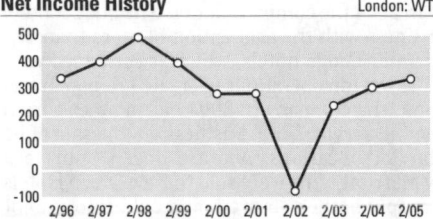

Wipro Limited

You might say this company has really cleaned up in the technology services business. Wipro is one of India's leading providers of system integration and outsourcing services, but it also manufactures a variety of consumer products, including hand soap. Operating in about 35 countries, its Wipro Technologies division offers software development and business process outsourcing (BPO) services, as well as management consulting and product engineering. Its Wipro Infotech unit focuses on providing IT services for customers in India and the Asia/Pacific region. Wipro's consumer products unit makes detergent, soap, and talcum powder along with light bulbs. Chairman Azim Premji owns more than 80% of Wipro.

Once highly diversified, Wipro has focused on expanding its technology services businesses, which now account for about 90% of its revenue. Wipro Technologies has benefited from cost-conscious companies, particularly in the US (which accounts for more than half its business), looking to outsourcing as a way to drive profits. Wipro has continued to maintain its position as a leading consumer products maker in India, however; it ranks #1 or #2 in several product categories, including shampoos, baby care products, and light bulbs.

In addition to technology and consumer products, Wipro manufactures hydraulic parts and equipment primarily for the automotive market through Wipro Fluid Power. It also provides support services for users of General Electric medical devices though Wipro GE Medical Systems, a joint venture 51% owned by GE.

Premji, whose stake in Wipro has made him the richest person in India and one of the wealthiest in the world, took his father's post as head of the company in 1968. A self-taught businessman who shuns publicity, he is known as a man who values integrity over extreme wealth: Wipro has suffered power outages and import confiscations in the past for its refusal to offer or accept bribes.

HISTORY

In 1947 M. H. Hasham Premji turned down an offer from the prime minister of Pakistan to migrate from India and become finance minister. Premji cited his loyalty to India as well as to his business, Western Indian Vegetable Products (Wipro), founded in 1946 to sell cooking oil. Wipro went public in 1947.

Like any proper Indian industrialist, Premji eventually diversified into other markets, including bath soap and hydraulic fluid. Instead of employing the customary tactic of courting Indian bureaucrats to help grow his business, Premji focused on customers. He kept costs low by branding generic products and selling directly to retailers instead of middlemen. When Premji died of a heart attack in 1966, he left behind a $2 million business.

Premji's 21-year-old son, Azim, who had only three months left in his engineering degree program at Stanford, returned home and took the reins in 1968. Although he had little idea how to run a business, he took a cue from his father's success and continued diversifying into new markets. In 1977 India asked computing giant IBM to leave the country after a dispute over investment and intellectual property, opening the door for Wipro to tackle computer manufacturing and distribution. Instead of plucking away ex-IBM employees, Premji hired managers from a truck maker and a refrigeration company, who together helped turn Wipro computers into a leading national brand.

In 1980 Wipro began offering information technology services in India. Three years later the company moved into software, offering branded products in the same market as US upstart Microsoft. Wipro entered the toilet soap and dot matrix printer markets in 1985.

It was in the late 1980s that Wipro finally discovered its growth business, software services. (It abandoned software sales in 1990.) The company's reputation as a software integrator was secured in 1989 when Wipro and General Electric, whose business model Premji admired and followed very carefully, formed Wipro GE Medical Systems as a joint venture. Possessing GE as a partner and long-term client over the next decade attracted scores of research and development contracts from blue-chip clients in the US (Cisco Systems), Japan (Hitachi), and Europe (Alcatel).

During the early 1990s Wipro began transitioning away from costly onsite software projects in the US to more profitable offshore development in India. It also entered the lighting business in 1992. With Taiwan-based Acer, Wipro formed a joint venture in 1995 to manufacture and sell computers and other peripherals in India.

The company reorganized in 1999 into four companies, each run separately: software, hardware and systems, consumer care and lighting, and hydraulic fluid. Wipro Net was also formed to offer e-commerce implementation services. In 2000 Wipro listed on the New York Stock Exchange, gaining an international investment audience for what few shares Premji didn't already own. The move caused his personal wealth to soar.

In 2002 Wipro launched genetic data software division Healthcare and Life Sciences. Also that year the company bought Indian call center operator Spectramind for $90 million and American Management Systems' global energy practice for $24 million to form Wipro BPO Solutions. The following year, though, it reorganized its operations, folding Wipro BPO into its global IT services division, Wipro Technologies, along with the technology-oriented parts of its Health-Sciences unit.

EXECUTIVES

Chairman, CEO, Managing Director: Azim H. Premji, age 59, $465,666 pay
COO: A. Lakshman Rao, age 56, $141,588 pay (prior to promotion)
EVP Finance and CFO: Suresh C. Senapaty, age 48, $158,745 pay
VP and CIO: Tamal Dasgupta, age 54, $102,496 pay
VP and Corporate Controller: Harish Shah, age 47
VP and General Counsel: Madhu Khatri, age 41
VP Corporate Communication, Brand, and Community Initiatives: Vijay Gupta, age 47
VP Corporate Taxation: P. V. Srinivasan, age 45
VP Human Resources: Pratik Kumar, age 39, $103,475 pay
VP Human Resources Development: Ranjan Acharya, age 47, $101,500 pay
VP Mission Quality: Jagdish Ramaswamy, age 41
President, Wipro Consumer Care & Lighting: Vineet Agrawal, age 43, $128,193 pay
President, Wipro Fluid Power: M. S. Rao
President, Wipro Infotech; President of Technology Infrastructure Services & Interops, Wipro Technologies: Suresh Vaswani, age 45, $147,704 pay
President of Embedded & Product Engineering Solutions, Wipro Technologies: Ramesh Emani, age 48, $147,152 pay
President of Enterprise Solutions, Wipro Technologies: Sudip Banerjee, age 45, $130,656 pay
President of Finance & Insurance, Wipro Technologies: Girish S. Paranjpe, age 47, $133,036 pay
CEO, Americas and Europe: P. R. (Sekar) Chandrasekhar
Investor Relation Officer: Sridhar Ramasubbu
Auditors: KPMG

LOCATIONS

HQ: Wipro Limited
Doddakannelli, Sarjapur Rd., Bangalore, Karnataka 560035, India
Phone: +91-80-2844-0011   **Fax:** +91-80-2844-0056
US HQ: 1300 Crittenden Ln., 2nd Fl., Mountain View, CA 94043
US Phone: 650-316-3555   **US Fax:** 650-316-3468
Web: www.wiprocorporate.com

Wipro has operations throughout India. Its technology services divisions have operations in more than 35 countries.

2005 Sales

	$ mil.	% of total
US	958	51
India	443	24
Europe	380	20
Other regions	82	5
Total	**1,863**	**100**

PRODUCTS/OPERATIONS

2005 Sales

	$ mil.	% of total
Global technology services	1,390	75
India & Asia/Pacific technology services	307	16
Consumer care & lighting	104	6
Other	62	3
Total	**1,863**	**100**

Selected Operations

Wipro Consumer Care & Lighting (consumer products manufacturing)
Wipro Fluid Power (hydraulic equipment manufacturing)
Wipro GE Medical Systems (49%, medical equipment support services)
Wipro Infotech (India and Asia/Pacific technology services)
Wipro Technologies (global technology services)

Selected Technology Services

Business process outsourcing (BPO)
Enterprise information technology
    Application development and re-engineering
    Business intelligence and data warehousing
    Consulting
    Enterprise application integration
Research and development
    Embedded systems
    Hardware design and development
    Internet access devices
    Software design and development
    Telecommunications and networking
Technology infrastructure support

Selected Products

Consumer care
    Chandrika (soap)
    Glucovita (vitamins)
    Milk & Roses (soap)
    Safewash (laundry detergent)
    Santoor (soap)
    Santoor Chandan (soap)
    Santoor Talc
    Wipro Active Talc
    Wipro BabySoft
    Wipro Shikakai (shampoo)
Lighting
    Wipro Smartlite
    Wipro Longlite
Office furniture
    Vibrant
    Wipro Sterling

COMPETITORS

Accenture	IBM Global Services
BearingPoint	Infosys
Capgemini	Johnson & Johnson
Cognizant Tech Solutions	Keane
Computer Sciences Corp.	Komatsu
Convergys	Perot Systems
Deloitte Consulting	Philips Electronics
EDS	Procter & Gamble
GE	Satyam
HCL Technologies	Sauer-Danfoss
Hindustan Lever	Siemens Medical
Hitachi	Tata Consultancy
HP Technology	TeleTech
Solutions Group	Unilever
Hyundai	

HISTORICAL FINANCIALS

Company Type: Public

Income Statement

FYE: March 31

	REVENUE ($ mil.)	NET INCOME ($ mil.)	NET PROFIT MARGIN	EMPLOYEES
3/05	1,863	363	19.5%	46,500
3/04	1,350	231	17.1%	32,000
3/03	904	171	18.9%	23,300
3/02	696	171	24.5%	13,800
3/01	662	138	20.8%	—
3/00	527	81	15.5%	—
3/99	437	26	6.0%	—
3/98	363	22	6.0%	—
Annual Growth	**26.3%**	**49.5%**	**—**	**49.9%**

2005 Year-End Financials

Debt ratio: 0.0%
Return on equity: 30.6%
Cash ($ mil.): 130
Current ratio: 3.49
Long-term debt ($ mil.): 0
No. of shares (mil.): 1,407
Dividends
Yield: 0.0%
Payout: —
Market value ($ mil.): 14,367

Stock History

NYSE: WIT

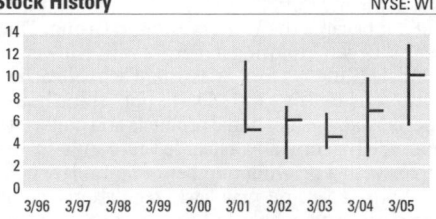

	STOCK PRICE ($) FY Close	P/E High/Low		PER SHARE ($) Earnings	Dividends	Book Value
3/05	10.21	49	22	0.26	0.00	0.92
3/04	7.02	58	18	0.17	0.00	0.77
3/03	4.68	56	31	0.12	0.00	0.54
3/02	6.20	61	24	0.12	0.00	0.40
3/01	5.34	114	52	0.10	0.00	0.29
Annual Growth	**17.6%**	**—**	**—**	**27.0%**	**—**	**33.4%**

Wolters Kluwer

This publisher is focused on the basics in life: death and taxes. One of Europe's leading professional publishers, Wolters Kluwer disseminates information on tax and legal affairs, business information, medical and scientific data, and education through print and electronic formats. Its operations include CCH Publishing, Ovid Technologies, Pharma Solutions, and Wolters-Noordhoff. The company has divested the businesses that made up its professional training division. Wolters Kluwer has operations in more than 25 countries, primarily in Europe and North America.

Under the direction of CEO Nancy McKinstry, the company is attempting to regain its financial health after battling a multi-year advertising slump. In 2003 McKinstry announced a three-year plan to turn the company around by focusing on key customer segments. She started the reorganization plan with an 8% cut in the company workforce announced in late 2003.

Wolters Kluwer has made a number of acquisitions to expand into new professional publishing market segments. Acquisitions in 2005 included Italian publishers De Agostini Professionale and Utet Professionale as well as Romanian legal publisher EON.

HISTORY

A pioneer of the Dutch publishing industry, J. B. Wolters founded his publishing house in 1836 to provide instructional material for Netherlands schools. The company later merged with educational publisher Noordhoff (founded in 1858). J. B. Wolters had no children, so the business went to his brother-in-law E. B. Horst in 1860. Dutch academic Anthony Schepman took over the management of Wolters-Noordhoff in 1917 and led the business' expansion. In 1920 it opened an office in the Dutch colony of Indonesia.

Wolters-Noordhoff and Information and Communication Union (ICU) merged in 1972. ICU had been formed by the 1970 merger of Samson (founded by Nicholaas Samson in 1883 to print government publications) and publisher A. W. Sijthoff. After the Wolters-Noordhoff-ICU merger, the company initially took the ICU name, but in 1983 it became the Wolters Samson Group. That year it began exploring a merger with Kluwer.

Abele Kluwer, a former assistant schoolteacher, became a publisher in 1889. His publishing house specialized in educational products and children's books. The company expanded its range in the 1920s with a growing number of up-to-date publications regarding new laws, regulations, court decisions, and scholarly texts. Kluwer hired its first non-family managing director, J. M. Gorter, in 1957 and went public in 1967.

Reed Elsevier (now called Reed Elsevier Group plc) made a bid to acquire Kluwer in 1987, buying a minority stake in the company. The Anglo-Dutch concern was rebuffed by the subsequent merger of Wolters Samson with Kluwer that year, however, and was left with about a third of the shares in the new Wolters Kluwer. Despite Reed Elsevier's repeated advances to work closely with Wolters Kluwer, the company pursued an independent growth strategy. In 1990 it acquired J.B. Lippincott, a US health care publisher. That year Reed Elsevier sold its stake in the firm.

In the early 1990s Wolters Kluwer began acquiring several medium-sized European companies and in 1995 bought Commerce Clearing House (with roots dating back to 1892). In 1997 it agreed to an $8.8 billion acquisition deal from Reed Elsevier; however, the deal fell apart the following year. (Both companies blamed regulatory hurdles for the pact's failure.) Meanwhile, Wolters Kluwer bought Waverly (medical and scientific books and magazines) and Plenum Publishing (scientific and technical trade books and journals). It also bought Ovid Technologies, a provider of electronic information retrieval services to the academic, medical, and scientific markets.

The following year Wolters Kluwer acquired US professional information publisher Bureau of Business Practice and search and retrieval service Accusearch. In late 1999 internal candidate Casper van Kempen replaced C.J. Brakel as chairman; he was out six months later, having clashed with the board over the company's Web strategy. Deputy chairman Robert Pieterse was tapped to replace him. Also in 2000 Wolters Kluwer announced that it would invest some $240 million in Internet-related operations. The company divested itself of its professional training business that year. In 2001 the company bought Cutter Environment, a unit of Cutter Information, which was folded into its Aspen Publishers unit.

Wolters Kluwer sold the health care book division of its Aspen Publishing unit in late 2002 to Jones and Bartlett Publishers. In addition, Wolters Kluwer sold its academic publishing unit (Kluwer Academic Publishers) for $582 million to two London-based equity firms. The company bought US financial services and information firm GainsKeeper Inc. in 2002.

Pieterse left the company in 2003 and was replaced by board member Nancy McKinstry. The company made two acquisitions in 2003: CEDAM, an Italian legal publisher, and TyMerix, a legal e-billing service in the US. In 2004 the company's corporate and financial services unit acquired software maker Summation Legal Technologies.

In 2005 the company announced it would group all of its financial businesses under the name Wolters Kluwer Financial Services.

EXECUTIVES

CEO and Chairman, Executive Board: Nancy McKinstry, age 46
CFO and Member, Executive Board: Boudewijn Beerkens
Member, Executive Board: Jean-Marc M. Detailleur
Member, Executive Board: Hugh J. Yarrington
Member, Supervisory Board: Leonard P. (Len) Forman, age 59
SVP Business Development: Dave Lampert
SVP Corporate Human Resources: Kathy Baker
SVP Strategy: Andres Sadler
VP Corporate Communications: Caroline Wouters
VP Investor Relations: Oya Yavuz
CEO, Corporate and Financial Services:
  Christopher Cartwright
CEO, Education: Harry Sterk
CEO, Legal, Tax & Business Europe: Rolv Eide, age 49
CEO, Wolters Kluwer Health: Jeffrey McCaulley
President and CEO, CCH: Kevin Robert
President, Ovid Technologies: Gary Foster
President, WK Legal: Robert (Bob) Becker, age 48
CTO, Education: Ilhan Aksoycan
Chief Human Resources Officer, North America:
  Mark Sherman
Sales and Marketing Director, Wolters Kluwer Legal, Tax, and Regulatory Europe: Haico Meijerink, age 41
Auditors: KPMG Accountants N.V.

LOCATIONS

HQ: Wolters Kluwer nv
  Apollolaan 153, P.O.Box 75248,
  NL-1070 AE Amsterdam, The Netherlands
Phone: +31-20-60-70-400   **Fax:** +31-20-60-70-490
US HQ: 161 N. Clark St., 48th Fl., Chicago, IL 60601
US Phone: 312-425-7000   **US Fax:** 312-425-7023
Web: www.wolterskluwer.com

2004 Sales

	% of total
Europe	52
North America	44
Asia/Pacific	3
Other countries	1
Total	**100**

PRODUCTS/OPERATIONS

2004 Sales

	% of total
Legal, Tax & Regulatory Europe	40
Health	19
Tax, Accounting & Legal	18
Corporate & Financial Services	13
Education	10
Total	**100**

2004 Sales

	% of total
Print	52
Electronic	
Internet/Online	18
CD-ROM/Offline	17
Services	13
Total	**100**

COMPETITORS

American Lawyer Media	John Wiley
Bertelsmann	McGraw-Hill
Blackwell Publishing	Pearson
Bureau of National Affairs	Reed Elsevier Group
Cadmus Communications	Thomson Corporation
Editis	VNU
IHS	

HISTORICAL FINANCIALS

Company Type: Public

Income Statement

FYE: December 31

	REVENUE ($ mil.)	NET INCOME ($ mil.)	NET PROFIT MARGIN	EMPLOYEES
12/04	4,448	184	4.1%	18,393
12/03	4,313	(87)	—	19,689
12/02	4,082	344	8.4%	20,833
12/01	3,399	124	3.6%	19,766
12/00	3,450	319	9.3%	19,009
12/99	3,103	361	11.6%	17,452
12/98	3,214	363	11.3%	17,431
12/97	2,571	286	11.1%	15,385
12/96	2,497	277	11.1%	14,948
12/95	1,830	281	15.4%	8,993
Annual Growth	**10.4%**	**(4.6%)**	**—**	**8.3%**

2004 Year-End Financials

Debt ratio: 270.1%
Return on equity: 17.2%
Cash ($ mil.): 937
Current ratio: 1.09
Long-term debt ($ mil.): 2,855

Net Income History

OTC: WTKWY

Woolworths

Chow down under with Australia's #1 food retailer, Woolworths (aka "Woolies"). The company operates 2,385 supermarkets, general merchandise, and electronics stores throughout Australia. (Its 700-plus supermarkets and nearly 575 liquor stores account for about 80% of sales.) In addition, Woolworths sells gasoline and leverages its distribution network to provide wholesale merchandise for third-party supermarkets. Australia's #2 retailer (after Coles Myer), Woolworths' general merchandise discount stores operate under the Big W name. The company also runs more than 200 Dick Smith Electronics stores and 18 Dick Smith Electronics PowerHouse superstores, and about 120 company-owned Tandy consumer electronics stores.

Woolworths (which has no relation to the five-and-dime chain once operated in the US) is trying not to choke on its own success, but it's hard to be humble. It has added gas pumps and banking to some supermarket locations, has opened Woolworths Metro (convenience stores), and acquired 72 Franklins supermarkets in 2001 (from a rival chain owned by Hong Kong-based Dairy Farm International Holdings). In a bid to fend off rival Coles Myer's entry into the food-and-fuel market, Woolworths has formed a joint venture with Caltex Australia to expand its network of discount fuel outlets to 450. Also, the retailer has overhauled its supply chain operations to become a low-cost operator after studying systems at US retail giant Wal-Mart and the UK's Tesco.

Woolworths has about 20% of Australia's take-home liquor market, compared to Coles Myers'

16% share. In a bid to increase liquor sales — which are growing faster than general merchandise or grocery sales — Woolworths and millionaire pubs owner Bruce Mathieson recently beat out Coles in a takeover battle for Australia's biggest pub operator, Australian Leisure & Hospitality (ALH), which has 263 liquor outlets, 154 of them in pubs, and a 5% share of the country's take-home liquor market.

Still hungry for acquisitions, CEO Roger Corbett has said Woolies would consider buying either of the Kmart or Target divisions from rival Coles Myer if they came up for sale. The company plans to add 25 supermarkets each year over the next two years. Woolworths' supermarkets operate under the flagship Woolworths and Safeway names.

HISTORY

Harold Percival Christmas first tried a mail-order dress business before opening the popular Frock Salon retail store. Christmas and his partners opened a branch store in the Imperial Arcade in Sydney in 1924, renaming it "Woolworths Stupendous Bargain Basement" and luring customers with advertisements calling it "a handy place where good things are cheap . . . you'll want to live at Woolworths." The company borrowed the name from Frank Woolworth's successful US chain, after determining that chain had no plans to open stores in Australia. Woolworths was listed on the Australian stock exchange in 1924.

Food sales came more than 30 years later. Woolworths opened its first freestanding, full-line supermarket in 1960, then diversified into specialty retail, buying the Rockmans women's clothing store chain the next year (sold, 2000). It expanded into discounting with the Big W chain in 1976 and further diversified when it bought 60% of the Dick Smith Electronics store chain in 1981 (buying the remainder in 1983).

The purchase of the Safeway grocery chain (the Australian operations of the US-based chain) put Woolworths on the top of the supermarket heap in 1985. But the company was hurting (it lost $13 million in 1985-86) because of a restructuring in the early 1980s that had weakened management by bulking up the front offices and dividing responsibilities. Woolworths got a shot in the arm from Paul Simons, who returned to the company in 1987 after running competitor Franklins. Simons cleaned house in the front offices, closed unprofitable stores, and began the successful "Fresh Food People" marketing strategy.

Industrial Equity Limited (IEL) bought Woolworths in 1989; IEL then became part of Adelaide Steamship group, which spun off Woolworths as a public company in 1993. The following year career Woolworths manager Reg Clairs took over as CEO, following the untimely death (on a golf course) in 1993 of Harry Watts, who was being groomed for the job. As a result, the company has an unwritten rule of avoiding CEOs older than 60. (Although Woolworths appears to be bending that rule for its current CEO, 61-year-old Roger Corbett.)

Clairs took the company in a variety of new directions. Woolworths began supplying fresh food to neighbor Asia in 1995. It added Plus Petrol outlets adjacent to Woolworths Supermarkets in 1996. It also started a superstore concept for its Dick Smith Electronics chain (Power House) that year. In 1997 the company launched its Woolworths Metro store chain, which targets commuters and other on-the-run shoppers in urban areas, and it aggressively jumped into wholesaling to independent grocers.

Clairs (who was turning 60 in 1999) stepped down in late 1998 and Roger Corbett took over as CEO. Woolworths also began offering banking services to its customers and bought Dan Murphy, a Victoria-based liquor chain, in 1998. It divested its Chisholm Manufacturing meat plants in 2000.

In 2001 Woolworths acquired two liquor store chains (Liberty Liquor, Booze Bros), more than 200 Tandy Electronics stores, and 72 Franklins supermarkets from Hong Kong-based Dairy Farm International Holdings (most of which were later converted to the Woolworths and Food for Less banners). It sold its Crazy Prices general merchandise stores, and began restructuring its liquor operations into four distinctive formats.

In 2002 Woolworths exited the New Zealand market when it sold its supermarkets group there to Foodland Associated for $690 million.

Supermarket division chief Bill Wavish resigned in 2003 and was replaced by former chief general manager of supermarket operations Tom Flood. Wavish was considered one of the top candidates to replace Corbett. Also in 2003 the company discontinued its Australian Independent Wholesalers (AIW) operations. Flood resigned abruptly in 2004. Flood, like Wavish, was considered a likely successor to Corbett.

In the fall of 2004, the board of directors of Australia's biggest pub owner, Australian Leisure & Hospitality (ALH), recommended the company accept a $985 million takeover bid by Woolworths and The Bruce Mathieson Group. Previously, the duo had acquired a 16% stake in ALH.

EXECUTIVES

Chairman: James A. Strong, age 60
Group Managing Director, CEO, and Board Member: Roger C. Corbett, age 61, $1,236,599 pay
CFO: Tom Pockett, $389,687 pay
Director, General Merchandise, BIG W and Consumer Electronics Businesses: Marty Hamnett, $345,899 pay
Director, Supermarkets: Michael Luscombe, $363,894 pay
Chief Logistics and Information Officer: Steve Bradley, $363,894 pay
Chief General Manager, Stage 3 of Project Refresh: Bernie Brookes, $363,894 pay
Chief General Manager, Free Standing Petrol and Liquor: Naum J. Onikul, $372,492 pay
General Manager, Human Resources: Julie Coates
General Manager, BIG W: Greg Foran
General Manager, Woolworths Academy: Judy Howard
General Manager, Corporate Services and Secretary: Rohan K. S. Jeffs
General Manager, Dick Smith Electronics: Alvin Ng
General Manager, Supermarket Operations: Peter Smith
General Manager, Property: Peter Thomas
General Manager, Mercury Program: Penny Winn
General Manager, Business Development: Gary Reid
Auditors: Deloitte Touche Tohmatsu

LOCATIONS

HQ: Woolworths Limited
540 George St., 5th Fl., Sydney 2000, Australia
Phone: +61-2-9323-1555   **Fax:** +61-2-9323-1599
Web: www.woolworths.com.au

2005 Sales

	% of total
New South Wales and Australian Capital Territory	32
Victoria	25
Queensland	20
South Australia and Northern Territory	10
Western Australia	9
Tasmania	4
Total	**100**

PRODUCTS/OPERATIONS

2005 Sales

	% of total
Food and liquor	76
Petrol	11
Big W	9
Consumer electronics	3
Hotels	1
Total	**100**

2005 Sales

	% of total
Supermarkets	30
Petrol stations	24
Liquor stores	19
Dick Smith Electronics stores	9
Hotels	7
Tandy stores	5
Big W stores	5
Dick Smith Electronics PowerHouse stores	1
Total	**100**

Selected Operations

Food stores
 Safeway
 Woolworths Metro
 Woolworths Supermarkets
General merchandise stores
 BIG W
Liquor stores
 BWS (neighborhood stores)
 Dan Murphy's (destination outlets)
 First Estate (fine wine stores)
 Woolworths Liquor (attached to supermarkets)
Specialty retail
 Dick Smith Electronics
 Dick Smith Electronics PowerHouse
 Tandy Electronics
Other
 Caltex/WOW Petrol (gas stations)
 GreenGrocer.com.au (online grocery store)
 Woolworths Ezy Banking
 Woolworths HomeShop (online grocery and liquor store)

COMPETITORS

ALDI	Harvey Norman Holdings
BP	Metcash
Coles Myer	Pick'n Pay
Foodland Associated	Royal Dutch/Shell Group
Harris Scarfe Holdings	

HISTORICAL FINANCIALS

Company Type: Public

Income Statement

	REVENUE ($ mil.)	NET INCOME ($ mil.)	NET PROFIT MARGIN	EMPLOYEES
6/05	23,875	602	2.5%	145,000
6/04	19,269	504	2.6%	140,000
6/03	17,551	434	2.5%	145,000
6/02	13,791	317	2.3%	145,000
6/01	10,908	243	2.2%	140,000
6/00	12,278	176	1.4%	125,000
6/99	12,510	170	1.4%	120,000
6/98	10,366	172	1.7%	100,000
6/97	11,629	193	1.7%	100,000
6/96	11,007	184	1.7%	95,000
Annual Growth	**9.0%**	**14.1%**	**—**	**4.8%**

2005 Year-End Financials

Debt ratio: 120.8%   Current ratio: 0.82
Return on equity: 45.3% Long-term debt ($ mil.): 1,991
Cash ($ mil.): 329

700
600
500
400
300
200
100
0

6/96 6/97 6/98 6/99 6/00 6/01 6/02 6/03 6/04 6/05

WPP Group

Marketing and advertising services bind this group together. WPP Group is the world's second largest media and communications services conglomerate (behind Omnicom Group), with operations in more than 100 countries. Its flagship agency networks, including Grey Worldwide, JWT, Ogilvy & Mather, and Young & Rubicam, offer creative campaign development and brand management services. WPP's holdings also include public relations firms, media buying and planning agencies, and many specialized marketing and communications units. In addition, its Kantar Group division is one of the world's leading market research organizations.

Having weathered a challenging recession, WPP is looking to position itself for growth in both the near- and long-term future. It completed a $1.75 billion acquisition of US-based rival Grey Global Group in 2005, beating out bids from private equity players (including Kohlberg Kravis Roberts & Co.) and rival advertising firm Havas. In addition to expanding the overall size of the company, the acquisition carried with it another important asset, Grey's long-standing relationship with Procter & Gamble. Soon after P&G's mega-merger with Gillette closed in 2005, however, the consumer products giant shifted about $800 million in media services assignments from WPP's Mindshare to Starcom MediaVest (a unit of Publicis).

The company is also keeping its eye open for additional acquisitions as it races to overtake Omnicom. WPP has long been speculated as a leading candidate to snatch up media planning and buying conglomerate Aegis Group. Other rumored acquisition targets include both of France's leading advertising companies, Havas and Publicis.

In the short term, though, WPP does have some headaches to take care of. Its Young & Rubicam network has become a consistent underperformer that has lost several big clients, including Burger King, Jaguar, and Sony. WPP also has a big challenge ahead to integrate the various operations of Grey into the rest of the holding company.

HISTORY

WPP Group began as Wire and Plastic Products, a maker of grocery baskets and other goods founded in 1958 by Gordon Sampson (who retired from the company in 2000). Investors led by former Saatchi & Saatchi advertising executive (and current WPP CEO) Martin Sorrell bought the company in 1985 and began acquiring marketing firms under the shortened name of WPP. In 1987 Sorrell used revenue from these busi-

nesses (and a sizable loan) to buy US advertising warhorse J. Walter Thompson (now JWT).

JWT was founded by William James Carlton as the Carlton & Smith agency in 1864. The New York City-based firm was bought by James Walter Thompson in 1877 and was later responsible for Prudential Insurance's Rock of Gibraltar symbol (1896). It began working for Ford (which is still a client) in 1943. JWT went public in 1969.

Following its acquisition of JWT, WPP formed European agency Conquest in 1988. The company (and its debt) grew the next year when it bought the Ogilvy Group (founded by David Ogilvy in 1948) for $860 million, making WPP the world's largest advertising company. But its acquisition frenzy also positioned the company for a fall in 1991, when depressed economies in the US and the UK slowed advertising spending. Saddled with debt, WPP nearly went into receivership before recovering the next year.

WPP began a period of controlled growth with no major acquisitions in 1993. It expanded internationally in 1994, opening new offices in South America, Europe, the Middle East, and Asia. Winning IBM's $500 million international advertising contract that year also aided WPP's financial recovery. However, this led to the loss of business from IBM's rivals, including AT&T, Compaq's European division (Compaq was purchased by Hewlett-Packard in 2002), and Microsoft.

By 1997 the company was again ready to flex its acquisition muscle. The firm bought 21 companies that year, including a stake in IBOPE (a market research firm in Latin America) and a share of Batey Holdings (the majority owner of Batey Ads, a prominent ad agency in the Asia/Pacific region). That year WPP also created its media planning unit MindShare.

More acquisitions followed in 1998, including a 20% stake in Asatsu (the #3 advertising agency in Japan). The next year the company bought Texas-based market research firm IntelliQuest Information Group, which was merged with WPP's Millward Brown unit. Along with its acquisitions, WPP snagged some significant new accounts in 1998 and 1999, lining up business with Kimberly-Clark, Merrill Lynch, and the embattled International Olympic Committee.

In 2000 the company bought US-based rival Young & Rubicam for about $4.7 billion — one of the largest advertising acquisitions ever. The move catapulted WPP to the top spot among the world's advertising firms. As if that wasn't enough, its MindShare unit later snagged the $700 million media planning account of consumer products giant Unilever. WPP also took a 49% stake in UniWorld Group, the largest African-American-owned ad agency in the US.

Hamish Maxwell, chairman since 1996, retired in 2001 and was replaced by Philip Lader, the former US ambassador to the UK. That year, however, WPP's top ranking was stolen away by Interpublic Group following its acquisition of True North Communications. It later sparked a bidding war with Havas Advertising when it offered $630 million to buy UK media services firm Tempus Group. WPP grudgingly completed its acquisition of Tempus in 2002. The following year the company acquired Cordiant Communications.

In 2005 WPP made another big splash in the industry when it acquired Grey Global Group for $1.75 billion.

EXECUTIVES

Chairman: Philip Lader, age 59
CEO and Director: Sir Martin S. Sorrell, age 60, $3,848,000 pay
Group Finance Director and Board Member: Paul W. G. Richardson, age 47, $1,254,000 pay
EVP Public Relations and Public Affairs and Director: Howard G. Paster
Group Strategy Director and Board Member: Mark Read, age 38
Group Communications Director: Feona McEwan
Chief Talent Officer: Mark Linaugh
Executive Chairman, Mediaedge:cia: Charles Courtier, age 40
Chairman, Berlin Cameron & Partners: Andy Berlin
Chairman, Fitch: Rodney Fitch
Chairman and CEO, Grey Global Group: Edward H. (Ed) Meyer, age 78
Chairman and CEO, Hill & Knowlton: Paul Taaffe
Chairman and CEO, JWT: Bob Jeffrey
Chairman and CEO, The Kantar Group: Eric Salama, age 41
Chairman and CEO, Ogilvy & Mather Worldwide: Rochelle B. (Shelly) Lazarus, age 57, $1,607,000 pay
Chairman and CEO, Young & Rubicam Brands and Y&R Advertising: Ann M. Fudge, age 53
President and CEO, CommonHealth: Matt Giegerich
President and CEO, Fitch:RPA: Todd Cameron
COO, Specialist Communications North America: Mary Ellen Howe
Investor Relations Director: Francis S. (Fran) Butera
Deputy Group Finance Director: Chris Sweetland
Auditors: Deloitte & Touche LLP

LOCATIONS

HQ: WPP Group plc
27 Farm St., London W1J 5RJ, United Kingdom
Phone: +44-20-7408-2204   **Fax:** +44-20-7493-6819
US HQ: 125 Park Ave., New York, NY 10017-5529
US Phone: 212-632-2200   **US Fax:** 212-632-2222
Web: www.wpp.com

WPP Group has operations in more than 100 countries.

2004 Sales

	$ mil.	% of total
Europe		
UK	1,397	17
Other countries	2,175	26
North America	3,167	39
Asia/Pacific, Latin America & Middle East	1,504	18
Total	8,243	100

PRODUCTS/OPERATIONS

2004 Sales

	$ mil.	% of total
Advertising & media services	3,806	46
Market research & consulting	1,428	17
Public relations & public affairs	854	11
Branding, health care communications & other	2,155	26
Total	8,243	100

COMPETITORS

Aegis Group
Dentsu
GfK
GfK NOP
Havas
Interpublic Group
Ipsos
Omnicom
Publicis
Taylor Nelson
VNU

HISTORICAL FINANCIALS

Company Type: Public

Income Statement

FYE: December 31

	REVENUE ($ mil.)	NET INCOME ($ mil.)	NET PROFIT MARGIN	EMPLOYEES
12/04	8,243	560	6.8%	59,932
12/03	7,323	372	5.1%	54,324
12/02	6,298	142	2.3%	49,439
12/01	5,856	395	6.7%	51,009
12/00	4,457	366	8.2%	55,000
12/99	3,511	279	8.0%	27,711
12/98	3,184	233	7.3%	25,589
12/97	2,885	192	6.6%	22,909
12/96	2,896	171	5.9%	21,166
12/95	2,412	107	4.4%	19,138
Annual Growth	14.6%	20.2%	—	13.5%

2004 Year-End Financials

Debt ratio: 33.7%
Return on equity: 7.6%
Cash ($ mil.): 2,630
Current ratio: 0.92
Long-term debt ($ mil.): 2,528
No. of shares (mil.): 237
Dividends
Yield: 0.4%
Payout: 9.6%
Market value ($ mil.): 12,961

Stock History

NASDAQ: WPPGY

	STOCK PRICE ($) FY Close	P/E High/Low		PER SHARE ($) Earnings	Dividends	Book Value
12/04	54.67	25	18	2.40	0.23	31.66
12/03	49.30	31	16	1.62	0.47	30.18
12/02	37.88	94	49	0.62	0.39	25.59
12/01	53.90	38	19	1.75	0.32	23.97
12/00	62.81	50	24	2.12	0.28	30.56
12/99	83.13	46	16	1.82	0.25	3.32
12/98	30.88	25	11	1.56	0.21	1.02
12/97	22.56	21	16	1.19	0.18	(0.14)
12/96	21.47	19	10	1.14	0.14	0.13
12/95	12.69	19	11	0.71	0.08	(0.33)
Annual Growth	17.6%	—	—	14.5%	12.5%	—

Yamaha

This company doesn't produce records, but it does help people make plenty of music. Yamaha is the world's leading maker of musical instruments, including pianos, electronic keyboards, and synthesizers. It also manufactures and distributes a wide variety of wind and percussion instruments, as well as guitars, violins, and other string instruments. Yamaha is a also a leading manufacturer of home audio and video equipment, and it makes a line professional audio gear. In addition, the company makes semiconductors and other electronic components. Yamaha owns more than 20% of Yamaha Motor Co., Japan's #2 motorcycle manufacturer.

While musical instruments has traditionally been Yamaha's largest businesses segment (accounting for almost 60% of revenue), its components business has been the top performer in terms of profits. Sales of digital signal processing chips for use in mobile phones has been the big driver in this segment, but Yahama is expanding into new applications for its chips, including automobile components and amusement equipment. Still, musical instruments remain at the core of the company's identity and growth plans. Beyond increased spending for marketing and product development, Yamaha continues to invest in its music instruction schools as a way to create future consumers for its products.

The company is also expanding beyond its manufacturing roots to become a leader in new digital content markets. It operates ringtone downloading services for mobile phone users in about a dozen countries, and it has launched Web sites that allow music fans to hear songs from up-and-coming artists. Yamaha is also leading the development of networked karaoke equipment that can download songs from the Internet and offer uploading features. To strengthen its position in the music-creation market, Yamaha acquired Steinberg Media Technologies (a division of Pinnacle Systems) in late 2004.

One segment that has struggled, though, is Yamaha's leisure business. Its six resorts across Japan have been impacted by adverse weather and a slowdown in domestic tourism spending. Yamaha continues to invest in upgraded facilities and marketing efforts while it evaluates a potential sale of the resort properties.

HISTORY

Torakusu Yamaha first repaired medical instruments. But while repairing a broken organ, he decided he could make his own. His first attempt did not have good sound, but continuous work over a four-month period led to a new organ — completed in 1887 — that was highly praised. He established Yamaha Organ Manufacturing Company in 1889. In 1897, as production grew, Yamaha incorporated the company as Nippon Gakki (Japan Musical Instruments). Nippon Gakki began producing upright pianos in 1900 and grand pianos in 1902.

In 1920 the company diversified into the production of wooden airplane propellers (based on woodworking skills used in making pianos) and added pipe organs (1932) and guitars (1946) to its line of musical instruments. Genichi Kawakami, whose father had managed the company since 1927, took over in 1950.

The company formed its first overseas subsidiary, Yamaha de Mexico, in 1958. Under Kawakami's leadership, Nippon Gakki became the world's largest producer of musical instruments, developing Japan's first electronic organ, the Electone, in 1959. Kawakami conducted the company's movements into wind instruments (1965), stereos (1968), microchips (1971), and furniture (1975). He established the Yamaha Music Foundation in 1966 to oversee the company's music schools. By 1982 people in the Americas, Europe, and Asia could buy Yamaha-brand products locally.

Nippon Gakki undertook further diversification, particularly into customized chips for CD players. In 1983 it introduced a powerful, but affordable synthesizer. The company changed its name to Yamaha in 1987. It opened a facility in China two years later. Yamaha emphasized exports of electronic instruments and the production of integrated circuits.

Until 1992 three generations of the Kawakami family dominated Yamaha. After a failed attempt by heir apparent Hiroshi Kawakami to cut back Yamaha's workforce through early retirement, the manufacturer's in-house labor union revolted. Kawakami was replaced by Seisuke Ueshima, a Yamaha veteran who set out to work on a combination of product innovation and corporate restructuring. Ueshima made a pact with the unions to keep most factory workers, lay off 30% of its Japanese administrative staff, and cut overseas employees.

In 1997 the company launched a joint licensing program with Stanford University for the Sondius-XG sound synthesis technology; the two institutions agreed to share royalties from the technology, which provides realistic sound quality for musical instruments and computer games.

Undergoing sluggish sales of electronic parts, in 1999 Yamaha stopped producing magnetic heads for hard disk drives, shut down a semiconductor plant, and trimmed its workforce by giving 11% of its employees early retirement. In 2000 the company introduced a bamboo guitar that could help slow the depletion of hardwoods and debuted its Super "Melo-Ring" for cellular phone users. That same year, Shuji Ito was named president of Yamaha. The company launched a high-resolution projector for home theater use in 2001. Genichi Kawakami, the 90-year-old former president of Yamaha, died in 2002.

In early 2003 the company decided to exit from the CD recorder market to focus more on high-end home theater systems. Also that year Yamaha's Electronics Marketing Corporation began operations and the Hangzhou Yamaha Musical Instruments Co. was founded in China.

EXECUTIVES

Chairman: Katsuhiko Kishida, age 64
President and Director: Shuji Ito, age 63
Managing Director, Digital Content, Digital Media, Development, and Technology Planning and Board Member: Hirokazu Kato, age 61
Managing Director, Corporate Planning, Personnel, and Information Systems, and Board Member: Tsuneo Kuroe, age 59
Director of General Administration and Environmental Management and Board Member: Shinya Hanamoto, age 59
Director of Accounting and Finance, Auditing, and Golf Products Division and Board Member: Tokihisa Makino, age 55
Director of Car Parts, Production Engineering, and Quality Assurance Divisions and Board Member: Yasushi Yahata
General Manager, Audio Visual and Information Technology Business Group: Hiroshi Sekiguchi
General Manager, Europe; President, Yamaha Music Holding Europe: Motoki Takahashi
General Manager, Legal and Intellectual Property Division: Kosuke Kamo
General Manager, Public Relations Division: Yoshikazu Tobe
President, Yamaha Corporation of America: Yoshihiro (Yoshi) Doi
Auditors: Ernst & Young ShinNihon

LOCATIONS

HQ: Yamaha Corporation
  10-1, Nakazawa-cho, Hamamatsu,
  Shizuoka 430-8650, Japan
Phone: +81-53-460-2800   **Fax:** +81-53-460-2802
US HQ: 6600 Orangethorpe Ave., Buena Park, CA 90620
US Phone: 714-522-9011   **US Fax:** 714-522-9961
Web: www.global.yamaha.com

2005 Sales

	$ mil.	% of total
Japan	2,909	59
North America	806	16
Europe	786	16
Asia & other regions	465	9
Total	**4,966**	**100**

PRODUCTS/OPERATIONS

2005 Sales

	$ mil.	% of total
Musical instruments	2,814	57
Audio visual & information technology	723	15
Electronic equipment & metal products	642	13
Lifestyle-related products	398	8
Recreation	170	3
Other	219	4
Total	**4,966**	**100**

Selected Products and Services

Musical instruments
- Digital and electronic musical instruments
  - Electronic pianos
  - Portable keyboards
  - Synthesizers
- Digital content distribution
- Educational musical instruments
- Educational services
  - English schools
  - Music schools
- Percussion instruments
- Pianos
- Pro audio equipment
- Soundproofing and acoustical design
- String instruments (guitars, violins)
- Wind instruments

Consumer audio visual and information technology products
- CD players
- DVD players
- Digital cinema projectors
- Home theater systems
- PC speakers
- Routers
- Stereo receivers
- Stereo speakers
- Video projectors

Electronic equipment and metal products
- Electronic devices
- Electronic alloys and other specialty metals
- Large-scale integration chips (LSIs)
- Semiconductors
- Thermoelectric materials

Lifestyle-Related Products
- Bathtubs and washstands
- Furniture
- System kitchens

Recreation
- Golf courses
- Leisure facilities
- Sightseeing facilities
- Ski resorts

Other
- Automobile interior components
- Golf equipment
- Industrial robots
- Metallic molds and components

COMPETITORS

CASIO COMPUTER	Roland
Creative Technology	Samick
Epson	Samsung Electronics
Fender Musica	Sharp
Gibson Guitar	Sony
Harman International	Steinway
Hoshino Gakki	TDK
Kawai	TEAC
Matsushita	Toshiba
Philips Electronics	Victor Company of Japan
Pioneer	Young Chang

HISTORICAL FINANCIALS

Company Type: Public

Income Statement

FYE: March 31

	REVENUE ($ mil.)	NET INCOME ($ mil.)	NET PROFIT MARGIN	EMPLOYEES
3/05	4,966	183	3.7%	23,828
3/04	5,107	412	8.1%	23,903
3/03	4,379	150	3.4%	23,563
3/02	3,803	(78)	—	23,020
3/01	4,109	105	2.6%	22,277
3/00	5,003	(387)	—	21,599
3/99	4,733	(0)	—	9,044
3/98	4,577	101	2.2%	9,281
3/97	4,884	114	2.3%	9,324
3/96	4,952	88	1.8%	9,872
Annual Growth	**0.0%**	**8.5%**	**—**	**10.3%**

2005 Year-End Financials

Debt ratio: 2.4%
Return on equity: 7.3%
Cash ($ mil.): 476
Current ratio: 1.55
Long-term debt ($ mil.): 61

Net Income History

Pink Sheets: YAMCY

YPF, S.A.

The largest company in Argentina answers to a Spanish parent: Integrated oil company YPF is 99%-owned by Repsol YPF, Spain's largest oil concern (formerly Repsol). YPF has proved reserves of 1.3 billion barrels of oil, and 8 trillion cubic feet of natural gas. It produces, refines, and markets petroleum, natural gas, and petrochemicals. The company's three Argentine refineries have an annual capacity of 116 million barrels, 51% of Argentina's total refining capacity. YPF distributes oil to its approximately 1,900 service stations in Argentina. Subsidiary YPF International has production interests in Indonesia, and also develops US oil and gas properties.

YPF also produces electricity and distributes LPG through interests in Bolivia, Brazil, Chile, Peru, and Russia.

Before its acquisition by Repsol, YPF had transformed itself from an inefficient state-owned firm into a streamlined international player. It has benefited from the Mercosur agreement, which set up an economic union in South America to promote regional trade.

HISTORY

An Argentine government team discovered oil while drilling for water in 1907. Determined to keep the oil under Argentine control, the government formed the world's first state-owned oil company, Direccion Nacional de los Yacimientos Petroliferos Fiscales (YPF), in 1922 to operate the newly discovered field. However, YPF lacked drilling equipment, capital, and staff; it found

that the only way to increase domestic oil production was to allow in foreign oil companies. Although YPF's activities ebbed in the 1920s, it made major oil discoveries across Argentina in the 1930s.

A major turning point came with Juan Peron's rise to power in 1945. Peron extended state control over broad sections of the economy, including oil. He nationalized British and US oil holdings and gave YPF a virtual monopoly. In 1945 YPF accounted for 68% of the country's oil production; by 1955 it produced 84%. The company discovered a huge gas field two years later in western Argentina, making YPF — and Argentina — a major gas producer.

However, YPF's production failed to keep pace with the demands of the growing economy, and imports still dominated Argentina's oil market. Over the next 30 years, YPF experienced radical swings in government policy as ultranationalist military regimes alternated with liberal, reformist governments. YPF grew into a bloated and inefficient conglomerate. Between 1982 and 1989, despite a World Bank-financed program to modernize YPF's refineries, the firm lost more than $6 billion.

In 1989 Carlos Menem became Argentina's president, and YPF was privatized as part of his economic reform plan to cut loose 50 state-owned companies. To prepare YPF for its IPO, the president brought in a former head of Baker Hughes, Jose Estenssoro, to draft a plan for privatization. The plan was so impressive that Menem gave him the job as CEO of the company in 1990. Estenssoro cut 87% of YPF's staff and sold off $2 billion of noncore assets. By 1993 YPF was profitable and went public as YPF Sociedad Anonima, selling 45% of its shares to raise $3 billion.

A year later YPF began expanding beyond Argentina by shipping crude oil to Chile through a new 300-mile pipeline. It bought woebegone Texas oil company Maxus Energy in 1995 and turned it around at great expense. Estenssoro and three other YPF executives died in a plane crash that year; in 1997 YPF selected Roberto Monti, who had headed Maxus, to serve as its CEO.

In 1997 YPF and Astra C.A.P.S.A. — in which Spanish oil firm Repsol had a controlling stake — jointly purchased a 67% stake in Mexpetrol Argentina (an affiliate of Mexican state oil company PEMEX). Repsol was aggressively moving overseas. In 1998 Repsol lobbied hard to buy part of YPF; Spain's King Juan Carlos himself phoned up Menem to promote Repsol's interests.

A year later the Argentine government auctioned off a 15% stake in YPF to Repsol for $2 billion; Repsol then bought another 83% of the company for $13.2 billion. Repsol became Repsol YPF, and its chairman, Alfonso Cortina, took over as chairman and CEO of YPF, while Monti was named VC and COO.

Monti retired the next year, after Repsol YPF increased its stake in YPF from 98% to 99%.

EXECUTIVES

Chairman and CEO, Repsol YPF and YPF: Alfonso Cortina de Alcocer, age 61
CFO and Director: Carlos A. Olivieri
General Manager and Director: Jose Maria Ranero Diaz
Director of External Relations: Fabian Falco
Director of General E&P, Argentina, Bolivia, and Brazil: Gonzalo López Fanjul
Director of Human Resources: Matteo Llurba
Director of Legal Affairs: Alejandro Quiroga Lopez
Director of Trading, Latin America: Alejandro Luchetta
Director of General Refining and Marketing, Latin America: Pascual Olmos

LOCATIONS

HQ: YPF, S.A.
Avenida Presidente Roque Sáenz Peña 777,
C. 1035 ACC Buenos Aires, Argentina
Phone: +54-11-4329-2000 **Fax:** +54-11-4329-2113
Web: www.repsol-ypf.com/eng/home/home.asp

YPF's oil and gas interests are primarily located in
Argentina, Indonesia, and the US.

PRODUCTS/OPERATIONS

2004 Sales

	% of total
Refining & marketing	49
Exploration & production	42
Chemicals	6
Other	3
Total	**100**

COMPETITORS

BP	PETROBRAS
COPEC	Petróleo Ipiranga
Exxon Mobil	Pioneer Natural Resources
Imperial Oil	Royal Dutch/Shell Group
PDVSA	TOTAL
PEMEX	Unocal

HISTORICAL FINANCIALS

Company Type: Public

Income Statement

FYE: December 31

	REVENUE ($ mil.)	NET INCOME ($ mil.)	NET PROFIT MARGIN	EMPLOYEES
12/04	6,757	1,653	24.5%	9,583
12/03	7,251	1,585	21.9%	9,395
12/02	5,833	995	17.1%	8,946
12/01	8,155	818	10.0%	8,900
12/00	8,674	1,231	14.2%	8,837
12/99	6,598	481	7.3%	9,000
12/98	5,501	589	10.7%	9,500
12/97	6,145	886	14.4%	10,000
12/96	5,944	845	14.2%	9,750
12/95	4,974	823	16.5%	9,350
Annual Growth	**3.5%**	**8.1%**	**—**	**0.3%**

2004 Year-End Financials

Debt ratio: 7.6%
Return on equity: 21.8%
Cash ($ mil.): 167
Current ratio: 1.74
Long-term debt ($ mil.): 571
No. of shares (mil.): 393
Dividends
Yield: 10.6%
Payout: 111.0%
Market value ($ mil.): 17,306

Stock History

NYSE: YPF

12/95 12/96 12/97 12/98 12/99 12/00 12/01 12/02 12/03 12/04

	STOCK PRICE ($) FY Close	P/E High/Low		PER SHARE ($) Earnings	Dividends	Book Value
12/04	44.00	11	8	4.20	4.66	19.04
12/03	37.02	9	3	4.03	2.65	19.51
12/02	12.17	9	3	2.53	1.12	15.35
12/01	19.75	15	8	2.08	4.22	21.55
12/00	29.94	12	8	3.49	0.88	23.53
12/99	36.94	33	20	1.35	0.66	20.89
12/98	27.94	22	11	1.64	0.66	20.43
12/97	34.19	15	10	2.48	0.42	19.66
12/96	25.25	11	8	2.31	0.60	18.08
12/95	21.63	10	6	2.30	0.60	16.73
Annual Growth	**8.2%**	**—**	**—**	**6.9%**	**25.6%**	**1.4%**

Zurich Financial Services

It's a wonder anyone would leave Zürich, nestled as it is in the beautiful Swiss Alps. But the business interests of Zurich Financial Services (Zurich) have crossed the mountains and spread to all but cover the globe. With operations in more than 50 countries worldwide, the company is the second-largest provider of general corporate insurance (after AIG). Focused on markets in Europe and in the US (through its North America Commercial unit), the company's General Insurance segment offers property/casualty and specialty insurance, while its Life Insurance segment offers life insurance, annuities, and other investment policies. The company was founded in 1872.

A strategic reorganization begun in 2004 has sought to consolidate Zurich's business under a single brand and refocus on its two principal segments — General Insurance and Life Insurance. The company operates through five divisions. Its Global Corporate unit focuses on risk management for large international and domestic clients. The Europe General Insurance division provides property/casualty and specialty lines for businesses and individuals; key markets are Germany, Italy, Spain, and Switzerland. The International Businesses unit has operations focused in Latin America, the Asia/Pacific region, China, Southern Africa, and other emerging markets.

In the US, Zurich serves business customers through its North America Commercial division, which includes Zurich American Insurance Company and its subsidiaries. Its Farmers Group operates the Farmers Management Services providing management to the Farmers Insurance Group, which provides auto and homeowners insurance. Zurich manages the Farmers Exchanges but holds no ownership stake.

The company's reorganization and efforts to refocus on its principal lines of business, as well as its expansion into markets deemed "underrepresented" have led to a financial turnaround.

HISTORY

The roots of Zurich Financial Services (ZFS) stretch back to the 1872 founding of a reinsurer for Switzerland Transport Insurance. The company soon branched out into accident, travel, and workers' compensation insurance and in 1875 it changed its name to Transport and Accident Insurance plc Zurich to reflect the changes. It then expanded into Berlin (the jumping-off point for its expansion into Scandinavia and Russia) and Stuttgart, Germany. The company exited marine lines in 1880; it later left the reinsurance business and expanded into liability insurance; in 1894 it changed its name to Zurich General Accident and Liability Insurance.

In 1912 Zurich crossed the Atlantic, expanding operations into the US. It agreed in 1925 to provide insurance for Ford cars at favorable terms. Zurich's business was hard hit during the wars years of the late 1930s and 1940s. In 1955 the company changed its name to Zurich Insurance.

Starting in the 1960s, Zurich began buying other insurers, including Alpina (1965, Switzerland), Agrippina (1969, Germany), and Maryland Casualty Group (1989, US). It also bought the property liability operations of American General.

In the early 1990s the company shifted its strategy, expanding into what it deemed underrepresented markets in the UK and the US. Being big wasn't enough; Zurich needed to find a focus. It also jettisoned such marginal or unprofitable business lines as commercial fire insurance in Germany.

In 1995 Zurich bought struggling Chicago-based asset manager Kemper and in 1997 bought lackluster mutual fund manager Scudder Stevens & Clark, forming Scudder Kemper. That year it also bought failed Hong Kong investment bank Peregrine Investment Holdings.

In 1998 Zurich merged with the financial services businesses of B.A.T Industries, formerly known as the British-American Tobacco Co., created in 1902 as a joint venture between UK-based Imperial Tobacco and American Tobacco. As public disapproval of smoking grew in the 1970s, British-American Tobacco began diversifying; it changed its name to B.A.T Industries in 1976 and moved into insurance. In 1984 it rescued UK insurer Eagle Star from a hostile offer by German insurance giant Allianz. The next year it bought Hambro Life Assurance, renaming it Allied Dunbar. Moving into the large US market in 1988, B.A.T bought Farmers Insurance Group.

While B.A.T battled the antismoking army of the 1990s, the insurance industry struggled with stagnant growth. In 1997 Europe's largest insurance firms were named as defendants in class action lawsuits that sought recovery for unpaid claims on Holocaust-era insurance policies. In 1998 Zurich became a founding member of the International Commission on Holocaust Era Insurance Claims (ICHEIC).

Also in 1998 Zurich and B.A.T's insurance units merged to create Zurich Financial Services. The firm reshuffled some of its holdings and sold Eagle Star Reinsurance. In 1999 Zurich spun off its real estate holdings into PSP Swiss Property and, at the turn of the century, it focused on expansion, buying the new business of insurer Abbey Life, which it merged into Allied Dunbar. In 2000, the holding companies formed to own Zurich (Zurich Allied and Allied Zurich) were merged into the firm.

In 2002 Zurich completed the spin off of reinsurance unit Zurich Re, which became Converium. It also sold troubled asset manager Zurich Scudder to Deutsche Bank and acquired the bank's life insurance operations in Italy, Spain, and Portugal. It also acquired life insurance firm Deutsche Herold, as well as German financial services provider Bonnfinanz and mutual fund distributor DGV. Zurich also sold a large holding in its US-based Zurich Life to BANK ONE and sold its operations in Hungary, Poland, and Slovakia, to Italian insurer Generali.

The write off of assets and strengthening of non-life reserves resulted in Zurich posting a $3.4 billion loss for 2002. Rolf Hüppi, Zurich's legendary chairman and CEO, stepped down while the company's asset management unit tumbled and investors pulled out. James Schiro, previously with PricewaterhouseCoopers, was named as the new chief executive and has guided a turnaround at the company. Zurich has seen growth in net income every year since 2002.

Zurich has paid out some $900 million in claims related to the September 11 terrorist attacks in the US.

EXECUTIVES

Chairman: Manfred Gentz, age 63
Vice Chairman: Philippe O. Pidoux, age 62
CEO: James J. (Jim) Schiro, age 59
COO: Peter Eckert, age 60
Group Finance Director: Patrick H. O'Sullivan, age 56
Chief Administrative Officer: Richard P. Kearns, age 55
Chief Information Technology Officer:
  Michael Paravicini, age 44
**Chief Investment Officer and Head, Group Strategic
  Planning:** David L. Wasserman, age 51
General Counsel and Company Secretary:
  Monica Mächler-Erne, age 49
CEO, Europe General Insurance: Dieter Wemmer,
  age 49
CEO, General Insurance: John Amore, age 57
CEO, Global Corporate Business:
  Geoffrey (Geoff) Riddell, age 50
CEO, Global Life Insurance: Paul van de Geijn, age 59
CEO, Zurich North America Commercial:
  Axel P. Lehmann, age 46
Head, Investor Relations & Rating Agencies:
  Seraina Maag-Gubler, age 37
Chief Economist and Head, Media and Public Relations:
  Daniel M. Hofmann, age 56
**Group Chief Marketing Officer and Head, Corporate
  Communications:** E. Randall Clouser, age 47
CEO, Farmers Insurance Group: Paul N. Hopkins,
  age 49
Chief Risk Officer: Wayne Fisher, age 60
Group Chief Actuary: Steve Wilson, age 39
Group Head, Human Resources: Harald P. Stoehr, age 54
CEO, US Small Business: John H. Lynch, age 54
Auditors: PricewaterhouseCoopers AG

LOCATIONS

HQ: Zurich Financial Services
  Mythenquai 2, 8022 Zurich, Switzerland
Phone: +41-1-625-2525   **Fax:** +41-1-625-2641
US HQ: North America Commercial, Zurich Towers,
  1400 American Ln., Schaumburg, IL 60196
US Phone: 847-605-6000   **US Fax:** 847-605-6011
Web: www.zurich.com

2004 Sales

	$ mil.	% of total
Continental Europe	20,828	34
North America		
Corporate	11,530	19
Consumer	6,046	10
UK, Ireland & South Africa	15,849	26
Centrally managed businesses	3,970	7
Other	2,393	4
Adjustments	(938)	—
Total	**59,678**	**100**

PRODUCTS/OPERATIONS

2004 Assets

	$ mil.	% of total
Investments		
Debt securities	130,512	38
Equity securities	58,740	17
Cash & cash equivalents	16,959	5
Trading equity portfolios in capital		
markets & banking activities	2,773	1
Investments in associates	645	—
Other investments	41,530	12
Investments held on account and		
at risk of life insurance		
policyholders	24,189	7
Reinsurance assets	23,004	7
Receivables	11,161	3
Deferred policy acquisition costs	13,344	4
Deferred tax assets	4,200	1
Mortgage loans given as collateral	4,135	1
Deposits made under assumed		
reinsurance contracts	3,312	1
Accrued investment income	2,614	1
Fixed assets	2,116	—
Goodwill	744	—
Derivative trading assets &		
other assets	3,515	1
Other intangible assets	2,590	1
Total	**346,083**	**100**

2004 Sales

	$ mil.	% of total
Net earned premiums & policy fees	41,804	77
Net investment income	9,114	14
Net capital gains on investments		
& impairments	4,934	
Management fees	2,030	4
Net gain on divestments of		
businesses	88	2
Other income	1,708	3
Total	**59,678**	**100**

2004 Sales

	$ mil.	% of total
General insurance	33,155	54
Life insurance	21,943	36
Farmers management services	2,084	4
Other business	2,631	4
Corporate & other	1,344	2
Adjustments	(1,479)	—
Total	**59,678**	**100**

COMPETITORS

AIG
Allianz
Aviva
AXA
CNA Financial
Generali
St. Paul Travelers
Winterthur

HISTORICAL FINANCIALS

Company Type: Public

Income Statement

FYE: December 31

	ASSETS ($ mil.)	NET INCOME ($ mil.)	INCOME AS % OF ASSETS	EMPLOYEES
12/04	346,083	2,587	0.7%	53,246
12/03	317,876	2,120	0.7%	62,000
12/02	285,856	(3,430)	—	67,824
12/01	231,605	(387)	—	70,000
12/00	231,363	2,328	1.0%	72,930
12/99	221,178	3,260	1.5%	71,390
12/98	214,651	802	0.4%	68,876
12/97	191,807	2,142	1.1%	68,000
Annual Growth	**8.8%**	**2.7%**	**—**	**(3.4%)**

2004 Year-End Financials

Equity as % of assets: 6.4%   Long-term debt ($ mil.): 6,859
Return on assets: 0.8%   Sales ($ mil.): 59,678
Return on equity: 12.4%

Net Income History

Swiss: ZURN

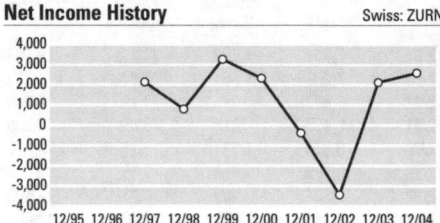

Hoover's Handbook of

World Business

The Indexes

Index by Industry

CONSUMER PRODUCTS MANUFACTURERS

Apparel
adidas-Salomon 24
LVMH 209
Tommy Hilfiger 352

Appliances
Electrolux 122

Cleaning Products
Henkel KGaA 151
Reckitt Benckiser 276

Consumer Electronics
CASIO COMPUTER 95
Creative Technology 103
Matsushita 213
Nintendo Co. 231
Philips Electronics (Royal Philips
    Electronics N.V.) 258
Pioneer 259
SANYO Electric 301
Sony 320

Housewares
Waterford Wedgwood 374

Jewelry & Watch Manufacturing
Swatch Group 328

Musical Equipment
Yamaha 381

Personal Care Products
Kao Corporation 185
L'Oréal SA 205
Shiseido 310
Unilever 361

Photographic & Optical Equipment/Supplies Manufacturers
Fuji Photo Film 139
Nikon 230

Tobacco
British American Tobacco 80
Gallaher Group 142
Imperial Tobacco Group 169
Japan Tobacco 183

Toys & Games
LEGO Holding 202

CONSUMER SERVICES

Travel Agencies & Services
Club Med 97
TUI AG 359

ELECTRONICS

Contract Electronics Manufacturing
Tatung Co. 333

Electrical Products
Schneider Electric 305

Electronic Components
Sharp 309

Semiconductor Equipment & Materials
Tokyo Electron 350

Semiconductors
Kyocera 199
Samsung Group 297
ST 323
TDK 334

ENERGY & UTILITIES
RWE 293
SUEZ S.A. 325

Electric Utilities
Electricité de France 121
Enel S.p.A. 124
Energias de Portugal (EDP - Energias
    de Portugal, S.A.) 126
E.ON AG 128
Scottish Power 306
Tokyo Electric Power 349

Energy Trading & Marketing
Centrica plc 96

Natural Gas Utilities
Gaz de France 143

Oil & Gas Exploration & Production
Gazprom) 144

Oil & Gas Refining, Marketing & Distribution
BP p.l.c. 76
Eni S.p.A. 127
Imperial Oil 168
LUKOIL (OAO LUKOIL) 208
Mitsui & Co. 220
MOL 224
OMV 248
PETROBRAS (PETRÓLEO
    BRASILEIRO S.A. -
    PETROBRAS) 253
Petróleos de Venezuela S.A. 255
Petróleos Mexicanos 256
PKN ORLEN (Polski Koncern Naftowy
    ORLEN SA) 262
Repsol YPF 280
Royal Dutch/Shell 292
Statoil ASA 322
TOTAL S.A. 356
YPF, S.A. 382

Water Utilities
Veolia Environnement 362

FINANCIAL SERVICES

Accounting
Deloitte 111
Ernst & Young 131
KPMG 195
PricewaterhouseCoopers 268

Asset Management
AMP Limited 40

Investment Firms
Ifi 165
SOFTBANK 318

Securities Brokers & Traders
Nomura Holdings 237

FOOD

Candy & Confections
Nestlé S.A. 228

Dairy Products
Danone) 110

Food Wholesale Distributors
ITOCHU 177

Foodservice
Compass Group 100
Sodexho Alliance 317

Sugar & Sweeteners
Tate & Lyle PLC 332

INDUSTRIAL MANUFACTURING

Agricultural Machinery Manufacturing
Kubota 197

Construction, Mining & Other Heavy Equipment Manufacturing
Komatsu Ltd. 192

Industrial Automation & Industrial Control Products Manufacturing
ABB Ltd. 20
Invensys plc 175

Industrial Contract Manufacturing
Mitsubishi 219

Industrial Machinery & Equipment Manufacturing
Hitachi, Ltd. 154
MAN 210

Paper & Paper Product Manufacturing
Stora Enso Oyj 324

Rubber & Plastic Product Manufacturing
Bridgestone 78
Michelin (Compagnie Générale des
    Établissements Michelin) 216
Pirelli & C. 261

INSURANCE

Insurance Brokers
Lloyd's 203

Life Insurance
AEGON N.V. 26
Assicurazioni Generali 44
Aviva plc 49
AXA 51
CNP Assurances 98
ING Groep 174
Legal & General Group 201
Nippon Life Insurance 232
Prudential plc 269

Property & Casualty Insurance
Allianz AG 37
Millea Holdings 218
Zurich Financial Services 383

Reinsurance
Munich Re (Münchener
    Rückversicherungs-Gesellschaft
    Aktiengesellschaft) 225

LEISURE
Rank Group 275

Gambling
Hilton Group 153

Lodging
Accor 22

Restaurants & Cafes
Whitbread PLC 375

MEDIA
Bertelsmann 68
Lagardère SCA 200
Televisa (Grupo Televisa, S.A.) 339
Thomson Corporation 347

Information Collection & Delivery
Reuters Group 281

Music
EMI Group 123

Publishing
Asahi Shimbun 43
Axel Springer 52
Hollinger Inc. 155
Pearson plc 251
Reed Elsevier 277
Wolters Kluwer 377

Television
BBC (British Broadcasting
    Corporation) 63
ITV plc 180

METALS & MINING
BHP Billiton 70

Aluminum Production
Alcan Inc. 31
Norsk Hydro 238

Industrial Metals & Minerals
Inco Limited 171
Lonmin Plc 204

Metals Distribution
Sojitz 319

Precious Metals Mining & Processing
Anglo American 41
Placer Dome 263

Steel Production
Corus Group 102
Mittal Steel 221
Nippon Steel 233
POSCO 265
ThyssenKrupp 348

PHARMACEUTICALS

Pharmaceuticals Manufacturers
AstraZeneca 46
GlaxoSmithKline 146
Novartis AG 241
Novo Nordisk 243
Roche Holding 284
Sanofi-Aventis 299

REAL ESTATE

Commercial Property Investment
Swire Pacific 329

Commercial Real Estate Development
Hopewell Holdings 158

RETAIL

Apparel & Accessories Retail
Benetton Group 67
PPR SA 267

Index by Headquarters

Index of Executives

A

Aasheim, Hilde 239
Abat, Jean-Raymond 51
Abbey, Scott G. 360
Abe, Tsutomu 223
Abercrombie, George B. 285
Abiteboul, Jean 143
Abramsky, Jenny 64
Abreu Aguiar, José A. 126
Abril Pérez, José María 65
Abril Pérez, Luis 338
Acharya, Ranjan 377
Acher, Franz-Josef 152
Achermann, Hubert 195
Achleitner, Paul 38
Acker, Rolf Dieter 61
Ackermann, Josef 115
Adachi, Seijiro 246
Adachi, Toshio 310
Adachi, Yoroku 89
Adami, Norman J. 295
Adams, Denis 272
Adams, George 188
Adams, Paul 81
Adams, Ralph G. 112
Aelick, Ronald C. 172
Agarwal, Bhikam C. 222
Agassi, Shai 303
Agemura, Yasuo 238
Agon, Jean-Paul 206
Agrawal, Vineet 377
Ågren, Christer 325
Agrusti, Raffaele 45
Aguilar, Alfonso Ballestero 280
Ahlers, Bernd 345
Ahmed, Javed 277
Ahn, Bok-Hyun 298
Ahn, Kyung-Soo 141
Ahrnell, Jan Henrik 341
Ahuja, Sanjiv 138
Aihara, Gempachiro 221
Aiken, Philip S. 71
Aimono, Minoru 37
Airey, Dawn 82
Aitken, Ian C. 287
Aizawa, Masatoshi 228
Akahane, Masao 309
Akashi, Masahiro 271
Akhurst, Bruce J. 344
Akikusa, Naoyuki 141
Akiyama, Kotaro 44
Akiyama, Masaki 213
Äkräs, Juha 237
Aksoycan, Ilhan 378
Alary, Pierre 74
Albrecht, Karl 35
Albrecht, Theo (ALDI) 35
Albrecht, Theo Jr. (ALDI) 35
Áldott, Zoltán 224
Alejandro Rojas, José 255
Alekperov, Vagit Y. 208
Alexander, Ralph C. 77
Alexander, William J. 294

Alexandre, Patrick 29
Alfaia de Carvalho, António P. 126
Alierta Izuel, César 338
Allamandi, Silvio 332
Allan, John 188
Allavena, Jean-Luc 200
Allen, Charles L. 180
Allen, David C. 77
Allen, Sharon L. 112
Allert, Richard H. 100
Allerton, John 344
Allgaier, Larry 242
Allgood, David 290
Almassy, Stephen E. 131
Almond, Stephen 112
Alonso Durán, Alfonso 338
Alphandéry, Edmond 98
Alphéus, Ingo 294
Alspaugh, Robert W. 195
Alsvik, Lars Christian 239
Altemark, Lars 203
Alvarez, José A. 56
Alves Pereira, Carlos 126
Alwan, Basil 34
Amador, Mercy Marie L. 299
Amano, Katsuyuki 351
Ambe Attar, Isidoro 342
Ambroso, Augusto 133
Amemiya, Hiroshi 218
Amore, John 384
Amssoms, Marianne 170
Ananenkov, Alexander G. 144
Ancierno, Ann 353
Andersen, Jørgen 91
Andersen, Kurt 68
Andersen, Lars Norman 203
Andersen, Nils S. 91
Andersen, Svein 322
Andersen, Thomas T. 43
Andersen, Ulrik 91
Anderson, Brad 103
Anderson, David 344
Anderson, Greg 368
Anderson, James 124
Anderson, Matthew 82
Anderson, Ruth 195
Anderson, Stephanie E. 172
Anderson, Toby 181
Andersson, Bengt 122
Andersson, Robert 237
Andrade, Flávio de 81
Andreassen, Arild 239
Andrews, Steve 83
Andruchow, Al 124
Ang, Ramon S. 299
Angelici, Bruno 46
Aninat, Cristián 337
Announ, Pascal 94
Ansell, Clive R. 83
Antinori, Thierry 207
Anzai, Fujio 177
Anzai, Takashi 179
Aoki, Satoshi 157
Apotheker, Leo 303

Appel, Frank 116
Ara, Yasuaki 141
Arai, Takao 233
Arakawa, Shoshi 78
Aramaki, Koichiro 189
Aramburuzabala Larregui, María A. 340
Aranha, Ashok 222
Arbola, Gérald 323
Arce, David 56
Archer-Shee, James B. 290
Ardeshir, Jehangir 331
Arendt, Axel 288
Argüelles, Raul 373
Argus, Don R. 70
Arima, Akira 245
Arlett, Julian 153
Armbruster, Jean-Claude 300
Armenio, Peter 290
Armour, Mark 278
Armstrong, Graeme D. 167
Armstrong, J. Gregory 161
Armstrong, T. Christian 354
Arnault, Bernard 209
Arteaga Carlebach, Maximiliano 340
Aruga, Shuji 309
Asada, Shunichi 223
Asahara, Takeshi 233
Asakawa, Osamu 37
Asami, Yasuo 78
Asano, Katsuhiko 189
Aschenbroich, Jacques 296
Ashby, Ian 71
Ashcroft, Charles P. 124
Ashton, Lynda 181
Ashton, Mike 153
Aso, Kotaro 140
Atay, Temel 192
Attal, Laurent 206
Au, Wai 60
Auci, Ernesto 133
Auguste, Georges 323
Augustine, Michael 332
Auque, François 120
Aurbach, Pamela 270
Avery, Kate 202
Axelrod, Mikhail A. 144
Ayuso, Javier 65
Azcárraga Jean, Emilio 340
Azuma, Kazunori 283
Azuma, Makoto 356

B

Baan, Roeland 222
Babeau, Emmanuel 253
Bacardi, Facundo L. 54
Bach, Herbert 225
Bach, Luis 54
Bacon, Gerry 369
Badalamenti, Salvatore 285
Badinter, Elisabeth 271
Badinter, Simon 271
Badke, Michael 187

Bahadur, Harsh 216
Bai, Dong-Man 298
Bailey, Michael J. 101
Baillie, Alistair 250
Bailly, Jean-Paul 98
Baird, Patrick S. 26
Baird, Richard L. 268
Baker, Ciaran 295
Baker, Kathy 378
Baker, Wendy 204
Bakker, Ruud H. 368
Balakrishnan, V. 173
Balbinot, Sergio 45
Balfour, Fergus 362
Balfour, Fiona 272
Bali, S. Ashish 112
Baltazar, Miguel 373
Bamba, Ryoichi 89
Bamford, Peter R. 369
Bandier, Martin N. 124
Bando, Aihiko 44
Banerjee, Gautam 268
Banerjee, Sudip 377
Banga, M. S. 362
Bangle, Chris 72
Bánhegyi, Ilona 224
Bantegnie, Pascal 34
Barbaroux, Olivier 121, 363
Barber, R. G. 159
Barberis, Joe 100
Barberot, Olivier 138
Barbosa, Fabio C. 22
Barclay, Mike 315
Barker, Ros 153
Barkov, Anatoly A. 208
Bärlocher, Urs 242
Barner, Marianne 166
Barnes, Kerry 25
Barrailler, Jacques 32
Barratt, Simon 376
Barrault, François 83
Barreto Pita de Abreu, António Manuel 126
Barrett, Matthew W. 60
Barrington, Jim 242
Barron, Laurence 30
Barrows, Charles 50
Bart, Pierre 121
Bartkiewicz, Jacek 262
Bartzokas, Robert J. 241
Bärve, Olof 304
Bassett, Edward H. 172
Bassetti, Victoria 124
Bassil, Alain 29
Bastón Patiño, José A. 340
Batni, Srinath 173
Baudin, Remí 318
Bauer, Walter 284
Bauer, Werner J. 229
Baujard, Olivier 34
Baumann, Ernst 72
Baur, Hans 265
Bauwens, Alain 152
Baxendale, Sonia A. 87

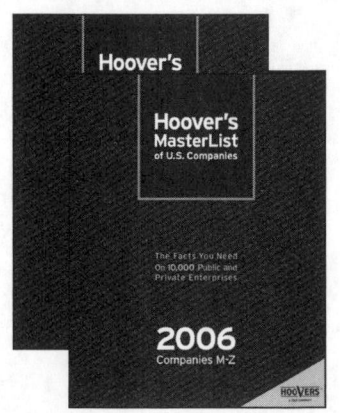